FEDERAL CRIMINAL LAW
AND
ITS ENFORCEMENT
Fourth Edition

By

Norman Abrams
Professor of Law Emeritus
University of California, Los Angeles

Sara Sun Beale
Charles L.B. Lowndes Professor of Law
Duke University School of Law

AMERICAN CASEBOOK SERIES®

Mat #40399541

Thomson/West have created this publication to provide you with accurate and authoritative information concerning the subject matter covered. However, this publication was not necessarily prepared by persons licensed to practice law in a particular jurisdiction. Thomson/West are not engaged in rendering legal or other professional advice, and this publication is not a substitute for the advice of an attorney. If you require legal or other expert advice, you should seek the services of a competent attorney or other professional.

American Casebook Series and West Group are trademarks registered in the U.S. Patent and Trademark Office.

COPYRIGHT © 1986, 1993 WEST PUBLISHING CO.
© West, a Thomson business, 2000
© 2006 Thomson/West
     610 Opperman Drive
     P.O. Box 64526
     St. Paul, MN 55164–0526
     1–800–328–9352

Printed in the United States of America

ISBN–13: 978–0–314–16306–6
ISBN–10: 0–314–16306–9

 TEXT IS PRINTED ON 10% POST CONSUMER RECYCLED PAPER

THIS BOOK IS DEDICATED TO
TOSHKA, HANNA, AND NAOMI ABRAMS
AND
DUNCAN, MATTHEW, AND STEVEN BEALE

*

Preface

Five years ago, the Preface to the Third Edition announced that "Federal Criminal Law has reached adulthood...," then noted the national attention focused on this subject and other developments such as the proliferation of federal drug prosecutions, and finally, highlighted the "great debate" that was taking place regarding the proper role of federal criminal law enforcement. All of these then-new developments have continued in the period since, and the great debate still goes on.

Since the publication of the previous edition, however, there has been a singular new development: The terrorism attacks on September 11, 2001 made the prevention and prosecution of, and the gathering of intelligence about, terrorism matters of the highest priority for the federal government. A military/"wartime" mode of proceeding against terrorism has been adopted along with an effort to intensify and make more effective civilian crime enforcement. Law enforcement personnel have been reassigned, investigative and intelligence agencies have been reorganized, authority has been centralized, new statutes have been enacted and some prosecutions have taken place. What impact these new developments in the terrorism arena are having on the overall effectiveness of federal criminal law enforcement is not yet definitively known, but the materials in this volume shed some light on that subject while continuing to provide a comprehensive, up-todate look at the federal criminal law operation.

The book is replete with new material. Not surprisingly, the subject of terrorism is revisited at a number of places in the volume. A new chapter on Ant-terrorism Enforcement (Ch. 12) has been added that provides an overview of some of the key statutes in the field and presents material on the kinds of cases that have been prosecuted and a window into the issues involved in dealing with U.S. civilians in a military/wartime mode. Anti-terrorism as a federal mission is addressed in detail both in Chapter 4's treatment of how the government targets its law enforcement resources, and in its description of the reorganization and centralization of the intelligence arms of the government in order to make them more effective in anti-terrorism work. The money laundering and currency reporting chapter takes account not only of new decisions, but also legislative and regulatory changes intended to adapting these laws to track terrorists and interrupt the flow of cash that supports their operations.

Three offense categories are now separately treated in Chapter 3 as in-depth illustrations of constitutional and statutory jurisdictional questions and substantive issues: Firerarms offenses, Violence against Women Act offenses and Travel Act and related offenses. The firearms material is new to the book and the VAWA material has been expanded from the previous edition.

Other new subjects have been added to the book: Perjury is newly treated in the same chapter (Ch. 15) in which the False Statement offense material appears. The offenses are closely related, and it is thought that while perjury is an important offense category that merits treatment on its own, studying it first will also help understanding of issues involved in the false statement area. A new extended Note has been added to the RICO chapter on Aiding and Abetting a RICO violation. It highlights a comparison and contrast with similar material relating to conspiracy to commit a RICO offense.

Every chapter has been revised to take account of major developments, both statutory and in the case law, including Supreme Court decisions involving federal commerce power jurisdiction, the mail and wire fraud statutes, federal program bribery, the Hobbs Act, the RICO statute and obstruction of justice. The drug chapter has been revised to include many new cases in the lower courts. Chapter 17, which deals with the choice between federal or state prosecution, as well as the possibility of dual prosecutions, has been revised to include new cases and examples, and also to make it a better teaching vehicle.

One of the most important changes in the book is a top to bottom revision of the Sentencing Guidelines chapter in response to the Supreme Court's decision in *Booker*. These materials are designed to provide students with a good introduction to the Guidelines themselves, as well as the *Booker* decision and the myriad of post *Booker* reform proposals.

This edition continues the organization and approach adopted in the previous edition. Once again, text notes in lieu of cases are used extensively with only the important cases, or in some instances, useful exemplar cases, being reproduced.

Federalism issues are addressed directly in Chapter 3 through extensive new material and a reorganization of the chapter, and the subject is then revisited as a recurring theme in the specific crime chapters. The overview chapters on Official Corruption and on Organizational Crimes have been retained because we think these chapters provide a way for students to understand the overlap and linkages between offenses in these two areas and to appreciate the commonalities and differences between related crime categories.

Once again, the Appendix contains statutory and Sentencing Guidelines materials too lengthy to include in the relevant chapters.

An effort has been made to make these materials as current and up-to-date as possible. Accordingly, the book includes material from the very end of the Supreme Court's 2004–2005 term as well as statutory, case law and other materials through the month of November, 2005.

This new edition, like previous editions, is for use in teaching courses in Federal Criminal Law, White Collar Crime, Organized Crime and similar offerings. The materials can be taught in a two or three hour semester (or equivalent course on the quarter system) in the second or third year of law school, or they can be used to teach a first year, second semester course, following a first semester, basic introductory Criminal Law course. The notion is that a first year, second semester Federal Criminal Law course provides an excellent follow-on to the basic Criminal Law course and provides the opportunity to examine the law of a specific jurisdiction applicable throughout the country with a unique combination of innovative crimes, complex issues of statutory interpretation, federalism issues, civil-criminal dichotomy and special policy and enforcement concerns.

N.A.
S.S.B.

December, 2005

*

Acknowledgements

A number of individuals helped us with the preparation of this edition. Norman Abrams would like to thank Corey F. Mostafa, UCLA Law, '07 for his thorough research assistance and Ayan Kayal, UCLA Law, '06, for his able assistance with the research and careful work on the preparation of the manuscript. He would also like to thank Tal Grietzer, UCLA Law School, for his able technical assistance with the manuscript. Sara Beale would like to thank Stacey McGavin Duke Law '07 and Jared Zane Duke Law '07 for their outstanding assistance with both research and manuscript preparation. She also thanks Joan Ashley, Duke Law, for assistance with the manuscript and technical details of all kinds.

In addition, we would like to thank the following individuals and organizations for permission to reprint excerpts from their publications:

Ann Althouse, *Theoretical and Constitutional Issues: Enforcing Federalism After* United States v. Lopez, 38 Ariz. L. Rev. 793 (1996). Copyright © 1996 by the Arizona Board of Regents. Reprinted by permission.

American Law Institute, Restatement (Third) of the Law of Foreign Relations of the United States, § 401. Copyright © 1987, the American Law Institute. Reproduced with the permission of the American Law Institute. All rights reserved.

Sara Sun Beale, *Too Many and Yet Too Few: New Principles to Define the Proper Limits for Federal Criminal Jurisdiction*, 46 Hastings L.J. 979 (1995). Copyright © 1995 by University of California, Hastings College of the Law. Reprinted from Hastings Law Journal, Volume 46, Number 4, April 1995, 979, by permission.

Sara Sun Beale, *The Unintended Consequences of Enhancing Gun Penalties: Shooting Down the Commerce Clause and Arming Federal Prosecutors*, 51 Duke, L.J. 1641 (2002). Reprinted with the permission of the Duke Law Journal.

Eric Blumenson & Eva Nilsen, *Policing for Profit: The Drug War's Hidden Economic Agenda*, 65 U. Chi. L. Rev. 35, 40–41 (1998). Reprinted with the permission of the University of Chicago Law Review.

Frank O. Bowman, III, *Playing "21" with Narcotics Enforcement: A Response to Professor Carrington*, 52 Wash. & Lee L. Rev. 937, 964–66 (1995). Reprinted with the permission of the Washington & Lee Law Review and Frank O. Bowman, III.

Frank O. Bowman, III & Michael Heise, *Quiet Rebellion II: An Empirical Analysis of Declining Federal Drug Sentences Including Data from the District Level*, 87 Iowa L. Rev. 477 (2002) (reprinted with permission).

Craig M. Bradley, *Federalism and Federal Criminal Law*. Reprinted from Hastings Law Journal, Volume 55, Number 3, February 2004, 573, by permission. © 2004 by University of California, Hastings College of Law.

Stephen Breyer, *The Federal Sentencing Guidelines and the Key Compromises Upon Which They Rest*, 17 Hofstra L. Rev. 1, 7–14 (1998). Reprinted with the permission of the Hofstra Law Review Association.

George D. Brown, *Constitutionalizing the Federal Criminal Law Debate:* Morrison, Jones, *and the ABA*, 2001 U. Ill. L. Rev. 983, 1014–1017. Copyright to the University of Illinois Law Review is held by the Board of Trustees of the University of Illinois. Reprinted by permission.

George D. Brown, *Putting Watergate Behind Us*—Salinas, Sun-Diamond *and Two Views of the Anti-Corruption Model*, 74 Tulane L. Rev. 747 (2000). Reprinted with permission of the author.

Harry A. Chernoff, et al., *The Politics of Crime*, 33 Harv. J. Legis. 527, 577 (1996). Copyright © 1996 by the President and Fellows of Harvard College. Reprinted with the permission of the President and Fellows of Harvard College.

Jesse H. Choper, *Taming Congress's Power under the Commerce Clause: What Does the Future Portend?*, Published originally in 55 Ark L Rev 731. Copyright 2003 by the Arkansas Law Review and Bar Association, Inc. Reprinted by permission.

Steven D. Clymer, Unequal Justice: *The Federalization of Criminal Law*, 70 S.Cal.L.Rev. 643–688 (1997). Reprinted with the permission of the Southern California Law Review.

Dennis E. Curtis, *Comment: Congressional Powers and Federal Judicial Burdens*, 46 Hastings L.J. 1019 (1995). Reprinted with the permission of the Hastings College Law Journal.

Dennis E. Curtis, *The Effect of Federalization on the Defense Function*, 543 Annals Am. Acad. Pol. & Soc. Sci. 85, 88–89, copyright © 1996 by Sage Publications, Inc. Reprinted by Permission of Sage Publications, Inc.

W. Kent Davis, *Swords Into Plowshares: the Dangerous Politicization of the Military in the Post-Cold War Era*, 33 Val. U. L. Rev. 61 (1998). Reprinted with the permission of W. Kent Davis.

Philip Frickey and William N. Eskridge, *The Supreme Court 1993 Term—Forward: Law as Equilibrium*, 108 Harv. L. Rev. 26 (1994). Reprinted with the permission of the Harvard Law Review Association, copyright © 1994 by the Harvard Law Review Association, Philip Frickey and William N. Eskridge.

Elizabeth Glazer, *Thinking Strategically: How Federal Prosecutors Can Reduce Violent Crime*, 26 Fordham Urb. L.J. 573 (1999). Reprinted with the permission of the Fordham University Urban Law Journal.

Jamie Gorelick & Harry Litman, *Prosecutorial Discretion and the Federalization Debate*, 46 Hastings L.J. 967, 976–77 (1995). © 1995 by University of California, Hastings College of the Law. Reprinted from Hastings Law Journal, Volume 46, Number 4, April 1995, 967, by permission.

Sandra Guerra, *Domestic Drug Interdiction Operations: Finding the Balance*, 82 Journal of Criminal Law and Criminology 1109, 1112–13 (1992). Reprinted by special permission of Northwestern University School of Law, Journal of Criminal Law and Criminology.

Sandra Guerra, *Family Values?: The Family as an Innocent Victim of Civil Drug Asset Forfeiture*, 81 Cornell L. Rev. 343 (1996). Reprinted with the permission of the Cornell Law Review.

Sandra Guerra, *The Myth of Dual Sovereignty: Multijurisdictional Drug Law Enforcement and Double Jeopardy*, 73 N.C.L. Rev. 1159 (1995). Reprinted from North Carolina Law Review, Volume 73, 1995, 1159, by permission.

Peter D. Hardy, *The Emerging Role of the Quid Pro Quo Requirement in Public Corruption Prosecutions Under the Hobbs Act*, 28 U. Mich. J. L. Ref. 409 (1995). Reprinted with the permission of the University of Michigan Journal of Law Reform.

Linda F. Harrrison, *The Law of Lying: The Difficulty of Pursuing Perjury under the Federal Perjury Statutes*, 35 U. Tol. L. Rev. 397 (2003). Reprinted with the permission of the University of Toledo Law Review, Volume 35, (2003) and Linda F. Harrison.

Peter J. Henning, *Federalism and the Federal Prosecution of State and Local Corruption*, 92 Ky. L.J. 75 (2003/2004). Reprinted with the permission of Kentucky Law Journal and Peter J. Henning.

Philip B. Heymann and Mark H. Moore, *The Federal Role in Dealing with Violent Crime*, 543 Annals Am. Acad. Pol. & Soc. Sci. 103, 107–08, copyright © 1996 by Sage Publications, Inc. Reprinted by permission of Sage Publications, Inc.

Asa Hutchinson, *An Effective Drug Policy to Protect America's Youth and Communities*, 30 Fordham Urb. L.J. 441, 462 (2003). This article was originally published in the Fordham Urban Law Journal as *An Effective Drug Policy to Protect America's Youth and Communities*, 30 Fordham Urb. L.J. 441, 462 (2003).

Dan M. Kahan, *Lenity and Federal Common Law Crimes*, 1994 Supreme Court Review 345 (1994). Reprinted with the permission of the University of Chicago Press.

Pamela Karlan, *Discrete and Relational Criminal Representation: The Changing Vision of the Right to Counsel*, 105 Harv. L. Rev. 6770 (1992). Copyright © 1992 by the Harvard Law Review Association. Reprinted with the permission of the Harvard Law Review Association and Pamela Karlan.

Susan R. Klein, *Independent-Norm Federalism in Criminal Law*, 90 Cal. L. Rev. 1541, 1554 n. 62 (2000). © 2002 by the California Law Review. Reprinted from California Law Review, Vol. 90, No. 5, p. 1154 by permission of the University of California, Berkeley and Susan R. Klein.

Renee M. Landers, *Prosecutorial Limits on Overlapping Federal and State Jurisdiction*, 543 Annals Am. Acad. Pol. & Soc. Sci. 64, 65, copyright © 1996 by Sage Publications, Inc. Reprinted by Permission of Sage Publications, Inc.

Harry Litman & Mark D. Greenberg, *Dual Prosecution: A Model for Concurrent Federal Jurisdiction*, 543 Annals Am. Acad. Pol. & Soc. Sci. 72, 75–77, 83–84 (1996). Copyright © 1996 by Sage Publications, Inc. Reprinted by Permission of Sage Publications, Inc.

Rory K. Little, *Myths and Principles of Federalization*, 46 Hastings L.J. 1029 (1995). Reprinted with the permission of the Hastings College Law Journal.

Tracey L. Meares, *Social Organization and Drug Law Enforcement*, 35 Am. Crim. L. Rev. 191, 206–07 (1998). Reprinted with permission of the publisher, Georgetown University and American Criminal Law Review. Copyright © 1998.

Geraldine Szott Moohr, *The Federal Interest in Criminal Law*, 47 Syracuse L. Rev. 1127 (1997). Reprinted with the permission of the Syracuse University Law Review.

Michael Edmund O'Neill, *Understanding Federal Prosecutorial Declinations: An Empirical Analysis of Predictive Factors*, 41 Am.Crim.L.Rev.1439 (2004). Reprinted with permission of the publisher, American Criminal Law Review, copyright © 2004.

Ellen S. Podgor, *Department of Justice Guidelines: Balancing "Discretionary Justice,"* 13 Cornell J.L. & Pub. Pol'y 167, 196 (2003). Reprinted with the permission of the Cornell Journal of Law and Public Policy.

Donald H. Regan, *How to Think About the Federal Commerce Power and Incidentally Rewrite United States v. Lopez*, 94 Mich. L. Rev. 554 (1995). Reprinted with the permission of the Michigan Law Review and Donald H. Regan.

Daniel C. Richman, *Federal Criminal Law, Congressional Delegation, and Enforcement Discretion*, 46 UCLA L. Rev. 757 (1999). Reprinted with the permission of the UCLA Law Review and Daniel C. Richman. Originally published in 46 UCLA L. Rev. 757. Copyright © 1999, The Regents of the University of California. All Rights Reserved.

Daniel C. Richman, *Prosecutors and Their Agents, Agents and Their Prosecutors*, 103 Columb. L.Rev. 749, 768–771 (2003). Reprinted with the permission of the Columbia Law Review.

Tom Rickhoff, Essay: *The U.S. Attorney: Fateful, Powers Limited*, 28 St. Mary's L.J. 499 (1997). Reprinted with the permission of St. Mary's Law Journal.

Gerald J. Russello, *Review of* GOTHAM UNBOUND: HOW NEW YORK CITY WAS LIBERATED FROM THE GRIP OF ORGANIZED CRIME by James B. Jacobs with Coleen Friel and Robert Radick, 10 Law and Politics Book Review 71–73 (January 2000). Reprinted with the permission of Gerald J. Russello.

L.B. Schwartz, *Federal Criminal Jurisdiction and Prosecutors' Discretion*, 13 Law & Contemp. Prob. 64 (1948). Reprinted with the permission of Law & Contemporary Problems.

Michael S. Simons, *Prosecutorial Discretion and Prosecutorial Guidelines: a Case Study in Controlling Federalization*, 75 N.Y.U.L.Rev. 893, 962 (2000). Reprinted with the permission of the New York University Law Review.

David A. Sklansky, *Cocaine, Race, and Equal Protection*, 47 Stan. L. Rev. 1283, 1308–09 (1995). Reprinted with permission.

Tom Stacy and Kim Dayton, *The Underfederalization of Crime*, 6 Cornell J. of Law & Soc. Pol. 247 (1997). Reprinted with the permission of the Cornell Journal of Law and Social Policy.

John K. Villa, A *Critical View of Bank Secrecy Act Enforcement and the Money Laundering Statute*, 37 Cath. U. L. Rev. 487, 500–02 (1988). Reprinted with the permission of The Catholic University of America Law Review.

Sarah N. Welling, Smurfs, *Money Laundering, and the Federal Criminal Law: The Crime of Structuring Transactions*, 41 Fla. L. Rev. 287, 290-92 (1989). Reprinted with the permission of the Florida Law Review.

Charles N. Whitaker, Note, *Federal Prosecution of State and Local Bribery: Inappropriate Tools and the Need for a Structured Aproach*, 78 Va. L. Rev. 1617 (1992). Reprinted with permission.

Gregory H. Williams, *Good Government by Prosecutorial Decree: The Use and Abuse of Mail Fraud*, 32 Ariz. L. Rev. 137 (1990). Copyright © 1990 by the Arizona Board of Regents, reprinted by permission and reprinted with permission of Gregory H. Williams.

Franklin M. Zimring and Gordon Hawkins, *Toward a Principled Basis for Federal Criminal Legislation*, 543 Annals Am. Acad. Pol. & Soc. Sci. 15, 22–23, copyright © 1996 by Sage Publications, Inc. Reprinted by Permission of Sage Publications, Inc.

*

Summary of Contents

Page
APPENDIX

Table of Contents

Table of Cases

The principal cases are in bold type. Cases cited or discussed in the text are roman type. References are to pages. Cases cited in principal cases and within other quoted materials are not included.

*

Table of Statutes

Table of Federal Sentencing Guidelines References

Titles have been abbreviated. **Bold** references indicate that the text of the Guideline has been reprinted.

*

FEDERAL CRIMINAL LAW
AND
ITS ENFORCEMENT

Fourth Edition

*

Part I

GENERAL PRINCIPLES

Chapter 1

INTRODUCTION

INTRODUCTION

The federal criminal enforcement system has numerous features that attest to its importance and distinguish it from the ordinary criminal law. The operations of the federal government in the realm of criminal law continue to be at center stage today. One can hardly pick up a newspaper without reading about a federal investigation or prosecution of some notoriety, about debate about the federal enforcement emphasis, or about congressional investigations of federal criminal enforcement operations or consideration of proposals for new crime legislation. It would surprise most people to learn that despite the amount of attention paid to the federal criminal system, in statistical terms, the federal criminal law is actually a very small part of the total criminal justice operation in this country. Yet its true importance is much greater than those numbers suggest.

Because of its geographic spread, visibility, symbolic value, importance as a model and usefulness in dealing with special crime problems in different parts of the country, federal operations arguably comprise the single most important criminal enforcement system in this country. Currently, in the wake of and as a result of the attacks that took place on September 11, 2001, major changes are occurring in the organization, functioning and focus of the Department of Justice, U.S. Attorney offices, and major law enforcement agencies such as the FBI, all designed to address the problem of terrorism. We anticipate that the changes will have a significant impact but, overall, the basic, traditional role and responsibilities of the federal government in this arena will continue. (See Chapter 4 where these issues are pursued in more detail.)

Congress and federal prosecutors and police agencies play a leadership role in crime enforcement very much like that of the Supreme Court of the United States in the judicial sphere, extending far beyond actual jurisdiction and authority. For example, enactment by the Congress of a new federal statute such as RICO or adoption of a new enforcement approach by the Department of Justice instantly provides a model nationwide that many states can emulate. Similarly, federal agencies through task forces and coordinating efforts bring together multiple agencies, federal, state and local, in joint and cooperative operations in which the federals typically play the lead role.

Terrorism has been elevated today to be the No. 1 priority of federal enforcement against crime, but other traditional federal enforcement priorities are not likely to be abandoned. In the past half century, much of the effort of federal enforcement has been directed nationwide against crimes and corruption in our basic institutions, in the business world and in government. By one measure or another, organized crime, including street gangs, and illicit drugs, continue to be problem areas whose unfettered growth continues to threaten the fabric of the nation.

There is a sense in which the importance of the federal criminal system is probably greater today than in the past. The system has been growing; there are more federal crimes on the books reaching more kinds of conduct; there are more agents in the major federal enforcement agencies; a stronger central administrative authority is being exercised from Washington over federal prosecutors and investigators; and a more activist enforcement posture has been adopted. As a result, the federal criminal system today is having considerably more impact.

For a time, the federal "war" on organized crime focused great attention on that sphere of criminal prosecution. Later there was a shift in emphasis toward white collar crime and political corruption. Later still, another change in Administration produced an apparent switch in emphasis toward fighting international drug trafficking. Still more recently, major corporate fraud and accounting scandals have shifted attention again toward business crime. And the "war" on terrorism has now become a central focus. In the past, there were ebbs and flows in the various "wars" against crime that affected the amount of investigatory work being done in particular areas with a corresponding impact on the kinds and numbers of cases being prosecuted in each category, the type of issues being litigated, and the development of the law in specific crime areas. Will the war on terrorism be subject to the same kind of ebb and flow, or does it signal a paradigm shift that will not easily be reversed? Only time will tell. In the meantime, all of these changes, nuances and complexities continue to add an element of vitality to the subject of Federal Criminal Law that makes it intrinsically interesting.

The subject matter of this volume is devoted largely, though not exclusively, to a detailed treatment of specific federal offenses—crimes such as RICO, mail fraud, the Hobbs Act, the drug laws, money laundering, obstruction of justice, and, now, terrorism. There is also an emphasis, however, on the features of our federal system of criminal enforcement that are unusual and present issues different from those typically seen at the state and local level. For example, the majority of crimes treated in this volume generally are not those that offend against direct federal interests but rather those that define conduct that could also be prosecuted in the state courts, variously denoted "auxiliary," "local" or "non-federal interest" crimes. The categories are not airtight, however, and some important federal interest offenses are included here—for example, bribery of federal officials, perjury, false statements to federal agencies and obstruction of justice.

The emphasis on the non-federal interest crimes should be explained. Of course, a major element in the federal criminal system is the protection of direct federal interests—money, property and persons associated with the federal government. However, in protecting such interests the federal criminal system functions like any state or local enforcement operation, and no special or unusual criminal law features attach. On the other hand, the criminal law involved in the federal government's role in investigating and prosecuting crimes which historically were handled only at the state-local level raises important issues of law and policy that warrant careful study. A major purpose of this volume is to stimulate thinking about such issues.

In studying these materials, one will encounter certain major themes suggestive of such questions as the following: Is the major shift of personnel to the field of anti-terrorism going to leave enough people for the federal agencies also to be able to staff the traditional areas of federal enforcement? Is the increasing number of federal prosecutions of crimes that do not offend against any direct federal interest warranted? Is there an acceptable rationale for such activity? Are there dangers associated with the present trends in the growth of the federal criminal law and federal agencies? If so, what are they, and what can be done to slow or reverse the trends? In connection with these issues, account must be taken of the strong tradition in this country that the primary responsibility for criminal enforcement rests with state and local government. What would be an ideal allocation of law enforcement responsibility between federal and state and local government? Is there a practical way to implement the ideal?

How well is the system functioning at the operational level? Given limited federal resources, a broad authority and extensive geographic jurisdiction, how does one select the relatively few cases to investigate and prosecute so as to make the federal effort reflect a consistent national policy? Is it wasteful to have two systems covering the same ground? There is much increased federal-state-local cooperation, but are there also inefficient competition, interference and duplication of investigative efforts?

In addition to the foregoing, numerous specific federalism concerns are also raised by these materials: for example, jurisdictional concerns—the constitutional and statutory bases for the exercise of a broad federal authority that in its genesis was deemed limited; the duplicative prosecutions issue—whether the federal government can and should pursue criminal conduct previously prosecuted by a state or vice versa; issues relating to the increased efforts to give the federal criminal law extraterritorial effect; and numerous issues relating to the state-federal relationship at the operational level—for example, how state prosecutorial interests are protected.

In reading these materials the student will also encounter and want to study carefully other notable features of our federal system, aspects that are perhaps not intrinsic to all federal systems. For example: (1) the system has an unusual number of broadly defined open-ended crime categories, such as mail fraud, that are adaptable to many, different types of fact situations. (2) conspiracy and the complex, organizational crimes, such as the Racketeering–Influenced and Corrupt Organizations (RICO) statute and the Continuing Criminal Enterprise (CCE) statute are being used very extensively; (3) there is a frequent practice of charging multiple counts of different crimes for essentially the same conduct; although state and local prosecutors also engage in this practice, it appears to be much more frequently done in the federal system. (5) civil treble damage actions based upon criminal conduct and authorized by statute are often being brought by private individuals; civil RICO particularly illustrates this; and the federal government in some landmark cases is filing private civil RICO actions seeking equitable relief. In connection with each of the foregoing, one should ask: why has this particular feature developed on the federal landscape? Is it a desirable development or practice that the states are likely to follow? What issues of law and policy does it raise?

At a minimum, careful study of these materials will give the student a detailed understanding of most of the important features of the Federal Criminal Law and the multi-faceted operations of the federal criminal system. The real challenge, however, is to think carefully about and begin to address the larger issues presented regarding the nature of the federal criminal enforcement role.

Chapter 2

FEDERAL, STATE AND LOCAL CRIMINAL ENFORCEMENT RESOURCES*

INTRODUCTORY NOTE—THE HISTORY OF FEDERAL LAW ENFORCEMENT

Federal law enforcement in the United States may be dated back to September 24, 1789, when the office of the Attorney General of the United States was created by Act of Congress, and Edmund Randolph was appointed to that position by President Washington. William Wirt, who served as Attorney General under President Monroe, established the first basic guidelines for the position. The same statute that established the office of Attorney General also created United States Attorneys for each judicial district, and in 1861 the Attorney General was given formal administrative control over them.

The first federal police agency was established in 1789, when the Revenue Cutter Service was established to help prevent smuggling. In 1868, Congress authorized a force of 25 detectives. In 1870, Congress established the Department of Justice with the Attorney General as its head. To finance the original Department of Justice, Congress appropriated $50,000 for the detection and prosecution of crimes. The internal organization of the Department evolved slowly. In 1908, the Bureau of Investigation, composed of a few special investigators, was established in the Department; in 1924, J. Edgar Hoover became the head of the renamed Federal Bureau of Investigation. It was not until 1915 that a nucleus of attorneys closely identified with federal criminal matters came into being within the Department. The Criminal Division of the Department was first mentioned in the 1919 Annual Report of the Attorney General. Prior to the establishment of the Criminal Division,

---

* The figures cited in this chapter have been derived, in some instances by extrapolation, from a variety of sources including *Annual Reports of the Attorney General of the United States;* the FBI's *Uniform Crime Reports: Crime in the United States; Source Book of Criminal Justice Statistics* issued by the Bureau of Justice Statistics in the U.S. Department of Justice; *Federal Judicial Workload Statistics* prepared by the Administrative Office of the United States Courts; and *Annual Report, State Court Caseload Statistics* prepared by the National Center for State Courts.

criminal matters were treated by the various Assistant Attorneys General with responsibility for particular substantive areas, e.g. Tax or Antitrust.

For a more detailed treatment of the Department of Justice and the office of Attorney General, see HOMER S. CUMMINGS & CARL McFARLAND, FEDERAL JUSTICE (1937); John A. Fairlie, *The United States Department of Justice*, 3 MICH.L.REV. 352 (1905); ALBERT LANGELUTTIG, THE DEPARTMENT OF JUSTICE OF THE UNITED STATES (Instit. for Govt. Research, 1927); LUTHER A. HUSTON, THE DEPARTMENT OF JUSTICE (1967). For an excellent treatment of the office of U.S. Attorney, see JAMES EISENSTEIN, COUNSEL FOR THE UNITED STATES (1978).

The remaining materials in this chapter describe the relative magnitude of criminal enforcement resources—that is, police forces and prosecutors' offices—and criminal caseloads on the federal and state levels.

A. FEDERAL CRIMINAL ENFORCEMENT AGENCIES

The principal criminal justice units of the Department of Justice are the Federal Bureau of Investigation, the Drug Enforcement Administration, the Criminal Division, the Bureau of Prisons, the U.S. Marshals Service and the Executive Office for United States Attorneys. Criminal matters are also prosecuted under the supervision of other Divisions in the Department—e.g. the Tax, Antitrust and Civil Rights Divisions.

There are numerous federal police agencies not attached to the Department of Justice, for example, the Secret Service and Postal Inspectors. There are over 50 major federal law enforcement agencies concerned with enforcement of federal criminal laws. Depending on which agencies are counted, there are as many as 200 federal agencies today that have some criminal enforcement role. As of 1997, the federal government employed in excess of 86,000 full-time employees involved in "police protection" including both investigative agents and administrative support personnel. (By way of illustration, it should be noted that the FBI employs approximately four administrative support persons for every three special agents.)

1. THE FBI

The FBI investigates violations of a majority of federal criminal statutes; its jurisdiction extends to over 200 categories of federal law. In the typical case, the results of an investigation are given to the appropriate U.S. Attorney or Department of Justice lawyer who determines whether further action is warranted. In recent years the Bureau's announced enforcement emphasis has been on the investigation of organized crime (including narcotics trafficking, loansharking, and pornography operations), white collar crime, foreign counter-intelligence and terrorism. Until 1982, the FBI did not conduct drug investigations.

Its move into that investigative arena led to extensive joint operations with the Drug Enforcement Administration.

The FBI is the largest federal criminal enforcement agency (excluding the military services, see *infra* pp. 609–621). It is organized into 9 Divisions, 56 field offices and 45 foreign liaison posts or Legal Attachés supervised from FBI Headquarters in Washington, D.C. The Field Divisions and their 400 ancillary offices are located throughout the U.S. and in Puerto Rico and Guam. The foreign liaison posts are useful for investigations that cross international lines. As of June 30, 2003, the FBI employed 27,537 persons, including 11,633 Special Agents.

2. THE DRUG ENFORCEMENT ADMINISTRATION (DEA)

Formerly called the Bureau of Narcotics and located in the Treasury Department, the DEA was shifted to the Justice Department in 1973. The DEA enforces controlled substances laws and regulations and is the agency primarily responsible for developing federal drug enforcement programs. Its responsibilities include the investigation and preparation for prosecution of cases involving major interstate and international drug traffickers, management of the national narcotic intelligence system, and coordination with international agencies and foreign governments to reduce the availability of illegal drugs in the U.S. market.

The federal drug enforcement effort has in recent years increased significantly, as has the reach of federal drug laws. In 1948, there were 150 federal narcotics agents; in 2005, the DEA employed 5,296 special agents and 5,598 support persons.

3. OTHER FEDERAL POLICE AGENCIES

The United States Marshals Service (also located in the Department of Justice) provides security for judicial proceedings including federal judges, jurors and other participants, is responsible for locating and arresting federal fugitives and maintaining custody of federal prisoners, and performs other law enforcement services at the request of other federal agencies. The Marshals Service is also responsible for the federal witness protection program. There are 94 U.S. Marshals, and 4,709 deputy U.S. Marshals and administrative personnel.

Some other major enforcement agencies are now located in the Department of Homeland Security: the Customs Service, which has grown from fewer than 150 agents in 1948 to approximately 11,000 agents in 2005; and the Secret Service (some 300 agents in 1948 and about 2,100 special agents in 1999) with responsibility for presidential protection and similar duties, as well as enforcement against counterfeiting and government check forgery. The Bureau of Alcohol, Tobacco and Firearms (ATF) with approximately 2,000 agents, all of whom have gun control, explosives, and arson responsibilities, has been shifted to the Department of Justice. The Internal Revenue Service, located in the Treasury Department, employs 2800 special agents for criminal investigations.

Many other government departments and agencies also have investigatory personnel to deal with criminal violations arising out of the administration of their regulatory programs. These include criminal law enforcement personnel functioning within the Department of Agriculture, the Department of Labor, the Department of the Interior, the Securities and Exchange Commission, and the Food and Drug Administration.

4. THE CRIMINAL DIVISION

For purposes of criminal law enforcement, the two most important organizational units within the Department of Justice are the Criminal Division and the United States Attorneys Offices (which are discussed below). The Criminal Division supervises the enforcement of all federal criminal laws, except for those criminal statutes specifically assigned to other Divisions, such as Antitrust, Tax, Civil Rights, and Environment and Natural Resources (environmental crimes). Over four hundred prosecutors work in the Criminal Division. Since the late 1960s, the Criminal Division has attempted to exercise greater supervisory control over decision-making by United States attorneys in the field, with a view to making federal prosecutive policy more uniform nationwide. The Division also functions in an advisory capacity to the United States attorneys, providing technical assistance of various kinds, and attorneys when needed in the trial of particular cases.

The Department's current organizational chart, reprinted below, reflects to some degree the present emphasis in federal law enforcement.

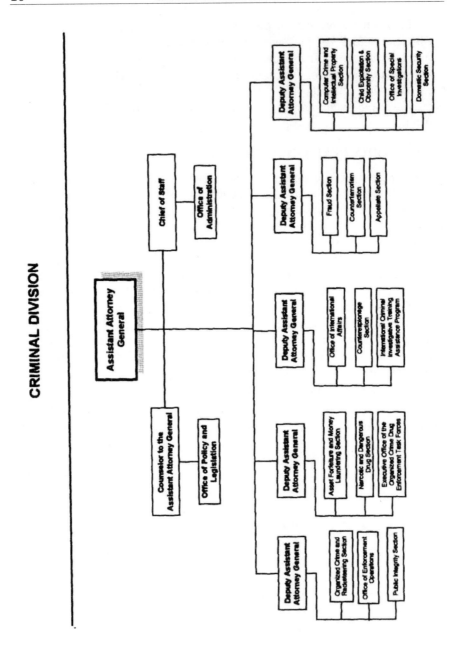

5. UNITED STATES ATTORNEYS

There are 93 offices of the U.S. Attorneys. The Executive Office for U.S. Attorneys in the Department of Justice provides them with general assistance. The offices are located within the federal judicial districts in the 50 states, Guam, Northern Mariana Islands, Puerto Rico, and the Virgin Islands. Within each district, the U.S. Attorney is the chief federal prosecutor enforcing federal criminal laws in the locale. (He or she also handles most of the civil litigation in which the United States is involved.)

U.S. Attorneys are appointed by the President for four-year terms. Assistant U.S. Attorneys are recommended by the U.S. Attorney and appointed by the Attorney General. In 2005 the Offices of the U.S. Attorneys ranged in size from eleven (in the E.D. Missouri) to over 350 (in D.C.) attorneys. As of August 1999, there were 4,773 Assistant U.S. Attorneys and approximately 6,000 non-attorney employees in these offices. In the ordinary case, the decision whether to prosecute is made by the assistant United States Attorney in the field upon referral of the matter by a federal investigative agency. In a few areas, the investigative agency may be required to refer the matter to the appropriate Division in the Justice Department.

The Department of Justice organizational chart reprinted below shows the Criminal Division, U.S. Attorneys, DEA, FBI, and other units.

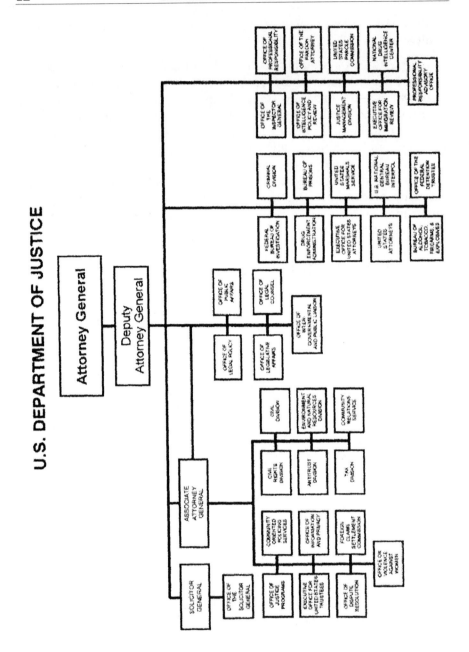

6. DRUG TASK FORCES AND ORGANIZED CRIME STRIKE FORCES

In addition to the divisions and agencies described above, there have also been efforts to employ joint federal-state task forces and other specialized units to attack particular types of criminal activity.

The task force concept has been used extensively in the context of drug enforcement. In 1982 the first regional task forces called Organized

Crime Drug Enforcement Task Forces (OCDETF) were established to target the higherups in organized criminal drug enterprises. The agencies involved are the DEA, FBI, IRS, ATF, Immigration and Naturalization, U.S. Marshals, Customs, and Coast Guard. The DEA also has a State and Local Task Force program in which DEA agents join with state and local police in drug enforcement units aimed at middle-level violators. In 1999, 134 DEA/State and Local Task Forces were operational in major cities throughout the country.

For more than two decades the Department of Justice maintained separate organizational units to deal with organized crime. From 1966 to 1990, many Justice Department attorneys assigned to the Organized Crime and Racketeering Section in the Criminal Division served in organized crime strike forces made up of government attorneys and representatives from federal investigative agencies; the strike forces had special responsibility for investigating and prosecuting persons connected to organized crime. Representatives from state agencies, although not formally part of the strike forces, were also involved in some instances. Strike forces operated in 25 cities. Because organized crime extends across state lines, the strike force attorneys reported directly to the Justice Department in Washington, not to the local United States Attorneys. In 1990 the strike forces were merged with the local United States Attorney's Offices. The move was intended to end occasional turf battles between prosecutors in the same district and streamline the government's attack on organized crime.

B. STATE AND LOCAL CRIMINAL ENFORCEMENT RESOURCES

1. POLICE

Estimates of the number of police agencies in the United States have varied. In 1967, in the Task Force Report: the Police, President's Commission on Law Enforcement and the Administration of Justice, a 40,000 figure was cited. In 1989, the figure given was approximately 12,000.[b] In the Uniform Crime Reports for 2003, it was noted that 14,072 city, county and state police agencies, representing a population of more than 274 million, existed.

Most of these agencies are found in small government units, and a great many have only a handful of law enforcement officers. In 2003, these state and local agencies employed approximately 663,796 police officers.

2. PROSECUTORS

The district or county attorney in most states is a locally elected official. In larger communities the prosecutor heads a large staff of assistants; most prosecutors however, work in very small offices, and in many jurisdictions, the entire prosecutor's office may function on a part-

---

b. Sourcebook of Criminal Justice Statistics (U.S. Dept. of Justice 1991) 44.

time basis. A rough estimate is that there are between 25 and 30 thousand state and local prosecutors nationwide.

The attorneys general in a few states have full responsibility for all criminal prosecutions in the state and directly supervise local prosecutors. While many state attorneys general have the formal authority (through constitutional or statutory provisions or the common law) to supervise and coordinate local law enforcement activity, in most states this authority is not exercised. Compare with this the more centralized organization of the prosecutorial function of the federal criminal justice system.

C. FEDERAL AND STATE CRIMINAL CASELOAD

In 2004, 71,022 criminal cases involving 93,349 defendants were filed in the U.S. District Courts. Based upon the experience in prior years, it is estimated that more than two thirds of these cases involved felonies. During the period from 1955 to 2004, total criminal filings in the district courts ranged from a low of about 28,000 cases (1956–61 and 1980) to a high of 71,022 (2004). During the period since 1930, although the nature of the crimes prosecuted and the types of cases have changed, total federal filings have remained within a limited range, averaging about 35,000 cases annually, though this figure may now be somewhat higher because of an increase in the number of filings in recent years. The total number of federal felony filings nationwide continues to be less than 10 percent of the total number of state filings for the entire country.

Countrywide, case filing data at the state level are very difficult to obtain because of incomplete reporting, inconsistent definitions used for defining felonies and counting cases filed, and the fact that some states report aggregated data for both felonies and misdemeanors. Reports from all 50 states indicate that in 1996 close to 998,000 felony cases were filed.

Data collected by the United States Sentencing Commission show the general breakdown of the types of cases prosecuted in each year and trends for selected types of cases. The figures below show the breakdown of case types in 2003 and the trends for selected offenses from 2000–2004.[c]

c. This data is published yearly on the Sentencing Commission's internet site, <http://www.ussc.gov> as part of the Commission's Sourcebook of Federal Sentencing Statistics.

Figure A

DISTRIBUTION OF OFFENDERS IN EACH PRIMARY OFFENSE CATEGORY[1]
Fiscal Year 2003

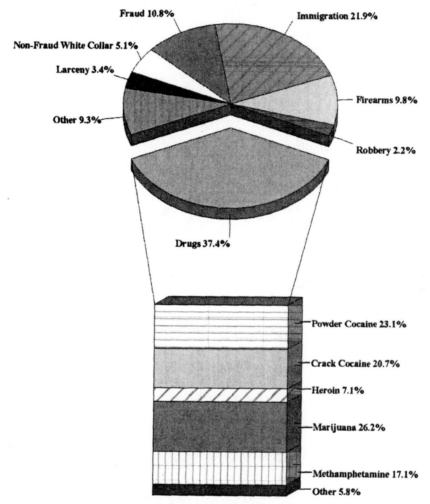

[1] Of the 70,258 guideline cases, 578 were excluded due to missing primary offense category. An additional 667 cases were excluded due to missing drug type. The Drug category includes the following offense types: Trafficking, Use of a Communication Facility, and Simple Possession. The Non–Fraud White Collar-category includes the following offense types: Embezzlement, Forgery/Counterfeiting, Bribery, Money Laundering, and Tax.

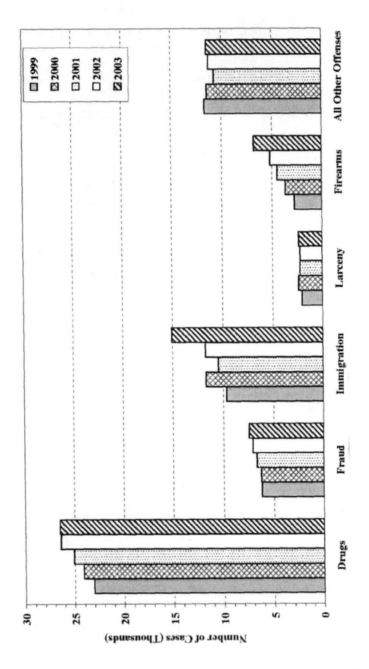

Figure B

NUMBER OF GUIDELINE OFFENDERS IN SELECTED OFFENSE TYPES[1]

Fiscal Years 1999 - 2003

[1] Drug offenses in this bar chart include: trafficking, use of a communication facility, and simple possession. Data in this figure represent information from USSC's ongoing data files; therefore, data points may vary from prior Source-books.

SOURCE: U.S. Sentencing Commission, 1999–2003 Datafiles, USSCFY99–USSCFY03.

More precise data are also available. The following table gives a breakdown according to crime category of federal criminal filings in the district courts from 2000 to 2004:

Table D–2

U.S. District Courts—Criminal Cases Commenced, by Major Offense (Excluding Transfers), During the 12–Month Periods Ending September 30, 2000 Through 2004

Table D-2. Cases
U.S. District Courts—Criminal Cases Commenced, by Major Offense (Excluding Transfers), During the 12-Month Periods Ending September 30, 2000 Through 2004

Nature of Proceedings and Offense	2000	2001	2002	2003	2004	Percent Change 2004 Over 2003
TOTAL	62,152	62,134	68,452	70,012	70,397	.4
PROCEEDINGS COMMENCED BY						
INDICTMENT	39,469	41,191	45,041	47,629	48,118	1.0
INFORMATION—INDICTMENT WAIVED	10,701	9,509	10,104	11,088	11,116	.3
INFORMATION—OTHER	8,160	8,058	7,975	7,653	8,473	10.7
REMANDED FROM APPELLATE COURT	83	64	123	96	47	-51.0
REMOVED FROM STATE COURT	30	36	24	30	26	-13.3
REOPENED/REINSTATED	66	38	61	69	78	13.0
APPEAL FROM U.S. MAGISTRATE JUDGE	83	113	105	81	59	-27.2
JUVENILE DELINQUENCY PROCEEDINGS	239	171	160	185	150	-18.9
CONSENT BEFORE MAGISTRATE JUDGE	978	1,019	1,071	1,442	1,239	-14.1
RETRIAL ON MISTRIAL	76	60	69	55	39	-29.1
RETRIAL—REMAND FROM APPEALS COURT	95	74	71	84	84	.
VIOLATION NOTICE	2,172	1,801	1,648	1,680	968	-42.4
GENERAL OFFENSES						
HOMICIDE, TOTAL [2]	370	329	370	311	200	-35.7
MURDER—FIRST DEGREE	334	292	313	261	151	-42.1
MURDER—SECOND DEGREE	7	9	15	13	11	-15.4
MANSLAUGHTER	29	28	42	37	38	2.7
ROBBERY, TOTAL	1,258	1,355	1,292	1,123	1,209	7.7
BANK	1,219	1,325	1,239	1,085	1,177	8.5
POSTAL	25	16	27	20	17	-15.0
OTHER	14	14	26	18	15	-16.7
ASSAULT [2]	685	622	633	811	955	17.8
BURGLARY—BREAKING AND ENTERING, TOTAL	69	52	44	46	60	30.4
BANK	.	.	.	.	.	.
POSTAL	13	11	12	13	16	23.1
INTERSTATE SHIPMENTS	.	1	1	.	3	.
OTHER	46	40	31	33	41	24.2

Table D-2. Cases (September 30, 2004—Continued)

Nature of Proceedings and Offense	2000	2001	2002	2003	2004	Percent Change 2004 Over 2003
LARCENY AND THEFT, TOTAL	3,414	3,242	3,138	3,103	2,878	-7.3
BANK	276	244	173	179	102	-43.0
POSTAL	455	445	489	438	389	-11.2
INTERSTATE SHIPMENTS	164	160	184	177	147	-16.9
OTHER U.S. PROPERTY	1,828	1,798	1,798	1,782	1,771	.5
TRANSPORTATION. ETC. OF STOLEN PROPERTY	249	209	212	166	155	-6.6
OTHER	442	386	302	361	314	-17.6
EMBEZZLEMENT, TOTAL	1,200	1,072	1,075	962	841	-12.6
BANK	667	580	516	403	329	-18.4
POSTAL	242	226	274	282	242	-14.2
OTHER	291	266	285	277	270	-2.5
FRAUD, TOTAL	7,788	7,585	8,204	8,092	7,539	-6.8
INCOME TAX	581	457	447	433	496	14.5
LENDING INSTITUTION	1,303	1,194	1,095	958	898	-6.1
POSTAL	1,117	1,129	1,118	1,039	1,031	-.8
VETERANS AND ALLOTMENTS	5	1	8	8	1	
SECURITIES AND EXCHANGE	94	88	120	109	90	-17.4
SOCIAL SECURITY	640	536	1,091	978	672	-31.3
FALSE PERSONATION	39	34	37	27	29	7.4
NATIONALITY LAWS	364	398	239	301	242	-19.6
PASSPORT FRAUD	281	253	261	411	449	9.2
FALSE CLAIMS AND STATEMENTS	1,258	1,394	1,845	1,661	1,646	-.9
OTHER	2,106	2,096	2,143	2,169	1,985	-8.5
AUTO THEFT	199	180	152	131	141	7.6
FORGERY AND COUNTERFEITING, TOTAL	1,203	1,212	1,193	1,078	889	-17.5
TRANSPORTATION OF FORGED SECURITIES	-	-	-	-	-	
POSTAL FORGERY	-	-	-	-	-	
OTHER FORGERY	131	100	111	93	83	-10.8
COUNTERFEITING	1,072	1,112	1,082	985	806	-18.2
SEX OFFENSES, TOTAL	944	1,017	1,187	1,325	1,638	23.6
SEXUAL ABUSE	431	428	514	552	607	10.0
OTHER	513	589	673	773	1,031	33.4

Table D-2. Cases (September 30, 2004—Continued)

Nature of Proceedings and Offense	2000	2001	2002	2003	2004	Percent Change 2004 Over 2003
DRUGS	17,585	18,425	19,215	18,996	18,440	-2.9
MISCELLANEOUS GENERAL OFFENSES, TOTAL	12,544	13,190	14,897	16,432	16,300	-.8
BRIBERY	145	131	118	101	137	35.6
DRUNK DRIVING AND TRAFFIC	4,679	4,958	5,148	5,084	4,593	-9.7
ESCAPE	635	582	562	519	435	-16.2
EXTORTION, RACKETEERING, AND THREATS	557	486	594	479	495	3.3
GAMBLING AND LOTTERY	17	6	10	11	9	-18.2
KIDNAPPING	111	104	96	124	117	-5.6
PERJURY	113	137	114	84	80	-4.8
WEAPONS AND FIREARMS	5,367	5,845	7,382	9,075	9,352	3.1
OTHER	900	961	960	955	1,082	13.3
SPECIAL OFFENSES						
IMMIGRATION LAWS	12,150	11,277	12,575	15,490	17,021	10.5
LIQUOR, INTERNAL REVENUE	9	3	2	1	-	-
FEDERAL STATUTES, TOTAL	2,944	2,573	2,384	2,281	2,286	.2
AGRICULTURE/CONSERVATION LAWS	316	262	232	226	258	14.2
ANTITRUST VIOLATIONS	43	28	24	11	12	9.1
FOOD AND DRUG LAW	52	70	59	46	46	-
MIGRATORY BIRD LAWS	52	56	74	126	81	-35.7
MOTOR CARRIER LAW	5	3	2	3	5	-
NATIONAL DEFENSE LAWS	535	464	147	76	50	-34.2
CIVIL RIGHTS	82	77	63	51	69	35.3
CONTEMPT	109	158	107	73	84	15.1
CUSTOMS LAWS	97	79	78	72	75	4.2
POSTAL LAWS	112	135	129	122	117	-4.1
OTHER	1,441	1,221	1,469	1,475	1,489	.9

NOTE: THIS TABLE INCLUDES ALL FELONY AND CLASS A MISDEMEANOR CASES, BUT INCLUDES ONLY THOSE PETTY OFFENSE CASES THAT HAVE BEEN ASSIGNED TO DISTRICT JUDGES.
PERCENT CHANGE IS COMPUTED ON 10 OR MORE CASES.
IN 2003, A CHANGE IN CODING CAUSED SOME CASES THAT PREVIOUSLY WOULD HAVE BEEN CLASSIFIED AS HOMICIDE CASES TO BE REPORTED AS AGGRAVATED ASSAULT CASES. THEREFORE, TOTALS FOR 2003 AND THEREAFTER ARE NOT COMPARABLE TO TOTALS FOR PREVIOUS YEARS.
INCLUDES ESCAPE FROM CUSTODY, AIDING OR ABETTING AN ESCAPE, FAILURE TO APPEAR IN COURT, AND BAIL JUMPING.
OBSTRUCTING MAIL, MAILING NONMAILABLE MATERIAL, AND OTHER POSTAL REGULATIONS.

Chapter 3

SCOPE OF THE FEDERAL CRIMINAL LAWS

As an introduction to the offenses that in subsequent chapters will be addressed in depth, we examine in this chapter the general scope of the federal criminal laws. Every federal offense has two dimensions—its jurisdictional reach and its substantive coverage. The federal criminal law differs from the usual state penal code insofar as the Congress does not have plenary authority to enact crime legislation; there are jurisdictional limits on what the federal government can do in dealing with crime. Two questions addressed in this chapter are: 1) what substantive limits are placed on the coverage of federal criminal statutes by jurisdictional limits (either constitutional in origin or based in statutory language)? 2) Do these limits result in criminal code coverage that is coherent and rational?

A. BASES FOR FEDERAL CRIMINAL JURISDICTION

In addressing the limits on federal authority, it is convenient to distinguish between those features that involve the protection of direct federal interests and those that do not. As we shall see later, the lines between these categories are not always clear. For present purposes, direct federal interests can be defined as those that involve the protection of federally-owned property, persons employed by the federal government or the federal purse.

Congress' authority to enact criminal statutes aimed at protecting the direct interests of the federal government is derived from certain of the enumerated powers set forth in Section 8 of the Constitution, e.g. the power "to provide for the Punishment of counterfeiting the Securities and * * * Coin of the United States," plus the power to "provide for * * * the general Welfare of the United States," and is supplemented by the last paragraph in Section 8, which provides that Congress shall have the power—

To make all Laws which shall be necessary and proper for carrying into Execution the foregoing Powers, and all other Powers vested by this Constitution in the Government of the United States, or in any Department or Officer thereof.

Because significant issues of law and policy are raised in connection with the federal system's role in protecting interests other than those that are directly federal, in this chapter we focus mainly on the use of federal criminal authority to protect such interests. Congress' authority to enact criminal statutes not aimed at protecting direct federal interests is always based in one of the enumerated powers. The three enumerated powers most frequently relied upon are the commerce power, the postal power and the taxing power. In modern times, the commerce power has been used more frequently than the other enumerated powers as the jurisdictional basis for federal crimes. An important early use of the postal power is the mail fraud statute, 18 U.S.C. § 1341. The taxing power was the jurisdictional base for most federal drug enforcement laws until 1970 when a new comprehensive federal drug statute based in the commerce power was substituted for the prior laws. We focus in this chapter on the commerce power.

The commerce power is set forth in Article I, Section 8 of the Constitution, which provides that "The Congress shall have Power * * * to regulate Commerce * * * among the several States * * * ". Jurisdiction under the commerce power has been based on various kinds of connections to interstate commerce.

In *United States v. Lopez*, 514 U.S. 549 (1995), the Supreme Court summarized the commerce power basis for federal jurisdiction in the following terms:

> In . . . [*NLRB v. Jones & Laughlin Steel Corp.*, 301 U.S. 1 (1937)] , the Court warned that the scope of the interstate commerce power "must be considered in the light of our dual system of government and may not be extended so as to embrace effects upon interstate commerce so indirect and remote that to embrace them, in view of our complex society, would effectually obliterate the distinction between what is national and what is local and create a completely centralized government." . . . * * *

Consistent with this structure, we have identified three broad categories of activity that Congress may regulate under its commerce power. First, Congress may regulate the use of the channels of interstate commerce. Second, Congress is empowered to regulate and protect the instrumentalities of interstate commerce, or persons or things in interstate commerce, even though the threat may come only from intrastate activities. Finally, Congress' commerce authority includes the power to regulate those activities having a substantial relation to interstate commerce, i. e., those activities that substantially affect interstate commerce.

Initially, we describe and summarize the different legislative approaches to commerce power jurisdiction in formulating federal crimes and present materials that address some of the special problems that arise under the different approaches. Later in this chapter, we shall examine in more depth three substantive crime areas—the Travel Act, the Violence Against Women Act, and firearms offenses—that illustrate the kinds of jurisdictional issues that can arise and how they interact with the substantive criminal law applied under the statutes in question.

1. TRANSPORTATION ETC. IN INTERSTATE COMMERCE

The earliest approaches to federal criminal jurisdiction under the commerce power typically were based on the direct crossing of an interstate boundary by way of the transporting or shipping of a physical object or the traveling of a person. Reliance on this type of commerce power basis for federal criminal jurisdiction was upheld by a majority of the Supreme Court in *Champion v. Ames (The Lottery Case)*, 188 U.S. 321 (1903) where the specific items, lottery tickets, were transported interstate. Four justices in dissent argued that a lottery ticket did not become an article of commerce simply because it was transported interstate; that "[t]his in effect breaks down all the differences between that which is, and that which is not, an article of commerce, and the necessary consequence is to take from the states all jurisdiction over the subject as far as interstate communication is concerned[;] * * * [that this] is a long step in the direction of wiping out all traces of state lines, and the creation of a centralized government."

Subsequently, the constitutionality of the exercise of federal criminal authority based on the transportation of the victim across a state line was firmly established by the decision in *Hoke v. United States*, 227 U.S. 308 (1913), in which the Supreme Court sustained the constitutionality of the Mann Act, 36 Stat. at L. 325, Ch. 395 enacted in 1910, which made it a federal crime knowingly to transport or aid or assist in obtaining transportation for, in interstate or foreign commerce any woman or girl for the purpose of prostitution or debauchery, or for any other immoral purpose.

The decisions in the *Lottery Case* and in *Hoke* laid the constitutional foundation for congressional enactment, in the 1930's and earlier, of a series of federal criminal statutes involving criminal conduct combined with interstate movement or transportation: e.g. the Dyer Act (interstate transportation of stolen motor vehicles), 18 U.S.C. §§ 2311–13; the Lindbergh Law (interstate transportation of a kidnapped person), 18 U.S.C. §§ 1201–02; the National Stolen Property Act, 18 U.S.C. §§ 2314–15; and the Fugitive Felon Act, 18 U.S.C. § 1073.

The transportation or movement in commerce approach to federal criminal jurisdiction has been used frequently in the decades since the 1930's, but in its modern guise, it has been expanded and is being used more imaginatively. The early statutes emphasized transportation or movement of a prohibited item or an element involved in the criminal activity, such as the victim. That approach is still being used, e.g. 18 U.S.C. § 2251—transporting in commerce a visual or print medium which depicts sexually explicit conduct involving children. The § 2251 offense also extends to instances where the accused knows or has reason to know that the material will be transported in commerce. Other modern examples include interstate travel in aid of specified criminal activity made criminal under 18 U.S.C. § 1952 (the Travel Act) and the federal carjacking statute that proscribes taking by force or violence a motor vehicle "that has been transported, shipped, or received in inter-state * * * commerce." 18 U.S.C. § 2119. Jurisdiction is also being based today on the transportation in commerce of items or parts of items that are not themselves prohibited or, on their face, connected to criminal activity. For example, jurisdiction under the electronic surveil-lance statute, 18 U.S.C. § 2511(1)(b)(iii), can be based upon the fact that the accused knows or has reason to know that the electronic device being used *or a component thereof* has been transported in commerce.

Jurisdiction has been expanded to apply not only to the transporta-tion of corporeal objects but also to the crossing of a state boundary by communications and electronic signals. Thus, jurisdiction under some statutes is based on the transmission in commerce of prohibited commu-nications—e.g. ransom or extortion communications under 18 U.S.C. § 875 or wagering information under 18 U.S.C. § 1084. The federal criminal net is spread even wider when jurisdiction is based merely on the use of a communication facility, e.g., a telephone call involving communications across a state border in aid of specified criminal activity again under 18 U.S.C. § 1952. A similar approach is found in 18 U.S.C. § 1343, transmission by means of wire, etc. communication in commerce in aid of a fraudulent scheme—that is, wire fraud. Until recently, case law under such provisions required that the transmission or communica-tion cross a state line, but that body of f law appears to be still evolving and may be undergoing an important change. See *infra*, p. 93.

Notes

1. Reliance on interstate travel or transportation as the jurisdictional element in federal criminal statutes has had a number of consequences:

a. From the very beginning of congressional enactment of federal offenses aimed essentially at ordinary crimes such as auto theft, prostitution, and kidnapping, the legislative approach has been to define these statutes in a rather odd way; the central element of the offense was, for example, transportation in interstate commerce, not the egregious conduct itself—viz. the theft etc. Thus as Professor Louis B. Schwartz wrote in a pioneering article, *Federal Criminal Jurisdiction and Prosecutors' Discretion*, 13 LAW & CONTEMP. PROBS. 64, 79 (1948):

Attention and controversy [have] tend[ed] to focus on the jurisdictional problem rather than the substantive issues of criminality.

b. There are also odd gaps in the legislative coverage. For example, a large scale auto theft ring whose activities affected commerce might not be the subject of federal prosecution if the vehicles were not in fact transported across a state line.

Professor Schwartz proposed a legislative approach to deal with both the problem of defining offenses in jurisdictional terms and the gaps in coverage:

> Rationalization of the federal penal code would call for definitions of federal crimes in terms of the significant criminal conduct. The jurisdictional features necessary to give federal authorities power to act should be brought together in a comprehensive definition. . . . Schwartz, *supra* at 80.

In 1970, he was able to give effect to these ideas as the principal drafter of a new Federal Criminal Code proposed by the National Commission on Reform of the Federal Criminal Laws, which he served as Director. This Code was not enacted, nor were subsequent codification bills that were introduced into the Congress over the course of the succeeding decade. *See* L.B. Schwartz, *Reform of the Federal Criminal Laws: Issues, Tactics, and Prospects*, 41 LAW & CONTEMP. PROBS. 1 (1977).

c. Despite such comments by academics and legislative proposals over the course of the last half century, Congress still continues in specific statutes to make a single jurisdictional element such as interstate travel, transportation or the like into the central element of the federal offense.

d. It should be noted, however, that increasingly federal criminal statutes are being drafted in a way to make the jurisdictional basis more comprehensive. Further, legislation such as the Racketeer Influenced and Corrupt Organizations (RICO) statute has also served to broaden and make more comprehensive the net of federal criminal liability. What is perplexing is the inconsistency in the congressional approach on this issue. What arguments are there against adopting a comprehensive jurisdictional approach in every federal criminal statute?

2. A related question is whether transportation or movement across a state line constitutes an adequate index of federal concern to warrant a federal prosecution of conduct traditionally dealt with at the local level. Professor Schwartz noted that, "The use of a particular jurisdictional circumstance in the definition of a federal crime only very crudely marks off the area in which . . . [there is justification for federal prosecution]." Schwartz, *supra* note 1 at p. 79. Of course, movement across a state line in the course of criminal conduct can be, and often is, merely a matter of happenstance. Is it relevant that the chances that criminal conduct will involve a crossing of a state boundary are likely to be greater in the geographically small states of the northeastern United States, or in those cities that lie across a state line such as Kansas City, or if the city, town or other locale in which the conduct arises happens to be close to a state border. Judge Henry Friendly has put the point more sharply:

> Why should the federal government care if a Manhattan businessman takes his mistress to sleep with him in Greenwich, Connecticut, although it would not if the lovenest were in Port Chester, N.Y.? Why should it make a difference that a New York pimp chooses Newark, N.J., rather than Nyack, N.Y., as the place where his employees transact their business? If the house is in Nyack, why is the United States interested because the girls have traveled over the

George Washington bridge and thence through New Jersey although it would not be if they crossed the Hudson over the New York Thruway? HENRY FRIENDLY, FEDERAL JURISDICTION, A GENERAL VIEW 58 (1973).

2. AFFECTING COMMERCE

a. *Inclusion of the Jurisdictional Element in the Definition of the Crime—The Hobbs Act*

Another jurisdictional basis derived from Congress' power to regulate commerce among the states is "effect" on commerce or, in the active voice, something that "affects" interstate commerce. Although in the earlier years of federal criminal legislation this basis was not used as frequently as the movement-across-a-state-line basis, in recent decades this jurisdictional approach in legislating federal crimes has gained increasing favor.

The earliest adoption in a major federal criminal statute of effect upon commerce as the jurisdictional peg was the enactment of the Anti–Racketeering Act in 1934, which provided in pertinent part: "Any person who, in connection with or in relation to any act in any way or in any degree affecting trade or commerce * * * [obtains money by force] commits a federal offense." 48 Stat. 979, ch. 569, section 2. This formula was carried forward when the Hobbs Act, 18 U.S.C. § 1951(a), amending the Anti–Racketeering Act, was passed. The Hobbs Act provides: "Whoever in any way or degree obstructs, delays, or affects commerce * * * by robbery or extortion * * *." 18 U.S.C. § 1951(a). For discussion of the history of the Hobbs Act and its relationship to its predecessor statute, see *United States v. Culbert*, 435 U.S. 371 (1978); *United States v. Local 807*, 315 U.S. 521 (1942).

Prior to its incorporation into federal criminal statutes, there was a substantial body of case law in the economic, non-criminal sphere addressing the constitutionality of various applications of the effect on commerce formula. This history is summarized in *Perez v. United States*, *infra* p. 26 and *United States v. Lopez*, *infra*, 30. For present purposes, it suffices to note that at an early date, it became clear that the Supreme Court was prepared to uphold federal regulation of local matters under the commerce power, provided that there was a sufficient demonstration of the effects of the intrastate activities on interstate commerce. *See Houston E. & W. Texas Ry. Co. v. United States*, 234 U.S. 342 (1914) (ICC authority upheld to order an end to an intrastate rate structure which discriminated against interstate traffic). *See generally*, Robert Cushman, *The National Police Power Under the Commerce Clause of the Constitution*, 3 MINN.L.REV. 289, 381 (1919).

Given this background, the constitutionality of the Hobbs Act had seemed clear. Finally in *United States v. Green*, 350 U.S. 415, 420–421 (1956), with a brief statement, the Supreme Court upheld this exercise of congressional power. A few years later, in *Stirone v. United States*, 361 U.S. 212 (1960), the Court commented that the language of the Hobbs

Act manifests "a purpose to use all the constitutional power Congress has to punish interference with interstate commerce by extortion, robbery, or physical violence." *Id.* at 215.

In the last several decades, the jurisdictional approach used in the Hobbs Act has been extended to a number of other crimes. For example, the credit card fraud statute, 15 U.S.C. § 1644, proscribes use of a forged, stolen or fraudulently obtained card in a transaction affecting commerce. Under the RICO statute, 18 U.S.C. §§ 1961–68, federal jurisdiction is based on the fact that an enterprise, which may be related in any one of several ways to a pattern of racketeering activity, is engaged in, or the activities of which affect, commerce. The electronic surveillance statute, 18 U.S.C. § 2511(1)(b)(iv), provides penalties for the willful use of an electronic device to intercept an oral communication when such use "takes place on the premises of any business or other commercial establishment the operations of which affect interstate * * * commerce * * * or is for the purpose of obtaining information relating to the operations of * * * [such a] business or other commercial establishment." Recall that the Hobbs Act applies to a robbery or extortion which affects commerce. Do RICO or the electronic surveillance provision extend federal jurisdiction farther than the Hobbs Act? If so, in what respect? For treatment of the jurisdictional issue under RICO, see *infra* pp. 498–499.

Issues that arise in connection with the "affecting commerce" formula and concerns about this approach are quite different from those that attach to the transportation or travel across a state line jurisdictional basis. Whereas in the latter category of cases, the principal issues relate to gaps in coverage and the fortuitous nature of the occurrence of the jurisdictional facts, in the affecting commerce cases, the main issues relate to identifying the theory on which effect on commerce can be based and how much effect is needed, both for constitutional purposes and as a matter of statutory interpretation.

Pre-*Lopez* case law

In describing how the "affecting commerce" formula in the Hobbs Act has been interpreted , it is convenient to describe the state of the law prior to the decision in *United States v. Lopez*, 514 U.S. 549 (1995) and subsequent to that decision. We describe the pre-Lopez case law here and the post-*Lopez* law following the opinion in *Lopez*, *infra*, p. 30. Pre-*Lopez*, the courts of appeals used a number of different theories, but generally, the concept of effect on commerce was given a very expansive interpretation. A central question in the post-*Lopez* period is whether and to what extent that expansive approach must be scaled back.

Under one of the prevalent theories, pre-*Lopez*, the question was posed, did the criminal activity deplete the assets of the victim so that the victim had less funds available to make purchases that would have involved goods shipped in interstate commerce? Numerous cases upheld the sufficiency of the jurisdictional element on a depletion of assets theory, that is, that there was an effect on a business's potential as a purchaser of "interstate" items. *United States v. DeMet*, 486 F.2d 816 (7th Cir.1973); *United States v. Mazzei*, 521 F.2d 639 (3d Cir.1975); *United States v. Crowley*, 504 F.2d 992 (7th Cir.1974) (alternate ground).

Another theory used was that commerce was interfered with because the extortion prevented use of an item that had been recently shipped in commerce. *Battaglia v. United States*, 383 F.2d 303 (9th Cir.1967). *See also United States v. Kuta*, 518 F.2d 947 (7th Cir.1975).

On occasion, a more elaborate and creative theory of cause and effect was relied upon. *See United States v. Wright*, 797 F.2d 245 (5th Cir. 1986) in which a city attorney was charged with violating the Hobbs Act by extorting money from a law firm and its clients in exchange for not prosecuting "driving while intoxicated" cases. The court of appeals affirmed a decision that there was proof of sufficient effect on interstate commerce, based upon expert testimony that failure to prosecute drunk driving cases encourages more drunk driving, which jeopardizes highway safety by causing more accidents and thereby interferes with travel on interstate highways.

The prevailing view was also that a minimal or de minimis effect on commerce is sufficient. *United States v. Demet*, *supra*. In *United States v. Jarrett*, 705 F.2d 198 (7th Cir.1983), a Hobbs Act conviction based on the robbery of a local retail store was upheld. The court rejected the argument that although a de minimis effect on commerce was sufficient in extortion cases, more of an effect was required in Hobbs Act robbery prosecutions. Are there any other reasons why such a distinction might be drawn?

For many years, there were relatively few prosecutions for robbery under the Hobbs Act. Department of Justice policy provided that the robbery provision of the statute was to be used "only in instances involving organized crime or wide-ranging schemes." In recent years, however, there have been an increasing number of robbery prosecutions based in the Hobbs Act.

The Supreme Court's opinion in *United States v. Lopez*, *infra* p. 30 precipitated a large number of challenges to the sufficiency of the showing of jurisdictional facts in Hobbs Act prosecutions, especially in the cases prosecuted under the robbery clause of the statute. We address the issues generated by *Lopez*, infra pp. 42–55.

b. Jurisdiction Based on Effect on Commerce Without Including the Jurisdictional Element in the Definition of the Offense: The Class of Activities Approach

The "affecting" commerce approach used in the Hobbs Act required the government to prove such effect in each individual prosecution. It was not until enactment of the of the Consumer Credit Protection Act of 1964, 18 U.S.C. § 891 et seq. and the decision in *Perez v. United States*, 402 U.S. 146 (1971) that the effect on commerce was applied and approved as a basis for jurisdiction over a traditional crime category without requiring proof of the effect in the particular case.

In *Perez*, the Supreme Court addressed the question of whether Title II of the Act was a valid exercise of congressional authority under the commerce clause. Section 892 declared it a federal crime punishable by a maximum of 20 years imprisonment to make an extortionate extension of credit or to conspire to do so. An extortionate extension of credit was defined in section 891(6) as one with respect to which it is the understanding of the creditor and the debtor that delay in or failure to make repayment could result in the use of violence or other criminal means. The statutory description of the offense did not contain a provision requiring proof of a connection to commerce in the individual prosecution. The congressional findings in the first section of the legislation did provide:

> "(1) Organized crime is interstate and international in character. Its activities involve many billions of dollars each year. It is directly responsible for murders, willful injuries to person and property, corruption of officials, and terrorization of countless citizens. A substantial part of the income of organized crime is generated by extortionate credit transactions.

> "(3) Extortionate credit transactions are carried on to a substantial extent in interstate and foreign commerce and through the means and instrumentalities of such commerce. Even where extortionate credit transactions are purely intrastate in character, they nevertheless directly affect interstate and foreign commerce."

The defendant in *Perez* was a loan shark who engaged in extortionate credit transactions, that is, he used the threat of violence (threatening to send his victim and his family to the hospital with a broken back or legs) as a method of collection of loans as to which he demanded ever-increasing payments.

Justice Douglas, speaking for the Court, reviewed several Supreme Court cases from the economic sphere on the reach of the commerce power, including *Wickard v. Filburn*, 317 U.S. 111 (1942) and *United States v. Darby*, 312 U.S. 100 (1941):

> [In] *Wickard* v. *Filburn*, 317 U.S. 111, a unanimous Court held that wheat grown wholly for home consumption was constitutionally within the scope of federal regulation of wheat production because, though never marketed interstate, it supplied the need of the grower which otherwise would be satisfied by his purchases in the open market. We said:

>> "Even if appellee's activity be local and though it may not be regarded as commerce, it may still, whatever its nature, be reached by Congress if it exerts a substantial economic effect on interstate commerce, and this irrespective of whether such effect is what might at some earlier time have been defined as 'direct' or 'indirect' ". 317 U.S., at 125.

In *United States v. Darby*, 312 U.S. 100, the decision sustaining an Act of Congress which prohibited the employment of workers in the production of goods "for interstate commerce" at other than prescribed wages and hours, a class of activities was held properly regulated by Congress without proof that the particular intrastate activity against which a sanction was laid had an effect on commerce. . . .

That case is particularly relevant here because it involved a criminal prosecution, a unanimous Court holding that the Act was "sufficiently definite to meet constitutional demands." Petitioner is clearly a member of the class which engages in "extortionate credit transactions" as defined by Congress and the description of that class has the required definiteness. * * *

Where the class of activities is regulated and that class is within the reach of federal power, the courts have no power "to excise, as trivial, individual instances" of the class. *Maryland v. Wirtz*, 392 U.S. 183, 193.

Extortionate credit transactions, though purely intrastate, may in the judgment of Congress affect interstate commerce. In an analogous situation, Mr. Justice Holmes, speaking for a unanimous Court, said: "[W]hen it is necessary in order to prevent an evil to make the law embrace more than the precise thing to be prevented it may do so." *Westfall v. United States*, 274 U.S. 256, 259. In that case an officer of a state bank which was a member of the Federal Reserve System issued a fraudulent certificate of deposit and paid it from the funds of the state bank. It was argued that there was no loss to the Reserve Bank. Mr. Justice Holmes replied, "But every fraud like the one before us weakens the member bank and therefore weakens the System." In the setting of the present case there is a tie in between local loan sharks and interstate crime.

The Court proceeded to describe various studies, reports and hearings, concluding:

The essence of all these reports and hearings was summarized and embodied in formal congressional findings. They supplied Congress with the knowledge that the loan shark racket provides organized crime with its second most lucrative source of revenue, exacts millions from the pockets of people, coerces its victims into the commission of crimes against property, and causes the takeover by racketeers of legitimate businesses.

We have mentioned in detail the economic, financial, and social setting of the problem as revealed to Congress. We do so not to infer that Congress need make particularized findings in order to legislate. We relate the history of the Act in detail to answer the impassioned plea of petitioner that all that is involved in loan sharking is a traditionally local activity. It appears, instead, that loan sharking in its national setting is one way organized interstate crime holds its guns to the heads of the poor and the rich alike and syphons funds from numerous localities to finance its national operations.

Notes

1. Could Congress, after *Perez*, have enacted federal criminal statutes dealing with a broad range of criminal activity without requiring a showing of a link to commerce in the individual case? What kind of legislative findings would Congress have to make? Consider the following statement:

> "[S]ince the total economic impact of almost any class of criminal activity substantially injures interstate business, most traditionally local crimes could be federalized, under a broad construction of the commerce power." Note, 49 Tex.L.Rev. 1100, 1111 (1971).

2. The broadest jurisdictional peg in the pre–1960's commerce power criminal statutes was found in the Hobbs Act. Did *Perez* appear to open the door to a more extensive use of the commerce power than was available under the Hobbs Act?

3. *Perez* relieves the prosecutor of the burden of having to prove a link to commerce in the individual case. Also, as an incident thereof, a possible mens rea issue with respect to the jurisdictional element is removed. How significant are these changes in prevailing doctrine? Are they necessarily a positive development? See Norman Abrams, *Report on Jurisdiction*, 1 Working Papers, Nat. Com'n on Reform of Fed.Crim.L. 33, 43 (1970).

4. As a result of *Perez*, did it appear that Congress could draft criminal offenses in the same form used in state penal codes? Stated another way, did it become easier for Congress to define offenses in terms of the harmful conduct rather than the jurisdictional element?

5. Which of the changes suggested in the preceding paragraphs—viz. enlargement of federal law enforcement authority; relieving prosecutors of having to prove federal jurisdiction in the individual case; or making it easier for Congress to define crimes in traditional criminal law terms—would be likely to have the most impact on the nature of the federal criminal law and its enforcement?

6. The statute involved in *Perez*, the Consumer Credit Protection Act, was enacted in 1964. Two other important federal criminal statutes which did not contain a jurisdictional commerce element but were based in the commerce power were enacted in 1970: the Comprehensive Drug Abuse Prevention and Control Act, (see ch. 9, pp. 330–333 infra) and the illegal gambling business statute, (*see* infra, p. 631). It is noteworthy that the RICO statute, enacted at the same time did contain a jurisdictional element in the statutory description of the offense. Until the 1990's, Congress did not use a class of activities approach very often in the enactment of other criminal statutes. In 1990, however, the Gun–Free School Zones Act was enacted; in 1992, The Child Support Recovery Act was passed. In 1994, The Freedom of Access to Clinic Entrances Act became law. A challenge to the constitutionality of the Gun–Free School Zones Act was the first of these statutes to reach the Supreme Court.

UNITED STATES v. LOPEZ

514 U.S. 549, 115 S.Ct. 1624, 131 L.Ed.2d 626 (1995).

CHIEF JUSTICE REHNQUIST delivered the opinion of the Court.

In the Gun–Free School Zones Act of 1990, Congress made it a federal offense "for any individual knowingly to possess a firearm at a place that the individual knows, or has reasonable cause to believe, is a school zone." 18 U.S.C. § 922 (q)(1)(A) (1988 ed., Supp. V). The Act neither regulates a commercial activity nor contains a requirement that the possession be connected in any way to interstate commerce. We hold that the Act exceeds the authority of Congress "to regulate Commerce * * * among the several States * * *."

On March 10, 1992, respondent, who was then a 12th-grade student, arrived at Edison High School in San Antonio, Texas, carrying a concealed .38 caliber handgun and five bullets. Acting upon an anonymous tip, school authorities confronted respondent, who admitted that he was carrying the weapon. He was arrested and charged under Texas law with firearm possession on school premises. The next day, the state charges were dismissed after federal agents charged respondent by complaint with violating the Gun–Free School Zones Act of 1990.

* * *

* * * The District Court conducted a bench trial, found him guilty of violating § 922(q), and sentenced him to six months' imprisonment and two years' supervised release. On appeal, respondent challenged his conviction based on his claim that § 922(q) exceeded Congress' power to legislate under the Commerce Clause. The Court of Appeals for the Fifth Circuit agreed and reversed respondent's conviction. It held that, in light of what it characterized as insufficient congressional findings and legislative history, "section 922(q), in the full reach of its terms, is invalid as beyond the power of Congress under the Commerce Clause." Because of the importance of the issue, we granted certiorari, and we now affirm.

* * * Congress' commerce authority includes the power to regulate those activities having a substantial relation to interstate commerce, i.e., those activities that substantially affect interstate commerce.

Within this final category, admittedly, our case law has not been clear whether an activity must "affect" or "substantially affect" interstate commerce in order to be within Congress' power to regulate it under the Commerce Clause. We conclude, consistent with the great weight of our case law, that the proper test requires an analysis of whether the regulated activity "substantially affects" interstate commerce.

We now turn to consider the power of Congress, in the light of this framework, to enact § 992(q). * * * [I]f § 922(q) is to be sustained, it must be * * * as a regulation of an activity that substantially affects interstate commerce.

First, we have upheld a wide variety of congressional Acts regulating intrastate economic activity where we have concluded that the activity substantially affected interstate commerce. Examples include the regulation of intrastate coal mining, intrastate extortionate credit transactions, restaurants utilizing substantial interstate supplies, inns and hotels catering to interstate guests, and production and consumption of home-grown wheat. These examples are by no means exhaustive, but the pattern is clear. Where economic activity substantially affects interstate commerce, legislation regulating that activity will be sustained.

Even *Wickard*, [Wickard v. Filburn, 317 U.S. 111 (1942)] which is perhaps the most far reaching example of Commerce Clause authority over intrastate activity, involved economic activity in a way that the possession of a gun in a school zone does not. Roscoe Filburn operated a small farm in Ohio, on which, in the year involved, he raised 23 acres of wheat. It was his practice to sow winter wheat in the fall, and after harvesting it in July to sell a portion of the crop, to feed part of it to poultry and livestock on the farm, to use some in making flour for home consumption, and to keep the remainder for seeding future crops. The Secretary of Agriculture assessed a penalty against him under the Agricultural Adjustment Act of 1938 because he harvested about 12 acres more wheat than his allotment. The Court said,

> "It can hardly be denied that a factor of such volume and variability as home-consumed wheat would have a substantial influence on price and market conditions. This may arise because being in marketable condition such wheat overhangs the market and, if induced by rising prices, tends to flow into the market and check price increases. But if we assume that it is never marketed, it supplies a need of the man who grew it which would otherwise be reflected by purchases in the open market. Home-grown wheat in this sense competes with wheat in commerce."

Section 922(q) is a criminal statute that by its terms has nothing to do with "commerce" or any sort of economic enterprise, however broadly one might define those terms. Section 922(q) is not an essential part of a larger regulation of economic activity, in which the regulatory scheme could be undercut unless the intrastate activity were regulated. It cannot, therefore, be sustained under our cases upholding regulations of activities that arise out of or are connected with a commercial transaction, which viewed in the aggregate, substantially affects interstate commerce.

Second, § 922(q) contains no jurisdictional element which would ensure, through case-by-case inquiry, that the firearm possession in question affects interstate commerce. * * *

Although as part of our independent evaluation of constitutionality under the Commerce Clause we of course consider legislative findings, and indeed even congressional committee findings, regarding effect on interstate commerce the Government concedes that "neither the statute nor its legislative history contain[s] express congressional findings regarding the effects upon interstate commerce of gun possession in a school zone." We agree with the Government that Congress normally is not required to make formal findings as to the substantial burdens that an activity has on interstate commerce. But to the extent that congressional findings would enable us to evaluate the legislative judgment that the activity in question substantially affected interstate commerce, even though no such substantial effect was visible to the naked eye, they are lacking here.

* * *

The Government's essential contention, in fine, is that we may determine here that § 922(q) is valid because possession of a firearm in a local school zone does indeed substantially affect interstate commerce. The Government argues that possession of a firearm in a school zone may result in violent crime and that violent crime can be expected to affect the functioning of the national economy in two ways. First, the costs of violent crime are substantial, and, through the mechanism of insurance, those costs are spread throughout the population. Second, violent crime reduces the willingness of individuals to travel to areas within the country that are perceived to be unsafe. The Government also argues that the presence of guns in schools poses a substantial threat to the educational process by threatening the learning environment. A handicapped educational process, in turn, will result in a less productive citizenry. That, in turn, would have an adverse effect on the Nation's economic well-being. As a result, the Government argues that Congress could rationally have concluded that § 922(q) substantially affects interstate commerce.

We pause to consider the implications of the Government's arguments. The Government admits, under its "costs of crime" reasoning, that Congress could regulate not only all violent crime, but all activities that might lead to violent crime, regardless of how tenuously they relate to interstate commerce. Similarly, under the Government's "national productivity" reasoning, Congress could regulate any activity that it found was related to the economic productivity of individual citizens: family law (including marriage, divorce, and child custody), for example. Under the theories that the Government presents in support of § 922(q), it is difficult to perceive any limitation on federal power, even in areas such as criminal law enforcement or education where States historically have been sovereign. Thus, if we were to accept the Government's arguments, we are hard pressed to posit any activity by an individual that Congress is without power to regulate.

Although JUSTICE BREYER argues that acceptance of the Government's rationales would not authorize a general federal police power, he is unable to identify any activity that the States may regulate but Congress may not. JUSTICE BREYER posits that there might be some limitations on Congress' commerce power, such as family law or certain aspects of education. These suggested limitations, when viewed in light of the dissent's expansive analysis, are devoid of substance.

JUSTICE BREYER focuses, for the most part, on the threat that firearm possession in and near schools poses to the educational process and the potential economic consequences flowing from that threat. Specifically, the dissent reasons that (1) gun-related violence is a serious problem; (2) that problem, in turn, has an adverse effect on classroom learning; and (3) that adverse effect on classroom learning, in turn, represents a substantial threat to trade and commerce. This analysis would be equally applicable, if not more so, to subjects such as family law and direct regulation of education.

For instance, if Congress can, pursuant to its Commerce Clause power, regulate activities that adversely affect the learning environment, then, a fortiori, it also can regulate the educational process directly. Congress could determine that a school's curriculum has a "significant" effect on the extent of classroom learning. As a result, Congress could mandate a federal curriculum for local elementary and secondary schools because what is taught in local schools has a significant "effect on classroom learning," and that, in turn, has a substantial effect on interstate commerce.

JUSTICE BREYER rejects our reading of precedent and argues that "Congress . . . could rationally conclude that schools fall on the commercial side of the line." Again, JUSTICE BREYER's rationale lacks any real limits because, depending on the level of generality, any activity can be looked upon as commercial. Under the dissent's rationale, Congress could just as easily look at child rearing as "falling on the commercial side of the line" because it provides a "valuable service—namely, to equip [children] with the skills they need to survive in life and, more specifically, in the workplace." We do not doubt that Congress has authority under the Commerce Clause to regulate numerous commercial activities that substantially affect interstate commerce and also affect the educational process. That authority, though broad, does not include the authority to regulate each and every aspect of local schools.

Admittedly, a determination whether an intrastate activity is commercial or noncommercial may in some cases result in legal uncertainty. But, so long as Congress' authority is limited to those powers enumerated in the Constitution, and so long as those enumerated powers are interpreted as having judicially enforceable outer limits, congressional legislation under the Commerce Clause always will engender "legal uncertainty."

* * *

These are not precise formulations, and in the nature of things they cannot be. But we think they point the way to a correct decision of this case. The possession of a gun in a local school zone is in no sense an economic activity that might, through repetition elsewhere, substantially affect any sort of interstate commerce. Respondent was a local student at a local school; there is no indication that he had recently moved in interstate commerce, and there is no requirement that his possession of the firearm have any concrete tie to interstate commerce.

To uphold the Government's contentions here, we would have to pile inference upon inference in a manner that would bid fair to convert congressional authority under the Commerce Clause to a general police power of the sort retained by the States. Admittedly, some of our prior cases have taken long steps down that road, giving great deference to congressional action. The broad language in these opinions has suggested the possibility of additional expansion, but we decline here to proceed any further. To do so would require us to conclude that the Constitution's enumeration of powers does not presuppose something not enumerated, and that there never will be a distinction between what is truly national and what is truly local. This we are unwilling to do.

For the foregoing reasons the judgment of the Court of Appeals is Affirmed.

JUSTICE KENNEDY, with whom JUSTICE O'CONNOR joins, concurring.

. . . . The statute makes the simple possession of a gun within 1,000 feet of the grounds of the school a criminal offense. In a sense any conduct in this interdependent world of ours has an ultimate commercial origin or consequence, but we have not yet said the commerce power may reach so far. If Congress attempts that extension, then at the least we must inquire whether the exercise of national power seeks to intrude upon an area of traditional state concern.

An interference of these dimensions occurs here, for it is well established that education is a traditional concern of the States. The proximity to schools, including of course schools owned and operated by the States or their subdivisions, is the very premise for making the conduct criminal. In these circumstances, we have a particular duty to ensure that the federal-state balance is not destroyed.

While it is doubtful that any State, or indeed any reasonable person, would argue that it is wise policy to allow students to carry guns on school premises, considerable disagreement exists about how best to accomplish that goal. In this circumstance, the theory and utility of our federalism are revealed, for the States may perform their role as laboratories for experimentation to devise various solutions where the best solution is far from clear.

If a State or municipality determines that harsh criminal sanctions are necessary and wise to deter students from carrying guns on school premises, the reserved powers of the States are sufficient to enact those measures. Indeed, over 40 States already have criminal laws outlawing the possession of firearms on or near school grounds.

Other, more practicable means to rid the schools of guns may be thought by the citizens of some States to be preferable for the safety and welfare of the schools those States are charged with maintaining. These might include inducements to inform on violators where the information leads to arrests or confiscation of the guns, programs to encourage the voluntary surrender of guns with some provision for amnesty, penalties imposed on parents or guardians for failure to supervise the child, laws providing for suspension or expulsion of gun-toting students, or programs for expulsion with assignment to special facilities.

The statute now before us forecloses the States from experimenting and exercising their own judgment in an area to which States lay claim by right of history and expertise, and it does so by regulating an activity beyond the realm of commerce in the ordinary and usual sense of that term. The tendency of this statute to displace state regulation in areas of traditional state concern is evident from its territorial operation. There are over 100,000 elementary and secondary schools in the United States. Each of these now has an invisible federal zone extending 1,000 feet beyond the (often irregular) boundaries of the school property. In some communities no doubt it would be difficult to navigate without infringing on those zones. Yet throughout these areas, school officials would find their own programs for the prohibition of guns in danger of displacement by the federal authority unless the State chooses to enact a parallel rule.

* * *

For these reasons, I join in the opinion and judgment of the Court.

[Justice Thomas also wrote a separate concurring opinion. Justice Breyer, with whom Justice Stevens, Souter and Ginsburg joined wrote a dissenting opinion, and Justice Souter also wrote a separate dissent.]

c. *Post–Lopez Developments*

Notes

1. Since the decision in *Lopez*, the Supreme Court has returned to the same issues in two cases, *United States v. Morrison*, 529 U.S. 598 (2000), and *Gonzales v. Raich*, 125 S.Ct. 2195 (2005).

a. Although not a criminal case, *Morrison*, like *Lopez*, held that a federal statute exceeded Congress' power under the Commerce Clause. Accordingly, the case has been repeatedly cited and relied upon by criminal defendants seeking to strike down the particular commerce power-based statute under which they had been prosecuted. Morrison involved a civil suit under the provisions of the Violence Against Women Act (VAWA), 42 U.S.C. § 13981. The plaintiff, alleging that she had been raped by the defendants all of whom were students at the Virginia Polytechnic Institute, sought a federal civil remedy under § 13981 as a victim of gender-motivated violence. Chief Justice Rehnquist wrote the Opinion of the Court:

> Petitioners * * * seek to sustain § 13981 as a regulation of activity that substantially affects interstate commerce. Given § 13981's focus on gender-motivated violence wherever it occurs (rather than violence directed at the instrumentalities of interstate commerce, interstate markets, or things or persons in interstate commerce), we agree that this is the proper inquiry. * * *

> Both petitioners and Justice SOUTER's dissent downplay the role that the economic nature of the regulated activity plays in our Commerce Clause analysis. But a fair reading of *Lopez* shows that the noneconomic,

criminal nature of the conduct at issue was central to our decision in that case. * * *

The second consideration that we found important in analyzing [the statute in Lopez] was that the statute contained "no express jurisdictional element which might limit its reach to a discrete set of firearm possessions that additionally have an explicit connection with or effect on interstate commerce." Such a jurisdictional element may establish that the enactment is in pursuance of Congress' regulation of interstate commerce.

Third, we noted that neither [the statute] 'nor its legislative history contain[s] express congressional findings regarding the effects upon interstate commerce of gun possession in a school zone.' "

Finally, our decision in *Lopez* rested in part on the fact that the link between gun possession and a substantial effect on interstate commerce was attenuated. The United States argued that the possession of guns may lead to violent crime, and that violent crime "can be expected to affect the functioning of the national economy in two ways. First, the costs of violent crime are substantial, and, through the mechanism of insurance, those costs are spread throughout the population. Second, violent crime reduces the willingness of individuals to travel to areas within the country that are perceived to be unsafe." The Government also argued that the presence of guns at schools poses a threat to the educational process, which in turn threatens to produce a less efficient and productive work force, which will negatively affect national productivity and thus interstate commerce.

We rejected these "costs of crime" and "national productivity" arguments because they would permit Congress to "regulate not only all violent crime, but all activities that might lead to violent crime, regardless of how tenuously they relate to interstate commerce." We noted that, under this but-for reasoning: "Congress could regulate any activity that it found was related to the economic productivity of individual citizens: family law (including marriage, divorce, and child custody), for example. Under the[se] theories ..., it is difficult to perceive any limitation on federal power, even in areas such as criminal law enforcement or education where States historically have been sovereign. Thus, if we were to accept the Government's arguments, we are hard pressed to posit any activity by an individual that Congress is without power to regulate."

With these principles underlying our Commerce Clause jurisprudence as reference points, the proper resolution of the present cases is clear. Gender-motivated crimes of violence are not, in any sense of the phrase, economic activity. While we need not adopt a categorical rule against aggregating the effects of any noneconomic activity in order to decide these cases, thus far in our Nation's history our cases have upheld Commerce Clause regulation of intrastate activity only where that activity is economic in nature.

Like the Gun–Free School Zones Act at issue in *Lopez,* § 13981 contains no jurisdictional element establishing that the federal cause of action is in pursuance of Congress' power to regulate interstate commerce. Although *Lopez* makes clear that such a jurisdictional element would lend support to the argument that § 13981 is sufficiently tied to interstate commerce,

Congress elected to cast § 13981's remedy over a wider, and more purely intrastate, body of violent crime.

* * *

In contrast with the lack of congressional findings that we faced in *Lopez*, § 13981 *is* supported by numerous findings regarding the serious impact that gender-motivated violence has on victims and their families. But the existence of congressional findings is not sufficient, by itself, to sustain the constitutionality of Commerce Clause legislation. As we stated in *Lopez*, " '[S]imply because Congress may conclude that a particular activity substantially affects interstate commerce does not necessarily make it so.' " * * * In these cases, Congress' findings are substantially weakened by the fact that they rely so heavily on a method of reasoning that we have already rejected as unworkable if we are to maintain the Constitution's enumeration of powers. Congress found that gender-motivated violence affects interstate commerce "by deterring potential victims from traveling interstate, from engaging in employment in interstate business, and from transacting with business, and in places involved in interstate commerce; . . . by diminishing national productivity, increasing medical and other costs, and decreasing the supply of and the demand for interstate products." Given these findings and petitioners' arguments, the concern that we expressed in *Lopez* that Congress might use the Commerce Clause to completely obliterate the Constitution's distinction between national and local authority seems well founded. The reasoning that petitioners advance seeks to follow the but-for causal chain from the initial occurrence of violent crime (the suppression of which has always been the prime object of the States' police power) to every attenuated effect upon interstate commerce. If accepted, petitioners' reasoning would allow Congress to regulate any crime as long as the nationwide, aggregated impact of that crime has substantial effects on employment, production, transit, or consumption. Indeed, if Congress may regulate gender-motivated violence, it would be able to regulate murder or any other type of violence since gender-motivated violence, as a subset of all violent crime, is certain to have lesser economic impacts than the larger class of which it is a part.

Petitioners' reasoning, moreover, will not limit Congress to regulating violence but may, as we suggested in *Lopez*, be applied equally as well to family law and other areas of traditional state regulation since the aggregate effect of marriage, divorce, and childrearing on the national economy is undoubtedly significant. Congress may have recognized this specter when it expressly precluded § 13981 from being used in the family law context. Under our written Constitution, however, the limitation of congressional authority is not solely a matter of legislative grace.[7]

* * *

7. Justice SOUTER's theory [in dissent] that *Gibbons v. Ogden*, 9 Wheat. 1, 6 L.Ed. 23 (1824), *Garcia v. San Antonio Metropolitan Transit Authority*, 469 U.S. 528, 105 S.Ct. 1005, 83 L.Ed.2d 1016 (1985), and the Seventeenth Amendment provide the answer to these cases, is remarkable because it undermines this central principle of our constitutional system. As we have repeatedly noted, the Framers crafted the federal system of Government so that the people rights would be secured by the division of power. * * * Departing from their parliamentary past, the Framers

Petitioner Brzonkala's complaint alleges that she was the victim of a brutal assault. * * * If the allegations here are true, no civilized system of justice could fail to provide her a remedy for the conduct of respondent Morrison. But under our federal system that remedy must be provided by the Commonwealth of Virginia, and not by the United States.

[Justice Thomas wrote a concurring opinion. Justices Souter, Stevens, Ginsburg and Breyer dissented, first in an opinion by Justice Souter and then in an opinion by Justice Breyer in which Justice Stevens joined and Justices Souter and Ginsburg partially joined.].

b. *Gonzales v. Raich*, 125 S.Ct. 2195 (2005) is another recent case raising a *Lopez*-like issue, but after two decisions striking down federal statutory provisions on the ground that they exceed Congress's power under the commerce clause, this time the Court sustained the application of the commerce power to a local activity. The respondents sought to enjoin enforcement of the federal drug laws insofar as they made criminal the possession or manufacturing of marijuana for personal medical use. Justice Stevens (joined by Justices Kennedy, Souter, Breyer and Ginsburg, with Justice Scalia concurring in the judgment) wrote the Opinion of the Court:

The case is made difficult by respondents' strong arguments that they will suffer irreparable harm because, despite a congressional finding to the contrary, marijuana does have valid therapeutic purposes. The question before us, however, is not whether it is wise to enforce the statute in these circumstances; rather, it is whether Congress' power to regulate interstate markets for medicinal substances encompasses the portions of those markets that are supplied with drugs produced and consumed locally. Well-settled law controls our answer. The CSA is a *valid* exercise of federal power, even as applied to the troubling facts of this case. We accordingly vacate the judgment of the Court of Appeals. * * *

Our case law firmly establishes Congress' power to regulate purely local activities that are part of an economic "class of activities" that have a substantial effect on interstate commerce .. As we stated in

adopted a written Constitution that further divided authority at the federal level so that the Constitution provisions would not be defined solely by the political branches nor the scope of legislative power limited only by public opinion and the Legislature self-restraint. * * *

No doubt the political branches have a role in interpreting and applying the Constitution, but ever since *Marbury* this Court has remained the ultimate expositor of the constitutional text. * * *

Contrary to Justice SOUTER's suggestion, *Gibbons* did not exempt the commerce power from this cardinal rule of constitutional law. His assertion that, from *Gibbons* on, public opinion has been the only restraint on the congressional exercise of the commerce power is true only insofar as it contends that political accountability is and has been the only limit on Congress' exer-

cise of the commerce power *within that power's outer bounds*. As the language surrounding that relied upon by Justice SOUTER makes clear, *Gibbons* did not remove from this Court the authority to define that boundary.

We accordingly reject the argument that Congress may regulate noneconomic, violent criminal conduct based solely on that conduct's aggregate effect on interstate commerce. The Constitution requires a distinction between what is truly national and what is truly local. In recognizing this fact we preserve one of the few principles that has been consistent since the Clause was adopted. The regulation and punishment of intrastate violence that is not directed at the instrumentalities, channels, or goods involved in interstate commerce has always been the province of the States.

Wickard, "even if appellee's activity be local and though it may not be regarded as commerce, it may still, whatever its nature, be reached by Congress if it exerts a substantial economic effect on interstate commerce." We have never required Congress to legislate with scientific exactitude. When Congress decides that the " 'total incidence' " of a practice poses a threat to a national market, it may regulate the entire class. * * *

Our decision in *Wickard*, is of particular relevance. In *Wickard*, we upheld the application of regulations promulgated under the Agricultural Adjustment Act of 1938, which were designed to control the volume of wheat moving in interstate and foreign commerce in order to avoid surpluses and consequent abnormally low prices. The regulations established an allotment of 11.1 acres for Filburn's 1941 wheat crop, but he sowed 23 acres, intending to use the excess by consuming it on his own farm. Filburn argued that even though we had sustained Congress' power to regulate the production of goods for commerce, that power did not authorize "federal regulation [of] production not intended in any part for commerce but wholly for consumption on the farm." Justice Jackson's opinion for a unanimous Court rejected this submission. He wrote:

> "The effect of the statute before us is to restrict the amount which may be produced for market and the extent as well to which one may forestall resort to the market by producing to meet his own needs. That appellee's own contribution to the demand for wheat may be trivial by itself is not enough to remove him from the scope of federal regulation where, as here, his contribution, taken together with that of many others similarly situated, is far from trivial."

Wickard thus establishes that Congress can regulate purely intrastate activity that is not itself "commercial," in that it is not produced for sale, if it concludes that failure to regulate that class of activity would undercut the regulation of the interstate market in that commodity.

The similarities between this case and *Wickard* are striking. Like the farmer in *Wickard*, respondents are cultivating, for home consumption, a fungible commodity for which there is an established, albeit illegal, interstate market.[28] Just as the Agricultural Adjustment Act was designed "to control the volume [of wheat] moving in interstate and foreign commerce in order to avoid surpluses ..." and consequently control the market price, a primary purpose of the CSA [Controlled Substance Act] is to control the supply and demand of controlled substances in both lawful and unlawful drug markets. In *Wickard*, we had no difficulty concluding that Congress had a rational basis for believing that, when viewed in the aggregate, leaving home-consumed wheat outside the regulatory scheme would have a substantial influence on price and market conditions. Here too, Congress had a rational basis

---

28. Even respondents acknowledge the existence of an illicit market in marijuana; indeed, Raich has personally participated in that market, and Monson expresses a willingness to do so in the future. * * *

for concluding that leaving home-consumed marijuana outside federal control would similarly affect price and market conditions.

More concretely, one concern prompting inclusion of wheat grown for home consumption in the 1938 Act was that rising market prices could draw such wheat into the interstate market, resulting in lower market prices. The parallel concern making it appropriate to include marijuana grown for home consumption in the CSA is the likelihood that the high demand in the interstate market will draw such marijuana into that market. While the diversion of homegrown wheat tended to frustrate the federal interest in stabilizing prices by regulating the volume of commercial transactions in the interstate market, the diversion of homegrown marijuana tends to frustrate the federal interest in eliminating commercial transactions in the interstate market in their entirety. In both cases, the regulation is squarely within Congress commerce power because production of the commodity meant for home consumption, be it wheat or marijuana, has a substantial effect on supply and demand in the national market for that commodity.[29]

In assessing the scope of Congress' authority under the Commerce Clause, we stress that the task before us is a modest one. We need not determine whether respondents' activities, taken in the aggregate, substantially affect interstate commerce in fact, but only whether a "rational basis" exists for so concluding. Given the enforcement difficulties that attend distinguishing between marijuana cultivated locally and marijuana grown elsewhere and concerns about diversion into illicit channels, we have no difficulty concluding that Congress had a rational basis for believing that failure to regulate the intrastate manufacture and possession of marijuana would leave a gaping hole in the CSA. Thus, as in *Wickard*, when it enacted comprehensive legislation to regulate the interstate market in a fungible commodity, Congress was acting well within its authority to "make all Laws which shall be necessary and proper" to "regulate Commerce ... among the several States." U.S. Const., Art. I, § 8. That the regulation ensnares some purely intrastate activity is of no moment. As we have done many times before, we refuse to excise individual components of that larger scheme.

To support their contrary submission, respondents rely heavily on two of our more recent Commerce Clause cases. In their myopic focus, they overlook the larger context of modern-era Commerce Clause jurisprudence preserved by those cases. Moreover, even in the narrow prism of respondents' creation, they read those cases far too broadly. Those two cases, of course, are *Lopez*, 514 U.S. 549, 131 L.Ed.2d 626, 115 S.Ct. 1624, and *Morrison*, 529 U.S. 598, 146 L.Ed.2d 658, 120 S.Ct. 1740. As an initial matter, the statutory challenges at issue in those cases were markedly different from the challenge respondents pursue in the case at hand. Here, respondents ask us to excise individual applications of a concededly valid statutory scheme. In contrast, in both *Lopez* and

29. To be sure, the wheat market is a lawful market that Congress sought to protect and stabilize, whereas the marijuana market is an unlawful market that Congress sought to eradicate. This difference, however, is of no constitutional import. It has long been settled that Congress' power to regulate commerce includes the power to prohibit commerce in a particular commodity.

Morrison, the parties asserted that a particular statute or provision fell outside Congress' commerce power in its entirety. This distinction is pivotal for we have often reiterated that where the class of activities is regulated and that class is within the reach of federal power, the courts have no power 'to excise, as trivial, individual instances' of the class."

At issue in *Lopez* was the validity of the Gun–Free School Zones Act of 1990, which was a brief, single-subject statute making it a crime for an individual to possess a gun in a school zone. 18 U.S.C. § 922(q)(1)(A). The Act did not regulate any economic activity and did not contain any requirement that the possession of a gun have any connection to past interstate activity or a predictable impact on future commercial activity. Distinguishing our earlier cases holding that comprehensive regulatory statutes may be validly applied to local conduct that does not, when viewed in isolation, have a significant impact on interstate commerce, we held the statute invalid.

We explained: "Section 922(q) is a criminal statute that by its terms has nothing to do with 'commerce' or any sort of economic enterprise, however broadly one might define those terms. Section 922(q) is not an essential part of a larger regulation of economic activity, in which the regulatory scheme could be undercut unless the intrastate activity were regulated. It cannot, therefore, be sustained under our cases upholding regulations of activities that arise out of or are connected with a commercial transaction, which viewed in the aggregate, substantially affects interstate commerce."

The statutory scheme that the Government is defending in this litigation is at the opposite end of the regulatory spectrum. * * * [T]he CSA, enacted in 1970 as part of the Comprehensive Drug Abuse Prevention and Control Act, 84 Stat. 1242–1284, was a lengthy and detailed statute creating a comprehensive framework for regulating the production, distribution, and possession of five classes of "controlled substances." Most of those substances—those listed in Schedules II through V—"have a useful and legitimate medical purpose and are necessary to maintain the health and general welfare of the American people." 21 U.S.C. § 801(1). The regulatory scheme is designed to foster the beneficial use of those medications, to prevent their misuse, and to prohibit entirely the possession or use of substances listed in Schedule I, except as a part of a strictly controlled research project.

While the statute provided for the periodic updating of the five schedules, Congress itself made the initial classifications. It identified 42 opiates, 22 opium derivatives, and 17 hallucinogenic substances as Schedule I drugs. 84 Stat. 1248. Marijuana was listed as the 10th item in the third subcategory. That classification, unlike the discrete prohibition established by the Gun–Free School Zones Act of 1990, was merely one of many "essential parts of a larger regulation of economic activity, in which the regulatory scheme could be undercut unless the intrastate activity were regulated." Our opinion in *Lopez* casts no doubt on the validity of such a program.

2. As the first decision in 60 years to strike down a federal statute on the ground that it violated the commerce clause, *Lopez* triggered a strong

reaction in the courts and in the law reviews. Constitutional challenges based on *Lopez* were mounted in cases involving criminal statutes that on their face did not directly involve commerce or economic enterprises (*e.g.* the Child Support Recovery Act and the Freedom of Access to Clinic Entrances Act), and *Lopez* was also relied upon as a basis for challenge in cases involving statutes that contained a jurisdictional element of affecting commerce (*e.g.* numerous Hobbs Act cases) or where the statutory definition made jurisdiction turn on the crossing of a state line There were *Lopez* challenges in the lower courts virtually to every criminal statute founded on the commerce clause.

While defendants had some initial success in the district courts in challenging the constitutional validity of some federal criminal statutes based on *Lopez*, the strong trend of decisions in the courts of appeal was to sustain the statutes against such attacks. Thus the courts of appeal consistently upheld the constitutionality of the Child Support Recovery Act and the Freedom of Access to Clinic Entrances Act, both of which contain congressional findings regarding the nexus to commerce but lacked any jurisdictional element in the description of the offense. As to the CSRA, *see, e.g. United States v. Bailey*, 115 F.3d 1222 (5th Cir.1997); *United States v. Mussari*, 95 F.3d 787 (9th Cir.1996); *United States v. Sage*, 92 F.3d 101 (2d Cir. 1996); and as to the FACEA, *see, e.g., United States v. Wilson*, 73 F.3d 675 (7th Cir.1995) and *United States v. Bird*, 124 F.3d 667 (5th Cir. 1997).

3. Is a substantial effect on commerce required under the Hobbs Act? *Lopez*, of course, did not involve a statute containing a jurisdictional-effect-on-commerce provision. Does the substantial effect approach taken in *Lopez* also apply where the definition of the crime contains such a jurisdictional element, as in the Hobbs statute? Post-*Lopez*, most of the courts of appeals did not change their view that it was not necessary that the charged extortion or robbery have a substantial effect on commerce. Thus some of the courts of appeal continued to rule that a de minimis effect on commerce is still the standard to be applied, *see, e.g., United States v. Smith*, 182 F.3d 452, 456 (6th Cir.1999) and cases cited therein. Some courts have continued to rely on the depletion of assets theory. See, e.g. *United States v. Nutall*, 180 F.3d 182, 186 (5th Cir.1999); *United States v. Woodruff*, 122 F.3d 1185 (9th Cir.1997). Another approach, which reaches the same conclusion but on a different rationale, is reflected in the following statement in *United States v. Guerra*, 164 F.3d 1358, 1361 (11th Cir.1999): "An individual defendant's conduct need not substantially affect commerce precisely because the Hobbs Act regulates general conduct—robberies and extortion—which in the aggregate affects commerce substantially."

4. Limits on the use of an aggregation approach—Whether individual similar instances can be automatically aggregated as suggested in *Guerra*, supra, note 3, or whether there must be some rational basis for finding sufficient connection between them is an issue that has split the Fifth Circuit Court of Appeals down the middle. The issues been addressed in two extensive en banc opinions, first in *United States v. Hickman*, 179 F.3d 230 (5th Cir.1999) and then in *United States v. McFarland*, 311 F.3d 376 (5th Cir. 2002). In both cases, Hobbs Act robbery convictions were affirmed by an equally divided court with only those judges who voted to reverse the convictions writing full opinions. In both cases, the Supreme Court denied

certiorari, *Hickman,* 530 U.S. 1203 (2000) and *McFarland,* 538 U.S. 962 (2003). We reproduce below the *McFarland* opinion which also quotes from the earlier *Hickman* case.

UNITED STATES v. McFARLAND

311 F.3d 376 (5th Cir. 2002).

Appeal from the United States District Court for the Northern District of Texas; TERRY R. MEANS, JUDGE.

Before KING, CHIEF JUDGE, GARWOOD, JOLLY, HIGGINBOTHAM, DAVIS, JONES, SMITH, WIENER, BARKSDALE, EMILIO M. GARZA, DEMOSS, BENAVIDES, STEWART, PARKER, DENNIS, and CLEMENT, CIRCUIT JUDGES.

PER CURIAM:

By reason of an equally divided *en banc* court, we affirm the district court's judgment of conviction and sentence.

* * *

GARWOOD, CIRCUIT JUDGE, with whom E. GRADY JOLLY, PATRICK E. HIGGINBOTHAM, EDITH H. JONES, JERRY E. SMITH, RHESA HAWKINS BARKSDALE, DEMOSS and CLEMENT, CIRCUIT JUDGES, join, dissenting:

We respectfully dissent from the evenly divided Court's per curiam, unexplained affirmance of these convictions. The nature of the case and our reasons for concluding that reversal is required are set forth below.

James McFarland, Jr. appeals his conviction of four counts of robbery of local convenience stores in Fort Worth, Texas, in violation of 18 U.S.C. § 1951 (the Hobbs Act) and four corresponding counts of using and carrying a firearm during and in relation to those robberies in violation of 18 U.S.C. § 924(c)(1). He challenges his conviction on the Hobbs Act counts, asserting that the evidence was insufficient to establish the constitutionally or statutorily required nexus to interstate commerce and that the jury charge respecting this element was defective.

* * *

Each of the four retail stores sold items of merchandise some of which the evidence showed were originally manufactured or processed outside of Texas. As to none of the three convenience stores was there any evidence indicating what fraction or percentage of their sales was of or allocable to items which had been manufactured or processed out of Texas, or what was the total dollar amount either of such sales or of all sales at the particular store.

* * *

The trial court's jury charge instructed, with reference to the Hobbs Act counts, that, among other things:

"If you decide that there is any effect at all of [sic] interstate commerce, then that is enough to satisfy this element. The effect can be minimal. A showing that a business regularly buys goods from out of state allows an inference that a robbery may impair a future purchase.... If you find beyond a reasonable doubt that the defendant's conduct affected interstate commerce, then you may conclude that the government has met its burden of proof as to the interstate commerce element of the offense."

McFarland objected to the word "any" in the first sentence above quoted, objected to the sentence "the effect can be minimal," and to the failure to include the word "substantially," as he had previously requested, between "conduct" and "interstate commerce" in the last above quoted sentence. These objections were all overruled.

... [T]he principal issue presented is whether the Hobbs Act extends, or may be applied consistent with the limitations of the Commerce Clause reflected by *Lopez* and *Morrison,* to these robberies of local retail stores.

The Hobbs Act, 18 U.S.C. § 1951, provides in relevant part:

"Whoever in any way or degree obstructs, delays, or affects commerce or the movement of any article or commodity in commerce, by robbery or extortion or attempts or conspires so to do, or commits or threatens physical violence to any person or property in furtherance of a plan or purpose to do anything in violation of this section shall be fined under this title or imprisoned not more than twenty years, or both.

* * *

(b) As used in this section—

(3) The term 'commerce' means commerce within the District of Columbia, or any Territory or Possession of the United States; all commerce between any point in a State, Territory, Possession, or the District of Columbia and any point outside thereof; all commerce between points within the same State through any place outside such State; and all other commerce over which the United States has jurisdiction."

* * *

We are aware of nothing in the legislative history relating or referring to the aggregation principle or anything comparable to it as applicable to discrete intrastate actions which individually have only a minimal, indirect and attenuated effect on interstate commerce.

This legislative history strongly suggests to us that Congress in enacting the Hobbs Act was concerned with protecting against relatively direct obstruction of the actual movement of goods in interstate commerce, and did not contemplate its application to robberies of local retail stores such as those here.[20] * * *

20. Moreover, so far as we are aware the 1934 Act was never applied to robberies of local retail stores such as those here, and for many years the Hobbs Act apparently was not either. *Cf. United States v. Enmons,* 410 U.S. 396, 93 S.Ct. 1007, 1015, 35 L.Ed.2d 379 (1973) (It is unlikely that if Congress had indeed wrought such a major

... [W]e conclude that to determine whether the Hobbs Act applies to these offenses we must examine the limits of the commerce power as articulated by the Supreme Court in *Lopez* and *Morrison*.

* * * In *Lopez* the Court "identified three broad categories of activity that Congress may regulate under its commerce power," namely:

"First, Congress may regulate the use of the channels of interstate commerce" * * *

"Second, Congress is empowered to regulate and protect the instrumentalities of interstate commerce, or persons or things in interstate commerce, even though the threat may come only from intrastate activities" (listing as examples " 'destruction of an aircraft,' " " 'thefts from interstate shipments,' " * * *

Third, "Congress' commerce authority includes the power to regulate those activities having a substantial relation to interstate commerce ... i.e. those activities that substantially affect interstate commerce....

Within this final category, admittedly, our case law has not been clear whether an activity must 'affect' or 'substantially affect' interstate commerce in order to be within Congress' power to regulate it under the Commerce Clause.... We conclude, consistent with the great weight of our case law, that the proper test requires an analysis of whether the regulated activity 'substantially affects' interstate commerce.' *United States v. Lopez*, 115 S.Ct. 1624 at 1629–30 (1995).

* * * *Morrison* held unconstitutional, as beyond Congress's power under the Commerce Clause, 42 U.S.C. § 13981, the civil action portion of the Violence Against Women Act of 1994. *Morrison* observes that "[p]etitioners do not contend that these cases fall within either of the first two categories of Commerce Clause regulation. They seek to sustain § 13981 as a regulation of activity that substantially affects interstate commerce.... [w]e agree that this is the proper inquiry." *Id.* at 1749. The Court held that section 13981 did not meet the requirements of the third *Lopez* category, stating "petitioners' reasoning would allow Congress to regulate any crime so long as the nationwide, aggregated impact

expansion of federal criminal jurisdiction in enacting the Hobbs Act, its action would have so long passed unobserved; also invoking principles of strict construction of criminal statutes and reluctance to assume significant change in relation between federal and state criminal jurisdiction in declining broad construction of Hobbs Act). Further, the "depletion of assets" theory, which is essentially the basis for Hobbs Act prosecutions such as that in this case, seems to have had its origin in *United States v. Provenzano*, 334 F.2d 678 (3d Cir.1964), where, in upholding a "depletion of assets" jury charge in a conviction for extorting $30,000 from an interstate trucking company to pre-

vent labor disruption of its terminal, the court stated:

"We can perceive no reason why extortive payments, *in substantial amounts*, paid as here from the treasury of a company *engaged in interstate* commerce in order *to avoid obstruction of the company interstate business* should not be deemed to affect commerce and therefore to lie within the proscription of the Hobbs Act.... This was the substance of the court charge. We hold it to have been a correct one in the light of *all the circumstances*." *Id.* at 693 (emphasis added).

of that crime has substantial effects on employment, production, transit, or consumption," contrary to the constitutionally required "distinction between what is truly national and what is truly local."

Th[e] ... category—"use of the channels of interstate commerce"—is clearly inapplicable to the present offenses, and the Government does not contend otherwise.

The Government contends that these offenses fall within *Lopez* category two because, according to the Government, the victim stores were engaged in interstate commerce, * * * and that therefore no "substantial" effect on interstate commerce had to be shown.

* * * [W]e reject the Government's contention that these are *Lopez* category two offenses. To begin with, simply because a business is engaged to any extent in interstate commerce does not alone suffice to bring regulation of any and all conduct involving it within category two. That category applies to "instrumentalities of interstate commerce," such as "an aircraft" or a railroad line, and to "persons or things in interstate commerce," such as "thefts from interstate shipments." Plainly, a local retail store is not analogous to any of those. The Government's argument would vastly expand *Lopez*'s category two, extending federal jurisdiction on a *per se,* categorical basis to a broad range of matters such as shoplifting of a candy bar from any business engaged in interstate commerce or children scuffling in any such business's parking lot, and would also blur the distinction between categories two and three.

* * *

We accordingly conclude that the issue of whether the Hobbs Act is properly applied to these robberies turns on whether such application meets the test of *Lopez* category three, as to which "the proper test requires an analysis of whether the regulated activity 'substantially affects' interstate commerce."

The evidence does not reflect any *particular, concrete* effect on interstate commerce that in fact *actually* resulted from any of the four robberies. But the evidence does support the conclusions that the victim stores each regularly used their funds to, among *other* things, purchase from local wholesalers inventory which *included* (but was *not* shown to be limited to) items manufactured out-of-state, and that the robberies reduced, by the amounts taken ($50, $100, $145, $1,500–2,000), the funds the stores would, but for the robbery, otherwise thereafter have had available for use in (or withdrawal from) their respective businesses, *including* (but not limited to) use for inventory purchasing. The evidence also shows that any reduction in a retailer's purchases from its wholesaler would reduce the funds the wholesaler would otherwise thereafter have had available for use in (or withdrawal from) its business, *including* (but *not* limited to) use for purchase of out-of-state merchandise. * * * Assuming that all this suffices to show that each individual robbery did probably or potentially have some minimal, attenuated and indirect affect on interstate commerce, it is clear that none individually had what could fairly be described as a "substantial" affect (actual, probable or potential).

The Government in this connection relies on the "aggregation" principle under which in determining whether the affect on interstate commerce is "substantial" the focus is not upon any one individual instance of the activity covered by the regulation but is rather upon whether the aggregate of all covered instances as a whole substantially affects interstate commerce. The validity of that general principle has long been clearly established, and is recognized in both *Lopez* and *Morrison.* At the same time, however, each of those decisions holds that the principle is not of universal or unlimited application, and refused to apply it to sustain the statutes there under consideration. Thus, in *Morrison* the Court recognized that the aggregate of instances of gender-motive violence within the scope of section 13981 did ultimately have a large effect on interstate commerce, but nevertheless held that the aggregation principle could not be applied. * * *

The central question in this case, then, is whether this Hobbs Act prosecution can be sustained under the aggregation theory. We now turn to that question.

Because the Hobbs Act has an interstate commerce related jurisdictional element and the statutes at issue in *Lopez* and *Morrison* contained no comparable provision, as the Supreme Court's opinions in those cases emphasized, some of our sister circuits have relied on this distinction (among other considerations) in holding that *Lopez* and *Morrison* are either largely inapplicable to Hobbs Act cases, or do not require that a substantial effect on interstate commerce be shown in Hobbs Act prosecutions falling under *Lopez* category three. We respectfully disagree. Such an approach would in effect either create a fourth category of commerce clause power, contrary to the plainly comprehensive three category approach taken in *Lopez* and *Morrison,* or would do away with the "substantially affect" requirement which those opinions so clearly state is constitutionally mandated in category three cases. Congress lacks the power to provide for a *lesser* relation to interstate commerce in *that* category of case simply by including a jurisdictional provision. Otherwise the principles enunciated in *Lopez* and *Morrison* would be essentially meaningless. * * *

This is not to say that the Hobbs Act jurisdictional element serves no function. It allows a determination in each case, based on its particular facts and characteristics, whether in that case application of the statute is consistent with Congress's Commerce Clause power. Because of that jurisdictional element the statute is not properly subject to being facially invalidated, which was essentially the result in *Lopez* and *Morrison* where the statutes involved lacked any jurisdictional element.

Some of our sister circuits have held that the refusal of *Lopez* and *Morrison* to apply the aggregation principle to sustain the statutes there under consideration is wholly inapplicable to the Hobbs Act because those statutes proscribed offenses which were not commercial or economic while robbery (or extortion, but we here deal only with robbery), which the Hobbs Act proscribes, is a commercial or economic activity as it always involves taking "personal property" from another person. * * *

We respectfully take a somewhat different view of the matter.

The approach of these cases seems to be that whenever the regulated activity is "economic," then, for purposes of *Lopez* category three cases, there are never any limits whatever to use of the aggregation theory and it may always be employed to satisfy (and as practical matter *will* always satisfy) the "substantially" affects requirement of *Lopez* category three. While this would seem, at least as a *practical* matter, to limit *Lopez* category three to cases where the regulated activity was non-economic and to obliterate any distinction in "economic" cases between the *Lopez* categories, we need not and do not reach that issue.

Assuming, *arguendo,* that there is a class of category three cases as to which there are no restraints whatever on aggregation, we conclude that such a class would *exclude* instances where "the regulated activity" is *not* properly described as "commercial" or "economic" *in the same general sense* as "commercial." [32]

Lopez and *Morrison* each refer to both "commercial" and "economic" activities and appear to use the terms synonymously. Thus *Lopez* states that section 922(q) does not "regulate[ ] a commercial activity" and that

> "Section 922(q) is not an essential part of a larger regulation of economic activity, in which the regulatory scheme could be undercut unless the intrastate activity were regulated. It cannot, therefore, be sustained under our cases upholding regulations of activities that arise out of or are connected with a *commercial transaction,* which viewed in the aggregate, substantially affects interstate commerce,"

and that

> "We do not doubt that Congress has authority under the Commerce Clause to *regulate* numerous *commercial activities* that substantially affect interstate commerce and also affect the educational process.... Admittedly, a determination *whether an* intrastate *activity* is *commercial or noncommercial* may in some cases result in legal uncertainty."

The last sentence above quoted is likewise quoted in *Morrison.*. Justice Kennedy, in his concurring opinion in *Lopez* (joined in by Justice

---

32. If "the regulated activity" is not "commercial" (or the regulation does not govern the conduct of a wholly or partially commercial enterprise or endeavor), that means merely that, in *Lopez* category three cases where there must be a "substantially affects" showing, then, whether or not aggregation is available depends on the considerations elaborated * * *below and in Judge Higginbotham's *Hickman* dissent. We need not and do not address whether such considerations (or similar ones) govern or limit the availability of aggregation for such purpose where the regulated intrastate activity is "commercial" (or the regulation does govern the conduct of a wholly or partially commercial enterprise or endeavor).

O'Connor and joining in Chief Justice Rehnquist's opinion for the Court) states:

> "Were the Federal Government to take over the regulation of entire areas of traditional state concern, areas having nothing to do with *the regulation* of *commercial activities,* the boundaries between the spheres of federal and state authority would blur and political responsibility would become illusory." *Id.* at 1638 (emphasis added).

The above passage is likewise quoted with approval in *Morrison.*

And, since what we are concerned with is the power of Congress under the Commerce Clause—the power "[t]o regulate Commerce with foreign Nations, and among the several States, and with the Indian Tribes"—"commercial" rather than simply any broadly understood concept of "economic" seems to be the appropriate concept.

Robbery is the "activity" regulated by the Hobbs Act, and we conclude that for these purposes robbery cannot be considered a commercial activity. Robbery does have an economic effect. But so, too, do not only all thefts of any kind from any victim but also, for example, virtually all criminal homicides. Moreover, the here relevant portion of the Hobbs Act, apart from simply specifying that the accused have committed a "robbery" which "in any way or degree . . . affects commerce" (although not requiring any intention to have or foreknowledge of such an effect), says nothing whatever about the identity, status or activity (whether as being engaged in any sort of commercial activity or otherwise) of either the victim or the robber, and does not purport to in any way regulate the conduct of any commercial activity. What is relevant in this connection under *Lopez* and *Morrison* is not the *effects* of the conduct which the statute proscribes but whether the statute may fairly be said to regulate commercial activity. * * *

We recognize that some decisions have taken the view that "the Hobbs Act regulates the interference with economic activity by robbery and for that reason alone an aggregation analysis is always *per se* appropriate and all that needs be shown is a depletion of assets.* * * However, as noted, the here relevant portion of the Hobbs Act says nothing about the victim being an "interstate entity." And, we are aware of no Commerce Clause case in which the Supreme Court has applied the aggregation principle to a class of activities where contours of the class are not reasonably inferable from the language of the challenged statute or regulation. Moreover, the approach of allowing aggregation simply because of "the infliction of economic harm" (or the "depletion of . . . assets") equally supports making a federal offense of any crime (say any criminal homicide or assault producing serious bodily injury) so long as it causes economic harm or depletes economic resources and hence in some way or degree affects interstate commerce—in the same sense as does a fifty dollar robbery or a fifty cent shoplifting from a victim (whether an individual or a local retailer) who purchases items made in another state-and so long as the aggregate effect of all such crimes on interstate commerce is substantial. Yet, *Morrison* rejects the notion that

Congress may regulate a crime simply because "the nationwide, aggregated impact of that crime has substantial effects on employment, production, transit, or consumption." *Lopez* and *Morrison* reflect that such a limitation on the aggregation principle is necessary because "[t]he Constitution requires a distinction between what is truly national and what is truly local," and "[t]he regulation and punishment of intrastate violence that is not directed at the instrumentalities, channels, or goods involved in interstate commerce has always been the province of the States." Certainly, none of the instant robberies can be characterized as "directed at the instrumentalities, channels, or goods involved in interstate commerce." Further, the several decisions refusing to find the Hobbs Act applicable to most robberies of individuals under theories of deletion of assets and aggregation of the effect on interstate commerce of all such robberies likewise support our view in this respect.

We turn now to the appropriate standards to determine whether in such a case the applicable *Lopez* category three "substantially affects" requirement can be met by aggregating the effects of all such robberies.

As previously observed, the aggregation principle has relevance only in *Lopez* category three cases, cases that are concerned only with regulation of intrastate conduct. As to such regulation, *Lopez's* explicit requirement that the regulated intrastate conduct not merely affect interstate commerce but that it do so "substantially" is obviously designed to insure that congressional power under the Commerce Clause is not wholly without meaningful limits and does not obliterate the "distinction between what is truly national and what is truly local."
* * *

Although the Supreme Court has on several occasions sustained federal statutes on the aggregation theory, it has never applied or even referred to it in a Hobbs Act case (nor is anything in the Hobbs Act legislative history supportive of such an approach). Nor since *Lopez* and *Morrison* has the Court made any general analysis or explanation of the contours of the doctrine.

* * * [I]n *United States v. Hickman,* 151 F.3d 446 (5th Cir.1998) (panel opinion), 179 F.3d 230 (5th Cir.1999) (en banc), we * * * addressed the requisite interstate commerce connection respecting Hobbs Act convictions for several robberies of retail establishments. The *Hickman* panel affirmed the convictions, * * * but expressed "serious questions" as to the propriety of applying the aggregation principle in that setting. The en banc court noted that "[b]y means of an equally divided en banc court, we affirm the counts of conviction," but no opinion for affirmance was issued. *Hickman,* 179 F.3d 230. Half the judges comprising the en banc court joined in a dissenting opinion by Judge Higginbotham urging reversal on the basis that, particularly in light of *Lopez,* the aggregation principle was not properly applicable to those Hobbs Act prosecutions.

Given the intervening decision in *Morrison* we revisit that issue and now express our essential agreement with the conclusions and underlying reasoning of Judge Higginbotham's *Hickman* opinion.[38] As stated in that opinion:

> "We would hold that substantial effects upon interstate commerce may not be achieved by aggregating diverse, separate individual instances of intrastate activity where there is no rational basis for finding sufficient connections among them. Of course, Congress may protect, enhance, or restrict some particular interstate economic market, such as those in wheat, credit, minority travel, abortion service, illegal drugs, and the like, and Congress may regulate intrastate activity as part of a broader scheme. The Hobbs Act is not a regulation of any relevant interstate economic market, nor are there other rational connections among nationwide robberies that would entitle Congress to make federal crimes of them all.

> The Hobbs Act does not target any class of product, process, or market, or indeed even commercial victims. It facially applies to any robbery, or its attempt, of any person or entity.... The Hobbs Act offers no 'regulatory scheme' which 'could be undercut' if individual robberies were not aggregated.... Thus, putting aside robberies as part of an effort to regulate particular interstate markets such as guns, drugs, or organized crime syndicates, a local robbery spree can be within Congress power only if it by itself has a substantial effect.

* * *

> "Where Congress has sought to regulate—protect, enhance, or restrict—some particular market such as wheat, credit, minority travel, or abortion service, it has pointed the way to a rational aggregation test. It has identified those things that affect that market, things which if not all subject to the regulation would erode the effort. Intrastate production and sales can be aggregated, because the prices of goods and services are determined in interstate markets. If, for example, the federal government enacts a price control to ensure sufficient income for producers, it will be thwarted if consumers switch to buying goods in intrastate commerce or produce the goods themselves. Because the instances of economic activity are intimately connected and in the aggregate substantially affect commerce, Congress can regulate such activity."

We also observe that not only does the Hobbs Act "not target any class of product, process or market or even commercial victims," but it has also been held to apply to robbery (or extortion) which adversely affects *illegal* commerce as well as to that which *beneficially* affects commerce. * * *

38. We recognize decisions of our sister circuits that continue after *Morrison* to apply an aggregation analysis to Hobbs Act prosecutions. *See, e.g., United States v. Elias,* 285 F.3d 183, 188–89 (2d Cir.2002); *United States v. Gray,* 260 F.3d 1267, 1273–74 (11th Cir.2001); *United States v. Peterson,* 236 F.3d 848, 852 (7th Cir.2001); *United States v. Malone,* 222 F.3d 1286, 1294–95 (10th Cir.2000). *But see United States v. Lynch,* 282 F.3d 1049, 1054 (9th Cir.2002); *United States v. Wang,* 222 F.3d 234, 240 (6th Cir.2000). For the reasons stated herein, we respectfully view the matter differently.

Where the Supreme Court has applied aggregation to uphold federal regulation of intrastate conduct against constitutional challenge under the Commerce Clause, there has always been a rational basis to find sufficient interrelationship or commonality of effect on interstate commerce among the discrete intrastate instances regulated and between them and a scheme of regulation (protection, enhancement or restriction) of some particular interstate market or activity such that the regulation of those intrastate activities can rationally be viewed as necessary to the effectiveness of or a meaningfully supporting part of the scheme of regulation of that particular interstate activity or market.

* * *

In *Perez v. United States,* 402 U.S. 146, 91 S.Ct. 1357, 28 L.Ed.2d 686 (1971), the Court sustained Perez's conviction for making an extortionate extension of credit contrary to the provisions of Title II of the Consumer Credit Protection Act of 1968, rejecting the contention that the statute was unconstitutional as not requiring proof that the particular transaction affected interstate commerce. The Court observed that "[p]etitioner is one of the species commonly known as 'loan sharks' which Congress found are in large part under the control of 'organized crime,' " citing congressional findings under Title II that "[o]rganized crime is interstate and international in character," that "[a] substantial part of the income of organized crime is generated by extortionate credit transactions," and that "[e]xtortionate credit transactions are carried on to a considerable extent in interstate and foreign commerce and through the means and instrumentalities of such commerce" and "[e]ven where ... purely intrastate in character ... directly affect interstate and foreign commerce." It also noted evidence before Congress that loan sharking was "the second largest source of revenue for organized crime" and is "controlled by organized criminal syndicates," that "through loan sharking the organized underworld has obtained control of legitimate businesses, including securities brokerages and banks," and concluded by stating that "loan sharking in its national setting is one way organized interstate crime ... syphons funds from numerous localities to finance its national operations."

The Court likewise noted that "[t]here was ample evidence showing petitioner was a 'loan shark' who used the threat of violence as a method of collection," and "[i]n the setting of the present case there is a tie-in between local loan sharks and interstate crime." * * *

Plainly, *Perez* dealt with a national market in credit, in which individual instances interact with each other by virtue of market forces. More significantly, perhaps, it dealt with a statute attempting to regulate a particular interstate activity, that of "organized interstate crime," which was financed by the both local and interstate loan sharking which it controlled. Moreover, *Perez* also relied on the principle that " 'when it is necessary in order to prevent an evil to make the law embrace more than the precise thing to be prevented it may do so' " and then observed "in the present case there is a tie-in between local loan sharks and interstate crime." This would appear to invoke the rule that where the same kind of trafficking is carried on both interstate and intrastate Congress in preventing the interstate trafficking may also proscribe the intrastate trafficking *where,* as a practical matter (for reasons such as the fungibility of the particular commodities or the like), it is necessary to regulate the intrastate trafficking in order to effectively regulate the interstate trafficking.

The present case does not involve the targeting of any particular interstate market or activity, and it is evident that the proscription of robberies which do not have the requisite effect on interstate commerce is in no sense necessary to effective regulation of those that do.

* * *

We recognize that "substantial" for purposes of *Lopez* category three has a qualitative as well as a quantitative aspect, though those two aspects are somewhat interrelated rather than being entirely independent of each other. Limits on the aggregation principle, necessary to give meaning to "substantial" so as to preserve the distinction between "what is truly national and what is truly local," should thus take into account both quantitative and qualitative considerations. We conclude that the limits we have outlined do so notwithstanding that their most obvious focus may be quantitative. To the extent that there is a meaningful, rational basis to aggregate, then the aggregated quantitative effect on interstate commerce tends to qualitatively justify viewing the matter as truly national rather than truly local. Conversely, that the regulated category three intrastate conduct is not a commercial activity but is rather essentially "the suppression of violent crime" is a qualitative consideration pointing towards the regulation being of a truly local nature *unless* there is a meaningful and rational basis for aggregation. There is no sufficient rational basis to aggregate the effects on interstate commerce of any of the four individual prototypically local crimes of violence here prosecuted with the effects on interstate commerce of all the undifferentiated mass of robberies covered by the Hobbs Act's general proscription of any and all robberies that "in any way or degree . . . affect [ ] commerce." * * *

The conviction on each of the Hobbs Act counts accordingly should be reversed. * * * We respectfully dissent from the affirmance of these convictions.

PATRICK E. HIGGINBOTHAM, CIRCUIT JUDGE, concurring in the dissent from the judgment affirming conviction, with whom GARWOOD, E. GRADY JOLLY and DeMOSS, CIRCUIT JUDGES, join:

For a second time this court has been unable to agree upon the bite of recent Supreme Court interpretations of the Commerce Clause. This should be no surprise. We are left adrift by a statute whose reach is at best no more fixed than a property line set at the latest low tide mark of an ocean tributary.

There is some certainty. The Supreme Court has turned away from the New Deal view that the reach of the Commerce Clause is to be largely defined by the political process. But the path it will follow and how far it will go are undecided. In turn, the respective roles of Congress and the courts in this enterprise remain uncertain. Add the Hobbs Act's unique effort to define its reach by proscribing all robberies over which there is federal jurisdiction—a wholly tautological statement made at the zenith of the judiciary's abandonment of the commerce field to the Congress—and we are left with three choices. We can take the Hobbs Act as a congressional punt and decide it ourselves, we can leave it to the political process, or we can invoke the dialogic process of the doctrine of clear statement. The first two options describe this court's division. Our court's impasse leads me to state the case for the third path. * * *

With the developing case law since *Hickman,* there is a step that principles of judicial restraint offer this inferior court before it decides if Congress has the authority under the Commerce Clause to make a federal crime of local robberies such as those before us here. It could insist that Congress first do what it has not done—make clear its purpose to reach the wholly intrastate activity charged in the crimes now before us. * * * [B]y the third path we ought to refuse to apply the Hobbs Act to this genre of local robberies until Congress clearly states its purpose to do so. Only then should the courts decide the commerce question now being pressed upon us.

The Supreme Court has long required that if Congress intends to alter "the usual constitutional balance between the States and the Federal Government," it must make an unmistakably clear statement of its intention to do so in the language of the statute. * * *

Notes

1. In *Hickman,* a half dozen robberies were committed by a small criminal group. In the original *Hickman* panel opinion, *United States v. Hickman,* 151 F.3d 446, 456 (5th Cir.1998), Judge Parker stated: "Without question, these robberies standing alone, or viewed cumulatively, do not substantially affect commerce." Judge Higginbotham in the *en banc* Hickman opinion stated, "if an organized criminal group committed various robberies that together substantially affected commerce, we would not doubt Congress's ability to prosecute a member of the group ... pursuant to an appropriate statute." At what point does a string of robberies committed by the same group have a substantial effect on commerce? What should be the significant determinants? The size of the group? the number of robberies? the kind of places robbed? the cumulative or individual "take" of the robberies? other factors? The U.S. Attorneys Manual Hobbs Act policy states that the robbery provision is to be utilized only in instances involving organized crime, or wide-ranging schemes. Do you think constitutional considerations were the basis for this policy limitation, or only conservation of prosecutorial resources? Was the *Hickman* or *McFarland* prosecution consistent with the USAM policy?

2. *Hickman* and *McFarland* deal with the effect of *Lopez* and subsequent Supreme Court cases on enforcement of the robbery provisions of the Hobbs Act.

a. What about other criminal statutes that include an effect on commerce as an element of the crime? The federal arson statute, 18 U.S.C. § 844(i) provides criminal penalties for "Whoever maliciously damages ... by means of fire or an explosive, any ... real or personal property used in interstate ... commerce or in any activity affecting interstate ... commerce." The early post-*Lopez* cases sustained the application of the affecting commerce formula against attacks based on *Lopez. See e.g. United States v. Tocco*, 135 F.3d 116 (2d Cir.1998) (*Lopez* did not elevate the government's burden in establishing jurisdiction under 844(i)); *United States v. Hicks*, 106 F.3d 187 (7th Cir.1997) (aggregation theory used in support of jurisdiction). In *Jones v. United States*, 529 U.S. 848 (2000), the Supreme Court avoided having to decide the effect of *Lopez* on a statutory effect-on-commerce jurisdiction provision by construing the statute not to reach the arson of an owner-occupied private residence. Justice Ginsburg writing for a unanimous Court stated:

> Construing the statute's text, we hold that an owner-occupied residence not used for any commercial purpose does not qualify as property "used in" commerce or commerce-affecting activity; arson of such a dwelling, therefore, is not subject to federal prosecution under § 844(i). Our construction of § 844(i) is reinforced by the Court's opinion in *United States v. Lopez*, 514 U.S. 549, 131 L.Ed.2d 626, 115 S.Ct. 1624 (1995), and the interpretive rule that constitutionally doubtful constructions should be avoided where possible....

* * *

> [T]he provision does, however, require that the building be "used" in an activity affecting commerce. That qualification is most sensibly read to mean active employment for commercial purposes, and not merely a passive, passing, or past connection to commerce.

b. *United States v. Robertson*, 514 U.S. 669 (1995), decided shortly after *Lopez*, has been frequently cited by the lower courts in addressing questions regarding the effect of *Lopez* on other commerce-based jurisdictional provisions. The following description of *Robertson* is taken from a portion of the *McFarland* case omitted from the case as reproduced supra, p. 43:

> The defendant was convicted ... and of violating 18 U.S.C. § 1962(a) (RICO) "by investing the proceeds of those unlawful activities in the 'acquisition of any interest in, or the establishment or operation of, any enterprise which is engaged in, or the activities of which affect, interstate or foreign commerce.'" The Ninth Circuit, in a pre-*Lopez* decision, ... reversed the RICO conviction, holding that the RICO enterprise—an Alaskan gold mine—was not shown to have "had more than an incidental effect on interstate commerce" and hence did not meet section 1962(a)'s "the activities of which affect, interstate ... commerce" requirement (without addressing the "engaged in ... interstate commerce" prong of section 1962(a)). *United States v. Robertson*,

15 F.3d 862, 868 (9th Cir.1994). The Ninth Circuit did not even mention, let alone discuss, the Commerce Clause or the limits of Congress's power thereunder. The Supreme Court, shortly after *Lopez*, reversed the Ninth Circuit's reversal of the RICO count, holding there was sufficient evidence that the gold mine was "engaged in ... interstate ... commerce" for purposes of section 1962(a). *Robertson*, 115 S.Ct. at 1733. It stated in this connection:

> ... *Robertson*, who resided in Arizona, made a cash payment of $125,000 for placer gold mining claims near Fairbanks. He paid approximately $100,000 (in cash) for mining equipment and supplies, some of which were purchased in Los Angeles and transported to Alaska for use in the mine. Robertson also hired and paid the expenses for seven out-of-state employees to travel to Alaska to work in the mine.... He again hired a number of employees from outside Alaska to work in the mine.

> * * *

> Furthermore, Robertson, the mine's sole proprietor, took $30,000 worth of gold, or 15% of the mine's total output, with him out of the State.

> Whether or not these activities met (and whether or not, to bring the gold mine within the 'affecting commerce' provision of RICO, they would have to meet) the requirement of substantially affecting interstate commerce, they assuredly brought the gold mine within 1962(a)'s alternative criterion of 'any enterprise ... engaged in ... interstate or foreign commerce.'

Robertson is a statutory construction case and does not purport to make any constitutional holding or to address (or recognize as being potentially before it) any constitutional issue, and it does not mention *Lopez* or discuss its three categories of Commerce Clause power.* * *

    c. Suppose the commerce-based jurisdictional element in a federal criminal statute is the crossing of a state line. After *Lopez* and its progeny, must there nevertheless be a substantial effect on commerce? In *United States v. Page*, 167 F.3d 325 (6th Cir. 1999), reproduced infra p. 84, the constitutionality of the criminal provisions of the Violence Against Women Act was challenged in reliance on *Lopez*. The statute contains the jurisdictional element of crossing a state line, but the defendant argued that after *Lopez* there must be a substantial effect on commerce to sustain a criminal statute that regulates non-economic activity, even one that contains a requirement that a crime victim must be taken across a state line. By an equally divided vote, the claim was rejected that *Lopez* had extended the "substantial effects" test to all commerce clause legislation, citing *United States v. Robertson*, supra note b.

    d. Federal criminal jurisdiction based on as little as one movement across a state boundary, can hardly be viewed as involving a "substantial" link to commerce. Thus, *United States v. Robertson* and *United States v. Page*, might be viewed as standing for the proposition that jurisdiction can be based on such an element even though it is not substantial. Does it make sense to require substantiality with respect to one kind of jurisdictional element, i.e. effect on commerce, but not with respect to another kind of jurisdictional element, namely the crossing of a state line? On what grounds might such a distinction be based? If a requirement of substantiality were added as a gloss on the crossing of a state line jurisdictional element, what would be the measure of substantiality?

3. The decision in *Lopez* and *Morrison* precipitated a substantial amount of scholarly writing in the law reviews (and it is anticipated that *Gonzales v. Raich* will have a similar effect). A few examples are set forth here:

a. Professor Robert Nagel sees *Lopez* as a response to the fundamental inconsistency between the principle that the federal government has only limited powers and the definition of some of those powers (e.g. the Commerce Clause) in a fashion that is impossible to limit. He argues that these kinds of conflicting principles pose a dilemma that the Supreme Court responds to by shifting between them, emphasizing one principle and then the other, without openly acknowledging the impossibility of harmonizing the irreconcilable principles. Robert F. Nagel, *The Future of Federalism*, 46 Case W. Res. L.Rev. 643 (1996).

b. Professor Ann Althouse expressed the following views regarding *Lopez*:

> Many matters that absorb Congress today do not represent any sort of considered analysis about whether a national *solution* is needed. Indeed, the practice of deferring to the judgment of Congress as to what affects interstate commerce is flawed for this very reason: members of Congress, inclined to pursue their personal political goals, commonly resort to legislative gestures designed to appeal to the passions of the electorate. The expansive federalization of criminal law shows this force in action. Anti-crime bills make good press, * * * These laws may pass even when they will undercut superior solutions arrived at by the states. * * *
>
> Uniformity is frequently a good thing, necessary to the solution of the kinds of problems involved in *Wickard v. Filburn*. Individual states cannot impose production caps or price controls without damaging the interests of their citizens in their commercial activities. But individualized state and local solutions to the problem of violence in schools do not have that dysfunctional quality. Laws of this kind do not create opportunities for states to seek their own advantage at the expense of other states or to sabotage the efforts of other states.

Ann Althouse, *Theoretical and Constitutional Issues: Enforcing Federalism After United States v. Lopez*, 38 Ariz. L.Rev. 793, 818–19 (1996).

c. Also consider the following comments by Professors Eskridge and Frickey, who, while commenting on the Supreme Court's construction of federal criminal statutes, stated:

> In this area, the Court and the Congress are at loggerheads, and the Court may feel that it must communicate its concern to Congress clearly, come what may. * * * [T]he Court may sense that it alone is left to confront Congress. These instincts may well represent good policy, but they more clearly represent a vision of law as institutional equilibri-

um. Whatever is driving these decisions, it is not values traditionally associated with the rule of law.

William N. Eskridge, Jr. & Philip P. Frickey, *The Supreme Court 1993 Term—Forward: Law as Equilibrium*, 108 Harv. L.Rev. 26, 71 (1994).

d. In a series of articles, Professors Grant Nelson and Robert Pushaw, writing both jointly and later, separately, have advanced and applied a new approach for the exercise of the constitutional commerce power that would substitute for the Supreme Court's economic/noneconomic approach as reflected in *Lopez, Morrison* (and more recently, *Raich*). One formulation of the approach would define commerce for constitutional purposes as, "the voluntary sale or exchange of property or services and all accompanying market-based activities, enterprise relationships, and interests." See Grant S. Nelson & Robert J. Pushaw, Jr., *Rethinking the Commerce Clause: Applying First Principles to Uphold Federal Commercial Regulations but Preserve State Control over Social Issues*, 85 Ia. L.Rev. 1 (1999); and Robert J. Pushaw, Jr., & Grant S. Nelson, *A Critique of the Narrow Interpretation of the Commerce Clause*, 96 Nev. U. L. Rev. 695 (2002). Professor Nelson further developed and applied the thesis in Grant S. Nelson, *A Commerce Clause Standard for the New Millennium: "Yes" to Broad Congressional Control over Commercial Transactions; "No" to Federal Legislation on Social and Cultural Issues*, 55 Ark.L.Rev. 1213 (2003). Professor Pushaw applied the thesis to support the constitutionality of federal legislation prohibiting partial birth abortions as well as protecting abortion clinics from violence on the ground that the provision of abortions constitutes a voluntary sale of services. Robert J. Pushaw, Jr., *Does Congress Have the Constitutional Power To Prohibit Partial–Birth Abortion?* 42 Harv. J. on Legis. 319 (2005).

Professor Jesse Choper summarized and critiqued the Nelson–Pushaw approach in Jesse H. Choper, *Taming Congress's Power under the Commerce Clause: What Does the Future Portend?*, 55 Ark. L. Rev. 731, 739–742 (2003):

In an admirably thoughtful effort, examining the original understanding of the Commerce Clause and seeking to develop an intellectually coherent test for drawing sound judicially enforceable restraints, Grant Nelson and Robert Pushaw attempt to breathe life into the economic/noneconomic distinction by confining the entire sphere of congressional regulation to "commerce," and then defining "commerce" as comprehending three areas:

The first includes buying and selling goods; the production of such merchandise through activities such as manufacturing, farming, and mining; and incidents of that production, such as environmental and safety effects. The second encompasses the compensated provision of services (such as labor, insurance, and banking), which have long been regarded as "commercial," and which form a vital element of our modern economy. The third consists of the means by which commerce is transacted—for example, the documents used to facilitate commerce (contracts, negotiable instruments, securities, letters of credit, security interests in property, etc.). Further, in an attempt to remove most "criminal law enforcement"—which the Rehnquist majority has identified, in addition to "family law (including marriage, divorce, and child custody) . . . [and] education, where States historically have been sovereign"—Nelson and Pushaw further limit "commerce" to "consensual transactions." Recognizing that a major concern for the Lopez and Morrison majorities was whether any limits on Congress's power to regulate crime would exist if GFSZA or VAWA had been upheld, Nelson and Pushaw concede that while most crime may be characterized as economic because it involves wealth transfer, it is not "commerce" because it does not involve a bargained relation between parties.

In my view, though, the major problem with their reasoning in respect to this point is that insurance comprises a "bargained for, consensual transaction." Indeed, Nelson and Pushaw agree that crimes against insured property, even though not themselves economic activities, fall within their definition of "commerce." As a result, Congress could make it unlawful to injure any individual or business that carries insurance to cover the economic effects of the criminal act. This would seemingly include many (probably most) acts of murder, arson, robbery, and burglary. Logically, even rape or other physical assaults would be covered if the victim called on her health insurance for medical treatment. If so, it seems intuitively problematic to make one class of crimes subject to federal power just because of the presence of insurance, while the exact offense would be outside the ambit of congressional authority in its absence.

Moreover, in determining what "commerce" means for these purposes, it is difficult to distinguish between committing arson against insured property (which Nelson and Pushaw count) and growing wheat for home consumption (which they do not). Neither act is "commerce" in itself, but both have a "direct" ("automatic" may be a less tainted word) economic consequence: imposing liability on an insurance company, and reducing the demand for wheat. These seem to be distinguishable from the gun law in Lopez, which did appear to require "pil[ing] inference upon inference" before reaching an economic impact, but not so clearly different from the statute in Morrison because of the "immediate" result of gender-motivated violence on absence from the work force. Similarly, the "direct" economic effect of a crime covered by insurance (i.e., insurer must pay) seems different by only the slightest degree from the "direct" economic effect of offenses against uninsured persons or property (e.g., replacing stolen or destroyed items, or obtaining medical care for personal injury).

Nelson and Pushaw's discussion of the Endangered Species Act ("ESA") provides a revealing illustration. They believe that Congress could forbid construction of a hospital on land that is the habitat of an endangered species "because the restriction on construction affects commercial land development.... ESA may even be applied where a landowner contracts with a builder to construct a single family home on a parcel that is the habitat of an endangered species." But suppose that the landowner decides to build the house himself. Although it is true that there is no "commercial" contract, still, it seems to me that the economic impact of the construction appears to be sufficiently similar to justify Commerce Clause coverage.

Ultimately, Nelson acknowledges that

[c]ongressional power fails, in our view, in only a few relatively discreet situations. For example, Congress probably lacks the power to regulate directly air pollution caused by home fireplaces, backyard barbeques, and lawnmowers. Even here, however, Congress probably could deal with the problem indirectly by regulating the construction or manufacturing [or sale] of such appliances.

Indeed, Nelson and Pushaw further observe that "Congress arguably should be permitted to regulate noncommercial activities because many of them have a great impact on interstate commerce," albeit one that requires a series of inferences.

This all leaves very little beyond national governance and comes very close to reinstating the all-encompassing pre-Lopez regime. In the end, Nelson and Pushaw's major effort to curtail the boundless commerce power that their analysis seems to imply is by urging the Court to "halt the increasing reliance by Congress on the Commerce Clause" to regulate a noncommercial activity for the purpose of imposing "a specific cultural or moral viewpoint," pointing out that "the Framers believed that national uniformity is good in commerce but bad in political, social, cultural, and moral matters."

This presents at least two significant difficulties. First, the areas of Congress's present Commerce Clause authority that would be primarily affected by application of this approach would be in respect to the "channels" and "instrumentalities" prongs. For it has been congressional use of the "jurisdictional nexus" that has most successfully allowed it to approach the creation of a national police power. Indeed, Nelson and Pushaw specifically urge elimination of these two prongs as independent sources of regulatory capacity....

The second difficulty, however, presents the major obstacle. The distinction between "economic" or "commercial" issues and "political, social, cultural, and moral matters" is exceedingly blurred. "All decisions about what the law should be are moral decisions in part. To which side of the 'moral economic' divide could we assign the question whether to have a minimum wage, or progressive taxation, or endangered species protection?" Is barring possession or use of marijuana an attempt by Congress to impose a political, moral, cultural, or social view? Or does it seek to regulate an international business? Into which category does use of faith-based organizations fall when Government enlists them to help solve such problems as drug addiction, juvenile delinquency, and teenage pregnancy? Questions such as these, among a number of others, highlight the range of quandaries presented by the economic/noneconomic distinction advanced by the Court and related theories of prominent commentators.

e. In the same article, Professor Choper also comments on Congress's use of a commerce nexus jurisdictional provision in federal statutes, id. at 755–759:

Although the Court's discussion of the "substantial effects" prong of the Commerce Clause in *Lopez* and *Morrison* runs deep, both rulings explicitly reaffirmed and left wholly unqualified the other two "broad categories of activity that Congress may regulate under its commerce power." Since neither *Lopez* nor *Morrison* involved a statute that included a jurisdictional element (or jurisdictional nexus), i.e., in which the subject of federal control itself is or has been in interstate commerce, the Court gave no indication of how elastic these might be to inoculate similar legislation from constitutional invalidation. Indeed, under the current state of the law, although less than fully developed, the "jurisdictional nexus" prong of Commerce Clause analysis seems to permit virtually unlimited congressional regulation. This dominion, clearly established in opinions of the Court well before the "substantial effects" approach, may be seen as even more threatening to the primary goals and ideas envisioned by the Framers.

Thus, in brief, the great purpose of the Commerce Clause, although assuredly limited in its ultimate reach, was to enable Congress to facilitate interstate trade, to promote development of national industries and markets and, generally, to encourage economic growth. Yet, in *Champion v. Ames*, the famous *Lottery Case*, the Court ruled that the commerce power authorized Congress to prohibit the transportation of lottery tickets across state lines, even though these articles were intrinsically harmless and the law's unambiguous purpose was the social regulation of public morals rather than some commercial or economic goal—a decision whose rationale led "to the conclusion that Congress may arbitrarily exclude from commerce among the States any article, commodity or thing, of whatever kind or nature, or however useful or valuable, which it may choose, no matter with what motive."

In my view, if the judicial branch took a wrong turn regarding the original understanding of the restricted scope of the Commerce Clause, this is where it occurred, when it sustained congressional power to hinder interstate trade and, effectively, to destroy those national industries and markets that it wished. Soon after the *Lottery Case*, and well before the New Deal revolution, the Court upheld federal provisions of the Mann Act that prohibited the transportation across state lines of women not just for prostitution, but also for noncommercial immoral purposes. The Court did dramatically alter this course in *Hammer v. Dagenhart*, invalidating a federal bar on the interstate transportation of goods produced by child labor on the ground that "[t]he grant of power to Congress over the subject of interstate commerce was to enable it to regulate such commerce, and not to give it authority to control the States in their exercise of the police power over local trade and manufacture." But after the New Deal switch in time, the Court emphatically reaffirmed the *Lottery Case*....

This "jurisdictional nexus" approach was subsequently relied on in cases such as *Scarborough v. United States*, which upheld federal criminalization of firearm possession by felons, and *Cleveland v. United States*, which upheld federal prohibition of polygamy.

If the Court allows this line of doctrine to continue unqualifiedly, Congress may well find that its ability to engage in social regulation will be little slowed. *Lopez* and *Morrison* notwithstanding, Congress still may use its control over the channels of interstate commerce to establish a "plenary police power that would authorize enactment of every type of legislation" in regard to noneconomic as well as economic conduct. To this day, for instance, under what has been termed "a fetishism of state-line crossings," it is a federal crime for a felon, living within a single state and never having crossed state lines, to possess a firearm. Even after *Lopez* and *Morrison*, this statute has been upheld by every federal court of appeals because of the presence of a jurisdictional element: the firearms have been shipped or transported in interstate or foreign commerce. At trial, the prosecution need only show that the gun was manufactured in another state, even if many years earlier.

Moreover, federal statutes today penalize persons who cross a state line with the intent to commit designated acts. Thus, to take VAWA, if Congress were to prohibit anyone from crossing state borders with the intention of committing gender-motivated violence, this would provide the "jurisdictional element" missing in both *Lopez* and *Morrison*. Even further, is it possible that Congress could (a) prohibit travel in (or use of) interstate commerce in the future by persons who have committed such violence in the past, and (b) prohibit such violence in the future by persons who have traveled in (or used) interstate commerce in the past? To take *Lopez*, could Congress pass a law prohibiting the possession within a school zone of any firearm that has ever traveled in interstate commerce—which would almost certainly include almost every firearm in the country?

There is precedent that may support such comprehensive national regulatory impact.

f. See also George D. Brown, *Constitutionalizing the Federal Criminal Law Debate: Morrison, Jones, and the ABA*, 2001 U. Ill. L. Rev. 983, 1014–1017:

In analyzing the constitutional problems posed by jurisdictional elements, I find it helpful to distinguish between those that I refer to as "nexus" elements, and "effects" elements. An example of the former would be the punishment of possession of, or interference with an object that had traveled in interstate commerce. The nexus is the fact of having been in interstate commerce. An example of the latter type is a statute that requires proof of an effect on interstate commerce from the defendant's proscribed conduct. Most of the language about the ease with which jurisdictional elements are satisfied is more readily applicable to elements of the first type than those of the second. ... It is certainly true that goods and people move across state lines, and that if such movement is treated as a nexus, it is potentially easy to satisfy in almost "every case." A hospitable approach to nexus jurisdictional elements can also be found in Supreme Court precedent.... It is also important to note that *Lopez* summarized existing Commerce Clause precedent as establishing the famous three categories of permissible regulation. The first is that of "the use of the channels of interstate commerce." Focusing on that category, it is easy to see that the fact of a person or thing having traveled in commerce can bring to bear Congress's power to regulate the channels. Indeed, the problem with nexus statutes is that they are so easy to satisfy that the spirit of *Lopez* can be totally circumvented. . . . As recently as *Morrison*, the federalist majority seemed to indicate approval of nexus elements involving travel in interstate commerce.

However, it is odd to construct a rationale for virtually unlimited national power out of *Lopez*—a case that was intended to, and did, impose limits in the name of federalism. If Congress were to move towards a broad use of nexus elements, the Court would have to take a second look. There is language in *Morrison* suggesting that jurisdictional elements "might" limit the reach of statutes to those with a connection to commerce, and that they "may" establish that a particular statute is in furtherance of the commerce power.

The problems posed by statutes that require an "effect" on commerce are more complex. After all, *Morrison* and *Lopez* involved the question of the effect on commerce of a class of activities and such important issues as whether the effect had to be substantial and the activity had to be either economic or commercial. If one assumes that effects element statutes are to be analyzed within the *Lopez* framework, they appear to fall squarely within the third category: "[T]he power to regulate those activities having a substantial relation to interstate commerce." A significant problem posed by a jurisdictional element statute that requires an effect on commerce is how to handle the criminalization of noneconomic activity that may, in individual cases, have some effect on interstate commerce, but not a substantial one. This problem can be broken down into several sets of issues. The first is whether noneconomic activity is out of bounds. Morrison appeared to leave this question slightly open. Moreover, the notion of protecting interstate commerce from "intrastate violence that is . . . directed at the instrumentalities, channels, or goods" involved in it appears to extend to noneconomic activity. A second issue is that of the quantifiable effect on interstate commerce. This is a complex question. On the one hand, the use of an effects element suggests a congressional desire to screen out small cases that do not justify the intervention of federal authority. On the other hand, there is the serious question of how frequently an individual noneconomic criminal act could possibly have an effect on interstate commerce that rises to the level of "substantial." It is one thing for an entire class of activities such as loan-sharking to meet this standard; it is quite another matter for an isolated act to meet it. This brings up a third issue raised by effects elements: Is it conceptually possible to aggregate the effects of individual instances so that an evaluation of the statute may look at its impact on commerce across a range of applications? There is a clear appeal to doing so, given the difficulty of meeting the substantiality test. On the other hand, utilization of any such technique would seem to obliterate the distinction between jurisdictional element statutes and those regulating classes of activity. Aggregating conduct to reach the desired threshold would turn the former type of statute into the latter.

The above discussion suggests that generalizations about jurisdictional-elements statutes need to draw a distinction between the types of statutes I have outlined here. Those who predict smooth sailing for nexus element statutes may well be correct. Effects-element statutes are another matter, both in theory and in practice. Indeed, it is these statutes that have caused the greatest amount of confusion and uncertainty in the lower courts.

3. ILLUSTRATIVE APPLICATIONS OF THE JURISDICTIONAL AND SUBSTANTIVE REACH OF SEVERAL STATUTORY CRIME AREAS

In this section, we examine the jurisdictional features and substantive reach of several federal statutory crime areas: the firearms laws, the Travel Act (and related criminal statutes that use a ''facilities of commerce'' jurisdictional approach) and crimes enacted as part of the Violence Against Women Act of 1994. The purpose is to examine in specific statutory contexts and in more depth some of the constitutional commerce power authority issues discussed in the previous section; to consider the kinds of issues of statutory interpretation issues that arise in applying the jurisdictional concepts used under the commerce power; and to explore some of the interplay between jurisdictional and substantive issues.

a. Firearms Offenses

Federal laws regulating the manufacture, distribution, sale, possession and use of guns, 18 U.S.C. §§ 921–931, are complex and engender controversy. The current legislative scheme and the predecessor legislation were described as follows in *United States v. Stewart*, 348 F.3d 1132, at n. 5 (9th Cir. 2003):

> The Federal Firearms Act, Pub. L. No. 75–785, 52 Stat. 1250 (1938) (repealed 1968), for example, required firearm manufacturers and dealers to obtain federal licenses before *engaging in interstate commerce*, permitted licensees to *ship firearms interstate* only to other licensees, mandated that licensees keep permanent records of firearm *transactions*, and prohibited the *interstate movement of firearms* by or to fugitives or persons indicted or convicted of violent crimes, or if the firearms were stolen or had altered serial numbers. §§ 2–3, 52 Stat. at 1250–52. The Omnibus Crime Control and Safe Streets Act (Omnibus Act) of 1968, Pub. L. No. 90–351, 82 Stat. 197 (1968) (current version at 18 U.S.C. §§ 921–30 (1994)), incorporated nearly all of the Federal Firearms Act and also required federal licenses for all persons in the *firearms business*, whether or not that business was conducted interstate. § 902, 82 Stat. at 231. With respect to machineguns, the Act prohibited licensees from *selling or delivering* them without first receiving affidavits from local law enforcement. § 902, 82 Stat. at 230. The Gun Control Act of 1968, Pub. L. No. 90–618, 82 Stat. 1213 (1968) (current version at 18 U.S.C. §§ 921–30 (1994)), added broader coverage of *transactions* in ammunition, strengthened restrictions on *deliveries and sales* of heavy firearms, including machineguns, and prohibited *interstate movement* of firearms by or to unlawful drug users. § 102, 82 Stat. at 1218–21.

See Sara Sun Beale, The Unintended Consequences of Enhancing Gun Penalties: Shooting Down the Commerce Clause and Arming Federal Prosecutors, 51 Duke, L.J. 1641 (2002):

> The modern era of federal firearms legislation began in 1968 after the assassinations of Robert Kennedy and Martin Luther King, Jr. That year, Congress expansively employed its authority under the Commerce Clause to reach a wide range of gun-related crime. For present purposes, the most important provision of the 1968 legislation made it a federal crime for a previously convicted felon to possess a firearm. The Department of Justice interpreted the statute as extending federal jurisdiction to any felon who possessed a firearm—with no showing required in individual cases of any connection to interstate commerce or any other basis for federal jurisdiction—and the lower courts accepted this interpretation. So interpreted, the federal felon-in-possession statute and the loan-sharking statute also enacted in 1968 were the first federal criminal statutes to employ the class-of-activities model to assert criminal jurisdiction under the Commerce Clause. In a pair of decisions in 1971, the Supreme Court upheld the class-of-activities approach in the loan-sharking statute, but it finessed the issue in a case involving the felon-in-possession statute.

The last-mentioned case to which Professor Beale refers was *United States v. Bass*, 404 U.S. 336 (1971). Bass involved a prosecution under a provision of the Act (then numbered as § 1202 (a)) which made it unlawful for felons to "receive ..., possess ... or transport ... in commerce or affecting commerce ... any firearm." The government argued that all possessions of firearms by felons were prohibited, that no connection with commerce had to be proved in the individual case. The Supreme Court construed the "in commerce or affecting commerce" phrase as modifying each of the statutory verbs, receiving, possessing and transporting, and set aside the conviction because the prosecution had failed to prove the nexus with commerce in the particular case. The Court stated:

> In the instant case, the broad construction urged by the Government renders traditionally local criminal conduct a matter for federal enforcement and would also involve substantial extension of federal police resources. Absent proof of some interstate commerce nexus in each case, § 1202(a) dramatically intrudes upon traditional state criminal jurisdiction.

Two other early Supreme Court decisions interpreting the 1968 legislation were *Barrett v. United States*, 423 U.S. 212 (1976) and *Scarborough v. United States*, 431 U.S. 563 (1977). In Scarborough, the Court ruled that in order to convict a felon under § 1202(a), the Government only had to prove that "the firearm possessed by the convicted felon traveled at some time in interstate commerce." See also the *Barrett* decision where the Court reached the same kind of conclusion under a different provision of the statute. In this connection, see *United States v. Coward*, 151 F.Supp.2d 544 (E.D. Pa. 2001):

> *Scarborough* may fairly be read to establish the legal fiction that has prevailed in these cases since it was announced. This is so even under the present ... [provision prohibiting possession of firearms by convicted felons]. Simply phrased, *Scarborough*'s legal fiction is that the transport of a weapon in interstate commerce, however remote in the distant past, gives its present intrastate possession sufficient interstate aspect to fall within the ambit of the statute. This fiction is indelible and lasts as long as the gun can shoot.

Our focus in this section is on those provisions rendering unlawful certain activities relating to guns, specifically the criminal provisions found in 922 and 924. The 922 criminal provisions proscribe various kinds of gun business-related activities such as manufacture, possession, transfer, sale, etc. by persons who are not licensed to engage in such activities as well as impermissible activities by those who are licensed. Most of these provisions contain express links to interstate commerce or involve licensed importers, manufacturers, dealers or collectors.

As to provisions relating to the latter group which do not contain express provisions requiring links to interstate commerce, see, e.g. *United States v. Crandall*, 453 F.2d 1216 (1st Cir. 1972) holding that § 922(b) (which regulates the activities of licensed importers, manufacturers, dealers and collectors but does not expressly mention interstate commerce) is not unconstitutional: The general involvement of the licensed individuals "with interstate commerce is ample to justify federal regulation of even their intrastate sales." Similarly, in *United States v. Petrucci*, 486 F.2d 329 (9th Cir. 1973), the court ruled that the intrastate business of unlicensed dealers substantially affects interstate commerce in firearms and thus the dealings in firearms by an unlicensed individual can be banned under § 922(a). See also *United States v. Redus*, 469 F.2d 185 (9th Cir.1972).

A similar approach and rationale probably supports the constitutionality under the commerce clause of a provision such as § 922(a) (7) prohibiting the manufacture of armor piercing ammunition or under (8), the sale of such ammunition by a manufacturer, without any statement of an explicit link to interstate commerce. Similarly, a provision such as subsec. (d) of § 922 which, while not containing express language requiring a nexus to interstate commerce, prohibits sale or disposal of firearms or ammunition to listed categories of persons (such as persons under indictment or having been convicted of a felony, fugitives from justice, users of controlled substances, mental defectives, illegal aliens, etc.), because it involves a commerce-linked activity, is sustainable under the commerce clause. To be contrasted with subsec. (d), subsec. (g) of § 922 prohibits the same listed categories of individuals from *possessing* firearms. Subsec. (g) does, however, contain an express provision that limits the prohibition to possession "in or affecting commerce" or receiving "any firearm or ammunition which has been shipped ... in interstate ... commerce." (Subsec.(g) is the successor provision to § 1202(a), the provision construed by the Supreme Court in the *Bass* and *Scarborough* cases, discussed supra.)

There are at least three provisions among those regulating gun control that are somewhat more problematic under the commerce clause, not including the provision that was at issue in *Lopez*, § 922 (q), which was amended by the Congress in 1996 and now reads as follows:

> It shall be unlawful for any individual knowingly to possess a firearm that has moved in or that otherwise affects interstate ... commerce at a place that the individual knows or has reasonable cause to believe is a school zone

The three provisions about which a commerce power question can be raised because they prohibit "possession" without expressly requiring a link to commerce, are: § 922(x)(2) which makes it unlawful for a juvenile to possess a handgun; § 922(p)(1)(A) which makes it a crime to, inter alia, possess a firearm not detectable by walk-through metal detectors; and § 922(*o*)(1) which prohibits transfer or possession of a machine gun. The constitutionality of the machine gun provision has been recently addressed by the courts.

UNITED STATES v. STEWART

348 F.3d 1132 (9th Cir. 2003).

KOZINSKI, CIRCUIT JUDGE:

We decide whether Congress can, under its Commerce Clause power, prohibit the mere possession of homemade machineguns.

Section 922(*o*) makes it unlawful to "transfer or possess a machinegun." Notably absent from this provision is any jurisdictional requirement that the machinegun has traveled in or substantially affected interstate commerce. We decide whether this statute, as applied to Stewart, offends the Commerce Clause.

* * *

In *United States v. Rambo*, 74 F.3d 948 (9th Cir. 1996), we held that section 922(*o*) was "a regulation of the use of the channels of interstate commerce" because "there can be 'no unlawful possession under section 922(*o*) without an unlawful transfer.' " We elaborated that, " 'in effect, the ban on such possession is an attempt to control the interstate market for machineguns by creating criminal liability for those who would constitute the demand-side of the market, i.e., those who would facilitate illegal transfer out of the desire to acquire mere possession.' " *Rambo* thus held section 922(*o*) was a valid exercise of the commerce power because a transfer or sale must have preceded the criminalized possession.

Stewart's case reveals the limits of *Rambo*'s logic. Contrary to *Rambo*'s assumption that an unlawful transfer must precede unlawful possession, Stewart did not acquire his machineguns from someone else: He fabricated them himself. The government has never contested Stewart's claim that the machineguns were entirely homemade, and the evidence supports his claim. The chief of the ATF Firearms Technology Branch, referring to one of the machineguns, testified that it was *"a unique type of firearm."* He explained that the machineguns were "based on a ... Sten gun design," which is a type of British machinegun, and had "certain [Sten gun] parts,", but "the rest of the parts ... [were] not ... conventional Sten gun parts," * * * None of the machineguns had original Sten receiver tubes (the part of the gun that houses the cartridge when the weapon is fired), and at least one was identified as having a "homemade receiver tube." On some of the machineguns, the trigger was "quite different" from "an ordinary Sten gun trigger." The ATF chief testified that "the only time [he'd] ever seen ... this [type of mechanism was] in conjunction with [a].... single-shot rifle."

The district court ruled against Stewart's Commerce Clause argument, reasoning that "the parts, at least, moved in interstate commerce." Indeed, some of the machinegun parts did move in interstate commerce. At some level, of course, everything we own is composed of something that once traveled in commerce. This cannot mean that *everything* is subject to federal regulation under the Commerce Clause, else that constitutional limitation would be entirely meaningless. As *Lopez* reminds us, Congress's power has limits, and we must be mindful of those limits so as not to " 'obliterate the distinction between what is national and what is local and create a completely centralized government.' " *Lopez*, 514 U.S. at 557 * * ** The difficult question is where to draw the line between a regulated object and the matter from which that object was created.

* * *

Some components of Stewart's machineguns had crossed state lines, but these components did not add up to a gun. Not even close. ... [M]any additional parts and tools, as well as expertise and industry, were needed to create functioning machineguns. This is quite different than if Stewart had ordered a disassembled gun and simply put the parts together, the way one might assemble a chair from IKEA. These machineguns were a "unique type of firearm," with legal parts mixed and matched from various origins; they required more than a simple turn of a screwdriver or a hit of a hammer to become machineguns. We therefore cannot say that the machineguns themselves—in any recognizable form—traveled in interstate commerce.

Because these firearms were genuinely homemade, we find that Stewart did not obtain his machineguns by "using the channels of interstate commerce." Thus, although *Rambo* found section 922(*o*) to be generally valid under the Commerce Clause, *Rambo*'s reasoning does not cover Stewart's case.

Even if Stewart did not *use* the channels of interstate commerce, his possession of machineguns may still have substantially *affected* interstate commerce. Several courts of appeals have held section 922(*o*) constitutional on this ground. *Wright*, 117 F.3d at 1268–71; *United States* v. *Rybar*, 103 F.3d 273, 276–85 (3d Cir. 1996); *United States v. Kenney*, 91 F.3d 884, 890–91 (7th Cir. 1996). We cannot agree that simple possession of machineguns—particularly possession of homemade machineguns—has a substantial effect on interstate commerce.

In *United States* v. *Morrison*, 529 U.S. 598, 146 L. Ed. 2d 658, 120 S. Ct. 1740 (2000), the Supreme Court set out the controlling test for determining whether a regulated activity "substantially affects" interstate commerce: We must consider (1) whether the regulated activity is commercial or economic in nature; (2) whether an express jurisdictional element is provided in the statute to limit its reach; (3) whether Congress made express findings about the effects of the proscribed activity on interstate commerce; and (4) whether the link between the prohibited activity and the effect on interstate commerce is attenuated.

We start by considering the first and fourth prongs of the *Morrison* test, as we have deemed them the most important. The first prong is not satisfied here. Possession of a machinegun is not, without more, economic in nature. Just like the statute struck down in *Lopez*, section 922(*o*) "is a criminal statute that by its terms has nothing to do with 'commerce' or any sort of economic enterprise, however broadly one might define those terms." Unlike in *Wickard* v. *Filburn*, 317 U.S. 111, 87 L. Ed. 122, 63 S. Ct. 82 (1942), where growing wheat in one's backyard could be seen as a means of saving money that would otherwise have been spent in the open market, a homemade machinegun may be part of a gun collection or may be crafted as a hobby. Or it may be used for illegal purposes. Whatever its intended use, without some evidence that it will be sold or transferred—and there is none here—its relationship to interstate commerce is highly attenuated.

Moreover, the regulation itself does not have an economic purpose: whereas the statute in *Wickard* was enacted primarily to control the market price of wheat, there is no evidence that section 922(*o*) was enacted to regulate commercial aspects of the machinegun business. More likely, section 922(*o*) was intended to keep machineguns out of the hands of criminals—an admirable goal, but not a commercial one.

We can also say with some confidence that the effect of Stewart's possession of homemade machineguns on interstate commerce was attenuated under the fourth prong of the *Morrison* test. *Lopez* already rejected the reasoning that, because the cost of violent crimes is spread through insurance, regulations intended to prevent violent crimes significantly affect the national economy .. Nor did *Lopez* buy the argument that violent crime substantially affects commerce by reducing people's willingness to travel to unsafe areas of the country. Though prohibition of all machinegun possession may have a greater chance of reducing violent crime than a prohibition that extends only to school zones, this does not change what the Court said in *Lopez*: that under these expansive theories, "it is difficult to perceive any limitation on federal power, even in areas such as criminal law enforcement ... where States historically have been sovereign." * * * This "cost of crime" rationale thus cannot save the government's case.

* * * Stewart's homemade machineguns did not stimulate a demand for anything illegal—all the components he bought were legally available from commercial sources.... Similarly, by crafting his own guns and working out of his own home, Stewart functioned outside the commercial gun market. His activities obviously did not increase machinegun demand. Nor can we say that Stewart's homemade machineguns reduced overall demand. Unlike wheat, for example, which is a staple commodity that Filburn would probably have had to buy, had he not grown it himself, there is no reason to think Stewart would ever have bought a machinegun from a commercial source, had he been precluded by law from building one himself. In fact, the evidence suggests that Stewart was cognizant of the law and made careful efforts not to come into conflict with it. Thus, the link between Stewart's activity and its effect on interstate commerce is simply too tenuous to justify federal regulation.

This case fails *Morrison*'s other requirements as well. * * *

Section 922(*o*) is quite different from previous firearms regulations. Whereas section 922(*o*) addresses *possession* of machineguns, all of the earlier legislation cited by the Third Circuit deals with *transactions*, *sales* or *deliveries* of firearms, and nearly all of the provisions specifically require that the transaction, sale or delivery be conducted interstate. All of these provisions are cut from the ordinary cloth of Commerce Clause regulation of interstate commerce, while section 922(*o*) is much closer to the statute struck down in *Lopez*. That statute criminalized gun possession in a particular location—a school zone. Section 922(*o*) criminalizes possession of a particular type of firearm—a machinegun. The latter no more has an inherent link to interstate commerce than the former. The Supreme Court found that the school zones statute " 'plowed thoroughly new ground and represented a sharp break with the long-standing pattern of federal firearms legislation,' " * * * Section 922(*o*) is no less of a "sharp break" from previous regulations.

Moreover, nothing in the legislative history of any of the earlier firearms statutes speaks to the relationship between mere possession of firearms and interstate commerce. Instead, the legislative findings focus primarily on the need for federal enforcement where firearms cross state and international borders, and are thus difficult for individual states to regulate on their own. * * * The Gun Control Act's findings * * * discuss only the need "to strengthen Federal controls over *interstate and foreign commerce in firearms* and to assist the States effectively to regulate firearms *traffic* within their borders." H.R. Rep. No. 90–1597 (1968) Nothing in the legislative history suggests that Congress ever considered the impact of purely intrastate possession of homemade machineguns on interstate commerce, and there is no reason to assume that prohibiting local possession of machineguns would have the same national and commercial consequences as prohibiting the interstate and foreign traffic in firearms. We therefore cannot import these earlier legislative findings to give section 922(*o*) constitutional grounding.

Based on the four-factor *Morrison* test, section 922(*o*) cannot be viewed as having a substantial effect on interstate commerce. We therefore conclude that section 922(*o*) is unconstitutional as applied to Stewart.

RESTANI, JUDGE, concurring in part, dissenting in part:

I dissent from that part of the majority's opinion which finds 18 U.S.C. § 922(*o*) unconstitutional as applied to a machine gun partially home manufactured from legal parts. I agree that this case is not controlled by prior circuit precedent, which relies on earlier illegal transfers. *See, e.g., United States v. Rambo*, 74 F.3d 948 (9th Cir. 1996). Rather, I adopt the reasoning of the Seventh Circuit in *United States v. Kenney*, 91 F.3d 884 (7th Cir. 1996), which finds that the regulation of possession, as well as transfer, of machine guns is part of Congress's long standing efforts to regulate the trade in machine guns, that is, to regulate the whole of the economic activity of trade in machine guns.(upholding the constitutionality of § 922(*o*) as a regulation of activity substantially affecting interstate commerce).

Unlike the majority, and like the court in *Kenney*, I find *Wickard v. Filburn*, 317 U.S. 111, 87 L. Ed. 122, 63 S. Ct. 82 (1942) controlling. Possession of machine guns, home manufactured or not, substantially interferes with Congress's long standing attempts to control the interstate movement of machine guns by proscribing transfer and possession. Congress's chosen method in § 922(*o*) was to totally eliminate the demand side of the economic activity by freezing legal possession at 1986 levels, "an effect that is closely entwined with regulating interstate commerce" even as applied to purely intrastate possession of machine guns resulting from home manufacture. Allowing home manufacture is clearly not within the intent of § 922(*o*) and would upset Congress's entirely lawful plan to regulate trade in machine guns. Accordingly, I dissent in part.

Notes

1. The Supreme Court granted review in the *Stewart* case and vacated the judgment below, 125 S. Ct. 2899 (2005), stating:

> On petition for writ of certiorari to the United States Court of Appeals for the Ninth Circuit. Motion of respondent for leave to proceed *in forma pauperis* and petition for writ of certiorari granted. Judgment vacated, and case remanded to the United States Court of Appeals for the Ninth Circuit for further consideration in light of *Gonzales v. Raich*, 545 U.S. ___, 125 S.Ct. 2195 (2005).

2. What is the significance of the Supreme Court's action in *Stewart*? Recall that the Court in *Gonzales v. Raich* in upholding the regulation of locally grown and locally used marijuana (for medical purposes) described

the regulatory scheme under the Controlled Substances Act in the following terms:

> * * * [T]he CSA, enacted in 1970 as part of the Comprehensive Drug Abuse Prevention and Control Act, 84 Stat. 1242–1284, was a lengthy and detailed statute creating a comprehensive framework for regulating the production, distribution, and possession of five classes of "controlled substances." * * *

> * * * [The marijuana] classification, unlike the discrete prohibition established by the Gun–Free School Zones Act of 1990, was merely one of many "essential parts of a larger regulation of economic activity, in which the regulatory scheme could be undercut unless the intrastate activity were regulated." Our opinion in *Lopez* casts no doubt on the validity of such a program.

Is the Supreme Court's action in *Stewart* subject to the interpretation that the Court views the regulatory scheme for firearms as roughly comparable to the "comprehensive framework" applicable to controlled substances; and that "the regulatory scheme could be undercut unless the [particular] intrastate activity [namely, possession of homemade machine guns] were regulated"?

Recall that in *Gonzales v. Raich*, the Court characterized the Lopez statute in the following terms:

> At issue in *Lopez* was the validity of the Gun–Free School Zones Act of 1990, which was a brief, single-subject statute making it a crime for an individual to possess a gun in a school zone. 18 U.S.C. § 922(q)(1)(A). The Act did not regulate any economic activity and did not contain any requirement that the possession of a gun have any connection to past interstate activity or a predictable impact on future commercial activity. * * *

> We explained: "Section 922(q) is a criminal statute that by its terms has nothing to do with 'commerce' or any sort of economic enterprise, however broadly one might define those terms. Section 922(q) is not an essential part of a larger regulation of economic activity, in which the regulatory scheme could be undercut unless the intrastate activity were regulated."

3. If firearms are under a comprehensive regulatory framework, why was the Gun Free School Zones provision at issue in *Lopez* not viewed as just one more provision in that scheme? How is it different from the provision making it a crime to possess a machine gun?

Was it significant that the *Lopez* statute was not enacted as part of the original regulatory scheme but was added later? Note, however that the Lopez provision § 922(q) was added to 922 and became thereby just one of a series of provisions (including the machine gun section) that made unlawful specific conduct relating to firearms. Is it fair to characterize it as "a brief, single-subject statute" that "did not regulate any economic activity . . .?"

4. Should it be constitutionally significant that the machine gun provision, § 922(*o*) penalizes "possession *or transfer*" of machine guns? [emphasis added].

5. Is it an adequate basis for distinguishing the *Lopez* gun-school zone provision from the machine gun provision that, as Judge Kozinski noted, the *Lopez* statute "criminalized gun possession in a particular location—a school zone" while section 922(*o*) "criminalizes possession of a particular type of firearm—a machinegun?" But recall that he further noted, "The latter no more has an inherent link to interstate commerce than the former."

Might the implication of the remand of *Stewart* be that the constitutional line is to be drawn between statutes that make punishment turn on the type of item possessed rather than statutes that focus on where the item is possessed. Initially at least, that seems a very fine line to draw for constitutional purposes.

6. If *Stewart* is different from *Lopez* because the former involves a crime that turns on regulating possession of a particular type of firearm whereas the latter turns on regulating where the firearm is possessed, what about a prohibition that turns on the characteristics of the person who possesses the weapon? We have in mind here, not the possession, for example, by felon or illegal alien provisions, which by statute require an express link to commerce, but rather, the provision prohibiting possession by juveniles, § 922(x), which contains no language requiring a link to commerce. See *United States v. Michael R.*, 90 F.3d 340 (9th Cir. 1996):

Read as a whole, § 922(x) by its terms regulates commerce: subsection (1) is targeted at curbing the supply of handguns and suitable ammunition, while subsection (2) restricts the demand for these firearms. We find that under the statute, Congress is in effect regulating interstate commerce by attacking both the supply and demand for firearms with respect to juveniles.

Second, we have no doubt that possession of a handgun by a juvenile, as a general matter, could have a substantial effect on interstate commerce.

* * *

The first two grounds are self-explanatory: possession of a handgun by a juvenile implicates interstate commerce through the manufacturing process and by its deterrent effect on interstate travel. We also find a nexus between this statute and Congress's efforts to control firearms and drug trafficking. In today's drug culture, it is not uncommon for runners to be under 18 years old. And as reflected by the crime statistics, many of them carry guns. It is logical, then, that a statute regulating the sale, transfer, and possession of handguns by juveniles could have a substantial effect in curbing the illegal flow in commerce of drugs and firearms.

7. Claims have been rejected that *Lopez* imposes a requirement that the nexus to commerce be substantial under provisions such as § 922(g) and 922(j) (which contain express language requiring a commerce connection). See, e.g., *United States v. Pritchett*, 327 F.3d 1183 (11th Cir. 2003):

Pritchett contends that the interstate commerce activity regulated by the Commerce Clause must now substantially affect interstate commerce. We disagree. In fact, we * * * concluded that "[n]othing in *Lopez* suggests that the 'minimal nexus' test should be changed." [United

States v.] *McAllister*, 77 F.3d at 390. Moreover, the Supreme Court's decision in *Lopez* does not apply to § 922(g) because § 922(g) contains a jurisdictional element absent in the statute invalidated by *Lopez. Id.* Thus, we conclude that *Lopez* does not apply to § 922(j) because § 922(j) contains the same jurisdictional element found in § 922(g), and this jurisdictional element is missing from the statute at issue in *Lopez*.

8. Consider in connection with the foregoing notes the comments of Professor Bradley on the constitutionality of the various federal firearms provisions. Craig M. Bradley *Federalism and Federal Criminal Law*, 55 Hastings L. J. 573, 601–602 (2004):

We distinguish *Lopez* on the ground that § 922(*o*), by contrast with § 922(q), is integral to a larger federal scheme for the regulation of trafficking in firearms—an economic activity with strong interstate effects.... [S]ection 922(*o*) fits into the overall regulation of the international and interstate market in weapons deemed particularly dangerous by Congress. Section 922(a) places restrictions on the international and interstate shipment of firearms generally. Section 922(b)(4) forbids the sale or delivery of machine guns by licensed importers, manufacturers, dealers, or collectors except as specifically authorized by the Secretary of Defense.

Indeed, *Lopez* noted that § 922(q) (the Gun Free School Zones Act) "represents a sharp break with the longstanding pattern of federal firearms regulation," suggesting that the Court is probably prepared to accept Congress's extensive regulation of certain particularly dangerous firearms, even though the link to interstate commerce in individual cases may be attenuated.

* * *

The states are not in a good position to regulate the national and international trade in especially dangerous weapons like machine guns and hand grenades, and having a federal offense for possession of such weapons, even if it cannot, or need not, be proved that the weapons have moved in or affected interstate commerce, seems like a reasonable aspect of that regulatory authority. Congress, moreover, has made findings about the effects of these weapons on commerce. On the other hand, criminalizing possession of handguns, which are not highly regulated, and as to which state laws vary, does not seem like such a compelling federal interest or to have such an obvious effect on commerce, though gun possession by felons and narcotics addicts certainly poses a more direct threat to commerce than does possession by someone in a school zone.

Admittedly, the above reasoning is not self-evident. The more obvious order of vulnerability of the statutes is that convictions under § 922(*o*), with no reference to commerce, are the most vulnerable. Convictions under § 922(g), with a requirement of affecting commerce that is not being proved, are also likely to be reversed, whereas convictions under the new § 922(q), which forbids possession of a weapon that has traveled in interstate commerce, are the safest. I am predicting, however, that § 922(q) and § 922(g) convictions are more likely to be reversed, whereas § 922(*o*) convictions will likely be upheld. This is based on the language of *Morrison* suggesting that the mere presence of a jurisdictional hook in a statute is not dispositive, as well as the political consideration that the Court is more likely to support Congress's findings and general authority in the area of particularly dangerous weapons rather than handguns. That is, regulation of hand grenades and machine guns is a "truly national" concern. Further, the Court may not accept Congress's attempt to "overrule" *Lopez.*

9. The issue of the constitutionality of the various laws regulating firearms under the Second Amendment has been frequently raised. See, e.g. *United States v. Haney,* 264 F.3d 1161 (10th Cir. 2001):

> John Lee Haney was convicted of possessing two machineguns in violation of 18 U.S.C. § 922(*o*). On appeal, he asserts that § 922(*o*) violates the Second Amendment

> * * *

> The Second Amendment reads, "A well regulated Militia, being necessary to the security of a free State, the right of the people to keep and bear Arms, shall not be infringed." Haney argues that by banning possession of machineguns, § 922(*o*) infringes his right to keep and bear arms and hence violates the Second Amendment. We reject this contention as inconsistent with governing case law.

> There are two twentieth-century Supreme Court cases discussing the Second Amendment in what appear to be holdings. In *United States v. Miller,* 307 U.S. 174, 59 S.Ct. 816, 83 L.Ed. 1206 (1939), the Court rejected a Second Amendment challenge to a criminal prosecution for transporting an unregistered firearm. The Court held,

> In the absence of any evidence tending to show that possession or use of a 'shotgun having a barrel of less than eighteen inches in length' at this time has some reasonable relationship to the preservation or efficiency of a well regulated militia, we cannot say that the Second Amendment guarantees the right to keep and bear such an instrument. Certainly it is not within judicial notice that this weapon is any part of the ordinary military equipment or that its use could contribute to the common defense.

> In *Lewis v. United States,* 445 U.S. 55, 100 S.Ct. 915, 63 L.Ed.2d 198 (1980), the Court held that the laws prohibiting a felon from possessing a firearm do not violate the Due Process Clause. The Court applied rational-basis scrutiny, noting that the laws "are neither based upon constitutionally suspect criteria, nor do they trench upon any constitutionally protected liberties." In support, the Court cited *Miller,* which it characterized as holding that "the Second Amendment guarantees no right to keep and bear a firearm that does not have some reasonable relationship to the preservation or efficiency of a well regulated militia."

> Our published Tenth Circuit opinions treat the Second Amendment similarly. In *United States v. Oakes,* 564 F.2d 384 (10th Cir.1977), we rejected a Second Amendment challenge to the federal law criminalizing possession of an unregistered machinegun, 26 U.S.C. § 5861(d). We

found no evidence that the firearm in question was connected with a militia, even though the defendant was nominally a member of the Kansas militia and the "Posse Comitatus," a militia-type organization registered with the state:

The purpose of the second amendment as stated by the Supreme Court in *United States v. Miller* was to preserve the effectiveness and assure the continuation of the state militia. The Court stated that the amendment must be interpreted and applied with that purpose in view. To apply the amendment so as to guarantee appellant's right to keep an unregistered firearm which has not been shown to have any connection to the militia, merely because he is technically a member of the Kansas militia, would be unjustifiable in terms of either logic or policy. This lack of justification is even more apparent when applied to appellant's membership in "Posse Comitatus," an apparently nongovernmental organization. We conclude, therefore, that this prosecution did not violate the second amendment.

Our most recent pronouncement on the Second Amendment is *United States v. Baer,* 235 F.3d 561 (10th Cir.2000). In *Baer,* we rejected a "time-worn" Second Amendment challenge to the federal felon-in-possession law, noting that "the circuits have consistently upheld the constitutionality of federal weapons regulations like [this one] absent evidence that they in any way affect the maintenance of a well regulated militia."

Consistent with these cases, we hold that a federal criminal gun-control law does not violate the Second Amendment unless it impairs the state's ability to maintain a well-regulated militia. This is simply a straightforward reading of the text of the Second Amendment. This reading is also consistent with the overwhelming weight of authority from the other circuits. * * *

Nor has Haney proven several facts logically necessary to establish a Second Amendment violation. As a threshold matter, he must show that (1) he is part of a state militia; (2) the militia, and his participation therein, is "well regulated" by the state; (3) machineguns are used by that militia; and (4) his possession of the machinegun was reasonably connected to his militia service. None of these are established.

The militia of the Second Amendment is a governmental organization: The Constitution elsewhere refers to "the Militia of the several States," Art. II, § 2, and divides regulatory authority over the militia between the federal and state governments, Art. I, § 8. Thus, the militia does not include the private anti-government groups that sometimes refer to themselves as "militias." Haney is not part of the "well regulated" militia, that is, a "militia actively maintained and trained by the states,". At best, Haney claims to be a member of the "unorganized" (and therefore not a "well regulated" state) militia* * * Haney does not claim to be a member of the National Guard or the Oklahoma State Guard, and he has submitted no evidence that the Oklahoma unorganized militia and his participation therein are well-regulated by the State of Oklahoma. * * * Nor has Haney submitted any evidence that machineguns of the sort he possessed are used by the militia, or that his possession was connected to any sort of militia service.

In sum, § 992(*o*) does not impair the state's ability to maintain a well-regulated militia and therefore does not violate the Second Amendment.

10.   Where the fact that a firearm moved at some point in interstate commerce is alleged, how is it proved? Of course, if manufacturing, sales or transportation records are available, or other forms of evidence directly bearing on the issue, those forms of proof are likely to be used. When such evidence is not available, prosecutors may be forced to use indirect and circumstantial methods of proof. See, e.g., *United States v. Corey*, 207 F.3d 84 (1st Cir. 2000).

11.   The issue of whether there is a sufficient link to commerce arises in federal gun laws that prohibit the use of a gun in connection with commission of other crimes. See, e.g. *United States v. Bell*, 90 F.3d 318 (8th Cir. 1996):

Bell next argues that the District Court erred in denying his motion to dismiss the firearm count under 18 U.S.C. § 924(c)(1), which applies to any person who "during and in relation to any crime of violence or drug trafficking crime ... uses or carries a firearm." Relying on *United States v. Lopez*, 514 U.S. 549, 115 S.Ct. 1624, 131 L.Ed.2d 626 (1995), Bell contends that Congress lacks the authority under the Commerce Clause to make the use of firearms in connection with drug trafficking a federal offense. * * * We reject Bell's attempt to extrapolate the reasoning and holding in *Lopez* to § 924(c)(1).

Section 924(c)(1), unlike § 922(q), is tied to interstate commerce. Section 924(c)(1) is not a free-standing statute; it imposes an additional penalty for using or carrying a firearm during or in relation to the violation of other federal statutes for which there plainly is a nexus to interstate commerce. One of the statutory predicates for a § 924(c)(1) violation is the commission of a federal drug-trafficking offense, which is defined by § 924(c)(2) as including any felony punishable under the Controlled Substances Act, 21 U.S.C. §§ 801–971 (1994). In this case, Bell pleaded guilty to violating 21 U.S.C. § 841(a)(1). It is beyond question that the activity § 841(a)(1) seeks to criminalize—the production and distribution of controlled substances—substantially affects interstate commerce. Congress has made explicit findings concerning the effect that the drug trade has on interstate commerce. *See, e.g.,* 21 U.S.C. § 801(2) ("The illegal importation, manufacture, distribution, and possession and improper use of controlled substances have a substantial and detrimental effect on the health and general welfare of the American people."); *id.* § 801(4) ("Local distribution and possession of controlled substances contribute to swelling the interstate traffic in such substances."); *id.* § 801(6) ("Federal control of the intrastate incidents of the traffic in controlled substances is essential to the effective control of the interstate incidents of such traffic."). In light of these findings, we have held that Congress may regulate both interstate and intrastate drug trafficking under the Commerce Clause. Although Bell's argument explicitly challenges the constitutionality of § 924(c)(1), the argument implicitly questions the constitutionality of § 841(a)(1) because § 924(c)(1) derives its interstate nexus from that underlying federal drug-trafficking provision. Courts have determined consistently (both before and after *Lopez*) that § 841(a)(1) is a valid exercise of congressional Commerce Clause power.

BAILEY v. UNITED STATES

516 U.S. 137 (1995).

JUSTICE O'CONNOR delivered the opinion of the Court.

These consolidated petitions each challenge a conviction under 18 U.S.C. § 924(c)(1). In relevant part, that section imposes a 5–year minimum term of imprisonment upon a person who "during and in relation to any crime of violence or drug trafficking crime ... uses or carries a firearm." We are asked to decide whether evidence of the proximity and accessibility of a firearm to drugs or drug proceeds is alone sufficient to support a conviction for "use" of a firearm during and in relation to a drug trafficking offense under 18 U.S.C. § 924(c)(1).

In May 1989, petitioner Roland Bailey was stopped by police officers after they noticed that his car lacked a front license plate and an inspection sticker. When Bailey failed to produce a driver's license, the officers ordered him out of the car. As he stepped out, the officers saw Bailey push something between the seat and the front console. A search of the passenger compartment revealed one round of ammunition and 27 plastic bags containing a total of 30 grams of cocaine. After arresting Bailey, the officers searched the trunk of his car where they found, among a number of items, a large amount of cash and a bag containing a loaded 9–mm. pistol.

Bailey was charged on several counts, including using and carrying a firearm in violation of 18 U.S.C. § 924(c)(1). A prosecution expert testified at trial that drug dealers frequently carry a firearm to protect their drugs and money as well as themselves. Bailey was convicted by the jury on all charges, and his sentence included a consecutive 60–month term of imprisonment on the § 924(c)(1) conviction.

The Court of Appeals for the District of Columbia Circuit rejected Bailey's claim that the evidence was insufficient to support his conviction under § 924(c)(1). The court held that Bailey could be convicted for "using" a firearm during and in relation to a drug trafficking crime if the jury could reasonably infer that the gun facilitated Bailey's commission of a drug offense. In Bailey's case, the court explained, the trier of fact could reasonably infer that Bailey had used the gun in the trunk to protect his drugs and drug proceeds and to facilitate sales. Judge Douglas H. Ginsburg, dissenting in part, argued that prior Circuit precedent required reversal of Bailey's conviction.

In June 1991, an undercover officer made a controlled buy of crack cocaine from petitioner Candisha Robinson. The officer observed Robinson retrieve the drugs from the bedroom of her one-bedroom apartment.

After a second controlled buy, the police executed a search warrant of the apartment. Inside a locked trunk in the bedroom closet, the police found, among other things, an unloaded, holstered .22–caliber Derringer, papers and a tax return belonging to Robinson, 10.88 grams of crack cocaine, and a marked $20 bill from the first controlled buy.

* * *

A divided panel of the Court of Appeals reversed Robinson's conviction on the § 924(c)(1) count. The court determined, "given the way section 924(c)(1) is drafted, even if an individual intends to use a firearm in connection with a drug trafficking offense, the conduct of that individual is not reached by the statute unless the individual actually uses the firearm for that purpose." The court held that Robinson's possession of an unloaded .22–caliber Derringer in a locked trunk in a bedroom closet fell significantly short of the type of evidence the court had previously held necessary to establish actual use under § 924(c)(1). The mere proximity of the gun to the drugs was held insufficient to support the conviction. Judge Henderson dissented, arguing, among other things, that the firearm facilitated Robinson's distribution of drugs because it protected Robinson and the drugs during sales.

In order to resolve the apparent inconsistencies in its decisions applying § 924(c)(1), the Court of Appeals for the District of Columbia Circuit consolidated the two cases and reheard them en banc. In a divided opinion, a majority of the court held that the evidence was sufficient to establish that each defendant had used a firearm in relation to a drug trafficking offense and affirmed the § 924(c)(1) conviction in each case.

As the debate within the District of Columbia Circuit illustrates, § 924(c)(1) has been the source of much perplexity in the courts. The Circuits are in conflict both in the standards they have articulated, ... and in the results they have reached. ... We granted certiorari to clarify the meaning of "use" under § 924(c)(1). 514 U.S. 1062 (1995).

Section 924(c)(1) requires the imposition of specified penalties if the defendant, "during and in relation to any crime of violence or drug trafficking crime ..., uses or carries a firearm." Petitioners argue that "use" signifies active employment of a firearm. The Government opposes that definition and defends the proximity and accessibility test adopted by the Court of Appeals. We agree with petitioners, and hold that § 924(c)(1) requires evidence sufficient to show an *active employment* of the firearm by the defendant, a use that makes the firearm an operative factor in relation to the predicate offense.

This action is not the first one in which the Court has grappled with the proper understanding of "use" in § 924(c)(1). In *Smith*, we faced the question whether the barter of a gun for drugs was a "use," and concluded that it was. *Smith* v. *United States*, 508 U.S. 223, 124 L. Ed. 2d 138, 113 S. Ct. 2050 (1993). As the debate in *Smith* illustrated, the word "use" poses some interpretational difficulties because of the different meanings attributable to it. Consider the paradoxical statement: "I *use* a gun to protect my house, but I've never had to *use* it." "Use" draws meaning from its context, and we will look not only to the word itself, but also to the statute and the sentencing scheme, to determine the meaning Congress intended.

We agree with the majority below that "use" must connote more than mere possession of a firearm by a person who commits a drug offense. Had Congress intended possession alone to trigger liability under § 924(c)(1), it easily could have so provided. This obvious conclusion is supported by the frequent use of the term "possess" in the gun-crime statutes to describe prohibited gun-related conduct. See, *e.g.,* §§ 922(g), 922(j), 922(k), 922(*o*)(1), 930(a), 930(b).

Where the Court of Appeals erred was not in its conclusion that "use" means more than mere possession, but in its standard for evaluating whether the involvement of a firearm amounted to something more than mere possession. Its proximity and accessibility standard provides almost no limitation on the kind of possession that would be criminalized; in practice, nearly every possession of a firearm by a person engaged in drug trafficking would satisfy the standard, "thereby erasing the line that the statutes, and the courts, have tried to draw." Rather than requiring actual use, the District of Columbia Circuit would criminalize "simple possession with a floating intent to use." ...

An evidentiary standard for finding "use" that is satisfied in almost every case by evidence of mere possession does not adhere to the obvious congressional intent to require more than possession to trigger the statute's application.

This conclusion—that a conviction for "use" of a firearm under § 924(c)(1) requires more than a showing of mere possession—requires us to answer a more difficult question. What must the Government show, beyond mere possession, to establish "use" for the purposes of the statute? We conclude that the language, context, and history of § 924(c)(1) indicate that the Government must show active employment of the firearm.

We start, as we must, with the language of the statute. The word "use" in the statute must be given its "ordinary or natural" meaning, a meaning variously defined as "to convert to one's service," "to employ," "to avail oneself of," and "to carry out a purpose or action by means of." ... These various definitions of "use" imply action and implementation.

We consider not only the bare meaning of the word but also its placement and purpose in the statutory scheme. " 'The meaning of statutory language, plain or not, depends on context.' " ... Here, Congress has specified two types of conduct with a firearm: "uses" or "carries."

Under the Government's reading of § 924(c)(1), "use" includes even the action of a defendant who puts a gun into place to protect drugs or to embolden himself. This reading is of such breadth that no role remains for "carry." The Government admits that the meanings of "use" and "carry" converge under its interpretation, but maintains that this overlap is a product of the particular history of § 924(c)(1). Therefore, the Government argues, the canon of construction that instructs that "a legislature is presumed to have used no superfluous words," is inapplicable. We disagree. Nothing here indicates that Congress, when it provided these two terms, intended that they be understood to be redundant.

We assume that Congress used two terms because it intended each term to have a particular, nonsuperfluous meaning. While a broad reading of "use" undermines virtually any function for "carry," a more limited, active interpretation of "use" preserves a meaningful role for "carries" as an alternative basis for a charge. Under the interpretation we enunciate today, a firearm can be used without being carried, e.g., when an offender has a gun on display during a transaction, or barters with a firearm without handling it; and a firearm can be carried without being used, e.g., when an offender keeps a gun hidden in his clothing throughout a drug transaction.

* * *

To illustrate the activities that fall within the definition of "use" provided here, we briefly describe some of the activities that fall within "active employment" of a firearm, and those that do not.

The active-employment understanding of "use" certainly includes brandishing, displaying, bartering, striking with, and, most obviously, firing or attempting to fire a firearm. We note that this reading compels the conclusion that even an offender's reference to a firearm in his possession could satisfy § 924(c)(1). Thus, a reference to a firearm calculated to bring about a change in the circumstances of the predicate offense is a "use," just as the silent but obvious and forceful presence of a gun on a table can be a "use."

The example given above—"I use a gun to protect my house, but I've never had to use it"—shows that "use" takes on different meanings depending on context. In the first phrase of the example, "use" refers to an ongoing, inactive function fulfilled by a firearm. It is this sense of "use" that underlies the Government's contention that "placement for protection"—i. e., placement of a firearm to provide a sense of security or to embolden—constitutes a "use." It follows, according to this argument, that a gun placed in a closet is "used," because its mere presence emboldens or protects its owner. We disagree. Under this reading, mere possession of a firearm by a drug offender, at or near the site of a drug crime or its proceeds or paraphernalia, is a "use" by the offender, because its availability for intimidation, attack, or defense would always, presumably, embolden or comfort the offender. But the inert presence of a firearm, without more, is not enough to trigger § 924(c)(1). Perhaps the nonactive nature of this asserted "use" is clearer if a synonym is used: storage. A defendant cannot be charged under § 924(c)(1) merely for storing a weapon near drugs or drug proceeds. Storage of a firearm, without its more active employment, is not reasonably distinguishable from possession.

A possibly more difficult question arises where an offender conceals a gun nearby to be at the ready for an imminent confrontation. ... Some might argue that the offender has "actively employed" the gun by hiding it where he can grab and use it if necessary. In our view, "use" cannot extend to encompass this action. If the gun is not disclosed or mentioned by the offender, it is not actively employed, and it is not "used." To conclude otherwise would distort the language of the statute as well as create an impossible line-drawing problem. How "at the ready" was the firearm? Within arm's reach? In the room? In the house? How long before the confrontation did he place it there? Five minutes or 24 hours? Placement for later active use does not constitute "use." An alternative rationale for why "placement at the ready" is a "use"—that such placement is made with the intent to put the firearm to a future active use—also fails. As discussed above, § 924(d)(1) demonstrates that Congress knew how to draft a statute to reach a firearm that was "intended to be used." In § 924(c)(1), it chose not to include that term, but instead established the 5–year mandatory minimum only for those defendants who actually "use" the firearm.

While it is undeniable that the active-employment reading of "use" restricts the scope of § 924(c)(1), the Government often has other means available to charge offenders who mix guns and drugs. The "carry" prong of § 924(c)(1), for example, brings some offenders who would not satisfy the "use" prong within the reach of the statute. And Sentencing Guidelines § 2D1.1(b)(1) provides an enhancement for a person convicted of certain drug-trafficking offenses if a firearm was possessed during the offense. United States Sentencing Commission, Guidelines Manual § 2D1.1(b)(1) (Nov. 1994). But the word "use" in § 924(c)(1) cannot support the extended applications that prosecutors have sometimes placed on it, in order to penalize drug-trafficking offenders for firearms possession.

... To sustain a conviction under the "use" prong of § 924(c)(1), the Government must show that the defendant actively employed the firearm during and in relation to the predicate crime.

Notes

1. Sara Sun Beale, The Unintended Consequences of Enhancing Gun Penalties: Shooting Down the Commerce Clause and Arming Federal Prosecutors, 51 Duke L.J. 1641 (2002):

> To deter gun violence and punish gun offenders, Congress—like state legislatures—has repeatedly increased the penalties for illegal gun possession and the use of guns in the commission of other crimes. After several rounds of statutory increases, the penalties are now much higher than penalties for criminal conduct that accompanies gun possession and also very high relative to penalties for other serious offenses. By

designating separate penalties for gun use, as high or higher than the penalties for many of the most serious traditional offenses, Congress has sent a deterrent message to would-be offenders and sought to incapacitate those who will not be deterred.

The volume of litigation concerning the definition of 924(c) has been extraordinary. The Supreme Court has decided eight cases involving different facets of the construction of 924(c) since its passage in 1968, and many other issues have been litigated extensively in the lower courts. This unusual volume of litigation results, at least in part, from especially aggressive efforts by federal prosecutors to impose harsher penalties in cases at—or beyond—the outer limits of the statute, as defined by the statutory terms enacted by Congress. The higher penalties that were intended to deter would-be criminals have given prosecutors a strong incentive to press the boundaries of the statute outward to capture more cases.

2.   See *Muscarello v. United States*, 524 U.S. 125 (1998):

Second, petitioners point out that, in *Bailey v. United States*, we considered the related phrase "uses ... a firearm" found in the same statutory provision now before us. See 18 U.S.C. § 924(c)(1) ("uses or carries a firearm"). We construed the term "use" narrowly, limiting its application to the "active employment" of a firearm. Petitioners argue that it would be anomalous to construe broadly the word "carries," its statutory next-door neighbor.

In *Bailey*, however, we limited "use" of a firearm to "active employment" in part because we assumed "that Congress ... intended each term to have a particular, non-superfluous meaning." A broader interpretation of "use," we said, would have swallowed up the term "carry." But "carry" as we interpret that word does not swallow up the term "use." "Use" retains the same independent meaning we found for it in *Bailey*, where we provided examples involving the displaying or the bartering of a gun. *Ibid.* "Carry" also retains an independent meaning, for, under *Bailey*, carrying a gun in a car does not necessarily involve the gun's "active employment." More importantly, having construed "use" narrowly in *Bailey*, we cannot also construe "carry" narrowly without undercutting the statute's basic objective. For the narrow interpretation would remove the act of carrying a gun in a car entirely from the statute's reach, leaving a gap in coverage that we do not believe Congress intended.

See also *Castillo v. United States*, 530 U.S. 120 (2000):

The question before us is whether Congress intended the statutory references to particular firearm types in § 924(c)(1) to define a separate crime or simply to authorize an enhanced penalty. If the former, the indictment must identify the firearm type and a jury must find that element proved beyond a reasonable doubt. If the latter, the matter need not be tried before a jury but may be left for the sentencing judge to decide. As petitioners note, our decision in *Jones* concluded, in a similar situation, that treating facts that lead to an increase in the maximum sentence as a sentencing factor would give rise to significant constitutional questions. See *Jones*, 526 U.S. at 239–252. Here, even apart from the doctrine of constitutional doubt, our consideration of § 924(c)(1)'s language, structure, context, history, and such other factors as typically help courts determine a statute's objectives, leads us to conclude that the relevant words create a separate substantive crime.

4. In 1998, the pertinent language of § 924(c) was amended to read: "uses or carries a firearm, or who, in furtherance of any such crime, possesses a firearm, ..." What effect does the addition of the clause, "or ... in furtherance of any such crime, possesses a firearm" have on the coverage of the mandatory minimum penalty? Which fact situations discussed in *Bailey* which were not covered by 924(c) as a result of that decision may now be covered as a result of the 1998 amendment? What problems of interpretation or application does the added language pose?

b. The Violence Against Women Act

Among the most recent examples of federal criminal statutes based on a jurisdictional element of movement across a state line are three statutes that are part of the 1994 Violence Against Women Act (VAWA): 18 U.S.C. § 2261(a) (interstate domestic violence); 18 U.S.C. § 2261A (interstate stalking); and 18 U.S.C. § 2262 (interstate violation of protection order). The following cases illustrate how a serious, traditionally local criminal problem can become the subject of federal criminal prosecution when linked to the jurisdictional element of interstate travel.

UNITED STATES v. PAGE

167 F.3d 325 (6th Cir.1999).

Before: MARTIN, CHIEF JUDGE; MERRITT, KENNEDY, WELLFORD, NELSON, RYAN, BOGGS, NORRIS, SUHRHEINRICH, SILER, BATCHELDER, DAUGHTREY, MOORE, COLE, CLAY, and GILMAN, CIRCUIT JUDGES.

PER CURIAM.

The en banc court is equally divided in this case. Eight members of the court favor affirmance of the district court and join in Judge Moore's concurring opinion. Seven members of the court agree with Judge Kennedy's dissent and would reverse; Judge Ryan, writing separately would also reverse; Judge Wellford would reverse for the reasons stated in his separate opinion as well as those stated in the opinions of Judges Kennedy and Ryan. Hence, as is customary under such circumstances, the appellant's conviction and sentence are affirmed by an equally divided vote.

KAREN NELSON MOORE, CIRCUIT JUDGE, concurring in the order.

As a response to the "escalating problem of violence against women" and in recognition of the severe toll such crimes have on our society in terms of "health care, criminal justice, and other social costs," Congress enacted in 1994 the Violence Against Women Act ("VAWA" or the "Act"). S. REP. NO. 103–138, at 37, 41 (1993). Among numerous other provisions, the Act criminalized interstate domestic violence and interstate violation of protection orders. While Congress was particularly concerned with those crimes that "disproportionately burden women," S. REP. NO. 103–138, at 37, the criminal provisions are gender-neutral, and enforcement has been gender-neutral as well. *See, e.g., United States v. Gluzman*, 953 F. Supp. 84 (S.D.N.Y.1997) (upholding the indictment of a wife for the murder of her estranged husband in violation of 18 U.S.C. § 2261), *aff'd*, 154 F.3d 49 (2d Cir.1998).

Derek Page, the defendant in this case, was convicted under 18 U.S.C. § 2261(a)(2), which makes it illegal for any person to "cause a spouse or intimate partner to cross a State line ... by force, coercion, duress, or fraud and, in the course or as a result of that conduct, intentionally commit a crime of violence and thereby cause bodily injury to the person's spouse or intimate partner." On appeal, he raises the questions whether physical violence that occurs before interstate travel begins can satisfy the "in the course ... of that conduct" requirement of § 2261(a)(2) and whether a threat of violence that results in the aggravation of pre-existing injuries can be a "crime of violence" causing "bodily injury" for purposes of the statute. I would answer both questions in the affirmative and conclude that there was sufficient evidence for the jury to convict Page under either theory. Finally, I would reject Page's argument that § 2261(a)(2) is unconstitutional and hold that the statute is a constitutional exercise of Congress's power to regulate interstate commerce.

The facts of this case are not unlike the stories of many women who attempt to leave abusive relationships. Carla Scrivens's relationship with Page started out on fairly blissful terms. Yet, Page soon became controlling, possessive, and even physically abusive, * * *. In light of the deterioration of their relationship, after less than three months together, Scrivens told Page that she was moving out and ending their relationship.

The planned attack against Scrivens took place when she attempted to retrieve her belongings, all of which were still in Page's condominium in Columbus, Ohio. Upon Scrivens's arrival, Page pushed her down, dragged her away from the door when she attempted to leave, and tried to spray her with mace. He then beat her with his fists, a claw hammer, and a pipe wrench over the course of several hours. * * * After the beating, Page carried his victim, ... and placed her into his car under threat of further violence from his stun gun. Page then drove around for approximately four hours, crossing state lines through West Virginia into Pennsylvania and intentionally passing several local hospitals on the way even though Scrivens pleaded with him to stop for medical treatment at either Riverside or Ohio State University, two hospitals in the Columbus area. * * *

Page eventually left her at a hospital in Washington, Pennsylvania, where, after she realized that Page would not return, Scrivens told emergency room personnel that Page had attacked her and agreed to report the incident to the police.

Page was charged with kidnaping and interstate domestic violence. After his first trial resulted in a hung jury, a second jury acquitted him of kidnaping under 18 U.S.C. § 1201 and convicted him of interstate domestic violence under 18 U.S.C. § 2261(a)(2). * * *

A divided panel of this court reversed, holding that Page could be convicted under § 2261(a)(2) only for violence committed during the time in which he and Scrivens were actually traveling in the car. Concluding that the jury improperly had been permitted to consider the attack inside the condominium as the "crime of violence" underlying the interstate domestic violence charge, the panel remanded for a new trial. See 136 F.3d at 488. We granted rehearing en banc and now affirm by an equally divided vote.

Page's conduct, as presented to the jury, falls within the scope of § 2261(a)(2) under at least two theories of liability. The evidence showed that he committed interstate domestic violence both: (1) when, by beating his ex-girlfriend into a state of semi-consciousness over the course of several hours, he was enabled to and did force her across state lines against her will in an attempt to evade the law, and (2) when he forced her to travel interstate under threat of violence, intentionally preventing her from obtaining medical treatment, thereby causing aggravation of her pre-existing injuries.

A. "IN THE COURSE OF": INFLICTION OF BODILY INJURY INTEGRALLY RELATED TO THE FORCIBLE TRANSPORTATION OF A VICTIM ACROSS STATE LINES

In order to escape liability under § 2261(a)(2), Page argues that "in the course * * * of that conduct" as used in the statute refers to the narrow act of "crossing a State line" rather than to all conduct involved in "causing a spouse or intimate partner to cross a State line ... by force, coercion, duress, or fraud." As he interprets the statute, it does not reach the violence he committed inside the condominium, even though that conduct was an integral part of his causing his victim to cross state lines by force. This construction not only distorts the plain language of the statute but also makes little sense given the reality of the crime and the very reasons why Congress believed federal involvement was necessary in this area that has traditionally been left to the states.

The crime of violence that took place inside Page's condominium—the beating and the use of a stun gun and mace—is precisely what enabled Page to force Scrivens to travel across state lines. The beating subdued his victim, rendered her in no condition to resist him physically as she was being placed into his car, and frightened her so severely that she agreed not to make any "commotion" that might attract attention and aid from others once they left his condominium. The attack also allowed Page to retain control over Scrivens during the forcible transportation. ... The beating was an integral part of the forcible transportation since it enabled Page to force Scrivens on an unwilling four-hour journey the destination of which was not revealed to Scrivens until much later. Consequently, the beating that took place inside Page's condominium clearly occurred "in the course" of Page forcibly "causing" Scrivens "to cross a State line."

Furthermore, evidence presented to the jury showed that Page removed Scrivens from the local area precisely because he feared the consequences of his having harmed her and knew that interstate travel would make it more difficult for police authorities to hold him liable for his crime. It is difficult to believe that Congress intended to exclude from this statute's purview the beating of an intimate partner by a batterer who then forcibly transports his victim across state lines under threat of further violence in order to avoid detection from the law. Gaps and inadequacies of state law enforcement were among the main reasons for which federal legislation dealing with domestic violence was thought to be necessary. The VAWA was intended to deal with the problem of batterers who make their crimes more difficult to discover and prosecute by carrying or forcing their intimate partners across state lines. . . . When batterers take their victims across state lines, local prosecutors often encounter difficulties subpoenaing hospital documents and witnesses from other states. Multi-state jurisdiction is also valuable during the investigative stage, in which local police officers encounter similar barriers.

* * *

The Supreme Court recently reiterated the well-settled principle that "the transportation of persons across state lines" is a "form of 'commerce.' " . . . *Caminetti v. United States*, 242 U.S. 470, 491, 61 L. Ed. 442, 37 S. Ct. 192 (1917)). In *Caminetti*, the Court upheld the White Slave Traffic Act of 1910, under which the defendant had been convicted of transporting a woman across state lines for the purpose of prostitution or debauchery. The Court rejected the argument that the statute exceeded Congress's powers under the Commerce Clause because the purpose of debauchery was unrelated to commerce. . . . Section 2261(a)(2) is similarly constitutional under the Commerce Clause because the interstate domestic violence provision's requirement of "the crossing of a state line . . . places the [commission of a crime of violence causing bodily injury] squarely in interstate commerce." . . . Any arguably intrastate nature or timing of the crime of violence is irrelevant, just as it was with respect to the debauchery in *Caminetti*.

Page contends that Congress nonetheless exceeded its constitutional authority because, after *Lopez*, a criminal statute that regulates non-economic activity must be analyzed under the third category. This argument is based on a mis-reading of *Lopez*. *Lopez* has caused some controversy over whether purely *intrastate*, non-commercial activities can ever have the substantial effect on interstate commerce that is necessary to bring them within Congress's power. *Lopez* did not, however, extend the "substantial effects" test to all Commerce Clause legislation. Congress retains plenary power to regulate the channels of interstate commerce. *See United States v. Robertson*, 514 U.S. 669, 670, 131

L. Ed. 2d 714, 115 S. Ct. 1732 (1995) (explaining that the "substantial effects" test defines the extent of Congress's power to regulate intrastate activity and does not apply when the regulated activity itself crosses state lines. To hold that § 2261(a)(2) is unconstitutional, we would have to hold that *Lopez* overruled a long line of cases upholding Congress's power to criminalize acts occurring in interstate commerce. . . .

Page tries to distinguish this case from *Caminetti* and other cases allowing congressional regulation of interstate transportation by arguing that the *actus reus* of his crime was the initial attack on Scrivens, which was purely intrastate, while under statutes such as the White Slave Act and the Mann Act the *actus reus* is the actual movement across state lines with immoral intentions. His complaint is that although purporting to criminalize an act of *inter*state travel, Congress has "really" criminalized *intra*state domestic violence. Such an analysis was the basis for the holding that Congress could not bar the interstate shipment of the products of child labor because it was "really" trying to prohibit child labor itself. *See Hammer v. Dagenhart,* 247 U.S. 251, 271–72, 62 L. Ed. 1101, 38 S. Ct. 529 (1918), overruled by *Darby,* 312 U.S. at 116–17. This approach to the interstate commerce power has long since been rejected. Congress undoubtedly has the power to criminalize the forcible transportation of a person across state lines. It may as easily focus its efforts on the smaller class of cases in which the forced transportation is part of an incident of domestic violence in which the victim suffers bodily injury.

Because 18 U.S.C. § 2261(a)(2) is a valid exercise of Congress's powers under the Commerce Clause and reaches those situations where a beating of an intimate partner is integrally related to the subsequent transportation of the victim across state lines by force, I concur in the order affirming Page's conviction and sentence.

Notes

1. In the principal case, would the actions of Page in relation to Scrivens have been any less serious or any less an appropriate target of criminal sanctions if he had driven around for four hours, came very close to the Pennsylvania border, but never left Ohio?

2. Why should the federal government care more about Scrivens being beaten because Page happened to drive across two state lines during the four hour trip? Note that in *Page,* Judge Moore called attention to the fact that where interstate travel is involved, it is more difficult for local prosecutors effectively to pursue the matter. Is this likely to be true in every case of interstate travel involving this kind of crime? Even if not, is the fact that that kind of difficulty may occur in some cases enough justification to warrant federal jurisdiction and the possibility of federal prosecution in every case of a similar crime involving interstate travel?

3. As has been described in the previous chapter, the resources available to federal criminal enforcement are quite limited. Unless there is to be a major expansion in those resources (which itself would mean a major change in the allocation of law enforcement responsibilities in this country), the

federal role must inevitably be limited. In recent years, many scholars have discussed and debated what the nature of that limited federal criminal role should be. In Chapter 4, *infra*, we address in more detail the kind of justifications that have been suggested for 1) legislating federal crimes that are not aimed at protecting direct federal interests; 2) determining which of those crimes that have been thus legislated should be prosecuted.

UNITED STATES v. AL–ZUBAIDY

283 F.3d 804 (6th Cir. 2002).

COLE, CIRCUIT JUDGE.

This action stems from an interstate stalking charge under 18 U.S.C. § 2261A brought against Defendant Appellant Emad Al–Zubaidy. Al–Zubaidy argues that his bench trial conviction was not supported by sufficient evidence that he had formed the requisite intent under the statute, and that 18 U.S.C. § 2261A is an unconstitutional exercise of Congress's Commerce Clause power. Al–Zubaidy now appeals from the conviction and sentence imposed by the district court.

This appeal presents two issues for our review: (1) Whether the district court properly denied Defendant's Fed.R.Crim.P. 29(c) Motion for Judgment of Acquittal because there was sufficient evidence that Defendant crossed state lines with the intent to injure or harass his ex-wife; and (2) Whether 18 U.S.C. § 2261A exceeds Congress's authority under the Commerce Clause of the U.S. Constitution. We conclude that the district court properly denied Defendant's Motion for Judgment of Acquittal and affirm the judgment of the district court. We also conclude that 18 U.S.C. § 2261A does not exceed Congress's authority under the Commerce Clause of the U.S. Constitution.

I.

Defendant Al–Zubaidy and his wife Aathra Al–Shimary were married in Saudi Arabia in 1992. In 1994, Al–Zubaidy and Al Shimary moved to Rockford, Illinois with their two children. Their marriage was pervaded with abuse, and the record indicates multiple instances of physical and emotional mistreatment of Al Shimary. Al–Zubaidy also appears to have had trouble holding a job, drank heavily, and often would not come home until late at night.

The couple later spent time in Kansas City, Missouri, and Lincoln, Nebraska. In both locations, Al–Zubaidy continued his pattern of emotional and physical abuse against Al–Shimary. This pattern included severe blows, one of which caused Al–Shimary to fall down a flight of steps while pregnant with the couple's third child. A later assault nearly sent Al–Shimary into premature labor. While still in Nebraska, Al–Zubaidy spent time in jail for sexually assaulting another woman. After discovering that her husband was having sexual relations with another woman, Al–Shimary obtained a Nebraska divorce in 1997. Al–Shimary then moved back to Rockford, Illinois with her three children-in part because she feared possible repercussions from her ex-husband because of the divorce.

Al–Zubaidy followed Al–Shimary back to Rockford and maintained a separate residence. Soon thereafter, Al–Zubaidy began threatening Al–Shimary with physical harm if she did not reconcile their marriage. In particular, he would show up at her apartment and harass her, and threatened to burn down Al–Shimary's apartment. After several months of abuse, Al–Shimary decided to move to Detroit, Michigan to be near to her parents and younger brother and to escape from Al–Zubaidy.

Al–Shimary moved to Detroit in late October, 1997. The parties stipulate that Al–Zubaidy moved to Detroit on October 28 or 29, 1997, which the district court found to be a few days to a week after Al–Shimary's move. However, only three days after Al–Shimary's move, Al–Zubaidy began making threatening calls to Al–Shimary's father in Detroit. These threatening calls occurred on a daily basis, late at night, and involved death threats to the father concerning him, his wife, and Al–Shimary and her children. * * *

Although Al–Shimary did not live with her parents and brother in Detroit for the bulk of this harassment, she was aware of this harassment to her family, and would often have them spend the night with her and her children out of fear of Al–Zubaidy. The record does not state when Al–Zubaidy first learned Al–Shimary's new address in Detroit, but his direct harassment of her began in December, 1997–just two months after his arrival in Detroit. On one occasion, Al–Zubaidy allegedly assaulted Al–Shimary with a baseball bat outside of her apartment. Another time, Al–Zubaidy arrived at Al–Shimary's apartment with the stated intention to see his children, but quickly hit her in the head with a heavy toy truck. Al–Zubaidy and an accomplice also tried to force Al–Shimary into their car on a third occasion. In March, 1998, Al–Shimary's apartment was set on fire by an unknown arsonist, and Al–Zubaidy warned Al–Shimary's father that his house was "also going to burn down." These events were not isolated: Al–Shimary testified that Al Zubaidy would come to her apartment every night, standing outside and screaming at her. Even after Al–Shimary had moved to a new apartment to escape Al–Zubaidy's constant harassment, she noticed him waiting outside her apartment late at night.

* * * Al–Zubaidy was charged with one count of interstate stalking, in violation of 18 U.S.C. § 2261A. He waived a jury trial, and was found guilty by the district court on February 25, 2000. He was sentenced to a prison term of forty-six months on October 24, 2000.

Defendant argues that the United States failed to establish at the bench trial that he had crossed state lines with the intent to injure or harass Al–Shimary. Section 2261A has three main elements: (a) that interstate travel occurred; (b) that Defendant's intent was to injure or harass another person; and (c) that the person he intended to harass or injure was placed in reasonable fear of death or serious bodily injury to herself or a member of her family as a result of that travel.[2]

The first element of 18 U.S.C. 2261A, that Al–Zubaidy crossed state lines, is established by the parties' stipulation that he traveled from Illinois to Michigan on October 28 or 29, 1997. The third element also weighs heavily against Al–Zubaidy; regardless of his intent, his actions as a result of his travel to Detroit certainly placed Al–Shimary in reasonable fear of death or serious bodily injury to herself or a member of her family. The district court's factual findings, that Al–Shimary's "fear was reasonable based on his [Al–Zubaidy] assaultive and abusive history, and he [Al–Zubaidy] expressly included death in his threats not only to her but to her father and mother, as well," easily survive our clear error review.

The second element of § 2261A looks to whether Al–Zubaidy's intent was to injure or harass Al–Shimary and her family when he crossed state lines. Al–Zubaidy is correct when he argues that § 2261A requires more than a showing that he crossed a state line and then later stalked Al–Shimary. He must have intended to harass or injure Al–Shimary at the time he crossed the state line. While the district court made a factual finding that Al–Zubaidy's interstate travel took place "several days" after that of Al–Shimary and that he followed her to Detroit, the record is somewhat unclear as to exactly when Al–Shimary made her move. Al–Shimary also told her father at one point that Al–Zubaidy had come to visit her in Rockford (after the divorce, but before her move to Detroit) to see his children. That he also followed Al–Shimary to Detroit to be near his children, rather than harass Al–Shimary and her family, is plausible. Finally, even though Al–Zubaidy's harassment of Al–Shimary's family began almost immediately upon his arrival to Detroit, his first confirmed harassment of Al–Shimary in person did not occur until late December 1997—almost two months after his arrival.

The evidence supporting the district court's finding that Al Zubaidy possessed the requisite intent certainly "would allow a rational trier of fact to find the defendant guilty beyond a reasonable doubt" and thus survives our *de novo* review of the district court's denial of the Rule 29(c) motion. The general rule in criminal cases is that "intent may be inferred from the totality of circumstances surrounding the commission of the prohibited act."

The district court's factual findings that Al–Zubaidy moved to Detroit only a few days after Al–Shimary returned there to be near her parents has considerable support in the record. Al–Zubaidy's professed motive of reconciliation with his wife and children for moving to Detroit

---

2. The statute provides:

Whoever travels in interstate ... commerce ... with the intent to kill, injure, harass, or intimidate another person and in the course of, or as a result of, such travel places that person in reasonable fear of the death of, or serious bodily injury to, that person, [or] a member of the immediate family ... of that person ... shall be punished as provided in section 2261(b).

18 U.S.C. § 2261A

also holds little weight. Al–Shimary's father encouraged Al–Zubaidy to reconcile with his wife, and on two separate occasions Al–Zubaidy showed no interest whatsoever in doing so. The district court found that "there's simply no evidence to suggest that he [Al–Zubaidy] made any attempt to, or had any interest in, reconciling with his former wife." Under the totality of the circumstances test, Al–Zubaidy's proffered alternative motives for following his ex-wife to Detroit—reconciling with Al–Shimary or visiting his children—are minimized relative to his intention to "kill, injure, harass, or intimidate".

Finally, it is true that the timeline of Al–Zubaidy's actions was staggered, and that his most severe assaults and threats directly on Al–Shimary did not begin until nearly two months after his first arrival in Detroit on October 29, 1997. However, Al–Zubaidy's phone calls to the home of Al–Shimary's father-involving threats of death and damage to property began only a few days after the move. The statute covers threats that cause reasonable fear of the death or serious bodily injury not only to Al–Shimary herself, but also to a member of her immediate family. 18 U.S.C. § 2261A. Even if the reasonable fear of death or serious bodily injury to Al–Shimary does not qualify in this case because of the two month delay, her reasonable fear for her family does. *Id.*

The district judge's findings that Al–Zubaidy's intent was to "injure, harass, and abuse her [Al–Shimary] as much as he could get away with" also support § 2261A's requirement of reasonable fear to oneself. This finding is well-supported in the record, and survives our clear error review of a district court's findings of fact. It also is the logical outcome of the totality of the circumstances test to ascertain intent, and is readily supported by the evidence viewed in a light most favorable to the government. A rational trier of fact would have no difficulty finding the defendant guilty beyond a reasonable doubt under this evidence. The district court correctly found this evidence sufficient for the conviction and denial of the Rule 29(c) motion for acquittal.

* * *

Plaintiff argues that 18 U.S.C. § 2261A exceeds Congress's authority under the Commerce Clause of Article I, Section 8, Clause 3 of the U.S. Constitution.

In endorsing the constitutionality of § 2261A, the interstate stalking statute, we are careful to distinguish it from the statute at issue in *Morrison*. Section 13981 punished intrastate activity, included no jurisdictional element, and relied on the prohibited conduct's aggregate effect on interstate commerce. *Morrison*, 529 U.S. at 617. That § 13981 provides for civil remedies and § 2261A provides for criminal remedies is not nearly as important as the Commerce Clause justification for those remedies. Section 2261A is spared the "substantial effects" test for Commerce Clause regulation because it regulates a *channel* of commerce—prohibiting persons from crossing state lines to engage in unlawful conduct. *Lopez* and *Morrison* both endorse Congress's power to regulate under this category. Our own precedent following *Morrison* is in agreement, and we now join the Eighth Circuit in extending it to include 18 U.S.C. § 2261A.

c. The Travel Act and Related Statutes

UNITED STATES v. MAREK

238 F.3d 310 (5th Cir. 2001), cert. denied 534 U.S.
813, 122 S.Ct. 37, 151 L.Ed.2d 11 (2001).

Before Reynaldo G. Garza, Politz, Jolly, Higginbotham, Davis, Jones, Smith, Wiener, Barksdale, Emilio M. Garza, Demoss, Benavides, Stewart, Parker and Dennis, Circuit Judges.

Wiener, Circuit Judge:

According to its title, the federal murder-for-hire statute, 18 U.S.C. § 1958 (" § 1958"), criminalizes the "[u]se of *interstate commerce facilities* in the commission of murder-for-hire." The statute proscribes paying another to commit murder, but only when the defendant either (1) "travels in or causes another (including the intended victim) to travel in interstate or foreign commerce," or (2) "uses or causes another (including the intended victim) to use the mail or any facility in interstate or foreign commerce." Both of the instant cases concern only the second prong of § 1958's jurisdictional element, the *use* of an interstate (or foreign) commerce facility.

In *United States v. Cisneros,* [203 F.3d 333 (5th Cir.2000), *vacating* 194 F.3d 626 (5th Cir.1999).] a panel of this court suggested in *dicta* that, to satisfy the jurisdictional element, a facility must be used in an *inter* state fashion, i.e., that *intra* state use of a facility would not suffice, even though that facility is one that generally is an interstate commerce facility. In contrast, a divided panel of this court held, in *United States v. Marek,* [198 F.3d 532 (5th Cir.1999), *reh'g granted,* 206 F.3d 449 (5th Cir.2000).] that wholly *intra* state use of a facility that is an interstate commerce facility is sufficient to satisfy § 1958's jurisdictional element. The *Marek* majority acknowledged Cisneros but *reasoned that it was not binding because, in furtherance of her murder-for-hire scheme, Cisneros had caused international telephone calls to be made, an activity that indisputably satisfied the jurisdictional element even if Marek's wholly* intra *state communic*ation might not. Thus, the portion of *Cisneros* that suggests that § 1958's application is limited to *interstate* use of an interstate commerce communication facility is *dicta*.

To reconcile these differences and announce a consistent position for this Circuit, we voted to rehear both cases en banc, which had the collateral effect of vacating both panel decisions. We now adopt the position taken by the panel majority in *Marek* and hold that § 1958's *use* of a "facility in interstate commerce" is synonymous with the use of an "interstate commerce facility" and satisfies the jurisdictional element of that federal murder-for-hire statute, irrespective of whether the particular transaction in question is itself *inter* state or wholly *intra* state.

The facts are not in dispute. Defendant–Appellant Betty Louise Marek pleaded guilty to paying an undercover FBI agent, who was posing as a hit-man, to murder her boyfriend's paramour. Marek was arrested after she used Western Union to transfer $500 to the putative hit-man. Marek initiated the wire transfer in Houston, Texas, and it was received in Harlingen, Texas. The government introduced no evidence to show that the Western Union transmission actually crossed the Texas state line en route from Houston to Harlingen, so we must assume that it did not.[8] After the district court had accepted Marek's guilty plea and subsequently sentenced her, she appealed her conviction, urging that the district court erred when it found that she had admitted to facts that satisfied each legal element of the crime charged. Convinced that Western Union is "a facility in interstate commerce," and that this phrase is synonymous with "interstate commerce facility," a divided panel of this court affirmed her conviction, holding that Marek's wholly *intra* state use of Western Union was sufficient to satisfy the jurisdictional element of § 1958.

The relevant facts in *Cisneros* also are undisputed at this juncture. Doris Cisneros wanted to have her daughter's erstwhile boyfriend killed. Cisneros told this to her fortune teller and asked if the seer would find someone to commit the murder for a price. Acting as Cisneros's agent, the clairvoyant—through another client—ultimately located and employed two hit-men for Cisneros. In doing so the oracle placed and received international phone calls between Texas and Mexico. The hit-men traveled from Mexico to Brownsville, Texas, where they shot and killed Cisneros's intended victim. A jury convicted Cisneros, and she appealed.

A panel of this court concluded that a reasonable jury could have found that (1) the fortune teller had participated in international telephone calls as Cisneros agent, and (2) those calls were sufficiently connected to the murder to be n furtherance of that crime. The panel therefore affirmed Cisneros conviction.

A crucial factual distinction between *Marek* and *Cisneros* exists: In *Cisneros* the subject telephone calls were unquestionably international so the *use* of the telephone facility was international ("foreign"), as is the telephone facility itself; in *Marek,* however, there was only an *intra* state communication (a wire transfer of funds between two Texas cities), albeit the communication facility, Western Union, is an interstate com-

---

8. As described in a recent Fifth Circuit case, however, the Western Union procedure for wiring money from one Texas city to another (in that case, from Lufkin to Beaumont) required Western Union agents in both cities to call the company's main computer in Bridgeton, Missouri. *See United States v. Brumley,* 79 F.3d 1430, 1432–33 (5th Cir.1996), *rev on other grounds en banc,* 116 F.3d 728, 731 (5th Cir.1997) (affirming convictions and noting that the wire transfers "were accomplished electronically through a Western Union facility located outside of Texas"); *see also United States v. Davila,* 592 F.2d 1261, 1263 (5th Cir.1979) (upholding wire fraud conviction under 18 U.S.C. § 1343 of defendant who used Western Union to send money between San Antonio and McAllen when all wire transfers were routed through Middletown, Virginia).

merce facility. Therefore, to affirm *Marek* we must conclude that § 1958 reaches *intra* state use of a facility in interstate commerce. In *Cisneros,* on the other hand, even if we assume *arguendo* that the statute should be accorded the narrowest interpretation possible, we must affirm Cisneros's conviction on the strength of the international (foreign) telephone calls.

In Marek's case we must ask whether, for purposes of satisfying the jurisdictional element of the federal murder-for-hire statute, it is sufficient that the defendant used an interstate commerce facility in an *intra state fashion. Asked differently, is it necessary that both (1) the facility and (2) the defendant*'s use of that facility be in interstate or foreign commerce? To answer this question, we will look first to the plain language of the statute and second to its statutory context.

§ 1958. Use of interstate commerce facilities in the commission of murder-for-hire

(a) Whoever travels in or causes another (including the intended victim) to travel in interstate or foreign commerce, *or uses or causes another (including the intended victim) to use the mail or any facility in interstate or foreign commerce*, with intent that a murder be committed in violation of the laws of any State or the United States as consideration for the receipt of, or as consideration for a promise or agreement to pay, anything of pecuniary value, or who conspires to do so, shall be fined [or imprisoned] under this title[.]

(b) As used in this section and section 1959—

(1) "anything of pecuniary value" means anything of value in the form of money, a negotiable instrument, a commercial interest, or anything else the primary significance of which is economic advantage;

(2) *"facility of interstate commerce"* includes means of *transportation* and *communication*; and

(3) "State" includes a State of the United States, the District of Columbia, and any

As is patent on the face of the statute, this crime can be committed by engaging in either of two distinct activities: (1) *travel* or (2) *use*. If, in *Marek* or *Cisneros* (or both), the jurisdictional element was satisfied, it must have been under the use prong, as the travel prong is nowhere implicated. The travel and use prongs are distinguishable by the divergent natures of the two activities: *Travel* requires the physical movement of a person, such as by walking, running, or riding in or on a bike, car, wagon, train, bus, or airplane; in contrast, *use* contemplates a perpetrator who remains essentially stationary while causing an inanimate object to be (1) communicated (e.g., a letter, telegram, or money order) or (2) transported (e.g., a gun, a bomb, or cash). The statute's definition of travel never mentions the facility; presumably a perpetrator could violate the travel prong on foot, using no "facility" at all, as, for example, by hiking cross-country to deliver the blood money.

The key question of statutory construction presented in *Marek* is whether, under the use prong of § 1958, the phrase "in interstate or foreign commerce" modifies "use" or modifies "facility." Purely from a structural viewpoint, we must conclude that "in interstate or foreign commerce" is an adjective phrase that modifies "facility," the noun that immediately precedes it—*not* an adverbial phrase that modifies the syntactically more remote verb, "[to] use." We see the former conclusion as the more natural and sensible reading of the relevant portion of the statute. Primarily because of the proximity of "in interstate or foreign commerce" to "facility," the word which that phrase modifies is facility and not use. A contrary conclusion—that "in interstate or foreign commerce" modifies "use"—would require a strained structural interpretation of the statute.

When it adopted § 1958, Congress was acting within the second of three broad categories identified by the Supreme Court in *United States v. Lopez* as conduct appropriately subject to regulation under the Commerce Clause. Of the second category, the Court wrote that "Congress is empowered to regulate and protect the instrumentalities of interstate commerce, or persons or things in interstate commerce, *even though the threat may come only from intrastate activities.*" When Congress regulates and protects under the second *Lopez* category, therefore, federal jurisdiction is supplied by the nature of the instrumentality or facility used, not by separate proof of interstate movement. Under statutes similar to § 1958, federal jurisdiction based on *intra* state use of *inter* state facilities is an appropriate exercise of the commerce power, as this and other circuit courts repeatedly have found.

In *United States v. Heacock,* [31 F.3d 249, 255 (5th Cir.1994)] this circuit concluded that the U.S. Post Office is a "facility in interstate commerce," and that intrastate mailings satisfied the jurisdictional requirement of the Travel Act.[29] Significant to our analysis today, the *Heacock opinion alludes to the mail*'s unique history but never mentions Congress's postal power, instead stressing the status of the mail as an interstate commerce facility:

> In other words, whenever a person uses the United States Post Office to deposit, to transport, and to deliver parcels, money, or other material by means of the mail, that person clearly and unmistakably has used a "facility in interstate commerce," irrespective of the intrastate destination of the item mailed.

Congress had made the sufficiency of intrastate mailings plain in a 1990 amendment entitled "Clarification of applicability of 18 U.S.C.1952 to all mailings in furtherance of unlawful activity." The amendment changed § 1952's wording slightly to mirror that of § 1958, targeting "[w]hoever travels in interstate or foreign commerce or uses the mail or

29. 18 U.S.C. § 1952. We have previously held that it is appropriate to interpret § 1958 in light of § 1952 given that the two sections employ similar language, and that § 1958 was intended to supplement § 1952. *United States v. Edelman,* 873 F.2d 791, 794 (5th Cir.1989).

any facility in interstate or foreign commerce."[33] As Congress thus expressly made clear that § 1952 applies to intrastate mailings, and did so by importing § 1958's wording into § 1952, logic dictates that precisely the same wording in § 1958 must apply equally to intrastate use of other interstate facilities, such as Western Union.

In a similar vein, through passage of a 1994 amendment to the federal mail fraud statute, Congress expanded 18 U.S.C. § 1341 to reach private interstate commercial carriers, such as Emery, DHL, and Federal Express, in addition to the U.S. Postal Service. Although no circuit court has addressed whether that amendment requires the crossing of state lines to establish jurisdiction, one district court recently held that the amended statute does cover "purely intrastate delivery of mails by private or commercial carriers as long as those carriers engage in interstate deliveries. . . . While jurisdiction lies only under the Commerce Clause for the use of private or commercial carriers, Congress may still regulate their intrastate activities because they are instrumentalities of interstate commerce."[34] Here again, the conclusion is appropriate because intrastate use of interstate facilities is properly regulated under Congress's second-category *Lopez* power.

Mail and delivery services are not the only "means of transportation and communication" amenable to congressional Commerce Clause protection under *Lopez* during wholly intrastate use. Interstate commerce facilities that have created a criminal federal jurisdictional nexus during intrastate use include telephones,[35] automobiles, and airplanes. Perhaps most analogous to Marek's use of Western Union are the facts of *United States v. Baker*, [82 F.3d 273 (8th Cir.1996), *cert. denied*, 519 U.S. 1020, 117 S.Ct. 538, 136 L.Ed.2d 423 (1996).] an Eighth Circuit case holding that an interstate network of automatic teller machines ("ATMs") is a facility in interstate commerce "squarely within the literal language of the Travel Act." In *Baker*, the Eighth Circuit upheld a Travel Act conviction based on an extortion victim's cash withdrawal from his local bank using another local bank's ATM. The *Baker* court noted that, even though the transaction at issue was strictly local, customers could use

---

33. Before amendment, § 1952 applied to "[w]hoever travels in interstate or foreign commerce or uses any facility in interstate or foreign commerce, including the mail." This is the language interpreted in *Heacock*.

34. *United States v. Photogrammetric Data Services, Inc.,* 103 F.Supp.2d 875, 882 (E.D.Va.2000).

35. *United States v. Weathers,* 169 F.3d 336, 341 (6th Cir.1999) ("It is well established that telephones, even when used intrastate, constitute instrumentalities of interstate commerce."), *cert. denied*, 528 U.S. 838, 120 S.Ct. 101, 145 L.Ed.2d 85 (1999); *United States v. Gilbert,* 181 F.3d 152, 158–59 (1st Cir.1999) (finding jurisdiction under 18 U.S.C. § 844(e), concerning threats made "through the use of the mail, tele-

phone, telegraph, or other instrument of interstate or foreign commerce, or in or affecting interstate or foreign commerce"); *United States v. Clayton,* 108 F.3d 1114, 1117 (9th Cir.1997) (cellular telephones); *United States v. Houlihan,* 92 F.3d 1271, 1292 (1st Cir.1996) (assuming that telephones are facilities in interstate commerce under § 1958); *Alley v. Miramon,* 614 F.2d 1372, 1379 (5th Cir.1980) (stating, in a securities case, that the court as consistently held that the intrastate use of the telephone may confer jurisdiction over a private action under Section 10(b) and Rule 10b–5. Rule 10b–5 supplies jurisdiction by the use of any means or instrumentality of interstate commerce or of the mails.

the ATM network to make interstate deposits and withdrawals, and the court noted: "Though [the victim's] withdrawal triggered an entirely intrastate electronic transfer between [the two local banks], the jury found that [the defendant] caused [the victim] to use a facility in interstate commerce."

The dissent notes that we are splitting with the Sixth Circuit's interpretation of 1958 in *United States v. Weathers,* [supra n. 35] in which that court found jurisdiction proper based on a defendant's in-state call using a cellular telephone that sent an interstate search signal. Although the holdings of this case and *Weathers* do not actually conflict with each other, it is true that our reasoning does. As noted above, however, the Sixth Circuit's reasoning that the use of an instrumentality *in* interstate commerce (i.e., the mail) requires the crossing of state lines was expressly rejected by congressional amendment of the Travel Act.[43] We did not follow that reasoning in *Heacock* and we decline to do so now, particularly given Congress's use of the very language of 1958 we interpret today to remove any possible doubt that the Travel Act applies even to intrastate mailings.[44]

We are satisfied that when § 1958 is read as a whole and viewed in context as part of the power of Congress to regulate and protect the instrumentalities of interstate commerce, even when the threat comes from intrastate activities, it becomes clear that the *facility,* not its use, is what must be "in interstate or foreign commerce." In the instant context, then, when a facility employed to advance murder-for-hire is in interstate or foreign commerce generally, the jurisdictional element of § 1958 is satisfied even though the particular *use* of the facility on the specific occasion in question is only *intra* state. Thus, both (1) Marek's intrastate use of Western Union—a quintessential facility *in* interstate commerce—to transfer funds within Texas, and (2) Cisneros's international telephone calls, are sufficient to satisfy the jurisdictional element of § 1958, and—more importantly—that jurisdictional element is present in the statute through a valid exercise of congressional Commerce Clause power under the second *Lopez* category. . . .

---

43. The Sixth Circuit reasons that a statute regulating a "facility *in* interstate commerce" governs channels of interstate commerce, the first *Lopez* category, while a "facility *of* interstate commerce" falls into the second *Lopez* category, comprising the instrumentalities of interstate commerce. We conclude that the "use of facilities (*in* or *of*) interstate commerce" in violation of § 1958 falls into the second category. Because it is not necessary to this case, we do not decide whether § 1958's "travel in interstate commerce" prong refers to the channels of interstate commerce, or to *Lopez*'s second-category "persons or things in interstate commerce." *See Lopez,* 514 U.S. at 558, 115 S.Ct. 1624.

44. The dissent, like the Sixth Circuit, would decide this case based on perceived differences in the meanings of "of" and "in." In *Dupuy v. Dupuy,* 511 F.2d 641, 642–43 (5th Cir.1975), we found significant that the Securities Act of 1933 based jurisdiction on the use of instruments *in* interstate commerce, while the Securities Exchange Act of 1934 required use of an instrumentality *of* interstate commerce. We do not contend that similarly varying phraseology never can have statutory significance; we merely conclude, based on the grammatical structure of § 1958 and the use of both phrases interchangeably in the statute and its legislative history, that Congress's particular deployment of these two prepositions in § 1958 is not dispositive of this case.

Marek nevertheless contends that subsection (b)(2) of § 1958—which explains that "facility of interstate commerce" includes both means of *transportation* and means of *communication*—introduces an ambiguity into the statute. Marek's argument goes as follows: There is an inconsistency between the statute's substantive subsection (§ 1958(a)), which uses the phrase "facility *in* interstate or foreign commerce," on the one hand, and subsection (b)(2)'s "defining" of the phrase "facility *of* interstate commerce," on the other. Marek contends that the phrase used in the substantive subsection ("facility *in* interstate commerce") implicates a more restricted class of facilities than does the phrase used in the "definitional" subsection ("facility *of* interstate commerce") because, she insists, for a facility to be *in* interstate commerce, there must be a nexus between the facility and its use in interstate commerce. In other words, in Marek's view, facilities are only *in* interstate commerce when they are employed in an interstate fashion, whereas a facility that is almost always used *in* interstate commerce (like Western Union) remains a facility *of* interstate commerce, even in instances when its use is intrastate. Given this inconsistency between the substantive provision of subsection (a) and the explanatory provisions of subsection (b)(2), urges Marek, the substantive subsection must predominate. Thus, continues Marek's argument, as her use of Western Union (which she admits is a facility *of* interstate commerce) was wholly *intra* state it was not the *use* of a facility *in* interstate commerce, even though the facility itself is an interstate commerce facility. Not surprisingly, we disagree.

First, we find the inconsistency between § 1958(a) and (b)(2) to be more apparent than real, and that use of slightly different phraseology in the clarification section ("of" rather than "in") was not intended by Congress to limit the scope of the statute. Subsection (b)(2) does not "define" facility; rather, it merely clarifies that a facility can be a means of transportation, such as an interstate delivery service, *or* a means of communication, such as a telegraph or telephone network. As the travel prong of the statute never mentions "facility," subsection (b)(2) applies only to the use prong, merely clarifying that it covers the sending of *things* as well as *messages*. For example, sending a bomb from Houston to Harlingen via UPS would involve *transportation* because a "thing" is sent, but sending a letter from Houston to Harlingen via Federal Express would involve *communication* because only a message is sent. In both instances, however, a "facility" is "used." Despite Marek's effort to create ambiguity out of whole cloth, we perceive none.

The legislative history of § 1958 is even more persuasive. A 1983 Senate Judiciary Committee report describes the offense punishable under the murder-for-hire statute as "the travel in interstate or foreign commerce or the use of the facilities of interstate or foreign commerce or of the mails, as consideration for the receipt of anything of pecuniary value, with the intent that a murder be committed." The report later explains that "[t]he gist of the offense is the travel in interstate commerce or the use of the facilities of interstate commerce or of the mails with the requisite intent and the offense is complete whether or not the murder is carried out or even attempted." Even though the statute was not intended to usurp the authority of state and local officials, the report states, "the option of Federal investigation and prosecution should be available when a murder is committed or planned as consideration for something of pecuniary value and the proper Federal nexus, such as interstate travel, use of the facilities of interstate commerce, or use of the mails, is present." In a discussion of the murder-for-hire portion of the bill extending over three pages, the Senate report uses the phrase "facility [or facilities] *of* interstate commerce" four times and "facility *in* interstate commerce" only once, drawing no apparent distinction between the two. We find inescapable the conclusion that "of" and "in" were considered and used by Congress as synonyms in regards to this particular statute.

We hold today that the statute is unambiguous and clear on its face. But even if we were to assume, for argument's sake, that the statute is ambiguous, any lingering doubt regarding the statute's meaning is laid to rest by the title of the section. The title of § 1958—"Use of interstate commerce facilities in the commission of murder-for-hire"—plainly eliminates any claim of ambiguity. The title is unambiguous and clearly employs "interstate commerce" to modify "facility," not "use." The Supreme Court has held that it is appropriate to consider the title of a statute in resolving putative ambiguities . . . .

Section 1958 employs three phrases to describe "facility" in the context of the statute: "interstate commerce facilities" in the title; "facility in interstate or foreign commerce" in subsection (a); and "facility of interstate commerce" in subsection (b)(2). A review of the statute, its legislative history, and the United States Code as a whole indicates that, at least in this statute, Congress used these terms interchangeably as synonyms.

Not to be dissuaded, Marek further contends that: (1) Even if we reject her construction of the statute in favor of the government's, we must nevertheless find that both constructions are reasonable and choose the narrower one pursuant to the rule of lenity; (2) the government's construction raises doubts about the statute's constitutionality, which must be resolved in a way that avoids potential constitutional infirmity; and (3) the federal murder-for-hire statute criminalizes conduct that is traditionally the province of state law enforcement, and Congress should not be presumed to have altered the federal-state balance unless it speaks with unmistakable clarity. We dispose of each of these contentions in turn.

The rule of lenity—rule of narrow construction rooted in concern for individual rights, awareness that it is the legislature and not the courts that should define criminal activity, and belief that fair warning should be accorded as to what conduct is criminal—applies when, but only when, "after seizing every thing from which aid can be derived, the Court is left with an ambiguous statute." We are convinced that this is not such a case and, under these circumstances, we will not "blindly incant the rule of lenity to 'destroy the spirit and force of the law which the legislature intended to and did enact.' "

Additionally, the rule of lenity should not be invoked here because it was no surprise to Marek that murder-for-hire is a serious crime with serious penalties. The principle behind the rule of lenity is that no one should be forced to speculate whether her conduct is prohibited. It would be absurd to say that Marek did not know that her conduct—hiring an assassin to commit murder—was prohibited.

The rule of constitutional doubt is likewise inapplicable. Marek contends that a broad application of § 1958 to intrastate activities would violate the Tenth Amendment, compelling adoption of the narrow interpretation of the statute she advocates to save it from constitutional infirmity. For all the reasons stated above, however, the statute's requirement that a perpetrator either travel in interstate commerce or use an interstate commerce facility confirms that the statute raises no constitutional concerns, given Congress's clear constitutional authority to regulate interstate commerce. "[T]he authority of Congress to keep the channels of interstate commerce free from immoral and injurious uses has been frequently sustained, and is no longer open to question."

Finally, Marek argues that the intention to alter the federal-state balance in this area—traditionally the province of state law enforcement—must be evidenced by unmistakable clarity. For the same reasons that we reject application of the rule of lenity hat (1) the statute is plain on its face, and (2) even if we concede for the sake of argument that there is some slight internal inconsistency in terminology, it is resolved by the statute legislative history and title—we reject the notion that Congress has not spoken with sufficient clarity to criminalize conduct traditionally the subject of state criminal laws.

Like Marek's, the dissent's lament over the perceived trampling of states' rights misses the mark by the palpable failure to include a crucial observation: Under § 1958, federal authorities have nothing more than *concurrent* jurisdiction over the subset of murders-for-hire that bear the requisite nexus with interstate commerce. The legislative history plainly states that federal investigation and prosecution should be no more than an "option" to be "used in appropriate cases" to assist state and local authorities, and that "Federal jurisdiction should be asserted selectively based on such factors as the type of defendants reasonably believed to be involved and the relative ability of the Federal and State authorities to investigate and prosecute."

The records in both of these cases eschew any possibility that federal authorities preemptively muscled aside local law enforcement; rather, federal law enforcement was invited by the locals to become involved. Cisneros first was tried and convicted of capital murder in state court. Only after a Texas appellate court reversed that conviction for insufficiency of the evidence did the state take the initiative and turn over her case to federal prosecutors. As for Marek, a county sheriff's deputy tipped to her quest for a mercenary killer referred the case to the Texas Rangers, who in turn referred the case to the FBI. The two cases before us illustrate the very "[c]ooperation and coordination between Federal and State officials" that Congress intended that § 1958 foster. The embodiment of such clear legislative intent in providing for concurrent jurisdiction and preemption must not be overlooked in analogizing the extent of congressional intrusion into spheres of state and local law enforcement. With all due respect, we believe that the dissent would be well advised to pull back its states' rights argument. Failure to acknowledge that § 1958 creates *concurrent* jurisdiction only subjects the dissent's objectivity to question. For despite its *power* to preempt this area when regulating commerce, Congress exercised restraint and comity, in the true spirit of Federalism, by creating only *concurrent* jurisdiction. . . .

AFFIRMED.

[E. GRADY JOLLY, CIRCUIT JUDGE, joined by EDITH H. JONES, JERRY E. SMITH, BARKSDALE and DEMOSS, CIRCUIT JUDGES, wrote a dissenting opinion.]

Notes

1. See also *Bertoldo v. United States*, 145 F.Supp.2d 111 (D. Mass. 2001):

> Bertoldo argues that he did not intend to commit a murder for hire when he traveled across interstate lines and, as a result, this court did not have jurisdiction over the crime. Bertoldo, however, misconstrues the relationship between the intent element and the jurisdictional element of 18 U.S.C. § 1958. The intent element of § 1958 relates to murder; it does not relate to interstate activity. *See, U.S. v. Winters*, 33 F.3d 720, 721 (6th Cir.1994). The interstate travel merely triggers federal jurisdiction. A defendant need not intend to travel across state lines to commit a murder for hire; instead, a defendant need only intend to commit a murder for hire and, in doing so, travel across state lines.

> As the *Winters* court pointed out, "[t]he significance of labeling a statutory requirement as 'jurisdictional' is not that the requirement is viewed as outside the scope of the evil Congress intended to forestall, but merely that the existence of the fact that confers federal jurisdiction need not be one in the mind of the actor at the time he perpetrates the act made criminal by the federal statute." *Id.* at 721 (internal quotations omitted). Here, Bertoldo's claim that the murder for hire was not on his mind when he drove from Connecticut to Massachusetts is of no jurisdictional significance.

2. The *Marek* case is important for a number of reasons.

a. The majority opinion takes a strong position on an issue that had caused a split among the circuits—whether jurisdiction based on the "use of a facility "in" or "of" commerce can be based on a purely intrastate act such as a local telephone call. If federal jurisdiction under one of the relevant statutes can be based on a local phone call, how broad is the coverage of the statutes that contain such jurisdictional language.

b. The majority treats use of the mails as a commerce power basis for jurisdiction rather than a postal power issue. Is this sound?

c. The court notes a number of different kinds of "facilities" of interstate commerce and their use. Can you think of any not mentioned by the court?

d. The court finds a basis for jurisdiction under the statute in the intrastate use of a facility of commerce. How does this compare with the basis for jurisdiction that the Supreme Court found in cases like *Wickard v. Filburn, Perez v. United States,* and *Gonzales v. Raich?* Are there parallels? Differences?

e. The case provides a good review of the several maxims of statutory construction that the courts invoke with relative frequency in federal criminal cases. What are the differences in the applicability and effects of these maxims?

f. The case points out the relationship between the Travel Act, 18 U.S.C. § 1952 and the Murder-for-Hire statute, 18 U.S.C. § 1958. While the jurisdictional provisions in the two statutes are quite similar, the substantive coverage of the Travel Act is much broader.

3. The Travel Act provides:

§ 1952. Interstate and foreign travel or transportation in aid of racketeering enterprises

(a) Whoever travels in interstate or foreign commerce or uses the mail or any facility in interstate or foreign commerce, with intent to

(1) distribute the proceeds of any unlawful activity; or

(2) commit any crime of violence to further any unlawful activity; or

(3) otherwise promote, manage, establish, carry on, or facilitate the promotion, management, establishment, or carrying on, of any unlawful activity,

and thereafter performs or attempts to perform—

(A) an act described in paragraph (1) or (3) shall be fined under this title, imprisoned not more than 5 years, or both; or

(B) an act described in paragraph (2) shall be fined under this title, imprisoned for not more than 20 years, or both, and if death results shall be imprisoned for any term of years or for life.

(b) As used in this section (i) "unlawful activity" means (1) any business enterprise involving gambling, liquor on which the Federal excise tax has not been paid, narcotics or controlled substances (as defined in section 102(6) of the Controlled Substances Act) [21 U.S.C. § 802(b)], or prostitution offenses in violation of the laws of the State in which they are committed or of the United States, (2) extortion, bribery, or arson in violation of the laws of the State in which committed or of the United States, or (3) any act which is indictable under subchapter II of chapter 53 of title 31, United States Code, or under section 1956 or 1957 of this title and (ii) the term "State" includes a State of the United

States, the District of Columbia, and any commonwealth, territory, or possession of the United States.

(c) Investigations of violations under this section involving liquor shall be conducted under the supervision of the Secretary of the Treasury.

4. The Travel Act was enacted in 1961, at the beginning of the Kennedy Administration as an outgrowth of concern about "organized crime," The bill was aimed at organized crime figures whose criminal activities crossed state lines; it originally covered only interstate travel but was amended in the course of the legislative process to cover the use of any facility in interstate commerce, including the mails and telephones.

The statute as finally enacted was innovative in a number of respects. It relied upon the commerce power to make criminal not just one but a number of major categories of crime heretofore only made criminal under state law. It utilized for the first time the technique of incorporating state crimes directly into a specific federal criminal statute where the conduct had some link to commerce. It adopted an expansive approach to the type of crime related deeds to be covered by the Act. It also adopted an expansive approach to the commerce connection, requiring interstate movement but covering all forms thereof including the absorption of the use of the mails into the commerce base.

The Travel Act can be viewed as the direct forerunner of the modern complex and organizational crime statutes: RICO, the illegal gambling business statute, and the continuing criminal enterprise statute. It was the first federal criminal statute that contained the principle components of a complex crime—that is, it expressly included multiple other crimes among its elements. Because the Travel Act incorporated into its terms crimes defined by reference to state law, the scope of the federal statute was to be determined in part by the breadth of interpretation given to such "state law" terms. See *Perrin v. United States*, 444 U.S. 37 (1979):

> The Travel Act was one of several bills enacted into law by the 87th Congress as part of the Attorney General's 1961 legislative program directed against "organized crime." Then Attorney General Robert Kennedy testified at Senate and House hearings that federal legislation was needed to aid state and local governments which were no longer able to cope with the increasingly complex and interstate nature of large scale, multiparty crime. The stated intent was to "dry up" traditional sources of funds for such illegal activities. . . .

> To remedy a gap in the authority of federal investigatory agencies, Congress employed its now familiar power under the Commerce Clause of the Federal Constitution to prohibit activities of traditional state and local concern that also have an interstate nexus . . . That Congress was consciously linking the enforcement powers and resources of the federal and state governments to deal with traditional state crimes is shown by its definition of "unlawful activity" as an "enterprise involving gambling, liquor . . ., narcotics or controlled substances . . ., or prostitution offenses in violation of the laws of the State in which they are committed or of the United States." The statute also makes it a federal offense to travel or use a facility in interstate commerce to commit "extortion

[or] bribery ... in violation of the laws of the State in which committed or of the United States." Because the offenses are defined by reference to existing state as well as federal law, it is clear beyond doubt that Congress intended to add a second layer of enforcement supplementing what it found to be inadequate state authority and state enforcement.

5.   In *Perrin v. United States, supra* note 4, the Court stated that "a major area of Congressional concern was with the infiltration by organized crime into legitimate activities." See, e.g., *United States v. Davis*, 780 F.2d 838 (10th Cir.1985) where the defendants argued that the Travel Act was "directed toward organized crime," and that their case fell outside the reach of the Act because "there was no evidence of any element of organized crime or of an association of their activities with a larger, ongoing enterprise." *Id.* at 843. The court responded that although "the legislative history of the Travel Act indicates it was aimed at combating organized crime, it has been clearly established that its reach is not limited to that end."

6.   The *Perrin* case, *supra* note 4, was a prosecution under the Travel Act involving a commercial bribery scheme in which an employee was paid to steal valuable confidential geological data from the geological exploration company for which he worked. The government alleged Travel Act jurisdiction based on interstate telephone calls and interstate transportation of materials in furtherance of the scheme. The defendant contended that "bribery" under the Travel Act should be limited to its common law meaning and not be extended to commercial situations involving the bribery of private individuals. The Supreme Court rejected the contention based on the ordinary meaning of the term bribery "at the time Congress enacted the statute in 1961," Congress's purposes in enacting the Travel Act, and its own precedent in a parallel case. Inter alia, the Court stated:

> There can be little doubt that Congress recognized in 1961 that bribery of private persons was widely used in highly organized criminal efforts to infiltrate and gain control of legitimate businesses, an area of special concern of Congress in enacting the Travel Act.

* * *

Our approach to ascertaining the meaning of "bribery" must be guided by our holding in *United States v. Nardello*, 393 U.S. 286 (1969), where the same provision of the Act under review in this case was before the Court. There, the respondents were charged with traveling in interstate commerce with the intent to engage in extortion contrary to the laws of Pennsylvania in violation of § 1952. Pennsylvania's "Extortion" statute applied only to acts committed by public officials. However, the State had outlawed the particular conduct engaged in by the respondents under a statute entitled "Blackmail." An opinion by Chief Justice Warren for a unanimous Court rejected the argument limiting the definition of extortion to its common law meaning, holding that Congress used the term in a generic and contemporary sense. We are similarly persuaded that the generic definition of bribery, rather than a narrow common law definition, was intended by Congress.

7.   To what extent does the concept of a "business enterprise" or other elements in section (b) of the Travel Act, supra, import an organizational or

commercial feature into the Act? There are several aspects to this question. Does the business enterprise element apply to all of the several different kinds of "unlawful activity" covered by the Act? If not, do the other kinds of "unlawful activity" under the Act have a "business" dimension? What is the meaning of "business enterprise" under the Act? The phrase has been held to mean "a continuous course of conduct, rather than a sporadic casual involvement in a proscribed activity." *United States v. Bates*, 840 F.2d 858 (11th Cir.1988). In *United States v. Kendall*, 766 F.2d 1426 (10th Cir.1985), the evidence supporting a "continuous course of unlawful conduct" included the fact that the defendants had discussed three future unlawful ventures. Compare the interpretation of the phrase in the Travel Act with the enterprise element in the RICO statute, *infra*, Chapter 11, and the continuing criminal enterprise element in the CCE statute, *infra*, Chapter 9.

8. Regarding the "unlawful activity" element, the court in *United States v. Woodward*, 149 F.3d 46, 66 (1st Cir.1998), stated:

> The Travel Act does not require the government to prove that the alleged unlawful activity violates the laws of the state ultimately traveled to or of the state where money actually changed hands.... A conviction may be sustained where the evidence demonstrates unlawful activity in violation of the laws of the state where the effects of the unlawful scheme are felt. * * * Here Woodward is a legislator from Massachusetts and the jury could have concluded that the gratuity, though paid in Florida, was paid for the purpose of influencing legislative activities in and affecting Massachusetts. * * * [T]hat is sufficient.

See also United States v. Falcon, 766 F.2d 1469 (10th Cir.1985); *United States v. Walsh*, 700 F.2d 846 (2d Cir.1983). Indeed, "[t]he legality of the immediate object of interstate travel * * * is irrelevant to the determination of coverage by the Travel Act where the interstate activities are part of a larger plan to engage in a prohibited activity." *United States v. Davis*, 780 F.2d 838, 843 (10th Cir.1985). Thus interstate travel to purchase lawfully obtained chemicals and paraphernalia to be used in the illegal manufacture of methamphetamine was held to violate the Act. *Ibid.*

9. The conduct comprising a violation of the Act can be inchoate with regard to the unlawful activity, that is, it consists of travel in commerce with intent to distribute, commit or promote. But "[u]nlike the crime of attempt, the Travel Act does not require that the government establish that the accuse took a substantial step in furtherance of the intended unlawful activity." *United States v. Jenkins*, 943 F.2d 167, 173 (2d Cir.1991). Rather, in addition to travel with the necessary intent, there is the requirement that "thereafter" the accused perform or attempt to perform one of the acts intended, that is, distribution of the proceeds of unlawful activity, commission of a crime of violence to further unlawful activity or facilitating the carrying on of the unlawful activity. The act that is performed "thereafter" has been likened to proof of an overt act. *United States v. Harris,* 903 F.2d 770, 773 (10th Cir.1990). In *United States v. Jenkins, supra,* one of the "facilitating" thereafter acts was use of the telephone by the accused's secretary to make foreign travel arrangements.

10. In *United States v. Altobella*, 442 F.2d 310 (7th Cir.1971), the defendants extorted money from a traveling businessman who on a Thurs-

day evening had been lured into a compromising situation by a female accomplice. To pay part of the extortion money (bargained down to $150), that same evening the victim wrote a check for $100 which he cashed at the desk of his hotel; he then delivered the cash to the defendant. The next day, Friday, the defendant paid $50 of the proceeds of the extortion to his female accomplice.

The victim was from another state, and the check that he had written was drawn on a bank in his home town. In accordance with banking practice, the check cleared through two local banks and then was forwarded on the following Tuesday by mail interstate to the victim's hometown bank. The use of the facilities of interstate commerce relied upon by the government in the case was this sending of the check through the mails interstate. Was the "thereafter" requirement met in this case?

The court (per then Judge, now Justice, John Paul Stevens) stated:

> To warrant federal intervention we believe the statute requires a more significant use of a facility of interstate commerce in aid of the defendants' unlawful activity than is reflected on this record.

> The use of the mails by the bank through which appellants' victim's check was cleared, a few days after it had been cashed at the ... [hotel], was purely incidental to appellants' sordid scheme. Their purpose would have been achieved equally well if the victim had borrowed $100 from associates at the hotel or had written a check on a local bank. Moreover, the unlawful activity which followed the cashing of the check was merely the payment of $50 to ... [the accomplice]. Unquestionably, the distribution of the proceeds of criminal activity may satisfy the "thereafter" requirement of the statute in a proper case. But when both the use of the interstate facility and the subsequent act are as minimal and incidental as in this case, we do not believe a federal crime has been committed.

> We do not believe Congress intended to authorize federal intervention in local law enforcement in a marginal case such as this.

11. Was Judge Stevens adding a requirement that the nexus to interstate commerce under the Travel Act must be substantial (i.e. "more significant"; not "purely incidental"; not "minimal and incidental")? Compare this view of his opinion in *Altobello* with the issue of whether the substantial connection to commerce element in *Lopez* applies in instances where the federal statute contains an express provision requiring a link to interstate commerce. See notes 2.b.–d., supra, pp. 55–57. Was Judge Stevens' gloss a constitutional requirement or added as a matter of statutory interpretation?

12. Must the travel or the use of the facility in commerce be done with the sole purpose of "distributing * * *, committing * * *, or otherwise facilitating" the unlawful activity? In *United States v. Walsh*, 700 F.2d 846, 854 (2d Cir.1983), it was stated: "Where travel is motivated by two or more purposes, some of which lie outside the ambit of the Travel Act, a conviction is still possible if the requisite illegal purpose is also present."

13. In *United States v. R.J.S., Jr.*, 366 F.3d 960 (8th Cir. 2004), the court ruled that a bomb threat call made over a telephone in a school's detention room (where the defendant and two others had been placed) to the

school secretary's telephone that was connected to a separate 10–digit interstate number constituted the use of an "instrument of interstate commerce" under 18 U.S.C. § 844(e). The court stated:

> Regardless of whether the call defendant made within the school required the use of an interstate telephonic system, both telephones were connected to an interstate telephonic system. Both were connected to separate ten-digit interstate numbers. In addition, defendant's call made both telephones unavailable to outside, interstate contact.

For a similar 8th Circuit decision, see *United States v. Corum,* 362 F.3d 489 (8th Cir.2004) (intrastate use of a telephone to communicate bomb threats to three houses of worship satisfies the interstate-commerce element of 18 U.S.C. § 844(e)).

Chapter 4

THE FEDERAL ROLE IN EN-FORCEMENT AGAINST CRIME

In this chapter, we address issues relating to the nature of the federal role in enforcement against crime. In part A, a selection of the many views that are reflected in the current debate on that subject is presented. These materials raise basic issues including such questions as: Should the existing scope of coverage of the federal criminal laws be modified and a different approach taken to legislating in this area? Can one derive general principles to govern what the role of the federal government should be in the nationwide addressing of crime? Should there be a single federal role, centrally determined, or should the federal approach be one that adapts to local needs?

The existing federal criminal laws are quite comprehensive, and it is hard to think of a crime under state law that cannot be prosecuted federally. At the same time, existing federal resources that may be brought to bear in crime enforcement—police, prosecutorial, defense, judicial and correctional—are quite small when compared with state enforcement systems and with the totality of crime in this country. The discrepancy between the broad range of applicability of the federal criminal law, as it is presently configured and the relatively limited federal resources suggests the need to examine both how these resources are, and how they can and should be, targeted. Part B contains materials that describe, and should be useful in evaluating, the methods that are being used for such targeting.

A. THE GREAT DEBATE

Discussion of the nature of the federal role in enforcement against crime is not new. For at least the past half century, the subject has been periodically addressed by scholars, judges and government agencies. What is new, however, is the extent of interest: In the last decade, reports have been issued by judicial, governmental and bar bodies addressing the subject; there have also been a large number of symposia and numerous individual articles devoted to it. A significant cottage industry on the federal role has developed. What is also new is the range of disagreement among those who have written on the subject. Whereas earlier, there was a basic position taken, with dissent generally only regarding means to achieve the goal, now the entire subject has been thrown open to being rethought. Truly, there is an ongoing great debate on the nature of the federal role.

What do you think has triggered this debate? Supreme Court decisions such as *Lopez* and *Morrison* and Raich, discussed in the previous chapter, undoubtedly has been one contributing factor. *See, e.g.,* Adam Kurland, *First Principles of American Federalism and the Nature of Federal Criminal Jurisdiction*, 45 EMORY L.J. 1 (1996). The very rapid growth over the course of the past four decades in the number of federal crimes that are not designed to protect a direct federal interest is another. Efforts by some legislators to enact even broader federal crimes is still another. The fact that the federal courts have been flooded by prosecutions involving illegal drugs is another. The effect of the Federal Sentencing Guidelines is still another. The interest in the subject stimulated by the creation of casebooks and courses in Federal Criminal Law and closely related subjects may also be playing a role. What effect the new emphasis on enforcement against terrorism will have in this debate is not yet clear. Overall, the interest in addressing issues relating to this subject may simply be the natural culmination of a process of growth in the federal criminal law enforcement machinery that causes us to ask: Where are we going? What do we want to be the respective roles of the federal and state crime enforcement systems?

The current debate can be over-simplified and characterized as a disagreement between the federalizers and the anti-federalizers—between those who want a comprehensive federal criminal code that largely duplicates the criminal law of the states and those who oppose that approach. But, of course, that view of the debate focuses more on the federal criminal code itself and less on the nature of the federal role, and does not take into account many of the great variety of different positions that have been expressed. We set forth below a sampling of the different views.

We should emphasize here that the difference between the federalizers and the anti-federalizers does not rest in significantly differing views about the appropriate magnitude of the federal criminal operation. Most of the participants in the debate prefer the continuation of a limited role for the national government in the enforcement efforts against crime. The main difference lies in whether they propose to achieve a limited role by restricting the scope of federal statutory coverage or by a targeting of the federal criminal enforcement machinery in some other way.

A basic federalizer position is espoused, for example, by Harry Litman and Mark Greenberg, both Department of Justice officials, who extol a system of federal criminal laws that largely duplicates the coverage of state penal codes: "[T]he federal government's ability to respond to national problems depends on a significant overlap between federal and state criminal jurisdiction." Harry Litman & Mark Greenberg, *Dual Prosecutions: A Model for Concurrent Federal Jurisdiction*, 543 ANNALS AM. ACAD. POL. & SOC. SCI. 72, 84 (1996). They also note that "enactment of federal criminal legislation manifests congressional intent that a federal criminal remedy be available but not that it be applied in all cases." *Id.* at 83. Renee M. Landers, another Justice Department official, similarly argues that such extensions of federal criminal jurisdiction do "not signal an attempt to supplant state authority but, rather, is an effort to supplement * * * [it] by invoking federal power and applying federal resources in strategic and limited ways." Renee M. Landers, *Prosecutorial Limits on Overlapping Federal and State Jurisdiction*, 543 ANNALS AM. ACAD. POL. & SOC. SCI. 64 (1996).

An anti-federalizer position is reflected in Franklin E. Zimring & Gordon Hawkins, *Toward a Principled Basis for Federal Criminal Legislation*, 543 ANNALS AM. ACAD. POL. & SOC. SCI. 15, 22 (1996): "If we can do better at specifying the conditions that justify federal crime, we are obligated to do so." *See also* the recommendations in the December 1994 Draft Proposed Long Range Plan for the Federal Courts prepared by a committee of the Judicial Conference of the United States, at p. 21, which similarly reflects a view of appropriate federal criminal jurisdiction based on categories of traditional federal crimes. For other expressions of anti-federalizing views, see Vaugh H. Walker, *Comment: Federalizing Organized Crime*, 46 HASTINGS L.J. 1127 (1995); Kathleen F. Brickey, *Criminal Mischief: the Federalization of American Criminal Law*, 46 HASTINGS L.J. 1135 (1995). *See also* Rory K. Little, *Myths and Principles of Federalization*, 46 HASTINGS L.J. 1029 (1995) for a proposal of a presumption against federalization of crime, one, however, that is rebuttable.

In 1998, a Task Force of the Criminal Justice Section of the American Bar Association issued a report, The Federalization of Criminal Law (1998). Professor Brown characterized and commented on the report in George D. Brown, *Constitutionalizing the Federal Criminal Law Debate: Morrison, Jones, and the ABA*, 2001 U. Ill. L. Rev. 983, 997–1001, 1023–1024:

> ... [T]he Task Force, like other commentators on the federal court system, such as Judge Richard Posner, sees the growing number of criminal cases as a threat to the unique role of the federal courts. The criticism can extend beyond the overlapping offenses to most criminal cases, but at least eliminating the former would make it easier for the federal courts to "play the distinctive and complementary role envisioned for them in the Constitution's federal scheme."
>
> In my view, this is one of the principal strengths of the overall position that the Task Force advocates. Article III Courts are not

meant to be courts of general jurisdiction, but to resolve the delineated set of matters that the Constitution envisions for them. Extensive prosecutions of the overlapping offenses blur any unique role, as well as undermine the status of the state courts as the only courts of general jurisdiction. In this sense, it can be argued that a vigorous federalism in the criminal law area protects both state and national institutions. One might take the argument a step further and argue that handling what ought to be essentially state prosecutions casts the federal courts somewhat in the role of villains.

Federal criminal law is here to stay. So is the debate it generates. The controversy arises not out of crimes involving clearly federal interests, such as theft of federal property, but out of statutes creating federal crimes duplicating offenses that the states already investigate and prosecute. The American criminal justice system has evolved into one of largely concurrent jurisdiction. This development creates the potential for federal prosecutors to step in whenever they conclude national interests require it. Defenders of national authority see this as a positive sign, especially in situations where states might be somehow unable to act.

However, there are serious negative consequences. There is certainly an erosion of state authority. There is a drain on federal resources, particularly those of the federal courts. Perhaps most seriously, the presence of concurrent criminal justice systems covering the same behavior creates serious problems of civil rights and civil liberties. . . . Some federal offenses carry the death penalty. It is not hard to imagine those on the victim's side arguing for federal prosecution, especially in a state that has abolished the death penalty. The debate has been going on for some time. What is new is the injection of a strong constitutional element. This development began with *Lopez*, and the notion that there are judicially enforceable limits to federal incursions into the domain of state criminal law. *Morrison* substantially reenforces this concept.

* * *

A quite different challenge is that facing the other participants in the debate: how to deal with the Court's forceful entry into it. The view that the whole question is one of legislative policy only seems hard to maintain after *Morrison* and *Lopez*. Yet it retains considerable appeal as the ABA Task Force Report shows. My sense of the matter is that the Court's new federalism is here to stay. If the "great debate" were to recognize that fact and build on it, the whole subject would be enriched.

Does the Great Debate revolve around the question of whether the federal law enforcement operation is growing too large or whether too many federal crimes are being enacted by the Congress? For the view that there has not been an expansion of the federal law enforcement operation in recent decades, see Thomas G. Stacy & Kimberley A.

Dayton, *The Underfederalization of Crime*, 6 Cornell J. of Law & Pub. Pol'y 247, 249–250, 252, 272, 285, 286, 318–319, 324 (1997):

> The image of a runaway national government increasingly taking away the enforcement of the criminal law from the States is essentially false. The available evidence indicates that the national government's share in the enforcement of criminal law has been actually diminishing for more than the last half century.... [C]onstitutional and policy considerations affirmatively support the opposite conclusion that the national government may (and probably should) exercise more authority, especially with respect to the street crime that plagues poor urban areas. It seems that crime, especially street crime, has been underfederalized.

> [A] considerable body of statistical evidence reveals that the national government's exercise of its concurrent authority has been so selective that its share of overall enforcement has actually declined for more than the last half century. * * *

> In 1980, which judges and scholars use as the base year for measuring the recent increase, the number of federal criminal filings was at an historic low, lower than in any year since 1917. Beyond this, a recent increase in federal filings does not and cannot, by itself, establish an expanding national share. To gauge changes in national and state crime fighting shares, one must try to compare federal filings with state filings and compare trends over a longer period of time.

One frequently finds in much of both the federalizer and antifederalizer literature statements of principles to guide us in this arena. The principles sought are designed to serve different functions, depending on the writer. For example, in some instances the principles are a basis for deciding when the federal criminal law can be invoked to prosecute crime that is also covered by state criminal law. In other instances, the principles are a basis for determining when it is appropriate to enact a federal criminal law. Although there are many similarities in the principles articulated by the different scholars and professionals, there are also important differences. We set forth below some examples of such principles and comments on the search for principles.

1. We begin with the early statement in L.B. Schwartz, *Federal Criminal Jurisdiction and Prosecutors' Discretion*, 13 Law & Contemporary Probs. 64, 73 (1948) indicating that federal prosecution would be deemed appropriate in the following cases, when: 1) the states are unable or unwilling to act; 2) the jurisdictional feature is an important ingredient to the success of the offense, and not merely incidental to it; 3) if the jurisdictional feature is incidental, another substantial federal interest is protected by the assertion of federal power; 4) the criminal operation extends into a number of states, transcending the local interests of any one state; 5) to refer a complicated case investigated and developed by federal prosecutors to state authorities would be inefficient.

2.   Franklin E. Zimring & Gordon Hawkins, *Toward a Principled Basis for Federal Criminal Legislation*, 543 ANNALS AM. ACAD. POL. & SOC. SCI. 15, 22–23 (1996): "There are * * * four different reasons why a particular behavior might be subject to a federal criminal prohibition: 1. The national government has a strong substantive interest in the suppression of a particular behavior. 2. The national government has a larger interest in the control of a behavior than do units of either state or local government. 3. The national government has a distinct advantage as compared to state criminal justice systems in detecting, prosecuting, or punishing a particular behavior. 4. State criminal justice systems are substantially ineffective, as compared to the potential of the federal government, in the detection, prosecution, or punishment of a particular behavior."

3.   Jamie S. Gorelick & Harry Litman, *Prosecutorial Discretion and the Federalization Debate*, 46 HASTINGS L.J. 967, 972 (1995): "[I]t is appropriate for Congress to provide for federal involvement in a particular crime area where: (1) there is a pressing problem of national concern; (2) state criminal jurisdiction is inadequate to solve significant aspects of the problem; and (3) the federal government—by virtue of its investigative, prosecutorial, or legal resources—is positioned to make a qualitative difference to the solution of the problem, i.e., a difference that could not be produced by the state's dedicating a similar amount of resources to the problem." These same authors, however, also suggest, "In order to allow sufficient flexibility to bring a federal prosecution when an aspect of a law enforcement problem requires it, federal criminal legislation will inevitably have to be over-inclusive." *Id.* at 972.

4.   Harry Litman & Mark D. Greenberg, *Dual Prosecutions: A Model for Concurrent Federal Jurisdiction*, 543 ANNALS AM. ACAD. POL. & SOC. SCI. 72, 81–82 (1995): " * * * Congress may appropriately provide for a federal role in an area largely regulated by the states in order to ensure the availability of a federal response in the few cases in which it is needed to protect compelling national interests. The federal government's special attributes give it the potential effectively to prosecute unusual cases—such as cases involving international or multistate criminal organizations or sensitive charges of local corruption—that states may have difficulty handling. For example, federal prosecutions have the benefits of the federal system's interstate jurisdictional and investigative reach; distance from local politics and a highly independent judiciary; expertise in particular areas such as securities and civil rights; specialized resources such as witness protection programs and advanced investigative techniques; and legal tools such as the federal preventive detention statute."

5.   Philip B. Heymann & Mark H. Moore, 543 ANNALS AM. ACAD. POL. & SOC. SCI. 103, 107–111 (1996): "[T]he nation * * * has several different traditions to guide it in determining the appropriate federal role. There is the traditional, conservative view, which seeks to restrain the federal role in dealing with ordinary street crime. There is the somewhat more aggressive stance that encourages the federal government to play a role

in financing, coordinating, and encouraging innovation in local criminal justice agencies. Finally, there is the most aggressive stance, which sanctions an active federal operational response to violent crime relying on federal agencies. * * * What falls within the category of federal responsibility because local law enforcement cannot handle it? The first is obvious. * * * [T]erritorial boundaries limit * * * ability to handle crimes that involve, in major ways, other jurisdictions. * * * [L]ocal jurisdictions are far less capable than the federal government in handling technically sophisticated or prolonged investigations. * * * There is one very debatable area within this broad category of what local law enforcement cannot handle. * * * [W]hat are being used by law enforcement are friendlier federal procedures and sentences, the difficult-to-duplicate investigative capabilities. * * * [F]ailure to change these aspects of [state] criminal law represents a state decision to, at best, strike a balance between the prosecution and the defense somewhat differently in the state. * * * [T]he extension of federal jurisdiction to a local matter [on this ground] seems unjustified. * * * Federal law enforcement resources should be used to deal with problems that everyone wants generally allocated to local law enforcement only when (1) there is an emergency requiring the specialized federal talents and (2) the federal efforts are directed, in large part, to helping local law enforcement develop for itself those missing capabilities."

6.　Sara Sun Beale, *Too Many and Yet Too Few: New Principles to Define the Proper Limits for Federal Criminal Jurisdiction*, 46 HASTINGS L.J. 979, 1005–1008 (1995): "Prior efforts to list the criteria for federal criminal jurisdiction have failed to match the case load to the federal courts' capacity because these efforts have generally treated the need for federal resources as a sufficient basis for federal criminal jurisdiction (at least for some classes of cases). Some commentators treat the need for federal resources as a justification for extending federal criminal jurisdiction to broad categories of cases. For example, one commentator supports federal criminal jurisdiction when there would be economies of scale, when the conduct in question threatens to overwhelm local authorities, and when states are unable or unwilling to face up to certain problems. Others reject any general reliance on the need for resources as a basis for federal criminal jurisdiction, but nonetheless base federal jurisdiction on the need for federal resources in some narrow class, or classes, of cases. This approach is taken in a draft long range plan prepared for the Judicial Conference in 1994, which supports federal criminal jurisdiction based on the need for federal resources in 'sophisticated criminal enterprises requiring federal resources or expertise to prosecute.'

"Any theory that bases federal criminal jurisdiction on the need for federal resources is likely to produce far more cases than can fit comfortably within the small federal judicial system. There is, for example, tremendous expansive potential in the suggestion that federal jurisdiction is appropriate when criminal conduct threatens to overwhelm local authorities. If state authorities are inadequately financed, they may be overwhelmed by even garden-variety crime. Authorities in many states say they presently are overwhelmed by drug and violent crime caseloads. Similarly, if federal intervention is warranted whenever the states have failed adequately to face up to some form of criminal activity, this criterion may be satisfied whenever state anticrime efforts are unsuccessful—particularly if it can be said that resource constraints hampered state enforcement efforts. In short, the federal courts do not have the capacity to accommodate all of the criminal cases in which there is a national interest and a need for federal resources.

" * * * Congress appropriately may ask why the availability of federal jurisdiction should turn on whether a few large enterprises are involved, rather than a large number of individuals or smaller groups. * * * [I]t is certainly arguable that there is as great a need for federal resources when the scope of crime is great in the aggregate, even though many of the individual cases are small. * * * It would be naive to deny that there is a federal interest—and, indeed, a significant effect on commerce—as a result of violent street crime.

"The key question * * * should not be when federal resources are needed, but rather when federal judicial resources are necessary to respond to some form of criminal activity."

7. Rory K. Little, *Myths and Principles of Federalization*, 46 Hastings L.J. 1029, 1074 (1995): "A principle of federalization that merely enshrines 'important' federal interests or some similar concept provides no useful guidance: instead it resonates of 'we know it when we see it' * * *. Thus, one person's concept of a 'strong federal interest' might well be another person's idea of a 'trivial local crime.'" *Id.* at 1074. "Another possible set of limiting federalization mechanisms might focus purely on workload objections and borrow from jurisdictional minimum concepts applied in federal civil statutes." *Id.* at 1075. "The challenge is to capture linguistically a comprehensible description of criminal conduct that is appropriately federal, rather than to simply roll up the federal courthouse drawbridges on a workload rationale." *Id.* at 1077. " 'Unique' federal interests is too limited; 'intrastate commerce' is too broad; and 'strong' federal interests is too manipulable. There is, however, a principle that both explains many past federalizations * * * and might realistically work to limit future federalization: demonstrated state failure." *Id.* at 1078.

8. Geraldine Szott Moohr, *The Federal Interest in Criminal Law*, 47 Syracuse L.Rev. 1127, 1138 (1997): "[T]hree proposals provide criteria, or models, to guide Congress in determining when a federal interest warrants the enactment of a federal criminal statute. * * * The 'prosecutorial discretion' model advises Congress to continue the federalization of criminal law and to delegate the determination of federal interest to executive branch prosecutors. The 'state failure' model advises Congress to pass criminal legislation only when there is demonstrated state failure to control criminal conduct. The Judicial Conference [Committee on Long Range Planning of the Judicial Conference of the United States,

Proposed Long Range Plan for the Federal Courts (1994)], or crime classification model advises Congress to rely on categories of traditional federal offenses to define the federal interest in criminal law."

9.   Elizabeth Glaser, *Thinking Strategically: How Federal Prosecutors Can Reduce Violent Crime*, 26 FORDHAM URB. L.J. 573, 591 (1999): "In the traditional model of joint federal and local efforts to combat violent crime, the federal role has been, for the most part, to prosecute the exemplary case. * * * That kind of role is an important one for federal prosecutors to play: with a minimum display of force, select a single target whose swift and certain prosecution and severe punishment will serve as an effective morality play for his associates."

10.   Daniel C. Richman, *Federal Criminal Law, Congressional Delegation, and Enforcement Discretion*, 46 U.C.L.A. L. REV. 757, 807–808 (1999): "This legislative enthusiasm for decentralized, and less moderated, prosecutorial power doubtless reflects some deep-seated political norms that extend beyond the peculiar circumstances of federal prosecutorial authority. After all, the entire American criminal justice system is characterized by an almost instinctive embrace of fragmented authority, with the tensions between police and prosecutors, attorneys general and district attorneys usually seen as a virtue, rather than a vice. And the ideal of locally based law enforcement is embedded in the system as well, reflected in the prevalence of elected district attorneys, venue rules, and jury composition doctrines. The U.S. Attorney system thus offers federal legislators the neat ability to criminalize conduct, with all the political advantages such legislation entails, without rejecting the virtues of localism in criminal enforcement."

11.   For a summary of various positions regarding the federalization of criminal law, consult Sara Sun Beale, *Reporter's Draft for the Working Group on Principles to Use When Considering the Federalization of Criminal Law*, 46 HASTINGS L.J. 1277 (1995).

———

Insofar as the debate regarding the scope of the federal criminal code focuses on whether or not it is desirable to expand the coverage in the code still further, or to try to limit the number of federal crimes, the issue may be largely moot or, rather, a classic case of locking the barn door after the horse has escaped. Those who argue for limiting the coverage seem generally to be thinking in terms of limiting expansion of the code. They do not seem to be thinking about "rolling back" the coverage, or whether such a rollback is feasible and how it might be done, or about the kinds of other issues that would be posed by such a development.

Similarly, many of those who argue for broad statutory coverage, with the selection of cases to be governed by prosecutorial discretion, fail also adequately to take into account the difficulties of regulating or controlling the exercise of discretion. Professor Dennis Curtis has described the problems associated with attempting to have "a national policy that sets forth the kinds of cases and the kinds of criminals that should be the targets of the federal effort * * *. [S]uch national coordination is undercut by the structure of federal prosecution which is diffused. In practice, individual United States Attorneys differ widely both in the selection of offenders to prosecute and in the choice of which crimes to charge. * * * While written Department of Justice guidelines exist, no national policy sufficiently curbs individual prosecutorial choices.

"One would think that * * * [the existing] increased cooperation by state and federal law enforcement personnel could provide an atmosphere in which coherent policy could develop about when to prosecute in state courts and when to prosecute in federal courts. No such overall policy has emerged, however. All prosecutors have pressures, including political needs to be reactive to criminal activity. Prosecutors need to be responsive to cooperating agencies who have done investigative work and who want to see and report the fruits of such efforts. * * * [T]he overall interrelations have not yielded a holistic approach to sort cases by jurisdiction, state and federal, or an approach that enables nuanced responsiveness to local needs." Dennis E. Curtis, *The Effect of Federalization on the Defense Function*, 543 ANNALS AM. ACAD. POL. & SOC. SCI. 85, 88–89 (1996). Compare the foregoing with the views expressed by Professors Podgor and Simon, respectively: Ellen S. Podgor, *Department of Justice Guidelines: Balancing "Discretionary Justice"* 13 Cornell J.L. & Pub. Pol'y 167 (2004); Michael A. Simon, *Prosecutorial Discretion and Prosecutorial Guidelines: A Case Study in Controlling Federalization*, 75 N.Y.U. L.Rev. 893 (2000).

B. METHODS OF TARGETING FEDERAL RESOURCES

None of the scholars and professionals whose works are quoted in the previous section argue in favor of a huge expansion of the federal role in criminal enforcement and the substitution of a plenary federal responsibility for the traditional state role. All accept the fact that federal resources are limited. For most, this suggests or implies the need for some methods of targeting or channeling the federal law enforcement efforts. In this section, we review the several ways in which such targeting is already being accomplished in practice and also discuss some alternative approaches. The premise underlying the materials in this section is that some centralized approach to targeting is needed.

One should keep in mind, however, another perspective reflected in a couple of the excerpts quoted in section A, that is, the notion that the federal enforcement system should be viewed as a localized system that is designed to permit adaptation to local needs by U.S. Attorneys' offices through prosecutorial decisions that are made there. Under this view the only targeting that needs to be done is accomplished through decisions regarding local needs made by the U.S. Attorneys. This perspective rejects the need for application by the U.S. Attorneys of an overriding federal approach. Of course, there is a sense in which this view reflects the reality of the way the system presently works. At the same time, there clearly is a centralized policy dimension to the existing system. There is a tension between these two views of the federal criminal operation—that it is at a certain level centralized and controlled at a policy level from Washington, or that it is essentially a local decision-making system.

There is still another dimension of how the federal enforcement system operates today, at least in certain areas, that should be mentioned. The advent and now-frequent use of joint task forces involving not only multiple federal agencies but also state and local law enforcement agency personnel has introduced at the operational level a type of state-federal cooperation that was not seen a half century ago. Thus, not only can the federal enforcement system be viewed as having a local decision-making aspect, but the decision-making may, in some contexts, involve extensive cooperation and communication with state and local counterparts. Often, the form of cooperation involves state or local officials investigating a matter, making the arrest(s) and then turning over the matter to federal officials for prosecution in the federal system. The reverse, of course, also occurs: federal agents may turn over a matter for prosecution in the state system.

There are several possible approaches to targeting and channeling of the federal enforcement effort against crime. The first would be constitutional. See the views of Professor George D. Brown, supra, p. 62. Since we have already addressed in some detail in the previous chapter the constitutional issues under the commerce power, we pause here only to identify in section 1 the essential question that would arise were heavy reliance placed on a constitutional approach to limiting the federal role. A second approach would be statutory in nature, targeting by various means the kind of conduct that is thought an appropriate subject for federal prosecution. In section 2, we identify issues relating to any effort to limit by statute the categories of conduct that are deemed appropriate for federal prosecution. Finally, in section 3, we survey a broad range of administrative approaches to achieving the desired modicum of targeting.

1. TARGETING USING A CONSTITUTIONAL APPROACH

As discussed in Chapter 3, until the decision in *United States v. Lopez, supra* pp. 57–64, there was little case law that imposed significant restrictions on the ability of Congress to use the commerce power as a jurisdictional base in ways that gave federal criminal statutes an extremely broad applicability. It remains unclear whether the decisions in *Lopez* and *Morrison* impose significant restrictions on the ability of the Congress to legislate criminal statutes with broad coverage.

The implications of the subsequent decision in *Gonzales v. Raich*; the possible use of an aggregation approach under statutes that use the "affecting commerce" jurisdictional base; the continuing viability of, and new broad interpretations given to jurisdictional pegs such as the use of a facility of interstate commerce; and the fact that a crossing of a state boundary at any time in the past has been upheld as a sufficient nexus to commerce under some statutory jurisdictional provisions all seem to indicate that Congress' broad power to legislate criminal statutes has not yet been significantly restricted.

Even were the Supreme Court to follow up and begin to impose significant restrictions on the ability of the Congress to use the commerce power, Congress has other means at its disposal, e.g. the taxing power. See Jesse H. Choper, *Taming Congress's Power under the Commerce Clause: What Does the Near Future Portend?* 55 Ark. L.Rev. 731 (2003). Further, if the Court limits Congress's power to legislate crimes under the commerce clause, how likely is it that the constitutional limits that would be imposed would restrict federal criminal authority appropriately? Or to repeat Professor Louis B. Schwartz's statement, quoted earlier, p. 23, would it "only crudely mark * * * off the area in which * * * [there is justification for federal prosecution]"?

2. TARGETING USING STATUTORY TECHNIQUES

As has been previously noted, the existing federal criminal laws are in many respects a patchwork, cover a wide range of subjects and are broadly applicable, largely overlapping with state criminal laws. Many federal crimes are cast in broad terms without many limiting statutory terms. *See* Dan M. Kahan, *Lenity and Federal Common Law Crimes*, 1994 S.Ct. Rev. 345. Even statutes that are not broadly phrased may have an extremely broad applicability because the crimes described therein, even taking into account the federal jurisdictional element, are committed so frequently. An example, of course, is the Hobbs Act robbery provision. A striking feature of the federal criminal law is in how many cases crimes may be prosecuted under more than one federal criminal statute. In many instances, for example, bribery can be prosecuted under as many as a half dozen statutes. This is so because: a) Congress tends to be careless and duplicate provisions; b) some provisions have different jurisdictional provisions but cover similar substantive offenses; c) the interpretative breadth of some provisions permits prosecution of several different kinds of crime categories; and d) some of the organizational crimes cover multiple crime categories.

Some of those writers quoted in the previous section have argued for a principled approach to the drafting of federal criminal statutes, keeping in mind appropriate spheres of federal and state criminal law or applying appropriate principles of federal interest. Even were such an approach taken with regard to new legislation, the existing broadly formulated federal criminal laws would remain on the books. Given the existing breadth and complexity of the federal criminal laws, it would not accomplish very much prospectively to try to mount a serious effort to target the federal criminal law more narrowly through legislative drafting. To be really effective, a major overhaul of the existing criminal laws would be required; a major new codification effort would be needed. Even then, one can be skeptical whether it is feasible significantly to improve the targeting of the federal role through a legislative approach. Furthermore, reviewing the history of federal criminal law reform suggests that a major reform effort would not easily succeed.

The simplest way to limit federal prosecution concerning particular categories of criminal conduct would, of course, be not to enact a federal crime on the subject. Thus, for example, had the federal carjacking statute, 18 U.S.C. § 2119 (3), not become law, questions would not be raised about the "nature of the federal concern addressed by this law." Kathleen F. Brickey, *The Commerce Clause and Federalized Crime, A Tale of Two Thieves*, 543 ANNALS AM. ACAD. POL. & SOC. SCI. 27, 30 (1996). The Congress, however, repeatedly reacts in a political way to high profile cases and particular concerns of the public, "expressing outrage over a local crime that attracted national media attention." *Ibid. See also* Sara Sun Beale, *What's Law Got to Do with It? The Political, Social, Psychological and Other Non-legal Factors Influencing the Development of (Federal) Criminal Law*, 1 BUFF. CRIM.L.REV. 23 (1997); Sanford H. Kadish, *Comment: The Folly of Overfederalization*, 46 HASTINGS L.J. 1247 (1995). Query whether it is possible to break this congressional pattern.

It has also been suggested that—

In general, * * * there is a reason why federal criminal jurisdiction cannot easily be delimited by statute to predefined "distinctively federal" cases. It is exceedingly difficult to draft a statute in a way that includes only those crimes that are sophisticated, inter-jurisdictional, or sensitive enough to require a federal solution.

Jamie S. Gorelick & Harry Litman, *Prosecutorial Discretion and the Federalization Debate*, 46 HASTINGS L.J. 967, 972 (1995).

Recall the various principles suggested by different writers in Part A of this chapter to govern the invocation of federal criminal jurisdiction. How many of those principles might lend themselves to being incorporated into the statutory descriptions of federal crimes?

Alternatively, consider, for example, whether including certain terms in a statutory offense that limits it to instances of a specified magnitude meet the "distinctively federal" criterion. (Recall Professor Beale's comment, *op cit supra*, p. 116, that "Congress may appropriately ask why the availability of federal jurisdiction should turn on whether a few large enterprises are involved, rather than a large number of individuals or smaller groups.") If criteria of magnitude are used to delimit specified federal offenses, they might include elements that require that the criminal conduct involves large scale activity, measured by one or more indices of scale—for example, based on the number of participants; the number of crimes, or other kinds of repeated activities connected to the commission of the crimes; the amount of money involved; the amount of time the criminal activity has been or is likely to be ongoing, the number of times that the federal jurisdictional element was involved or, alternatively, the substantiality of the federal jurisdictional element, and the like. Suppose, for example, the federal carjacking statute described an offense that required a minimal number of carjacking episodes or a minimal number of participants. Of course, such an approach requires resolution of the question, what is a distinctively federal concern? Is large scale activity by itself an adequate index of federal concern? *Also see* Rory K. Little, *Myths and Principles of Federalization*, 46 HASTINGS L.J. 1029, 1075–1076 (1995) rejecting the use of jurisdictional minima amounts and the like as a principled basis for limiting the federal statutory role.

In subsequent chapters, we shall be examining some federal statutes, e.g. the RICO statute, the Continuing Criminal Enterprise statute, and the Credit Card Fraud statute, that contain some indices of scale, but in general, Congress has not seen fit often to impose such limits in drafting criminal legislation. Are there other ways to identify through statutory language "distinctively federal" cases?

Any thought that might be given to trying to address federalization issues through a general revision of the federal criminal code should take into account the history of federal criminal code reform efforts. In 1971, the National Commission on Reform of the Federal Criminal Laws published its Final Report containing a draft of a proposed Federal Criminal Code that was submitted to the Congress. The Commission was chaired by Edmund G. "Pat" Brown (and often referred to as the Brown Commission) and was directed by Professor Louis B. Schwartz. The goal of the Commission's work was to "improve" and "reform" the federal law of crimes. It represented the first time that an effort was made to adopt a comprehensive, integrated and logical approach to the drafting of the federal criminal code which has historically grown piecemeal and ad hoc.

The Commission's approach was to define criminal conduct "in a manner similar to that in which offenses are defined in state codes" (Comment to § 201, Final Report) and to set forth the jurisdictional bases separately, indicating with respect to each offense the jurisdictional base(s) applicable to it. The result of this approach was to create a proposed federal criminal code that generally resembled a state criminal code with similar plenary crime coverage, and only differed from a state code insofar as federal jurisdictional bases restricted the applicability of its particular provisions. The Commission's approach with respect to federal role issues was to rely very heavily on the exercise of discretion by federal prosecutors. *See* the comments to section 201, *and see* section 207. No particular effort was thus made in this codification project to draft federal crimes in a manner that captured for each a distinctively federal interest.

Although considered in the Congress on several occasions, the Commission's draft was not enacted into law. Over the next ten years, a series of bills containing versions of comprehensive codes, most of them to a greater or lesser extent influenced by the Commission's draft, were introduced into the Congress. None were enacted, and in the 1980's, efforts to enact a comprehensive code were abandoned. Why the codification efforts failed despite the investment of a great deal of time and work into the project is itself a subject worthy of study. Instead of enacting a comprehensive code, Congress, every few years since, has enacted broad crime bills that contain a wide range of subjects. *See generally Symposium, Toward a New Federal Criminal Code*, 2 BUFFALO CRIM.L.REV. (1998).

3. TARGETING THROUGH JUDICIAL INTERPRETATION

The terms of broadly-phrased federal criminal statutes are, of course, subject to judicial interpretation. Whenever a statutory term is narrowed by interpretation, it affects the range of application of the statute and has implications for the role the statute plays in federal criminal enforcement; contrariwise, broad interpretations extend the reach of the statute and extend the applicability of the federal law of crimes. In considering such interpretative issues, the courts generally look to the specific statutory language, often consider the legislative history and the purposes of the legislation and sometimes refer to maxims of statutory interpretation. In effect, materials in each of the chapters in this volume, beginning with Chapter 5, are devoted to the judicial interpretation of significant federal criminal statutes.

Sometimes, too, a defendant may argue, relying on the legislative history, the asserted purpose of the statute, and federalism concerns, that the scope of a federal statute should be narrowed by adding an interpretative gloss that is not tied to any particular statutory language. The history of the Mann Act, for example, is an interesting case study in how efforts can be made to limit the substantive reach of a broad statute. The case history of this statute involved the rejection by the Supreme Court of an interpretative gloss that would have restricted the application of the statute to instances of some degree of scale. Subsequently, efforts were made judicially to narrow the statute in other ways by describing more precisely the prohibited activity. Later still, the underlying statute was amended so as to narrow its scope through a measure of scale. Finally, the statute was revised again and the particular measure of larger scale criminal activity was deleted.

The Mann Act, enacted in 1910, codified at 18 U.S.C. § 2421, is one of Congress' early ventures into legislating a federal crime in an area thought to be traditionally reserved to state and local law enforcement, namely, prostitution and immoral sexual activity. In *Caminetti v. United States*, 242 U.S. 470 (1917), the Supreme Court addressed the question of the scope of the statute. Caminetti was charged with traveling across a state line for an amorous purpose, to have sexual relations with his travel partner. The statute in pertinent part made it a federal crime for—

> "any person * * * to knowingly transport, * * * in interstate or foreign commerce, * * * any woman or girl for the purpose of prostitution or for any other immoral purpose * * *."

Caminetti argued that the statute was intended to reach only commercial vice; that the Court should therefore narrow the scope of the statute (and thus make it inapplicable to him) through a judicial gloss on the statutory language. The legislative history and the title of the statute provided some support for the argument, but the fact was that the language of the statute was broadly phrased, and a majority of the Court rejected the claim, concluding, "when words are free from doubt they must be taken as the final expression of legislative intent. * * * "

Does it make more sense for the federal government to be prosecuting commercial vice, that is, prostitution, than for it to be pursuing private immorality (albeit, that which crosses a state line) that has no commercial feature? Is this a kind of criterion of magnitude? Is either subject an appropriate target for the federal government, or is this an area that should be left entirely to state law enforcement? If the Court had been inclined to interpret the statute in accordance with the defendant's argument, what would it have said in its opinion? What kind of criteria of interpretation might it have presented to the lower federal courts and prosecutors?

Caminetti is an early decision reflecting one type of pattern that has repeated itself in a significant number of instances down to the present: Congress is presented with information suggesting that there is a type of serious crime problem of sufficient magnitude and occurring on a national scale so as to warrant federal intervention through the legislating of a new federal crime. Congress sometimes then proceeds to legislate a statute that is drafted in terms that extend more broadly than the kind of criminal activity that was the perceived reason for the legislation. The legislative history is nevertheless replete with statements indicating that the purpose of the statute was to deal with the perceived kind of large scale criminal activity.

Subsequently, a prosecution is brought under the new statute, involving a mundane, local situation rather than the type of large scale criminal activity that was the perceived national crime problem. Because of the absence of limiting language in the statute, the prosecution appears to be a permissible invocation of the statute, and the defendant is convicted. The defendant appeals, claiming that the statute should be limited to the purposes behind the statute as delineated in the legislative history. The courts uphold the broad interpretation of the statute, consistent with its actual language, concluding that while the statute was "primarily" aimed at the indicated large scale criminal activity, the plain meaning of its express language is controlling.

You will find in reading the materials in subsequent chapters, that the pattern just described is repeated again and again. Indeed, it has been relatively infrequent for the Supreme Court significantly to narrow by interpretation the reach of a federal criminal statute. As you reflect further on this pattern, consider how much it helps to account for the various special characteristics of the federal criminal law. Consider, too, whether, if in cases like *Caminetti* the Court were consistently to adopt a narrowing interpretation, the overall scope of the federal criminal law might be reduced.

4. ADMINISTRATIVE TARGETING OF AREAS OF PROSECU-TION AND CASES TO PROSECUTE

In Part A of this chapter, it was suggested by a number of the scholars who have written on the federal role, that the principal targeting, in the context of a broadly applicable federal criminal code and limited federal enforcement resources must be done by the executive branch, that is, through administrative targeting. In the context of the federal system, at the national level this means that formally, the Attorney General and his representatives in the U.S. Department of Justice have the responsibility to select the areas to emphasize for investigation and prosecution. As we shall, the process of selecting an area involves identifying issues of importance and appropriateness to the federal role, describing and characterizing the area, and allocating resources, including personnel, to support the emphasis on the area.

The selection of areas of prosecution, that is, enforcement missions and priorities, is a means to target the areas of prosecution, but because it defines allocation of resources and general goals, it does not determine which specific cases to prosecute and which statutes to use in particular cases. The development of prosecutorial policies by the Department of Justice or the U.S. Attorneys has the potential partially to fill this gap. But even where there are applicable policies, there is a need for an informed and sensitive exercise of prosecutorial discretion in the individual case. Ultimately, it is the decision-making that takes place in the U.S. Attorney's office that ends up being decisive in the choice of cases to prosecute.

But the choices made by U.S. Attorneys and their Assistant USA's, is often heavily influenced by and depend on the investigations that are carried on by the various federal police agencies—which cases are investigated and how well they are developed. *See* Elizabeth Glazer, *Thinking Strategically: How Federal Prosecutors Can Reduce Violent Crime*, 26 FORDHAM URB. L.J. 573 (1999): " * * * [T]he federal prosecutor still operates to a large extent in an arena constructed by federal investigative agencies. A prosecutor can have a dramatic impact within any particular case, but which cases and what areas will be selected for federal attention remain an area of largely undisputed agency discretion * * *." Of course, the goal of emphasizing a particular area requires that the emphasis be communicated to the relevant investigating agencies.

In this section, we survey these various topics of administrative targeting by the executive branch. It will be useful at this time for the student to review the descriptions of the various federal enforcement agencies set forth *supra*, Chapter 2. In particular, salient characteristics of the federal law enforcement arm should be kept in mind, the fact that: a) it consists of numerous investigative agencies of different size, each with its own investigative jurisdiction; b) although the larger agencies are directed from Washington, they operate through regional or local offices; c) some of these investigative agencies are within the Department of Justice (e.g. FBI, DEA, ATF and U.S. Marshalls), while others are located in other Departments (e.g. postal inspectors, immigration enforcement and customs agents, and Secret Service) and do not come under the jurisdiction of the Attorney General; d) the prosecutorial component is composed mainly of 94 U.S. Attorney's offices, each headed by a presidential appointee, sometimes with his/her own local political base, and some unevenness exists in the role different U.S. Attorneys play in the prosecutorial system with some offices setting their own priorities; the problem of unevenness is also complicated by wide differences in the size of the offices; e) the Washington component of the federal prosecutorial operation consists mainly of the Criminal Division, but also includes the Tax Division and other Divisions of the Department of Justice with criminal enforcement responsibilities, and each Division relates to the U.S. Attorneys' offices in its own way.

Our main focus with be on the approaches that involve the setting of enforcement priorities and federal missions and the means of targeting and controlling the exercise of prosecutorial discretion. In addition, however, we shall also describe various subsidiary techniques and methods that also assist in the targeting function. In the materials that follow, the student should try to judge the efficacy of the setting of federal missions and priorities as well as the efforts to control prosecutorial discretion while also taking into account the fragmented and geographically widespread character of the federal criminal enforcement operation. Inevitably, such an assessment must be preliminary at this stage, but you should keep in mind the issues raised here as you study the materials in the remainder of this volume.

a. *Enforcement Priorities or Missions*

1. Introductory Overview—The Elevation of the Anti-Terrorism Mission and Its Implications

The simplest, most direct method by which the Department of Justice has attempted to focus the federal criminal enforcement effort has been to announce enforcement priorities or federal missions. Taking a broad, historical view, one can see an evolution in the targets chosen and the areas of criminality emphasized. Each time a new emphasis was announced it was followed, at least for a time, by special efforts to implement the new announced priority[ies]. Typically, changes in enforcement emphases or priorities occur when a new Administration takes office but changes have also been made midstream in the course of a presidential term. The evolution of targets between the 1930's and the new millennium largely focused the federal criminal enforcement effort on organized crime, white collar crime, drug offenses, official corruption, violent crime, and, to a lesser extent, espionage and terrorism. At any given time, during this 70 year period one or more of these areas was highlighted, and more attention was paid to it, but overall, all of these areas were being targeted during all of this period.

Post–September 11, 2001, however, there occurred what could turn out to be (but may not be) a quantum shift in the federal criminal enforcement role, especially in regard to the role and the functions of the FBI. At least that is how it appears on the surface, but there are also counter-indications.

Post 9/11, both the Attorney General and the Director of the FBI announced a major shift in the focus of the Bureau, from crime investigation to terrorism prevention. The FBI defines terrorism as "the unlawful use of force or violence against persons or property to intimidate or coerce a government or the civilian population thereof in furtherance of political or social objectives."

Early indications were that as many as 674 agents had been shifted from crime investigation to counterterrorism and that more than one fourth of the FBI's domestic agents were working in the terrorism field. See Gary Fields and John R. Wilke, The Ex Files: FBI's New Focus Places Big Burden on Local Police, The Wall Street Journal, June 30, 2003, at A1.

In September, 2004, the Inspector General of the Department of Justice issued a report entitled, *The Internal Effects of the Federal Bureau of Investigations Reprioritization* (Audit Rept 04–39 OIG). The Inspector General found that whereas there had been 890 FBI agents working on drug matters in 2001, by 2003, the number had been reduced to 335. id. On the other hand, the number of agents assigned to organized crime matters remained stable during that period; similarly the agents working in Organized Crime/Drug Enforcement Task Forces also was not reduced, but similar to the reduction in agents working on drugs, the Inspector General found that "the FBI utilized 413 fewer agents on violent crime matters [bank robberies, extortions, kidnappings, violent gangs and criminal enterprises involved in major thefts] in FY 2003 than in FY 2000. Regarding white collar crime matters, in FY 2000, 2426 agents were involved in such investigations; in FY 2003, the number had dropped to 1952.

Given these reductions, one would expect a substantial impact on the number of non-terrorism cases initiated, in selected areas, for example, drug cases, since 2001. Here, however, the evidence is somewhat conflicting. Thus, a significant drop in the number of new drug cases was reported during the period from 2000 to 2002—namely 1825 reduced to 944. Id. However, the U.S. district court data on the number of drug prosecutions initiated during the period from 2001 to 2004 do not show a similar reduction. Indeed the number of such cases commenced rose slightly between 2001 and 2002 from 18,425 to 19,215 in 2002, dropped slightly to 18,996 in 2003, and then dropped again to 18,440 in 2004, almost the identical number initiated in 2001. All in all, this data suggests that the number of drug cases commenced during the period in question remained relatively stable.

There are a number of possible explanations for the fact that at least some of the available data do not show the expected drop in the number of drug prosecutions initiated. The data could be in error. More likely, the fact that the FBI reduced the number of agents who investigate drug cases does not necessarily mean that the number of drug cases prosecuted federally would drop. Those FBI agents who still work on drug cases may increase their productivity, or the type of cases worked on may result in more prosecutions per agent (e.g. working on a greater number of smaller cases rather than larger more complex cases that require more agent hours per single case). Also, other agencies, both federal and state, work on drug enforcement, and the slack left by a reduction in the FBI role may have been picked up by an increase in the number of cases initiated through the work of other agencies (e.g. the DEA or state and local agencies). This seems the most likely explanation, and there are some indications that this has been occurring. See, e.g., Wash. Post, May 29, 2002, AO1 reporting that the DEA and state and local police would have to fill the gap created by the diversion of FBI agents from narcotics investigations. On the other hand, the head of the DEA's Los Angeles office indicated that the DEA and the FBI will continue to work major drug cases in the area with other police agencies, stating, "We will hope that doesn't change much, because the drug problem is so enormous in the area. On the other hand, we also realize that their primary mission is terrorism. LA Times, June 13, 2002, Pt. 2, p. 7. See also Wall Street Journal, July 5, 2002, A4 reporting that the DEA had shifted 40 agents to the Mexican border to replace FBI agents in that region who had been switched to terrorism work.

For various reasons, it is important to determine the actual effects of what might herald a major change in the nature of the federal role in criminal enforcement. At about the time this volume went to press, the Inspector General of the Department of Justice testified that his office is "currently is working on a ... review examining how the FBI's reprioritization efforts and the shift of resources from more traditional criminal investigative areas such as drugs and white collar crime to terrorism has affected other federal, state, and local law enforcement organizations." Testimony of Glenn A. Fine, Inspector General, US DOJ, Senate Committee on the Judiciary, July 27, 2005.

Previous changes in emphasis seemed simply to change which enforcement areas stand out as "first among equals." Whereas antiterrorism efforts had always been an element in the federal law enforcement set of missions, since 9/11, terrorism prevention has become the number one target of the FBI resulting in a significant shift in federal law enforcement focus, the exact long-term effects of which still remain to be determined. Thus, the activity surrounding the goal of fighting terrorism since 9/11 has given the appearance of elevating the terrorism enforcement effort to be on a par with criminal enforcement in all of the other areas combined. Thus, in the latest five year strategic plan for the Department of Justice for the period, 2003–2008, among the Goals and Objectives, were the following federal law enforcement priorities: I.

Prevent Terrorism and Promote the Nation's Security; and. II. Enforce Federal Laws and Represent the Rights and Interests of the American People. The criminal law enforcement areas listed under the second heading were violent crime, illegal drugs and white collar, economic and cybercrime.

In addition to the foregoing, account should also be taken of a series of developments within and around the FBI that occurred in the spring and early summer of 2005. In April, 2005, a special presidential commission on intelligence filed a report highly critical of the FBI and urging the creation of a National Security Service within the Bureau that would unite the Bureau's counterintelligence and counterterrorism divisions and make them accountable to the Director of National Intelligence. LA Times, April 1, 2005, A13 (The FBI had always had a separate counterintelligence division and elevated counterterrorism to the level of a division in the 1990's. [Regarding the FBI's jurisdiction over foreign counter intelligence, see Executive Order 12065, § 1.14, reproduced at 50 U.S.C.A. § 401.] After 9/11, a separate intelligence directorate was established within the Bureau with a director of intelligence who reported to the Director of the FBI.). The Bureau had earlier resisted the creation of a new domestic intelligence agency modeled on Britain's MI–5, which does not have law enforcement authority, NY Times, June 10, 2005, A1. Critics of the Bureau had suggested that without a fully dedicated service, the Bureau would not get ahead of the terrorist threat; that what was required was a massive culture change within the FBI because "the guns and badges and the mind-set of the F.B.I. don't totally fit with the challenges of countering terrorism." NY Times, June 30, 2005, A1. The intelligence panel had criticized the FBI for a "bureaucratic culture that naturally resists change"; it reported that it interviewed agents who even after 9/11 said that the Bureau considered helping local police to be one of its key functions while another stated that law enforcement is more important than catching terrorist leaders like Osama bin Laden. LA Times, April 30, 2005.

On June 29, 2005, President Bush issued a directive to implement the recommendation of the Intelligence Commission to create a new National Security Service within the FBI. That same day the Director of the FBI and the Attorney General announced the proposal to create such a Service that would combine the counterintelligence, counterterrorism and intelligence units and create a semi-autonomous service within a service headed by a chief who reports both to the FBI Director and to the Director of National Intelligence. The DNI will have coordination and budget powers in regard to the new Service. The establishment of the new NSS within the Bureau was designed, inter alia, to improve cooperation and communication between the CIA and the FBI and "elevates intelligence operations to new prominence within the FBI" to counter the continuing orientation of the FBI toward traditional law enforcement. NY Times, June 30, 2005, A1.

At the press conference announcing the establishment of the National Security Service, the Director of the FBI stated: "We are establishing a career path, starting October 1st, where every one of our new agents coming out of new agents class will spend three years at a small- or mid-sized office learning about the criminal justice system, learning about the parameters under which we gather information and intelligence within the United States, before they then go and specialize in one of the intelligence specialties that is set up by this National Security Service." Also relevant to this subject are some statements made by the Intelligence Commission:

> The FBI's hybrid nature is one of its strengths. In today's world of transnational threats, the line between 'criminal activity' and 'national security information' is increasingly blurred, as is well-illustrated by the use of illegal drug proceeds to fund terrorist activity.

> Personnel in the service would take advantage of its specialized career options, but agents in the service would go through law enforcement training along with their counterparts in the FBI's criminal divisions. Agents could laterally transfer between the service and the FBI's other divisions mid-career.

> Ensuring continuing coordination between the FBI's two halves is critical for at least two reasons: such coordination is necessary to optimize the FBI's performance in both national security and criminal investigations, ...

> As long as the Bureau continues to expose Special Agents to a tour of criminal work, as it should, its agents will have experience in criminal justice matters and continue to be extensively trained to uphold the Constitution and protect civil liberties.

So what does all of this portend for the federal role in criminal enforcement and the great debate on that subject? The FBI continues to subscribe to its traditional crime enforcement agenda while elevating terrorism to a preeminent place. When the dust has settled and the situation has stabilized, will its enforcement in the traditional areas be reduced significantly as a result of this change in mission? Will the emphasis on intelligence work and fighting terrorism remake the self-image of FBI agents and relegate traditional enforcement against crime to second-place status? The returns on this are not yet in, but what evidence there is suggests that enforcement in the traditional areas may not be reduced significantly. While the FBI is the largest of the federal crime enforcement agencies, there are other agencies that can take up some of the slack. If a significant reduction in the federal effort occurs, it seems likely that it would be more or less across-the-board and not involve eliminating entirely a particular enforcement area.

There is also, of course, the possibility that a heavy focus of the FBI on terrorism investigations will in various ways produce a diminishing of the importance of the federal role in traditional criminal enforcement and reverse the trend toward the federal government expanding its role in the traditional crime areas. Here, too, it is too soon to tell.

The great debate was, in part, triggered by Congress legislating more crimes and the incremental growth and extension of the federal role in crime enforcement. With the shift of the focus to terrorism, the issues involved in the great debate may seem to be less important, and Congress may focus more on terrorism-related matters and less on traditional crime. In any event, the great debate is not likely to challenge the proposition that the primary responsibility for fighting terrorism lies in the federal domain.

As mentioned above, an important question is whether the new emphasis on terrorism is similar to earlier "wars," for example, on organized crime or white collar crime, or is it qualitatively different. Generally, in the past, addition of a new priority or mission did not result in the dropping of any of the others from the list, although given limited federal resources, some of the earlier emphases inevitably were diminished by addition of a new one. In the past, the adding of a new priority sometimes did not result so much in the addition of something new as it did in the reshaping of something old. Thus when the Justice Department began its war on white collar crime during the Administration of President Jimmy Carter, it may simply have produced an increased emphasis on crimes under that label as part of its earlier declared war against organized crime. Similar, the recent addition of cybercrime and international financial crimes as Justice Department targets has added those areas to the focus on white collar and economic crime. Are Justice Department changes in priorities sometimes symbolic; influenced by political considerations, or other factors? Consult generally, NANCY E. MARION, A HISTORY OF FEDERAL CRIME CONTROL INITIATIVES, 1960–1993 (1994); Nancy E. Marion, *Symbolic Policies in Clinton's Crime Control Agenda*, 1 BUFF. CRIM. L.REV. 67 (1997). *See also* Sara Sun Beale, *What's Law Got to Do with It? The Political, Social, Psychological and Other Non-legal Factors Influencing the Development of (Federal) Criminal Law*, 1 BUFF. CRIM. L. REV. 23 (1997).

We turn now to a brief introduction to some of the principal federal criminal enforcement priorities in addition to terrorism. In thinking about each of the priority areas described below, consider how a priorities approach for focusing the federal criminal enforcement effort compares with some of the other methods of administrative control described further along in these materials. What are the advantages of the priorities approach? The disadvantages?

It is one thing to announce a law enforcement priority; it is quite another task to implement it. Implementation requires, at the least, attention to issues of allocation of resources, including personnel, cooperation among federal agencies and with state and local (and in some contexts, international) agencies, the legal framework and the functions of investigation and prosecution. How, for example, does one focus investigative resources on organized crime or white collar crime? What steps must be taken in that connection relating to personnel, investigative techniques, organization, and the like?

2. *Organized Crime*

Organized crime has been a special federal target for more than five decades. It particularly became a subject of governmental attention as a result of hearings conducted by Senator Kefauver in the early 1950's and has been mentioned in the Annual Reports of the Attorney General of the United States since 1950. Various steps have been taken since then, e.g. in 1954–55, the establishment of the Organized Crime and Racketeering Section in the Department of Justice; in 1967, the opening of Organized Crime Strike Forces offices in major cities (but note that in 1990, the Strike Forces were merged with the U.S. Attorneys offices); and in 1970, enactment of the Organized Crime Control Act in aid of an enlarged federal role in this area, and various other administrative steps implemented in the ensuing years. Recall, too, that as stated above, the recent elevation of the terrorism mission did not result in any significant change in the number of FBI agents addressing organized crime.

The starting point for analysis of the federal government's role in criminal enforcement aimed at organized crime is to define the target. The definition used can, of course, influence the approach taken to the problem. An illustrative sampling of definitions and the groups that have spawned them follows:

a) La Cosa Nostra (LCN)—the most popular of the definitions used, referring to 24 families of Italian descent composed of about 5,000 members (with another 50,000 people associated), each family organized in a hierarchy with several managerial levels. It is also perhaps the narrowest and most traditional of the meanings.

b) The President's Crime Commission described organized crime as "a society that seeks to operate outside the control of the American people and their governments," TASK FORCE REPORT: ORGANIZED CRIME, PRESIDENT'S COMM'N ON LAW ENFORCEMENT & THE ADM'N OF JUSTICE (1967), and as involving thousands of criminals, complex structures, intricate conspiracies, engaged in supplying illegal goods and services, using illegitimate methods and the corrupting of public officials, using private and secret procedures.

c) Congressman Poff in discussing the proposed legislation that became the RICO statute stated: "[A]s if organized crime were a precise and operative legal concept, like murder, rape or robbery. Actually, of course, it is a functional concept like white collar or street crime, serving simply as a shorthand method of referring to a large and varying group of individual criminal offenses committed in diverse circumstances." 116 Cong. Rec. at 35, 344 (1970).

d) In 1979, the National Organized Crime Planning Council (NOCPC), formulated the following definition which appears to be the definition being applied by a number of federal investigative agencies:

> "Organized Crime" refers to those self perpetuating, structured and disciplined associations of individuals or groups, combined together for the purpose of obtaining monetary or commercial gains or

profits, wholly or in part by illegal means, while protecting their activities through a pattern of graft and corruption. Organized crime groups possess certain characteristics which include but are not limited to the following: A) Their illegal activities are conspiratorial; B) In at least part of their activities, they commit or threaten to commit acts of violence or other acts which are likely to intimidate; C) They conduct their activities in a methodical, systematic, or highly disciplined and secret fashion; D) They insulate their leadership from direct involvement in illegal activities by their intricate organizational structure; E) They attempt to gain influence in Government, politics, and commerce through corruption, graft, and legitimate means; F) They have economic gain as their primary goal, not only from patently illegal enterprises such as drugs, gambling and loansharking, but also from such activities as laundering illegal money through and investment in legitimate business.

This definition was reported to have been criticized by the Chief of the Organized Crime and Racketeering Section of the Justice Department as "too general and not sufficient for developing targets * * * that instead, this definition must be used in conjunction with national priorities developed by NOCPC." Report by the Comptroller General of the U.S., Stronger Federal Effort Needed in Fight Against Organized Crime (GAO, 1981). NOCPC developed five national priorities for organized crime investigations—labor racketeering, infiltration of legitimate business, police corruption, narcotics conspiracies, and violence.

e) Ethnic gangs and organizations. However, the phrase is defined, organized crime today has been broadened to include groups similar to La Cosa Nostra but which come from other ethnic backgrounds. The 2003–2008 DOJ Strategic Plan reports that "Non-traditional organized crime groups from Russia, Eastern Europe, Asia, Central and South America, Africa, and many other parts of the world have begun to operate in the United States.... They are not as firmly established as the domestic, traditional organized crime syndicates, although some of them have emulated the LCN in the way they have structured their operations.... For well-entrenched international organized crime, our strategy is to identify the most significant organizations operating in the United States; ... and initiate joint investigations designed to curtail their emergence." An increase in the number and size of ethnic street gangs also in part reflects recent patterns of immigration. The Strategic Plan reports that according to one recent survey, more than 13,700 gangs with 750,000 members were active in the United States while another survey published in 2000 found more than 30,000 gangs and 800,000 members. The Strategic Plan comments, "While gang membership is difficult to estimate, experts agree that the numbers are much higher than they were a decade ago." *See generally* NATIONAL INSTITUTE OF JUSTICE, GANG CRIME AND LAW ENFORCEMENT (1994); FELIX M. PADILLA, THE GANG AS AN AMERICAN ENTERPRISE (1992). As part of the federal efforts against organized crime, there seems to be increasing attention to anti-gang enforcement. See, e.g. L.A. Times, August 2, 2005, A12, describing a nationwide federal crackdown involving the arrest of 582 alleged gang members most of whom were subject to deportation for immigration violations. According to this report, law enforcement officials and Congress are placing renewed emphasis on immigration law as a tool for combating gangs, and new legislation is in the works to strengthen the tools that law enforcement can use against gangs.

f) There are other approaches that can be taken to the definitional issue. One might, for example, attempt to define the concept in terms of types of crimes. What crimes should be included under such an approach? See, for example, the list of state and federal predicate offenses included under the RICO statute, 18 U.S.C.A. § 1961(1), *infra* pp. 478–480, which was enacted with organized crime as one of its primary targets. Or consider a description that has been used by the FBI in describing its Organized Crime Program priorities: "labor racketeering, narcotics, official corruption, illegal infiltration of business, loansharking, illegal gambling, arson for profit, gangland slayings, and adult and child pornography." Annual Rept., Atty. Gen. of the U.S. 35 (1983).

For a earlier survey of various attempts to define organized crime, see H. ABADINSKY, THE MAFIA IN AMERICA 35–39 (1981).

What justifies the large federal effort aimed at organized crime (must such a role be justified)? *See generally*, John C. Jeffries, Jr. & John Gleeson, *The Federalization of Organized Crime: Advantages of Federal Prosecution*, 46 HASTINGS L.J. 1095 (1995). However defined, organized crime is a less precise target than, let us say, bank robbery. Enforcement in this field poses special problems and requires the use of creative law enforcement techniques.

3. *White Collar Crime*

White collar crime has long been a focus of federal criminal enforcement. By 1975, it was described as an enforcement area of "high priority," and the Attorney General's Committee on White Collar Crime was established. By 1980 it was elevated into a "war" and described as "the highest investigative priority." William H. Webster, *An Examination of FBI Theory and Methodology Regarding White Collar Crime Investigation and Prevention*, 17 AM.CRIM.L.REV. 275, 279 (1980). *See also* U.S. DEPARTMENT OF JUSTICE, NATIONAL PRIORITIES FOR THE INVESTIGATION AND PROSECUTION OF WHITE COLLAR CRIMES (1980). The priority on this area continues: In the 2003–2008 DOJ Strategic Plan, Strategic Objective 2.3 identifies the combating of "white collar crime, economic crime, and cybercrime" as an important goal. "... [T]he internet and other global network computer systems ... have ... provided a powerful new medium in which to commit unlawful acts ... provides.... [a] formidable tool to commit traditional and new crimes.... Combating computer crime requires investigators, forensic experts, and prosecutors who must all have technical expertise." Recall that as stated above, probably as a result of the increase focus on terrorism, almost 500 fewer agents were reported to be working on white collar crime in 2003 than there were in the year 2000. Corporate fraud accounting scandals toward the beginning of the millennium led to the formation of a Corporate Fraud Task Force, an interagency group established by the President in January, 2002, and the prosecution of more than 1300 individuals for various related white collar crimes. Wall Street Journal, August 4, 2005, A4.

Questions regarding this enforcement priority parallel those raised under the Organized Crime heading. There is the matter of definition. The writings on the subject are voluminous and numerous definitions can be found therein. They can be categorized in terms of the characteristics of the offenders, the relationship between offenders and their occupations, or according to the character of the criminality. The ANNUAL REPT, ATT. GEN. OF THE U.S. 39 (1983) used the following approach:

> White collar crimes are illegal acts that use deceit and concealment—rather than the application or threat of physical force or violence—to obtain money, property, or service; to avoid the payment or loss of money; or to secure a business or personal advantage. White collar criminals occupy positions of responsibility and trust in government, industry, the professions, and civic organizations.

Similar language is used in the 2003–2008 DOJ Strategic Plan.

What justifies a large federal role in prosecuting white collar crime that does not involve a defrauding of the federal government or federal officials? Consider in this connection the following claims:

a) The federal government has a special responsibility under the commerce clause to insure the economic well-being of the country;

b) Federal intervention is necessary because state and local governments are not adequately dealing with this form of criminality;

c) Federal enforcement agencies are better equipped than state and local agencies to deal with white collar crime;

d) State and local enforcement agencies are at a disadvantage in prosecuting white collar crime which often involves more than one state or may involve actions or actors outside of the United States.

Should federal prosecution of white collar crime be limited to cases of a certain magnitude? Based upon what kinds of factors? Consult generally, JOACHIM J. SAVELSBERG & PETER BRUHL, CONSTRUCTING WHITE-COLLAR CRIME: RATIONALITIES, COMMUNICATION, POWER (1994); Simon & Swart, *The Justice Department Focuses on White Collar Crime: Promises and Pitfalls*, 30 CRIME & DELINQUENCY 107 (1984); Norman Abrams, *Assessing the Federal Government's "War" on White Collar Crime*, 53 TEMP. L.Q. 984 (1980).

4. *Official Corruption*

Official corruption, sometimes called public or political corruption, can be subsumed under white collar crime (as illustrated by the material under the white collar heading quoted above), or it can be viewed as a separate enforcement priority. Official corruption which has long been an enforcement priority of the federal government covers, of course, corruption of federal officials but also has been generally defined to include the corruption of state and local officials. Although there is no generally applicable provision that makes it a federal crime to bribe a state or local official, there are a number of federal criminal statutes that deal with bribery or have been interpreted to include bribery under which state and local officials can be prosecuted: the Travel Act, 18 U.S.C. § 1952, and the Hobbs Act, 18 U.S.C. § 1951; mail and wire fraud, 18 U.S.C. §§ 1341, 1343; the RICO statute, 18 U.S.C. § 1962; and, where federal moneys are involved, 18 U.S.C. §§ 666 and 201.

The rationale for making official corruption at the state and local level a matter of federal concern would seem to be that federal investigation and prosecution are desirable because state or local law enforcement may have broken down as a result of the corruption, or state and local police and prosecutors may be disinclined or find it awkward to proceed against their colleagues. The 2003–2008 DOJ Strategic Plan stated: "The Department recognizes that a strong deterrent capability is necessary to prevent criminals from defrauding, and therefore, weakening the Nation's industries and institutions. . . ." Should state and local agencies be given an opportunity to deal with the matter before proceeding federally? Is it preferable for a state to handle such matters itself, if necessary by appointment of a special prosecutor? Should the federal government prosecute in all such cases or only those of a certain magnitude? *See generally*, Charles F.C. Ruff, *Federal Prosecution of Local Corruption: A Case Study in the Making of Law Enforcement Policy*, 65 Geo. L.J. 1171 (1977).

5. *Drug Enforcement*

The federal law enforcement effort against the criminal drug trade has been using a significant proportion of federal investigatory, prosecutorial, judicial and correctional resources, but as noted supra, there has been a significant shift in the number of FBI personnel devoted to this enforcement effort. The overall effects of this shift which is quite recent are still developing. Is a concentration on the drug trade an appropriate allocation of federal resources? For a detailed description of federal goals, strategy and treatment of administrative priorities in the drug area, see infra, Chapter 9.

6. *Violent Crime*

Prior to the administration of Lyndon Johnson in the decade of the 1960's, although the federal government focused on certain crime areas that indirectly affected the amount of street crime, such as illegal drugs and organized crime, it did not attempt directly to address the problem of violent crime at the local level. Even during the Johnson administration when the government began to pay attention to street crime, its approach was not via criminal enforcement but rather in the form of the first large-scale federal grant program to state and local governments in aid of their crime reduction efforts, a program that was authorized by The Safe Streets and Crime Control Act of 1968. During this period, it was thought, that ordinary street crime did not provide the jurisdictional links to interstate commerce that could provide a basis for a broad-based federal enforcement attack on violent crime. Also, given the magnitude of the task of dealing with such crime, it was hard to see how the limited federal resources that were available could make a significant dent in the problem. And violent crime at the local level was seen as a local problem within the historical and traditional purview of state and local governments.

In 1991 Attorney General Richard Thornburg announced a major change in the federal approach, Operation Triggerlock, the cornerstone of a new emphasis in the Department of Justice on violent crime. The Attorney General characterized Operation Triggerlock as "a comprehensive effort to use federal laws pertaining to firearm violence to target the most dangerous offenders in each community and put them away for hard time in federal prisons." *Text of Triggerlock Implementation Memo*, DOJ ALERT, vol. 1, No. 1, p. 17 (July 1991). U.S. Attorneys said that the program came at a time when "some overburdened state criminal justice systems were ready to collapse." *Triggerlock Stats Impressive, Questions Remain*, DOJ ALERT, vol. 1, No. 6, p. 5 (December 1991). A follow-up memorandum by the head of the Criminal Division commented that "[t]he initiative is intended to be carried out in a manner which complements, rather than supplants, state and local enforcement efforts." *Id.* at 17. The implementation memorandum instructs each United States Attorney to appoint a Triggerlock task force involving federal, state, and local representatives to develop an enforcement strategy for the district. *Ibid.* The primary statutes applicable to Triggerlock are 18 U.S.C. §§ 922(g)(1) & (2) (felon in possession of a firearm), 924(e)(1) (armed career criminal penalty enhancement), and 924(c)(1) (possession of a firearm during the commission of a federal crime of violence or drug trafficking crime). See Chapter 3, supra at pp. 78–84.

The Triggerlock implementation memo suggests several strategies to identify potential targets, including screening of all state and local arrests within each district of felons (a) who were in possession of a firearm at the time of their arrest, or (b) whose arrest was for an offense that involved the possession or use of a firearm. *Id.* at 19. The memo also suggests that such strategies may be supplemented by obtaining from the state prison a list of all person about to be released from prison who qualify for armed career criminal prosecution. *Id.* Since such strategies have the potential to generate a very large number of targets, federal prosecutors are advised to have "articulable objective standards" to determine which cases will be prosecuted. *Id.* Federal prosecutors are also required to coordinate with state and local counterparts through the task force. *Ibid.*

Triggerlock was implemented aggressively. In the first six months after the announcement of the initiative 2,651 defendants were charged, and by that point approximately 650 defendants were being charged each month *Id.* at 5. The prosecutions resulted in stiff sentences: the average sentence for a defendant convicted under § 924(e) (the career offender provision) was 17 years, and the average sentence under § 924(c) (possession of a firearm during commission of a federal crime or a crime of violence) was 6 years. *Ibid.* While federal officials claimed that the program was successfully removing violent criminals from the streets, some criminal defense lawyers charged that the administration was merely trying to present itself as tough on gun violence while at the same time opposing gun control. *Ibid.*

The Department of Justice 1993 budget request continued this new emphasis on violent crime. While the budget also sought increases for traditional areas of emphasis such as white collar crime, these increases were small compared to the requests for programs aimed at combating violent crime. The Department sought a 24% increase in funding for programs to combat violent crime. *Federal Push on Violent Crime Stressed in Budget*, DOJ ALERT, vol. 2, No. 3, 2 (March 1992). The Department planned to assign 2,000 FBI agents to violent crime by the end of fiscal 1993. *Ibid*

In the 1990s some lawmakers proposed a significant additional expansion of the federal role in the prosecution of violent crime. Senator Alphonse D'Amato proposed the creation of two new crimes that would expand the application of federal law still further and federalize virtually all violent street crime, adding still further to the number of cases from among which federal prosecutors could chose to prosecute, and potentially increasing the total number of federal prosecutions of violent crime offenders. D'Amato proposed making any murder committed with a handgun that had traveled in commerce a federal crime. He also introduced a provision—dubbed Son of Triggerlock—that would have made the possession of a handgun a federal crime if it were used to commit a state felony. In 1991 a bill passed the Senate that would have punished this new federal crime with a mandatory sentence or 10 or 20 years, depending on whether the gun was discharged. *Federal Push on Violent Crime Stressed in Budget*, DOJ ALERT, vol. 2, no. 3, p. 2 (March 1992). Chief Justice William Rehnquist took the unusual step of opposing D'Amato's proposals, arguing that they would swamp the federal courts with routine cases that belong in state court, while hampering the courts from dealing with cases that require the resources of the federal system. *Id.* at 2–3.

Given its limited resources, can the federal government make a significant contribution to the fight against violent crime? What is the rationale for federal involvement in this area. Consult generally, Elizabeth Glazer, *Thinking Strategically: How Federal Prosecutors Can Reduce Violent Crime*, 26 FORDHAM URB. L. J. 573 (1993); Philip B. Heymann & Mark H. Moore, *Legislating Federal Crime and Its Consequences: The Federal Role in Dealing with Violent Street Crime: Principles, Questions and Cautions*, 543 ANNALS AM. ACAD. POL. & SOC. SCI. 103 (1996). *See also* GENERAL ACCOUNTING OFFICE, GAO/GDD–96–

150, REPORT TO THE ATTORNEY GENERAL: VIOLENT CRIME–FEDERAL LAW EN-FORCEMENT ASSISTANCE IN FIGHTING LOS ANGELES GANG VIOLENCE (1996).

In her *Thinking Strategically* article, *supra*, Elizabeth Glazer, the Chief of Crime Control Strategies in the U.S. Attorney's Office for the Southern District of New York, argues that federal prosecutors should adopt a strategic rather than a case-oriented approach to crime reduction and crime control:

> This Article explores some of the assets that federal prosecutors bring to the table in assisting a federal effort to reduce violent crime through the analysis of data, the strategic use of federal laws and the coordination of federal, state, local and private resources. First, because federal prosecutors sit at the center of agency investigations, they have a panoramic view of the agencies' often overlapping investigative efforts; and because they see those efforts, without the filter of any single agency's jurisdictional interests, they can evaluate the direction of those efforts dispassionately. Second, prosecutors are familiar with the array of laws—criminal, civil and administrative—that could be used in a strategic attempt to reduce crime. Although as currently employed, federal laws have had a scattershot effect on crime, they could provide an unparalleled opportunity for federal prosecutors to move towards a comprehensive and strategic approach to combating crime in both geographic and subject matter areas.

In the wake of Triggerlock, a dizzying array of national and locally based imaginatively-named federal programs have sprouted. The most significant of these is Project Safe Neighborhoods which is described on its own website:

> Project Safe Neighborhoods is a comprehensive, strategic approach to reducing gun crime in America. The various crime reduction initiatives in the past decade have taught us that, to have a truly significant impact, the federal government must do more than just increase its arrest and prosecution numbers. Our efforts must be comprehensive. We must build effective partnerships with our state and local counterparts. We must enhance our capacity to obtain and analyze crime and other data that should guide our strategies and afford us the opportunity to measure the impact of our efforts. We must maintain an edge in the attack on gun crime by providing expansive and comprehensive training for federal, state, and local law enforcement officers and prosecutors. We must convey the priorities, message, and results of our efforts to the media and community members. And we must build a powerful and lasting coalition with our citizens—one that empowers them to be agents of change in their own communities.
>
> This Administration is committed to an all-out assault on gun crime and will provide the resources necessary for Project Safe Neighborhoods' success. The Administration has committed over one billion dollars to this effort over four years. This funding is

being used to hire new federal and state prosecutors, support investigators, provide training, distribute gun lock safety kits, deter juvenile gun crime, and develop and promote community outreach efforts as well as to support other gun crime reduction strategies.

Despite an overall decline in the number of gun homicides during the last fifteen years, gun crime in America remains intolerably high. All told, two-thirds of the nation's 16,000 homicides in 2002 were committed with guns.

Nearly half a million people are victims of non-fatal firearm crime each year. Of particular alarm is the high toll gun crime takes on young people. . . .

Individual cities and states have begun to respond effectively to this epidemic of gun crime. Model firearms programs, such as Project Exile in Richmond, VA, and Operation Ceasefire in Boston, MA, have achieved success in many large cities throughout the country. It is this Administration's task to expand upon these successes by giving all United States Attorneys both a mandate and a framework for creating an effective gun crime reduction program.

* * *

Each United States Attorney is also encouraged to create a specialized unit within his or her office to target the most significant gun crime problems within the district to maximize the impact of this initiative and help ensure the safety of our nation's communities.

To complement the efforts of these specialized units, the Department of Justice created a Firearms Enforcement Assistance Team (FEAT) network comprised of persons with expertise in the core elements of Project Safe Neighborhoods. This network will assist the districts with their implementation efforts.

* * *

Although the specific approach to combating gun crime will accordingly vary from district to district, this initiative asks each United States Attorney to incorporate three national priorities in his or her strategic plan. Those priorities are as follows:

- increased prosecution of violent organizations using federal conspiracy, racketeering, narcotics, and all other available laws aggressively to attack and punish violent drug traffickers, violent street gangs, and violent robbery rings;

- heightened enforcement of all federal laws against illegal gun traffickers, as well as corrupt federal firearms licensees that supply them, with an emphasis on those gun traffickers who supply illegal firearms to violent organizations and to juveniles; and,

- renewed aggressive enforcement of federal firearms laws against those persons prohibited from possessing firearms or who use firearms in furtherance of illegal activities, including those persons denied under the Brady Act.

Other colorfully-named programs with goals related to Triggerlock and Project Safe Neighborhoods include:

a) the Weed and Seed Strategy which focuses on a targeted area and involves law enforcement and prosecutors cooperating in "weeding out" criminals who participate in violent crime and drug abuse, and attempting to prevent their return to the area; and "seeding," bringing relevant human services to and restoring the area.

b) locally-based programs such as Triggerlock II, Project Exile, Total Mission and Operation SafeHome, all of which happen to be initiatives in the Northern District of California. Specifically, Triggerlock II is an expanded version of Triggerlock, developed at the federal district level to vigorously prosecute firearms offenders in federal court and to heighten awareness of the violence associated with firearms. Project Exile is essentially the same program but called by a different name in another part of the federal district. Total Mission is a gun/gang violence reduction program in the Mission District of San Francisco. Operation Safe Home is a joint initiative with HUD to reduce crime and violence in public housing through interagency cooperative efforts.

Viewing these various programs and strategies in their entirety, one sees the following characteristics that, however named, they appear to share in common: enhanced federal prosecution of violent crime offenders, usually using federal gun laws; a community-based strategy for bringing people together to discuss and identify non-prosecution methods for reducing crime and violence and improving the quality of life in their area; marketing and advertising the program to make people aware and to involve them in relevant activities. Under this federal approach to dealing with local crime and violence the U.S. Attorney has assumed a central role:

> We promote the idea that, in this context, the U.S.Attorney's Office is a neutral third party that tries to bring participants to the table in a nonthreatening forum to address crime reduction strategies.

Weed and Seed link, U.S. Department of Justice, Northern District of California Website

It appears that in certain parts of the country, the federal government has assumed unto itself a significant responsibility for taking locally based and directed actions to reduce local crime through cooperative actions with other agencies and local communities. It remains to be seen whether: a) there are sufficient federal resources to support these activities, particularly at a time when terrorism has been elevated to be a major target of federal law enforcement efforts; b) these efforts turn out to be viewed as successful at the local level; and c) these activities have any negative effects, including drawing resources from other important areas of federal enforcement.

b. *Policy Statements and Prosecutorial Discretion*

1. *Policy Issued by the Criminal Division*

Another approach used to focus federal law enforcement authority, through controls over the exercise of investigatory and prosecutorial discretion, is the formulation of policy statements. Those statements of policy, quasi-legislative in form, that are issued by the Criminal Division in the U.S. Department of Justice are designed to provide guidance and limits beyond those imposed by relevant governing statutes to U.S. Attorneys' offices throughout the country. These policies are usually set forth in the U.S. Attorneys' Manual (USAM) which is available online at http://www.usdoj.gov/usao/eousa/foia_reading_room/usam/. One should also be aware of the Criminal Resource Manual portion of the USAM that contains useful background material relating to enforcement under particular federal criminal statutes.

Policy contained in the USAM is of several types: a) general policy statements that are not tied to particular criminal statutes and are applicable across-the-board in all federal criminal prosecutions; b) crime-specific prosecutorial policy statements (these policies sometimes involve a requirement of consultation or approval by the Criminal Division; in some instances they severely limit the scope of enforcement of particular criminal statutes); and c) statements that deal with procedural and other matters that do not involve substantive policies limiting the scope of enforcement or prosecutorial discretion.

An important issue with respect to both the general and the crime-specific policy statements are whether they are being adhered to in the field by U.S. Attorneys' offices and whether there are effective mechanisms in place to ensure that they are followed. As noted *supra*, p. 117, there is a tension between the view of the federal criminal operation as one that is at a certain level centralized, that is, controlled at a policy level from Washington, and the view that it is a localized system, where the actual decisions to prosecute and the handling of prosecutions take place in the field, that is, in the U.S. Attorneys' offices. This tension comes into sharp focus in connection with the subject of adherence by U.S. Attorneys to approval requirements and substantive policy statements issued by the Criminal Division in Washington.

a) *General policies*

In 1980, then Attorney General Benjamin Civiletti issued a document, Principles of Federal Prosecution, that is now incorporated into the U.S. Attorneys' Manual, § 9–27.001 et seq. (Sept. 1997). Some excerpts from these Principles and the accompanying comments are reproduced below. Additional excerpts are set forth at pp. 805–806.

These Principles of Federal Prosecution have been designed to assist in structuring the decision making process of attorneys for the government. For the most part, they have been cast in general terms with a view to providing guidance rather than to mandating results. The intent is to assure regularity without regimentation, to prevent unwarranted disparity without sacrificing flexibility.

[T]hey will contribute to more effective management of the government's limited prosecutorial resources by promoting greater consistency among the prosecutorial activities of the * * * United States Attorney's offices and between their activities and the Department's law enforcement priorities * * *.

Different offices face different conditions and have different requirements. In recognition of these realities, and in order to maintain the flexibility necessary to respond fairly and effectively to local conditions, each U.S. Attorney is specifically authorized to modify or depart from the principles set forth herein, as necessary in the interests of fair and effective law enforcement within the district. In situations in which a modification or departure is contemplated as a matter of policy or regular practice, the appropriate Assistant Attorney General and the Deputy Attorney General must approve the action before it is adopted.

The attorney for the government should commence or recommend federal prosecution if he/she believes that the person's conduct constitutes a federal offense and that the admissible evidence will probably be sufficient to obtain and sustain a conviction, unless, in his/her judgment, prosecution should be declined because: 1. No substantial federal interest would be served by prosecution; 2. The person is subject to effective prosecution in another jurisdiction; or 3. There exists an adequate non-criminal alternative to prosecution.

In determining whether prosecution should be declined because no substantial federal interest would be served by prosecution, the attorney for the government should weigh all relevant considerations, including: 1. Federal law enforcement priorities; 2,. The nature and seriousness of the offense; 3. The deterrent effect of prosecution; 4. The person's culpability in connection with the offense; 5. The person's history with respect to criminal activity; 6. The person's willingness to cooperate in the investigation or prosecution of others; and 7. The probable sentence or other consequences if the person is convicted.

Federal law enforcement resources and federal judicial resources are not sufficient to permit prosecution of every alleged offense over which federal jurisdiction exists. Accordingly, in the interest of allocating its limited resources as to achieve an effective nationwide law enforcement program, from time to time the Department establishes national investigative and prosecutorial priorities. These priorities are designed to focus federal law enforcement efforts on those matters within the federal jurisdiction that are most deserving of federal attention and are most likely to be handled effectively at the federal level. In addition, individual U.S. Attorneys may establish their own priorities, within the national priorities, in order to concentrate their resources on problems of particular local or regional significance. In weighing the federal interest in a particular prosecution, the attorney for the government should give careful consideration to the extent to which prosecution would accord with established priorities.

The Department of Justice has promulgated other general prosecutorial policy statements. Most notable among these are the Petite policies relating to duplicate state and federal prosecutions for essentially the same conduct (treated in detail, *infra* p. 822 et seq.) and relating to successive federal prosecutions growing out of the same conduct. *See generally* U.S. ATTORNEYS MANUAL § 9–2.001 et seq.

b) Crime-specific substantive policies

There are, in fact, not a great many significant crime-specific substantive policy statements in the USAM. We have already seen one of these, namely the Hobbs Act policy quoted *supra*, p. 54. One of the most detailed such crime-specific policies is the RICO policy statement. In the chapters, *infra*, that address specific crimes, the relevant crime-specific policy statements are reproduced at appropriate points.

Crime-specific policy statements, where they exist, take many different forms. For example, in connection with the carjacking statute, USAM § 9–60.1010 (Sept. 1997) provides:

> In view of the increase of motor vehicle theft and the use of violence in connection with that offense, the Attorney General was directed by the Congress to have the * * * FBI and the United States Attorneys' Offices cooperate with State and local officials to investigate carjacking, and, when appropriate and consistent with prosecutorial discretion and resources, prosecute violators in federal court.

Regarding federal prosecutorial policy for bank robbery, USAM § 9–61.610 (Sept. 1997) provides:

> It continues to be Department policy to reduce Federal involvement in the bank robbery area, and make deliberate progress toward maximum feasible deferral of bank robbery matters to those State and local law enforcement agencies which are prepared to handle them. However, no case should be deferred in favor of State/local investigation or prosecution where the state/local law enforcement authorities will not adequately handle it.

The policy relating to 18 U.S.C. § 1959 (violent crimes in aid of racketeering) provides in USAM § 9–110.812 (Sept. 1997):

> * * * The statutory language is extremely broad, in that it covers such conduct as a threat to commit an assault, and other relatively minor conduct normally prosecuted by local authorities. Thus, although the involvement of traditional organized crime will not be a requirement for approval of proposed prosecutions, a prosecution will not be authorized unless the violent crimes involved are sub-

stantial because of the seriousness of the injuries, the number of incidents, or other aggravating factors.

As one can see from these illustrations, the crime specific policies tend to formulated in broad language that do not tie the hands of federal prosecutors and promote the exercise of discretion in deciding whether to prosecute. Many, such as the bank robbery policy, only go so far as to provide a direction, one might say a presumption, for federal action. Others, such as the car jacking statute, do not even go that far, leaving the decision whether to prosecute federally to a judgment that it is "appropriate and consistent with prosecutorial discretion and resources," meanwhile not providing any specific criteria for how to exercise that "discretion."

Query: How limiting are these policies? Do you think that crime-specific policies should provide more guidance? What kind of criteria might you suggest? Why do you think that the government has failed in most instances to formulate policies that provide more guidance than these?

c) *Approval and consultation requirements*

In connection with the prosecution of some offenses, the Department of Justice requires that a U.S. Attorney obtain approval before filing the charge and in other instances that there be consultation with the Department. A requirement of centralized administrative review can help to maintain consistency in the interpretation of relevant prosecutorial priorities and policies and is a way to aid in the focussing of federal enforcement authority.

Prior approval by the Attorney General or Deputy or Assistant Attorney General of the initiation of prosecution is required by statute in connection with certain offenses. *See, e.g.*, 18 U.S.C. §§ 245, 1073. Prior approval by the Criminal Division is required, as a matter of Justice Department policy, in connection with certain offenses—e.g. RICO, see *infra* p. 577, and subversive activities prosecutions, see § 9–2.132, USAM. The requirement that a U.S. Attorney "consult" with the Criminal Division prior to initiating prosecution is applicable to a number of offenses, including, for example: air piracy outside the special aircraft jurisdiction of the United States, 49 U.S.C. § 1472(n); counterfeit substance and continuing criminal enterprise prosecutions under 21 U.S.C. §§ 841(a)(2) and 848; specified categories of Hobbs Act prosecutions; obscenity prosecutions; and mail fraud cases involving election fraud.

In 1995, Attorney General Janet Reno promulgated approval procedures relating to seeking the death penalty in federal criminal cases. These procedures were codified in the U.S. Attorney's Manual in 1997, USAM §§ 10.010 et seq. Prior authorization by the Attorney General is required before a federal prosecutor may seek the death penalty. Before seeking such approval the U.S. Attorney must first notify the defense and then make a submission in writing to the Attorney General discussing aggravating and mitigating factors, the defendant's background and criminal history, the basis for the federal prosecution and any other relevant information. Within the Department, these submissions are reviewed by a Committee that also gives the defense counsel an opportunity to make a written or oral presentation in opposition to the death penalty. (Note the unusual nature of this provision in the setting of a Department of Justice approval process.) The Committee makes a recommendation to the Attorney General regarding the application of the death penalty.

For a useful detailed description of the Department's death penalty review process, see Rory K. Little, *The Federal Death Penalty: History, and Some Thoughts about the Department of Justice's Role*, 26 FORDHAM URB. L.REV. 347 (1999). Professor Little had served as a member of the Department's Capital Cases Review Committee.

d) Adherence to Criminal Division policies

There are differing views of the relationship between U.S. Attorneys offices and the Department of Justice and, particularly in regard to the subject of adherence to departmental policies. See, for example, the suggestion that departmental directives to U.S. Attorneys' offices are "most often honored in the breach." Charles F.C. Ruff, *Federal Prosecution of Local Corruption, A Case Study in the Making of Law Enforcement Policy*, 65 GEO. L.J. 1171, 1207–08 (1977) (attributing the statement to a former Justice Department official). *See also* Dennis E. Curtis, *Comment: Congressional Powers and Federal Judicial Burdens*, 46 HASTINGS L.J. 1019, 1027 (1995):

> * * * [T]here are at least two serious questions to ask about the ability of the Attorney General to constrain charging decisions by individual U.S. Attorneys. First, United States Attorneys have a long history of at least some independence from Washington. Moreover, some U.S. Attorneys are powerful political players in their own right, jealous of their independence and confident of their own prosecutorial agenda. Second, courts have in the past been exceedingly reluctant to circumscribe the discretion of federal prosecutors * * * in charging. * * * Apart from the questions of political feasibility, there is some doubt whether any charging regulations can be effectively enforced by defendants, which in my opinion is the only way in which such regulations could be both effective and fair.

As some corroboration of these observations, one can take note of instances of a failure or apparent failure to adhere to departmental policies. See, for example, *Rinaldi v. United States*, 434 U.S. 22 (1977), involving a prosecution initiated by a U.S. Attorney in violation of the *Petite* policy. There have been numerous such cases. *See* Chapter 17, at p. 828. Consider also the Hobbs Act robbery cases discussed in Chapter 3, *supra*, pp. 42–54. On the surface at least, these cases do not appear to be consistent with the Hobbs Act robbery policy quoted *supra* at p. 54.

On the other hand, there is another view that presents quite a different picture of the department-U.S. Attorney relationship:

[S]truggles between the Attorney General's attempts to execute a cohesive national policy and the U.S. Attorney's efforts to respond to the needs of the local communities often challenge, and in certain instances eliminate, a U.S. Attorney's prosecutorial discretion. In addition, the Attorney General's authority to select Assistant U.S. Attorneys and to dispatch Special Attorneys to assist U.S. Attorneys in designated prosecutions inhibits the U.S. Attorney's ability to control his or her office. Furthermore, the Attorney General's ability to audit cases, coupled with the extensive reporting system which U.S. Attorneys are required to follow, creates a stringent watchdog system which prevents the U.S. Attorney from exercising independent judgment. Tom Rickhoff, *The U.S. Attorney: Fateful, Powers Limited*, 28 St. Mary's L.J. 499, 504–05 (1997).

Both views could be accurate. *See* JAMES EISENSTEIN, COUNSEL FOR THE UNITED STATES: U.S. ATTORNEYS IN THE POLITICAL AND LEGAL SYSTEMS 116 (1978): "The size of the office provides the best single indication of the relationship between a U.S. Attorney and the department." (Note that Judge Rickhoff was writing about the U.S. Attorney's office in the Western District of Texas.)

What kind of enforcement mechanisms does the Department of Justice have available to ensure adherence to departmental policies? Several devices have already been mentioned in the preceding paragraphs—namely, approval and consultation requirements, the ability to audit cases, and certain reporting requirements. Professor Curtis in the excerpt quoted above mentioned his preference for enforcement by defendants, that is, by giving defendants the right to litigate a failure to follow departmental policy. Note that departmental policies contain a clause that the policies are for internal purposes only and are non-litigable. The courts have consistently upheld this restriction. On the issue of giving defendants a right to litigate prosecutorial policy, see Norman Abrams, *Internal Policy: Guiding the Exercise of Prosecutorial Discretion*, 19 U.C.L.A. L. REV. 1 (1971); James Vorenberg, *Decent Restraint of Prosecutorial Power*, 94 HARV. L.REV. 1521 (1981). Professor Podgor has proposed a limited program of judicial oversight:

> First, it is suggested that there should be closer review by courts when there is guideline noncompliance. This can be accomplished by allowing defendants to use DOJ violations as evidence to support allegations of prosecutorial misconduct. Second, it is recommended that prosecutors should bear the burden of showing that they did not engage in misconduct, when there has been a violation of a department guideline. Finally, courts should consider reporting violations through the existing internal process, the Office of Professional Responsibility, to enhance overall compliance.

Ellen S. Podgor, *Department of Justice Guidelines: Balancing "Discretionary Justice,"* 13 Cornell J.L. & Pub. Pol'y 167, 196 (2003).

Compare Michael S. Simons, *Prosecutorial Discretion and Prosecutorial Guidelines: A Case Study in Controlling Federalization*, 75

N.Y.U.L.REV. 893, 962 (2000): "If prosecution guidelines were to create enforceable rights, they simply would not be drafted at all. Alternatively, if they were drafted, the guidelines would be drafted so broadly as to provide no meaningful guidance."

In several instances involving violations of the *Petite* policy or the department's obscenity prosecution policy, where the matter has come to the Supreme Court, the Solicitor General has moved to have the case remanded to allow the Government to dismiss the indictment. *See, e.g., Watts v. United States,* 422 U.S. 1032 (1975); *Redmond v. United States,* 384 U.S. 264 (1966).

Professor Kahan has proposed an innovative approach—that Congress delegate authority to the Department of Justice to interpret broadly phrased federal criminal statutes (or such statutes should be construed to involve such delegations of authority) and that the courts defer to the departmental interpretations unless they are unreasonable, applying the doctrine of *Chevron U.S.A., Inc. v. Natural Resources Defense Council, Inc.* 467 U.S. 837 (1984). Dan M. Kahan, *Is Chevron Relevant to Federal Criminal Law?* 110 HARV. L.REV. 469 (1996). Compare Kahan's proposal with the Department's promulgation of prosecutorial policy and the question of whether it should be subject to litigation by defendants? Are these two systems different? Interestingly, Kahan contends that this scheme would bring greater expertise to the task of interpretation, and result in both more uniformity and greater moderation in enforcement. Query: Is it appropriate to delegate to a prosecutorial office authority to interpret criminal statutes and to require the courts to defer to those interpretations? Note that such authority is commonly given to administrative agencies with responsibility for enforcing certain statutes such as those designed to protect the environment. Is there a difference between the Department of Justice and other administrative agencies? See Norman Abrams, *Exploring Limits on the Use of Administrative Agencies in the Felony Criminal Process,* 33 ISR. L.REV. 539, 573 (1999): "[T]here is a question whether the Department of Justice has the requisite degree of neutrality and objectivity to exercise the kind of authority that Kahan would give to it.... The fact that the Criminal Division does not, in the main, itself directly prosecute cases, does not mean that it does not have the psychology and culture of a prosecutorial unit."

Professor Clymer has commented on the fact that prosecution in the federal court of defendants who could have been charged in state court often results in harsher penalties and other disadvantages, but that the discretion whether to prosecute some individuals federally is not generally governed by administrative guidelines. Steven D. Clymer, *Unequal Justice: The Federalization of Criminal Law,* 70 S.Cal.L.Rev. 643, 650–651 (1997):

> ... [D]ramatic sentencing differentials and other disparities routinely occur when some offenders are prosecuted in state court and others, who may not be their partners but have engaged in the

same criminal conduct and are otherwise similarly situated, are instead selected for federal prosecution and the often harsher treatment that it entails. Such disparate treatment occurs nationwide on a daily basis when some defendants, engaged in drug transactions, weapons offenses, or other crimes over which there is overlapping federal and state criminal jurisdiction, happen to be among the unlucky ones selected for federal prosecution. Despite the significant ramifications of the forum selection decision, there is little administrative direction or judicial oversight to guide federal prosecutors in exercising their discretion to choose among offenders eligible for federal prosecution.

* * *

Even if courts refuse to enforce it, equal protection obligates prosecutors to have a rational basis for distinguishing between offenders who are charged and those who are not. Both the letter and the spirit of that command mandate that federal prosecutors have valid reasons for distinguishing between offenders who are subjected to harsher treatment as a result of federal prosecution and those who are instead charged in state court. The Department of Justice should amend its administrative guidelines to ensure compliance with equal protection principles.

The judiciary's role in limiting federalization-induced disparity also merits examination. One scholar has noted that, to date, 'no participants in the current federalization debate suggest a change in [the] doctrine' precluding judicial oversight of charging decisions absent proof of intentional discrimination. Critical examination of the underpinnings of this doctrinal limitation reveals, however, that the possibility of judicial oversight should be a topic of debate. If the Department of Justice does not require that its prosecutors make principled charging decisions, and if courts are confronted with evidence that federal prosecutors' selection decisions may be wholly unprincipled, courts should rethink their reluctance to scrutinize those decisions. Although courts should, at most, conduct limited review that would rarely afford defendants a judicial remedy, such oversight would promote principled charging decisions.

Professor Richman has listed a number of other "mechanisms" through which departmental authority can be asserted over "a recalcitrant [U.S. Attorney] office": reduction in funding; resolving jurisdictional conflicts in favor of other offices; using the disciplinary or removal power; and giving "the cold shoulder to U.S. Attorneys when they return to private practice." Daniel C. Richman, *Federal Criminal Law, Congressional Delegation, and Enforcement Discretion*, 46 U.C.L.A. L REV. 757, 781 (1999).

2. *U.S. Attorneys' Local Exercise of Prosecutorial Discretion*

a) *Declinations*

Examining only policies promulgated in Washington may lead one to overlook the fact that the U.S. Attorneys often develop their own local general and crime-specific policies. In some instances they are mandated to do so by policies formulated in the Department. *See, e.g.* § 9–101.600B., USAM.

An early Department of Justice study titled United States Attorneys' Written Guidelines for the Declination of Alleged Violations of Federal Criminal Laws (1979), noted "both notable similarities and striking differences across the various United States Attorneys' offices with respect to written declination policies." *Id.* at 4–5. The study revealed, for example, that in many districts for a number of crimes, declination policies include as a factor the value of the property or loss involved and that the specific declination cut off point, formulated in dollar amounts, varies markedly from district to district. Thus, for example, cases involving interstate transportation of stolen checks or money orders under 18 U.S.C.A. § 2314 may be declined if they involve a value of less than $5,000 in some districts, $2,000 in others, $1,000 in still others, etc. while in some districts whether the prosecution will be declined turns on both the amount and the number of the checks. Similar cut-off points are established in connection with other offenses, for example, amount of drugs in drug cases, and how long ago the underlying felony occurred in cases involving a charge of possession of a firearm by a convicted felon, etc. *See generally,* Richard Frase, *The Decision to File Federal Criminal Charges: A Quantitative Study of Prosecutorial Discretion,* 47 U. of Chi.L.Rev. 246 (1980); and two articles based on a study done more recently by Michael Edmund O'Neill, *Understanding Federal Prosecutorial Declinations: An Empirical Analysis of Predictive Factors,* 41 Am.Crim.L.Rev. 1439 (2004); and *When Prosecutors Don't: Trends in Federal Prosecutorial Discretion,* 79 Notre Dame L.Rev. 221 (2003). Professor O'Neill writes:

> [T]he number of matters referred to U.S. Attorneys' Offices for prosecution grew from 94,980 in 1994 to 117,450 in fiscal year 2000. ... It might be expected that with a substantial increase in referrals, the number of matters declined for prosecution might increase as well, given the foreseeable strain on available resources. Such is clearly not the case, however. In fact, the proportion of those matters that were declined for prosecution dropped from thirty-six percent in 1994 to twenty-six percent in 2000. ...

> These trends combine in an interesting fashion to demonstrate that although more matters were referred for prosecution, fewer of them were declined. It is difficult to imagine the emergence of these trends without an increase in investigative and prosecutorial resources during this time period. On this theory, the increase in investigative resources presumably led to an increase in the number of matters referred, while a corresponding increase in prosecutorial resources presumably resulted in a decrease in declinations.

* * *

However, it is interesting to note that while the DEA refers the second highest number of matters for prosecution, it has a substantially lower declination rate than many other agencies—only nineteen percent. Explaining the stark difference in the declination rates of the DEA and the FBI is no easy task. Although one could argue that the DEA's cases are better prepared and easier to prosecute because they generally involve illegal narcotics, it is difficult to draw such conclusions from the data alone. The discrepancy may also be a reflection of the fact that narcotics cases during the examined time period have merely been a higher priority for the various U.S. Attorneys' Offices. If that is the case, then it is possible that—all other things being equal—prosecutors afford priority to matters referred by the DEA when it comes to committing the use of available resources.

41 Am.Crim.L.Rev. 1439, 1445, 1449–1450.

b) *Relationships with investigative agencies*

The effect and role of investigative agencies on the exercise of the prosecutor's charging discretion and the corresponding influence of the prosecutor on the agency's investigative choices is garnering increasing attention. See Daniel C. Richman, *Prosecutors and Their Agents, Agents and Their Prosecutors*, 103 Colum. L.Rev. 749, 768–771 (2003):

> Why haven't federal prosecutors reduced their reliance on federal agencies by dealing directly with state and local agencies, trading the advantages of federal jurisdiction for investigative support? This has occurred, and may occur more, as the federal government reaches out for more local assistance in terrorism investigations. But there are obstacles. Although agents and police have their rivalries, they have similar professional perspectives. After Attorney General Ashcroft placed U.S. Attorneys in charge of joint terrorism task forces around the country, a former FBI executive expressed his concern that the move would " 'undermine[] the effectiveness of the FBI's relationship with state and local authorities,' " and noted that "several police chiefs" had advised that they were " 'not comfortable in such a relationship led by U.S. Attorneys.' "

> In any event, federal prosecutors are bound to federal agencies by asset specialization. Federal agents have a special familiarity with federal law, and because they cater primarily to federal prosecutors, they are likely to have developed informational networks with prosecutorial demands in mind. As in any long-term contractual relation, each side is likely to have developed structures that make exit difficult.

> Yet prosecutors, too, can take advantage of overlapping jurisdictions to play their federal counterparts against one another. The FBI dominates traditional organized crime cases, but when a group engages in drug dealing or gun running, the DEA or ATF may have an interest as well. In the white collar area, the Postal Inspection Service's jurisdiction over mail fraud makes that low profile agency a fit instrument for prosecutors seeking to go where the FBI would

prefer not to venture (or to control an investigation to a degree that the FBI would not tolerate). Thus, when Rudolph Giuliani's U.S. Attorney's Office pursued Wall Street cases in the late 1980s, it initially would create ad hoc investigative teams from the Postal Inspection Service, the IRS, and the SEC. Only after these cases garnered considerable positive media coverage did the FBI enter the area. In another district, a U.S. Attorney recently explained why he liked the overlap between FBI and Secret Service jurisdiction in white collar cases: The U.S. Attorney's Office, he noted, "doesn't want to put all their investigative eggs in one basket" because "at different times [the two agencies] have different resources and different commitments to different types of white collar cases."

Over time, the costs of competition have led agencies, or their political sponsors, to clarify these jurisdictional boundaries. Yet such clarifications have their own costs, and the current degree of blurriness may reflect some recognition of its advantages, which include the benefits of competition and the deterrence of corruption.

Interagency competition is not the only source of prosecutorial bargaining power at this structural level. Where an agency is particularly weak and poorly organized, prosecutors may be able to gain substantial control over its agenda.

c. Strike Forces, Task Forces, and Special Purpose Units

In addition to the statement of priorities, a method being used in different forms to channel the federal law enforcement effort is the establishment of special teams—i.e. personnel with a specific investigative-prosecutive mission. Of course, there have long been many standing federal investigative agencies that are relatively specialized in what they do—e.g. the DEA and Secret Service. Indeed it can be argued that the only federal investigative agency not specialized in some degree is the FBI with its broad ranging investigative jurisdiction. But beginning in the 1960's, special teams such as the organized crime strike forces and various drug task forces were established. In addition, the Justice Department established special purpose prosecutors' units in some of the U.S. attorneys' offices, e.g. Controlled Substances Units to coordinate drug prosecutions, and Economic Crime Units, to coordinate and oversee white collar crime prosecutions. As noted *supra* at p. 132, the organized crime task forces, which originally were free standing operations with lawyers assigned directly from Washington who maintained an office and an operation separate from the U.S. Attorneys were later absorbed into those offices.

Each approach to specialization varies somewhat in its details but the general purpose is always the same—to concentrate personnel on a specialized task in order to focus and coordinate investigations and prosecutions on a targeted area. The organized crime strike forces have been described as a form of "institutionalized cooperation," see Note, *The Strike Force: Organized Law Enforcement v. Organized Crime*, 6

COL. J. OF L. & SOC. PROBS. 496, 521 (1970); Meredith J. Rund, *Notes: Breathing Life into the "Working Arrangement" Rule: Maintaining a Federal Deterrent in Joint Federal–State Law Enforcement Operations,* 66 UMKC L.REV. 469 (1997).

As previously noted, supra, p. 127, the shifting of FBI agents into terrorism work has not resulted in the reduction of the number of FBI agents assigned to work on the Organized Crime/Drug Enforcement Task Forces.

Post 9/11, as part of making counterterrorism its highest priority, the Department of Justice "directed the formation or expansion of terrorism task forces and councils (with members from many federal, state, and local agencies and private industry) that coordinate and integrate intelligence and law enforcement functions to achieve the Department's counterterrorism goal. The Department of Justice's Terrorism Task Forces U.S. Dept. of Just., Office of the Inspector General Report No. 1–2005–007 (June, 2005). This OIG report found the following:

> The JTTFs [FBI's Joint Terrorism Task Forces] are operational units that conduct field investigations of actual or potential terrorism threats. Unlike the other entities reviewed in this report, the JTTFs existed before September 11, 2001. The FBI has established 103 JTTFs nationwide.

* * *

> We found that the JTTFs had inadequate administrative and analytical support, had high turnover in task force leadership, and exceeded their authorized staffing levels. ... [T]he FBI Director mandated that every terrorism lead must be addressed.... [A]ddressing every lead results in a demanding workload that is surpassing ... [the] resources available to the task forces. At all sites we visited, we found that the JTTFs were exceeding their authorized staffing levels for FBI agents by 75 to 125 percent by borrowing personnel from other FBI programs (such as drugs or white collar crime) within the field or resident agency office....

* * *

> We also found that the JTTFs do not have adequate connectivity to information technology systems to support the members' needs.

* * *

> Although Congress, the DEA, and the Department's leadership recognize the link between drug trafficking and terrorism (often called narcoterrorism), in comparison with other Department law enforcement components, the DEA has the lowest membership on the JTTFs.

* * *

Most JTTF ... members and supervisors ... stated that additional ICE [Department of Homeland Security's Bureau of Immigration and Customs Enforcement] agents, particularly former immigration agents, are needed on ... [the] task forces since most international terrorism cases have some link to immigration.

d. Coordination Bodies

The fragmented character of the federal law enforcement operation involving numerous agencies in different departments and the problem of rationalizing the state-federal relationship have created an urgent need for coordination. At various times, different types of coordination bodies have been established. Some examples of such bodies are described below.

In 1970 the National Council on Organized Crime was established to formulate a strategy to eliminate organized crime. The Council, which was chaired by the Attorney General, failed in its attempts to formulate a national strategy to fight organized crime. In November 1976, the National Organized Crime Planning Council (NOCPC) was formed to facilitate detailed planning and coordination between the strike forces and Federal law enforcement agencies. The intent of the Council was to facilitate the exchange of information among these agencies in order to provide a more coordinated approach to the Federal efforts to combat organized crime. *See* Report of the Comptroller General of the U.S., Stronger Federal Effort Needed in Fight Against Organized Crime (GAO 1981).

One of the recommendations of the August 1981 Report of the Attorney General's Task Force on Violent Crime was to establish Law Enforcement Coordinating Committees (LECC) in all federal districts to improve coordination of federal, state, and local law enforcement. The LECC's spawned a wide variety of cooperative law enforcement activities, ranging from bank robbery task forces to cross designation of prosecutors to sharing law enforcement intelligence.

The Attorney General's Advisory Committee of U.S. Attorneys made up of 15 U.S. Attorneys was established in 1973 and formalized in 1976 by order of the Attorney General, to make recommendations with respect to: developing Department policies and procedures; improving management, particularly with respect to the relationships between the Department and the U.S. Attorneys; operating the Law Enforcement Coordinating Committees (LECC); cooperating with state attorneys general and other state and local officials to improve the quality of justice in the United States; promoting greater consistency in the application of legal standards throughout the nation and at various levels of government; and aiding the Attorney General, Deputy Attorney General, and Associate Attorney General in formulating new programs.

Post 9/11, the Attorney General directed that each of the US Attorney Office's operate an ATAC [Anti-terrorism Advisory Council]. "The purpose of the ATACs is to 1) facilitate the exchange of information at the federal, state, and local levels and between the public and private sectors; 2) conduct counterterrorism training; and 3) coordinate terrorism prosecutorial and investigative strategies within the Department." Id.

e. *Investigative Techniques*

The development of investigative prosecutive priorities such as organized crime or white collar crime has generated a need for investigative tools and techniques that can be used in building cases against those who engage in these forms of criminal activity. It is not surprising therefore to find that in the same period when these priorities were being formulated, federal enforcement agencies were extensively using investigative techniques such as: electronic surveillance; grand jury investigations, including the convening of special grand juries that function over a longer period than the ordinary grand jury; grants of use immunity to obtain information from witnesses involved in criminality; the witness protection program, to protect witnesses who have given testimony; sting operations and other kinds of undercover operations; the use of informants; the offering of large rewards for crime related information; and obtaining tax related information and information from financial reporting applicable to banks, businesses and individuals engaged in a business or trade.

The need for such tools reflects the fact that the resources of the federal law enforcement operation are limited and require efficient means to generate crime related information, and that the priorities set involve crimes that are often not reported and are extremely difficult to uncover. The techniques may also be seen as a way to focus the federal law enforcement effort, and in a limited sense some of these tools are helpful in this regard: they do often serve to provide the needed crime-related information. But the techniques do not provide answers to questions such as: Which categories of crime should the federal government investigate? Within each category, what kinds of investigative criteria should be established? If the target is formulated in terms of business, occupations, or individuals, on which should emphasis be placed and how are the specific targets to be identified?

f. *Other Methods*

What other methods can you think of that might be used to focus and channel federal investigatorial and prosecutorial resources? Can you add to the following list?

1) Congressional control both through review of departmental funding and through continuing committee oversight. Consult generally Daniel C. Richman, *Federal Criminal Law, Congressional Delegation, and Enforcement Discretion*, 46 U.C.L.A. L. REV. 757 (1999) for a thoughtful, textured analysis of the reasons why Congress may prefer broad criminal statutes and decentralized prosecutorial power.

2) Internal management review programs.

3) A monitoring system involving an internal audit that would review prosecutorial decisions on a regular basis. *See generally*, Rabin, *Agency Criminal Referrals in the Federal System: An Empirical Study of Prosecutorial Discretion*, 24 STAN.L.REV. 1036 (1972).

4) Setting up arrangements whereby state or local prosecutors may participate in or influence individual decisions whether to prosecute federally.

g. The Use of Improper Criteria in Deciding to Investigate or Prosecute

1. In General

There is an additional set of problems pertaining to the prosecutorial and investigative function not addressed in the foregoing materials—the devising of methods to insure that decisions to investigate and prosecute in criminal cases are made only on a professional basis, untainted by political considerations or influence or other improper basis. For a useful study of the issues and a set of findings and recommendations growing out of Watergate and the FBI's COINTEL-PRO program, see ABA SPECIAL COMMITTEE TO STUDY FEDERAL LAW ENFORCEMENT AGENCIES, PREVENTING IMPROPER INFLUENCE ON FEDERAL LAW ENFORCEMENT AGENCIES (1976). What kinds of institutionalized methods to prevent abuses are likely to work? Is there any way to prevent improper influence by the White House in federal prosecutorial or investigative decision-making? What constitutes improper influence? Was it improper for the Justice Department to concentrate its resources on investigating and prosecuting James Hoffa during the attorney generalship of Robert Kennedy? *See* Monroe H. Freedman, *The Professional Responsibility of the Prosecuting Attorney*, 55 GEO. L.J. 1030 (1967); Richard Uviller, *The Virtuous Prosecutor in Quest of an Ethical Standard: Guidance from the ABA*, 71 MICH. L.REV. 1145 (1973). Should Justice be able to target for investigation particular individuals who it believes to be involved in La Cosa Nostra? *See United States v. Polizzi*, 500 F.2d 856, 857 (9th Cir.1974), and 115 Cong.Rec. Pt. 17, 23440–23441 (Aug. 12, 1969).

The Independent Counsel Statute was one kind of solution to the potential for improper influence over prosecutorial decisions where high government officials were the target. Consult generally the articles in: *The Independent Counsel Statute: A Symposium*, 49 MERCER L.REV. No 2 (1998); *Symposium, The Independent Counsel Act: From Watergate to Whitewater and Beyond*, 86 GEO. L.J. No. 6 (1998).

2. The Defense of Selective Prosecution

A claim that a prosecutor used an improper basis in deciding to prosecute is cognizable in the courts under the heading of selective prosecution. In recent years, the Supreme Court has decided two selective prosecution cases, *Wayte v. United States*, 470 U.S. 598 (1985), and *United States v. Armstrong*, 517 U.S. 456 (1996), the end result of which has been to make it very difficult to prove or succeed on a defense of selective prosecution.

In *Wayte*, the prosecution was for knowingly and willfully failing to register for the draft with the Selective Service System. The defendant was a vocal opponent of the draft who announced his opposition by writing to government officials stating that he had not registered and did not intend to do so. The defendant moved to dismiss on the ground of selective prosecution. The Court applied a two-pronged test: the petitioner was required to show both that the enforcement system the government used had a discriminatory effect and that it was motivated by a discriminatory purpose. The Court stated:

> All petitioner has shown here is that those eventually prosecuted, along with many not prosecuted, reported themselves as having violated the law. He has not shown that the enforcement policy selected nonregistrants for prosecution on the basis of their speech. * * * The Government did not prosecute those who reported themselves but later registered. Nor did it prosecute those who protested registration but did not report themselves or were not reported by others. In fact, the Government did not even investigate those who wrote letters to Selective Service criticizing registration unless their letters stated affirmatively that they had refused to comply with the law. * * * The Government, on the other hand, did prosecute people who reported themselves or were reported by others but who did not publicly protest. These facts demonstrate that Government treated all reported nonregistrants similarly. It did not subject vocal nonregistrants to any special burden. Indeed, those prosecuted in effect selected themselves for prosecution by refusing to register after being reported and warned by the Government.

Even if the passive policy had a discriminatory effect, petitioner has not shown that the Government intended such a result.

In *Armstrong*, the defendants had been indicted on crack charges and filed a motion for discovery alleging that they were selected for federal rather than state prosecution because they were Black. In support of their motion, they had offered an affidavit prepared by the Federal Public Defender's Office stating that in every one of the 24 crack cases closed by the office during 1991 the defendants were Black. The district court had granted the motion, ordering the Government to provide the defense with a list of the cases from the past three years in which the government had charged both cocaine and firearms offenses, to identify the race of the defendants, and to explain its criteria for deciding to prosecute those defendants for federal drug offenses.

The Supreme Court ruled that to obtain discovery on the claim that he was singled out for prosecution because of his race a defendant must make a threshold showing that the government declined to prosecute similarly situated suspects of other races. Since the defendants had not made such a showing, it was error to order the Government to provide information.

Did this ruling leave defendants who wish to make out a claim of selective prosecution with any practical avenues to succeed? Note that normally the relevant evidence is in the hands of the prosecutor.

Consider in connection with the foregoing, the views of Professor Clymer. Steven D. Clymer, *Unequal Justice: The Federalization of Criminal Law*, 70 S.Cal L.Rev. 643, 688 (1997):

> ... [In] *Wayte v. United States*, in which the defendant challenged his prosecution for failure to register for the draft by claiming that his vocal protest of Selective Service laws made it more likely that he would be charged, the Court rejected the claim, holding that in order to prevail on a selective prosecution claim a defendant must prove that the prosecutor selected him because of his exercise of his First Amendment rights. From this, lower courts apparently reason that *Wayte* imposes a 'proof-of-improper-purpose' threshold for all selective prosecution claims. A defendant who only questions the rationality of a charging decision can never satisfy this requirement because a rationality challenge tacitly concedes an inability to prove that the prosecutor has an improper discriminatory purpose. However, *Wayte* does not impose such a threshold. Although *Wayte* does require proof of an improper prosecutorial purpose, it does so only in those cases in which the defendant's equal protection claim is predicated on an allegation that an exercise of a constitutional right (or membership in a suspect class) played a role in the charging decision. *Wayte* never challenged the decision to prosecute him but not others who had also failed to register as simply irrational. Thus, the Court had no occasion to address the viability of such a claim.
>
> Whatever force lower courts' interpretations of ... *Wayte* may have once had, it is unlikely that they survived *Wade v. United States*, [504 U.S. 181 (1992)] a more recent Supreme Court decision. In *Wade*, a unanimous Court concluded that the Constitution requires that all prosecutorial decisions, including charging decisions, be rationally related to legitimate government ends. The Court did not suggest equal protection prohibits only improper discriminatory decisions. ...

Part II

FRAUD AND POLITICAL CORRUPTION

Chapter 5

MAIL FRAUD

INTRODUCTION

The federal crime of mail fraud has had an unusual history. Enacted in 1872, it is the oldest federal criminal statute being used extensively to prosecute crimes that are within the province of state and local law enforcement. For purposes of this chapter, we will use the term "mail fraud" generically to cover both mail fraud (18 U.S.C.A. § 1341) and its younger sibling, the wire fraud statute (18 U.S.C.A. § 1343). The two statutes are parallel in all respects except the jurisdictional provisions, which are discussed *infra* at 219–28. Although many fraud and related types of cases are being prosecuted today under other specific federal statutes, the government continues to make frequent use of the mail and wire fraud statutes.[a]

The durability of the crime of mail fraud—despite the enactment over the years of a series of related, more specific criminal statutes—is largely explained by the unusual flexibility that the courts have accorded it. As a former federal prosecutor explained:

> To federal prosecutors of white collar crime, the mail fraud statute is . . . our true love. We may flirt with RICO, show off with 10b–5, and call the conspiracy law "darling," but we always come home to the virtues of 18 U.S.C. § 1341, with its simplicity, adaptability, and comfortable familiarity.

Jed Rakoff, *The Federal Mail Fraud Statute (Part I)*, 18 Duq. L. Rev. 771, 771 (1980). Of course, a "flirtation" with RICO need not compromise at all the relationship with mail fraud, which is the most frequently used predicate offense in civil RICO cases.

Today, as in the past, most mail fraud prosecutions are based upon facts that show fraud in the traditional sense—conduct amounting to the

---

a. The number of defendants charged with postal and wire fraud has been declining, dropping from 1,046 in 2001 to 928 in 2005. Though mail fraud defendants still outnumber wire fraud defendants (573 to 355 in 2005), proportionately there seems to have been a slight shift toward wire fraud in recent years. ADMINISTRATIVE OFFICE OF THE UNITED STATES COURTS, JUDICIAL BUSINESS OF THE UNITED STATES COURTS, The 12–month periods ending March 31, 2001 to 2005, Table D–2.

crime of obtaining property by false pretenses. However, the statute is increasingly being used to prosecute conduct not amounting to traditional criminal fraud but which may involve other crimes such as bribery or extortion. In other cases, the mail fraud statute has been used to prosecute conduct that does not show fraud in a classic sense and does not violate any other provision of the state or federal penal laws. The conduct involved may take place in a commercial or corporate setting or involve a state or local government official; increasingly the mail fraud statute is being used to prosecute various forms of commercial bribery and political corruption. A few cases involve bizarre scenarios, such as a recent case in which the defendant was convicted of mail fraud after killing two of her husbands and her boyfriend in order to collect their life insurance benefits. *United States v. Gray*, 405 F.3d 227 (4th Cir. 2005).

Section A examines the scope of the "scheme to defraud" element, introducing the general subject of the role of the mail fraud statute in protecting against deprivations of intangible rights and breaches of fiduciary duties. Sections B and C explore two kinds of prosecutions for intangible rights: prosecutions for political corruption and for breaches of fiduciary duties in the private sector. Section D takes up the question what counts as "property" for purposes of the mail and wire fraud statutes, and Section E deals with issues relating to "use of the mails." Finally, Section F explores the issues arising out of the overlap between mail fraud and a host of other federal criminal statutes.

18 U.S.C.

§ 1341. Frauds and swindles

Whoever, having devised or intending to devise any scheme or artifice to defraud, or for obtaining money or property by means of false or fraudulent pretenses, representations, or promises, or to sell, dispose of, loan, exchange, alter, give away, distribute, supply, or furnish or procure for unlawful use any counterfeit or spurious coin, obligation, security, or other article, or anything represented to be or intimated or held out to be such counterfeit or spurious article, for the purpose of executing such scheme or artifice or attempting so to do, places in any post office or authorized depository for mail matter, any matter or thing whatever to be sent or delivered by the Postal Service, or deposits or causes to be deposited any matter or thing whatever to be sent or delivered by any private or commercial interstate carrier, or takes or receives therefrom, any such matter or thing, or knowingly causes to be delivered by mail or such carrier according to the direction thereon, or at the place at which it is directed to be delivered by the person to whom it is addressed, any such matter or thing, shall be fined under this title or imprisoned not more than 20 years, or both. If the violation affects a financial institution, such person shall be fined not more than $1,000,000 or imprisoned not more than 30 years, or both.

18 U.S.C.

§ 1343. Fraud by wire, radio, or television

Whoever, having devised or intending to devise any scheme or artifice to defraud, or for obtaining money or property by means of false or fraudulent pretenses, representations, or promises, transmits or causes to be transmitted by means of wire, radio, or television communication in interstate or foreign commerce, any writings, signs, signals, pictures, or sounds for the purpose of executing such scheme or artifice, shall be fined under this title or imprisoned not more than 20 years, or both. If the violation affects a financial institution, such person shall be fined not more than $1,000,000 or imprisoned not more than 30 years, or both.

18 U.S.C.

§ 1346. Definition of "scheme or artifice to defraud"

For the purposes of this chapter, the term "scheme or artifice to defraud" includes a scheme or artifice to deprive another of the intangible right of honest services

A. THE BREADTH OF THE CONCEPT OF SCHEME TO DEFRAUD

The mail fraud act was passed as part of an overall recodification of the postal laws, and there is little indication of Congress's intention, beyond the statement of a sponsor of the legislation that measures were needed "to prevent the frauds which are mostly gotten up in the large cities ... by thieves, forgers, and rapscallions generally, for the purpose of deceiving and fleecing the innocent people in the country." CONG. GLOBE, 41st Cong., 3d Sess., 35 (1870) (Rep. Farnsworth) (commenting on same proposal in prior session of Congress).

So who are the mail and wire fraud defendants, the "rapscallions," of the 21st century? A glance at the daily newspaper reveals the tremendous range of these statutes. From the leaders of industry to high-ranking government officials, mail and wire fraud have been used against some of the most notorious defendants of the past few years. In the wave of corporate scandals that began with Enron, the fraud statutes have been used to prosecute many of the corporate executives. Enron's Kenneth Lay, Adelphia's John and Timothy Rigas, HealthSouth's Richard Scrushy, Rite Aid's Martin Grass, and Cendant's E. Kirk Shelton have all been charged with mail or wire fraud.[b] The fraud statutes have

b. Kenneth Lay was indicted on conspiracy, securities fraud, and wire fraud, and trial is scheduled for 2006. John and Timothy Rigas were convicted of conspiracy, securities fraud, and bank fraud, but were acquitted on the wire fraud charges in 2004. Richard Scrushy was acquitted of all charges, including conspiracy, securities fraud, mail fraud, and money laundering in 2005. Martin Grass pled guilty to conspiracy to defraud and obstruct justice in 2004. E. Kirk Shelton was convicted of conspiracy, securities fraud, wire fraud, and mail fraud in 2005.

also been used to bring down some powerful government officials, such as former Governor John Rowland of Connecticut, who in 2004 pled guilty of conspiring to deprive residents of honest services by engaging in tax and mail fraud, and former Governor George Ryan of Illinois, who faces numerous corruption charges including mail fraud. At the federal level, Republican fund raiser and lobbyist Jack Abramoff, a close associate of House Speaker Tom Delay, has been charged with wire fraud, though Delay appears to have had no involvement in the transaction in question, the purchase of a shipping line. And recently, the fraud statutes have made it onto the world stage in the U.N. oil-for-food program in Iraq. In August 2005, former U.N. procurement officer Aleksandr Yakovlev pled guilty to charges of conspiracy, wire fraud, and money laundering for his role of soliciting bribes in the scandal.

So just how did §§ 1341 and 1343 go from a recodification of the postal laws to such powerful tools for prosecutors? The material in this section explains the development of these statutes over the years. Keep in mind this history as you read through the rest of the chapter.

The *Durland* case excerpted below provided the Supreme Court with its first opportunity to interpret the mail fraud act. Federal prosecutors had charged the defendants with selling bonds though the mail upon which they never intended to make the promised repayments. Under the common law rule only misrepresentations as to present or past facts constituted a basis for a charge of obtaining property by false pretenses, and this was the prevailing rule in the United States at the time of the *Durland* case. Consequently, in most state courts a person could not be convicted of obtaining property by false pretenses if he had only made a false promise, i.e. stated an intention to pay money at some future date without intending in fact to make the payment. *Durland* thus presented the Supreme Court with an opportunity to explore the question how the mail fraud act compares with common law fraud and with the state law of fraud and false pretenses.

DURLAND v. UNITED STATES
161 U.S. 306, 16 S.Ct. 508, 40 L.Ed. 709 (1896).

MR. JUSTICE BREWER delivered the opinion of the court:

Inasmuch as the testimony has not been preserved, we must assume that it was sufficient to substantiate the charges in the indictments; that this was a scheme and artifice to defraud, and that the defendant did not intend that the bonds should mature, or that although money was received any should be returned, but that it should be appropriated to his own use. In other words he was trying to entrap the unwary, and to secure money from them on the faith of a scheme glittering and attractive in form, yet unreal and deceptive in fact, and known to him to be such. So far as the moral element is concerned it must be taken that the defendant's guilt was established.

But the contention on his part is that the statute reaches only such cases as, at common law, would come within the definition of "false pretenses," in order to make out which there must be a misrepresentation as to some existing fact and not a mere promise as to the future. It is urged that there was no misrepresentation as to the existence or solvency of the corporation, the Provident Bond & Investment Company, or as to its modes of doing business, no suggestion that it failed to issue its bonds to any and every one advancing the required dues, or that its promise of payment according to the conditions named in the bond was not a valid and binding promise. And, then, as counsel say in their brief, "it [the indictment] discloses on its face absolutely nothing but an intention to commit a violation of a contract. If there be one principle of criminal law that is absolutely settled by an overwhelming avalanche of authority it is that fraud either in the civil courts or in the criminal courts must be the misrepresentation of an existing or a past fact, and cannot consist of the mere intention not to carry out a contract in the future."

The question thus presented is one of vital importance, and underlies both cases. We cannot agree with counsel. The statute is broader than is claimed. Its letter shows this: "Any scheme or artifice to defraud." Some schemes may be promoted through mere representations and promises as to the future, yet are none the less schemes and artifices to defraud. Punishment because of the fraudulent purpose is no new thing. As said by Mr. Justice Brown in *Evans v. United States* (No. 1), 153 U.S. 584, 592: "If a person buys goods on credit in good faith, knowing that he is unable to pay for them at the time, but believing that he will be able to pay for them at the maturity of the bill, he is guilty of no offense even if he be disappointed in making such payment. But if he purchases them, knowing that he will not be able to pay for them, and with an intent to cheat the vendor, this is a plain fraud, and made punishable as such by statutes in many of the states."

But beyond the letter of the statute is the evil sought to be remedied, which is always significant in determining the meaning. It is common knowledge that nothing is more alluring than the expectation of receiving large returns on small investments. Eagerness to take the chances of large gains lies at the foundation of all lottery schemes, and, even when the matter of chance is eliminated, any scheme or plan which holds out the prospect of receiving more than is parted with appeals to the cupidity of all.

In the light of this the statute must be read, and so read it includes everything designed to defraud by representations as to the past or present, or suggestions and promises as to the future. The significant fact is the intent and purpose. The question presented by this indictment to the jury was not, as counsel insist, whether the business scheme suggested in this bond was practicable or not. If the testimony had shown that this Provident company, and the defendant, as its president, had entered in good faith upon that business, believing that out of the moneys received they could by investment or otherwise make enough to justify the promised returns, no conviction could be sustained, no matter how visionary might seem the scheme. The charge is that in putting forth this scheme it was not the intent of the defendant to make an honest effort for its success, but that he resorted to this form and pretense of a bond without a thought that he or the company would ever make good its promises. It was with the purpose of protecting the public against all such intentional efforts to despoil, and to prevent the postoffice from being used to carry them into effect, that this statute was passed; and it would strip it of value to confine it to such cases as disclosed an actual misrepresentation as to some existing fact, and exclude those in which is only the allurement of a specious and glittering promise. This, which is the principal contention of counsel, must be overruled. * * *

Notes

1. **The implications of *Durland*.** In one sense *Durland* merely anticipated a desirable change in the scope of fraud that was ultimately adopted by the states as well. There has been a general movement throughout the United States toward making false promises the subject of criminal prosecution. *See, e.g., People v. Ashley*, 42 Cal.2d 246, 267 P.2d 271 (1954); MODEL PENAL CODE § 223.3 (1962).

In another sense, however, *Durland* was a much more radical decision, since it cut the mail fraud statute loose from its common law moorings and established that federal mail fraud was not limited to the scope of frauds punishable under state law. In considering the implications of *Durland*, remember that the states retain their jurisdiction over fraudulent behavior, and the vast majority of fraud prosecutions continue to be brought by the states. Mail fraud prosecutions thus constitute an adjunct to the states' general jurisdiction over fraud. This raises the question why Congress deemed it necessary to supplement the states' jurisdiction over fraud. What is the justification for having a federal provision dealing with fraud that may have broader coverage than the comparable crime under state law? Should the Court have conformed federal law to state law? If so, what if the law varies from state to state?

What are the drawbacks in having a discrepancy between state and federal penal law on this subject? This is a fundamental question that you should reconsider after you have reviewed all of the material in this chapter.

2. **A signal that *Durland* might be reconsidered?** In *Neder v. United States*, 527 U.S. 1 (1999), the defendant was charged with filing false income tax returns and with mail, wire, and bank fraud. Although materiality is undeniably an element of the tax offense and most courts had also held it to be an element of the fraud offenses, the trial court failed to submit the issue to the jury. The Supreme Court focused principally on the question whether the failure to submit the element of materiality to the jury could be harmless in light of the Sixth Amendment. However, in the closing portion of its opinion the majority discussed the question whether materiality is an element of mail, wire, and bank fraud. The Court relied on the "the rule that Congress intends to incorporate the well-settled meaning of the common-law terms it uses." 527 U.S. at 21. Concluding that the well-settled common law meaning of fraud required materiality, the Court found no evidence to rebut

the presumption that Congress meant to incorporate this element into the fraud statutes in question.

In response to the argument that *Durland* "unmoor[ed] the mail fraud statute from its common-law analogs," the Court commented that *Durland* "held that the mail fraud statute reaches conduct that would not have constituted 'false pretenses' at common law, [but] it did not hold, as the Government argues, that the statute encompasses more than common-law fraud." 527 U.S. at 24. The Court recognized that to some degree the language and structure of the fraud statutes is incompatible with the common law definition of fraud (focusing, for example, on the use of the mails to effectuate a fraudulent scheme, rather than on the completion of the fraudulent scheme), but it suggested that otherwise the courts should look to the common law definition of fraud. Since *Neder* was decided in the end-of-term rush and the Court's attention was principally directed to other issues within the case, it is hard to say whether it really portends a major change. If the lower courts take this opinion at face value, they may begin to read the mail and wire fraud statutes more conservatively. In reading the materials that follow, consider the question whether the courts' approaches are consistent with *Durland* or with *Neder*.

3. **Garden variety mail and wire fraud cases**. In the wake of *Durland* and *Neder*, the mail and wire fraud statutes can and are used to prosecute a wide variety of conduct involving a material falsehood or misrepresentation. Most of the cases in sections B and C involve conduct at the farthest reach of these statutes, but there are also plenty of cases closer to the center. For example, in *United States v. Daniel*, 329 F.3d 480 (6th Cir.2003), a wire fraud charge grew out of a senior employee's unauthorized receipt of company money to cover margin calls from his personal stock broker. Daniel claimed that he intended to pay the money back when—as he hoped—the price of his stock bounced back up, but the stock never bounced back. Although Daniel was able to get access to the initial funds without making any misstatements, as the market price dropped further and further, he sought funds that eventually totaled more than $3 million on nine additional occasions. To get the funds, Daniel was forced to provide explanations that became increasingly detailed and further from the truth. The appellate court had no trouble affirming the jury's finding that Daniel made a variety of statements that were both false and material, and it also rejected his claim that he lacked intent to defraud because he believed he could ultimately repay the loans. As the court explained:

> [N]either law nor policy supports this approach, which would have the jury look beyond his bad conduct to his overall motives. It is sufficient that the defendant by material misrepresentations intends the victim to accept a substantial risk that otherwise would not have been taken. The government had only to establish that Daniel intended to deprive Century of money in the short-term, and it presented sufficient evidence for the jury so to find.

Daniel is an example of a traditional case where the victim was actually defrauded of money by the defendant. As you read Sections B and C, which explore the application of the fraud statutes in the context of honest services, keep in mind that the majority of fraud cases are still of the more traditional sense.

1. THE EVOLVING CONCEPT OF SCHEME TO DEFRAUD— THE BIRTH, DEATH, AND REBIRTH OF THE INTANGIBLE RIGHTS THEORY

By cutting the concept "scheme to defraud" free of its common law antecedents, *Durland* set the stage for a series of developments that profoundly altered the scope of the Mail Fraud Act, extending it to reach cases of public corruption, election fraud, and private breaches of fiduciary duty. What has come to be called the "intangible rights doctrine" developed in a series of cases in lower federal courts. Before considering the current cases we will review briefly the development of the intangible rights theory, its renunciation by the Supreme Court, and its reaffirmation by Congress.

a. The Development of the Intangible Rights Theory in the Lower Courts

The intangible rights doctrine originated in the 1940s and developed in the next few decades in the lower courts. Intangible rights prosecutions from every circuit extended the mail fraud statute to cases in which the victims were deprived of some intangible right or interest, rather than of money or property. In *McNally* (discussed below) Justice Stevens described these cases as follows:

> In the public sector, judges, State Governors, chairmen of state political parties, state cabinet officers, city aldermen, Congressmen and many other state and federal officials have been convicted of defrauding citizens of their right to the honest services of their governmental officials. In most of these cases, the officials have secretly made governmental decisions with the objective of benefitting themselves or promoting their own interests, instead of fulfilling their legal commitment to provide the citizens of the State or local government with their loyal service and honest government. Similarly, many elected officials and their campaign workers have been convicted of mail fraud when they have used the mails to falsify votes, thus defrauding the citizenry of its right to an honest election. In the private sector, purchasing agents, brokers, union leaders, and others with clear fiduciary duties to their employers or unions have been found guilty of defrauding their employers or unions by accepting kickbacks or selling confidential information. In other cases, defendants have been found guilty of using the mails to defraud individuals of their rights to privacy and other nonmonetary rights.

The intangible rights cases substantially extended the concept of fraud. The cases typically involved neither an express misrepresentation, nor the loss of any money or tangible property by the victim of the scheme. The element of deceit or misrepresentation was generally satisfied by nondisclosure of dishonest or corrupt actions, and the loss of an intangible right obviated the necessity to determine whether the scheme caused any economic loss. For example, former governor Otto Kerner of Illinois was convicted of mail fraud on the theory that his failure to disclose a sweetheart deal with the racing industry deprived the public of his faithful services as an elected official. The governor had reaped a large profit after being permitted to buy stock in certain racing operations below the market price. In return, he supported a statutory increase in the number of days horse racing was permitted in the state. The prosecution did not allege that the state (or any group of citizens within the state) had suffered any financial loss. To the contrary, the increased racing days produced additional racing revenues and thus additional taxes. Moreover, no competitors were injured, since the racing days were available throughout the state.

During this period courts also sustained intangible rights convictions in the private sector. One of the classic examples in this genre is *United States v. George*, 477 F.2d 508 (7th Cir.1973). In that case, Yonan, an employee of Zenith Radio Corporation who was in charge of buying cabinets for the company's new "Circle of Sound" product, had negotiated a contract with the Accurate Box Corporation in which he received a $1 kickback from Accurate for every cabinet that Zenith purchased. The court noted that Zenith had paid a fair price for the cabinets and that the profit Accurate made was within the 10% allowed by Zenith. Furthermore, the record indicated that Yonan had always insisted on quality and efficiency and had never requested any preferential treatment for Accurate. However, Yonan had twice signed documents that embodied Zenith's policy against accepting gratuities from suppliers. In upholding the conviction, the court stated:

> We need not accept the Government's far ranging argument that anytime an agent secretly profits from his agency he has committed criminal fraud. Not every breach of every fiduciary duty works a criminal fraud. But here Yonan's duty was to negotiate the best price possible for Zenith or at least to apprise Zenith that [Accurate] was willing to sell his cabinets for substantially less money. Not only did Yonan secretly earn a profit from his agency, but also he deprived Zenith of material knowledge that [Accurate] would accept less profit. There was a very real and tangible harm to Zenith in losing the discount or losing the opportunity to bargain with a most relevant fact before it.

Id. at 512–13.

Although the intangible rights theory originated in mail fraud cases, it soon became equally well established in wire fraud cases.

b. The Supreme Court's Renunciation of the Intangible Rights Doctrine in McNally

In *McNally v. United States*, 483 U.S. 350 (1987), the Supreme Court rejected the intangible rights interpretation of the mail fraud statute, bringing what turned out to be only a temporary halt in the application of the mail and wire fraud statutes to intangible rights cases. *McNally* involved Kentucky state officials who were receiving commissions from insurance agencies in return for insurance contracts with the state. Subsequently, these officials were charged and convicted for "violating § 1341 by devising a scheme to defraud the Commonwealth's citizens and government of their 'intangible right' to have the Commonwealth's affairs conducted honestly, and to obtain money by means of false pretenses and the concealment of material facts." *Id.* at 350. Over the dissent of Justices Stevens and O'Connor, the Court held that the mail fraud statute reaches only the deprivation of "property" rights. The Court interpreted the legislative history as indicating that "the original impetus behind the mail fraud statute was to protect the people from schemes to deprive them of their money or property." *Id.* at 356. *Durland*, the Court said, held that the phrase scheme or artifice to defraud "is to be interpreted broadly insofar as property rights are concerned, but it did not indicate that the statute had a more extensive reach." *Id.* The Court also rejected the structural argument relied upon by lower courts, which had held that the two clauses of the act could be read in the disjunctive, distinguishing a "scheme or artifice to defraud" from a scheme for "obtaining money or property by false or fraudulent pretenses." *Id.* at 357. The Court held that this language was not intended to depart from the general understanding of the term defraud, which it said refers to " 'wronging one in his property rights by dishonest methods or schemes,' and 'usually signif[ies] the deprivation of something of value by trick, deceit, chicane, or overreaching.' " *Id.* at 358.

Finally, the Court cited two other general considerations that buttressed its conclusion, the rule of lenity and considerations of federalism. It concluded:

> Rather than construe the statute in a manner that leaves its outer boundaries ambiguous and involves the Federal Government in setting standards of disclosure and good government for local and state officials, we read § 1341 as limited in scope to the protection of property rights. If Congress desires to go further, it must speak more clearly than it has.

Id. at at 360.

In dissent Justice Stevens argued that the intangible rights doctrine accorded with the intent of Congress and was firmly grounded in the disjunctive structure and language of the act. He rejected the view that the enacting Congress had intended the statute to have a narrow reach:

> Statutes like the Sherman Act, the civil rights legislation, and the mail fraud statute were written in broad general language on the understanding that the courts would have wide latitude in construing them to achieve the remedial purposes that Congress had identified. The wide open spaces in statutes such as these are most appropriately interpreted as implicit delegations of authority to the courts to fill in the gaps in the common-law tradition of case-by-case

adjudication. The notion that the meaning of the words "any scheme or artifice to defraud" was frozen by a special conception of the term recognized by Congress in 1872 is manifestly untenable.

Id. at 372. Justice Stevens found no basis for the application of the rule of lenity, since any ambiguity in the language of the statute had long since been removed by the many lower court decisions adopting the intangible rights theory. He ended his opinion provocatively, asking "why a Court that has not been particularly receptive to the rights of criminal defendants in recent years has acted so dramatically to protect the elite class of powerful individuals who will benefit from this decision." *Id.* at 376.

c. The Enactment of § 1346 and the Rebirth of Intangible Rights

The *McNally* decision provoked a swift legislative response. One year later Congress accepted the Court's invitation to "speak more clearly" by enacting 18 U.S.C. § 1346, which provides:

> For the purposes of this chapter, the term "scheme or artifice to defraud" includes a scheme or artifice to deprive another of the intangible right of honest services.

Section 1346 (which applies to the mail, wire, and bank fraud statutes) was adopted as part of the Anti–Drug Abuse Act of 1988. Because of its inclusion in this much larger piece of legislation, it did not generate floor debate. Senator Biden, the chair of the Judiciary Committee, did provide a section-by-section analysis, which states:

> This section overturns the decision in *McNally v. United States* in which the Supreme Court held that the mail and wire fraud statutes protect property but not intangible rights. Under the amendment, those statutes will protect any person's intangible right to the honest services of another, including the right of the public to the honest services of public officials. The intent is to reinstate all of the pre-*McNally* caselaw pertaining to the mail and wire fraud statutes without change.

134 Cong.Rec. S17360–02 (daily ed., Nov. 10, 1988).

Other proposals were introduced into Congress in response to *McNally*, including a proposal by Representative Conyers to define the word "fraud" throughout the United States code to include the deprivation of "intangible rights of any kind whatsoever in any manner or for any purpose whatsoever,"[c] and a Justice Department proposal for a new statute prohibiting public corruption.[d] For a discussion of these proposals, see Craig M. Bradley, *Foreword: Mail Fraud After McNally and Carpenter: The Essence of Fraud*, 79 J. CRIM. L. & CRIMINOLOGY 573, 618–

---

c. H.R. 3089, 100th Cong., 1st Sess., 133 Cong. Rec. E3240–02 (Aug. 4, 1987).

d. The Anti–Corruption Act of 1988, S. 2793, 100th Cong., 2d Sess., 134 Cong. Rec. S12581–04 (Sept. 15, 1988).

621 (1988). The question of legislative alternatives to the expansion of the mail fraud statute is considered further in Chapter 8.

2. QUESTIONS CONCERNING THE CONTEMPORARY SCOPE OF THE MAIL AND WIRE FRAUD STATUTES

With these developments in mind, we turn to the contemporary cases applying the mail and wire fraud statutes, as amended by § 1346. The cases in the sections that follow probe the meaning of two statutory terms. First, what does the term "honest services" mean in the context of mail and wire fraud? Do honest services prosecutions raise any special problems? Should this term mean something different when the defendant was a public employee or public official, rather than a private person? Second, what is "property" for purposes of the mail and wire fraud statutes? In interpreting these statutes, does it make a difference if the conduct in question arguably falls within the ambit of some other federal regulatory scheme? What if it is legal under state law?

B. PROSECUTING PUBLIC FIDUCIARIES: USING THE MAIL AND WIRE FRAUD STATUTES TO POLICE POLITICAL CORRUPTION UNDER § 1346

In the decade since the adoption of § 1346 the lower courts have taken up the task of defining the meaning of the term "honest services."

UNITED STATES v. LOPEZ–LUKIS
102 F.3d 1164 (11th Cir.1997).

Before TJOFLAT, CIRCUIT JUDGE, and RONEY and CAMPBELL, SENIOR CIRCUIT JUDGES.

TJOFLAT, CIRCUIT JUDGE:

Sections 1341 and 1346 of Title 18 of the United States Code, the federal mail fraud statutes, make it unlawful to deprive the electorate of a governmental office holder's "honest services." This interlocutory appeal presents the question of whether these statutes make criminal a scheme in which a county commissioner, in addition to selling her own votes to a lobbyist, takes steps to ensure that a majority of commissioners vote for projects favored by the lobbyist. In this mail fraud prosecution, the district court, ruling on a defense motion in limine, answered this question in the negative and struck the portion of the indictment alleging that the defendants' scheme to defraud included an attempt to control the composition of the commission. The court's order also precluded the Government from introducing evidence that would establish this objective. The Government appealed; we now reverse.

I.

Defendant Vicki Lopez–Lukis is a former member of the five-person Board of County Commissioners for Lee County, Florida ("the Board").

She served on the Board from her election to office in November 1990 until her resignation in January 1993. Defendant Sylvester Lukis is a lobbyist who represents clients before the Board. The defendants engaged in a romantic relationship during Lopez–Lukis' term in office and were married subsequent to the events giving rise to this case.

A.

Lopez–Lukis and Lukis were indicted by a federal grand jury on March 10, 1995. Count one of the indictment, which is supplemented by a bill of particulars, charges both defendants with violating the federal mail fraud statutes, 18 U.S.C. §§ 1341, 1346. The indictment alleges that during Lopez–Lukis' term on the Board, the defendants devised a scheme "to deprive the citizens of Lee County and the State of Florida of their intangible right to [Lopez–Lukis'] honest services . . . in her official capacity as Lee County Commissioner." Specifically, the defendants are charged with using Lopez–Lukis' position for the benefit of Lukis' clients, two of whom—Ogden Projects, Inc., and Goldman–Sachs and Company—are identified by name in the indictment.[4]

The indictment alleges that Lukis paid Lopez–Lukis in order to influence her actions as a county commissioner and that, to facilitate their scheme, the defendants concealed their "monetary and intimate relationship" from the public. More important for this appeal, however, paragraph fourteen of the mail fraud count alleges that the defendants tried to prevent Susan Anthony, a candidate for the Board who opposed the interests of Lukis' clients, from unseating Lopez–Lukis' fellow Board member John Manning in the 1992 primary election.[5] The alleged purpose of this endeavor was to control the composition of the Board to ensure that it would continue to vote in favor of the interests of Lukis' clients.

To secure Manning's victory, the defendants allegedly threatened that, unless she withdrew from the race, they would disseminate to several media organizations a videotape that depicted Anthony, who was campaigning as a family-values candidate, engaging in an extramarital affair. The Government's proffer to the district court alleges that both defendants told Manning that they were preparing videotapes that would "derail" Anthony's campaign. When Anthony did not withdraw from the

---

4. In its bill of particulars ordered by the district court, the Government contends that the defendants helped Ogden Projects, a contractor, retain its contract to construct a multimillion-dollar waste-to-energy incinerator in Lee County and ensure that the Board would allow the project to move forward. Lukis and Lopez–Lukis were apparently successful in their efforts on behalf of Ogden Projects: a final notice to proceed with construction of the project was issued by the Board on October 21, 1992. The defendants also enjoyed apparent success in promoting the interests of Goldman–Sachs,

a brokerage house. The Board voted to select Goldman–Sachs to perform underwriting work for public projects in Lee County, including an airport.

5. The indictment alleges that Anthony ran as "an anti-incinerator candidate"; in other words, she opposed the incinerator project being undertaken by Lukis' client, Ogden Projects. According to the proffer made by the Government at the hearing on the defendants' motion in limine, Lukis and his clients supported Manning in the election.

race, the defendants distributed the videotape to the media. Manning subsequently defeated Anthony in the primary's run-off election. We refer to this series of events collectively as the "videotape incident."

B.

Early in the case, the defendants moved to strike paragraph fourteen from the indictment. As grounds for their motion, the defendants argued that the allegations of paragraph fourteen were irrelevant to the crime charged (i.e., mail fraud under sections 1341 and 1346), that their conduct described in that paragraph was protected by the First Amendment, and that litigation of its allegations would "needlessly complicate and lengthen the process of trying this case." The district court summarily denied their motion on June 20, 1995.

The defendants later moved in limine to exclude "any and all evidence relating to any surveillance videotape of Susan Anthony on the same grounds as they presented in support of their earlier motion to strike. The district court heard this motion on September 1, 1995. Ruling from the bench on September 5, the day before the trial was to commence, the court concluded that because the videotape incident did not involve Lopez–Lukis' official duties as county commissioner, it was not the sort of conduct proscribed by sections 1341 and 1346. In granting the defendants' motion to suppress all evidence related to the videotape incident, the court vacated its earlier order denying the motion to strike and granted that motion as well, striking paragraph fourteen from the indictment. The Government immediately announced that it would appeal the court's ruling; it took this interlocutory appeal the next day, the day the trial was to begin. The district court stayed further proceedings in the case pending the outcome of this appeal.

We hold that the district court misconstrued section 1346 and improperly narrowed the scope of the scheme alleged by the Government. We therefore reverse its order striking paragraph fourteen from the indictment and excluding all evidence relating to the videotape incident.

II.

The district court apparently based its decision that the videotape incident could not be used to prove mail fraud not on the question of factual relevance, but on the question of whether this conduct "fit" within the parameters of section 1346.[11] We review this question of statutory interpretation de novo.

---

11. The district judge stated:

While [the videotape incident] is, indeed, reprehensible and illegal, it is simply outside the framework of the subject mail fraud charge under Section 1346.

The Court has simply not been able to fit this transaction into the mail fraud scheme which is the subject of Count 1. It

stands out as a peculiarly inappropriate part of this mail fraud count.

The district court also noted that the mailing upon which the mail fraud charge is based was sent almost a year before the videotape incident and shared "no connection" with the videotape incident. The degree to which the district court consid-

A proper understanding of the scheme alleged is essential to the resolution of this appeal. The heart of count one is an allegation of a broad bribery scheme: Lukis paid Lopez–Lukis for political favors. The present controversy centers on exactly what Lukis' money bought. The indictment alleges that Lukis bribed Lopez–Lukis because he thought that she would give him two things: (1) her vote on key matters and (2) control of the Board—that is, her influence to deliver a majority of the Board's votes on those matters. The central question in this appeal is whether sections 1341 and 1346 reach such a bribery scheme.

We believe the answer to this question should be self-evident: if it is illegal for a public official to sell her own vote, it also must be illegal for her to sell her vote and her influence over other's votes as well. After all, because the Board consists of five members and presumably acts by majority vote, it would do Lukis little good if all that his money purchased was Lopez-Lukis' single vote.

In this section, we first explain why a scheme by a legislator to deliver control of a majority of legislative votes for a price constitutes a scheme to defraud, as defined by sections 1341 and 1346. We then address the district court's reasoning and demonstrate why it is erroneous. Finally, we examine the allegations against the defendants and show why they manifest an attempt to deliver control of the Board.

A.

A brief review of the mail fraud statutes and their interpretation by the courts is helpful to understanding why they proscribe a scheme for a legislator to sell control of a legislative body when that scheme includes use of the mails. To establish a violation of sections 1341 and 1346, the Government must prove that the defendants "(1) intentionally participated in a scheme or artifice to defraud and (2) used the United States mails to carry out that scheme or artifice."

At common law, the prohibition of fraud generally was regarded as protecting property rights only. *See McNally v. United States*, 483 U.S. 350, 358 n. 8 (1987). As early as the 1940s, however, federal prosecutors seeking to combat government corruption began using section 1341 to prosecute schemes to defraud the public of the honest and faithful services of government officials. In the 1987 *McNally* case, the Supreme Court rejected this practice by holding that section 1341 was "limited in scope to the protection of property rights" and therefore did not prohibit schemes to defraud the citizens of their intangible right to honest and impartial government.

Section 1346 was enacted in 1988 to revive the "honest-services" theory of mail fraud. We have recognized that Congress passed this

ered this to be determinative is unclear, but to the extent that it relied on this observation as grounds for excluding the evidence, it was in error. There is no requirement that every piece of evidence of the scheme to defraud somehow relate to the mailing. The only requirement is that the mailing be related to some "step in the plot."

provision to overrule *McNally* and reinstate prior law. Consequently, we consider pre-*McNally* cases as persuasive authority in evaluating the scope of honest-services fraud. Both the former Fifth Circuit] before *McNally* and this circuit after *McNally* consistently have held that schemes by government officials to deprive the public of its right to their honest services, when a mailing is involved, constitute mail fraud.

The crux of this theory is that when a political official uses his office for personal gain, he deprives his constituents of their right to have him perform his official duties in their best interest. Elected officials generally owe a fiduciary duty to the electorate. When a government officer decides how to proceed in an official endeavor—as when a legislator decides how to vote on an issue—his constituents have a right to have their best interests form the basis of that decision. If the official instead secretly makes his decision based on his own personal interests—as when an official accepts a bribe or personally benefits from an undisclosed conflict of interest—the official has defrauded the public of his honest services.

The appellees concede that a county commissioner commits honest-services fraud when she sells her vote. It is no less a violation of sections 1341 and 1346, however, for that commissioner, in addition to selling her vote, to take steps to ensure that a majority of commissioners vote with her. In both scenarios, the commissioner deprives her constituents of their right to her honest services by deciding how to vote based on her own interests. The second scenario simply makes this deprivation more concrete. In addition to depriving her constituents of their right to her honest services, she seeks to ensure that the actions the Board takes are in her own best interests instead of the best interests of the public.[13]

One commissioner's vote, without more, does not guarantee that a particular legislative proposal favored by the briber will succeed. Any such measure generally requires a majority vote from the commission. While we do not mean to suggest that the bribery of a single official for a vote cannot sustain a conviction for mail fraud, that an official took steps to ensure that her fraudulent scheme would yield results makes the case against her more compelling. Such actions increase the likelihood that the scheme to defraud the electorate of their right to the commissioner's honest services will bear fruit. Surely section 1346 was intended to prohibit just this sort of conduct, and today we hold that it does.

B.

The district court construed section 1346 to proscribe conduct aimed at obtaining an individual legislator's vote, but no more. By excluding

13. This analysis does not suggest that, under such a scenario, the other commissioners are necessarily depriving their constituents of the right to honest services. It is entirely possible that they will decide that proposals that she supports are in fact in the best interest of the electorate and vote accordingly. In this case, only the bribed commissioner would be depriving her constituents of their right to honest services.

That the result of the bribed commissioner's vote actually benefits the electorate would not change the fraudulent nature of her conduct. Sections 1341 and 1346 do not address the wisdom or results of a legislative decision; rather, they concern the manner in which officials make their decisions.

evidence necessary to prove the existence of a larger scheme, it narrowed the scheme's scope from an attempt to obtain control of the Board to an attempt to procure a single vote. This narrow interpretation of the mail fraud statutes was erroneous.

The court ruled that the videotape incident was outside the scope of section 1346 because it did not involve Lopez–Lukis' official duties. As the court noted, "[Lopez–Lukis'] duties and responsibilities as a County Commissioner simply [did] not include the determination as to who is elected to serve on the County Commission." Even if we assume that honest-services fraud involving a public official can be predicated only on the performance of services in an official capacity, the court's ruling misconceives the nature of the scheme alleged in the indictment.

The object of the alleged scheme was not to keep Anthony off the Board or otherwise determine who would serve on the Board. Rather, the goal was for Lopez–Lukis to receive personal benefits in exchange for her efforts to secure Board action that favored the interests of Lukis' clients. The videotape incident is relevant for at least two reasons. First, because the incident was allegedly designed to keep Manning, who would likely vote for projects favored by Lukis' clients, on the Board, it tends to show that Lopez–Lukis had an agenda to serve the interests of Lukis' clients instead of the interests of her constituents.

Second, the videotape incident also demonstrates that the scheme embraced more than just the compromising of one vote on the Board. The scheme involved efforts to influence decisions of the entire Board. Lopez–Lukis' single vote, without more, could not carry out the objectives of the defendants' scheme to procure Board action favorable to Lukis' clients. To pass, any measure favorable to Lukis' clients required a majority of the Board's votes—that is, the votes of Lopez–Lukis and at least two others. To the extent she exercised influence over the composition and voting of the Board, Lopez–Lukis made the deprivation of her constituents' right to her honest services more complete and profitable. In this regard, the videotape incident may be viewed merely as a means to an end. Thus, the Government does not seek to predicate mail fraud liability on the videotape incident itself; it is merely attempting to use the incident as circumstantial proof of a broad scheme to defraud.

While we need not and do not decide the issue, it may be true that the videotape incident, standing alone, could not support criminal liability under section 1346 because it did not directly involve conduct in Lopez–Lukis' official capacity. If true, this proposition would not mean, however, that the Government cannot introduce such evidence to demonstrate a broad scheme to control and obtain favorable votes from the Board. Because the videotape incident tends to show both that Lopez–Lukis intended to benefit Lukis' clients instead of the public and that the scheme was more likely to succeed, it is clearly relevant to the charge of honest-services fraud and properly was charged in the indictment as part of her overall scheme.[16]

---

16. For this reason, two other arguments that the appellees stress in their brief are misguided. In addition to agreeing with the district court's official-duty analy-

Any hard and fast rule that the government cannot use a public official's conduct that is not in an official capacity as evidence of a scheme to defraud the public of an official's honest services would impermissibly narrow the scope of section 1346 and "would belie a clear congressional intent to construe the mail fraud statute broadly." Therefore, we decline to read such a rule into the statute.

C.

The appellees argue in their brief that regardless of whether the district court erred in its interpretation of section 1346, we should affirm its ruling because the Government failed to proffer any evidence that keeping Anthony off the Board would further the interests of Lukis' clients. While any implication that the videotape incident was part of a scheme to control the Board might hinge to some degree on such evidence, the appellees' characterization of the Government's evidence is not supported by the record. The Government has offered to prove several facts that could persuade a rational factfinder that Lopez–Lukis could control a majority of Board votes more easily with Manning, instead of Anthony, on the Board.

For example, the Government has proffered that Lopez–Lukis told Manning that she was going to "derail" Anthony's campaign against him. This allegation, if proven, would support an inference that Manning owed a political debt to Lopez-Lukis and likely would vote with her on key issues. Thus, Lopez–Lukis could better obtain votes favorable to Lukis' present or future clients with Manning on the Board.

Moreover, the record is replete with evidence that, without Anthony, the Board would be more likely to vote in favor of the interests of at least two of Lukis' current clients—Ogden Projects and Goldman–Sachs. First, the indictment specifically alleges that Anthony opposed Ogden Projects' incinerator project. Had she been elected, she posed a serious threat to the project. Second, in its proffer the Government offered to prove that Lukis helped raise funds for Manning's campaign and that officials from Goldman–Sachs and Ogden Projects contributed to Man-

---

sis, the appellees offer two other, alternative arguments that would justify affirming its order even though the district court did not address them. They first point to the line of cases beginning with *Fasulo v. United States*, 272 U.S. 620 (1926), which hold[s] that extortion cannot be the basis for a mail fraud conviction. The appellees argue that the videotape incident, as alleged, constitutes extortion and thus is not covered by § 1346. Second, they argue that their actions constitute political speech and thus deserve protection under the First Amendment.

Again, we need not decide whether the videotape incident alone can support a mail fraud conviction. The Government is seek-ing to punish the defendants not because they tried to keep a candidate from being elected to the Board, but because they used Lopez–Lukis' office for personal benefit. Evidence of the videotape incident tends to show both that Lopez–Lukis intended to ensure that the Board would vote for the interests of Lukis' clients and that their scheme was likely to succeed.

Even if the videotape incident could not serve as a proper independent basis for imposing criminal liability—either because of the rule set down in Fasulo or because of First Amendment concerns—the Government may use it as evidence that the defendants engaged in a broad scheme to defraud the public.

ning's campaign fund. This evidence suggests that Manning would further the interests of Lukis' clients if re-elected, or at least that Lukis' clients assumed he would. In short, keeping Anthony off the Board formed an important step in effectuating the defendants' alleged scheme to sell control of the Board.

UNITED STATES v. MARGIOTTA

688 F.2d 108 (2d Cir.1982).

[*Margiotta* is a pre-*McNally* case revived by the enactment of § 1346. A divided court upheld the mail fraud conviction of the Republican Committee Chairman of Nassau County for a breach of honest services arising out of the distribution of commissions from insurance purchased by the government. The evidence established that numerous brokers, lawyers, and friends of Margiotta who did no legitimate work received thousands of dollars in commissions, and that Margiotta controlled this patronage. The majority held that Margiotta owed the public a fiduciary duty, and that his failure to disclose material information about the commissions breached this duty and constituted a violation of the mail fraud statute. The dissenting opinion, excerpted below, is a classic critique of the honest services theory of mail fraud.]

RALPH K. WINTER, CIRCUIT JUDGE (concurring in part and dissenting in part):

* * *

I

It should be emphasized at the outset that, while a kickback scheme is relevant to Margiotta's conviction for mail fraud, it is not essential. Nor is the government required to prove any loss whatsoever to taxpayers or a violation of New York law. Reduced to essentials, the majority holds that a mail fraud conviction will be upheld when a politically active person is found by a jury to have assumed a duty to disclose material facts to the general citizenry and deliberately failed to do so. Margiotta's conviction is based upon his failure as a partisan political leader with great influence to disclose to the citizens of the Town of Hempstead and Nassau County his knowledge that the Williams Agency would have been willing to act as Broker of Record for considerably smaller commissions than were actually paid. Because those citizens might have compelled the municipalities to reduce these costs had they been given this information, it is a material fact.

* * *

The indictment itself demonstrates the scope of the theory underlying Margiotta's conviction. It charged him with defrauding the State, the Town of Hempstead and Nassau County and their citizens (i) "of the right to have (their) affairs ... conducted honestly, impartially, free from bribery, corruption, fraud, dishonesty, bias, and deceit" and (ii) "of the honest and faithful participation of (Margiotta) in (their) affairs.'' Given this sweeping charge and the majority opinion, no amount of rhetoric seeking to limit the holding to the facts of this case can conceal that there is no end to the common political practices which may now be swept within the ambit of mail fraud. Since the doctrine adopted by the majority applies to candidates as well as those holding office, a candidate who mails a brochure containing a promise which the candidate knows cannot be carried out is surely committing an even more direct mail fraud than what Margiotta did here. An elected official who for political purposes performs an act imposing unnecessary costs on taxpayers is guilty of mail fraud if disclosure is not made to the public. A partisan political leader who throws decisive support behind a candidate known to the leader to be less qualified than his or her opponent because that candidate is more cooperative with the party organization, is guilty of mail fraud unless that motive is disclosed to the public. A partisan political leader who causes elected officials to fail to modernize government to retain jobs for the party faithful is guilty of mail fraud unless that fact is disclosed. In each of these cases the undisclosed fact is as ''material'' as the facts which Margiotta failed to disclose, the harm to the public is at least as substantial as the harm resulting from Margiotta's scheme, and the dishonesty, partiality, bias and deceit in failing to disclose those facts is equally present. This is not to say that Margiotta's conduct as a whole is not more odious than the conduct described in these hypotheticals. That is not the issue. The point is that the actions taken by Margiotta deemed relevant to mail fraud by the majority are present in each case: a relationship calling for disclosure, a material fact known to the candidate, official or party leader, and a failure to disclose it.

The majority is quite simply wrong in brushing aside the First Amendment issues. The theory they adopt subjects politically active persons to criminal sanctions based solely upon what they say or do not say in their discussions of public affairs. The majority explicitly bottoms Margiotta's mail fraud conviction on his failure to say something. Its logic would easily extend to the content of campaign literature. Indeed, it takes no great foresight to envision an indictment framed on the theory adopted by the majority and alleging mail fraud based on public speeches.

II

* * * The proposition that any person active in political affairs who fails to disclose a fact material to that participation to the public is guilty of mail fraud finds not the slightest basis in Congressional intent, statutory language or common canons of statutory interpretation. This wholly impermissible result is brought about, I believe, by drawing an erroneous analogy between fiduciary relationships involving private parties based on express or implied contract and relationships between politically active persons and the general citizenry in a pluralistic, partisan, political system.

Mr. Justice Frankfurter quite appropriately underlined the fact that to say that a man is a fiduciary only begins an analysis; it gives direction to further inquiry. To whom is he a fiduciary? What obligations does he owe as a fiduciary? In what respect has he failed to discharge these obligations? And what are the consequences of his deviation from duty?

The words fiduciary duty are no more than a legal conclusion and the legal obligations actually imposed under that label vary greatly from relationship to relationship. Nevertheless, because fiduciary relationships in the private sector have been the subject of centuries of common law development, there is a considerable body of law based on implied or express contract governing whether particular behavior is legal. Its most notable feature, however, is the degree to which fiduciary obligations vary from relationship to relationship. Partners, employees, trustees and corporate directors are all fiduciaries, yet their legal obligations may be wholly dissimilar. While an hourly employee usually may quit a job without fearing legal action even though he leaves at a time which makes it difficult for the employer to continue business, a trustee may not so easily abandon his beneficiaries. While a trustee's actions are void or voidable if tainted by a conflict of interest, the corporate officer generally can act even if he is personally interested so long as the action is fair to the corporation.

To transfer this complex, variable body of law to the political context, simply by mouthing the word fiduciary, makes the very mistake underlined by Mr. Justice Frankfurter * * *. Although the courts have, with precious little analysis, brought virtually all participants in government and politics under the rubric fiduciary, the obligations imposed are wholly the creation of recent interpretations of the mail fraud statute itself. A reading of the cases in this area, however, shows how little definition there is to these newly created obligations which carry criminal sanctions. For all one can find in the case law, no distinction is made between the fiduciary obligations of a civil servant, political appointee, elected official, candidate or partisan political leader. Juries are simply left free to apply a legal standard which amounts to little more than the rhetoric of sixth grade civics classes. One searches in vain for even the vaguest contours of the legal obligations created beyond the obligation to conduct governmental affairs "honestly" or "impartially," to ensure one's "honest and faithful participation" in government and to obey "accepted standards of moral uprightness, fundamental honesty, fair play and right dealing." The present case is no exception. While there is talk of a line between legitimate patronage and mail fraud, there is no description of its location. With all due respect to the majority, the quest for legal standards is not furthered by reference to "the right to good government" and the duty "to act in a disinterested manner."

Of course, we should all hope that public affairs are conducted honestly and on behalf of the entire citizenry. Nevertheless, we should recognize that a pluralistic political system assumes politically active persons will pursue power and self-interest. Participation in the political process is not limited to the pure of heart. Quite frankly, I shudder at the prospect of partisan political activists being indicted for failing to act "impartially" in influencing governmental acts.[5] Where a statute, particularly a criminal statute, does not regulate specific behavior, enforcement of inchoate obligations should be by political rather than criminal sanctions. Where Congress has not passed legislation specifying particular acts by the politically active as criminal, our reliance rather should be on public debate, a free press and an alert electorate. In a pluralistic system organized on partisan lines, it is dangerous to require persons exercising political influence to make the kind of disclosure required in public offerings by the securities laws.

III

My concerns in this case thus extend far beyond a disagreement over statutory interpretation. The limitless expansion of the mail fraud statute subjects virtually every active participant in the political process to potential criminal investigation and prosecution. It may be a disagreeable fact but it is nevertheless a fact that political opponents not infrequently exchange charges of "corruption," "bias," "dishonesty," or deviation from "accepted standards of ... fair play and right dealing." Every such accusation is now potentially translatable into a federal indictment. I am not predicting the imminent arrival of the totalitarian night or the wholesale indictment of candidates, public officials and party leaders. To the contrary, what profoundly troubles me is the potential for abuse through selective prosecution and the degree of raw political power the freeswinging club of mail fraud affords federal prosecutors.

* * *

Even as to the partisan distribution of insurance commissions, the government concedes that Margiotta's conduct, so far as relevant to mail fraud, was hardly unique; in fact, it was a statewide practice. For example, Margiotta's Democratic counterpart in Long Island diverted commissions to brokers recommended by him when he was in power. One presumes he made no public announcement that he was doing so even though the practice imposed unnecessary costs on taxpayers. And the government brief states, as to insurance purchased by the State, "New York State employees performed all the work that a broker of record would perform; when policies were awarded, a politically designat-

---

5. Among the truths assumed by the founders was that self-interest would be a major generating force in democratic politics. The concern over "faction" motivated by "passion ... adverse ... to the interests of the community" appears again and again in The Federalist Papers. The founders suffered under no illusion that only "enlightened statesmen" would hold the reins of power. They sought safety in checks and balances and a separation of powers which would prevent the assertion of too much power in a single hand. The majority decision vests federal prosecutors with largely unchecked power to harass political opponents. It may be that we should expect only "enlightened statesmen" to hold such office, but, with Madison, I would prefer not to take such a risk.

ed broker was named the broker for each particular policy and received the commission." While the government seeks to distinguish this scheme by saying there was no sale of office—a point irrelevant to the theory of the mail fraud count—the New York State scheme was, if anything, more harmful so far as the taxpayers were concerned. In Nassau County, the Williams Agency did perform some services in return for the commissions. The state practice was to pay state employees to do the work and distribute the commissions to brokers who did nothing at all. Notwithstanding the statewide existence of what in the majority's view was mail fraud, only Margiotta was indicted.

In arguing this case, the United States Attorney left no doubt that he prosecuted Margiotta for political corruption generally. The problem is that in stretching the mail fraud statute to fit this case, we create a crime which applies equally to persons who have not done the evil things Margiotta is said to have done, a catch-all political crime which has no use but misuse. After all, the only need served by resort to mail fraud in these cases is when a particular corruption, such as extortion, cannot be shown or Congress has not specifically regulated certain conduct. But that use creates a danger of corruption to the democratic system greater than anything Margiotta is alleged to have done. It not only creates a political crime where Congress has not acted but also lodges unbridled power in federal prosecutors to prosecute political activists. When the first corrupt prosecutor prosecutes a political enemy for mail fraud, the rhetoric of the majority about good government will ring hollow indeed.

Notes

Lopez–Lukis involved the prosecution of a county commissioner based upon charges that she failed to disclose her receipt of payments from a lobbyist—whom she later married—in return for her promotion of certain projects, her agreement to oppose another candidate for the commission, and her release—during an electoral campaign—of a videotape showing that candidate in a compromising situation. Although the video tape is a unique element, many other prosecutions for mail and wire fraud statutes are based upon similar allegations. In 2005, for example, mail and wire fraud charges were brought against a variety of past and present officials of local government, including the mayors of Norristown, Pennsylvania and Lynwood, California, the treasurer of Philadelphia, and a member of the Santa Ana city council. What are the dangers involved in using the mail fraud act to police the ethics of local politicians?

Judge Winters and other critics of the use of mail fraud to prosecute political corruption have identified a number of concerns, which are closely interrelated. In considering the issues discussed below, keep in mind the hypotheticals posed by Judge Winter, *supra* at 179:

> a. A candidate mails a political brochure containing a promise that the candidate knows he cannot carry out. (For example, the statement "Read my lips: no new taxes."[e])

---

e. The "Read my lips" hypothetical was suggested in Ellen S. Podgor, *Mail Fraud:* *Opening Letters*, 43 S.C. L. Rev. 223, 238–39 (1992).

b. A partisan political leader throws her support behind a candidate the leader knows to be less qualified than his opponent because the leader knows this candidate will cooperate with the party.

1. **Prosecutorial Discretion**: Does the current breadth of the mail fraud statute give federal prosecutors undesirable leeway? Critics have expressed concern that ambitious federal prosecutors may succumb to the desire to chalk up a "big kill"—the conviction of a prominent political figure—even when the evidence shows relatively inconsequential misconduct.[f] There is also a potential for politically motivated prosecutions. The prosecution of former governor Otto Kerner is described above as an example of the intangible rights theory. Professor Gregory Williams notes that Kerner was prosecuted during the Nixon Administration, which brought no charges against 13 key legislators who were also known to have been involved in the conduct that gave rise to Kerner's prosecution. Gregory H. Williams, *Good Government by Prosecutorial Decree: The Use and Abuse of Mail Fraud*, 32 Ariz. L. Rev. 137, 148 (1990) (hereinafter *Government by Prosecutorial Decree*).[g] Why was Kerner alone prosecuted? In 1960 Kerner's statehouse victory had helped elect John Kennedy and defeat Nixon. The Kerner prosecution also suggests how a high profile political corruption case can serve as a stepping stone to a political career for the prosecutor. James Thompson, the United States Attorney who prosecuted Kerner, was himself subsequently elected governor. One commentator suggested that "Kerner was but the innocent victim of a vindictive president."[h]

Federal prosecutors can select a small number of persons for prosecution from a very large pool of potential offenders. In the early 1980's, for example, Professor Williams calculated that only 1.3% of the complaints about postal fraud resulted in investigations, though 46% of those investigations resulted in an arrest. *Good Government by Prosecutorial Decree* at 144. This figure varies widely from the norm of prosecuting 40–60% of the potential offenders that was suggested by one of the leading scholars of discretion.[i]

There are no specialized administrative checks in place to prevent ambitious or politically motivated prosecutors from abusing the mail fraud act. In contrast to its treatment of RICO, see *infra* at 577, the United States Attorney's Manual provides little direction regarding prosecutions for mail and wire fraud. The only guidance regarding the exercise of prosecutorial discretion is provided by the following passage:

---

f. John C. Coffee, Jr., *The Metastasis of Mail Fraud: The Continuing Story of White Collar Crime*, 21 Am. Crim. L. Rev. 1, 21–22 (1983).

g. Professor Williams also suggests that the 1949 prosecution of independent automobile manufacturer Preston Tucker, which helped to crush Tucker's dream of competing with the industry giants, was influenced by associates of Senator Warren Ferguson, who had received substantial campaign support from the big three auto manufacturers. *Good Government by Prosecutorial Decree* at 147. This charge is dramatized in the movie "Tucker: The Man and His Dreams" (1988), starring Jeff Bridges.

h. H. Messick, The Politics of Prosecution: Jim Thompson, Marje Everett, Richard Nixon and the Trial of Otto Kerner 220 (1978).

i. Kenneth C. Davis, Police Discretion 155 (1975).

Prosecutions of fraud ordinarily should not be undertaken if the scheme employed consists of some isolated transactions between individuals, involving minor loss to the victims, in which case the parties should be left to settle their differences by civil or criminal litigation in the state courts. *Serious consideration, however, should be given to the prosecution of any scheme which in its nature is directed to defrauding a class of persons, or the general public, with a substantial pattern of conduct.*

UNITED STATES ATTORNEYS' MANUAL § 9–43.100 (Oct. 1997) (emphasis added). Note that § 9–85.210 of the UNITED STATES ATTORNEYS MANUAL also requires requires prior consultation with the Public Integrity Section in all federal criminal matters that focus on violations of federal *or state* campaign financing laws, federal patronage crimes, and corruption of the electoral process. This provision refers explicitly to prosecutions under the mail fraud and wire fraud statutes, but—rather surprisingly—it does not mention the Hobbs Act. For a discussion of the use of the Hobbs Act to prosecute state and local corruption, see Chapter 6.

A recent economic study provides some support for the argument that federal prosecutors systematically employ their charging discretion in a manner that enhances their own career prospects. *See* Edward L. Glaser, et al., *What Do Prosecutors Maximize? An Analysis of the Federalization of Drug Crimes*, 2 AM. L. & ECON. REV. 259 (2000). Studying federal and state inmates convicted of drug offenses, the authors found that the federal prisoners had higher education and income, were more often white, were more likely to be represented by retained counsel, and were less likely to have prior offenses than their state counterparts. The authors suggest that this pattern may indicate that federal prosecutors choose cases with wealthier more prestigious defendants represented by more prestigious counsel.

A former Assistant U.S. Attorney argues that the ambiguous nature of the honest services doctrine makes the use of mail and wire fraud statutes in public corruption cases particularly vulnerable to political pressures. Thomas M. DiBiagio, *Politics and the Criminal Process: Federal Public Corruption Prosecutions of Popular Public Officials Under the Honest Services Component of the Mail and Wire Fraud Statutes*, 105 DICK. L. REV. 57 (2000). To reduce this uncertainty, DiBiagio advocates tying the honest services doctrine to a specified underling activity such as bribery, conflict of interest, illegal gratuity, and extortion offenses. What do you think of this proposal?

2. **Vagueness**: Does the way the mail fraud statute has been used in the political corruption context raise serious questions under the constitutional void-for-vagueness doctrine? Although the cases permit no litmus test for determining whether a criminal statute is void for vagueness, they generally reflect two principal concerns: whether the statute gives fair warning to those potentially subject to prosecution, and whether it is susceptible to abuse by arbitrary and discriminatory enforcement.[j] Is the concept of the public fiduciary's duty sufficiently well defined to provide adequate notice to potential defendants or to place meaningful limits on the

---

j. For a general introduction to the void-for vagueness doctrine in criminal cases, see 1 WAYNE R. LAFAVE, CRIMINAL LAW § 2.3 (4th ed. 2003), and John Calvin Jeffries, Jr., *Legality, Vagueness, and the Construction of Penal Statutes*, 71 VA. L. REV. 189 (1985).

discretion of federal prosecutors? Professor Williams considers this issue and concludes:

> Politics is infused with personal judgments about public policy matters, and to suggest that "fair notice" concerns can be automatically inferred from a so-called common understanding of the "rightness" of those judgments defies belief. While George Washington Plunkitt's characterization of inappropriate action of politicians as the difference between "honest graft and dishonest graft," may be wide of the mark, there is considerable variation of views on the political acceptability of failing to implement campaign promises or using patronage to develop a cadre of party loyalists. To require state and local politicians to know exactly what political behavior might constitute mail fraud places far too much guesswork in the interpretation of criminal statutes.

Good Government by Prosecutorial Decree at 151–52. Several other commentators have suggested that Section 1346 may be subject to a successful attack on the grounds of vagueness.[k] In contrast, Professor John Coffee has suggested that public officials have little to complain about because "the expectations of public officials are deeply ingrained in our culture, and unfair surprise does not result when the criminal law enforces these expectations." John C. Coffee, Jr., *Modern Mail Fraud: The Restoration of the Public/Private Distinction*, 35 AM. CRIM. L. REV. 427, 463–64 (1998). Are the values that Professor Coffee mentions the ones taught in sixth grade civics classes as feared by Judge Winters dissent in *Margiotta*? Does this give too much discretion to the jury?

One issue that plays a role in applying the void-for-vagueness doctrine is whether the provision in question could be made clearer. It would certainly be possible to draft a provision more closely tailored to political corruption, as demonstrated by the existing federal bribery provisions applicable to federal officials, which are discussed in Chapter 7, and by the Department of Justice's legislative proposal in response to *McNally*. The development of such an alternative federal statute is considered in Chapter 8.

Another aspect that traditionally plays a significant role in the application of the vagueness doctrine is the potential for chilling protected constitutional rights. Judicial scrutiny under the vagueness doctrine is most rigorous when First Amendment rights are implicated. Does the breadth of the mail fraud statute violate the First Amendment, either because it penalizes protected political speech or because it implicates the protected associational rights of political figures? Are you satisfied with the majority's conclusion in *Margiotta* that these arguments are a mere chimera?[l]

The vagueness issue has been discussed at length in two Second Circuit cases involving defendants in the private sector, rather than public employees or elected officials.

In *United States v. Handakas*, 286 F.3d 92 (2d Cir.2002), a divided panel held that the honest services provision of the mail fraud statute was void for

k. Craig M. Bradley, *Foreword: Mail Fraud after* McNally *and* Carpenter: *The Essence of Fraud*, 79 J. CRIM. L. & CRIMINOLOGY 573, 620–21 (1988); Ellen S. Podgor, *supra* n.e, at 269–70.

l. For a discussion of the First Amendment issues, see Coffee, *supra* note f, at 13–17, and *Good Government by Prosecutorial Decree* at 152–53.

vagueness as applied to the defendant in question. The defendant was a contractor whose conviction was based on the claim that he deprived the New York City School Construction Authority (SCA) of his honest services by failing to pay his employees the prevailing wage required by state law. The majority held the honest services provision to be constitutionally inadequate both for its failure to provide a clear indication on its face of what conduct is forbidden, and its failure to provide adequate standards to enforcement authorities, thereby creating the opportunity for the misuse of government power. The majority noted that the government had, in essence, relied on the defendant's breach of his contract as the basis for its claim that he had deprived the SCA of his honest services. The court found this interpretation unprecedented and far too sweeping:

> If the "honest services" clause can be used to punish a failure to honor the SCA's insistence on the payment of prevailing rate of wages, it could make a criminal out of anyone who breaches any contractual representation: that tuna was netted dolphin-free; that stationery is made of recycled paper; that sneakers or T-shirts are not made by child workers; that grapes are picked by union labor—in sum so called consumer protection law and far more.

Even someone familiar with the cases construing the mail fraud statute would, the court concluded, "lack any comprehensible notice that federal law has criminalized breaches of contract." The court declined to define the key terms and coverage of the statute. It also noted that the "absence of discernible standards in the 'honest services' doctrine implicates principles of federalism." In effect, federal authorities had exercised prosecutorial discretion to sharpen the penalty for state laws that these authorities believed had been insufficiently policed or punished by the state.

Handakas was overruled by a divided en banc court in *United States v. Rybicki*, 354 F.3d 124 (2d Cir.2003), *cert. denied*, 125 S.Ct. 32 (2004). The defendants were personal injury lawyers whose agents paid insurance claims adjusters to expedite settlements. There was no evidence that the settlements were inflated above what would have been a reasonable range for the claims, but the insurance companies had written policies prohibiting the acceptance of such payments, which were not disclosed. The defendants were convicted of 22 counts of mail and wire fraud and conspiracy to commit mail fraud by a scheme to defraud the insurance companies of the adjusters' honest services. The en banc court affirmed the conviction by a vote of 7 to 4, rejecting the claim that § 1346 was unconstitutionally vague either on its face or as applied. The majority reasoned that when Congress legislates it is presumed to incorporate the settled meaning of common law terms, and thus the enactment of § 1346 incorporated the pre-*McNally* cases defining the scope of the intangible right to honest services under the mail and wire fraud statutes. After reviewing the private sector honest services cases, the majority found that the case before it fell squarely within these prior precedents, and hence the defendants had adequate warning that their conduct fell within the ambit of the statute. The court's summary of the prior cases from the private sector is reprinted *infra* at 199–200.

The dissenters argued that § 1346 was facially invalid. First, no lay person could know what was proscribed, since he or she would be unable to undertake the extended legal analysis the majority found necessary to determine the scope of the statute from the prior cases. Moreover, a review of the cases revealed that the lower courts remain divided on many key issues, and accordingly the statute as construed provides insufficient notice to potential defendants and guidance to limit prosecutorial discretion. The dissenters identified the following issues as ones upon which the circuits are split, which in the dissenters' view made it clear that the phrase fraudulent deprivation of the right to honest services has no settled meaning:

(1) the requisite mens rea to commit the crime,

(2) whether the defendant must cause actual tangible harm,

(3) the duty that must be breached,

(4) the source of that duty, and

(5) which body of law informs us of the statute's meaning.

For an analysis of the circuits' approaches to the limits on the honest services doctrine, see Carrie A. Tendler, Notes, *An Indictment of Bright Line Tests for Honest Services Mail Fraud,* 72 FORDHAM L. REV. 2729 (2004). Rather than using a bright line test as a limit on the honest services doctrine, Tendler suggests a case-by-case balancing of numerous factors, such as materiality, intended gain to the defendant, and reasonable forseeability of harm. She claims such an approach would provide adequate notice to potential defendants while still following the intent of Congress for a flexible application of the mail fraud statute.

3. **Federalism:** Is federal prosecution of state and local officials consistent with the appropriate division of responsibility between the federal, state, and local governments? Although federal officials have accounted for the largest number of prosecutions of offenses involving abuse of public office since the early 1980's, state and local officials still comprise a substantial portion (approximately 42% of those charged in 2003).[m] For many years mail and wire fraud were the most common charges against state and local officials prosecuted for corruption in the federal courts, and these statutes are still employed to prosecute state and local corruption, though other statutes have risen in favor as well.[n] For an overview of prosecution of state and local corruption, see Chapter 8.

What is the constitutional source of authority for federal prosecutions of political corruption at the state and local level? It has been suggested that the federal government has an obligation under the Republican government clause of the constitution to ensure that states are free of public corruption,[o] and that authority was cited in the Congressional debates that led to the

m. U.S. DEPT. OF JUSTICE, REPORT TO CONGRESS ON THE ACTIVITIES AND OPERATIONS OF THE PUBLIC INTEGRITY SECTION FOR 2003, 51 (2003).

n. For example, in 1981, 34% of state officials and 45% of local officials against whom federal corruption charges were brought were charged with mail or wire fraud. *Good Government by Prosecutorial Decree* at 145. In contrast, the Executive Office of United States Attorneys reports that in fiscal year 1997 only 11% of state

officials and 12% of local officials who were charged with corruption were prosecuted under the mail fraud act.

o. "The United States shall guarantee to every State in this Union a Republican form of government * * *." U.S. Const. Art. IV, Sec. 4, cl. 1. *See generally* Adam H. Kurland, *The Guarantee Clause as a Basis for Federal Prosecutions of State and Local Officials,* 62 S. CAL. L. REV. 369 (1989).

enactment of § 1346.[p] Alternatively, one might plausibly argue that corruption in state and local government has a negative effect on interstate commerce. Whatever the merits of those arguments, it seems clear that the majority in *Margiotta* was correct: even if Congress did not have the power directly to regulate these matters, it has the constitutional authority to do so insofar as the conduct involves a use of the mails.

Thus the question ultimately is one of policy, and several arguments are typically made in favor of federal prosecutions. It has been argued that successful prosecution of government corruption requires investigation and prosecution by an outside agency with capability and objectivity.[q] Since state and local prosecutors are drawn from, work with, and may be responsible to the local political establishment, they may not want to rock the boat by prosecuting their colleagues. Moreover, the resources available to federal prosecutors (including the investigative resources of the F.B.I.) are generally superior to those available to local prosecutors. And, finally, it has been suggested that the importance of prosecuting public corruption is so great that it is desirable to have at least auxiliary federal jurisdiction in cases of extreme corruption or laxity in state or local law enforcement itself.

On the other hand, there are strong arguments against the federal government acting as *parens patriae* to ensure the proper functioning of state and local government. Arguably federal intervention is less effective than local prosecution would be, since it does not necessarily mark any fundamental change in the local system of government. Occasional federal intervention may simply reduce the incentive for state and local governments to clean up their own houses.[r] States also have a significant interest in controlling their own political forums; some states may see benefits in machine politics and political patronage systems of which federal officials may disapprove. State legislation may also seek to draw a clear distinction between legislative compromises and political payoffs, and to define terms like "corruptly."

4. **Defining the scope of public fiduciary duties:** Professor Williams criticizes the use of the mail and wire fraud statutes "to develop an *ad hoc* Federal Code of Political Conduct." *Good Government by Prosecutorial Decree* at 157. Both *McNally* and *Margiotta* involved aspects of a well-entrenched state political patronage system, and the federal prosecutors were not required to show that the conduct in question violated any state criminal statute or indeed any state law. Is the establishment of standards of conduct for state and local officials a matter that should be governed by federal law? And if so, is a series of innovative prosecutions under § 1346 an acceptable way to develop those standards?

Although most circuits continue to adhere to the rule that no violation of state law is required in an honest services prosecution, in *United States v.*

---

p. 134 Cong. Rec. H11251 (daily ed. Oct. 21, 1988) (comments of Rep. Conyers introducing legislation to overrule *McNally*).

q. WHITNEY N. SEYMOUR, UNITED STATES ATTORNEY 174–75 (1975). Mr. Seymour served as United States Attorney for the Southern District of New York.

r. For a sophisticated discussion of the considerations noted above, and an argument that federal prosecutions are seldom justified except at the gubernatorial level, see Charles Ruff, *Federal Prosecution of Local Corruption: A Case Study in the Making of Federal Law Enforcement Policy*, 65 GEO. L. J. 1171 (1977).

Brumley, 116 F.3d 728, 734 (5th Cir.1997), the en banc court disagreed, and grounded its opinion on bedrock principles of federalism:

> Despite its rhetorical ring, the rights of citizens to honest government have no purchase independent of rights and duties locatable in state law. To hold otherwise would offer § 1346 as an enforcer of federal preferences of "good government" with attendant potential for large federal inroads into state matters and genuine difficulties of vagueness. Congress did not use those words, and we will not supply them. * * * The federalism arguments that inform the definition of "honest services" under federal criminal law are powerful, and we acknowledge them in our holdings today.

116 F.3d at 734. *Brumley* left open the question whether a violation of a state *criminal* law was a prerequisite for an honest services prosecution, or whether a violation of some civil standard would be sufficient.

The Fifth Circuit's position obviously gives deference to state autonomy and to the policies implicit in state law, and it also ensures that the defendant has notice of the applicable standards. But reliance on state law also has disadvantages. It means that federal enforcement is less able to serve as a check on corruption at the state level. Some states or localities may have relatively lax standards for state and local officials. Indeed, it could be argued that federal enforcement is needed most where state standards are insufficient, judged by broad national standards. Moreover, reliance on state standards also means that the mail fraud statute means different things in different states. Is this position consistent with *Durland*? Do you really think it a good idea?

In the circuits that do not require a violation of state law, what limits should be imposed to restrain prosecutors and provide fair warning to would-be defendants? In *United States v. Bloom*, 149 F.3d 649 (7th Cir.1998), the court commented:

> No one can be sure how far the intangible rights theory of criminal responsibility really extends, because it is a judicial gloss on § 1341. Congress told the courts in § 1346 to go right on glossing the mail fraud and wire fraud statutes along these lines. Given the tradition (which verges on constitutional status) against common-law federal crimes, and the rule of lenity that requires doubts to be resolved against criminalizing conduct, it is best to limit the intangible rights approach to the scope it held when the Court decided (and Congress undid) *McNally*. *An employee deprives his employer of his honest services only if he misuses his position (or the information he obtained in it) for personal gain.*

149 F.3d at 656 (emphasis added). What do you think of the court's suggestion? Are these limitations sufficient? Too restrictive? If the defendant does not violate § 1346 unless she is seeking personal gain, is there really any difference between an honest services prosecution and one based upon a deprivation money or property?

In *United States v. Murphy*, 323 F.3d 102 (3d Cir.2003), the court explicitly rejected *Margiotta*'s holding that a local party official could be prosecuted under the mail and wire fraud statute for depriving the state and its citizens of his own honest services. The court agreed with many of the concerns Judge Winter expressed in his dissenting opinion in *Margiotta*. Holding that it was improper to allow the jury to conjure a duty of honest services to the public "out of a fog of assumptions," a divided panel of the court of appeals also endorsed the need for a "state law limiting principle for honest services fraud." The court did not reach the question whether a state-law created duty is required to sustain an honest services conviction, because it found no basis in state law for the recognition of a fiduciary relationship of any nature. In so doing, the court recognized that the defendant's conduct may have violated the state bribery law (as the jury had found in reaching its verdict on the Travel Act count), but it concluded that the bribery law did not to create a fiduciary relationship between the county political chair and the public.

C. PROSECUTING PRIVATE FIDUCIARIES: USING THE MAIL AND WIRE FRAUD STATUTES TO POLICE THE PRIVATE SECTOR UNDER § 1346

As noted *supra* at 167–68, prior to *McNally* numerous mail fraud cases were based on the breach of fiduciary duties by corporate officers and employees, union officials, attorneys, and others. By amending the definition of fraud to include deprivations of the right of honest services, section 1346 appears to reinstate the law in these cases as it stood before *McNally*. This section explores the distinctive issues that arise when honest services prosecutions are brought in the private sector.

UNITED STATES v. HAUSMANN

345 F.3d 952 (7th Cir.2003).

Before BAUER, MANION, and WILLIAMS, CIRCUIT JUDGES.

BAUER, CIRCUIT JUDGE.

Charles P. Hausmann pleaded guilty to a charge of conspiracy to commit mail and wire fraud. A jury convicted Scott J. Rise of the same offense. Each defendant appeals from the district court's denial of his pretrial motion for dismissal of the indictment. Rise also challenges the district court's jury instructions and Hausmann appeals from his sentence based on his challenge to the district court's calculation of the loss amount attributable to the fraud. For the reasons set forth herein, we affirm the decisions of the district court and, consequently, Hausmann's sentence and Rise's conviction.

BACKGROUND

Hausmann, a Milwaukee, Wisconsin, personal injury lawyer, referred certain of his clients to Rise, a chiropractor, for chiropractic services paid from insurance settlement proceeds, in return for which Rise made corresponding payments, equal to twenty percent of the fees he collected for those services, to third-party recipients at Hausmann's direction. Recipients included (i) individuals who had provided miscellaneous personal services to Hausmann or his relatives, (ii) a marketing firm providing services at Hausmann's direction, (iii) business entities (or their agents) in which Hausmann held some interest, and (iv) charities that Hausmann supported.[1] Between October 1999 and June 2001, these payments totaled $77,062.87. Hausmann did not disclose this kickback arrangement to his clients, ordinarily victims of automobile accidents. The typical client signed a retainer agreement providing that, in exchange for the services of Hausmann's law firm, Hausmann–McNally, S.C., he or she would pay the firm one third of "whatever total sum is collected." The standard agreement also provided as follows:

> The client further authorizes his attorney to pay medical and other bills incurred as a result of this accident directly to the doctors and hospitals. *It is further understood and agreed that said money to pay these bills shall come from the client's portion of the settlement.*

(Emphasis in original).

In January 2002, Hausmann and Rise were indicted on charges of conspiracy to commit mail and wire fraud, in violation of 18 U.S.C. § 371. Both defendants moved for pretrial dismissal of the indictment, which they argued failed to allege a criminal offense or the essential elements thereof. The motions were heard by a magistrate judge, upon whose recommendation the district court denied them. Hausmann then entered a conditional plea of guilty on the conspiracy charge, preserving his right to appeal the denial of his motion to dismiss.

A jury convicted Rise of the conspiracy charge. At Rise's trial, his former employee testified that Rise used the term "kickback" to describe the payments. Rise filed unavailing motions for a judgment of acquittal and for arrest of judgment. The district court sentenced Hausmann and Rise each to sixty-day terms of imprisonment (stayed pending the disposition of this appeal) and twelve-month terms of supervised release, and ordered them to pay restitution in the joint and several amount of $77,062.87.

This appeal ensued.

Analysis

I. *Sufficiency of the Indictment and Evidence of Rise's Guilt*

Appellants challenge the sufficiency of the indictment, asserting that it fails adequately to allege the elements of the underlying mail and wire

---

1. For example, Rise paid (i) a total of $31,692.00 to a marketing firm with whom Hausmann, but not Rise, contracted to market the services of lawyers and chiropractors as part of a planned "Accident Care Network"; (ii) at least $2000, nominally to a charity, but effectively as consideration for landscaping work performed at Hausmann's residence; (iii) a total of $14,900 to a full-time handyman who provided services at Hausmann's direction to Hausmann's firm, Rise's practice, Hausmann personally, a business jointly owned by Hausmann and his law partner in their individual capacities, and Hausmann's sister; and (iv) $850 to a company that refinished the wood floors of a contract employee involved in Hausmann's marketing project.

fraud offense. Rise further argues that the government failed to prove the aforementioned elements and that, consequently, the district court improperly denied his motion for judgment of acquittal pursuant to Rule 29 of the Federal Rules of Criminal Procedure.

We review de novo both the sufficiency of a criminal indictment and the denial of a motion for judgment of acquittal. A valid indictment must (I) state each element of the alleged offense, (ii) provide the defendant with information adequate for the preparation of his defense, and (iii) provide sufficient basis for a judgment that would bar any subsequent prosecution for the same offense. "The test for validity is not whether the indictment could have been framed in a more satisfactory manner, but whether it conforms to minimal constitutional standards." Denial of a motion for judgment of acquittal is appropriate unless "the evidence is insufficient to sustain a conviction," Fed. R. Crim. P. 29(a). "In considering the sufficiency of the evidence, we review it in the light most favorable to the prosecution, and as long as any rational jury could have returned a guilty verdict, the verdict must stand."

Rise's appeal from the denial of his motion for judgment of acquittal is duplicative of Appellants' challenge to the sufficiency of the indictment. Both theories allege that the government failed to allege or prove, respectively, the following purported elements of the mail and wire fraud offenses underlying the conspiracy charge: (i) actual or foreseeable harm to Hausmann's clients; (ii) Hausmann's fiduciary duty in excess of that memorialized in the retainer agreements; (iii) that Hausmann's conflict of interest adversely affected his clients; (iv) intent to defraud; (v) the materiality of the nondisclosure to clients of the scheme; and (vi) the scheme's interstate jurisdictional nexus.

Where "two or more persons conspire ... to commit any offense" under Title XVIII of the United States Code "one or more of such persons [who commit] any act to effect the object of the conspiracy" may be held criminally liable therefor under 18 U.S.C. § 371. It is a violation of 18 U.S.C. §§ 1341, 1343, and 1346 to use the United States Postal Service, a private interstate courier, or an interstate wire communications service in order to implement a "scheme or artifice to defraud [by depriving] another of the intangible right of honest services." 18 U.S.C. § 1346. Despite our doubts as to the applicability of these "intangible-rights theory" provisions of the mail and wire fraud statutes to cases of breach of fiduciary duty with nothing more, this Court has suggested that liability under this theory may nonetheless result where a defendant misuses his fiduciary relationship (or information acquired therefrom) for personal gain. *See United States v. Bloom*, 149 F.3d 649, 655–56 (7th Cir. 1998). We have held, moreover, that an employee's undisclosed derivation of profits from business he transacted on his employer's behalf amounted to a deprivation of the employer's intangible right to honest services in violation of 18 U.S.C. §§ 1341 and 1346. *United States v. Montani*, 204 F.3d 761, 768–69 (7th Cir. 2000). Accordingly, under the intangible-rights theory of federal mail or wire fraud liability, a valid indictment need only allege, and a finder of fact need only believe, that a defendant used the interstate mails or wire communications system in furtherance of a scheme to misuse his fiduciary relationship for gain at the expense of the party to whom the fiduciary duty was owed.

Here, the indictment clearly and correctly stated the fiduciary relationship between Hausmann and his clients:

> During the time period of the scheme, Hausmann–McNally, S.C., including defendant Hausmann and other agents and employees under his direction, owed a fiduciary duty to the clients of the law firm, . . . [including] the obligation of Haussman–McNally to disclose to the client any financial interest that the law firm may have involving the representation; to advise the client in a conflict-free manner; . . . to negotiate in the best interest of the client [; and] *to provide accurate and complete information to the clients regarding the financial terms of personal injury case settlements, as well as the amount of compensation taken by the lawyers involved in the case.*

(Emphasis added). Furthermore, at Rise's trial, the government presented the testimony of Hausmann's law partner, John McNally, describing the clients' dependence upon legal representation by the firm in order to settle their claims, as well as testimony from several clients describing Hausmann's written representations regarding their settlements and the firm's compensation and the reliance they placed thereupon.

The Wisconsin Supreme Court Rules of Professional Conduct for Attorneys provide that "[a] lawyer may not allow related business interests to affect representation, for example, by referring clients to an enterprise in which the lawyer has an undisclosed interest." Comment to Wis. Sup. Ct. R. 20:1.7(b). Thus, the indictment's statement that "[t]he kickback arrangement was concealed from the clients of Hausmann–McNally in violation of the fiduciary duty described above" clearly alleges Hausmann's misuse of the fiduciary relationship. Testimony of clients that were unaware of the kickback scheme served as evidence at Rise's trial of the misuse of the fiduciary relationship.

The indictment also clearly alleged, and the government demonstrated at Rise's trial, that Hausmann gained over $70,000 in kickback payments made to third parties for his personal benefit or entities in which he had some interest, including, for example, "at least $2000 in landscaping improvements performed at Hausmann's personal residence," and that such concealed payments deprived clients of the intangible right of honest services. At trial, for example, the government produced evidence that Rise signed a check in the amount of $1000 as a direct payment for such landscaping work.

Appellants contend that Rise's third-party payments were not kickbacks, but rather constituted the legitimate spending of income derived from use of fees to which Rise was legally entitled. They maintain that Hausmann's clients had no right to the settlement funds paid to Rise nor, consequently, to the allocation of twenty percent of those funds to expenditures designated by Hausmann. In this sense, reason Appellants, no harm resulted to Hausmann's clients, who were deprived of nothing to which they were entitled. This reasoning ignores the reality that Hausmann deprived his clients of their right to know the truth about his compensation: In addition to one third of any settlement proceeds he negotiated on their behalf, every dollar of Rise's effective twenty percent fee discount went to Hausmann's benefit. Insofar as Hausmann misrepresented this compensation, that discount should have inured to the benefit of his clients. It is of no consequence, despite Appellants' arguments to the contrary, that Rise's fees (absent his discount) were competitive, or that clients received the same net benefit as they would have absent the kickback scheme. The scheme itself converted Hausmann's representations to his clients into misrepresentations, and Hausmann illegally profited at the expense of his clients, who were entitled to his honest services as well as their contractually bargained-for portion of Rise's discount.

Appellants also contend that the indictment did not properly allege their use of the interstate mails or wire communications systems in furtherance of the kickback scheme. However, the indictment plainly states that Appellants,

> and others acting on their behalf, for the purpose of executing and attempting to execute a scheme to defraud: (a) did cause and intend to cause matter to be delivered by the United States Postal Service and commercial interstate carrier according to the directions thereon ... ; and (b) did cause or intend to cause sounds to be transmitted in interstate commerce by means of wire communications....
> The matter included: (a) solicitations and communications from Hausmann–McNally to clients; (b) communications between Hausmann–McNally lawyers and [Rise's clinic] regarding billings; and (c) communications between Hausmann and certain recipients of the kickback checks. The interstate wire communications included telephone calls, facsimiles and emails between Hausmann and certain recipients of the kickback checks; and telephone calls from Hausmann to others regarding the flow of kickback payments.

The indictment thus sufficiently alleges the interstate element of Appellants' conspiracy to commit mail and wire fraud.

Finally, Rise challenges his culpability based on his lack of awareness that Hausmann was defrauding his clients. However, the knowing payer of an illegal kickback is criminally liable for conspiracy to commit mail or wire fraud to the same extent as the recipient of such a payment. Insofar as Rise knowingly signed checks payable to third-party recipients (in order to conceal the scheme) equal in total amount to twenty percent of the fees he collected in connection with referrals from Hausmann, Rise acted in furtherance of the conspiracy to defraud the clients. His guilt as a co-conspirator is clear.

For all of these reasons, the indictment sufficiently alleges the elements of the mail and wire fraud offenses underlying the conspiracy charge against Appellants: that Hausmann used the required interstate means in order to misuse his fiduciary relationship for his gain and at his clients' expense. Furthermore, we find that a rational jury could have found Rise guilty based upon the evidence produced at his trial.

II. Constitutionality of the Application of the Mail and Wire Fraud States to Appellants' Conduct

Appellants further challenge the constitutionality of the application of 18 U.S.C. §§ 1341, 1343, and 1346 as void for vagueness and based on principles of federalism. The constitutionality of a federal statute is an issue of law subject to de novo review.

"Vagueness may invalidate a criminal law for either of two independent reasons. First, it may fail to provide the kind of ordinary notice that will enable ordinary people to understand what conduct it prohibits; second, it may authorize and even encourage arbitrary and discriminatory enforcement." *City of Chicago v. Morales,* 527 U.S. 41, 56 (1999) (citing *Kolender v. Lawson,* 461 U.S. 352, 357 (1983)). Appellants claim both, that the mail and wire fraud statutes did not provide them with adequate notice of the criminality of their kickback scheme, and that application of the mail and wire fraud statutes to the facts of this case invites the government arbitrarily to police the fairness of private business transactions through enforcement of criminal statutes. With respect to the first of these two arguments, this Court's decision in *Bloom,*[3] placed Appellants on notice that criminal liability under the mail and wire fraud statutes—particularly under an intangible-rights theory—attaches to the misuse of one's fiduciary position for personal gain. *See* 149 F.3d at 655–56. With respect to the second, the existence of Hausmann's fiduciary duty owed to his clients distinguishes this case from one where the government arbitrarily and impermissibly relies upon the mail and wire fraud statutes to enforce merely the terms of a private contract. *Cf. United States v. Handakas,* 286 F.3d 92, 107 (2d Cir. 2002) (refusing to expand the application of 18 U.S.C. § 1346 and thereby render "[e]very breach of a contract or state law . . . punishable as a felony in federal court"). We therefore find that the mail and wire fraud statutes, 18 U.S.C. §§ 1341, 1343, and 1346, are not unconstitutionally vague, as applied under the intangible-rights theory to a kickback scheme enabled by the offender's misuse of his fiduciary position gain.

Appellants further contend that the indictment violates principles of federalism because it "overreaches" the scope of the federal criminal law by criminalizing conduct which is regulated by state law. Unlike the cases that Appellants cite for this proposition, such as *Handakas,* 286 F.3d 92 (misrepresentations by defendant contractor violated state wage laws); *Cleveland v. United States,* 531 U.S. 12 (2000) (defendants made false statements in state gaming license applications); and *United States v. Lopez,* 514 U.S. 549 (1995) (invalidating Gun–Free School Zones Act of

---

3. *Bloom* was decided in July 1998, more than one year prior to the alleged   commencement of the kickback scheme.

1990 as insufficiently related to regulation of interstate commerce); in which federalization of state laws or state regulated conduct was held unconstitutional, this case casts no meaningful doubt on Congress's authority to regulate use of the interstate mails and wire communications systems in furtherance of fraudulent conduct.[4] The indictment alleged such use of the interstate mail and wire communications systems, including an allegation that kickback payment checks were mailed out of state. Moreover, as the magistrate judge aptly noted in his recommendation to deny Appellants' motions to dismiss the indictment, "[w]ithout some showing that either the statutes in question or the prosecution of this case contravene some specific rule of constitutional or statutory law, the mere fact that the conduct in question is of a sort traditionally dealt with through state law cannot serve as a basis for dismissing [the] indictment." Appellants have made no such showing, and we are unpersuaded by the argument.

III. Jury Instructions

As an alternative basis for appealing his conviction, Rise claims that the district court failed to instruct the jury that, in order to convict him, it must find that (i) Rise reasonably contemplated harm to Hausmann's clients and (ii) the scheme was intended not only as a gain to Hausmann, but also a loss to his clients. Here, Rise alleges an error of law in the jury instructions, which we review de novo.

The district court instructed the jury, in relevant part, as follows:

To find that there existed a scheme to deprive one or more clients of the Hausmann–McNally law firm of his or her right to the honest services of that firm you must find beyond a reasonable doubt, first, that a fiduciary relationship existed between one or more of the clients of the Hausmann–McNally firm. Second, that Scott Rise and Charles Hausmann knowingly engaged in a scheme to deprive one or more clients of the Hausmann–McNally law firm of the right to honest services of the Hausmann–McNally law firm as charged in Count 1. And, third, that through such scheme, Charles Hausmann misused his fiduciary relationship with one or more clients of the Hausmann–McNally law firm for personal gain.

This instruction adequately and accurately communicates the elements of Rise's offense. There is no requirement under the law as articulated in *Bloom* and reiterated today that a co-conspirator to a wire and mail fraud scheme contemplate actual or foreseeable harm to the victim. Also, though the law does not require the court to instruct a jury that the scheme is intended to cause a loss to the victims *as well as* a gain to the offender, the loss element is implicit in the district court's references both to a deprivation of one or more clients' right to honest services—a type of loss in and of itself—and to Hausmann's gain. As

---

4. This authority is established in the Postal Power of Article I, Section 8, Clause 7 of the Constitution. *See also United States* v. *Elliott,* 89 F.3d 1360, 1363–64 (8th Cir. 1996).

discussed above, once Rise opted to discount his fees for chiropractic services, Hausmann's clients shared Rise's economic loss-a corollary to their entitlement to a portion of Hausmann's gain. Finding no error in the district court's instruction of the jury that convicted him, we reject Rise's jury instruction claim.

AFFIRMED.

Notes

1. Although the First Amendment concerns noted at 178-87 are not applicable in private sector cases, the mail and wire fraud statutes—amplified by § 1346—generate distinctive concerns in private sector cases. In the 1990s many courts were sympathetic to these concerns, reversing several private sector cases on a variety of grounds. In *United States v. Frost*, 125 F.3d 346 (6th Cir.1997), the court explained why the application of the honest services doctrine to the private sector is more "problematic" than its application to public officials, and it gave the mail fraud act a more limited reading in this context than its language would suggest. The court held that in private sector prosecutions a breach of fiduciary duty cannot constitute mail fraud unless it creates at least a risk of economic harm to the party to whom the duty was owed. The court stated:

> The right of the public to the honest services of its officials derives at least in part from the concept that corruption and denigration of the common good violates "the essence of the political contract." Enforcement of an intangible right to honest services in the private sector, however, has a much weaker justification because relationships in the private sector generally rest upon concerns and expectations less ethereal and more economic than the abstract satisfaction of receiving "honest services" for their own sake.

>   * * *

> We recognize that the literal terms of the "intangible right to honest services" doctrine do not indicate that the prosecution must prove that a fiduciary breach has created a risk of economic harm to the employer. Rather, the literal terms suggest that dishonesty by an employee, standing alone, is a crime. Courts, however, have refused to interpret the doctrine so broadly. For example, the Tenth Circuit has commented that, "[a]ssuming without deciding that § 1346 has application where a private actor or quasi-private actor is deprived of honest services in the context of a commercial transaction, it would give us great pause if a right to honest services is violated by every breach of contract or every misstatement made in the course of dealing." *United States v. Cochran*, 109 F.3d 660, 667 (10th Cir.1997); see also *Czubinski*, 106 F.3d at 1077 (when holding that IRS employee who performed unauthorized searches of confidential files did not commit wire fraud, explaining that Congress did not enact § 1346 "to create what amounts to a draconian personnel regulation," and cautioning against interpreting § 1346 so as to "transform[ ] governmental workplace violations into felonies"); *Jain*, 93 F.3d at 442 (stating that "prior intangible rights convictions involving private sector relationships have almost

invariably included proof of actual harm to the victims' tangible interests"). This refusal to carry the intangible rights doctrine to its logical extreme stems from a need to avoid the over-criminalization of private relationships: "[I]f merely depriving the victim of the loyalty and faithful service of his fiduciary constitutes mail fraud, the ends/means distinction is lost. Once the ends/means distinction is abolished and disloyalty alone becomes the crime, little remains before every civil wrong is potentially indictable."

125 F.3d at 365, 368. In light of the language and history of § 1346, is it appropriate for courts to limit its application to cases in which the defendant creates a risk of economic harm? Wasn't the honest services language added to reach cases where there was no scheme to defraud the victims of money or property?

2. Mail fraud prosecutions of private fiduciaries potentially overlap with a number of other legal regimes: including the federal securities laws, state corporate laws, and state laws regulating other fiduciaries, such as attorneys.

a. *Federal securities law.* A number of cases exemplify the potential for both overlap and divergence between the federal securities laws and mail fraud. As noted earlier, many of the defendants in the recent wave of corporate scandals have been charged with both mail fraud and securities or bank fraud. In *Carpenter v. United States*, 484 U.S. 19 (1987) (discussed at 202–06, and 214), the defendants were convicted not only of wire and mail fraud, but also of securities fraud. The Supreme Court had little difficulty with the mail fraud conviction, which it affirmed unanimously, but it split 4–4 on the securities fraud charge and affirmed without opinion.

Is it desirable to have such divergence between the federal securities laws and the federal law developed under the mail fraud statute? Michael Dreeben notes that in formulating the securities laws the SEC and the federal courts seek to strike "a delicate balance between fairness to investors and the practical realities of the market" that may not be considered in a mail fraud prosecution. Michael Dreeben, *Insider Trading and Intangible Rights: The Redefinition of the Mail Fraud Statute*, 26 AM. CRIM. L. REV. 181, 210 (1988). This balance is reflected in various limitations on the insider trading rules, but there are no parallel limitations under the mail fraud statute. *Id.* at 209–214. Thus mail fraud prosecutions can reach conduct that falls outside the carefully crafted limits of the federal securities laws.

b. *State corporate law.* Much of the behavior subject to prosecution as mail and wire fraud is also regulated by state corporate law. Congress has never attempted to regulate intra-corporate affairs, and the Supreme Court has declined to interpret the federal securities laws as creating a general rule of federal fiduciary duties. In *United States v. Siegel,* 717 F.2d 9 (2d Cir.1983), the court upheld the wire fraud convictions of corporate officers who received cash proceeds of corporate sales and used them for non-corporate purposes without recording these transactions in the corporate books. Total corporate sales ranged from $30 million to $100 million per year, and these off-the-books transactions amounted to $100,000 over the course of several years. In dissent, Judge Winter objected to the use of the wire fraud "to create a federal law of fiduciary obligations imposed on corporate directors and officers, thereby setting the stage for the development of an expandable body of criminal law regulating intracorporate affairs." 717 F.2d at 23.

Where a mail fraud prosecution is based upon the theory that a corporate officer or employee breached a fiduciary duty owed to the corporation, does state or federal law define the standard of duty? *See Durland, supra* at 163. One commentator argues that allowing federal law developed in mail fraud prosecutions to define these duties will undermine the efficiency of the state regimes that are currently based upon a sound view of the economic function of the modern corporation, shifting decision making about the best rule of corporate law to individual federal prosecutors and juries, acting after the fact. Peter R. Ezersky, Note, *Intra-Corporate Mail and Wire Fraud: Criminal Liability for Fiduciary Breach*, 94 YALE L.J. 1427, 1442–43 (1985). Thus federal mail fraud prosecutions displace the varied rules that different states developed to attract corporate charters and inhibit desirable experimentation.

3. Professor John Coffee argues that the potential for overbroad and unanticipated applications of § 1346 is even greater in private sector cases than in prosecutions of public officials, and that different standards should apply depending upon the context. Coffee advocates a more restrictive standard for private sector cases under § 1346 than for cases involving public fiduciaries. In his view the shared culture provides public fiduciaries with the necessary knowledge of the standards of conduct, and no independent violation of state or federal law should be required as a prerequisite for a mail or wire fraud conviction of a public fiduciary. Coffee argues that private fiduciaries lack such a shared understanding except as it arises from state and federal law, and accordingly that mail fraud prosecutions in the private sector should be limited to cases in which the prosecution can demonstrate a violation of state law (e.g., state corporate law) or a violation of an independent federal statute (e.g., the securities laws). John C. Coffee, Jr., *Modern Mail Fraud: The Restoration of the Public/Private Distinction*, 35 AM. CRIM. L. REV. 427, 463 (1998). Is this argument persuasive? Note that in the private sector the effect of Coffee's proposal would be to protect individual defendants, and also to prevent independent bodies of state and federal law (securities law, corporate law, etc.) from being effectively overridden by mail and wire fraud. Are these arguments sufficient to warrant more protective treatment than that given to political actors, who may claim the special protections of the First Amendment?

4. In *United States v. Rybicki*, 354 F.3d 124 (2d Cir.2003) (en banc), *cert. denied*, 125 S.Ct. 32 (2004), the defendants were personal injury lawyers whose agents made payments to insurance claims adjusters to expedite settlement of their clients' claims. The defendants were convicted of 22 counts of mail and wire fraud, and conspiracy to commit mail fraud by a scheme to defraud the insurance companies of the adjusters' honest services. In the course of rejecting the claim (discussed *supra* at 186-87) that the statute was unconstitutionally vague, the court reviewed all of the pre-*McNally* honest services cases involving the private sector, summarizing them as follows:

the term "scheme or artifice to deprive another of the intangible right to honest services" in section 1346, when applied to private actors, means a scheme or artifice to use the mails or wires to enable an officer or employee of a private entity purporting to act for and in the interests of his or her employer secretly to act in his or her or the defendant's own interests instead, accompanied by a material misrepresentation made or omission of information disclosed to the employer or other person. [I]n self-dealing cases, unlike bribery or kickback cases, there may also be a requirement of proof that the conflict caused, or at least was capable of causing, some detriment.

The defendants' conduct, the court concluded, fell squarely within the definition of honest services fraud as defined by these prior cases. The court also noted that the same standard applied to persons who are not employees but who have assumed a duty of loyalty comparable to that owed by an officer or employee of a private entity.

5. As noted in the introduction to this chapter, federal prosecutors adapt their use of the mail and wire fraud statutes to reach new kinds of fraud, and *Hausmann* is not an isolated case. Note, however, that federal prosecutors also have other tools for going after health care fraud, including the health care fraud act, 18 U.S.C. § 1347 (discussed in the next note), and the Medicare/Medicaid anti-kickback statute, 42 U.S.C. § 1320a–7b. The latter has proven particularly effective.

One of the FBI's largest Medicare fraud investigations led to a series of highly publicized 1997 raids to obtain documentary evidence from the offices of the nation's largest health care chain, Columbia/HCA Healthcare Corp. After the raids, the corporation's stock price plummeted and it responded by replacing top executives and scaling back its operations substantially. In 1999 two Columbia/HCA executives in Florida were convicted of violating the Medicare/Medicaid anti-kickback statute in a scheme that prosecutors say led to overpayments of more than $3 million. Earlier in 1999 the Olsten Corp. agreed to pay a $61 million fine and a subsidiary plead guilty to undisclosed charges to settle an investigation into its business with Columbia/HCA in connection with home health care. Additional indictments, as well as civil suits under the False Claims Act, were anticipated.

More recently, federal prosecutors have focused on the pharmaceutical hospital supply industries. For example, in 2003 British pharmaceutical maker AstraZeneca plead guilty to medicare fraud charges, agreeing to pay a $64 million criminal fine, a $291 million civil settlement, and $25 million to settle allegations of fraud against Medicare in connection with the prostate cancer drug Zoladex, admitting that it gave doctors free samples of the drug knowing that the government would be billed. A Taxpayers Against Fraud report states that drug companies AstraZeneca, Bayer, Dey, GlaxoSmithKline, Pfizer, and TAP Pharmaceuticals paid $1.6 billion between 2001 and 2003 to settle suits accusing them of marketing fraud and overbilling Medicare and Medicaid. In 2004 the Justice Department opened a criminal investigation of the medical-supply industry to determine whether hospitals and other medical providers are fraudulently overcharging Medicare, Medicaid, and other federal and state health programs for a wide array of goods, and over a dozen medical-supply companies received subpoenas. The investigation focused on the industry's use of rebates, discounts, barter arrangements, and refunds to hospitals and other medical centers in connection with goods ranging from rubber gloves and drugs to x-ray machines.

The focus on health care fraud is politically popular and it now brings in substantial revenues,[s] but some critics charge that the government is employing criminal charges to change well-established industry practices, and that many of the cases arise out of good faith disputes over the meaning of the highly complex Medicaid billing regulations.[t] In *United States v. Jain*, 93 F.3d 436 (8th Cir.1996), the court of appeals affirmed the defendant's conviction for violating the anti-kickback statute, rejecting his claim that the jury should have been instructed that he must have acted to intentionally violate a known legal duty. It upheld the instruction that the defendant must have acted willfully, which means "unjustifiably and wrongfully, known to be such by the defendant." 93 F.3d at 440. The court commented that "[b]oth the plain language of that statute, and respect for the traditional principle that ignorance of the law is no defense, suggest that a heightened mens rea standard should only require proof that Dr. Jain knew that his conduct was wrongful, rather than proof that he knew it violated 'a known legal duty.'" 93 F.3d at 441. Other courts have given the term "willful" a more generous reading in this context. Note that the more narrowly the anti-kickback statute is read, the more prosecutors have an incentive to rely on broad provisions such as the mail fraud act. Of course prosecutors do not have to choose one charge rather than another: as in *Jain*

they can combine charges under the mail or wire fraud statute with charges under the more specialized health care and Medicare fraud statutes.

6. Congress enacted a specific health care fraud statute, 18 U.S.C. § 1347, as part of the Health Insurance Portability and Accountability Act of 1996, Public Law No. 104–191. This statute extends the principles of mail fraud to schemes "to defraud any health care benefit program." 18 U.S.C. § 1347(a). One of the first cases involving a prosecution under § 1347 was *United States v. Lauersen*, 1999 WL 637237 (S.D.N.Y.1999), in which two doctors were charged with submitting false invoices that indicated patients had undergone gynecological procedures, when in fact the patients were being treated for infertility. More recently, in *United States v. Lucien*, 347 F.3d 45 (2d Cir.2003), the defendants were convicted of health care fraud for staging car accidents in order to collect insurance benefits under New York's no-fault automobile insurance regime. The court rejected the defendants' argument that § 1347 applied only to health care professionals, and also

s. In 2003, the federal government won or negotiated more than $1.8 billion in judgments and settlements in health care fraud matters. *See* THE DEPARTMENT OF HEALTH AND HUMAN SERVICES AND THE DEPARTMENT OF JUSTICE, HEALTH CARE FRAUD AND ABUSE PROGRAM ANNUAL REPORT FOR FY 2003.

t. For example, in a kick-back prosecution involving a physician who billed the government for time he was "available" to see patients, the court reversed the conviction, commenting that the government's theory would criminalize a practice common among lawyers:

Professionals, including lawyers, sometimes bill for simply being available if needed. One may disagree with the practice because the professional may be doing other billable work at the time. However, billing is nevertheless arguably appropriate because to be available, the professional must forego the opportunity to go fishing or worship in Mecca at the same time. Absent some affirmative reason to believe that use of code 96500 does not cover being available, billing under that code is at worst an attempt to bill at the outer limits permitted, not fraud.

Siddiqi v. United States, 98 F.3d 1427, 1439 (2d Cir.1996).

held that the no-fault automobile insurance regime qualified as a "health care benefit program" under the statute. It seems that prosecutors have been making use of § 1347, as there were 220 health care fraud defendants in 2005–nearly one-fourth as many defendants as mail and wire fraud.[u]

7. To some degree, health care fraud investigations have been casualties of the 9/11 attacks. In 2005 the Government Accounting Office reported that money earmarked by Congress to investigate fraud in the Medicare and Medicaid programs appears to have been improperly shifted to other purposes, particularly antiterrorism efforts. The FBI admitted that it was unable to show that it had used the money for the intended purpose, noting that agents previously assigned to health care fraud investigations had been shifted to counterterrorism activities. The GAO said that the number of agents assigned to health care investigations was 31 percent below the number budgeted in 2002, and 26 percent below the budgeted number in 2003. An FBI spokesman said that the bureau is now focusing again on health care fraud, which is one of its top white collar investigative priorities.

8. FBI investigations are not the only way the government learns of fraud involving health care (or other types of fraud against government programs). The False Claims Act, 31 U.S.C. § 3729 et seq., provides financial incentives for individuals to come forward as "whistleblowers." The law provides that the government can recover treble damages in a civil action, and it gives whistleblowers a financial reward when their information leads to the discovery and proof of fraudulent conduct. It also protects whistleblowers from being fired. In recent years, whistleblowers have been responsible for federal fraud cases against many well known companies, including Tenet Healthcare, Lockheed Martin, TAP Pharmaceutical Products, Inc., and Boeing. Taxpayers Against Fraud Education Fund maintains an excellent web site that provides information about the False Claims Act, describes ongoing cases, and explains how to bring a claim. *See* http://www.taf.org/ . For an interesting discussion of some of the issues raised by the False Claims Act and the role of private citizens in these actions, see Pamela H. Bucy, *Private Justice*, 76 S. Cal. L. Rev. 1 (2002), and Marc I. Steinberg & Seth A. Kaufman, *Minimizing Corporate Liability Exposure When the Whistle Blows in the Post Sarbanes–Oxley Era*, 30 J. Corp. L. 445 (2005).

D. WHAT IS PROPERTY?

Unless a case can be recast as one involving the right to honest services under § 1346, *McNally* holds that the mail and wire fraud statutes reach only schemes to defraud the victim of property. Within a few months of its decision in *McNally* the Supreme Court was faced with the following case, which raised the question what kinds of "property" rights fall within the scope of these statutes.

CARPENTER v. UNITED STATES
484 U.S. 19, 108 S.Ct. 316, 98 L.Ed.2d 275 (1987).

Justice White delivered the opinion of the Court.

[Defendant Winans was a reporter for the Wall Street Journal, and one of the two writers for its "Heard on the Street" column. The column

---

u. *See supra* note 2, p. 160.

discussed selected stocks, giving positive and negative information and opinions, but no inside information. Because of its perceived quality and integrity, the column affected the price of the stocks discussed.

The Journal had an official policy and practice that prior to publication the contents of the column were the Journal's confidential information. Despite his awareness of this rule, Winans entered a scheme with two brokers to give them advance information about the contents and timing of the column. The brokers would then buy and sell based on the predicted impact of the column and share the profits. Over four months the brokers made trades netting $690,000 on the basis of prepublication information about 27 columns.

Winans and one of the brokers were convicted of mail and wire fraud, securities fraud[a] and conspiracy. Defendant Carpenter, Winans' roommate, was convicted of aiding and abetting.]

* * *

Petitioners assert that their activities were not a scheme to defraud the Journal within the meaning of the mail and wire fraud statutes; and that in any event, they did not obtain any "money or property" from the Journal, which is a necessary element of the crime under our decision last Term in *McNally v. United States*, 483 U.S. 350 (1987). We are unpersuaded by either submission and address the latter first.

We held in *McNally* that the mail fraud statute does not reach "schemes to defraud citizens of their intangible rights to honest and impartial government," and that the statute is "limited in scope to the protection of property rights." Petitioners argue that the Journal's interest in prepublication confidentiality for the "Heard" columns is no more than an intangible consideration outside the reach of § 1341; nor does that law, it is urged, protect against mere injury to reputation. This is not a case like *McNally*, however. The Journal, as Winans' employer, was defrauded of much more than its contractual right to his honest and faithful service, an interest too ethereal in itself to fall within the

---

a. One of the two questions presented in the Supreme Court was whether criminal liability could be imposed under the securities laws when the newspaper, the only alleged victim of the fraud, had no interest in the securities traded. The courts below held that the fraud was "in connection with" a purchase or sale of securities because the scheme's sole purpose was to buy and sell securities at a profit based on advance information of the column's contents. The Supreme Court was equally divided on this issue, and it affirmed the securities fraud convictions without opinion. The

Court returned to the issue it had left open in *Carpenter* in United States v. O'Hagan, 521 U.S. 642, 649 (1997). It endorsed the misappropriation theory of criminal liability under § 10(b) of the Securities Act, upholding the conviction of a lawyer who purchased stock on the basis of inside information acquired as a member of a law firm representing a corporation making a tender offer. In light of the decision in *O'Hagan*, prosecutors no longer need to employ the mail and wire fraud statutes to reach conduct of this nature.

protection of the mail fraud statute, which "had its origin in the desire to protect individual property rights." Here, the object of the scheme was to take the Journal's confidential business information—the publication schedule and contents of the "Heard" column—and its intangible nature does not make it any less "property" protected by the mail and wire fraud statutes. *McNally* did not limit the scope of § 1341 to tangible as distinguished from intangible property rights.

Both courts below expressly referred to the Journal's interest in the confidentiality of the contents and timing of the "Heard" column as a property right, and we agree with that conclusion. Confidential business information has long been recognized as property. * * * The Journal had a property right in keeping confidential and making exclusive use, prior to publication, of the schedule and contents of the "Heard" column. As the Court has observed before: "[N]ews matter, however little susceptible of ownership or dominion in the absolute sense, is stock in trade, to be gathered at the cost of enterprise, organization, skill, labor, and money, and to be distributed and sold to those who will pay money for it, as for any other merchandise." *International News Service v. Associated Press*, 248 U.S. 215 (1918).

Petitioners' arguments that they did not interfere with the Journal's use of the information or did not publicize it and deprive the Journal of the first public use of it, miss the point. The confidential information was generated from the business, and the business had a right to decide how to use it prior to disclosing it to the public. Petitioners cannot successfully contend based on Associated Press that a scheme to defraud requires a monetary loss, such as giving the information to a competitor; it is sufficient that the Journal has been deprived of its right to exclusive use of the information, for exclusivity is an important aspect of confidential business information and most private property for that matter.

We cannot accept petitioners' further argument that Winans' conduct in revealing prepublication information was no more than a violation of workplace rules and did not amount to fraudulent activity that is proscribed by the mail fraud statute. Sections 1341 and 1343 reach any scheme to deprive another of money or property by means of false or fraudulent pretenses, representations, or promises. As we observed last Term in *McNally*, the words "to defraud" in the mail fraud statute have the "common understanding" of " 'wronging one in his property rights by dishonest methods or schemes,' and 'usually signify the deprivation of something of value by trick, deceit, chicane or overreaching.' " 483 U.S., at 358 (quoting *Hammerschmidt v. United States*, 265 U.S. 182, 188 (1924)). The concept of "fraud" includes the act of embezzlement, which is " 'the fraudulent appropriation to one's own use of the money or goods entrusted to one's care by another.' " *Grin v. Shine*, 187 U.S. 181, 189 (1902).

The District Court found that Winans' undertaking at the Journal was not to reveal prepublication information about his column, a promise that became a sham when in violation of his duty he passed along to his co-conspirators confidential information belonging to the Journal, pursuant to an ongoing scheme to share profits from trading in anticipation of the "Heard" column's impact on the stock market. In *Snepp v. United States*, 444 U.S. 507, 515, n. 11 (1980) (per curiam), although a decision grounded in the provisions of a written trust agreement prohibiting the unapproved use of confidential Government information, we noted the similar prohibitions of the common law, that "even in the absence of a written contract, an employee has a fiduciary obligation to protect confidential information obtained during the course of his employment." As the New York courts have recognized: "It is well established, as a general proposition, that a person who acquires special knowledge or information by virtue of a confidential or fiduciary relationship with another is not free to exploit that knowledge or information for his own personal benefit but must account to his principal for any profits derived therefrom." *Diamond v. Oreamuno*, 24 N.Y.2d 494, 497, 301 N.Y.S.2d 78, 80, 248 N.E.2d 910, 912 (1969); *see also* RESTATEMENT (SECOND) OF AGENCY §§ 388, Comment c, 396 (1958).

We have little trouble in holding that the conspiracy here to trade on the Journal's confidential information is not outside the reach of the mail and wire fraud statutes, provided the other elements of the offenses are satisfied. The Journal's business information that it intended to be kept confidential was its property; the declaration to that effect in the employee manual merely removed any doubts on that score and made the finding of specific intent to defraud that much easier. Winans continued in the employ of the Journal, appropriating its confidential business information for his own use, all the while pretending to perform his duty of safeguarding it. In fact, he told his editors twice about leaks of confidential information not related to the stock-trading scheme, demonstrating both his knowledge that the Journal viewed information concerning the "Heard" column as confidential and his deceit as he played the role of a loyal employee. Furthermore, the District Court's conclusion that each of the petitioners acted with the required specific intent to defraud is strongly supported by the evidence.

Lastly, we reject the submission that using the wires and the mail to print and send the Journal to its customers did not satisfy the requirement that those mediums be used to execute the scheme at issue. The courts below were quite right in observing that circulation of the "Heard" column was not only anticipated but an essential part of the scheme. Had the column not been made available to Journal customers, there would have been no effect on stock prices and no likelihood of profiting from the information leaked by Winans.

Note

Although *Carpenter* established that the mail and wire fraud statutes reached schemes to defraud the victim of intangible property, the Court provided little guidance on how to define the term property. The crucial distinction is between intangible property rights and all other intangible rights.

Since the decisions in *McNally* and *Carpenter* the lower courts have been asked to characterize a wide variety of rights as property for purposes of the mail or wire fraud statute, including frequent flyer mileage, market share, lost business opportunities, employees' rights under a collective bargaining agreement, union ballots, shareholders' rights to the information necessary to monitor the behavior of the corporation and its officers, the right to control spending, the right to control one's exposure to tort liability, the right to make an informed lending decision, and the government's right to collect taxes and fees for postal services.[b] One of the most hotly litigated issues has been the application of the mail fraud statute to fraudulent schemes to obtain government licenses and permits. The reported cases have involved everything from licenses for school bus drivers and physicians to arms export licenses and patents.[c] In 2000, the Supreme Court addressed the issue in the case that follows.

CLEVELAND v. UNITED STATES

531 U.S. 12, 121 S.Ct. 365, 148 L.Ed.2d 221 (2000).

JUSTICE GINSBURG delivered the opinion of the Court.

This case presents the question whether the federal mail fraud statute, 18 U.S.C. § 1341, reaches false statements made in an application for a state license. Section 1341 proscribes use of the mails in furtherance of "any scheme or artifice to defraud, or for obtaining money or property by means of false or fraudulent pretenses, representations, or promises." Petitioner Carl W. Cleveland and others were prosecuted under this federal measure for making false statements in

---

b. United States v. Loney, 959 F.2d 1332 (5th Cir. 1992) (frequent flyer coupons are property, and scheme was also intended to deprive airline of revenues); Lancaster Community Hosp. v. Antelope Val. Hosp. Dist., 940 F.2d 397, 405–06 (9th Cir. 1991) (scheme to increase one's market share at expense of another is too amorphous, and customers are not property); Israel Travel Advisory Service, Inc. v. Israel Identity Tours, Inc., 61 F.3d 1250, 1258 (7th Cir. 1995) (lost business opportunities are property); United States v. Rastelli, 870 F.2d 822, 830–31 (2d Cir. 1989) (union rights under collective bargain agreement); United States v. DeFries, 43 F.3d 707, 710 (D.C.Cir. 1995) (union ballots are property); United States v. D'Amato, 39 F.3d 1249, 1259 (2d Cir. 1994); United States v. Wallach, 935 F.2d 445, 464–66 (2d Cir. 1991) (shareholders' right is property); United States v. Shyres, 898 F.2d 647, 651–52 (8th Cir.1990) (right to pay for services without paying kickbacks is property); United States v. Granberry, 908 F.2d 278, 280 (8th Cir. 1990) (ability to avoid tort liability that might arise from hiring murderer to drive school buses is not property); United States v. DiNome, 86 F.3d 277, 284 (2d Cir. 1996)

(material information that a bank needs to make an informed lending decision is property); United States v. Lewis, 67 F.3d 225, 232–33 (9th Cir. 1995) (a bank's right to make informed lending choices is not a property right); Ginsburg v. United States, 909 F.2d 982, 987 (7th Cir. 1990) (federal government has property right to income taxes); United States v. Gelb, 881 F.2d 1155, 1162 (2d Cir. 1989) (Postal Service has property interest in postage).

c. *See, e.g.,* United States v. Schwartz, 924 F.2d 410, 417–18 (2d Cir. 1991) (arms export licenses are not property); United States v. Granberry, 908 F.2d 278, 280 (8th Cir. 1990) (unissued license to drive school bus is not property); United States v. Martinez, 905 F.2d 709, 713–14 (3d Cir. 1990) (medical license is property); Semiconductor Energy Laboratory Co., Ltd. v. Samsung Electronics Co., Ltd., 4 F.Supp.2d 473, 475 (E.D. Va. 1998) (holding that in granting a patent, the Patent and Trademark Office cannot be the victim of fraud because the PTO does not forfeit any money or property).

applying to the Louisiana State Police for permission to operate video poker machines. We conclude that permits or licenses of this order do not qualify as "property" within § 1341's compass. It does not suffice, we clarify, that the object of the fraud may become property in the recipient's hands; for purposes of the mail fraud statute, the thing obtained must be property in the hands of the victim. State and municipal licenses in general, and Louisiana's video poker licenses in particular, we hold, do not rank as "property," for purposes of § 1341, in the hands of the official licensor.

I

Louisiana law allows certain businesses to operate video poker machines. La.Rev.Stat. Ann. §§ 27:301 to 27:324 (West Supp.2000). The State itself, however, does not run such machinery. The law requires prospective owners of video poker machines to apply for a license from the State. § 27:306. The licenses are not transferable, § 27:311(G), and must be renewed annually, La. Admin. Code, tit. 42, § 2405(B)(3) (2000). To qualify for a license, an applicant must meet suitability requirements designed to ensure that licensees have good character and fiscal integrity.

In 1992, Fred Goodson and his family formed a limited partnership, Truck Stop Gaming, Ltd. (TSG), in order to participate in the video poker business at their truck stop in Slidell, Louisiana. Cleveland, a New Orleans lawyer, assisted Goodson in preparing TSG's application for a video poker license. The application required TSG to identify its partners and to submit personal financial statements for all partners. It also required TSG to affirm that the listed partners were the sole beneficial owners of the business and that no partner held an interest in the partnership merely as an agent or nominee, or intended to transfer the interest in the future.

TSG's application identified Goodson's adult children, Alex and Maria, as the sole beneficial owners of the partnership. It also showed that Goodson and Cleveland's law firm had loaned Alex and Maria all initial capital for the partnership and that Goodson was TSG's general manager. In May 1992, the State approved the application and issued a license. TSG successfully renewed the license in 1993, 1994, and 1995 pursuant to La. Admin. Code, tit. 42, § 2405(B)(3) (2000). Each renewal application identified no ownership interests other than those of Alex and Maria.

In 1996, the FBI discovered evidence that Cleveland and Goodson had participated in a scheme to bribe state legislators to vote in a manner favorable to the video poker industry. The Government charged Cleveland and Goodson with multiple counts of money laundering under 18 U.S.C. § 1957, as well as racketeering and conspiracy under § 1962. Among the predicate acts supporting these charges were four counts of mail fraud under § 1341. The indictment alleged that Cleveland and Goodson had violated § 1341 by fraudulently concealing that they were the true owners of TSG in the initial license application and three renewal applications mailed to the State. They concealed their ownership interests, according to the Government, because they had tax and financial problems that could have undermined their suitability to receive a video poker license.

Before trial, Cleveland moved to dismiss the mail fraud counts on the ground that the alleged fraud did not deprive the State of "property" under § 1341. The District Court denied the motion, concluding that "licenses constitute property even before they are issued." A jury found Cleveland guilty on two counts of mail fraud (based on the 1994 and 1995 license renewals) and on money laundering, racketeering, and conspiracy counts predicated on the mail fraud. The District Court sentenced Cleveland to 121 months in prison.

On appeal, Cleveland again argued that Louisiana had no property interest in video poker licenses, relying on several Court of Appeals decisions holding that the government does not relinquish "property" for purposes of § 1341 when it issues a permit or license. The Court of Appeals for the Fifth Circuit nevertheless affirmed Cleveland's conviction and sentence, *United States v. Bankston*, 182 F.3d 296, 309 (1999), considering itself bound by its holding in *United States v. Salvatore*, 110 F.3d 1131, 1138 (1997), that Louisiana video poker licenses constitute "property" in the hands of the State. Two other Circuits have concluded that the issuing authority has a property interest in unissued licenses under § 1341. *United States v. Bucuvalas*, 970 F.2d 937, 945 (C.A.1 1992) (entertainment and liquor license); *United States v. Martinez*, 905 F.2d 709, 715 (C.A.3 1990) (medical license).

We granted certiorari to resolve the conflict among the Courts of Appeals, and now reverse the Fifth Circuit's judgment.

* * *

III

In this case, there is no assertion that Louisiana's video poker licensing scheme implicates the intangible right of honest services. The question presented is whether, for purposes of the federal mail fraud statute, a government regulator parts with "property" when it issues a license. For the reasons we now set out, we hold that § 1341 does not reach fraud in obtaining a state or municipal license of the kind here involved, for such a license is not "property" in the government regulator's hands. Again, as we said in *McNally*, "[i]f Congress desires to go further, it must speak more clearly than it has."

To begin with, we think it beyond genuine dispute that whatever interests Louisiana might be said to have in its video poker licenses, the State's core concern is regulatory. Louisiana recognizes the importance of "public confidence and trust that gaming activities ... are conducted honestly and are free from criminal and corruptive elements." La.Rev. Stat. Ann. § 27:306(A)(1) (West Supp. 2000). The video poker licensing statute accordingly asserts the State's "legitimate interest in providing strict regulation of all persons, practices, associations, and activities related to the operation of ... establishments licensed to offer video draw poker devices." Ibid. The statute assigns the Office of State Police, a part of the Department of Public Safety and Corrections, the responsibility to promulgate rules and regulations concerning the licensing process. § 27:308(A). It also authorizes the State Police to deny, condition, suspend, or revoke licenses, to levy fines of up to $1,000 per violation of any rule, and to inspect all premises where video poker devices are offered for play. §§ 27:308(B), (E)(1). In addition, the statute defines criminal penalties for unauthorized use of video poker devices, and prescribes detailed suitability requirements for licensees.

In short, the statute establishes a typical regulatory program. It licenses, subject to certain conditions, engagement in pursuits that private actors may not undertake without official authorization. In this regard, it resembles other licensing schemes long characterized by this Court as exercises of state police powers.

Acknowledging Louisiana's regulatory interests, the Government offers two reasons why the State also has a property interest in its video poker licenses. First, the State receives a substantial sum of money in exchange for each license and continues to receive payments from the licensee as long as the license remains in effect. Second, the State has significant control over the issuance, renewal, suspension, and revocation of licenses.

Without doubt, Louisiana has a substantial economic stake in the video poker industry. The State collects an upfront "processing fee" for each new license application ($10,000 for truck stops), a separate "processing fee" for each renewal application ($1,000 for truck stops), an "annual fee" from each device owner ($2,000), an additional "device operation" fee ($1,000 for truck stops), and, most importantly, a fixed percentage of net revenue from each video poker device (32.5% for truck stops). It is hardly evident, however, why these tolls should make video poker licenses "property" in the hands of the State. The State receives the lion's share of its expected revenue not while the licenses remain in its own hands, but only after they have been issued to licensees. Licenses pre-issuance do not generate an ongoing stream of revenue. At most, they entitle the State to collect a processing fee from applicants for new licenses. Were an entitlement of this order sufficient to establish a state property right, one could scarcely avoid the conclusion that States have property rights in any license or permit requiring an upfront fee, including drivers' licenses, medical licenses, and fishing and hunting licenses. Such licenses, as the Government itself concedes, are "purely regulatory."

Tellingly, as to the character of Louisiana's stake in its video poker licenses, the Government nowhere alleges that Cleveland defrauded the State of any money to which the State was entitled by law. Indeed, there is no dispute that TSG paid the State of Louisiana its proper share of revenue, which totaled more than $1.2 million, between 1993 and 1995. If Cleveland defrauded the State of "property," the nature of that property cannot be economic.

Addressing this concern, the Government argues that Cleveland frustrated the State's right to control the issuance, renewal, and revocation of video poker licenses under La.Rev.Stat. Ann. §§ 27:306, 27:308 (West Supp. 2000). The Fifth Circuit has characterized the protected interest as "Louisiana's right to choose the persons to whom it issues video poker licenses." But far from composing an interest that "has long been recognized as property," *Carpenter*, these intangible rights of allocation, exclusion, and control amount to no more and no less than Louisiana's sovereign power to regulate. Notably, the Government overlooks the fact that these rights include the distinctively sovereign authority to impose criminal penalties for violations of the licensing scheme, including making false statements in a license application. Even when tied to an expected stream of revenue, the State's right of control does not create a property interest any more than a law licensing liquor sales in a State that levies a sales tax on liquor. Such regulations are paradigmatic exercises of the States' traditional police powers.

The Government compares the State's interest in video poker licenses to a patent holder's interest in a patent that she has not yet licensed. Although it is true that both involve the right to exclude, we think the congruence ends there. Louisiana does not conduct gaming operations itself, it does not hold video poker licenses to reserve that prerogative, and it does not "sell" video poker licenses in the ordinary commercial sense. Furthermore, while a patent holder may sell her patent, see 35 U.S.C. § 261 ("patents shall have the attributes of personal property"), the State may not sell its licensing authority. Instead of a patent holder's interest in an unlicensed patent, the better analogy is to the Federal Government's interest in an unissued patent. That interest, like the State's interest in licensing video poker operations, surely implicates the Government's role as sovereign, not as property holder.

The Government also compares the State's licensing power to a franchisor's right to select its franchisees. On this view, Louisiana's video poker licensing scheme represents the State's venture into the video poker business. Although the State could have chosen to run the business itself, the Government says, it decided to franchise private entities to carry out the operations instead. However, a franchisor's right to select its franchisees typically derives from its ownership of a trademark, brand name, business strategy, or other product that it may trade or sell in the open market. Louisiana's authority to select video poker licensees rests on no similar asset. It rests instead upon the State's sovereign right to exclude applicants deemed unsuitable to run video poker operations. A right to exclude in that governing capacity is not one appropriately labeled "property." Moreover, unlike an entrepreneur or business partner who shares both losses and gains arising from a business venture, Louisiana cannot be said to have put its labor or capital at risk through its fee-laden licensing scheme. In short, the State did not decide to venture into the video poker business; it decided typically to permit, regulate, and tax private operators of the games.

We reject the Government's theories of property rights not simply because they stray from traditional concepts of property. We resist the Government's reading of § 1341 as well because it invites us to approve a sweeping expansion of federal criminal jurisdiction in the absence of a clear statement by Congress. Equating issuance of licenses or permits with deprivation of property would subject to federal mail fraud prosecution a wide range of conduct traditionally regulated by state and local authorities. We note in this regard that Louisiana's video poker statute typically and unambiguously imposes criminal penalties for making false statements on license applications. As we reiterated last Term, " 'unless Congress conveys its purpose clearly, it will not be deemed to have significantly changed the federal-state balance' in the prosecution of crimes." *Jones v. United States*, 529 U.S. 848, 858 (2000) (quoting *United States v. Bass*, 404 U.S. 336, 349 (1971)).

Moreover, to the extent that the word "property" is ambiguous as placed in § 1341, we have instructed that "ambiguity concerning the ambit of criminal statutes should be resolved in favor of lenity." *Rewis v. United States*, 401 U.S. 808, 812 (1971). This interpretive guide is especially appropriate in construing § 1341 because, as this case demonstrates, mail fraud is a predicate offense under RICO, 18 U.S.C. § 1961(1), and the money laundering statute, § 1956(c)(7)(A). In deciding what is "property" under § 1341, we think "it is appropriate, before we choose the harsher alternative, to require that Congress should have spoken in language that is clear and definite."

Finally, in an argument not raised below but urged as an alternate ground for affirmance, the Government contends that § 1341, as amended in 1909, defines two independent offenses: (1) "any scheme or artifice to defraud" and (2) "any scheme or artifice ... for obtaining money or property by means of false or fraudulent pretenses, representations, or promises." Because a video poker license is property in the hands of the licensee, the Government says, Cleveland "obtain[ed] ... property" and thereby committed the second offense even if the license is not property in the hands of the State.

Although we do not here question that video poker licensees may have property interests in their licenses,[d] we nevertheless disagree with the Government's reading of § 1341. In *McNally*, we recognized that "[b]ecause the two phrases identifying the proscribed schemes appear in the disjunctive, it is arguable that they are to be construed independent-

---

d. Notwithstanding the State's declaration that "[a]ny license issued or renewed ... is not property or a protected interest under the constitutions of either the United States or the state of Louisiana," "[t]he question whether a state-law right constitutes 'property' or 'rights to property' is a matter of federal law," *Drye v. United States*, 528 U.S. 49, (1999). In some contexts, we have held that individuals have constitutionally protected property interests in state-issued licenses essential to pursuing an occupation or livelihood. *See, e.g., Bell v. Burson*, 402 U.S. 535, 539 (1971) (driver's license).

ly." But we rejected that construction of the statute, instead concluding that the second phrase simply modifies the first by "ma[king] it unmistakable that the statute reached false promises and misrepresentations as to the future as well as other frauds involving money or property." Indeed, directly contradicting the Government's view, we said that "the mail fraud statute ... had its origin in the desire to protect individual property rights, and any benefit which the Government derives from the statute must be limited to the Government's interests as property holder." We reaffirm our reading of § 1341 in *McNally*. Were the Government correct that the second phrase of § 1341 defines a separate offense, the statute would appear to arm federal prosecutors with power to police false statements in an enormous range of submissions to state and local authorities. For reasons already stated, we decline to attribute to § 1341 a purpose so encompassing where Congress has not made such a design clear.

IV

We conclude that § 1341 requires the object of the fraud to be "property" in the victim's hands and that a Louisiana video poker license in the State's hands is not "property" under § 1341. Absent clear statement by Congress, we will not read the mail fraud statute to place under federal superintendence a vast array of conduct traditionally policed by the States. Our holding means that Cleveland's § 1341 conviction must be vacated. Accordingly, the judgment of the United States Court of Appeals for the Fifth Circuit is reversed, and the case is remanded for further proceedings consistent with this opinion.

Notes

1. Note that the issue in *Cleveland* was the nature of *the government's* interest in the licenses that it issues. What if the case involves an effort to defraud a *licensee*? For many purposes licenses or permits in the hands of grantees are treated as their property. And, as a matter of policy, licensees stand on a far different footing than the government that issues a license. The *Cleveland* Court recognized this distinction, noting, *supra* at 211, that "we do not here question that video poker licensees may have property interests in their licenses."

2. Notwithstanding *Cleveland*, some government interests are property for purposes of the mail fraud act. In *United States v. Pasquantino*, 125 S.Ct. 1766 (2005), the Supreme Court upheld the use of the wire fraud statute to prosecute a scheme to deprive a foreign government of tax revenues. The defendants ordered large quantities of liquor over the telephone from discount package stores in Maryland, and then hired third parties to pick up the liquor and drive it across the Canadian border without paying the required excise taxes. The liquor was hidden in the vehicles, and the drivers did not declare it. The applicable taxes were roughly double the purchase price of the liquor. Under the common law the right to be paid money was a form of property, and fraud included a scheme to deprive the victim of his entitlement to money. Moreover, "[t]he fact that the victim of the fraud

happens to be the Government, rather than a private party, does not lessen the injury." The Court distinguished *Cleveland* on the ground that the government had not alleged that the state had been defrauded of any money to which it was entitled; the injury the state suffered was purely regulatory and not economic. In contrast, "Canada's entitlement to tax revenue is a straight-forward 'economic' interest."

3. At a policy level, what do you think of the results in *Pasquantino* and *Cleveland*? This is another way of asking whether limiting mail and wire fraud to cases involving deprivations of "property" helps to focus the statutes on cases involving a strong federal interest. Is there a substantial federal interest in making sure Canada collects all of its liquor taxes? The United States has an indirect interest in the reciprocity such a prosecution may engender, which may encourage Canadian officials to assist in enforcing American customs laws. But note there are some interests cutting the other way. The Maryland retailers were making a profit on these transactions, and the drivers who transported the liquor probably spend money in the U.S. as well. What about *Cleveland*? Of course the federal prosecutors were trying, in effect, to enforce the Louisiana laws that were intended to prevent corruption in the gaming industry. Is that a significant problem? Louisiana has a history of serious government corruption, and gambling has been associated with corruption in many jurisdictions. If you were calling the shots at the federal level, would you be more interested in helping Canada police its borders, or in using federal prosecutions to clean up corruption in Louisiana and other states?

4. A host of difficult questions regarding the definition of property have bedeviled the lower courts. In some cases, the courts have concluded that there was no property right. *See, e.g., United States v. Lewis,* 67 F.3d 225, 232–33 (9th Cir. 1995) (bank's right to make informed lending decisions is not property); *United States v. Henry,* 29 F.3d 112, 115 (3d Cir. 1994) (competing banks' interest in fair bidding opportunity to serve as depositories not a property right). Other cases, in contrast, characterize various interests as property rights. *See, e.g., United States v. DeFries,* 43 F.3d 707, 710 (D.C. Cir. 1995) (union merger ballots were property because they embodied information about member preferences that was costly to produce and would be costly to recreate); *United States v. Ashman,* 979 F.2d 469, 477–78 (7th Cir. 1992) (except for transactions on "limit days" when no other price was being traded in the pit, manipulation of matching commodities futures trades deprived customers of property right consisting of opportunity to obtain a better price, even though each customer's order was filled within the relevant range).

In *United States v. Catalfo,* 64 F.3d 1070 (7th Cir. 1995), the defendant was a futures and options trader who formed a relationship with a clearing firm by leading it to believe that he contemplated only small trades with little risk, when in fact he and his cohorts intended to trade in such massive quantities on a single day that their own trading would influence prices and permit them to reap a fortune. When their plan fell apart after they had begun their massive trades, one of the firms they had duped had lost $8.5 million, $2 million more than its net worth. Catalfo argued that he intended only to make his money by trading on the floor of the Chicago Board of Trade, and not to defraud the clearing firm. The court of appeals upheld his wire fraud convictions, reasoning that he intended to fraudulently obtain the collateral or credit upon which he based his trades from the clearing firm, imposing the enormous risk of loss on them by means of his misrepresentations. He deprived the clearing firm "of the right to control its risk of loss, which had a real and substantial value." Catalfo also argued that nothing in his contract with the clearing firm prevented him from trading beyond his own limited capital outlay and no margin limit had been placed on him. In other words, he did not even violate his contract with the clearing firm. The court brushed this argument aside with the comment that "[f]raud remains fraud even if the victim should have acted more prudently."

What do you think of *Catalfo*? Is a clearing firm's interest in "control[ing] its risk of loss" really any different than some of the interests that other lower courts have rejected, such as a bank's right to make informed lending decisions? Which way would you come down if you were a judge, and why? Perhaps the context matters. Are mail fraud prosecutions like *Ashman* and *Catalfo* the best way to regulate commodities trading? It seems likely that the size of the loss Mr. Catalfo caused influenced the thinking of the federal prosecutors and perhaps the court as well. Do you agree that is a proper consideration in determining whether the defendant's conduct fell within the ambit of the wire fraud statute?

Of course *Catalfo* was decided prior to *Cleveland*. Does *Cleveland* compel a different result? On the one hand, the Court's focus in *Cleveland* was on distinguishing between property rights and the government's sovereign regulatory interests (which are not property), and the cases noted above don't raise those issues. On the other hand, the Court did make some comments that have broader applicability. It noted that the government's arguments "stray[ed] from traditional concepts of property," and would bring about "a sweeping expansion of federal criminal jurisdiction in the absence of a clear statement by Congress." In the absence of such a clear statement, the *Cleveland* Court declined to significantly alter the federal-state balance. The Court also invoked the rule of lenity. So, do you think that the Court would see *Catalfo* as just as problematic as *Cleveland*? Remember that *Carpenter*, *supra* 202-06, was decided just a year or so after *McNally*, and it gave the mail fraud statute an expansive reading. For examples of post-*Cleveland* cases finding property rights, see *United States v. Coffey*, 361 F.Supp.2d 102 (E.D.N.Y. 2005) (union welfare fund's right to know that suppliers' firms were tied to organized crime constituted property right), and *United States v. Duff*, 336 F.Supp.2d 852 (N.D. Ill. 2004) (city's right to control how its money was spent and to contract with minority and women owned firms constituted property right).

5. Should the issue whether the state has a "property" right be analyzed under federal or state law? Before the decision in *Cleveland*, most of the federal courts relied on state authorities, and some decisions treated state law as dispositive of the question whether a particular issue is property. But in footnote 4, *supra* at 211, the *Cleveland* Court characterized this as an issue of federal law, without explaining why. Writing before *Cleveland*, Judge Frank Easterbrook asked why the existence of a federal felony should turn on "language in musty state cases," and noted that the interpretation of federal antitrust law does not depend upon state property law. *Borre v. United States*, 940 F.2d 215, 226 (7th Cir. 1991) (Easterbrook, J., concurring

and dissenting). Moreover, as the court noted in *United States v. Shotts*, 145 F.3d 1289, 1294 & n.6 (11th Cir. 1998), resort to state law is one source of the conflicts between circuits and even within circuits. If the courts are now going to develop a federal definition of property for purposes of the mail fraud statute, what distinctive principles should govern such a definition?

6. In *United States v. Walters*, 997 F.2d 1219 (7th Cir. 1993), an entertainment agent sought to enter the lucrative business of representing professional athletes by giving college athletes money and other valuables in exchange for exclusive agency contracts. Knowing that under NCAA regulations the signing of such a contract would end the athletes' eligibility, Walters agreed to keep the contracts secret until the athletes left school. The government charged Walters with mail fraud, claiming that he defrauded the schools that the athletes attended out of their athletic scholarships, which would not have been paid had the schools known of the secret contracts. While the schools were certainly deprived of property, the property went to the athletes, and not to defendant Walters. The court reversed Walters' conviction, articulating a new requirement for mail and wire fraud cases: to fall within the wire and mail fraud statutes, the defendant must have a scheme to obtain property *from the victim*. Writing for the court, Judge Easterbrook reasoned as follows:

> According to the United States, neither an actual nor a potential transfer of property from the victim to the defendant is essential. It is enough that the victim lose; what (if anything) the schemer hopes to gain plays no role in the definition of the offense. We asked the prosecutor at oral argument whether on this rationale practical jokes violate § 1341. A mails B an invitation to a surprise party for their mutual friend C. B drives his car to the place named in the invitation. But there is no party; the address is a vacant lot; B is the butt of a joke. The invitation came by post; the cost of gasoline means that B is out of pocket. The prosecutor said that this indeed violates § 1341, but that his office pledges to use prosecutorial discretion wisely. Many people will find this position unnerving (what if the prosecutor's policy changes, or A is politically unpopular and the prosecutor is looking for a way to nail him?). Others, who obey the law out of a sense of civic obligation rather than the fear of sanctions, will alter their conduct no matter what policy the prosecutor follows. Either way, the idea that practical jokes are federal felonies would make a joke of the Supreme Court's assurance that § 1341 does not cover the waterfront of deceit.

> Practical jokes rarely come to the attention of federal prosecutors, but large organizations are more successful in gaining the attention of public officials. In this case the mail fraud statute has been invoked to shore up the rules of an influential private association. Consider a parallel: an association of manufacturers of plumbing fixtures adopts a rule providing that its members will not sell "seconds" (that is, blemished articles) to the public. The association proclaims that this rule protects consumers from shoddy goods. To remain in good standing, a member must report its sales monthly. These reports flow in by mail. One member begins to sell "seconds" but reports that it is not doing so. These sales take business away from other members of the association, who lose profits as a result. So we have mail, misrepresentation, and the

loss of property, but the liar does not get any of the property the other firms lose. Has anyone committed a federal crime? The answer is yes—but the statute is the Sherman Act, 15 U.S.C. § 1, and the perpetrators are the firms that adopted the "no seconds" rule. *United States v. Trenton Potteries Co.*, 273 U.S. 392 (1927). The trade association we have described is a cartel, which the firm selling "seconds" was undermining. Cheaters depress the price, causing the monopolist to lose money. Typically they go to great lengths to disguise their activities, the better to increase their own sales and avoid retaliation. The prosecutor's position in our case would make criminals of the cheaters, would use § 1341 to shore up cartels.

Fanciful? Not at all. Many scholars understand the NCAA as a cartel, having power in the market for athletes. The NCAA depresses athletes' income—restricting payments to the value of tuition, room, and board, while receiving services of substantially greater worth. The NCAA treats this as desirable preservation of amateur sports; a more jaundiced eye would see it as the use of monopsony power to obtain athletes' services for less than the competitive market price. Walters then is cast in the role of a cheater, increasing the payments to the student athletes. Like other cheaters, Walters found it convenient to hide his activities. If, as the prosecutor believes, his repertory included extortion, he has used methods that the law denies to persons fighting cartels, but for the moment we are concerned only with the deceit that caused the universities to pay stipends to "professional" athletes. For current purposes it matters not whether the NCAA actually monopsonizes the market for players; the point of this discussion is that the prosecutor's theory makes criminals of those who consciously cheat on the rules of a private organization, even if that organization is a cartel. We pursue this point because any theory that makes criminals of cheaters raises a red flag.

Cheaters are not self-conscious champions of the public weal. They are in it for profit, as rapacious and mendacious as those who hope to collect monopoly rents. Maybe more; often members of cartels believe that monopoly serves the public interest, and they take their stand on the platform of business ethics, while cheaters' glasses have been washed with cynical acid. Only Adam Smith's invisible hand turns their self-seeking activities to public benefit. It is cause for regret if prosecutors, assuming that persons with low regard for honesty must be villains, use the criminal laws to suppress the competitive process that undermines cartels.... [W]hat is it about § 1341 that labels as a crime all deceit that inflicts any loss on anyone? Firms often try to fool their competitors, surprising them with new products that enrich their treasuries at their rivals' expense. Is this mail fraud because large organizations inevitably use the mail? "[A]ny scheme or artifice to defraud, or for obtaining money or property by means of false or fraudulent pretenses, representations, or promises" reads like a description of schemes to get money or property by fraud rather than methods of doing business that incidentally cause losses.

None of the Supreme Court's mail fraud cases deals with a scheme in which the defendant neither obtained nor tried to obtain the victim's property. It has, however, addressed the question whether 18 U.S.C. § 371, which prohibits conspiracies to defraud the United States, criminalizes plans that cause incidental loss to the Treasury. *Tanner v. United States*, 483 U.S. 107, 130 (1987), holds that § 371 applies only when the United States is a "target" of the fraud; schemes that cause indirect losses do not violate that statute. *McNally* tells us that § 371 covers a broader range of frauds than does § 1341, and it follows that business plans causing incidental losses are not mail fraud. We have been unable to find any appellate cases squarely resolving the question whether the victim's loss must be an objective of the scheme rather than a byproduct of it, perhaps because prosecutions of the kind this case represents are so rare. * * *

Many of our cases ask whether a particular scheme deprived a victim of property. They do so not with an emphasis on "deprive" but with an emphasis on "property"—which, until the enactment of 18 U.S.C. § 1346 after Walters' conduct, was essential to avoid the "intangible rights" doctrine that *McNally* jettisoned. No one doubted that the schemes were designed to enrich the perpetrators at the victims' expense; the only difficulty was the proper characterization of the deprivation. Not until today have we dealt with a scheme in which the defendants' profits were to come from legitimate transactions in the market, rather than at the expense of the victims. Both the "scheme or artifice to defraud" clause and the "obtaining money or property" clause of § 1343 contemplate a transfer of some kind. Accordingly, following both the language of § 1341 and the implication of *Tanner*, we hold that only a scheme to obtain money or other property from the victim by fraud violates § 1341. A deprivation is a necessary but not a sufficient condition of mail fraud. Losses that occur as byproducts of a deceitful scheme do not satisfy the statutory requirement.

The Supreme Court accepted a similar argument in a recent Hobbs Act case, *Scheidler v. National Organization for Women, Inc.*, 537 U.S. 393 (2003). The Court concluded that under the Hobbs Act it's not sufficient to prove that the defendant caused the victim to lose property. The defendant must "obtain" the property that the victim has lost. The defendants who sought to drive abortion providers out of business with violent protests did not seek to obtain their property, and hence no extortion occurred within the meaning of the Hobbs Act. But note that the Court relied on specific language in the Hobbs Act and on the legislative history of the Act, so this conclusion will not necessarily carry over to the mail and wire fraud statutes. For a discussion of *NOW v. Scheidler*, see *infra* 243.

7. *Pasquantino*, discussed in note 2, involved not only the definition of property, but also some special doctrines that may be applicable in cases with international elements. The Court concluded that "the wire fraud statute punishes fraudulent use of domestic wires, whether or not such conduct constitutes smuggling, occurs aboard a vessel, or evades foreign taxes." It rejected the argument that the prosecution was barred by the common law revenue rule which "at its core ... prohibited the collection of tax obligations of foreign nations." As the Court explained:

An action by a domestic sovereign enforces the sovereign's own penal law. A prohibition on the enforcement of foreign penal law does not plainly prevent the Government from enforcing a domestic criminal law.

The Court acknowledged that in an attenuated sense the prosecution "enforces" the Canadian revenue laws, but not in a manner that contravened the policies underlying the rule, which was to "prevent judicial evaluations of the policy-laden enactments of other sovereigns." Because the prosecution was brought by the Executive branch, which has the general responsibility for foreign affairs, there was little risk of the courts unknowingly causing international friction. The Court also noted that the statute punishes fraud executed "in interstate or *foreign* commerce," so this is not a statute in which Congress had only domestic concerns in mind.

Four members of the Court dissented in an opinion written by Justice Ginsburg, charging that the Court had "ascribed an exorbitant scope to the wire fraud statute, in disregard of our repeated recognition that 'Congress legislates against the backdrop of the presumption against extraterritoriality.'" The dissenters noted that when Congress explicitly addressed international smuggling it provided for criminal enforcement of the customs laws of other nations only when that nation has reciprocal laws criminalizing smuggling into the United States. Canada has no such reciprocal law. The dissenters also noted that prosecution was not authorized by the tax treaty between the U.S. and Canada, and that Canada could extradite a U.S. citizen for violating Canadian tax laws. Finally, the dissenters read the revenue tax rule to cover the case, particularly in light of requirement of victim restitution.

The government tried to push the envelope even more in a prosecution in the Southern District of New York. In *United States v. Giffen*, 326 F.Supp.2d 497 (S.D. N.Y. 2004), the indictment charged a U.S. citizen with making unlawful payments of $78 million in cash and luxury items to past and present senior officials–including the current president—of the Republic of Kazakhstan pursuant to a scheme to deprive the citizens of Kazakhstan of the honest services of their officials. At the time of the events charged, the defendant held the semi-official title of "Counselor" to the President of Kazakhstan. The indictment charged that he used this position to engineer a complex series of oil and gas transactions that generated the payments to the Kazak officials, business worth $67 million in fees for his New York-based company, and millions of dollars in unreported income to himself and others. The district court dismissed this portion of the indictment, holding that (1) Congress did not intend that the intangible right to honest services encompass bribery of foreign officials in foreign countries, (2) the application of the honest services provision of 18 U.S.C. § 1346 to Giffin was unconstitutionally vague, and (3) in light of the principles of international comity, the court would not without a clear statement from Congress seek to determine the duties owed by Kazak officials to their own citizens. Indeed, the court noted, the government of Kazakhstan had opposed the prosecution, and had appealed to officials in the Departments of State and Justice for assistance.

What do you think of these developments from the perspective of either broad policy considerations or a more technical legal analysis. Doesn't the reference to "foreign commerce" in the wire fraud statute send a signal that at least in appropriate cases Congress intended to allow prosecutions with a substantial international component? If so, does that authorize extraterritorial jurisdiction? Note that *Giffen* and *Pasquantino* both involved U.S. citizens and some conduct in the U.S., as well as related conduct in other countries. *Giffen* illustrates the point that even if you have no qualms about applying the statute to cases in which a substantial part of the case arose outside of the U.S., it may still be difficult to define with certainty the applicable standards of behavior. Should the U.S. use wire and mail fraud prosecutions to export its view of ethics and good government to very different settings, such as those in developing countries? How should the court go about defining the standard of honest services in a developing country like Kazakhstan? Should the judiciary leave the ball in the court of Congress, which has already addressed related questions in the Foreign Corrupt Practices Act (FCPA), 15 U.S.C. § 78dd–2 et seq.?[g] What do you think of the recent wire fraud charges against U.N. officials involved in the Iraqi oil-for-food scandal, discussed *supra* p. 163?

And finally, if this is what the mail and wire fraud statutes mean, are they unconstitutionally vague, at least as applied to *some* cases? (*See supra* 184 for more discussion of vagueness.)

Note that the general topic of the extraterritorial application of federal criminal statutes is addressed in connection with terrorism, *infra* at 403–21.

E.   USE OF THE MAILS

SCHMUCK v. UNITED STATES

489 U.S. 705, 109 S.Ct. 1443, 103 L.Ed.2d 734 (1989).

JUSTICE BLACKMUN delivered the opinion of the Court.

I

In August 1983, petitioner Wayne T. Schmuck, a used-car distributor, was indicted in the United States District Court for the Western District of Wisconsin on 12 counts of mail fraud, in violation of 18 U.S.C. §§ 1341 and 1342.

The alleged fraud was a common and straightforward one. Schmuck purchased used cars, rolled back their odometers, and then sold the automobiles to Wisconsin retail dealers for prices artificially inflated because of the low-mileage readings. These unwitting car dealers, relying on the altered odometer figures, then resold the cars to customers, who in turn paid prices reflecting Schmuck's fraud. To complete the resale of each automobile, the dealer who purchased it from Schmuck would submit a title-application form to the Wisconsin Department of Transportation on behalf of his retail customer. The receipt of a Wisconsin title was a prerequisite for completing the resale; without it, the dealer could not transfer title to the customer and the customer could not

---

g. The indictment also contained counts alleging violations of the FCPA, money laundering, and the federal income tax laws.

obtain Wisconsin tags. The submission of the title-application form supplied the mailing element of each of the alleged mail frauds.

II

"The federal mail fraud statute does not purport to reach all frauds, but only those limited instances in which the use of the mails is a part of the execution of the fraud, leaving all other cases to be dealt with by appropriate state law." *Kann v. United States*, 323 U.S. 88, 95, 65 S.Ct. 148, 151, 89 L.Ed. 88 (1944). To be part of the execution of the fraud, however, the use of the mails need not be an essential element of the scheme. *Pereira v. United States*, 347 U.S. 1, 8, 74 S.Ct. 358, 362, 98 L.Ed. 435 (1954). It is sufficient for the mailing to be "incident to an essential part of the scheme," ibid., or "a step in [the] plot," *Badders v. United States*, 240 U.S. 391, 394, 36 S.Ct. 367, 368, 60 L.Ed. 706 (1916).

Schmuck, relying principally on this Court's decisions in *Kann*, supra, *Parr v. United States*, 363 U.S. 370, 80 S.Ct. 1171, 4 L.Ed.2d 1277 (1960), and *United States v. Maze*, 414 U.S. 395, 94 S.Ct. 645, 38 L.Ed.2d 603 (1974), argues that mail fraud can be predicated only on a mailing that affirmatively assists the perpetrator in carrying out his fraudulent scheme. The mailing element of the offense, he contends, cannot be satisfied by a mailing, such as those at issue here, that is routine and innocent in and of itself, and that, far from furthering the execution of the fraud, occurs after the fraud has come to fruition, is merely tangentially related to the fraud, and is counterproductive in that it creates a "paper trail" from which the fraud may be discovered. We disagree both with this characterization of the mailings in the present case and with this description of the applicable law.

We begin by considering the scope of Schmuck's fraudulent scheme. Schmuck was charged with devising and executing a scheme to defraud Wisconsin retail automobile customers who based their decisions to purchase certain automobiles at least in part on the low-mileage readings provided by the tampered odometers. This was a fairly large-scale operation. Evidence at trial indicated that Schmuck had employed a man known only as "Fred" to turn back the odometers on about 150 different cars. Schmuck then marketed these cars to a number of dealers, several of whom he dealt with on a consistent basis over a period of about 15 years. Indeed, of the 12 automobiles that are the subject of the counts of the indictment, 5 were sold to "P and A Sales," and 4 to "Southside Auto." Thus, Schmuck's was not a "one-shot" operation in which he sold a single car to an isolated dealer. His was an ongoing fraudulent venture. A rational jury could have concluded that the success of Schmuck's venture depended upon his continued harmonious relations with, and good reputation among, retail dealers, which in turn required the smooth flow of cars from the dealers to their Wisconsin customers.

Under these circumstances, we believe that a rational jury could have found that the title-registration mailings were part of the execution of the fraudulent scheme, a scheme which did not reach fruition until the retail dealers resold the cars and effected transfers of title. Schmuck's scheme would have come to an abrupt halt if the dealers either had lost faith in Schmuck or had not been able to resell the cars obtained from him. These resales and Schmuck's relationships with the retail dealers naturally depended on the successful passage of title among the various parties. Thus, although the registration-form mailings may not have contributed directly to the duping of either the retail dealers or the customers, they were necessary to the passage of title, which in turn was essential to the perpetuation of Schmuck's scheme. As noted earlier, a mailing that is "incident to an essential part of the scheme," *Pereira*, 347 U.S., at 8, 74 S.Ct., at 363, satisfies the mailing element of the mail fraud offense. The mailings here fit this description.

Once the full flavor of Schmuck's scheme is appreciated, the critical distinctions between this case and the three cases in which this Court has delimited the reach of the mail fraud statute—*Kann*, *Parr*, and *Maze*—are readily apparent. The defendants in *Kann* were corporate officers and directors accused of setting up a dummy corporation through which to divert profits into their own pockets. As part of this fraudulent scheme, the defendants caused the corporation to issue two checks payable to them. The defendants cashed these checks at local banks, which then mailed the checks to the drawee banks for collection. This Court held that the mailing of the cashed checks to the drawee banks could not supply the mailing element of the mail fraud charges. The defendants' fraudulent scheme had reached fruition. "It was immaterial to them, or to any consummation of the scheme, how the bank which paid or credited the check would collect from the drawee bank." 323 U.S., at 94, 65 S.Ct., at 151.

In *Parr*, several defendants were charged, inter alia, with having fraudulently obtained gasoline and a variety of other products and services through the unauthorized use of a credit card issued to the school district which employed them. The mailing element of the mail fraud charges in *Parr* was purportedly satisfied when the oil company which issued the credit card mailed invoices to the school district for payment, and when the district mailed payment in the form of a check. Relying on *Kann*, this Court held that these mailings were not in execution of the scheme as required by the statute because it was immaterial to the defendants how the oil company went about collecting its payment. 363 U.S., at 393, 80 S.Ct., at 1184.

Later, in *Maze*, the defendant allegedly stole his roommate's credit card, headed south on a winter jaunt, and obtained food and lodging at motels along the route by placing the charges on the stolen card. The mailing element of the mail fraud charge was supplied by the fact that the defendant knew that each motel proprietor would mail an invoice to the bank that had issued the credit card, which in turn would mail a bill to the card owner for payment. The Court found that these mailings could not support mail fraud charges because the defendant's scheme had reached fruition when he checked out of each motel. The success of his scheme in no way depended on the mailings; they merely determined which of his victims would ultimately bear the loss.

The title-registration mailings at issue here served a function different from the mailings in *Kann, Parr,* and *Maze.* The intrabank mailings in *Kann* and the credit card invoice mailings in *Parr* and *Maze* involved little more than post-fraud accounting among the potential victims of the various schemes, and the long-term success of the fraud did not turn on which of the potential victims bore the ultimate loss. Here, in contrast, a jury rationally could have found that Schmuck by no means was indifferent to the fact of who bore the loss. The mailing of the title-registration forms was an essential step in the successful passage of title to the retail purchasers. Moreover, a failure of this passage of title would have jeopardized Schmuck's relationship of trust and goodwill with the retail dealers upon whose unwitting cooperation his scheme depended. Schmuck's reliance on our prior cases limiting the reach of the mail fraud statute is simply misplaced.

To the extent that Schmuck would draw from these previous cases a general rule that routine mailings that are innocent in themselves cannot supply the mailing element of the mail fraud offense, he misapprehends this Court's precedents. In *Parr* the Court specifically acknowledged that "innocent" mailings—ones that contain no false information—may supply the mailing element. In other cases, the Court has found the elements of mail fraud to be satisfied where the mailings have been routine. *See, e.g., Carpenter v. United States,* 484 U.S. 19, 28, 108 S.Ct. 316, 322, 98 L.Ed.2d 275 (1987) (mailing newspapers).

We also reject Schmuck's contention that mailings that someday may contribute to the uncovering of a fraudulent scheme cannot supply the mailing element of the mail fraud offense. The relevant question at all times is whether the mailing is part of the execution of the scheme as conceived by the perpetrator at the time, regardless of whether the mailing later, through hindsight, may prove to have been counterproductive and return to haunt the perpetrator of the fraud. The mail fraud statute includes no guarantee that the use of the mails for the purpose of executing a fraudulent scheme will be risk free. Those who use the mails to defraud proceed at their peril.

For these reasons, we agree with the Court of Appeals that the mailings in this case satisfy the mailing element of the mail fraud offenses.

JUSTICE SCALIA, with whom JUSTICE BRENNAN, JUSTICE MARSHALL, and JUSTICE O'CONNOR join, dissenting.

The purpose of the mail fraud statute is "to prevent the post office from being used to carry [fraudulent schemes] into effect." *Durland v. United States,* 161 U.S. 306, 314, 16 S.Ct. 508, 511, 40 L.Ed. 709 (1896); *Parr v. United States,* 363 U.S. 370, 389, 80 S.Ct. 1171, 1182, 4 L.Ed.2d 1277 (1960). The law does not establish a general federal remedy against fraudulent conduct, with use of the mails as the jurisdictional hook, but reaches only "those limited instances in which the use of the mails is *a part of the execution of the fraud,* leaving all other cases to be dealt with by appropriate state law." *Kann v. United States,* 323 U.S. 88, 95, 65 S.Ct. 148, 151, 89 L.Ed. 88 (1944) (emphasis added). In other words, it is mail fraud, not mail and fraud, that incurs liability. This federal statute is not violated by a fraudulent scheme in which, at some point, a mailing happens to occur—nor even by one in which a mailing predictably and necessarily occurs. The mailing must be in furtherance of the fraud.

In *Kann v. United States,* we concluded that even though defendants who cashed checks obtained as part of a fraudulent scheme knew that the bank cashing the checks would send them by mail to a drawee bank for collection, they did not thereby violate the mail fraud statute, because upon their receipt of the cash "[t]he scheme ... had reached fruition," and the mailing was "immaterial ... to any consummation of the scheme." We held to the same effect in *United States v. Maze,* 414 U.S. 395, 400–402, 94 S.Ct. 645, 648–649, 38 L.Ed.2d 603 (1974), declining to find that credit card fraud was converted into mail fraud by the certainty that, after the wrongdoer had fraudulently received his goods and services from the merchants, they would forward the credit charges by mail for payment. These cases are squarely in point here. For though the Government chose to charge a defrauding of retail customers (to whom the innocent dealers resold the cars), it is obvious that, regardless of who the ultimate victim of the fraud may have been, the fraud was complete with respect to each car when petitioner pocketed the dealer's money. As far as each particular transaction was concerned, it was as inconsequential to him whether the dealer resold the car as it was inconsequential to the defendant in *Maze* whether the defrauded merchant ever forwarded the charges to the credit card company.

Nor can the force of our cases be avoided by combining all of the individual transactions into a single scheme, and saying, as the Court does, that if the dealers' mailings obtaining title for each retail purchaser had not occurred then the dealers would have stopped trusting petitioner for future transactions. (That conclusion seems to me a non sequitur, but I accept it for the sake of argument.) This establishes, at most, that the scheme could not technically have been consummated if the mechanical step of the mailings to obtain conveyance of title had not occurred. But we have held that the indispensability of such mechanical mailings, not strictly in furtherance of the fraud, is not enough to invoke the statute. For example, when officials of a school district embezzled tax funds over the course of several years, we held that no mail fraud had occurred even though the success of the scheme plainly depended on the officials' causing tax bills to be sent by mail (and thus tax payments to be received) every year. *Parr v. United States,* 363 U.S., at 388–392, 80 S.Ct., at 1182–1184. Similarly, when those officials caused the school district to pay by mail credit card bills—a step plainly necessary to enable their continued fraudulent use of the credit card—we concluded that no mail fraud had occurred.

I find it impossible to escape these precedents in the present case. Assuming the Court to be correct in concluding that failure to pass title to the cars would have threatened the success of the scheme, the same could have been said of failure to collect taxes or to pay the credit card bills in *Parr*. * * *

Notes

1. Prior to *Schmuck* there were several lines of authority upon which defendants could rely to attack the sufficiency of a mailing. Mailings could be attacked on the ground that they were counterproductive to the fraudulent scheme, that they occurred prior to the commencement of the scheme, or that they occurred after the fruition of the scheme (though mailings designed to lull the victims into a false sense of security could be an exception to the latter limitation). *Schmuck* rejects these objective tests in favor of a subjective standard reaching any mailing that is part of the scheme as conceived by the perpetrator. However, some of the previous issues can still arise under a *Schmuck* analysis. In *United States v. Pierce*, 409 F.3d 228 (4th Cir. 2005), the court rejected the defendant's argument that the mailing was not in furtherance of the scheme. The defendant conducted bingo games for a charitable organization, and would purchase extra cases of instant games from the supplier, selling these "off-the-books" games which were not included in the sales reports mailed to the organization. The court held that the inaccurate reports lulled the organization into a false sense of security and was conceived as part of the scheme to conceal the fraud. The dissent argued that the scheme was completed when the "off-the-books" sales were omitted, and the mailing of the report did not further or conceal the fraud. *See also United States v. Strong*, 371 F.3d 225 (5th Cir. 2004) (rejecting government's argument that defendant's mailings had a lulling effect). For a general discussion of the mailing element, see 2 SARAH N. WELLING ET AL., FEDERAL CRIMINAL LAW AND RELATED CIVIL ACTIONS §§ 17.27–17.31 (1998).

The issue of the sufficiency of the mailing was raised by Whitewater figure Susan McDougal. McDougal was prosecuted for mail fraud by Independent Counsel Kenneth Starr in connection with the mailing of a Small Business Administration loan documentation form. The court of appeals rejected McDougal's argument that the form was mailed after she received the loan, on the grounds that "even a mailing that became necessary after the defendant 'has successfully fleeced his victim' can come within the statue if the mailing is necessary to permit the defendant to 'retain the fruits of [the] fraud.'" *United States v. McDougal*, 137 F.3d 547, 555 (8th Cir. 1998). The court concluded that the mailing in question met this standard for several reasons, including the fact that failure to submit the expected form might have prompted an SBA investigation.

2. One issue *Schmuck* treated only in a footnote is whether a mail fraud charge may be based upon a mailing that was required by state or federal law. In *Parr v. United States*, 363 U.S. 370, 391 (1960), the Court stated: "we think it cannot be said that mailings made or caused to be made under the imperative command of duty imposed by state law are criminal under the federal mail fraud statute." *Parr* involved the allegation that

school board members had misappropriated school revenues; the mailings were tax statements, checks, and receipts.[h]

Schmuck distinguished *Parr* in a short footnote. Whereas the required mailings in *Parr* "would have been made regardless of the defendants' fraudulent scheme, the mailings in the present case, though in compliance with Wisconsin's car-registration procedure, were derivative of Schmuck's scheme to sell 'doctored' cars and would not have occurred but for that scheme." 489 U.S. at 713 n.7. The Court also noted that the tax notices themselves had not been increased as part of the fraud. *Ibid.*

In light of *Schmuck*, consider the following lines of lower court authority construing *Parr*.

a. Several circuits have held that legally required mailings can be prosecuted as mail fraud only if they contain false statements. *United States v. Curry*, 681 F.2d 406, 412–13 (5th Cir. 1982), *United States v. Gray*, 790 F.2d 1290, 1298 (6th Cir. 1986), *rev'd on other grounds, sub nom. McNally v. United States*, 483 U.S. 350 (1987).

The Second Circuit's opinion upholding Leona Helmsley's mail fraud conviction is a variation on this theme. Helmsley, the owner of many luxury hotels in New York and the wife of a real estate billionaire, avoided paying more than $1.7 million in federal and state taxes by billing personal expenses to business accounts. (She was widely quoted as stating, "We don't pay taxes. The little people pay taxes.") In addition to federal tax evasion, Helmsley was also charged with mail fraud in connection with her false state tax returns. She was convicted and sentenced to four years in prison. On appeal the Second Circuit assumed that she had been required by circumstances to mail her state return, but it nonetheless upheld her mail fraud conviction. *United States v. Helmsley*, 941 F.2d 71, 95 (2d Cir. 1991). The court emphasized that Helmsley's mailings contained false representations that were part of the execution of her scheme to defraud; in contrast, *Parr* involved a scheme to steal funds that had been mailed, not a scheme to defraud. *Accord United States v. Kellogg*, 955 F.2d 1244, 1247–48 (9th Cir. 1992).

b. In *United States v. Green*, 786 F.2d 247, 249–50 (7th Cir. 1986), Judge Easterbrook noted that the legal duty language of *Parr* was not its holding, since the Court also focused on the prosecutor's failure to tie the mailings to the success of the scheme or to connect the defendants' conduct to the size of the taxes. He concluded that a mail fraud prosecution may be based on legally-required mailings that are important to the success of the scheme to defraud, and left open the question whether it would also be necessary to show that legally required mailings were made with the specific intent to defraud the recipients of the mail. 786 F.2d at 250.

3. It is not necessary to show specific intent to use the mails. However, when the defendant is charged with having caused an innocent third party to make the mailing in question, an inquiry into the defendant's state of mind is required to determine causation. In *Pereira v. United States*, 347 U.S. 1, 8–

---

h. This is another aspect of the *Parr* case discussed in the *Schmuck* decision reprinted *supra*. The *Parr* defendants had two fraudulent schemes: the fraudulent use of credit cards, discussed in *Schmuck*, and the misappropriation of school board revenues by other means, including writing and then cashing checks made out to fictitious persons and converting and cashing checks sent in payment of taxes.

9 (1954), the Supreme Court explained that one "causes" a mailing when "one does an act with knowledge that the use of the mails will follow in the ordinary course of business, or where such use can reasonably be foreseen, even though not actually intended." The wire fraud statute has parallel language covering anyone who "causes" a wire transmission, and the lower courts recognize that *Pereira* requires proof that the defendant knew or could have foreseen that there would be a wire transmission by a third party.

The wire fraud statute requires a transmission "by means of wire, radio, or television communication *in interstate or foreign commerce* [of] any writings, signs, signals, pictures, or sounds for the purpose of executing such scheme or artifice." Although it might be possible to read this language as reaching any transmission over interstate telephone or telegraph lines, the statute has consistently been interpreted to require that the transmission in question be interstate in character.[i] In contrast, the mail fraud statute applies to intrastate as well as interstate mailings. This disparity can yield anomalous results. For example, in *United States v. Bryant*, 766 F.2d 370 (8th Cir. 1985), the defendants used both mailings and telegrams to effectuate a fraudulent scheme to obtain preferential bookings at the St. Louis Convention Center. All of the communications went from one city in Missouri to another. The intrastate mailings clearly established the jurisdictional predicate under Section 1341, but intrastate telegrams were not sufficient under Section 1343. Ultimately, however, federal jurisdiction was sustained on two wire fraud counts because of a bizarre fortuity. Unbeknownst to the defendants, two of their telegrams had been routed electronically through a Western Union installation in Virginia. Since the interstate nexus was a jurisdictional requirement unrelated to culpability, the court held that the government was not required to show that the defendants had any knowledge or foresight of the interstate character of the transmission. 766 F.2d at 374–75.

Is there any good reason for this disparity in the jurisdictional scope of these two parallel statutes? Does Congress have the constitutional authority to extend the reach of the wire fraud statute to any telephone or telegraph transmission that effectuates a scheme to defraud? What is the rationale for not requiring the government to prove a defendant's culpability in regard to jurisdictional elements? See also Chapter 3 at 107–08 for a discussion of the inter-/intra-state issue in regard to the Travel Act.

4. What if the government agent maneuvers a defendant into making a mailing in order to create federal jurisdiction for mail fraud? In *United States v. Kaye*, 586 F.Supp. 1395 (N.D. Ill. 1984), the indictment alleged that defendant was a deputy sheriff who solicited and received bribes to fix divorce cases. An undercover federal agent sought defendant's assistance in obtaining a divorce from his fictitious wife, giving a fictitious Virginia

---

i. The legislative history provides some support for this restrictive interpretation. The original language of Section 1343 reached only transmissions "by means of interstate wire, radio, or television communications." Act of July 16, 1952, ch. 879, § 18(a), 66 Stat. 722. The 1956 legislation adopting the current language was intended solely to expand the statute to reach transmissions in foreign commerce, which had been held to be outside the scope of the original language. *See* H.R. Rep. No. 84–2835 at 2 (1956), *reprinted in* 1957 U.S.C.C.A.N. 3091, 3091.

address for her. A summons addressed to a local person would have been served in person, but because the agent's "wife" supposedly lived in Virginia, the defendant mailed the summons. Relying on *United States v. Archer*, 486 F.2d 670, 682 (2d Cir. 1973), the defendant moved to dismiss on the ground that the government had manufactured jurisdiction. Leaving open the possibility that this claim might be stronger after trial, the district court refused to dismiss the indictment before trial. It noted that most courts had been "disinclined to apply such equitable notions with a broad brush," and that the Seventh Circuit had not met the concept of manufactured jurisdiction head on, but had seemed to signal disapproval. 586 F.Supp. 1401–02.

Archer was a Travel Act prosecution in which the court found that all of the interstate and foreign calls were either casual and incidental, or engineered by federal investigators solely to provide a basis for federal jurisdiction. The court reversed the conviction, concluding that Congress did not intend the Travel Act to reach such a case. Does this analysis apply equally well to mail fraud prosecutions? For a case upholding mail fraud counts while dismissing Travel Act counts, see *United States v. Isaacs*, 493 F.2d 1124 (7th Cir. 1974).

5. Although it is still universally called the mail fraud statute, in fact § 1341 is no longer limited to cases involving the use of the mails. It was amended in 1994 to include cases in which the defendant "deposits or causes to be deposited any matter or thing whatever to be sent or delivered by any private or commercial interstate carrier, or takes or receives therefrom, any such matter or thing, or knowingly causes to be delivered by * * * such carrier according to the direction thereon." Although the amendment was justified by the need to protect senior citizens against scams involving the sale of overpriced (or nonexistent) goods using private carriers for delivery and payment, the amendment is not limited to cases involving senior citizens. Rather, the amendment extends the statute to cover a gap created by the widespread use of private delivery services such as Federal Express and UPS that have to some degree displaced the Postal Service. Of course the amended language cannot be justified by the Postal Power, and is based instead upon the commerce clause. Given the Supreme Court's interpretation of Congress's power under the commerce clause, is it necessary that the interstate carrier transport the item across state lines? Several courts have said no. *See United States v. Hasner*, 340 F.3d 1261 (11th Cir. 2003); *United States v. Gil*, 297 F.3d 93 (2d. Cir. 2002); *United States v. Photogrammetric Data Servs., Inc.*, 259 F.3d 229 (4th Cir. 2001). For a discussion of this provision and the interpretative issues it raises, see Peter J. Henning, *Maybe It Should Just Be Called Federal Fraud: The Changing Nature of the Mail Fraud Statute*, 36 B.C. L. Rev. 435, 469–76 (1995).

The 1994 Crime Bill also added a penalty enhancement provision, 18 U.S.C. § 2326, which provides, inter alia, for an additional penalty of up to five years for a conviction of mail or wire fraud "in connection with telemarketing," and an additional penalty of up to ten years if the offense under these sections "victimized ten or more persons over the age of 55" or "targeted persons over the age of 55." With the addition of these provisions, the mail and wire fraud statutes have become even more potent tools to attack telemarketing and scams directed against senior citizens.

6. The materials in this section may have persuaded you that the jurisdictional predicates in mail and wire fraud are construed more broadly than they should be. But before you reach that conclusion, consider the argument that these jurisdictional predicates are actually too narrow, rather than too broad. A good case can be made that the current scope of federal jurisdiction over fraud is unduly narrow, omitting many forms of fraud where there is a clear federal interest. For example, there is no federal jurisdiction over fraudulent schemes based upon their size or their demonstrated effect on interstate commerce. Similarly, no federal jurisdiction presently exists over a fraudulent scheme spanning several states if it is executed by means of personal delivery, even if the delivery crossed state lines. Is there a sufficient federal interest to justify federal prosecution of some additional classes of fraud? If so, what should an expanded federal fraud statute cover?

The federal code proposed by the National Commission on Reform of the Federal Criminal Law, referred to *infra* at 1034, consolidated fraud with other theft offenses and established federal jurisdiction over all of the consolidated offenses on numerous grounds, including use of the mails *or a facility in interstate or foreign commerce* in the commission of the offense, movement of any person across state lines in the commission of the offense, federal ownership of the property in question, and movement of the property in question in interstate or foreign commerce. FINAL REPORT § 1740.[j] It did not, however, extend jurisdiction over these offenses whenever there was an effect on commerce (though it retained this basis for jurisdiction over extortion, thereby preserving the jurisdiction that already existed under the Hobbs Act). FINAL REPORT § 1740(3). It also provided for a number of special bases for jurisdiction based upon the federally protected or regulated character of the victim or the defendant.[k]

The fraud offense proposed by the National Commission did not contain any jurisdictional provisions focusing on the prosecution of state and local government officials. If Congress determines that there is a federal interest in the prosecution of fraud and corruption in state and local government, how should the jurisdictional predicate be defined? See the proposed federal anti-corruption act, *infra* at 319.

Note on the Unit of Prosecution in Mail Fraud Cases

Because the use of mails, rather than the fraudulent scheme itself, is the gist of a mail fraud violation, each use of the mails in furtherance of a fraudulent scheme is a violation of the act. *Badders v. United States*, 240 U.S. 391, 394 (1916). This means that the prosecutor often has the option of charging a large number of counts of mail fraud, which greatly increases the

---

j. Section 1740 provided for jurisdiction under paragraphs (a), (b), (d), (e), (h), (i), (j), (k), and (*l*) of Section 201, which is reprinted at 1034 *infra*.

k. For example, it provided for jurisdiction when the offense was committed by a federal public servant acting under color of office or by an officer or employee of a common carrier, and when the offense was committed by a misrepresentation of United States ownership, guarantee, or issuance of insurance, when the subject of the offense was an employee benefit plan or a registered investment company. FINAL REPORT § 1740(4).

maximum potential penalty. In some cases a large number of counts and a long sentence are clearly justified by the size of the scheme and the number of victims involved. For example, in *United States v. Helms*, 897 F.2d 1293, 1295 (5th Cir. 1990), the defendants were convicted of 41 counts of mail and wire fraud for mailings in connection with a scheme to sell distributorships in nonexistent businesses. There were 629 identified victims who had been defrauded of a total of more than five million dollars. The defendants were sentenced to 60 and 75 years imprisonment.

In other cases, however, there may be no relationship between the number of mailings and the size of the fraud or the number of victims involved. In the context of a fraudulent disability claim, for example, a separate count may be based upon the mailing of each monthly check to the claimant. In *United States v. Brown*, 948 F.2d 1076 (8th Cir. 1991), a defendant who obtained larger Veteran's benefits by fraudulently claiming total rather than partial disability was convicted of 41 counts of mail and wire fraud, permitting a maximum sentence of 205 years.[1] While the payments involved in Brown were substantial and they continued over a period of years, this analysis permits stacking of counts regardless of the size of the payments involved, the number of victims, or the complexity or duration of the scheme.

The Sentencing Guidelines scheme, discussed in Chapter 18 *infra*, decreases the importance of the prosecutor's discretion to charge a large number of counts. Although the maximum penalty is still controlled by the number of counts, subject to that limitation the penalty actually imposed will be determined based upon a series of criteria that focus on nature of the offense (the amount of money involved in the scheme, the impact on the victims, etc.), and on the defendant's criminal history. Should the significance of basing the number of counts on the number of mailings be entirely eliminated? How might this be done?

F.   MAIL FRAUD AND OTHER CRIMES

UNITED STATES v. MAZE

414 U.S. 395, 94 S.Ct. 645, 38 L.Ed.2d 603 (1974).

* * *

MR. CHIEF JUSTICE BURGER, with whom MR. JUSTICE WHITE joins, dissenting.

I join in the dissent of Mr. Justice White * * * but add a few observations on an aspect of the Court's holding which seems of some importance. Section 1341 of Title 18 U.S.C., has traditionally been used against fraudulent activity as a first line of defense. When a "new" fraud develops—as constantly happens—the mail fraud statute becomes a stopgap device to deal on a temporary basis with the new phenomenon, until particularized legislation can be developed and passed to deal

---

1. The defendant's actual sentence, based upon both the mail fraud convictions and one count of obstruction of justice, was 57 months and a three year term of supervised release.

directly with the evil. "Prior to the passage of the 1933 [Securities] Act, most criminal prosecutions for fraudulent securities transactions were brought under the Federal Mail Fraud Statute." Mathews, *Criminal Prosecutions Under the Federal Securities Laws and Related Statutes: The Nature and Development of SEC Criminal Cases*, 39 Geo.Wash. L. Rev. 901, 911 (1971). Loan sharks were brought to justice by means of 18 U.S.C. § 1341, Lynch, *Prosecuting Loan Sharks Under the Mail Fraud Statute*, 14 Ford L. Rev. 150 (1945), before Congress, in 1968, recognized the interstate character of loansharking and the need to provide federal protection against this organized crime activity, and enacted 18 U.S.C. § 891 et seq., outlawing extortionate extensions of credit. Although inadequate to protect the buying and investing public fully, the mail fraud statute stood in the breach against frauds connected with the burgeoning sale of undeveloped real estate, until Congress could examine the problems of the land sales industry and pass into law the Interstate Land Sales Full Disclosure Act, 82 Stat. 590, 15 U.S.C. § 1701 et seq. Coffey & Welch, *Federal Regulation of Land Sales: Full Disclosure Comes Down to Earth*, 21 Case W. Res. L. Rev. 5 (1969). Similarly, the mail fraud statute was used to stop credit card fraud, before Congress moved to provide particular protection by passing 15 U.S.C. § 1644.

The mail fraud statute continues to remain an important tool in prosecuting frauds in those areas where legislation has been passed more directly addressing the fraudulent conduct. Mail fraud counts fill pages of securities fraud indictments even today. Mathews, 39 Geo. Wash. L. Rev., at 911. Despite the pervasive Government regulation of the drug industry, postal fraud statutes still play an important role in controlling the solicitation of mail-order purchases by drug distributors based upon fraudulent misrepresentations. Hart, *The Postal Fraud Statutes: Their Use and Abuse*, 11 Food Drug Cosm. L.J. 245, 247, 261 (1956). Maze's interstate escapade—of which there are numberless counterparts—demonstrates that the federal mail fraud statute should have a place in dealing with fraudulent credit card use even with 15 U.S.C. § 1644 on the books.

The criminal mail fraud statute must remain strong to be able to cope with the new varieties of fraud that the ever-inventive American "con artist" is sure to develop. Abuses in franchising and the growing scandals from pyramid sales schemes are but some of the threats to the financial security of our citizenry that the Federal Government must be ever alert to combat. Comment, *Multi-Level or Pyramid Sales Systems: Fraud or Free Enterprise*, 18 S.D. L. Rev. 358 (1973). * * *

Notes

1. Chief Justice Burger's dissenting statement in *Maze* raises an interesting question. Why did Congress on numerous occasions see fit to enact specific legislation if the conduct was already a federal crime under the mail fraud statute? As Justice Burger noted, the mail fraud statute has been used by federal prosecutors to deal with diverse categories of fraudulent con-

duct—e.g. securities, real estate and credit card frauds. In several such instances Congress subsequently also enacted specific legislation to deal with the particular problem area. In each instance, what did the new statute add or change?

The legislation dealing with the fraudulent use of credit cards is a good example of this process. As originally enacted in 1970, 15 U.S.C. § 1644, made it a federal crime to use any counterfeit, lost, stolen, or fraudulently obtained credit card to obtain goods or services having a retail value aggregating $5,000 in a transaction affecting interstate or foreign commerce. Various amendments were adopted in 1974 that lowered the jurisdictional amount to $1,000, clarified the mens rea requirement, and added five additional sections, creating a series of new offenses related to counterfeit, altered, forged, lost, stolen, or fraudulently obtained credit cards. The sections added later made it an offense to 1) transport such a card in interstate commerce; 2) use interstate commerce to sell such a card; 3) receive, conceal, or use either tickets for interstate or foreign commerce or goods that had moved in interstate commerce if the tickets or goods had been purchased with such a card; and 4) furnish money or property through knowing use of such a card. The jurisdictional amounts in these sections varied.

A comparison of the two versions of § 1644 and the mail fraud act raises a number of interesting questions. What is the federal interest, and does it depend upon the amount of goods and services involved? In exploring the rationale for the $5,000 minimum in the original statute, the Fifth Circuit explained that "Congress ... was concerned for jurisdictional purposes that the credit card transaction affect interstate or foreign commerce ... [and] that federal courts not be involved in frauds involving small amounts that might be handled readily in the state courts." *United States v. Mikelberg*, 517 F.2d 246, 251 (5th Cir. 1975) (holding that aggregation of purchases in interstate commerce was allowed to reach the $5,000 requirement). The 1974 revision extended the statute to cases in which credit cards that had been lost, stolen, etc., were used "to obtain money, goods, services, or anything of value which within any one-year period has a value aggregating $1,000 or more." In one sense this merely recognized the economic impact might be equally severe if credit cards were used in many smaller transactions rather than a single large transaction. However, the statute also reduced the minimum amount to $1,000. Is this amount too small to justify a federal prosecution?

2. Justice Burger's opinion also raises a second important question. After enactment of more specific legislation, such as § 1644, is it appropriate for a federal prosecutor to charge mail fraud as well as a violation of the more specific statute in question? *See United States v. Green*, 494 F.2d 820, 827–28 (5th Cir. 1974) (§ 1644 was intended to expand government capacity to deal with fraudulent credit card schemes, and did not preclude prosecution under mail fraud statute). *See also* Chief Justice Burger's dissent in *Maze*, *supra*. What kinds of problems, if any, arise from bringing such overlapping charges? Should any limitation on penalties be imposed in such cases? One commentator argued that there is a difference between "good gapfilling" and "bad gapfilling:"

Broad statutes such as the mail fraud statute enable prosecutors and courts to fill gaps in the criminal law. Such gapfilling is good when the illicit activity is a new form of fraud that Congress has yet to consider. * * *

In contrast, "bad" gapfilling occurs when prosecutors and courts use the mail fraud statute to fill gaps in existing statutes, undermining the congressional judgment embodied in those statutory gaps. Once Congress has passed "particularized legislation," the mail fraud statute is no longer needed to act as a stopgap. Suppose Congress enacts a credit card statute with a requirement that the fraud be for at least five thousand dollars. Congress has made a specific judgment that credit card fraud for amounts below five thousand dollars does not merit the attention of federal authorities. But if a prosecutor now elects to prosecute a case of credit card fraud involving three hundred dollars under the mail fraud statute, she has undone that congressional judgment. She has used the mail fraud statute to fill a statutory gap intentionally created by Congress. Such gapfilling is bad because it blocks the ability of Congress to place certain conduct beyond the reach of federal criminal law.

Todd E. Molz, Note, *The Mail Fraud Statute: An Argument for Repeal by Implication*, 64 U. Chi. L. Rev. 983, 985–86 (1997). Do you find this distinction convincing? Suppose the purpose of § 1341 is to protect the integrity of the postal system and to prevent its use as an instrument for propagating fraud. Does this affect Molz's distinction?

Following the wave of corporate scandals in 2002, Congress passed the Sarbanes–Oxley Act, which added new business crimes to the federal code as well as increased the penalties for mail and wire fraud. Considering that these increased penalties were part of an act directed at corporate misdeeds, do you think Congress was in some sense indicating to prosecutors that mail and wire fraud should be used against corporate executives? It seems that prosecutors have taken up the call, as the mail and wire fraud statutes have been used in conjunction with the securities and bank fraud offenses in many of the recent prosecutions, *see supra* n. b, p. 162. For a discussion of prosecutorial tactics in these business scandals, see Dale A. Oesterle, *Early Observations on the Prosecutions of the Business Scandals of 2002–03: On Sideshow Prosecutions, Spitzer's Clash with Donaldson over Turf, the Choice of Civil or Criminal Actions, and the Tough Tactic of Coerced Cooperation*, 1 Ohio St. J. Crim. L. 443 (2004). Oesterle points out that in order to avoid the complexity, cost, and risk of prosecuting the "main" charges, prosecutors often use "sideshow" charges, such as mail and wire fraud, technical disclosure violations, money laundering, and obstruction of justice, which are far easier to prove. If a prosecutor doesn't want to—or can't—charge a defendant with the offense that has been tailored for that type of behavior, do you think it is a fair tactic to use these "sideshow" charges?

The next case considers these issues in the context of another statute that overlaps with mail fraud.

UNITED STATES v. COMPUTER SCIENCES CORP.

689 F.2d 1181 (4th Cir. 1982).

Before Murnaghan and Ervin, Circuit Judges, and Wilkins, District Judge.

Murnaghan, Circuit Judge.

* * *

The trial court's approach involved a determination that there had existed a legislative intent, when Congress enacted 18 U.S.C. § 287, the statute outlawing false claims against the government, to make prosecution under 18 U.S.C. § 287 exclusive, and to preclude prosecution thereafter under the subsequently enacted mail fraud and wire fraud statutes for the same activities even though they might, viewed without regard to 18 U.S.C. § 287, meet the description of the crimes of mail and wire fraud.[g] The mail fraud statute, 18 U.S.C. § 1341, was originally enacted in 1872, the wire fraud statute, 18 U.S.C. § 1343, in 1952.

The statute punishing false claims against the United States began its life in 1863,[j] was reenacted as part of a comprehensive revision of the Criminal Code in 1909, and in 1948 was divided into two parts. One of the parts became 18 U.S.C. § 287,[k] which makes it criminal to present false claims against the government. The other part, which punishes false statements to the government, was codified as 18 U.S.C. § 1001.[l]

Perusal of the false claims statute, on the one hand, and of the mail fraud and wire fraud statutes, on the other, discloses no language suggesting mutual exclusivity insofar as prosecution is concerned. The district court placed great reliance on the cases of *Simpson v. United States*, 435 U.S. 6, 98 S.Ct. 909 (1978), and *Busic v. United States*, 446 U.S. 398, 100 S.Ct. 1747 (1980). However, those cases dealt with situations where a statute includes within its language its own enhanced

g. An implication of the district court's rationale is that, even if 18 U.S.C. § 287 were, for some reason, ruled invalid or inapplicable, or if it were repealed, there could still be no mail fraud or wire fraud prosecution, where the government is the defrauded person, although all the requirements spelled out in the mail and wire fraud statutes would be fully satisfied.

j. Since the mail fraud and wire fraud statutes did not exist in 1863, it requires a great stretch of imagination to attribute an intent to Congress in 1863 prospectively to render inapplicable to frauds against the government any statute which might later be enacted by a subsequent Congress or Congresses.

k. Whoever makes or presents to any person or officer in the civil, military, or naval service of the United States, or to any department or agency thereof, any claim upon or against the United States, or any department or agency thereof, knowing such claim to be false, fictitious, or fraudulent, shall be fined not more than $10,000 or imprisoned not more than five years, or both.

l. Whoever, in any matter within the jurisdiction of any department or agency of the United States knowingly and willfully falsifies, conceals or covers up by any trick, scheme, or device a material fact, or makes any false, fictitious or fraudulent statements or representations, or makes or uses any false writing or document knowing the same to contain any false, fictitious or fraudulent statement or entry, shall be fined not more than $10,000 or imprisoned not more than five years, or both.

punishment provisions (for example, bank robbery with a dangerous weapon has an enhanced punishment as compared to bank robbery alone). Since the particular statute controls and rules out the more general, those cases reach the sensible result that a general enhancement statute (applying to all crimes involving use of firearms) is ineffective as a second enhancer.

Here, however, we have the situation not at all uncommon, as the case of *Block burger v. United States*, 284 U.S. 299, 52 S.Ct. 180 (1932), and its numerous close relatives, demonstrate, of more than one statute infringed by a single act or combination of acts. Dismissal by the district judge of the indictment as to the counts charging wire fraud and mail fraud occurred at a very early stage of the case, before the taking of any evidence and, of course, before any adjudication of guilt. It will be time enough to determine whether the *Blockburger* test,[m] calling for a restriction to a single *punishment,* applies if and when the time should ever arrive when the defendants or some of them are found guilty both of wire fraud or mail fraud, on the one hand, and of false claims against the United States, on the other. Whatever the answer to that question may be, however, it does not relate to the right of the government to prosecute under both a wire fraud or mail fraud statute and the false claims statute. Guilt and punishment are two distinct and separate considerations. Finding nothing in the statutory language itself or in the legislative history of the wire fraud, mail fraud and false claims statutes to require a determination that prosecution under one must be at the expense of prosecuting under the other, or any evidence of an intent to withdraw from one statute a coverage it obviously has standing alone because of a coverage also afforded by another statute, we conclude that dismissal of the wire fraud and mail fraud charges was in error.

* * *

Notes

1. In *United States v. Weatherspoon*, 581 F.2d 595 (7th Cir. 1978), the court rejected an argument that mail fraud could not be charged where the same conduct also violated 18 U.S.C. § 1001 (the false statement statute):

> * * * there is nothing in either the language or the legislative history of the false statements statute, 18 U.S.C. § 1001, reflecting any Congressional intent to create a hierarchy of sanctions that would preempt the application of the mail fraud statute, 18 U.S.C. § 1341, to the submission of false statements to a government agency through the use of the mails. We note that the mail fraud statute has long been used in concert with statutes proscribing the making of false statements to a government agency, and no question has heretofore been raised as to the propriety of doing so as far as we know. After all, the mail fraud statute proscribes different conduct and requires proof of different elements than the false statements statute, and Congress has the right

m. For a statement of the *Blockburger* test, see *infra*, p. 397.

to authorize additional sanctions for abuse of the mails in connection with a scheme to defraud the Government even though the fraud may be separately punished under another federal statute. Finally, we note that Weatherspoon received concurrent sentences under the mail fraud and false statements counts, and thus has little to gain as a practical matter even if we were to adopt her novel view that she could not be prosecuted under the mail fraud statute if her conduct could be reached, in whole or part, under another federal criminal statute. We hold that, by using the mails to submit false statements to a government agency, Weatherspoon subjected herself to separate prosecution and punishment under both the mail fraud and false statements statutes.

581 F.2d at 599–600. Regarding the false statement statute, see generally *infra* pp. 715–56.

2.   Although this position was never adopted by a majority of the lower federal courts, an influential district court decision refused to allow the government to prosecute income tax offenses as fraud. In *United States v. Henderson*, 386 F.Supp. 1048 (S.D.N.Y. 1974), the court observed that the mail fraud act's stopgap function was not applicable in light of specialized "legislation that affords adequate protection of the public interest in the collection of income taxes." 386 F.Supp. at 1053. Each of the numerous tax offenses carried a different penalty and together these provisions evinced a "congressional purpose to confine tax violations to prohibitions and sanctions contained in the comprehensive Internal Revenue Code statutory scheme." 386 F.Supp. at 1054. Judge Weinfeld concluded:

> The policy of the prosecution of fragmentizing charges which center about the filing of an alleged false tax return, by applying the mail fraud statute under three separate counts, two of which include the mailing of the very income tax returns at issue, with the result that a conviction would permit multiple sentences reaching staggering, if not utterly unrealistic, years of imprisonment has its outer limits. In my view the outer limits were set by Congress by grouping the various tax violations and delinquencies in the one chapter of the Internal Revenue Code, referred to as the "hierarchical system of sanctions," which has been recognized by the Supreme Court as "the capstone of a system of sanctions which singly or in combination were calculated to induce prompt and forthright fulfillment of every duty under the income tax law and to provide a penalty suitable to every degree of delinquency."

386 F.Supp. at 1054 (footnotes omitted). Most courts either distinguished *Henderson* or declined to follow it. The majority view is criticized in Ellen S. Podgor, *Tax Fraud–Mail Fraud: Synonymous, Cumulative, or Diverse?*, 57 U. Cin. L. Rev. 903, 925–29 (1989). Professor Podgor argues that allowing prosecutors to charge tax fraud as mail fraud not only enhances the sentence, but also facilitates conviction and effectively incorporates tax fraud as a predicate offense for RICO. The issue has less practical importance, however, because the Department of Justice has issued a guideline stating that only in "exceptional circumstances" will tax fraud prosecutions be approved as prosecutions for mail fraud (and hence as a RICO predicate). United States Attorneys' Manual § 6–4.210 (Mar. 2001). Citing *Henderson*, the Manual states the position "that Congress intended that tax crimes be

charged as tax crimes and that the specific criminal law provisions of the Internal Revenue Code should form the focus of prosecutions when essentially tax law violation motives are involved, even though other crimes may technically have been committed." The MANUAL also notes that exceptions may be made in narrowly defined circumstances. For example, in a tax shelter case where investors were victimized, mail fraud charges might be added in addition (not in lieu of) tax charges in order to support the government's claim for restitution to individual victims of the scheme.

3.   If the prosecutor's motives in "stacking" mail fraud on top of other more specialized charges is to increase the potential sentence, this strategy will generally be less effective under the Sentencing Guidelines system, which focuses more on the conduct involved and less on the charging structure of the indictment. *See infra* 842-53.

4.   One of the other weapons in the Government's arsenal against mail fraud is the use of injunctions under 18 U.S.C. § 1345. This act allows the Attorney General to seek an injunction when a person has violated or is about to violate the mail fraud or wire fraud statutes in order to prevent "a continuing and substantial injury to the United States or to any person or class of persons." 18 U.S.C. § 1345. One of the most bizarre cases involving § 1345 is *United States v. Quadro Corp.*, 928 F.Supp. 688 (E.D. Tex. 1996), in which the Government sought to enjoin Quadro Corporation from marketing a device for detecting missing or hidden objects. Quadro had been successfully selling the Quadro Tracker to schools, police departments, prisons, and interested individuals, claiming that the Tracker could find guns or drugs hidden in lockers, missing people at a distance of 500 miles, explosives hidden in a house, drugs inside the body of an addict, lost golf balls, and even the virus that causes AIDS. *Id.* at 693–94. However, inspection of the device by a team of nuclear physicists revealed only a hollow plastic shell fitted with a retractable antenna; in addition, the computer circuitry that supposedly controlled the device was a piece of paper sealed between two sheets of plastic. *Id.* at 692. After hearing testimony from Government experts that under no known scientific principle could a hollow plastic tube detect a hidden object, the court permanently enjoined Quadro from using the mails or interstate wires to market any device that resembled the Tracker. *Id.* at 699.

Chapter 6

THE HOBBS ACT

INTRODUCTION

The Hobbs Act, 18 U.S.C. § 1951, criminalizes at least three distinct forms of criminal conduct: 1) robbery, 2) extortion by force, threat or fear, and 3) extortion under color of law. In each case, federal jurisdiction exists if the conduct "affects commerce or the movement of any article or commodity in commerce." Note that the Act criminalizes inchoate as well as completed conduct, reaching any conspiracy or attempt to affect commerce by robbery or extortion, as well as any violence or threat of violence in furtherance of a plan to violate the statute.

The Hobbs Act traces its ancestry back to the Anti–Racketeering Act of 1934. In *United States v. Culbert*, 435 U.S. 371 (1978), the Supreme Court rejected the contention that racketeering is an element of the offense under the Hobbs Act, upholding the conviction of a lone individual who attempted to extort money from bank officials. (In a nice bit of irony, he demanded that the money be left at a Goodwill drop box.) The Court discussed the legislative history in some detail. The 1934 Act was part of a package of New Deal legislation intended to respond to increased lawlessness during the Depression (and to the weakness of state and local governments at the time). Although it was enacted at a time when Congress was very concerned about racketeering activities, the 1934 Act was nonetheless written in broad language that nowhere mentioned racketeering. Since the drafters of the legislation had recognized that the term had a broad and amorphous meaning, their failure to include the term racketeering was deliberate. Although the Act referred to "force, violence or coercion" it did not define extortion or robbery.

The Hobbs Act was enacted in response to a decision of the Supreme Court giving the 1934 Act a narrow interpretation.[a] *United States v. Teamsters*, 315 U.S. 521 (1942), held that the 1934 Act did not cover the actions of union truck drivers who exacted money by threats or violence

---

a. The Hobbs Act was named after Representative Samuel F. Hobbs, who introduced the bill.

from out-of-town drivers in return for undesired and often unutilized services. Congress responded by enacting the Hobbs Act. As the *Culbert* Court explained:

> The bill that eventually became the Hobbs Act deleted the exception on which the Court had relied in *Teamsters* and substituted specific prohibitions against robbery and extortion for the Anti–Racketeering Act's language relating to the use of force or threats of force. The primary focus in the Hobbs Act debates was on whether the bill was designed as an attack on organized labor. Opponents of the bill argued that it would be used to prosecute strikers and interfere with labor unions. The proponents of the bill steadfastly maintained that the purpose of the bill was to prohibit robbery and extortion perpetrated by anyone. Although there were many references in the debates to "racketeers" and "racketeering," none of the comments supports the conclusion that Congress did not intend to make punishable all conduct falling within the reach of the statutory language. To the contrary, the debates are fully consistent with the statement in the Report of the House Committee on the Judiciary that the purpose of the bill was "to prevent anyone from obstructing, delaying, or affecting commerce, or the movement of any article or commodity in commerce by robbery or extortion *as defined in the bill.*"

The text, even as illuminated by the legislative history, gives little sense of the breadth of the Hobbs Act's application. As the chapter that follows indicates, there are still controversies about the application of the Hobbs Act in the context of labor relations, and the Act is also used to prosecute a range of conduct, from gas station hold ups to corruption of state governors. Recently, the Act provided the basis for federal jurisdiction over the snipers who terrorized the Washington. D.C. area in 2002. The snipers were originally arrested on Hobbs Act charges based on an extortion note demanding $10 million that was found at the scene of one of the killings. The Attorney General eventually permitted the defendants to be transferred to Virginia state authorities to be prosecuted for capital murder. For a discussion of this case and the jurisdictional issues involved, see Chapter 17 *supra* pp. 802–03.

The materials in this chapter focus primarily on the use of the Hobbs Act to prosecute extortion. Section A addresses the first prong of the statute, which criminalizes extortion by force or threat. Section B considers extortion under color of official right, and its relationship to bribery and political corruption. Section C discusses the jurisdictional requirements under the Hobbs Act, in the context of both extortion and robbery.

Because the federal bribery and gratuities laws apply only to federal officials, federal prosecutions of state and local corruption must be brought under some other provision. The Hobbs Act now appears to be the statute of choice in prosecutions for the acceptance of official gratuities by state and local officials. As you review the materials that follow, consider the implications of charging bribery and gratuities cases under the Hobbs Act, rather than other federal provisions.

18 U.S.C.

§ 1951. Interference with commerce by threats or violence

(a) Whoever in any way or degree obstructs, delays, or affects commerce or the movement of any article or commodity in commerce, by robbery or extortion or attempts or conspires so to do, or commits or threatens physical violence to any person or property in furtherance of a plan or purpose to do anything in violation of this section shall be fined under this title or imprisoned not more than twenty years, or both.

(b) As used in this section—

(1) The term "robbery" means the unlawful taking or obtaining of personal property from the person or in the presence of another, against his will, by means of actual or threatened force, or violence, or fear of injury, immediate or future, to his person or property, or property in his custody or possession, or the person or property of a relative or member of his family or of anyone in his company at the time of the taking or obtaining.

(2) The term "extortion" means the obtaining of property from another, with his consent, induced by wrongful use of actual or threatened force, violence, or fear, or under color of official right.

(3) The term "commerce" means commerce within the District of Columbia, or any Territory or Possession of the United States; all commerce between any point in a State, Territory, Possession, or the District of Columbia and any point outside thereof; all commerce between points within the same State through any place outside such State; and all other commerce over which the United States has jurisdiction.

(c) This section shall not be construed to repeal, modify or affect section 17 of Title 15, sections 52, 101–115, 151–166 of Title 29 or sections 151–188 of Title 45.

———

Although we began this chapter by stating that the Hobbs Act criminalizes three different forms of criminal conduct (robbery and extortion by force as well as extortion under color of official right), and we focus on those aspects of the Hobbs Act in the remainder of the chapter, the Supreme Court has granted certiorari to consider whether the Act also includes an another type of case. One of the questions presented in *National Organization for Women v. Scheidler*, 396 F.3d 807 (7th Cir.), *cert. granted*, 125 S.Ct. 2991 (2005), is whether the Hobbs Act "can be read to punish acts or threats of physical violence against 'any person or property' in a manner that 'in any way or degree * * * affects commerce,' even if such acts or threats of violence are wholly unconnected to either extortion or robbery?" We discuss this issue *infra* at 245.

A. EXTORTION BY FORCE, VIOLENCE, OR FEAR

UNITED STATES v. EDWARDS

303 F.3d 606 (5th Cir. 2002).

Before HIGGINBOTHAM, WEINER, and BENAVIDES, CIRCUIT JUDGES.

BENAVIDES, CIRCUIT JUDGE:

After a long, complex trial, the former governor of Louisiana, his son, and several of his associates were convicted for their roles in various schemes to make money from Louisiana's riverboat gambling license process by exploiting the former governor's apparent ability to influence that process. [This was the third prosecution of governor Edwin Edwards, who had previously won re-election despite being the subject of multiple federal corruption prosecutions. One part of the complicated scheme at issue in this case was a claim that two of the governor's associates–Cecil Brown and Bobby Johnson–had ostensibly represented the governor in extorting money from various individuals who sought approval of riverboat casinos, promising to help them obtain licenses in exchange for money and threatening to make obtaining licenses impossible if they did not pay. Brown and Johnson were convicted of extortion in schemes involving two of the license applicants, LRGC/NORC and Jazz Enterprises, Inc. After discussing various other claims, the court turned to the force, violence or fear prong of extortion.]

A.

The jury also had sufficient evidence on the theory of extortion by wrongful use of fear. Extortion by wrongful use of fear includes fear of economic harm. This harm must take the form of a particular economic loss, not merely the loss of a potential benefit. Brown argues that he did not exploit LRGC/NORC's fear of not receiving a license, as the evidence merely demonstrates that LRGC/NORC willingly paid him in the hope of receiving an extra benefit not available to others. He analogizes the situation to the facts of *United States v. Garcia*, 907 F.2d 380, 385 (2d Cir. 1990), in which the Second Circuit reasoned that a congressman who had taken money from a company could not be convicted of extortion absent any evidence that the company was making the payments out of fear. By paying the congressman, the Second Circuit held, the victim "was purchasing an advocate, not buying off a thug." This was "not the stuff of which extortion is made."

We disagree that this case is similar to *Garcia*. Instead, we find *United States v. Collins*, 78 F.3d 1021 (6th Cir. 1996), more instructive. In *Collins*, the Sixth Circuit refused to follow *Garcia* in light of evidence that the persons making the payments had indeed acted out of fear.

Similarly, in the present case, the jury had ample evidence that the victims were acting out of fear of economic loss. For example, it could have credited the testimony of several persons who stated that as a result of Brown's threats, they believed that they would not even have an opportunity to obtain a license. One such person, Allan Morse, testified that: "We all felt the same way. Everybody at every meeting felt that if these payments were not made, then it would automatically shut off any chance that we would receive a license." In light of this evidence we conclude that this is not a situation like *Garcia*, in which the payees were merely attempting to obtain preferential access and thought that, even without the payments, they would have a fair opportunity to compete for the license. To the contrary, unlike *Garcia*, this is the stuff of which extortion is made.

* * *

B.

Like Brown, Johnson argues that the evidence supporting the government's theory of extortion by wrongful use of fear relating to the Jazz scheme was insufficient. He contends that, at most, Jazz principals were placed in fear of the loss of a potential economic benefit, which is insufficient to support an extortion conviction. *See Tomblin*, 46 F.3d at 1384 (stating that "fear of losing a potential benefit does not suffice"). As with Brown, this argument is unavailing. The jury had ample evidence that Johnson capitalized on Jazz's fear that by not making the payments, it would lose the right to compete at all, not merely preferential treatment in an otherwise fair competition. For example, the jury heard Johnson threaten Jazz that if it did not give him a 12.5% cut, "that was all there was to it. You gone with Edwin.... And you know it too and [expletive] you'll be walking the streets." He also stated, "I just hate to see you all lose the license. I mean it's gone and you can write that off you know." At one point, Johnson brought Brown to meet Bradley and introduced Brown as his "partner." He renewed his demand of 12.5%, and pointed to Brown, saying, "You wasn't gonna get none, you was gone, 'til I got in there and got him involved." Bradley testified that he interpreted Johnson's and Brown's statements as threats that Jazz would not receive a license if it did not pay. Based on this evidence, the jury's verdict regarding the Jazz scheme extortion was well supported.

* * *

Notes

1. This case involved the governor of Louisiana, and accordingly charges could have been—and were—also brought against Governor Edwards and his cronies under the color of official right prong of the statute, which is discussed *infra* at 246–61. But the force and fear prong of the Hobbs Act is not limited to the cases arising in the public sector. Indeed

Congress was principally concerned with private sector extortion, and many force and fear prosecutions under the Hobbs Act arise in the private sector.

The application of Hobbs Act extortion to private sector cases raises distinctive policy issues, particularly in cases involving labor disputes (discussed in note 5 below) and commercial bribery. There is no federal law making commercial bribery illegal, and some federal prosecutors have tried to use the Hobbs Act to fill the gap, arguing that these cases fall within extortion by fear. A frequently cited example is *United States v. Capo*, 817 F.2d 947 (2d Cir. 1987) (en banc), which involved a group of employees at Eastman Kodak Company who accepted bribes in exchange for referring individuals for lucrative jobs within the company. Like the *Edwards* court, the *Capo* majority stressed the need to distinguish between mere bribery to get a benefit, and extortion—as the *Edwards* court put it, the difference between buying an advocate or buying off a thug. According to this reasoning, the Hobbs Act applies only when the victim is buying off a thug. In *Capo* the majority took the rather unusual step of finding the evidence insufficient to support the jury's finding that the "victims" felt fear that failure to pay the kickbacks would result in harm, concluding that it showed only that they were seeking preferential treatment. Why is this distinction so important, indeed important enough that the en banc court itself reweighed the evidence?

The *Capo* majority expressed concern that Hobbs Act jurisdiction in such cases would erode the thin line between extortion and garden variety commercial bribery and disrupt the balance between federal and state law:

> It is the sensitive duty of federal courts to review carefully the enforcement of our federal criminal statutes to prevent their injection into unintended areas of state governance. Exercising that duty, we find it necessary to nullify this attempted application of the Hobbs Act to circumstances it was never meant to reach. Incremental extensions of federal criminal jurisdiction arguably present a more pernicious hazard for our federal system than would a bold accretion to the body of federal crimes. At a minimum, a clear extension of federal responsibility is likely to be sufficiently visible to provoke inquiries and debate about the propriety and desirability of changing the state-federal balance. Less abrupt, more subtle expansions, however, such as nearly occurred here, are less likely to trigger public debate, and, yet, over time cumulatively may amount to substantial intrusions by federal officials into areas properly left to state enforcement. By holding that the Hobbs Act does not encompass state-law commercial bribery, we seek to demarcate a point beyond which congress intended federal prosecutors not to pass.

817 F.2d at 955. Two judges dissented, stressing that it is not the role of the court to second guess the jury's interpretation of the evidence. Is the majority's concern justified?

2.   Cases like *Edwards* raise another interesting question: assuming the requisite fear on the part of the victim, does it matter what the victim is afraid of? If the purpose of payments is to obtain *more than* merely fair treatment, should they be treated only as bribery, or may they constitute extortion as well? Professor James Lindgren has suggested that there are three relevant baselines in extortion cases: fair treatment, expected treat-

ment, and status quo. James Lindgren, *The Theory, History, and Practice of the Bribery–Extortion Distinction*, 141 U. PA. L. REV. 1695, 1699 (1993). The victim may fear an economic loss if he does not receive fair treatment, but he may also fear that he will get less than the expected treatment or will lose the status quo. Lindgren's three baselines provide another way to analyze *Capo*. As the en banc court interpreted the evidence, the victims did not fear the loss of fair treatment or expected treatment, or any detriment to the status quo; what they sought was to improve upon the status quo. In *Edwards*, in contrast, the court found that the applicants feared the loss of fair treatment, or a level playing field in consideration for a license.

How does this apply to "victims" who obtained their property interest illicitly? If the baseline against which loss is measured is expected treatment or the status quo, it may not matter that the victim previously sought or obtained preferential treatment. A few cases appear to fit this model, upholding extortion charges under the Hobbs Act where the victim feared that he would lose preferential treatment or a property interest that he had obtained illicitly. *See, e.g., United States v. Rivera Rangel*, 396 F.3d 476 (1st Cir. 2005) (government contractors feared loss of continued preferential treatment from government insider); *United States v. Tomblin*, 46 F.3d 1369 (5th Cir. 1995) (bankers who had fraudulently acquired interest in savings and loan feared losing their interest in the S & L). On the other hand, other courts frame the question in a way that might exclude cases where the defendant seeks to preserve an interest that was gained improperly, asking whether the victims would lose an opportunity "to which they were legally entitled." *United States v. Collins*, 78 F.3d 1021, 1030 (6th Cir. 1996) (discussed in *Edwards*).

3.   As long as a defendant exploits his victim's fear it is not necessary that the defendant make any threat, nor that he have created the fear. *See United States v. Abelis*, 146 F.3d 73, 82 (2d Cir. 1998) (a "defendant need only attempt to exploit a fear to be guilty of attempted extortion; he need not attempt to create it"); *United States v. Collins*, 78 F.3d 1021, 1030 (6th Cir. 1996); *United States v. Knox*, 68 F.3d 990, 996 (7th Cir. 1995).

4.   Efforts to use the Hobbs Act and civil RICO to challenge abortion clinic violence led to a Supreme Court decision giving a limited meaning to the phrase "obtaining property" under the Hobbs Act.

In *Scheidler v. National Organization for Women, Inc.*, 537 U.S. 393 (2003), after a seven week civil trial, the jury found defendants responsible for a pattern of racketeering activity including 21 violations of the Hobbs Act, as well as many violations of state extortion law, the Travel Act, and related attempt and conspiracy counts. The Hobbs Act defines extortion as "the obtaining of property from another, with his consent, induced by wrongful use of actual or threatened force, violence, or fear. . . ." Writing for eight members of the Court, the Chief Justice concluded that the defendants' conduct did not fall within this definition because they did not "obtain" property from the plaintiffs. The Court emphasized both the language of the act and its legislative history. Both of the two sources upon which Congress based the Hobbs Act—the New York Penal Code and the Field Code— defined extortion as obtaining property from another, and this entailed both deprivation and acquisition of property. Although the defendants interfered with, disrupted, and in some cases completely deprived the plaintiffs of their ability to exercise their property rights, they did not acquire the property. They "neither pursued nor received 'something of value from' respondents that they could exercise, transfer, or sell." Defining the defendants' conduct as extortion would eliminate the requirement that property must be obtained, and also erase the distinction between extortion and the distinct crime of coercion. Under the New York Penal Code coercion was a separate and lesser offense when Congress drafted the Hobbs Act. The distinction between extortion and coercion was "clearly drawn in New York law," and the Anti–Racketeering Act of 1934 (based on New York law) included both extortion and coercion. But when Congress replaced the Anti–Racketeering Act with the Hobbs Act, it included extortion but not coercion.

The Court recognized the apparent tension between its statements in prior Hobbs Act cases, and explained how they should be reconciled. In *Culbert* (discussed *supra* at 237) the Court stated that Congress intended to use all of its constitutional power in the Hobbs Act, but other Hobbs Act cases apply the rule of lenity. The Court noted that the statement in *Culbert* referred to Congress's intention to employ the full scope of its power under the commerce clause. Here, however, there was no claim that the conduct in question did not affect interstate commerce, and the rule of lenity was appropriate to determine which of two rational readings of the statute to adopt. Accordingly the Court concluded that "[i]f the distinction between extortion and coercion, which we find controls these cases, is to be abandoned, such a significant expansion of the law's coverage must come from Congress, and not from the courts."

Justice Ginsburg concurred in an opinion joined by Justice Breyer. She emphasized that the principal effect of the Court's decision would be in other cases pursued under RICO. In light of the severe criminal penalties and hefty civil liability available under RICO, she stated her view that the Court was "rightly reluctant" to extend RICO's domain further by endorsing the lower courts' expansive definition of extortion. In a footnote she noted the possibility that the plaintiffs' interpretation would have made the Hobbs Act—and thus RICO—applicable to the civil rights sit-ins.

Justice Stevens dissented, arguing that the majority appeared to limit extortion under the Hobbs Act to the acquisition of tangible property, despite decades of lower court decisions to the contrary. He quoted at length from *United States v. Tropiano*, 418 F.2d 1069 (2d Cir. 1969), which held that threats of physical violence aimed at deterring the owners of a competing trash removal company from soliciting customers in certain areas violated the Hobbs Act. The *Tropiano* court concluded that the right to solicit customers was a property right under the Hobbs Act. This analysis has been widely followed by the lower federal courts, and Stevens argued that uniform construction of the Act should remain the law unless Congress decides to amend the statute. That is especially true, he reasoned, since both the Supreme Court and lower courts have recognized that Congress intended the Hobbs Act to be given a broad construction. Justice Stevens predicted that the principal beneficiaries of the Court's decision would be the professional criminals who were the original target of the Hobbs Act and the legislation it superseded. In a footnote, he noted that Congress had overturned the Supreme Court's narrow reading of the mail fraud statute despite a similar unbroken pattern of lower court decisions (see *supra* at 168–71), and he commented that "Congress remains free to correct the Court's error in these cases as well."

As noted *supra* at 239, the Supreme Court has granted certiorari again in the *Scheidler* case to resolve the question whether the Hobbs Act covers not only robbery and extortion, but also acts or threats of physical violence against person or property in a manner that obstructs or affects commerce, even if such acts or threats of violence are wholly unconnected to either extortion or robbery. If you reread the statutory language, *supra* at 239, you will see that there's a good argument that cases like *Scheidler* still fall within the Hobbs Act if force or violence was used or threatened in a way that would affect interstate commerce, even though this conduct does not constitute extortion as that term was defined by *Scheidler II*.

5. In the context of labor disputes, the major concern is reconciling the Hobbs Act and the complex statutory scheme, administered by the National Labor Relations Board, that regulates labor relations and contemplates that rough tactics may sometimes be used. In *United States v. Enmons*, 410 U.S. 396 (1973), the Supreme Court held that the Hobbs Act "does not apply to the use of force to achieve legitimate labor ends." *Id.* at 401. On the other hand, the Court also made it clear that even in the labor context the Hobbs Act would reach violence and threats aimed at securing a wrongful purpose, such as obtaining wages for unwanted or fictitious services. The lower courts have continued to observe this distinction, finding some purposes such as personal payoffs to union leaders to be improper, and emphasizing the role of the collective bargaining agreement in determining the legitimacy or wrongfulness of various demands. For example, in *United States v. Douglas*, 398 F.3d 407 (6th Cir. 2005), the indictment charged that union representatives violated the Hobbs Act when they demanded jobs for their friends in exchange for ending a strike. The court held that the indictment was sufficient to state a Hobbs Act violation because the jobs in question contradicted a provision of the collective bargaining agreement and were illegitimate. *See generally* 1 SARAH N. WELLING ET AL., FEDERAL CRIMINAL LAW AND RELATED CIVIL ACTIONS: CRIMES, FORFEITURE, THE FALSE CLAIMS ACT AND RICO § 15.13 (1998).

6. Should the Hobbs Act ever be used to punish litigation abuses? If so, how extreme would the conduct have to be? In *United States v. Pendergraft*, 297 F.3d 1198 (11th Cir. 2002), the court considered whether the threat of a lawsuit supported by false evidence rose to the level of a Hobbs Act violation. The defendants were a doctor and his business associate who opened an abortion clinic amidst resistance from the county government. What at first glance looked like a case of a fight over abortion rights and the county's use of power to stop the clinic became more complicated when the doctor used false affidavits to threaten a lawsuit against the county. (It was clear the affidavits were false, because they were in direct conflict with the evidence from federal wire taps.) Federal prosecutors indicted the defendants, charging them with attempted extortion for using the false affidavits in an attempt to obtain a monetary settlement from the county. The court found that though "not 'rightful,'" the defendants' fabrication of evidence did not rise to the level of a Hobbs Act violation:

We recognize that the fabrication of evidence is criminalized by the perjury statute. While the same conduct can violate several statutes, we do not think that Pendergraft and Spielvogel's conduct does. The law jealously guards witnesses who participate in judicial proceedings; witnesses should be "unafraid to testify fully and openly." Because the rigors of cross-examination and the penalty of perjury sufficiently protect the reliability of witnesses, courts have been unwilling to expand the scope of witness liability, since, by doing so, " 'the risk of self-censorship becomes too great.' "

Criminalizing false testimony via the Hobbs Act would expand the scope of witness liability. Witnesses might decline to provide affidavits in questionable lawsuits against a government, fearing that they could be charged with conspiracy to commit extortion if the lawsuit fails. Such a possibility is unsettling, and we do not believe that Congress intended to expand the scope of witness liability in this way. The fabrication of evidence, then, does not make a threat to sue a government "wrongful" within the meaning of the Hobbs Act.

Id. at 1207. As the court notes, it is not clear that the Hobbs Act is the right tool to use against this type of conduct, because other statutes exist to handle abuse of litigation. These include sanctioning perjury and false statements, discussed *infra* Chapter 15, and obstruction of justice, discussed *infra* Chapter 16. Note that the statutes specifically dealing with perjury and false statements are rich with precedents, but neither the language of the Hobbs Act nor any prior case law provides any standards for dealing with the issues that arise in the litigation context. Trying to fit the round peg of litigation abuse into the square hole of the Hobbs Act could lead to conflicts with more fine-tuned bodies of law.

B. EXTORTION UNDER COLOR OF OFFICIAL RIGHT

Though presented as a discussion of the force and fear prong of the Hobbs Act, *Edwards* is also a case of extortion under color of official right. In the following case, the Supreme Court defines the limits of what conduct is necessary for a violation of the official right prong.

EVANS v. UNITED STATES

504 U.S. 255, 112 S.Ct. 1881, 119 L.Ed.2d 57 (1992).

JUSTICE STEVENS delivered the opinion of the Court.

* * *

I

Petitioner was an elected member of the Board of Commissioners of DeKalb County, Georgia. During the period between March 1985 and October 1986, as part of an effort by the Federal Bureau of Investigation (FBI) to investigate allegations of public corruption in the Atlanta area, particularly in the area of rezonings of property, an FBI agent posing as a real estate developer talked on the telephone and met with petitioner on a number of occasions. Virtually all, if not all, of those conversations were initiated by the agent and most were recorded on tape or video. In those conversations, the agent sought petitioner's assistance in an effort to rezone a 25–acre tract of land for high-density residential use. On July 25, 1986, the agent handed petitioner cash totaling $7,000 and a check, payable to petitioner's campaign, for $1,000. Petitioner reported the check, but not the cash, on his state campaign-financing disclosure form; he also did not report the $7,000 on his 1986 federal income tax return. Viewing the evidence in the light most favorable to the Government, as we must in light of the verdict, *see Glasser v. United States*, 315 U. S. 60, 80 (1942), we assume that the jury found that petitioner accepted the cash knowing that it was intended to ensure that he would vote in favor of the rezoning application and that he would try to persuade his fellow commissioners to do likewise. Thus, although petitioner did not initiate the transaction, his acceptance of the bribe constituted an implicit promise to use his official position to serve the interests of the bribe-giver.

official doesn't have to solicit payment

In a two-count indictment, petitioner was charged with extortion in violation of 18 U. S. C. § 1951 and with failure to report income in violation of 26 U. S. C. § 7206(1). He was convicted by a jury on both counts. With respect to the extortion count, the trial judge gave the following instruction:

> "The defendant contends that the $8,000 he received from agent Cormany was a campaign contribution. The solicitation of campaign contributions from any person is a necessary and permissible form of political activity on the part of persons who seek political office and persons who have been elected to political office. Thus, the acceptance by an elected official of a campaign contribution does not, in itself, constitute a violation of the Hobbs Act even though the donor has business pending before the official.

> However, if a public official demands or accepts money in exchange for [a] specific requested exercise of his or her official power, such a demand or acceptance does constitute a violation of the Hobbs Act regardless of whether the payment is made in the form of a campaign contribution."

In affirming petitioner's conviction, the Court of Appeals noted that the instruction did not require the jury to find that petitioner had demanded or requested the money, or that he had conditioned the performance of any official act upon its receipt. The Court of Appeals held, however, that "passive acceptance of a benefit by a public official *is* sufficient to form the basis of a Hobbs Act violation if the official knows that he is being offered the payment in exchange for a specific requested exercise of his official power. The official need not take any specific action to induce the offering of the benefit."

This statement of the law by the Court of Appeals for the Eleventh Circuit is consistent with holdings in eight other Circuits. Two Circuits, however, have held that an affirmative act of inducement by the public official is required to support a conviction of extortion under color of official right. Because the majority view is consistent with the common-law definition of extortion, which we believe Congress intended to adopt, we endorse that position.

II

It is a familiar "maxim that a statutory term is generally presumed to have its common-law meaning." As we have explained, "where Congress borrows terms of art in which are accumulated the legal tradition and meaning of centuries of practice, it presumably knows and adopts the cluster of ideas that were attached to each borrowed word in the body of learning from which it was taken and the meaning its use will convey to the judicial mind unless otherwise instructed. In such case, absence of contrary direction may be taken as satisfaction with widely accepted definitions, not as a departure from them." *Morissette v. United States*, 342 U. S. 246, 263 (1952).

At common law, extortion was an offense committed by a public official who took "by colour of his office" money that was not due to him for the performance of his official duties. A demand, or request, by the public official was not an element of the offense. Extortion by the public official was the rough equivalent of what we would now describe as "taking a bribe." It is clear that petitioner committed that offense. The question is whether the federal statute, insofar as it applies to official extortion, has narrowed the common-law definition.

* * *

Although the present statutory text is much broader than the common-law definition of extortion because it encompasses conduct by a private individual as well as conduct by a public official, the portion of the statute that refers to official misconduct continues to mirror the common-law definition. There is nothing in either the statutory text or the legislative history that could fairly be described as a "contrary direction," *Morissette v. United States*, 342 U. S., at 263, from Congress to narrow the scope of the offense.

* * *

The two courts that have disagreed with the decision to apply the common-law definition have interpreted the word "induced" as requiring a wrongful use of official power that "begins with the public official, not with the gratuitous actions of another." *United States v. O'Grady*, 742 F. 2d, at 691; *see United States v. Aguon*, 851 F. 2d, at 1166 ("'inducement' can be in the overt form of a 'demand,' or in a more subtle form such as 'custom' or 'expectation' "). If we had no common-law history to guide our interpretation of the statutory text, that reading would be plausible. For two reasons, however, we are convinced that it is incorrect.

First, we think the word "induced" is a part of the definition of the offense by the private individual, but not the offense by the public official. In the case of the private individual, the victim's consent must be "induced by wrongful use of actual or threatened force, violence or fear." In the case of the public official, however, there is no such requirement. The statute merely requires of the public official that he obtain "property from another, with his consent, ... under color of official right." The use of the word "or" before "under color of official right" supports this reading.

Second, even if the statute were parsed so that the word "induced" applied to the public officeholder, we do not believe the word "induced" necessarily indicates that the transaction must be initiated by the recipient of the bribe. Many of the cases applying the majority rule have concluded that the wrongful acceptance of a bribe establishes all the inducement that the statute requires. They conclude that the coercive element is provided by the public office itself. And even the two courts that have adopted an inducement requirement for extortion under color of official right do not require proof that the inducement took the form of a threat or demand.

Petitioner argues that the jury charge with respect to extortion allowed the jury to convict him on the basis of the "passive acceptance of a contribution."[18] He contends that the instruction did not require the jury to find "an element of duress such as a demand," and it did not properly describe the quid pro quo requirement for conviction if the jury found that the payment was a campaign contribution.

We reject petitioner's criticism of the instruction, and conclude that it satisfies the quid pro quo requirement of *McCormick v. United States*, 500 U. S. 257 (1991), because the offense is completed at the time when the public official receives a payment in return for his agreement to perform specific official acts; fulfillment of the quid pro quo is not an element of the offense. We also reject petitioner's contention that an affirmative step is an element of the offense of extortion "under color of official right" and need be included in the instruction. As we explained above, our construction of the statute is informed by the common-law

---

18. Petitioner also makes the point that "[t]he evidence at trial against [petitioner] is more conducive to a charge of bribery than one of extortion." Although the evidence in this case may have supported a charge of bribery, it is not a defense to a charge of extortion under color of official right that the defendant could also have been convicted of bribery. Courts addressing extortion by force or fear have occasionally said that extortion and bribery are mutually exclusive, *see, e.g., People v. Feld*, 262 App. Div. 909, 28 N.Y.S.2d 796, 797 (1941); while that may be correct when the victim was intimidated into making a payment (extortion by force or fear), and did not offer it voluntarily (bribery), that does not lead to the conclusion that extortion under color of official right and bribery are mutually exclusive under either common law or the Hobbs Act.* * *

* * * We agree with the Seventh Circuit in *United States v. Braasch*, 505 F.2d 139, 151, n. 7 (1974), cert. denied, 421 U. S. 910 (1975), that " 'the modern trend of the federal courts is to hold that bribery and extortion as used in the Hobbs Act are not mutually exclusive.' "

tradition from which the term of art was drawn and understood. We hold today that the Government need only show that a public official has obtained a payment to which he was not entitled, knowing that the payment was made in return for official acts. [20]

Our conclusion is buttressed by the fact that so many other courts that have considered the issue over the last 20 years have interpreted the statute in the same way. Moreover, given the number of appellate court decisions, together with the fact that many of them have involved prosecutions of important officials well known in the political community, it is obvious that Congress is aware of the prevailing view that common-law extortion is proscribed by the Hobbs Act. The silence of the body that is empowered to give us a "contrary direction" if it does not want the common-law rule to survive is consistent with an application of the normal presumption identified in *Taylor* and *Morissette*.

III

An argument not raised by petitioner is now advanced by the dissent. It contends that common-law extortion was limited to wrongful takings under a false pretense of official right. It is perfectly clear, however, that although extortion accomplished by fraud was a well-recognized type of extortion, there were other types as well. As the court explained in *Commonwealth v. Wilson*, 30 Pa. Super. 26 (1906), an extortion case involving a payment by a would-be brothel owner to a police captain to ensure the opening of her house:

> "The form of extortion most commonly dealt with in the decisions is the corrupt taking by a person in office of a fee for services which should be rendered gratuitously; or when compensation is permissible, of a larger fee than the law justifies, or a fee not yet due; but this is not a complete definition of the offense, by which I mean that it does not include every form of common-law extortion."

* * *

The dissent's theory notwithstanding, not one of the cases it cites holds that the public official is innocent unless he has deceived the payor by representing that the payment was proper. Indeed, none makes any reference to the state of mind of the payor, and none states that a "false pretense" is an element of the offense. Instead, those cases merely support the proposition that the services for which the fee is paid must be official and that the official must not be entitled to the fee that he collected-both elements of the offense that are clearly satisfied in this case. The complete absence of support for the dissent's thesis presumably explains why it was not advanced by petitioner in the District Court

---

20. The dissent states that we have "simply made up" the requirement that the payment must be given in return for official acts. On the contrary, that requirement is derived from the statutory language "under color of official right," which has a well-recognized common-law heritage that distinguished between payments for private services and payments for public services. See, for example, *Collier v. State*, 55 Ala. 125 (1877), which the dissent describes as a "typical case."

or the Court of Appeals, is not recognized by any Court of Appeals, and is not advanced in any scholarly commentary.

[JUSTICE O'CONNOR concurred in Parts I and II of the Court's opinion, but expressed no view on the issue raised in Part III because it had not been briefed or argued.]

JUSTICE KENNEDY, concurring in part and concurring in the judgment.

The Court gives a summary of its decision in these words: "We hold today that the Government need only show that a public official has obtained a payment to which he was not entitled, knowing that the payment was made in return for official acts." In my view the dissent is correct to conclude that this language requires a quid pro quo as an element of the Government's case in a prosecution under 18 U. S. C. § 1951, and the Court's opinion can be interpreted in a way that is consistent with this rule. Although the Court appears to accept the requirement of a quid pro quo as an alternative rationale, in my view this element of the offense is essential to a determination of those acts which are criminal and those which are not in a case in which the official does not pretend that he is entitled by law to the property in question. Here the prosecution did establish a quid pro quo that embodied the necessary elements of a statutory violation. I join part III of the Court's opinion and concur in the judgment affirming the conviction. I write this separate opinion to explain my analysis and understanding of the statute.

With regard to the question whether the word "induced" in the statutory definition of extortion applies to the phrase "under color of official right," 18 U. S. C. § 1951(b)(2), I find myself in substantial agreement with the dissent. Scrutiny of the placement of commas will not, in the final analysis, yield a convincing answer, and we are left with two quite plausible interpretations. Under these circumstances, I agree with the dissent that the rule of lenity requires that we avoid the harsher one. We must take as our starting point the assumption that the portion of the statute at issue here defines extortion as "the obtaining of property from another, with his consent, induced ... under color of official right."

I agree with the Court, on the other hand, that the word "induced" does not "necessarily indicat[e] that the transaction must be *initiated* by the" public official. (emphasis in original). Something beyond the mere acceptance of property from another is required, however, or else the word "induced" would be superfluous. That something, I submit, is the quid pro quo. The ability of the official to use or refrain from using authority is the "color of official right" which can be invoked in a corrupt way to induce payment of money or to otherwise obtain property. The inducement generates a quid pro quo, under color of official right, that the statute prohibits. The term "under color of" is used, as I think both the Court and the dissent agree, to sweep within the statute those corrupt exercises of authority that the law forbids but that nevertheless cause damage because the exercise is by a governmental official.

The requirement of a quid pro quo means that without pretense of any entitlement to the payment, a public official violates § 1951 if he intends the payor to believe that absent payment the official is likely to abuse his office and his trust to the detriment and injury of the prospective payor or to give the prospective payor less favorable treatment if the quid pro quo is not satisfied. The official and the payor need not state the quid pro quo in express terms, for otherwise the law's effect could be frustrated by knowing winks and nods. The inducement from the official is criminal if it is express or if it is implied from his words and actions, so long as he intends it to be so and the payor so interprets it.

* * *

The requirement of a quid pro quo in a § 1951 prosecution such as the one before us, in which it is alleged that money was given to the public official in the form of a campaign contribution, was established by our decision last Term in *McCormick v. United States*, 500 U. S. (1991). Readers of today's opinion should have little difficulty in understanding that the rationale underlying the Court's holding applies not only in campaign contribution cases, but all § 1951 prosecutions. That is as it should be, for, given a corrupt motive, the quid pro quo, as I have said, is the essence of the offense.

Because I agree that the jury instruction in this case complied with the quid pro quo requirement, I concur in the judgment of the Court.

JUSTICE THOMAS, with whom the CHIEF JUSTICE and JUSTICE SCALIA join, dissenting.

The Court's analysis is based on the premise, with which I fully agree, that when Congress employs legal terms of art, it " 'knows and adopts the cluster of ideas that were attached to each borrowed word in the body of learning from which it was taken and the meaning its use will convey to the judicial mind.' " (quoting *Morissette v. United States*, 342 U. S. 246, 263 (1952)). Thus, we presume, Congress knew the meaning of common-law extortion when it enacted the Hobbs Act, 18 U. S. C. § 1951. Unfortunately, today's opinion misapprehends that meaning and misconstrues the statute. I respectfully dissent.

I

[After examining a variety of sources, Justice Thomas concluded that common law extortion under color of office required a pretense that the public officer was entitled to the money or property in question.]

Perhaps because the common-law crime—as the Court defines it—is so expansive, the Court, at the very end of its opinion, appends a qualification: "We hold today that the Government need only show that a public official has obtained a payment to which he was not entitled, *knowing that the payment was made in return for official acts*." (emphasis added). This quid pro quo requirement is simply made up. The Court does not suggest that it has any basis in the common law or the language of the Hobbs Act, and I have found no treatise or dictionary that refers to any such requirement in defining "extortion."

Its only conceivable source, in fact, is our opinion last Term in *McCormick v. United States*, 500 U. S. 257 (1991). Quite sensibly, we insisted in that case that, unless the Government established the existence of a quid pro quo, a public official could not be convicted of extortion under the Hobbs Act for accepting a campaign contribution. We did not purport to discern that requirement in the common law or statutory text, but imposed it to prevent the Hobbs Act from effecting a radical (and absurd) change in American political life.

Because the common-law history of extortion was neither properly briefed nor argued in *McCormick*, the quid pro quo limitation imposed there represented a reasonable first step in the right direction. Now that we squarely consider that history, however, it is apparent that that limitation was in fact overly modest: at common law, McCormick was innocent of extortion not because he failed to offer a quid pro quo in return for campaign contributions, but because he did not take the contributions under color of official right. Today's extension of *McCormick's* reasonable (but textually and historically artificial) quid pro quo limitation to all cases of official extortion is both unexplained and inexplicable-except insofar as it may serve to rescue the Court's definition of extortion from substantial overbreadth.

II

As serious as the Court's disregard for history is its disregard for well-established principles of statutory construction. The Court chooses not only the harshest interpretation of a criminal statute, but also the interpretation that maximizes federal criminal jurisdiction over state and local officials. I would reject both choices.

A

The Hobbs Act defines "extortion" as "the obtaining of property from another, with his consent, *induced* by wrongful use of actual or threatened force, violence, or fear, or *under color of official right*." 18 U. S. C. § 1951(b)(2) (emphasis added). Evans argues, in part, that he did not "induce" any payment. The Court rejects that argument, concluding that the verb "induced" applies only to the first portion of the definition. Thus, according to the Court, the statute should read: " 'The term "extortion" means the obtaining of property from another, with his consent, *either* [1] induced by wrongful use of actual or threatened force, violence, or fear, or [2] under color of official right.' "

* * *

Our duty in construing this criminal statute, then, is clear: "The Court has often stated that when there are two rational readings of a criminal statute, one harsher than the other, we are to choose the harsher only when Congress has spoken in clear and definite language." *McNally v. United States*, 483 U. S. 350, 359–360 (1987). Because the Court's expansive interpretation of the statute is not the only plausible one, the rule of lenity compels adoption of the narrower interpretation. That rule, as we have explained on many occasions, serves two vitally important functions:

> "First, 'a fair warning should be given to the world in language that the common world will understand, of what the law intends to do if a certain line is passed. To make the warning fair, so far as possible the line should be clear.' Second, because of the seriousness of criminal penalties, and because criminal punishment usually represents the moral condemnation of the community, legislatures and not courts should define criminal activity." *United States v. Bass*, 404 U. S. 336, 348 (1971) (citations omitted; footnote omitted).

Given the text of the statute and the rule of lenity, I believe that inducement is an element of official extortion under the Hobbs Act.

Perhaps sensing the weakness of its position, the Court suggests an alternative interpretation: even if the statute does set forth an "inducement" requirement for official extortion, that requirement is always satisfied, because "the coercive element is provided by the public office itself." I disagree. A particular public official, to be sure, may wield his power in such a way as to coerce unlawful payments, even in the absence of any explicit demand or threat. But it ignores reality to assert that every public official, in every context, automatically exerts coercive influence on others by virtue of his office. If the Chairman of General Motors meets with a local court clerk, for example, whatever implicit coercive pressures exist will surely not emanate from the clerk. In *Miranda v. Arizona*, 384 U. S. 436 (1966), of course, this Court established a presumption of "inherently compelling pressures" in the context of official custodial interrogation. Now, apparently, we assume that all public officials exude an aura of coercion at *all* places and at *all* times. That is not progress.

B

The Court's construction of the Hobbs Act is repugnant not only to the basic tenets of criminal justice reflected in the rule of lenity, but also to basic tenets of federalism. Over the past 20 years, the Hobbs Act has served as the engine for a stunning expansion of federal criminal jurisdiction into a field traditionally policed by state and local laws-acts of public corruption by state and local officials. See generally Ruff, *Federal Prosecution of Local Corruption: A Case Study in the Making of Law Enforcement Policy*, 65 Geo. L.J. 1171 (1977). That expansion was born of a single sentence in a Third Circuit opinion: "[The 'under color of official right' language in the Hobbs Act] repeats the common law definition of extortion, a crime which could only be committed by a public official, and which did not require proof of threat, fear, or duress." *United States v. Kenny*, 462 F.2d 1205, 1229, cert. denied, 409

U. S. 914 (1972). As explained above, that sentence is not necessarily incorrect in its description of what common-law extortion did not require; unfortunately, it omits an important part of what common-law extortion did require. By overlooking the traditional meaning of "under color of official right," *Kenny* obliterated the distinction between extortion and bribery, essentially creating a new crime encompassing both.

> "As effectively as if there were federal common law crimes, the court in *Kenny* ... amend[ed] the Hobbs Act and [brought] into existence a new crime—local bribery affecting interstate commerce. Hereafter, for purposes of Hobbs Act prosecutions, such bribery was to be called extortion. The federal policing of state corruption had begun." J. Noonan, Bribes 586 (1984).

After *Kenny*, federal prosecutors came to view the Hobbs Act as a license for ferreting out all wrongdoing at the state and local level— " 'a special code of integrity for public officials.' " *United States v. O'Grady*, 742 F. 2d 682, 694 (CA2 1984) (en banc) (quoting letter from Raymond J. Dearie, U. S. Attorney for the Eastern District of New York, to the United States Court of Appeals for the Second Circuit, dated Jan. 21, 1983). In short order, most other circuits followed *Kenny's* lead and upheld, based on a bribery rationale, the Hobbs Act extortion convictions of an astonishing variety of state and local officials, from a state governor down to a local policeman.

Our precedents, to be sure, suggest that Congress enjoys broad constitutional power to legislate in areas traditionally regulated by the States—power that apparently extends even to the direct regulation of the qualifications, tenure, and conduct of state governmental officials. As we emphasized only last Term, however, concerns of federalism require us to give a narrow construction to federal legislation in such sensitive areas unless Congress' contrary intent is "unmistakably clear in the language of the statute." *Gregory v. Ashcroft*, 501 U. S. 452, 460 (1991). "This plain statement rule is nothing more than an acknowledgment that the States retain substantial sovereign powers under our constitutional scheme, powers with which Congress does not readily interfere." *Gregory's* teaching is straightforward: because we "assume Congress does not exercise lightly" its extraordinary power to regulate state officials, we will construe ambiguous statutory provisions in the least intrusive manner that can reasonably be inferred from the statute.

Gregory's rule represents nothing more than a restatement of established law:

> "Congress has traditionally been reluctant to define as a federal crime conduct readily denounced as criminal by the States.... As this Court emphasized only last Term in *Rewis v. United States*, [a case involving the Hobbs Act's counterpart, the Travel Act] we will not be quick to assume that Congress has meant to effect a significant change in the sensitive relation between federal and state criminal jurisdiction. In traditionally sensitive areas, such as legislation affecting the federal balance, the requirement of clear state-

ment assures that the legislature has in fact faced, and intended to bring into issue, the critical matters involved in the judicial decision." *United States v. Bass*, 404 U. S., at 349 (footnote omitted).

Similarly, in *McNally v. United States*, 483 U. S. 350 (1987)—a case closely analogous to this one—we rejected the Government's contention that the federal mail fraud statute, 18 U. S. C. § 1341, protected the citizenry's "intangible right" to good government, and hence could be applied to all instances of state and local corruption. Such an expansive reading of the statute, we noted with disapproval, would "leav[e] its outer boundaries ambiguous and involv[e] the Federal Government in setting standards of disclosure and good government for local and state officials."

The reader of today's opinion, however, will search in vain for any consideration of the principles of federalism that animated *Gregory, Rewis, Bass*, and *McNally*. It is clear, of course, that the Hobbs Act's proscription of extortion "under color of official right" applies to all public officials, including those at the state and local level. As our cases emphasize, however, even when Congress has clearly decided to engage in some regulation of the state governmental officials, concerns of federalism play a vital role in evaluating the scope of the regulation. The Court today mocks this jurisprudence by reading two significant limitations (the textual requirement of "inducement" and the common-law requirement of "under color of office") out of the Hobbs Act's definition of official extortion.

III

I have no doubt that today's opinion is motivated by noble aims. Political corruption at any level of government is a serious evil, and, from a policy perspective, perhaps one well suited for federal law enforcement. But federal judges are not free to devise new crimes to meet the occasion. Chief Justice Marshall's warning is as timely today as ever: "It would be dangerous, indeed, to carry the principle that a case which is within the reason or mischief of a statute, is within its provisions, so far as to punish a crime not enumerated in the statute, because it is of equal atrocity, or of kindred character, with those which are enumerated."

Whatever evils today's opinion may redress, in my view, pale beside those it will engender. "Courts must resist th[e] temptation [to stretch criminal statutes] in the interest of the long-range preservation of limited and even-handed government." *United States v. Mazzei*, 521 F. 2d 639, 656 (CA3 1975) (en banc) (Gibbons, J., dissenting). All Americans, including public officials, are entitled to protection from prosecutorial abuse. * * *

* * *

Our criminal-justice system runs on the premise that prosecutors will respect and courts will enforce the boundaries on criminal conduct set by the legislature. Where, as here, those boundaries are breached, it becomes impossible to tell where prosecutorial discretion ends and prosecutorial abuse, or even discrimination, begins. The potential for abuse, of course, is particularly grave in the inherently political context of public-corruption prosecutions.

In my view, Evans is plainly innocent of extortion. With all due respect, I am compelled to dissent.

Notes

1. As noted in *Evans*, the Supreme Court concluded in *McCormick v. United States*, 500 U.S. 257 (1991), that proof of a quid pro quo—a promise or undertaking—is an essential element of a Hobbs Act prosecution based upon payments identified as campaign contributions.[b] Writing for the majority, Justice White explained:

> Serving constituents and supporting legislation that will benefit the district and individuals and groups therein is the everyday business of a legislator. It is also true that campaigns must be run and financed. Money is constantly being solicited on behalf of candidates, who run on platforms and who claim support on the basis of their views and what they intend to do or have done. Whatever ethical considerations and appearances may indicate, to hold that legislators commit the federal crime of extortion when they act for the benefit of constituents or support legislation furthering the interests of some of their constituents, shortly before or after campaign contributions are solicited and received from those beneficiaries, is an unrealistic assessment of what Congress could have meant by making it a crime to obtain property from another, with his consent, "under color of official right." To hold otherwise would open to prosecution not only conduct that has long been thought to be well within the law but also conduct that in a very real sense is unavoidable so long as election campaigns are financed by private contributions or expenditures, as they have been from the beginning of the Nation. It would require statutory language more explicit than the Hobbs Act contains to justify a contrary conclusion. Cf. *United States v. Enmons*, 410 U.S. 396, 411 (1973).

> This is not to say that it is impossible for an elected official to commit extortion in the course of financing an election campaign. Political contributions are of course vulnerable if induced by the use of force, violence, or fear. The receipt of such contributions is also vulnerable under the Act as having been taken under color of official right, but only if the payments are made in return for an explicit promise or undertaking by the official to perform or not to perform an official act. In such situations the official asserts that his official conduct will be controlled by the terms of the promise or undertaking.

> This formulation defines the forbidden zone of conduct with sufficient clarity. As the Court of Appeals for the Fifth Circuit observed in

b. Quid pro quo is a Latin phrase meaning the exchange of one thing (quid) for another (quo).

United States v. Dozier, 672 F.2d 531, 537 (1982): "A moment's reflection should enable one to distinguish, at least in the abstract, a legitimate solicitation from the exaction of a fee for a benefit conferred or an injury withheld. Whether described familiarly as a payoff or with the Latinate precision of quid pro quo, the prohibited exchange is the same: a public official may not demand payment as inducement for the promise to perform (or not to perform) an official act."

500 U.S. at 272–73.

2. If a quid pro quo is required, what exactly must the government prove? In *McCormick*, Justice White wrote of "an explicit promise or undertaking by the official to perform or not to perform an official act." 500 U.S. at 257. But in *Evans*, Justice Stevens, writing for the majority, reviewed the evidence and concluded that under those circumstances the official's "acceptance of the bribe constituted an implicit promise to use his official position to serve the interests of the bribe-giver." 504 U.S. at 257. And note that Justice Kennedy's concurring opinion in *Evans* states that "[t]he official and the payor need not state the quid pro quo in express terms, for otherwise the law's effect could be frustrated by knowing winks and nods." 504 U.S. at 274. On the other hand, if nothing explicit is required, will it be too easy for the government to establish an implicit undertaking?

3. Does the quid pro quo requirement apply only to cases involving campaign contributions or does it apply to all Hobbs Act prosecutions based upon color of official right? All the circuits that have considered the issue have adopted the view that the standard for quid pro quo varies, depending on whether the case involved a public official's receipt of a campaign contribution. *Evans* establishes a modified or relaxed implicit quid pro quo standard to be applied to non-campaign contribution cases, but the comparatively strict standard of *McCormick* still governs a public official's receipt of campaign contributions. The prevailing view that *Evans* applies only to non-campaign contribution cases is difficult to reconcile with the fact that *Evans* itself arose out of a payment made to a county commissioner during his reelection campaign. Troubled by this paradox, some courts have recognized that there may be a policy rationale for drawing a distinction depending on whether a case involves payments that are claimed to be campaign contributions:

> We are not convinced that *Evans* clearly settles the question. And we recognize a policy concern which might justify distinguishing campaign contributions from other payments. After all, campaign contributions often are made with the hope that the recipient, if elected, will further interests with which the contributor agrees; there is nothing illegal about such contributions. To distinguish legal from illegal campaign contributions, it makes sense to require the government to prove that a particular contribution was made in exchange for an explicit promise or undertaking by the official. Other payments to officials are not clothed with the same degree of respectability as ordinary campaign contributions. For that reason, perhaps it should be easier to prove that those payments are in violation of the law.

United States v. Giles, 246 F.3d 966, 972 (7th Cir. 2001).

Note that Justice Kennedy's concurring opinion in *Evans* asserts that "[r]eaders of today's opinion should have little difficulty in understanding that the rationale underlying the Court's holding applies not only in campaign contribution cases, but all § 1951 prosecutions." 504 U.S. at 278 (Kennedy, J., concurring). Justice Kennedy's position has the advantage of avoiding the need to characterize payments to determine whether they are subject to a quid pro quo requirement (or a stricter quid pro quo requirement). It has also been suggested that a quid pro quo requirement should be applicable to all Hobbs Act prosecutions in order to parallel the treatment in the federal bribery and gratuities statute, which treats a payment made without any quid pro quo as a far less serious offense than a bribe. Medrith Lee Hager, Note, *The Hobbs Act: Maintaining the Distinction Between a Bribe and a Gift*, 83 Ky. L.J. 197 (1995). The federal bribery and gratuities statute, 18 U.S.C. § 201, is discussed in Chapter 7.

4. Another commentator has suggested that a different set of considerations may play a role in how the Hobbs Act is interpreted:

> Ultimately, how strictly a judge will interpret the quid pro quo requirement will depend partly upon her particular moral and political viewpoints. Professor Lowenstein has drawn a parallel between three theories of political representation and three theories of corruption. The first political theory, the trusteeship theory, regards outside pressure as harmful to the extent that it interferes with a legislator's ability to pursue the objective public interest. This parallels a view of corruption as being that which is immoral. The second political theory, the mandate theory, regards outside pressure as harmful to the extent that it interferes with a legislator's willingness to enact popular preferences. This parallels a view of corruption as being that which thwarts public opinion. The third political theory, pluralism, stresses the importance of a legislator's ability to register accurately the various forces exerted by competing groups. This parallels a view of corruption as being that which is legally defined as such.

> Professor Lowenstein's discussion is useful because it provides a backdrop for understanding how one's political and moral philosophy can affect how rigorous one thinks laws against political corruption should be. Individuals who subscribe to either of the first two political theories, the trusteeship or the mandate theories, presumably will be more alarmed by the fact that wealthy individuals may purchase disproportionate political influence—regardless of whether they do so through exchanges involving quid pro quo arrangements—because disproportionate influence by the wealthy tends to deter a legislator from exercising independent judgment or responding to popular preferences. Conversely, pluralists will be less alarmed by the purchasing of political influence. As Professor Lowenstein explains, under the pluralism model of politics,

> > [t]he public official is seen as a purely passive agent, who responds more or less perfectly to group pressures. Under this conception, preoccupation with the integrity of representatives is beside the point, and there is little sense in a concept like corruption, at least at the policy-making level. Any practice that seriously interferes with the accuracy with which official register the strength of con-

tending forces is perhaps a source of concern, but the pluralist conception of policy as the outcome of a mechanical process provides no basis for assessing the accuracy of the registering of group forces. Accuracy is assumed.

What pluralism considers corrupt, therefore, is simply that which traditionally has been prohibited, such as quid pro quo exchanges with officials, rather than what newer, more expansive theories of public accountability may consider unacceptable.

Peter D. Hardy, *The Emerging Role of the Quid Pro Quo Requirement in Public Corruption Prosecutions Under the Hobbs Act*, 28 U. MICH. J.L. REF. 409, 454–55 (1995). Do you agree that such considerations are likely to play a role in the interpretation of the Hobbs Act? Should they?

5. In *United States v. McLeczynsky*, 296 F.3d 634 (7th Cir. 2002), a private citizen was convicted of extortion under color of official right. McLeczynsky was a private driving instructor who acted as an intermediary between state officials and private individuals who paid the officials to obtain fraudulent permits. What limits, if any, should be placed on the theory that *private citizens* may be prosecuted for aiding and abetting Hobbs Act extortion *under color of official right*? Could the payors themselves be charged with aiding and abetting the government officials who committed the extortion under color of official right? Note that the Hobbs Act is not structured as a bribery statute per se, but rather as an extortion statute, with the payors implicitly treated as the victims of the official's extortionate scheme. In general, victims cannot be charged with aiding and abetting. *See generally* Model Penal Code § 2.06(6)(a) (unless otherwise provided, a person is not an accomplice in the commission of an offense if he is a victim of that offense). Some courts have evaded this principle by defining the payor in Hobbs Act cases as a "non-victim" or "victimizer" when he or she has taken a more active role "beyond the mere acquiescence of a victim," such as soliciting or inducing the payment. *United States v. Spitler*, 800 F.2d 1267, 1276 n. 5, 1277, 1278 (4th Cir. 1986) (affirming conviction for aiding and abetting extortion and conspiracy to commit extortion when defendant authorized his employees to accede to a government official's demands for payments in exchange for awarding his company a government contract and approved their inflated invoices); *see also United States v. Cornier–Ortiz*, 361 F.3d 29, 40 (1st Cir. 2004) (affirming conviction for aiding and abetting extortion because there was evidence that defendant, a manager of a private management corporation, had a payment arrangement with a HUD official in exchange for benefits and therefore "was not an innocent victim at all").

Is there a principled way to distinguish between a true victim and a "non-victim"? Or is this merely another improper extension of the Hobbs Act to cover cases that are really state-law bribery?

6. *Evans* adopted the views advanced Professor James Lindgren in an article entitled *The Elusive Distinction Between Bribery and Extortion: From the Common Law to the Hobbs Act*, 35 UCLA L. REV. 815 (1988). This article contains an excellent review of the law of extortion in England and the United States, as well as a review of the development of the Hobbs Act as a tool for the prosecution of political corruption.

7.   What are the consequences of prosecuting political corruption on the part of state and local officials under the Hobbs Act rather than a statute aimed specifically at bribery and the illegal gratuities? What difference, if any, does it make whether the prosecutor attempts to characterize such conduct as mail or wire fraud, rather than a violation of the Hobbs Act? Note that prosecutions under the Hobbs Act, like those under the mail and wire fraud acts, raise again the question whether corruption in state and local government is an appropriate subject of *federal* enforcement efforts. These issues are explored in Chapter 5 at pp. 171–90 and in Chapter 8.

C. AFFECTING INTERSTATE COMMERCE

The Hobbs Act reaches conduct that "in any way or degree obstructs, delays or affects interstate commerce or the movement of any article or commodity in commerce." 18 U.S.C. § 1951(a). In *Stirone v. United States*, 361 U.S. 212, 215 (1960), the Supreme Court concluded that the Act "speaks in broad language, manifesting a purpose to use all the constitutional power Congress has to punish interference with interstate commerce by extortion, robbery or physical violence." The Act defines commerce in the broadest possible terms, reaching "all . . . commerce over which the United States has jurisdiction." 18 U.S.C. § 1951(b)(3).

In view of the statutory language and the Supreme Court's acknowledgment that the Hobbs Act is intended to employ the fullest extent of federal authority under the commerce clause, the lower federal courts have traditionally held that an actual impact on commerce is sufficient if it is small or even "de minimis."

Can this interpretation of the Hobbs Act be reconciled with the Supreme Court's recent Commerce Clause decisions in *Lopez* and *Morrison, supra* at 30–42? This point is discussed in *United States v. McFarland*, 311 F.3d 376 (5th Cir. 2002), *supra* at pp. 43–54, which should be reviewed at this point. In *McFarland*, a Hobbs Act robbery case, the en banc court—which split 8 to 8—struggled to define the limits of the aggregation principle. Although eight members of the court proposed a test that would allow the aggregation principle to be applied in only a limited category of cases, neither that principle—nor any other—has achieved general acceptance.

Although some concurring and dissenting opinions (and half of the en banc court in *McFarland*) seek to cut back on the reach of the Hobbs Act, all of the courts of appeals at present adhere to the view that a de minimis or slight effect on commerce is still sufficient under the Hobbs Act. In *United States v. Stillo*, 57 F.3d 553, 558 n.2 (7th Cir. 1995), the court explained:

> In invalidating the federal ban on guns in school zones, *Lopez* made clear that not everything is possible under the Commerce Clause. In so holding the Court did not call into question the Hobbs Act which—unlike the school gun ban—is aimed at a type of economic activity, extortion, and contains an express jurisdictional element.

Nor did the *Lopez* decision undermine this Court's precedents that minimal potential effect on commerce is all that need be proven to support a conviction. "Where a general regulatory statute bears a substantial relation to commerce, the de minimis character of individual instances arising under that statute is of no consequence." *Lopez*, 115 S. Ct. at 1629, *quoting Maryland v. Wirtz*, 392 U.S. 183, 197 n. 27.

Stillo is a good example of how far the lower courts have allowed prosecutors to carry this principle. The defendant was a Cook County judge who accepted bribes from defense attorneys to fix cases. The indictment included a Hobbs Act conspiracy charge based upon the judge's agreement to take a bribe to fix a sham case presented by a lawyer who was cooperating with an FBI informant. Although the judge agreed through an intermediary to suppress the evidence against the fictitious defendant in return for an unspecified fee, no bribe was ever paid because the judge decided that the man purporting to be the defendant looked like an FBI plant. The government's theory was that if the judge had accepted the bribe it would have depleted the assets of the lawyer's firm. The court upheld the conviction, noting that the law firm had purchased numerous items in interstate commerce, including a calculator and covers for wills. Since the previous bribes accepted by the judge were $1000–2000 for a felony case, this is the amount by which the firm's assets would have been depleted. Obviously there would have been a negligible effect on interstate commerce.

Other lower court decisions have upheld Hobbs Act convictions involving sums as small or smaller. This is especially apparent in cases involving Hobbs Act robbery charges. *See, e.g., United States v. Brennick*, 405 F.3d 96, 100 (1st Cir. 2005) (upholding Hobbs Act robbery conviction for robbery of a Wal–Mart store where $522.37 was taken from a business with monthly sales of $8.5 million based upon store manager's testimony that the money would have been reinvested in the purchase of goods manufactured outside the state); *United States v. Haywood*, 363 F.3d 200, 202, 210(3d Cir. 2004) (upholding Hobbs Act conviction for robbery of $50 to $70 from a bar that sold beer that had traveled in interstate commerce).

Many of the cases emphasize the principle of aggregation and the "depletion of assets" theory, which finds an effect on commerce where a robbery or extortion deprives the victim of assets that would otherwise have been used for purchases in interstate commerce. For example, in *United States v. Curtis*, 344 F.3d 1057 (10th Cir. 2003), the court rejected a constitutional challenge to a Hobbs Act robbery conviction arising out of eight robberies of retail outlets in which the amounts taken ranged from $15 to $700. The court explained:

> We have repeatedly interpreted the "broad language" of the Hobbs Act to mean that for the Government to obtain a conviction under the Act, the evidence need show only a potential or de minimis effect

on interstate commerce. Simply proving that a robbery depleted the assets of a business engaged in interstate commerce will suffice.

The lower courts are in agreement that the Hobbs Act covers cases where a robbery depletes the assets of a business engaged in interstate commerce, but what about the robbery of an individual? Do the courts treat the depletion of an individual's assets differently than those of a business? If not, what qualifies as a business? The following case explores these issues and illustrates just how far the Hobbs Act can reach.

UNITED STATES v. WILKERSON

361 F.3d 717 (2d Cir. 2004).

Before: MINER, CALABRESI and STRAUB, CIRCUIT JUDGES.

MINER, CIRCUIT JUDGE:

In the early evening hours of September 8, 1997, Bilberto Lopez and his brother, Natividad, were the victims of a "hold up" while they were moving a stove into the basement of a multi-dwelling residential building that they owned in Brooklyn. Instead of complying with their assailant's demand for money, the Lopez brothers resisted. Consequently, both brothers were shot, and Bilberto died on the basement floor from a gunshot wound. Their assailant fled without recovering the $350 to $400 in cash that Bilberto was carrying on his person.

Qasim Duffy and defendant-appellant Linwood Wilkerson were subsequently tried separately in the United States District Court for the Eastern District of New York (Block, J.) for their respective roles in the hold up: Duffy, for being the hold up man who allegedly attempted to rob the Lopez brothers and for killing Bilberto; and Wilkerson, for his alleged role in [among other things, planning the robbery, aiding in the hold up, and driving the getaway car]. Duffy was acquitted. Wilkerson was convicted on: (i) one count of conspiring with Duffy to interfere with commerce by robbery, in violation of the Hobbs Act, 18 U.S.C. §§ 1951 & 3551 et seq.; (ii) one count of aiding and abetting Duffy's attempt to interfere with commerce by robbery, in violation of the Hobbs Act, 18 U.S.C. §§ 2, 1951 & 3551 et seq.; [and other counts].

[On appeal, Wilkerson argued, inter alia, that] the evidence was legally insufficient to support the jury's finding that the attempted robbery/conspiracy, if successful, would have affected interstate commerce, as required by the Hobbs Act. * * * For the reasons that follow, we find all of these arguments to be without merit and affirm the judgment of conviction.

BACKGROUND

Viewing the evidence in the light most favorable to the Government, the evidence presented at trial was as follows: The Lopez brothers owned an eight-unit residential building located at 141 Hull Street in Brooklyn, New York. Two of the eight dwellings were occupied by the Lopez brothers and their families, and the remaining six units were rented out to residential tenants. The basement of the building was used exclusively by the Lopez brothers to store materials used in their local landscaping business as well as personal items. In addition to their landscaping business, the Lopez brothers also worked as part-time dishwashers at a TGI Friday's restaurant on the weekends.

Wilkerson was a plumber who lived in an apartment located at 139 Hull Street. The Lopez brothers had hired Wilkerson several times in the past to perform plumbing work at their building and to repair the van that they used in their landscaping business.

At around 6:50 p.m. [on the night of the hold up], the Lopez brothers and a twelve-year-old boy named Martin "David" Nunez were moving a stove from the hallway of their building into the basement. When they reached the basement, they closed behind them the door leading to the outside. Shortly thereafter, Natividad heard a knock at the basement door and then a voice from behind the door—a person inquiring about renting one of the apartments in the building. When Natividad opened the door, a man entered the basement, pointed a gun at them, announced that "this [was] a hold up," and demanded that they give him whatever money they had. Instead of complying, the Lopez brothers attempted to wrestle the gun away from their assailant while Nunez ran up the stairs. During the ensuing struggle, each of the brothers was shot, and Bilberto was fatally wounded. The robber then ran out of the building without having taken any money. Natividad could not recall whether his assailant was wearing a jacket and was unable to identify Duffy as the robber. Nunez, however, did identify Duffy as the robber.

A few minutes later, [a neighbor] heard the superintendent of her building yelling at her to get the children out of the street because the superintendent had heard gun shots coming from the basement of the Lopez brothers' building. While she was telling the children to get out of the street and go inside, [the neighbor] looked toward the corner of Hull and Rockaway and saw Duffy running around the corner. Immediately thereafter, she saw Wilkerson get into his brown Cadillac and drive off in the same direction.

In late January/early February of 2001, Wilkerson and Duffy were indicted and arraigned for the hold up of the Lopez brothers. The Government later stipulated to a severance, and the two were tried separately in early 2002. While Wilkerson was incarcerated pending trial, he befriended Richard Toney, a federally-sentenced prisoner who taught Bible studies at the prison chapel. Toney testified that Wilkerson asked him for legal advice concerning the latter's upcoming trial and subsequently made several incriminating statements to Toney when he asked Wilkerson to tell him about the facts of Wilkerson's case. When Toney asked Wilkerson if [Duffy] had been involved in the robbery, Wilkerson responded: "[W]e did [it,] me and Duffy did it, but I can't be placed in the basement, they can't place me inside the basement. I didn't actually pull the trigger but they can't place me inside the basement." According to Toney, Wilkerson then told him that "Duffy [had run] out of the basement, run down the street, around the block" and that Wilkerson had gone "around the block, picked Duffy up, [and taken] Duffy somewhere."

Wilkerson's judgment of conviction and sentence was entered on March 18, 2003, and this timely appeal followed.

* * *

II. Interstate Commerce Element of the Hobbs Act Counts

Wilkerson next argues that the evidence supporting his Hobbs Act conviction was legally insufficient in that it did not satisfy the interstate commerce element of the Act. . . .

A. Sufficiency of the Evidence

The Hobbs Act proscribes, inter alia, robberies, attempted robberies, and conspiracies to commit robberies that "in any way or degree obstruct[ ], delay[ ], or affect[ ]" interstate commerce. 18 U.S.C. § 1951(a), (b)(3). "In a Hobbs Act prosecution, proof that 'commerce [wa]s affected is critical since the Federal Government's jurisdiction of this crime rests only on that interference.'" Indeed, "[t]here is nothing more crucial, yet so strikingly obvious, as the need to prove the jurisdictional element of a crime." This "jurisdictional nexus transforms the quintessential state crimes of robbery and extortion into federal crimes." Nevertheless, "it is well established that the burden of proving a nexus to interstate commerce is minimal." Indeed, "[t]he jurisdictional requirement of the Hobbs Act may be satisfied by a showing of a very slight effect on interstate commerce. Even a potential or subtle effect will suffice."

Before turning to the evidence supporting Wilkerson's Hobbs Act conviction and our examination of whether that evidence was legally sufficient, we provide a brief summary of our recent Hobbs Act jurisprudence in which the legal sufficiency of the evidence was challenged. We do so because all of these cases were decided after Wilkerson was convicted, and the outcomes of these cases (and the reasoning supporting those outcomes) explain our conclusion that Wilkerson's Hobbs Act conviction must be affirmed, notwithstanding the exceedingly thin evidence concerning the interstate commerce element.

In *United States v. Elias*, 285 F.3d 183 [(2d Cir. 2002)], the defendant was convicted of robbing $1400 in cash, along with cigarettes, subway MetroCards, telephone calling cards, and food stamps from a neighborhood grocery store in Queens. The evidence that this robbery affected interstate commerce was that the grocery story sold beer that had been brewed in Mexico and the Dominican Republic and fruit that had been grown in Florida and California. In affirming the defendant's conviction, we rejected the argument that the Government was required to show that some of the products sold at the grocery store were purchased directly from out-of-state suppliers. Specifically, we held that "a robbery of a local distribution or retail enterprise may be said to affect interstate commerce if the robbery impairs the ability of the local enterprise to acquire—whether from out-of-state or in-state suppliers—goods originating out-of-state." The rationale for our holding was that the grocery store

> furnished an outlet for goods that move[d] in interstate commerce, and the robbery impaired its financial capacity to draw goods from interstate origins for local resale. Since the evidence at trial established that the [grocery store] stocked goods originating out-of-state, the requisite indirect, minimal effect on interstate commerce was thereby sufficiently established.

In *United States v. Jamison*, 299 F.3d 114 [(2d Cir. 2002)], a divided panel of our court affirmed a Hobbs Act conviction arising out of the attempted murder and robbery of a businessman at his home. The victim was "a part owner of an incorporated retail business ... , which sold clothing, shoes, [pagers], cell phones, CDs, and tapes," and a trafficker in cocaine. The attempted robbery occurred shortly after the victim had returned home from purchasing $15,000 worth of merchandise for his business, carrying approximately $3300 in unspent cash from his shopping trip. In addition to the cash he was carrying with him when he returned home, the victim also had stored approximately $18,000 in cash in a safe in his house.

The defendant showed up at the victim's house with a gun, demanding to know "[w]here[ ] the money" was. At the defendant's trial, the Government sought to satisfy the interstate commerce element of the Hobbs Act by demonstrating the effect that the robbery would have had on the victim's clothing and narcotics businesses. "The [G]overnment's theory was that [the defendant's] attempted robbery, if successful, would have depleted cash that [the victim had] regularly used to purchase items in interstate commerce as inventory for his clothing and cocaine businesses."[5] On appeal, the defendant argued that "the evidence did not allow the inference that [the victim had] intended to use the money in his possession to purchase goods in interstate commerce," and that "where the robbery victim is a private individual, rather than a business, the robbery is less likely to affect commerce, and the [G]overnment must therefore show a 'substantial' effect, rather than a minimal effect," on interstate commerce.

We rejected the first argument and declined to reach the second. In particular, in concluding that the victim had "commingled the moneys coming to him from all sources to be used for all purposes," we relied on his testimony that he had "intended to use the approximately $21,000 he had in cash ... for 'drugs or clothing, whatever.'" With respect to the defendant's argument that the victim's use of the word "whatever" indicated that the victim had intended to use the money for personal expenses, we found that the victim's testimony (when viewed in the light

---

5. The Government established that the items in the victim's clothing inventory were manufactured, inter alia, outside the United States and that the cocaine sold by the victim originated outside of New York. 299 F.3d at 117.

most favorable to the Government) established that "he [had] used [the money] primarily to purchase business inventory for both businesses." Thus, "[t]he jury could draw the inference that, had [the] robbery attempt succeeded in depriving [the victim] of the $21,000 ... he had on hand at his house, this would have substantially diminished his inventory purchases of clothing manufactured [out of state], and cocaine originating [out of state]." Furthermore, because we concluded that "[r]obbing [this particular victim] in his home was no different in its effect on commerce from robbing a place of business," we declined to reach the defendant's argument that a stricter standard should apply for satisfying the interstate commerce element in Hobbs Act prosecutions arising out of the robbery of an individual as opposed to a business.

In *United States v. Fabian*, 312 F.3d 550[(2d Cir. 2002)], another divided panel of our court affirmed a Hobbs Act conviction arising out of the robbery of (and conspiracy to rob) two separate victims, one of whom was a retired taxi cab driver. The defendant, believing that the retired taxi driver was a loan shark, broke into the victim's house and stole several thousand dollars and some jewelry. In affirming the defendant's conviction, we rejected the argument that the interstate commerce element was not met because the retired taxi driver was not, in fact, a loan shark involved in interstate commerce. "What [was] legally relevant [was] whether at the time of the crime, [the defendant] believed he was robbing a loan shark ... , not whether the crimes *actually* involved a loan shark."

On the same day that we affirmed the Hobbs Act conviction in *Fabian*, we reversed the Hobbs Act conviction in *United States v. Perrotta*, 313 F.3d 33 [(2d Cir. 2002)], where the "only connection to interstate commerce [was] that the victim work[ed] for a company engaged in interstate commerce." Such a "link between the crime and interstate commerce," we held, was "simply too attenuated to support federal Hobbs Act jurisdiction." In reaching this conclusion, we "join[ed] our sister circuits in drawing a distinction between the extortion of an individual and the extortion of a business for the purposes of establishing Hobbs Act jurisdiction."[6] To permit the defendant's Hobbs Act

---

6. *See United States v. Lynch*, 282 F.3d 1049, 1053 (9th Cir. 2002) ("the taking of small sums of money from an individual has its primary and direct impact only on that individual and not on the national economy"); *United States v. Nghia Le*, 256 F.3d 1229, 1234–36 (11th Cir. 2001), *cert. denied*, 534 U.S. 1145, 122 S.Ct. 1103, 151 L.Ed.2d 999 (2002); *United States v. Min Nan Wang*, 222 F.3d 234, 239 (6th Cir. 2000) ("a small sum stolen from a private individual does not, through aggregation, affect interstate commerce merely because the individual happens to be an employee of a national company"); *United States v. Quigley*, 53 F.3d 909, 910 (8th Cir. 1995) (no jurisdiction where robbery victims were two indi-

viduals who were en route to a liquor store to make a purchase); *United States v. Collins*, 40 F.3d 95, 100 (5th Cir. 1994) (no jurisdiction found where defendant robbed a computer company executive of his car and his cell phone, even though the robbery might have prevented the victim from attending business meetings or making business phone calls) ("Criminal acts directed toward individuals may violate [§] 1951(a) only if: (1) the acts deplete the assets of an individual who is directly and customarily engaged in interstate commerce; (2) if the acts cause or create the likelihood that the individual will deplete the assets of an entity engaged in interstate commerce; or (3) if the number of individuals victimized or the conviction to stand, we concluded, "would expand the reach of the Hobbs Act to include every robbery or extortion committed." Finally, we identified circumstances in which the interstate commerce element of the Hobbs Act would be satisfied when the target of the defendant was an individual instead of a business: (i) where the victim directly participated in interstate commerce; (ii) where the defendant targeted the victim "because of her status as an employee at a company participating in interstate commerce"; (iii) where the assets of a company engaged in interstate commerce were, or would have been, depleted as a result of the harm or potential harm, respectively, to the individual victim; or (iv) where the defendant targeted the assets of a business engaged in interstate commerce rather than an individual. But we also held that "[m]erely showing employment with a company that [did] business in interstate commerce, without more, stretch[ed] the Hobbs Act too far."

Finally, in *United States v. Silverio*, 335 F.3d 183 (2d Cir. 2003) (per curiam), we affirmed the Hobbs Act conviction of a defendant who attempted to rob a doctor in his apartment, in the belief that the doctor kept a substantial amount of cash from his medical practice there. Specifically, we held that the evidence demonstrated an "interstate nexus because [the doctor] was a direct participant in interstate commerce through his business of treating a worldwide celebrity clientele, because the robbery would have depleted the assets of [the doctor's] business, and because the robbery targeted the assets of his business rather than his personal property." We explained that "in the absence of an actual effect on interstate commerce, a defendant's belief about the nature of his crime may be determinative. But when ... ample effects on interstate commerce [have been] demonstrated, the state of mind of the defendant is not relevant."

With the above precedents in mind, we turn to the evidence introduced by the Government to support the interstate commerce element of Wilkerson's Hobbs Act conviction. At the time of the hold up, the Lopez brothers had been operating their landscaping business for about five years. According to Natividad, the landscaping business was an "informal" business, i.e., it was not incorporated; there was no separate bank account for the business; the business' phone number was the home phone number of one of the Lopez brothers; the income from the business was not reported to the Internal Revenue Service; and no written records were kept for the business. The services performed by the business were clipping trees and mowing and fertilizing lawns for residential, in-state customers. The demands of the business varied with the changing of the seasons, but during the summer, the Lopez brothers worked nine-to-ten hours a day, six days a week.

sum at stake is so large that there will be some 'cumulative effect on interstate commerce' " (footnotes omitted)); *United States v. Buffey*, 899 F.2d 1402, 1406 (4th Cir. 1990) ("Extorting money to be devoted to personal use from an individual does not affect interstate commerce."); *United States v. Mattson*, 671 F.2d 1020, 1025 (7th Cir. 1982) (drawing a nexus by linking an employee with a corporation's ability to purchase goods in interstate commerce "is too indirect").

The Lopez brothers purchased the supplies used in their landscaping business from two local retail stores: Home Depot and Cale Brothers. The Lopez brothers typically purchased their supplies every week or two, typically on Mondays. Natividad testified that items shown in photographs of the basement taken shortly after the hold up were supplies that had been purchased for the landscaping business that were being stored in the basement. These items included clippers, fertilizer, landscaping bags, peat moss, and a lawnmower. A Home Depot employee (who for nine years had managed the garden department in the Brooklyn Home Depot store in which he worked) testified that several of the landscaping supplies contained in the photographs of the basement were carried by his store and other Home Depot stores, although he could not confirm that the items in the photographs had, in fact, been purchased from Home Depot. The Home Depot employee further testified that most of the supplies featured in the photographs of the basement had originated outside New York. For example, the peat moss came from Canada; the lawnmower, from Minnesota; the lawnmower oil, from North Carolina; the fertilizer, from Ohio; and the lime, from somewhere in the southwestern United States.

Natividad also testified about the $350 to $400 Bilberto was carrying when he was killed. Although the hold up occurred on a Monday evening, the Lopez brothers had not yet purchased landscaping supplies for the week. According to Natividad, they were "putting the money in the bank and cashing the checks ... in order to be able to make some payments that [they] had to make." Natividad further testified that they had intended to use this money to "buy the equipment that [they] used in gardening" and to pay for other, family-related expenses. There is no evidence in the record to indicate the source of the money Bilberto was carrying (e.g., the landscaping business, rental income from their building, salary from TGI Friday's, etc.). Finally, Toney testified that Wilkerson had given him a number of reasons for robbing the Lopez brothers:

> [Wilkerson] ... knew these guys because they owned a landscaping company or lawn service or something, that he had worked with these guys before but he did not like the guy that had got killed, they [were] having confrontations as far as money or something but he didn't like the guy that had gotten killed and he knew they always kept money inside this establishment, large amounts of money.

In light of the Hobbs Act cases described above, the totality of this evidence, when viewed in the light most favorable to the Government, establishes a sufficient nexus between the charged offenses and interstate commerce to satisfy the interstate commerce element of the Hobbs Act, albeit barely. Specifically, this evidence would permit a rational juror to infer that: (i) Wilkerson conspired (and aided and abetted an attempt) to rob the assets of the Lopez brothers' landscaping business; (ii) the landscaping business, although it serviced only in-state customers, purchased supplies from an in-state retailer, which had purchased those same supplies from out-of-state wholesalers; and (iii) if the attempted robbery had been successful, it would have depleted assets from the landscaping business that would have been used to buy supplies that traveled in interstate commerce. Under the Hobbs Act precedents discussed above, this evidence was legally sufficient to support Wilkerson's conviction.

Admittedly, several factual anomalies converged to make this a somewhat unusual case. First, the Lopez brothers' landscaping business was not a traditional, incorporated business, such as the grocery store in *Elias*. But we have affirmed Hobbs Act convictions where the victims' businesses did not comply with all of the formalities observed in the legitimate business world and, indeed, even where the victims engaged in the buying and selling of contraband. *See, e.g., Fabian*, 312 F.3d 550 (drug trafficking by one victim and alleged loansharking by the other victim); *Jamison*, 299 F.3d 114 (cocaine trafficking); *cf. United States v. Jones*, 30 F.3d 276 (2d Cir. 1994) (robbery victim was an undercover narcotics officer whose depleted assets were to be used to purchase narcotics). Second, the robbery took place at an individual's residence instead of at his place of business, in contrast to the robbery in *Elias*. But as we observed in *Jamison, Fabian*, and *Silverio*, the fact that a robbery takes place at a residence does not transform the robbery from the robbery of a business into the random robbery of an individual (as was the case in *Perrotta*), so long as the evidence supports the conclusion that the robbery targeted the assets of a business. Third, the amount of money found on the victim was only a few hundred dollars. Given that Wilkerson was charged with the inchoate offenses of conspiracy and attempted robbery, however, the relevant inquiry is not how much money was at the crime scene (or indeed whether there was any money at the crime scene at all), but rather how much money Wilkerson intended to steal and what effect the theft of that amount of money would have had on interstate commerce.

On appeal, Wilkerson argues that there was insufficient evidence to satisfy the interstate element of the Hobbs Act, because "[t]he [G]overnment offered no evidence as to the source of [the] money; [i.e.,] whether it was from [the Lopez brothers'] dishwashing job, from rent, from lawn mowing, or from all of these sources." Given the evidence discussed above, however, this is a red herring. That some or all of the money Bilberto was carrying may have come from a source other than the landscaping business is of no moment, given that a rational juror could have inferred that Wilkerson had targeted the assets of the Lopez brothers' landscaping business and that at least some of the money Bilberto was carrying at the time of the hold up would have been used to purchase out-of-state supplies for that business.

Wilkerson also argues that there was insufficient proof that the money Bilberto was carrying would have been used to purchase out-of-state gardening supplies. Specifically, Wilkerson points to the facts that the Lopez brothers purchased their supplies from both Home Depot and Cale Brothers and that no evidence was introduced concerning the origins of the landscaping materials sold at Cale Brothers. Nevertheless, the testimony from the Home Depot employee established not only that the supplies depicted in the photographs taken of the basement had been shipped to Home Depot from out-of-state suppliers, but also that several of these items (e.g., lime) could have been purchased only from an out-of-state supplier, as there were no local suppliers of these products in New York. Consequently, a rational juror could have inferred that the targeted funds would have been used to purchase landscaping supplies that could have come only from out of state.

Finally, Wilkerson argues that the evidence failed to establish that the Lopez brothers were "targeted" because of their landscaping business. In support of this argument, Wilkerson relies on the fact that, in Toney's testimony, he testified in separate sentences that (i) Wilkerson knew that the Lopez brothers owned a landscaping business, and (ii) Wilkerson knew that they always kept large sums of money inside their house. While Toney's testimony was not a model of grammatical clarity, a rational juror could have inferred from his testimony that Wilkerson had planned to rob the Lopez brothers at their home because he believed they kept large sums of money from their landscaping business there.

In affirming Wilkerson's Hobbs Act conviction based on the evidence that was presented to the jury, we are mindful that we stand on the metaphorical slippery slope, dangerously close to "expand[ing] the reach of the Hobbs Act to include nearly every robbery ... committed." Indeed, were we the first panel to rule on this type of sufficiency-of-the-evidence challenge, we might well reach a different conclusion. But we are not the first panel to address this issue and are bound by the decisions of prior panels until such time as they are overruled either by an en banc panel of our Court or by the Supreme Court. Accordingly, we find that the Government provided sufficient evidence for a rational juror to have "found the essential elements of [the § 1951 count] beyond a reasonable doubt."

Notes

1. As noted in *Wilkerson*, the majority of courts distinguish between the depletion of the assets of an individual and a business when finding an effect on interstate commerce for Hobbs Act purposes. Does this distinction make sense? If an individual is robbed of money they would have used to by a hamburger at McDonald's, is there any less of a de minimis effect on interstate commerce than the court found sufficient in *Stillo, supra* at 261, where a law firm was deprived of funds that it could have used to buy covers for wills? Where does this distinction come from? Recall that the Hobbs Act prohibits robbery and extortion that *"in any way or degree obstructs, delays, or affects commerce or the movement of any article or commodity in commerce."* 18 U.S.C. § 1951(a) (emphasis added). Nothing in this language distinguishes between the robbery of a business and an individual. It appears that the courts are making a policy choice, selecting a point at which to cut off the reach of the Hobbs Act. Indeed, courts have justified the individual/business distinction by arguing that to hold otherwise "would expand the

reach of the Hobbs Act to include every robbery or extortion committed."
United States v. Perrotta, 313 F.3d 33, 37 (2d Cir. 2002). Perhaps there is
also a constitutional rationale to the distinction. One court noted that the
line between individuals and businesses

> is supported by the "noncommercial" character of the activity involved
> in *Lopez* itself (schooling), and by the Supreme Court's recent decision
> interpreting the federal arson statute to be limited to commercial
> buildings, an interpretation adopted in part at least to avoid having to
> decide Congress's power under the commerce clause to make burning
> down a private residence a federal crime, *Jones v. United States*, 529
> U.S. 848, 858–59 (2000).

United States v. Marrero, 299 F.3d 653, 656 (7th Cir. 2002). Are you
persuaded? What if the individual is Donald Trump, whose personal transactions almost certainly exceed those of many small businesses?

2.   Once courts decide to distinguish between individuals and businesses for this purpose, they have to determine what counts as a business. In
Wilkerson, the court found that the robbery of two individuals in their home
was the robbery of a business because the victims had an informal landscaping business. How far do you think this idea would carry—to a teen's
occasional lawn mowing business? A kid's lemonade stand? In what might
seem to be a bizarre twist, some courts have treated individual drug dealers
as a "business enterprise," making it easier to prosecute robberies of drug
dealers under the Hobbs Act. Where the victim was a drug dealer, the courts
have accepted the argument a robbery has depleted the assets of the
narcotics trafficking operation. For example, in *United States v. Williams*,
342 F.3d 350 (4th Cir. 2003), the court upheld a Hobbs Act conviction arising
out of the robbery of a cocaine dealer in which $1,000 was stolen and the
dealer was killed.

It seems clear that the purpose of the Hobbs Act was not to make the
streets safe for drug dealers, and these cases don't make much sense if their
only function is to protect such illegal businesses. In one case involving the
robbery of a drug dealer, the court noted:

> Of course, there is an element of paradox in a prosecution for
> obstructing *illegal* commerce . . . ; one might as an original matter have
> thought that were it not for concerns about encouraging violent activities, such as armed robbery, the obstruction of illicit commerce should
> be rewarded rather than punished. The less protection the law gives
> drug dealers, the higher the price of illegal drugs and so the smaller the
> quantity consumed–the very aim of the "war on drugs."

United States v. Marrero, 299 F.3d 653, 654 (7th Cir. 2002). Is there any way
to make sense of the prosecutors' decision to bring these cases and the
courts' interpretation of the Hobbs Act to permit them? These prosecutions
are often used to reach the violence associated with drug trafficking: the
defendants in both *Williams* and *Marrero* were themselves drug dealers.
Drug violence and turf wars often have collateral consequences such as
random drive-by shootings. Hobbs Act prosecutions are a way to get federal
jurisdiction over these associated crimes, enhancing the sentence of violent
drug offenders. For example, in *Williams* the Hobbs Act charge was part of
an indictment that also included drug trafficking and firearms charges, and

the defendant was sentenced to concurrent terms totaling 45 years. Particularly since federal prisoners must serve at least 87.5% of their sentences, this is likely a much stiffer sentence than the defendant would have received in the state system.

3.   As is the case under other federal statutes, see 23-24, jurisdiction under the Hobbs Act sometimes turns on factors that seem a poor measure of whether there is a federal interest. In *United States v. McCarter*, 406 F.3d 460 (7th Cir. 2005), the defendant was convicted of Hobbs Act attempted robbery after he held up a woman at gunpoint in a parking garage. Finding that the victim was carrying only $13 in cash, the defendant ordered her to drive him to an ATM machine to withdraw additional funds. The robbery was foiled when the victim alerted two bystanders and the defendant ran away. The court found there was jurisdiction solely based on the fact that the ATM card would have been used:

> Had the crime not been interrupted, and [the victim] been forced to withdraw money from the ATM, she would have done so by inserting her card into the ATM, causing an electronic signal to be sent to Ohio, where the transaction would have been processed and a signal dispatched back to the ATM to enable her to withdraw cash from the machine.

> * * * Had [the victim] been forced to withdraw money from an ATM, the withdrawal would have been an interstate transaction, a transaction in commerce.

Is this a good interpretation of the language "affecting commerce"? The court seems to suggest that if the victim had been carrying only cash there would not have been federal jurisdiction. Why not? Wouldn't that cash itself at some point have come from an interstate transaction, such as the use of an ATM machine or a check? As your parents probably told you on more than one occasion, cash doesn't grow on trees, and all of it circulates through the banking system. So where does that analysis take us? Does it mean that taking *any* cash (perhaps the $13 dollars here) affects interstate commerce? Most courts are not going to go that far. Note that the prosecutor didn't charge a completed robbery in this case, even though it appears that the defendant took the $13. Note also that the argument that the ATM withdrawal provided a link to interstate commerce was used as an alternative to the depletion of assets theory, which was not available because the victim was an individual.

4.   The Hobbs Act does not require an actual effect on interstate commerce; a potential effect on commerce is sufficient to trigger jurisdiction. The statute covers anyone who "in any way or degree ... affects commerce ... by robbery or extortion or attempts or conspires so to do...." 18 U.S.C. § 1951(a). Not only does the Hobbs Act proscribe attempted robbery or extortion, but, if the offense is completed, "the government need only prove that the Hobbs Act extortion *potentially* affected commerce." *United States v. Urban*, 404 F.3d 754, 767 (3d Cir. 2005). In *Urban*, city plumbing inspectors were convicted of extorting payments from plumbers whose work they inspected. The court upheld the conviction using the depletion of assets theory, even though many of the plumbers testified that the payments did not actually affect the amount they spent in interstate commerce, because

"extortion which depletes the assets of persons or businesses engaged in interstate commerce is, as a matter of law, a Hobbs Act violation."

What if an effect on commerce is impossible because the "victim" is really a government sting operation? In *United States v. Rodriguez*, 360 F.3d 949, 957 (9th Cir. 2004), the defendant was caught in an undercover sting operation in which he agreed to rob the stash house of a supposed drug dealer. Convicted of conspiracy to interfere with commerce by robbery, the defendant argued that, because the intended robbery victims were non-existent, the government could not show that there was a de minimis effect on commerce. In rejecting this argument, the court stressed that impossibility is not a defense:

> The government need not show "certainty of effect on commerce; a reasonable probability is enough." It is well-established that, for there to be federal jurisdiction, the government need not show that the actual criminal activity had an impact on commerce; rather, the government need only show that "the class of acts has such an impact."

5. Is there a greater justification for stretching the Hobbs Act to cover cases of public corruption? Does it matter which officials are involved? A divided court of appeals held that the government demonstrated a sufficient effect on interstate commerce in the prosecution of a city attorney and his crony in private practice who took bribes to fix DWI cases. In *United States v. Wright*, 797 F.2d 245 (5th Cir. 1986), the government presented expert testimony that "local failure to prosecute DWI cases encourages more drunken driving, which jeopardizes highway safety by causing more accidents, and thus interferes with interstate travel on interstate highways." Judge Brown dissented, arguing:

> The tawdry activities brought to light at trial were undoubtedly unethical, probably criminal, and should not be tolerated in a democratic society. But not every case of small-town corruption is an appropriate target for federal prosecution, and the Hobbs Act appears to be a particularly inappropriate vehicle for the present prosecution.

> The case law under the Hobbs Act requires that it is the illegal act—here the extortion—which must affect interstate commerce. *See United States v. Elders*, 569 F.2d 1020, 1025 (7th Cir.1978) ("more than a speculative attenuated 'one step removed' kind of effect"). I do not take issue with the Court's conclusion that only a minimal connection between the extortion and the effect on interstate commerce is required, but the tenuous connection between "fixed" DWI prosecutions in Monroe, Louisiana and interstate commerce in this case strains even the sturdy lines with which we suspend the legal fictions termed "interstate commerce analysis." Since it must be the effect which the extortion has on interstate commerce, not all of the farfetched contingent consequences, I think we should sound once and for all to United States Attorneys and District Courts not to reach out to the Hobbs Act to bring every crooked small-town officeholder to justice.

After *Lopez* and *Morrison*, courts have continued to affirm convictions in similar cases involving corruption affecting the judicial system. For example, in *United States v. Rubio*, 321 F.3d 517 (5th Cir. 2003) the court found a sufficient nexus to interstate commerce when a bail bondsman and another official conspired with district attorneys to take bribes to fix a variety of cases. The court agreed with *Wright* that fixing DUI cases could affect commerce by causing accidents, and it concluded that fixing drug cases affects commerce because drugs are traded on an international market. *See also United States v. Castleberry*, 116 F.3d 1384 (11th Cir. 1997) (upholding Hobbs Act conviction of a private attorney who took money from DUI clients and paid a cut to the local prosecutor to fix the cases).

Think about the context of these prosecutions: corruption of the state judicial system. On the one hand, the state has a strong interest in its own institutions, which heightens federalism concerns. On the other hand, the involvement of local prosecutors (or the state courts) can make it difficult if not impossible for state and local officials to take action, which certainly strengthens the argument in favor of federal intervention. Perhaps equally important, it seems likely that cases such as *Wright* and *Rubio* are far less numerous than the robbery cases that have excited the greatest resistance from the federal courts in cases such as *McFarland*. It is one thing to open the federal courts to cases involving state and local corruption, especially corruption involving the judicial system, and another to use the federal courts to handle street crime and crimes of violence. Of course these considerations are not reflected in the text of the statute, which provides the same jurisdictional predicate for robbery, extortion by force and fear, and extortion under color of official right. What role should—and do—these considerations play? Do you see any evidence that they are important to federal prosecutors? Do the courts seem any more willing to accept (or cut back on) Hobbs Act jurisdiction in different kinds of cases?

6. Should there be administrative regulation of the use of the Hobbs Act? If so, which kinds of cases should be restricted, and what kinds of guidelines would be appropriate? At present, the United States Attorneys Manual imposes relatively few restrictions on Hobbs Act cases. Consultation with the Organized Crime and Racketeering Section's Labor–Management Unit is required prior to the commencement of prosecution in cases arising out of labor-management disputes. U.S. Dep't of Justice, United States Attorneys Manual 9–131.030 (Oct. 1997). In addition, the Manual states the policy that Hobbs Act robbery "is to be utilized only in instances involving organized crime, gang activity, or wide-ranging schemes." *Id.* at 9–131.040.

The previous version of the Manual, in contrast, also required consultation with the Criminal Division prior to the filing of cases involving extortion under color of official right by a public official's misuse of office, and required written approval of the Assistant Attorney General of the Criminal Division before the filing of Hobbs Act robbery charges, after solicitation of the views of the local prosecutor. U.S. Dep't of Justice, United States Attorneys Manual 9–131.030 (Oct. 1988).

If you were Attorney General, would you reinstitute controls on extortion cases involving public officials? Robbery cases? If you favor more control of prosecutorial discretion in this context, consider whether it is sufficient simply to require consultation, or whether—as was once the case with robbery charges—prior approval should be required before a prosecution is instituted.

Chapter 7

OFFICIAL BRIBERY AND GRATUITIES

INTRODUCTION

The principal federal provision criminalizing bribery of federal officials and the payment or receipt of official gratuities by such officials is 18 U.S.C. § 201. Section 201 is supplemented with a variety of more specific provisions,[a] the most important of which is the federal program bribery provision, 18 U.S.C. § 666.

Section 201(b) covers bribery and 201(c) covers the lesser illegal gratuities offense. Bribery is punishable by up to 15 years of imprisonment, a fine of at least three times the value of the bribe, and disqualification from holding federal office; the lesser gratuities offense is punishable by up to two years imprisonment and a fine. Both bribery and the gratuities offense require proof that 1) something of value was requested, offered, or given, 2) to a federal public official, (3) with illicit intent (though the intent requirement for the two offenses varies). The key distinction between bribery and illegal gratuities is the presence or absence of a quid pro quo. Bribery requires a quid pro quo, official action in exchange for a bribe. The bribery section, 201(b), requires proof that something of value was requested, offered, or given in order to influence an official act. This is a quid pro quo. In contrast, the gratuities provision, 201(c), requires that the thing of value was offered or solicited "otherwise than as provided by law for the proper discharge of official

---

a. There are also a myriad of statutes that deal with the bribery of specific federal officials and bribery in particular settings of federal concern. See, e.g., 7 U.S.C. § 60 (bribery of persons licensed under cotton standards); 7 U.S.C. §§ 85, 87b (bribery of grain inspectors); 15 U.S.C. § 80b–3(e)(2)(a) (bribery of investment advisers); 18 U.S.C. § 152 (bribery in bankruptcy proceedings); 18 U.S.C. §§ 210–11 (1988) (bribery for purpose of obtaining appointive public office); 18 U.S.C. §§ 212–13 (bribery of bank examiners); 18 U.S.C. §§ 214–15 (bribery for purpose of obtaining bank loans); 18 U.S.C. § 217 (bribery to adjust farm indebtedness); 18 U.S.C. § 224 (bribery in sporting contests); 18 U.S.C. § 1510 (bribery of persons engaged in criminal investigations of violations of United States statutes); 29 U.S.C. § 186 (bribery of employees regarding rights in labor disputes and related bargaining); 33 U.S.C. § 447 (bribery of harbor supervisors); 42 U.S.C. § 1320a–7b (bribery of persons administering funds in federal or state health care programs); 47 U.S.C. § 509(a)(2) (bribery of contestants in broadcasted contests of intellectual skill).

duty * * * for or because of any official act performed or to be performed by such public official." In *United States v. Sun Diamond Growers*, reprinted below, the Supreme Court explained this language and compared it to the bribery provisions of the act.

Both the bribery and illegal gratuities provisions criminalize the conduct of both the corrupt public official and the person who pays the bribe or gratuity. As noted in Chapters 5 and 6, that is not the case when official bribery is prosecuted under the Hobbs Act as extortion under color of law or under the mail fraud act.

The bribery and gratuities provisions have been used to prosecute a wide variety of cases. In one case, the director of the Treasury Department's Executive Office for Asset Forfeiture ended up on the wrong side of the law when she was convicted of soliciting jobs for her paramour and his friend in exchange for favorable action on government contracts to update the asset tracking system. *See United States v. Quinn*, 359 F.3d 666 (4th Cir. 2004). The nature of the cases varies over time. For example, there has been a rash of recent prosecutions involving the bribery of immigration officials. For example, *United States v. Carroll*, 346 F.3d 744, 745 (7th Cir. 2003), involved the prosecution of a U.S. foreign service officer in Guyana who was involved in a scheme in which "he coordinated the illegal sale of hundreds of fraudulent visas through local brokers with whom he shared an average of $10,000 in bribe proceeds per visa." In the post–9/11 period, immigration cases of all kinds are receiving greater attention because of increased concerns over public safety and national security, and this is reflected in bribery cases as well as other types of prosecutions.

In the materials that follow, Sections A, B, and C focus on § 201. Section A examines the difference between the crimes of bribery and illegal gratuities, which lies in the intertwined concepts of quid pro quo and corrupt intent. Section B discusses the other two main elements of § 201, the requirement that a "thing of value" be offered, requested, or given to a "federal official." Section C explores the distinction between the offenses under § 201 and campaign contributions and legitimate fees for services. Section D explores the reach of the federal program bribery provision, 18 U.S.C. § 666.

Section 201 is aimed at the bribery of federal officials. There is no general federal statute that addresses the bribery of state and local officials, though (as noted in Sections B and D) bribery of local officials who receive federal grant moneys may be reached either under § 201 or 18 U.S.C. § 666. Rather, the Hobbs Act, mail fraud statute, and Travel Act have been used with great frequency to prosecute such conduct. Bribery of federal officials is punishable under the necessary and proper clause because it interferes with the conduct of the federal program in question. The exercise of federal jurisdiction over the federal official involved (or the official receiving federal funds) is thus part and parcel of the exercise of jurisdiction over the program in question. Thus the federal interest in the bribery of federal officials is quite substantial and direct, and the same is true of federal program bribery involving state and local officials participating in federally funded programs. In contrast, though the federal interest in interstate commerce and the regulation of the mails provided a sufficient basis for the enactment of the Hobbs Act, Travel Act, and mail fraud statute, the federal interest in the prevention of bribery, extortion, and fraud directed against private individuals is less direct and substantial.

In Chapter 8, infra, we consider a proposal to adopt a general federal statute, modeled on § 201, proscribing the bribery of state and local officials. How would such a provision differ from § 666? Is such a provision either necessary or desirable?

§ 201. Bribery of public officials and witnesses[b]

(a) For the purpose of this section—

(1) the term "public official" means Member of Congress, Delegate, or Resident Commissioner, either before or after such official has qualified, or an officer or employee or person acting for or on behalf of the United States, or any department, agency or branch of Government thereof, including the District of Columbia, in any official function, under or by authority of any such department, agency, or branch of Government, or a juror;

(2) the term "person who has been selected to be a public official" means any person who has been nominated or appointed to be a public official, or has been officially informed that such person will be so nominated or appointed; and

(3) the term "official act" means any decision or action on any question, matter, cause, suit, proceeding or controversy, which may at any time be pending, or which may by law be brought before any public official, in such official's official capacity, or in such official's place of trust or profit.

(b) Whoever—

(1) directly or indirectly, corruptly gives, offers or promises anything of value to any public official or person who has been selected to be a public official, or offers or promises any public official or any person who has been selected to be a public official to give anything of value to any other person or entity, with intent—

(A) to influence any official act; or

(B) to influence such public official or person who has been selected to be a public official to commit or aid in committing, or collude in, or allow, any fraud, or make opportunity for the commission of any fraud, on the United States; or

b. Subsections (b)(3)–(4) and (c)(2)–(3), which are omitted, make it a crime to offer a bribe or gratuity to a witness for the purpose of influencing his testimony before a federal court, house of Congress, or agency, and make it a crime for the witness to accept such a bribe or gratuity. Subsections (d) and (e), which are also omitted, contain additional material relevant to (b)(3)–(4) and (c)(2)–(3).

(C) to induce such public official or such person who has been selected to be a public official to do or omit to do any act in violation of the lawful duty of such official or person;

(2) being a public official or person selected to be a public official, directly or indirectly, corruptly demands, seeks, receives, accepts, or agrees to receive or accept anything of value personally or for any other person or entity, in return for: *"in return for"*

(A) being influenced in the performance of any official act;

(B) being influenced to commit or aid in committing, or to collude in, or allow, any fraud, or make opportunity for the commission of any fraud, on the United States; or

(C) being induced to do or omit to do any act in violation of the official duty of such official or person;

* * *

shall be fined under this title or not more than three times the monetary equivalent of the thing of value, whichever is greater, or imprisoned for not more than fifteen years, or both, and may be disqualified from holding any office of honor, trust, or profit under the United States.

Gratuities (c) Whoever— *Gratuities*

(1) otherwise than as provided by law for the proper discharge of official duty—

(A) directly or indirectly gives, offers, or promises anything of value to any public official, former public official, or person selected to be a public official, for or because of any official act performed or to be performed by such public official, former public official, or person selected to be a public official; or

(B) being a public official, former public official, or person selected to be a public official, otherwise than as provided by law for the proper discharge of official duty, directly or indirectly demands, seeks, receives, accepts, or agrees to receive or accept anything of value personally for or because of any official act performed or to be performed by such official or person; *"for or because of"*

* * *

shall be fined under this title or imprisoned for not more than two years, or both.

A. THE DISTINCTION BETWEEN BRIBERY AND GRATUITIES

UNITED STATES v. SUN–DIAMOND GROWERS OF CALIFORNIA

526 U.S. 398, 119 S.Ct. 1402, 143 L.Ed.2d 576 (1999).

JUSTICE SCALIA delivered the opinion of the Court.

Talmudic sages believed that judges who accepted bribes would be punished by eventually losing all knowledge of the divine law. The

Federal Government, dealing with many public officials who are not judges, and with at least some judges for whom this sanction holds no terror, has constructed a framework of human laws and regulations defining various sorts of impermissible gifts, and punishing those who give or receive them with administrative sanctions, fines, and incarceration. One element of that framework is 18 U.S.C. § 201(c)(1)(A), the "illegal gratuity statute," which prohibits giving "anything of value" to a present, past, or future public official "for or because of any official act performed or to be performed by such public official." In this case, we consider whether conviction under the illegal gratuity statute requires any showing beyond the fact that a gratuity was given because of the recipient's official position.

I

Respondent is a trade association that engaged in marketing and lobbying activities on behalf of its member cooperatives, which were owned by approximately 5,000 individual growers of raisins, figs, walnuts, prunes, and hazelnuts. Petitioner United States is represented by Independent Counsel Donald Smaltz, who, as a consequence of his investigation of former Secretary of Agriculture Michael Espy, charged respondent with, inter alia, making illegal gifts to Espy in violation of § 201(c)(1)(A). That statute provides, in relevant part, that anyone who

> "otherwise than as provided by law for the proper discharge of official duty ... directly or indirectly gives, offers, or promises anything of value to any public official, former public official, or person selected to be a public official, for or because of any official act performed or to be performed by such public official, former public official, or person selected to be a public official ... shall be fined under this title or imprisoned for not more than two years, or both."

Count One of the indictment charged Sun–Diamond with giving Espy approximately $5,900 in illegal gratuities: tickets to the 1993 U.S. Open Tennis Tournament (worth $2,295), luggage ($2,427), meals ($665), and a framed print and crystal bowl ($524). The indictment alluded to two matters in which respondent had an interest in favorable treatment from the Secretary at the time it bestowed the gratuities. First, respondent's member cooperatives participated in the Market Promotion Plan (MPP), a grant program administered by the Department of Agriculture to promote the sale of U.S. farm commodities in foreign countries. The cooperatives belonged to trade organizations, such as the California Prune Board and the Raisin Administrative Committee, which submitted overseas marketing plans for their respective commodities. If their plans were approved by the Secretary of Agriculture, the trade organizations received funds to be used in defraying the foreign marketing expenses of their constituents. Each of respondent's member cooperatives was the largest member of its respective trade organization, and each received significant MPP funding. Respondent was understandably concerned, then, when Congress in 1993 instructed the Secretary to promulgate regulations giving small-sized entities preference in obtaining MPP funds. If the Secretary did not deem respondent's member cooperatives to be small-sized entities, there was a good chance they would no longer receive MPP grants. Thus, respondent had an interest in persuading the Secretary to adopt a regulatory definition of "small-sized entity" that would include its member cooperatives.

Second, respondent had an interest in the Federal Government's regulation of methyl bromide, a low-cost pesticide used by many individual growers in respondent's member cooperatives. In 1992, the Environmental Protection Agency announced plans to promulgate a rule to phase out the use of methyl bromide in the United States. The indictment alleged that respondent sought the Department of Agriculture's assistance in persuading EPA to abandon its proposed rule altogether, or at least to mitigate its impact. In the latter event, respondent wanted the Department to fund research efforts to develop reliable alternatives to methyl bromide.

Although describing these two matters before the Secretary in which respondent had an interest, the indictment did not allege a specific connection between either of them—or between any other action of the Secretary—and the gratuities conferred. The District Court denied respondent's motion to dismiss Count One because of this omission. The court stated:

> "[T]o sustain a charge under the gratuity statute, it is not necessary for the indictment to allege a direct nexus between the value conferred to Secretary Espy by Sun–Diamond and an official act performed or to be performed by Secretary Espy. It is sufficient for the indictment to allege that Sun–Diamond provided things of value to Secretary Espy because of his position."

At trial, the District Court instructed the jury along these same lines. It read § 201(c)(1)(A) to the jury twice (along with the definition of "official act" from § 201(a)(3)), but then placed an expansive gloss on that statutory language, saying, among other things, that "[i]t is sufficient if Sun–Diamond provided Espy with unauthorized compensation simply because he held public office," and that "[t]he government need not prove that the alleged gratuity was linked to a specific or identifiable official act or any act at all." The jury convicted respondent on, inter alia, Count One (the only subject of this appeal), and the District Court sentenced respondent on this count to pay a fine of $400,000.

The Court of Appeals reversed the conviction on Count One and remanded for a new trial, stating:

> "Given that the 'for or because of any official act' language in § 201(c)(1)(A) means what it says, the jury instructions invited the jury to convict on materially less evidence than the statute demands—evidence of gifts driven simply by Espy's official position."

In rejecting respondent's attack on the indictment, however, the court stated that the Government need not show that a gratuity was given "for or because of" any particular act or acts: "That an official has an abundance of relevant matters on his plate should not insulate him or his benefactors from the gratuity statute—as long as the jury is required to find the requisite intent to reward past favorable acts or to make future ones more likely."

II

Initially, it will be helpful to place § 201(c)(1)(A) within the context of the statutory scheme. Subsection (a) of § 201 sets forth definitions applicable to the section—including a definition of "official act," § 201(a)(3). Subsections (b) and (c) then set forth, respectively, two separate crimes—or two pairs of crimes, if one counts the giving and receiving of unlawful gifts as separate crimes—with two different sets of elements and authorized punishments. The first crime, described in § 201(b)(1) as to the giver, and § 201(b)(2) as to the recipient, is bribery, which requires a showing that something of value was corruptly given, offered, or promised to a public official (as to the giver) or corruptly demanded, sought, received, accepted, or agreed to be received or accepted by a public official (as to the recipient) with intent, inter alia, "to influence any official act" (giver) or in return for "being influenced in the performance of any official act" (recipient). The second crime, defined in § 201(c)(1)(A) as to the giver, and § 201(c)(1)(B) as to the recipient, is illegal gratuity, which requires a showing that something of value was given, offered, or promised to a public official (as to the giver), or demanded, sought, received, accepted, or agreed to be received or accepted by a public official (as to the recipient), "for or because of any official act performed or to be performed by such public official."

The distinguishing feature of each crime is its intent element. Bribery requires intent "to influence" an official act or "to be influenced" in an official act, while illegal gratuity requires only that the gratuity be given or accepted "for or because of" an official act. In other words, for bribery there must be a quid pro quo—a specific intent to give or receive something of value in exchange for an official act. An illegal gratuity, on the other hand, may constitute merely a reward for some future act that the public official will take (and may already have determined to take), or for a past act that he has already taken. The punishments prescribed for the two offenses reflect their relative seriousness: Bribery may be punished by up to 15 years' imprisonment, a fine of $250,000 ($500,000 for organizations) or triple the value of the bribe, whichever is greater, and disqualification from holding government office. See 18 U.S.C. §§ 201(b) and 3571. Violation of the illegal gratuity statute, on the other hand, may be punished by up to two years' imprisonment and a fine of $250,000 ($500,000 for organizations). See §§ 201(c) and 3571.

The District Court's instructions in this case, in differentiating between a bribe and an illegal gratuity, correctly noted that only a bribe requires proof of a quid pro quo. The point in controversy here is that the instructions went on to suggest that § 201(c)(1)(A), unlike the bribery statute, did not require any connection between respondent's intent and a specific official act. It would be satisfied, according to the instructions, merely by a showing that respondent gave Secretary Espy a gratuity because of his official position—perhaps, for example, to build a reservoir of goodwill that might ultimately affect one or more of a multitude of unspecified acts, now and in the future. The United States, represented by the Independent Counsel, and the Solicitor General as amicus curiae, contend that this instruction was correct. The Independent Counsel asserts that "section 201(c)(1)(A) reaches any effort to buy favor or generalized goodwill from an official who either has been, is, or may at some unknown, unspecified later time, be *in a position to act favorably* to the giver's interests." (emphasis added). The Solicitor General contends that § 201(c)(1)(A) requires only a showing that a "gift was motivated, at least in part, by the recipient's *capacity to exercise governmental power or influence* in the donor's favor" without necessarily showing that it was connected to a particular official act. (emphasis added).

In our view, this interpretation does not fit comfortably with the statutory text, which prohibits only gratuities given or received "for or because of *any official act* performed or to be performed" (emphasis added). It seems to us that this means "for or because of some particular official act of whatever identity"—just as the question "Do you like any composer?" normally means "Do you like some particular composer?" It is linguistically possible, of course, for the phrase to mean "for or because of official acts in general, without specification as to which one"—just as the question "Do you like any composer?" could mean "Do you like all composers, no matter what their names or music?" But the former seems to us the more natural meaning, especially given the complex structure of the provision before us here. Why go through the trouble of requiring that the gift be made "for or because of any official act performed or to be performed by such public official," and then defining "official act" (in § 201(a)(3)) to mean "any decision or action on any question, matter, cause, suit, proceeding or controversy, which may at any time be pending, or which may by law be brought before any public official, in such official's official capacity," when, if the Government's interpretation were correct, it would have sufficed to say "for or because of such official's ability to favor the donor in executing the functions of his office"? The insistence upon an "official act," carefully defined, seems pregnant with the requirement that some particular official act be identified and proved.

Besides thinking that this is the more natural meaning of § 201(c)(1)(A), we are inclined to believe it correct because of the peculiar results that the Government's alternative reading would produce. It would criminalize, for example, token gifts to the President based on his official position and not linked to any identifiable act—such as the replica jerseys given by championship sports teams each year during ceremonial White House visits. Similarly, it would criminalize a high school principal's gift of a school baseball cap to the Secretary of Education, by reason of his office, on the occasion of the latter's visit to the school. That these examples are not fanciful is demonstrated by the fact that counsel for the United States maintained at oral argument that a group of farmers would violate § 201(c)(1)(A) by providing a complimentary lunch for the Secretary of Agriculture in conjunction with his speech to the farmers concerning various matters of USDA policy—so long as the Secretary had before him, or had in prospect, matters affecting the farmers. Of course the Secretary of Agriculture always has before him or in prospect matters that affect farmers, just as the President always has before him or in prospect matters that affect college and professional sports, and the Secretary of Education matters that affect high schools.

It might be said in reply to this that the more narrow interpretation of the statute can also produce some peculiar results. In fact, in the above-given examples, the gifts could easily be regarded as having been conferred, not only because of the official's position as President or Secretary, but also (and perhaps principally) "for or because of" the official acts of receiving the sports teams at the White House, visiting the high school, and speaking to the farmers about USDA policy, respectively. The answer to this objection is that those actions—while they are assuredly "official acts" in some sense—are not "official acts" within the meaning of the statute, which, as we have noted, defines "official act" to mean "any decision or action on any question, matter, cause, suit, proceeding or controversy, which may at any time be pending, or which may by law be brought before any public official, in such official's official capacity, or in such official's place of trust or profit." 18 U.S.C. § 201(a)(3). Thus, when the violation is linked to a particular "official act," it is possible to eliminate the absurdities *through the definition of that term*. When, however, no particular "official act" need be identified, and the giving of gifts by reason of the recipient's mere tenure in office constitutes a violation, nothing but the Government's discretion prevents the foregoing examples from being prosecuted.

The Government insists that its interpretation is the only one that gives effect to all of the statutory language. Specifically, it claims that the "official position" construction is the only way to give effect to § 201(c)(1)(A)'s forward-looking prohibition on gratuities to persons who have been selected to be public officials but have not yet taken office. Because, it contends, such individuals would not know of specific matters that would come before them, the only way to give this provision effect is to interpret "official act" to mean "official position." But we have no trouble envisioning the application of § 201(c)(1)(A) to a selectee for federal office under the more narrow interpretation. If, for instance, a large computer company that has planned to merge with another large computer company makes a gift to a person who has been chosen to be Assistant Attorney General for the Antitrust Division of the Department of Justice and who has publicly indicated his approval of the merger, it would be quite possible for a jury to find that the gift was made "for or because of" the person's anticipated decision, once he is in office, not to challenge the merger. The uncertainty of future action seems to us, in principle, no more an impediment to prosecution of a selectee with respect to some future official act than it is to prosecution of an officeholder with respect to some future official act.

Our refusal to read § 201(c)(1)(A) as a prohibition of gifts given by reason of the donee's office is supported by the fact that when Congress has wanted to adopt such a broadly prophylactic criminal prohibition upon gift giving, it has done so in a more precise and more administrable fashion. For example, another provision of Chapter 11 of Title 18, the chapter entitled "Bribery, Graft, and Conflicts of Interest," criminalizes the giving or receiving of any "supplementation" of an Executive official's salary, without regard to the purpose of the payment. See 18 U.S.C. § 209(a). Other provisions of the same chapter make it a crime for a bank employee to give a bank examiner, and for a bank examiner to receive from a bank employee, "any loan or gratuity," again without regard to the purpose for which it is given. *See* §§ 212–213. A provision of the Labor Management Relations Act makes it a felony for an employer to give to a union representative, and for a union representative to receive from an employer, anything of value. 29 U.S.C. § 186 (1994 ed. and Supp. III). With clearly framed and easily administrable provisions such as these on the books imposing gift-giving and gift-receiving prohibitions specifically based upon the holding of office, it seems to us most implausible that Congress intended the language of the gratuity statute—"for or because of any official act performed or to be performed"—to pertain to the office rather than (as the language more naturally suggests) to particular official acts.

Finally, a narrow, rather than a sweeping, prohibition is more compatible with the fact that § 201(c)(1)(A) is merely one strand of an intricate web of regulations, both administrative and criminal, governing the acceptance of gifts and other self-enriching actions by public officials. For example, the provisions following § 201 in Chapter 11 of Title 18 make it a crime to give any compensation to a federal employee, or for the employee to receive compensation, in consideration of his representational assistance to anyone involved in a proceeding in which the United States has a direct and substantial interest, § 203; for a federal employee to act as "agent or attorney" for anyone prosecuting a claim against the United States, § 205(a)(1); for a federal employee to act as "agent or attorney" for anyone appearing before virtually any Government tribunal in connection with a matter in which the United States has a direct and substantial interest, § 205(a)(2); for various types of federal employees to engage in various activities after completion of their federal service, § 207; for an Executive employee to participate in any decision or proceeding relating to a matter in which he has a financial interest, § 208; for an employee of the Executive Branch or an independent agency to receive "any contribution to or supplementation of salary . . . from any source other than the Government of the United States,"

§ 209; and for a federal employee to accept a gift in connection with the "compromise, adjustment, or cancellation of any farm indebtedness," § 217. A provision of the Internal Revenue Code makes it criminal for a federal employee to accept a gift for the "compromise, adjustment, or settlement of any charge or complaint" for violation of the revenue laws. 26 U.S.C. § 7214(a)(9).

And the criminal statutes are merely the tip of the regulatory iceberg. In 5 U.S.C. § 7353, which announces broadly that no "employee of the executive, legislative, or judicial branch shall solicit or accept anything of value from a person ... whose interests may be substantially affected by the performance or nonperformance of the individual's official duties," § 7353(a)(2), Congress has authorized the promulgation of ethical rules for each branch of the Federal Government, § 7353(b)(1). Pursuant to that provision, each branch of Government regulates its employees' acceptance of gratuities in some fashion. *See, e.g.,* 5 CFR § 2635.202 et seq. (1999) (Executive employees); Rule XXXV of the Standing Rules of the Senate, Senate Manual, S. Doc. No. 104–1 (rev. July 18, 1995) (Senators and Senate Employees); Rule XXVI of the Rules of the House of Representatives, 106th Cong. (rev. Jan. 7, 1999) (Representatives and House employees); 1 Research Papers of the National Commission on Judicial Discipline & Removal, Code of Conduct for U.S. Judges, Canon 5(C)(4), pp. 925–927 (1993) (federal judges).

All of the regulations, and some of the statutes, described above contain exceptions for various kinds of gratuities given by various donors for various purposes. Many of those exceptions would be snares for the unwary, given that there are no exceptions to the broad prohibition that the Government claims is imposed by § 201(c)(1). In this regard it is interesting to consider the provisions of 5 CFR § 2635.202 (1999), issued by the Office of Government Ethics (OGE) and binding on all employees of the Executive Branch and independent agencies. The first subsection of that provision, entitled "General prohibitions," makes unlawful approximately (if not precisely) what the Government asserts § 201(c)(1)(B) makes unlawful: acceptance of a gift "[f]rom a prohibited source" (defined to include any person who "[h]as interests that may be substantially affected by performance or nonperformance of the employee's official duties," 5 CFR S 2635.203(d)(4) (1999)) or "[g]iven because of the employee's official position," § 2635.202(a)(2). The second subsection, entitled "Relationship to illegal gratuities statute," then provides:

> "Unless accepted in violation of paragraph (c)(1) of this section [banning acceptance of a gift 'in return for being influenced in the performance of an official act'], a gift accepted under the standards set forth in this subpart *shall not constitute an illegal gratuity otherwise prohibited by 18 U.S.C. S 201(c)(1)(B)."*

§ 2635.202(b) (emphasis added).

We are unaware of any law empowering OGE to decriminalize acts prohibited by Title 18 of the United States Code. Yet it is clear that many gifts "accepted under the standards set forth in [the relevant] subpart" will violate 18 U.S.C. § 201(c)(1)(B) if the interpretation that the Government urges upon us is accepted. The subpart includes, for example—as § 201(c)(1)(B) does not—exceptions for gifts of $20 or less, aggregating no more than $50 from a single source in a calendar year, see 5 CFR § 2635.204(a) (1999), and for certain public-service or achievement awards and honorary degrees, see § 2635.204(d). We are frankly not sure that even our more narrow interpretation of 18 U.S.C. § 201(c)(1)(B) will cause OGE's assurance of nonviolation if the regulation is complied with to be entirely accurate; but the misdirection, if any, will be infinitely less.

More important for present purposes, however, this regulation, and the numerous other regulations and statutes littering this field, demonstrate that this is an area where precisely targeted prohibitions are commonplace, and where more general prohibitions have been qualified by numerous exceptions. Given that reality, a statute in this field that can linguistically be interpreted to be either a meat axe or a scalpel should reasonably be taken to be the latter. Absent a text that clearly requires it, we ought not expand this one piece of the regulatory puzzle so dramatically as to make many other pieces misfits. As discussed earlier, not only does the text here not require that result; its more natural reading forbids it.

* * *

We hold that, in order to establish a violation of 18 U.S.C. § 201(c)(1)(A), the Government must prove a link between a thing of value conferred upon a public official and a specific "official act" for or because of which it was given. We affirm the judgment of the Court of Appeals, which remanded the case to the District Court for a new trial on Count One. Our decision today casts doubt upon the lower courts' resolution of respondent's challenge to the sufficiency of the indictment on Count One—an issue on which certiorari was neither sought nor granted. We leave it to the District Court to determine whether that issue should be reopened on remand.

It is so ordered.

Notes

1. *Sun Diamond* held that under § 201 both bribery and illegal gratuity require a nexus between the offer or receipt of something of value and some particular official act, and that bribery, but not gratuities, requires a quid pro quo (a Latin phrase meaning the exchange of one thing (quid) for another (quo)). In attempting to explain the distinction between bribery and gratuities after *Sun Diamond*, one lower court commented:

> The two prohibitions differ in two fundamental respects. First, bribery requires a quid pro quo, and accordingly can be seen as having a two-way nexus. That is, bribery typically involves an intent to affect the future actions of a public official through giving something of value, and receipt of that thing of value then motivates the official act. A gratuity,

by contrast, requires only a one-way nexus; "the gratuity guideline presumes a situation in which the offender gives the gift without attaching any strings...."

The two provisions additionally differ in their temporal focus. Bribery is entirely future-oriented, while gratuities can be either forward or backward looking. In other words, whereas bribery involves the present giving, promise, or demand of something in return for some action in the future, an unlawful gratuity can take one of three forms. First, a gratuity can take the form of a reward for past action—i.e. for a performed official act. Second, a gratuity can be intended to entice a public official who has already staked out a position favorable to the giver to maintain that position. Finally, a gratuity can be given with the intent to induce a public official to propose, take, or shy away from some future official act. This third category would additionally encompass gifts given in the hope that, when the particular official actions move to the forefront, the public official will listen hard to, and hopefully be swayed by, the giver's proposals, suggestions, and/or concerns.

United States v. Schaffer, 183 F.3d 833, 841–42 (D.C. Cir. 1999)

Since gratuities are given with no strings attached, i.e., no quid pro quo, why is the offer or acceptance of a gratuity prohibited? For example, why make it a federal crime to give a public official a gift because of his conduct in office? The court in *United States v. Evans*, 572 F.2d 455, 480 (5th Cir. 1978), gave a classic statement of the rationale: "Even if corruption is not intended by either the donor or the donee, there is still a tendency in such a situation to provide conscious or unconscious preferential treatment of the donor by the donee, or the inefficient management of public affairs." For a further discussion of the policy issues raised by the prosecution of gratuities, see Chapter 8 at 311, 314–17.

There is often no direct proof of the *quid pro quo* element, which relates to the subjective intent of the parties and an agreement that may never have been explicit. This evidentiary difficulty suggests an additional reason for the adoption of gratuity penalties, which impose criminal liability when no quid pro quo can be proved. On the other hand, it is relevant to ask how hard it is in practice to prove a quid pro quo. In that regard, see the materials on the Hobbs Act in Chapter 6 and *United States v. Biaggi, infra* at 294.

2. Does *Sun Diamond* reach the correct result? At the Supreme Court argument in *Sun Diamond* one justice asked whether it would be an illegal gratuity if a regulated company made a multimillion dollar gift to the chairman of the FCC because of his official position, but *not* with any particular act in mind. *See* 1999 WL 135163 at * 43. The Supreme Court adopted a construction of § 201 that does not reach this hypothetical. Shouldn't such conduct be illegal? The Supreme Court concluded that § 201(c) doesn't reach this conduct, but it emphasized that such conduct does fall within other civil and criminal provisions. For example, 5 U.S.C. § 7353, provides that no "employee of the executive, legislative, or judicial branch shall solicit or accept anything of value from a person ... whose interests may be substantially affected by the performance or nonperformance of the individual's official duties." A violation of § 7353 is punished by "appropriate disciplinary and other remedial action." 5 U.S.C. § 7353(c).

The Court's decision thus serves as a reminder that Congress has supplemented the general provisions in § 201 with a variety of narrower criminal and civil provisions. Some of these provisions are listed in footnote a, supra at 276.

3. The concept of the quid pro quo is intertwined with the concept of the corrupt intent required to sustain a bribery conviction under § 201. In *United States v. Traitz*, 871 F.2d 368, 396 (3d Cir. 1989), the court explained:

> [Section 201] has been said to require that the alleged briber offer the bribe with a "corrupt intent" to influence official conduct. This requires the government to show that the "money was knowingly offered to an official with the intent and expectation that, in exchange for the money, some act of a public official would be influenced." Provided that the money is offered with corrupt intent, "the official does not necessarily even need to be aware of the bribe . . . so long as a bribe is offered or promised with the required intent to influence any official act the crime is committed."

As reflected in this quotation, the intention of the payor and the payee will not necessarily be the same in bribery and gratuity cases. While both may be liable under section 201 if each had the requisite intent, it is also possible for only one of the parties to be guilty of the offense. *See United States v. Evans*, 572 F.2d 455, 480 (5th Cir. 1978) (giving and receiving gratuity are not interdependent offenses; donee's intent may be different from the donor's).

What exactly does the term "corruptly" in § 201(b)(1) mean? That issue was raised in *United States v. Alfisi*, 308 F.3d 144 (2d. Cir. 2002). The defendant, an employee for a produce wholesaler, had been convicted of bribery for payments he made to a USDA produce inspector. At trial, Alfisi's primary defense was that he had been extorted by the inspector and was paying him merely to perform his duty legally. On appeal, he attacked a jury charge which defined the term "corruptly" as entailing the "specific intent to influence [the inspector's] official acts of performing inspections and certifying the condition and grade of fruits and vegetables." Alfisi argued that the instruction was erroneous because it allowed the jury to convict him for bribery even if the quid pro quo sought from the inspector was simply the faithful execution of his duties.

After mentioning in a footnote that the "proper response to coercion" is "to go to the authorities, not to make the payoff," the court rejected Alfisi's argument. First, the court defined the "corrupt intent" required as the intention "to procure a quid pro quo agreement—'to influence an official act,'" and concluded that "[i]t cannot be seriously argued that Alfisi's payments did not fall within that broad language, even if he was paying [the inspector] solely to make accurate inspections." Second, the court determined that "sound legislative purpose" favored reading the statute broadly, as the danger of an underinclusive interpretation was much greater than that of an overinclusive one.

The dissent argued that the majority's definition of "corruptly" was too broad:

> Our cases * * * provide that a payment made in the course of a shakedown * * * is not a bribe. A person who makes a payment

pursuant to such extortion intends not to cultivate such corruption, but only to avoid the tendrils of a corruption already sprouted. Such a person does not act "corruptly" within the meaning of the statute because he does not seek the lawlessness that the bribery statute seeks to prevent.

Further, the dissent argued that the definition of "corruptly" used by the district court and the majority, "the specific intent to influence ... official acts," if inserted in place of the term "corruptly" in § 203 (b)(1), would render the term superfluous:

> The district court effectively instructed the jury that Alfisi committed bribery if he "directly or indirectly, *with the specific intent to influence official acts* [the court's definition of "corruptly"], [gave], offered, or promised something of value to [a] public official with the *intent to influence any official act.*" (emphasis added; ellipses omitted).

Which construction of the statute seems more plausible? Which is better policy? The government charged Alfisi under § 203 (b)(1)(A), which requires proof that the defendant had intent to "influence any official act." Note that § 203 (b)(1)(C) criminalizes the making of corrupt payments with the intent "to induce * * * [a public official] to do or omit to do any act in violation of the lawful duty of such official or person." Neither the majority nor the dissent discussed § 203 (b)(1)(C). How is that provision, an alternative to § 203 (b)(1)(A), relevant to the construction of § 203 (b)(1)(A)?

4.   Under § 201 the offense is considered complete when a bribe or gratuity is either offered or solicited. In that sense, § 201 defines an inchoate offense. Accordingly, it is not surprising that the lower courts have held that the statute is violated even if the official never performs the requested action, or has no authority to take the requested action.

5.   The courts have read broadly the requirement that the bribe relate to official acts. For example, in *United States v. Biaggi*, 853 F.2d 89, 97–99 (2d Cir. 1988), the court rejected the claim that a congressman's only official acts occur within the legislative process itself, noting that the congressman's letters to municipal authorities were written on congressional letterhead, and that he opened a file in his congressional office and used congressional office personnel. The court rejected Biaggi's claim that § 201 is limited to official acts directed toward federal officials, noting that the statute "refers to 'any' action taken on a matter brought before the public official in his official capacity." Id. at 98.

6.   Members of Congress charged with violations of the bribery laws have invoked the Speech or Debate Clause of the United States Constitution, which states that "for any Speech or Debate in either House, they [Senators or Representatives] shall not be questioned in any other place." U.S. Const., Art I, § 6, Cl 1. In *United States v. Brewster*, 408 U.S. 501 (1972), the Supreme Court held that the Speech and Debate Clause does not bar prosecution under Section 201, because the acceptance of a bribe is not a legislative act. On the other hand, in *United States v. Helstoski*, 442 U.S. 477 (1979), the Court held that the Speech and Debate Clause precludes the government from introducing evidence of a member's legislative act in a prosecution under Section 201.

B. OTHER ELEMENTS OF A VIOLATION OF § 201

Both the bribery and gratuities provisions in § 201 prohibit giving a "thing of value" to a "public official." How have those terms been defined?

1. THING OF VALUE

Because § 201 is aimed at misuse of public office in expectation of some gain or reward, the phrase "thing of value" has generally been construed to encompass anything that has subjective value to the recipient, and the cases run the gamut from golf clubs to unsecured loans. *See generally* 1 SARAH N. WELLING ET AL., FEDERAL CRIMINAL LAW AND RELATED CIVIL ACTIONS § 7.3 (1998). Section 201 has even been held to reach a case where the defendant was tricked into accepting a bribe that had no actual commercial value. Senator Harrison Williams was convicted of bribery under § 201 in connection with Abscam, an elaborate undercover sting operation conducted by the FBI. He accepted stock in three sham corporations, anticipating that they would receive $100 million in loans from a fictitious entity created by the FBI. In return, the Senator agreed to help the corporations obtain government mining contracts. In *United States v. Williams*, 705 F.2d 603 (2d Cir. 1983), a bribery prosecution under § 201, the court upheld his conviction, despite the recognition that the stock has no commercial value, because Williams subjectively believed that it had value. The court commented that "[c]orruption of office occurs when the officeholder agrees to misuse his office in the expectation of gain, whether or not he has correctly assessed the worth of the bribe." *Id.* at 623.

The phrase "thing of value" also includes intangible benefits. As in the case of tangible benefits, the question is whether an intangible benefit has subjective value to the public official in question.[c] For example, one district court accepted the argument that providing a public official's girlfriend with the funds to purchase an airline ticket so that she could accompany the official on an international trip might be a "thing of value" from the official's point of view. *United States v. Sun–Diamond Growers*, 941 F.Supp. 1262, 1269 (D.D.C. 1996). (This is another aspect of the Independent Counsel investigation that led to the Supreme Court's decision on 279–87.)

Although it is not unusual for a public official to accept a specific offer of future employment in the private sector, a public official may be

---

c. The phrase "thing of value" is also used in a number of other statutes, where it has generally been given a similarly broad interpretation, encompassing various intangibles. *See, e.g., United States v. Schwartz*, 785 F.2d 673, 679–81 (9th Cir.1986) (assistance in arranging union mergers constitutes thing of value under 18 U.S.C. § 1954, reviews cases under other statutes); *United States v. Girard*, 601 F.2d 69, 71 (2d Cir. 1979) (information constitutes thing of value under 18 U.S.C. § 641; reviews prior cases under various statutes holding thing of value could encompass sexual intercourse, the promise to reinstate an employee, and an agreement not to run in an election).

bribed by a promise of future employment if there is a specific quid pro quo. In *United States v. Biaggi*, 909 F.2d 662, 684–85 (2d Cir. 1990), a prosecution growing out of the Wedtech government procurement scandal, the court upheld the conviction of an SBA official who was bribed by the promise of a lucrative job with a law firm. The court noted that in the absence of a specific quid pro quo the conflict of interest statutes regulate the subsequent employment of public officials.

Although the principal provisions of § 201 deal with the corruption of public officials, as noted in footnote b on page 278, § 201(c)(2) also criminalizes offering a thing of value to a federal witness for or because of his testimony. In *United States v. Singleton*, 144 F.3d 1343 (10th Cir. 1998), a panel of the Tenth Circuit created a major stir when it concluded that a federal prosecutor's promise of leniency is a "thing of value" within the meaning of § 201, and accordingly that the prosecutor had violated § 201(c)(2) by entering into a plea agreement to exchange leniency for a co-conspirator's agreement to testify against the defendant. *Id.* at 1348–49. The panel characterized its interpretation as a straightforward application of the plain language of § 201, which applies to "whoever" offers or promises a witness a thing of value and contains no exception for government agents. The panel reasoned that "[i]f justice is perverted when a criminal defendant seeks to buy testimony from a witness, it is no less perverted when the government does so." *Id.* at 1346. The government's interest in the fair administration of the judicial system would be advanced rather than hampered, the court concluded, by applying § 201(c) to all parties. Indeed, if § 201 were not so construed, the statute would allow a prosecutor to bribe a witness with money in exchange for favorable testimony. The panel rejected the argument that its interpretation was inconsistent with the federal sentencing laws–which provide for a downward departure for substantial assistance to the government—since those provisions merely reward assistance after it is given, and do not provide for an agreement in advance to provide leniency in return for testimony. The court concluded that the testimony obtained in violation of § 201(c) should be suppressed.

A divided en banc court reversed, agreeing with a host of decisions from other circuits that had rejected the panel opinion. *United States v. Singleton*, 165 F.3d 1297 (10th Cir. 1999). The majority concluded that a literal reading of the statute to include prosecutors ignores the fact that in entering into a plea agreement a federal prosecutor acts as a representative of the United States in its sovereign capacity. Even the broad word "whoever" does not encompass the United States as sovereign, particularly where the application of the statute in question would deprive the government of its established practice of granting leniency in exchange for testimony against the witness's criminal associates. If Congress had intended to criminalize this long established prosecutorial practice, it would have done so in clear unmistakable language. The majority noted, however, that the established practice provides no authority for paying a witness for his testimony or other abusive conduct. All circuits that have since decided the issue have found that the government's promise of leniency in exchange for testimony is not a thing of value for the purposes of § 201(c)(2). *See United States v. Johnson*, 136 F.Supp.2d 553, 563 (W.D. Va. 2001) (collecting cases).

2. PUBLIC OFFICIAL

Since the relevant provisions of § 201 are aimed at public corruption, they require that the bribe or gratuity be offered requested or received by a "public official" or a "person who has been selected to be a public official." This language has created no special difficulty as applied to federal officers or employees. However, Section 201(a)(1) also defines "public official" to include any "person acting for or on behalf of the United States, or any department, agency or branch of Government thereof, including the District of Columbia, in any official function, under or by authority of any such department, agency, or branch of Government."

The Supreme Court's decision in *Dixson v. United States*, 465 U.S. 482 (1984), signaled that § 201 can reach employees of state and local government, as well as employees of private corporations carrying out federal responsibilities. The Court stated:

> section 201(a) has been accurately characterized as a "comprehensive statute applicable to all persons performing activities for or on behalf of the United States," whatever the form of delegation of authority. To determine whether any particular individual falls within this category, the proper inquiry is not simply whether the person had signed a contract with the United States or agreed to serve as the Government's agent, but rather whether the person occupies a position of public trust with official federal responsibilities. Persons who hold such positions are public officials within the meaning of section 201 and liable for prosecution under the federal bribery statute.

465 U.S. at 496. Applying this standard, the Court determined that employees of a private nonprofit corporation that administered a subgrant from Peoria's federal urban renewal block grant were subject to § 201, even though neither the individual defendants nor their employer had ever entered into any agreement with any federal agency. The Court stated that defendants had the operational responsibility for the administration of the grant, and that they were required to follow federal guidelines which governed where and how the funds could be spent. The Court concluded that "[b]y accepting the responsibility for distributing these federal fiscal resources, petitioners assumed the quintessentially official role of administering a social service program established by the United States Congress." 465 U.S. at 497. The Court observed that "[t]he federal government has a strong and legitimate interest in prosecuting petitioners for their misuse of government funds," and that that these officials had the sort of national trust Congress intended to reach in § 201. *Id.* at 482. Justice O'Connor dissented, arguing that grants-in-

aid should be treated as categorically different than other types of federal activity in recognition of the principle of grantee autonomy, and grantee autonomy has its greatest significance in the case of federal block grants, like those involved in the present case.

As *Dixson* demonstrates, the phrase "public officer or employee" is not limited to persons employed by the federal government. State and local officials are subject to § 201 if they occupy a position of public trust with federal responsibilities. *See, e.g., United States v. Strissel,* 920 F.2d 1162 (4th Cir. 1990) (executive director of city housing authority who distributed HUD funds); *United States v. Velazquez,* 847 F.2d 140 (4th Cir. 1988) (county deputy who worked in local jail with contract to house federal prisoners). A similar issue arises under the false statement statute, 18 U.S.C. § 1001, when courts seek to determine whether the statement in question was within the jurisdiction of a federal department of agency. *See infra* at 725–27. In many cases federal program bribery may involve false statements that can be prosecuted under § 1001. For a discussion of the false statements statute, see Chapter 15, infra.

Private citizens who perform some delegated governmental function may also be subject to prosecution under 18 U.S.C. § 201. *See, e.g., United States v. Thomas,* 240 F.3d 445 (5th Cir. 2001) (prison guard who was employed by private company contracted by INS to run prison and who performed the same duties and had the same responsibilities as a federal prison guard); *United States v. Kenney,* 185 F.3d 1217 (11th Cir. 1999) (employee of defense contractor who did not have any decision-making authority but did advise on technical issues and whose advice was given great weight).

C. DISTINGUISHING BRIBERY AND EXTORTION FROM CAMPAIGN CONTRIBUTIONS AND FEES FOR LEGITIMATE SERVICES

Although the typical bribery case involves a payment to a public official who has no colorable claim to a legitimate purpose for the payment, other cases involve payments that might be characterized as being a campaign contribution or a fee for legitimate services. For example, in *United States v. Biaggi,* 909 F.2d 662 (2d Cir. 1990), the government charged a Congressman who maintained an "of counsel" relationship with a law firm and others in the firm with bribery and extortion in connection with payments the defendants characterized as fees for legal services. The government charged that Congressman Biaggi wielded his influence to help Wedtech obtain nearly $50 million in defense contracts under a program that permitted the award of contracts to minority-owned businesses without competitive bidding, and that Wedtech's payments to Biaggi were disguised as a retainer and fees to the law firm.

Where there is a colorable basis for claiming that a payment was made for a legitimate purpose, how does a court determine whether it can constitute an illegal gratuity or the quid pro quo required for bribery? And what happens if the evidence suggests that a payment had mixed purposes, both legitimate and illegitimate? In the *Biaggi* case, for example, some of the charges focused on a $50,000 payment that the defendants characterized as legal fees for negotiating and drafting a three-year lease for $50,000 per year. The law firm clearly did perform some legal services in connection with the lease.

The *Biaggi* court concluded that the evidence would support a finding that the $50,000 payment had both a lawful and an unlawful purpose, and it concluded that the evidence was sufficient to uphold the defendants' convictions for bribery (as well as extortion):

> It thus appears, and surely the jury was entitled to find, that the $50,000 payment had two purposes. * * * Thus, the issue as to the $50,000 payment becomes whether a payment may be found to constitute a bribe and an extortion where it is sought and paid for both lawful and unlawful purposes. We think it may. A valid purpose that partially motivates a transaction does not insulate participants in an unlawful transaction from criminal liability.... In such cases, however, the evidence must suffice to permit the jury to find beyond a reasonable doubt that the unlawful purposes were of substance, not merely vague possibilities that might attend an otherwise legitimate transaction. A client paying his law firm's legal fee does not commit bribery simply because a Congressman is "of counsel" to the firm and the client hopes the Congressman will some day be helpful. * * *

> In the pending case, several factors permitted the jury to find the $50,000 payment unlawful. It followed a prior extortionate demand by Biaggi and Ehrlich for a five percent stock interest. It was discussed with a Congressman while matters were pending on which the Congressman's assistance was urgently needed. The bill was submitted just one week after the need for the Congressman's assistance became apparent. The bill was paid the day after the governmental action on which the Congressman had assisted. The bill was not accompanied by normal law firm time records and, though perhaps justified in part by the legal services rendered, was in addition to a substantial retainer. Under all the circumstances the jury was entitled to conclude that the $50,000 was demanded and paid, at least in part, to obtain the political services of Congressman Biaggi. * * *

909 F.2d at 683–84.

Another aspect of the *Biaggi* case concerned payments that defendants characterized as campaign contributions, but the government characterized as bribes and extortion. Do the current definitions of bribery and the receipt of gratuities adequately distinguish campaign contributions? Are these statutes adequate in view of the realities of financing modern political campaigns? How do these concepts relate to other common political techniques such logrolling, i.e., vote trading by legislators? Observing that "American politics consists largely of pressures and deals," Professor Daniel Lowenstein critiques the adequacy of the current definitions of bribery and gratuities, and offers some suggestions for a reconceptualization of these offenses. Daniel Hayes Lowenstein, *Political Bribery and the Intermediate Theory of Politics*, 32 UCLA L. Rev. 784 (1985). *See also* Lydia Segal, *Can We Fight the New Tammany Hall? Difficulties of Prosecuting Political Patronage and Suggestions for Reform*, 50 Rutgers L. Rev. 507 (1998); Joseph R. Weeks, *Bribes, Gratuities, and the Congress: The Institutionalized Corruption of the Political Process, The Impotence of Criminal Law to Reach It, and a Proposal for Change*, 13 J. Leg. 123 (1986); William M. Welch, Comment, *The Federal Bribery Statute and Special Interest Campaign Statutes*, 79 J. Crim. L. & Criminology 1347 (1989).

How do the bribery and gratuities offenses compare to mail fraud and the Hobbs Act, which are also used to prosecute political corruption? For a discussion of the Hobbs Act, see Chapter 6; for an overview of the political corruption offenses, see Chapter 8.

D. FEDERAL PROGRAM BRIBERY

The federal program bribery statute, 18 U.S.C. § 666 provides an increasingly important mechanism for the federal prosecution of bribery and corruption of persons who are not federal employees. Its development has been explosive,[d] but it has received so little attention that one scholar called it a stealth statute. As you read § 666, consider what limitations the statute places upon the government's ability to prosecute corruption of state and local officials, and whether the statute may also be used to prosecute third parties who receive payments of some sort that can be traced to the government.

18 U.S.C. § 666. Theft or bribery concerning programs receiving Federal funds[e]

(a) Whoever, if the circumstance described in subsection (b) of this section exists–

(1) being an agent of an organization, or of a State, local, or Indian tribal government, or any agency thereof—

* * *

d. Despite recent decisions interpreting the statute broadly, there are not yet a large number of prosecutions. According to the Federal Justice Statistics Database (available online at http://fjsrc.urban.org) in 2003 there were only 168 prosecutions in which § 666 was the most serious filing offense.

e. Subsection (a)(1)(A) also criminalizes the conduct of one who:

embezzles, steals, obtains by fraud, or otherwise without authority knowingly converts to the use of any person other than the rightful owner or intentionally misapplies, property that—

(i) is valued at $5,000 or more, and

(ii) is owned by, or is under the care, custody, or control of such organization, government, or agency....

(B) corruptly solicits or demands for the benefit of any person, or accepts or agrees to accept, anything of value from any person, intending to be influenced or rewarded in connection with any business, transaction, or series of transactions of such organization, government, or agency involving anything of value of $5,000 or more; or

(2) corruptly gives, offers, or agrees to give anything of value to any person, with intent to influence or reward an agent of an organization or of a State, local or Indian tribal government, or any agency thereof, in connection with any business, transaction, or series of transactions of such organization, government, or agency involving anything of value of $5,000 or more;

shall be fined under this title, imprisoned not more than 10 years, or both.

(b) The circumstance referred to in subsection (a) of this section is that the organization, government, or agency receives, in any one year period, benefits in excess of $10,000 under a Federal program involving a grant, contract, subsidy, loan, guarantee, insurance, or other form of Federal assistance.

(c) This section does not apply to bona fide salary, wages, fees, or other compensation paid, or expenses paid or reimbursed, in the usual course of business.

(d) As used in this section—

(1) the term "agent" means a person authorized to act on behalf of another person or a government and, in the case of an organization or government, includes a servant or employee, and a partner, director, officer, manager, and representative;

(2) the term "government agency" means a subdivision of the executive, legislative, judicial, or other branch of government, including a department, independent establishment, commission, administration, authority, board, and bureau, and a corporation or other legal entity established, and subject to control, by a government or governments for the execution of a governmental or intergovernmental program * * *.

* * *

(5) the term 'in any one-year period' means a continuous period that commences no earlier than twelve months before the commission of the offense or that ends no later than twelve months after the commission of the offense. Such period may include time both before and after the commission of the offense.

SALINAS v. UNITED STATES
522 U.S. 52, 118 S.Ct. 469, 139 L.Ed.2d 352 (1997).

JUSTICE KENNEDY delivered the opinion of the Court.

The case before us presents two questions: First, is the federal bribery statute codified at 18 U.S.C. § 666 limited to cases in which the bribe has a demonstrated effect upon federal funds? Second, does the conspiracy prohibition contained in the Racketeer Influenced and Corrupt Organizations Act (RICO) apply only when the conspirator agrees to commit two of the predicate acts RICO forbids?[f] * * * Ruling against the petitioner on both issues, we affirm the judgment of the Court of Appeals for the Fifth Circuit.

I

This federal prosecution arose from a bribery scheme operated by Brigido Marmolejo, the Sheriff of Hidalgo County, Texas, and petitioner Mario Salinas, one of his principal deputies. In 1984, the United States Marshals Service and Hidalgo County entered into agreements under which the county would take custody of federal prisoners. In exchange, the Federal Government agreed to make a grant to the county for improving its jail and also agreed to pay the county a specific amount per day for each federal prisoner housed. Based on the estimated number of federal prisoners to be maintained, payments to the county were projected to be $915,785 per year. The record before us does not disclose the precise amounts paid. It is uncontested, however, that in each of the two periods relevant in this case the program resulted in federal payments to the county well in excess of the $10,000 amount necessary for coverage under 18 U.S.C. § 666. (We denied certiorari on the question whether the monies paid to the county were "benefits" under a "Federal program" under § 666(b), and we assume for purposes of this opinion that the payments fit those definitions.)

Homero Beltran–Aguirre was one of the federal prisoners housed in the jail under the arrangement negotiated between the Marshals Service and the county. He was incarcerated there for two intervals, first for 10 months and then for 5 months. During both custody periods, Beltran paid Marmolejo a series of bribes in exchange for so-called "contact visits" in which he remained alone with his wife or, on other occasions, his girlfriend. Beltran paid Marmolejo a fixed rate of six thousand dollars per month and one thousand dollars for each contact visit, which occurred twice a week. Petitioner Salinas was the chief deputy responsible for managing the jail and supervising custody of the prisoners. When Marmolejo was not available, Salinas arranged for the contact visits and on occasion stood watch outside the room where the visits took place. In return for his assistance with the scheme, Salinas received from Beltran a pair of designer watches and a pickup truck.

Salinas and Marmolejo were indicted and tried together, but only Salinas' convictions are before us. Salinas was charged with one count of violating RICO, 18 U.S.C. § 1962(c), one count of conspiracy to violate RICO, § 1962(d), and two counts of bribery in violation of § 666(a)(1)(B). The jury acquitted Salinas on the substantive RICO count but convicted him on the RICO conspiracy count and the bribery

---

f. The Court's discussion of this issue is omitted here, but is discussed infra at 552–55.

counts. A divided panel of the Court of Appeals for the Fifth Circuit affirmed. To resolve the case, we consider first the bribery scheme * * *.

II

Salinas contends the Government must prove the bribe in some way affected federal funds, for instance by diverting or misappropriating them, before the bribe violates § 666(a)(1)(B).* * *

The enactment's expansive, unqualified language, both as to the bribes forbidden and the entities covered, does not support the interpretation that federal funds must be affected to violate § 666(a)(1)(B). Subject to the five-thousand-dollar threshold for the business or transaction in question, the statute forbids acceptance of a bribe by a covered official who intends "to be influenced or rewarded in connection with any business, transaction, or series of transactions of [the defined] organization, government or agency." § 666(a)(1)(B). The prohibition is not confined to a business or transaction which affects federal funds. The word "any," which prefaces the business or transaction clause, undercuts the attempt to impose this narrowing construction.

Furthermore, the broad definition of the "circumstances" to which the statute applies provides no textual basis for limiting the reach of the bribery prohibition. The statute applies to all cases in which an "organization, government, or agency" receives the statutory amount of benefits under a federal program. § 666(b). The language reaches the scheme alleged, and proved, here.

Neither does the statute limit the type of bribe offered. It prohibits accepting or agreeing to accept "anything of value." § 666(a)(1)(B). The phrase encompasses all transfers of personal property or other valuable consideration in exchange for the influence or reward. It includes, then, the personal property given to Salinas in exchange for the favorable treatment Beltran secured for himself. The statute's plain language fails to provide any basis for the limiting § 666(a)(1)(B) to bribes affecting federal funds.

Salinas attempts to circumscribe the statutory text by pointing to its legislative history. "Courts in applying criminal laws generally must follow the plain and unambiguous meaning of the statutory language. '[O]nly the most extraordinary showing of contrary intentions' in the legislative history will justify a departure from that language." *United States v. Albertini*, 472 U.S. 675, 680 (1985) (citations omitted) (quoting *Garcia v. United States*, 469 U.S. 70, 75(1984)); *see also Ardestani v. INS*, 502 U.S. 129, 135 (1991) (courts may deviate from the plain language of a statute only in " 'rare and exceptional circumstances' ").

The construction Salinas seeks cannot stand when viewed in light of the statutory framework in existence before § 666 was enacted and the expanded coverage prescribed by the new statute. Before § 666 was enacted, the federal criminal code contained a single, general bribery provision codified at 18 U.S.C. § 201. Section 201 by its terms applied only to "public official[s]," which the statute defined as "officer[s] or employee[s] or person [s] acting for or on behalf of the United States, or any department, agency or branch of Government thereof, including the District of Columbia, in any official function, under or by authority of any such department, agency, or branch." § 201(a). The Courts of Appeals divided over whether state and local employees could be considered "public officials" under § 201(a). *Compare United States v. Del Toro*, 513 F.2d 656, 661–662(2d Cir.), cert. denied, 423 U.S. 826 (1975), with *United States v. Mosley*, 659 F.2d 812, 814–816 (C.A.7 1981), and *United States v. Hinton*, 683 F.2d 195, 197–200 (C.A.7 1982), *aff'd. sub nom.Dixson v. United States*, 465 U.S. 482, 104 S.Ct. 1172, 79 L.Ed.2d 458 (1984). Without awaiting this Court's resolution of the issue in *Dixson*,[g] Congress enacted § 666 and made it clear that federal law applies to bribes of the kind offered to the state and local officials in *Del Toro*, as well as those at issue in *Mosley* and *Hinton*.

As this chronology and the statutory language demonstrate, § 666(a)(1)(B) was designed to extend federal bribery prohibitions to bribes offered to state and local officials employed by agencies receiving federal funds. It would be incongruous to restrict § 666 in the manner Salinas suggests. The facts and reasoning of *Del Toro* give particular instruction in this respect. In that case, the Second Circuit held that a city employee was not a "public official" under § 201(a) even though federal funds would eventually cover 100% of the costs and 80% of the salaries of the program he administered. Because the program had not yet entered a formal request for federal funding, the Second Circuit reasoned, "[t]here were no existing committed federal funds for the purpose." The enactment of § 666 forecloses this type of limitation. Acceptance of Salinas' suggestion that a bribe must affect federal funds before it falls within § 666(a)(1)(B) would run contrary to the statutory expansion that redressed the negative effects of the Second Circuit's narrow construction of § 201 in *Del Toro*. We need not consider whether the statute requires some other kind of connection between a bribe and the expenditure of federal funds, for in this case the bribe was related to the housing of a prisoner in facilities paid for in significant part by federal funds themselves. And that relationship is close enough to satisfy whatever connection the statute might require.

Salinas argues in addition that our decisions in *Gregory v. Ashcroft*, 501 U.S. 452 (1991), and *McNally v. United States*, 483 U.S. 350 (1987), require a plain statement of congressional intent before § 666(a)(1)(B) can be construed to apply to bribes having no effect on federal funds. In so arguing, however, Salinas makes too much of *Gregory* and *McNally*. In each of those cases, we confronted a statute susceptible of two plausible interpretations, one of which would have altered the existing balance of federal and state powers. We concluded that, absent a clear indication of Congress' intent to change the balance, the proper course was to adopt a construction which maintains the existing balance.

---

g. The Supreme Court's decision in *Dixson* is discussed supra at 293.

"No rule of construction, however, requires that a penal statute be strained and distorted in order to exclude conduct clearly intended to be within its scope. . . ." As we held in *Albertini, supra,* at 680.

"Statutes should be construed to avoid constitutional questions, but this interpretative canon is not a license for the judiciary to rewrite language enacted by the legislature. Any other conclusion, while purporting to be an exercise in judicial restraint, would trench upon the legislative powers vested in Congress by Art. I, § 1, of the Constitution."

These principles apply to the rules of statutory construction we have followed to give proper respect to the federal-state balance. As we observed in applying an analogous maxim in *Seminole Tribe of Florida v. Florida,* 517 U.S. 44 (1996), "[w]e cannot press statutory construction to the point of disingenuous evasion even to avoid a constitutional question." *Gregory* itself held as much when it noted the principle it articulated did not apply when a statute was unambiguous. A statute can be unambiguous without addressing every interpretive theory offered by a party. It need only be "plain to anyone reading the Act" that the statute encompasses the conduct at issue. *Compare United States v. Bass,* 404 U.S. 336, 349–350 (1971) (relying on Congress' failure to make a clear statement of its intention to alter the federal-state balance to construe an ambiguous firearm-possession statute to apply only to firearms affecting commerce), with *United States v. Lopez,* 514 U.S. 549, 561–562 (1995) (refusing to apply *Bass* to read a similar limitation into an unambiguous firearm-possession statute). The plain-statement requirement articulated in *Gregory* and *McNally* does not warrant a departure from the statute's terms. The text of § 666(a)(1)(B) is unambiguous on the point under consideration here, and it does not require the Government to prove federal funds were involved in the bribery transaction.

Furthermore, there is no serious doubt about the constitutionality of § 666(a)(1)(B) as applied to the facts of this case. Beltran was without question a prisoner held in a jail managed pursuant to a series of agreements with the Federal Government. The preferential treatment accorded to him was a threat to the integrity and proper operation of the federal program. Whatever might be said about § 666(a)(1)(B)'s application in other cases, the application of § 666(a)(1)(B) to Salinas did not extend federal power beyond its proper bounds.

In so holding, we do not address § 666(a)(1)(B)'s applicability to intangible benefits such as contact visits, because that question is not fairly included within the questions on which we granted certiorari. Nor do we review the Court of Appeals' determination that the transactions at issue "involv[ed] any thing of value of $5,000 or more," since Salinas does not offer any cognizable challenge to that aspect of the Court of Appeals' decision. We simply decide that, as a matter of statutory construction, § 666(a)(1)(B) does not require the Government to prove the bribe in question had any particular influence on federal funds and that under this construction the statute is constitutional as applied in this case.

* * *

Notes

1. It seems fair to assume that every state and virtually every city and county receive federal funds of more than $10,000 per year. Indeed, the reported prosecutions involve not only states and large cities, but cities with populations of less than 10,000. *See* George D. Brown, *Stealth Statute— Corruption, The Spending Power, and the Rise of 18 U.S.C. § 666*, 73 NOTRE DAME L. REV. 247, 276 (1998). *Salinas* suggested that the corruption of *any* state or local government employee is now within the reach of § 666, as long as the threshold amount of $5,000 is met.

2. In the wake of *Salinas*, the circuits split on the question whether § 666 required any type of nexus between the bribe and a risk to government funds. In *Sabri v. United States*, 541 U.S. 600 (2004), the Supreme Court granted review to resolve the split and to decide whether § 666 exceeds the scope of Congress's power under the Spending Clause. The defendants—a real estate developer and a member of the Minneapolis Community Development Agency (MCDA)—were accused of kickbacks and bribes in connection with regulatory approvals and eminent domain proceedings. They were charged with violating § 666(a)(2). The city received $29 million per year in federal funds, and MCDA received $23 million, but the indictment did not allege any nexus between the defendant's conduct and the federal funds.

The *Sabri* Court rejected the constitutional challenge in fairly broad terms. It stated:

> Congress has authority under the Spending Clause to appropriate federal monies to promote the general welfare, Art. I, § 8, cl. 1, and it has corresponding authority under the Necessary and Proper Clause, Art. I, § 8, cl. 18, to see to it that taxpayer dollars appropriated under that power are in fact spent for the general welfare, and not frittered away in graft or on projects undermined when funds are siphoned off or corrupt public officers are derelict about demanding value for dollars. Congress does not have to sit by and accept the risk of operations thwarted by local and state improbity. Section 666(a)(2) addresses the problem at the sources of bribes, by rational means, to safeguard the integrity of the state, local, and tribal recipients of federal dollars.

The Court observed that the government has an interest in bribery and corruption affecting a federal grant recipient, even if the bribe is not directly tied to the federal funds:

> Money is fungible, bribed officials are untrustworthy stewards of federal funds, and corrupt contractors do not deliver dollar-for-dollar value. Liquidity is not a financial term for nothing; money can be drained off here because a federal grant is pouring in there. And officials are not any the less threatening to the objects behind federal spending just because they may accept general retainers. It is certainly enough that

the statutes condition the offense on a threshold amount of federal dollars defining the federal interest, such as that provided here, and on a bribe that goes well beyond liquor and cigars.

The legislative history buttressed the conclusion that Congress acted within the scope of the Necessary and Proper Clause when it dispensed with a nexus requirement; § 666 was enacted to fill in gaps in narrower statutes that had hampered efforts to protect the integrity of the money distributed through federal programs.

In contrast to *Lopez* and *Morrison*,[h] it was not necessary to pile inference upon inference to show a link to Congressional authority, because "[t]he power to keep a watchful eye on expenditures and on the reliability of those who use public money is bound up with congressional authority to spend in the first place." The Court summarily rejected Sabri's argument that § 666(a)(2) amounts to an unduly coercive, and impermissibly sweeping, condition on the grant of federal funds as judged under the criterion applied in *South Dakota v. Dole,* 483 U.S. 203 (1987). The Court explained that § 666(a)(2) "is authority to bring federal power to bear directly on individuals who convert public spending into unearned private gain, not a means for bringing federal economic might to bear on a State's own choices of public policy."

There were no dissents, but Justice Thomas concurred in the judgment. He agreed that § 666 is a valid exercise of Congress' authority (at least under the Court's current precedents) to regulate interstate commerce, but questioned the Court's application of the Necessary and Proper Clause to the spending power. He disagreed with the Court's characterization of *McCulloch v. Maryland,* 17 U.S. (4 Wheat.) 316 (1819), "as having established a 'means-ends rationality' test." Showing that a statute is "plainly adapted" to a legitimate end, he argued, requires more than that a particular statute is a "rational means" to safeguard that end. Rather, it is "necessary to show some obvious, simple, and direct relation between the statute and the enumerated power." Applying this standard, Justice Thomas expressed doubt that § 666(a)(2) is a proper use of the Necessary and Proper Clause as applied to Congress' power to spend:

> [S]imply noting that "[m]oney is fungible," for instance, does not explain how there could be any federal interest in "prosecut[ing] a bribe paid to a city's meat inspector in connection with a substantial transaction just because the city's parks department had received a federal grant of $10,000," *United States v. Santopietro,* 166 F.3d 88, 93 (C.A.2 1999). It would be difficult to describe the chain of inferences and assumptions in which the Court would have to indulge to connect such a bribe to a federal interest in any federal funds or programs as being "plainly adapted" to their protection. And, this is just one example of many in which any federal interest in protecting federal funds is equally attenuated, and yet the bribe is covered by the expansive language of § 666(a)(2). Overall, then, § 666(a)(2) appears to be no more plainly adapted to protecting federal funds or federally funded programs than a hypothetical federal statute criminalizing fraud of any kind perpetrated on any individual who happens to receive federal welfare benefits

h. For a general discussion of those cases, see *supra* at 30–38.

Two other members of the Court also disassociated themselves from a portion of the opinion of the Court. In the third section of the opinion—"an afterword on Sabri's technique for challenging his indictment by facial attack on the underlying statute"—the Court expressed the view that facial challenges "are best when infrequent" and "should be discouraged." Justices Kennedy and Scalia did not join this section of the opinion, noting that in both *Lopez* and *Morrison* the Court resolved the basic question whether Congress in enacting the statute in question had exceeded its constitutional authority.

4.   In light of *Salinas* and *Sabri*, how far *does* § 666 go? Does it really reach a bribe to a city meat inspector just because the parks department received federal funds? Given the size and complexity of the municipal governments in large cities like New York and Los Angeles, is it conceivable that the courts would uphold such a prosecution merely because those cities, like all others, receive amounts far in excess of the threshold level? The lower courts have read *Sabri* broadly, rejecting as-applied challenges to § 666 where there is no connection between the bribe and the federal funds. *See, e.g., United States v. Caro–Muniz*, 406 F.3d 22, 27 (1st Cir. 2005) (upholding a mayor's conviction for bribery in connection with a contract to install lights at a municipal sports complex because the city had received unrelated funds from the Federal Emergency Management Agency).

On the other hand, the Department of Justice currently advises federal prosecutors not to push the envelope in prosecutions under § 666. The DEPARTMENT OF JUSTICE CRIMINAL RESOURCE MANUAL notes that the "very broad language of the statute.... seemingly permits the prosecution of any state agent, regardless of whether his or her specific agency received the necessary Federal assistance, as long as the state received the required Federal assistance," and notes that "[t]his broad reading, while statutorily permissible, would Federalize many state offenses in which the Federal interest is slight or nonexistent." To ensure that only "significant" Federal interests are protected and to follow Congressional intent, the MANUAL "strongly suggest[s]" that government attorneys adopt a narrower reading of § 666 requiring "that the agent must have illegally obtained cash or property from the agency that received the necessary Federal assistance." *See* DEPARTMENT OF JUSTICE, CRIMINAL RESOURCE MANUAL at 1001, *available at* http://www.usdoj.gov/usao/eousa/foia_reading_room/usam/title9/crm01001.htm (last visited August 23, 2005).

For a critique of *Sabri* and an interesting analysis of that decision in the context of the Supreme Court's new federalism decisions, as well as a broader look at the constitutional underpinnings of the federal government's role in fighting corruption at the state and local level, see George D. Brown, *Carte Blanche: Federal Prosecutions of State and Local Officials after* Sabri, 54 CATH. U. L. REV. 403 (2005). This article also provides a helpful summary of other major articles that examine *Salinas* and *Sabri,* including Richard W. Garnett, *The New Federalism, the Spending Power, and Federal Criminal Law,* 89 *Cornell L. Rev.* 1 (2003), Roderick W. Hills, Jr., *Corruption and Federalism: (When) Do Federal Criminal Prosecutions Improve Non–Federal Democracy,* 6 THEORETICAL ENQUIRIES L. 113 (2005), and Peter J. Henning, *Federalism and the Federal Prosecution of State and Local Corruption,* 92

KY. L.J. 75 (2003/04). These articles are discussed in Chapter 8, *infra* at 315–17, where we discuss the issues common to public corruption cases.

5. Note that the constitutional and policy questions raised by the Supreme Court's decisions concerning § 666 may just be the tip of a very large iceberg. If the Court is prepared to take § 666 this far, the combined force of the Necessary and Proper Clause and the Spending Clause is so sweeping that Congress may wish to rely on them much more frequently in the future. Why take the risk of grounding a statute on some other power—like the Commerce Clause—that may be more carefully policed by the courts, if the spending power, backed by the Necessary and Proper Clause, can reach the same result on a more certain constitutional footing? If you were a congressional staffer bent upon drafting new criminal legislation (or civil legislation), you might be thinking about how you could tie it, even loosely, to some form of federal funding. For a thoughtful discussion of the risks of pushing the Spending Clause too far, see Lynn A. Baker & Mitchell N. Berman, *Getting Off the Dole, Why the Court Should Abandon Its Spending Doctrine, and How a Too-Clever Congress Could Provoke It To Do So*, 78 IND. L.J. 459 (2003).

6. Section 666(a)(2) makes it a crime to "corruptly" offer or give anything of value "with intent to influence or reward." This language raises another fundamental question on which the lower courts are divided: does it reach only bribery, or does it also reach illegal gratuities where there is no quid pro quo? The term corruptly is generally associated with bribery, and the statute speaks of an intent to influence. On the other hand, it is also sufficient if the donor has only the "intent to * * * reward," and this language seems broad enough to encompass gratuities. The Second Circuit has concluded that § 666 reaches gratuities. *See United States v. Bonito*, 57 F.3d 167, 171 (2d Cir. 1995), but it has been suggested that the court's analysis blurs the distinction between bribery and gratuities by referring to gratuities given corruptly. *See United States v. Jennings*, 160 F.3d 1006, 1015 n.4 (4th Cir. 1998). Of course if the statute reaches gratuities as well as bribery this would substantially increase its impact. It would also subject defendants in gratuities cases to a sentence of up to 10 years, in contrast to the maximum 2 year sentence for a gratuities violation under § 201. This issue is discussed in Professor Brown's article cited in note 4 above, and in Stephen F. Smith, *Proportionality and Federalism*, 91 VA. L. REV. 879, 920–21 (2005). Using the Hobbs Act's incorporation of both bribery and extortion an example of the proportionality problems that arise from excessively broad interpretations of federal criminal statutes, Professor Smith argues for a reinvigorated rule of lenity sensitive to the need to avoid disproportionate punishments.

7. Section 666(b) provides that the prohibitions defined in (a) apply only to an organization or government agency that receives "benefits in excess of $10,000 under a Federal program involving a grant, contract, subsidy, plan, guarantee, insurance, or other form of Federal assistance." This language raises a variety of issues.

In *Fischer v. United States*, 529 U.S. 667 (2000), the Supreme Court considered whether § 666 applies to Medicare funds received by hospitals or physicians, since the benefits are payable to the individual recipients who may assign them to the medical providers. The Court held that a health care provider who received Medicare payments received "benefits" and thus was subject to prosecution under § 666. The Court did not announce any broad principles for the interpretation of the program bribery statute, though it did provide some guidance for future cases.

The Court declined to adopt the broadest possible interpretation of the statute, which would reach any receipt of federal funds, saying this would give the statute a virtually limitless reach and upset the proper federal-state balance. It stated that in order to determine whether an organization is receiving "benefits" under § 666 the courts should "examine the program's structure, operation, and purpose," as well as the conditions under which the organization receives federal payments. Applying this test, the Court concluded that "the Government has a legitimate and significant interest in prohibiting financial fraud or acts of bribery being perpetrated on Medicare providers," and that fraud "threatens the program's integrity." The Court concluded that medical providers as well as patients are beneficiaries of the Medicare program.

Justice Thomas dissented. He argued that medical providers engage in a market transaction and are compensated, and thus do not receive government benefits. Similarly, grocery stores that receive food stamps—though they are regulated by the government like health care providers—are not recipients of a government benefit. Thomas's opinion contains an interesting footnote (n.3) in which he comments on the constitutional significance of provisions to ensure that the exercise of the spending power is related to a federal interest.

Other knotty questions can arise in determining whether the bribe is offered or accepted "in connection with any business, transaction, or series of transactions * * * involving anything of value of $5,000 or more" as required by § 666(a)(1)(B) & (2). For example, the issue in *Salinas* was whether the conjugal visits met this standard. The court of appeals, recognizing that intangible benefits are covered by the statute, sought to determine the "market value" of the visits, and concluded that they exceeded the threshold amount. *United States v. Marmolejo*, 89 F.3d 1185, 1193–94 (5th Cir. 1996). If a policeman accepts $4,000 in bribes to look the other way and not investigate a drug dealer, does this meet the $5,000 standard? Is the value here limited to the amount of the bribe, or can it be measured by the value from the perspective of the briber (who remained living at home with his family and continued his activities) or from the perspective of the police department (which lost the honest services of the policeman)? *See United States v. McCormack*, 31 F.Supp.2d 176, 182–83 (D. Mass. 1998).

8. Although this chapter focuses on the bribery provisions of § 666, subsection (a)(1)(A) also criminalizes the conduct of one who "embezzles, steals, obtains by fraud, or otherwise without authority knowingly converts to the use of any person other than the rightful owner or intentionally misapplies" property valued at $5,000 or more that is in the care, custody, or control of one of the designated governments, agencies or organizations. These provisions have not been used much to date, but in the long run they too may add significantly to the broad sweep of § 666. Consider, for example, the breadth of the term "fraud" as it has been defined in the context of mail

and wire fraud. Could § 666 also provide a basis for a general "honest services" theory as applied to all of the covered individuals? Can you think of any reason that federal prosecutors might prefer to bring an honest services indictment under § 666 than under mail or wire fraud? Each count of mail and wire fraud is punishable by twenty years, whereas the maximum punishment under § 666 is ten years. But of course the actual sentences to be meted out will be determined by the Guidelines. For a discussion of sentencing under the various statutes that punish official corruption, *see* *infra* p. 311 et seq.

Chapter 8

AN OVERVIEW OF FEDERAL CRIMES DEALING WITH POLITICAL CORRUPTION

The preceding chapters have discussed the main federal statutes used to prosecute political corruption: the Hobbs Act, the mail and wire fraud statutes, the federal bribery and gratuities provisions, and the federal program bribery statute. In addition, interstate travel to facilitate bribery can be prosecuted under the Travel Act, 18 U.S.C. § 1952, which is discussed *supra*, pp. 93–108. What accounts for the multiplicity of provisions used to prosecute bribery and political corruption? What are the consequences of prosecution under one provision rather than another?

The narrow scope of the federal bribery and gratuities provisions, which apply only to federal officials,[a] has generated pressure for expansive readings of the other federal statutes in question in order to allow federal prosecution of corruption in state and local government. In the case of the Hobbs Act and mail and wire fraud, this pressure has been felt on two fronts. First, conduct that fits the classic mold of bribery or the receipt of an illegal gratuity has been recharacterized as a form of fraud or extortion, which requires a substantial extension of these concepts. Second, there has also been pressure to stretch the jurisdictional predicates, i.e., the use of the mails and the effect of commerce. In Travel Act prosecutions, the pressure has been felt principally on the jurisdictional element—interstate travel or the use of interstate facilities—because the Act borrows the definition of "bribery" from other federal or state statutes.

This chapter considers the consequences of prosecuting local political corruption in the federal courts. We explore the effects of recharacterizing bribery and gratuities cases as fraud or extortion, and probe the distinctions between fraud and extortion. This material may be used to

---

a. Note, however, that state or local officials administering federal funds may be prosecuted for federal program bribery under 18 U.S.C. § 666, and that this provision is being used with increasing frequency. *See supra* at 296–307.

stimulate class discussion of the material in one or all of these chapters, or for review.

1. Many cases could be brought under one—or more—of the statutes discussed in Chapters 5, 6, and 7, and it is useful to compare the elements—and the potential punishments—as they apply to particular facts. In many cases, prosecutors charge the same conduct, or different elements of the conduct, under more than one of the statutes. For example, in *United States v. Antico*, 275 F.3d 245 (3d Cir. 2001), the defendant was convicted of RICO, Hobbs Act extortion, and honest services mail fraud violations. Moreover, in reviewing the conviction, the court also addresses the standards applicable under the federal bribery and gratuity statute. For another example of political corruption charges that run the statutory gamut, see the press release infra at 323–28, which describes a 30 count indictment including mail fraud, Hobbs Act, RICO and bribery charges arising out of Operation Plunder Dome. The indictment alleges that various officials in Providence, Rhode Island (including the mayor, the mayor's chief of staff and his former director of administration, and the former chair of the city board of tax assessment review) conducted city government and the mayor's campaign organization as a criminal enterprise.[b] (For a discussion of RICO, see chapter 11, infra.) What do you think of the prosecutorial choices in these cases? What do they tell you about the scope of the various statutory provisions?

2. Characterizing corrupt political conduct as fraud or extortion generates pressure to enlarge these concepts. Are the enlarged concepts of fraud and extortion coherent? Do they have clear boundaries? What problem areas exist?

a. The scope of the mail and wire fraud statutes is determined by judicial decisions such as *McNally, Carpenter,* and *Cleveland,* as well as 18 U.S.C. § 1346. The prosecution must prove a scheme to defraud the victim of either a property right or the "intangible right of honest services." Both options give rise to many questions.

As discussed at pages 202–19, the Supreme Court and the lower courts have struggled to define the term property for purposes of the mail and wire fraud statutes. The cases involving fraudulent schemes to obtain government licenses or permits exemplify this difficulty. Does it make sense to have the determination whether such a scheme is subject to federal prosecution turn on whether the license or permit is property? Is this a good measure of the presence or absence of a federal interest? Or is it a good measure of whether the conduct in question should be criminalized at all? On the other hand, if we leave the concept of property and the traditional law of fraud behind, what will determine the scope of the mail and wire fraud statutes? Is there any other textual

---

b. For various news stories about the case, and the governor's conviction, see George D. Brown, *New Federalism's Unanswered Questions: Who Should Prosecute* *State and Local Officials for Political Corruption*, 60 WASH. & LEE L. REV. 417, 419 & nn.1–3 (2003).

or historical way to give content to the concept of fraud? Of course every state prosecutes fraud, and it has been defined in their statutes (and by the Model Penal Code as part of a consolidated offense). Should federal law conform to state law on this point?

Section 1346 provides an additional basis for mail and wire fraud prosecutions. It states that these statutes reach any scheme or artifice to deprive another of "the intangible right of honest services." This legislation raises a host of difficult questions about the scope of the honest services owed by a member of the state legislature or city council. Here again one of the fundamental questions is the relationship between federal and state law. Which should determine the boundaries of these duties? Suppose we say the statutes do (and perhaps must) impose a federal standard. Do they effectively create a federal conflict of interest standard—enforced by criminal prosecutions—for state and local officials? If so, what is the scope of this standard? Do these statutes also impose federal limitations on campaign financing? On campaign promises and rhetoric?

b. *Evans* and *McCormick* delineate the scope of the Hobbs Act as it applies to extortion under color of official right. *Evans*, *supra* at p. 246, held that no inducement or explicit request by the public official is required. What exactly is required? In the case of campaign contributions, *McCormick*, *supra* at pp. 257–58, held that a quid pro quo is required. The Supreme Court plainly intended the quid pro quo requirement to insulate the solicitation and receipt of ordinary campaign contributions from criminal prosecutions. Did the Court go further in *Evans* and extend the quid pro quo requirement to all Hobbs Act prosecutions for extortion under color of official right? The opinion is not crystal clear, though Justice Kennedy, *supra* at p. 258, interprets it as imposing a quid pro quo requirement across the board. As noted at 258–59, most lower courts have concluded that a quid pro quo is required in all color of official rights cases, but that a more relaxed standard applies in cases not involving campaign contributions.

Should a quid pro quo be required in all official extortion cases under the Hobbs Act? Is a quid pro quo requirement necessary when the official in question is appointed rather than elected, and thus has no need to solicit campaign contributions? Should the same standard apply to all color of official rights cases (and if so, which standard—the relatively strict standard in *McCormick*, or the easier to meet standard in *Evans*)?

But of course in many cases a federal prosecutor could recharacterize the "extortion" as "fraud" under the mail and wire fraud statutes. Is a quid pro quo required to demonstrate a deprivation of the right of honest services under the mail and wire fraud statute? If not, are you comfortable with the disparity between the requirements under the Hobbs Act and the mail and wire fraud statutes? Perhaps a quid pro quo should also be required in mail and wire fraud prosecutions. Could the courts impose that limitation, or would it take legislation?

3. The enlargement of the Hobbs Act and the mail and wire fraud statutes reaches conduct that might otherwise be characterized as bribery or the receipt of illegal gratuities. How do the requirements for a prosecution under either the Hobbs Act or the mail and wire fraud acts compare with the elements of the crime of bribery? As discussed in Chapter 7, *supra* at 282–83, 287–88, a prosecution for bribery under 18 U.S.C. § 201 requires proof of corrupt intent and a quid pro quo, but a prosecution for the lesser offense of receipt of an illegal gratuity does not. The structure of the federal bribery and gratuities offenses highlight the importance of the presence or absence of a quid pro quo requirement in Hobbs Act and mail fraud prosecutions.

No scheme of lesser and greater offenses exists under either the Hobbs Act or the mail and wire fraud statutes. Should these latter offenses be treated as the equivalent of bribery offenses, or should they be construed to reach gratuities offenses as well? Do you think that the receipt of illegal gratuities should constitute a deprivation of the "right to honest services" under the mail and wire fraud statutes? If so, should such conduct be insulated from prosecution simply because no mail or wire communications occurred, or should prosecution be available under the Hobbs Act if the requisite effect on commerce can be shown? *See generally* Charles N. Whitaker, Note, *Federal Prosecution of State and Local Bribery: Inappropriate Tools and the Need for a Structured Approach*, 78 VA. L. REV. 1617 (1992); William M. Welch II, Comment, *The Federal Bribery Statute and Special Interest Campaign Statutes*, 79 J. CRIM. L. & CRIMINOLOGY 1347 (1989). Of course as noted in point 1 above, *Evans* and *McCormick* impose a quid pro quo requirement in some, or perhaps all, extortion under color of right cases.

Is this a question solely of the presence or absence of a federal interest? Perhaps is it also a question of an appropriate penalty structure. Professor Stephen Smith argues interpreting federal crimes such as mail fraud broadly rather than narrowly promotes disproportionate punishment. Prosecutors who are dissatisfied with the penalties available under a variety of federal statutes can too easily reformulate their charges to fall within mail and wire fraud, bringing the 20 year penalty into play instead of the lower penalties Congress selected for the specific forms of criminal conduct. *See* Stephen F. Smith, *Proportionality and Federalism*, 91 U. VA. L. REV. 879, 921–25 (2005).

4. The penalty structure of the statutes in question and the Sentencing Guidelines should be considered in evaluating the effect of these provisions.

In recent years, both Congress and the Sentencing Commission have substantially revised the penalty provisions applicable to political corruption. At the statutory level, Congress increased the basic penalty for mail and wire fraud from 5 years to 20 years. This brings those statutes into line with the Hobbs Act (maximum penalty 20 years) and into rough parity with the bribery provisions of § 201 (maximum penalty 15 years). The maximum penalty for a gratuity violation under § 201 is 2 years.

Higher penalties are available under the mail and wire fraud statutes for cases involving financial institutions. These statutes merely set the maximum penalties. The penalties actually imposed are determined by the Sentencing Guidelines. Note, however, that the Supreme Court has held that the Guidelines may only be applied in an advisory fashion. See *infra* at 854–69.

The Commission recently reorganized, revised, and rationalized the provisions applicable to the Hobbs Act, the mail and wire fraud statutes, and the bribery and gratuities provisions, and substantially increased the applicable penalties.

A single guideline, U.S.S.G. § 2C1.1, now applies to all bribery cases, whether charged as Hobbs Act extortion under color of official right, fraudulent deprivation of honest services under the mail fraud and wire fraud statutes, or bribery under 18 U.S.C. § 201. In 2004 the Sentencing Commission amended § 2C1.1 to significantly increase sentences for all of these offenses. The amended guideline varies the penalty depending on whether the defendant was an elected public official, a public official, or a non-public official, imposing the highest penalties on elected public officials and other public officials in "high-level decision-making or sensitive positions." Under § 2C1.1 the minimum offense level for these officials is 18. The amount of the bribe is a specific offense characteristic that increases the offense level using the chart in the fraud guideline (reprinted, *infra,* at 997–1005). There is also an upward adjustment for cases involving more than one bribe. The Commission expected that under the 2004 amendments the average sentence for a public official who takes a bribe would increase by more than 50 percent. In announcing the changes, the Commission called public corruption offenses crimes of "internal terrorism" that strike at the heart of our democratic government. At the request of the Department of Homeland Security, the 2004 amendments also included an enhancement for bribery cases involving the facilitation of entry into the United States or the obtaining of passports or other government identification documents.

The 2004 amendments also increased penalties for gratuities cases under 18 U.S.C. § 201, which are governed by U.S.S.G. § 2C1.2. This provision has lower base offense levels than bribery (11 for public officials, 9 for other officials), subject to the same adjustments as the provisions governing bribery.

Because the reorganization applies the same guideline regardless of the statute under which public corruption charges are brought, sentencing considerations are less likely to play a major role in determining which statute prosecutors will employ. Or, to look at the matter from the defendant's perspective, the sentence imposed isn't likely to vary depending on which statute is charged. Note, however, that in cases at the highest end of the range, the statutory maximum for these offenses still varies, with the penalties under § 201 topping out at 15 years. Note also that the gratuities guideline, § 2C1.2, refers only to cases brought under 18 U.S.C. § 201. If cases that would be gratuities under § 201 can also be brought under the Hobbs Act or the mail and wire fraud statutes (see note 3, page 311), using those statutes may substantially increase the sentence—though a defendant might argue that the case *should* be governed by § 2C1.2, or that a downward departure would be appropriate. (And, as long as the Guidelines are advisory, the defendant could also argue that this is a situation where the court should not follow the Guideline if the facts reveal only a gratuity.)

U.S.S.G. §§ 2C1.1 and 2C1.2 are reprinted *infra* at 1010–19. For a comprehensive discussion of the Sentencing Guidelines, see Chapter 18 *infra*.

4. The jurisdictional predicates of the applicable federal statutes have been read broadly. Both courts and prosecutors have read each of these statutes expansively. In general, Hobbs Act convictions are upheld if there is a minimal effect on commerce, and the wire and mail fraud statutes reach fraudulent schemes even if the use of the mails or wire communications was not a central feature of the scheme. Prosecutors have aggressively pursued prosecutions for political corruption under each of these statutes when the minimal jurisdictional predicate could be established. *See supra* at 171–90, 261–62, 273–75. In the case of the Travel Act, *supra* at p. 103, federal prosecutors and investigators have sometimes gone further, seeking to maneuver a suspect into using a facility of interstate commerce in order to create federal jurisdiction. See *supra* at pp. 226–27. As a result most acts of state and local political corruption probably fall within the ambit of at least one federal statute.

However, though the combined sweep of federal jurisdiction is extremely broad, the scope of each of the statutes in question is more restricted. If a political bribery and kickback case is characterized as fraud, it falls within the mail and wire fraud statutes if letters are mailed in furtherance of the scheme, but not if the same communications are made by local telephone calls. The hypothetical case falls within the Hobbs Act if the prosecution can characterize it as extortion under color of official right and establish the requisite effect on commerce. But what if the prosecution is unable to establish a sufficient effect on commerce (which would be much more likely if the Supreme Court sides with the lower court judges who think that *Lopez* and *Morrison* require a cutback in Hobbs Act jurisdiction)? Would such a case constitute a violation of the Travel Act? It might, but new factors would enter the analysis. First, it would be necessary to show that the conduct in question violated the state bribery statute. Second, there must be proof of interstate travel or the use of an interstate facility. How difficult is it to meet this requirement? A few decisions require that the use of an interstate facility be related "significantly" to the illegal activity, see, e.g., *United States v. O'Hara*, 301 F.3d 563, 570 (7th Cir. 2002), *United States v. Altobella*, 442 F.2d 310, 314 (7th Cir. 1971), and *United States v. Archer*, 486 F.2d 670, 682 (2d Cir. 1973). Others hold that any conduct that facilitates the illegal activity is sufficient. *See United States v. Peveto*, 881 F.2d 844, 860–61 (10th Cir. 1989); *United States v. Lozano*,

839 F.2d 1020, 1022 (4th Cir. 1988). Finally, the order of events is important: the Travel Act requires that the defendant use the interstate facility and "thereafter" engage in the prescribed conduct. Although the distinction between the use of a local letter or a local telephone call—or whether interstate travel occurs before or after prescribed conduct—is not necessarily a good measure of the extent of a federal interest in a case, it may determine whether there is federal jurisdiction.

Are there significant jurisdictional gaps in the existing structure? For example, is corruption of the local judicial system covered? Does the type of case matter? *See, e.g., United States v. Wright, supra* at p. 274, holding that fixing drunken driving cases affects commerce because it makes interstate highway travel more dangerous. What if the bribes were taken in divorce court? Even if there were no impact on commerce in such a case and no mailing or use of an interstate facility, is it possible to argue that a federal interest is present?

5. Many Hobbs Act and mail and wire fraud prosecutions involve low level and in some cases petty bribery or gratuities offenses by state and local officials. A student note compiled the following examples:

> * * * One notable example involved a successful prosecution under RICO and the Hobbs Act (which both carry twenty-year penalties) of inspectors in the Chicago Department of Sewers who received $10 to $20 "tips." Other Hobbs Act prosecutions of low-level local bribery include cases brought against the following government employees: state transportation department employees who received vacations from highway contractors, a New York City Transit Authority official who passively accepted meals and vacations from contractors doing business with the city, an Alcoholic Beverage Control Commissioner who received substantial quantities of liquor, the Director of the Department of Education of Guam who received clothes and appliances from vendors, and a school board member who received payments and airline tickets from contractors who transacted business with the board. Prosecutions under the mail fraud statute include cases against the following local officials: a city tax official who received gratuities from a company that he was auditing, a landfill operator who gave a series of cash "tips" to a local sanitation department official who had power to decide where the city would dump its trash, and a city council member who used city automobile supplies for his personal use.

Charles N. Whitaker, Note, *Federal Prosecution of State and Local Bribery: Inappropriate Tools and the Need for a Structured Approach*, 78 Va. L. Rev. 1617, 1627–28 (1992) (citations omitted).

Is there a substantial federal interest in the prosecution of such low-level corruption at the state and local level? Are you convinced that federal jurisdiction over all types of corruption in state and local government is desirable? Prosecutions of this nature pose starkly the issue of the proper relationship between federal and state authority. Federal enforcement offers two main advantages: it brings in investigators and prosecutors who are not a part of the allegedly corrupt local political establishment, and it provides a desirable second line of defense against corruption in government.

What are the negative consequences of federal jurisdiction in this context? Political corruption prosecutions raise concerns about both political motivations and the desire to garner publicity by going after "big game." Recent events in Maryland seemed to have elements of both concerns: the press reported that the U.S. Attorney for Maryland had instructed his staff in July 2004 that he wanted three front page white collar or public corruption cases by November 6—in other words, right before election day.[c] But is there any evidence or any reason to believe that the availability of a federal prosecution enhances the danger of politically motivated prosecutions, or that federal prosecutors any more likely than their state counterparts to go gunning for "big game"? Indeed, federal prosecutors, unlike state prosecutors, are not elected, and there is some supervision available from "Main Justice" in Washington. The Justice Department responded by making public a letter informing the U.S. Attorney for Maryland that he must submit any proposed public corruption indictment to the Deputy Attorney General until further notice.

What about resource considerations? It seems unlikely that there are there sufficient federal resources to prosecute all low-level corruption throughout the United States. Another important facet of the problem is how federal prosecutions will affect state enforcement efforts. Will federal prosecutions serve as a spur to state enforcement efforts, or a disincentive? It has also been suggested that the expansion of federal jurisdiction threatens a significant loss of political autonomy at the state and local level. Are there important local variations that ought to be preserved? Consider in this light the intangible rights prosecutions under the mail fraud and wire fraud statutes, *supra* at pp. 171–90, which frequently involved challenges to well-established patronage practices.

Several recent articles debate this issue, and are well worth reading. Some authors argue that there is a substantial federal interest in prosecuting state and local corruption.

Professor George Brown is a leading advocate of a federal role in prosecuting state and local corruption. He advocates a "protective" federal role, and articulates a vision of a general right to good government. He argues that corruption undermines the rule of law, equal access to government, and the right to cast an equally weighted vote. Corruption is undemocratic because it gives special access to certain private interests. Brown argues that his view is consistent with the Supreme Court's recent First Amendment cases on campaign finance reform, which recognize that political patronage can be violative of the First Amendment. Prosecuting state and local corruption can be seen as

c. These events are described in George D. Brown, *Carte Blanche: Federal Prosecu-* *tion of State and Local Officials After* Sabri, 54 CATHOLIC U. L. REV. 403, 403 (2005).

another example of the national role in preserving the democratic system. *See generally* George D. Brown, *Carte Blanche: Federal Prosecution of State and Local Officials After* Sabri, 54 CATHOLIC U. L. REV. 403 (2005), and George D. Brown, *New Federalism's Unanswered Question: Who Should Prosecute State and Local Officials For Political Corruption?*, 60 WASH. & LEE L. REV. 417 (2003). In *Carte Blanche* Professor Brown also relates his views to some of the other key scholarship.

Professor Peter Henning argues that the constitution reflects a deep concern with preventing corruption—what he calls its "Anti–Corruption Legacy"–that justifies a federal role in the prosecution of misconduct by state and local officials (as well as federal officials). He identifies a number of constitutional provisions that reflect this Anti–Corruption Legacy and create structural features to limit corruption at the federal level, and a smaller number of provisions that in his view reflect a concern with state or local corruption. More importantly, he argues that the Constitution reflects a concern with a federal-state balance as a means of protecting liberty by limiting the powers at each level of government. Corruption interferes with the federal-state balance by undermining state and local governments, and hence weakening the protection for liberty. As he explains:

> The constitutional design to eliminate corruption demonstrates the Framers' intent to guard against the threat to liberty from the misuse of public authority.
>
> . . . . In analyzing Congress' constitutional power to enact a statute, the Anti–Corruption Legacy supports a broad interpretation of congressional authority to reach the conduct of state and local officials, regardless of whether the crime could also be prosecuted by the state.
>
> . . . . [T]he individual liberty afforded by federalism is enhanced when the integrity of government is protected through federal prosecution.

Peter J. Henning, *Federalism and the Federal Prosecution of State and Local Corruption*, 92 KY. L.J. 75, 82 (2003/2004).

But not everyone is persuaded that federal prosecution of state and local corruption will promote democracy. To the contrary, Professor Roderick Hills fears that federal prosecutors may impose a federal conflict of interest system that is fundamentally incompatible with a distinctive style of democracy that flourishes at the state and local level. The federal government has adopted what he calls "bureaucratic populism," which is characterized by full time bureaucrats who are rigidly insulated from private interests. But most states have "participatory populism," which rejects the separation of public and private spheres, and mixes lay and professional decision making. Both elected officials and administrative officers generally serve only part time, and maintain substantial private interests in the community. Hills argues that each style of democracy has advantages and disadvantages, and that an uncritical adoption of norms of bureaucratic populism through a notion of "honest services" under the mail and wire fraud statutes threatens the operation of participatory populism. *See* Roderick M. Hills, *Corruption and Federalism: (When) Do Federal Criminal Prosecutions Improve Non–Federal Democracy*, 6 THEORETICAL INQUIRIES 113 (2005). Hills makes the interesting suggestion that to impose at least a modest restraint on federal prosecutions it might be wise to require central approval of all state and local corruption prosecutions.

Finally, for a broader perspective, see Peter J. Henning, *Public Corruption: A Comparative Analysis of International Corruption Conventions and United States Law*, 18 ARIZ. J. INT'L & COMPARATIVE L. 793 (2001).

6. If there is a substantial federal interest in the prosecution of state and local political corruption, is there a need for a new federal statute explicitly aimed at such conduct? How satisfactory is the current stopgap system, where statutes originally aimed at other concerns have been pressed into service? Does it make sense to have the definition of the offense and the penalty turn not on the nature of the misconduct in question, but the jurisdictional provision that it triggered? Is the answer a new federal statute aimed explicitly at state and local political corruption? Such a statute would raise several issues:

a. **Jurisdiction** What should the jurisdictional base of such a statute be? Is there any reason not to assert federal jurisdiction over state and local corruption under all of the available jurisdictional predicates, i.e., mail, effect on commerce, travel in commerce, use of interstate facilities, etc.? Or are there some jurisdictional predicates that should not be employed in this context?

As a constitutional matter, is there a more all-encompassing theoretical basis for federal jurisdiction? Might such a basis be found in the constitutional guarantee of a republican government in each state? *See* Adam H. Kurland, *The Guarantee Clause as a Basis for Federal Prosecutions of State and Local Officials*, 62 S. CAL. L. REV. 367 (1989). Or could Congress make a finding that state and local political corruption has an effect on interstate commerce? How might political corruption affect commerce? Adding to the cost of doing business? Interfering with the market by providing special benefits to entities that pay bribes? Do you think that findings such as these could be supported by empirical evidence? Could Congress legitimately make a finding that these activities—as a class—have a sufficiently significant impact on commerce to warrant federal jurisdiction over the whole class of conduct, without a showing in each individual case? *See supra* at p. 26 et seq. Assuming that Congress could assert jurisdiction over this entire class of conduct, should it do so? Or should federal jurisdiction be targeted far more narrowly, leaving some—or all—of these problems for state enforcement?

Are there some forms of corruption that are too de minimis to be of federal concern? If so, would you measure this concern in dollars? If a penalty structure based on the dollars involved does not seem entirely satisfactory, can you suggest another measure or measures?

b. **The elements of the offense** What existing substantive offense should serve as the model for the new federal offense? Bribery seems to be the most natural starting point. Would there be any advantages of employing the framework of fraud or extortion instead? Should the new federal statute distinguish between bribery and gratuities offenses? If so, can the framework of either fraud or extortion accommodate this distinction?

(1) Gratuities pose different issues than bribery. As George Brown explained:

Once one leaves the domain of bribery, one encounters the fundamental nature of a pluralistic system in which it is taken as a given that a large variety of interests will attempt to secure influence of means. Gifts are common in the private sector and may represent nothing more than an attempt by lobbyists to secure a healthy working relationship with policymakers. Even if they raise ethical questions, these might be better dealt with through civil and administrative processes than the criminal law. The latter presents the danger, particularly in the political corruption context, of prosecutorial abuse, and may, depending upon the working of any given statute, present "snares for the unwary."

George D. Brown, *Putting Watergate Behind Us—* Salinas, Sun–Diamond *and Two Views of the Anti–Corruption Model*, 74 Tulane L. Rev. 747, 770 (2000).

(2) Would it be desirable to make any special provisions for campaign contributions? If so, what would you suggest? *See generally* Daniel Hays Lowenstein, *Political Bribery and the Intermediate Theory of Politics*, 32 UCLA L. Rev. 784 (1985); Joseph R. Weeks, *Bribes, Gratuities and the Congress: The Institutionalized Corruption of the Political Process, The Impotence of Criminal Law to Reach It, and a Proposal for Change*, 13 J. Legis. 123 (1986); William M. Welch II, Comment, *The Federal Bribery Statute and Special Interest Campaign Statutes*, 79 J. Crim. L. & Criminology, 1347 (1989).

(3) To whom should such a statute apply? Any employee or official of state or local government? Or only a smaller group of high level officials? Should it apply to persons running for political office? To party officials or others who exercise de facto influence over governmental decisions? For a discussion of this issue in the context of mail fraud, see *supra* at pp. 182–90.

(4) How should these decisions, and others, affect the penalty or penalties to be prescribed? *Cf.* U.S.S.G. § 2C1.1(b)(2) (increasing penalty for bribery offenses according to "the value of the payment, the benefit received or to be received in return for the payment, the value of anything obtained or to be obtained by a public official or others acting with a public official, or the loss to the government from the offense,

whichever is greatest''); U.S.S.G. § 2C1.1(b)(3) (increasing the base level to a minimum of 18 if the offense involved a payment intended to influence ''an elected official or any public official in a high-level decision-making or sensitive position'').

c. **The relationship between state and federal standards** Should a new federal statute incorporate state law in any form, or set a uniform federal standard? On the one hand, the mail fraud statute has been interpreted to override state law on issues such as the duty of fiduciaries. *See supra* at pp. 188–90. On the other hand, the Travel Act allows federal prosecution of bribery in violation of state law if federal jurisdictional predicates are met. This allows some variation state to state in terms of the conduct expected on the part of state and local officials. Would it be desirable to follow this model in the new statute? Or should the new statute create a federal code of minimum conduct? If a federal standard is needed, should it follow the law applicable to federal officials, 18 U.S.C. § 201? Why or why not?

d. **A new statute or wholesale recodification?** The strained interpretations of the Hobbs Act and the mail and wire fraud statute illustrate vividly one consequence of the failure to enact a comprehensive revision of the federal criminal code. The current federal code is a hodgepodge that grew up willy-nilly as Congress enacted a series of provisions dealing with the problem of the moment. If a comprehensive revision of the federal code were undertaken, how might it differ from the enactment of a single statute aimed at the problem of state and local political corruption? See, for example, the comprehensive jurisdictional provisions proposed by the Brown Commission, *infra* at p. 1034.

e. **Evaluating one proposal: H.R. 3371** The Department of Justice supported Title 48 of the Violent Crime Prevention Act of 1991, H.R. 3371, 102nd Cong., which would have created two new offenses, public corruption and narcotic-related public corruption. These proposals are reprinted below. Why are there two provisions? What distinguishes each? How would these proposals deal with the issues identified here? Would they introduce new problems? If legislation is needed, would you support the adoption of either or both of these provisions? If these provisions were adopted, should any other provisions currently in force be repealed or amended to narrow their scope? Do you think the Department would still support this provision? What changes have occurred since 1991 that might affect its thinking?

H. R. 3371

TITLE XLVIII—PUBLIC CORRUPTION

SEC. 4801. SHORT TITLE.

This title may be cited as the ''Anti–Corruption Act of 1991''.

SEC. 4802. OFFENSE.

Chapter 11 of title 18, United States Code, is amended by adding at the end thereof the following new section:

226. Public corruption

(a) Whoever, in a circumstance described in subsection (d), deprives or defrauds, or endeavors to deprive or to defraud, by any scheme or artifice, the inhabitants of a State or political subdivision of a State of the honest services of an official or employee of such State, or political subdivision of a State, shall be fined under this title, or imprisoned for not more than 10 years, or both.

(b) Whoever, in a circumstance described in subsection (d), deprives or defrauds, or endeavors to deprive or to defraud, by any scheme or artifice, the inhabitants of a State or political subdivision of a State of a fair and impartially conducted election process in any primary, run-off, special, or general election—

(1) through the procurement, casting, or tabulation of ballots that are materially false, fictitious, or fraudulent or that are invalid, under the laws of the State in which the election is held;

(2) through paying or offering to pay any person for voting;

(3) through the procurement or submission of voter registrations that contain false material information, or omit material information; or

(4) through the filing of any report required to be filed under State law regarding an election campaign that contains false material information or omits material information, shall be fined under this title or imprisoned for not more than ten years, or both.

(c) Whoever, being a public official or an official or employee of a State, or political subdivision of a State, in a circumstance described in subsection (d), deprives or defrauds, or endeavors to deprive or to defraud, by any scheme or artifice, the inhabitants of a State or a political subdivision of a State of the right to have the affairs of the State or political subdivision conducted on the basis of complete, true, and accurate material information, shall be fined under this title or imprisoned for not more than 10 years, or both.

(d) The circumstances referred to in subsections (a), (b), and (c) are that—

(1) for the purpose of executing or concealing such scheme or artifice or attempting to do so, the person so doing—

(A) places in any post office or authorized depository for mail matter, any matter or thing whatever to be sent or delivered by the Postal Service, or takes or receives therefrom, any such matter or thing, or knowingly causes to be delivered by mail according to the direction thereon, or at the place at which it is directed to be delivered by the person to whom it is addressed, any such matter or thing;

(B) transmits or causes to be transmitted by means of wire, radio, or television communication in interstate or foreign commerce any writings, signs, signals, pictures, or sounds;

(C) transports or causes to be transported any person or thing, or induces any person to travel in or to be transported in, interstate or foreign commerce; or

(D) uses or causes to use of any facility of interstate or foreign commerce;

(2) the scheme or artifice affects or constitutes an attempt to affect in any manner or degree, or would if executed or concealed so affect, interstate or foreign commerce; or

(3) as applied to an offense under subsection (b), an objective of the scheme or artifice is to secure the election of an official who, if elected, would have some authority over the administration of funds derived from an Act of Congress totaling $10,000 or more during the 12–month period immediately preceding or following the election or date of the offense.

(e) Whoever deprives or defrauds, or endeavors to deprive or to defraud, by any scheme or artifice, the inhabitants of the United States of the honest services of a public official or person who has been selected to be a public official shall be fined under this title, imprisoned for not more than 10 years, or both.

* * *

(h) For purposes of this section—

(1) the term 'State' means a State of the United States, the District of Columbia, Puerto Rico, and any other commonwealth, territory, or possession of the United States;

(2) the terms 'public official' and 'person who has been selected to be a public official' have the meaning set forth in section 201 of this title; the terms 'public official' and 'person who has been selected to be a public official' shall also include any person acting or pretending to act under color of official authority;

(3) the term 'official' includes—

(A) any person employed by, exercising any authority derived from, or holding any position in the government of a State or any subdivision of the executive, legislative, judicial, or other branch of government thereof, including a department, independent establishment, commission, administration, authority, board, and bureau, and a corporation or other legal entity established and subject to control by a government or governments for the execution of a governmental or intergovernmental program;

(B) any person acting or pretending to act under color of official authority; and

(C) includes any person who has been nominated, appointed or selected to be an official or who has been officially informed that he or she will be so nominated, appointed or selected;

(4) the term 'under color of official authority' includes any person who represents that he or she controls, is an agent of, or otherwise acts on behalf of an official, public official, and person who has been selected to be a public official; and

(5) the term 'uses any facility of interstate or foreign commerce' includes the intrastate use of any facility that may also be used in interstate or foreign commerce.''.

* * *

SEC. 4805. NARCOTICS–RELATED PUBLIC CORRUPTION.

(a) IN GENERAL.—CHAPTER 11 OF TITLE 18, UNITED STATES CODE, IS AMENDED BY INSERTING AFTER SECTION 219 THE FOLLOWING NEW SECTION:

220. Narcotics and public corruption

(a) Any public official who, directly or indirectly, corruptly demands, seeks, receives, accepts, or agrees to receive or accept anything of value personally or for any other person in return for—

(1) being influenced in the performance or nonperformance of any official act; or

(2) being influenced to commit or to aid in committing, or to collude in, or to allow or make opportunity for the commission of any offense against the United States or any State; shall be guilty of a class B felony.

(b) Any person who, directly or indirectly, corruptly gives, offers, or promises anything of value to any public official, or offers or promises any public official to give anything of value to any other person, with intent—

(1) to influence any official act;

(2) to influence such public official to commit or aid in committing, or to collude in, or to allow or make opportunity for the commission of any offense against the United States or any State; or

(3) to influence such public official to do or to omit to do any act in violation of such official's lawful duty;

shall be guilty of a class B felony.

(c) There shall be Federal jurisdiction over an offense described in this section if such offense involves, is part of, or is intended to further or to conceal the illegal possession, importation, manufacture, transportation, or distribution of any controlled substance or controlled substance analogue.

(d) For the purpose of this section—

(1) the term 'public official' means—

(A) an officer or employee or person acting for or on behalf of the United States, or any department, agency, or branch of Government thereof in any official function, under or by authority of any such department, agency, or branch of Government;

(B) a juror;

(C) an officer or employee or person acting for or on behalf of the government of any State, territory, or possession of the United States (including the District of Columbia), or any political subdivision thereof, in any official function, under or by the authority of any such State, territory, possession, or political subdivision; or

(D) any person who has been nominated or appointed to be a public official as defined in subparagraph (A), (B), or (C), or has been officially informed that he or she will be so nominated or appointed;

(2) the term 'official act' means any decision, action, or conduct regarding any question, matter, proceeding, cause, suit, investigation, or prosecution which may at any time be pending, or which may be brought before any public official, in such official's official capacity, or in such official's place of trust or profit; and

(3) the terms 'controlled substance' and 'controlled substance analogue' have the meaning set forth in section 102 of the Controlled Substances Act.''

News Release
U.S. Department of Justice
United States Attorney
District of Rhode Island

Contact: Thomas Connell, 401–528–5224, thomas.connell@usdoj.gov
April 2, 2001

Cianci, Frank Corrente, Richard Autiello, Edward Voccola, and Joseph Pannone are accused of conducting city government and the mayor's campaign organization as a criminal enterprise; aide Artin Coloian is charged in bribery conspiracy.

A federal grand jury has indicted Providence Mayor Vincent A. Cianci, Jr. and four others on racketeering charges. The indictment alleges that they operated city government and the Mayor's campaign organization as a criminal enterprise designed to enrich Cianci and his campaign fund. A sixth defendant is charged with engaging in one of the bribery schemes alleged in the indictment.

United States Attorney Margaret E. Curran and Charles S. Prouty, Special Agent in Charge of the Federal Bureau of Investigation, announced the 30–count indictment, which was returned today in U.S.

District Court, Providence. It alleges that bribery, extortion, and other criminal conduct permeated city government in violation of the Racketeer Influenced Corrupt Organizations Act (RICO). The indictment also seeks the forfeiture of assets, including the Mayor's campaign fund.

The indictment is the latest to result from Operation Plunder Dome, an investigation into Providence municipal government that was initiated and led by the Federal Bureau of Investigation. The Rhode Island State Police also participated in the investigation and the Internal Revenue Service Criminal Investigation Division provided assistance.

Charged in the indictment with RICO conspiracy and RICO conduct are:

- Cianci;
- Frank E. Corrente, the mayor's former Director of Administration;
- Richard E. Autiello, a member of the Providence Towing Association;
- Edward E. Voccola, a businessman who has leased real estate to the city;
- and Joseph A. Pannone, former Chair of the city Board of Tax Assessment Review.

Artin H. Coloian, the mayor's Chief of Staff, is charged with engaging in a bribery conspiracy but is not charged with RICO offenses.

The indictment was placed under seal until FBI agents arrested Voccola, who will be held overnight pending arraignment Tuesday in U.S. District Court, Providence. The other defendants, who were not arrested, will be summoned to appear for arraignment.

Charges against Corrente and Pannone that were alleged in an indictment returned last June are contained in this indictment, which supercedes the earlier one.

The indictment alleges that Cianci used his office to obtain cash, often in the guise of campaign contributions, and other consideration from city employees and vendors. It alleges that those who paid money to Cianci or his campaign, or otherwise complied with his demands, were rewarded with leases, contracts, employment and promotions, business, or other benefits.

A synopsis of the allegations follows. Some conduct is charged both as acts that furthered the RICO enterprise and as separate criminal offenses.

Tow List

The indictment alleges that, between 1991 and 1999, Cianci, Corrente, and Autiello obtained approximately $250,000 in campaign contributions from members of the Providence Towing Association to ensure their continuance on the Tow List, from which the city Police Department selects towers to tow cars. Cianci, Corrente, and Autiello are charged with extortion conspiracy and extortion as a RICO act and, in separate counts, with conspiracy, extortion, and federal bribery.

Jere Lease

Edward Voccola, through his company, Jere Realty, Inc., is alleged to have corruptly leased property on West Fountain Street to the city School Department in 1991. Over the course of several years, Voccola allegedly paid Corrente and Cianci some of the proceeds of the lease payments, allegedly converting Jere Realty checks into cash for the illicit payments. Cianci, Corrente, and Voccola are charged with mail fraud and bribery as a RICO act. Voccola is also charged with conspiracy and money laundering as a RICO act. Corrente is also charged with witness tampering, as a RICO act and in a separate count.

Ronci Estate

In 1998, Cianci, Corrente, and Pannone allegedly extorted $15,000 from the heirs of Fernando Ronci in exchange for reducing back taxes due on Ronci-owned property on Reservoir Avenue. The three are charged with conspiracy to commit extortion and extortion, both as a RICO act and in separate counts.

Planning Department Job

Cianci is alleged to have directed the Department of Planning and Development to hire Christopher Ise in exchange for a $5,000 payment that was allegedly paid through Cianci's Executive Assistant, Coloian. Cianci is charged with a RICO act of extortion conspiracy and bribery, and Cianci and Coloian are charged in separate counts with conspiracy and federal bribery.

City-owned Lots

The indictment alleges that Cianci attempted to extort $10,000 from Anthony Freitas so that Freitas could buy two city-owned lots for $1,000 each. Cianci is charged with extortion conspiracy, attempted extortion, and mail fraud, all as a RICO act and in separate counts. Freitas, who was cooperating with the FBI during this investigation, did not buy the lots.

Freitas Lease

The indictment alleges that, between April 1998 and April 1999, Corrente and Pannone attempted to extort money from Freitas in exchange for helping him lease buildings on Westminster Street to the city. According to the indictment, Freitas twice gave Corrente $1,000 to facilitate the lease. Corrente and Pannone are charged with extortion conspiracy and two attempts at extortion, both as a RICO act and in separate counts.

"Pay to Get Paid"

The indictment alleges that, between June and October 1998, Corrente and Pannone tried to extort bribes from Anthony Freitas in exchange for facilitating payment to Freitas and his company, JKL Engineering, for services that had been rendered to the city. Corrente and Pannone are charged with conspiracy to commit extortion, attempted extortion, mail fraud conspiracy, and mail fraud, all as a RICO act and in separate counts.

University Club

The indictment alleges that, in 1998, Cianci used city agencies to pressure the University Club to admit him as a member, holding up approval of the club's renovation plans. In September 1998, the club gave Cianci a free, lifetime, honorary membership. The indictment also alleges that Cianci tried to hinder a witness from providing information to the FBI and to a federal grand jury. Cianci is charged with extortion, mail fraud, and witness tampering, all as RICO acts and in separate counts.

Police Department Hire

Corrente and Autiello are alleged to have demanded a $5,000 payment for Joseph Maggiacomo III to be hired onto the Providence Police Department in 1996. Corrente and Autiello are charged with a bribery conspiracy and bribery as a RICO act and, in separate counts, with conspiracy and federal bribery.

Forfeiture

The indictment alleges that certain assets controlled by the defendants should be forfeited because they were derived from the criminal conduct of the racketeering enterprise. Among the assets being sought through forfeiture:

- three accounts belonging to Cianci's campaign organization, Friends of Mayor Cianci—a brokerage account at Credit Suisse First Boston in New York City, a partnership interest in T.G.T. Capital Partners of New York City, and an account at First Bank and Trust Company, Providence;

- assets controlled by Edward Voccola—the assets of Jere Realty Co., Inc., and real estate at (1) 425 Washington Street and 400–406 Washington Street, and (2) 15 & 19 Penelope Street and 403 West Fountain Street;

- $1,373,358 allegedly linked to Cianci, Corrente, and Voccola through the Jere Realty lease with the School Department; and the amounts of money allegedly obtained by the RICO defendants through various schemes alleged in the indictment: $250,000 by Cianci, Corrente, and Autiello; $15,000 by Cianci, Corrente, and Pannone; $5,000 by Cianci; $3,100 by Corrente and Pannone; and $5,000 by Corrente and Autiello.

The case is being prosecuted by Assistant U.S. Attorneys Richard W. Rose and Terrence P. Donnelly. FBI Special Agent W. Dennis Aiken is the lead agent in the Operation Plunder Dome investigation.–30–

News Release Attachment A

UNITED STATES v. VINCENT A. CIANCI, JR. et. al.

SUMMARY OF CHARGES

Vincent A. Cianci, 59, Providence Biltmore Hotel—RICO conspiracy, RICO, seven criminal RICO acts, three counts of Hobbs Act extortion conspiracy, three counts of Hobbs Act extortion, two counts of federal bribery conspiracy, two counts of federal bribery, one count of attempted extortion, one count of mail fraud conspiracy, two counts of mail fraud, and two counts of witness tampering.

Frank E. Corrente, 72, One Dean Ridge Boulevard, Cranston—RICO conspiracy, RICO, seven criminal RICO acts, four counts of Hobbs Act extortion conspiracy, two counts of Hobbs Act extortion, two counts of federal bribery conspiracy, two counts of federal bribery, four counts of attempted extortion, one count of mail fraud conspiracy, two counts of mail fraud, and one count of witness tampering.

Artin H. Coloian, 36, 360 Adelaide Avenue, Providence—one count of federal bribery conspiracy and one count of federal bribery.

Richard E. Autiello, 62, 88 Cathedral Avenue, Providence—RICO conspiracy, RICO, two criminal RICO acts, one count of Hobbs Act extortion conspiracy, one count of Hobbs Act extortion, two counts of federal bribery conspiracy, and two counts of federal bribery.

Edward E. Voccola, 72, 165 Glen Hills Drive, Cranston—RICO conspiracy, RICO, and two criminal RICO acts, one of those acts allegedly including 74 instances of money laundering.

Joseph A. Pannone, 73, 86 Lucille Street, Providence—RICO conspiracy, RICO, three criminal RICO acts, three counts of Hobbs Act extortion conspiracy, one count of Hobbs Act extortion, four counts of attempted extortion, one count of mail fraud conspiracy, and two counts of mail fraud.

News Release Attachment B

UNITED STATES v. VINCENT A. CIANCI, JR. et. al.

STATUTORY MAXIMUM PENALTIES

Upon conviction, the statutory maximum penalties for the offenses charged in the indictment are as follows:

RICO conspiracy—20 years imprisonment, a fine of $250,000 or twice the gross profit or proceeds from the offense, forfeiture of property that is part of or has been derived from the offense;

RICO—20 years imprisonment, a fine of $250,000 or twice the gross profit or proceeds from the offense;

Hobbs Act extortion conspiracy—20 years imprisonment, $250,000 fine;

Hobbs Act extortion and attempted extortion—20 years imprisonment, $250,000 fine;

Witness tampering—10 years imprisonment, $250,000 fine;

Federal bribery conspiracy—5 years imprisonment, $250,000 fine;

Federal bribery—10 years imprisonment, $250,000 fine;

Mail fraud conspiracy—5 years imprisonment, $250,000 fine;

Mail fraud—5 years imprisonment, $250,000 fine.

These are the maximum penalties specified in the relevant statutes. Upon a defendant's conviction, exact sentencing would be calculated on the basis of guidelines that take into account such factors as the specific nature and impact of an offense and a defendant's criminal background, if any. An indictment is merely an allegation and a defendants is presumed innocent unless and until proven guilty in court.

Part III

DRUG TRAFFICKING AND
MONEY LAUNDERING

Chapter 9

DRUG OFFENSE ENFORCEMENT

INTRODUCTION

Beginning in the early part of last century, the Federal Government assumed significant—though not exclusive—responsibility for regulating and controlling the use of addictive and other harmful drugs. Federal drug enforcement activities have increased dramatically in recent years, and in 2004, drug cases accounted for 27% of the federal criminal docket. Accordingly, drug legislation and policy are a topic of great importance in the federal criminal justice system.

The first federal anti-drug statute aimed directly and comprehensively at limiting domestic traffic in narcotic drugs was enacted in 1914. Prior to the adoption of this legislation, heroin, opium, morphine and cocaine could be freely purchased in the United States in local drug stores. Relying on the taxing power, Congress required persons who dealt with opium or coca leaves to register, keep records and pay a special tax. Criminal penalties applied to a failure to comply with any of these requirements. Over the next 55 years, Congress enacted piecemeal legislation adding new drugs—such as marijuana, cocaine, and barbiturates—to its list of controlled substances, establishing a licensing and quota system for narcotic drug manufacturers, and authorizing the forfeiture of vehicles used to transport contraband drugs. Although all of the early statutes continued to rely on the taxing power, several of the later statutes were grounded on the commerce power.

The Comprehensive Drug Abuse Prevention and Control Act of 1970, 21 U.S.C. §§ 801 et seq., was the first comprehensive effort to create a single all-encompassing scheme covering both narcotic and dangerous drugs. In enacting this provision Congress employed its authority under the Commerce Clause, but the statute requires no proof of a nexus to commerce in individual cases. Rather, jurisdiction is based upon the following findings by Congress, 21 U.S.C. § 801(3)–(6):

> (3) A major portion of the traffic in controlled substances flows through interstate and foreign commerce. Incidents of the traffic which are not an integral part of the interstate or foreign flow, such

as manufacture, local distribution, and possession, nonetheless have a substantial and direct effect upon interstate commerce because—

(A) after manufacture, many controlled substances are transported in interstate commerce,

(B) controlled substances distributed locally usually have been transported in interstate commerce immediately before their distribution, and

(C) controlled substances possessed commonly flow through interstate commerce immediately prior to such possession.

(4) Local distribution and possession of controlled substances contribute to swelling the interstate traffic in such substances.

(5) Controlled substances manufactured and distributed intrastate cannot be differentiated from controlled substances manufactured and distributed interstate. Thus, it is not feasible to distinguish, in terms of controls, between controlled substances manufactured and distributed interstate and controlled substances manufactured and distributed intrastate.

(6) Federal control of the intrastate incidents of the traffic in controlled substances is essential to the effective control of the interstate incidents of such traffic.

The 1970 statute remains in force (with various amendments described below) and thus these legislative findings provide the basis for all contemporary federal drug laws. For a discussion of the constitutional issues posed by Congress's class-of-activities approach, see *Perez v. United States*, 402 U.S. 146 (1971), *supra* 26.

The 1970 statute established five classes of controlled substances, each with its own sentencing schedule. Drugs were classified according to their potential for abuse and whether they have an accepted medical use, with schedule I drugs having the highest potential for abuse, no accepted medical use and therefore subject to the strictest controls. For example, marijuana, heroin, and LSD are listed as schedule I drugs, cocaine, crack and opium as schedule II drugs, while amphetamines and PCP are schedule III drugs. The Attorney General was given power to add or remove a drug from a schedule after making findings under criteria set forth in the statute; the Secretary of Health, Education, and Welfare was empowered to make scientific evaluations and recommendations regarding the classification of a drug.[a] (As noted later at 337–38, many people believe that marijuana does have medical benefits, but it has not been reclassified.)

The Act of 1970 made it criminal (when not in compliance with statutory requirements) to manufacture, distribute, dispense, import,

---

a. When the authority of the Attorney General and the Secretary to classify drugs was challenged under the non-delegation doctrine, the U.S. courts of appeals in a series of cases consistently upheld the constitutionality of the statutory delegation. *See, e.g.,* United States v. Pastor, 557 F.2d 930 (2d Cir. 1977); United States v. Davis, 564 F.2d 840 (9th Cir. 1977).

export, possess with intent to manufacture, distribute, or dispense, or knowingly possess narcotics or attempt or conspire to do any of the foregoing. Thus, for example, manufacturers and distributors of controlled substances were required to register, make inventories, keep records, stay within quotas, and file reports. The standards for registration varied depending on the class of controlled substance being manufactured. Provisions of the 1970 statute also penalized manufacturing or distributing drugs abroad with the intent to illegally import the substance into the United States. In addition, the Act criminalized participation in a continuing criminal drug-related enterprise, imposed additional penalties for distributing drugs to persons under 21 years of age, and provided asset forfeiture procedures.

In the 1980's Congress increased the penalties for most existing drug offenses, prescribing mandatory minimum sentences for most offenses. For example, 21 U.S.C. § 841 was amended to require a 10 year minimum sentence for anyone convicted of distributing, manufacturing, or possessing with the intent to distribute one kilogram of heroin or five kilograms of cocaine. For persons who have previously been convicted of a felony drug offense, the mandatory minimum increases to 20 years. Several new criminal provisions were enacted at this time, including 21 U.S.C. § 856, commonly known as the crack house statute, which makes it an offense to open or maintain a place for the purpose of manufacturing, distributing, or using a controlled substance, or to manage or control a building and knowingly or intentionally make it available for these purposes. During the same period Congress also created new non-drug offenses that were intended to make a major contribution to federal drug control strategy. The most important of these offenses dealt with money laundering. For a discussion of money laundering, see Chapter 10.

New civil and criminal drug penalties were also enacted in the 1980s. The new criminal penalty provision, codified as 21 U.S.C. § 862, provides that a defendant convicted of either trafficking or possession of a controlled substance may be declared ineligible for certain federal benefits. This provision is of interest for several reasons. First, it applies to state as well as federal convictions, and thus implements the goal of integrating federal and state anti-drug efforts. Second, because this provision applies to possession as well as trafficking offenses, it targets users. Prior federal enforcement efforts focused principally if not exclusively on reducing supply; by providing a penalty applicable to users, this provision could also serve to decrease demand. A list of over 460 deniable federal benefits was compiled, and enforcement efforts began in September of 1990. The new civil penalty provision, codified as 21 U.S.C. § 844a, also targets users, authorizing the imposition of a penalty of up to $10,000 for possession of a controlled substance in an amount indicating solely personal use.[b] The civil penalty provision is not applicable to

b. In order to assess a civil penalty pursuant to § 844a the Attorney General must provide an opportunity for a hearing on the record. 21 U.S.C. § 844a(c). If an assessment is ordered after such a hearing, the individual against whom the assessment was issued may then bring an action in federal district court at which the law and

individuals who have already been convicted of any state or federal offense relating to a controlled substance.

The summary given above demonstrates a substantial commitment by Congress to increase federal involvement in drug offense enforcement. As you read the sections that follow, consider whether these tactics are an appropriate use of federal muscle. Section A contains materials relating to federal enforcement policies in the drug field—the so-called "federal strategy." Section B considers the application of the core domestic provision, 21 U.S.C. § 841, which criminalizes the manufacture, distribution, or possession with intent to distribute a controlled substance. In dealing with these core offenses we focus on the features that are unique to the federal system, rather than features that are shared with state law (such as the definitions of possession or distribution). Section B also focuses on the issues raised by the grading criteria under § 841, the piggyback enhancement statutes, and the discretionary selection of core drug cases for prosecution in the federal system. In Section C we discuss 21 U.S.C. § 848, the continuing criminal enterprise (or "CCE") statute that Congress enacted to deal with drug kingpins. Sections D considers the issues arising from attempts to give extraterritorial application to federal drug control statutes.

A. FEDERAL STRATEGY

1. OVERVIEW OF THE FEDERAL DRUG STRATEGY

Federal drug enforcement activities have increased dramatically in recent years. The principal emphasis has been on reducing supply—stopping illicit manufacturing enterprises in this country, interdicting narcotics being imported from abroad, and apprehending large-scale dealers. But federal enforcement policies continue to evolve. Today, for example, there is a large emphasis on the use of a task force approach—that is, concentrating teams of federal, state, and local enforcement personnel in geographic areas where large quantities of drugs are being imported. Although such efforts often appear to bear fruit in terms of arrests, seizure of drugs, and prosecutions, it is less clear whether they can stem the overall flow of drugs into this country. The government now also appears to be putting a greater emphasis on the demand side of the drug problem, with over a third of the 2006 proposed budget to be spent on drug treatment and prevention.

Traditionally the Drug Enforcement Administration (DEA), located in the Department of Justice, carried major responsibility for enforcement of criminal drug laws. DEA is now aided by the FBI (which until 1982 had no authority to investigate drug cases), and DEA and FBI agents may conduct joint investigations.

facts shall be determined de novo at a jury trial and the government must prove a violation beyond a reasonable doubt. § 844a(g). If the individual does not request a hearing or seek judicial review before a penalty is assessed, the Attorney General may enforce the penalty in a civil action at which neither the decision to issue the order nor the amount of the penalty are subject to review. § 844a(h).

Though some commentators support legalization or decriminalization (see infra at 338–40), these sentiments have found virtually no support in Congress. The Anti–Drug Abuse Act of 1988 assessed the impact of drugs in society, finding the estimated total cost of drugs on the United States economy to be over $100 billion annually as a result of adverse health effects, increased health care costs, job-related accidents, lost productivity, increased crime, increased costs for law enforcement, and other factors. By 2000 this cost was estimated at over $160 billion a year. The Anti–Drug Abuse Act stated the policy of the federal government "to create a Drug–Free America," and included the following declaration of the sentiments of Congress:

> The Congress finds that legalization of illegal drugs, on the Federal or State level, is an unconscionable surrender in a war in which, for the future of our country and the lives of our children, there can be no substitute for total victory.

Anti–Drug Abuse Act of 1988, Pub. L. No. 100–690, § 5011, 102 Stat. 4181, 4296 (1988). This statement still seems to sum up Congress's position on legalization.

The 1988 Act also introduced the requirement of the yearly promulgation of a National Drug Control Strategy to provide quantified objectives. The National Drug Control Strategy in 2005 noted that the Administration's 2002 two-year goal of a 10% reduction in current use of illegal drugs by youths—defined as any illegal drug use within the past month—had been met and exceeded, and the program was ahead of schedule for the five-year goal of a 25% reduction in overall current drug use. The 2005 Strategy also detailed the Administration's plan for a balanced strategy in drug control, with the following three priorities: preventing drug use, "healing" America's drug users, and disrupting drug markets. OFFICE OF NATIONAL DRUG CONTROL POLICY, NATIONAL DRUG CONTROL STRATEGY: 2005, 1, 4.

To achieve these goals, the Office of National Drug Control Policy has consistently sought larger budgets. For example, the $12.4 billion FY 2006 budget request represented a 2.2% increase over FY 2005 and an 8.2% increase over FY 2002.[c] The 2005 Strategy stressed the use of program performance data in budgeting decisions. Each program's effectiveness in contributing to the Strategy's three national priorities will help determine how resources are allocated.

One of the more popular strategies in the war on drugs continues to be the use of task forces. In addition to receiving direct federal funds, local and state law enforcement enjoy substantial indirect assistance:

c. *Id.* at 5. The proposed budget represented the Administration's balanced strategy with 38.7% of the proposed budget to be spent on drug treatment and prevention, and 61.3% to be spent on law enforcement, international programs, drug-related intelligence spending, and interdiction activities. It should also be noted that in 2003 the Administration restructured the federal drug budget to better reflect actual dollars spent on reducing drug use. Therefore, budget statistics before 2002 cannot be readily compared to statistics from 2002 on.

The DEA assumes the costs of investigative overtime for non-federal personnel, an expense which can amount to hundreds of thousands of dollars annually. The DEA also provides "investigative expenses, such as payments to informants and 'buy money' to purchase contraband, as well as undercover vehicles and surveillance equipment." In addition, the state and local participants share in the assets, such as vehicles, seized under the federal asset forfeiture program. Moreover, state and local agents not involved in task forces can enlist DEA cooperation in the investigation of a particular case on an informal, ad hoc basis, and can also share in any assets forfeited as a result of the case. This type of informal cooperative effort has become an increasingly popular activity.

Sandra Guerra, *Domestic Drug Interdiction Operations: Finding the Balance*, 82 J. Crim. L. & Criminology 1109, 1112–13 (1992).

2. EVALUATING THE EFFECTIVENESS OF THE FEDERAL STRATEGY

How successful has the federal drug strategy been? Developing a fair and accurate evaluation is difficult, as the statistics can often be manipulated or misleading. Some of the data are not encouraging. Despite the government's efforts to disrupt the supply of drugs, the price of powder cocaine has actually dropped 80% from 1981 to 2003, and marijuana prices remain near their 20–year average.[d] Statistics on the demand side are also disappointing, as the annual number of marijuana initiates is at roughly the same level as in the early 1980's, and cocaine initiation has been steadily increasing since 1993.[e] However, Stephen D. Easton (a former U.S. Attorney) argues that the federal drug laws have worked and reduced drug usage when pursued actively. Stephen D. Easton, *Everybody Knows It, But Is It True? A Challenge to the Conventional Wisdom that the War on Drugs Is Ineffective*, 14 Fed. Sent. Rep. 132 (2002). He concludes that there is a correlation between the drug policies of the past three Administrations and drug use among high school seniors over that time period (a decrease in use under Presidents Reagan and George H.W. Bush, whose Administrations escalated the war on drugs through increased spending and criminal prosecutions, and an increase in use under President Clinton, who Easton claims de-escalated the war on drugs).[f]

The current federal strategy of being tough on drug offenders has had a substantial impact on the federal justice system itself. The first impact is felt in the federal courts, where the drug caseload has increased dramatically. The number of criminal cases involving drug offenses commenced in the U.S. District Courts grew from 3,745 cases in

d. Office of National Drug Control Policy, The Price and Purity of Illicit Drugs: 1981 Through the Second Quarter of 2003, v.

e. 2003 National Survey on Drug Use and Health, 44–45.

f. A review of more recent versions of the studies used by Easton suggests that drug use has declined slightly under President George W. Bush, who has increased total federal drug control spending.

1978, to 12,592 in 1990, to 18,996 in 2003. Bureau of Justice Statistics, Sourcebook of Criminal Justice Statistics Online-2002 < http://www.albany.edu/sourcebook/pdf/t510.pdf >. These numbers represent 11%, 22%, and 27%, respectively, of the total criminal caseload for that year.

Not surprisingly, the number of sentenced drug offenders in the federal prison population has tracked the growing federal caseload. In 1970 only 16.3% of the federal prison population were drug offenders. Drug offenders made up more than half of federal prisoners in 1990, and by 2005 there were 89,949 drug offenders in federal prisons, accounting for 53.6% of the total inmate population. Bureau of Prisons, Quick Fact Sheet (last modified July 2, 2005) <http://www.bop.gov>.

The policy of incarcerating large numbers of drug offenders has high costs. One facet of the cost is financial. For example, in fiscal year 2005 the estimated cost of housing drug offenders in the federal prison system was $2.5 billion.[g] Other costs are social. African Americans made up 45.2% of the prison population convicted for drug offenses in 2003,[h] and Professor Tracey Meares explains that this extraordinarily high rate of incarceration has had a tremendous impact within the African–American community:

> High rates of imprisonment of young African–American men and women translate into many broken families in African–American communities. It is difficult to measure how family ties and connections and individual psyches may be devastated when family members and close friends are removed from communities. Although quantification of emotional harm is practically impossible, some judgments about the ways in which high incarceration levels affect the vitality of families, the life chances of children left behind, and the economic circumstances of African–American communities are possible.
>
> First, imprisonment contributes to the already high percentage of families headed by single African–American women. Because the mortality rate for African–American men is somewhat higher than that for African–American women, the female to male ratio is already quite high in some African–American communities. High levels of incarceration of African–American men add to this ratio. Increases in the ratio of African–American women to African–American men are likely to lead to a lower probability of marriage and formation of two-parent families.
>
> Second, the removal of young adults from the community means fewer adults to monitor and supervise children. Inadequate supervi-

g. Assuming that the $4.7 billion requested by the President for the Federal Prison System in his 2005 Budget would be distributed on a pro rata basis throughout the prison system, then the cost of housing drug offenders in federal prisons is more than $2.5 billion. *See* Office of Management and budget, Budget of the United States Government, FY 2006, Department of Justice <http://www.whitehouse.gov/ omb/budget/fy2006/justice.html>.

h. This information was acquired from the Federal Justice Statistics Research Database at <http://fjsrc.urban.org> (visited July 26, 2005).

sion leads to increased opportunities for children to become involved in delinquency and crime. The increasing rate of African–American women sentenced to prison presents an additional hazard to poor African–American communities and especially to the children growing up in them, although the absolute numbers are small compared to the numbers of African–American men imprisoned. * * * Because African–American women often are the primary caretakers of children in poor communities, there is a growing risk that children are in danger of losing both parents to the criminal justice system. As a result, these children face a very high risk of future criminal involvement. Moreover, communities will suffer a loss because each additional incarcerated adults erodes the important community adult/child ratio that is a predictor of greater neighborhood supervision.

In addition to the negative consequences that high rates of imprisonment undoubtedly have on the amount of emotional support and caregiving available to the families of incarcerated individuals, high imprisonment rates are also likely to have a detrimental effect on the economic well-being of families in impoverished neighborhoods. The prevalence of low economic status and unemployment among families predicts low levels of community social organization. Given the well-established association between poverty and families headed by single women, there can be little doubt that high rates of incarceration of African–American men will contribute to the deepening poverty in the African–American community.

Tracey L. Meares, *Social Organization and Drug Law Enforcement*, 35 Am. Crim. L. Rev. 191, 206–207 (1998).

3. SUPPORT FOR LEGALIZATION

As mentioned previously, the call for reconsidering the federal drug strategy has been growing, and there is support both for limited measures that would legalize particular drugs and for wholesale decriminalization. Laws purporting to legalize the use of particular drugs in contravention of the federal scheme have been enacted in several states, and been immediately challenged by federal authorities. There is also support for wholesale decriminalization, though no jurisdiction has yet incorporated those ideas into legislation.

a. *The Federal Challenge to Narrow State Initiatives*

The federal government has aggressively challenged state efforts to permit limited medical use of particular drugs governed by the Controlled Substances Act (CSA), seeking a declaration in each case that federal law barred the state initiatives. These cases have raised interpretative questions under the CSA as well as constitutional issues.

The first set of challenges concerned state ballot initiatives in Arizona and California authorizing the use of marijuana to alleviate pain and suffering under the supervision of a physician. In two cases involving California's Compassionate Medical Use Act the Supreme Court rebuffed the state's efforts. In the first case, *United States v. Oakland Cannabis Buyers' Cooperative*, 532 U.S. 483 (2001), the Court upheld an injunction permanently banning cannabis dispensaries from providing marijuana for any purpose, rejecting the claim that the Controlled Substances Act was subject to an implied medical necessity exception. In *Gonzales v. Raich*, 125 S.Ct. 2195 (2005), users and growers of marijuana under the California Compassionate Use Act sought injunctive and declaratory relief on the ground that the CSA exceeds Congress' authority under the Commerce Clause. Following the advice of their doctors, the plaintiff patients—who suffered from severe medical conditions including an inoperable brain tumor and chronic back pain and muscle spasms—used marijuana for medical purposes. Their marijuana was grown in state using only California products. One plaintiff grew the marijuana solely for her own use. Two anonymous caregivers cultivated the marijuana for the other plaintiff, who was too ill to do so herself. However, the Controlled Substances Act does not recognize state statutes of this type, and makes possession of marijuana or other controlled substance illegal except as authorized by the *federal* law. The Supreme Court upheld the federal statutory scheme as a valid exercise of the Commerce Clause. The Court, relying on a 1942 decision regarding the intrastate production and consumption of wheat,[i] held that Congress had a rational basis for concluding that taken in the aggregate the intrastate manufacture and possession of marijuana, even for medical uses, substantially affects interstate commerce.

In *Oregon v. Ashcroft*, 368 F.3d 1118 (9th Cir. 2004), the state brought action seeking declaratory and injunctive relief preventing federal enforcement or application of the Attorney General's directive indicating that physicians who assist the suicide of terminally ill patients pursuant to Oregon's Death with Dignity Act would be violating the federal Controlled Substances Act. The district court enjoined the enforcement of the directive, and the court of appeals upheld that decision. The appellate court found that given the primacy of the states' role in regulating professional medical conduct, the courts would interpret a federal statute to intrude upon the states' authority only if Congress clearly intended to shift the federal state balance. The court found no such clear Congressional statement, and accordingly it concluded that the Ashcroft directive also conflicted with the language of the CSA. The Supreme Court has granted certiorari. *Gonzales v. Oregon*, 125 S.Ct. 1299 (2005).

b. Decriminalization

Another approach that opponents of the federal drug policy have advocated is the wholesale legalization or decriminalization of drugs.

---

i. Wickard v. Filburn, 317 U.S. 111 (1942) (holding that farmer exceeding quota on wheat production, even when was used for personal consumption, taken in the aggregate, could substantially affect interstate commerce, and so could be regulated by Congress).

Proponents argue that prohibition and criminalization are doomed to failure because making drugs illegal creates a lucrative market. The costs and risks associated with trafficking illegal drugs essentially impose a value-added tax on drugs that is imposed by the government, but collected by the traffickers. Given the persistent demand for drugs in the United States, when successful enforcement reduces the supply of a drug, its price and potential profits will rise, drawing suppliers to the market who will then act to fill the gap. For example, the government's effort to eliminate the production of Turkish heroin in the 1970's merely shifted the production of heroin to Mexico and Southeast Asia.[j] Likewise, the efforts to intercept marijuana coming into Miami in the 1980's resulted in a shift to smuggling more concealable cocaine. This phenomenon can be seen locally as well, where the removal of one supplier merely creates an attractive opportunity for others. As one commentator noted:

> The publicized conviction of a drug dealer, by instantly creating a vacancy in the lucrative drug market, has the same effect as hanging up a help-wanted sign saying, "drug dealer needed—$5,000 a week to start—exciting work."

The War on Drugs, Is It Time To Surrender?, 9 INST. FOR PHIL. & PUB. POLICY 1, 4 (1989).

Can tougher federal sentences change this equation? Critics of the federal policy say no. Assuming that traffickers are rational decisionmakers, the new sentences merely increase the price and hence the profit. Moreover, drug trafficking involves features that may limit the deterrent effect of criminal sanctions.[k] For example:

> One reason that tough sanctions may be associated with low levels of specific deterrence is that despite a high lifetime likelihood of arrest, the probability that an individual will be caught committing a particular offense is incredibly low. [Inciardi and Pottieger's research] provides an especially striking example of this phenomenon. In their sample of 254 crack dealers from Miami, approximately 87% had been arrested at some point within the year of the survey. However, out of over 220,000 offenses, the likelihood of arrest for each particular incident was less than 1%!

Tracey L. Meares, *Social Organization and Drug Law Enforcement*, 35 AM. CRIM. L. REV. 191, 212 (1998).

j. For an in-depth historical and economic analysis of the global opium trade, see Alfred W. McCoy, *From Free Trade to Prohibition: A Critical History of the Modern Asian Opium Trade*, 28 FORDHAM URB. L.J. 307 (2000).

k. Many of those involved are adolescents, and psychological studies show that adolescents frequently do not assess the risks of their behavior or respond to incremental increases in risks. Dwight L. Greene, *Foreword, Drug Decriminalization: A Chorus in Need of Masterrap's Voice*, 18 HOFSTRA L. REV. 457, 463–64 n.17 (1990). Moreover, deterrence theory may not be valid for those most economically and socially disadvantaged: in some segments of society "jail time is viewed as part of a man's right of passage and is referred to simply as 'going away,' a normal part of life." *Id.* Professor Greene also notes that for some of the most disadvantaged members of society jail—with adequate food and shelter—would represent an improvement in their living conditions. *Id.*

Proponents of legalization charge that the current federal policy of prohibition has many other indirect costs. Street crime by drug users seeking to support their habits is at least partially attributable to prohibition, which increases the price of drugs. Black market transactions foster the use of violence to eliminate competition and remove suspected informants. While the principal targets of such violence are themselves involved in drug trafficking, numerous bystanders—including children—have lost their lives as well.[1] The enormous profits generated by drug trafficking also pose an enormous risk of government corruption. Other problems associated with prohibiting drugs are the health risks associated with uncertain potency and purity, and the spread of AIDS through the use of dirty needles.

The legalization debate also raises the question how much control the government should have over individual decisions. Proponents of legalization believe that the individual should be able to make his own decisions over his mind and body, and that the government's attempts to regulate morality in criminalizing drugs often cause more harm than benefit. *See* John Tierney, *Debunking the Drug War*, N.Y. TIMES, Aug. 9, 2005; *Set It Free*, THE ECONOMIST, July 26, 2001.

For a detailed and balanced analysis of both sides of the decriminalization argument, see DOUGLAS N. HUSAK, LEGALIZE THIS! THE CASE FOR DECRIMINALIZING DRUGS (Colin McGinn ed., 2002). Husak concludes that the current drug policy is not only ineffective but more importantly is unjust.

4. OTHER APPROACHES

Commentators have presented other approaches besides outright legalization. Professors Rasmussen and Benson advocate the decentralization of the drug policy to the state and local governments. David W. Rasmussen & Bruce L. Benson, *Rationalizing Drug Policy Under Federalism*, FLA. ST. U. L. REV. 679, 700–702 (2003). They argue that the federal drug policy—which is formulated in the best interests of politically powerful groups, such as law enforcement bureaucracies, prosecutors, and legislators—relies too heavily on criminal enforcement that "aggravates rather than mitigates the social consequences of drug use." Decentralizing the drug policy would force local decision-makers to take more responsibility for the costs of their policies, leading to policies that generate greater social benefits. In addition, they argue, since the type and extent of drug abuse varies tremendously across the nation, localizing policy-making would allow states and local jurisdictions to develop more innovative and better-suited solutions.

Judge John T. Curtin, who sits in the Western District of New York, has criticized the current federal drug strategy and advocated greater reliance on harm-reduction measures. John T. Curtin, *Drug Policy*

---

1. In other countries the violence associated with drug trafficking has threatened to overcome the government itself: a few years ago Columbia's entire Supreme Court was assassinated in an attack, along with its attorney general and minister of justice, and judges who order extradition to the United States were threatened with death.

Alternatives—A Response from the Bench, 28 Fordham Urb. L.J. 263 (2000). These changes include freely available clean needles, convenient methadone treatments for heroin users, treatment instead of jail for drug users and low-level sellers, expanded educational and job opportunities in urban neighborhoods, and research into methods to take the profit out of the drug distribution system. Judge Curtin also noted the political obstacles to change, as legislators who propose reform are often accused of being soft on crime. Therefore, he advocates a grass roots movement to increase public knowledge of the problems with the current drug policy in hopes of eventually forcing a change.

5. DEFENSE OF THE FEDERAL STRATEGY

Many people reject legalization and believe that the federal strategy is working. Professor Frank Bowman defends the current federal policy and argues that the rhetoric of the "war on drugs" has created a false measure of success:

> * * * Americans expect that their wars will be of limited duration. They expect that the short-term application of maximum human, industrial, and technological effort will produce a complete victory, after which the war machine will be dismantled and everyone will get to go home. Any law enforcement initiative, whether against drugs or jaywalking, that invites measurement by that yardstick will fail.
>
> People sell and use drugs for the same reasons they commit the other crimes in the criminal code—satisfaction of physical and psychic appetites, lust, greed—the gamut of discreditable human motivations. Until men become angels, some people will continue to break narcotics laws, in just the same way they continue to break the laws against rape, robbery, and murder. There is never "victory" in the criminal law. The bad guys never strike their colors, stack their arms, and surrender in a body so we can live happily ever after. Neither does society have the luxury of surrender. If, despite our best efforts, people keep on shoplifting, tapping the till, and sticking up 7–11's, we do not repeal the laws against theft, embezzlement, and robbery.
>
>   * * *
>
> So let us beat an orderly retreat from the shot-torn fields of the rhetorical "war on drugs." The beginning of rational discussion of drug policy is agreement that enforcement of narcotics laws is no different than enforcing other criminal laws. Therefore, those who support narcotics prohibitions should stop suggesting, or even implying, that whatever new measure they happen to be promoting will be the increment of escalation that will finally result in "victory" over the drug pushers. Conversely, those who oppose the direction drug policy in America has taken should stop declaring that we have "lost" the "war on drugs" because stern enforcement measures have not eradicated the drug trade.

Frank O. Bowman, III, *Playing "21" with Narcotics Enforcement: A Response to Professor Carrington*, 52 WASH. & LEE L. REV. 937, 964–66 (1995). When viewed in this light, Bowman argues that the federal strategy has not failed.

More recently, former DEA Administrator Asa Hutchinson defended the federal drug strategy:

> People who know the facts and understand the problem realize that a small percentage of the population uses drugs. The solution to drug abuse is vigilance coupled with thoughtful planning and action; we should not surrender to the problem. It is always interesting to look at issues from a theoretical standpoint. The reality is that drugs are illegal because they are dangerous. They cause pain and suffering to individuals and families, as well as neighborhoods and communities, and cost our society substantial sums of money. There is no reason to think that allowing the free flow of any mind altering illegal drug in America would reduce the number of users or addicts, or reduce the overall cost of protecting our citizens from its harms.

> Common sense tells us that we must work to reduce the number of people using illegal drugs. Legalization would substantially increase the number of people in school or college, at work, or in business, who would suffer the residual effects of a drug that has no useful purpose. At a time when we are working to improve public health by reducing alcohol and tobacco use by teens, when we check identification before we sell cigarettes or alcohol to someone, it seems counterintuitive that a small but vocal minority is working to create a society in which there is free access to the chemicals that we know are dangerous to individuals and society.

> The facts on this issue make a strong case for a national policy geared toward effective drug abuse education and prevention, and treatment for people dependent on illegal drugs. Our nation should also continue to conduct research to determine the most effective means of educating children and youth about the dangers of illegal drugs and the best ways to rehabilitate illegal drug users. On the supply side, the criminal justice system should continue to impose sanctions on people and organizations that are in the business of growing, manufacturing, transporting, and distributing illegal drugs.

Asa Hutchinson, *An Effective Drug Policy to Protect America's Youth and Communities*, 30 FORDHAM URB. L.J. 441, 462 (2003).

If, as Bowman argues, the "war on drugs" is a bad metaphor, what would be better? Consider the following proposal:

> Cancer is a more appropriate metaphor for the nation's drug problem. Dealing with cancer is a long-term proposition. It requires the mobilization of support mechanisms—medical, educational, and societal—to check the spread of the disease and improve the prognosis. The symptoms of the illness must be managed while the root cause

is attacked. The key to reducing both drug abuse and cancer is research-driven prevention coupled with cutting-edge treatment.

See OFFICE OF NATIONAL DRUG CONTROL POLICY, NATIONAL DRUG CONTROL STRATEGY: 1999, 7. Does the term "cancer" improve the debate? After considering all of the above materials, what is your opinion of the federal drug strategy? What changes would you make?

B. THE CORE OFFENSES: MANUFACTURE, DISTRIBUTION, AND POSSESSION WITH INTENT TO DISTRIBUTE

In the materials that follow, we begin with a focus on what we call the core domestic drug offenses: manufacture, distribution, and possession with intent to distribute, all of which are defined by 21 U.S.C. § 841 (reprinted below). Because the concepts of manufacture, distribution, and possession do not, in general, differ from those utilized in state law, these definitions present no issues of special interest in a course on federal criminal law. Accordingly, we focus on the special features unique to or characteristic of federal law.

The most significant and characteristic feature of the core offenses in § 841 is the sentencing provisions. As you read the statute, note that the definition of the offenses in section (a) comprises only a few lines, which are then followed by several pages dealing in great detail with sentencing. Section 841 provides for sentences (many of which are mandatory minimum sentences) based upon the type and quantity of drug involved, with increases provided for repeat offenders and cases where injury or death resulted. These provisions are the focus of Section 1. In Section 2 we discuss another distinctive feature of the federal drug laws: the piggyback enhancement statutes that come into play when the core offenses under § 841 are committed under defined circumstances (e.g., near a school). In Section 3 we present the criteria that currently govern the exercise of prosecutorial discretion in the selection of cases for prosecution under the core statutes and the enhancement provisions, and consider the effect of those prosecutorial policies on the federal courts.

21 U.S.C.

§ 841. Prohibited acts A

(a) Unlawful acts

Except as authorized by this subchapter, it shall be unlawful for any person knowingly or intentionally—

> (1) to manufacture, distribute, or dispense, or possess with intent to manufacture, distribute, or dispense, a controlled substance; or

> (2) to create, distribute, or dispense, or possess with intent to distribute or dispense, a counterfeit substance.

(b) Penalties

Except as otherwise provided in section 859, 860, or 861 of this title, any person who violates subsection (a) of this section shall be sentenced as follows:

(1)(A) In the case of a violation of subsection (a) of this section involving—

(i) 1 kilogram or more of a mixture or substance containing a detectable amount of heroin;

(ii) 5 kilograms or more of a mixture or substance containing a detectable amount of—

(I) coca leaves, except coca leaves and extracts of coca leaves from which cocaine, ecgonine, and derivatives of ecgonine or their salts have been removed;

(II) cocaine, its salts, optical and geometric isomers, and salts of isomers;

(III) ecgonine, its derivatives, their salts, isomers, and salts of isomers; or

(IV) any compound, mixture, or preparation which contains any quantity of any of the substances referred to in subclauses (I) through (III);

(iii) 50 grams or more of a mixture or substance described in clause (ii) which contains cocaine base;

(iv) 100 grams or more of phencyclidine (PCP) or 1 kilogram or more of a mixture or substance containing a detectable amount of phencyclidine (PCP);

(v) 10 grams or more of a mixture or substance containing a detectable amount of lysergic acid diethylamide (LSD);

* * *

(vii) 1000 kilograms or more of a mixture or substance containing a detectable amount of marijuana, or 1,000 or more marijuana plants regardless of weight;

* * *

such person shall be sentenced to a term of imprisonment which may not be less than 10 years or more than life and if death or serious bodily injury results from the use of such substance shall be not less than 20 years or more than life, a fine not to exceed the greater of that authorized in accordance with the provisions of Title 18, or $4,000,000 if the defendant is an individual or $10,000,000 if the defendant is other than an individual, or both. If any person commits such a violation after a prior conviction for a felony drug offense has become final, such person shall be sentenced to a term of imprisonment which may not be less than 20 years and not more than life imprisonment and if death or serious bodily injury results from the use of such substance shall be sentenced to life imprisonment, a fine not to exceed the greater of twice that authorized in accordance with the provisions of Title 18, or $8,000,000 if the defendant is an individual or $20,000,000 if the defendant is other than an individual, or both. If any person commits a violation of this subparagraph or of section 849, 859, 860, or 861 of this title after two or more prior convictions for a felony drug offense have become final, such person shall be sentenced to a mandatory term of life imprisonment without release and fined in accordance with the preceding sentence. Any sentence under this subparagraph shall, in the absence of such a prior conviction, impose a term of supervised release of at least 5 years in addition to such term of imprisonment and shall, if there was such a prior conviction, impose a term of supervised release of at least 10 years in addition to such term of imprisonment. Notwithstanding any other provision of law, the court shall not place on probation or suspend the sentence of any person sentenced under this subparagraph. No person sentenced under this subparagraph shall be eligible for parole during the term of imprisonment imposed therein.

* * *

[The remaining sections of § 841 are reprinted at 949–56 in the appendix. They contain provisions setting lower penalties for smaller amounts of the substances listed in (b)(1)(A), penalties for other schedule II substances not separately listed and for substances listed on schedules IV and V, penalties for even smaller amounts of marijuana, and offenses regarding listed precursor chemicals, cultivation of drug crops on federal lands, booby traps on federal properties, etc.]

The penalty scheme established in § 841 (including the enhancement provisions of § 841(b)) applies to the offenses of attempt and conspiracy as well. 21 U.S.C. § 846 provides:

Any person who attempts or conspires to commit any offense defined in this subchapter shall be subject to the same penalties as those prescribed for the offense, the commission of which was the object of the attempt or conspiracy.

1. THE GRADING SCHEME APPLICABLE TO THE CORE OFFENSES

In the case that follows, the Eleventh Circuit considers the interpretation of the weight-based sentencing provisions governing manufacture and distribution of LSD. The question is whether the court must base the sentence on the weight of the pure drug, or on the combined weight of the drug and the water in which it was contained. The answer is critically important because the applicability of the mandatory minimum sentences turns on the weight of the drug for which the defendant is responsible. Based on the weight of the pure drug, Grant's sentence would be 15 to 22 months, but including the water as well would make the 10 year mandatory minimum applicable. *Grant* and the notes that follow explore the issues that arise from reliance on drug type and weight as the primary measure of the seriousness of drug offenses.

UNITED STATES v. GRANT

397 F.3d 1330 (11th Cir. 2005).

Before CARNES, HULL and HILL, CIRCUIT JUDGES.

HILL, CIRCUIT JUDGE:

This case is one of first impression in this circuit. It involves the weight of drugs used in re-sentencing the defendant, Dorian Grant, in a drug conspiracy.

Grant pled guilty to one count of conspiracy to possess with intent to distribute and conspiracy to distribute 10 grams or more of a "mixture or substance" containing a detectable amount of lysergic acid dietyhlamide (LSD) in violation of 18 U.S.C. § 2; 21 U.S.C. §§ 841(a)(1), 841(b)(1)(A)(v), and 846. The LSD that Grant and his co-conspirators trafficked in was in liquid form.

The district court sentenced Grant to 108 months' imprisonment. Subsequently, that sentence was vacated and Grant was sentenced to 54 months' imprisonment.

Grant now appeals his re-sentencing. We affirm the judgment of the district court.

I. BACKGROUND

A. *Factual Background*

The facts are not in dispute. The LSD distributed by college senior Grant and his co-conspirators was contained in water. The weight of the pure LSD alone was 0.1263 grams, the equivalent of 2526 dosage units or "hits." The aggregate weight of the water and the pure LSD was 103.7 grams (liquid LSD), or approximately one-third of the liquid contents found in a soda can.

B. *Procedural Background*

1. *Initial Sentencing*

Grant's indictment charged, and Grant pleaded guilty to, a count containing a specific drug quantity, i.e., 10 grams or more of a mixture or substance containing a detectable amount of LSD. Accordingly, Grant faced a statutory minimum sentence of 10 years. Sections 841(b)(1)(A)(v) and 846.[3] Using the December 16, 2000, edition of the sentencing guidelines manual, the probation officer, in his presentence investigation report (PSI), attributed 103.7 grams of LSD to Grant, the weight of the liquid LSD. Grant did not object to the PSI.[4]

---

3. Section 841(b)(1)(A)(v) reads in part: "[i]n the case of a violation of subsection (a) of this section involving ... 10 grams or more of a mixture or substance containing a detectable amount of [LSD].... such person shall be sentenced to a term of impris- onment which may not be less than 10 years or more than life...."

4. Based upon this calculation, the maximum statutory penalty Grant faced was imprisonment for not less than ten years and not more than life; not more than a

Prior to hearing, the government filed a motion for downward departure pursuant to 18 U.S.C. § 3553(e) and U.S.S.G. § 5K1.1, for Grant's substantial assistance to authorities in investigating and prosecuting others involved in the LSD conspiracy. In response, the district court departed downwardly from the 120–month statutory minimum sentence and sentenced Grant to 108 months' imprisonment. Sections 841(b)(1)(A)(v), 846; Section 3553(e); Sections 5K1.1 and 5G1.1(b).[5] He was specially assessed $100 and given five years' supervised release.

While Grant's appeal was pending, his defense counsel alerted the government and the court to a case that had been overlooked at sentencing. *See United States v. Camacho*, 261 F.3d 1071 (11th Cir.2001) (for sentencing guideline purposes, the weight of pure LSD alone should be used to determine a defendant's base offense level). In response, the government filed a motion for summary remand. This court construed the government's motion as a confession of error, vacated Grant's sentence, and remanded the case for re-sentencing.

2. *Re-sentencing*

At re-sentencing, over objections of defense counsel, the district court again found the 120–month statutory minimum sentence under Section 841(b)(1)(A)(v) to be the baseline from which to sentence Grant a second time. At hearing, the district court stated that, "[i]n the Court's opinion there's no question that liquid LSD is a *mixture* or substance containing a detectable amount of LSD, thereby triggering Section 841(b)(1)(A)(v) ... I agree with the probation officer that the total weight of the liquid LSD solution must be used to determine the mandatory minimum sentence." (Emphasis added.)

This time the district court departed downwardly, not by twelve months, but by sixty-six months. It imposed a sentence upon Grant of fifty-four months, half his original sentence. *See* Sections 841(b)(1)(A)(v), 846; Section 3553(e); Sections 5K1.1, 5G1.1(b). Grant now appeals his re-sentencing.

II. ISSUES PRESENTED

A. In applying the mandatory statutory minimum penalty provision, should the district court consider the weight of the liquid LSD, as "a mixture or substance containing a detectable amount of LSD" under Section 841(b)(1)(A)(v), or the weight of the pure LSD alone?

* * *

$4,000,000 fine; and at least five years' supervised release. His projected guideline sentencing range was 151 to 188 months' imprisonment.

5. U.S.S.G. § 5G1.1(b), entitled "Sentencing on a Single Count of Conviction,"

reads in full: "Where a statutorily required minimum sentence is greater than the maximum of the applicable guideline range, the statutorily required minimum sentence shall be the guideline sentence."

IV. Discussion

A. Contentions of the Parties

1. The First Issue

a. Grant's Contentions as to the Weight of Liquid LSD Issue

Grant contends that he should be sentenced to no more than fifteen to twenty-one months' imprisonment under the sentencing guidelines, based upon his criminal history, with adjustment for acceptance of responsibility. *See Camacho,* 261 F.3d at 1074. He argues that, "as he was convicted of" selling .1234 grams of pure LSD, this is the amount of drugs in which he trafficked under *Camacho.* He claims that in this circuit only the weight of the pure LSD alone, not the liquid LSD, can be used in determining his sentence under the sentencing guidelines.

In making this argument, Grant acknowledges that the analysis set forth in *Camacho* stopped short at the sentencing guidelines, and did not reach the drug weight issue in the context of the penalty statute. Nevertheless, he claims the same result should occur. He does this by trying to distinguish *Chapman v. United States,* 500 U.S. 453 (1991) and *Neal v. United States,* 516 U.S. 284 (1996), from his case.

The Supreme Court held in both *Chapman* and *Neal* that LSD impregnated into blotter paper is a "mixture or substance" containing LSD within the meaning of the penalty statute; therefore the weight of the carrier medium should be included in determining the appropriate sentence for trafficking in LSD. Grant avers, however, that neither *Chapman* nor *Neal* involved liquid LSD and should be read only in the context of LSD mounted on a carrier medium such as blotter paper.

In essence, Grant is arguing that the LSD here was in an intermediate wholesale distribution form, unlike the retail consumer form found in *Chapman* and *Neal.* He claims it is much too bulky and much too diluted to be marketed directly to consumers.[7] It is merely two separate substances contained together in a vial, with no fixed ratio between them. He asserts that there is no enfolding, no bonding, no impregnating. Similar to clothes contained in a suitcase, or individuals confined by a courtroom, the LSD is merely encased in water, not mixed with it or in it.

b. The Government's Contentions as to the Weight of the LSD Issue

The government avers that this is a straightforward case. The statute provides for a 10–year mandatory minimum sentence for possession with intent to distribute 10 grams or more of a mixture or substance containing a detectable amount of LSD. Section 841(b)(1)(A)(v). Insofar as the penalty statute is concerned, Grant pled guilty to conspiracy to distribute a specific amount of drugs, i.e., 10 grams or more.

---

7. Grant concedes that consumers can get high by drinking liquid LSD, although this is not the way LSD is typically marketed.

Although the facts in *Chapman* involved LSD mounted on a carrier medium, i.e., blotter paper, the government argues that the Supreme Court nevertheless defined "mixture" according to its plain and ordinary terms. In the case of liquid LSD, the two components are intermingled, although they can perhaps be regarded as having a separate existence (where Webster's Third New International Dictionary 1449 (1986) defines a "mixture" to include "a portion of matter consisting of two or more components that do not bear a fixed proportion to one another and that however thoroughly commingled are regarded as retaining a separate existence").

The government claims that what Grant distributed, what he was charged with, and what he pled guilty to, meet the statutory criteria for the imposition of the ten year mandatory minimum sentence. In addition, the government argues that it is the weight of the liquid LSD that should be considered, not the weight of the pure LSD, because the weight of the pure LSD is so minuscule that it does not adequately reflect the seriousness of the crime, i.e., 2526 drug-induced highs. *See Camacho,* 261 F.3d at 1075.

In support of its argument that the district court acted properly in this case, the government cites case law from other circuits holding that liquid LSD is a "mixture or substance" for purposes of the statutory mandatory minimum sentence, and that the guidelines range is trumped by Section 5G1.1(b). *See United States v. Morgan,* 292 F.3d 460, 461 (5th Cir. 2002) (vacating guidelines sentence in liquid LSD case and remanding for imposition of 10–year minimum sentence mandated by Section 841(b)(1)(A)(v)); *see also United States v. Ingram,* 67 F.3d 126, 129 (6th Cir. 1995).

* * *

B. *The First Issue—The Weight of the LSD*

1. *The Statutes and the Sentencing Guidelines*

Section 841(b)(1)(A)(v) provides for a mandatory minimum of 10 years' imprisonment for a violation of subsection (a) [making it unlawful to knowingly or intentionally manufacture, distribute, dispense, or possess with intent to manufacture, distribute, or dispense, a controlled substance] involving "10 grams or more of a mixture or substance containing a detectable amount of [LSD]." The sentencing guidelines parallel the statutory language and require[ ] the base offense level to be determined based upon the weight of a "mixture or substance containing a detectable amount of" LSD. Section 2D1.1(c).

2. *Supreme Court Cases and Sentencing Guidelines' Amendment 488*

In 1991, in *Chapman,* the Supreme Court held that the phrase "mixture or substance containing. . . . LSD" in Section 841(b)(1) refers to "the weight of the carrier medium upon which the drug is mounted. Two years later, the sentencing commission promulgated an amendment to the guidelines, reducing the penalties for trafficking in carrier-mounted LSD by calculating base offense levels, not at the weight of the LSD plus carrier medium as in *Chapman,* but by using a standard dosage formula of 0.4 mg. per dose of LSD (amendment 488). *See* U.S.S.G. § 2D1.1(c), n. (H).

In 1996, in *Neal,* the Supreme Court held that, when calculating penalties under the statute, amendment 488 does not overcome *Chapman's* definition of "mixture or substance," and principles of *stare decisis* require that it adhere to its earlier decision in *Chapman.* In sum, the sentencing commission has no authority to amend the penalty statute, the guidelines' calculation is independent of the statutory calculation, and the statute controls if they conflict. The sentencing commission's dose-based method cannot be squared with *Chapman.*

3. Eleventh Circuit Precedent

Grant's initial sentence was vacated and remanded by this court for re-sentencing by the district court in light of *Camacho,* at that time, a case of first impression. This court held in *Camacho* that, as to the sentencing guidelines, with regard to LSD contained in a liquid solution, the weight of the pure LSD alone should be used to ascertain the appropriate base offense level. As *Camacho* did not examine the drug weight issue in the context of the penalty statute, as is present in this appeal, this is an issue of first impression in this circuit.

4. Other Circuits' Precedent

Two circuits have held in liquid LSD cases that, although the weight of the pure LSD alone should be used in determining a defendant's base offense level under the sentencing guidelines, a district court could consider the weight of the liquid LSD when determining the applicability of the mandatory statutory minimum. *See Morgan,* 292 F.3d 460; *Ingram,* 67 F.3d 126. Both cases are distinguished from the case before us, as *Morgan* was reviewed by the Fifth Circuit for plain error and *Ingram* was decided prior to *Neal.* Nevertheless we find them helpful in our discussion.

5. The Facts Before Us

Morgan most closely aligns with the facts before us. Although the amount of pure LSD in *Morgan* was less than 10 grams, Morgan's guilty plea included his possessing, with intent to distribute, 10 grams or more of LSD, triggering the ten-year minimum sentence mandated by Section 841(b)(1)(A)(v). Under Section 5G1.1(b), the *Morgan* court used the statutory minimum because it was greater than the maximum sentence under the guidelines. *Id.* (holding that the market-oriented approach used in *Chapman* warrants including the weight of the liquid solution in determining a mandatory minimum sentence).

The same is true in Grant's case. Unlike the defendant in *Camacho,* Grant's indictment charged, and Granted pleaded guilty to, a count containing a specific drug quantity, i.e., 10 or more grams. Accordingly, Grant faced a statutory minimum sentence of ten years. Section 841(b)(1)(A)(v); Section 5G1.1(b).

Similarly to the defendant in *Morgan,* Grant was informed by the district court at his initial sentencing that the maximum statutory penalty it could impose would be a sentence of imprisonment of "not less than ten years nor more than life." Grant acknowledged to the court that he understood. While Grant earnestly urges us to extend the weight of the pure LSD rationale of *Camacho* to statutory minimum cases, our reading of *Chapman* makes it clear that we may not do so.

We conclude that the district court should use the weight of the liquid LSD in applying Grant's statutory minimum sentence. Under *Chapman,* liquid LSD can be characterized as the carrier medium of choice at the wholesale level. LSD on blotter paper, LSD in gel form or LSD on a sugar cube can be characterized as the carrier mediums of choice at the retail end of the distribution chain. As the Supreme Court noted, LSD drug dealers are free to choose their own carrier medium, scrutinize its weight, and, by so doing, act to minimize their potential sentences.

* * *

V. Conclusion

The judgment of the district court is affirmed.

Notes

1. **Problems measuring drug quantities in sentencing:** The court in *Grant* discusses the *Chapman* case and the differences between calculating the statute's mandatory minimum sentences as interpreted by the Supreme Court and the Sentencing Guidelines as promulgated by the Sentencing Commission.

Most people thought that the Supreme Court reached the wrong result in *Chapman* (one court quipped that it would make just as much sense to weigh the defendant as the blotter paper). *Chapman* subjected defendants in some LSD cases to much longer sentences just because they used a heavier carrier, and it also distorted their sentences in comparison to dealers who sold other drugs. As the court explained in *United States v. Marshall*, 908 F.2d 1312, 1334 (7th Cir. 1990):

> That irrationality is magnified when we compare the sentences for people who sell other drugs prohibited by 21 U.S.C. § 841. Marshall, remember, sold fewer than 12,000 doses [of LSD] and was sentenced to twenty years. Twelve thousand doses sounds like a lot, but to receive a comparable sentence for selling heroin Marshall would have had to sell ten kilograms, which would yield between one and two million doses. To receive a comparable sentence for selling cocaine he would have had to sell fifty kilograms, which would yield anywhere from 325,000 to five

million doses. While the corresponding weight is lower for crack—half a kilogram—this still translates into 50,000 doses.

The Commission responded to *Chapman* by amending the Guidelines to calculate the base offense level for LSD on the basis of a dosage formula rather than by the weight of the "mixture." Unfortunately, this did not solve the whole problem. In *Neal* the Supreme Court concluded that the amended Guideline had no effect on the statutory language in § 841 that imposes mandatory minimum sentences.

The net result is that where the inclusion of the carrier medium drives the weight of the "mixture" of LSD up to the level that triggers the mandatory minimums under § 841(b), the minimum sentence required by the statute trumps the Guidelines calculation. *Neal* makes clear the limitations on the Sentencing Commission's ability to fine tune sentencing in the context of drug offenses, because Congress has incorporated mandatory minimums into most of the relevant statutes. It also raises questions about Congress's competence to make the findings necessary for the fine-grained policy judgments incorporated in the sentencing provisions of § 841 and the other drug statutes. For a general discussion of the role of the Sentencing Commission, see Chapter 18, *infra*.

The lower courts have divided on the proper application of the mixture standard as it governs the calculation of the statutory minimums under *Chapman*. In *United States v. Lopez–Gil*, 965 F.2d 1124 (1st Cir. 1992), the defendant had dissolved cocaine into the sides of two fiberglass suitcases. The First Circuit held that the trial court had properly taken into account the weight of the suitcase after the metal parts had been removed. Judge Brown dissented, arguing that the suitcases "were more like traditional containers than ingestible carriers." He noted that the mix of fiberglass and cocaine was not usable as a narcotic; given the majority's resolution of the case, he wondered why the weight of the metal frames had been excluded. He dissented again on denial of the petition for rehearing on this issue, noting that Lopez–Gil would spend approximately five additional years in prison because of the inclusion of the weight of the suitcase. In contrast, the Seventh Circuit reversed a sentence calculated on the basis of a mixture that included methamphetamine, unreacted chemicals and by-products, the latter two of which were poisonous when ingested. *United States v. Stewart*, 361 F.3d 373 (7th Cir. 2004). Similarly, the Eleventh Circuit held that the weight of a nonusable non-drug liquid should be excluded when calculating the weight to determine the sentence. *United States v. Rolande–Gabriel*, 938 F.2d 1231 (11th Cir. 1991). The court concluded that whether or not the entire mixture should be weighed depended on usability, consumability, and readiness for wholesale or retail distribution. But in *United States v. Berroa–Medrano*, 303 F.3d 277 (3d Cir. 2002), the Third Circuit rejected the defendant's argument that a mixture was not consumable because it contained only a trace amount of heroin, and was actually a "gag bag" meant to fool the consumer.

2. **Factors other than drug quantities:** In the current drug sentencing scheme, Congress has focused on mandatory minimum sentences based on drug type and quantity. It is well-accepted that certain drugs are more dangerous than others, and that dealing in larger quantities is more

serious behavior. So the broad outline of the current drug scheme makes sense. However, as discussed above, in practice the problem of determining the quantity upon which the sentence should be based has been fraught with problems. Moreover, even assuming that the quantities can be measured and scaled in a reliable fashion, drug type and weight may still not be a satisfactory basis for determining sentences.

There has been a widespread recognition that at least in some cases mandatory minimum sentences based upon drug type and weight are too harsh. Accordingly, the effect of these mandatory minimum statutes has been ameliorated, to a degree, by the statutory "safety valve" provision, 18 U.S.C. § 3553(f). Section § 3553(f) provides that in cases brought under 21 U.S.C. §§ 841, 844, 846, and 21 U.S.C. §§ 960 and 963, the court shall impose a sentence pursuant to guidelines "without regard to any statutory minimum sentence" if the court makes the following findings at sentencing:

(1) the defendant does not have more than 1 criminal history point, as determined under the sentencing guidelines;

(2) the defendant did not use violence or credible threats of violence or possess a firearm or other dangerous weapon (or induce another participant to do so) in connection with the offense;

(3) the offense did not result in death or serious bodily injury to any person;

(4) the defendant was not an organizer, leader, manager, or supervisor of others in the offense, as determined under the sentencing guidelines and was not engaged in a continuing criminal enterprise, as defined in section 408 of the Controlled Substances Act; and

(5) not later than the time of the sentencing hearing, the defendant has truthfully provided to the Government all information and evidence the defendant has concerning the offense or offenses that were part of the same course of conduct or of a common scheme or plan, but the fact that the defendant has no relevant or useful other information to provide or that the Government is already aware of the information shall not preclude a determination by the court that the defendant has complied with this requirement.

How broad (or narrow) is the safety valve provision? Note that a defendant must meet all five criteria to be eligible. In your view, does this provision correctly define the universe of defendants who should receive more lenient treatment? Of course that question assumes that having a safety valve is a good idea. Does the existence of such a safety valve undermine the deterrent effect, or the social meaning that Congress intended to produce when it enacted mandatory minimum statutes? Note that the Guidelines also provide something that is referred to as a "safety valve provision," § 2D1.1(b)(6), which reduces the sentence otherwise applicable by 2 levels.

Just as the safety valve provision recognized that there are certain cases where the mandatory minimum sentences were not appropriate, other provisions provide for greater sentences in cases where the behavior is deemed to be more dangerous. For example, as discussed later in this section, pp. 369–75, various provisions increase the maximum penalty for a drug offense where the defendant distributed drugs near a school, employed a minor in the commission of the offense, or sold drugs to a pregnant woman. Similarly, as discussed in Section C, pp. 389–403, the continuing criminal enterprise offense targets the so-called drug kingpins. The Guidelines mimic the statutory pattern: they base the sentence primarily on the type and weight of the drug involved, but also allow some adjustments (e.g., an upward adjustment for the leaders or organizers of drug rings).

There is evidence that many front-line participants in the federal criminal justice system now view the drug sentencing laws as unnecessarily harsh, and that they are quietly exercising their discretion in ways that have significantly reduced federal drug sentences. Frank Bowman and Michael Heise have presented data showing a downward trend in drug sentence length since 1992, and they argue their data shows:

> (1) at virtually every point in the Guidelines sentencing process where prosecutors and judges can exercise discretionary authority to reduce drug sentences, they have done so; and (2) where we can measure trends, the trend since roughly 1992 has always been toward exercising discretion in favor of leniency with increasing frequency.

Frank O. Bowman & Michael Heise, *Quiet Rebellion II: An Empirical Analysis of Declining Federal Drug Sentences Including Data from the District Level*, 87 Iowa L. Rev. 477, 480–81 (2002). There is, of course, still discretion left in the system, even with mandatory minimums. For example, a prosecutor can choose what offenses to charge, and whether to accept a plea to a lesser included offense. A court has discretion to go above a mandatory minimum, and discretion to determine where to sentence within the range provided for by the Sentencing Guidelines.

How large has the decline in drug sentences been? Bowman and Heise found a decrease in the average sentence of nearly two years (or 22%) as measured by data from the Administrative Office of the U.S. Courts, and a decrease of 13 months (or 14%) as measured by the Sentencing Commission's data. Moving from national data to data at the district and circuit level, they found:

> a remarkable degree of variation in both sentence length and change in average sentence length. For example, in 1992, the average drug sentence within a district ranged from 22 months to 176 months, and forty-one of the ninety-four judicial districts actually had higher average drug sentences in 1999 than in 1992.

> * * * [N]either population density nor district size as expressed by the number of Assistant United States Attorneys employed by the district shows a statistically significant relationship to the increase or decrease of the average drug sentence within a district.

> * * * [I]ncreases in prosecutorial workload correlate consistently with decreases in drug sentence length, but oddly, increases in judicial workload demonstrate virtually no such relationship. Events in the Mexican border districts exerted particular influence from 1996–1999.

Id. at 482–83. For a different view of the decline, see John Scalia, Jr., *The Impact of Changes in Federal Law and Policy on the Sentencing Of, and Time Served in Prison By, Drug Defendants Convicted in U.S. District Courts*, 14 Fed. Sent. Rep. 152 (2002). Scalia believes that the decline did not begin until 1995, and attributes it, at least in part, to different factors: the greater influence of sentences for marijuana defendants, the increase in the number of defendants receiving a downward departure for substantial assistance and other reasons, and the impact of the 'safety valve' that exempted certain defendants from otherwise applicable mandatory penalties and reduce the guideline range by two levels.

3. **Constitutional issues with using drug quantities in sentencing:** We have seen some of the problems with the current focus on drug type and quantity. This scheme has faced numerous constitutional challenges as well.

The Sixth Amendment right to a jury trial has been a major issue in determining what procedures must be followed when the government seeks to impose enhanced penalties under § 841(b). Prior to the Supreme Court's decision in *Apprendi v. New Jersey*, 530 U.S. 466 (2000), it was generally held that drug type and quantity were not elements of the offense, but rather sentencing factors relevant to determining the penalty. For that reason, neither proof beyond a reasonable doubt nor a right to jury trial were regarded as applicable. In *Apprendi* the Supreme Court held that any fact that increases the penalty beyond the ordinary statutory maximum must be submitted to the jury and proved beyond a reasonable doubt. Subsequently, the Court ruled in *Harris v. United States*, 536 U.S. 545 (2002), that mandatory minimum sentences do not have to be submitted to the jury and proved beyond a reasonable doubt. The most recent decision in this line of cases is *United States v. Booker*, 543 U.S. 220 (2005), which reaffirmed and extended the principle announced in *Apprendi*, finding two key provisions of the Sentencing Reform Act unconstitutional.

Laying aside guidelines issues, how do *Apprendi* and *Booker* affect drug cases under § 841? The structure of § 841 is extremely complex, and it includes several statutory maxima. As one court explained:

> Section 841(b) delineates several different default statutory maximums based on drug quantity (and other factors not relevant here, such as drug type and whether or not seriously bodily injury resulted): 20 years if no drug quantity is specified, 40 years for five or more grams of cocaine base, and life for fifty or more grams of cocaine base. 21 U.S.C. § 841(b)(1)(A)–(C); *See also United States v. Martinez–Medina*, 279 F.3d 105, 121 (1st Cir.) (identifying default statutory maximum under § 841(b)(1)(A) as life); *Robinson*, 241 F.3d at 119 (identifying default statutory maximum as twenty years under § 841(b)(1)(C), where no quantity had been determined beyond a reasonable doubt); *United States v. Baltas*, 236 F.3d 27, 41 (1st Cir. 2001) (same); *Smith*, 308 F.3d at 741 (finding a default statutory maximum of 20 years for more than fifty kilograms of marijuana under § 841(b)(1)(C)).

United States v. Goodine, 326 F.3d 26, 32 (1st Cir. 2003). Under *Apprendi* the facts necessary to increase the sentence above the relevant default must be proven to the jury beyond a reasonable doubt.[m] *Apprendi* thus requires

---

m. Note, however, that some courts do not label these facts "elements," reasoning that Congress did not intend them to be elements, even if the Constitution requires some heightened procedures. *Cf.* United States v. Villarce, 323 F.3d 435, 439 (6th Cir. 2003) (drug type and quantity are not elements for purposes of mens rea analysis).

the courts to parse the statutory language of the various subsections of § 841 to discover the default statutory penalties for each offense. This is sometimes rather challenging.

As long as drug quantity and type affect sentencing but do not raise the statutory maximum, they are not subject to the heightened procedures under *Apprendi*. Accordingly, for purposes of determining the applicability of mandatory *minimum* sentences *Harris* holds that the judge can find the facts using the preponderance standard at sentencing as long as the sentence is below the statutory maximum authorized by the jury's factual findings. Although some commentators think *Harris* is fundamentally inconsistent with *Booker*, the Supreme Court has not given any indication that it will overrule *Harris*.

Under the Sentencing Guidelines drug type and quantity are the most important factor in determining the sentence for defendants convicted of violating § 841 and other drug statutes. For a discussion of the guidelines regime, see Chapter 17. The *Booker* opinion is reprinted *infra* at 854–69.

As reflected in *Grant*, Congress has significantly increased the penalties for drug offenses and relied increasingly on mandatory sentencing. Many states have followed the same course. Constitutional challenges to these sentencing schemes have generally been unsuccessful. In *Harmelin v. Michigan*, 501 U.S. 957 (1991), the Supreme Court upheld a life sentence without possibility of parole under a state statute that made such a sentence mandatory for possession of 650 grams or more of any mixture containing cocaine. The Court rejected the defendant's claim that his sentence violated the cruel and unusual punishment clause because it was significantly disproportionate to the crime and because it precluded the consideration of the particularized circumstances and the criminal. The Court split 5 to 4. Justice Scalia announced the judgement of the Court, but only the Chief Justice joined the central portion of Justice Scalia's opinion. Justice Kennedy filed an opinion concurring in part and concurring in the judgment, and there were three dissenting opinions. Although the case did not produce agreement on the appropriate analysis, it did indicate that a majority of the Court was unwilling to override a legislative judgment that more severe sentences—up to and including mandatory life sentences without parole—are the best way to deal with one or more aspects of the drug problem. On remand, the Michigan Supreme Court found that the sentence violated the state constitutional guarantee against cruel and unusual punishment. *People v. Bullock*, 485 N.W.2d 866 (Mich. 1992). More recently, in *United States v. Angelos*, 345 F.Supp.2d 1227 (D. Utah 2004), a 24–year old first offender who possessed (but did not use or display) a gun during three drug deals was sentenced to 55 years. The court reluctantly rejected the defendant's cruel and unusual punishment challenge, but called on the President to commute his sentence and on Congress to modify its harsh mandatory minimum sentences. *Id.* at 1230–31.

As mentioned earlier, most would agree that certain drugs should be treated differently than others. But as the next case and the notes that follow indicate, not everyone agrees with the designations Congress has made, and many have raised constitutional challenges. Most criticism has been directed at § 841(b)(1)(B), which specifies the same sentence for possession of 500 grams of powdered cocaine as for 5 grams of cocaine base, or "crack." Is this 100 to 1 ratio good policy? Is it constitutional? The next case explores these questions.

UNITED STATES v. SMITH

73 F.3d 1414 (6th Cir. 1996).

RYAN, CIRCUIT JUDGE.

* * *

On December 6, 1993, police officers David Barnes and Scott White were on routine patrol near a high school in Martins Ferry, Ohio, when they observed Smith seated in a vehicle parked on the side of the road. While passing the vehicle, Officer Barnes observed Smith slumped down in the driver's seat drinking a can of beer. The officers drove around the block in order to approach the vehicle from behind. When they returned to the place where the car had been parked, it was gone. After a brief search of the area, the officers spotted and stopped the vehicle. Officer Barnes exited his patrol car and approached Smith who had exited his vehicle. Officer Barnes asked Smith for his driver's license and Smith responded that he did not have it with him. When Officer Barnes asked Smith for his name and social security number, Smith allegedly turned and attempted to flee. Officer Barnes stopped Smith after Smith had taken only a few steps.

Before placing Smith under arrest, Officer Barnes looked into Smith's car and saw an open beer can sitting on the floor of the driver's side, marijuana scattered throughout the car, and additional unopened containers. Officer Barnes arrested Smith for possessing an open beer can in a motor vehicle, and for consumption of alcohol in a motor vehicle. At the police station, a search of Smith revealed a black film container containing over five grams of cocaine and $138.

* * * On September 23, 1994, Smith was sentenced on the drug possession offense to 60 months imprisonment to be followed by a three-year period of supervised release.

* * *

[Smith] challenges the constitutionality of the 100:1 ratio for crack cocaine and powder cocaine in section 2D1.1 of the Sentencing Guidelines. The defendant urges this court to reverse the law of this circuit and follow a recent decision by the United States District Court for the Northern District of Georgia, *United States v. Davis*, 864 F.Supp. 1303 (N.D.Ga.1994), which held that crack cocaine enhancements are unconstitutionally vague. The defendant urges this court to do so in light of new scientific evidence which suggests that there is no meaningful distinction between crack cocaine and powder cocaine.

The defendant therefore raises a constitutional challenge to his sentence, over which, as a question of law, this court exercises de novo review.

Section 841 contains the same ratio as that contained in section 2D1.1 of the Sentencing Guidelines. 21 U.S.C. § 841. This circuit has heard and rejected vagueness challenges to the 100:1 ratio in § 841 on several occasions based on the same reasoning used by Smith. In *United States v. Levy*, 904 F.2d 1026 (6th Cir.1990), the defendant challenged the 100:1 ratio in 21 U.S.C. § 841 and alleged that the term "cocaine base" was unconstitutionally vague. This court rejected the challenge. *Id.* at 1033. In so holding, this court explained: "It is undisputed that Congress amended [21 U.S.C. § 841(b)(1)(B)] out of concern that cocaine base is 'more dangerous to society than cocaine [powder] because of crack's potency, its highly addictive nature, its affordability, and its increasing prevalence.'" *Id.* at 1032 (brackets added and in original) (quoting *United States v. Buckner*, 894 F.2d 975, 978 (8th Cir.1990)).

The court further found:

> In broad terms, cocaine base and cocaine hydrochloride may be distinguished by their texture and chemical composition. Cocaine hydrochloride is water soluble, formed in crystals or flakes, and is generally snorted by users. Cocaine base is not water soluble, is concentrated in rock-hard forms of various sizes, and is generally smoked. Thus, the phrase cocaine base defines a substance that is distinguishable from other forms of cocaine based upon appearance, texture, price, means of consumption, the character and immediacy of the effects of use, and chemical composition.

Also, in *United States v. Pickett*, 941 F.2d 411 (6th Cir.1991), this circuit held that the 100:1 ratio in 21 U.S.C. § 841 does not violate substantive due process because Congress did not act arbitrarily or irrationally when it established the ratio. Relevant to Smith's arguments on appeal, the *Pickett* court found that

> there is sufficient difference of opinion in the scientific community regarding the different likelihoods of becoming addicted to crack or cocaine to justify the Congressional distinction between the two.... [E]xperts believe that the speed with which crack gets to the brain produces a significantly different effect that increases the likelihood of addiction. There was also evidence produced [at the sentencing hearing] that crack is usually a purer drug than is cocaine.

Most notably, this court in *United States v. Salas*, No. 93–5897, 1994 WL 24982, 1994 U.S.App. LEXIS 1515 (6th Cir. Jan. 27, 1994) (unpublished disposition), held:

> The Sentencing Guidelines do not establish the illegality of any conduct. Rather, they are directives to judges and not to citizens. As such, they are not susceptible to a vagueness attack. Since there is no constitutional right to sentencing guidelines, the limitations

placed on judges' discretion by the Guidelines do not violate a defendant's right to due process by reason of vagueness.

* * *

Accordingly, the judgment of the district court is AFFIRMED.

NATHANIEL R. JONES, CIRCUIT JUDGE, concurring.

I concur in the result, but am compelled to discuss my concerns regarding the impact of the 100:1 sentencing ratio for crack and powdered cocaine ("100:1 ratio") that exists in both statutory law and the Sentencing Guidelines. The ratio has an acute societal impact which continues to expand. Nevertheless, this court has determined that the ratio passes constitutional muster. I believe that with the benefit of new information and the application of the ratio, the time has come for the court to reexamine its supporting analysis. As judges, we should no longer remain wedded to that which experience shows is neither rational nor fair.

The 100:1 ratio was created by the Anti–Drug Abuse Act of 1986 ("Act"). Congress passed the Act in order to respond to the public's growing fear of the "crack epidemic." In 1988, Congress amended the Act to establish a mandatory minimum penalty for possession of crack, which is "the only such federal penalty for a first offense of simple possession of a controlled substance." The United States Sentencing Commission subsequently incorporated the ratio into the Sentencing Guidelines.

Since the Act's passage, the African–American community has borne the brunt of enforcement of the 100:1 ratio. From 1985 to 1986, the number of minority youth detained for drug offenses increased 71%. By 1994, blacks comprised 90.4% of all federal crack cocaine drug offenders. From 1992 to 1994, the percentage of drug prosecutions involving crack offenses increased from 14.6% to 21.2%. Therefore, the Act has resulted in an increasingly disproportionate number of young black males being prosecuted and incarcerated for a considerable amount of time, to the point that blacks, who comprise 12% of the population, now make up 57.7% of the prisoners in federal jails for drug offenses.

The racial disproportionality of crack-related prosecutions is even more disturbing in light of the harsher sentences for crack offenses. The mean sentence for crack traffickers, most of whom are black, is 133.4 months. In contrast, powdered cocaine traffickers receive a mean sentence of approximately ninety months. The majority of these offenders are white. Similarly, for simple possession offenses, crack offenders receive a sentence which is nearly ten times longer than that received for cocaine offenders: the mean sentence for crack possession offenders is 30.6 months, while that for cocaine offenders is 3.2 months. Yet 73.8% of cocaine possession offenders obtain supervised release while only 32% of crack possession defenders are granted parole. Thus, the numbers clearly illustrate the disparities in prosecutions, sentencing, and probation between cocaine offenders, who are mostly white, and crack offenders, who are mostly black, since the 100:1 ratio came into being.

In recent years we have rejected a variety of constitutional claims against the 100:1 ratio. [*United States v. Levy*, 904 F.2d 1026, 1033 (6th Cir.1990); *United States v. Pickett*, 941 F.2d 411, 419 (6th Cir.1991); *United States v. Williams*, 962 F.2d 1218 (6th Cir.)].

In rejecting these challenges to the 100:1 ratio, we have relied on three premises. The first premise is that crack cocaine is "a substance that is distinguishable from other forms of cocaine based on appearance, texture, price, means of consumption, the character and immediacy of the effects of use, and chemical composition." *Levy*, 904 F.2d at 1033. The second premise is that "crack is a purer drug than cocaine and the speed with which it progresses to the brain 'produces a significantly different effect that increases the likelihood of addiction.'" *Williams*, 962 F.2d at 1227 (quoting *Pickett*, 941 F.2d at 418). The final premise is that the cheapness and accessibility of crack " 'could create other societal problems which required remedying,' " including the exposure of children to the drug. *Id.* The ever-expanding body of evidence, however, suggests that these premises lack saliency so as to cast considerable doubt on this court's legal analysis.

The first premise requires us to conclude that crack cocaine and powdered cocaine are pharmacologically distinct drugs. *Levy*, 904 F.2d at 1033. The empirical and scientific data suggests the contrary. Crack and powdered cocaine are each comprised of cocaine hydrochloride. Powdered cocaine is consumed intranasally, while crack is smoked. Crack, however, is mixed with solvents such as baking soda, and this mixture produces a concentrated crystalline substance. The distinction in the physical properties of crack cocaine notwithstanding, "[c]ocaine in any form—paste, powder, freebase, or crack—produces the same physiological and psychotropic effects." Dr. Charles Shuster, former Director of the National Institute on Drug Abuse, puts it more bluntly: " 'cocaine is cocaine, whether you take it in intranasally, intravenously, or smoked.' " Therefore, while crack and powdered cocaine are distinguishable in form and in price, they are essentially the same drug.

The second premise is that crack is more addictive than powdered cocaine. *Williams*, 962 F.2d at 1227. This premise is also suspect. Experts have noted that crack users absorb the cocaine into their bloodstream more quickly than those who snort powdered cocaine. In turn, a "high" produced by smoking crack peaks within a minute of smoking, while the "high" produced by powdered cocaine peaks after twenty minutes. The crack high decreases within forty minutes while the powdered cocaine high lasts for two hours. Because crack produces quicker highs and lows than does powdered cocaine, it is estimated that the likelihood of addiction to crack is fifty times higher than that of powdered cocaine.

Although crack's addictive qualities are not at issue, the assertion that crack is a more dangerous drug than cocaine is suspect. According to Dr. George Schwartz, a noted expert in the field of pharmacology and toxicology, crack is no more or less addictive than powdered cocaine. In fact, much of the data on crack cocaine suggests that the contrary might be true. Government statistics show that cocaine is a more popular drug than crack: as of 1994, there were five times more powdered cocaine users than crack users. The death rate among powdered cocaine users is three times higher than the rate for crack users. In addition, powdered cocaine poses a greater risk of heart and lung disease than crack. Thus, while crack has some undeniably addictive and dangerous qualities, the evidence on powdered cocaine makes it increasingly difficult for me to understand why crack cocaine offenders receive significantly higher sanctions than powdered cocaine offenders.

The final, and perhaps most controversial, premise is that crack cocaine poses a greater threat to the fabric of our society than powdered cocaine. *See Pickett*, 941 F.2d at 418. Concededly, this premise is not totally meritless. * * * Crack is distributed through open-air sales, couriers, and crack houses. One gram of crack provides approximately twenty to twenty-five "hits", thus enabling crack vendors to carry and sell their illicit product more easily than powdered cocaine dealers. These characteristics make the crack trade lucrative, and breed violent competition. This danger is reflected in the statistic which reveals that while 27.9% of all crack offenders carry weapons, only 15.1% of powdered cocaine offenders do so.

Other commonly held perceptions about the evils of crack, however, may be exaggerated. For example, a key factor in the passage of the Act was the impression held by many lawmakers that crack addicts are wont to commit violent crimes.[1] The Sentencing Commission, however, found that while crack addicts resort to drug dealing and petty crimes to support their habits, "the stereotype of a drug-crazed addict committing heinous crimes is not true for either [crack or powdered] cocaine."

Another perception is that crack is responsible for a marked increase in the births of "boarder babies"—commonly called "crack babies"— particularly among African–American women. The Sentencing Commission found that pregnant women who use crack put their babies at a greater health risk because they consume greater quantities of cocaine than powdered cocaine users. But the Sentencing Commission also found that there is no reliable data to establish that crack contributes to more births of "cocaine-exposed babies" than powdered cocaine. Further com-

---

1. A number of legislators spoke of crack's link to crime during the passage of the Act. In his support of the Act, Senator Lawton Chiles expressed concern over the "growing crime rates in urban as well as rural areas." 132 Cong. Rec. S12169–01 (daily ed. Sept. 9, 1986) (statement of Sen. Chiles). Congressman Craig Biaggi maintained that the crack epidemic was "sending our crime rates sky high." 132 Cong. Rec. at 15659 (daily ed. June 26, 1986) (statement of Rep. Biaggi). Furthermore, in his testimony before the House Judiciary Subcommittee on Crime, Wade Henderson, Director of the Washington, D.C. Bureau of the NAACP, invoked the testimony of Eric Sterling, who served as the subcommittee's counsel during passage of the Act. Henderson at 12–13. According to Mr. Sterling, members of the House of Representatives submitted articles about " 'crazed black men killing innocent people while on cocaine' " into the Congressional Record during deliberations over the Act. *Id.*

plicating this issue is the fact that doctors are ten times more likely to report black women for abusing drugs during pregnancy than white women.

Of all the perceptions that exist about the societal impact of crack, the most significant perception is that crack is directly responsible for the deterioration of the African–American community. Although crack has undoubtedly taken its toll on this community, powdered cocaine may have an equally devastating, if not more devastating, impact. Powdered cocaine is the illicit ingredient in crack cocaine; crack cannot be manufactured without it. Powdered cocaine reaches the open-air crack distribution market "at the wholesale and retail levels." It also pervades the more discreet markets in mostly white, suburban communities. Despite the ubiquity of powdered cocaine, however, powdered cocaine dealers are not punished as harshly as crack cocaine dealers. As the Sentencing Commission succinctly noted, "the substantial differential in the ratio between crack and powder cocaine punishes the retail dealer of crack far more severely than the powder cocaine supplier who may have sold the powder cocaine from which multiple street dealers made crack."

The emphasis on crack and its contribution to urban decay also diverts attention from the other socioeconomic symptoms which contribute to the deterioration of the African–American community. There exists a common perception that "the drug trade has overwhelmed many urban black communities, wiping out legitimate businesses and steering young men to crime." Other commentators, however, suggest the opposite: "past discrimination in housing, employment, and education has contributed to the creation of a black underclass...." As a result, the young black males who are overwhelmingly attracted to the drug trade "are too often socialized to believe that they can only achieve the American dream through illegal activities ..." Consequently, "[c]rack distribution.... provide[s] inner-city black males with a unique chance to make money and attain stature in their community." Thus, it is quite possible that Judge Heaney was right when he wrote in his concurrence in *United States v. Willis*, 967 F.2d 1220, 1227 (8th Cir.1992) (Heaney, J. concurring), that "until young black men have equal opportunities for a decent education and jobs, [the drug problem] will only get worse."

The current enforcement and sentencing policies may in fact be substantial factors in the persistence of the "crack epidemic" in the African-American community. These policies have resulted in the incarceration of scores of young black males, many of whom will remain in prison until they reach middle age. During their extended periods of incarceration, " 'their peers are beginning families, learning constructive life skills, and starting careers.' Thus, the longer [they are] in jail, the greater the competitive disadvantage they will suffer upon their release." Therefore, these young men will lack the wherewithal to help later generations avoid the perils of illegal activity, thereby exposing the community to continued drug-related crime.

Finally, the crack sentencing policies may perpetuate the problems they seek to resolve because of their provocative racial overtones. The longer the policies exist, the greater the risk that we send a message to the public that "the lives of white criminals are considered by the U.S. justice system to be at least 100 times more valuable and worthy of preservation than those of black criminals." This sentencing inequity presents a greater danger that black males will hold our judicial system in greater contempt and become increasingly attracted to the crack distribution as a career opportunity. With one-third of our black males already under the supervision of the criminal justice system, the 100:1 ratio may drive a wedge between our young black males and our justice system which will inure to the benefit of neither. We can ill afford this costly disconnect.

Therefore, with the benefit of this further examination, I regard the premises which drive our constitutional analysis of the 100:1 ratio with great suspicion. Each of these premises is subject to challenge, and we must not ignore this fact. I urge my colleagues to don a more realistic set of lenses. Otherwise, we risk substantial harm to the integrity of our constitutional jurisprudence. Continued use of the law to perpetuate a result at variance with rationality and common sense—even in a war on drugs—is indefensible. We have seen instances of this being done in our nation's past that have come back to haunt us. I predict that unless we apply the lesson of *Toyosaburo Korematsu v. United States*, 323 U.S. 214, 65 S.Ct. 193, 89 L.Ed. 194 (1944),[3] for instance, we will be forced to relive that tragedy.

Once again, I offer Lord Atkins' warnings to his fellow countrymen during World War II: "In England, amidst the clash of arms the laws are not silent. They may be changed, but they speak the same language in war as in peace." I argue for change with respect to imposing sentences that yield a wretchedly unfair result. I do this as a virtual single voice. Yet, as Lord Atkins also said, "I protest, even if I do it alone, against a strained construction put upon words, with the effect giving uncontrolled power of imprisonment to the minister." As a court, in the name of justice, we must revisit without delay this issue, in light of its impact on imprisonments.

Notes

1. Is there something fundamentally wrong with the constitutional analysis applicable to the cases challenging the 100:1 ratio on equal protection grounds? David Sklansky argues that what the law misses is unconscious racism:

3. In *Korematsu*, the Court upheld the constitutionality of Executive Order No. 34, which resulted in the internment of Japanese–Americans. *Id.* The Court found that the Executive Branch and Congress had sufficient grounds to promulgate such an order. *Id.* at 218, 65 S.Ct. at 194–95. It explained that "there were disloyal members of [the Japanese-American] population, whose number and strength could not be readily ascertained ... such persons ... constituted a menace to the national defense and security, which demanded that prompt and adequate measures be taken against it." *Id.*

The federal crack penalties provide a paradigmatic case of unconscious racism. While these penalties may reflect some degree of affirmative antipathy toward blacks, the evidence of that is at best suggestive and anecdotal. What the legislative history of the Anti–Drug Abuse Act and its predecessors provide a good deal more reason to suspect is that, regardless of the objectives Congress was pursuing, it would have shown more restraint in fashioning the crack penalties, or more interest in amending them in ensuing years, if the penalties did not apply almost exclusively to blacks. In the words of one defense attorney, "Maybe I'm cynical, but I think that if you saw a lot of young white males getting five-and 10-year minimums for dealing powder cocaine, you'd have a lot more reaction."

Because of the blindness equal protection doctrine shows to the danger of unconscious racism, the federal crack sentences have been assessed only for "rational basis." The nature of that assessment, in turn, has blinded our law to a second troubling feature of the sentences—the severity of the difference between the penalties for crack and those for cocaine powder. The rational-basis test asks only whether the line Congress has drawn is rationally related to a legitimate governmental interest; the test entirely ignores how and to what extent Congress has made the line count. Current doctrine thus directs courts to inquire whether it is reasonable for Congress to distinguish between crack and powder cocaine, but not whether it is reasonable to distinguish between them by treating an ounce of one the same as 100 ounces of the other.

Unfortunately, it is precisely here, in the extent of the differential treatment, that one would most expect unconscious racism to manifest itself. The problem of "racially selective sympathy and indifference" becomes most acute not when Congress divides people into classes, but when it determines what treatment people in each class should receive. Far from operating independently, then, the blindness of current doctrine to unconscious racism and to the extent of differential treatment reinforce each other. Together they render virtually invisible to equal protection analysis much of what is most troubling about the federal crack sentences.

David A. Sklansky, *Cocaine, Race, and Equal Protection*, 47 STAN. L. REV. 1283, 1308–09 (1995). Sklansky concludes that the root of the problem is the Supreme Court's one-size-fits-all approach to equal protection analysis. He argues that equal protection should be disaggregated, permitting the courts to take different approaches in different contexts. In the context of a federal sentencing rule shown to have a seriously disproportionate impact on black defendants, the courts should shift the burden and require the government to rebut the inference of conscious or unconscious racism by providing an alternative explanation for the rule. The government should be required "to provide a neutral explanation not just for the distinction Congress drew, but also for what it did with that distinction—a neutral explanation, for example, not just for setting separate quantity thresholds for crack, but also for setting them at one percent of the thresholds for its precursor, powder cocaine." 47 STAN. L. REV. at 1319. Sklansky suggests that the crack penalties would fail this test because there is no racially neutral explanation for the capriciously selected 100:1 ratio.

2. No federal appellate court has yet found the crack to cocaine sentencing ratio unconstitutional;[n] although many commentators have attacked the ratio as evidence of racial bias.[o] Change, if it occurs, will likely come through the actions of the Sentencing Commission or Congress. On three occasions the Commission has proposed eliminating or ameliorating the distinction between crack and powder cocaine, but Congress has rebuffed these proposals. The response to the Commission's first proposal was particularly acrimonious, and it led to the first Congressional rejection of a proposed Guideline.

The Commission first took up the issue in 1995, when it proposed amending both the Guidelines and the relevant federal statutes to eliminate the 100:1 crack to powdered cocaine ratio, and equalize the treatment of crack and powdered cocaine. Although the Commission was unanimous in its conclusion that the 100:1 ratio should be eliminated, it divided 4 to 3 on the question whether the Guidelines for crack and powdered cocaine should be equalized or the ratio should be lowered to 10:1 or 5:1. Focusing on the fairness of the system, the majority's report concluded:

> When a sentencing policy has a severe disproportionate impact on a minority group, it is important that sufficient bases exist for the policy. The law should not draw distinctions that single out some offenders for harsher punishment unless these distinctions are clearly related to a legitimate policy goal. For the reasons described above, we do not believe that a sufficient policy basis for the current penalty differential exists.

The Justice Department opposed the crack amendment, and Congress passed legislation disapproving these guidelines and instructing the Commission to submit new recommendations for cocaine sentencing. Pub. L. 104–38, 109 Stat. 334 (1995). Not surprisingly, Congress also declined to enact the statutory changes proposed by the Commission.

The Sentencing Commission responded to this congressional directive in a second special report to Congress issued in April 1997. *See* UNITED STATES

---

n. Every appellate court has upheld the constitutionality of the 100:1 crack-to-powder cocaine sentencing ratio. *See* United States v. Singleterry, 29 F.3d 733 (1st Cir. 1994); United States v. Jackson, 59 F.3d 1421 (2d Cir. 1995); United States v. Frazier, 981 F.2d 92 (3d Cir. 1992); United States v. Fisher, 58 F.3d 96 (4th Cir. 1995); United States v. Galloway, 951 F.2d 64 (5th Cir. 1992); United States v. Shorter, 54 F.3d 1248 (7th Cir. 1995); United States v. Williams, 982 F.2d 1209 (8th Cir. 1992); United States v. Jackson, 84 F.3d 1154 (9th Cir. 1996); United States v. Williams, 45 F.3d 1481 (10th Cir. 1995); United States v. Sloan, 97 F.3d 1378 (11th Cir. 1996); United States v. Thompson, 27 F.3d 671 (D.C. Cir. 1994).

o. *See* RANDALL KENNEDY, RACE, CRIME, AND THE LAW 364–86 (1997); Paul Butler, *(Color)*

Blind Faith: The Tragedy of Race, Crime, and the Law, 111 HARV. L. REV. 1270, 1276–79 (1998); David H. Angeli, A *"Second Look" at Crack Cocaine Sentencing Policies: One More Try for Federal Equal Protection*, 34 AM. CRIM. L. REV. 1211 (1997). *But see* Elizabeth Tison, Comment, *Amending the Sentencing Guidelines for Cocaine Offenses: The 100–to–1 Ratio is Not as "Cracked" Up as Some Suggest*, 27 S. Ill. U.L.J. 413 (2003) (arguing that claims of a racial bias in the crack/cocaine ratio are not substantiated by conclusive statistics, and that the sentencing scheme should be amended by raising penalties for cocaine rather than lowering penalties for crack, which would be a retreat in the war on drugs and a failure to protect vulnerable members of society from the greater dangers of crack).

Sentencing Commission, Special Report to the Congress: Cocaine and Federal Sentencing Policy, *reprinted in* 10 Fed. Sent. R. 184 (1998). With respect to mandatory minimum sentences for possession with intent to distribute, the Commission recommended unanimously that the 500–gram trigger for powder cocaine should be reduced to a level between 125 and 375 grams, while the 5–gram trigger for crack cocaine should be increased to a level between 25 and 75 grams. Alterations within these ranges would produce a reduction in the current 100:1 ratio to a level somewhere between 1.6:1 and 15:1. Although the current 100:1 ratio has been criticized primarily for its grossly disparate impact on minorities, the Commission did not frame the rationale for its new recommendations in terms of this disparity, and it devoted less than a paragraph to a discussion of this observation despite a scathing concurrence by Vice–Chairman Gelacek. Instead, the Commission grounded its analysis in terms of the appropriate allocation of state and federal law enforcement resources.

The Commission conceded that crack cocaine represented a greater public danger than powder at the consumer level, but maintained that federal resources should remain focused on echelons above street-level distribution. *See id.* at 185–186. The increase in the powder cocaine trigger was justified primarily on the ground that crack cocaine is derived from powder; thus, increasing the trigger would reflect the dangers posed by this possible conversion while reserving the mandatory minimum sentence to a quantity targeted more directly at mid-level distributors and above. *See id.* at 186–188. The recommended reduction in the crack trigger was similarly justified as a means of targeting distributors above street-level based on quantity considerations alone. *See id.* Finally, for the same reasons, the Commission recommended unanimously that the penalties for simple possession of crack and powder cocaine should be equalized. *See id.* at 188. Although this recommendation did not indicate how equalization should be achieved, the most likely inference would be that the Commission favored equalization by eliminating the unique mandatory minimum for first-offense simple possession of crack rather than imposing a new minimum for the simple possession of powder cocaine.

Notwithstanding the recommendation of the Commission or the support expressed by senior administration officials, Congress has taken a dim view of raising the crack trigger. Although a number of key federal legislators on the House and Senate Judiciary Committees have shown an interest in legislation to eliminate the 100:1 ratio, Republicans and Democrats have not agreed on the appropriate substitute. In the 109th Congress, Democrats have favored bringing the crack penalties down to those applicable to powdered cocaine, while Republicans has favored increasing the penalties for powdered cocaine to those now available for crack.[p]

Most recently, in 2002 the Sentencing Commission provided a report to Congress, entitled Cocaine and Federal Sentencing Policy, that set forth recommendations for statutory and guideline modifications to the federal sentencing structure for cocaine offenses. By providing a recommendation

---

p. *Compare* H.R. 48, 109th Cong. (2005) (Republican sponsored bill), *with* H.R. 2456, 109th Cong. (2005) (Democratic sponsored bill). In earlier legislation, Republicans fa- vored a 10:1 ratio, rather than equivalency. *See* S. 146, 106th Cong. (1999) and S. 5 106th Cong. (1999).

rather than promulgating its own proposed legislation and guidelines—which might suggest a lack of deference to Congress on the underlying policy issues—the Commission seems to have been attempting to avoid a confrontation and to cultivate a more productive relationship with Congress. Unfortunately, this proposal did not garner support, and the events surrounding the PROTECT Act of 2003, see *infra*, pp. 868 and 888, indicate that the relationship between the Commission and Congress is severely frayed.

The Commission's 2002 press release summarized its recommendations as follows:

The Sentencing Commission recommends that Congress adopt a three-pronged approach for revising federal cocaine sentencing policy:

(1) increase the quantity of crack cocaine required that triggers an automatic mandatory minimum sentence. Specifically, the five-year mandatory minimum threshold quantity for crack cocaine offenses should be adjusted from the current 5 grams trigger to at least 25 grams and the current ten-year threshold quantity from 50 grams to at least 250 grams (and repeal the mandatory minimum for simple possession of crack cocaine);

(2) direct the Sentencing Commission to provide appropriate sentencing enhancements to increase penalties should the drug crime involve: (a) a dangerous weapon (including a firearm); (b) bodily injury resulting from violence; (c) distribution to protected individuals and/or locations; (d) repeat felony drug trafficking offenders; and (e) importation of drugs by offenders who do not perform a mitigating role in the offense; and

(3) maintain the current statutory minimum threshold quantities for powder cocaine offenses at 500 grams triggering the five-year mandatory minimum penalty and 5,000 grams for the ten-year mandatory minimum penalty (understanding that the contemplated specific guideline sentencing enhancements would effectively increase penalties for the more dangerous and more culpable powder cocaine offenders).

The recommendations, if adopted, would narrow the difference between average sentences for crack cocaine and powder cocaine offenses from 44 months to approximately one year. Specifically, the Commission estimates that the average sentence for crack cocaine offenses would decrease from 118 months to 95 months, and the average sentence for powder cocaine offenses would increase from 74 months to 83 months. Importantly, the guideline sentencing range based solely on drug quantity for crack cocaine offenses still would be significantly longer (approximately two-to-four times longer) than powder cocaine offenses involving equivalent drug quantities.

* * *

In justifying its recommendations, the Commission made the following major findings about cocaine offender profiles examined between fiscal years 1995 and 2000:

● Contrary to the general objective of the 1986 legislation to target "serious" and "major" traffickers, two-thirds of federal crack cocaine offenders were street-level dealers. Only 5.9 percent of federal crack cocaine offenders performed trafficking functions most consistent with the functions described in the legislative history of the Anti–Drug Abuse Act of 1986 as warranting a five-year penalty, and 15.2 percent performed trafficking functions most consistent with the functions described as warranting a ten-year penalty;

● The current penalty structure was based on beliefs about the association of crack cocaine offenses with certain harmful conduct—particularly violence—that are no longer accurate. In 2000, for example, three quarters of federal crack cocaine offenders had no personal weapon involvement, and only 2.3 percent discharged a weapon. Therefore, to the extent that the 100–to–1 drug quantity ratio was designed in part to account for this harmful conduct, it sweeps too broadly by treating all crack cocaine offenders as if they committed those more harmful acts, even though most crack cocaine offenders, in fact, had not;

● The negative effects of prenatal crack cocaine exposure are identical to the negative effects of prenatal powder cocaine exposure and are significantly less severe than previously believed;

● The overwhelming majority of offenders subject to the heightened crack cocaine penalties are black, about 85 percent in 2000. This has contributed to a widely held perception that the current penalty structure promotes unwarranted disparity based on race. Although this assertion cannot be scientifically evaluated, the Commission finds even the perception of racial disparity problematic because it fosters disrespect for and lack of confidence in the criminal justice system. These conclusions led the Commission to unanimously conclude that the various congressional objectives can be achieved more effectively by decreasing the 100–to–1 drug quantity ratio.

3. Following the Supreme Court's decision in *United States v. Booker*, 543 U.S. 220 (2005), which made the Sentencing Guidelines advisory rather than mandatory, some district judges have used this new freedom in sentencing to grant defendants convicted of crack offenses below-Guidelines sentences, often by using ratios less than 100:1. *See, e.g., Simon v. United States*, 361 F.Supp.2d 35 (E.D.N.Y. 2005); *United States v. Smith*, 359 F.Supp.2d 771 (E.D. Wis. 2005). However, at least one judge does not agree:

Congress has made a choice regarding crack cocaine. To my way of thinking, it is not the best choice, but it is not a crazy one either. As a judge, I should defer to the choice of penalties that Congress has made for crack cocaine even though I would quickly do something different if it were within my proper role to choose. This is because judge-made changes to the crack Guidelines, while sometimes principled, are (1) undemocratic, and (2) not plainly superior to the judgments of Congress. We should maintain the status quo when exercising our *Booker* discretion within the context of the crack cocaine Guidelines because we are judges and not legislators and because the status quo is what Congress has chosen. When it comes to the severity of punishment, Congress has the right to be wrong.

* * *

Let us suppose, however, that I have not convinced the reader that we should maintain the status quo. What is the alternative?

I have my favorite, and that would be the 20–to–1 proposal set forth in the *2002 Report*. But, we might also adopt the Clinton administration's 10–to–1 ratio or the 5–to–1 ratio set out in the *1997 Report*. Or, I have an idea, let us really make things fair and impose the mandatory minimum sentence whenever the pertinent crack Guidelines call for a sentence exceeding that minimum. Wait a minute—perhaps we should merely mimic the powder cocaine Guidelines. Better yet, let us put together a hybrid of all these approaches. Now, here's the ticket, forget about drug quantities altogether and impose no sentence that is greater than necessary. The permutations are as numerous as there are federal judges who sentence crack dealers.

Come to think of it, why should we limit ourselves to fiddling with the crack Guidelines? While we are at it, perhaps we should increase, or maybe we should decrease, the punishments we impose for methamphetamine trafficking. Incidentally, if we are going to rewrite the law for meth-sentencing, I might vote for an increase. You cannot understand the horror of this particular drug trade until you see what methamphetamine trafficking does to the people who use the drug, the communities that must deal with the resulting social costs, and the poor and vulnerable Mexican mules who frequently truck it up from the super labs across the border in exchange for a ride to an American meat-packing plant where they hope to find legitimate (but incredibly hard) work.

Simply stated, unlike Congress or the Commission, we judges lack the institutional capacity (and, frankly, the personal competence) to set and then enforce one new, well-chosen, theoretically coherent, national standard. As opposed to a uniform, albeit flawed, Guideline, it would make things far worse to have a bunch of different standards for crack sentencing. For that reason alone, we should sit on our collective hands and give the crack Guidelines substantial or heavy weight until Congress decides otherwise.

United States v. Tabor, 365 F.Supp.2d 1052, 1060–61 (D. Neb. 2005). For a further discussion on the Sentencing Guidelines post-*Booker*, see Chapter 18.

2. SUPPLEMENTATION OF THE CORE OFFENSES—THE SCHOOLYARD STATUTE AND OTHER PIGGYBACK EN-HANCEMENT PROVISIONS

Congress has supplemented the standard offenses under 21 U.S.C. § 841—manufacturing, distribution, and possession with intent to distribute—with a variety of provisions that increase the maximum sentences applicable to the underlying conduct when one or more additional criteria are met. For example, the schoolyard statute, 21 U.S.C. § 860, provides that the maximum penalties for manufacturing, distribution, or possession with intent to distribute shall be doubled for the first offense and tripled for any subsequent offense that is committed within 1,000 feet of a school. Similar doubling and trebling provisions apply if the defendant employs or uses a person under the age of eighteen in the commission of a drug offense, or knowingly distributes drugs to a pregnant woman. *See* 21 U.S.C. §§ 860(f) & 861 (a)(1)-(2). In addition, 18 U.S.C. § 924 (c) provides for an additional consecutive sentence of five years if the defendant uses or carries a firearm "in the commission of a crime of violence or drug trafficking."

Using the schoolyard statute as a model, this section explores some of the issues raised by the piggyback enhancement provisions. Although these provisions raise some interesting questions, it should be noted that they come up in very few actual prosecutions. For example, in 1999, the most recent year for which data were reported, the number of suspects in which these offenses were the most serious offense investigated amounted to less than 1% of all drug suspects.[q] It may be the case that the standard offense—21 U.S.C. § 841—can now carry such harsh sentences that prosecutors rarely have a need to charge these additional piggyback provisions.

21 U.S.C.

§ 860.[r] Distribution or manufacturing in or near schools and colleges.

(a) Penalty

Any person who violates [21 U.S.C.] 841(a)(1) or [21 U.S.C.] 856 ... by distributing, possessing with intent to distribute, or manufacturing a controlled substance in or on, or within one thousand feet of, the real property comprising a public or private elementary, vocational, or secondary school or a public or private college, junior college, or university, or a playground, or housing facility owned by a public housing authority, or within 100 feet of a public or private youth center, public swimming pool, or video arcade facility, is (except as provided in subsection (b) of this section) subject to (1) twice the maximum punishment authorized by section 841(b) of this title; and (2) at least twice any term of supervised release authorized by section 841(b) of this title for a first offense. A fine up to twice that authorized by section 841(b) of this title may be imposed in addition to any term of imprisonment authorized by this subsection.

* * *

(c) Employing children to distribute drugs near schools and playgrounds

q. This statistic was obtained from a 2001 Bureau of Justice Statistics Special Report on Federal Drug Offenders, available online at <http://www.ojp.usdoj.gov/bjs/pub/pdf/fdo99.pdf> (visited July 25, 2005).

r. This provision was originally codified as 21 U.S.C. § 845a. For convenience we refer to the schoolyard statute as § 860, even when the prosecution was brought under § 845a.

Notwithstanding any other law, any person at least 21 years of age who knowingly and intentionally—

(1) employs, hires, uses, persuades, induces, entices, or coerces a person under 18 years of age to violate this section; or

(2) employs, hires, uses, persuades, induces, entices, or coerces a person under 18 years of age to assist in avoiding detection or apprehension for any offense under this section by any Federal, State, or local law enforcement official,

is punishable by a term of imprisonment, a fine, or both, up to triple those authorized by section 841 of this title.

Notes

1. The lower courts are divided on a question that has a very significant bearing on the scope of the schoolyard statute, which is whether it applies to cases where the defendant possessed drugs within 1,000 feet of a school, but intended to distribute them elsewhere. Interpreting the statute to require only possession within the schoolyard zone greatly enhances the prosecutor's discretionary authority to subject a large class of defendants to enhanced penalties. Several of the early cases involved defendants who were in a bus or train station, intending to pass through the school zone on their way to another destination. Though the stations were located within 1,000 feet of a school, none of the defendants were planning to distribute any drugs at these schools. The district courts dismissed the charges under § 860 because of the government's inability to prove that the defendants intended to distribute within 1,000 feet of a school. These decisions reflect not only technical judgments about the language of § 860 and its legislative history, but also reluctance to allow the fortuity of a school's location significantly to increase a defendant's sentence.

The courts of appeals to consider the issue, however, have concluded—albeit on facts more favorable to the government—that Congress intended "to create a 'drug free zone' around our nation's schools." *United States v. Wake*, 948 F.2d 1422, 1430 (5th Cir. 1991). *Accord United States v. Harris*, 313 F.3d 1228 (10th Cir. 2002); *United States v. Ortiz*, 146 F.3d 25 (1st Cir. 1998); *United States v. Rodriguez*, 961 F.2d 1089 (3d Cir. 1992). As originally adopted the schoolyard statute applied only to distribution within the school zone. The statute was amended in 1986 to add manufacturing, and in 1988 to add possession with intent to distribute. The sectional analysis provided by the Senate Judiciary Committee in 1988 stated that the enhanced penalties would apply to anyone "apprehended near a school with a quantity of drugs sufficient to indicate an intent to distribute." 134 CONG. REC. S17,360, S17,365 (daily ed. Nov. 10, 1988) (statement of Senator Biden). Finding neither the language of the statute nor the legislative history created any ambiguity, the courts of appeals have refused to apply the rule of lenity.

Writing for the Third Circuit in *Rodriguez*, Judge Alito responded at length to "extreme" hypotheticals, such as the application of a the statute "to a defendant who speeds by school in a train or other vehicle on the way to a narcotics sale":

> The argument implicitly made by advancing such hypothetical cases appears to be the following. The schoolyard statute was intended to provide enhanced penalties for certain criminal conduct that poses an increased risk for students while in or near their schools. The hypothetical cases noted do not involve any such increased risk. * * *
>
> No matter how interpreted, the coverage of the schoolyard provision would not correspond precisely with the class of cases involving increased risk to students. The interpretation adopted by these district courts—requiring proof that a drug possessor intended to distribute drugs within 1000 feet of a school—would make the statute inapplicable in several situations in which the mere possession of sizeable quantities of drugs near a school would create an increased risk for students. For example, Congress undoubtedly knew that the mere presence of substantial quantities of drugs increases the risk of gunfire and other violence. In addition, a person possessing drugs may abandon them while fleeing from the police * * *. The drugs may also be lost or stolen near a school and may then find their way into students' hands.
>
> Furthermore, the interpretation of the schoolyard statute adopted by these district courts would still include some cases involving no increased risk to students. To take a hypothetical case perhaps no more fanciful than those cited in these courts' opinions, a drug smuggler, during a period when school is not in session, might possess a large quantity of drugs with the intent to sell them to a major buyer in an apartment at the top of a high-rise building that is located within 1000 feet of a school but is separated from the school by a limited access highway that cannot be crossed at any point nearby. The selection of this site for the transaction might not realistically involve any increased risk to the school's students, but this conduct would still fall within the schoolyard statute even if proof of an intent to distribute within 1000 feet of a school were required.
>
> In short, the schoolyard statute, no matter how interpreted, involves some degree of imprecision. Therefore, in deciding whether to require proof that a drug possessor intended to distribute drugs within 1000 feet of a school, Congress had to decide whether (a) to require proof of such intent and thus make the statute inapplicable in the situations noted above in which the mere possession of sizeable quantities of drugs near a school would pose an increased risk to students or (b) to dispense with proof of such intent and thus make the statute applicable in a few situations, such as the hypothetical cases posed by some of the district court judges, involving no increased risk to students. We certainly cannot say that the latter choice is so clearly preferable that Congress must have selected that option. Therefore, we do not think that the extreme hypothetical cases cited in some of the district court decisions support those courts' interpretation of the schoolyard provision.

961 F.2d at 1094–95. A recent case illustrates one of the possibilities foreseen by Judge Alito. In *United States v. Harris*, 313 F.3d 1228 (10th Cir.

2002), the defendant was stopped on the street when a police officer smelled marijuana. While being searched, the defendant fled, and during the subsequent chase threw a wrapped package of crack cocaine over the fence of a local school playground. Not surprisingly in light of the fact that the drugs actually landed on the school playground, the court rejected the defendant's contention that the statute was inapplicable because there was no proof that he had intended to distribute the drugs near the school.

2. The appellate courts in both *Wake* and *Rodriguez* suggested that there might be ways of dealing with the hypothetical extreme cases—which may not seem so hypothetical in light of the district court cases noted above. After noting that the courts are obliged to apply the intent of Congress "even if it may lead to anomalous results," Judge Barksdale dropped a footnote observing that the present case was a paradigm of those Congress sought to deter, and therefore the court had no occasion to consider whether there might be an "implied exception * * * where, for example, the possessing defendant merely speeds underneath a school in a subway train." *United States v. Wake*, 948 F.2d at 1433, n. 9. *Cf. United States v. Archer*, 486 F.2d 670 (2d Cir.1973) (dismissing prosecution where jurisdiction was based on acts that were either casual and incidental, or engineered by authorities).

Judge Alito suggested another response to the concern that a fortuity should not dramatically increase a defendant's sentence. In footnote 8 he commented:

> If a trial court is actually presented with one of these extreme cases, we believe the Sentencing Guidelines would generally permit the court to eliminate any unwarranted increase in the sentence that would otherwise be imposed. In most cases involving convictions under the school-yard statute for possession with intent to distribute, the only effect of the schoolyard statute is a one-or two-point increase in the offense level under U.S.S.G. § 2D1.2(a). If a case technically qualifies for such an increase but it is clear that the defendant's conduct did not create any increased risk for those whom the schoolyard statute was intended to protect, we believe that a one-or two-point downward departure to eliminate this increase would be permissible.

United States v. Rodriguez, 961 F.2d at 1095 n.8. For a discussion of the Sentencing Guidelines, see Chapter 18.

3. In *United States v. Pitts*, 908 F.2d 458, 460 (9th Cir. 1990), the defendant offered to prove that 80% of Spokane fell within the schoolyard zone, which includes not only schools and playgrounds, but also pools, video arcades, and other places where youth congregate. In New York and other major metropolitan areas with extremely high population density, the whole city may actually fall within the schoolyard statute.

What standards govern the exercise of prosecutorial charging discretion under the schoolyard statute? In *Wayte, supra* at 156–57, the Supreme Court held that the exercise of prosecutorial discretion does not violate equal protection unless distinctions are drawn on the an invidious basis such as race, religion, or the exercise of constitutionally protected rights. Since the defendant in *Pitts* had not alleged that he had been selected for prosecution under § 860 on the basis of race or some other invidious criteria, the court of appeals affirmed his conviction.

Taken together, *Rodriguez, Wake,* and *Pitts* appear to provide federal prosecutors with largely unreviewable discretion to impose the enhanced penalties available under § 860 on virtually any defendant—or virtually all defendants—charged with a violation of § 841 in a major metropolitan area. Does the legislative history indicate that Congress intended the schoolyard statute to sweep this broadly?

4.   Does the Supreme Court's decision that the Gun Free Schools Zones Act exceeded the commerce power (see *supra* pp. 30–35) cast any doubt on the constitutionality of the federal drug laws, particularly the schoolyard statute? The lower courts have generally concluded that it does not. Whereas the law struck down in *Lopez* punished mere possession of a firearm in or near a school, 21 U.S.C. § 860 punishes drug *trafficking*: distribution, possession with intent to distribute, and manufacturing. "Drug trafficking is inherently commercial in nature; firearm possession is not." *United States v. Garcia–Salazar*, 891 F.Supp. 568, 572 (D. Kan. 1995). *See also United States v. Koons*, 300 F.3d 985 (8th Cir. 2002) (collecting cases). The Supreme Court has given no hint that *Lopez* undercuts the Controlled Substances Act. To the contrary, as discussed *supra*, p. 38, in *Gonzales v. Raich*, 125 S.Ct. 2195 (2005), the Court held that the application of the Controlled Substances Act to intrastate growers and users of marijuana for medical purposes in compliance with state law did not violate the Commerce Clause.

5.   What if government agents arrange matters so that a particular drug transaction takes place within a school zone (by, for example, having an undercover agent make a buy and request delivery close to a school)? This is not an attempt to manufacture federal jurisdiction, *cf. Altobella, supra* at 106, because there is plainly federal jurisdiction over the drug transaction, regardless of its location. Is it entrapment? *See Jacobson v. United States*, 503 U.S. 540 (1992) (defendant is not entrapped if he was predisposed to commit the crime and the government merely afforded the opportunity).

6.   The maximum penalties for drug offenses may also be doubled (or trebled for repeat offenses) if the defendant "knowingly and intentionally" employs a minor in the course of a drug offense. 21 U.S.C. § 861 (a)-(c). Does this wording require the government to prove the defendant had knowledge of the minor's age? Most courts have said no. *See United States v. Frazier*, 213 F.3d 409 (7th Cir. 2000) (collecting cases). The court in *United States v. Chin*, 981 F.2d 1275 (D.C. Cir. 1992) found that Congress intended to protect juveniles with § 861, and meant to place the burden on the drug dealer to know who is working for him. This interpretation may have an impact comparable to that of the interpretation of the schoolyard statute in *Rodriguez* and *Wake*. What percentage of drug rings would you expect to include the participation of at least one person under the age of 18? Does this statute meaningfully restrict the class of defendants whose sentences may be enhanced? If there is no evidence that the defendant has already employed a minor, is there anything wrong with government investigators setting up a sting using an undercover agent or informant who is under the age of 18?

Whether the age of a minor is a strict liability element is an issue that can arise in other offenses as well. For example, Congress is considering new legislation that targets criminal street gangs. See H.R. 1279, 109th Cong., which was approved by the House on May 11, 2005. A Senate version of the bill makes it an offense to recruit any person to become a member of a criminal street gang with the intent that the person will act to effect the criminal activities of the gang. S. 1322, 109th Cong. § 1 (2005). The bill provides for an increased penalty (up to 10 years imprisonment rather than a maximum of 3 years) if the recruited person is a minor and the defendant is over 18. If this law is enacted, do you think it should be interpreted to require knowledge of the minor's age?

3.   PROSECUTORIAL DISCRETION AND THE CORE FEDERAL DRUG OFFENSES: THE CRITIQUE AND THE SEARCH FOR A SOLUTION

The core federal drug offenses are defined in the broadest possible terms: it is a federal offense to manufacture, distribute, or possess with the intent to distribute any quantity of heroin, cocaine, marijuana, PCP, LSD, or methamphetamines, or to attempt or conspire to do so. 21 U.S.C. §§ 841, 846; § 841 is excerpted *supra* at 343, and reprinted in full in the appendix at 949. It is also a federal crime to import or export any of these drugs. 21 U.S.C. § 960. The existence of this broad jurisdictional grant does not, however, mean that drug trafficking should be prosecuted exclusively or even predominantly in the federal courts, any more than the broad jurisdictional grant in the Hobbs Act means that every robbery affecting interstate commerce should be tried in federal court. The very large increase in the number of federal drug prosecutions over the last few decades has given rise to a lively debate on the principles that should govern the selection of the drug cases that will be prosecuted in federal rather than state court.

At present the U.S. Attorneys Manual does not specify the criteria for the exercise of prosecutorial discretion in drug cases (though the Manual does address the exercise of discretion in general terms, see *supra* at 142–43). Indeed, the current manual deletes the criteria stated in an earlier version. Until the revision in 1997 the Manual provided:

9–101.200 REFERRAL OF CONTROLLED SUBSTANCE CASES TO STATE OR LOCAL PROSECUTORS

The following factors should be considered in deciding whether controlled substance cases should be charged in federal court or referred to state or local prosecutors for action: (1) sufficiency of the evidence; (2) degree of federal involvement; (3) effectiveness of state and local prosecutors; (4) willingness of state or local authorities to prosecute cases investigated primarily by federal agents; (5) amount of controlled substances involved; (6) violator's background; (7) possibility that prosecution will lead to disclosure of violations committed by other persons; and (8) the district court's backlog of cases.

A.   Declination of federal prosecution on evidentiary grounds is understandable and justified. However, absent unusual circumstances, declination should not be based solely on any of the other factors. The amount involved is only one of several factors which should be considered before deciding whether to prosecute in federal court. In considering the amount involved attention should be paid to the purity of the controlled substance and the method of packaging.

B. When a U.S. Attorney declines to prosecute a controlled substance case and thereafter a state or local prosecutor also declines prosecution, the Drug Enforcement Administration should be afforded an opportunity to request federal prosecutive consideration and such cases should be accepted unless it is not in the public interest to do so. Federal prosecution might not be warranted, for example, where the violator qualifies for processing under a deferred prosecution plan.

C. In appraising the effectiveness of nonfederal authorities, consideration should be given to the professional competence of local and state prosecutors and the length of time it takes to try a case in local and state courts. Consideration should also be given to the penalties provided by local or state law, the sentencing practices of local and state judges and the applicable parole eligibility standards of nonfederal jurisdictions.

D. In assessing the background of a violator, consideration should be given to the offender's age, degree of culpability, and prior criminal record. The prosecutor should also consider whether significant mitigating circumstances exist, whether the offender has cooperated with the government, and whether the offender is dependent on drugs. For example, if an offender is young, has no previous record, is a narcotic addict, and was arrested for possession for the offender's personal use, it may be appropriate to defer prosecution conditioned upon the offender's enrollment in a drug treatment program.

E. Serious consideration should always be given to the question of whether an offender would, if federally charged, cooperate and furnish evidence of narcotic violations committed by the offender's confederates or by others.

F. U.S. Attorneys are urged to cooperate fully with state and local prosecutors and investigators and to encourage them in actively combating drug trafficking. There will be instances where state or local prosecution of controlled substance offenders would be warranted even when there has been significant federal involvement in the case. However, since the federal government has significant responsibilities in the area of drug law enforcement, care should be taken in deciding which is the most appropriate judicial forum in which to prosecute a controlled substance case.

G. U.S. Attorneys should confer with special agents in charge of DEA field offices in their districts regarding standards and procedures to be utilized in determining whether controlled substance cases should be prosecuted federally or referred to state or local prosecutors.

H. Periodically, U.S. Attorneys should meet or confer with state and local prosecutors in connection with referral of federal cases for prosecution.

————

As this excerpt indicates, when the Department published criteria to guide the exercise of federal charging discretion it did not restrict federal prosecutions to drug offenses involving large drug organizations or interstate offenses, or even to offenses involving large quantities of drugs—though the amount "is one of several factors that should be considered." Subsection C specifically directed federal prosecutors to consider whether a state prosecution would be timely and effective, and whether the state penalties would be adequate. Since most state court systems were (and still are) overloaded, and since federal penalties were (and still are) typically more severe than state penalties, these directives were consistent with federal prosecution of a very large number of drug cases.

In the absence of any written national guidelines, what currently governs the number and type of drug prosecutions brought in the federal courts? As noted in the introduction to this chapter, *supra* at 334, additional resources were provided for drug law enforcement and the number of drug cases in the federal courts increased rapidly throughout the 1980s and 1990s; drug cases now account for approximately 27% of federal prosecutions and 55% of the inmates in federal prisons. This dramatic increase raises a number of questions. Is the increase in federal drug prosecutions a good use of federal resources? Exactly what kind of drug cases are being brought in the federal system? And what impact has the increase had on the federal courts? Two conflicting views on these issues were highlighted by the report of the Federal Courts Study Committee, a blue ribbon committee composed primarily of members of Congress and federal judges authorized by Congress to "examine the problems and issues" facing the federal courts and "develop a long-range plan for the future of the federal judiciary." The Committee issued its final report, a portion of which is excerpted below, in 1990.[s]

REPORT OF THE FEDERAL COURTS STUDY COMMITTEE, APRIL 2, 1990

Part I, pp. 35–37.

A. Federal and State Prosecution of Narcotics Violations

Federal prosecuting authorities should limit federal prosecutions to charges that cannot or should not be prosecuted in the state courts and

---

s. One of the authors, Sara Beale, was an associate reporter for the Workload Sub- committee of the Federal Courts Study Committee.

should forge federal-state partnerships to coordinate prosecution efforts. Congress should direct additional funds to the states to help them to assume their proper share of the responsibilities for the war on drugs, including drug crime adjudication.

The federal courts' most pressing problems—today and for the immediate future—stem from unprecedented numbers of federal narcotics prosecutions. The committee cannot overstate the urgency of Congress's authorizing the judgeships requested by the Judicial Conference since 1984, including those in the consolidated proposal of October 1989. Nor can it overstate the importance of the executive and legislative branches' filling the vacancies that exist today.

More judgeships are essential. But they are not the ultimate solution to the federal courts' caseload crisis. Both the principles of federalism and the long-term health of the federal judicial system require returning the federal courts to their proper, limited role in dealing with crime. Many of the new drug cases now flooding the federal system could be prosecuted just as effectively in state courts, under state laws. Over-reliance on federal courts for drug prosecutions will either force Congress to bloat the federal courts beyond recognition or force the federal courts to stop meeting their other constitutional and statutory responsibilities.

It is well to understand how much things have changed. Since 1980, federal criminal filings have risen by well over 50 percent, outpacing civil filings. Drug filings have fueled this increase, growing 280 percent in the same period. In fact, drug filings increased more than 15 percent in 1987 and again in 1988, while other criminal filings decreased. The Chief Justice noted in his 1989 year-end report on the judiciary that drug filings now constitute more than a quarter of all new criminal filings, and, in some districts, almost two-thirds. Drug cases now account for 44 percent of the federal criminal trials, and almost all of these are jury trials. Roughly 50 percent of federal criminal appeals are drug cases. And the Judicial Conference last year reported to Congress that by 1991 drug filings will increase from 20 to 50 percent over 1988 levels.

Drug filings not only increase the federal court workload; they distort it. The Speedy Trial Act in effect requires that federal courts give criminal cases priority over civil cases. As a result, some districts with heavy drug caseloads are virtually unable to try civil cases and others will soon be at that point. And when courts cannot set realistic trial dates, parties lose much of their incentive to settle and civil cases drag on in limbo.

At some point, moreover, the federal civil docket will not be the only casualty of the war on drugs. At some point, the war on drugs will be a casualty of itself. Overload causes backlog. Backlog threatens timely prosecution and, under the Speedy Trial Act, can lead to dismissals. The Chief Justice has warned against "an hour-glass-shaped law enforcement system." It will have increased prosecutorial and correctional resources; "but without the judge-power to handle the added workload there will be a bottleneck in the middle of the system substantially lessening our ability to win the war on drugs.''

We recognize the magnitude of the drug problems now facing our nation, and the significant role that federal prosecutions must play in a comprehensive solution to these problems. But we urge the Department of Justice to exercise greater selectivity in bringing drug prosecutions in the federal courts and to develop clear national policies governing which drug cases to prosecute in the federal courts. We concur in the President's January 1990 drug control strategy, which acknowledges that state and local law enforcement have primacy in drug control and which would provide a substantial increase in Bureau of Justice Assistance funds for state and local law enforcement efforts. The federal system must not be overwhelmed with cases that could be prosecuted in the state courts. Federal drug enforcement strategy should target the relatively small number of cases that state authorities cannot or will not effectively prosecute—cases, for example, that involve international or interstate elements. We recognize that there are occasions when small drug cases appropriately appear in federal court. Such a case might, for example, be the first stage in the prosecution of a larger multi-state drug organization. Unfortunately, at the present time minor cases that lack such a connection are being brought in many districts.

We realize that the Department of Justice has initiated programs to build relationships with local prosecutors and has established drug task forces that include federal, state and local prosecutors. We also endorse a Department policy that gives due credit to agents of the Federal Bureau of Investigation when their work results in successful state prosecutions, just as it does when the work results in successful federal prosecutions. We applaud these efforts but are convinced that they have not solved the critical problem identified here: too many prosecutions that do not require the unique resources of the federal judicial system are still finding their way into federal court. We are told that state prosecutors often ask their federal counterparts to begin prosecutions that lack interstate or foreign elements. Given the current overload within the federal system, federal prosecutors must resist the urge to dedicate the scarce resources of the federal judicial system to problems that can be dealt with effectively at the state and local level.

Minor drug cases also find their way into federal court because Congress has provided funds for federal and not for state prosecutions. We urge Congress to provide additional resources to enable the federal courts to process the drug cases that belong in those courts. But federal funding should no longer serve as an incentive to bring cases into federal courts that could and should be prosecuted in the state courts. Some of the funds that Congress has approved for drug enforcement should be used to provide assistance for drug enforcement at the critical state and local level, including resources for state courts, public defenders and assigned counsel.

* * *

Dissenting statement of MR. DENNIS, in which CONGRESSMAN MOOR-
HEAD joins:

Drug abuse and drug trafficking are severely taxing the resources of
many of our government institutions. Police, prosecutors, courts and
prisons are hard pressed to satisfy the steadily increasing demands of a
society facing this threat to its fundamental wellbeing. Our society is
looking to its law enforcement agencies to be vigorous in bringing to
justice those who are violating our drug laws, because the future of our
nation is at stake.

The federal judiciary must not shrink from its critical responsibility
to lobby for an adequate capacity in the federal courts to judge drug
cases brought into the federal forum. The role of the federal courts is
crucial to drug law enforcement, for without their authority federal law
enforcement loses its nationwide subpoena power, its electronic surveillance authority, its contempt and immunity powers, and its forfeiture
authority to name a few. The federal judiciary must not neglect assuming its share of the workload for fear that the federal judiciary will
become too large. The state courts are not substitutes for the federal
judiciary and tinkering with the budgets of federal and state law enforcement agencies will not change that reality.

The Federal Courts Study Committee should be recommending more
federal judgeships to create a greater capacity in our federal judiciary to
meet its responsibilities and leave the choice of forum to the prosecutors.

Notes

The Federal Courts Study Committee's recommendation for greater
prosecutorial selectivity in instituting federal drug cases ultimately rested on
two bases. First, as stated in the excerpt noted above, the federal courts'
resources have not kept pace with the demands of the increased drug
caseload, and drug cases have overtaxed the system. This problem, however,
could be remedied merely by increasing the federal courts' resources to
match the increase in the drug caseload.

While the Federal Courts Study Committee called for increased resources, it ultimately rejected the view that increased resources are the
whole solution. The other basis for the Committee's recommendation regarding drug prosecutions was its conclusion that the size of the federal judiciary
cannot be significantly expanded without a fundamental revision of the
federal judicial structure. In the Committee's view, the present federal
judicial structure is perilously close to its maximum capacity, especially at
the appellate level. The Committee argued that neither the number of
circuits nor the number of judges within each circuit can be increased
indefinitely without producing a negative impact on the quality of federal
decisional law. A greater number of circuits and a larger number of federal
judges inevitably increase the likelihood of inter-and intracircuit conflicts.
Failure to resolve large numbers of such conflicts means that federal law will
be incoherent and no longer uniform. Moreover, a significant and rapid
increase in the number of federal judges—especially to hear a docket of drug

cases—would have an obvious effect on the profile of the persons who would be willing to accept an appointment to the federal bench. On the other hand, if the size of the federal courts is not substantially increased, a larger drug caseload can be accommodated only by a reduction in the cases presently on the federal docket, or by a reduction in the resources allocated to those cases. This would decrease the resources for what has been the core function of the federal courts for the last 200 years: interpreting federal laws and construing federal rights. Civil litigants—from corporations to taxpayers to civil rights plaintiffs—could find that as a practical matter the federal courthouse door is closed to them.

The Federal Courts Study Committee argued that there is no justification for diverting resources from the core functions of the federal courts or for dramatically enlarging—and in so doing fundamentally changing—the federal courts in order to hear a large number of drug cases that could be handled effectively in the state courts if they had adequate resources. There is, however, ample justification for increased federal funding of state law enforcement and the state courts, so that those institutions are equipped to handle the simple drug cases that do not require the specialized resources of the federal courts. This would, as the Committee stated, have the effect of returning the federal courts to a more limited role in dealing with crime, which is largely the province of the states.

What should one make of the argument in the dissenting statement that there are many advantages to federal prosecution applicable to all drug cases: electronic surveillance and forfeiture authority, powers of contempt and immunity, and nationwide service of process. Many states have already enacted laws that parallel federal law on these subjects, and Congress can ensure the adoption of similar laws in the remaining states. This could be accomplished by conditioning the allocation of federal drug prosecution grants upon a state's adoption of similar laws (as, for example, the grant of federal highway funds was conditioned on the adoption of a 55 m.p.h. speed limit). Thus the Committee did not view these procedural advantages as an appropriate basis for bringing simple drug prosecutions in the federal courts. Perhaps equally important, in light of the mandatory minimum sentences applicable to most federal drug offenses, prosecuting a drug case in federal rather than state court ordinarily yields a longer sentence.

The excerpt that follows considers the consequences of the current decentralized and unstructured approach to the exercise of prosecutorial discretion in the federal system. As you read this material, consider the following questions. Is there any harm done if individual prosecutors or United States Attorneys follow different approaches in deciding which drug cases to prosecute federally, and if some bring relatively minor cases in the federal courts that could have been prosecuted effectively in the state courts? If federal prosecutors do bring relatively minor drug cases in the federal courts, do the courts have the authority to dismiss such prosecutions? Does it matter whether a federal rather than a state prosecution was initiated precisely because federal law is more favorable to the prosecution on several points, including the law of electronic surveillance? What if a federal drug prosecution is brought in order to obtain a longer sentence?

SARA SUN BEALE, TOO MANY AND YET TOO FEW: NEW PRINCIPLES TO DEFINE THE PROPER LIMITS FOR FEDERAL CRIMINAL JURISDICTION

46 Hastings L.J. 979, 996–1004 (1995).

II. TOO FEW CRIMINAL PROSECUTIONS: INEQUALITY BETWEEN DEFENDANTS PROSECUTED FOR THE SAME CONDUCT IN THE STATE AND FEDERAL SYSTEMS

* * *

A. Disparity Among Defendants

The expansion of federal criminal jurisdiction has led to serious inequalities among similarly situated defendants with regard to sentencing as well as significant procedural rights. Disparity has been fostered because the contemporary expansion of federal jurisdiction has not been accompanied by preemption of existing state criminal laws. Federal law has simply been layered over existing state law to produce dual jurisdiction. Despite the phenomenal expansion of dual federal-state jurisdiction, federal law differs from state law on significant matters of procedure, the definition of the relevant crimes and defenses, and, perhaps most importantly, the sentences applicable to various offenses.[70] Dual jurisdiction means that offenders are subject to a kind of cruel lottery, in which a small minority of the persons who commit a particular offense is selected for federal prosecution and subjected to much harsher sentences—and often to significantly less favorable procedural or substantive standards—than persons prosecuted for parallel state offenses. The structural disparity fostered by the new regime of dual jurisdiction is at odds with the premise of the federal Sentencing Guidelines.

Dual federal-state criminal jurisdiction is now the rule rather than the exception. Federal law reaches at least some instances of each of the following state offenses: theft, fraud, extortion, bribery, assault, domestic violence, robbery, murder, weapons offenses, and drug offenses. In many instances, federal law overlaps almost completely with state law, as is the case with drug offenses.

The sentences available in a federal prosecution are generally higher than those available in state court—often ten or even twenty times higher. For example, in one drug case the recommended state sentence was eighteen months, while federal law required a mandatory minimum sentence of ten years, and the applicable federal sentencing guidelines range was 151 to 188 months for one defendant and 188 to 235 months for the other. Another defendant subject to a five-year mandatory

---

70. Of course, the precise content of state law varies between jurisdictions on many of the matters in question here. Despite this variance, some generalizations may be made. First, federal sentences are generally longer than state sentences for the same conduct. Second, the Federal Rules of Criminal Procedure provide a defendant with fewer procedural rights related to joinder, severance, and pretrial discovery than the rules in force in many states. * * *

minimum in federal court would have been eligible for a sentence of zero to ninety days in state court as a first offender. A defendant who was placed on two years probation in state court was later sentenced to sixty-three months for the same conduct in federal court. Similarly, a defendant who received a diversionary state disposition to a thirty-day inpatient drug rehabilitation program, followed by expungement of his conviction upon successful completion of the program and follow-up, was subject to forty-six to fifty-seven months of imprisonment under the applicable federal guidelines. It is not unusual for codefendants whose conduct is identical to receive radically different sentences, depending upon whether they are prosecuted in state or federal court. For example, one defendant whose codefendant received no jail time in a state prosecution received a ten-year federal sentence.

Generally, the decision to bring charges in federal rather than state court is made on an ad hoc basis. The United States Attorneys' Manual (the Manual) does contain some general standards for the exercise of prosecutorial discretion, but they are written so broadly that they provide little guidance. The Manual also contains some standards applicable to specific offenses, but, in general, these too are stated in very broad terms. * * * In the case of the remaining offenses, charging discretion and any regulation of that discretion occur in the United States Attorney's office for each district. While some offices have charging guidelines for some of these remaining offenses, in many cases there are no standards to guide individual prosecutors. When standards are adopted in individual districts, the standards may vary significantly among districts.

On occasion, federal prosecutors have publicly pursued a deliberate strategy of taking only a fraction of similar or identical cases, with the hope that the severe results in those federal cases will result in general deterrence. For example, in the Southern District of New York, then-United States Attorney Rudolph Giuliani initiated 'federal day,' one day chosen at random each week in which all street-level drug dealers apprehended by local authorities would be prosecuted in federal court. Giuliani stated that '[t]he idea was to create a Russian-roulette effect.' Prosecutors in the Eastern District of Pennsylvania issued a press release in 1992 describing a case that was intended to serve as an example that would persuade defendants to plead guilty in state court to avoid the possibility of federal charges. The defendant who was to serve as this example to others was a small-time drug dealer who had rejected a state plea offer of a four-year sentence; he was sentenced in federal court to life without parole.

In each of these cases, federal law overlapped with state law and federal law provided for higher penalties. While many cases fell within the ambit of the federal statute in question, only a few of those cases were prosecuted in federal court. While in some instances an effort may have been made to identify particularly serious cases for federal prosecution, in other cases the selection was random or the criteria for selection were unrelated to the defendant's culpability.[92] For purposes of this Article, the resulting differences among defendants prosecuted in federal and state courts will be referred to as structural inequalities.

B. Lack of Judicial Remedies for Inequalities Resulting from Intermittent Federal Prosecutions

Under present law there is no basis to challenge these structural inequalities. The federal courts have uniformly rejected equal protection challenges to such disparate sentences and have held that they have no jurisdiction to review federal prosecutors' charging decisions absent a claim of discrimination on the basis of suspect characteristics, such as race. Judicial review is unavailable even if the prosecutor's decision to file in federal court was motivated by a desire to impose a harsher sentence and was inconsistent with the treatment of other offenders.

One district court concluded that, in light of the enormous disparity in federal and state sentencing laws, due process requires that there be articulated or written standards for referral to federal authorities, but that decision was reversed on appeal, and it has been rejected by the other circuits.

C. Structural Disparities Among Defendants Violate Federal Sentencing Policy

The prosecutorial policy of employing harsh sanctions in a few cases for deterrent effect stands in sharp contrast with federal sentencing policy. The Sentencing Reform Act of 1984 (the Act) provides that one of the factors to be considered in imposing federal sentences is 'the need to avoid unwarranted sentence disparities among defendants with similar records who have been found guilty of similar conduct.' The Act directs the Federal Sentencing Commission to establish policies and practices that ameliorate such disparities.

The legislative history stresses the importance of eliminating sentencing disparity:

> Sentencing disparities that are not justified by differences among offenses or offenders are unfair both to offenders and to the public. A sentence that is unjustifiably high compared to sentences for similarly situated offenders is clearly unfair to the offender; a sentence that is unjustifiably low is just as plainly unfair to the public. Such sentences are unfair in more subtle ways as well. Sentences that are disproportionate to the seriousness of the offense create a disrespect for the law. Sentences that are too severe create unnecessary tensions among inmates and add to disciplinary problems in the prisons.

92. For example, federal prosecutors frequently agree to take cases if their state counterparts are particularly overburdened. This cooperation would be entirely admirable if it did not have the effect of arbitrarily imposing far higher sentences on particular defendants for reasons wholly unrelated to their individual culpability.

Presumably, Congress must have been aware of the overlap of federal and state criminal jurisdiction when it enacted the current sentencing regime and aware that federal sentences would vary from those available under state law. The legislative history gives no indication, however, that Congress was made aware of the degree to which these factors could undermine its stated goal of ending unjustified sentencing disparities. Further, there is ample evidence that Congress had a second major goal in enacting sentencing reform: enhancing sentencing severity, particularly in the case of drug offenses and violent crimes. While the goal of enhancing sentencing severity grew steadily more important during the time Congress had sentencing reform under consideration, it never displaced the goal of reducing sentencing disparity. To the contrary, the passage of the Sentencing Reform Act would not have been possible without the sponsorship of both political conservatives (who sought harsher sentences) and political liberals such as Senator Kennedy, whose principal concern was the elimination of unjustified sentencing disparity.

While there is an economic argument that the arbitrary selection of a few cases for harsh sentencing is the most efficient, i.e., least expensive, means of promoting deterrence, such a practice is incompatible with the federal Sentencing Guidelines regime. The current policy of removing only a few of the many identical cases for harsher treatment in the federal system—leaving the remainder in the state system where they will receive more lenient treatment—is the practical equivalent of selecting 1 case in 100 (or 1000) within the federal system and increasing the sentence three-, four-, or tenfold in order to obtain increased deterrence. Such a cruel lottery would make a mockery of the enormous time and energy now being devoted in the federal system to equalizing the sentences for offenders whose conduct and criminal history are the same.

If we are on the right track with the Guidelines, and if it is important to eliminate unjustified sentencing disparity within the federal system, we can no longer afford to blind ourselves to the consequences of failing to use the same care in selecting the class of cases to which we apply the Guidelines as we use in applying the Guidelines to the cases that we select for federal prosecution.

D. The Policy of Intermittent Federal Prosecutions Also Results in the Ad Hoc Denial of State Procedural Rights to Certain Defendants

While sentencing is probably the most important factor that motivates prosecutors to bring federal charges when there is dual jurisdiction, other factors provide the prosecution with an advantage in particular cases. In one case, for example, the district court employed its supervisory authority to dismiss a case that had no federal ties, but had been transferred to federal court to avoid state constitutional restrictions on the use of informants, wiretaps, and search warrants. The court of appeals reversed, concluding that while such systematic transfers to federal court were a source of concern, the federal courts may not interfere with the executive's discretionary power to control criminal prosecutions. In addition, other provisions of the Federal Rules of Criminal Procedure also favor the prosecution more than the comparable state rules. For example, the federal discovery rules are far more restrictive than those in many states, such as Florida, and federal joinder rules are more permissive than those applicable in many states. These procedural differences sometimes motivate federal prosecutors to bring a case that would otherwise be pursued by state authorities. In effect, prosecutors may forum shop in order to gain a procedural advantage.

Notes

1. Are you convinced that the "cruel lottery" is really that bad? In any case, what kind of solutions can you come up with? One can envision responses from all three branches of government. Perhaps the most straight-forward solution is for the Executive Branch, via the Attorney General, to issue prosecutorial guidelines. Do you think the Department of Justice should promulgate guidelines in the U.S. Attorneys Manual for drug cases? If you favor the adoption of specific guidelines, consider the following questions. What purpose would the guidelines be intended to serve? Is judicial enforcement necessary to attain that purpose? What criteria should be included? Would you be satisfied with the statement of criteria that governed prior to 1997 (see *supra* at 375–77)? Note that these criteria give individual prosecutors a great deal of discretion, and they do not provide for judicial review. What changes, if any, would you make in these guidelines?

2. For an example of a case discussing the question whether the federal courts have any inherent authority to place some limits on prosecutorial discretion, see *United States v. Uccifferri*, 960 F.2d 953 (11th Cir. 1992). Uccifferri was charged with conspiring to distribute cocaine. He moved to dismiss on the grounds that the case was a product of a state investigation, lacked any federal ties, and was being brought in federal court solely to take advantage of procedural rules favorable to the prosecution. The district court agreed and dismissed the case, citing its supervisory power over the integrity of the federal justice system. The court of appeals reversed in a per curiam opinion, holding that the federal courts have no authority to dismiss on public policy grounds an indictment that alleges a violation of the federal criminal code. Although it recognized that the transfer of state cases to federal court raises legitimate concerns, the court of appeals held that "it is the prerogative of the executive to initiate criminal proceedings" and that "courts should not interfere with the executive's discretionary power to control criminal prosecutions."

Would giving courts some discretion to dismiss cases of insufficient federal interest be a good idea? If so, it would probably require legislation granting this authority. For a discussion of the concept of the federal courts' supervisory power and an argument that supervisory power would not justify the dismissal of cases on this ground, see Sara Sun Beale, *Reconsidering Supervisory Power in Criminal Cases: Constitutional and Statutory Limits on the Authority of the Federal Courts*, 84 COLUM. L. REV. 1433 (1984).

3. For a case raising the question whether there is any constitutional impediment to the selection of federal charges to secure a harsher penalty

that that available in state court, see *United States v. Ortiz*, 783 F.Supp. 507 (C.D. Cal. 1992), where (as in *Ucciferri*) the federal charges arose out of a state investigation and the first charges were filed in state court. The district court rejected the defendant's motion to dismiss:

> The Supreme Court has long recognized that, when a criminal act violates more than one statute, the Government may prosecute either crime as long as the decision is not based upon an unjustifiable standard such as race, religion, or other arbitrary classification. *See, e.g., Bordenkircher v. Hayes*, 434 U.S. 357, 364 (1978). Consequently, under most circumstances, the decision whether to prosecute and what to charge or bring before a grand jury rests in the prosecutor's discretion. Such prosecutorial discretion is not a violation of due process.

> The defendant argues the rule should be different in the case of a prosecutor's discretion to select the forum, as opposed to selecting the statute. He contends it violates due process for the prosecutor to proceed with this case in federal court because it started in state court and was transferred to federal court solely because the federal penalty is more severe. Defendant asserts his case is entirely and exclusively a state-based claim: it originated with a citizen's tip to a Garden Grove police officer; the investigation was conducted by the Garden Grove police department's narcotics unit; the surveillance of the suspected activity was conducted by state officers; the search warrant was issued by a state judge; the search was executed by Garden Grove police officers; he was initially charged with violations of California law; and he was originally held at the Orange County Jail. Based on these factors, defendant concludes the case properly belongs in state court.

> Similar to the discretion of prosecutors to select the particular crimes to prosecute, federal prosecutors have the discretion to prosecute a defendant in federal court for conduct which may also be a crime under state law. The government may even seek a federal indictment for criminal conduct after prosecution has already commenced in state court or after a conviction has been obtained there. Thus, the transfer of the case from California state court to the federal court does not, by itself, violate defendant's due process rights.

> Moreover, a transfer to federal court solely to obtain an increased sentence does not violate a defendant's due process rights. The analogy to the "choice of statute" cases is again appropriate: When evidence supports prosecution under different statutes, the "prosecutor may be influenced by the penalties available upon conviction, but this fact, standing alone, does not give rise to a violation of the Equal Protection or Due Process Clause." *United States v. Batchelder*, 442 U.S. 114, 125 (1979). The Court reasoned that a defendant has no constitutional right to elect which of two applicable federal statutes shall be the basis of the indictment and prosecution, and should similarly not be entitled to chose the penalty scheme under which the sentence will be imposed.

> Although *Batchelder* dealt with prosecutorial selection among applicable federal statutes, this same principle has been applied by several courts outside the Ninth Circuit to prosecutorial selection of forum. These courts have found that a prosecutor's decision to transfer a case

from state to federal court, thereby subjecting the defendant to a heavier potential penalty, does not violate constitutional due process.

* * * [I]t is no violation of constitutional due process for what would otherwise be a state prosecution to be transferred to federal court solely to obtain an increased federal sentence.

Id. at 509–10.

4. What about a legislative solution? As noted above, Congress could authorize the federal courts to dismiss cases where there is no sufficient federal interest. It could also repeal or amend legislation to narrow the scope of federal jurisdiction over smaller drug offenses (and other essentially local crime). Although past hearings may indicate some Congressional concern for this issue,[t] a sustained legislative push for reform is difficult to envision, because legislators are painfully aware of the consequences of being labeled "soft on crime." As one article noted:

From 1968 to 1988, Republicans controlled the crime issue. They won six out of seven Presidential elections during that time. In 1992, the Republicans failed to stress crime, and lost. In 1994, Democrats failed to stress crime, and lost. Political consultants and commentators continue to argue whether economic or social issues like crime are more important to electoral success. Results, however, suggest a simple rule: control of the crime issue is a necessary, though perhaps not sufficient, requirement for political victory in America.

Harry A. Chernoff, et al., *The Politics of Crime*, 33 Harv. J. Legis. 527, 577 (1996). *See also* Sara Sun Beale, *What's Law Got to Do With It? The Political, Social, Psychological and Other Non–Legal Factors Influencing the Development of (Federal) Criminal Law*, 1 Buff. Crim. L. Rev. 23 (1997).

At the end of the day, which branch of government do you think is best equipped for limiting prosecutorial discretion? How likely is it that change will actually occur?

5. For a study of the trends and predictive factors on prosecutorial declinations, see Michael Edmund O'Neill, *Understanding Federal Prosecutorial Declinations: An Empirical Analysis of Predictive Factors*, 41 Am. Crim. L. Rev. 1439 (2004). O'Neill found that drug prosecutions are the least likely of all federal crimes to be declined for prosecution, and that drug cases with lower drug weight were more likely to be declined. Given the rising numbers of drug charges being brought in federal courts over the past several decades, and the federal sentencing scheme based on drug weight, do these findings surprise you? One interesting fact is that among drug types, marijuana cases were the least likely to be declined. However, this might be due to the fact that investigators are aware that lower drug weight cases are more often declined, and so they may only refer marijuana cases with a high drug weight. The issue of the choice between federal and state prosecution is examined in more general context in Chapter 17, *infra* at pp. 795–807.

t. *Federalization of Criminal Law: Hearing Before the Senate Committee on Governmental Affairs*, 106th Cong., 1999 WL 279565 (May 6, 1999) (testimony of former Assistant Attorney General Edwin Meese III) (summarizing the findings of the American Bar Association's Task Force on the Federalization of Crime).

C. CONTINUING CRIMINAL ENTERPRISE—CCE

The Comprehensive Drug Abuse Prevention and Control Act of 1970 created a new kind of drug offense, the continuing criminal enterprise— or CCE–21 U.S.C. § 848. As the Supreme Court explained, CCE is "designed to reach the 'top brass' in drug rings, not the lieutenants and foot soldiers." *Garrett v. United States*, 471 U.S. 773, 781 (1985). The statute requires proof of "a continuing series of violations" of the federal drug laws that (1) were undertaken by a person who occupies a position of organizer, supervisor, or manager with respect to five or more persons, and (2) from which the organizer or supervisor "obtains substantial income." The penalties for a CCE violation are severe: 20 years imprisonment and a fine of $2,000,000 for the first offense, and 30 years and $4,000,000 for any subsequent offense, plus forfeiture of the proceeds of the crimes and property used in carrying out the crime. As a result of a 1986 amendment CCE also includes a provision authorizing life imprisonment for "principal administrators, organizers, or leaders" of very large scale drug organizations. Section 848 includes a federal death penalty provision.

The materials that follow develop the meaning of the statutory elements—management or organization of five or more persons, substantial income, and a series of violations—as well as the problems that arise from the structure of the statute. Like RICO, CCE is a compound-complex statute, which requires proof of other violations and thereby raises double jeopardy and multiple punishment issues. In addition, like 18 U.S.C. § 1955 (the gambling business statute), CCE requires the participation of a minimum number of people working in concert. This structure resembles a conspiracy in some respect, and raises questions about the relationship between CCE and conspiracy.

Like the piggyback enhancement provisions, discussed *supra* 369–75, the CCE offense raises a number of interesting issues, but is only charged in a small number of cases. In 1999, the most recent year for which data were reported, only 214 suspects were prosecuted for CCE as the most serious offense, amounting to less than 1% of all federal drug suspects. Given the fact that drug prosecutions make up more than one quarter of the federal caseload, why are there so few CCE-kingpin prosecutions? One possibility is that it's just too hard to prove a CCE violation. On the other hand, perhaps prosecutors could prove CCE violations in many more cases, but they don't try to do so because adding a CCE charge doesn't have much of an impact. As you read the materials in this section, keep these two basic questions in mind: (1) how difficult is it to prove a CCE violation, and (2) how often does adding a CCE charge give the prosecution something that it can't otherwise get?

21 U.S.C.A.

§ 848. Continuing criminal enterprise

(a) Penalties; forfeitures

Any person who engages in a continuing criminal enterprise shall be sentenced to a term of imprisonment which may not be less than 20 years and which may be up to life imprisonment, to a fine not to exceed the greater of that authorized in accordance with the provisions of Title 18, or $2,000,000 if the defendant is an individual or $5,000,000 if the defendant is other than an individual, and to the forfeiture prescribed in section 853 of this chapter; except that if any person engages in such activity after one or more prior convictions of him under this section have become final, he shall be sentenced to a term of imprisonment which may not be less than 30 years and which may be up to life imprisonment, to a fine not to exceed the greater of twice the amount authorized in accordance with the provisions of Title 18, or $4,000,000 if the defendant is an individual or $10,000,000 if the defendant is other than an individual, and to the forfeiture prescribed in section 853 of this chapter.

(b) Conditions for life imprisonment for engaging in continuing criminal enterprise

Any person who engages in a continuing criminal enterprise shall be imprisoned for life and fined in accordance with subsection (a) of this section if—

(1) such person is the principal administrator, organizer, or leader of the enterprise or is one of several such principal administrators, organizers, or leaders; and

(2)(A) the violation referred to in subsection (d)(1) of this section involved at least 300 times the quantity of a substance described in subsection 841(b)(1)(B) of this title, or

(B) the enterprise, or any other enterprise in which the defendant was the principal or one of several principal administrators, organizers, or leaders, received $10 million dollars in gross receipts during any twelve-month period of its existence for the manufacture, importation, or distribution of a substance described in section 841(b)(1)(B) of this title.

(c) Continuing criminal enterprise defined

For purposes of subsection (a) of this section, a person is engaged in a continuing criminal enterprise if—

(1) he violates any provision of this subchapter or subchapter II of this chapter the punishment for which is a felony, and

(2) such violation is a part of a continuing series of violations of this subchapter or subchapter II of this chapter—

(A) which are undertaken by such person in concert with five or more other persons with respect to whom such person occupies a position of organizer, a supervisory position, or any other position of management, and

(B) from which such person obtains substantial income or resources.

(d) Suspension of sentence and probation prohibited

In the case of any sentence imposed under this section, imposition or execution of such sentence shall not be suspended, probation shall not be granted, and the Act of July 15, 1932 (D.C.Code, secs. 24–203 to 24–207), shall not apply.

(e) Death penalty

(1) In addition to the other penalties set forth in this section—

(A) any person engaging in or working in furtherance of a continuing criminal enterprise, or any person engaging in an offense punishable under section 841(b)(1)(A) or section 960(b)(1) who intentionally kills or counsels, commands, induces, procures, or causes the intentional killing of an individual and such killing results, shall be sentenced to any term of imprisonment, which shall not be less than 20 years, and which may be up to life imprisonment, or may be sentenced to death; and

(B) any person, during the commission of, in furtherance of, or while attempting to avoid apprehension, prosecution or service of a prison sentence for, a felony violation of this subchapter or subchapter II of this chapter who intentionally kills or counsels, commands, induces, procures, or causes the intentional killing of any Federal, State, or local law enforcement officer engaged in, or on account of, the performance of such officer's official duties and such killing results, shall be sentenced to any term of imprisonment, which shall not be less than 20 years, and which may be up to life imprisonment, or may be sentenced to death.

(2) As used in paragraph (1)(b), the term "law enforcement officer" means a public servant authorized by law or by a Government agency or Congress to conduct or engage in the prevention, investigation, prosecution or adjudication of an offense, and includes those engaged in corrections, probation, or parole functions.

* * *

The provisions dealing with procedures for the imposition of the death penalty are included in the statutory appendix at 957–66.

1. THE ELEMENTS OF THE OFFENSE

UNITED STATES v. CHURCH

955 F.2d 688 (11th Cir. 1992).

KRAVITCH, CIRCUIT JUDGE.

[Defendant Coppola was convicted of three predicate drug violations involving the purchase and distribution of cocaine, and of engaging in a continuing criminal enterprise in violation of 21 U.S.C. § 848. In addition, Coppola and defendant Church were convicted of conducting the affairs of an enterprise through a pattern of racketeering activity and conspiring to do so in violation of RICO, 18 U.S.C. 1962(c),(d). Coppola was sentenced to 40 years on the CCE violation and 15 years for the cocaine and RICO violations. Seventy witnesses testified at the trial, which lasted three months. The government presented evidence that from 1973 to approximately 1981 Coppola and others imported and distributed large quantities of marijuana. Coppola headed the enterprise that imported the marijuana, funneled the marijuana profits into legitimate businesses, and used violence to protect his interests.]

* * *

Coppola next contends that the government failed to prove that (1) he acted in concert with five or more persons (2) with respect to whom he held a position as an organizer, supervisor, or manager. According to the CCE statute, the government must prove that the defendant "occupies a position of organizer, a supervisory position, or any other position of management" with respect to five or more other persons. 21 U.S.C. § 848(b)(2)(A). The Supreme Court has given this definition a "common-sense reading," finding that it "is designed to reach the 'top brass' in the drug rings, not the lieutenants and foot soldiers." *Garrett v. United States*, 471 U.S. 773, 781 (1985).

In *United States v. Apodaca*, 843 F.2d 421 (10th Cir.), cert. denied, 488 U.S. 932 (1988), the Tenth Circuit examined the statutory definition, noting the significance of the fact that the statute is phrased in the disjunctive: The government can prove a defendant's role as an organizer or a supervisor or any other type of manager, and the terms "can denote differing levels of managerial control and coordination."

The Second Circuit has stated that "[i]n ordinary parlance, a relationship of supervision is created when one person gives orders or directions to another person who carries them out."

An organizer, on the other hand, is not "necessarily able to control those whom he or she organizes." Rather, "an organizer can be defined as a person who puts together a number of people engaged in separate activities and arranges them in their activities in one essentially orderly operation or enterprise." *Apodaca*, 843 F.2d at 426 (quoting 2 E. Devitt & C. Blackmar, Federal Jury Practice and Instructions § 58.21 (1977)).

The defendant need not be the only, or even the dominant, organizer, supervisor, or manager, and the government need not show that the defendant had the same type of relationship with respect to each of the five or more persons. Further, to satisfy the in-concert element the government need not prove that Coppola conspired with the five other persons at the same time or that the five conspired with one another.

The government presented evidence that in the New York conspiracy, which formed the basis for Count Five, Coppola acted as a supervisor of Biscuiti and as a supervisor or organizer of Tribiano and Papanier. Biscuiti, for instance, reported to Coppola on the ongoing negotiations with the potential source and had to await Coppola's approval before going ahead with the deal.

With respect to Counts Six and Seven and other CCE predicate acts, the government presented evidence that Coppola acted either as a supervisor or organizer of Lee and Rodovich, organizing the scheme, telling Lee and Rodovich what their roles would be, telling Lee when to acquire cocaine, how to dispose of the profits, and whom to contact as a source. Although the three agreed to split the profits equally, Coppola financed the scheme. Lee, whose role was to transport the cocaine, testified that he considered that he worked for Coppola.

Further, this court has held that "[a]n individual need not have direct communications with participants in order to be their supervisor.... [I]f a defendant personally hires only the foreman, that defendant is still responsible for organizing the individuals hired by the foreman to work as the crew." Adding Lee underlings Caswell, Ray Fosberg ("Fosberg"), and Marilyn Jones ("Jones") for their part in the Kansas City distributions brings the total of persons acting in concert with Coppola to eight. Several other individuals arguably could be added to this total. A reasonable trier of fact could therefore find from the evidence that Coppola held a position as organizer, manager, or supervisor with respect to five or more persons.

Finally, Coppola claims that the government failed to prove that he derived "substantial income or resources" from the CCE. The Ninth Circuit, noting that "[i]n applying the CCE statute, other courts have wisely refrained from establishing a precise definition of what constitutes 'substantial' income or resources," has found that "[t]he practical meaning of [this term] will normally be a question for the trier of fact and its scope will develop case by case." *United States v. Medina*, 940 F.2d 1247, 1251 (9th Cir.1991). This court has held that "evidence that large amounts of cocaine and tens of thousands of dollars passed through the operation" satisfies this element.

The government offered evidence that in the first three Kansas City distributions and the May, 1984 transaction with Edelstein, the organization reaped approximately $140,000. "The jury may reasonably conclude that the supervisors and managers of such a lucrative operation derived income from it." Large portions of the kilos of cocaine remaining in the possession of members of the organization count as "resources" under the statute. Under any definition, Coppola's share of this income and these resources was substantial.

Notes

1. What does it mean to organize, manage, or supervise others? Are there some common relationships that do—or do not—satisfy this criteria? Courts generally construe the management element liberally, but agree that a mere buyer-seller relationship is not sufficient. In *United States v. Jackson*, 345 F.3d 638, 646 (8th Cir. 2003), the court stated that the management

element is satisfied if "the defendant exerted some type of influence over another individual as exemplified by that individual's compliance with the defendant's directions, instructions, or terms." The court upheld the conviction of a defendant who directed others to purchase, process, transport, deliver, and sell drugs on his behalf. Do you think a liberal interpretation of the management element reflects a desirable flexibility in the application of CCE, or does it extend the statute to little fish that are a far cry from the top brass referred to by the Supreme Court in *Garrett*?

2. In *United States v. Jenkins*, 904 F.2d 549 (10th Cir. 1990), the defendant claimed that he had acted as a subordinate, not a manager. The court upheld his conviction, commenting that "the defendant need not be the dominant organizer or manager of the enterprise; he need only occupy some managerial position with respect to five or more persons." It also observed that "simply because Jenkins was not the 'king pin' does not mean that he did not have his share of minions."

Is the application of CCE to a person who is concededly not the dominant manager consistent with the notion of CCE as aimed at the top brass of the drug trade? Note that § 848(b) (added in 1986) imposes mandatory life imprisonment on "the principal administrator, organizer or leader of the enterprise or one of several such principal administrators, organizers, or leaders" of very large scale drug organizations. To satisfy subsection (b) the organization in question must have gross receipts of at least $10,000,000 in one year or deal in drug quantities at least 300 times the amount specified in 21 U.S.C. § 841(b)(1)(B). Has Congress recognized that CCE is being applied to what might be called the middle brass, and added subsection (b) to deal with the top brass? Or is CCE still aimed at drug king pins, and subsection (b) targeted to super kingpins?

3. What if the defendant is alleged to have associated with more than five people, and the involvement of some or all of them is contested? Is the defendant entitled to an instruction that the jury must unanimously agree on which five individuals the defendant organized, managed, or supervised? At least seven circuits have concluded that the jury need not agree on the identity of the five persons whom the defendant organizes, manages, or supervises. In *United States v. Moorman*, 944 F.2d 801, 803 (11th Cir. 1991), the court summarized the cases:

> The common rationale which runs through the decisions of the other Circuits is twofold. First, there is no general unanimity requirement as to a "specific fact underlying an element" of an offense. Second, the criminal enterprise statute is concerned only with the size of the enterprise, not with the identities of the subordinates, which is irrelevant. The requirement that the defendant has managed five subordinates, regardless of their identity, merely establishes that the defendant played a leadership role in an enterprise sufficiently large to merit the enhanced punishment provided by the statute.

> "While the jury must reach a consensus on the fact that there were five or more underlings, which is an essential element of the CCE offense, there is no logical reason why there must be unanimity on the identities of these underlings."

4. What if the cast of characters changes over time? The courts have generally agreed that it is irrelevant if the identity of the persons organized or supervised changes, as long as there are a sufficient number of individuals involved. Limiting CCE exclusively to cases where the identity of the individuals did not change would make it easy to evade the statute by regular personnel changes. On the other hand, what if the cast of characters changes and there are not at least five people involved at all times? In *United States v. Bafia*, 949 F.2d 1465 (7th Cir. 1991), the Seventh Circuit rejected the defendant's claim that CCE requires the defendant to manage five persons simultaneously. The majority reaffirmed an earlier holding:

> The government need not establish that the defendant managed five people at once, that the five acted in concert with each other, that the defendant exercised the same kind of control over each of the five, or even that the defendant had personal contact with each of the five.

Id. at 1471. Judge Posner dissented on this point:

> To be convicted of being a drug kingpin, defendant Cappas had to be found to have supervised five or more persons. Not any five persons, though. The court notes that the kingpin statute does not "apply to a small-time drug dealer who uses one courier in January, a second in February, and so on, until five couriers have taken part." That would be a two-man operation, not a six-man one. The five underling slots needn't all be occupied at the same time, however, so Cappas is wrong to argue that the kingpin must supervise all five underlings at once. Suppose the kingpin presided over a drug ring that employed underlings A, B, and C to manufacture the drug and D, E, and F to distribute it. And suppose that during the manufacturing phase D and E were on layoff, so that the kingpin was supervising only four persons, while during distribution A and B were on layoff, so that again the kingpin was supervising only four persons. It would still be a six-man, not a four-man, operation, and the kingpin statute would apply.
>
> So far so good, but my colleagues go on to say that it is "irrelevant that underlings came and went," and that it is "sufficient that the [kingpin] had a conspiratorial agreement with each of the five underlings"—and in the setting of this case these statements are misleading. That underlings come and go is irrelevant if there are more than five slots, and on that assumption the relation among the underlings is also irrelevant. But if the question is how many slots there are, it becomes crucial whether the underlings are merely replacements for the second fiddle in the two-man band or whether they fill out a table of organization that, however informal, has at least five spaces on it.
>
> The only way to reconcile the principle that mere replacements can't get you up to five and the principle that simultaneous supervision of all five is not required is to insist that the defendant's criminal organization have five or more positions, whether or not they're all filled at any particular moment. The focus on positions is consistent with, indeed I think required by, the court's observation that the kingpin statute "is intended to combat large criminal organizations." A two-man band is not a large organization no matter how many times the second player is replaced. A six-man band is a large organization within the

sense of the statute even if not all six players are playing at once. I assume that if through electronic wizardry two players can play all six instruments at once it's still not a six-piece band within the meaning of the statute but that is not an issue here.

Id. at 1481.

Who has the better argument? If Judge Posner's argument is accepted, will the jury be able to draw the necessary distinctions? Compare the treatment of similar issues under 18 U.S.C. § 1955, the gambling business statute, *supra* at 629–31.

5. Although the circuits have generally decided that the jury need not unanimously agree as to which five people the defendant associated with, the Supreme Court in *Richardson v. United States*, 526 U.S. 813 (1999), held that the jury must be unanimous as to which specific violations made up the "continuing series of violations." The Court decided that statute's phrase "series of violations" referred to several elements, rather than a single element with multiple underlying facts. Because the jury must unanimously agree on each element of the offense, they must agree about which predicate crimes the defendant committed. The Court rejected the dissent's argument that requiring jury unanimity would make CCE too difficult to prove. It appears that the majority may have been correct, as the vast majority of convictions that have been appealed after *Richardson* because of an inadequate jury unanimity instruction have been upheld. In most cases, the jury also found the defendant guilty of the underlying crimes, leading courts to conclude that the failure to instruct regarding unanimity on the "series of violations" phrase of the CCE charge was harmless error. *See, e.g., United States v. Almaraz*, 306 F.3d 1031 (10th Cir. 2002).

The *Richardson* Court sidestepped the question whether the unanimity requirement will be applicable to the requirement that the defendant organize, manage, or supervise five or more other persons. Do you think there is a good reason to require proof of unanimity for the offenses that make up the series, but not for the identity of the persons who are organized, managed, or supervised by the defendant? In a case decided before *Richardson*, the Third Circuit concluded that predicate offenses, the conduct which the CCE statute is designed to punish and deter, should be treated quite differently from the identity of the defendant's underlings, which "is peripheral to the statute's other primary concern, which is the defendant's exercise of the requisite degree of supervisory authority over a sizeable enterprise." *United States v. Jackson*, 879 F.2d 85, 87–88 (3d Cir. 1989). Do you agree?

6. The issue of the minimum duration, if any, required for a "continuing" criminal enterprise has received relatively little attention. In *United States v. Jones*, 801 F.2d 304, 307 (8th Cir. 1986), the court observed that "[c]ontinuing' requires that the course of illicit conduct span a definite period of time." Compare the treatment of the continuity issue under RICO, where this issue has been litigated extensively. *See infra* at 538–44. Should the courts tighten up their interpretation of the continuity elements in CCE cases?

7. The statute establishes no dollar amount necessary to constitute substantial income for a CCE violation. As indicated in the principal case, the courts too have refused to identify a minimum amount. *See, e.g., United*

States v. Henderson, 78 Fed. Appx. 91, 93 (10th Cir. 2003) ("We have declined to define "substantial" as any particular amount, leaving this judgment up to the trier of fact."). The court in *Henderson* held that the jury could have found $486,000 in revenue over four years was substantial. The court also rejected the defendant's argument that the revenue did not constitute "substantial income or resources" because it was reinvested in drugs, not retained as profit. Therefore, it was acceptable for the jury to consider the $486,000 in revenue even though the defendant owned only one significant asset, a Cadillac Escalade valued at $21,000 and no other luxury items, had $27,000 of debt, and had court-appointed counsel for his trial.

Why doesn't the statute specify a definite amount? Given the illegal nature of all of the transactions and the secrecy that surround them, would the prosecutor ordinarily be able to prove with any precision how much net income the defendant received? Would it be easier to show gross income? Note that § 848(b), which provides for a mandatory life sentence for the principal administrators of very large drug enterprises, specifies that one criteria for size is the "gross receipts" of the enterprise. Is that a workable approach? Should it be extended to § 848(c)?

2. CCE AND DOUBLE JEOPARDY

Compound complex statutes, such as CCE and RICO, require proof of one or more violations of other criminal statutes (the predicate offenses), plus additional elements. This structure naturally raises Double Jeopardy issues. As the Supreme Court has explained, there are multiple facets to Double Jeopardy analysis:

> Our cases have recognized three separate guarantees embodied in the Double Jeopardy Clause: It protects against a second prosecution for the same offense after acquittal, against a second prosecution for the same offense after conviction, and against multiple punishments for the same offense.

Justices of Boston Municipal Court v. Lydon, 466 U.S. 294 (1984).

Unfortunately—for both students and courts—the Supreme Court's Double Jeopardy caselaw is both complex and difficult. Indeed, the Court itself has referred to its decisions as "a veritable Sargasso Sea which could not fail to challenge the most intrepid judicial navigator." *Albernaz v. United States*, 450 U.S. 333, 343 (1981). Without undertaking a full explication of the Double Jeopardy clause, we will sketch out some of its ramifications for CCE prosecutions.

The Double Jeopardy clause prohibits successive prosecutions and multiple punishments only for "the same offense," and the definition of what constitutes the same offense is an important issue in Fifth Amendment cases. The Supreme Court has long recognized that offenses that fall under different sections of the federal criminal code (or a state code) may nonetheless be "the same offense" for purposes of the Double Jeopardy clause. The principal test employed by the Court to determine what constitutes the same offense was announced in *Blockburger v. United States*, 284 U.S. 299 (1932), which states that two distinct statutory provisions constitute separate offenses as long as "each provision requires proof of a fact that the other does not." Under this test, a greater offense and a lesser included offense (e.g., assault with a deadly weapon and assault), constitute the *same* offense for constitutional purposes, because the lesser offense does not require proof of any fact not also required for proof of the greater offense.

Given this general definition of "the same offense," it is easy to see why CCE appears to raise constitutional questions. Under *Blockburger*, each of the predicate offenses appear to be lesser included offenses and thus for Double Jeopardy purposes "the same offense" as CCE. Does that mean that a defendant may not be punished for both CCE and the underlying predicate offenses, and that a prosecution for a predicate offense would bar a later prosecution for CCE? Although there are some Double Jeopardy limitations applicable to CCE prosecutions, the complex Double Jeopardy case law gives federal prosecutors far more leeway than the *Blockburger* test might suggest.

a. CCE and Multiple Punishments

In the context of multiple punishments, the Supreme Court has placed an important limitation on the application of the Double Jeopardy clause. The Court has held that the Double Jeopardy clause prohibits the imposition of *multiple punishments* for "the same offense" *only* when that has the effect of exceeding the punishment intended by the legislature. Multiple punishments for separate violations that constitute the same offense are permissible, however, when authorized by the legislature. Thus the main question is what the legislature intended. The Supreme Court has adopted a rule of thumb; applying what is often called the *"Blockburger"* standard, it presumes that where two statutory provisions proscribe 'the same offense,' a legislature does not intend to impose two punishments for that offense. *Blockburger* is used to determine what constitutes the same offense for this purpose, and hence to trigger the presumption regarding the legislature's intent. But the Court has made it clear that this presumption may be overcome.

In *Garrett v. United States*, 471 U.S. 773, 782 (1985), the Supreme Court reviewed both the language of CCE and its legislative history, concluding that Congress's intent to make CCE a separate offense from the predicate violations and allow cumulative punishments "could hardly be clearer." Since it does not violate Congress's intent to impose separate punishments for both CCE and the predicate offenses, the Double Jeopardy clause imposes no bar. For a case reaffirming that *Garrett* permits a defendant to be sentenced for both a substantive offense and CCE, see *United States v. Riddick*, 156 F.3d 505, 512 (3d Cir. 1998). (It should be noted, however, that this holding applies only when the issue arises in the context of a single prosecution. Successive prosecutions are discussed below.)

But what if one of the predicate offenses is a drug conspiracy? Doesn't organizing a series of drug offenses involving a group of five or more persons working "in concert" sound like it would be a conspiracy under 21 U.S.C. § 846? In *Rutledge v. United States*, 517 U.S. 292 (1996), the Supreme Court held that multiple punishments are *not* permitted for both CCE and a predicate drug conspiracy under § 846 because the conspiracy is a lesser included offense. The Court explained:

> For the reasons set forth in *Jeffers*, [432 U.S. 137 (1977),] and particularly because the plain meaning of the phrase "in concert" signifies mutual agreement in a common plan or enterprise, we hold that this element of the CCE offense requires proof of a conspiracy that would also violate § 846. Because § 846 does not require proof of any fact that is not also a part of the CCE offense, a straightforward application of the *Blockburger* test leads to the conclusion that conspiracy as defined in § 846 does not define a different offense from the CCE offense defined in § 848. Furthermore, since the latter offense is the more serious of the two, and because only one of its elements is necessary to prove a § 846 conspiracy, it is appropriate to characterize § 846 as a lesser included offense of § 848.

Id. at 297. Applying the rule of thumb that Congress does not intend to allow multiple punishments for the same offense, the *Rutledge* Court held that a defendant could not be sentenced for both CCE and a predicate conspiracy under § 846.

b. CCE and Successive Prosecutions

In the context of successive prosecutions, the Supreme Court has held that Double Jeopardy bars a second prosecution after either an acquittal or a conviction for the same offense (though it has recognized a few exceptions to that rule). The *Garrett* case noted above also raised the issue of successive prosecutions, but the Supreme Court did not definitively resolve the issue. Garrett pled guilty to importing marijuana in the Western District of Washington. Subsequently he was indicted in Florida on CCE charges, and the government introduced evidence not only of drug offenses that occurred in Florida, but also the Washington offense. A majority of the Supreme Court upheld the defendant's CCE conviction, rejecting the claim that Double Jeopardy barred the second prosecution because the CCE conviction constituted the same offense under *Blockburger*. Although it did not rest its holding on this ground, the Court suggested that ordinary Double Jeopardy principles do not apply to compound-complex offenses. Noting that the *Blockburger* test was designed to apply to a single course of conduct that occurs within a relatively short time period, the Court commented that these principles could not necessarily be transposed from this "classically simple situation" to "the multilayered conduct, both as to time and to place, involved in this case." 471 U.S. at 789. However the Court found it unnecessary to resolve this issue, for it concluded that even if CCE and the Washington drug charge were the same offense one of the exceptions to Double Jeopardy applied in the case before it. The Court relied upon an exception developed in *United States v. Diaz*, 223 U.S. 442 (1912), where the Court held that Double Jeopardy did not bar a murder conviction when the victim died after his attacker was convicted of assaulting him. Since the victim was still alive at the time of the first prosecution, the government could not have brought the murder charge at that time. Similarly, the Court suggested that the CCE conduct continued after Garrett's conviction on the Washington charge.

What if the *Diaz* exception does not apply? The Supreme Court has never returned to this issue, though a later decision supports the view that ordinary Double Jeopardy principles will not apply to CCE because of its character as a multi-layered offense.[u] The lower courts have generally concluded that Double Jeopardy does not bar successive prosecutions for CCE and its predicate offenses.[v] The only cases that have caused the lower courts difficulty are those in which the predicate offense in question was a drug conspiracy. The courts were divided on the proper resolution of this issue before the Supreme Court's decision in *Rutledge* (which held as noted above that multiple punishments may not be imposed for both CCE and a conspiracy under § 846); a majority of the lower courts permitted successive prosecutions under a variety of theories. The lower courts have not yet resolved the question whether *Rutledge* requires a change of analysis, or whether it is limited to the context of multiple punishments. A footnote in the *Rutledge* opinion makes it clear that the Court left open the question of successive prosecutions. The Court noted that the facts before it did not present the kind of case that might warrant a successive prosecution, e.g., a case in which the government first prosecuted the defendant for a drug conspiracy without being aware of the additional facts that would permit prosecution of CCE. 517 U.S. at 307.

Several commentators support somewhat greater restrictions— though not a bar–on the government's power to bring successive prosecutions in CCE cases. In an article providing an excellent discussion of the application of Double Jeopardy principles to CCE (and RICO), Susan Klein and Katherine Chiarello advocate a new test that would neither exempt CCE cases from Double Jeopardy/successive prosecution analysis nor subject it to the same limitations as applicable to ordinary offenses. Susan R. Klein & Katherine P. Chiarello, *Successive Prosecutions and Compound Criminal Statutes: A Functional Test*, 77 TEX. L. REV. 333, 352–53 nn.97–99 (1998). They favor a presumption that Double Jeopardy bars a successive prosecution, which may be rebutted if the prosecution can demonstrate a legitimate reason for a second prosecution consistent with the values of the Double Jeopardy clause. Anne Bowen Poulin reaches a similar conclusion by a different route. Poulin sees no need for any special double jeopardy analysis for CCE or other compound of-

u. In United States v. Felix, 503 U.S. 378 (1992), the Court noted that *Blockburger* was developed for cases involving a single course of conduct and may not be readily transposed to offenses of a different character; it held that (1) conspiracy and its object offense are separate offenses for Double Jeopardy purposes, and (2) conspiracy and its object offense may be prosecuted successively and separate punishments may be imposed.

v. For a collection of cases involving CCE, RICO, and other compound offenses, see Susan R. Klein & Katherine P. Chiarello, *Successive Prosecutions and Compound Criminal Statutes: A Functional Test*, 77 Tex. L. Rev. 333, 352–53 nn.97–99 (1998).

fenses. Instead, she favors imposing greater limitations on all successive prosecutions, defining the term "same offense" broadly, but then balancing the government's interest in a successive prosecution against the defendant's Double Jeopardy interests on a case by case basis. Successive prosecutions involving CCE or other compound offenses would not be permitted in the absence of "specific and strong justification." Anne Bowen Poulin, *Double Jeopardy Protection From Successive Prosecution: A Proposed Approach*, 92 GEO. L.J. 1183, 1272–78 (2004).

3. THE FUTURE OF CCE

Why is the number of CCE prosecutions so small? It's time to return to the questions posed at the beginning of this section and to consider some related legislative initiatives.

First, how difficult it is to prove a CCE violation? Recall that more than one quarter of the roughly 60,000 federal prosecutions each year are for drug offenses. In light of the material on pp. 391–97, do you think it should be possible for the prosecution to establish the requisite series of predicate offenses, leadership, and income in more than 214 cases each year? Assuming that there were three or more drug offenses, how much more does it take to establish the requisite elements of leadership and income?

If you conclude—as we do—that these elements have been construed in a fashion that is quite favorable to the prosecution, then you might be justifiably puzzled that the government makes so little use of this powerful weapon. Despite the analytical complexity, as explained at 397–401, Double Jeopardy does not really limit prosecutions under CCE. Yet CCE is seldom used. Why? We think the CCE weapon is less powerful than it seems. To see why, you have to understand key changes in the sentencing laws after the CCE statute was enacted in 1970. In 1970, the terms of imprisonment available for CCE were much higher than those for the predicate drug offenses, and forfeiture was available *only* for CCE and RICO, to strip drug kings and racketeers of their illicit assets. Later legislation, however, brought the sentences for the predicate drug offenses much closer to the sentences authorized for CCE. Congress made forfeiture available for all drug offenses, and it ratcheted up the terms of imprisonment available for CCE's predicate drug offenses, adding mandatory minimums that served as a floor for the Sentencing Guidelines ranges.

Now prosecutors can get forfeiture without charging CCE, and may be able to get to the top of the sentencing chart (360 months to life, or life) on the basis of drug quantity and other sentencing factors—without charging CCE. Indeed, the Guidelines themselves incorporate a CCE-like enhancement provision, increasing the sentence of any defendant convicted of drug (and other) offenses by 4 levels if he was "an organizer or leader of a criminal activity that involved five or more participants or was otherwise extensive." U.S.S.G. § 3B1.1(a). Since this is a sentencing enhancement, not a separate criminal charge, the procedural hurdles facing the prosecution are far lower than they would be for proof of a CCE charge.[w]

If this analysis is correct, the number of CCE charges is likely to remain small unless Congress readjusts the sentencing consequences, either lowering sentences for other drug offenses (which seems unlikely at least in the short run), or significantly increasing the sentence for CCE. Even that, however, might not be sufficient to make much of a difference. As noted at 354–55 *supra*, there is some evidence that drug penalties are already so high that prosecutors (as well as judges) no longer seek the highest possible sentences in drug cases, making numerous discretionary decisions that tend to lower sentences in individual cases and in the aggregate.

Although Congress has not focused on CCE in recent years, it is now showing significant interest in a related problem: that of street gangs, many—if not all—of which are involved in drug trafficking. The gang bills, like CCE, are intended to function as sentence enhancers, but with three key differences. First, the gang bills do not focus on kingpins, though they are worded broadly enough to reach anyone from the upper echelon to the lowest level. Second, they incorporate federal drug offenses as predicate gang crimes, but most of the provisions treat crimes of violence—rather than drug offenses—as the defining characteristic of a street gang. And, finally, the gang bills do more than just increase federal sentences; they also extend federal jurisdiction because the list of predicate crimes under the gang bills includes state crimes.

The gang bill receiving the greatest legislative support to date is H.R. 1279, 109th Cong. § 1 (2005), which passed the House of Representatives on May 11, 2005. It defines a criminal street gang as any group of three or more individuals who commit two or more "gang crimes," at least one of which must be a crime of violence. The definition of gang crime includes numerous state crimes—including any "crime of violence." Therefore, one can be subject to serious federal punishment—no less than 10 years imprisonment—for the commission of certain state crimes if they are committed in furtherance of a criminal street gang.

Even without new legislation, the Justice Department and Homeland Security are seeking to crack down on violent gangs. Over a two week period in July 2005, Homeland Security reported that it had made 500 gang-related arrests, and the Attorney General has formed an Anti–Gang Coordination Committee and requested that each United States Attorney prepare and implement a comprehensive, district-wide strategy—in consultation with state and local law enforcement—to coordinate anti-gang activity across the board.

w. As discussed in Chapter 18, *infra* at 854–69, the Supreme Court concluded that the procedures under the Sentencing Reform Act were inconsistent with the Sixth Amendment right to trial by jury and the Due Process right to proof beyond a reasonable doubt, but it concluded that judicial fact-finding by a preponderance of the evidence was permissible if the Guidelines were merely advisory, and that this remedy best comported with the intent of Congress in establishing the Guidelines system.

We discuss the common problems raised by organizational crime statutes—including CCE—in Chapter 13 *infra* at 622.

D. EXTRATERRITORIAL JURISDICTION

A large proportion of drug offenses under the Comprehensive Drug Abuse Prevention and Control Act of 1970 and subsequent federal enactments involve conduct that takes place partly or wholly outside the United States. Intercepting drugs before they reach the borders of the United States, aiding foreign nations in their attempts to eradicate indigenous drug cartels, and bringing drug lords to justice are all key elements of the federal drug strategy.

The use of federal resources to combat conduct that occurs outside the borders of the United States raises important questions about the extraterritorial reach of federal criminal law under principles of international law, under the constitution, and as a matter of statutory construction.

There are several distinct aspects of extraterritorial jurisdiction. Section 401 of the RESTATEMENT (THIRD) OF THE LAW OF FOREIGN RELATIONS OF THE UNITED STATES (1986) identifies three aspects of jurisdiction. It states:

> Under international law, a state is subject to limitations on
>
> (a) jurisdiction to prescribe, *i.e.,* to make its law applicable to the activities, relations, or status of persons * * * by legislation * * *;
>
> (b) jurisdiction to adjudicate, *i.e.,* to subject persons or things to the process of its courts or administrative tribunals, whether in civil or criminal proceedings, whether or not the state is a party to the proceedings;
>
> (c) jurisdiction to enforce, *i.e.,* to induce or compel compliance or punish noncompliance with its laws or regulations. whether through the courts or by use of executive, administrative, police, or other nonjudicial action.

These limitations raise some interesting questions. Upon what basis can Congress define conduct that occurs wholly within another sovereign country as criminal? What if the conduct were entirely legal in that other country? Assuming that Congress has enacted legislation that is intended to reach extraterritorial conduct involving drug trafficking, what special limitations, if any, does international law impose on the activities of federal agencies such as the F.B.I. and the D.E.A.? And what are the consequences under domestic law if there is a breach of international law?

Some drug legislation, such as 21 U.S.C. § 959, explicitly provides for extraterritorial jurisdiction. Consider the application of that provision and the questions raised above in the following case concerning a famous—or infamous—character, General Manuel Noriega.

UNITED STATES v. NORIEGA

746 F.Supp. 1506 (S.D. Fla. 1990).

HOEVELER, DISTRICT JUDGE.

* * *

The case at bar presents the Court with a drama of international proportions, considering the status of the principal defendant and the difficult circumstances under which he was brought before this Court. The pertinent facts are as follows:

On February 14, 1988, a federal grand jury sitting in Miami, Florida returned a twelve-count indictment charging General Manuel Antonio Noriega with participating in an international conspiracy to import cocaine and materials used in producing cocaine into and out of the United States. Noriega is alleged to have exploited his official position as head of the intelligence branch of the Panamanian National Guard, and then as Commander-in-Chief of the Panamanian Defense Forces, to receive payoffs in return for assisting and protecting international drug traffickers, including various members of the Medellin Cartel, in conducting narcotics and money laundering operations in Panama.

Specifically, the indictment charges that General Noriega protected cocaine shipments from Colombia through Panama to the United States; arranged for the transshipment and sale to the Medellin Cartel of ether and acetone, including such chemicals previously seized by the Panamanian Defense Forces; provided refuge and a base for continued operations for the members of the Medellin Cartel after the Colombian government's crackdown on drug traffickers following the murder of the Colombian Minister of Justice, Rodrigo Lara–Bonilla; agreed to protect a cocaine laboratory in Darien Province, Panama; and assured the safe passage of millions of dollars of narcotic proceeds from the United States into Panamanian banks. Noriega also allegedly traveled to Havana, Cuba and met with Cuban president Fidel Castro, who, according to the indictment, mediated a dispute between Noriega and the Cartel caused by the Panamanian troops' seizure of a drug laboratory that Noriega was paid to protect. All of these activities were allegedly undertaken for General Noriega's own personal profit. Defendant Del Cid, in addition to being an officer in the Panamanian Defense Forces, was General Noriega's personal secretary. He is charged with acting as liaison, courier, and emissary for Noriega in his transactions with Cartel members and other drug traffickers.

Because of the activities alleged, Defendants are charged with engaging in a pattern of racketeering activity, in violation of the RICO statutes, 18 U.S.C. §§ 1962(c) and 1962(d); conspiracy to distribute and import cocaine into the United States, in violation of 21 U.S.C. § 963; and distributing and aiding and abetting the distribution of cocaine, intending that it be imported into the United States, in violation of 21

U.S.C. § 959 and 18 U.S.C. § 2. Defendant Noriega is further charged with aiding and abetting the manufacture of cocaine destined for the United States, in violation of 21 U.S.C. § 959 and 18 U.S.C. § 2; conspiring to manufacture cocaine intending that it be imported into the United States, in violation of 21 U.S.C. § 963; and causing interstate travel and use of facilities in interstate commerce to promote an unlawful activity, in violation of 18 U.S.C. § 1952(a)(3) and 18 U.S.C. § 2.

* * *

[At the time the indictment was returned by the grand jury in Miami, General Noriega was still the head of the Panamanian Defense Forces and the head of state of Panama. After the indictment relations deteriorated between the United States and Panama. On December 15, 1989, General Noriega declared that a "state of war" existed between the United States and Panama. Tension increased as one American serviceman was shot and killed and several others were beaten by Panamanian troops. On December 20, 1989 President Bush ordered U.S. Troops into combat in Panama City. General Noriega eluded United States troops for several days, eventually taking refuge in the Papal Nunciature in Panama City. After an eleven day stand-off, General Noriega finally surrendered to the American forces on January 3, 1990. From Panama, he was flown to Florida and formally arrested by agents of the Drug Enforcement Agency.]

* * *

I. JURISDICTION OVER THE OFFENSE

The first issue confronting the Court is whether the United States may exercise jurisdiction over Noriega's alleged criminal activities. Noriega maintains that "the extraterritorial application of the criminal law is unreasonable under the unique facts of this case, and cannot be relied upon to secure jurisdiction over a leader of a sovereign nation who has personally performed no illegal acts within the borders of the United States." Although the defendant attempts to weave his asserted status as a foreign leader into his challenge to the extraterritorial application of this country's criminal laws, the question of whether the United States may proscribe conduct which occurs beyond its borders is separate from the question of whether Noriega is immune from prosecution as a head of state. This distinction is made clear in the defendant's own discussion of the applicable international law on extraterritorial jurisdiction, which does not look to a foreign defendant's official status but rather to the nature and effect of the conduct at issue. The Court therefore reserves analysis of Noriega's claim to head of state immunity and confines its discussion here to the ability of the United States to reach and prosecute acts committed by aliens outside its territorial borders.[4] While the indictment cites specific instances of conduct occurring within the Unit-

---

4. No jurisdictional obstacle would be present were the defendant a United States citizen, since a country may regulate the acts of its citizens wherever they occur.

ed States, including the shipment of cocaine from Panama to Miami and several flights to and from Miami by Noriega's alleged co-conspirators, the activity ascribed to Noriega occurred solely in Panama with the exception of the one trip to Cuba. Noriega is charged with providing safe haven to international narcotic traffickers by allowing Panama to be used as a location for the manufacture and shipment of cocaine destined for this country's shores.

Where a court is faced with the issue of extraterritorial jurisdiction, the analysis to be applied is 1) whether the United States has the power to reach the conduct in question under traditional principles of international law; and 2) whether the statutes under which the defendant is charged are intended to have extraterritorial effect. As Noriega concedes, the United States has long possessed the ability to attach criminal consequences to acts occurring outside this country which produce effects within the United States. *Strassheim v. Daily*, 221 U.S. 280, 285 (1911); *Restatement (Third) of the Foreign Relations Law of the United States* [hereinafter *Restatement (Third)*] § 402(1)(c). For example, the United States would unquestionably have authority to prosecute a person standing in Canada who fires a bullet across the border which strikes a second person standing in the United States. *See Restatement (Third)* § 402, Comment d. "All the nations of the world recognize 'the principle that a man who outside of a country willfully puts in motion a force to take effect in it is answerable at the place where the evil is done ...'" The objective territorial theory of jurisdiction, which focuses on the effects or intended effects of conduct, can be traced to Justice Holmes' statement that "[a]cts done outside a jurisdiction, but intended to produce or producing effects within it, justify a State in punishing the cause of the harm as if he had been present at the effect, if the State should succeed in getting him within its power." *Strassheim v. Daily*, 221 U.S. at 285, 31 S.Ct. at 560. Even if the extraterritorial conduct produces no effect within the United States, a defendant may still be reached if he was part of a conspiracy in which some co-conspirator's activities took place within United States territory. The former Fifth Circuit, whose decisions establish precedent for this Court, has on numerous occasions upheld jurisdiction over foreigners who conspired to import narcotics into the United States but never entered this country nor personally performed any acts within its territorial limits, as long as there was proof of an overt act committed within the United States by a co-conspirator.

More recently, international law principles have expanded to permit jurisdiction upon a mere showing of *intent* to produce effects in this country, without requiring proof of an overt act or effect within the United States. According to the *Restatement (Third)*:

> Cases involving intended but unrealized effect are rare, but international law does not preclude jurisdiction in such instances, subject to the principle of reasonableness. When the intent to commit the proscribed act is clear and demonstrated by some activity, and the effect to be produced by the activity is substantial and foreseeable,

the fact that a plan or conspiracy was thwarted does not deprive the target state of jurisdiction to make its law applicable.

§ 402, Comment d.

In the drug smuggling context, the 'intent doctrine' has resulted in jurisdiction over persons who attempted to import narcotics into the United States but never actually succeeded in entering the United States or delivering drugs within its borders. The fact that no act was committed and no repercussions were felt within the United States did not preclude jurisdiction over conduct that was clearly directed at the United States.

These principles unequivocally support jurisdiction in this case. The indictment charges Noriega with conspiracy to import cocaine into the United States and alleges several overt acts performed within the United States in furtherance of the conspiracy. Specifically, the indictment alleges that co-conspirators of Noriega purchased a Lear jet in Miami, which was then used to transport drug proceeds from Miami to Panama. Moreover, Noriega's activities in Panama, if true, undoubtedly produced effects within this country as deleterious as the hypothetical bullet fired across the border. The indictment alleges that, as a result of Noriega's facilitation of narcotics activity in Panama, 2,141 pounds of cocaine were illegally brought into Miami from Panama. While the ability of the United States to reach and proscribe extraterritorial conduct having effects in this country does not depend on the amount of narcotics imported into the United States or the magnitude of the consequences, the importation of over 2,000 pounds of cocaine clearly has a harmful impact and merits jurisdiction. Finally, even if no overt acts or effects occurred within the territorial borders, the object of the alleged conspiracy was to import cocaine into the United States and therefore an intent to produce effects is present.

The defendant's argument that the exercise of jurisdiction over his alleged activities in Panama is unreasonable is simply unsupportable in light of established principles of international law and the overwhelming case law in this Circuit upholding jurisdiction under similar circumstances. Other than asserting his status as a foreign leader, which presents a different question from the one posed here, Noriega does not distinguish this case from those cited above. He cites the principle of reasonableness recently articulated in the *Restatement (Third)* § 403, but fails to say how extending jurisdiction over his conduct would be unreasonable. In fact, the defendant's invocation of a reasonableness requirement supports rather than undermines the application of jurisdiction in the present case. * * * [T]he same section of the *Restatement* establishes that narcotics offenses provide the strong justification meriting criminal jurisdiction: "Prosecution for activities committed in a foreign state have generally been limited to serious and universally condemned offenses, such as treason or traffic in narcotics, and to offenses by and against military forces. In such cases the state in whose territory the act occurs is not likely to object to regulation by the state concerned." *Id.* (citations omitted). The *Restatement* therefore explicitly recognizes the reasonableness of extending jurisdiction to narcotics activity such as that alleged here. Even if another state were likely to object to jurisdiction here, the United States has a strong interest in halting the flow of illicit drugs across its borders. In assessing the reasonableness of extraterritorial jurisdiction, one of the factors to be considered is the character of the activity to be regulated, including the importance of regulation to the regulating state and the degree to which the desire to regulate is generally accepted. *Restatement (Third)* § 403(1)(c). The consensus of the American public on the need to stem the flow of drugs into this country is well publicized and need not be elaborated upon in detail. Further, the Court notes that the United States has an affirmative duty to enact and enforce legislation to curb illicit drug trafficking under the Single Convention on Narcotics Drugs, 18 U.S.T. 1409, T.I.A.S. No. 6298, New York, March 30, 1961, ratified by the United States, 1967, amended 26 U.S.T. 1441, T.I.A.S. No. 8118. Given the serious nature of the drug epidemic in this country, certainly the efforts of the United States to combat the problem by prosecuting conduct directed against itself cannot be subject to the protests of a foreign government profiting at its expense. In any case, the Court is not made aware of any instance in which the Republic of Panama objected to the regulation of drug trafficking by the United States. In sum, because Noriega's conduct in Panama is alleged to have resulted in a direct effect within the United States, the Court concludes that extraterritorial jurisdiction is appropriate as a matter of international law.

This conclusion does not end the Court's analysis, however, since a further requirement is that the criminal statutes under which the defendant is charged be intended to apply to conduct outside the United States. Noriega is charged with violations of 21 U.S.C. § 959 (distributing a controlled substance with the knowledge that it would be unlawfully imported into the United States); 21 U.S.C. § 952 (importing a controlled substance into the United States from a place outside thereof); 21 U.S.C. § 963 (conspiring to commit the above offenses); and 18 U.S.C. § 2 (aiding and abetting the violation of § 959). The indictment also alleges that Noriega participated in a pattern of racketeering activity consisting of the above crimes, in violation of the Racketeer Influenced and Corrupt Organizations Act (RICO), §§ 1962(c) and 1962(d), and caused the travel and use of facilities in interstate and foreign commerce in furtherance of a narcotics conspiracy, in violation of 18 U.S.C. § 1952(a)(3).

Section 959, prohibiting the distribution of narcotics intending that they be imported into the United States, is clearly meant to apply extraterritorially. The statute expressly states that it is "intended to reach acts of manufacture or distribution committed outside the territorial jurisdiction of the United States." 21 U.S.C. § 959(c). The remaining statutes, by contrast, do not on their face indicate an express intention that they be given extraterritorial effect. Where a statute is silent as to its extraterritorial reach, a presumption against such application normally applies. However, "such statutes may be given extraterritorial effect if the nature of the law permits it and Congress intends it. Absent an express intention on the face of the statutes to do so, the exercise of that power may be inferred from the nature of the offenses and Congress' other legislative efforts to eliminate the type of crime involved."

With respect to 21 U.S.C. § 952, it is apparent from the very nature of the offense that the statute was intended to reach extraterritorial acts. Section 952 makes it unlawful to import narcotics "into the United States from *any place outside* thereof." (emphasis added). Because importation by definition involves acts originating outside of the territorial limits of the United States, the Court can only infer that § 952 applies to conduct which begins abroad; any interpretation to the contrary would render the statute virtually meaningless. With jurisdiction over the substantive violations of §§ 959 and 952 established, jurisdiction over the conspiracy and aiding and abetting counts likewise follows. Since a conspiracy to commit an offense is closely related to the offense itself, courts have regularly inferred the extraterritorial reach of the § 963 conspiracy statute on the basis of a finding that the substantive statutes apply abroad. The same must be said for an aiding and abetting charge; if anything, the act of aiding and abetting is even more intimately connected to the underlying crime. In short, the Court perceives no sound jurisdictional reason for distinguishing the conspiracy and aiding and abetting charges from the substantive offense for purposes of extraterritorial application. Section 963 and 18 U.S.C. § 2 must therefore be given extraterritorial effect as well.

* * *

Notes

1. Section 401 of the Restatement on Foreign Relations describes the customary rationales upon which jurisdiction to prescribe may be based. The two most common bases for assertions of extraterritorial jurisdiction are nationality and territoriality. Under the **nationality principle**, states may assert jurisdiction over their own nationals for conduct that occurs outside that state's borders. The **territorial principle** asserts jurisdiction over conduct that occurred within the state's borders, but it has also been extended to cover conduct outside its territory that has or is intended to have substantial effects within its territory. Restatement (Third) of the Law of Foreign Relations § 402(1)(c). A third well-recognized basis of extraterritorial jurisdiction is the **protective principle**, which permits a state to exercise jurisdiction over conduct outside its territory that threatens the state's national security. The **passive personality principle**, which would give a state jurisdiction over offenses committed against its nationals, is still controversial, though it is gaining increasing acceptance where the victims have been selected because of their nationality. Finally, a long-established principle of international law provides jurisdiction over crimes "recognized by the community of nations as of universal concern, such as piracy, slave trade, attacks on or hijacking of aircraft, genocide, war crimes and perhaps

certain acts of terrorism," even when there is no territorial or nationality basis for asserting jurisdiction. *Id.* § 404. Which principle(s) did the Noriega court rely upon?

2. The protective principle allows a sovereign state to assert jurisdiction over individuals whose conduct affects the national interest and security of the state. Although this theory is traditionally used to assert jurisdiction over only a few crimes (most notably espionage), the Eleventh Circuit has recognized the possibility that the protective principle might be used to assert jurisdiction over drug traffickers:

> The district court in *Marino-Garcia* found that jurisdiction over stateless vessels exists under the "protective principle." The protective principle requires proof that the illegal activity threatens the security or governmental functions of the United States. The district court reasoned that drug trafficking amounts to a threat to this country's security. Our disposition of this case renders consideration of the protective principle unnecessary. Nonetheless, we note that if drug trafficking is found to be a threat to the security of the United States this country would have jurisdiction under the protective principle over all vessels engaged in the illicit practice, including those flying foreign flags.

United States v. Marino-Garcia, 679 F.2d 1373, 1378, n.4 (11th Cir. 1982). There has also been some support for treating drug trafficking as one of the universal offenses against the law of nations, like piracy, slavery, and genocide.

3. On what basis have courts found the exercise of jurisdiction to prescribe insufficient? In *United States v. Medjuck*, 48 F.3d 1107 (9th Cir. 1995), Canadian and American members of an international drug conspiracy challenged the application of the Maritime Drug Law Enforcement Act (MDLEA), 46 U.S.C. § 1903–04, to conduct outside of the United States. The Navy intercepted the conspirators' ship (which was registered in St. Vincent) in international waters and discovered hashish. At the time of the interception, the ship was returning to Asia after offloading part of its cargo onto a smaller ship operated by undercover U.S. agents. The Act prohibits drug activity by "any person on board a vessel subject to the jurisdiction of the United States," which is defined to include a vessel registered to a foreign nation which had consented to the enforcement of U.S. law. St. Vincent had given such consent. The court held that due process required a showing of "a sufficient nexus between the conduct condemned and the United States." 48 F.3d at 1110–11. Because the district court had not required the government to make such a showing nor given the defendants an opportunity for rebuttal, the court of appeals reversed their convictions. In 1996, Congress amended MDLEA by adding § 1903(f), which provided that jurisdiction is not an element of the offense, but a preliminary question of law for the court, and so does not need to be proven to the jury. *See United States v. Moreno-Morillo*, 334 F.3d 819 (9th Cir. 2003).

In *United States v. Ledesma-Cuesta*, 347 F.3d 527 (3d Cir. 2003), the defendant challenged the court's jurisdiction under MDLEA where he had been found in possession of cocaine on a ship bound for the United States, but apprehended in international waters. The court held that jurisdiction under MDLEA was proper where the defendant has attempted to enter the

United States with the intent to distribute a controlled substance. Requiring law enforcement to wait for traffickers to enter U.S. waters would contradict Congress' purpose in drafting the statute. For a case analyzing the same issue in the context of an attempted airplane bombing, see *United States v. Yousef*, 327 F.3d 56 (2d Cir. 2003).

4. Though some provisions, such as Section 959, explicitly provide for extraterritorial jurisdiction, other provisions are silent on this question. The courts use theories of international law, as well as various tools of statutory interpretation, to determine the scope of the statute. One of the leading decisions on the extraterritorial application of criminal statutes is *United States v. Bowman*, 260 U.S. 94, 97–98 (1922):

> We have in this case a question of statutory construction. The necessary locus, when not specially defined, depends upon the purpose of Congress as evinced by the description and nature of the crime and upon the territorial limitations upon the power and jurisdiction of a government to punish crime under the law of nations. Crimes against private individuals or their property, like assaults, murder, burglary, larceny, robbery, arson, embezzlement, and frauds of all kinds, which affect the peace and good order of the community must, of course, be committed within the territorial jurisdiction of the government where it may properly exercise it. If punishment of them is to be extended to include those committed outside of the strict territorial jurisdiction, it is natural for Congress to say so in the statute, and failure to do so will negative the purpose of Congress in this regard. * * *

> But the same rule of interpretation should not be applied to criminal statutes which are, as a class, not logically dependent on their locality for the government's jurisdiction, but are enacted because of the right of the government to defend itself against obstruction, or fraud wherever perpetrated, especially if committed by its own citizens, officers, or agents. Some such offenses can only be committed within the territorial jurisdiction of the government because of the local acts required to constitute them. Others are such that to limit their locus to the strictly territorial jurisdiction would be greatly to curtail the scope and usefulness of the statute and leave open a large immunity for frauds as easily committed by citizens on the high seas and in foreign countries as at home. In such cases, Congress has not thought it necessary to make specific provision in the law that the locus shall include the high seas and foreign countries, but allows it to be inferred from the nature of the offense. * * *

5. The *Bowman* analysis was recently applied in a case involving a Canadian citizen charged, under 21 U.S.C. § 963, with conspiring to export cocaine *from* the United States (21 U.S.C. § 953). *United States v. MacAllister*, 160 F.3d 1304 (11th Cir. 1998). The government claimed that the defendant financially backed a scheme to transport cocaine from Jacksonville, Florida to Montreal. After the American contingent had been arrested, Canadian authorities, pursuant to a treaty request, extradited MacAllister to the United States to stand trial. After his conviction, the defendant appealed, challenging the district court's subject matter jurisdiction. While agreeing that §§ 963 and 953 did not explicitly provide for extraterritorial application,

the court held that "[l]ogic dictates that Congress would not have passed a drug conspiracy statute that prohibits international drug smuggling activities, while simultaneously undermining the statute by limiting its extraterritorial application." *Id.* at 1308. Furthermore,

> Coconspirators committed acts in furtherance of the conspiracy within the territorial boundaries of the United States. This conduct has a detrimental effect on our nation. We conclude that extraterritorial application is permitted under the objective territorial principle of international law.

Id. Are you comfortable with the United States having criminal jurisdiction over any person whose conspirator commits some acts in furtherance of the crime within the United States?

6.   Another portion of the district court's opinion in *Noriega, supra* at 404, held that both RICO and the Travel Act apply to conduct outside the United States that produces or is intended to produce effects in this country. 746 F.Supp. at 1516–19. With regard to RICO the court concluded:

> Given the Act's broad construction and equally broad goal of eliminating the harmful consequences of organized crime, it is apparent that Congress was concerned with the effects and not the locus of racketeering activities. The Act thus permits no inference that it was intended to apply only to conduct within the United States. Such a narrow construction would frustrate RICO's purpose by allowing persons engaged in racketeering activities directed at the United States to escape RICO's bite simply by moving their operations abroad. Yet in the context of narcotics activities, perhaps the greatest threat to this country's welfare comes from enterprises outside the United States such as the Colombian cocaine cartels. Keeping in mind Congress' specific instruction that RICO be applied liberally to effect its remedial purpose, the Court cannot suppose that RICO does not reach such harmful conduct simply because it is extraterritorial in nature. As long as the racketeering activities produce effects or are intended to produce effects in this country, RICO applies.

Id. at 1517. Do you see any special difficulties in giving RICO extraterritorial effect? RICO authorizes civil actions for treble damages. If the *Noriega* court is right, that presumably means that RICO authorizes private plaintiffs to bring treble damages in the federal courts for conduct that occurred outside the U.S., even in jurisdictions in which that conduct was legal. Such private plaintiffs are not, of course, restrained by other foreign policy goals as federal prosecutors might be. For a general discussion of RICO, see Chapter 11.

7.   The first part of the district court's opinion, reprinted above, concerns U.S. jurisdiction to prescribe and adjudicate Noriega's conduct. The second part of the district court's opinion, reprinted below, addresses Noriega's claims relating to U.S. jurisdiction to enforce.

UNITED STATES v. NORIEGA

746 F.Supp. 1506 (S.D. Fla. 1990).

HOEVELER, DISTRICT JUDGE.

* * *

IV. ILLEGAL ARREST

Noriega also moves to dismiss the indictment on the ground that the manner in which he was brought before this Court—as a result of the United States government's invasion of Panama—is "shocking to the conscience and in violation of the laws and norms of humanity." He argues that the Court should therefore divest itself of jurisdiction over his person. In support of this claim, Noriega alleges that the invasion of Panama violated the Due Process Clause of the Fifth Amendment of the United States Constitution, as well as international law. Alternatively, he argues that even in the absence of constitutional or treaty violations, this Court should nevertheless exercise its supervisory authority and dismiss the indictment so as to prevent the Court from becoming a party to the government's alleged misconduct in bringing Noriega to trial.

A. *The Fifth Amendment Due Process Argument*

It is well settled that the manner by which a defendant is brought before the court normally does not affect the ability of the government to try him. The *Ker–Frisbie* doctrine, as this rule has come to be known, provides that a court is not deprived of jurisdiction to try a defendant on the ground that the defendant's presence before the court was procured by unlawful means. *Ker v. Illinois*, 119 U.S. 436 (1886); *Frisbie v. Collins*, 342 U.S. 519 (1952). This Circuit's adherence to the *Ker–Frisbie* doctrine was firmly established in *United States v. Winter*, in which the former Fifth Circuit declared:

> [W]e are convinced that under well established case law of the Supreme Court and this Circuit, a defendant in a criminal trial whether citizen or alien, whether arrested within or beyond the territory of the United States, may not successfully challenge the District Court's jurisdiction over his person on the grounds that his presence was unlawfully secured.

509 F.2d at 985–86. Thus, in order to divest the Court of jurisdiction, it is not enough for the defendant to assert, without more, that his arrest was illegal.

Noriega does not challenge the validity of the *Ker–Frisbie* rule but instead relies on what is commonly referred to as the *Toscanino* exception carved out by the Second Circuit. *United States v. Toscanino*, 500 F.2d 267 (2d Cir.1974). In that case, which also involved a challenge to a court's exercise of personal jurisdiction, the defendant contended that his presence was illegally obtained through torture and abuse. In support of his claim, the defendant offered to prove that United States officials abducted him from Uruguay and subjected him to extensive and continuous torture, including pinching his fingers with metal pliers, flushing alcohol into his eyes and nose, forcing other fluids up his anal passage, and attaching electrodes to his extremities and genitals. *Id.* at 270. Confronted with these allegations, the court refused to permit the government the fruits of its misconduct, holding that "we view due process as now requiring a court to divest itself of jurisdiction over the person of a defendant where it has been acquired as the result of the government's deliberate, unnecessary and unreasonable invasion of the accused's constitutional rights." *Id.* at 275. In so holding, the court relied on the Supreme Court's decision in *Rochin v. California*, where the Due Process Clause was applied to "the whole course of the proceedings in order to ascertain whether they offend those canons of decency and fairness which express the notions of justice of English-speaking peoples even toward those charged with the most heinous offenses." 342 U.S. 165, 172–73 (1952).

The type of governmental conduct necessary to invoke the *Toscanino* exception and warrant the drastic remedy of dismissal was subsequently clarified and narrowed by the Second Circuit in *United States ex rel. Lujan v. Gengler*, 510 F.2d 62 (2d Cir.), *cert. denied*, 421 U.S. 1001 (1975) [hereinafter *Lujan v. Gengler*]. There, the Court held that due process is violated and dismissal warranted only where the defendant proves "torture, brutality, and similar outrageous conduct." *Id.* at 65. The conduct must "shock the conscience." *Id.* Noriega asserts that the deaths, casualties, and destruction of property caused by the United States military action in Panama is "shocking to the conscience" and therefore falls within the *Toscanino* exception as narrowed by *Lujan v. Gengler*.

* * * The case at bar, however, does not present such a situation, since Noriega does not, and presumably cannot, allege that the Government's invasion of Panama violated any right personal to him, as required by the Due Process Clause of the Fifth Amendment. The defendant does not claim that he was personally mistreated in any manner incident to his arrest, at least not in any manner nearly approaching the egregious physical abuse stated in *Toscanino*.[27] Rather, Noriega bases his due process claim on the rights of third parties, to wit, those Panamanian citizens who were killed, injured, or had their property destroyed as a consequence of the invasion. The applicable cases suggest, however, that the limitations of the Due Process Clause "come into play only when the Government activity in question violated some protected right of the *defendant*." *United States v. Payner*, 447 U.S. 727,

---

27. On the present record, the only incident which comes close to any kind of personal mistreatment is the above-mentioned event in which American troops blasted the Papal Nunciature in Panama City with loud rock-and-roll music in an apparent effort to drive Noriega out. While there are those who might consider continued exposure to such music an Eighth Amendment violation, it is the opinion of the Court that such action does not rise to the level of egregious misconduct sufficient to constitute a due process violation.

737 n. 9 (1980). Nothing in *Toscanino* or in the other decisions cited by Noriega undermines that principle or in any way suggests that the due process rights of third parties may be vicariously asserted, as those cases all involve physical violation of the defendant's person. * * *

B. *Violations of International Law*

In addition to his due process claim, Noriega asserts that the invasion of Panama violated international treaties and principles of customary international law. * * *

Initially, it is important to note that individuals lack standing to assert violations of international treaties in the absence of a protest from the offended government. Moreover, the *Ker–Frisbie* doctrine establishes that violations of international law alone do not deprive a court of jurisdiction over a defendant in the absence of specific treaty language to that effect. To defeat the Court's personal jurisdiction, Noriega must therefore establish that the treaty in question is self-executing in the sense that it confers individual rights upon citizens of the signatory nations, and that it by its terms expresses "a self-imposed limitation on the jurisdiction of the United States and hence on its courts." *United States v. Postal, supra.*

As a general principle of international law, individuals have no standing to challenge violations of international treaties in the absence of a protest by the sovereign involved. The rationale behind this rule is that treaties are "designed to protect the sovereign interests of nations, and it is up to the offended nations to determine whether a violation of sovereign interests occurred and requires redress." *United States v. Zabaneh,* 837 F.2d 1249, 1261 (5th Cir.1988). Consistent with that principle, a treaty will be construed as creating enforceable private rights only if it expressly or impliedly provides a private right of action.

No such rights are created in the sections of the U.N. Charter, O.A.S. Charter, and Hague Convention cited by Noriega. Rather, those provisions set forth broad general principles governing the conduct of nations toward each other and do not by their terms speak to individual or private rights. Thus, under the applicable international law, Noriega lacks standing to challenge violations of these treaties in the absence of a protest by the Panamanian government that the invasion of Panama and subsequent arrest of Noriega violated that country's territorial sovereignty.

C. *Supervisory Authority*

Having determined that Defendant Noriega fails to state a valid defense based on due process and international law principles, this Court's inquiry is nonetheless unfinished, as Defendant Noriega alternatively bases his motion on the inherent supervisory power of the Court. Noriega alleges that, by asserting jurisdiction over him, this Court would thereby sanction and become party to the Government's alleged misconduct in invading Panama and bringing Noriega to trial.

The supervisory power doctrine, while it may serve to vindicate a defendant's rights in an individual case, "is designed and invoked primarily to preserve the integrity of the judicial system" and "to prevent the federal courts from becoming accomplices" to government misconduct. Courts have consequently invoked the doctrine to suppress evidence and dismiss indictments in the face of severe or pervasive prosecutorial abuse. Thus, supervisory authority is in essence a judicial vehicle to deter conduct and correct injustices which are neither constitutional nor statutory violations, but which the court nonetheless finds repugnant to fairness and justice and is loathe to tolerate. As invocation of supervisory power to dismiss an indictment is a harsh remedy, it is reserved only for flagrant or repeated abuses which are outrageous or shock the conscience. It is certainly not to be applied as a remedy for mere technical illegalities or inadvertent violations, as "[t]hese powers should not permit the criminal to go free because the constable blundered." Thus, a higher threshold of government misconduct is imposed for invocation of the supervisory power than that required to state a constitutional or statutory violation. Noriega argues that his arrest and presence before the Court was secured as a result of deliberate and indiscriminate atrocities committed by the United States in the course of its invasion of Panama, and that such conduct "shocking to the conscience" calls for an exercise of the Court's inherent supervisory authority resulting in dismissal of the indictment.

In response, the Government argues that, even pursuant to the Court's inherent supervisory authority, Noriega may not seek dismissal of the indictment based on alleged violations of the rights of third parties—in this case, the rights of individual Panamanians or of the Panamanian state. The Government's position thus seems to be that a defendant's own constitutional or statutory rights must be violated in order to trigger the exercise of a court's supervisory power. This stance blurs the critical distinction between the use of supervisory authority on the one hand and the courts' rulings based on violations of constitutional and statutory law on the other. Since, as stated earlier, use of supervisory authority presents an independent body of law and does not depend on the existence of a constitutional or statutory violation, the fact that a defendant's own such rights have not been violated is not decisive. A contrary result would indeed render the doctrine meaningless, since dismissal of an indictment or other remedy would thus flow from the required constitutional or statutory violation and invocation of the supervisory authority would therefore be unnecessary. Contrary to the suggestion implicit in the Government's position, "supervisory powers cases ... are not constitutional cases in disguise." *United States v. Payner*, 447 U.S. at 749 (Marshall, J., dissenting).

The majority ruling in *Payner, supra*, cited by the Government, is distinguishable on its facts and thus does not constrict this Court's exercise of its supervisory authority in the instant case. In *Payner*, the Supreme Court held that the supervisory power doctrine could not be used to suppress evidence obtained in violation of a third party's Fourth

Amendment rights. Because evidence is excluded under the Fourth Amendment only where an unlawful search or seizure violates the defendant's own constitutional rights, the Court refused to allow a different result under the supervisory power doctrine as that approach would circumvent "the careful balance of interests embodied in the Fourth Amendment decisions of this Court." 447 U.S. at 733. The Court's concern was simply to prevent supervisory powers from being used as an 'end run' around settled Fourth Amendment law, but its decision explicitly did not "limit the traditional scope of the supervisory power in any way; nor ... render that power 'superfluous.'" 447 U.S. at 735, n. 8. Since the illegal search at issue in *Payner* did not rise to the level of pervasive or shocking misconduct imposed under the doctrine of supervisory authority, the Court's narrow holding can hardly be construed to render that doctrine meaningless and the judicial system helpless in the face of inhumane conduct shocking to the conscience merely because technical standing requirements are not met. If, for example, we were confronted with a pure law enforcement effort in which government agents deliberately killed and tortured individuals for the sole purpose of discovering a fugitive's whereabouts in order to secure his arrest, the Court would face a situation which properly calls for invocation of its supervisory powers. It would also call to mind Justice Brandeis' eloquent dissent in *Olmstead v. United States*, 277 U.S. 438, 485 (1928):

> Decency, security, and liberty alike demand that government officials shall be subjected to the same rules of conduct that are commands to the citizen. In a government of laws, existence of the government will be imperilled if its fails to observe the law scrupulously. Our government is the potent, the omnipresent teacher. For good or for ill, it teaches the whole people by its example. Crime is contagious. If the government becomes a lawbreaker, it breeds contempt for law; it invites every man to become a law unto himself; it invites anarchy. To declare that in the administration of the criminal law the end justifies the means—to declare that the government may commit crimes in order to secure the conviction of a private criminal—would bring terrible retribution. Against that pernicious doctrine this Court should resolutely set its face.

This Court may someday have occasion to apply Justice Brandeis' wise words, but this is not that day, for we are confronted not with the above hypothetical but rather a military war in which innocent lives were unfortunately lost in the pursuit of foreign policy objectives. Although the motives behind the military action are open to speculation, the stated goals of the invasion were to protect American lives, support democracy, preserve the Panama Canal Treaties, and bring Noriega to the United States to stand trial for narcotics offenses. Because the President ordered Noriega arrested "in the course of carrying out the military operations in Panama," the capture of Noriega was incident to the broader conduct of foreign policy. While the Government's asserted rationales for the invasion are not beyond challenge and need not be blindly accepted by this Court, counsel for Noriega have offered no evidence to the contrary and the evidence they have offered in fact bolsters the conclusion that the invasion was primarily an exercise in foreign policy.

That foreign policy objectives rather than just law enforcement goals are implicated radically changes the Court's consideration of the government conduct complained of and, consequently, its willingness to exercise supervisory power. For the question then posed is whether a court may, under the guise of its supervisory authority, condemn armed conflict as "shocking to the conscience." Any such declaration not only runs squarely into the political question doctrine, which precludes courts from resolving issues more properly committed to the political branches, but would indeed constitute unprecedented judicial interference in the conduct of foreign policy.

Although the judiciary clause of the Constitution does not limit the ability of federal courts to adjudicate issues merely because they present political questions, judges have nevertheless defined a category of executive and legislative branch actions as beyond the scope of judicial inquiry ever since the Supreme Court first claimed the power of judicial review in *Marbury v. Madison*, 5 U.S. (1 Cranch) 137, 165–66 (1803). The nonjusticiability of political questions is therefore not so much a product of constitutional doctrine but primarily a recognition of the separation of powers and the system of checks and balances provided for in the Constitution. *Baker v. Carr*, 369 U.S. 186, 210 (1962).

* * *

Notes

1. The *Noriega* saga continued to play throughout the 1990's.[x] In *United States v. Noriega*, 764 F.Supp. 1480 (S.D. Fla. 1991), Noriega moved to dismiss his indictment based on the Government's interference with his Sixth Amendment right to counsel. While awaiting his trial in prison, Noriega had been provided with a telephone that bore a notice that all conversations, except properly placed calls to an attorney, would be monitored. After 9 months of calls, the Government subpoenaed the taped conversations. One of the Government's witnesses listened to 22 of these tapes, including some in which Noriega discussed potential government witnesses with his attorney. All of this became public when CNN, after obtaining the tapes from an unknown source, approached Noriega's lead attorney and played portions of the tapes.[y] Despite these problems, the judge held that there had been no Sixth Amendment violation because the intrusion had been unintentional, had provided no benefit to the prosecution, and had incurred no harm to Noriega's defense. *Id.* at 1489.

x. In addition to the district court cases mentioned in the note, Noriega's conviction was upheld on appeal. *See* United States v. Noriega, 117 F.3d 1206 (11th Cir. 1997).

y. *See also* United States v. Cable News Network, Inc., 865 F.Supp. 1549 (S.D. Fla. 1994) (CNN held guilty of criminal contempt after repeatedly broadcasting Noriega's conversation with his attorney following a court-ordered injunction).

Subsequently, after being convicted, Noriega challenged the right of the court to sentence him because of his standing as a prisoner of war under the Geneva Convention III. *See United States v. Noriega*, 808 F.Supp. 791 (S.D. Fla. 1992). The court held that although Noriega was a prisoner of war and entitled to the full range of rights under the treaty, he could serve his sentence in a civilian prison as long as these benefits were honored. *Id.* at 803. After reaching its decision, the court admonished:

> Whether or not those rights can be fully provided in a maximum security penitentiary setting is open to serious question. For the time being, however, that question must be answered by those who will determine Defendant's place and type of confinement. In this determination, those charged with that responsibility must keep in mind the importance to our own troops of faithful and, indeed, liberal adherence to the mandates of Geneva III. Regardless of how the government views the Defendant as a person, the implications of a failure to adhere to the Convention are too great to justify departures.

Id.

Although Noriega lost nearly every court decision, after nearly 10 years in confinement, he finally did achieve a small victory. In *United States v. Noriega*, 40 F. Supp. 2d 1378 (S.D. Fla. 1999), the court held that Noriega's 40 year sentence should be reduced to 30 years. The court cited two factors that influenced its decision: the considerable disparity between Noriega's sentence and the sentences actually served by his co-conspirators, and the fact that Noriega was being held, for security reasons, essentially in solitary confinement. *Id.* at 1380.

2. Although General Noriega did not challenge the validity of the *Ker-Frisbie* doctrine, the Supreme Court subsequently reexamined its validity. The case arose out of the Attorney General's reversal of the government's traditional policy regarding extraterritorial arrests carried out or ordered by United States law enforcement agencies. The Attorney General concluded that United States agents could arrest suspects abroad even if there was a valid extradition treaty between the United States and the country in question.

The issue came before the Supreme Court in the prosecution of Dr. Alvarez–Machain, a citizen of Mexico who was forcibly kidnapped from his home and flown to Texas, where he was arrested for his participation in the kidnapping and murder of DEA Special Agent Enrique Camerena–Salazar and his pilot. Dr. Alvarez–Machain was suspected of prolonging Agent Camerena's life while others tortured him. Frustrated by the perceived lack of interest in prosecuting the case on the part of Mexican officials, the DEA paid Mexican nationals to kidnap Dr. Alvarez–Machain and bring him to the United States. He was arrested by the DEA on arrival in the United States. The lower courts rejected Alvarez–Machain's motion to dismiss based upon outrageous government conduct, but held that the district court lacked jurisdiction to try him because the conduct of the United States violated the extradition treaty.

In a 6 to 3 decision, *United States v. Alvarez–Machain*, 504 U.S. 655 (1992), the Supreme Court upheld the *Ker-Frisbie* doctrine and rejected the claim that the extradition treaty stripped the courts of jurisdiction. Writing for the majority, the Chief Justice held that the extradition treaty was merely an option, not the sole means by which a suspect could be brought into the United States. Since there was no treaty violation, *Ker-Frisbie* governed. Under those circumstances, even if the abduction of Dr. Alvarez–Machain was shocking or in violation of general principles of international law, the decision whether to hold him for trial or return him to Mexico was a matter for the executive branch, not the courts.

Justice Stevens dissented, calling the majority's decision "monstrous." 504 U.S. at 670. He argued that the extradition treaty was the exclusive mechanism, and that the abduction violated the treaty, thus depriving the courts of jurisdiction.

Dr. Alvarez–Machain returned to the Supreme Court. After being acquitted of murder, he brought suit under the Alien Tort Statute (ATS) and the Federal Tort Claims Act (FTCA) seeking damages against the United States, DEA agents, former Mexican policemen, and Mexican civilians, alleging that his arrest violated his civil rights. The Supreme Court held that Alvarez–Machain was not entitled to a remedy under either statute. Writing for the majority, Justice Souter found that, because the FTCA claim was based on harm that occurred in Mexico, it fell within the "foreign country" exception to waiver of government immunity, regardless of whether the tortious acts or omissions leading to the injury occurred in the United States. Although the jurisdictional scope of the ATS does allow a cause of action for some violations of norms of customary international law, the Court held that a brief illegal detention prior to transfer to legal custody did not amount to such a violation. *Sosa v. Alvarez–Machain*, 542 U.S. 692 (2004).

3.   Are the constitutional limits on domestic police investigations equally applicable when governmental investigators go abroad? The Supreme Court considered this question most recently in *United States v. Verdugo–Urquidez*, 494 U.S. 259 (1990). The defendant was a Mexican citizen. The DEA believed that the defendant was the leader of an organization that smuggled narcotics into the United States, and that he had been involved in the murder of DEA agent Camerena–Salazar. A warrant was issued in the United States for defendant's arrest, and after discussion with federal officials, Mexican authorities apprehended the defendant in that country and transported him to the United States. DEA agents, working with Mexican officials, then searched his Mexican residence and seized incriminating documents. The district court granted defendant's motion to suppress this evidence on the ground that the warrantless search violated the Fourth Amendment, and a divided panel of the court of appeals affirmed.

The Supreme Court reversed, holding that the Fourth Amendment does not apply to a search and seizure of property located in a foreign country when that property is owned by a citizen of that country who has no voluntary attachment to the United States. Writing for the majority, the Chief Justice concluded that the fourth amendment phrase "the people"—in contrast with the words "person" and "accused" used in the Fifth and Sixth amendments—was a term of art referring to persons who are part of the national community or who have developed a sufficient connection to be considered a part of that community. Moreover, the history of the Fourth

Amendment demonstrates that it was intended to protect the people of the United States against the action of their own government, and not to restrain the government's actions against aliens outside its borders. Any restrictions on searches and seizures incident to American action abroad must therefore be imposed by the political branches through diplomatic understandings, treaties, or legislation. Although Justice Kennedy was one of the five members of the Court who joined the majority opinion, he also filed a concurring opinion making the more limited point that the Fourth Amendment warrant clause should not apply in Mexico as it does in this country. *See* 494 U.S. at 278. Justice Stevens concurred in the judgment. He concluded that the warrant clause of the Fourth Amendment does not apply to searches of noncitizens' homes in foreign jurisdictions, and that the search in question, with the approval and cooperation of Mexican authorities, was not unreasonable under the Fourth Amendment. *See id.* at 279. Justice Brennan and Justice Blackmun dissented.

Chapter 10

CURRENCY REPORTING OFFENSES AND MONEY LAUNDERING

INTRODUCTION

The laws requiring the reporting of large cash transactions and prohibiting money laundering are of relatively recent vintage. In 1970 Congress enacted the first statute, codified at 31 U.S.C. §§ 5311–5322, requiring financial institutions to report cash transactions over $10,000 to the government, and making failure to report a crime. Parallel provisions required persons transporting more than $5,000[a] in cash into or out of the United States to file a report. In the mid 1980's Congress created three new crimes to supplement this regulatory framework: structuring a financial transaction to avoid the reporting laws, 31 U.S.C. § 5324, and two money laundering offenses, 18 U.S.C. §§ 1956–57. Congress also enacted a provision codified as 26 U.S.C. § 6050I requiring individuals engaged in trade or business to report the receipt of cash payments in excess of $10,000. In 1992 Congress enacted a provision making it a federal offense to conduct, manage, or own an illegal money transmitting business transferring funds by wire, check, facsimile, or courier. 18 U.S.C. § 1960.

In 2001, Congress passed Title III of the USA PATRIOT Act, which was designed to improve the government's anti-money laundering efforts by both strengthening the reporting requirements and revising the money laundering offenses. Primary changes made by Title III include:

> Expanding the list of predicate crimes for money laundering offenses, which now include foreign crimes, operation of an illegal money remission business, and bulk cash smuggling;

> Requiring financial institutions to take further precautions when dealing with foreign countries or institutions considered to be of primary money laundering concern;

---

a. This amount was raised to $10,000 by an amendment contained in the Compre- hensive Crime Control Act of 1984.

Expanding the procedural tools that can be used in the prosecution of money laundering crimes, particularly by amending the federal government's authority for asset forfeiture by allowing the civil forfeiture of any person, entity, or property engaged in terrorism.

The penalties for the money laundering and currency reporting offenses are substantial, ranging from 5 years for a single willful currency reporting violation to 20 years for money laundering under 18 U.S.C. § 1956. Fines up to $500,000 or twice the value of the property in question are also authorized for the most serious offenses, and criminal forfeiture is a mandatory part of every criminal sentence under these provisions.

These statutes are attempts to deal with the phenomenon of money laundering. What is money laundering and why is Congress interested? Professor Sarah Welling explains:

Money laundering begins with dirty money. Money can get dirty in two ways. One way is through tax evasion; people make money legally, but they make more than they report to the government. Money also gets dirty through illegal generation. Common techniques include drug sales, gambling, and bribery. Once money is dirty, it must be converted into an apparently legitimate form, or "laundered" before it can be invested or spent. ' "Money laundering' is the process by which one conceals the existence, illegal source, or illegal application of income, and then disguises that income to make it appear legitimate.' "

Laundering has several goals. One is to hide or sanitize the property so the tax collector does not get it. This aspect of the laundering process has been chronicled in detail. Another goal is to convert the cash into a physically manageable and inconspicuous form. That form often is a postal money order or cashier's check, but it also could be gold, stamps, or any form of property. The importance of converting cash into a manageable physical form is illustrated by the case of Anthony Castelbuono. Castelbuono somewhat conspicuously brought $1,187,450 in small bills to a casino. The cash had an estimated volume of 5.75 cubic feet and weighed 280 pounds.

Whatever its goal, money laundering is harmful. Underground money absorbs no portion of the tax burden. More importantly, laundering is harmful because it allows the underlying criminal activity to thrive. Drug sales, gambling, or other crimes that generate cash are pointless if the cash cannot be invested or spent. Without laundering, the risk/reward ratio for the underlying crime is unattractive. Thus, success of the criminal venture depends on laundering. Efficient laundering renders the underlying crime lucrative, and therefore perpetuates it.

Money laundering has become a major concern recently because of the thriving drug trade. Laundering is required only if large amounts of cash are involved, because smaller amounts of dirty cash can be absorbed inconspicuously into a criminal's lifestyle. Huge amounts of cash require attention to disposal, and the drug trade currently generates such huge amounts. For example, in August 1988, five-thousand pounds of cocaine were seized in New York; the estimated street value was $355 million. Had this cocaine reached the streets, that $355 million would exist originally as cash. To put that cash to its best use, it would have to be laundered.

Aside from combating these measurable harms, putting a halt to money laundering also is emotionally appealing. The existence of laundering schemes indicates that some people get rich unfairly because they pay no taxes. Furthermore, the people who need laundering schemes often get rich because they sell drugs in the United States. Drug money laundering is especially unsavory on an intuitive level, considering the source of the cash that drives it.

Sarah N. Welling, *Smurfs, Money Laundering, and the Federal Criminal Law: The Crime of Structuring Transactions*, 41 FLA. L. REV. 287, 290–92 (1989).

What is the volume of money being laundered? The International Monetary Fund estimates that money laundering amounts to between 2 to 5 percent of the global gross domestic product, or roughly $590 billion to $1.5 trillion per year. In 1999 it was estimated that drug trafficking alone produces approximately $48 billion in profits per year to be laundered in the U.S. The dollars generated by drugs weigh considerably more than the drugs themselves, and the disposal of such a large volume of cash presents drug traffickers with significant practical problems. The wholesale sale of an imported kilogram (2.2 pounds) of heroin for $200,000 would generate approximately 50 pounds of $10 bills, or 5 pounds of $100 bills. The retail sale of the same amount of heroin would generate up to $1 million in cash, which would weigh up to 50 pounds. The retail sale of a kilogram of cocaine broken down into crack—which sells for between $5 and $10 on the street—could generate hundreds of pounds of cash.

Although drug traffickers head the list of those who need to dispose of large sums of illegally obtained currency, many other individuals also seek to launder money. These include persons who are evading taxes and various white collar criminals who have received bribes, kickbacks, and illegal campaign contributions. Thus the currency reporting and money laundering laws perform a crucial supporting role in drug enforcement and provide significant aid in the enforcement of the tax laws and the suppression of other criminal activity.

Money laundering enforcement has traditionally been concerned with eliminating criminals' ability to realize a usable profit, but the terrorist attacks of September 11, 2001 and the subsequent emphasis on tracking terrorist financing have led to a paradigm shift in the focus of anti-money laundering efforts. Now, the primary targets are not only those who launder "dirty" money to make a profit, but also those who funnel money—often from legitimate sources—into the hands of those carrying out terrorist objectives. Whereas money laundering investigations are initiated to achieve prosecutions and forfeitures, the ultimate goal of terrorist financing investigations is to stop the flow of funds to terrorists regardless of whether a prosecution is made.

Terrorist financing utilizes many of the same methods as traditional money laundering, such as shell companies and numbered bank accounts, and many of the executive, legislative, and regulatory changes that have been made since 9/11 have merged the counter-terrorism financing and anti-money laundering enforcement measures. Despite the similarities, the detection of terrorist financing presents its own unique challenges. First, terrorists usually do not need to launder substantial sums of money. For example, the 9/11 Commission estimated that the terrorists who carried out the attacks of September 11 required only $400,000–500,000 to plan and conduct their attacks. Second, terrorists often utilize underground banking systems that are difficult to detect. Third, the funds used to support terrorists are often included with legitimate sources of funding for charitable organizations and legitimate businesses. Finally, most of the transactions in the financing of terrorists do not involve the placement of cash, which is the easiest point of detection in money laundering. For further discussion of anti-terrorism enforcement, see chapter 12.

Forfeiture is an important aspect of the enforcement of the currency reporting and money laundering laws. With an exception for property held by banks and other financial institutions, 18 U.S.C. § 982(a) provides that the sentence of any person convicted under the currency reporting or bank secrecy laws "shall order that the person forfeit to the United States any property, real or personal, involved in such offense or any property traceable to such property." A parallel provision, 18 U.S.C. § 981(a), provides for civil forfeiture of property "involved in" the offenses in question. The availability of forfeiture—as well as stiff sentences of imprisonment—gives prosecutors a powerful incentive to charge money laundering in addition to or instead of other offenses. For a discussion of forfeiture, see Chapter 19.

Section A considers the regulatory offenses of failing to file a currency transaction report and structuring a financial transaction to avoid the currency reporting laws. Section B addresses the money laundering offenses, 18 U.S.C. §§ 1956 and 1957.

A. CURRENCY REPORTING OFFENSES

1. AN OVERVIEW OF THE LEGISLATIVE RESPONSE

The currency reporting legislation adopted in 1970 reflected a new approach. In contrast to the preceding chapters, which deal with harmful conduct, the currency reporting laws create a kind of "regulatory offense." Information is sought that is intended to be used in criminal enforcement, but the information does *not necessarily* relate to criminal activity. Congress adopted a regulatory scheme requiring reports of currency transactions to be filed and records to be kept which may be useful in criminal, tax, and regulatory investigations. The House report accompanying the original legislation stated:

> Criminals deal in money—cash or its equivalent. The deposit and withdrawal of large amounts of currency or its equivalent ... under unusual circumstances may betray a criminal activity. The money in many of these transactions may represent anything from the proceeds of a lottery racket to money for the bribery of public officials.

H.R. Rep. No. 875, 91st Cong. 2d Sess., reprinted in 1970 U.S. Code Cong. & Ad. News 4394, 4396. The 1970 legislation was part of a statute popularly known as the Bank Secrecy Act. The popular name of the act refers to other provisions dealing with foreign jurisdictions with bank secrecy laws. Cases and commentators often use the designation Bank Secrecy Act or BSA to refer to the currency reporting laws.

It should be emphasized that it is not criminal to deal in large amounts of money. It is not a crime to deposit cash in excess of $10,000 in a bank, or to transport more than $10,000 in cash into or outside of the country. However, the Bank Secrecy Act does require that reports must be filed: (1) for specified currency transactions with banks or other financial institutions (CTRs), and (2) in connection with transportation of moneys in excess of the specified amount across the international border (CMIRs). Criminal or civil penalties can be imposed for a failure to make such reports or for making them falsely.

Financial institutions are not the only ones required to file currency reports on domestic cash transactions. In 1984 Congress added a broad new currency reporting requirement: all persons are required to report the receipt of $10,000 in cash "in 1 transaction (or 2 or more related transactions)" in the course of one's trade or business. 26 U.S.C. § 6050I(a). Subsection (b) of that section provides that the report is to contain the name, address and tax identification number of the person from whom the cash was received, the amount of the cash, and the date and nature of the transaction. Section 6050I is found in the Internal Revenue Code, and its legislative history implies that this law has a tax revenue purpose—to identify taxpayers with large cash incomes and reduce the amount of revenue lost through the underreporting of income. There is little doubt, however, that the information may also be useful in criminal investigations. The USA PATRIOT Act integrated this requirement with other currency reporting provisions, incorporating it in 31 U.S.C. § 5331.[b] Dual reporting of this information will now be made to both the IRS and the Treasury Department's Financial Crimes Enforcement Network (FinCEN).

---

b. Because § 6050I originated as part of the tax code, prior to the adoption of the PATRIOT Act all violations were prosecuted under the tax code. The application of § 6050I to attorneys who receive cash fees from clients generated substantial controversy and left the circuits divided on the proper analysis. *Compare* Lefcourt v. United States, 125 F.3d 79 (2d Cir. 1997) (upholding penalty for law firm's failure to disclose client's name on Form 8300), *and* United States v. Goldberger & Dubin, 935 F.2d 501 (2d Cir. 1991) (§ 6050I does not violate Sixth Amendment right to counsel or attorney client privilege, and disclosure of name of client who made cash payments

With the addition of § 6050I the regulatory framework required the reporting of every major category of currency transaction: a deposit or withdrawal from a financial institution (§ 5313), the purchase of goods or services from a business or individual (§ 6050I), a transaction involving cash in or out of a casino, and the movement of currency into or out of the United States (§ 5316), plus any suspicious activity or transaction.

Compliance with these regulations generates a staggering number of reports. In 2003, financial institutions filed approximately 12.5 million CTRs under 31 U.S.C. §§ 5311–5322, and an additional 451,457 casino CTRs (IRS form 8362) were filed. The number of filings of IRS Form 8300s, though, which are filed pursuant to section 6050I, remained relatively low; only 129,816 were filed in 2003.[c] Do the benefits of the current reporting system outweigh its costs? For an article estimating that it costs a bank from $3 to $15 to file each CTR (depending on the technology used) and concluding that CTRs seldom lead to criminal prosecutions, see John J. Byrne, *The Bank Secrecy Act: Do Reporting Requirements Really Assist the Government?*, 44 ALA. L. REV. 801 (1993).

2. THE LIABILITY OF A FINANCIAL INSTITUTION FOR FAILURE TO FILE CURRENCY TRANSACTION REPORTS

The willful failure to file a financial report required under 31 U.S.C. §§ 5313[d] or 5316[e] is a felony under 31 U.S.C. § 5322. Financial institutions and their employees are the direct targets of § 5322 because the currency reporting statutes and regulations impose the reporting duty upon those institutions, and not upon their customers.

a. Establishing "Willfulness"

How can a bank's willfulness be established? The leading case on this question is *United States v. Bank of New England*, 821 F.2d 844 (1st

---

would not ordinarily be disclosure of privileged information); *with* United States v. Gertner, 873 F.Supp. 729 (D. Mass. 1995) (holding that client identifying information is protected by attorney client privilege and quashing summons seeking name of client attorneys omitted from Form 8300), *aff'd other grounds*, 65 F.3d 963 (1st Cir. 1995), *and* Formal Opinion 89–1, Ethics Advisory Committee of the National Association of Criminal Defense Attorneys, THE CHAMPION, 45 (Jan.–Feb. 1990) (absent informed consent, attorney should assert that identity of client is confidential on Form 8300 and related IRS enquiries). For a discussion of the ethical issues, see Eugene R. Gaetke & Sarah N. Welling, *Money Laundering and Lawyers*, 43 SYRACUSE L. REV. 1165 (1993), and Ellen S. Podgor, *Form 8300: The Demise of Law as a Profession*, 5 GEO. J. L. ETHICS 485 (1992). Because the enforcement of § 6050I under the tax code raises issues not common to the other currency reporting and money laundering prosecutions, we have not treated § 6050I in detail.

c. These figures were reported by the IRS in *FY2004 Money Laundering Tax Fraud Alert*. No figures were provided for CMIRS filed by persons entering or leaving the U.S. In 1991, more than 200,000 CMIRs were filed.

d. Section 5313(a) requires a domestic financial institution to report transactions for the payment, receipt or transfer of coins or currency as provided by the regulations prescribed by the Secretary of the Treasury. The text of § 5313(a) is reprinted in the Appendix, *infra* at 948.

e. Section 5316(a) requires a person who is about to or has transported monetary instruments of more than $10,000 at one time into or out of the United States to file a report. The text of § 5316(a) is reprinted in the Appendix, *infra* at 948–49.

Cir. 1987), in which the court adopted a collective knowledge standard. The Bank argued on appeal that the evidence did not show willfulness, but only a poor communications network that prevented the bank from consolidating the information held by various employees that would have revealed an obligation to file CTRs. The court rejected that argument, approving an instruction that held the bank responsible for the " 'sum of the knowledge of all of the employees,' " i.e., " 'the totality of what all of the employees know within the scope of their employment.' " *Id.* at 855. The court explained:

> A collective knowledge instruction is entirely appropriate in the context of corporate criminal liability. The acts of a corporation are, after all, simply the acts of all of its employees operating within the scope of their employment. The law on corporate criminal liability reflects this. Similarly, the knowledge obtained by corporate employees acting within the scope of their employment is imputed to the corporation. Corporations compartmentalize knowledge, subdividing the elements of specific duties and operations into smaller components. The aggregate of those components constitutes the corporation's knowledge of a particular operation. It is irrelevant whether employees administering one component of an operation know the specific activities of employees administering another aspect of the operation:
>
> > [A] corporation cannot plead innocence by asserting that the information obtained by several employees was not acquired by any one individual who then would have comprehended its full import. Rather the corporation is considered to have acquired the collective knowledge of its employees and is held responsible for their failure to act accordingly.
>
> Since the Bank had the compartmentalized structure common to all large corporations, the court's collective knowledge instruction was not only proper but necessary.

Id. at 856.

How far does the collective knowledge standard of *Bank of New England* go? Would there be a criminal violation if a bank could learn of its duty to report only by pooling information known to five or six employees who work in branches in different parts of the same city? In different cities? What if the customer deliberately sought to keep the bank in the dark as to the whole picture, and succeeds in doing so?

What are the policy implications of the *Bank of New England* standard? John Villa sees a risk that the government will prosecute morally neutral conduct and erode the industry's respect for the processes of administering justice. "If financial institutions perceive that the government is arbitrarily prosecuting banks for violating statutes which the banks are attempting to obey, then some banks will for the first time divert effort from attempting to obey the law to attempting to escape detection of the inevitable violations." John K. Villa, *A Critical View of Bank Secrecy Act Enforcement and the Money Laundering Statutes*, 37

CATH. U. L. REV. 487, 505–506 (1988). In Villa's view the short term gains the government might achieve from the use of the collective knowledge doctrine would be outweighed by the long run damage the use of this doctrine would do to attitudes toward the law.

The United States Attorneys Manual requires Criminal Division approval before a financial institution can be indicted for money laundering under 18 U.S.C. §§ 1956 & 1957, though it does not state the criteria that will determine whether a prosecution will be approved. USAM ¶ 9–105.300(4) (July 2005). Should similar approval be required in currency reporting prosecutions? If so, should any criteria be stated? Sections 1956 and 1957 are discussed in Section B, *infra*.

b. *The Relevance of Corporate Policies Requiring Reporting*

Banks may have criminal liability for failure to file CTRs even in cases where an employee acted without specific authority, or in violation of a specific bank policy. For example, in *United States v. Beusch*, 596 F.2d 871 (9th Cir. 1979), the court of appeals held that the district court did not err in instructing the jury that the corporation could be responsible for its agent's failure to file currency reports even if the agent's actions were contrary to the corporation's policies or instructions. The court explained that the acts of an agent may be imputed to the principal if it is the agent's purpose to benefit the principal and the agent's acts fall within the scope of his employment. The court recognized that the existence of corporate policies is relevant to a determination whether an agent acted to benefit the corporation, but it held that merely stating or publishing policies or instructions without diligent enforcement would not be sufficient to demonstrate that the agent did not act to benefit the corporation, or acted outside the scope of his employment. *Cf.* Model Penal Code § 2.07(c), which provides that a corporation may be convicted of the commission of an offense if—

> the commission of the offense was authorized, requested, commanded, performed, or recklessly tolerated by the board of directors or by a high managerial agent acting in behalf of the corporation within the scope of his employment.

Should liability under the currency reporting laws be limited to instances where the actor was a "high managerial agent" acting with within the scope of her employment and on behalf of the corporation? Or should it be sufficient simply to show that a lower level corporate agent, such as a teller, was acting within the scope of her employment? For a general discussion of the principles of corporate criminal liability, see 1 SARAH N. WELLING ET AL., FEDERAL CRIMINAL LAW AND RELATED ACTIONS: CRIMES, FORFEITURE, THE FALSE CLAIMS ACT AND RICO § 5.2 et seq. (1998). The Justice Department has promulgated general guidelines on the prosecution of corporations, which emphasize factors such as the risk of harm to the public and the pervasiveness of the conduct in question, and state that "it may not be appropriate to impose liability upon a corporation, particularly one with a compliance program in place, under a strict respondeat superior theory for the single isolated act of a rogue employee." Justice Department Guidance on Prosecution of Corporations (June 16, 1999), *reprinted at* 66 CRIM. L. REP. 189, 191 (1999).

c. SARs and "Know Your Customer" Reporting Requirements

Beginning in 1996 banks were required to file a new form, the SAR (suspicious activity report).[f] This form replaced the old criminal referral form as well as a question on the CTRs that asked whether the transaction was "suspicious." In contrast to the CTRs, which require the financial institutions to report all transactions above a certain dollar threshold, the SAR requires financial institution to identify and then report particular "suspicious" transactions to authorities, effectively conscripting these institutions into the government's investigative team. The SAR regulations raise a number of policy issues. First, is the SAR requirement consistent with the general rule that Americans have no duty to report crimes? A closely related question is whether it's a good idea to require financial institutions to serve as informants against their customers. Indeed, regulators have begun to see that the financial institutions may respond to these requirements in ways that do more harm than good. Despite these concerns, in 2001 Congress imposed additional requirements, referred to colloquially as "know your customer" regulations.

The SAR filing requirements have traditionally been a regulatory matter, but the added focus on terrorist financing since 9/11 has put banks under an increasing threat of criminal investigations for SAR filing failures. In January 2005, Riggs Bank in Washington, D.C. was prosecuted for failing to report highly suspicious cash transactions in the accounts of the Saudi Arabian embassy and foreign dictators. It agreed to pay a $16 million dollar fine and plead guilty to one count of failing to report suspicious activity. While Riggs came under suspicion for its dealings in the exotic banking business, in 2004 AmSouth Bank, a more traditional bank, was investigated for failing to detect signs that two of its customers were using AmSouth accounts as part of a scheme that defrauded more than 60 investors of millions of dollars. AmSouth was ultimately forced to enter into a deferred prosecution agreement, which required it to pay a $40 million civil forfeiture, acknowledge responsibility, cooperate with the investigation, and demonstrate future compliance. If AmSouth meets these obligations, the government agreed it will dismiss the allegations with prejudice after 12 months.

The enhanced scrutiny and increased risks produced two institutional responses that regulators see as counterproductive: financial institutions are now filing large numbers of unnecessary SARs, and they have begun to terminate accounts they regard as risky, particularly those of money services businesses. SAR filings for 2005 are now running 37%

---

f. For a description of the SAR filing process and the legal issues it raises, see Matthew R. Hall, Note, *An Emerging Duty* *to Report Criminal Conduct: Banks, Money Laundering, and the Suspicious Activity Report*, 84 KY. L.J. 643 (1995–96).

over filings in 2004, and it appears that financial institutions are filing even in cases where the account activity does not meet threshold requirements for reporting. Such defensive SAR filings are problematic for two reasons: they dilute the value of information being reported, and they implicate privacy concerns. Terminating the accounts of money services businesses—such as check cashing and money order businesses—is also problematic because it may drive them out of the formal banking sector, forcing them underground and making detection of money laundering and terrorist financing through these channels more difficult. In June 2005 federal regulators responded to these developments by publishing new anti-money laundering guidelines intended to lead to more consistent and predictable application of BSA requirements, and to a reduction in defensive SAR filings. The new guidelines focus on a bank's SAR decision-making process rather than individual SAR decisions.

The USA PATRIOT Act of 2001 directed the Secretary of Treasury to promulgate "know your customer" regulations requiring financial institutions to implement reasonable procedures for verifying the identify of persons opening an account, maintaining records of the information used to verify the person's identity, and determining whether the person appears on any lists of known or suspected terrorists or terrorist organizations provided to the financial institution by any government agency. 31 U.S.C. § 5318(I) (2003). This may not be the end of the matter, and regulators may want to impose more demanding requirements. A few years earlier the Federal Reserve Board and the FDIC published and then withdrew proposed regulations requiring financial institutions to be even more proactive. Those proposed regulations— which generated a storm of protest from Congress and the general public—were intended to uncover money laundering by drug dealers and other criminals by requiring financial institutions to determine their customers' fund sources, monitor their transactions, and report any suspicious activity. It remains to be seen whether these types of regulations will be reconsidered in the changed post–9/11 political landscape.

d. Civil and Regulatory Mechanisms to Ensure Reporting

Criminal prosecutions are not the only mechanism provided by Congress to ensure that financial institutions comply with the currency reporting requirements. The Treasury Department has imposed large civil fines in some cases. In response to a Freedom of Information request the government disclosed that between 1985 and 1997 Treasury had imposed 100 penalties totaling more than $30 million; the average penalty was $299,115 and the largest was $4.75 million, imposed on Bank of America in 1986. *Seven Newly Disclosed BSA Penalties Bring Total Over 100 Mark*, 8 MONEY LAUNDERING ALERT no. 8, p.6 (May 1997). The number of penalties had dropped in the two years prior to this report, and more than 100 penalty referrals were still pending, some dating back to 1987. *Id.*

Regulators also have other options, which may be used in tandem with criminal prosecutions: the termination of the charters, insurance, and offices of financial institutions convicted of money laundering, i.e., violations of 31 U.S.C. § 5322 or 18 U.S.C. §§ 1956 and 1957. *See* 12 U.S.C. § 93 (revoking charter of federal depositary institution), 12 U.S.C. § 1464 (forfeiting franchise of federal savings association), 12 U.S.C. § 1752 et seq. (forfeiting franchise of credit union), 12 U.S.C. § 1818(w) (terminating federal deposit insurance of state banks and savings associations). In addition, the 1992 legislation also provides that if a party affiliated with a financial institution is convicted of money laundering, that party, and any officers or directors who had knowledge of such violations, may be removed from office. 12 U.S.C. § 1818(e)(2).

These new provisions raise the general question when it's most effective to use criminal penalties and when it's preferable to use civil fines or other regulatory measures (including harsh measures such as the termination of a financial institution's charter—the corporate "death penalty"). Note that the existence of these alternative measures will also require coordination between federal prosecutors and regulators in the Treasury Department.

3. LIABILITY OF BANK CUSTOMERS IN CONNECTION WITH CURRENCY REPORTING REGULATIONS: THE NEW OFFENSE OF STRUCTURING

On its face the original legislative scheme had two key limitations: it imposed a duty solely on financial institutions (and not upon their customers), and the duty was triggered only by cash transactions exceeding $5,000 (later raised to $10,000). These limitations encouraged customers who did not want their transactions reported to avoid the reporting threshold. Customers manipulated many different variables, using different banks, different branches of the same bank, different teller stations at the same branch, different accounts, and transactions at different times. In many instances one or more third parties were employed to conduct these transactions on behalf of the owner of the currency. The numerous low level operatives who scurried from bank to bank became know as "smurfs," after the little blue cartoon characters.

In the first instance the Justice Department took the position that the banks had a duty to aggregate the transactions, and the customers could be prosecuted as accomplices if they sought to prevent the filing of CTRs on the basis of the aggregated transactions. These theories met with mixed reactions in the lower courts, where the circuits were split on both issues. Congress and the Secretary of the Treasury responded with statutory and regulatory amendments.

The regulatory amendments clarified the reporting duty of the banks, requiring aggregation. 31 C.F.R. § 103.22(c)(1) (2005) provides that "[a] financial institution includes all of its domestic branch offices * * * for the purpose of this paragraph's reporting requirements." 31 C.F.R. § 103.22(c)(2) (2005) further provides that "[m]ultiple currency transactions shall be treated as a single transaction if the financial institution has knowledge that they are by or on behalf of any person and result in either cash in or cash out totaling more than $10,000 during any one business day."

Congress also created a new offense of "structuring" to evade the currency reporting laws. Although the original statute covered only domestic currency transactions, a 1992 amendment broadened its scope to apply to structuring to avoid reporting on international monetary exchanges as well.[g] The statute was then amended by the USA PATRI-OT Act to impose stricter prohibitions on evading reporting requirements for transactions involving financial institutions.

§ 5324. Structuring transactions to evade reporting requirement prohibited

(a) Domestic coin and currency transactions involving financial institutions.—No person shall, for the purpose of evading the reporting requirements of section 5313(a) or 5325 or any regulation prescribed under any such section, the reporting or record keeping requirements imposed by any order issued under section 5326, or the record keeping requirements imposed by any regulation prescribed under section 21 of the Federal Deposit Insurance Act or section 123 of Public Law 91–508—

(1) cause or attempt to cause a domestic financial institution to fail to file a report required under section 5313(a) or 5325 or any regulation prescribed under any such section, to file a report or to maintain a record required by an order issued under section 5326, or to maintain a record required pursuant to any regulation prescribed under section 21 of the Federal Deposit Insurance Act or section 123 of Public Law 91–508;

(2) cause or attempt to cause a domestic financial institution to file a report required under section 5313(a) or 5325 or any regulation prescribed under any such section, to file a report or to maintain a record required by any order issued under section 5326, or to maintain a record required pursuant to any regulation prescribed under section 5326, or to maintain a record required pursuant to any regulation prescribed under section 21 of the Federal Deposit Insurance Act or section 123 of Public Law 91–508, that contains a material omission or misstatement of fact; or

(3) structure or assist in structuring, or attempt to structure or assist in structuring, any transaction with one or more domestic financial institutions.

* * *

(d) Criminal penalty.—

g. 31 U.S.C. § 5324(b) contains provisions dealing with international monetary transactions that track the domestic transaction provisions in 5324(a).

(1) In general.—Whoever violates this section shall be fined in accordance with title 18, United States Code, imprisoned for not more than 5 years, or both.

(2) Enhanced penalty for aggravated cases.—Whoever violates this section while violating another law of the United States or as part of a pattern of any illegal activity involving more than $100,000 in a 12–month period shall be fined twice the amount provided in subsection (b)(3) or (c)(3) (as the case may be) of section 3571 of title 18, United States Code, imprisoned for not more than 10 years, or both.

————

What does the statute cover? When courts and commentators speak of structuring, they are generally referring to section (a)(3).[h] Section (a)(3) makes it illegal to "structure" any transaction with one or more banks for the purpose of evading the reporting requirement. It clearly imposes liability on the customer, and is intended to deal with the problem of customers manipulating transactions in order to evade the reporting requirements. It does not, however, include any definition of the key term structuring. Regulations adopted by the Secretary of the Treasury define structuring as follows:

> (gg) Structure (structuring). For purposes of section 103.53, a person structures a transaction if that person, acting alone, or in conjunction with, or on behalf of, other persons, conducts or attempts to conduct one or more transactions in currency, in any amount, at one or more financial institutions, on one or more days, in any manner, for the purpose of evading the reporting requirements under section 103.22 of this Part. "In any manner" includes, but is not limited to, the breaking down of a single sum of currency exceeding $10,000 into smaller sums, including sums at or below $10,000, or the conduct of a transaction, or series of currency transactions, including transactions at or below $10,000. The transaction or transactions need not exceed the $10,000 reporting threshold at any single financial institution on any single day in order to constitute structuring within the meaning of this definition.

31 C.F.R. § 103.11(gg) (2005).

As Professor Sarah Welling explains, § 5324(a)(3) covers the main techniques used by launders to avoid reporting:

---

h. Section 5324(a)(1) extends liability for a bank's criminal failure to file a report to any person who causes that failure. This amounts to a specialized accomplice liability provision, enacted in response to decisions in some lower courts finding that this situation was not covered by the general accomplice liability provisions. Section 5324(a)(2) makes it a crime to cause a bank to file a report containing a material omission or misstatement. Note that the false statement act, 18 U.S.C. § 1001, also covers this conduct. In addition, both sections (a)(1) and (a)(2) contain attempt provisions, which are necessary because federal law contains no general attempt provision.

* * * [L]aunderers have three methods available under the revised regulations to avoid aggregation and the duty to report. Clause (3) covers each of these. First, the crime of structuring is not limited to transactions accomplished in a particular time period. Thus, transactions that would avoid aggregation under the regulations because $10,000 or less was transferred during one day would still qualify as structured transactions under clause (3). Second, because the crime of structuring does not depend on the bank's knowledge, using multiple agents and multiple accounts to keep the bank in the dark on the total transactions would not defeat liability under clause (3). Third, the crime of structuring includes transactions accomplished at "one or more domestic financial institutions,'" so conducting the transactions at multiple banks will not avoid liability. This clause is independent of the aggregation regulation, thus it prohibits all structuring regardless of whether the bank has a duty to file a report.

Sarah N. Welling, *Smurfs, Money Laundering, and the Federal Criminal Law: The Crime of Structuring Transactions*, 41 FLA. L. REV. 287, 304–07 (1989). Note that the definition in 31 C.F.R. § 103.11(gg) *"includes*, but is not limited to, the breaking down of a single sum of currency exceeding $10,000 into smaller sums * * *." (Emphasis added.) The same section also makes it clear that structuring can include actions by one person alone or in conjunction with others, and transactions at more than one financial institution on more than one day. What are the outer limits of the concept of structuring? Would it include structuring a contractual relationship to provide small frequent payments of amounts less than $10,000? Would it include setting prices at less than $10,000? What else might it include? Does the open-ended nature of the definition raise due process problems?

The elements of the offense of structuring are (1) knowledge of the reporting requirements, and (2) action intended to evade the requirements. The defendant must act for the purpose of evading the reporting requirements, but it is not necessary to prove that the defendant also knew that structuring itself is a crime. This point was clarified by an amendment to § 5324 that was enacted to override the Supreme Court's decision in *Ratzlaf v. United States*, 510 U.S. 135 (1994).

Why is structuring transactions to avoid taxes—which is legal— treated so differently than structuring financial transactions to avoid the currency reporting requirements? It is generally assumed that taxpayers have a legitimate interest in reducing their tax liability, and tax planning—including structuring transactions—is permitted to achieve that objective. While the amount of taxes paid is reduced by the structuring of transactions, information about the transactions is still provided to the government. In contrast, in the case of structuring to avoid the currency reporting requirements the purpose is to deny the government information about the transactions in question. Is this purpose inevitably suspect? Are criminals the only ones who are loathe have their cash transactions recorded? As noted above, Congress immediately nullified the Supreme Court's decision in *Ratzlaf* (which held that structuring requires knowledge that evading the reporting requirements is a crime). In explaining its reading of the statute, the *Ratzlaf* majority tried to provide examples of legitimate reasons for structuring, such as reducing the likelihood that the IRS would audit a legitimate business, reducing the likelihood of a burglary motivated by reports of cash transactions, and preventing a former spouse from learning of an increase in wealth that might affect spousal support. 510 U.S. at 144–45. It appears that Congress was not persuaded of the importance of protecting behavior of this nature from criminal liability. *See also* Welling, *supra*, at 309–10 (in enacting § 5324 Congress concluded that the societal threat from drug trafficking and money laundering outweighed the minimal threat to privacy from reporting).

4. THE ROLE OF THE CURRENCY REPORTING LAWS IN THE DEVELOPMENT OF THE MONEY LAUNDERING ENFORCEMENT REGIME

In the context of the overall money laundering enforcement plan, the currency reporting laws play the vital role in helping to detect money launderers and financiers of terrorists. The currency reporting laws have been largely successful in preventing drug traffickers and other money launderers from placing large sums of illegally generated cash directly into the U.S. banking system. Accordingly, although there are still some prosecutions for currency reporting violations and for structuring, the major prosecutorial focus is now on the money laundering statutes, 18 U.S.C. §§ 1956 and 1957. In 2003 the Department of Justice issued a statistical report analyzing its money laundering and currency reporting prosecutions from 1994 to 2001.[i] The pattern of enforcement for 2001 of the currency reporting, anti-structuring, and money laundering statutes when they are the most serious crime charged is represented in the chart below. As the chart indicates, money laundering charges are much more common than currency reporting and anti-structuring.

   i. The report is available online at
http://www.ojp.usdoj.gov/bjs/pub/pdf/mlo01.
pdf (visited July 19, 2005).

Defendants charged, by most serious charge filed, for FY 2001*

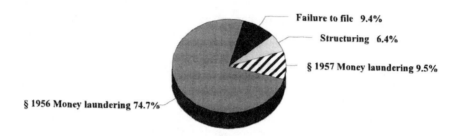

Failure to file 9.4%

Structuring 6.4%

§ 1957 Money laundering 9.5%

§ 1956 Money laundering 74.7%

Offenses under 1% omitted

Money laundering and currency reporting charges are not always the most serious charge; these offenses can also be added as secondary charges in cases involving a more serious crime. About one-third of all money laundering cases involved such secondary charges, and more than 90% of these secondary cases involved drug-related charges. Who were the defendants? Most were individuals. In 2001, for example, businesses comprised less than 2% of money laundering defendants. The 22 business defendants that were prosecuted included auto dealerships, grocery stores, banks, furniture stores, restaurants, physicians' offices, and beauty shops. The report also revealed that money laundering cases during this period were highly concentrated geographically; nearly half of all matters were referred in six areas designated as High Intensity Financial Crime Areas by the Departments of Treasury and Justice.

What do these statistics indicate? Are the prosecutions targeting the most serious kinds of conduct? Looking not only at prosecutions, but also at the rules administered by regulators and the detection systems run primarily by investigators, Mariano–Florentino Cuellar (a former Treasury official) concludes that the current regime has only limited effectiveness. In his view, it imposes disproportionately severe penalties on predicate offenders who are easily detected, and suffers from a limited capacity to detect a range of chargeable domestic and international offenses and from global diffusion that leaves authorities with room for both discretion and lax enforcement. *See* Mariano–Florentino Cuellar, *The Tenuous Relationship Between the Fight Against Money Laundering and the Disruption of Criminal Finance*, 93 J. Crim. L. & Criminology 311 (2003). As you read through the materials that follow, keep his critique in mind, and ask yourself whether the prosecutions discussed here seem to be the kinds of cases Congress had in mind when it enacted these laws.

The behavior of money launderers continues to evolve, and as discussed earlier, the post–9/11 focus on detecting terrorist financing has presented its own unique problems. New responses are required to meet these challenges. For example, in 2001 Congress dealt with the increasing use of bulk cash shipments out of the U.S. by creating a new money laundering offense, bulk cash smuggling, 18 U.S.C. § 5332, which prohibits the concealment and transfer of more than $10,000 across the border with the intent to evade reporting requirements. Similarly, regulators and investigators have stepped up their efforts to respond to the use of money service businesses, charities that have ties to terrorist organizations, informal value transfer systems (such as the hawala, where a hawala broker transfers funds for an individual to a counterpart broker, usually of the same ethnic group, in another country and outside the regulated financial system), and trade-based schemes that convert illicit proceeds into exported goods (such as the Columbia Black Market Peso Exchange). Technological advances have created new issues, and cyberlaundering, which includes the use of Internet banks, online transfers, transmission of electronic money, and stored value cards, has become increasingly problematic.

In 2005 an initiative was undertaken within the Treasury Department to expand the government's access to logs of international wire transfers into and out of American banks, because such transfers are widely used by terrorists to move money quickly and cheaply around the world. But with at least a half-billion international wire transfers a year totaling trillions of dollars, methods will be needed to develop clearer data and minimize disruption to banks.

Recognizing the dynamic nature of money laundering techniques and the need for an evolving and integrated federal strategy, Congress directed the President to publish a national strategy for combating money laundering and related financial crimes, and it established a program of grants to support local law enforcement efforts to detect and suppress money laundering. The fifth National Money Laundering Strategy, a joint effort of the Treasury and Justice Departments, was published in 2003. It focused on cutting off access to the international finance system by money launderers and terrorist financiers, enhancing the government's ability to target major money laundering organizations, and strengthening the anti-money laundering regulatory regime to improve its effectiveness.[j]

The global reach of money laundering and terrorist financing has led to greater international cooperation. The Financial Action Task Force on Anti–Money Laundering (FATF) was established at the G–7 in 1989 to combat money laundering more effectively, and thirty-one countries and two regional organizations are now members. The FATF published its Forty Recommendations on Money Laundering in 1990, and most recently revised them in June 2003. In addition, following the attacks of 9/11, the FATF released Nine Special Recommendations on Terrorist Financ-

j. The 2003 NATIONAL MONEY LAUNDERING STRATEGY is available at http://www. treas.gov/offices/enforcement/publications/ ml2003.pdf (visited June 22, 2005).

ing. A primary mission of the organization is to monitor the implementation of these recommendations in its member countries. While the FATF is the global standard-setter on anti-money laundering and counter-terrorist financing, numerous FATF-style regional bodies have been created that perform a similar mission on a regional level.

B. MONEY LAUNDERING:
18 U.S.C. §§ 1956 AND 1957

In the 1990s money laundering charges became increasing popular with federal prosecutors, who relied principally on § 1956. One Justice Department spokesman commented "that U.S. attorneys around the country see the future as lying in the money-laundering statutes, rather than RICO" because "Section 1956 gets you everything that RICO gets you, and more.'" Barry Tarlow, *RICO Report*, THE CHAMPION, August 1990 at 32. What more could a prosecutor want? First, Departmental approval is required for RICO prosecutions, but not for money laundering prosecutions. *See infra*, p. 577. Second, the list of predicate crimes that give rise to money laundering is even more extensive than the list of predicates for RICO. But other factors may be even more important. A Justice Department spokesman explained that the money laundering statutes are attractive to prosecutors because "the sentence for money laundering is, except in drug cases, about four times the sentence for the crime that generates the proceeds," and both the laundered funds and any property that facilitates the laundering are forfeitable. *Money Laundering Conference Focuses on Additions to Government's Arsenal*, 49 CRIM. L. REP. 1018, 1019 (1991). For example, absent special features, a simple fraud case generating $110,000 is likely to result in a combination of probation and home confinement if it is prosecuted as mail fraud (or some other form of federal fraud), but the same conduct will result in a sentence of several years in prison plus mandatory forfeiture if it is prosecuted as money laundering.[k] For a discussion of forfeiture, see Chapter 19.

The basic money laundering offense is defined in § 1956(a)(1)(A) and (B). The key term "financial transaction" is defined in § 1956(c)(4). The many offenses that qualify as "specified unlawful activity" are listed in subsection (c)(7). Note that subsection (f) provides for extraterritorial application under certain circumstances.

---

k. *See* B. FREDERICK WILLIAMS, JR. & FRANK D. WHITNEY, FEDERAL MONEY LAUNDERING: CRIMES AND FORFEITURES § 1.6 (1999) (concluding that the sentence for fraud would be at level 10, but the sentence for money laundering under § 1956 or § 1957 would be at level 15, 18, or 21, depending on whether the government proved that the funds were spent, hidden, or plowed back into the criminal enterprise; the most severe fraud sentence would be 12 months, and the most severe money laundering sentence would be 46 months). Williams and Whitney, who are federal prosecutors, also discuss other reasons prosecutors charge money laundering offenses, including "the ability to prosecute a wrongdoer when there is either insufficient evidence of the underlying criminal conduct or insufficient evidence connecting the wrongdoer to the underlying criminal conduct." *Id.* at § 1.7.

As you read the provision that follows, note that there are really four different offenses covered by § 1956, each defined by the intent with which the transaction in question is undertaken. These four variants are spelled out in §§ (a)(1)(A) and (a)(1)(B). They are "financial transactions" undertaken—

- with the intent to promote specified unlawful activity—(a)(1)(A)(I); or

- with the intent to evade taxes—(a)(1)(A)(ii); or

- with knowledge that the transaction is intended to conceal information about the proceeds of unlawful activity—(a)(1)(B)(I); or

- with knowledge that the transaction is intended to evade a currency reporting requirement—(a)(1)(B)(ii).

Section 1956(h) criminalizes conspiracies to violate the substantive provisions of § 1956, and thus subjects conspiracies to the same stiff penalties as completed offenses. In addition, § 1956 also includes provisions not reprinted below that criminalize international transfers of funds with similar intent and undercover operations where the transaction is made with government money that appears to be criminal proceeds (such as in government sting operations). *See* 18 U.S.C. § 1956 (a)(2) & (a)(3).

18 U.S.C.

§ 1956. Laundering of monetary instruments

(a)(1) Whoever, knowing that the property involved in a financial transaction represents the proceeds of some form of unlawful activity, conducts or attempts to conduct such a financial transaction which in fact involves the proceeds of specified unlawful activity—

(A)(i) with the intent to promote the carrying on of specified unlawful activity; or

(ii) with intent to engage in conduct constituting a violation of section 7201 or 7206 of the Internal Revenue Code of 1986; or

(B) knowing that the transaction is designed in whole or in part—

(i) to conceal or disguise the nature, the location, the source, the ownership, or the control of the proceeds of specified unlawful activity; or

(ii) to avoid a transaction reporting requirement under State or Federal law,

shall be sentenced to a fine of not more than $500,000 or twice the value of the property involved in the transaction, whichever is greater, or imprisonment for not more than twenty years, or both.

* * *

(b) Penalties.—[1]

(1) In general.—Whoever conducts or attempts to conduct a transaction described in subsection (a)(1) or (a)(3), or section 1957, or a transportation, transmission, or transfer described in subsection (a)(2), is liable to the United States for a civil penalty of not more than the greater of—

(A) the value of the property, funds, or monetary instruments involved in the transaction; or

(B) $10,000.

* * *

(c) As used in this section—

(1) the term "knowing that the property involved in a financial transaction represents the proceeds of some form of unlawful activity" means that the person knew the property involved in the transaction represented proceeds from some form, though not necessarily which form, of activity that constitutes a felony under State, Federal, or foreign law, regardless of whether or not such activity is specified in paragraph (7);

(2) the term "conducts" includes initiating, concluding, or participating in initiating, or concluding a transaction;

(3) the term "transaction" includes a purchase, sale, loan, pledge, gift, transfer, delivery, or other disposition, and with respect to a financial institution includes a deposit, withdrawal, transfer between accounts, exchange of currency, loan, extension of credit, purchase or sale of any stock, bond, certificate of deposit, or other monetary instrument, use of a safety deposit box, or any other payment, transfer, or delivery by, through, or to a financial institution, by whatever means effected;

(4) the term "financial transaction" means (A) a transaction which in any way or degree affects interstate or foreign commerce (i) involving the movement of funds by wire or other means or (ii) involving one or more monetary instruments, or (iii) involving the transfer of title to any real property, vehicle, vessel, or aircraft, or (B) a transaction involving the use of a financial institution which is engaged in, or the activities of which affect, interstate or foreign commerce in any way or degree;

(5) the term "monetary instruments" means (i) coin or currency of the United States or of any other country, travelers' checks, personal checks, bank checks, and money orders, or (ii) investment securities or negotiable instruments, in bearer form or otherwise in such form that title thereto passes upon delivery;

---

1. Subsection (b)(2) also provides for jurisdiction over foreign persons in order to adjudicate an action or enforce a penalty under § 1956. Subsections (b)(3) and (b)(4) also authorize pretrial restraint and the appointment of a federal receiver in these cases.

(6) the term "financial institution" includes—

(A) any financial institution, as defined in section 5312(a)(2) of title 31, United States Code, or the regulations promulgated thereunder; and

(B) any foreign bank, as defined in section 1 of the International Banking Act of 1978 (12 U.S.C. 3101);

(7) the term "specified unlawful activity" means—

(A) any act or activity constituting an offense listed in section 1961(1) of this title except an act which is indictable under subchapter II of chapter 53 of title 31;

(B) with respect to a financial transaction occurring in whole or in part in the United States, an offense against a foreign nation involving—

(i) the manufacture, importation, sale, or distribution of a controlled substance (as such term is defined for the purposes of the Controlled Substances Act);

(ii) murder, kidnapping, robbery, extortion, destruction of property by means of explosive or fire, or a crime of violence (as defined in section 16);

(iii) fraud, or any scheme or attempt to defraud, by or against a foreign bank (as defined in paragraph 7 of section 1(b) of the International Banking Act of 1978));

(iv) bribery of a public official, or the misappropriation, theft, or embezzlement of public funds by or for the benefit of a public official;

(v) smuggling or export control violations involving—

(I) an item controlled on the United States Munitions List established under section 38 of the Arms Export Control Act (22 U.S.C. 2778); or

(II) an item controlled under regulations under the Export Administration Regulations (15 C.F.R. Parts 730—774); or

(vi) an offense with respect to which the United States would be obligated by a multilateral treaty, either to extradite the alleged offender or to submit the case for prosecution, if the offender were found within the territory of the United States;

(C) any act or acts constituting a continuing criminal enterprise, as that term is defined in section 408 of the Controlled Substances Act (21 U.S.C. 848);

(D) an offense under section 32 (relating to the destruction of aircraft), section 37 (relating to violence at international airports), section 115 (relating to influencing, impeding, or retaliating against a Federal official by threatening or injuring a family member), section 152 (relating to concealment of assets; false oaths and claims; bribery), section 175c (relating to the variola virus), section 215 (relating to commissions or gifts for procuring loans), section 351 (relating to congressional or Cabinet officer assassination), any of sections 500 through 503 (relating to certain counterfeiting offenses), section 513 (relating to securities of States and private entities), section 541 (relating to goods falsely classified), section 542 (relating to entry of goods by means of false statements), section 545 (relating to smuggling goods into the United States), section 549 (relating to removing goods from Customs custody), section 641 (relating to public money, property, or records), section 656 (relating to theft, embezzlement, or misapplication by bank officer or employee), section 657 (relating to lending, credit, and insurance institutions), section 658 (relating to property mortgaged or pledged to farm credit agencies), section 666 (relating to theft or bribery concerning programs receiving Federal funds), section 793, 794, or 798 (relating to espionage), section 831 (relating to prohibited transactions involving nuclear materials), section 844(f) or (I) (relating to destruction by explosives or fire of Government property or property affecting interstate or foreign commerce), section 875 (relating to interstate communications), section 922(1) (relating to the unlawful importation of firearms), section 924(n) (relating to firearms trafficking), section 956 (relating to conspiracy to kill, kidnap, maim, or injure certain property in a foreign country), section 1005 (relating to fraudulent bank entries), 1006 (relating to fraudulent Federal credit institution entries), 1007 (relating to fraudulent Federal Deposit Insurance transactions), 1014 (relating to fraudulent loan or credit applications), section 1030 (relating to computer fraud and abuse), 1032 (relating to concealment of assets from conservator, receiver, or liquidating agent of financial institution), section 1111 (relating to murder), section 1114 (relating to murder of United States law enforcement officials), section 1116 (relating to murder of foreign officials, official guests, or internationally protected persons), section 1201 (relating to kidnaping), section 1203 (relating to hostage taking), section 1361 (relating to willful injury of Government property), section 1363 (relating to destruction of property within the special maritime and territorial jurisdiction), section 1708 (theft from the mail), section 1751 (relating to Presidential assassination), section 2113 or 2114 (relating to bank and postal robbery and theft), section 2280 (relating to violence against maritime navigation), section 2281 (relating to violence against maritime fixed platforms), section 2319 (relating to copyright infringement), section 2320 (relating to trafficking in counterfeit goods and services), section 2332 (relating to terrorist acts abroad against United States nationals), section 2332a (relating to use of weapons of mass destruction), section 2332b (relating to international terrorist acts transcending national boundaries), section 2332g (relating to missile systems designed to destroy aircraft), section 2332h (relating to radiological dispersal devices), or section 2339A or 2339B (relating to providing material support to terrorists) of this title, section 46502 of title 49, United States Code, a felony violation of the Chemical Diversion and Trafficking Act of 1988 (relating to precursor and essential chemicals), section 590 of the Tariff Act of 1930 (19 U.S.C. 1590) (relating to aviation smuggling), section 422 of the Controlled Substances Act (relating to transportation of drug paraphernalia), section 38(c) (relating to criminal violations) of the Arms Export Control Act, section 11 (relating to violations) of the Export Administration Act of 1979, section 206 (relating to penalties) of the International Emergency Economic Powers Act, section 16 (relating to offenses and punishment) of the Trading with the Enemy Act, any felony violation of section 15 of the Food Stamp Act of 1977 [7 U.S.C.A. § 2024] (relating to food stamp fraud) involving a quantity of coupons having a value of not less than $5,000, any violation of section 543(a)(1) of the Housing Act of 1949 [42 U.S.C.A. § 1490s(a)(1)] (relating to equity skimming), any felony violation of the Foreign Agents Registration Act of 1938, any felony violation of the Foreign Corrupt Practices Act, or section 92 of the Atomic Energy Act of 1954 (42 U.S.C. 2122) (relating to prohibitions governing atomic weapons);

(E) a felony violation of the Federal Water Pollution Control Act (33 U.S.C. 1251 et seq.), the Ocean Dumping Act (33 U.S.C. 1401 et seq.), the Act to Prevent Pollution from Ships (33 U.S.C. 1901 et seq.), the Safe Drinking Water Act (42 U.S.C. 300f et seq.), or the Resources Conservation and Recovery Act (42 U.S.C. 6901 et seq.); or

(F) any act or activity constituting an offense involving a Federal health care offense;

(8) the term "State" includes a State of the United States, the District of Columbia, and any commonwealth, territory, or possession of the United States.

(d) Nothing in this section shall supersede any provision of Federal, State, or other law imposing criminal penalties or affording civil remedies in addition to those provided for in this section.

* * *

(f) There is extraterritorial jurisdiction over the conduct prohibited by this section if—

(1) the conduct is by a United States citizen or, in the case of a non-United States citizen, the conduct occurs in part in the United States; and

(2) the transaction or series of related transactions involves funds or monetary instruments of a value exceeding $10,000.

(g) Notice of conviction of financial institutions.—If any financial institution or any officer, director, or employee of any financial institution has been found guilty of an offense under this section, section 1957 or 1960 of this title, or section 5322 or 5324 of title 31, the Attorney General shall provide written notice of such fact to the appropriate regulatory agency for the financial institution.

(h) Any person who conspires to commit any offense defined in this section or section 1957 shall be subject to the same penalties as those prescribed for the offense the commission of which was the object of the conspiracy.

UNITED STATES v. CORCHADO—PERALTA

318 F.3d 255 (1st Cir. 2003).

Before BOUDIN, CHIEF JUDGE, HOWARD, CIRCUIT JUDGE, and SHADUR, SENIOR DISTRICT JUDGE.

BOUDIN, CHIEF JUDGE.

Between 1987 and 1996, Ubaldo Rivera Colon ("Colon") smuggled over 150 kilograms of cocaine into Puerto Rico, yielding some $4 million in profits, which he then laundered through a variety of investments and purchases. Colon was indicted on drug, bank fraud, and conspiracy charges and, based on a plea agreement, was sentenced in June 2002 to over 20 years in prison. This case concerns not Colon but three peripheral figures, including his wife.

Colon's wife, Elena Corchado Peralta ("Corchado"), and two associates, Basilio Rivera Rodriguez ("Rivera") and Oscar Trinidad Rodriguez ("Trinidad") were indicted and tried together on one count of conspiring with Colon to launder money. 18 U.S.C. §§ 1956(a)(1)(B) and (h). Corchado was also indicted on one count of bank fraud. 18 U.S.C. § 1344 (2000). During their eight-day trial, Colon provided extensive testimony about his money laundering methods, which included a variety of transactions (purchases, investments, and loans) involving the defendants.

All three defendants were convicted on the charges against them. Corchado received a 27–month sentence, Rivera, 57 months, and Trinidad, 63 months. All three defendants appealed, each arguing that the evidence was not sufficient to support conviction. Trinidad and Rivera raise other issues as well and we address their claims in a companion opinion. Corchado appeals alone, but it is helpful to begin by outlining the criminal offense that was the principal charge against all of them.

The money laundering statute, 18 U.S.C. § 1956 (2000), among other things makes it criminal for anyone, "knowing that the property involved in a financial transaction represents the proceeds of some form of unlawful activity" to "conduct ... such a financial transaction which in fact involves the proceeds of specified unlawful activity"—

(A)(i) with the intent to promote the carrying on of specified unlawful activity; or

. . . .

(B) knowing that the transaction is designed in whole or in part—

(i) to conceal or disguise the nature, the location, the source, the ownership or the control of the proceeds of specified unlawful activity;

. . . .

Id. § 1956(a)(1).

The three defendants in this case were charged under subsection (B)(i), based on knowledge of "design[ ]", and not under (A)(i), based on an "intent to promote." In each instance, there is no doubt that the defendant did engage in one or more financial transactions involving Colon's drug proceeds. The issue turns, rather, on state of mind elements. Pertinently, as to Corchado, she disputes knowing either that the "property" represented proceeds of drug dealing or that "the transaction" was "designed . . . to conceal or disguise. . . ." The evidence, taken most favorably to the government, showed the following.

Elena Corchado Peralta met Colon sometime in the early 1990s and they were married in 1994. Corchado, then about 25 years old, was a student when they met and later worked part-time in her mother's jewelry store. She has a college degree in business administration and some training in accounting. Colon testified that he held himself out as a successful legitimate businessman throughout their relationship and that his wife knew about neither his drug smuggling nor his own money laundering activities.

Corchado performed many transactions involving Colon's drug proceeds. These transactions fell into two broad categories—expenditures and deposits. On the expenditure side, Colon directed Corchado to write and endorse checks to purchase a cornucopia of expensive cars, boats, real estate, and personal services. Colon maintained that his wife thought that the money was derived from legitimate businesses.

The purchases themselves were extensive and expensive, affording the couple a fancy lifestyle. For example, Corchado purchased a BMW, a Mercedes Benz, and a Porsche for the couple. At another time, she made a single monthly payment to American Express of $18,384 for interior decorating purchases. And on another day, she signed three checks totaling $350,000 that were used to purchase land for one of Colon's businesses. In total, Corchado signed the majority of 253 checks, representing many hundreds of thousands of dollars of purchases.

With respect to deposits, Corchado's main responsibility was to deposit $6,000 checks on a monthly basis into one of Colon's accounts. Colon testified that he had made a $700,000 loan to an associate using his drug profits with the understanding that the associate was to pay him back over the course of many months so as to dissociate Colon from the illegal proceeds. Under the terms of the arrangement, the checks came from legitimate businesses, and Colon testified that his wife was not aware of the circumstances underlying the monthly payments. At trial, the government also presented evidence showing that on one occasion Corchado wired $40,000 to a Florida company at Colon's request.

Tax records signed by Corchado showed that she knew that her husband's reported income from his legitimate businesses was far less than the money she was handling. For example, the joint tax return that Corchado signed for 1995 listed a total amount of claimed income of only $12,390. The government presented evidence showing that the couple's total reported income between 1992 and 1997 was only approximately $150,000. Corchado did not testify at trial.

We begin with the first knowledge requirement—namely, that Corchado was aware, at the time of the transactions she conducted, that the money she was handling, at least much of the time, was derived from drug dealings.[2] Corchado argues, correctly, that there is no direct evidence of her knowledge (say, by an admission by her or testimony from Colon that he told her about his business). Indeed, he testified repeatedly that she was unaware of his drug business; that in response to a question from her he had denied doing anything unlawful; that he never allowed her to attend meetings involving his drug business; and that he stopped distributing drugs when they were married.

Needless to say, the jury did not have to accept Colon's exculpatory testimony. It was clearly self-interested since Corchado was his wife and mother of their two children. But here, at least, the jury's disbelief could not count for much in the way of affirmative proof. Rather, whether there was knowledge of drug dealing, or so much awareness that ignorance was willful blindness, turns in this case on the same circumstantial evidence.

What the evidence shows is that Corchado knew that the family expenditures were huge, that reported income was a fraction of what was being spent and that legitimate sources were not so obvious as to banish all thoughts of possible illegal origin—as demonstrated by Colon's testimony that Corchado once raised the issue. Interviewed by an FBI agent, Corchado told him that her husband had been involved in the cattle business and, more recently, in real estate development but that none of the businesses had employees and that Colon had worked mainly out of his house. And, as the government fairly points out, Corchado was herself well educated and involved in the family bookkeeping.

This might seem to some a modest basis for concluding—beyond a reasonable doubt—that Corchado knew that her husband's income was

---

2. Formally, the charge is "conspiracy," under subsection (h) to violate subsection (a)(1)(B)(i); but the "agreement" requirement is undisputed: many, if not all, of the transactions were performed at Colon's request or with his consent. Thus, the open issue is Corchado's state of mind.

badly tainted. But the issue turns on judgments about relationships within families and about inferences that might be drawn in the community from certain patterns of working and spending. Further, it is enough to know that the proceeds came from "some form, though not necessarily which form," of felony under state or federal law. 18 U.S.C. § 1956(c)(1). The jury's judgment on this factual issue cannot be called irrational.

The other knowledge requirement is harder for the government. Here, the statute requires, somewhat confusingly, that Corchado have known that "the transaction" was "designed," at least in part, "to conceal or disguise the nature, the location, the source, the ownership or the control of the proceeds." 18 U.S.C. § 1956(a)(1)(B)(i). We will assume that it would be enough if Corchado herself undertook a transaction for her husband, knowing that her husband had such a design to conceal or disguise the proceeds, or if she undertook a transaction on her own having such a design herself. Other variations might exist, but these two seem the foremost possibilities.

It may help to treat separately the purchases on the one hand and the check deposits (and in one case a transfer) on the other. Any purchase of goods or services, whether by cash or by check, has a potential to conceal or disguise proceeds simply because it transforms them from money into objects or dissipates them in the performance of the services. But if this were enough, every expenditure of proceeds known to be tainted would itself be unlawful. Instead, the statute requires that someone—the instigator or spender—must have an intent to disguise or conceal and the spender must share or know of that intent.

Here, the government showed that from their marriage onward Corchado wrote most of the checks used by the couple to purchase expensive items (*e.g.,* several high-priced cars) and pay off credit card bills and that some of these payments were very large (one credit card bill exceeded $18,000). And, for reasons already given, it is assumed that the jury permissibly found that Corchado knew that some of the money she was spending was criminally derived. Finally, the government stresses that she must have known that Colon was bringing in and spending far more than he reported on his income tax returns. Is this enough for the jury to infer a specific intent to conceal or disguise and impute the intent itself, or knowledge of it, to Corchado?

In this case, nothing about the purchases, or their manner, points toward concealment or disguise beyond the fact that virtually *all expenditures* transform cash into something else. Here, the purchased assets were not readily concealable (*e.g.,* diamonds) nor peculiarly concealed (*e.g.,* buried in the garden) nor acquired in someone else's name nor spirited away to a foreign repository (*e.g.,* a Swiss bank deposit box). Indicia of this kind have been stressed in cases upholding money laundering charges and their absence noted in cases coming out the other way.

To hold that a jury may convict on this evidence—that Corchado spent her husband's money knowing that the money was tainted—is to make it unlawful wherever a wife spends any of her husband's money, knowing or believing him to be a criminal. That the purchases here were lavish or numerous hardly distinguishes this case from one in which a thief's wife buys a jar of baby food; if anything, Corchado's more flamboyant purchases were less likely than the baby food to disguise or conceal. Perhaps a hard-nosed Congress might be willing to adopt such a statute, *compare* 18 U.S.C. § 1957 (2000), but it did not do so here.

Less need be said about the deposit and transfer side. So far as we can tell, Corchado mostly did no more than make large regular deposits in an account given to her by her husband; there was no inference of concealment or disguise. As for the single transfer she made to another person at her husband's request, nothing suspicious about the circumstances is cited to us, let alone anything that would suggest knowledge on Corchado's part that the transfer was meant to conceal or disguise proceeds—as opposed to merely paying off a debt, making an investment, or conducting some other transaction incident to a business, lawful or otherwise.

* * *

Notes

1. As this case makes clear, mens rea is the key to many money laundering cases, and the mens rea structure of § 1956 is complex. In *Corchado–Peralta*, the court noted that the statute requires two levels of mens rea. It stated that a jury could have found the defendant knew her husband's income was derived from some form of unlawful activity. However, the court reversed Corchado's money laundering conviction because there was insufficient evidence to satisfy the second knowledge requirement: that she intended or knew the transactions were designed to conceal or disguise the proceeds. In *United States v. Rivera–Rodriguez*, 318 F.3d 268 (1st Cir. 2003), one of Corchado's co-defendants, Oscar Trinidad Rodriguez, challenged the government's proof of the other mens rea requirement. He conceded that he knew transactions he performed for Colon were designed to conceal the source of the funds involved, but argued that he did not know the transactions involved illegal proceeds. The court rejected this argument, explaining:

> Here, Colon engaged in very large cash transactions involving Trinidad (the initial purchase and the Florida delivery) and more than one such venture occurred. With Trinidad's help, Colon patently splintered the deposits to amounts just under $10,000, a step serving only to avoid bank reporting. And Colon placed the boat in Trinidad's name even though Trinidad had contributed nothing.

> Sometimes one of these red-flag events—cash, concealment, false ownership—can occur even with lawfully derived income (*e.g.*, to foster tax evasion or the concealment of income from a spouse). But taken together, the pattern was surely that of an effort to launder illegally

obtained proceeds, or at least a jury could reasonably so conclude. The case law is consistent with this view.

Id. at 272.

2.   Section 1956 requires proof that the defendant engaged in a "financial transaction." The definition of financial transaction provides the jurisdictional basis by requiring a connection to interstate commerce. Subsection (c)(4) defines financial transaction:

> the term "financial transaction" means (A) a transaction which in any way or degree affects interstate or foreign commerce (i) involving the movement of funds by wire or other means or (ii) involving one or more monetary instruments, or (iii) involving the transfer of title to any real property, vehicle, vessel, or aircraft, or (B) a transaction involving the use of a financial institution which is engaged in, or the activities of which affect, interstate or foreign commerce in any way or degree;

Note that this provision is worded in the alternative. It is sufficient to show *either* that the transaction or the instrument affects commerce in any way or degree, *or* that the transaction involved the use of a financial institution whose activities affect interstate commerce. Accordingly, in *United States v. Koller*, 956 F.2d 1408, 1411–12 (7th Cir. 1992), the court held that "the use of the financial institution involved in the transaction may be incidental, as it was here, and need not be shown to have been a part of, contributed to, or facilitated the design to conceal."

3.   Should § 1956 be used to increase the penalties for conduct that falls squarely within the ambit of other federal crimes? This issue has arisen in drug cases, and divided the federal circuits on two questions regarding the "financial transaction" requirement: (1) whether the payment for drugs with the proceeds of drug trafficking constitutes a "financial transaction" in violation of § 1956(a), and (2) whether the transportation of drug proceeds by the drug seller or his courier constitutes a "financial transaction" in violation of § 1956(a). For example, in one case the defendant received cocaine by Express Mail from a source in Alaska. She sold the cocaine to buyers in Vermont and used the proceeds of those sales to purchase money orders which she mailed to pay her supplier. Her conviction for violating § 1956(a) was affirmed by the Second Circuit, *United States v. Skinner*, 946 F.2d 176 (2d Cir. 1991), but would have been overturned in several other circuits, *see, e.g., United States v. Heaps*, 39 F.3d 479, 485–86 (4th Cir. 1994). *See also United States v. Dovalina*, 262 F.3d 472, 476 (5th Cir. 2001) (collecting cases). This issue has also come up in mail fraud cases, where the question is typically whether a particular financial transaction occurs after the fraud has been completed, or is, instead, part of the fraud itself. *See United States v. Lee*, 232 F.3d 556 (7th Cir. 2000). Professor Jimmy Gurule—who later became Under Secretary of Enforcement in the Treasury Department—has argued that the money laundering laws were intended to punish criminal activity not otherwise proscribed by federal law, and that § 1956 targets the "*post-crime* hiding and reinvesting of illegal profits to continue proscribed activity." Jimmy Gurule, *The Money Laundering Control Act of 1986: Creating a New Federal Offense or Merely Affording Federal Prosecutors an Alternative Means of Punishing Specified Unlawful Activity?*, 32 AM. CRIM. L. REV. 823 (1995) (emphasis added).

4. The defendant in *Corchado–Peralta* was charged with money laundering for engaging in financial transactions involving her husband's drug proceeds, in part by writing checks to make large purchases. What if these checks were drawn on accounts that contained not only the drug proceeds, but also funds from other legitimate sources? Addressing that issue, the Seventh Circuit upheld a money laundering conviction in *United States v. Jackson*, 935 F.2d 832, 840 (7th Cir. 1991). The court reasoned that it was sufficient to show that the *transaction in question involved* the proceeds of one of the types of criminal conduct specified. The court buttressed its conclusion with the observation that Congress could not have meant the money laundering statute to be easily evaded by commingling criminal proceeds with legitimate funds. The other circuits have generally agreed with this conclusion. *See* 2 SARAH N. WELLING ET AL., FEDERAL CRIMINAL LAW AND RELATED ACTIONS: CRIMES, FORFEITURE, THE FALSE CLAIMS ACT AND RICO § 18.14(B)(iii)(b) (1998) (collecting cases). Is this construction faithful to the language of § 1956? Section 1956 requires proof that (1) the defendant knew that "the property involved" in a transaction "represents the proceeds" of unlawful activity, and (2) the financial transaction "in fact involves the proceeds."

5. How specific must the evidence be to show that the property in question constitutes "proceeds" of specified unlawful activity (SUA)? The courts have generally rejected the argument that the government must demonstrate that the funds in question can be traced to a specific SUA, such as a particular drug transaction. *Id.* Since the offense focuses on the conversion of criminal proceeds into other less easily identifiable forms, the particular nature of the earlier crimes has been deemed to be unimportant. *See, e.g., United States v. Gabel*, 85 F.3d 1217, 1224 (7th Cir. 1996). Indeed, where the indictment charges both substantive offenses and money laundering, several courts have held that an acquittal on the substantive counts does not preclude a conviction on the money laundering, which does not depend upon proof of the specific predicate offenses listed in the indictment. *See, e.g., United States v. Mankarious*, 151 F.3d 694, 703 (7th Cir. 1998). The government does have to prove that the property was the proceeds of unlawful activity, but that is often accomplished by circumstantial proof of a general nature. *See generally* B. FREDERICK WILLIAMS, JR. & FRANK D. WHITNEY, FEDERAL MONEY LAUNDERING: CRIMES AND FORFEITURES § 4.4.3 (1999). Is there anything wrong with predicating criminal liability under § 1956 on proof that does not establish any particular criminal violation, as long as the evidence establishes in general terms that the defendant has been involved in criminal activity? Can you establish this point as a general matter without any proof of specific violations? *Cf. Richardson v. United States*, 526 U.S. 813 (1999) (holding that jury in CCE case must unanimously agree not only that defendant committed some "continuing series of violations," but also which specific violations make up that series). *Richardson* is discussed *supra* p. 396.

6. In refusing to uphold the defendant's conviction under § 1956, the court in *Corchado-Peralta* states:

> To hold that a jury may convict on this evidence—that Corchado spent her husband's money knowing that the money was tainted—is to make it unlawful wherever a wife spends any of her husband's money, knowing or believing him to be a criminal.... Perhaps a hard-nosed

Congress might be willing to adopt such a statute, *compare* 18 U.S.C. § 1957 (2000), but it did not do so here.

318 F.3d at 259.

This implicitly suggests that § 1957 comes close to the kind of statute that would make spending any property derived from a specified unlawful activity illegal. Keep this in mind as you read *Rutgard, infra* at p. 453, and the notes that follow, which discuss the differences between § § 1956 and 1957.

§ 1957. Engaging in monetary transactions in property derived from specified unlawful activity

(a) Whoever, in any of the circumstances set forth in subsection (d), knowingly engages or attempts to engage in a monetary transaction in criminally derived property that is of a value greater than $10,000 and is derived from specified unlawful activity, shall be punished as provided in subsection (b).

(b)(1) Except as provided in paragraph (2), the punishment for an offense under this section is a fine under title 18, United States Code, or imprisonment for not more than ten years or both.

(2) The court may impose an alternate fine to that imposable under paragraph (1) of not more than twice the amount of the criminally derived property involved in the transaction.

(c) In a prosecution for an offense under this section, the Government is not required to prove the defendant knew that the offense from which the criminally derived property was derived was specified unlawful activity.

(d) The circumstances referred to in subsection (a) are—

(1) that the offense under this section takes place in the United States or in the special maritime and territorial jurisdiction of the United States; or

(2) that the offense under this section takes place outside the United States and such special jurisdiction, but the defendant is a United States person (as defined in section 3077 of this title, but excluding the class described in paragraph (2)(D) of such section).

(e) Violations of this section may be investigated by such components of the Department of Justice as the Attorney General may direct, and by such components of the Department of the Treasury as the Secretary of the Treasury may direct, as appropriate and, with respect to offenses over which the United States Postal Service has jurisdiction, by the Postal Service. Such authority of the Secretary of the Treasury and the Postal Service shall be exercised in accordance with an agreement which shall be entered into by the Secretary of the Treasury, the Postal Service, and the Attorney General.

(f) As used in this section—

(1) the term "monetary transaction" means the deposit, withdrawal, transfer, or exchange, in or affecting interstate or foreign commerce, of funds or a monetary instrument (as defined in section

1956(c)(5) of this title) by, through, or to a financial institution (as defined in section 1956 of this title), including any transaction that would be a financial transaction under section 1956(c)(4)(B) of this title, but such term does not include any transaction necessary to preserve a person's right to representation as guaranteed by the sixth amendment to the Constitution;

(2) the term "criminally derived property" means any property constituting, or derived from, proceeds obtained from a criminal offense; and

(3) the term "specified unlawful activity" has the meaning given that term in section 1956 of this title.

UNITED STATES v. RUTGARD

116 F.3d 1270 (9th Cir. 1997).

Before GOODWIN, WIGGINS, and NOONAN, CIRCUIT JUDGES.

NOONAN, CIRCUIT JUDGE.

Jeffrey Jay Rutgard appeals his conviction of numerous counts of mail fraud on, and false claims to, Medicare, of counts of mail fraud on other insurers, and of transactions in money derived from the frauds. He appeals as well a judgment of forfeiture. He also appeals his sentence, challenging the enhancements and the calculation of loss that led to the imposition of a sentence of 11 1/4 years and an order of restitution of over $16 million embracing virtually the entire proceeds of his practice as an ophthalmologic surgeon between 1988 and April, 1992.

* * *

BACKGROUND

The Insurers. Medicare is the federal health insurance program for persons over the age of 65 who meet its qualifications. As Medicare beneficiaries are 65 years of age or older, medical treatment of their eyes is a significant part of Medicare coverage. For example, in 1991, a year involved in this case, it is estimated that 45 percent of the approximately thirty million beneficiaries of Medicare received eye care paid for by Medicare, which processed thirty-five million claims for such care. The cost demonstrated by these statistics underlines the importance to the government and to taxpayers of honest billing in the practice of ophthalmologists, and they illustrate the prevalence of conditions among those over the age of 65 that necessitate treatment of their eyes.

Medicare pays only for services that are "reasonable and necessary for the diagnosis or treatment of illness or injury or to improve the functioning of a malformed body member." Participating providers are required to ensure that any services rendered to Medicare recipients are supported by sufficient evidence of medical necessity.

* * *

Jeffrey Jay Rutgard. Dr. Rutgard, the defendant, was born in Chicago, Illinois, in 1951. His father was a physician. He attended the College of Medicine of the University of Illinois. He also enrolled in the university's graduate school where he was a James Scholar. On the basis of his proficiency in these schools he skipped internship and moved directly to a three-year residency in ophthalmology at the Medical School of the University of Iowa. In 1981 he came from this residency to practice in San Diego, California.

In 1982 he secured his own medical practice by the purchase of Dr. Amos Root's in San Diego. Four years later he bought Dr. John Bickerton's in La Jolla and thereafter had two offices. In 1989 he opened as well an ambulatory surgery center in La Jolla. His practice flourished. He kept an extraordinary schedule of working 6 ½ days per week, 16 hours a day, with trips to medical meetings but without vacations. He also made a great deal of money. From 1988 through May, 1992 he received from Medicare (80% of his practice) over $15 ½ million.

His skill as a surgeon was recognized. The success of his practice he attributed in large measure to word-of-mouth recommendation by satisfied patients. Dr. Bickerton and several other ophthalmologists sent members of their families to him for surgery. Members of the staff who were government witnesses at trial had only praise for his surgical abilities.

Rutgard was also an active promoter of his practice. One-third of his practice he estimated came from his "community relations" program. He employed staff to hold free screening at senior citizen centers and nursing and retirement homes and, although without professional qualifications, to diagnose cataract and eyelid problems, suggesting Rutgard as the doctor who could cure them. Vans arranged by Rutgard brought this kind of clientele to his clinics for further examination. Members of his staff, including the van drivers and the receptionist, were paid bonuses or qualified for raises by the number of the persons they successfully recruited to have surgery by him. In pursuit of these rewards some staff would tell strangers wearing glasses whom they saw in a supermarket that they should see Dr. Rutgard.

* * *

Rutgard was not shy about self-promotion. Staff was instructed to say, "Doctor is the best eye doctor in San Diego." Staff was told to tell patients, "The Lord guides his work and skills." Rutgard was rebuked by the American College of Eye Surgeons for putting out a resume stating that he was a fellow rather than a member of that college. He was criticized in 1991 by the chairman of the ethics committee of the American Academy of Ophthalmology for an advertisement stating that he was "board-certified" by this academy, which does not do such certification. He gave patients *Cataracts And Implants. A Guide For Patients And Their Families.* The front, inside and back covers all showed him as the co-author of the book with Dr. Phillip C. Hoopes, and the book was dedicated by the two authors to their wives. In fact only

Dr. Hoopes was the author, and Rutgard's name appeared as author because he paid Hoopes to have his name displayed as author.

PROCEEDINGS

[After dismissing of a number of counts the government went to trial on 132 counts alleging various forms of fraud, false claims, and money laundering. The charges on which Rutgard was convicted included billing for medically unnecessary cataract surgery, post-operative laser procedures, and eyelid surgery; billing for more expensive procedures than those actually performed and for procedures patients never received; falsifying patient complaints on medical charts; and one count of money laundering involving more than $7 million in proceeds of the fraud. The government introduced evidence regarding the medical condition and treatment of 17 patients, as well as information about billing practices for various procedures. After a detailed review of the evidence regarding each patient and each billing procedure, the court of appeals reversed several counts on the ground of evidentiary insufficiency, but affirmed the remainder of the counts.

The court then turned to the government's contention that Rutgard's entire practice was a fraud. Conceding that Rutgard had engaged in some "extremely questionable practices," the court pointed out that the government had neither charged nor proven that Rutgard's practice was a criminal enterprise under RICO or that any conspiracy to defraud the government had existed. In fact, based on the total number of patients Rutgard saw, and the fact that his employees only testified as to certain, isolated instances of fraud, the court reached the "inescapable inference that a fair amount of recording and billing in the Rutgard practice was performed without fraud." The court bolstered this conclusion with the absence of any counts of fraud charged in other areas of Rutgard's practice, such as his treatments for glaucoma and retina problems, and with the counts of fraud that the court itself determined to be unsupported by the evidence. From these findings the court determined that the government had failed to prove that Rutgard's entire practice was a fraud. Therefore, the court also rejected the claim that the entire proceeds of Rutgard's practice were derived from fraudulent activity. As a result of this conclusion, the court considered only the funds received as a direct result of the proven counts of fraud, a total of $46,000, for purposes of the money laundering charge.]

The Monetary Transactions Count. In May, 1992 after the government's search of Rutgard's office, his wife Linda, at his direction, made two wire transfers to the National Westminster Bank on the Isle of Man, one of $5,629,220.74 on May 5 and one of $1,935,220.48 on May 6. The transfers were made from the Rutgard Family Trust, whose accounts were at the Imperial Trust Company in San Diego.

The government's accounting expert noted $15.8 million paid by Medicare to Rutgard entities between the beginning of 1988 and April, 1992. He testified that Rutgard deposited $3,754,056 derived from these entities into the family trust account during this period and deposited $1.9 million in municipal bonds so that a total of $5,654,056 entered this account from October 29, 1990, when Rutgard opened the account with a personal check for $560,000, to May, 1992. He testified that the balance of the account came from municipal bonds delivered to the trust account at unspecified times. On appeal the government argues that the jury could take into account the first year, 1987, when insurance fraud began, and come to the conclusion that the entire amount transferred by wire transfers on May 5 and 6 was the proceeds of insurance fraud.

To prove this contention the government advanced the theory that all of Rutgard's practice was a fraud. If the government had succeeded in this proof, it would have properly convicted him of the monetary transaction counts. But we have just determined that the government's proof was deficient. The government, as we have also held, established Rutgard's guilt of particular counts of fraud. The proceeds of that fraud come to over $46,000. Can the convictions under § 1957 be sustained on the theory that at least $20,000 of fruits of fraud were incorporated in the wire transfers of May 6 and 7? To answer that question requires a consideration of the terms and purpose of § 1957 and a close look at the companion statute, § 1956.

These statutes govern monetary transactions in criminally derived property. The standard money laundering statute is 18 U.S.C. § 1956. The other statute, the one under which Rutgard was convicted, is 18 U.S.C. § 1957. In construing § 1956, we referred to § 1957 as "a companion money laundering statute," *United States v. Garcia*, 37 F.3d 1359, 1365 (9th Cir. 1994), without having occasion to mark the differences between the two. We now have occasion to mark those differences.

Section 1956, alone at issue in *Garcia*, bears the title "Laundering of monetary instruments." It punishes by imprisonment of up to 20 years and a fine a defendant who:

> knowing that the property involved in a financial transaction represents the proceeds of some form of unlawful activity, conducts or attempts to conduct such a financial transaction which in fact involves the proceeds of specified unlawful activity—
>
> > (A)(i) with the intent to promote the carrying on of specified unlawful activity; or
> >
> > (ii) with intent to engage in conduct constituting a violation of section 7201 or 7206 of the Internal Revenue Code of 1986; or
> >
> > (B) knowing that the transaction is designed in whole or in part—
> >
> > > (i) to conceal or disguise the nature, the location, the source, the ownership, or the control of the proceeds of specified unlawful activity; or
> > >
> > > (ii) to avoid a transaction reporting requirement under State or Federal law.

18 U.S.C. § 1956(a)(1). For present purposes, five elements of § 1956 differentiate it from § 1957, the statute at issue here—its title, its requirement of intent, its broad reference to "the property involved," its satisfaction by a transaction that "in part" accomplishes the design, and its requirement that the intent be to commit another crime or to hide the fruits of a crime already committed.

Section 1957 has a different heading: "Engaging in monetary transactions in property derived from specified unlawful activity." It punishes by up to ten years' imprisonment and a fine anyone who:

> knowingly engages or attempts to engage in a monetary transaction in criminally derived property that is of a value greater than $10,000 and is derived from specified unlawful activity.

18 U.S.C. § 1957(a). The description of the crime does not speak to the attempt to cleanse dirty money by putting it in a clean form and so disguising it. This statute applies to the most open, above-board transaction. *See* 18 U.S.C. § 1957(f)(1) (broadly defining "monetary transaction"). The intent to commit a crime or the design of concealing criminal fruits is eliminated. These differences make violation of § 1957 easier to prove. But also eliminated are references to "the property involved" and the satisfaction of the statute by a design that "in part" accomplishes the intended result. These differences indicate that proof of violation of § 1957 may be more difficult.

Section 1957 could apply to any transaction by a criminal with his bank. Two years after its enactment an amendment was necessary to provide that the term "monetary transaction" does not include "any transaction necessary to preserve a person's right to representation as guaranteed by the sixth amendment to the Constitution." Without the amendment a drug dealer's check to his lawyer might have constituted a new federal felony.

Section 1957 was enacted as a tool in the war against drugs. It is a powerful tool because it makes any dealing with a bank potentially a trap for the drug dealer or any other defendant who has a hoard of criminal cash derived from the specified crimes. If he makes a "deposit, withdrawal, transfer or exchange" with this cash, he commits the crime; he's forced to commit another felony if he wants to use a bank. This draconian law, so powerful by its elimination of criminal intent, freezes the proceeds of specific crimes out of the banking system. As long as the underlying crime has been completed and the defendant "possesses" the funds at the time of deposit, the proceeds cannot enter the banking system without a new crime being committed. A type of regulatory crime has been created where criminal intent is not an element. Such a powerful instrument of criminal justice should not be expanded by judicial invention or ingenuity. We "should not enlarge the reach of enacted crimes by constituting them from anything less than the incriminating components contemplated by the words used in the statute."

For these reasons we do not find helpful in interpreting § 1957 the cases applying § 1956, which speaks of design "in whole or in part" and of "a financial transaction involving property." Other circuits, however, have used the § 1956 precedents to eliminate any tracing of funds in a § 1957 case. *See United States v. Moore*, 27 F.3d 969, 976–77 (4th Cir. 1994); *United States v. Johnson*, 971 F.2d 562 (10th Cir. 1992). They have reasoned that otherwise § 1957 could be defeated by a criminal mingling innocently-obtained funds with his ill-gotten moneys.

This reasoning rests on the fungibility of money in a bank. That fungibility, destroying the specific identity of any particular funds, makes the commingling of innocent funds with criminal funds an obvious way to hide the criminal funds. If § 1956 required tracing of specific funds, it could be wholly frustrated by commingling. For that reason, the statute not only proscribes any transaction whose purpose is to hide criminal funds but reaches any funds "involved" in the transaction. Neither the same reasoning nor the same language is present in § 1957, the statute here applied.

The monetary transaction statute cannot be made wholly ineffective by commingling. To prevail, the government need show only a single $10,000 deposit of criminally-derived proceeds. Any innocent money already in the account, or later deposited, cannot wipe out the crime committed by the deposit of criminally-derived proceeds. Commingling with innocent funds can defeat application of the statute to a withdrawal of less than the total funds in the account, but ordinarily that fact presents no problem to the government which, if it has proof of a deposit of $10,000 of criminally-derived funds, can succeed by charging the deposit as the crime; or the government may prevail by showing that all the funds in the account are the proceeds of crime. Commingling will frustrate the statute if criminal deposits have been kept under $10,000. But that is the way the statute is written, to catch only large transfers. Moreover, if the criminal intent was to hide criminal proceeds, as would presumably be the case any time criminally derived cash was deposited with innocently derived funds to hide its identity, § 1956 can kick in and the depositor of amounts under $10,000 will be guilty of a § 1956 crime.

The government did not take its possible course of charging Rutgard with deposits of over $10,000 of fraudulent proceeds. The government had the means of doing so because its accounting expert identified the large deposits Rutgard made. But as Rutgard was neither charged nor convicted of deposits in violation of § 1957, we cannot uphold his convictions on that basis.

Rutgard's convictions may be upheld if he transferred out of the account all the funds that were in it or if there was a rule or presumption that, once criminally-derived funds were deposited, any transfer from the account would be presumed to involve them for the purpose of applying § 1957. Rutgard did not transfer all the funds in the family trust account, however. The government showed that the account held $8.5 million on April 2, 1992 and $13,901 on July 2, 1992, the dates of the quarterly bank statements. But so far as evidence at trial goes, more than $46,000 remained in the account after the May 5 and 6 transfers.

These transfers therefore did not necessarily transfer the $46,000 of fraudulent proceeds.

The alternative way of sustaining the convictions depends on a presumption, which the Fourth Circuit created in *Moore*, 27 F.3d at 976–77, but which we decline to create. The statute does not create a presumption that any transfer of cash in an account tainted by the presence of a small amount of fraudulent proceeds must be a transfer of these proceeds. Unlike § 1956, § 1957 does not cover any funds "involved." To create such a presumption in order to sustain a conviction under § 1957 would be to multiply many times the power of that draconian law. It would be an essay in judicial lawmaking, not an application of the statute. As the government did not prove that any fraudulently-derived proceeds left the account on May 5 or May 6, 1992, the monetary transfer counts, Counts 216 and 217, were not proved beyond a reasonable doubt.

* * *

Notes

1. What are the differences between sections 1956 and 1957?

a. As the *Rutgard* court noted, one significant difference is the intent requirement. Section 1956(a) requires that the defendant have *either* "the intent to promote the carrying on of specified unlawful activity" or "know[lege] that the transaction is designed in whole or part—(i) to conceal or disguise the nature, the location, the source, the ownership, or control of the proceeds of specified unlawful activity, or (ii) to avoid a transaction reporting requirement * * *." In contrast, § 1957 requires only that the defendant have "knowingly engage[ ] * * * in a monetary transaction in criminally derived property."

b. A second significant difference is that § 1956 applies to "financial transactions," and § 1957 applies to "monetary transactions." What's the difference? The term "monetary transactions in § 1957 is narrower. It is defined in § 1957(f)(1) to include only deposits, withdrawals, transfers, and exchanges of funds through a "financial institution" engaged in interstate commerce. In contrast, § 1956 defines the term financial transaction more broadly to include not only the kind of monetary transactions covered in § 1957, but also the transfer of title to any real property, vehicle, vessel or aircraft. 18 U.S.C. § 1956(c)(4)(iii). This gives § 1956 additional breadth.

c. Finally, § 1957 applies to "criminally derived property that is of a value greater than $10,000," and defines this as "any property constituting, or derived from, proceeds obtained from a criminal offense." 18 U.S.C. § 1957(a) & (f)(1). In contrast, § 1956 refers simply to "the proceeds of some form of unlawful activity." Section 1956 doesn't specify any minimal dollar amount, but otherwise it's not clear whether the difference in wording is significant. A good argument can be made that § 1957 is broader because it applies not only to "proceeds" but also to property "derived from" proceeds, whereas § 1956 makes no reference to property derived from proceeds. Under this interpretation, § 1956 would be limited to direct fruits, but

§ 1957 would allow greater latitude to trace the proceeds through subsequent transactions and exchanges, and base criminal liability on later transactions. *But see United States v. Savage*, 67 F.3d 1435, 1442 (1995) (stating that "criminally derived property" means the same thing as "proceeds" under § 1956), and B. Frederick Williams, Jr. & Frank D. Whitney, Federal Money Laundering: Crimes and Forfeitures § 6.1 n.8 (1999) (stating that the use of different terminology in §§ 1956 and 1957 is "quite probably an artifact of the fact that the House and Senate bills were too hastily assembled in conference at the end of a contentious session and enacted into law" and "there is no indication that Congress intended different meanings").

d. *Rutgard* holds that a prosecution under § 1957 (unlike a prosecution under § 1956) may not be based upon funds drawn from a commingled account unless those funds can be traced and shown to be the proceeds of unlawful activity. As the court recognized, *supra* p. 458, other circuits have disagreed. *Rutgard* specifically disagreed with *United States v. Moore*, 27 F.3d 969, 976–77 (4th Cir. 1994), where the court allowed the government to meet its burden under § 1957 by showing that the transaction involved funds drawn from an account in which proceeds were commingled with legitimate funds, and recognized a presumption in the government's favor. The court explained:

> Money is fungible, and when funds obtained from unlawful activity have been combined with funds from lawful activity into a single asset, the illicitly-acquired funds and the legitimately-acquired funds (or the respective portions of the property purchased with each) cannot be distinguished from each other; that is, they cannot be traced to any particular source, absent resort to accepted, but arbitrary, accounting techniques. As a consequence, it may be presumed in such circumstances, as the language of section 1957 permits, that the transacted funds, at least up to the full amount originally derived from crime, were the proceeds of the criminal activity or derived from that activity. A requirement that the government trace each dollar of the transaction to the criminal, as opposed to the non-criminal activity, would allow individuals effectively to defeat prosecution for money laundering by simply commingling legitimate funds with criminal proceeds.

Id. at 976–77.

Should tracing be required under either or both statutes, in order to establish that a predicate transaction actually involves criminal proceeds? If so, how would that work? What accounting principles should be applied? In the forfeiture context, one circuit has allowed the government to choose among various rules for characterizing commingled assets, with the result that the government may treat *either* the first assets drawn from commingled funds, or the last remaining assets, as the proceeds. *United States v. Banco Cafetero Panama*, 797 F.2d 1154, 1158–59 (2d Cir. 1986).[o] Is this option preferable to the presumption in *Moore*?

o. For a general discussion of the various means to prove tracing under the forfeiture statutes, see B. Frederick Williams, Jr. & Frank D. Whitney, Federal Money Laundering: Crimes and Forfeitures § 4.4.2 et seq. (1999).

Another circuit has suggested an approach based on the proportion of "clean" and "dirty" money in the account drawn upon. *United States v. Loe*, 248 F.3d 449, 467 (5th Cir. 2001). The court, while following the *Rutgard* rule until the issue could be considered en banc, explained in a footnote:

> There is much to be said in favor of a "proportionality" rule. Under such a rule, courts would treat any withdrawal from an account as containing proportional fractions of clean and dirty money. Applying the facts of the instant case, "dirty" funds ($470,790.22) comprised approximately 21 per cent of the total amount in the account ($2,205,00). Applying this same proportion to the withdrawal in question ($776,742), $165,842.42 of the funds withdrawn would be "dirty." As this amount exceeds the $10,000 threshold articulated in section 1957, LHI's conviction would be justified.
>
> A proportionality rule would avoid some of the oddities associated with the *Davis* approach. Under *Davis,* if aggregate withdrawals are less than the amount of clean funds in the account, the statute is not violated. However, once withdrawals exceed the clean funds in the account, all subsequent transactions (including the transaction by which the defendant exceeds the clean-funds threshold) are transformed into "dirty" transfers warranting conviction. A proportionality rule avoids this somewhat mechanistic result.
>
> Moreover, a proportionality rule is more sensitive to the fungible nature of money. Whereas the *Davis* rule engages in a presumption that clean money is spent before dirty money, a proportionality rule recognizes that a withdrawal mirrors the sources of the money in the account. If the account is the product of clean and dirty money, a withdrawal should reflect this arrangement in equal proportions.
>
> Finally, this rule would be more faithful to the plain language of the statute. The *Davis* rule allows a court to look at the total number of withdrawals from an account, aggregating a series of transactions. *See United States v. Davis*, 226 F.3d 346, 357 (5th Cir. 2000). However, section 1957 imposes liability on a transaction-by-transaction basis. *See* 18 U.S.C.A. § 1957 ("Whoever ... knowingly engages ... in a monetary transaction in [dirty money] of a value greater than $10,000 ... shall be punished."). A proportionality rule would avoid the aggregation mechanism condoned in *Davis* and more accurately reflect the language and purpose of the statute. However, as the *Davis* rule is binding on this panel, we must apply it to the case at bar, leaving change to a case appropriately before the en banc court.

Id. at 467.

For additional discussions of the tracing issue, see *United States v. Braxtonbrown–Smith*, 278 F.3d 1348, 1352–55 (D.C. Cir. 2002) (rejecting requirement of full tracing and reviewing cases from all circuits); Joseph R. Miller, Note, *Federal Money Laundering Crimes—Should Direct Tracing of Funds Be Required?*, 90 Ky. L.J. 441 (2002).

2. Some courts have found that the phrase "criminally derived property" limits the application of § 1957 in another way. In *United States v. Piervinanzi*, 23 F.3d 670 (2d Cir. 1994), a defendant who worked at Morgan

Guaranty succeeded in having $24 million dollars from a customer's account wired to an account he had set up at Banker's Trust. A supervisor had the transfer reversed, foiling the scheme, when the clerk who took the order said that the person who telephoned did not sound like the customer. Was the $24 million dollars "criminally derived" property? Because the statute defines criminally derived property as "proceeds *obtained* from a criminal offense," the court of appeals concluded that the proceeds of a crime must first be in the defendant's possession and then be transferred for § 1957 to apply. Accordingly, it reversed Piervinanzi's conviction. Similarly, *United States v. Johnson*, 971 F.2d 562 (10th Cir. 1992), held that § 1957 was inapplicable where the defendant's fraudulent scheme caused his victims to wire funds to his account, since the funds were not yet "proceeds" when the wire transfers were made. Note that this construction is faithful to the wording of the statute and also makes it harder to use § 1957 to drive up the penalty for the underlying criminal offense. Should this analysis be applied to § 1956, which requires a financial transaction involving the "proceeds" of unlawful activity?

3. What does § 1957 really add to the federal arsenal? Section 1957 bars drug traffickers and persons who commit the other specified offenses from using the banking system in the United States to store or transfer any large sums derived from their illegal activities. Accordingly, virtually any spending of illegal proceeds in an amount in excess of $10,000 will constitute a new offense if the transaction involves a financial institution. For example, payment by check for housing or personal living expenses will constitute a violation of § 1957 if the expenses if payment is made by a check for more than $10,000. Moreover, since anyone who participates in a prohibited monetary transaction falls within the scope of § 1957, liability extends to banks and their employees, and also to third parties who knowingly come into possession of criminally derived proceeds. The next case illustrates this aspect of § 1957, and also explores the question whether willful blindness is a sufficient basis for liability under § 1957.

UNITED STATES v. CAMPBELL

977 F.2d 854 (4th Cir. 1992).

ERVIN, CHIEF JUDGE.

* * *

The relevant facts are comprehensively set out in the district court's published opinion. We will only summarize them here. In the summer of 1989, Ellen Campbell was a licensed real estate agent working at Lake Norman Realty in Mooresville, North Carolina. During the same period, Mark Lawing was a drug dealer in Kannapolis, North Carolina. Lawing decided to buy a house on Lake Norman. He obtained Campbell's business card from Lake Norman Realty's Mooresville office, called Campbell, and scheduled an appointment to look at houses.

Over the course of about five weeks, Lawing met with Campbell approximately once a week and looked at a total of ten to twelve houses. Lawing and Campbell also had numerous phone conversations. Lawing represented himself to Campbell as the owner of a legitimate business, L & N Autocraft, which purportedly performed automobile customizing services. When meeting with Campbell, Lawing would travel in either a red Porsche he owned or a gold Porsche owned by a fellow drug dealer, Randy Sweatt, who would usually accompany Lawing. During the trips to look at houses, which occurred during normal business hours, Lawing would bring his cellular phone and would often consume food and beer with Sweatt. At one point, Lawing brought a briefcase containing $20,000 in cash, showing the money to Campbell to demonstrate his ability to purchase a house.

Lawing eventually settled upon a house listed for $191,000 and owned by Edward and Nancy Guy Fortier. The listing with the Fortiers had been secured by Sara Fox, another real estate agent with Lake Norman Realty. After negotiations, Lawing and the Fortiers agreed on a price of $182,500, and entered into a written contract. Lawing was unable to secure a loan and decided to ask the Fortiers to accept $60,000 under the table in cash and to lower the contract price to $122,500.[1] Lawing contacted Campbell and informed her of this proposal. Campbell relayed the proposal to Fox, who forwarded the offer to the Fortiers. The Fortiers agreed, and Fox had the Fortiers execute a new listing agreement which lowered the sales price and increased the commission percentage (in order to protect the realtors' profits on the sale).

Thereafter Lawing met the Fortiers, Fox and Campbell in the Mooresville sales office with $60,000 in cash. The money was wrapped in small bundles and carried in a brown paper grocery bag. The money was counted, and a new contract was executed reflecting a sales price of $122,500. Lawing tipped both Fox and Campbell with "a couple of hundred dollars."

William Austin, the closing attorney, prepared closing documents, including HUD–1 and 1099–S forms, reflecting a sales price of $122,500, based on the information provided by Campbell. Campbell, Fox, Austin, Lawing, Lawing's parents and the Fortiers were all present at the closing. The closing documents were signed, all reflecting a sales price of $122,500.

Campbell was indicted on a three count indictment alleging: 1) money laundering, in violation of 18 U.S.C. § 1956(a)(1)(B)(i); 2) engaging in a transaction in criminally derived property, in violation of 18 U.S.C. § 1957(a); and 3) causing a false statement (the HUD–1 form) to be filed with a government agency, in violation of 18 U.S.C. § 1001. She was tried and convicted by a jury on all three counts. After the verdict, the district court granted Campbell's motion for judgment of acquittal with respect to the money laundering and transaction in criminally

---

1. Lawing's explanation to Campbell of this unorthodox arrangement was that the lower purchase price would allow Lawing's parents to qualify for a mortgage. Lawing would then make the mortgage payments on his parent's behalf. Lawing justified the secrecy of the arrangement by explaining that his parents had to remain unaware of the $60,000 payment because the only way he could induce their involvement was to convince them he was getting an excellent bargain on the real estate.

derived property counts. The district court also conditionally ordered a new trial on these counts if the judgment of acquittal was reversed on appeal. The Government appeals.

II.

In reviewing a district court's grant of a post-verdict acquittal, this court must decide "whether, viewing the evidence in the light most favorable to the government, any rational trier of facts could have found the defendant guilty beyond a reasonable doubt." * * *

The money laundering statute under which Campbell was charged applies to any person who:

> knowing that the property involved in a financial transaction represents the proceeds of some form of unlawful activity, conducts or attempts to conduct such a financial transaction which in fact involves the proceeds of specified unlawful activity ... knowing that the transaction is designed in whole or in part ... to conceal or disguise the nature, the location, the source, the ownership, or the control of the proceeds of specified unlawful activity....

18 U.S.C. § 1956(a)(1). The district court found, and Campbell does not dispute, that there was adequate evidence for the jury to find that Campbell conducted a financial transaction which in fact involved the proceeds of Lawing's illegal drug activities. The central issue in contention is whether there was sufficient evidence for the jury to find that Campbell possessed the knowledge that: (1) Lawing's funds were the proceeds of illegal activity, and (2) the transaction was designed to disguise the nature of those proceeds.

In assessing Campbell's culpability, it must be noted that the statute requires actual subjective knowledge. Campbell cannot be convicted on what she objectively should have known. However, this requirement is softened somewhat by the doctrine of willful blindness. In this case, the jury was instructed that:

> The element of knowledge may be satisfied by inferences drawn from proof that a defendant deliberately closed her eyes to what would otherwise have been obvious to her. A finding beyond a reasonable doubt of a conscious purpose to avoid enlightenment would permit an inference of knowledge. Stated another way, a defendant's knowledge of a fact may be inferred upon willful blindness to the existence of a fact. It is entirely up to you as to whether you find any deliberate closing of the eyes and inferences to be drawn from any evidence. A showing of negligence is not sufficient to support a finding of willfulness or knowledge. I caution you that the willful blindness charge does not authorize you to find that the defendant acted knowingly because she should have known what was occurring when the property at 763 Sundown Road was being sold, or that in the exercise of hindsight she should have known what was occurring or because she was negligent in failing to recognize what was occurring or even because she was reckless or

foolish in failing to recognize what was occurring. Instead, the Government must prove beyond a reasonable doubt that the defendant purposely and deliberately contrived to avoid learning all of the facts.

Neither party disputes the adequacy of these instructions on willful blindness or their applicability to this case.

As outlined above, a money laundering conviction under section 1956(a)(1)(B)(i) requires proof of the defendant's knowledge of two separate facts: (1) that the funds involved in the transaction were the proceeds of illegal activity; and (2) that the transaction was designed to conceal the nature of the proceeds. In its opinion supporting the entry of the judgment of acquittal, the district court erred in interpreting the elements of the offense. After correctly reciting the elements of the statute, the court stated, "in a prosecution against a party other than the drug dealer," the Government must show *"a purpose of concealment"* and "knowledge of the drug dealer's activities." This assertion misstates the Government's burden. The Government need not prove that the defendant had the *purpose* of concealing the proceeds of illegal activity. Instead, as the plain language of the statute suggests, the Government must only show that the defendant possessed the *knowledge* that the transaction was designed to conceal illegal proceeds.

This distinction is critical in cases such as the present one, in which the defendant is a person other than the individual who is the source of the tainted money. It is clear from the record that Campbell herself did not act with the purpose of concealing drug proceeds. Her motive, without question, was to close the real estate deal and collect the resulting commission, without regard to the source of the money or the effect of the transaction in concealing a portion of the purchase price. However, Campbell's motivations are irrelevant. Under the terms of the statute, the relevant question is not Campbell's purpose, but rather her knowledge of Lawing's purpose.[4]

The sufficiency of evidence regarding Campbell's knowledge of Lawing's purpose depends on whether Campbell was aware of Lawing's status as a drug dealer. Assuming for the moment that Campbell knew that Lawing's funds were derived from illegal activity, then the under the table transfer of $60,000 in cash would have been sufficient, by itself, to allow the jury to find that Campbell knew, or was willfully blind to the fact, that the transaction was designed for an illicit purpose. Only if Campbell was oblivious to the illicit nature of Lawing's funds could she credibly argue that she believed Lawing's explanation of the under the table transfer of cash and was unaware of the money laundering poten-

---

4. We have no difficulty in finding that Lawing's purpose satisfied the statutory requirement that the transaction be "designed in whole or in part ... to conceal or disguise the nature, the location, the source, the ownership, or the control of the proceeds of specified unlawful activity...." 18 U.S.C. § 1956(a)(1)(B). The omission of $60,000 from all documentation regarding the sales price of the property clearly satisfies this standard—concealing both the nature and the location of Lawing's illegally derived funds. * * *

tial of the transaction. In short, the fraudulent nature of the transaction itself provides a sufficient basis from which a jury could infer Campbell's knowledge of the transaction's purpose, if, as assumed above, Campbell also knew of the illegal source of Lawing's money.[5] As a result, we find that, in this case, the knowledge components of the money laundering statute collapse into a single inquiry: Did Campbell know that Lawing's funds were derived from an illegal source?

The Government emphasizes that the district court misstated the Government's burden on this point as well, by holding that the Government must show Campbell's "knowledge of the drug dealer's activities." As the text of the statute indicates, the Government need only show knowledge that the funds represented "the proceeds of some form of unlawful activity." 18 U.S.C. § 1956(a)(1). Practically, this distinction makes little difference. All of the Government's evidence was designed to show that Campbell knew that Lawing was a drug dealer. There is no indication that the jury could have believed that Lawing was involved in some form of criminal activity other than drug dealing. As a result, the district court's misstatement on this point is of little consequence.

The evidence pointing to Campbell's knowledge of Lawing's illegal activities is not overwhelming. First, we find that the district court correctly excluded from consideration testimony by Sweatt that Lawing was a "known" drug dealer. Kannapolis, where Lawing's operations were located, is approximately fifteen miles from Mooresville, where Campbell lived and worked, and, as the district court pointed out, there was no indication that Lawing's reputation extended over such an extensive "community."

However, the district court also downplayed evidence that we find to be highly relevant. Sara Fox, the listing broker, testified at trial that Campbell had stated prior to the sale that the funds "may have been drug money." The trial court discounted this testimony because it conflicted with Fox's grand jury testimony that she did not recall Campbell ever indicating that Lawing was involved with drugs. In evaluating the testimony in this manner, the trial court made an impermissible judgment on witness credibility—a judgment that was clearly within the exclusive province of the jury. When ruling on a motion for judgment of acquittal the district court is obligated to weigh the evidence in the light most favorable to the Government. Under that standard, Fox's testimony regarding Campbell's statement that the

---

5. In this respect the present case is completely distinguishable from the principal case relied upon by the district court, *United States v. Sanders*, 929 F.2d 1466 (10th Cir. 1991). In that case, the court overturned two money laundering convictions of a defendant who, with funds admittedly derived from an illegal source, had purchased two automobiles. Unlike the present case, there was nothing irregular about the transactions themselves. The court found the transactions to be devoid of any attempt "to conceal or disguise the source or nature of the proceeds" and found that application of the money laundering statute to "ordinary commercial transactions" would "turn the money laundering statute into a 'money spending statute,' "a result clearly not intended by Congress. The present case, by contrast, presents a highly irregular financial transaction which, by its very structure, was designed to mislead onlookers as to the amount of money involved in the transaction.

funds "may have been drug money" should have been accepted as completely true.

In addition, the Government presented extensive evidence regarding Lawing's lifestyle. This evidence showed that Lawing and his companion both drove new Porsches, and that Lawing carried a cellular phone, flashed vast amounts of cash, and was able to be away from his purportedly legitimate business for long stretches of time during normal working hours. The district court conceded that this evidence "is not wholly [sic] irrelevant" to Campbell's knowledge of Lawing's true occupation, but noted that Lawing's lifestyle was not inconsistent with that of many of the other inhabitants of the affluent Lake Norman area who were not drug dealers. Again, we find that the district court has drawn inferences from the evidence which, while possibly well-founded, are not the only inferences that can be drawn. It should have been left to the jury to decide whether or not the Government's evidence of Lawing's lifestyle was sufficient to negate the credibility of Campbell's assertion that she believed Lawing to be a legitimate businessman.

We find that the evidence of Lawing's lifestyle, the testimony concerning Campbell's statement that the money "might have been drug money," and the fraudulent nature of the transaction in which Campbell was asked to participate were sufficient to create a question for the jury concerning whether Campbell "deliberately closed her eyes to what would otherwise have been obvious to her." As a result, we find that a reasonable jury could have found that Campbell was willfully blind to the fact that Lawing was a drug dealer and the fact that the purchase of the Lake Norman property was intended, at least in part, to conceal the proceeds of Lawing's drug selling operation. Accordingly, we reverse the judgment of acquittal on the money laundering charge.

III.

The statute under which Campbell was charged in Count 2 provides:

> Whoever ... knowingly engages or attempts to engage in a monetary transaction in criminally derived property that is of a value greater than $10,000 and is derived from specified unlawful activity, shall be punished as provided in subsection (b).

18 U.S.C. § 1957(a). The parties do not dispute that Campbell engaged in a monetary transaction in property of a value in excess of $10,000 or that the property was derived from "specified unlawful activity" as defined by the statute. Once again, the dispositive question is whether Campbell knew that Lawing's funds were the proceeds of criminal activity. As such, the discussion above with regard to the money laundering charge is completely applicable here. Because a jury could reasonably find that Campbell knew of, or was willfully blind to, Lawing's true occupation, it was error for the district court to grant a judgment of acquittal on this count as well.

[The final portion of the opinion affirmed the district court's conditional grant of a new trial in the interests of justice. In ruling on such a

motion the district court is permitted to weigh the credibility of witnesses, and to grant such a motion if it determines that the verdict was
against the weight of the evidence.]

Notes

1. The legislative history supports the conclusion that willful blindness
can satisfy the knowledge requirements in §§ 1956 and 1957. S. Rep. No.
433, 99th Cong. 2d Sess. 9–10 (1986) states:

> The "knowing" scienter requirements are intended to be construed, like
> existing scienter requirements, to include instances of "willful blind-
> ness." Thus, a currency exchanger who participates in a transaction
> with a known drug dealer involving thousands of dollars in cash, and
> accepts a commission far above the market rate, could not escape
> conviction, from the first tier of the offense, simply by claiming that he
> did not know for sure that the currency involved in the transaction was
> derived from crime. On the other hand, an automobile dealer who sells a
> car at market rates to a person whom he merely suspects of involvement
> with crime, cannot be convicted of this offense in the absence of a
> showing that he knew something more about the transaction or the
> circumstances surrounding it.

The adoption of the knowledge requirement came after the rejection of
previous bills employing a "reason to know" or "reckless disregard" standard. G. Richard Strafer, *Money Laundering: The Crime of the '90's*, 22 AM.
CRIM. L. REV. 149, 166 (1989). Is the knowledge standard—incorporating
willful blindness—significantly different than a recklessness standard? The
leading federal case on the willful blindness doctrine is *United States v.
Jewell*, 532 F.2d 697 (9th Cir. 1976).

What are the consequences of applying the willful blindness standard to
money laundering? Is there a danger that bankers, real estate brokers and
other business people will rely on stereotypes, and be less willing to engage
in transactions with racial minorities? *See* Rachel Ratliff, *Third-Party Money
Laundering: Problems of Proof and Prosecutorial Discretion*, 7 STAN. L. &
POL'Y REV. 173, 176 (1996).

2. How far will §§ 1956 and 1957 liability extend in the case of banks
and other financial institutions?

Will filing a CTR be sufficient to shield bank employees from liability?
What if the bank goes further and files a criminal referral regarding a
suspicious transaction: is that enough? Some federal prosecutors apparently
believe that neither action necessarily protects a banker from criminal
liability. Two Texas bankers were indicted for laundering drug money even
though they had reported their suspicions to regulatory authorities, though
the district judge granted the defense motion to dismiss the charges at the
close of the government's case. *Norwest Probe Signals Tough New Theory*,
DOJ ALERT, Vol. 2, No. 9, p. 4, 5 (Sept. 1992). Though the bankers had filed a
CTR and even called a Treasury official to report their concern, the government argued that they had accepted cash of suspicious origin, listed a straw
man on the CTR, and then helped hide the origin of the funds by making
loans, secured by the deposit. *Ibid.* Though the criminal charges were

dismissed, the issue of civil forfeiture of the funds in question was settled only when the bank conceded the liability of two bankers and the chairman (and largest shareholder) of the bank, effectively ending the banking careers of the former. *Ibid.* Another prosecution under the false statements statute, 18 U.S.C. § 1001, was instituted against a Montana bank that filed a criminal referral regarding a suspicious transaction; prosecutors reportedly believe that the information provided was incomplete and hence false. *Id.* at 4. Are these attempts to extend the reach of § 1957 appropriate?

The United States Attorneys Manual takes the unusual step of requiring Criminal Division approval before a financial institution can be indicted for money laundering under 18 U.S.C. §§ 1956 & 1957 (though it does not state the criteria that will determine whether a prosecution will be approved). USAM ¶ 9–105.300(4) (July 2005). Do you agree that this is a sensitive area that requires some restraint on prosecutorial discretion? If so, what kind of criteria should be applied in determining whether a prosecution should be instituted against a financial institution (and should these criteria be published)? Should there be a requirement that the relevant federal regulatory agencies be consulted? Note that the government has a variety of non-criminal mechanisms available to deal with misconduct in financial institutions. *See supra* p. 431, n. 32. Perhaps because of these safeguards and alternative means of enforcement, very few actual prosecutions of financial institutions for money laundering actually take place. However, the potential for enormous liability under these provisions casts a large shadow over bank operations, and often leads to the problem of defensive SARs filing, *see supra* pp. 430–31.

3. Is § 1957 good policy? Are its terms sufficiently clear to give fair notice? John Villa says no on both counts:

> The [currency reporting laws], as well as the more recent laundering statutes, implicitly reflect a congressional judgment that law enforcement goals can be achieved more effectively by severely punishing federally regulated financial institutions than by developing cooperative programs with the banking industry. The wisdom of this approach is open to serious question because financial institutions historically have been close allies with the law enforcement community, and have cooperated with federal law enforcement authorities almost to a fault. Moreover, in its headlong rush to be tough on the banks, Congress adopted legislative changes that have created insoluble problems for financial institutions without any corresponding benefit to law enforcement interests.

> A case in point is section 1957 of title 18 of the United States Code. Before analyzing the flaws in the statute, it is worth observing that the statute presents a clear departure from traditional concepts of criminal behavior. Although the criminal law has long forbidden the receipt of stolen goods, it has not generally prohibited a person from doing business with or for another simply because unlawful conduct served as the source of the funds for the transaction. One has the right to sell his house to a gangster as freely as to a clergyman as long as the parties perform the transaction at arm's length with no intent to assist the gangster in the commission of a crime.

Section 1957, by contrast, reflects a new approach and one that seems likely to exact unanticipated social costs. One who suspects a person of offering stolen goods for sale may protect himself by merely declining to purchase the suspect goods. The social cost of declining that purchase is minimal. If, on the other hand, it is a crime to do any business at all with one who deals in the proceeds of illegal activity, then those who are merely suspected of crimes will find that they cannot engage in everyday commerce; fearing criminal liability, no one will risk dealing with them. The impact on the suspected individual can be severe because no knowledgeable person will transact business with him, yet there may be no means by which the suspected individual can clear himself. The social cost of imposing such a stigma on individuals—especially those who have not been convicted of, let alone charged with, any crime—should present grave civil liberties concerns even for the most ardent law-and-order legislator. It is disappointing to find that Congress did not seriously debate these important issues at the time it enacted section 1957.

Putting to one side the serious policy questions presented by section 1957, the statute itself is riddled with ambiguities that present enormous problems for financial institutions. As bank officers confront these ambiguities, they may well choose to read the statute broadly—thus minimizing their own risk of criminal prosecution—which would cause the statute to have an even greater impact than Congress expected. A direct result of loose draftsmanship will, therefore, cause the denial of financial services to some innocent customers by justifiably cautious bankers.

Section 1957 prohibits conducting transactions that involve 'criminally derived property.' Yet, neither section 1957 nor section 1956 define these 'proceeds' concepts, thus, inviting a wide range of interpretation. Do the statutes only apply to the direct fruits of illegal activity or do they also apply to the products of those fruits which are reinvested and thereby change form? If $25,000 in illegal proceeds are placed into a bank account containing $75,000 in legal monies, does every check subsequently written on that account consist of 25% illegal proceeds? If a bank lends a customer $50,000 and subsequently learns that an unlawful activity created his source of funds, can it accept repayment of the loan? If an individual has legal and illegal sources of income, can a bank transact any business with him without fear of prosecution?

Even with adequate definition of the key statutory terms, there is little chance that financial institutions could apply them accurately. Financial institutions are ill-equipped to decide whether a particular customer obtains his funds from illegal sources. It typically takes a trained federal prosecutor, using experienced investigators and the unparalleled power of a federal grand jury, months or even years to identify criminal activity. An inexperienced banker applying an unintelligible statute like section 1957 has little hope of making a correct decision while a customer transaction is pending. If the financial institution incorrectly decides to terminate business activities with the suspected customer, a major civil lawsuit is inevitable.

The impossible choices that face many financial institutions demonstrate that Congress has simply dropped the problem in the lap of the financial services industry and walked away. None of the options are attractive, but some financial institutions will ultimately decide that unless a customer clearly and openly engages in illegal activity, they will not terminate business contacts with him. While this may be a realistic solution, it is not a happy one. It means that many financial institutions will, for the first time, knowingly operate on the fringe of the criminal law.

John K. Villa, *A Critical View of Bank Secrecy Act Enforcement and the Money Laundering Statutes*, 37 CATH. U. L. REV. 487, 500–02 (1988). *See also* G. Richard Strafer, *Money Laundering: The Crime of the '90's*, 27 AM. CRIM. L. REV. 149 (1989) (identifying several "defects" in the money laundering statutes and advocating various amendments).

4. *Campbell* demonstrates the reach of § 1957 to third parties. For a decision applying this provision to an accountant who assisted drug traffickers who funneled drug money into legitimate commercial transactions, see *United States v. Bornfield*, 145 F.3d 1123 (10th Cir. 1998).

What about cash paid to attorneys? Section 1957 was amended in 1988 to add a provision dealing expressly with the application of that section to attorneys fees. Section 1957(f) provides that the term monetary transaction—

> does not include any transaction necessary to preserve a person's right to representation as guaranteed by the sixth amendment to the Constitution * * *.

This provision was enacted before the Supreme Court's decision in *Caplin & Drysdale v. United States*, *infra* at 931–35. As discussed in greater detail in Chapter 19, *Caplin & Drysdale* held that a criminal defendant has no Sixth Amendment right to use the proceeds of criminal activity to pay for defense counsel where those funds were subject to forfeiture. In light of the decision in *Caplin & Drysdale*, what is the effect, if any, of the attorneys fee provision in § 1957(f)(1)? For a discussion of this provision, see Note, *Indirect Deprivation of the Effective Assistance of Counsel: The Prospective Prosecution of Criminal Defense Attorneys for 'Money Laundering,'* 34 N.Y. L. SCH. L. REV. 303 (1989).

There were a number of high profile money laundering prosecutions of attorneys in the 1990s, including the prosecution of former federal prosecutors who were charged with aiding the Cali drug cartel after attempting to extradite the same individuals in their role as prosecutors. *See* Rachel Ratliff, *Third-Party Money Laundering: Problems of Proof and Prosecutorial Discretion*, 7 STAN. L. & POL'Y REV. 173, 178–183 (1996).

For a more general treatment of the subject of money laundering and defense lawyers see Eugene R. Gaetke & Sarah N. Welling, *Money Laundering and Lawyers*, 43 SYRACUSE L. REV. 1165 (1993), and *Protecting Yourself and Your Fee: A Defense Lawyer's Practice Guide in a New Age of Federal Law*, ABA RICO Cases Comm., July 1991.

5. The U.S. Attorneys Manual provides that the approval of the Assistant Attorney General of the Criminal Division is required before an indict-

ment under § 1957 may be presented charging an attorney with a violation of that section where "the criminally derived property is or purports to be attorneys' fees paid to the attorney for providing representation to a client in a criminal or civil matter." USAM ¶ 9–105.300 (July 2005). Section 9–105.600 provides:

> Because the Department firmly believes that attorneys representing clients in criminal matters must not be hampered in their ability to effectively and ethically represent their clients within the bounds of the law, the Department, as a matter of policy, will not prosecute attorneys under § 1957 based upon the receipt of property constituting bona fide fees for the legitimate representation in a criminal matter, except if (1) there is proof beyond a reasonable doubt that the attorney had actual knowledge of the illegal origin of the specific property received (prosecution is not permitted if the only proof of knowledge is evidence of willful blindness); and (2) such evidence does not consist of (a) confidential communications made by the client preliminary to and with regard to undertaking representation in the criminal matter; or (b) confidential communications made during the course of representation in the criminal matter; or (c) other information obtained by the attorney during the course of the representation and in furtherance of the obligation to effectively represent the client.

* * *

> This prosecution standard applies only to fees received for legal "representation in a criminal matter." Attorneys who receive criminally derived property in exchange for carrying out or engaging in other commercial transactions unrelated to the representation of a client in a criminal matter or for representing a client in a civil matter should be treated the same as any other person.

Note that this policy does not exempt fees paid for representation in connection with civil matters.

The question whether the attorney-client relationship should be subject to limitations imposed by the currency reporting, money laundering, and forfeiture laws has been hotly debated. *See supra* at 426 n. b, and *infra* at 931–38. A controversial "gatekeeper" proposal has been made to require lawyers and accountants who participate in the financial system to put systems in place to detect and prevent money laundering. In May 2002, the FATF issued a report (a "consulting paper") including a "gatekeeper initiative" extending to lawyers and accountants. The Departments of Justice and Treasury had been working with the FATF to develop a recommendation on the role that U.S. attorneys may be required to play. The key elements under discussion were whether attorneys will be required to file suspicious activity reports when they engage in financial transactions on behalf of their clients and become aware of illegal client activity, as well as requirements that attorneys know their clients, and inquire about the source of the client's funds associated with any financial transaction. An American Bar Association Task Force strongly opposed the requirement that lawyers report suspicious activity reports as well as the "no tipping" rule that would also prevent lawyers from notifying their client if they provide such a report. The Task Force contended that such requirements would be contrary to the ethical rules governing lawyers, would impair client compliance with the law, and could ultimately undermine the fundamental principles underlying the United States legal system.[p]

The FATF's revised Forty Recommendations, issued in 2003, included a narrower gatekeeper proposal applying to lawyers, notaries, and independent legal professionals only when they "prepare for or carry out" transactions for their client concerning particular activities including buying and selling real estate; managing client money, securities, or other assets; managing bank, savings, or securities accounts; creating, operating, or managing legal persons or arrangements; and buying and selling business entities. Lawyers are not required to report their suspicions if the relevant information was obtained in circumstances where they are subject to professional secrecy or legal professional privilege. Did this provision strike the right balance, or is there a need to make an exception to the attorney-client privilege in this context?

6. Despite—or perhaps because of—the breadth of § 1957, the Department of Justice has brought relatively few cases under that provision. For example, the Department of Justice reported that in 2001, the most recent year for which data is available, it completed 140 prosecutions under § 1957, compared with nearly 1,245 prosecutions under § 1956. Do you have any idea what factors might explain this pattern? Note that the penalty for violation of § 1956 is 20 years, while the maximum under § 1957 is only 10 years.

p. The American Bar Association's Task Force Report is available online at http:// www1.oecd.org/fatf/pdf/REV_US-American-BarAssn.pdf (visited July 19, 2005).

*

Part IV

GROUP AND ORGANIZATIONAL CRIME

Chapter 11

RICO—THE RACKETEER INFLU-
ENCED AND CORRUPT OR-
GANIZATIONS STATUTE

INTRODUCTION

The Racketeer Influenced and Corrupt Organizations (RICO) statute, 18 U.S.C. §§ 1961–1968, was enacted in 1970 as part of the
Organized Crime Control Act. It defined an unusually innovative and
adaptable statutory scheme.

The statute describes a complex crime, somewhat similar to conspiracy insofar as the crime usually involves group activity and is committed
when the commission of other "predicate" crimes is involved. It is aimed
at both criminal activity that takes over legitimate business and criminal
activity that is carried on in a business-like way. It carries forward,
builds upon, and elaborates on earlier tentative federal efforts to define
racketeering. *See, e.g.* 18 U.S.C. § 1952. It provides for very severe
traditional prison and money penalties and also makes available a
diverse set of other remedies such as forfeiture, treble damages, divestiture, reorganization and other equitable measures.

Generally speaking, the statute makes criminal four types of conduct:

- using or investing income derived from a pattern of racketeering
  activity to acquire an enterprise engaged in or affecting commerce, § 1962(a);

- acquiring an interest in such an enterprise through a pattern of
  racketeering activity, § 1962(b);

- conducting the affairs of an enterprise through a pattern of
  racketeering activity, § 1962(c); and

- conspiring to commit any of the first three violations, 1962(d).

The key concepts in the foregoing offenses, namely "enterprise,"
and "pattern of racketeering activity" are not traditional or common law
concepts and are newly defined in § 1961 of the statute. Section 1961(1),

for example, contains a very long list of federal crimes and a shorter list of state crimes that are defined as "racketeering activity."

Section 1963 provides a maximum penalty of 20 years imprisonment for a RICO violation; most of the predicate offenses listed as racketeering activity have lesser penalties assigned to them. An individual convicted of RICO may end up with penalties imposed for the RICO violation, for the predicate offenses and for conspiracy to commit a RICO violation under § 1962(d). A successful RICO prosecution can thus add enormously to the maximum penalties that can be imposed under the applicable criminal statutes. Of course, one should be attentive to the impact of the Sentencing Guidelines on the punishment for RICO and related crimes.

As you study the materials in this Chapter, it will be helpful to keep in mind the following questions:

- Is RICO essentially a conspiracy or super-conspiracy statute? What might be meant by the concept of a super-conspiracy?

- Is RICO primarily a penalty enhancement statute? If so, what justifies the higher penalties?

- Is the RICO statute primarily aimed at "organized crime,"—what does that mean? At "racketeering"—what does that mean? At the infiltration of legitimate business?

- Is the RICO statute also an effective weapon for use against terrorism organizations and terrorist activities? The USA PATRI- OT Act enacted in the wake of the terrorist attacks on September 11, 2001 amended section 1961 by adding specific terrorist crimes to the long list of offenses in that section; and the Intelligence Reform and Terrorism Prevention Act of 2004 added offenses relating to biological, chemical and nuclear weapons.

A special feature of RICO is that the statute provides that a private person injured by the commission of a criminal RICO violation has the basis for a civil treble damage suit. A RICO violation is also a basis for the government to seek civil equitable relief. Because the bases for these civil remedies are criminal RICO violations, the courts address the criminal law issues in civil RICO cases as well as in criminal RICO judicial opinions. Criminal RICO is a key prosecutorial tool , and there have been a significant number of criminal RICO cases. The number of cases, however, in which private civil plaintiffs seek to invoke RICO dwarfs the criminal caseload. The result is that the law of criminal RICO has been developing in both criminal and civil RICO cases at an unusually fast pace, much faster than the pattern of judicial interpretation applicable to other federal criminal statutes. Would you expect the content of the judicial interpretations of the RICO statute to be affected by the fact that many of these interpretations are occurring in civil cases?

RICO has generated much controversy and a substantial literature, and there have been a number of proposals to reform the statute. Thus far, Congress has declined to enact any major changes in the RICO statute, although there have been some relatively minor amendments of the original statute. RICO has also been used as a model in many states which have adopted "little RICO" statutes.

One should keep in mind that the full impact of RICO cannot be appreciated until one also studies the most frequently-used predicate offenses, some of which, e.g. mail fraud, are themselves quite open-ended crimes. RICO has been challenged on various constitutional grounds, e.g. double jeopardy, ex post facto, and vagueness, but all of these challenges have been rejected by the courts.

Most of the RICO cases involve charges under § 1962(c) or (d), that is conducting the affairs of an enterprise through a pattern of racketeering activity or conspiring to do so, and, accordingly, these materials mainly focus on cases brought under those sections. In Section A, we introduce a central element of a RICO charge, the "enterprise," and in section B, we examine the concept of the "person" who can be charged with a RICO violation and the issue of distinguishing between the person and the enterprise. In Section C, we address the "pattern of racketeering activity" concept, breaking it into its two component parts, that is the "pattern" requirement and the issues that arise with respect to "racketeering activity."

In Sections D and E, we examine RICO conspiracy and civil RICO, and we conclude in Section F with a review of the Department of Justice's RICO Prosecutorial Guidelines.

TITLE 18 U.S.C. CHAPTER 96—RACKETEER INFLUENCED AND CORRUPT ORGANIZATIONS

§ 1961. Definitions

As used in this chapter—

(1) "racketeering activity" means (A) any act or threat involving murder, kidnapping, gambling, arson, robbery, bribery, extortion, dealing in obscene matter, or dealing in a controlled substance or listed chemical (as defined in section 102 of the Controlled Substances Act), which is chargeable under State law and punishable by imprisonment for more than one year; (B) any act which is indictable under any of the following provisions of title 18, United States Code: Section 201 (relating to bribery), section 224 (relating to sports bribery), sections 471, 472, and 473 (relating to counterfeiting), section 659 (relating to theft from interstate shipment) if the act indictable under section 659 is felonious, section 664 (relating to embezzlement from pension and welfare funds), sections 891–894 (relating to extortionate credit transactions), section 1028 (relating to fraud and related activity in connection with identification documents), section 1029 (relating to fraud and related activity in connection with access devices), section 1084 (relating to the transmission of gambling information), section 1341 (relating to mail fraud), section 1343 (relating to wire fraud), section 1344 (relating to financial institution fraud), section 1425 (relating to the procure-

ment of citizenship or nationalization unlawfully), section 1426 (relating to the reproduction of naturalization or citizenship papers), section 1427 (relating to the sale of naturalization or citizenship papers), sections 1461–1465 (relating to obscene matter), section 1503 (relating to obstruction of justice), section 1510 (relating to obstruction of criminal investigations), section 1511 (relating to the obstruction of State or local law enforcement), section 1512 (relating to tampering with a witness, victim, or an informant), section 1513 (relating to retaliating against a witness, victim, or an informant), section 1542 (relating to false statement in application and use of passport), section 1543 (relating to forgery or false use of passport), section 1544 (relating to misuse of passport), section 1546 (relating to fraud and misuse of visas, permits, and other documents), sections 1581–1591 (relating to peonage, slavery, and trafficking in persons), section 1951 (relating to interference with commerce, robbery, or extortion), section 1952 (relating to racketeering), section 1953 (relating to interstate transportation of wagering paraphernalia), section 1954 (relating to unlawful welfare fund payments), section 1955 (relating to the prohibition of illegal gambling businesses), section 1956 (relating to the laundering of monetary instruments), section 1957 (relating to engaging in monetary transactions in property derived from specified unlawful activity), section 1958 (relating to use of interstate commerce facilities in the commission of murder-for-hire), sections 2251, 2251A, 2252, and 2260 (relating to sexual exploitation of children), sections 2312 and 2313 (relating to interstate transportation of stolen motor vehicles), sections 2314 and 2315 (relating to interstate transportation of stolen property), section 2318 (relating to trafficking in counterfeit labels for phonorecords, computer programs or computer program documentation or packaging and copies of motion pictures or other audiovisual works), section 2319 (relating to criminal infringement of a copyright), section 2319A (relating to unauthorized fixation of and trafficking in sound recordings and music videos of live musical performances), section 2320 (relating to trafficking in goods or services bearing counterfeit marks), section 2321 (relating to trafficking in certain motor vehicles or motor vehicle parts), sections 2341–2346 (relating to trafficking in contraband cigarettes), sections 2421–24 (relating to white slave traffic), sections 175–178 (relating to biological weapons), sections 229–229F (relating to chemical weapons), section 831 (relating to nuclear materials), (C) any act which is indictable under title 29, United States Code, section 186 (dealing with restrictions on payments and loans to labor organizations) or section 501(c) (relating to embezzlement from union funds), (D) any offense involving fraud connected with a case under title 11 (except a case under section 157 of this title), fraud in the sale of securities, or the felonious manufacture, importation, receiving, concealment, buying, selling, or otherwise dealing in a controlled substance or listed chemical (as defined in section 102 of the Controlled Substances Act), punishable under any law of the United

States, (E) any act which is indictable under the Currency and Foreign Transactions Reporting Act, (F) any act which is indictable under the Immigration and Nationality Act, section 274 (relating to bringing in and harboring certain aliens), section 277 (relating to aiding or assisting certain aliens to enter the United States), or section 278 (relating to importation of alien for immoral purpose) if the act indictable under such section of such Act was committed for the purpose of financial gain, or (G) any act that is indictable under any provision listed in section 2332b(g)(5)(B)*;

* * *

(3) "person" includes any individual or entity capable of holding a legal or beneficial interest in property;

(4) "enterprise" includes any individual, partnership, corporation, association, or other legal entity, and any union or group of individuals associated in fact although not a legal entity;

(5) "pattern of racketeering activity" requires at least two acts of racketeering activity, one of which occurred after the effective date of this chapter and the last of which occurred within ten years (excluding any period of imprisonment) after the commission of a prior act of racketeering activity;

(6) "unlawful debt" means a debt (A) incurred or contracted in gambling activity which was in violation of the law of the United States, a State or political subdivision thereof, or which is unenforceable under State or Federal law in whole or in part as to principal or interest because of the laws relating to usury, and (B) which was incurred in connection with the business of gambling in violation of the law of the United States, a State or political subdivision thereof, or the business of lending money or a thing of value at a rate usurious under State or Federal law, where the usurious rate is at least twice the enforceable rate;* * *

§ 1962. Prohibited activities

(a) It shall be unlawful for any person who has received any income derived, directly or indirectly, from a pattern of racketeering activity or through collection of an unlawful debt in which such person has participated as a principal within the meaning of section 2, title 18, United States Code, to use or invest, directly or indirectly, any part of such income, or the proceeds of such income, in acquisition of any interest in, or the establishment or operation of, any enterprise which is engaged in, or the activities of which affect, interstate or foreign commerce. A purchase of securities on the open market for purposes of investment, and without the intention of controlling or participating in the control of the issuer, or of assisting another to do so, shall not be unlawful under this subsection if

---

* Section 2332b(g)(5)(B) lists 59 offenses that it defines as federal crimes of terrorism including hostage taking, assassinating the president and using plastic explosives.

the securities of the issuer held by the purchaser, the members of his immediate family, and his or their accomplices in any pattern or racketeering activity or the collection of an unlawful debt after such purchase do not amount in the aggregate to one percent of the outstanding securities of any one class, and do not confer, either in law or in fact, the power to elect one or more directors of the issuer.

(b) It shall be unlawful for any person through a pattern of racketeering activity or through collection of an unlawful debt to acquire or maintain, directly or indirectly, any interest in or control of any enterprise which is engaged in, or the activities of which affect, interstate or foreign commerce.

(c) It shall be unlawful for any person employed by or associated with any enterprise engaged in, or the activities of which affect, interstate or foreign commerce, to conduct or participate, directly or indirectly, in the conduct of such enterprise's affairs through a pattern of racketeering activity or collection of unlawful debt.

(d) It shall be unlawful for any person to conspire to violate any of the provisions of subsection (a), (b), or (c) of this section.

§ 1963. Criminal penalties

(a) Whoever violates any provision of section 1962 of this chapter shall be fined under this title or imprisoned not more than 20 years (or for life if the violation is based on a racketeering activity for which the maximum penalty includes life imprisonment), or both, and shall forfeit to the United States, irrespective of any provision of State law—

(1) any interest the person has acquired or maintained in violation of section 1962;

(2) any—

(A) interest in;

(B) security of;

(C) claim against; or

(D) property or contractual right of any kind affording a source of influence over;

any enterprise which the person has established, operated, controlled, conducted, or participated in the conduct of, in violation of section 1962; and

(3) any property constituting, or derived from, any proceeds which the person obtained, directly or indirectly, from racketeering activity or unlawful debt collection in violation of section 1962.

The court, in imposing sentence on such person shall order, in addition to any other sentence imposed pursuant to this section, that the person forfeit to the United States all property described in this subsection. In lieu of a fine otherwise authorized by this section, a defendant who derives profits or other proceeds from an offense may be fined not more than twice the gross profits or other proceeds.

(b) Property subject to criminal forfeiture under this section includes—

(1) real property, including things growing on, affixed to, and found in land; and

(2) tangible and intangible personal property, including rights, privileges, interests, claims, and securities.

* * *

[RICO forfeiture under 18 U.S.C. § 1963 is discussed infra, p. 915. 18 U.S.C. § 1964 which authorizes civil remedies is reprinted at pp. 559–560 in this chapter.]

A. THE ENTERPRISE ELEMENT

UNITED STATES v. TURKETTE

452 U.S. 576, 101 S.Ct. 2524, 69 L.Ed.2d 246 (1981).

JUSTICE WHITE delivered the opinion of the Court.

Chapter 96 of Title 18 of the United States Code, 18 U. S. C. §§ 1961–1968, entitled Racketeer Influenced and Corrupt Organizations (RICO), was added to Title 18 by Title IX of the Organized Crime Control Act of 1970, Pub. L. 91–452, 84 Stat. 941. The question in this case is whether the term "enterprise" as used in RICO encompasses both legitimate and illegitimate enterprises or is limited in application to the former. The Court of Appeals for the First Circuit held that Congress did not intend to include within the definition of "enterprise" those organizations which are exclusively criminal. 632 F.2d 896 (1980). This position is contrary to that adopted by every other Circuit that has addressed the issue. We granted certiorari to resolve this conflict.

I.

Count Nine of a nine-count indictment charged respondent and 12 others with conspiracy to conduct and participate in the affairs of an enterprise engaged in interstate commerce through a pattern of racketeering activities, in violation of 18 U. S. C. § 1962(d). The indictment described the enterprise as "a group of individuals associated in fact for the purpose of illegally trafficking in narcotics and other dangerous drugs, committing arsons, utilizing the United States mails to defraud insurance companies, bribing and attempting to bribe local police officers, and corruptly influencing and attempting to corruptly influence the outcome of state court proceedings...." The other eight counts of the indictment charged the commission of various substantive criminal acts by those engaged in and associated with the criminal enterprise, including possession with intent to distribute and distribution of controlled substances, and several counts of insurance fraud by arson and other means. The common thread to all counts was respondent's alleged leadership of this criminal organization through which he orchestrated and participated in the commission of the various crimes delineated in the RICO count or charged in the eight preceding counts.

After a 6–week jury trial, in which the evidence focused upon both the professional nature of this organization and the execution of a number of distinct criminal acts, respondent was convicted on all nine counts. He was sentenced to a term of 20 years on the substantive counts, as well as a 2–year special parole term on the drug count. On the RICO conspiracy count he was sentenced to a 20–year concurrent term and fined $20,000.

On appeal, respondent argued that RICO was intended solely to protect legitimate business enterprises from infiltration by racketeers and that RICO does not make criminal the participation in an association which performs only illegal acts and which has not infiltrated or attempted to infiltrate a legitimate enterprise. The Court of Appeals agreed. We reverse.

II.

In determining the scope of a statute, we look first to its language. If the statutory language is unambiguous, in the absence of "a clearly expressed legislative intent to the contrary, that language must ordinarily be regarded as conclusive * * *.

Section 1962 (c) makes it unlawful "for any person employed by or associated with any enterprise engaged in, or the activities of which affect, interstate or foreign commerce, to conduct or participate, directly or indirectly, in the conduct of such enterprise's affairs through a pattern of racketeering activity or collection of unlawful debt." The term "enterprise" is defined as including "any individual, partnership, corporation, association, or other legal entity, and any union or group of individuals associated in fact although not a legal entity." § 1961 (4). There is no restriction upon the associations embraced by the definition: an enterprise includes any union or group of individuals associated in fact. On its face, the definition appears to include both legitimate and illegitimate enterprises within its scope; it no more excludes criminal enterprises than it does legitimate ones. Had Congress not intended to reach criminal associations, it could easily have narrowed the sweep of the definition by inserting a single word, "legitimate." But it did nothing to indicate that an enterprise consisting of a group of individuals was not covered by RICO if the purpose of the enterprise was exclusively criminal.

* * *

Section 1961(4) describes two categories of associations that come within the purview of the "enterprise" definition. The first encompasses organizations such as corporations and partnerships, and other "legal entities." The second covers "any union or group of individuals associated in fact although not a legal entity." The Court of Appeals assumed that the second category was merely a more general description of the first. Having made that assumption, the court concluded that the more generalized description in the second category should be limited by the specific examples enumerated in the first. But that assumption is untenable. Each category describes a separate type of enterprise to be covered by the statute—those that are recognized as legal entities and those that are not. The latter is not a more general description of the former. The second category itself not containing any specific enumeration that is followed by a general description, *ejusdem generis* has no bearing on the meaning to be attributed to that part of § 1961(4).

A second reason offered by the Court of Appeals in support of its judgment was that giving the definition of "enterprise" its ordinary meaning would create several internal inconsistencies in the Act. With respect to § 1962(c), it was said:

> "If 'a pattern of racketeering' can itself be an 'enterprise' for purposes of section 1962 (c), then the two phrases 'employed by or associated with any enterprise' and 'the conduct of such enterprise's affairs through [a pattern of racketeering activity]' add nothing to the meaning of the section. The words of the statute are coherent and logical only if they are read as applying to legitimate enterprises."

This conclusion is based on a faulty premise. That a wholly criminal enterprise comes within the ambit of the statute does not mean that a "pattern of racketeering activity" is an "enterprise." In order to secure a conviction under RICO, the Government must prove both the existence of an "enterprise" and the connected "pattern of racketeering activity." The enterprise is an entity, for present purposes a group of persons associated together for a common purpose of engaging in a course of conduct. The pattern of racketeering activity is, on the other hand, a series of criminal acts as defined by the statute. The former is proved by evidence of an ongoing organization, formal or informal, and by evidence that the various associates function as a continuing unit. The latter is proved by evidence of the requisite number of acts of racketeering committed by the participants in the enterprise. While the proof used to establish these separate elements may in particular cases coalesce, proof of one does not necessarily establish the other. The "enterprise" is not the "pattern of racketeering activity"; it is an entity separate and apart from the pattern of activity in which it engages. The existence of an enterprise at all times remains a separate element which must be proved by the Government.

Apart from § 1962(c)'s proscription against participating in an enterprise through a pattern of racketeering activities, RICO also proscribes the investment of income derived from racketeering activity in an enterprise engaged in or which affects interstate commerce as well as the acquisition of an interest in or control of any such enterprise through a pattern of racketeering activity. The Court of Appeals concluded that these provisions of RICO should be interpreted so as to apply only to legitimate enterprises. If these two sections are so limited, the Court of Appeals held that the proscription in § 1962 (c), at issue here, must be similarly limited. Again, we do not accept the premise from which the Court of Appeals derived its conclusion. It is obvious that §§ 1962 (a) and (b) address the infiltration by organized crime of legitimate businesses, but we cannot agree that these sections were not also aimed at preventing racketeers from investing or reinvesting in wholly illegal enterprises and from acquiring through a pattern of racketeering activity wholly illegitimate enterprises such as an illegal gambling business or a loan-sharking operation. There is no inconsistency or anomaly in recognizing that § 1962 applies to both legitimate and illegitimate enterprises. Certainly the language of the statute does not warrant the Court of Appeals' conclusion to the contrary.

Similarly, the Court of Appeals noted that various civil remedies were provided by § 1964, including divestiture, dissolution, reorganization, restrictions on future activities by violators of RICO, and treble damages. These remedies it thought would have utility only with respect to legitimate enterprises. As a general proposition, however, the civil remedies could be useful in eradicating organized crime from the social fabric, whether the enterprise be ostensibly legitimate or admittedly criminal. The aim is to divest the association of the fruits of its ill-gotten gains. Even if one or more of the civil remedies might be inapplicable to a particular illegitimate enterprise, this fact would not serve to limit the enterprise concept. Congress has provided civil remedies for use when the circumstances so warrant. It is untenable to argue that their existence limits the scope of the criminal provisions.

Finally, it is urged that the interpretation of RICO to include both legitimate and illegitimate enterprises will substantially alter the balance between federal and state enforcement of criminal law. This is particularly true, so the argument goes, since included within the definition of racketeering activity are a significant number of acts made criminal under state law. 18 U. S. C. § 1961 (1) But even assuming that the more inclusive definition of enterprise will have the effect suggested the language of the statute and its legislative history indicate that Congress was well aware that it was entering a new domain of federal involvement through the enactment of this measure. Indeed, the very purpose of the Organized Crime Control Act of 1970 was to enable the Federal Government to address a large and seemingly neglected problem. The view was that existing law, state and federal, was not adequate to address the problem, which was of national dimensions. That Congress included within the definition of racketeering activities a number of state crimes strongly indicates that RICO criminalized conduct that was also criminal under state law, at least when the requisite elements of a RICO offense are present. As the hearings and legislative debates reveal, Congress was well aware of the fear that RICO would "[move] large substantive areas formerly totally within the police power of the State into the Federal realm." In the face of these objections, Congress nonetheless proceeded to enact the measure, knowing that it would alter somewhat the role of the Federal Government in the war against organized crime and that the alteration would entail prosecutions involving acts of racketeering that are also crimes under state law. There is no argument that Congress acted beyond its power in so doing. That being the case, the courts are without authority to restrict the application of the statute.

Contrary to the judgment below, neither the language nor structure of RICO limits its application to legitimate "enterprises." Applying it also to criminal organizations does not render any portion of the statute superfluous nor does it create any structural incongruities within the framework of the Act. The result is neither absurd nor surprising. On the contrary, insulating the wholly criminal enterprise from prosecution under RICO is the more incongruous position.

Section 904 (a) of RICO, 84 Stat. 947, directs that "[the] provisions of this Title shall be liberally construed to effectuate its remedial purposes." With or without this admonition, we could not agree with the Court of Appeals that illegitimate enterprises should be excluded from coverage. We are also quite sure that nothing in the legislative history of RICO requires a contrary conclusion.

III.

The statement of findings that prefaces the Organized Crime Control Act of 1970 reveals the pervasiveness of the problem that Congress was addressing by this enactment:

* * *

In light of the * * * findings, it was the declared purpose of Congress "to seek the eradication of organized crime in the United States by strengthening the legal tools in the evidence-gathering process, by establishing new penal prohibitions, and by providing enhanced sanctions and new remedies to deal with the unlawful activities of those engaged in organized crime."

* * * In view of the purposes and goals of the Act, as well as the language of the statute, we are unpersuaded that Congress nevertheless confined the reach of the law to only narrow aspects of organized crime, and, in particular, under RICO, only the infiltration of legitimate business.

This is not to gainsay that the legislative history forcefully supports the view that the major purpose of Title IX is to address the infiltration of legitimate business by organized crime. The point is made time and again during the debates and in the hearings before the House and Senate. But none of these statements requires the negative inference that Title IX did not reach the activities of enterprises organized and existing for criminal purposes.

On the contrary, these statements are in full accord with the proposition that RICO is equally applicable to a criminal enterprise that has no legitimate dimension or has yet to acquire one. Accepting that the primary purpose of RICO is to cope with the infiltration of legitimate businesses, applying the statute in accordance with its terms, so as to reach criminal enterprises, would seek to deal with the problem at its very source. Supporters of the bill recognized that organized crime uses its primary sources of revenue and power—illegal gambling, loan sharking and illicit drug distribution—as a springboard into the sphere of legitimate enterprise. * * *

As a measure to deal with the infiltration of legitimate businesses by organized crime, RICO was both preventive and remedial. Respondent's view would ignore the preventive function of the statute. If Congress had intended the more circumscribed approach espoused by the Court of Appeals, there would have been some positive sign that the law is not to reach organized criminal activities that give rise to the concerns about infiltration. The language of the statute, however—the most reliable evidence of its intent—reveals that Congress opted for a far broader definition of the word "enterprise," and we are unconvinced by anything in the legislative history that this definition should be given less than its full effect.

The judgment of the Court of Appeals is accordingly

Reversed.

JUSTICE STEWART agrees with the reasoning and conclusion of the Court of Appeals as to the meaning of the term "enterprise" in this statute. Accordingly, he respectfully dissents.

1. AN ASSOCIATION IN FACT AS THE ENTERPRISE

Notes

1. Although the RICO statute was enacted in 1970, for a number of years after there were few prosecutions under the statute. *Turkette* was the first case to reach the Supreme Court, and the decision in the case and the language of the Court's opinion became foundational. Subsequently, RICO cases came to be prosecuted more frequently.

2. The primary ruling in *"Turkette"* is that the term *"enterprise"* under the RICO statute includes associations that commit only illegal acts. This ruling had several consequences: 1) RICO is not restricted to infiltration of legitimate businesses by criminal elements as reflected in 18 U.S.C.§§ 1962(a) and (b), although one form of "enterprise" under the statute could be a legitimate business or corporation. 2) An informal criminal association could be an enterprise in a prosecution under the statute. In fact the bulk of RICO criminal prosecutions have been under § 1962(c) and have involved informal criminal associations. 3) Thus two forms of "enterprise" are covered by the statute. Each presents a different set of problems.

3. *Turkette* makes the point that "the legislative history forcefully supports the view that the major purpose of Title IX [the RICO statute] is to address the infiltration of legitimate business by organized crime." Professor James Jacobs concludes that RICO has been used very effectively to address the problem of organized crime in New York City, particularly within the labor unions. James B. Jacobs, *Gotham Unbound: How New York City Was Liberated from the Grip of Organized Crime* (NYU Press 1999). See a review of the Jacobs book by Gerald J. Russello, Law and Politics Book Review (Law & Courts Section, APSA) online at http://www.bsos.umd.edu/gvpt/lpbr /sub-pages/reviews/jacobs.html:

> Organized crime emerges from this study as a concrete and identifiable entity in the city's economic framework. It is structured, highly organized, economically intelligent and extremely flexible and opportunistic. Indeed, in some industries, control by organized crime may have had certain economic benefits, for example in the Fulton Fish Market, which further assisted its dominance These characteristics made organized crime highly resistant to traditional law enforcement techniques, and arrests and long prison terms did not restrict its activity or reduce its allure to potential recruits. The law enforcement approach changed upon the enactment, in 1970, of the Racketeer Influenced and Corrupt Organizations Act (RICO). RICO provided an avenue to reach organized crime, both as an entity itself and as an influence on other organizations such as labor unions. The statute enabled law enforcement to engage organized crime in the one area in which it could suffer significant short and long-term damage: its economics.

4. Another conclusion advanced by the Court in *Turkette* is that the "enterprise" is separate from the "pattern of racketeering activity"; that "proof of one does not necessarily establish the other." At the same time, the Court stated that "the proof used to establish these separate elements may in particular cases coalesce." Further consideration of the implications of this language as it bears on the issue of what must be proved to establish an enterprise is contained in notes 8, 9, and 10, *infra*. The interpretation of "pattern of racketeering activity" is addressed in section C, *infra*.

5. The definition of "enterprise" is set forth in § 1961(4) and includes a "group of individuals associated in fact" and "not a legal entity." On its face, that definition of enterprise, when characterized as a criminal association, calls to mind a criminal conspiracy. Given the difference in penalties—a simple criminal conspiracy under 18 U.S.C. § 371 has a maximum penalty of five years, while a RICO violation carries with it a maximum penalty of 20 years on a substantive RICO charge and another 20 for conspiracy to violate RICO—the question is posed, how does a RICO enterprise—in its informal criminal association version—differ, if it does, from a simple criminal conspiracy? Why is it treated as a much more serious criminal violation than conspiracy?

6. Recall that the Court in *Turkette* elaborated on the elements of an informal criminal association: First it referred to "a group of persons associated together for a common purpose of engaging in a course of conduct." Does this characterization differ from the usual definition of a conspiracy? Second, the Court described it as an "ongoing organization,

formal or informal" in which "the various associates function as a continuing unit." This formulation has been repeatedly cited by the lower courts in interpreting the enterprise concept. A number of questions can be raised about this formulation. Was it simply a dictum issued by the Court while deciding other issues in *Turkette* or was it necessary to the Court's decision? From where did the Court derive the formulation? Is it implicit in the concept of an enterprise or in any other words in § 1961(4), or is it entirely a judicial creation not necessarily compelled by the language of the statute? Apart from whether it follows from the terms of the statute, does it provide a useful, functional basis for distinguishing simple conspiracies from enterprises under RICO, and provide warrant for the severe penalties provided for under RICO?

7. In comparing simple conspiracies and the RICO enterprise as characterized in *Turkette*, consider the following excerpts that discuss the rationale for permitting cumulative sentences for a conspiracy and its object crime:

> * * * [A conspiracy] may and often does have criminal objectives that transcend any particular offenses that have been committed in pursuance of its goals. In the latter case, we think that cumulative sentences for conspiracy and substantive offenses ought to be permissible. * * * [T]aking due account of a combination when it has a real bearing on the sentence that should imposed * * * in our view [should be] limited to situations in which organized professional criminality is involved. Herbert Wechsler, et al., *The Treatment of Inchoate Crimes in the Model Penal Code of the American Law Institute: Attempt, Solicitation, and Conspiracy*, 61 COLUM. L. REV. 957, 960 (1961).

> * * * [When the defendant has been sentenced for the object offense,] sentence for the conspiracy should be varied according to the propensity of the particular combination to produce further unlawful activity * * *. [T]he imposition of cumulative sentences should be left to the discretion of the trial judge. In exercising * * * discretion, a judge should take account of the number of persons involved in the conspiracy, the number and gravity of the offenses contemplated, the continuing or temporary nature of the organization, and the past criminal behavior of the conspirators. *Developments in the Law—Criminal Conspiracy*, 72 HARV. L.REV. 920, 970 (1959).

Do the foregoing rationales for permitting cumulative sentences for both a conspiracy and its object crime provide any guidance in determining the kind of criminal associations that warrant heavier penalties than simple criminal conspiracies? How many of the elements in the *Turkette* formulation are similar to the elements in the foregoing excerpts? To what extent do the elements in the *Turkette* formulation indicate the likelihood of the commission of crimes in addition to those already committed? The nature and number of future crimes? That the combination is otherwise dangerous? How dangerous it is?

8. In the wake of *Turkette*, the lower federal courts have tried to put more content into the *Turkette* language quoted in note 5, *supra*. In the paragraphs that follow, we examine some of the interpretations and applications of the informal criminal association meaning of enterprise in the lower

federal courts. Consider in connection with these formulations whether the courts have been paying adequate attention to the appropriate concerns in defining the nature of an informal criminal enterprise.

9. A leading Eighth Circuit decision on the meaning of enterprise is *United States v. Bledsoe*, 674 F.2d 647 (8th Cir.1982). Twenty two defendants were charged with violating §§ 1962 (c) and (d) by a pattern of racketeering activity consisting of fraud in the sale of securities of four agricultural cooperatives. The court stated:

Bledsoe

> The primary intent of Congress in enacting 18 U.S.C. § 1962 (c) was to prevent organized crime from infiltrating businesses and other legitimate economic entities* * *. Legitimate businesses and other legitimate organizations tend to have a definite structure and clear boundaries which limit the applicability of a criminal statute aimed at the infiltration of criminal elements into these entities. Infiltration of legitimate entities also warrants the Act's severe sanctions. The Act's drafters perceived a distinct threat to the free market in organized criminal groups gaining control of enterprises operating in that market * * *. The bill's sponsors also believed that such infiltration was a source of power and protection for organized crime and gave it a permanent base from which it was more likely to perpetrate a continuing pattern of criminal acts.

> But Congress did not draft the statute to apply solely to infiltration of legitimate enterprises. The statute also reaches wholly criminal organizations. However, the Act was not intended to reach any criminals who merely associate together and perpetrate two of the specified crimes, rather it was aimed at "organized crime." * * *

> Obviously, no statute could and this statute was not intended to require direct proof that individuals are engaged in something as ill defined as "organized crime." * * *

> The word "enterprise" ordinarily means an undertaking or project or a unit of organization established to perform any such undertaking or project. However, under RICO, an enterprise cannot simply be the undertaking of the acts of racketeering, neither can it be the minimal association which surrounds these acts. Any two criminal acts will necessarily be surrounded by some degree of organization and no two individuals will ever jointly perpetrate a crime a without some degree of association apart from the commission of the crime itself. Thus unless the inclusion of the enterprise element requires proof of some structure separate from the racketeering activity and distinct from the organization which is a necessary incident to the racketeering, the Act simply punishes the commission of two of the specified crimes within a 10–year period. Congress clearly did not intend such an application of the Act.

> A comparison of the severe penalties authorized by RICO with those for conspiracy indicates that the Act must have been directed at participation in enterprises consisting of more than simple conspiracies to perpetrate the predicate acts of racketeering.* * *

> Although commonality of purpose may the sine qua non of a criminal enterprise, in many cases this singular test fails to distinguish

enterprises from individuals merely associated together for the commission of sporadic crime. Any two wrongdoers who through concerted action commit two or more crimes share a purpose. This suggests that an enterprise must exhibit each of three basic characteristics.

In addition to having a common or shared purpose which animates those associated with it, it is fundamental that the enterprise "function as a continuing unit." * * * What is essential, however, is that there is some continuity of both structure and personality. * * *

Finally, an enterprise must have an "ascertainable structure" distinct from that inherent in the conduct of a pattern of racketeering activity. This distinct structure might be demonstrated by proof that a group engaged in a diverse pattern of crimes or that it has an organizational pattern or system of authority beyond what was necessary to perpetrate the predicate crimes. The command system of a Mafia family is an example of this type of structure as is the hierarchy, planning, and division of profits within a prostitution ring. * * *

* * * [Applying this test] the evidence reveals loose and discontinuous patterns of associations and agreements * * * contemplating illegal use of the co-ops. We find no real evidence of a structure, a pattern of authority or control, or of a continuity in the pattern of association or the common purpose of all defendants.

10. The District of Columbia Circuit in *United States v. Perholtz*, 842 F.2d 343, 363 (D.C.Cir.1988) declined to follow *Bledsoe* and similar decisions:

The same group of individuals who repeatedly commit predicate offenses do not necessarily comprise an enterprise. An extra ingredient is required: organization. To the extent, however, these cases suggest that the organization cannot be inferred from the pattern (or even more, that the organization cannot exist unless it does something more than commit predicate acts), we cannot agree. *Turkette* specifically recognizes that the proof of the enterprise may "coalesce" with the proof of the pattern, i.e. that the different conclusions may be inferred from proof of the same predicate acts.

Those courts imposing a strict separateness requirement appear to be concerned that RICO could be expanded to encompass even a "sporadic and temporary criminal alliance." They need "the enterprise, on the one hand, and the "continuity plus relationship" requirement for the pattern of racketeering, on the other hand. [The Court here cited *Sedima v. Imrex* and the interpretation of the pattern requirement in the RICO offense. *See infra* sections C and D infra.]

We therefore follow those courts that have held that the government satisfies its burden if it proves the existence of the enterprise and of the pattern, and refuse to require the government to prove each by separate evidence.

11. In a Ninth Circuit civil RICO suit, *Chang v. Chen*, 80 F.3d 1293, 1297–1300 (9th Cir.1996), adopting the majority (i.e. the Eighth Circuit) position, the court stated:

At a minimum, to be an enterprise, an entity must exhibit "some sort of structure * * * for the making of decisions, whether it be hierarchical or consensual." The structure should provide "some mechanism for controlling and directing the affairs of the group in an ongoing, rather than an ad hoc basis."

It also is not necessary to show that the organization "has some function wholly unrelated to the racketeering activity." Rather, it is sufficient to show that the organization has an existence beyond that which is merely necessary to commit the predicate acts of racketeering. "The function of overseeing and coordinating the commission of several different predicate offenses and other activities on an on-going basis is adequate to satisfy the separate existence requirement."

The * * * complaint did not allege the existence of a system of authority that guided the operation of the alleged enterprise. Although each Appellee performed the same specific functions in each transaction, * * * there was no decision-making apparatus that limited or guided Appellees in the performance of their respective duties. Each Appellee conducted his or her role in the alleged fraudulent transactions autonomously. * * *

In addition to lacking a structure for decision making, there was no allegation that Appellees utilized a structure separate and apart from the predicate acts to distribute the proceeds of the transactions. The proceeds were allocated to Appellees in a manner consistent with ordinary real estate transactions. Appellees did not use the profits to purchase equipment to allow them to commit the predicate acts. * * * Appellees also did not utilize a management company to divert funds.

12.   The Second and later, the First Circuit, rejected the *Bledsoe* court's ascertainable structure requirement. *United States v. Coonan*, 938 F.2d 1553, 1559 (2d Cir. 1991): "Common sense suggests that the existence of an association-in-fact is oftentimes more readily proven by what it does, rather than by an abstract analysis of structure."

And see United States v. Patrick, 248 F.3d 11 (1st Cir. 2001):

"While 'enterprise' and 'pattern of racketeering activity' are separate elements of a RICO offense, proof of these two elements need not be separate.... Since ... [criminal enterprises] may not observe the niceties of legitimate organizational structures, we refuse to import an 'ascertainable structure' requirement into jury instructions."

Also *see United States v. Cianci*, 378 F.3d 71 (1st Cir. 2004):

"Courts following the 'ascertainable structure' approach do so out of concern that the factfinder not be misled into 'collapsing ... the enterprise element with the separate pattern of racketeering activity element of a RICO offense.... This circuit has cast its lot with courts that have declined to make Bledsoe's 'ascertainable structure' criterion a mandatory component of a district court's jury instructions explaining RICO associated-in-fact enterprises.... [W]e have read Turkette to impose a requirement that those associated in fact 'function as an ongoing unit' and constitute an 'ongoing organization.' Also important to such an enterprise is that its members share a 'common purpose.' '"

13.   Note that in each of the following cases, the issue was whether the evidence was sufficient to support the verdict. The two lines of cases

reflected in *Bledsoe* (Eighth Circuit) and *Perholtz* (District of Columbia Circuit) articulate a difference in approach, but in practice are they producing different results?

 a. *United States v. Davidson*, 122 F.3d 531, 534–535 (8th Cir.1997):

  Witnesses at the * * * trial portrayed Davidson as the leader of a local criminal organization. His auto lot and body shop were the base for theft and disassembly of stolen cars and trucks. His associates burglarized houses, defrauded insurers, sold drugs, and committed arson and murder to punish Davidson's enemies and protect his criminal enterprise. * * * On appeal, Davidson argues that the government failed to present sufficient evidence of a RICO "enterprise."

* * *

  Davidson argues that the government proved only "sporadic criminal predicate acts," not the requisite common purpose, and that there was no proof of an organization having the requisite continuity and a structure distinct from that inherent in the pattern of racketeering offenses. We disagree. Davidson ran a small but prolific crime ring. Initially, stepson * * * Scarbrough and Rollet were the foot soldiers, stealing cars and trucks and burglarizing homes. Davidson "chopped" the stolen cars in his shop and fenced the other stolen goods. But Davidson was more than an outlet for stolen goods. He instructed Scarbrough and Rollet to burn cars and houses, both for insurance proceeds and for intimidation. He financed their drug activities and provided other support for his criminal associates. * * *

  The length of these associations, the number and variety of crimes the group jointly committed, and Davidson's financial support of his underlings demonstrate an ongoing association with a common purpose to reap the economic rewards flowing from the crimes rather than a series of ad hoc relationships. Davidson's continued leadership provided continuity of personnel at the top of the criminal organization. Its members had the "family and social relationships" that helped define a criminal RICO enterprise. Numerous acts of retaliation and intimidation committed at Davidson's direction, and his attempt to involve the local sheriff in a murder-for-hire evidence a criminal enterprise broader than and distinct from its constituent criminal activities.

 b. *United States v. Richardson*, 167 F.3d 621, 623–625 (D.C.Cir.1999):

  A grand jury indicted appellant Billy Richardson and his codefendants Harold Cunningham and Percy Barron on RICO, RICO conspiracy and other charges flowing from their alleged participation in an armed robbery ring * * *. Their crime spree began with armed robbery of money and guns and escalated to shootings of robbery victims, bystanders, and rivals in crime. They killed five people. The indictment charged them with conducting their crimes as an informal criminal enterprise with Cunningham as its leader and primary decisionmaker.

  Richardson does not claim that the government failed to prove a common purpose among the participants (the first *Perholtz* factor), and for good reason: As the district court observed, the government presented "undeniable" evidence that their common purpose was "to obtain money or other property by robbery." Focusing instead on the second and third *Perholtz* factors, Richardson contends that the government presented only minimal evidence of "organization" and "continuity" beyond that necessary to commit the individual predicate crimes. We disagree.

* * * [T]he evidence showed that Richardson and his codefendants organized themselves hierarchically and planned their activities. According to trial witnesses, Cunningham served as the leader. He was usually first through the door and first to display a firearm. He announced the robbery, gave orders to the victims, and directed Richardson and Barron during the course of the robberies. Additional evidence of organization and continuity comes from the robberies' consistent pattern; from testimony that Richardson and his codefendants borrowed or rented cars to commit their crimes and attempted to switch license plates to avoid detection; from ballistics analysis establishing that they used guns stolen in earlier crimes to facilitate later robberies and shootings; from testimony that they committed acts of violence and retaliation to protect their armed robbery enterprise; and from evidence that the three had social ties and were often seen together during the summer of 1993, thus further supporting the existence of an association independent of their individual crimes.

Query: Did the *Richardson* court point to elements bearing on hierarchy and organization in addition to the predicate crimes? Did the *Davidson* court also rely on the predicate crimes as evidence of structure and organization? Did both courts rely on factors other than the predicate crimes for this purpose? What additional factors were relied upon in each case? Was it significant in *Davidson* that a number of different kinds of crimes were committed by the criminal group? Did *Richardson* et al. also commit a diversity of crimes? Would the *Davidson* court or any court that adhered to *Bledsoe* have been likely to uphold the finding in *Richardson* that the enterprise had sufficient "structure?"

    c. *United States v. White*, 116 F.3d 903, 923–924 (D.C.Cir.1997):

White argues that there was insufficient evidence that the conspiracy had the requisite degree of structure apart from its pattern of substantive offenses and that the district court incorrectly charged the jury on the enterprise element of the first Street Crew's * * * RICO conspiracy. We conclude that considerable evidence indicates that the conspiracy possessed a structure that extended beyond the substantive offenses. * * *

Specifically, White contends that the evidence established only that White and Hicks supplied drugs to others, who then acted as independent drug sellers and retained their own profits. He adds that there was no proof of a hierarchy or decision-making process within the conspiracy and asserts that the government's evidence at best "proved a loosely knit association of neighborhood drug dealers."

In response, the government points to a wide range of evidence about the organization of the First Street Crew and its operations. Among other things, the conspiracy gave itself a name, protected a geographic marketing area, and ran centralized crack storage and preparation operations. In addition, the evidence demonstrated that White and Hicks occupied positions superior to the conspiracy's retail-level drug sellers.

To what extent did the court in *White* point to factors in addition to the pattern of racketeering activity in support of its conclusion that there was an enterprise within the meaning of the RICO statute? What were these factors?

d. *See also United States v. Korando*, 29 F.3d 1114, 1116–1119 (7th Cir.1994):

> The government's theory at trial was that Korando was a henchman in a small outfit specializing in insurance fraud—murder and arson for profit. * * * Buskohl—owner of Frontier Realty * * * was alleged to be at the center of this clique. In addition to Korando, Buskohl allegedly had a handful of other men who would actually carry out the operation's work, and would receive a share of the profit.
>
> * * *
>
> The hallmark of an enterprise is a "structure." The import of this requirement is that the enterprise, to be an enterprise, needs to have "a structure and goals separate from the predicate acts themselves." We have noted, though, that RICO applies not only to formal enterprises, but also to informal ones like criminal gangs. "There must be some structure, to distinguish an enterprise from a mere conspiracy, but there need not be much." *Burdett v. Miller*, 957 F.2d 1375, 1379 (7th Cir. 1992). We have also noted that the continuity of an informal enterprise, and the differentiation of roles can provide the necessary "structure" to satisfy RICO's statutory requirement. * * *
>
> The government now contends that the "enterprise in the instant case had a loose but discernable structure," with Buskohl through his realty business finding property to burn. He would place the property in the names of the straw parties. Korando's role in all of this was (1) to help find the properties, (2) to help find the people in whose name to place the properties and (3) actually to burn the properties down. In addition, Steve Hecht, through his construction company, would rebuild the properties following the arsons.
>
> The evidence adduced at trial can be read to support such a theory. While this is not much of a structure, the division of labor that we emphasized in *Burdett* does appear to be present. And there is also evidence that this enterprise persisted over a period of many years, which is also a factor to which *Burdett* draws our attention. Though this is a close question, we conclude that a rational jury could find that this arrangement had a structure as that word is understood in this context.

14. The Seventh Circuit follows *Bledsoe* and requires an ascertainable structure. Did the court in *Korando* infer the structure from the racketeering activity? Might the government have alleged that Buskohl's realty business was the enterprise? If it had done so, would there have been a need to inquire into the "structure" issue? In light of the foregoing cases, how much of a difference in practice is there between the *Bledsoe* and *Perholtz* approaches? Can it be said that the courts that require proof of ascertainable

structure independent of the proof of the racketeering activity are likely to require a stronger evidentiary showing of the existence of the organization than is required under the minority view?

15. Are the courts in addressing the "structure" and "continuity" issues, as reflected in the foregoing cases identifying factors that warrant treating a RICO enterprise as different from a simple conspiracy? That justify the severe RICO penalties? When you study the *H.J. Inc. v. Northwestern Bell Telephone Company* case, *infra* p. 528, consider the meaning that the Court gives to the "pattern of racketeering activity" phrase. Does that meaning supplant or supplement the *Turkette-Bledsoe–Perholtz* test for an enterprise? Does it introduce additional factors into the determination that are helpful in assessing the dangerousness of the group?

2. A LEGAL ENTITY AS THE ENTERPRISE

The definition of enterprise includes "any individual, partnership, corporation, association, or other legal entity." A legal entity necessarily has some built-in legal structure and organizational features. (We defer for the moment consideration of the notion that an individual can be an enterprise. *See infra* p. 505). Accordingly, the type of issues relating to structure and organization that were discussed above regarding association in fact enterprises are unlikely to arise in connection with legal entity enterprises. But other kinds of issues are generated by the legal entity RICO cases.

It should be noted at the outset that the majority of legal entity RICO cases are civil RICO suits. Is that significant?

In any case, civil or criminal, where a legal entity that might be viewed as a RICO enterprise is involved, the prosecutor or plaintiff may, depending on the factual circumstances, have the option of alleging a legal entity enterprise, for example, the corporation on whose premises or through whose offices the crimes are being perpetrated; or an association in fact enterprise (composed of the individual participants in the criminal activities allegedly carried on by the enterprise), and there may be other possibilities. What kinds of factors might lead one, where choice is available, to allege an association in fact rather than a legal entity as the enterprise, or vice versa? Recall in this connection the language of § 1962 (c):

> It shall be unlawful for any person employed by or associated with any enterprise engaged in, or the activities of which affect, interstate or foreign commerce, to conduct or participate, directly or indirectly, in the conduct of such enterprise's affairs through a pattern of racketeering activity. * * *

As you study the materials in the remainder of this chapter, in any case where a choice was available as to which kind of enterprise to allege, consider what factors may have influenced the choice that was made, and whether you would have made the same choice.

Notes

1. A foreign corporation can be an enterprise under RICO. *Alfadda v. Fenn*, 935 F.2d 475, 479 (2d Cir.1991). *See United States v. Parness*, 503 F.2d 430, 439 (2d Cir.1974) where the court stated: "[T]he salutary purposes of the Act would be frustrated" if "those whose actions ravage the American economy * * * [could] escape prosecution simply by investing the proceeds of their ill-gotten gains in a foreign enterprise."

2. A combination of more than one legal entity, or legal entities combined with individuals can also be the enterprise on the theory that they comprise an association in fact. For example, in *United States v. London*, 66 F.3d 1227 (1st Cir.1995) the defendant operated a bar (Heller's Café) and in a small enclosed area in the bar, a check cashing service (M & L Associates), which he used to launder the proceeds of illegal gambling for his bookmaking customers. Both Heller's and M & L had at least one other employee other than the defendant. The enterprise charged in the indictment was the association in fact between Heller's Café, a corporation, and M & L Associates, a sole proprietorship. The court stated:

> The jury reasonably * * * could have found that * * * [the defendant] used the privacy afforded by Heller's to shield M & L from close scrutiny, to arrange meetings between * * * [an organized crime figure] and his bookmaking customers, and to collect "rent" [i.e. protection money] for * * * [the organized crime figure]. The jury also could have found that the enterprise functioned as a continuing unit and had an ascertainable structure distinct from that inherent in the conduct of a pattern of racketeering activity. As to the latter of these two requirements, M & L and Heller's were legitimate entities that did a significant amount of business completely separate from the pattern of racketeering activity at issue in this case. Heller's was a bar where drinks and food were sold. M & L was a check-cashing business—located inside of Heller's * * *. As to the former requirement, the jury could reasonably have surmised that M & L and Heller's operated as a symbiotic unit (M & L providing a ready source of cash for Heller's customers; Heller's customers taking advantage of M & L's convenience), and that they existed for a common purpose: the economic gain of [the defendant].

See also United States v. Masters, 924 F.2d 1362 (7th Cir.1991) where the enterprise was composed of a combination of legal entities and individuals.

How many different "enterprises" might possibly have been charged in the *London* case? Why did the prosecutor chose the particular combination that was alleged in the indictment?

3. Another application of RICO has been to use it against alleged government corruption, and the issue posed in that connection is whether a governmental agency—or indeed, a city or state—can be an enterprise under § 1962(c). The courts have uniformly upheld treating governmental agencies or government entities as enterprises under RICO, although not without some expressions of concern. *See, e.g. United States v. Thompson*, 685 F.2d

993 (6th Cir.1982) where the court, while upholding an indictment that alleged the office of the state governor as the RICO enterprise, also stated:

> We also, however, question the wisdom of continued employment of this form of indictment. The language of the RICO statute allows for but does not compel use of this device. We believe that identifying "The Office of Governor" (or for that matter any other governmental office) as the "enterprise" under RICO unnecessarily tends to disrupt comity in federal-state relationships and ... the statute itself provides readily available unobjectionable substitute language.
>
> ... [T]he language which could and we believe preferably should have been employed, would have alleged that the three defendants constituted a "group of individuals associated in fact although not a legal entity which made use of the Office of Governor of the State of Tennessee" for particular racketeering activities alleged in the indictment.

4. Another case illustrating the use of the flexibility and breadth of the concept of a RICO enterprise to focus on government corruption is *United States v. Cianci,* 378 F.3d 71 (1st Cir. 2004). The prosecutor alleged as the enterprise: the city of Providence and thirteen of its departments including the office of Mayor); the political organization of the defendant Cianci; and three individuals (Cianci among them) who were also charged as defendants:

> Defendants attempt to expose what they deem an error by the government in charging an overly broad enterprise that places a criminal onus on a largely innocent City. They warn that an enterprise such as that charged here implicates non-culpable municipal parties in associations which they had little or no idea were engaged in illicit activities. But this fear is misplaced. * * * Those employees of a city that do not exhibit the requisite mens rea with regard to enterprise's illicit purposes will not be criminally or civilly implicated. In the present litigation, the City was named a member of the charged enterprise, not a defendant. The City "shared" in the enterprise's purpose only to the extent of the defendants' considerable influence and control over the relevant municipal agencies, and to the extent of those officials and departments who were wittingly or unwittingly involved in the various schemes.

5. Section 1962 (a), (b) and (c) each require proof of "an enterprise which is engaged in, or the activities of which affect, interstate or foreign commerce." In connection with the choice between alleging a legal entity as the enterprise or alleging an association in fact, is it likely to be easier to prove the link to commerce in the one case than in the other? In *United States v. Thompson, supra* note 3, a dissenting judge stated the following in a footnote,

> The proof in this record which is treated as sufficient to establish activities in or affecting interstate commerce is slight. However, these are activities of individuals which would probably establish a sufficient nexus with commerce to support their prosecution as an enterprise of individuals associated in fact. It is quite a different thing to hold that the normal operations of the office of the chief executive of a state may be the basis of treating the office as an enterprise engaged in commerce

for the purpose of prosecuting individuals who have misused their connections with that office.

6.   In connection with the RICO jurisdictional issue discussed in note 5 supra, consider *United States v. Garcia,* 143 F.Supp.2d 791 (E.D. Mich. 2000). The enterprise alleged was a street gang known as the Cash Flow Posse, and the predicate acts alleged as racketeering activity were a series of murders. On the issue of jurisdiction, the court stated:

> If the court were to accept the Government's argument that the enterprise here engaged in interstate commerce because its members drove on I–94 within the state, because the members used a gun manufactured in another state, because the gun was purchased from a business that frequently has out-of-state customers, because the enterprise possibly had chapters in other states, and because two members of the enterprise discussed the case pending against them on a trip to Mexico, the distinction between what is truly national and what is truly local would be obliterated.

> * * *

> The Government contends that because the Cash Flow Posse resisted these efforts [i.e. out of state infiltration by gangs that wanted to engage in drug trafficking in Michigan] the Cash Flow Posse affected interstate commerce. This court disagrees. At best, the Government's evidence may show that the Cash Flow Posse stopped interstate commerce from occurring. . . .

For a detailed discussion of jurisdictional approaches based on the commerce power, see Chapter 3, supra.

3.   ENTERPRISES WITH IDEOLOGICAL GOALS

Assuming that required elements of a RICO enterprise and the other elements of the offense can be proven, can RICO be used to prosecute political terrorists or other ideological groups that use criminal means to advance their goals? Can RICO be used to prosecute political groups that engage in criminal activities even though they have no economic motive? The issue first came before the Supreme Court in the case that follows.

NATIONAL ORGANIZATION FOR WOMEN v. SCHEIDLER

510 U.S. 249, 114 S.Ct. 798, 127 L.Ed.2d 99 (1994).

CHIEF JUSTICE REHNQUIST delivered the opinion of the Court.

We are required once again to interpret the provisions of the Racketeer Influenced and Corrupt Organizations Act (RICO). * * * We granted certiorari to determine whether RICO requires proof that either the racketeering enterprise or the predicate acts of racketeering were motivated by an economic purpose. We hold that RICO requires no such economic motive.

Petitioner National Organization for Women, Inc. (NOW), is a national nonprofit organization that supports the legal availability of abortion; petitioners Delaware Women's Health Organization, Inc. (DWHO), and Summit Women's Health Organization, Inc. (SWHO), are health care centers that perform abortions and other medical procedures. Respondents are a coalition of antiabortion groups called the Pro–Life Action Network (PLAN), Joseph Scheidler and other individuals and organizations that oppose legal abortion, and a medical laboratory that formerly provided services to the two petitioner health care centers.

Petitioners sued respondents in the United States District Court for the Northern District of Illinois, * * * stemming from the activities of antiabortion protesters at the clinics. According to respondent Scheidler's congressional testimony, these protesters aim to shut down the clinics and persuade women not to have abortions. * * * Petitioners sought injunctive relief, along with treble damages, costs, and attorney's fees. They later amended their complaint, and pursuant to local rules, filed a "RICO Case Statement" that further detailed the enterprise, the pattern of racketeering, the victims of the racketeering activity, and the participants involved.

The amended complaint alleged that respondents were members of a nationwide conspiracy to shut down abortion clinics through a pattern of racketeering activity including extortion in violation of the Hobbs Act, 18 U.S.C. § 1951. * * * Petitioners alleged that respondents conspired to use threatened or actual force, violence, or fear to induce clinic employees, doctors, and patients to give up their jobs, give up their economic right to practice medicine, and give up their right to obtain medical services at the clinics.

Petitioners claimed that this conspiracy "has injured the business and/or property interests of the [petitioners]." According to the amended complaint, PLAN constitutes the alleged racketeering "enterprise" for purposes of § 1962(c).

We granted certiorari to resolve a conflict among the Courts of Appeals on the putative economic motive requirement of 18 U.S.C. §§ 1962(c) and (d).

We turn to the question whether the racketeering enterprise or the racketeering predicate acts must be accompanied by an underlying economic motive. Section 1962(c) makes it unlawful "for any person employed by or associated with any enterprise engaged in, or the activities of which affect, interstate or foreign commerce, to conduct or participate, directly or indirectly, in the conduct of such enterprise's affairs through a pattern of racketeering activity or collection of unlawful debt." Section 1961(1) defines "pattern of racketeering activity" to include conduct that is "chargeable" or "indictable" under a host of state and federal laws. RICO broadly defines "enterprise" in § 1961(4) to "include any individual, partnership, corporation, association, or other legal entity, and any union or group of individuals associated in fact although not a legal entity." Nowhere in either § 1962(c) or the RICO definitions in § 1961 is there any indication that an economic motive is required.

The phrase "any enterprise engaged in, or the activities of which affect, interstate or foreign commerce" comes the closest of any language in subsection (c) to suggesting a need for an economic motive. Arguably an enterprise engaged in interstate or foreign commerce would have a profit-seeking motive, but the language in § 1962(c) does not stop there; it includes enterprises whose activities "affect" interstate or foreign commerce. Webster's Third New International Dictionary 35 (1969) defines "affect" as "to have a detrimental influence on—used especially in the phrase affecting commerce." An enterprise surely can have a detrimental influence on interstate or foreign commerce without having its own profit-seeking motives.

We do not believe that the usage of the term "enterprise" in subsections (a) and (b) leads to the inference that an economic motive is required in subsection (c). The term "enterprise" in subsections (a) and (b) plays a different role in the structure of those subsections than it does in subsection (c). Section 1962(a) provides that it "shall be unlawful for any person who has received any income derived, directly or indirectly, from a pattern of racketeering activity . . . to use or invest, directly or indirectly, any part of such income, or the proceeds of such income, in acquisition of any interest in, or the establishment or operation of, any enterprise which is engaged in, or the activities of which affect, interstate or foreign commerce." Correspondingly, § 1962(b) states that it "shall be unlawful for any person through a pattern of racketeering activity or through collection of an unlawful debt to acquire or maintain, directly or indirectly, any interest in or control of any enterprise which is engaged in, or the activities of which affect, interstate or foreign commerce." The "enterprise" referred to in subsections (a) and (b) is thus something acquired through the use of illegal activities or by money obtained from illegal activities. The enterprise in these subsections is the victim of unlawful activity and may very well be a "profit-seeking" entity that represents a property interest and may be acquired. But the statutory language in subsections (a) and (b) does not mandate that the enterprise be a "profit-seeking" entity; it simply requires that the enterprise be an entity that was acquired through illegal activity or the money generated from illegal activity.

By contrast, the "enterprise" in subsection (c) connotes generally the vehicle through which the unlawful pattern of racketeering activity is committed, rather than the victim of that activity. Subsection (c) makes it unlawful for "any person employed by or associated with any enterprise . . . to conduct or participate . . . in the conduct of such enterprise's affairs through a pattern of racketeering activity. . . ." Consequently, since the enterprise in subsection (c) is not being acquired, it need not have a property interest that can be acquired nor an economic motive for engaging in illegal activity; it need only be an association in fact that engages in a pattern of racketeering activity. Nothing in subsections (a) and (b) directs us to a contrary conclusion.

The Court of Appeals also relied on the reasoning of *United States v. Bagaric*, 706 F.2d 42 (2d Cir.), *cert. denied*, 464 U.S. 840 (1983), to support its conclusion that subsection (c) requires an economic motive. In upholding the convictions, under RICO, of members of a political terrorist group, the *Bagaric* court relied in part on the congressional statement of findings which prefaces RICO and refers to the activities of groups that " 'drain billions of dollars from America's economy by unlawful conduct and the illegal use of force, fraud, and corruption.' " The Court of Appeals for the Second Circuit decided that the sort of activity thus condemned required an economic motive.

We do not think this is so. Respondents and the two Courts of Appeals, we think, overlook the fact that predicate acts, such as the alleged extortion, may not benefit the protesters financially but still may drain money from the economy by harming businesses such as the clinics which are petitioners in this case.

We also think that the quoted statement of congressional findings is a rather thin reed upon which to base a requirement of economic motive neither expressed nor, we think, fairly implied in the operative sections of the Act. As we said in *H. J. Inc. v. Northwestern Bell Telephone Co.*, 492 U.S. 229, 248 (1989): "The occasion for Congress' action was the perceived need to combat organized crime. But Congress for cogent reasons chose to enact a more general statute, one which, although it had organized crime as its focus, was not limited in application to organized crime."

In *United States v. Turkette*, 452 U.S. 576 (1981), we faced the analogous question whether "enterprise" as used in § 1961(4) should be confined to "legitimate" enterprises. Looking to the statutory language, we found that "there is no restriction upon the associations embraced by the definition: an enterprise includes any union or group of individuals associated in fact." Accordingly, we resolved that § 1961(4)'s definition of "enterprise" "appears to include both legitimate and illegitimate enterprises within its scope; it no more excludes criminal enterprises than it does legitimate ones." We noted that Congress could easily have narrowed the sweep of the term "enterprise" by inserting a single word, "legitimate." Instead, Congress did nothing to indicate that "enterprise" should exclude those entities whose sole purpose was criminal.

The parallel to the present case is apparent. Congress has not, either in the definitional section or in the operative language, required that an "enterprise" in § 1962(c) have an economic motive.

The Court of Appeals also found persuasive guidelines for RICO prosecutions issued by the Department of Justice in 1981. The guidelines provided that a RICO indictment should not charge an association as an enterprise, unless the association exists " 'for the purpose of maintaining operations directed toward an *economic* goal....' " *United States v. Ivic*, 700 F.2d at 64, quoting U.S. Dept. of Justice, United States Attorneys' Manual § 9–110.360 (1984) (emphasis added). The Second Circuit believed these guidelines were entitled to deference under administrative law principles. Whatever may be the appropriate deference afforded to such internal rules, * * * for our purposes we need note only that the

Department of Justice amended its guidelines in 1984. The amended guidelines provide that an association-in-fact enterprise must be "directed toward an economic *or other identifiable goal.*" U.S. Dept. of Justice, United States Attorney's Manual § 9–110.360 (Mar. 9, 1984) (emphasis added).

Both parties rely on legislative history to support their positions. We believe the statutory language is unambiguous and find in the parties' submissions respecting legislative history no such "clearly expressed legislative intent to the contrary" that would warrant a different construction.

Respondents finally argue that the result here should be controlled by the rule of lenity in criminal cases. But the rule of lenity applies only when an ambiguity is present; " 'it is not used to beget one. . . . The rule comes into operation at the end of the process of construing what Congress has expressed, not at the beginning as an overriding consideration of being lenient to wrongdoers.' " We simply do not think there is an ambiguity here which would suffice to invoke the rule of lenity.

We therefore hold that petitioners may maintain this action if respondents conducted the enterprise through a pattern of racketeering activity. The questions whether respondents committed the requisite predicate acts, and whether the commission of these acts fell into a pattern, are not before us. We hold only that RICO contains no economic motive requirement.

The judgment of the Court of Appeals is accordingly

Reversed.

Notes

1. The saga of NOW v. Scheidler continues. Following the Supreme Court's decision in *NOW v. Scheidler, supra,* (Scheidler *I*), the case returned to the trial court. In 2003, after a jury verdict in favor of the plaintiffs, the matter was again appealed. The Seventh Circuit affirmed, and the case then again went to the Supreme Court which held that the defendant protestors had not obtained property from the plaintiffs and therefore had not committed extortion under the Hobbs Act. The Court stated: "We further hold that our determination with respect to extortion under the Hobbs Act renders insufficient the other bases or predicate acts of racketeering supporting the jury's conclusion that petitioners violated RICO. Therefore, we reverse . . . ." *Scheidler v. NOW,* 537 U.S. 393 (2003) (Scheidler *II*). (For further discussion of the Court's treatment of the obtaining property issue under the Hobbs Act, see infra, p. 245.)

Following the decision in *Scheidler II,* the case was returned to the U.S. Court of Appeals where the plaintiffs noted that the earlier circuit affirmance had concluded that the 21 extortion-based Hobbs Act violations were sufficient to affirm the judgment while acknowledging that the jury had also found four acts of physical violence among the numerous predicate acts of RICO racketeering activity. They argued that the grant of certiorari that led to the Scheidler II ruling had not encompassed those four predicate acts involving "acts or threats of physical violence to any person or property" and had not addressed whether those acts were sufficient to supply racketeering activity that would support injunctive relief under the RICO cause of action. [Note: the Hobbs Act provides: "Whoever ... affects commerce ... by robbery or extortion ... *or commits or threatens physical violence to any person or property in furtherance of a plan or purpose to do anything in violation of this section* ..." (emphasis added) The issue of whether the italicized language describes a third offense under the Hobbs Act (i.e. in addition to robbery and extortion) or is only an incident of the robbery or extortion offenses described in the Act has not been definitively decided.]

The Seventh Circuit agreed that the two offense/ three offense issue under the Hobbs Act had not been decided and remanded the case to the district court for consideration of the issue, 91 Fed.Appx. 510 (7th Cir. 2004) (unpublished opinion). The protestors immediately filed a petition for certiorari with the Supreme Court. In their reply brief, the plaintiffs contended: "... [T]he proper interpretation of the physical violence prong of § 1951(a) was not before this Court in *Scheidler II*." The Supreme Court once again granted certiorari. *Scheidler v. NOW*, 125 S.Ct. 2991 (2005) setting the stage for a *Scheidler III* decision by the Supreme Court.

2.   In 1994, Congress had directly addressed the issue of clinic violence that was the target of the civil action in *NOW v. Scheidler* and enacted the Freedom of Access to Clinic Entrances Act, which, using a civil rights model, makes the relevant conduct a federal crime, establishes a right to bring a private civil action and provides that a civil action can be brought by the Attorney General of the United States or state attorneys general. Specifically, the statute prohibits the use or threat of force or physical obstruction against a person seeking to obtain or provide reproductive health services, including abortions. Comparing the choice between pursuing prosecution or a civil remedy under RICO or FACEA, the former establishes the possibility of heavier penalties in a criminal prosecution and treble damages in a civil suit, while the FACEA penalty scheme provides for the possibility in a civil suit context of a fixed minimum civil damage amount, punitive damages and civil money penalties.

B.   THE "PERSON" WHO MAY BE CHARGED AS A RICO DEFENDANT: DISTINGUISHING BETWEEN THE PERSON AND THE ENTERPRISE

Under the criminal RICO provisions, § 1962, criminal charges may not be brought against the "enterprise" but rather only against "any person" who has the necessary relationship to the enterprise—namely, under subsection (a), a person who invests income derived from a pattern of racketeering activity in the enterprise; under subsection (b), a person who acquires or maintains an interest in an enterprise through a pattern of racketeering activity; and under subsection (c), a person who, associated with an enterprise, conducts its affairs through a pattern of racketeering activity. Query, is any action permitted directly against the enterprise under § 1964, which deals with civil remedies? *See infra*, pp. 573–577.

The issue of who or what qualifies as a "person" and that person's relationship to the enterprise pose a variety of different issues which are treated in the materials that follow.

Notes

1. "Person" in the several subsections of § 1962 is the one who engages in the criminal violation and is thus chargeable as the RICO defendant. "Person" is defined under § 1961(3) to include "any individual or entity capable of holding a legal or beneficial interest in property." Under § 1961 (4), an enterprise can be an individual or a legal entity as well as an association in fact. Presumably therefore, both the person and the enterprise can be legal entities or individuals. This suggests the possibility of choice about, and perhaps some confusion over, who might be the "person" charged and who might be the "enterprise."

2. If a state or a governmental agency can be a RICO enterprise, does that mean that the governmental entity can be a "person" for purposes of a RICO prosecution and hence a RICO defendant? Of course, a governmental entity cannot be convicted and sentenced in any meaningful way. Accordingly, the issue may have significance only in a civil context. The issue, at bottom, is whether government entities are subject to either treble damages or various forms of equitable relief under § 1964.

3. A related but distinguishable issue is whether the same entity can be both the person charged with the RICO violation and the RICO enterprise. Subsection (c) of § 1962 requires that the defendant be employed by or associated with the enterprise and conduct or participate in the affairs of the enterprise. Reasoning that one cannot associate with oneself, most of the circuits concluded that the same entity cannot be both the enterprise and the person who violated RICO through association with the enterprise. *See, e.g., Bennett v. United States Trust Co. of New York*, 770 F.2d 308 (2d Cir. 1985). The Eleventh Circuit had disagreed with this majority view in *United States v. Hartley*, 678 F.2d 961 (11th Cir.1982), but finally joined the rest of the circuits, overruling *Hartley* in *United States v. Goldin Industries*, 219 F.3d 1268 (11th Cir. 2000)(en banc).

4. Neither subsection (a) or (b) of § 1962 contains language similar to that found in subsection (c) which is interpreted to suggest that the person and the enterprise must be distinct. Accordingly, the courts have generally concluded that the same entity can be charged as both the person and the enterprise under subsection (a) or (b). *See, e.g., Haroco, Inc. v. American National Bank & Trust Co.*, 747 F.2d 384 (7th Cir.1984), *aff'd on other grounds*, 473 U.S. 606 (1985). Apart from the language of the three subsections, does the distinction drawn by the courts on this issue, as to the difference between subsection (c) on the one hand, and subsections (a) and (b) on other hand, make sense as a matter of policy?

5. A variation on the theme of note 3, *supra* is the question whether an individual can be prosecuted as an enterprise under § 1962 (c) for conduct-

ing his or her own affairs through a pattern of racketeering activity? From the case law in note 3, it should follow that such a prosecution cannot be sustained. *See United States v. DiCaro,* 772 F.2d 1314 (7th Cir.1985). Compare, however, Judge Posner in *McCullough v. Suter,* 757 F.2d 142, 144 (7th Cir.1985):

> If the one-man band incorporates, it gets some legal protections from the corporate form, such as limited liability; and it is just this sort of legal shield for illegal activity that RICO tries to pierce. A one-man band that does not incorporate, that merely operates as a proprietorship, gains no legal protections from the form in which it has chosen to do business; the man and the proprietorship really are the same entity in law and fact. But if the man has employees or associates, the enterprise is distinct from him, and it then makes no difference, so far as we can see, what legal form the enterprise takes. The only important thing is that it be either formally (as when there is incorporation) or practically (as when there are people besides the proprietor working in the organization) separable from the individual.

6. How does the issue decided in the following case relate to the question of whether the same entity can be both the enterprise and the person who violates RICO?

CEDRIC KUSHNER PROMOTIONS LTD. v. KING

533 U.S. 158, 121 S.Ct. 2087, 150 L.Ed.2d 198 (2001).

JUSTICE BREYER delivered the opinion of the Court.

This case focuses upon a person who is the president and sole shareholder of a closely held corporation. The plaintiff claims that the president has conducted the corporation's affairs through the forbidden "pattern," though for present purposes it is conceded that, in doing so, he acted within the scope of his authority as the corporation's employee. In these circumstances, are there two entities, a "person" and a separate "enterprise"? Assuming, as we must given the posture of this case, that the allegations in the complaint are true, we conclude that the "person" and "enterprise" here are distinct and that the RICO provision applies.

Petitioner, Cedric Kushner Promotions, Ltd., is a corporation that promotes boxing matches. Petitioner sued Don King, the president and sole shareholder of Don King Productions, a corporation, claiming that King had conducted the boxing-related affairs of Don King Productions in part through a RICO "pattern," *i.e.,* through the alleged commission of at least two instances of fraud and other RICO predicate crimes. ... In the appellate court's view, § 1962(c) applies only where a plaintiff shows the existence of two separate entities, a "person" and a distinct "enterprise," the affairs of which that "person" improperly conducts. In this instance, "it is undisputed that King was an employee" of the corporation Don King Productions and also "acting within the scope of his authority." Under the Court of Appeals' analysis, King, in a legal sense, was part of, not separate from, the corporation. There was no "person," distinct from the "enterprise," who improperly conducted the "enterprise's affairs." . . .

Other Circuits, applying § 1962(c) in roughly similar circumstances, have reached a contrary conclusion. We granted certiorari to resolve the conflict. We now agree with these Circuits and hold that the Second Circuit's interpretation of § 1962(c) is erroneous.

. . . The Act says that it applies to "person[s]" who are "employed by or associated with" the "enterprise." § 1962(c). In ordinary English one speaks of employing, being employed by, or associating with others, not oneself. . . . In addition, the Act's purposes are consistent with that principle. Whether the Act seeks to prevent a person from victimizing, say, a small business, . . . or to prevent a person from using a corporation for criminal purposes, the person and the victim, or the person and the tool, are different entities, not the same.

The [Government] reads § 1962(c) "to require some distinctness between the RICO defendant and the RICO enterprise." And it says that this requirement is "legally sound and workable." We agree with its assessment, particularly in light of the fact that 12 Courts of Appeals have interpreted the statute as embodying some such distinctness requirement without creating discernible mischief in the administration of RICO. . . . Indeed, this Court previously has said that liability "depends on showing that the defendants conducted or participated in the conduct of the *enterprise's* affairs,' not just their *own* affairs." *Reves v. Ernst & Young,* 507 U.S. 170, 185, 113 S.Ct. 1163, 122 L.Ed.2d 525 (1993).

While accepting the "distinctness" principle, we nonetheless disagree with the appellate court's application of that principle to the present circumstances—circumstances in which a corporate employee, "acting within the scope of his authority," allegedly conducts the corporation's affairs in a RICO-forbidden way. The corporate owner/employee, a natural person, is distinct from the corporation itself, a legally different entity with different rights and responsibilities due to its different legal status. And we can find nothing in the statute that requires more "separateness" than that. . . .

Linguistically speaking, an employee who conducts the affairs of a corporation through illegal acts comes within the terms of a statute that forbids any "person" unlawfully to conduct an "enterprise," particularly when the statute explicitly defines "person" to include "any individual . . . capable of holding a legal or beneficial interest in property," and defines "enterprise" to include a "corporation." 18 U.S.C. §§ 1961(3), (4). And, linguistically speaking, the employee and the corporation are different "persons," even where the employee is the corporation's sole owner. After all, incorporation's basic purpose is to create a distinct legal entity, with legal rights, obligations, powers, and privileges different from those of the natural individuals who created it, who own it, or whom it employs. . . . We note that the Second Circuit relied on earlier Circuit precedent for its decision. But that precedent involved quite different circumstances which are not presented here. . . .

Further, to apply the RICO statute in present circumstances is consistent with the statute's basic purposes as this Court has defined them. The Court has held that RICO both protects a legitimate "enterprise" from those who would use unlawful acts to victimize it, *United States v. Turkette,* 452 U.S. 576, 591, 101 S.Ct. 2524, 69 L.Ed.2d 246 (1981), and also protects the public from those who would unlawfully use an "enterprise" (whether legitimate or illegitimate) as a "vehicle" through which "unlawful . . . activity is committed," *National Organization for Women, Inc., supra,* at 259, 114 S.Ct. 798. A corporate employee who conducts the corporation's affairs through an unlawful RICO "pattern . . . of activity," § 1962(c), uses that corporation as a "vehicle" whether he is, or is not, its sole owner. Conversely, the appellate court's critical legal distinction—between employees acting within the scope of corporate authority and those acting outside that authority—is inconsistent with a basic statutory purpose. . . . It would immunize from RICO liability many of those at whom this Court has said RICO directly aims— *e.g.,* high-ranking individuals in an illegitimate criminal enterprise, who, seeking to further the purposes of that enterprise, act within the scope of their authority.

* * *

Finally, we have found nothing in the statute's history that significantly favors an alternative interpretation. That history not only refers frequently to the importance of undermining organized crime's influence upon legitimate businesses but also refers to the need to protect the public from those who would run "organization[s] in a manner detrimental to the public interest." S.Rep. No. 91–617, at 82. This latter purpose, as we have said, invites the legal principle we endorse, namely, that in present circumstances the statute requires no more than the formal legal distinction between "person" and "enterprise" (namely, incorporation) that is present here.

In reply, King argues that the lower court's rule is consistent with (1) the principle that a corporation acts only through its directors, officers, and agents, (2) the principle that a corporation should not be liable for the criminal acts of its employees where Congress so intends, Brief for Respondents 20–21, and (3) the Sherman Act principle limiting liability under 15 U.S.C. § 1 by excluding "from unlawful combinations or conspiracies the activities of a single firm," *Copperweld Corp. v. Independence Tube Corp.,* 467 U.S. 752, 769–770, n. 15, 104 S.Ct. 2731, 81 L.Ed.2d 628 (1984). The alternative that we endorse, however, is no less consistent with these principles. It does not deny that a corporation acts through its employees; it says only that the corporation and its employees are not legally identical. It does not assert that ordinary *respondeat superior* principles make a corporation legally liable under RICO for the criminal acts of its employees; that is a matter of congressional intent not before us. See, *e.g., Gasoline Sales, Inc.,* 39 F.3d, at 73 (holding that corporation cannot be "vicariously liable" for § 1962(c) violations committed by its vice president). Neither is it inconsistent with antitrust law's intracorporate conspiracy doctrine; that doctrine turns on specific antitrust objectives. See *Copperweld Corp., supra,* at 770–771, 104 S.Ct. 2731. Rather, we hold simply that the need for two distinct entities is satisfied; hence, the RICO provision before us applies when a corporate employee unlawfully conducts the affairs of the corporation of which he is the sole owner—whether he conducts those affairs within the scope, or beyond the scope, of corporate authority.

Notes

1. What is the difference, if any, between Judge Posner's decision in *McCullough v. Suter,* supra, note 5, p. 506, and the decision in the *Cedric Kushner* case?

2. What is the difference, if any, between the *Cedric Kushner* decision and the decision in the *Fitzgerald* case that follows?

FITZGERALD v. CHRYSLER CORPORATION

116 F.3d 225 (7th Cir.1997).

Before POSNER, CHIEF JUDGE, and KANNE and EVANS, CIRCUIT JUDGES.

POSNER, CHIEF JUDGE.

This is a consumer class action for warranty fraud, brought under the RICO ("Racketeer Influenced and Corrupt Organizations") statute, 18 U.S.C. §§ 1961 et seq., against the Chrysler Corporation. The district judge dismissed the suit for failure to state a claim under RICO, and we therefore take the facts alleged in the complaint as true, of course without vouching for their truth. According to these allegations, Chrysler sold to the consumers of its motor vehicles extended warranties promising all sorts of warranty protection that Chrysler had secretly determined not to provide, so that when a consumer would bring in his Chrysler to a dealer for repairs covered by the express terms of the extended warranty and later sought reimbursement from Chrysler for the expense of the repairs, Chrysler refused to pay.

So far as bears on this case, RICO prohibits a "person . . . associated with any enterprise . . . to conduct . . . such enterprise's affairs through a pattern of racketeering activity." 18 U.S.C. § 1962(c). The "person" need not be a natural person, 18 U.S.C. § 1961(3), so Chrysler is a person within the meaning of the Act. "Racketeering activity" is a term of art that includes violating the federal mail and wire fraud statutes, and the complaint charges Chrysler with a number of such violations all in furtherance of the scheme of warranty fraud. We may assume, though without having to decide, that the complaint alleges a "pattern" of such violations, leaving only the question whether Chrysler may be said to have been "associated with an enterprise" and to have "conducted . . . such enterprise's affairs through" the wire and mail frauds. The enterprise alleged, taken most broadly, is a "Chrysler family" consisting of subsidiaries of the Chrysler Corporation engaged in various facets of production, financing, and marketing of Chrysler automobiles, plus

Chrysler's dealers, plus trusts controlled by Chrysler that in essence resell retail installment contracts for the purchase of Chrysler automobiles to the investing public. The plaintiffs argue that all these affiliates and agents participate directly or indirectly in the retail sale of Chrysler automobiles and accessories, of which the extended warranty is one; hence the affairs of the entire "enterprise" may be said to be conducted through the alleged pattern of fraudulent acts. Actually the plaintiffs carve up the medley of Chrysler entities into three different enterprises; but as none of the combinations of different members of the Chrysler family adds up to a RICO enterprise, it makes no difference how they are sorted.

Read literally, RICO would encompass every fraud case against a corporation, provided only that a pattern of fraud and some use of the mails or of telecommunications to further the fraud were shown; the corporation would be the RICO person and the corporation plus its employees the "enterprise." The courts have excluded this far-fetched possibility by holding that an employer and its employees cannot constitute a RICO enterprise. *E.g., Discon, Inc. v. NYNEX Corp.*, 93 F.3d 1055, 1063 (2d Cir.1996); *Jaguar Cars, Inc. v. Royal Oaks Motor Car Co.*, 46 F.3d 258, 268 (3d Cir.1995). We do not understand the plaintiffs to be quarreling with this exclusion, even though it doesn't emerge from the statutory language; it emerges from a desire to make the statute make sense and have some limits.

When a statute is broadly worded in order to prevent loopholes from being drilled in it by ingenious lawyers, there is a danger of its being applied to situations absurdly remote from the concerns of the statute's framers. Courts find it helpful, in interpreting such statutes in a way that will avoid absurd applications—a conventional office of statutory interpretation, even under "plain language" approaches, to identify the prototype situation to which the statute is addressed. That need not be the most common case to which it is applied; the prototype may be effectively deterred because its legal status is clear. The second step is to determine how close to the prototype the case before the court is—how close, in other words, the family resemblance is between the prototypical case and the case at hand. The prototypical RICO case is one in which a person bent on criminal activity seizes control of a previously legitimate firm and uses the firm's resources, contacts, facilities, and appearance of legitimacy to perpetrate more, and less easily discovered, criminal acts than he could do in his own person, that is, without channeling his criminal activities through the enterprise that he has taken over.

A step away from the prototypical case is one in which the criminal uses the acquired enterprise to engage in some criminal activities but for the most part is content to allow it to continue to conduct its normal, lawful business—and many of the employees of the business may be unaware that it is controlled and being used by a criminal. In the next step beyond that, and now coming as close to this case as any case has yet done, the criminal seizes control of a subsidiary of a corporation and perverts the subsidiary into a criminal enterprise that manages in turn to wrest sufficient control or influence over the parent corporation to use it to commit criminal acts; and the issue is whether the subsidiary can be deemed the RICO "person." * * *

What we cannot imagine, and what we do not find any support for in appellate case law, is applying RICO to a free-standing corporation such as Chrysler merely because Chrysler does business through agents, as virtually every manufacturer does. If Chrysler were even larger than it is and as a result had no agents, but only employees (it might own all its dealerships), it could not be made liable for warranty fraud under RICO. What possible difference, from the standpoint of preventing the type of abuse for which RICO was designed, can it make that Chrysler sells its products to the consumer through franchised dealers rather than through dealerships that it owns, or finances the purchases of its motor vehicles through trusts, or sells abroad through subsidiaries? We have never heard it suggested that RICO was intended to encourage vertical integration, yet that is the only effect that we can imagine flowing from a reversal of the district court's judgment.

In the prototypical case with which we began, it is easy to see how the defendant gains additional power to do evil by taking over a seemingly legitimate enterprise. How, though, was Chrysler empowered to perpetrate warranty fraud by selling through dealers rather than directly to the public? The warranty was issued by Chrysler, not by the dealers, and certainly not by the other members of the Chrysler "family." The dealers were merely a conduit, and the trusts and foreign subsidiaries were not even that. The dealers did not, by their incidental role in the alleged fraud (the other members of the "family," other than Chrysler itself, had no role), lend an air of legitimacy to a person or entity that unless masked by a legitimate seeming enterprise would be quickly discovered to be engaged in criminal acts. Chrysler has a greater appearance of probity than any automobile dealer. It has not established dealerships in order to fool car buyers into thinking that they are not dealing with the "racketeer" Chrysler, or to enable Chrysler to engage in fraud on a scale that would be impossible if it internalized the dealership function.

Maybe a manufacturer could use its dealers or other agents or affiliates in such a way as to bring about the sort of abuse at which RICO is aimed, in which event it might be possible to characterize the assemblage as a RICO enterprise. And we recognize the frequent asymmetry in the legal treatment of integrated and nonintegrated firms: under antitrust conspiracy law, for example, a firm can conspire with its dealers, but it cannot conspire with its subsidiaries or employees. *Copperweld Corp. v. Independence Tube Corp.*, 467 U.S. 752 (1984). (Outside the antitrust area, the law on this issue is less clear. *See id.* at 775 n. 24.) RICO, however, is not a conspiracy statute. Its draconian penalties are not triggered just by proving conspiracy. "Enterprise" connotes more. Just how much more is uncertain; but it is enough to decide this case that where a large, reputable manufacturer deals with its dealers and other agents in the ordinary way, so that their role in the manufacturer's illegal acts is entirely incidental, differing not at all from what it would be if these agents were the employees of a totally integrated enterprise, the manufacturer plus its dealers and other agents (or any subset of the members of the corporate family) do not constitute an enterprise within the meaning of the statute.

AFFIRMED.

Notes

1. In the *Cedric Kushner* case, Justice Breyer also stated: "This case concerns a claim that a corporate employee is the "person" and the corporation is the "enterprise." It is natural to speak of a corporate employee as a "person employed by" the corporation. § 1962(c). The earlier Second Circuit precedent concerned a claim that a corporation was the "person" and the corporation, together with all its employees and agents, were the "enterprise." See *Riverwoods Chappaqua Corp. v. Marine Midland Bank, N. A.*, 30 F.3d 339, 344 (1994) (affirming dismissal of complaint). It is less natural to speak of a corporation as "employed by" or "associated with" this latter oddly constructed entity. . . ."

2. For a decision similar to that in the principal case, see *Emery v. American General Finance, Inc.*, 134 F.3d 1321, 1324 (7th Cir.1998): "The firm must be shown to use its agents or affiliates in a way that bears at least a family resemblance to the paradigmatic RICO case in which a criminal obtains control of a legitimate (or legitimate-appearing) firm and uses the firm as the instrument of his criminality."

3. *See Bachman v. Bear, Stearns & Co.*, 178 F.3d 930, 932 (7th Cir. 1999) ("A firm and its employees, or a parent and its subsidiaries, are not an enterprise separate from the firm itself. To add the corporations to . . . their employees . . . is thus to add nothing").

4. *Bucklew v. Hawkins, Ash, Baptie & Co. LLP*, 329 F.3d 923 (7th Cir. 2003), per Posner, J.:

> The RICO claim is another loser. RICO provides a remedy against conducting the activities of an enterprise through a pattern of racketeering activity, and the definition of racketeering includes criminal copyright infringement. But apart from whether Bucklew could show that HAB has engaged in a pattern of such crimes, the RICO claim fails because the enterprise alleged to have been conducted through a pattern of racketeering activity (defendant HAB, Inc.) is a wholly owned subsidiary of the alleged racketeer (the other defendant, Hawkins, Ash, Baptie & Co.). The claim is that the parent stole the software and gave it to the subsidiary to market. A parent and its wholly owned subsidiaries no more have sufficient distinctness to trigger RICO liability than to trigger liability for conspiring in violation of the Sherman Act, unless the enterprise's decision to operate through subsidiaries rather than divisions somehow facilitated its unlawful activity, which has not been shown here.

5. *Baker v. IBP*, 357 F.3d 685 (7th Cir. 2004) per Easterbrook, J.:

... [W]e add that there is another fatal problem in this complaint: specification of the "enterprise....For purposes of ... [1962(c)], the "person" must be IBP, the only defendant. But how is IBP conducting the affairs of an enterprise through a pattern of racketeering activity? The complaint alleges that the "enterprise" is IBP plus the persons and organizations who help it find aliens to hire. We may assume that this congeries is a "group of individuals associated in fact although not a legal entity"—though the complaint comes perilously close to alleging that IBP plus its agents and employees is the "enterprise," a theory that won't fly. And it is not altogether clear how this "association in fact" has a common purpose, an essential ingredient. IBP wants to pay lower wages; the recruiters want to be paid more for services rendered (though IBP would like to pay them less); the Chinese Mutual Aid Association wants to assist members of its ethnic group. These are divergent goals.

6. In *Chen v. Mayflower Transit, Inc.*, 315 F.Supp.2d 886 (N.D. Ill. 2004), the defendant interstate moving company moved for summary judgment. The racketeering activity alleged as the basis for the RICO complaint was, in connection with a cross country move, the alleged extorting of money for additional origin and destination service charges and providing fraudulently low estimates. The defendant carrier, Mayflower, had agreements with approximately 400 local movers who were permitted to use Mayflower's name and logo. The actual moving work was done by drivers employed by the affiliated local companies:

> ... [T]he fact that the local moving companies may be deemed "agents" or "affiliates" of Mayflower does not by itself preclude Chen from establishing her RICO claim.

       * * *

The court finds that Chen has produced evidence establishing that Mayflower and the enterprise may be distinct entities. First, the enterprise is not simply Mayflower by another name. The relationship between Mayflower and the other participants in the enterprise is not employer-employee or parent-subsidiary. The agreement between Mayflower and its affiliates specifically notes that "[t]he parties agree that they have not established a partnership, cooperative, joint venture, franchise or any other business relationship." In addition, Chen has produced evidence that the affiliates associated with her move do significant business entirely apart from their relationship with Mayflower ...

Further, Chen has produced evidence that Mayflower and the enterprise each play a distinct role within the purported scheme. For instance, the evidence shows that the local moving companies conduct activities for the enterprise such as booking shipments, issuing estimates, providing local marketing services, determining (within an authorized range) what discounts to offer, performing physical services such as packing, unpacking, hauling, loading, unloading, storing the goods, and contributing movers and trucks, which Mayflower does not do. Conversely, Mayflower provides the centralized communication system via interstate wire to coordinate moves, provides a customer service department for the shippers, oversees operations, provides guidelines regarding discounts that may be offered by the affiliates, processes payments in connection with the moves (*e.g.*, processes credit transactions and collects and disburses the receipts from the shipments to other participants in the enterprise), provides the federal authority to operate interstate and contributes its name. The evidence that the two entities play distinct roles and had different rights and responsibilities is important in the distinctness analysis. ... The enterprise does not constitute Mayflower's regular business because Mayflower does not physically conduct moves, decide to impose the additional charges or share in the charges collected from the "additional services," including shuttles, long carries, and stair and elevator charges; only the enterprise does. ...

Indeed, the evidence produced shows that the success of the enterprise may *depend* on the distinctness between Mayflower and the enterprise; specifically, the use of the local moving companies as agents or affiliates permitted the enterprise to take Chen's goods under the representation that certain terms would be met, and then use the fact that her goods were being handled by a different local company as a basis to refuse to honor the agreement made with Chen and to require additional improper payments from Chen. That evidence indicates that by working through the enterprise, Mayflower was enabled to engage in the alleged racketeering activity in a way that would be impossible if Mayflower had internalized the agent-affiliate function. Put differently, the person-enterprise relationship in this case may have "empowered [Mayflower] to perpetrate ... fraud by selling through [its affiliates] rather than directly to the public."

7. Regarding the distinctiveness requirement, i.e. that the person and the enterprise must be distinct, see *Jaguar Cars v. Royal Oaks*, 46 F.3d 258, 268 (3d Cir.1995):

* * * [W]e conclude that the essential holding * * * [of our earlier precedent] remains undisturbed—a claim simply against one corporation as both "person" and "enterprise" is not sufficient. Instead, a viable § 1962 (c) action requires a claim against defendant "persons" acting through a distinct "enterprise." But, alleging conduct by officers or employees who operate or manage a corporate enterprise satisfies this requirement. A corporation is an entity legally distinct from its officers or employees, which satisfies the "enterprise" definition of * * * § 1961 (4) * * * Accordingly, Jaguar has satisfied the distinctiveness requirement of § 1962 (c). Jaguar has not brought a claim against Royal Oaks, but instead seeks recovery from the defendants, as persons operating and managing the Royal Oaks enterprise through a pattern of racketeering activity.

8. The cases in the preceding notes, from different vantage points, provide a window into the variety of different combinations that may be explored in deciding, in a corporate setting involving management, employees, subsidiaries, agents and the like, "what" to allege as the "enterprise" and "whom" to charge as the "person" under § 1962 (c). The cases indicate that not all the logical possibilities are legally acceptable. As suggested in Judge Posner's opinion in *Fitzgerald*, there are some parallels in the law of conspiracy, but, as he indicates, the conspiracy analogue may not be control-

ling in the setting of RICO. The complexities of this subject are made even more complicated when one adds to the picture the fact that the "person" may be inside or outside of the corporation, and the fact that the Supreme Court has added another requirement—that liability under § 1962 (c) is limited to those who "participate in the operation or management of the enterprise."

REVES v. ERNST & YOUNG

507 U.S. 170, 113 S.Ct. 1163, 122 L.Ed.2d 525 (1993).

[BLACKMUN, J., delivered the opinion of the Court, in which REHNQUIST, C.J., and STEVENS, O'CONNOR, and KENNEDY, JJ., joined, and in all but Part IV–A of which SCALIA and THOMAS, JJ., joined. SOUTER, J., filed a dissenting opinion, in which WHITE, J., joined.]

JUSTICE BLACKMUN delivered the opinion of the Court.

This case requires us once again to interpret the provisions of the Racketeer Influenced and Corrupt Organizations (RICO) chapter of the Organized Crime Control Act of 1970, Pub. L. 91–452, Title IX, 84 Stat. 941, as amended, 18 U. S. C. §§ 1961–1968 (1988 ed. and Supp. II). Section 1962(c) makes it unlawful "for any person employed by or associated with any enterprise engaged in, or the activities of which affect, interstate or foreign commerce, to conduct or participate, directly or indirectly, in the conduct of such enterprise's affairs through a pattern of racketeering activity. . . . " The question presented is whether one must participate in the operation or management of the enterprise itself to be subject to liability under this provision.

I

The Farmer's Cooperative of Arkansas and Oklahoma, Inc. (Co–Op), began operating in western Arkansas and eastern Oklahoma in 1946. To raise money for operating expenses, the Co–Op sold promissory notes payable to the holder on demand. Each year, Co–Op members were elected to serve on its board. The board met monthly but delegated actual management of the Co–Op to a general manager. In 1952, the board appointed Jack White as general manager.

In January 1980, White began taking loans from the Co–Op to finance the construction of a gasohol plant by his company, White Flame Fuels, Inc. By the end of 1980, White's debts to the Co–Op totaled approximately $4 million. In September of that year, White and Gene Kuykendall, who served as the accountant for both the Co–Op and White Flame, were indicted for federal tax fraud. At a board meeting on November 12, 1980, White proposed that the Co–Op purchase White Flame. The board agreed. One month later, however, the Co–Op filed a declaratory action against White and White Flame in Arkansas state court alleging that White actually had sold White Flame to the Co–Op in February 1980. The complaint was drafted by White's attorneys and led to a consent decree relieving White of his debts and providing that the Co–Op had owned White Flame since February 15, 1980.

White and Kuykendall were convicted of tax fraud in January 1981. Harry Erwin, the managing partner of Russell Brown and Company, an Arkansas accounting firm, testified for White, and shortly thereafter the Co–Op retained Russell Brown to perform its 1981 financial audit. Joe Drozal, a partner in the Brown firm, was put in charge of the audit and Joe Cabaniss was selected to assist him. On January 2, 1982, Russell Brown and Company merged with Arthur Young and Company, which later became respondent Ernst & Young.

One of Drozal's first tasks in the audit was to determine White Flame's fixed-asset value. After consulting with White and reviewing White Flame's books (which Kuykendall had prepared), Drozal concluded that the plant's value at the end of 1980 was $4,393,242.66, the figure Kuykendall had employed. Using this figure as a base, Drozal factored in the 1981 construction costs and capitalized expenses and concluded that White Flame's 1981 fixed-asset value was approximately $4.5 million. Drozal then had to determine how that value should be treated for accounting purposes. If the Co–Op had owned White Flame from the beginning of construction in 1979, White Flame's value or accounting purposes would be its fixed-asset value of $4.5 million. If, however, the Co–Op had purchased White Flame from White, White Flame would have to be given its fair market value at the time of purchase, which was somewhere between $444,000 and $1.5 million. If White Flame were valued at less than $1.5 million, the Co–Op was insolvent. Drozal concluded that the Co–Op had owned White Flame from the start and that the plant should be valued at $4.5 million on its books.

On April 22, 1982, Arthur Young presented its 1981 audit report to the Co–Op's board. In that audit's Note 9, Arthur Young expressed doubt whether the investment in White Flame could ever be recovered. Note 9 also observed that White Flame was sustaining operating losses averaging $100,000 per month. Arthur Young did not tell the board of its conclusion that the Co–Op always had owned White Flame or that without that conclusion the Co–Op was insolvent.

On May 27, the Co–Op held its 1982 annual meeting. At that meeting, the Co–Op, through Harry C. Erwin, a partner in Arthur Young, distributed to the members condensed financial statements. These included White Flame's $4.5 million asset value among its total assets but omitted the information contained in the audit's Note 9. Cabaniss was also present. Erwin saw the condensed financial statement for the first time when he arrived at the meeting. In a 5–minute presentation, he told his audience that the statements were condensed and that copies of the full audit were available at the Co–Op's office. In response to questions, Erwin explained that the Co–Op owned White Flame and that the plant had incurred approximately $1.2 million in losses but he revealed no other information relevant to the Co–Op's true financial health.

The Co–Op hired Arthur Young also to perform its 1982 audit. The 1982 report, presented to the board on March 7, 1983, was similar to the

1981 report and restated (this time in its Note 8) Arthur Young's doubt whether the investment in White Flame was recoverable. The gasohol plant again was valued at approximately $4.5 million and was responsible for the Co–Op's showing a positive net worth. The condensed financial statement distributed at the annual meeting on March 24, 1983, omitted the information in Note 8. This time, Arthur Young reviewed the condensed statement in advance but did not act to remove its name from the statement. Cabaniss, in a 3–minute presentation at the meeting, gave the financial report. He informed the members that the full audit was available at the Co–Op's office but did not tell them about Note 8 or that the Co–Op was in financial difficulty if White Flame were written down to its fair market value.

In February 1984, the Co–Op experienced a slight run on its demand notes. On February 23, when it was unable to secure further financing, the Co–Op filed for bankruptcy. As a result, the demand notes were frozen in the bankruptcy estate and were no longer redeemable at will by the noteholders.

II

On February 14, 1985, the trustee in bankruptcy filed suit against 40 individuals and entities, including Arthur Young, on behalf of the Co–Op and certain noteholders. The court then granted summary judgment in favor of Arthur Young on the RICO claim. The District Court applied the test established by the Eighth Circuit in *Bennett v. Berg*, 710 F.2d 1361, 1364 (en banc), that 1962(c) requires "some participation in the operation or management of the enterprise itself." The court ruled: "Plaintiffs have failed to show anything more than that the accountants reviewed a series of completed transactions, and certified the Co–Op's records as fairly portraying its financial status as of a date three or four months preceding the meetings of the directors and the shareholders at which they presented their reports. We do not hesitate to declare that such activities fail to satisfy the degree of management required by *Bennett v. Berg*."

The only part of the Court of Appeals' decision that is at issue here is its affirmance of summary judgment in favor of Arthur Young on the RICO claim. Like the District Court, the Court of Appeals applied the "operation or management" test articulated in *Bennett v. Berg* and held that Arthur Young's conduct did not "rise to the level of participation in the management or operation of the Co-op." The Court of Appeals for the District of Columbia Circuit also has adopted an "operation or management" test. *See Yellow Bus Lines, Inc. v. Drivers, Chauffeurs & Helpers Local Union 639*, 913 F.2d 948, 954 (1990) (en banc). We granted certiorari to resolve the conflict between these cases and *Bank of America National Trust & Savings Assn. v. Touche Ross & Co.*, 782 F.2d 966, 970 (11th Cir.1986) (rejecting requirement that a defendant participate in the operation or management of an enterprise).

III

"In determining the scope of a statute, we look first to its language. If the statutory language is unambiguous, in the absence of 'a clearly expressed legislative intent to the contrary, that language must ordinarily be regarded as conclusive.' "

The narrow question in this case is the meaning of the phrase "to conduct or participate, directly or indirectly, in the conduct of such enterprise's affairs." The word "conduct" is used twice, and it seems reasonable to give each use a similar construction. As a verb, "conduct" means to lead, run, manage, or direct. Webster's Third New International Dictionary 474 (1976). Petitioners urge us to read "conduct" as "carry on," so that almost any involvement in the affairs of an enterprise would satisfy the "conduct or participate" requirement. But context is important, and in the context of the phrase "to conduct . . . [an] enterprise's affairs," the word indicates some degree of direction.

The dissent agrees that, when "conduct" is used as a verb, "it is plausible to find in it a suggestion of control." The dissent prefers to focus on "conduct" as a noun, as in the phrase "participate, directly or indirectly, in the conduct of [an] enterprise's affairs." But unless one reads "conduct" to include an element of direction when used as a noun in this phrase, the word becomes superfluous. Congress could easily have written "participate, directly or indirectly, in [an] enterprise's affairs," but it chose to repeat the word "conduct." We conclude, therefore, that as both a noun and a verb in this subsection "conduct" requires an element of direction.

The more difficult question is what to make of the word "participate." This Court previously has characterized this word as a "ter[m] . . . of breadth." Petitioners argue that Congress used "participate" as a synonym for "aid and abet." That would be a term of breadth indeed, for "aid and abet" "comprehends all assistance rendered by words, acts, encouragement, support, or presence." Black's Law Dictionary 68 (6th ed. 1990). But within the context of § 1962(c), "participate" appears to have a narrower meaning. We may mark the limits of what the term might mean by looking again at what Congress did not say. On the one hand, "to participate . . . in the conduct of . . . affairs" must be broader than "to conduct affairs" or the "participate" phrase would be superfluous. On the other hand, as we already have noted, "to participate . . . in the conduct of . . . affairs" must be narrower than "to participate in affairs" or Congress' repetition of the word "conduct" would serve no purpose. It seems that Congress chose a middle ground, consistent with a common understanding of the word "participate"—"to take part in." Webster's Third New International Dictionary 1646 (1976).

Once we understand the word "conduct" to require some degree of direction and the word "participate" to require some part in that direction, the meaning of § 1962(c) comes into focus. In order to "participate, directly or indirectly, in the conduct of such enterprise's affairs," one must have some part in directing those affairs. Of course, the word "participate" makes clear that RICO liability is not limited to those with primary responsibility for the enterprise's affairs, just as the phrase "directly or indirectly" makes clear that RICO liability is not limited to those with a formal position in the enterprise,[4] but some part in directing the enterprise affairs is required. The "operation or management" test expresses this requirement in a formulation that is easy to apply.

IV

A

This test finds further support in the legislative history of § 1962. [The Court reviewed here various statements in the legislative history describing § 1962 as a prohibition on the operation or management of an enterprise through racketeering.]

Of course, the fact that Members of Congress understood § 1962(c) to prohibit the operation or management of an enterprise through a pattern of racketeering activity does not necessarily mean that they understood § 1962(c) to be limited to the operation or management of an enterprise. *Cf. Turkette*, 452 U.S. at 591 (references to the infiltration of legitimate organizations do not "require the negative inference that [RICO] did not reach the activities of enterprises organized and existing for criminal purposes"). It is clear from other remarks, however, that Congress did not intend RICO to extend beyond the acquisition or operation of an enterprise. While S. 30 was being considered, critics of the bill raised concerns that racketeering activity was defined so broadly that RICO would reach many crimes not necessarily typical of organized crime. *See* 116 Cong. Rec. 18912–18914, 18939–18940 (1970) (remarks of Sen. McClellan). Senator McClellan reassured the bill's critics that the critical limitation was not to be found in § 1961(1)'s list of predicate crimes but in the statute's other requirements, including those of § 1962:

> "... Unless an individual not only commits such a crime but engages in a pattern of such violations, and uses that pattern to obtain or operate an interest in an interstate business, he is not made subject to proceedings under title IX." 116 Cong. Rec., at 18940.

Thus, the legislative history confirms what we have already deduced from the language of § 1962(c)—that one is not liable under that provision unless one has participated in the operation or management of the enterprise itself.

B

RICO's "liberal construction" clause does not require rejection of the "operation or management" test. * * *

---

4. For these reasons, we disagree with the suggestion of the Court of Appeals for the District of Columbia Circuit that § 1962(c) requires "significant control over or within an enterprise." *Yellow Bus Lines, Inc. v. Drivers, Chauffeurs & Helpers Local Union 639*, 913 F.2d 948, 954 (1990) (en banc).

Petitioners argue that the "operation or management" test is flawed because liability under § 1962(c) is not limited to upper management but may extend to "any person employed by or associated with [the] enterprise." We agree that liability under § 1962(c) is not limited to upper management, but we disagree that the "operation or management" test is inconsistent with this proposition. An enterprise is "operated" not just by upper management but also by lower rung participants in the enterprise who are under the direction of upper management.[9] An enterprise also might be "operated" or "managed" by others "associated with" the enterprise who exert control over it as, for example, by bribery.

The United States also argues that the "operation or management" test is not consistent with § 1962(c) because it limits the liability of "outsiders" who have no official position within the enterprise. The United States correctly points out that RICO's major purpose was to attack the "infiltration of organized crime and racketeering into legitimate organizations," but its argument fails on several counts. First, it ignores the fact that § 1962 has four subsections. Infiltration of legitimate organizations by "outsiders" is clearly addressed in subsections (a) and (b), and the "operation or management" test that applies under subsection (c) in no way limits the application of subsections (a) and (b) to "outsiders." Second, § 1962(c) is limited to persons "employed by or associated with" an enterprise, suggesting a more limited reach than subsections (a) and (b), which do not contain such a restriction. Third, § 1962(c) cannot be interpreted to reach complete "outsiders" because liability depends on showing that the defendants conducted or participated in the conduct of the "enterprise's affairs," not just their own affairs. Of course, "outsiders" may be liable under § 1962(c) if they are "associated with" an enterprise and participate in the conduct of its affairs—that is, participate in the operation or management of the enterprise itself—but it would be consistent with neither the language nor the legislative history of § 1962(c) to interpret it as broadly as petitioners and the United States urge.

In sum, we hold that "to conduct or participate, directly or indirectly, in the conduct of such enterprise's affairs," § 1962(c), one must participate in the operation or management of the enterprise itself.

* * *

The judgment of the Court of Appeals is affirmed. * * *

Notes

1. Since the decision in *Reves*, a large number of circuit courts have addressed questions relating to the application and interpretation of the

---

9. At oral argument, there was some discussion about whether low-level employees could be considered to have participated in the conduct of an enterprise's affairs. We need not decide in this case how far § 1962(c) extends down the ladder of operation because it is clear that Arthur Young was not acting under the direction of the Co–Op's officers or board.

operation or management test. Indeed, it has become one of the most hotly contested of the various RICO issues.

An initial question is whether the *Reves* test applies only to outsiders, i.e. those outside the enterprise (such as the defendant accounting firm in *Reves)* or also applies to those inside the enterprise. One first circuit case has ruled: "*Reves*' analysis does not apply where a party is determined to be inside a RICO enterprise." *United States v. Owens*, 167 F.3d 739 (1st Cir.1999). Other first circuit cases have given a textured interpretation of the insider-outsider distinction. For example, in *United States v. Oreto*, 37 F.3d 739 (1st Cir.1994), the court stated: "Special care is required in translating *Reves*' concern with 'horizontal' connections—focusing on the liability of an outside adviser—into the 'vertical' question of how far RICO liability may extend within the enterprise." The court ruled that low level employees could be held liable; that an employee of the enterprise who is within the chain of command, could be held liable even if he only knowingly implemented management decisions made by others: "We think that Congress intended to reach all who participate in the conduct of [an] enterprise, whether they are generals or foot soldiers." *Id.* at 750–751.

For a defendant who was outside the enterprise (a loansharking operation's debtor who ended up aiding the operation), the First Circuit has held that "a defendant who is plainly integral to carrying out the enterprise's activities may be held criminally liable under RICO." *United States v. Shifman*, 124 F.3d 31, 36 (1st Cir.1997).

2. The Second Circuit has taken a different view, concluding that "the simple taking of directions and performance of tasks that are 'necessary or helpful' to the enterprise, without more, is insufficient to bring a defendant within the scope of § 1962(c)." *United States v. Viola*, 35 F.3d 37, 41 (2d Cir.1994). In *Viola*, a janitor-handyman who worked for the head of a drug-contraband trafficking operation transported stolen goods to buyers and returned most of the proceeds from the sales of the goods to the head of the operation:

> [A]lthough *Reves* still attaches liability to those down the "ladder of operation" who nonetheless played some management role * * * § 1962(c) liability cannot cover [the janitor for he] * * * was not on the ladder at all, but rather as the janitor and handyman, was sweeping up the floor "underneath it." Id. at 43.

Another second circuit case, *United States v. Diaz*, 176 F.3d 52, 92 (2d Cir.1999), has stated its view of what is necessary to bring a defendant under the *Reves* test:

> Under the *Reves* operation-management test, even if a defendant is not acting in a managerial role, we have held that he can still be liable for directing the enterprise affairs if he "exercised broad discretion" in carrying out the instructions of his principal.

Still another Second Circuit case suggests that the law of the Circuit on this issue is far from clear. In *United States v. Allen*, 155 F.3d 35 (2d Cir.1998), the issue arose on a motion for summary judgment in a RICO civil action brought by the government seeking injunctive relief and the disgorgement of illegal profits against 112 defendants involved in the trash hauling business, including organized crime families, a trade association, a labor union, carting firms and their officers and directors and a number of town employees alleged to have taken bribes. After citing statements in second circuit cases that seem to point in different directions and also referring to cases similar to the first circuit decision in *Oreto, supra* note 1, Judge Newman stated:

> We think that the only principle to be drawn from this array of holdings and statements is that the commission of crimes by lower level employees of a RICO enterprise may be found to indicate participation in the operation or management of the enterprise but does not compel such a finding. * * * Unless a civil RICO defendant is indisputably directing the affairs of the enterprise, his commission of crimes that advance its objectives must be assessed by a fact-finder to determine whether or not his criminal activity, assessed in the context of all the relevant circumstances, constitutes participation in the operation or management of the enterprise's affairs.

The court concluded that summary judgment was not warranted on the issue of the defendant's RICO liability. See generally, Scott Paccagnini, How Low Can You Go (Down the Ladder): The Vertical Reach of RICO, 37 J. Marshall L.Rev.1 (2003).

3. An eighth circuit case, *Handeen v. Lemaire*, 112 F.3d 1339 (8th Cir.1997) involved an alleged manipulation of the bankruptcy system to fraudulently obtain a discharge of the plaintiff's earlier judgment obtained against one of the defendants. The defendant law firm was alleged to have been actively advising the debtor regarding the fraudulent steps to be taken. (Recall that *Bennett v. Berg*, the case that originally developed the operation or management test was an eighth circuit decision.) Regarding the law firm's possible liability under RICO, the court stated:

> The Supreme Court's approval and refinement of our operation or management test has had far-reaching implications, particularly in the area of professional liability under RICO. * * *

> In our view, the *Reves* decision represents a fairly uncomplicated application of the operation or management test. * * * Furnishing a client with ordinary professional assistance, even when the client happens to be a RICO enterprise, will not normally rise to the level of participation sufficient to satisfy the Supreme Court's pronouncements in *Reves*. * * *

> Appreciation for the unremarkable notion that the operation or management test does not reach persons who perform routine services for an enterprise should not, however, be mistaken for an absolute edict that an attorney who associates with an enterprise can never be liable under RICO. An attorney's license is not an invitation to engage in racketeering. * * * [W]e will not shrink from finding an attorney liable when he crosses the line between traditional rendition of legal services and active participation in directing the enterprise. The polestar is the activity in question, not the defendant's status. "The cases reveal an underlying distinction between acting in an advisory professional capacity (even if in a knowingly fraudulent way) and acting as a direct participant in [an enterprise's] affairs." Bearing these principles in

mind, we are confident that * * * [the] Complaint could support a verdict against the firm.

4. The operation or management issue sometimes gets involved with the question of whether the person and the enterprise are sufficiently distinct. See *Baker v. IBP*, 357 F.3d 685 (7th Cir. 2004), also discussed supra note 5, p. 512:

> Even if the congeries is an enterprise, how is it that IBP operates or manages *that enterprise* through a pattern of racketeering activity? The nub of the complaint is that IBP operates *itself* unlawfully—it is IBP that supposedly hires, harbors, and pays the unlawful workers, for the purpose of reducing its payroll. IBP does not manage or operate some other enterprise by violating § 274; the complaint does not allege—and on appeal plaintiffs do not seek an opportunity to show—that IBP has infiltrated, taken over, manipulated, disrupted, or suborned a distinct entity or even a distinct association in fact. Contrast *United States v. Neapolitan,* 791 F.2d 489, 500 (7th Cir.1986). Without a difference between the defendant and the "enterprise" there can be no violation of RICO.

5. Like the issue of distinctiveness, the matter of operation or management of a RICO enterprise has many permutations depending on the nature of the enterprise alleged and the relationship of the defendant(s) person(s) to that enterprise. Consider, e.g., *Chen v. Mayflower Transit, Inc.* 315 F.Supp.2d 886 (N.D. Ill. 2004) (the facts of the case are presented, supra, note 6, p. 513.

> Mayflower also argues that it does not direct or control the enterprise. Mayflower asserts that, in fact, it is the local moving company *affiliates* who committed the predicate acts alleged and that those affiliates are not controlled by Mayflower. Citing *Reves,* Chen argues that the purpose of the "operation or management" test is to prevent the RICO statute from reaching "complete outsiders," and that Mayflower is not a "complete outsider" to the enterprise, but rather its "center point."

> * * *

> In the present case, Chen has established facts indicating that ... Mayflower does participate in the operation or management of the enterprise. The evidence produced shows that Mayflower develops policies and procedures, which its affiliates are required to follow. Mayflower directly controls the customer service department and the disbursement of funds to the local moving company affiliates, including the disbursement of the amounts received for the additional origin and destination charges. Mayflower also provides its name to the enterprise. Mayflower is the link between the booking agent who provides the allegedly fraudulent estimate and the hauling agent who extracts the additional charges.

> In addition, although Mayflower argues that its participation was limited to merely performing services for the enterprise because it was the local moving company agents who committed the alleged predicate acts (*e.g.,* issued fraudulent estimates and unilaterally imposed higher charges at the point of origin or destination), the evidence shows

otherwise. Mayflower issues the policies, procedure and guidelines which permits the alleged predicate acts to be committed. Mayflower's argument that the agents who committed the alleged predicate acts are not controlled by Mayflower because they "are all independent corporations, incorporated in different states, with different ownership from Mayflower" and because "[t]here is no evidence in the record of any relationship between the members of the Mayflower-enterprise ... no shared ownership and no shared employees" is also at odds with Mayflower's argument, discussed above, that the affiliates are acting as Mayflower's agents. And, significantly, Mayflower recruits and has the power to admit affiliates at will and, when dissatisfied, end its relationship with an affiliate "without cause." Mayflower's role in the enterprise therefore goes far beyond the mere giving of directions or performance of tasks helpful to the enterprise. Indeed, without Mayflower's involvement, it appears the enterprise would fail to exist altogether. Thus, the evidence produced suggests that Mayflower participates in the enterprise's operation and "t[akes] some part in directing [the enterprise's] affairs." Mayflower is not the "complete outsider" that the operation or management test seeks to exclude. Accordingly, summary judgment cannot be granted on this ground, either.

6. A further issue that has arisen is the extent to which, in a prosecution for conspiracy to violate the RICO statute under § 1962(d), the agreement of the defendants must contemplate or include participation in the operation or management of the RICO enterprise. The issue is addressed in more detail, *infra*, pp. 555–558, in the section on RICO Conspiracy. Suffice to note here that resolution of that issue bears on how wide the RICO net of liability extends.

7. It has been suggested that there is a conflict between *Reves'* narrowing of liability and the notion that RICO is to be liberally construed to effectuate its remedial purposes; that the tension arises because the courts are interpreting RICO narrowly in civil cases to restrict its overuse in such cases, and broadly in criminal cases to implement its remedial purposes; that this tension places the courts on the horns of a dilemma since *Reves* and other RICO doctrines are equally applicable to civil and criminal cases. *See Recent Case*, 108 HARV. L. REV. 1405, n. 8 (1995). *Compare* Brian Camp, *Dual Construction of RICO: The Road Not Taken in Reves*, 51 WASH. & LEE L. REV. 61 (1994).

NOTE ON THE USE OF AIDING & ABETTING LIABILITY AS A WAY TO AVOID THE IMPACT OF THE REVES DOCTRINE

Reves involved the question of whether an accounting firm that provided auditing information to a corporation could be held liable for a § 1962(c) RICO violation as a "person ... associated with ... [the] enterprise [that is, the corporation]. ..." The *Reves'* test was used to determine the liability of "person" under the language of § 1962(c); it thus addressed the liability of a principal in a RICO violation. *Reves* established that in order to violate the statute as a principal, one must participate in the operation or management of the enterprise.

Suppose, however, that a criminal prosecutor charges an accounting firm or a law firm (or any similar outside-of-the-enterprise operation that provides a service to the enterprise) not as a principal in a RICO violation but rather as an aider and abettor? If a RICO violation is a substantive crime, one would assume that ordinary accomplice liability applies to it. An accomplice is one who, (using the Model Penal Code formulation) "with the purpose of promoting or facilitating the commission of the offense ... aids ... [an]other person in planning or committing it ...." Even though, as the Supreme Court concluded, Arthur Young, the auditing firm, did not participate in the operation or management of the enterprise within the meaning of Reves, might not the firm nevertheless be held criminally liable as an aider and abettor to the violation of the RICO statute by, let us say, Jack White, the general manager who arguably did operate or manage the enterprise? Under this revised theory of the case, White would be the RICO "person"? Of coursed, in order to be viewed as an accomplice in this setting, Arthur Young would have to have the mens rea required to make a person an accomplice. We return to that issue below.

Imposing criminal liability on Arthur Young as an accomplice to a RICO violation rather than as the principal in the violation would seem to be a way to avoid the limiting effect of the Reves "operation or management" test. Moreover, it would seem potentially to apply both to "outsiders" who aid and abet the RICO person who operates or manages the enterprise and also to "insiders" who are too low in the enterprise hierarchy to be deemed to operate or manage but nevertheless assist the RICO person.

Why did the plaintiff in *Reves* not also use an aiding and abetting theory in pursuing the action? The barrier to the use of an accomplice theory of liability lies in a difference between civil and criminal RICO. Recall that Reves was a civil RICO case. Until now, we have generally assumed equivalence between the law applied in civil and criminal RICO cases, although it was suggested earlier (note 7, p. 524) that there may be different leeways of interpretation at work in the two arenas.

Section 1964(c), Title 18, U.S.C., provides that any "person injured in his business or property by reason of a violation of section 1962 ... may sue therefore ...." A RICO civil suit thus requires that one of the subsections of § 1962, a criminal provision, have been violated; in most instances, it would be § 1962(c). However, the aider and abettor theory under which Arthur Young might be held liable for a violation of § 1962(c) would require invocation not only of 18 U.S.C. § 1962(c), the RICO provision, but also of Title 18, U.S.C.'s accomplice provision, § 2. Section 2 provides "Whoever ... aids, abets ... commission [of an offense against the United States] is punishable as a principal."

Therefore, if in a civil RICO case, one wishes to hold Arthur Young liable on an accomplice theory, as stated above, one must at the outset demonstrate criminal liability through invocation of both § 1962(c) and § 2 of Title 18, U.S.C. But § 1964(c), through which ultimately civil RICO liability is imposed, only refers to § 1962, and not to § 2. Whether aiding and abetting liability can be imposed through a combination of 1964(c) and 1962(c) involves a matter of statutory interpretation. Do the words in 1964(c), "by reason of a violation of section 1962," carry with them the implication that liability based on § 2 is included? (Note: If the civil liability is based in § 1962(a), the issue may be different since 1962(a) mentions § 2.)

The RICO case law involving aiding and abetting issues typically has involved civil suits, not criminal prosecutions. Two Third Circuit cases illustrate the prevailing view that aiding and abetting liability for RICO is not available in a civil suit. In *Rolo v. City Investing Co. Liquidating Trust,* 155 F.3d 644 (3d Cir. 1998), the court ruled that "because RICO's statutory text does not provide for a private cause of action for aiding and abetting and 18 U.S.C. § 2 cannot be used to imply this private right, no such cause of action exists under RICO," quoted from *Pennsylvania Ass'n of Edwards Heirs v. Rightenhour,* 235 F.3d 839 (3d Cir. 2000). In the *Rightenhour* case, because they were barred by the *Rolo* decision from pursuing a statutory civil RICO aiding and abetting claim, the plaintiffs tried to persuade the court to recognize a civil aiding and abetting RICO claim as a common law civil remedy. The court rejected the claim. The Rolo and Rightenhour decisions both relied heavily on the Supreme Court's reasoning in *Central Bank of Denver v. First Interstate Bank of Denver,* 511 U.S. 164 (1994) in which the Court had held that private aiding and abetting suits were not authorized by § 10(b) of the Securities Exchange Act of 1934. In *Central Bank,* the Supreme Court had addressed the § 10(b) issue in the following terms:

> With respect ... to ... the scope of conduct prohibited by § 10(b), the text of the statute controls our decision.... We have refused to allow [§ 10(b)] challenges to conduct not prohibited by the text of the statute....
>
> Congress knew how to impose aiding and abetting liability when it chose to do so. If ... Congress intended to impose aiding and abetting liability, we presume it would have used the words "aid" and "abet" in the statutory text. But it did not.
>
> We reach the uncontroversial conclusion, ... that the text of the 1934 Act does not itself reach those who aid and abet a § 10(b) violation. [W]e think that conclusion resolves the case. It is inconsistent with settled methodology in § 10(b) cases to extend liability beyond the scope of conduct prohibited by the statutory text. To be sure, aiding and abetting a wrongdoer ought to be actionable in certain instances. The issue, however, is not whether imposing private civil liability on aiders and abettors is good policy but whether aiding and abetting is covered by the statute.

The foregoing analysis is applicable to civil RICO suits but what about criminal RICO? We initiated the analysis of the civil RICO issue by stating: "If a RICO violation is a substantive crime, one would assume that ordinary accomplice liability applies to it." The issue of statutory interpretation raised by the language in 1964(c) does not arise if an aiding and abetting theory is used in a criminal RICO case. So, it would appear that indeed *Reves* could be circumvented in a criminal RICO prosecution by the use of aiding and abetting theory. The fact is, however, that there appear to be no cases to support this conclusion, and there is little or no criminal RICO case law involving application of the operation or management test? Why indeed are these issues not arising more frequently in criminal RICO prosecutions? What might account for the fact that these issues have been raised repeatedly in civil RICO cases but not in criminal RICO prosecutions?

Suppose civil RICO liability is based in § 1962(d), that is, conspiring to violate one of the other subsections of 1962, let us say, § 1962(c). Is this a viable alternative to relying on aiding and abetting. Consider in this connection, *Salinas v. United States*, infra, p. 552, and particularly note 2, p. 555. Also consider the implications of *Salinas* and the material in note 2, p. 555 for the mens rea that an aider and abettor to a RICO violation must have in order to impose criminal liability. Unlike the aider and abettor RICO issue, it would seem that there should not be a difference in the treatment of the conspiracy issue depending on whether the case involves civil or criminal RICO. Why not?

The issue of aiding and abetting other kinds of complex crimes, e.g., a CCE or super CCE violation, also has arisen in the case law. See infra, p. 630, Chapter 13.

Notes

1. *Hayden v. Paul, Weiss, Rifkind, Wharton & Garrison*, 955 F.Supp. 248 (S.D.N.Y. 1997) is another case that illustrates the interplay of the *Reves* doctrine with the RICO-aiding and abetting issue:

> In this case, plaintiffs concede, as they must, that their aiding and abetting claims under § 10(b) and Rule 10b–5 must be dismissed in light of the Supreme Court's holding in *Central Bank of Denver v. First Interstate Bank of Denver*. . . . Plaintiffs' primary RICO claims under 18 U.S.C. § 1962(c) must also be dismissed because plaintiffs have neither alleged nor presented facts permitting a rational inference that Price participated in the "operation or management" of a RICO enterprise. . . . Indeed, it is well established that the provision of professional services by outsiders, such as accountants, to a racketeering enterprise, is insufficient to satisfy the participation requirement of RICO, since participation requires some part in directing the affairs of the enterprise itself. This remains true even if the accountants, such as Price, provided services which were essential to the success of the enterprise. . . .

> Nor does RICO's proscription of participation "directly or indirectly" in a RICO enterprise give rise to private civil liability for aiding and abetting. The Court in Central Bank noted that § 10(b) and Rule 10b–5 employ the term "directly or indirectly" and expressly rejected the argument that this language creates a private right of action for aiding and abetting. *Central Bank*, 511 U.S. at 176. The Court reasoned that "aiding and abetting liability extends beyond persons who engage, even indirectly, in a proscribed activity; aiding and abetting liability reaches persons who do not engage in the proscribed activities *at all*, but who give a degree of aid to those who do." *Id.* (emphasis added). The Court adopted similar reasoning in *Reves. See Reves*, 507 U.S. at 179 (requiring affirmative directing of enterprise affairs before imposing RICO liability).

> Plaintiffs also argue that since civil liability under RICO turns on whether a criminal violation has occurred, that criminal concepts of aiding and abetting should be construed to be applicable to RICO even if they are not applicable to securities violations. However, this argument,

if accepted, would undermine *Central Bank*, since its holding could be circumvented by the simple expedient of alleging a pattern of criminal securities law violations as predicate acts, and based upon that pattern seek to impose civil liability under RICO on the basis of aiding and abetting a RICO violation when, under *Central Bank*, that conduct could not be a basis for civil liability under the securities laws. In any event, since the arguments for inferring aiding and abetting liability under § 10(b) are stronger than in the case of RICO because the common law doctrine of aiding and abetting is presumably more readily applied to a judicially implied cause of action under § 10(b) than a statutory right of action under RICO, the reasoning of *Central Bank should have even more force when applied to RICO.*

2.   The *Hayden* case, *supra* note 1 also contained the following footnote discussion of another kind of interplay between *Reves* and aiding and abetting liability:

> Plaintiffs' reliance upon *131 Main Street Associates v. Manko*, 897 F.Supp. 1507 (S.D.N.Y.1995) is also misplaced. In that case, the court held that aiding and abetting a violation of § 10(b) and Rule 10b–5 may constitute predicate acts for a primary RICO violation by those who manage the affairs of a RICO enterprise. The Manko court reasoned that even after *Reves*, a person who *operates or manages an enterprise,* but who merely aids or abets the commission of predicate acts, may still be liable for a RICO violation. Nothing in this case suggests that persons who do not participate in the operation or management of the enterprise are subject to civil liability merely because they aid or abet predicate acts.

3.   For other decisions that have applied the effects of *Reves* and *Central Bank* on RICO aiding and abetting, see, e.g.: *American Automotive Accessories, Inc. v. Fishman*, 175 F.3d 534 (7th Cir. 1999); *Goldfine v. Sichenzia*, 118 F.Supp.2d 392 (S.D.N.Y. 2000); *Wuliger v. Liberty Bank,* 2004 WL 3377416 (N.D. Ohio); *In re: MasterCard International Inc. v. Internet Gambling Litigation,* 132 F.Supp.2d 468 (E.D. La. 2001), aff'd, 313 F.3d 257 (5th Cir. 2002) (without reaching aiding and abetting issue).

4.   In response to *Central Bank*, in the year 2000, Congress amended 15 U.S.C. § 78t, the section 10(b) provision, to extend liability to aiders and abettors. Should the RICO statute be amended in a similar manner?

C. THE PATTERN OF RACKETEERING ACTIVITY

1. THE PATTERN REQUIREMENT

H. J. INC. v. NORTHWESTERN BELL TELEPHONE COMPANY
492 U.S. 229, 109 S.Ct. 2893, 106 L.Ed.2d 195 (1989).

JUSTICE BRENNAN delivered the opinion of the Court.

We are called upon in this civil case to consider what conduct meets RICO's pattern requirement.

* * *

Petitioners, customers of respondent Northwestern Bell Telephone Co., filed this putative class action in 1986 in the District Court for the District of Minnesota. Petitioners alleged violations of §§ 1962(a), (b), (c), and (d) by Northwestern Bell and the other respondents—some of the telephone company's officers and employees, various members of the Minnesota Public Utilities Commission (MPUC), and other unnamed individuals and corporations—and sought an injunction and treble damages under RICO's civil liability provisions, §§ 1964(a) and (c).

The MPUC is the state body responsible for determining the rates that Northwestern Bell may charge. Petitioners' five-count complaint alleged that between 1980 and 1986 Northwestern Bell sought to influence members of the MPUC in the performance of their duties—and in fact caused them to approve rates for the company in excess of a fair and reasonable amount—by making cash payments to commissioners, negotiating with them regarding future employment, and paying for parties and meals, for tickets to sporting events and the like, and for airline tickets. * * * They * * * raised four separate claims under § 1962 of RICO. Count II alleged that, in violation of § 1962(a), Northwestern Bell derived income from a pattern of racketeering activity involving predicate acts of bribery and used this income to engage in its business as an interstate "enterprise." Count III claimed a violation of § 1962(b), in that, through this same pattern of racketeering activity, respondents acquired an interest in or control of the MPUC, which was also an interstate "enterprise." In Count IV, petitioners asserted that respondents participated in the conduct and affairs of the MPUC through this pattern of racketeering activity, contrary to § 1962(c). Finally, Count V alleged that respondents conspired together to violate §§ 1962(a), (b), and (c), thereby contravening § 1962(d).

* * *

In *Sedima, S. P. R. L. v. Imrex Co.*, 473 U.S. 479 (1985), this Court rejected a restrictive interpretation of § 1964(c) that would have made it a condition for maintaining a civil RICO action both that the defendant had already been convicted of a predicate racketeering act or of a RICO violation, and that plaintiff show a special racketeering injury. In doing so, we acknowledged concern in some quarters over civil RICO's use against "legitimate" businesses, as well as "mobsters and organized criminals"—a concern that had frankly led to the Court of Appeals' interpretation of § 1964(c) in *Sedima*. But we suggested that RICO's expansive uses "appear to be primarily the result of the breadth of the predicate offenses, in particular the inclusion of wire, mail, and securities fraud, and the failure of Congress and the courts to develop a meaningful concept of 'pattern' "—both factors that apply to criminal as well as civil applications of the Act. Congress has done nothing in the interim further to illuminate RICO's key requirement of a pattern of racketeering; and as the plethora of different views expressed by the Courts of Appeals since *Sedima* demonstrates, developing a meaningful concept of "pattern" within the existing statutory framework has proved to be no easy task.

* * *

A

We begin, of course, with RICO's text, in which Congress followed a "pattern [of] utilizing terms and concepts of breadth." As we remarked in *Sedima*, the section of the statute headed "definitions," does not so much define a pattern of racketeering activity as state a minimum necessary condition for the existence of such a pattern. Unlike other provisions in § 1961 that tell us what various concepts used in the Act "mean," 18 U.S.C. § 1961(5) says of the phrase "pattern of racketeering activity" only that it "requires at least two acts of racketeering activity, one of which occurred after [October 15, 1970,] and the last of which occurred within ten years (excluding any period of imprisonment) after the commission of a prior act of racketeering activity." It thus places an outer limit on the concept of a pattern of racketeering activity that is broad indeed.

Section 1961(5) does indicate that Congress envisioned circumstances in which no more than two predicates would be necessary to establish a pattern of racketeering—otherwise it would have drawn a narrower boundary to RICO liability, requiring proof of a greater number of predicates. But, at the same time, the statement that a pattern "requires at least" two predicates implies "that while two acts are necessary, they may not be sufficient." Section 1961 (5) concerns only the minimum number of predicates necessary to establish a pattern; and it assumes that there is something to a RICO pattern beyond simply the number of predicate acts involved. The legislative history bears out this interpretation, for the principal sponsor of the Senate bill expressly indicated that "proof of two acts of racketeering activity, without more, does not establish a pattern." Section 1961(5) does not identify, though, these additional prerequisites for establishing the existence of a RICO pattern.

In addition to § 1961(5), there is the key phrase "pattern of racketeering activity" itself, from § 1962, and we must "start with the assumption that the legislative purpose is expressed by the ordinary meaning of the words used." In normal usage, the word "pattern" here would be taken to require more than just a multiplicity of racketeering predicates. A "pattern" is an "arrangement or order of things or activity," 11 Oxford English Dictionary 357 (2d ed. 1989), and the mere fact that there are a number of predicates is no guarantee that they fall into any arrangement or order. It is not the number of predicates but the relationship that they bear to each other or to some external organizing principle that renders them "ordered" or "arranged." The text of RICO conspicuously fails anywhere to identify, however, forms of relationship or external principles to be used in determining whether racketeering activity falls into a pattern for purposes of the Act.

It is reasonable to infer, from this absence of any textual identification of sorts of pattern that would satisfy § 1962's requirement, in combination with the very relaxed limits to the pattern concept fixed in § 1961(5), that Congress intended to take a flexible approach, and envisaged that a pattern might be demonstrated by reference to a range of different ordering principles or relationships between predicates, within the expansive bounds set. For any more specific guidance as to the meaning of "pattern," we must look past the text to RICO's legislative history, as we have done in prior cases construing the Act.

The legislative history, which we discussed in *Sedima,* shows that Congress indeed had a fairly flexible concept of a pattern in mind. A pattern is not formed by "sporadic activity," S. Rep. No. 91–617, p. 158 (1969), and a person cannot "be subjected to the sanctions of title IX simply for committing two widely separated and isolated criminal offenses," 116 Cong. Rec. 18940 (1970) (Sen. McClellan). Instead, "[t]he term 'pattern' itself requires the showing of a relationship" between the predicates, and of " 'the threat of continuing activity,' " quoting S. Rep. No. 91–617, supra, at 158. "It is this factor of *continuity plus relationship* which combines to produce a pattern." 116 Cong. Rec., at 18940 (emphasis added). RICO's legislative history reveals Congress' intent that to prove a pattern of racketeering activity a plaintiff or prosecutor must show that the racketeering predicates are related, and that they amount to or pose a threat of continued criminal activity.

B

For analytic purposes these two constituents of RICO's pattern requirement must be stated separately, though in practice their proof will often overlap. The element of relatedness is the easier to define, for we may take guidance from a provision elsewhere in the Organized Crime Control Act of 1970 (OCCA), of which RICO formed Title IX. OCCA included as Title X the Dangerous Special Offender Sentencing Act. Title X provided for enhanced sentences where, among other things, the defendant had committed a prior felony as part of a pattern of criminal conduct or in furtherance of a conspiracy to engage in a pattern of criminal conduct. As we noted in *Sedima,* Congress defined Title X's pattern requirement solely in terms of the relationship of the defendant's criminal acts one to another: "[C]riminal conduct forms a pattern if it embraces criminal acts that have the same or similar purposes, results, participants, victims, or methods of commission, or otherwise are interrelated by distinguishing characteristics and are not isolated events." § 3575(e). We have no reason to suppose that Congress had in mind for RICO's pattern of racketeering component any more constrained a notion of the relationships between predicates that would suffice.

RICO's legislative history tells us, however, that the relatedness of racketeering activities is not alone enough to satisfy § 1962's pattern element. To establish a RICO pattern it must also be shown that the predicates themselves amount to, or that they otherwise constitute a threat of, continuing racketeering activity. As to this continuity requirement, § 3575(e) is of no assistance. It is this aspect of RICO's pattern element that has spawned the "multiple scheme" test adopted by some lower courts, including the Court of Appeals in this case * * * . But although proof that a RICO defendant has been involved in multiple criminal schemes would certainly be highly relevant to the inquiry into the continuity of the defendant's racketeering activity, it is implausible to suppose that Congress thought continuity might be shown only by proof of multiple schemes. The Eighth Circuit's test brings a rigidity to the available methods of proving a pattern that simply is not present in the idea of "continuity" itself; and it does so, moreover, by introducing a concept—the "scheme"—that appears nowhere in the language or legislative history of the Act. We adopt a less inflexible approach that seems to us to derive from a commonsense, everyday understanding of RICO's language and Congress' gloss on it. What a plaintiff or prosecutor must prove is continuity of racketeering activity, or its threat, simpliciter. This may be done in a variety of ways, thus making it difficult to formulate in the abstract any general test for continuity. We can, however, begin to delineate the requirement.

"Continuity" is both a closed-and open-ended concept, referring either to a closed period of repeated conduct, or to past conduct that by its nature projects into the future with a threat of repetition. It is, in either case, centrally a temporal concept—and particularly so in the RICO context, where *what* must be continuous, RICO's predicate acts or offenses, and the *relationship* these predicates must bear one to another, are distinct requirements. A party alleging a RICO violation may demonstrate continuity over a closed period by proving a series of related predicates extending over a substantial period of time. Predicate acts extending over a few weeks or months and threatening no future criminal conduct do not satisfy this requirement: Congress was concerned in RICO with long-term criminal conduct. Often a RICO action will be brought before continuity can be established in this way. In such cases, liability depends on whether the *threat* of continuity is demonstrated.

Whether the predicates proved establish a threat of continued racketeering activity depends on the specific facts of each case. Without making any claim to cover the field of possibilities—preferring to deal with this issue in the context of concrete factual situations presented for decision—we offer some examples of how this element might be satisfied. A RICO pattern may surely be established if the related predicates themselves involve a distinct threat of long-term racketeering activity, either implicit or explicit. Suppose a hoodlum were to sell "insurance" to a neighborhood's storekeepers to cover them against breakage of their windows, telling his victims he would be reappearing each month to collect the "premium" that would continue their "coverage." Though the number of related predicates involved may be small and they may occur close together in time, the racketeering acts themselves include a specific threat of repetition extending indefinitely into the future, and thus supply the requisite threat of continuity. In other cases, the threat of continuity may be established by showing that the predicate acts or offenses are part of an ongoing entity's regular way of doing business. Thus, the threat of continuity is sufficiently established where the predicates can be attributed to a defendant operating as part of a long-term association that exists for criminal purposes. Such associations include, but extend well beyond, those traditionally grouped under the phrase "organized crime." The continuity requirement is likewise satisfied where it is shown that the predicates are a regular way of conducting defendant's ongoing legitimate business (in the sense that it is not a business that exists for criminal purposes), or of conducting or participating in an ongoing and legitimate RICO "enterprise."

The limits of the relationship and continuity concepts that combine to define a RICO pattern, and the precise methods by which relatedness and continuity or its threat may be proved, cannot be fixed in advance with such clarity that it will always be apparent whether in a particular case a "pattern of racketeering activity" exists. The development of these concepts must await future cases, absent a decision by Congress to revisit RICO to provide clearer guidance as to the Act's intended scope.

III

Various amici urge that RICO's pattern element should be interpreted more narrowly than as requiring relationship and continuity in the senses outlined above, so that a defendant's racketeering activities form a pattern only if they are characteristic either of organized crime in the traditional sense, or of an organized-crime-type perpetrator, that is, of an association dedicated to the repeated commission of criminal offenses. Like the Court of Appeals' multiple scheme rule, however, the argument for reading an organized crime limitation into RICO's pattern concept, whatever the merits and demerits of such a limitation as an initial legislative matter finds no support in the Act's text, and is at odds with the tenor of its legislative history.

* * *

Representative Poff, another sponsor of the legislation, also answered critics who complained that a definition of "organized crime" was needed:

> "It is true that there is no organized crime definition in many parts of the bill. This is, in part, because it is probably impossible precisely and definitively to define organized crime. But if it were possible, I ask my friend, would he not be the first to object that in criminal law we establish procedures which would be applicable only to a certain type of defendant?"

The thrust of these explanations seems to us reasonably clear. The occasion for Congress' action was the perceived need to combat organized crime. But Congress for cogent reasons chose to enact a more general statute, one which, although it had organized crime as its focus, was not limited in application to organized crime. In Title IX, Congress picked out as key to RICO's application broad concepts that might fairly indicate an organized crime connection, but that it fully realized do not either individually or together provide anything approaching a perfect fit with "organized crime." (Sen. McClellan) ("It is impossible to draw an effective statute which reaches most of the commercial activities of organized crime, yet does not include offenses commonly committed by persons outside organized crime as well").

It seems, moreover, highly unlikely that Congress would have intended the pattern requirement to be interpreted by reference to a concept that it had itself rejected for inclusion in the text of RICO at least in part because "it is probably impossible precisely and definitively to define." * * *

As this Court stressed in *Sedima*, in rejecting a pinched construction of RICO's provision for a private civil action, adopted by a lower court because it perceived that RICO's use against non-organized-crime defendants was an "abuse" of the Act, "Congress wanted to reach both 'legitimate' and 'illegitimate' enterprises." Legitimate businesses "enjoy neither an inherent incapacity for criminal activity nor immunity from its consequences"; and, as a result, § 1964(c)'s use "against respected businesses allegedly engaged in a pattern of specifically identified criminal conduct is hardly a sufficient reason for assuming that the provision is being misconstrued." If plaintiffs' ability to use RICO against businesses engaged in a pattern of criminal acts is a defect, we said, it is one "inherent in the statute as written," and hence beyond our power to correct. RICO may be a poorly drafted statute; but rewriting it is a job for Congress, if it is so inclined, and not for this Court. There is no more room in RICO's "self-consciously expansive language and overall approach" for the imposition of an organized crime limitation than for the "amorphous 'racketeering injury' requirement" we rejected in *Sedima*. We thus decline the invitation to invent a rule that RICO's pattern of racketeering concept requires an allegation and proof of an organized crime nexus.

IV

We turn now to the application of our analysis of RICO's pattern requirement. Petitioners' complaint alleges that at different times over the course of at least a 6-year period the noncommissioner respondents gave five members of the MPUC numerous bribes, in several different forms, with the objective—in which they were allegedly successful–of causing these commissioners to approve unfair and unreasonable rates for Northwestern Bell. RICO defines bribery as a "racketeering activity," so petitioners have alleged multiple predicate acts.

Under the analysis we have set forth above, and consistent with the allegations in their complaint, petitioners may be able to prove that the multiple predicates alleged constitute "a pattern of racketeering activity," in that they satisfy the requirements of relationship and continuity. The acts of bribery alleged are said to be related by a common purpose, to influence commissioners in carrying out their duties in order to win approval of unfairly and unreasonably high rates for Northwestern Bell. Furthermore, petitioners claim that the racketeering predicates occurred with some frequency over at least a 6–year period, which may be sufficient to satisfy the continuity requirement. Alternatively, a threat of continuity of racketeering activity might be established at trial by showing that the alleged bribes were a regular way of conducting Northwestern Bell's ongoing business, or a regular way of conducting or participating in the conduct of the alleged and ongoing RICO enterprise, the MPUC.

The Court of Appeals thus erred in affirming the District Court's dismissal of petitioners' complaint for failure to plead "a pattern of racketeering activity." The judgment is reversed, and the case is remanded for further proceedings consistent with this opinion.

It is so ordered.

JUSTICE SCALIA, with whom THE CHIEF JUSTICE, JUSTICE O'CONNOR, and JUSTICE KENNEDY join, concurring in the judgment.

Four Terms ago, in *Sedima, S. P. R. L. v. Imrex Co.*, 473 U.S. 479 (1985), we gave lower courts the following four clues concerning the meaning of the enigmatic term "pattern of racketeering activity." First, we stated that the statutory definition of the term in 18 U.S.C. § 1961(5) implies "that while two acts are necessary, they may not be sufficient." Second, we pointed out that "two isolated acts of racketeering activity," "sporadic activity," and "proof of two acts of racketeering activity, without more" would not be enough to constitute a pattern. Third, we quoted a snippet from the legislative history stating "[i]t is this factor of *continuity plus relationship* which combines to produce a pattern." Finally, we directed lower courts' attention to 18 U.S.C. § 3575(e), which defined the term "pattern of conduct which was criminal" used in a different title of the same Act, and instructed them that "[t]his language may be useful in interpreting other sections of the Act. Thus enlightened, the District Courts and Courts of Appeals set out" to develop a meaningful concept of 'pattern,' and promptly produced the widest and most persistent Circuit split on an issue of federal law in recent memory. Today, four years and countless millions in damages and attorney's fees later (not to mention prison sentences under the criminal provisions of RICO), the Court does little more than repromulgate those hints as to what RICO means, though with the caveat that Congress intended that they be applied using a "flexible approach."

Elevating to the level of statutory text a phrase taken from the legislative history, the Court counsels the lower courts: " 'continuity plus relationship.' "This seems to me about as helpful to the conduct of their affairs as "life is a fountain." Of the two parts of this talismanic phrase, the relatedness requirement is said to be the "easier to define," yet here is the Court's definition, in toto: " '[C]riminal conduct forms a pattern if it embraces criminal acts that have the same or similar purposes, results, participants, victims, or methods of commission, or otherwise are interrelated by distinguishing characteristics and are not isolated events.' "This definition has the feel of being solidly rooted in law, since it is a direct quotation of 18 U.S.C. § 3575(e). Unfortunately, if normal (and sensible) rules of statutory construction were followed, the existence of § 3575(e)—which is the definition contained in another title of the Act that was explicitly not rendered applicable to RICO—suggests that *whatever* "pattern" might mean in RICO, it assuredly *does not* mean that. "[W]here Congress includes particular language in one section of a statute but omits it in another section of the same Act, it is generally presumed that Congress acts intentionally and purposely in the disparate inclusion or exclusion." But that does not really matter, since § 3575(e) is utterly uninformative anyway. It hardly closes in on the target to know that "relatedness" refers to acts that are related by "purposes, results, participants, victims, . . . methods of commission, *or* [just in case that is not vague enough] *otherwise*." Is the fact that the victims of both predicate acts were women enough? Or that both acts had the purpose of enriching the defendant? Or that the different coparticipants of the defendant in both acts were his coemployees? I doubt that the lower courts will find the Court's instructions much more helpful than telling them to look for a "pattern"—which is what the statute already says.

The Court finds "continuity" more difficult to define precisely. "Continuity," it says, "is both a closed-and openended concept, referring either to a closed period of repeated conduct, or to past conduct that by its nature projects into the future with a threat of repetition." I have no idea what this concept of a "closed period of repeated conduct" means. Virtually all allegations of racketeering activity, in both civil and criminal suits, will relate to past periods that are "closed" (unless one expects plaintiff or the prosecutor to establish that the defendant not only committed the crimes he did, but is still committing them), and all of them must relate to conduct that is "repeated," because of RICO's multiple-act requirement. I had thought, initially, that the Court was seeking to draw a distinction between, on the one hand, past repeated conduct (multiple racketeering acts) that is "closed-ended" in the sense that, in its totality, it constitutes only one criminal "scheme" or "episode"—which would not fall within RICO unless in its nature (for one or more of the reasons later described by the Court), it threatened future criminal endeavors as well—and, on the other hand, past repeated conduct (multiple racketeering acts) that constitutes several separate schemes—which is alone enough to invoke RICO. But of course that cannot be what it means, since the Court rejects the "multiple scheme" concept, not merely as the *exclusive* touchstone of RICO liability, but in all its applications, since it "introduc[es] a concept . . . that appears nowhere in the language or legislative history of the Act," and is so vague and "amorphous" as to exist only "in the eye of the beholder." Moreover, the Court tells us that predicate acts extending, not over a "substantial period of time," but only over a "few weeks or months and threatening no future criminal conduct" do not satisfy the continuity requirement. Since the Court has rejected the concept of separate criminal "schemes" or "episodes" as a criterion of "threatening future criminal conduct," I think it must be saying that at least a few months of racketeering activity (and who knows how much more?) is generally for free, as far as RICO is concerned. The "closed period" concept is a sort of safe harbor for racketeering activity that does not last too long, no matter how many different crimes and different schemes are involved, so long as it does not otherwise "establish a threat of continued racketeering activity." A gang of hoodlums that commits one act of extortion on Monday in New York, a second in Chicago on Tuesday, a third in San Francisco on Wednesday, and so on through an entire week, and then finally and completely disbands, cannot be reached under RICO. I am sure that is not what the statute intends, but I cannot imagine what else the Court's murky discussion can possibly mean.

Of course it cannot be said that the Court's opinion operates only in the direction of letting some obvious racketeers get out of RICO. It also makes it clear that a hitherto dubious category is included, by establishing the rule that the "multiple scheme" test applied by the Court of Appeals here is not only nonexclusive but indeed nonexistent. This is, as far as I can discern, the Court's only substantive contribution to our prior guidance—and it is a contribution that makes it *more* rather than *less* difficult for a potential defendant to know whether his conduct is covered by RICO. Even if he is only involved in a single scheme, he may still be covered if there is present whatever is needed to establish a "threat of continuity." The Court gives us a nonexclusive list of three things that do so. Two of those presumably polar examples seem to me extremely difficult to apply—whether "the predicates can be attributed to a defendant operating as part of a long-term association that exists for criminal purposes," and whether "the predicates are a regular way of conducting defendant's ongoing legitimate business." What is included beyond these examples is vaguer still.

It is, however, unfair to be so critical of the Court's effort, because I would be unable to provide an interpretation of RICO that gives significantly more guidance concerning its application. It is clear to me from the prologue of the statute, which describes a relatively narrow focus upon "organized crime," that the word "pattern" in the phrase "pattern of racketeering activity" was meant to import some requirement beyond the mere existence of multiple predicate acts. Thus, when § 1961(5) says that a pattern "requires at least two acts of racketeering activity" it is describing what is needful but not sufficient. (If that were not the case, the concept of "pattern" would have been unnecessary, and the statute could simply have attached liability to "multiple acts of racketeering activity"). But what that something more is, is beyond me. As I have suggested, it is also beyond the Court. Today's opinion has added nothing to improve our prior guidance, which has created a kaleidoscope of Circuit positions, except to clarify that RICO may in addition be violated when there is a "threat of continuity." It seems to me this increases rather than removes the vagueness. There is no reason to believe that the Courts of Appeals will be any more unified in the future, than they have in the past, regarding the content of this law.

That situation is bad enough with respect to any statute, but it is intolerable with respect to RICO. For it is not only true, as Justice Marshall commented in *Sedima*, that our interpretation of RICO has "quite simply revolutionize[d] private litigation" and "validate[d] the federalization of broad areas of state common law of frauds," so that clarity and predictability in RICO's civil applications are particularly important; but it is also true that RICO, since it has criminal applications as well, must, even in its civil applications, possess the degree of certainty required for criminal laws. No constitutional challenge to this law has been raised in the present case, and so that issue is not before us. That the highest Court in the land has been unable to derive from this statute anything more than today's meager guidance bodes ill for the day when that challenge is presented. However unhelpful its guidance may be, however, I think the Court is correct in saying that nothing in the statute supports the proposition that predicate acts constituting part of a single scheme (or single episode) can never support a cause of action under RICO. Since the Court of Appeals here rested its decision on the contrary proposition, I concur in the judgment of the Court reversing the decision below.

Notes

1. We have previously encountered the notion of continuity that the Court in *H.J., Inc.* makes an attribute of a "pattern of racketeering activity." Under *Turkette, supra,* p. 482, continuity is an attribute of the "enterprise." Does introducing it into the pattern requirement mean that it does not have to be considered as part of the enterprise element? *Compare United States v. Indelicato,* 865 F.2d 1370, 1381 (2d Cir.1989) (relatedness and continuity are attributes of activity, not of a RICO enterprise). Is it a duplicative requirement? How is the continuity element different, if it is, in the two elements of a RICO charge. Is it performing the same function? Recall in connection with the discussion of the enterprise element, the factors that were described in note 7, *supra* p. 489 that are deemed to indicate the dangerousness of a conspiracy. Does the continuity factor in connection with the pattern element add something more to the notion of the dangerousness in the combination than is provided by the continuity attribute of the enterprise element?

Note that in many cases the enterprise helps to establish the necessary continuity aspect of the pattern of racketeering activity. *See, e.g., United States v. Church,* 955 F.2d 688 (11th Cir.1992) (it is the association's long-term existence and regular way of doing business that poses the threat of continued racketeering activity). Certain kinds of RICO enterprises, like corrupt governmental agencies, may enable the continuity requirement to be proven more easily. *See, e.g., United States v. Stodola*, 953 F.2d 266 (7th Cir. 1992) (ongoing bribes of public officials, even if pertinent to only a single continuing service contract, may establish a pattern).

2. Some courts have added glosses to the *H.J., Inc.* closed and open-end continuity concepts.

a. A Second Circuit panel has suggested that the seriousness and nature of the crimes that comprise the racketeering activity may influence the interpretation of the continuity requirement. Thus in *United States v. Aulicino*, 44 F.3d 1102, 1111 (2d Cir.1995), the court reviewed a number of precedents and stated:

> [I]n cases where the acts of the defendant or the enterprise were inherently unlawful, such as murder or obstruction of justice, and were in pursuit of inherently unlawful goals, such as narcotics trafficking or embezzlement, the courts generally have concluded that the requisite threat of continuity was adequately established by the nature of the activity, even though the period spanned by the racketeering acts was short. In contrast, in cases concerning alleged racketeering activity in furtherance of endeavors that are not inherently unlawful, such as frauds in the sale of property, the courts generally have found no threat of continuing criminal activity arising from conduct that extended over even longer periods.

Is the *Aulicino* gloss consistent with *H.J., Inc.*? Does it follow from the notion that a function of the continuity requirement is to be an index of the dangerousness of the enterprise? In reviewing the cases below that interpret and apply the continuity requirement, consider the extent to which the Aulicino gloss helps to explain the results.

b. It has also been held that predicate acts that occur as part of a single, discrete and otherwise lawful transaction do not meet the continuity prong of the *H.J.* case. In *Word of Faith World Outreach Center Church, Inc. v. Sawyer*, 90 F.3d 118, 123 (5th Cir.1996), the Church which had been the subject of an investigatory reporting broadcast by ABC (PrimeTime Live), filed a civil RICO suit against the Broadcasting Company, alleging that the defendants sought to drive the Church out of business. The alleged racketeering activity included mail and wire fraud (the latter referred to false statements made during the broadcast). In addressing the continuity issue, the court stated:

> It is unnecessary to delve into the arcane concepts of closed-end or open-ended continuity under RICO. * * * [Our previous decisions] make clear that where alleged RICO predicate acts are part and parcel of a single, otherwise lawful transaction, a "pattern of racketeering activity" has not been shown. In this case, the alleged predicate acts occurred during the production and airing of PrimeTime broadcasts concerning Tilton and his Church. The alleged acts were part of a single, lawful endeavor—namely the production of television news reports concerning a particular subject. We agree with the district court that the Church has failed to plead a "continuity of racketeering activity, or its threat."

c. In *Edmondson & Gallagher v. Alban Towers*, 48 F.3d 1260, 1265 (D.C.Cir.1995), the court seemed to fuse the issues of relatedness and continuity:

> Plaintiffs here have alleged only a single scheme—to prevent or delay the sale of Alban Towers, or to secure a ransom for allowing the sale to proceed. Moreover, the scheme entails but a single discrete injury, the loss of the sale (or payment of the ransom) suffered by the small number of victims. The latter number only three. * * * We think that the combination of these factors (single scheme, single injury, and few victims) makes it virtually impossible for plaintiffs to state a RICO claim. The number of alleged predicate acts (fifteen), and the most generous estimate of the length of time the acts continued (three years, but with almost all occurring in December 1986–January 1987 and the fall of 1988), are not enough to overwhelm the three narrowing factors.

d. The District of Columbia Circuit subsequently followed up the decision in *Edmondson* with *Western Assocs. Ltd. P'ship v. Mkt. Square Assocs.*, 235 F.3d 629, 636–37 (D.C. Cir. 2001), in which the court characterized the *Edmonson* decision in the following terms:

> *Edmondson* identified six factors that a court should consider "in deciding whether a [RICO] pattern has been established." These factors are: "the number of unlawful acts, the length of time over which the acts were committed, the similarity of the acts, the number of victims, the number of perpetrators, and the character of the unlawful activity." *Edmondson* does not establish a rigid test, but rather presents a flexible guide for analyzing RICO allegations on a case by case basis. The court in *Edmondson* acknowledged that in some cases "some factors will weigh so strongly in one direction as to be dispositive." Id. The court also indicated that if a plaintiff alleges only a single scheme, a single injury, and few victims it is "virtually impossible for plaintiffs to state a RICO claim." Id.

e. Also see *Waddell & Reed Financial, Inc. v. Torchmark Corp.*, 223 F.R.D. 566 (D. Kan. 2004):

> Defendants argue that they are entitled to summary judgment because plaintiffs cannot show continuity under RICO. Without any analysis of how they satisfy the continuity element (either closed-ended or open-ended), plaintiffs conclude that defendants' scheme to improperly control them began in March of 1998, at the time of the initial IPO and spin-off, and that "predicate acts were performed continuously in 1999, 2000, 2001, 2002, 2003, and 2004." *See* Plaintiffs' Opposition Memorandum at 80 (citing list of 459 predicate acts). Plaintiffs' conclusory response is insufficient to survive summary judgment.
>
> The Court first considers the duration of the scheme. Viewing the evidence in a light most favorable to plaintiffs, if a scheme existed, a jury could infer that it lasted 26 months—from March 4, 1998 until May 4, 2000, when the last individual defendants resigned from the board of W & R Financial.
>
> Despite the alleged duration of the scheme, no reasonable jury would find continuity based on these allegations. To evaluate the exten-

siveness of the scheme, the Court first examines the number of victims. Here, the alleged predicate acts were directed solely at W & R Financial and its subsidiaries. Plaintiffs have not argued or produced any evidence of other victims. RICO is not aimed at the isolated offender. Instead, it is concerned with long-term criminal conduct. The isolated number of victims strongly weighs against a finding of continuity in this case. *See Duran v. Carris,* 238 F.3d 1268, 1271 (10th Cir.2001) (single victim); *Efron v. Embassy Suites (Puerto Rico), Inc.,* 223 F.3d 12, 18 (1st Cir.2000) (closed group of targeted victims), *cert. denied,* 532 U.S. 905, 121 S.Ct. 1228, 149 L.Ed.2d 138 (2001); *Edmondson & Gallagher v. Alban Towers Tenants Ass'n,* 48 F.3d 1260, 1265 (D.C.Cir.1995) (few victims); *Boone v. Carlsbad Bancorporation, Inc.,* 972 F.2d 1545, 1556 (10th Cir.1992) (finite group of victims); *SIL-FLO, Inc. v. SFHC, Inc.,* 917 F.2d 1507, 1516 (10th Cir.1990) (one victim); *U.S. Textiles,* 911 F.2d at 1269 (no indication of other potential victims).

The Court next considers the number and variety of racketeering acts. Plaintiffs allege numerous acts of mail and wire fraud. Courts have cautioned that mail fraud and wire fraud may deceptively create the appearance of a pattern, however, because often the mailing or use of wires is "only tangentially related to the underlying fraud" and is only "a matter of happenstance." "[T]he raw number of predicate acts has never been determinative, especially when only mail and wire fraud are alleged." *Ashland Oil,* 875 F.2d at 1278. Here, the mail fraud and wire fraud activities were totally normal business communications only tangentially related to the underlying fraud. For example, many of the predicate acts involve public filings and ordinary board meetings of Torchmark. These communications would be expected to continue before, during and even after the alleged scheme to defraud—acquisition of improper control of plaintiffs—was complete. Accordingly, the number and variety of racketeering acts does not suggest any continuity of the alleged scheme.

The Court next examines whether the alleged scheme caused distinct injuries. Distinct injuries ordinarily favor a finding of continuity. Plaintiffs have alleged injuries such as the costs of the Alabama and California litigation, the loss of compensation under the letter of July 8, 1999 and the loss of investment management fees. Although plaintiff has alleged distinct injuries, the injuries do not signal, or by themselves constitute, a threat of continuing criminal activity. All of plaintiffs' injuries derive from one failed business deal and one alleged scheme to control them. Accordingly, the distinct nature of plaintiffs' injuries by itself does not permit a reasonable jury to find continuity.

The Court next evaluates the complexity and size of the scheme, and the number of schemes alleged. Here, the scheme involved Torchmark and the three individual defendants. It required very limited planning—if any—to keep the scheme afloat. Defendants simply had to keep quiet from July 22 to September 28, 1999 about the fact that Torchmark viewed the agreement of July 8, 1999 as "not final." Absent some threat that criminal activity will continue, allegations of a single scheme directed at a discrete goal are insufficient to establish continuity.

Finally, the Court evaluates the nature and character of the alleged scheme. Plaintiffs claim that all of the alleged predicate acts were directed at one scheme—to improperly control W & R Financial and its subsidiaries. The nature and character of the scheme and underlying predicate acts do not suggest a threat of future illegal activity. . . . All predicate acts of mail fraud and wire fraud are based on a single contract negotiation. Even if the Court assumes that Torchmark and the common directors committed fraud, plaintiffs have not shown any threat of long-term racketeering activity. The fact that the parties and counsel have managed to keep this dispute alive for more than five years does not transform the limited nature of defendants' alleged scheme into a continuous pattern of racketeering activity.

In sum, plaintiff has not presented evidence from which a reasonable jury would find either closed-ended or open-ended continuity. While plaintiffs may have alleged a closed-ended series of predicate acts, they constitute a single scheme to accomplish one discrete goal, directed solely at plaintiffs, with no credible potential to extend to other persons or entities. Likewise, plaintiffs have not established open-ended continuity because the predicates themselves do not "involve a distinct threat of long-term racketeering activity, either implicit or explicit," and the predicates are not a regular way of conducting Torchmark's ongoing legitimate business or the RICO enterprise. For these reasons, the Court sustains defendants' motion for summary judgment on plaintiffs' RICO claim.

3. In *United States v. Richardson,* 167 F.3d 621, 626 (D.C.Cir.1999), applying the open-ended continuity approach, the court ruled that a series of robberies committed over a three and one-half month period met the pattern requirement:

The "fortuitous interruption of the * * * [racketeering] activity such as by an arrest" does not grant defendants a free pass to evade RICO charges. * * * As the district court observed, the sheer number of serious crimes, "which victimized dozens of persons and led to five deaths during the course of one summer, with no abatement of activity in sight," made the "threat of future criminality * * * palpable."

4. A civil RICO suit was brought against the leaders of several anti-abortion groups that on five occasions over a period of three and a half months had staged blockades of clinics. On a motion for summary judgment, the district court found that five blockades over a three month period did not constitute a closed-end period of continued criminal conduct and that the record did not reveal "a realistic prospect that the activity challenged in this suit will resume with enduring effects." The Court of Appeals reversed, based on the fact that defendants' "regular way of conducting their affairs involves the illegal acts conducted at . . . blockade, and that the . . . [defendants] have admitted [one of them had issued a press release threatening more actions] that they plan to continue their efforts." The court also noted that the defendants' strategy was "to strike randomly with little or no warning of which clinic they will target, making it inherently difficult or impossible to determine whether and when they will blockade again." *Libertad v. Welch,* 53 F.3d 428, 445–446 (1st Cir.1995).

5. Regarding the minimum period for closed-end continuity, see *Wisdom v. First Midwest Bank, of Poplar Bluff*, 167 F.3d 402, 407 (8th Cir.1999) (ten months is too short to satisfy closed-end analysis). *See also Primary Care Investors, Seven, Inc. v. PHP Healthcare Corp.* 986 F.2d 1208, 1215 (8th Cir.1993) (eleven months is insufficient to satisfy closed-end continuity, and noting that other Circuits hold that schemes less than one year are too short); *Corley v. Rosewood Care Center, Inc. of Peoria*, 142 F.3d 1041, 1049 (7th Cir.1998) ("considerable difficulty" in satisfying the continuity requirement where predicate racketeering acts were directed to a single victim for twelve to fourteen months). In *United States v. Pelullo*, 964 F.2d 193, 209–10 (3d Cir.1992), the court stated:

> * * * [M]ost courts that have found continuity in a closed period did so in cases involving periods of several years. * * *

> * * * [S]ince *H.J. Inc.*, it appears that we have not found continuity in a closed-ended case on the basis of duration alone.

> In our view, 19 months is sufficiently longer than a few weeks or months and indicates the type of long-term criminal conduct Congress sought to eradicate in enacting RICO. * * * While the Court in *H.J., Inc.* rejected the requirement of proving multiple schemes in favor of a more rigid approach in demonstrating continuity, the number of schemes remains a relevant factor.

Also see *Waddell & Reed Financial Inc*, supra note 2 e. where 26 months was in the circumstances not sufficient for closed-end continuity.

6. The *Corley* case, supra note 5 also involved an open-ended issue, with the court indicating that continuity depends on the existence of a threat that the conduct will recur in the future. The court also stated:

> Such a threat is present when: (1) a specific threat of repetition exists, (2) the predicates are a regular way of conducting [an] ongoing legitimate business, or (3) the predicates can be attributed to a defendant operating as part of a long-term association that exists for criminal purposes. Id. at 1049.

The court proceeded to characterize the facts in the case as follows:

> It is not entirely clear to us, in fact, that the scheme as alleged by *Corley* could not be described as "open-ended" in the sense that it reflects defendants' ongoing way of conducting a legitimate business enterprise. But in any event, the scheme clearly does not have the natural end point that has caused us to find a lack of continuity in some closed ended cases. Rather, the nature of the conduct alleged here would seem to carry with it the threat that defendants may continue to conduct business at their various nursing homes in what may be a fraudulent way.

7. In *Heller Financial, Inc. v. Grammco Computer Sales, Inc.*, 71 F.3d 518, 523–524 (5th Cir.1996), Grammco was alleged: 1) to have bribed an employee of a medical center that leased its computer equipment; and 2) to have fraudulently obtained financing from the plaintiff for the lease transaction. The court held that the predicate acts were not sufficiently related:

Heller essentially complains of two types of criminal activity: Grammco's alleged commercial bribery of Santa Rosa employee Joseph Dixon and his use of mail land wires to fraudulently induce Heller into extending him credit. According to Heller's pleadings, the purpose of the bribery scheme was to maintain Grammco's exclusive business relationship with Santa Rosa free of competition that might have caused Santa Rosa to take its computer business elsewhere. The alleged mail and wire fraud, on the other hand, sought to induce Heller into making a loan on terms that would have not otherwise been available. The purposes of the alleged predicate acts were distinct and dissimilar.

* * *

The predicate acts also had dissimilar results.

* * *

The difference in the "methods of commission" further supports our conclusion that the alleged predicate acts were not related.

* * *

We also note that the participants in the two types of criminal activity alleged by Heller were different.

* * *

Finally, we note that the two types of conduct which Heller seeks to connect into a pattern were directed at different victims.

* * *

* * * [W]e interpret the relationship prong to require more than an articulable factual nexus.

Might the court in *Heller* have based its conclusion on a ground other than the absence of relatedness? How persuasive is its relatedness analysis?

8. There is a another aspect to the relatedness requirement. RICO requires at least two distinct acts of racketeering activity. Occasionally the predicate acts alleged by the prosecution are so factually entangled with one another that there is a genuine issue as to whether they are separate. Many of the factors that are relevant in establishing a pattern—such as similarity of purposes, results, participants, victims, and methods of commission—encourage the filing of charges that are entangled to a lesser or greater degree. Violations of multiple statutes resulting from a single criminal transaction have been held to satisfy the pattern requirement despite the factual entanglement. *See, e.g., United States v. Gonzalez,* 921 F.2d 1530 (11th Cir.1991) (cocaine possession and Travel Act predicates, though flowing from a single narcotics importation, violated two statutes and could fulfill the RICO pattern requirement). *Compare United States v. Walgren,* 885 F.2d 1417 (9th Cir.1989) where the Ninth Circuit vacated a RICO conviction supported by only a single act (a telephone call) in violation of two statutes, a state bribery law and federal extortion law. *See also United States v. Biaggi,* 909 F.2d 662 (2d Cir.1990) where the predicate acts proven were bribery and obstruction of justice and the latter charge rested on a false denial of the bribery. In reversing the conviction, the court reasoned:

The "pattern" element guards against permitting RICO to be used against sporadic criminal activity. * * * If the commission of an offense and its false denial could establish a "pattern," then every offense related to a criminal enterprise would be eligible for inclusion in a pattern whenever the offender falsely denied its commission. *Id.* at 686.

9. A number of defendants have taken up Justice Scalia's invitation in *H.J, Inc.* to challenge RICO as unconstitutionally vague, but the courts have generally rejected pleas to examine the facial constitutional validity of the RICO statute, examining instead the legitimacy of its application to the facts in the case at hand. *See, e.g., Columbia Natural Resources v. Tatum*, 58 F.3d 1101 (6th Cir.1995) where the court rejected the vagueness claim, principally on the ground that there is a clear standard of conduct initially proscribed by the pattern requirement since a defendant must commit two of the enumerated federal or state offenses within ten years and a person of ordinary intelligence would know that committing "dozens if not hundreds" of acts of wire and mail fraud, over the course of almost a decade against the same victim, might constitute a pattern of racketeering activity. *See also United States v. Angiulo*, 897 F.2d 1169, 1180 (1st Cir.1990) (" * * * [A]lthough RICO's "pattern" element may be vague in some contexts, a matter on which we express no opinion, it is not vague in the context before us.")

2. RACKETEERING ACTIVITY

a. *In General*

Section 1961 (1) of Title 18, United States Code, lists the various crimes that are deemed "racketeering activity" under the RICO statute. The list includes nine state crimes and 38 federal crime categories, or 61 different federal statutory offenses, depending on how one counts—even these numbers are subject to debate, depending on how one counts. The important point is that the list is very long. The format of listing in the statute those offenses that are deemed racketeering activity makes it easy for the Congress to simply add new offenses to the list, and since the RICO statute was enacted in 1970, periodically, it has done so.

The current RICO statute now lists so many offenses as "racketeering activity" that there is hardly an important federal crime that is not listed in 1961(1). Insofar as the RICO statute was intended primarily to attack organized crime, is it appropriate to list so many offenses? Are there any offenses that organized crime does not commit? Compare Congressman Poff's remarks discussing legislation that eventually became the RICO statute, quoted *supra* p. 132.

Are there any state offenses not listed in § 1961 (1) (A) that in your judgment should be listed? The prevailing view is that the designations of these state crimes are generic, and that any state offense—regardless of the label under state law—that falls within the generic description may be a RICO predicate crime. *United States v. Garner*, 837 F.2d 1404 (7th Cir.1987). *Accord: United States v. Kotvas*, 941 F.2d 1141 (11th Cir.1991). This interpretative approach requires the federal courts to construe state statutes to determine whether they fit into one of the generic categories.

Note the breadth of the state offense provisions in § 1961(1). The statutory language refers to "any act or threat involving" the listed offenses. Is this language broad enough to cover attempts or conspiracies to engage in one of the listed offenses? See pp. 549–558, *infra*. Note also that § 1961 (1) requires that the predicate state crimes be "chargeable under State law" and "punishable by imprisonment for more than one year." Since the offense need only be "chargeable" the courts have usually concluded that state rules that preclude conviction—even though the substantive offense was committed—do not prevent reliance on the offense as a predicate act of racketeering. Thus, for example, the fact that the state statute of limitations has run on a state offense does not prevent its being used as a RICO predicate crime. *United States v. Davis*, 576 F.2d 1065 (3d Cir.1978); *United States v. Forsythe*, 560 F.2d 1127 (3d Cir. 1977). Only the conduct—not the individual—must be "chargeable" under state law.

Regarding the federal offenses listed in § 1961(1), note first that they are categorized under subsections (B), (C), (D), (E) and (F) of § 1961(1); that subsections (B), (C), (E) and (F) are introduced by the phrase, "any act which is indictable under [listing the relevant statutory offenses]" while subsection (D) is introduced by the phrase, "any offense involving [specifying the categories of criminal conduct], punishable under any law of the United States." Does any legal issue turn on the difference in phrasing? See *infra*. Is it likely that Congress was attentive to the nuances of this difference in phrasing? Finally, note that following each listed statutory citation or series of citations a parenthetical description of the nature of the offense is included—for example, "section 659 (relating to theft from interstate shipment)."

The crimes listed as racketeering activity include "open-ended" federal offenses such as mail fraud and some offenses that are themselves complex crimes such as the Travel Act. These offenses are themselves the subject of separate substantive treatment in this volume. Because of the flexibility of such offenses and their adaptability to different factual contexts it is not surprising to find them used frequently as the basis for RICO criminal charges. Note that mail and wire fraud, because of their breadth, are quite frequently alleged as the predicate racketeering activity in civil RICO suits.

b. *Conspiracy as a Predicate Offense*

Conspiracy may become an element of a RICO charge as one or more of the predicate offenses. The analysis differs depending on which of the aforementioned subsections of § 1961 (1) the case involves. Thus, conspiracy (or attempt) to commit murder can be a state offense predicate under subsection (A) since said conspiracy is an "act * * * involving" one of the listed offenses. *United States v. Licavoli*, 725 F.2d 1040 (6th Cir.1984). A similar analysis applies to a conspiracy to commit one of the offenses listed in subsection (D). *See, e.g., United States v. Weisman*, 624 F.2d 1118 (2d Cir.1980).

On the other hand, the introductory phrase for the other subsections of § 1961 (1) requires that the act be "indictable" under one of the enumerated federal statutes. Thus, if an enumerated statute contains within it a conspiracy clause (e.g. the Hobbs Act, 18 U.S.C. § 1951), conspiracy can be charged as a racketeering activity predicate crime, but if the enumerated offense in question does not include an internal conspiracy provision, it would appear that a conspiracy to commit the enumerated offense could not be used as a predicate offense. Suppose a conspiracy charge to commit one of the enumerated offenses (that does not have an internal conspiracy provision) listed in subsection (B), (C), (E) or (F) is filed under the general federal conspiracy provision, 18 U.S.C. § 371. Would that qualify as a RICO predicate offense? Since § 371 is not one of the enumerated statutes, that would seem not to qualify, and the Fifth Circuit so held, in *United States v. Martino*, 648 F.2d 367, 400 (5th Cir.1981), *aff'd sub nom. Russello v. United States*, 464 U.S. 16 (1983).

In situations where a conspiracy qualifies as one of the predicate crimes, there is authority to support the view that the crime which is the object of the conspiracy may be used as the other predicate crime. The result is that a single completed conspiracy can supply both of the predicate acts for a RICO charge. *See United States v. Licavoli*, 725 F.2d 1040 (6th Cir.1984) which held that conspiracy to commit murder and the object crime murder were separate crimes that could be used as the two predicate crimes, even though a state statute barred conviction of, or sentence for, both conspiracy to murder and murder. See *United States v. Warneke*, 310 F.3d 542 (7th Cir. 2002) for a more recent recognition of the use of conspiracy to commit a RICO violation along with conspiracy as a predicate offense.

Two conspiracies that otherwise qualified as enumerated racketeering activity can constitute the required two predicate crimes, provided only that they are sufficiently separate. *See, e.g. United States v. Benevento*, 836 F.2d 60,72–73 (2d Cir.1987). Of course, in all of these cases, the pattern requirements must also be satisfied.

The fact that inchoate conspiracies can be the predicate crimes for a RICO charge would seem to mean that in theory a substantive RICO charge could be entirely inchoate—a creature of criminal organizational activity that had not yet achieved fruition in the commission of object crimes. Can the harsh RICO penalties be justified where no substantive crimes have yet been committed?

c. *Predicate Acts Which Have Previously Been the Subject of a Criminal Prosecution*

Suppose the predicate offenses relied upon in a RICO prosecution had been the subject of a prior prosecution. Does that bar their use as a basis for a RICO charge? Should it matter whether the defendant was previously acquitted? Should it matter whether the prior prosecution took place in a state or federal court?

The courts have construed the RICO statute to allow the use of predicate offenses that had been the subject of prior prosecutions. The rationale is that the pattern of racketeering activity may have extended over a period of years, and the authorities may not have realized the full extent of the defendant's criminality when he was first prosecuted. Therefore it should be possible to base RICO charges on the entire pattern of racketeering offenses including those previous prosecuted. The language of § 1961 (1) (A) has been construed to be broad enough to include even charges for which the defendant has been acquitted in state courts. *See, e.g., United States v. Coonan*, 938 F.2d 1553 (2d Cir.1991). In *Coonan*, Judge Newman wrote a concurring opinion suggesting that inclusion of conduct for which the defendant had been acquitted is such an extraordinary result that the courts should construe the statute narrowly to avoid a result not foreseen by Congress.

As suggested above, the constitutional double jeopardy issue arises in a number of contexts. Where the first prosecution was for one of the predicate offenses, was in a state court and the defendant was acquitted, is a subsequent federal RICO prosecution barred by the double jeopardy clause of the Constitution? Held: The second prosecution does not run afoul of the double jeopardy clause; under the dual sovereignty doctrine, a federal prosecution based on the same facts as a prior state prosecution—whether the defendant had been acquitted or convicted in the state proceeding—is not barred by the double jeopardy clause because the state and federal governments have significantly different interests in the matter which their respective prosecutions vindicate. *United States v. Pungitore*, 910 F.2d 1084 (3d Cir.1990); *United States v. Frumento*, 563 F.2d 1083 (3d Cir.1977).

What result where the predicate crime is prosecuted first in a federal court, the defendant is convicted, and a RICO prosecution is then brought relying on the previous prosecuted predicate offense? Encouraged by the decision in *Grady v. Corbin*, 495 U.S. 508 (1990), in a series of cases, defendants had argued that double jeopardy was violated by prosecuting the RICO charge and including the previously prosecuted offense as one of the predicate acts. *Grady* had established a new test for double jeopardy in a successive prosecution context: A subsequent prosecution is barred if, to establish an essential element of an offense charged in the second prosecution, the government has to prove conduct that constitutes an offense for which the defendant was previously prosecuted. Even with *Grady* on the books, however, the double jeopardy claim was consistently rejected by a number of circuit courts. *See, e.g. United States v. Pungitore, supra* at 1109:

> The reasoning in [*Grady*] logically extends only to offenses arising from a single discrete event. We do not think that the Supreme Court meant to imply that the double jeopardy clause forecloses successive prosecutions in cases of compound-complex felonies such

as RICO, which involve several criminal acts occurring at different times in different places.

The court in *Pungitore* relied in part on *Garrett v. United States*, 471 U.S. 773 (1985), where the Supreme Court had ruled that double jeopardy was not violated where the government had used a previously convicted drug offense as a predicate crime in a prosecution for a violation of 21 U.S.C. § 848, continuing criminal enterprise. The *Pungitore* approach was also consistent with the Supreme Court's decision in *United States v. Felix*, 503 U.S. 378 (1992), where the Court had held that *Grady* did not bar a subsequent trial for conspiracy after a conviction for one of the overt acts.

Subsequently, the stir that *Grady* had created was laid to rest by the decision in *United States v. Dixon*, 509 U.S. 688 (1993): *Grady v Corbin* was overruled, and the *Blockburger* standard was reinstated as the exclusive test for double jeopardy in a successive prosecution context. [*Blockburger v. United States*, 284 U.S. 299 (1932) had ruled that if each of the statutes involved in the successive prosecutions contained an element that the other did not, the second prosecution was not violative of the Double Jeopardy clause.]

Cases involving an acquittal in a previous federal prosecution present a different issue from the foregoing cases. In the federal context, collateral estoppel principles–which are incorporated into the double jeopardy clause—would bar the government from relitigating the defendant's guilt of the previously acquitted predicate offense. Compare, however, *United States v. Esposito*, 912 F.2d 60, 62 (3d Cir.1990): Held: A subsequent prosecution of predicate drug offenses, after the defendant has been prosecuted and acquitted on the RICO charge is not barred by the Double Jeopardy clause.

For a general discussion of double jeopardy, see WAYNE R. LAFAVE, JEROLD H. ISRAEL, & NANCY J. KING, *CRIMINAL PROCEDURE* § 17.4 (3d ed. 2000).

D. RICO CONSPIRACY

The RICO offense is a crime that generally involves a group insofar as it is built around the concept of an enterprise, and enterprise is defined in terms that usually involves group activity. The RICO crime thus can be viewed as a substantive offense that also has some of the characteristics of a conspiracy violation. We have previously seen how the predicate crimes that comprise the required racketeering activity may also involve conspiracies.

Section 1962 (d) adds still another conspiracy dimension to RICO insofar as it makes it a separate federal crime to conspire to violate one of the substantive RICO violations defined in §§ 1962 (a), (b), and (c). It is another instance where Congress has adopted a specialized conspiracy provision to supplement the general conspiracy provision, 18 U.S.C.

§ 371. Like most of the specialized conspiracy provisions, the penalty provision applicable to 1962 (d) is tailored to the nature of the object crime. Given the nature of the substantive offense object, the question that has been raised is whether using a conspiracy charge in a RICO prosecution has other kinds of special procedural implications.

Notes

1. In an often-cited case, *United States v. Elliott*, 571 F.2d 880 (5th Cir.1978), the court addressed the procedural advantages of a RICO prosecution:

> The evidence in this case demonstrated the existence of an enterprise—a myriopod criminal network, loosely connected but connected nonetheless. By committing arson, actively assisting a car theft ring, fencing thousands of dollars worth of goods stolen from interstate commerce, murdering a key witness, and dealing in narcotics, * * * [two of the five defendants] directly and indirectly participated in the enterprise's affairs through a pattern * * * of racketeering activity. * * *

> Applying pre-RICO conspiracy concepts to the facts of this case, we doubt that a single conspiracy could be demonstrated. [The court here noted that a number of the defendants had no contact during the conspiracy, and the activities were too diverse to be tied together on the theory that participation in one implied awareness of the others.] * * *

> [W]e are convinced that, through RICO, Congress intended to authorize the single prosecution of a multi-faceted, diversified conspiracy by replacing the inadequate "wheel" and "chain" rationales with a new statutory concept: the enterprise.

> * * *

> In the context of organized crime, [the use of traditional conspiracy principles] * * * inhibited mass prosecutions because a single agreement or "common objective" cannot be inferred from the commission of highly diverse crimes by apparently unrelated individuals. RICO helps to eliminate this problem by creating a substantive offense which ties together these diverse parties and crimes. * * * The gravamen of the conspiracy charge in this case is not that each defendant agreed to commit arson, to steal goods from interstate commerce, to obstruct justice, and to sell narcotics; rather, it is that each agreed to participate, directly and indirectly, in the affairs of the enterprise by committing two or more predicate crimes. * * *

2. Professor Gerard Lynch has argued that traditional conspiracy law could theoretically reach a case like *Elliott*; that RICO is better viewed as having brought about a shift in practice, not in theory; that though under traditional conspiracy principles, courts might have accepted prosecutions of the breadth of some RICO prosecutions, such cases were generally not filed; "RICO thus may be better seen as the occasion for a change in judicial and prosecutorial policy than as a provider of new theoretical concepts." Gerard Lynch, *RICO: The Crime of Being a Criminal, Parts III & IV*, 87 Colum. L. Rev. 920, 951 (1987). Professor Lynch went on to suggest:

Three points need to be made about this analysis, however. First, the change in policy is itself significant. * * * [T]he prosecutions that result are distinctly broader than had previously been undertaken. * * *

Second, by incorporating state crimes as predicate activity, RICO does in fact expand the range of criminal objects that can be prosecuted in a single federal prosecution. * * * This is particularly significant in organized crime cases, where it permits unified prosecution of multiple crimes of violence that would previously have been regarded as unrelated.

Third, by creating a substantive offense worded in terms of a course of conduct, RICO constitutes a theoretical break with the transactional model of crime.... Although conspiracy prosecutions in practice permit presentation of a course of conduct in a single trial, in theory at least the crime remains defined in terms of a single act of agreement.

This conceptual change may have practical consequences. * * * The fiction that all of the crimes charged were part of a specific agreement could only be maintained if it plausibly could be imagined that the core players at least could have sat together and agreed—even if it was clear that they did not in the particular instance do so. "Participation in the affairs of an enterprise" more accurately captures the reality of what fringe participants in a conspiracy do than "agreeing" to the overall objectives of its core members, and therefore permits easier inferences of guilt. Ibid. at 951–953

3. To what extent is it necessary to include a RICO conspiracy count in the charge in order to obtain the advantages discussed in the *Elliott* case? Similarly, to what extent are the points made by Professor Lynch tied to a charge of conspiracy to violate RICO or are they implied in the substantive RICO offense itself? Does the use of § 1962(d) add procedural advantages (whether they be practical or theoretical), or is the principal effect of 1962 (d) to multiply penalties?

4. The RICO statute does not distinguish among participants in a § 1962 (c) or (d) violation: all are subject to the same maximum 20 year prison term. In contrast, the continuing criminal (illegal drug) enterprise, 21 U.S.C. § 848 (see supra, p. 389) attaches penalties only to drug kingpins who manage large drug rings and earn substantial income. Would it be desirable to use measures of scale that would vary penalties based on the nature of the participation, the size of the group or the magnitude of the criminal operation? *See, e.g., United States v. Yeager*, 210 F.3d 1315 (11th Cir. 2000) (holding that a sentencing enhancement for a criminal's leadership role can be based on defendant's role in the over-all RICO conspiracy, and it is not necessary to find that the defendant played a leadership role in the underlying drug conspiracy).

5. In discussing the extent of liability for substantive prostitution offenses of the participants in a large-scale prostitution ring, the drafters of the Model Penal Code argued:

Liability was properly imposed with respect to [those] defendants who directed and controlled the combination. They solicited and aided the commission of numberless specific crimes, including the ones for which they were held. But would so extensive a liability be just for each of the prostitutes or runners involved in the plan? They have, of course, committed their own crimes. * * * A court would and should hold that they are parties to a conspiracy: this is itself a crime. * * * However, laws would lose all sense of just proportion if simply because of the conspiracy itself each were held accountable for thousands of additional offenses of which he was completely unaware and which he did not influence at all. Model Penal Code § 2.06 commentary at 307 (1985).

Does the foregoing quotation have any implications for the possibility of differential liability under the RICO statute?

6.   What must a person charged with a RICO conspiracy have agreed to in order to be guilty of the offense? This issue was addressed by the Supreme Court in the following case.

SALINAS v. UNITED STATES

522 U.S. 52, 118 S.Ct. 469, 139 L.Ed.2d 352 (1997).

JUSTICE KENNEDY delivered the opinion of the Court.

This federal prosecution arose from a bribery scheme operated by Brigido Marmolejo, the Sheriff of Hidalgo County, Texas, and petitioner Mario Salinas, one of his principal deputies. In 1984, the United States Marshals Service and Hidalgo County entered into agreements under which the county would take custody of federal prisoners. In exchange, the Federal Government agreed to make a grant to the county for improving its jail and also agreed to pay the county a specific amount per day for each federal prisoner housed. Based on the estimated number of federal prisoners to be maintained, payments to the county were projected to be $915,785 per year. The record before us does not disclose the precise amounts paid. It is uncontested, however, that in each of the two periods relevant in this case the program resulted in federal payments to the county well in excess of the $10,000 amount necessary for coverage under 18 U.S.C. § 666.

Homero Beltran–Aguirre was one of the federal prisoners housed in the jail under the arrangement negotiated between the Marshals Service and the county. He was incarcerated there for two intervals, first for 10 months and then for 5 months. During both custody periods, Beltran paid Marmolejo a series of bribes in exchange for so-called "contact visits" in which he remained alone with his wife or, on other occasions, his girlfriend. Beltran paid Marmolejo a fixed rate of six thousand dollars per month and one thousand dollars for each contact visit, which occurred twice a week. Petitioner Salinas was the chief deputy responsible for managing the jail and supervising custody of the prisoners. When Marmolejo was not available, Salinas arranged for the contact visits and on occasion stood watch outside the room where the visits took place. In return for his assistance with the scheme, Salinas received from Beltran a pair of designer watches and a pickup truck.

Salinas and Marmolejo were indicted and tried together, but only Salinas' convictions are before us. Salinas was charged with one count of violating RICO, 18 U.S.C. § 1962(c), one count of conspiracy to violate RICO, § 1962(d), and two counts of bribery in violation of § 666(a)(1)(B). The jury acquitted Salinas on the substantive RICO count but convicted him on the RICO conspiracy count and the bribery counts. A divided panel of the Court of Appeals for the Fifth Circuit affirmed.

* * *

Salinas directs his second challenge to his conviction for conspiracy to violate RICO. There could be no conspiracy offense, he says, unless he himself committed or agreed to commit the two predicate acts requisite for a substantive RICO offense under § 1962(c). Salinas identifies a conflict among the Courts of Appeals on the point. Decisions of the First, Second, and Tenth Circuits require that, under the RICO conspiracy provision, the defendant must himself commit or agree to commit two or more predicate acts. * * * Eight other Courts of Appeals, including the Fifth Circuit in this case, take a contrary view * * *.

Before turning to RICO's conspiracy provision, we note the substantive RICO offense, which was the goal of the conspiracy alleged in the indictment. It provides:

> "It shall be unlawful for any person employed by or associated with any enterprise engaged in, or the activities of which affect, interstate or foreign commerce, to conduct or participate, directly or indirectly, in the conduct of such enterprise's affairs through a pattern of racketeering activity or collection of unlawful debt." 18 U.S.C. § 1962(c).

The elements predominant in a subsection (c) violation are: (1) the conduct (2) of an enterprise (3) through a pattern of racketeering activity. * * * The Government's theory was that Salinas himself committed a substantive § 1962(c) RICO violation by conducting the enterprise's affairs through a pattern of racketeering activity that included acceptance of two or more bribes, felonies punishable in Texas by more than one year in prison. The jury acquitted on the substantive count. Salinas was convicted of conspiracy, however, and he challenges the conviction because the jury was not instructed that he must have committed or agreed to commit two predicate acts himself. His interpretation of the conspiracy statute is wrong.

The RICO conspiracy statute, simple in formulation, provides:

> "It shall be unlawful for any person to conspire to violate any of the provisions of subsection (a), (b), or (c) of this section." 18 U.S.C. § 1962(d).

There is no requirement of some overt act or specific act in the statute before us, unlike the general conspiracy provision applicable to federal crimes, which requires that at least one of the conspirators have committed an "act to effect the object of the conspiracy." § 371. The RICO conspiracy provision, then, is even more comprehensive than the general conspiracy offense in § 371.

In interpreting the provisions of § 1962(d), we adhere to a general rule: When Congress uses well-settled terminology of criminal law, its words are presumed to have their ordinary meaning and definition. The relevant statutory phrase in § 1962(d) is "to conspire." We presume Congress intended to use the term in its conventional sense, and certain well-established principles follow.

A conspiracy may exist even if a conspirator does not agree to commit or facilitate each and every part of the substantive offense. The partners in the criminal plan must agree to pursue the same criminal objective and may divide up the work, yet each is responsible for the acts of each other. If conspirators have a plan which calls for some conspirators to perpetrate the crime and others to provide support, the supporters are as guilty as the perpetrators. A person, moreover, may be liable for conspiracy even though he was incapable of committing the substantive offense.

The point Salinas tries to make is in opposition to these principles, and is refuted by *Bannon v. United States*, 156 U.S. 464 (1895). There the defendants were charged with conspiring to violate the general conspiracy statute, which requires proof of an overt act. One defendant objected to the indictment because it did not allege he had committed an overt act. We rejected the argument because it would erode the common-law principle that, so long as they share a common purpose, conspirators are liable for the acts of their co-conspirators. We observed in *Bannon*: "To require an overt act to be proven against every member of the conspiracy, or a distinct act connecting him with the combination to be alleged, would not only be an innovation upon established principles, but would render most prosecutions for the offence nugatory." The RICO conspiracy statute, § 1962(d), broadened conspiracy coverage by omitting the requirement of an overt act; it did not, at the same time, work the radical change of requiring the Government to prove each conspirator agreed that he would be the one to commit two predicate acts.

Our recitation of conspiracy law comports with contemporary understanding. When Congress passed RICO in 1970, the American Law Institute's Model Penal Code permitted a person to be convicted of conspiracy so long as he "agrees with such other person or persons that they or one or more of them will engage in conduct that constitutes such crime." American Law Institute, Model Penal Code § 5.03(1)(a) (1962). As the drafters emphasized, "so long as the purpose of the agreement is to facilitate commission of a crime, the actor need not agree 'to commit' the crime." American Law Institute, Model Penal Code, Tent. Draft No. 10, p. 117 (1960). The Model Penal Code still uses this formulation. *See* Model Penal Code § 5.03(1)(a), 10 U. L. A. 501 (1974).

A conspirator must intend to further an endeavor which, if completed, would satisfy all of the elements of a substantive criminal offense, but it suffices that he adopt the goal of furthering or facilitating the criminal endeavor. He may do so in any number of ways short of agreeing to undertake all of the acts necessary for the crime's completion. One can be a conspirator by agreeing to facilitate only some of the acts leading to the substantive offense. It is elementary that a conspiracy may exist and be punished whether or not the substantive crime ensues, for the conspiracy is a distinct evil, dangerous to the public, and so punishable in itself.

It makes no difference that the substantive offense under subsection (c) requires two or more predicate acts. The interplay between subsections (c) and (d) does not permit us to excuse from the reach of the conspiracy provision an actor who does not himself commit or agree to commit the two or more predicate acts requisite to the underlying offense. True, though an "enterprise" under § 1962(c) can exist with only one actor to conduct it, in most instances it will be conducted by more than one person or entity; and this in turn may make it somewhat difficult to determine just where the enterprise ends and the conspiracy begins, or, on the other hand, whether the two crimes are coincident in their factual circumstances. In some cases the connection the defendant had to the alleged enterprise or to the conspiracy to further it may be tenuous enough so that his own commission of two predicate acts may become an important part of the Government's case. Perhaps these were the considerations leading some of the Circuits to require in conspiracy cases that each conspirator himself commit or agree to commit two or more predicate acts. Nevertheless, that proposition cannot be sustained as a definition of the conspiracy offense, for it is contrary to the principles we have discussed.

In the case before us, even if Salinas did not accept or agree to accept two bribes, there was ample evidence that he conspired to violate subsection (c). The evidence showed that Marmolejo committed at least two acts of racketeering activity when he accepted numerous bribes and that Salinas knew about and agreed to facilitate the scheme. This is sufficient to support a conviction under § 1962(d).

As a final matter, Salinas says his statutory interpretation is required by the rule of lenity. The rule does not apply when a statute is unambiguous or when invoked to engraft an illogical requirement to its text. The judgment of the Court of Appeals is

Affirmed.

Notes

1. In light of *Salinas*, is the following a correct statement of the law? "Thus, defendant who did not agree to the commission of crimes constituting a pattern of racketeering activity is not in violation of section 1962(d), even though he is somehow affiliated with a RICO enterprise * * *." *United States v. Neapolitan*, 791 F.2d 489, 498 (7th Cir.1986).

2. After the decision in *Reves, supra,* p. 515 and, particularly after *Salinas*, the question has arisen as to how to treat the *Reves'* operation or

management test in the context of a prosecution for a RICO conspiracy under § 1962(d). To be liable under 1962(d), must a defendant conspire to operate or manage the enterprise, or simply conspire with someone who is operating or managing the enterprise. The issue initially divided the circuits. The split was characterized in *United States v. Posada–Rios*, 158 F.3d 832, 857 (5th Cir.1998):

> [The defendants] * * * argue that the direction and control requirements of *Reves* also apply to a RICO conspiracy charge. * * * To date five circuits have addressed whether the management and control test set forth in Reves applies to a RICO conspiracy. The Second, Seventh, and Eleventh Circuits have held that *Reves'* management and control test does not apply to a RICO conspiracy, concluding that "*Reves* addressed only the extent of conduct or participation necessary to violate a substantive provision of the statute; the holding in that case did not address the principles of conspiracy law undergirding § 1964(d)." The Third and Ninth Circuits, however, have held that *Reves'* management and control test must necessarily apply to a RICO conspiracy because to hold otherwise would render *Reves* nugatory.
>
> We conclude that the better-reasoned rule is the one adopted by the Second, Seventh, and Eleventh Circuits, especially in light of the Supreme Court's recent decision in *Salinas* * * *

In what way would declining to require that the defendant must have conspired to operate or manage the enterprise render *Reves* nugatory? Clearly, the *Posada-Rios* court was not persuaded by that argument? Are you persuaded?

3.   a. In *Smith v. Berg*, 247 F.3d 532 (3d Cir. 2001), the Third Circuit subsequently changed its mind and adopted the majority position:

> *Reves* is not a conspiracy decision; its holding focuses solely on what is required to violate § 1962(c) as a principle in the first degree. *Reves* says nothing about the scope of § 1962(d).
>
> In *Salinas*, the defendant was charged with criminal violations of both section 1962(c) and section 1962(d) but convicted on the conspiracy charge alone. The Supreme Court resolved a conflict among the Courts of Appeals, finding—as had the majority of our sister Courts of Appeals—that a RICO conspiracy defendant need not himself commit or agree to commit predicate acts. In upholding the result in the *Salinas* case, the Supreme Court found that a violation of section 1962(c) was not a prerequisite to a violation of section 1962(d). Rather, the Court found that for purposes of conspiracy it "suffices that [defendant] adopt the goal of furthering or facilitating the criminal endeavor." Moreover, the Supreme Court provided an extensive discussion indicating that RICO's conspiracy section—section 1962(d)—is to be interpreted in light of the common law of criminal conspiracy and that all that is necessary for such a conspiracy is that the conspirators share a common purpose.
>
> Thus, as the District Court observed, *Salinas* makes "clear that § 1962(c) liability is not a prerequisite to § 1962(d) liability." The plain implication of the standard set forth in *Salinas* is that one who opts into or participates in a conspiracy is liable for the acts of his co-conspirators

which violate section 1962(c) even if the defendant did not personally agree to do, or to conspire with respect to, *any* particular element. . . .

In accord with the general principles of criminal conspiracy law, a defendant may be held liable for conspiracy to violate section 1962(c) if he knowingly agrees to facilitate a scheme which includes the operation or management of a RICO enterprise.

b. Later, the Ninth Circuit, the last remaining holdout, followed in the footsteps of the *Smith* case in *United States v. Fernandez*, 388 F.3d 1199 (9th Cir. 2004):

We adopt the Third Circuit's *Smith* test, which retains *Reves'* operation or management test in its definition of the underlying substantive § 1962(c) violation, but removes any requirement that the defendant have actually conspired to operate or manage the enterprise herself. Under this test, a defendant is guilty of conspiracy to violate § 1962(c) if the evidence showed that she "knowingly agreed to facilitate a scheme which includes the operation or management of a RICO enterprise."

Schoenberg's role in the activities of the Eme enterprise is enough to justify her § 1962(d) conspiracy conviction . . . The evidence at trial showed that Schoenberg collected protection money for the Eme on behalf of her husband, an Eme member; passed messages to her husband and other Eme members in order to facilitate communication between murder conspirators; smuggled drugs into prison; and accepted payment for drugs sold on the street. We affirm her conviction for conspiracy to violate RICO.

4. What led the Third and Ninth Circuits to change their collective minds in *Smith* and *Fernandez,* supra? The *Salinas* decision? Did these courts take account of the concern about rendering *Reves* "nugatory" raised in note 2 *supra*? Should they at least have discussed the issue?

5. We previously learned, supra, p. 524, that the case law indicates that an aiding and abetting theory cannot be used as a basis for civil RICO liability although there appears to be no impediment to its use in connection with criminal RICO. The same type of avoidance of the operation or management test would seem to be possible in a RICO 1964 (c) civil suit by alleging a conspiracy to violate RICO under 1962 (d) rather than charging under 1962 (c), given the cases discussed in notes 2–4, supra. Compare: David B. Smith & Terrance G. Reed, CIVIL RICO, § 5.04, p. 5–45 (Mathew Bender & Co. 2000): ". . . [I]f Congress' restriction of 1962(c) liability to those who operate or manage the enterprise can be avoided simply by alleging that a defendant aided and abetted or conspired with someone who operated or managed the enterprise, then Reves would be rendered almost useless." Of course, if conspiracy began to be used to avoid the effect of *Reves,* the courts might reconsider the issue, or it might eventually have to be addressed by the Supreme Court. Consider, e.g., *Wuliger v. Liberty Bank,* 2004 WL 3377416 (N.D. Ohio) where in a RICO civil suit, the district court found that the defendants had not operated or managed the enterprise, rejected an aiding and abetting theory because it was not available in a civil context, and also rejected liability founded on conspiracy under 1962(d):

As the court has determined there has been a failure to plead the conduct or participation in a racketeering enterprise under § 1962 (c), the Plaintiff's claim of conspiracy, which is dependent upon the viability of (c), must also fail as a matter of law.

Does the court's conclusion reflect an inherent weakness in the case in regard to conspiracy or might the flaw be curable by an amended pleading?

6. The courts have permitted convictions and cumulative sentences when the same conduct is charged as both a RICO conspiracy and a violation of the general conspiracy statute, 18 U.S.C. § 371. *See, e.g., United States v. Barton*, 647 F.2d 224 (2d Cir. 1981). Cumulative sentences have also been allowed where other conspiracy charges are combined with a RICO conspiracy charge. *See, e.g., United States v. Kragness*, 830 F.2d 842 (8th Cir. 1987) (RICO conspiracy and various drug conspiracies); *United States v. Kimble*, 719 F.2d 1253 (5th Cir. 1983) (RICO conspiracy and civil rights conspiracy under 18 U.S.C. § 241). Regarding cumulative sentencing in RICO conspiracy cases, see Nancy L. Ickler, Note, *Conspiracy to Violate RICO: Expanding Traditional Conspiracy Law*, 58 NOTRE DAME L. REV. 587 (1983).

7. Can RICO conspiracies and general conspiracies have different statute of limitations dates? If so, it may then be possible to be prosecuted for RICO conspiracy after the statute of limitations for general conspiracy has passed. Is this a sound result? *See* Ellen Jancko–Baken, Note, *When Will the Idling Statute of Limitations Start Running in RICO Conspiracy Cases?*, 10 CARDOZO L. REV. 2167 (1989).

E. CIVIL RICO

RICO enables a private civil complainant to sue for treble damages plus attorney's fees based on an injury arising out of a violation of the (criminal) RICO provisions. The statute also authorizes the government to proceed civilly and pursue equitable remedies against a RICO violator, in addition to authorizing criminal prosecutions (which have been examined in the previous sections of this Chapter). We examine the civil dimension of RICO in this section.

Other federal laws provide for civil and criminal remedies based on essentially the same conduct—for example, in the spheres of antitrust, securities laws, and civil rights. Compare the relationship between civil and criminal claims in these other areas of the law with the civil–criminal dichotomy under RICO. Is it different? In what respect?

Consider the following questions in regard to the relationship between civil and criminal RICO:

1. In deciding issues in both civil and criminal RICO cases, as we have seen in the previous sections, the courts generally follow precedents from both the civil and criminal RICO arenas. Is it feasible or desirable for RICO doctrine to develop along different lines depending on whether the issue arises in a civil or criminal context? Is there anything in the statutory scheme that militates against drawing such a distinction? Would you expect a judge to react differently to a civil RICO claim

brought against a stock broker than to a criminal RICO charge, brought against operators of a illegal drug ring? In the previous sections, have you seen any judicial decisions that you believe may have been influenced by the fact that the issues arose in a civil rather than a criminal context, or vice versa? See generally, Paul Edgar Harold, *Quo Vadis, Association in Fact? The Growing Disparity Between How Federal Courts Interpret RICO's Enterprise Provision in Criminal And Civil Cases (With A Little Statutory Background To Explain Why)*, 80 Notre Dame L.Rev. 781 (2005).

2. A large number of private civil RICO claims are filed each year: in most instances, they consist of RICO claims added to civil business litigation. What accounts for this frequent use of civil RICO? Consider the following:

a. "What gives civil RICO a potentially broad scope is that many of the incorporated predicate criminal statutes are even broader, on their face, than any comparable civil actions." Strafer, Massumi & Skolnick, *Civil RICO in the Public Interest: Everybody's Darling*, 19 AM. CRIM. L. REV. 655, 657–58 (1982).

b. "According to conventional wisdom, . . . adding a civil RICO count to a complaint serves as a potential inducement for defendants to settle the case and avoid the stigma of being publicly associated with nefarious 'racketeering activities.' " 1 KATHLEEN BRICKEY, CORPORATE CRIMINAL LIABILITY: A TREATISE ON THE CRIMINAL LIABILITY OF CORPORATIONS, THEIR OFFICERS AND AGENTS § 7A:02 at 427 (1992)(footnote omitted).

§ 1964. Civil remedies

(a) The district courts of the United States shall have jurisdiction to prevent and restrain violations of section 1962 of this chapter by issuing appropriate orders, including, but not limited to: ordering any person to divest himself of any interest, direct or indirect, in any enterprise; imposing reasonable restrictions on the future activities or investments of any person, including, but not limited to, prohibiting any person from engaging in the same type of endeavor as the enterprise engaged in, the activities of which affect interstate or foreign commerce; or ordering dissolution or reorganization of any enterprise, making due provision for the rights of innocent persons.

(b) The Attorney General may institute proceedings under this section. Pending final determination thereof, the court may at any time enter such restraining orders or prohibitions, or take such other actions, including the acceptance of satisfactory performance bonds, as it shall deem proper.

(c) Any person injured in his business or property by reason of a violation of section 1962 of this chapter may sue therefor in any appropriate United States district court and shall recover threefold the damages he sustains and the cost of the suit, including a reasonable attorney fee, except that no person may rely upon any conduct that would have been actionable as fraud in the purchase or sale of securities to establish a violation of section 1962. The exception contained in the preceding sentence does not apply to an action against any person that is criminally convicted in connection with the fraud, in which case the statute of limitations shall start to run on the date on which the conviction becomes final.

(d) A final judgment or decree rendered in favor of the United States in any criminal proceeding brought by the United States under this chapter [18 U.S.C. §§ 1961 et seq.] shall estop the defendant from denying the essential allegations of the criminal offense in any subsequent civil proceeding brought by the United States.

1. PRIVATE CIVIL REMEDIES

SEDIMA, S.P.R.L. v. IMREX CO., INC., ET AL.

473 U.S. 479, 105 S.Ct. 3275, 87 L.Ed.2d 346 (1985).

[WHITE, J., delivered the opinion of the Court, in which BURGER, C. J., and REHNQUIST, STEVENS, and O'CONNOR, JJ., joined. MARSHALL, J., filed a dissenting opinion, in which BRENNAN, BLACKMUN, and POWELL, JJ., joined. POWELL, J., filed a dissenting opinion.]

JUSTICE WHITE delivered the opinion of the Court.

The Racketeer Influenced and Corrupt Organizations Act (RICO), Pub. L. 91–452, Title IX, 84 Stat. 941, as amended, 18 U. S. C. §§ 1961–1968, provides a private civil action to recover treble damages for injury "by reason of a violation of" its substantive provisions. 18 U. S. C. § 1964(c). The initial dormancy of this provision and its recent greatly increased utilization are now familiar history. In response to what it perceived to be misuse of civil RICO by private plaintiffs, the court below construed § 1964(c) to permit private actions only against defendants who had been convicted on criminal charges, and only where there had occurred a "racketeering injury." While we understand the court's concern over the consequences of an unbridled reading of the statute, we reject both of its holdings.

I

RICO takes aim at "racketeering activity," which it defines as any act "chargeable" under several generically described state criminal laws, any act "indictable" under numerous specific federal criminal provisions, including mail and wire fraud, and any "offense" involving bankruptcy or securities fraud or drug-related activities that is "punishable" under federal law. § 1961(1). Section 1962, entitled "Prohibited Activities," outlaws the use of income derived from a "pattern of racketeering activity" to acquire an interest in or establish an enterprise engaged in or affecting interstate commerce; the acquisition or maintenance of any interest in an enterprise "through" a pattern of racketeering activity;

conducting or participating in the conduct of an enterprise through a pattern of racketeering activity; and conspiring to violate any of these provisions.

Congress provided criminal penalties of imprisonment, fines, and forfeiture for violation of these provisions. § 1963. In addition, it set out a far-reaching civil enforcement scheme, 1964, including the following provision for private suits:

> "Any person injured in his business or property by reason of a violation of section 1962 of this chapter may sue therefor in any appropriate United States district court and shall recover threefold the damages he sustains and the cost of the suit, including a reasonable attorney's fee." 1964(c).

In 1979, petitioner Sedima, a Belgian corporation, entered into a joint venture with respondent Imrex Co. to provide electronic components to a Belgian firm. The buyer was to order parts through Sedima; Imrex was to obtain the parts in this country and ship them to Europe. The agreement called for Sedima and Imrex to split the net proceeds. Imrex filled roughly $8 million in orders placed with it through Sedima. Sedima became convinced, however, that Imrex was presenting inflated bills, cheating Sedima out of a portion of its proceeds by collecting for nonexistent expenses.

In 1982, Sedima filed this action in the Federal District Court for the Eastern District of New York. The complaint set out common-law claims of unjust enrichment, conversion, and breach of contract, fiduciary duty, and a constructive trust. In addition, it asserted RICO claims under 1964(c) against Imrex and two of its officers. Two counts alleged violations of 1962(c), based on predicate acts of mail and wire fraud. See 18 U. S. C. §§ 1341, 1343, 1961(1)(B). A third count alleged a conspiracy to violate 1962(c). Claiming injury of at least $175,000, the amount of the alleged over-billing, Sedima sought treble damages and attorney's fees.

II

As a preliminary matter, it is worth briefly reviewing the legislative history of the private treble-damages action. RICO formed Title IX of the Organized Crime Control Act of 1970, Pub. L. 91–452, 84 Stat. 922. The civil remedies in the bill passed by the Senate, S. 30, were limited to injunctive actions by the United States and became §§ 1964(a), (b), and (d). Previous versions of the legislation, however, had provided for a private treble-damages action in exactly the terms ultimately adopted in § 1964(c).

During hearings on S. 30 before the House Judiciary Committee, Representative Steiger proposed the addition of a private treble-damages action "similar to the private damage remedy found in the anti-trust laws. [Those] who have been wronged by organized crime should at least be given access to a legal remedy. In addition, the availability of such a remedy would enhance the effectiveness of title IX's prohibitions." The

American Bar Association also proposed an amendment "based upon the concept of Section 4 of the Clayton Act."

Over the dissent of three members, who feared the treble-damages provision would be used for malicious harassment of business competitors, the Committee approved the amendment. In summarizing the bill on the House floor, its sponsor described the treble-damages provision as "another example of the antitrust remedy being adapted for use against organized criminality." The full House then rejected a proposal to create a complementary treble-damages remedy for those injured by being named as defendants in malicious private suits. Representative Steiger also offered an amendment that would have allowed private injunctive actions, fixed a statute of limitations, and clarified venue and process requirements. The proposal was greeted with some hostility because it had not been reviewed in Committee, and Steiger withdrew it without a vote being taken. The House then passed the bill, with the treble-damages provision in the form recommended by the Committee.

The Senate did not seek a conference and adopted the bill as amended in the House. The treble-damages provision had been drawn to its attention while the legislation was still in the House, and had received the endorsement of Senator McClellan, the sponsor of S. 30, who was of the view that the provision would be "a major new tool in extirpating the baneful influence of organized crime in our economic life."

III

The language of RICO gives no obvious indication that a civil action can proceed only after a criminal conviction. The word "conviction" does not appear in any relevant portion of the statute. *See* §§ 1961, 1962, 1964(c). To the contrary, the predicate acts involve conduct that is "chargeable" or "indictable," and "[offenses]" that are "punishable," under various criminal statutes. § 1961(1). As defined in the statute, racketeering activity consists not of acts for which the defendant has been convicted, but of acts for which he could be. *See also* S. Rep. No. 91–617, p. 158 (1969): "a racketeering activity ... must be an act in itself *subject to* criminal sanction" (emphasis added). Thus, a prior-conviction requirement cannot be found in the definition of "racketeering activity." Nor can it be found in § 1962, which sets out the statute's substantive provisions. Indeed, if either § 1961 or § 1962 did contain such a requirement, a prior conviction would also be a prerequisite, nonsensically, for a criminal prosecution, or for a civil action by the Government to enjoin violations that had not yet occurred.

The Court of Appeals purported to discover its prior-conviction requirement in the term "violation" in § 1964(c). However, even if that term were read to refer to a criminal conviction, it would require a conviction under RICO, not of the predicate offenses. That aside, the term "violation" does not imply a criminal conviction. It refers only to a failure to adhere to legal requirements. This is its indisputable meaning elsewhere in the statute. Section 1962 renders certain conduct "unlawful"; § 1963 and § 1964 impose consequences, criminal and civil, for "violations" of § 1962. We should not lightly infer that Congress intended the term to have wholly different meanings in neighboring subsections.

The legislative history also undercuts the reading of the court below. The clearest current in that history is the reliance on the Clayton Act model, under which private and governmental actions are entirely distinct. The only specific reference in the legislative history to prior convictions of which we are aware is an objection that the treble-damages provision is too broad precisely because "there need *not* be a conviction under any of these laws for it to be racketeering." 116 Cong. Rec. 35342 (1970) (emphasis added). The history is otherwise silent on this point and contains nothing to contradict the import of the language appearing in the statute. Had Congress intended to impose this novel requirement, there would have been at least some mention of it in the legislative history, even if not in the statute.

The Court of Appeals was of the view that its narrow construction of the statute was essential to avoid intolerable practical consequences. First, without a prior conviction to rely on, the plaintiff would have to prove commission of the predicate acts beyond a reasonable doubt. This would require instructing the jury as to different standards of proof for different aspects of the case. To avoid this awkwardness, the court inferred that the criminality must already be established, so that the civil action could proceed smoothly under the usual preponderance standard.

We are not at all convinced that the predicate acts must be established beyond a reasonable doubt in a proceeding under § 1964(c). In a number of settings, conduct that can be punished as criminal only upon proof beyond a reasonable doubt will support civil sanctions under a preponderance standard. There is no indication that Congress sought to depart from this general principle here. *See* Measures Relating to Organized Crime, Hearings on S. 30 et al. before the Subcommittee on Criminal Laws and Procedures of the Senate Committee on the Judiciary, 91st Cong., 1st Sess., 388 (1969) (statement of Assistant Attorney General Wilson); House Hearings, at 520 (statement of Rep. Steiger); id., at 664 (statement of Rep. Poff); 116 Cong. Rec. 35313 (1970) (statement of Rep. Minish). That the offending conduct is described by reference to criminal statutes does not mean that its occurrence must be established by criminal standards or that the consequences of a finding of liability in a private civil action are identical to the consequences of a criminal conviction. But we need not decide the standard of proof issue today. For even if the stricter standard is applicable to a portion of the plaintiff's proof, the resulting logistical difficulties, which are accepted in other contexts, would not be so great as to require invention of a requirement that cannot be found in the statute and that Congress, as even the Court of Appeals had to concede, did not envision.

The court below also feared that any other construction would raise severe constitutional questions, as it "would provide civil remedies for offenses criminal in nature, stigmatize defendants with the appellation 'racketeer,' authorize the award of damages which are clearly punitive, including attorney's fees, and constitute a civil remedy aimed in part to avoid the constitutional protections of the criminal law." We do not view the statute as being so close to the constitutional edge. As noted above, the fact that conduct can result in both criminal liability and treble damages does not mean that there is not a bona fide civil action. The familiar provisions for both criminal liability and treble damages under the antitrust laws indicate as much. Nor are attorney's fees "clearly punitive." As for stigma, a civil RICO proceeding leaves no greater stain than do a number of other civil proceedings. Furthermore, requiring conviction of the predicate acts would not protect against an unfair imposition of the "racketeer" label. If there is a problem with thus stigmatizing a garden variety defrauder by means of a civil action, it is not reduced by making certain that the defendant is guilty of fraud beyond a reasonable doubt. Finally, to the extent an action under § 1964(c) might be considered quasi-criminal, requiring protections normally applicable only to criminal proceedings, the solution is to provide those protections, not to ensure that they were previously afforded by requiring prior convictions.

Finally, we note that a prior-conviction requirement would be inconsistent with Congress' underlying policy concerns. Such a rule would severely handicap potential plaintiffs. A guilty party may escape conviction for any number of reasons—not least among them the possibility that the Government itself may choose to pursue only civil remedies. Private attorney general provisions such as § 1964(c) are in part designed to fill prosecutorial gaps. This purpose would be largely defeated, and the need for treble damages as an incentive to litigate unjustified, if private suits could be maintained only against those already brought to justice.

In sum, we can find no support in the statute's history, its language, or considerations of policy for a requirement that a private treble-damages action under § 1964(c) can proceed only against a defendant who has already been criminally convicted. To the contrary, every indication is that no such requirement exists. Accordingly, the fact that Imrex and the individual defendants have not been convicted under RICO or the federal mail and wire fraud statutes does not bar Sedima's action.

IV

In considering the Court of Appeals' second prerequisite for a private civil RICO action—"injury ... caused by an activity which RICO was designed to deter"—we are somewhat hampered by the vagueness of that concept. Apart from reliance on the general purposes of RICO and a reference to "mobsters," the court provided scant indication of what the requirement of racketeering injury means. It emphasized Congress' undeniable desire to strike at organized crime, but acknowledged and did not purport to overrule Second Circuit precedent rejecting a requirement of an organized crime nexus. The court also stopped short of adopting a "competitive injury" requirement; while insisting that the plaintiff show "the kind of economic injury which has an effect on competition," it did not require "actual anticompetitive effect."

The court's statement that the plaintiff must seek redress for an injury caused by conduct that RICO was designed to deter is unhelpfully tautological. Nor is clarity furnished by a negative statement of its rule: standing is not provided by the injury resulting from the predicate acts themselves. That statement is itself apparently inaccurate when applied to those predicate acts that unmistakably constitute the kind of conduct Congress sought to deter. The opinion does not explain how to distinguish such crimes from the other predicate acts Congress has lumped together in § 1961(1). The court below is not alone in struggling to define "racketeering injury," and the difficulty of that task itself cautions against imposing such a requirement.

We need not pinpoint the Second Circuit's precise holding, for we perceive no distinct "racketeering injury" requirement. Given that "racketeering activity" consists of no more and no less than commission of a predicate act, 1961(1), we are initially doubtful about a requirement of a "racketeering injury" separate from the harm from the predicate acts. A reading of the statute belies any such requirement. Section 1964(c) authorizes a private suit by "[any] person injured in his business or property by reason of a violation of 1962." Section 1962 in turn makes it unlawful for "any person"—not just mobsters—to use money derived from a pattern of racketeering activity to invest in an enterprise, to acquire control of an enterprise through a pattern of racketeering activity, or to conduct an enterprise through a pattern of racketeering activity. §§ 1962(a)-(c). If the defendant engages in a pattern of racketeering activity in a manner forbidden by these provisions, and the racketeering activities injure the plaintiff in his business or property, the plaintiff has a claim under § 1964(c). There is no room in the statutory language for an additional, amorphous "racketeering injury" requirement.

A violation of § 1962(c), the section on which Sedima relies, requires (1) conduct (2) of an enterprise (3) through a pattern of racketeering activity. The plaintiff must, of course, allege each of these elements to state a claim. Conducting an enterprise that affects interstate commerce is obviously not in itself a violation of § 1962, nor is mere commission of the predicate offenses. In addition, the plaintiff only has standing if, and can only recover to the extent that, he has been injured in his business or property by the conduct constituting the violation. As the Seventh Circuit has stated, "[a] defendant who violates section 1962 is not liable for treble damages to everyone he might have injured by other conduct, nor is the defendant liable to those who have not been injured." *Haroco, Inc. v. American National Bank & Trust Co. of Chicago*, 747 F.2d 384, 398 (1984), *aff'd*, 473 U.S. 606.

But the statute requires no more than this. Where the plaintiff alleges each element of the violation, the compensable injury necessarily is the harm caused by predicate acts sufficiently related to constitute a pattern, for the essence of the violation is the commission of those acts in connection with the conduct of an enterprise. Those acts are, when committed in the circumstances delineated in 1962(c), "an activity which RICO was designed to deter." Any recoverable damages occurring by reason of a violation of 1962(c) will flow from the commission of the predicate acts.

This less restrictive reading is amply supported by our prior cases and the general principles surrounding this statute. RICO is to be read broadly. This is the lesson not only of Congress' self-consciously expansive language and overall approach, see *United States v. Turkette*, 452 U.S. 576, 586–587 (1981), but also of its express admonition that RICO is to "be liberally construed to effectuate its remedial purposes," The statute's "remedial purposes" are nowhere more evident than in the provision of a private action for those injured by racketeering activity. Far from effectuating these purposes, the narrow readings offered by the dissenters and the court below would in effect eliminate 1964(c) from the statute. RICO was an aggressive initiative to supplement old remedies and develop new methods for fighting crime. While few of the legislative statements about novel remedies and attacking crime on all fronts were made with direct reference to 1964(c), it is in this spirit that all of the Act's provisions should be read. The specific references to 1964(c) are consistent with this overall approach. Those supporting 1964(c) hoped it would "enhance the effectiveness of title IX's prohibitions." Its opponents, also recognizing the provision's scope, complained that it provided too easy a weapon against "innocent businessmen," and would be prone to abuse. It is also significant that a previous proposal to add RICO-like provisions to the Sherman Act had come to grief in part precisely because it "could create inappropriate and unnecessary obstacles in the way of ... a private litigant [who] would have to contend with a body of precedent—appropriate in a purely antitrust context—setting strict requirements on questions such as 'standing to sue' and 'proximate cause.' "In borrowing its "racketeering injury" requirement from antitrust standing principles, the court below created exactly the problems Congress sought to avoid.

Underlying the Court of Appeals' holding was its distress at the "extraordinary, if not outrageous," uses to which civil RICO has been put. Instead of being used against mobsters and organized criminals, it has become a tool for everyday fraud cases brought against "respected and legitimate 'enterprises.' "Yet Congress wanted to reach both "legitimate" and "illegitimate" enterprises. The former enjoy neither an inherent incapacity for criminal activity nor immunity from its consequences. The fact that 1964(c) is used against respected businesses allegedly engaged in a pattern of specifically identified criminal conduct is hardly a sufficient reason for assuming that the provision is being misconstrued. Nor does it reveal the "ambiguity" discovered by the court below. "[The] fact that RICO has been applied in situations not expressly anticipated by Congress does not demonstrate ambiguity. It demonstrates breadth." *Haroco, Inc. v. American National Bank & Trust Co. of Chicago*, supra.

It is true that private civil actions under the statute are being brought almost solely against such defendants, rather than against the archetypal, intimidating mobster. Yet this defect—if defect it is—is inherent in the statute as written, and its correction must lie with Congress. It is not for the judiciary to eliminate the private action in situations where Congress has provided it simply because plaintiffs are not taking advantage of it in its more difficult applications.

We nonetheless recognize that, in its private civil version, RICO is evolving into something quite different from the original conception of its enactors. Though sharing the doubts of the Court of Appeals about this increasing divergence, we cannot agree with either its diagnosis or its remedy. The "extraordinary" uses to which civil RICO has been put appear to be primarily the result of the breadth of the predicate offenses, in particular the inclusion of wire, mail, and securities fraud, and the failure of Congress and the courts to develop a meaningful concept of "pattern." We do not believe that the amorphous standing requirement imposed by the Second Circuit effectively responds to these problems, or that it is a form of statutory amendment appropriately undertaken by the courts.

V

Sedima may maintain this action if the defendants conducted the enterprise through a pattern of racketeering activity. The questions whether the defendants committed the requisite predicate acts, and whether the commission of those acts fell into a pattern, are not before us. The complaint is not deficient for failure to allege either an injury separate from the financial loss stemming from the alleged acts of mail and wire fraud, or prior convictions of the defendants. The judgment below is accordingly reversed, and the case is remanded for further proceedings consistent with this opinion.

It is so ordered.

Notes

1. *Sedima* swept away two possible limitations on civil RICO actions. More importantly, it signaled the Court's unwillingness to restrict the reach of civil RICO, the Court having concluded that the breadth was inherent in the statutory scheme, and therefore any reforms are matters for Congress.

2. Civil RICO claims have been brought based on a remarkably broad range of complaints. Allegations which have been held to state a claim under civil RICO include: deprivation of inheritance and the honest and faithful performance of trustee's duties, *Norris v. Wirtz*, 703 F.Supp. 1322 (N.D.Ill. 1989); fraudulent assistance by a law firm to a client whose activities were

fraudulent, *Thomas v. Ross & Hardies*, 9 F.Supp.2d 547 (D.Md.1998); fraudulent misrepresentation of the education offered at a beauty college, *Rosario v. Livaditis*, 963 F.2d 1013 (7th Cir.1992); overcharging for architectural services, *Arabian American Oil Co. v. Scarfone*, 939 F.2d 1472 (11th Cir.1991); patent infringement and acts of unfair competition, *A. Stucki Co. v. Buckeye Steel Castings Co.*, 963 F.2d 360 (Fed Cir. 1992); the use of eminent domain, condemnation, and zoning by officials of a village to obtain property for favored developers, *Pelfresne v. Village of Rosemont*, 22 F.Supp.2d 756 (N.D.Ill.1998); wife in pending divorce action filed a RICO suit, alleging that the husband and other defendants fraudulently concealed separate and marital property to prevent her from sharing in the assets, *DeMauro v. DeMauro*, 115 F.3d 94 (1st Cir.1997). Complaints involving unions, either brought by union members against employers or brought by plaintiffs against the unions themselves, have also proven particularly conducive to civil RICO claims, *See*, e.g., *Tho Dinh Tran v. Alphonse Hotel Corp.*, 281 F.3d 23 (2d Cir. 2002); *Wall v. Roman*, 18 Fed.Appx. 41 (2d Cir. 2001) (unpublished opinion); *Forbes v. Eagleson*, 228 F.3d 471 (3d cir. 2000).

3.   Do you think it likely that a federal prosecutor would think criminal charges warranted in all of the cases cited in the previous note. It has been suggested that many RICO civil suits facially allege a criminal violation and yet turn out to be cases that would not have warranted criminal prosecution. What might account for this? *See* Norman Abrams, *A New Proposal for Limiting Private Civil RICO*, 37 UCLA L. REV. 1, 4–7 (1989).

4.   In 1995 Congress added the following language to § 1964 in order to restrict the application of RICO in securities frauds cases:

> except that no person may rely upon any conduct that would have been actionable as fraud in the purchase or sale of securities to establish a violation of section 1962. The exception contained in the preceding sentence does not apply to an action against any person that is criminally convicted in connection with the fraud, in which case the statute of limitations shall start to run on the date on which the conviction becomes final.

Why do you think Congress imposed this limitation and not others? *See generally Holmes v. Securities Investor Protection Corp.*, 503 U.S. 258 (1992).

5.   Civil RICO suits continue to be filed in significant numbers, but the courts have not been reluctant to deny relief on a variety of grounds: e.g. plaintiff's injuries did not flow from the harms that the predicate crimes were intended to cause, *Abrahams v. Young & Rubicam, Inc.*, 79 F.3d 234 (2d Cir.1996); predicate offenses were not sufficiently related to constitute a pattern of racketeering activity, *Heller Financial, Inc. v. Grammco Computer Sales, Inc.*, 71 F.3d 518 (5th Cir.1996); depositors in banks allegedly looted by owners of banks lack standing to sue those who induced them to deposit money through false representations regarding the banks' solvency, *Hamid v. Price Waterhouse*, 51 F.3d 1411 (9th Cir.1995); business rivals may not use RICO to complain about injuries derivatively caused by mail frauds perpetrated against customers, *Israel Travel Advisory Service, Inc. v. Israel Identity Tours, Inc.*, 61 F.3d 1250 (7th Cir.1995); some courts have also construed civil RICO's statute of limitations to bar many claims by holding that civil RICO accrues at the time a plaintiff knew, or should have known,

of his or her injury, e.g., *Lares Group, II v. Tobin*, 221 F.3d 41 (1st Cir. 2000), *Scott v. Boos*, 215 F.3d 940 (9th Cir. 2000).

6. The Ninth Circuit has decided a series of cases in which the court's view of the kind of harms that constitute injury to "business or property" within the meaning of 18 U.S.C. § 1964 (c) has evolved in the direction of a more expansive reading of that phrase. See O*scar v. University Students Cooperative Ass'n*, 965 F.2d 783 (9th Cir. 1992) (loss of use and enjoyment of rental apartment not sufficiently concrete financial loss); *Mendoza v. Zirkle Fruit Co.*, 301 F.3d 1163 (9th Cir. 2002) (agricultural laborers' wages depressed by illegal hiring of undocumented workers at wages below market; injury caused to property interest consisting of legal entitlement to non-interference with business relations: intentional interference with prospective business relations is a tort under California law). And see *Diaz v. Gates*, 420 F.3d 897 (9th Cir.2005) (en banc):

> Diaz claims to be a victim of the Los Angeles Police Department's infamous Rampart scandal. He sued over two hundred people connected with the Los Angeles Police Department (LAPD) or Los Angeles city government under the Racketeer Influenced and Corrupt Organizations Act (RICO), alleging that LAPD officers had "fabricated evidence" that he had committed assault with a deadly weapon, and that they had "tampered with witnesses and conspired to obtain [a] false conviction" against him, As a consequence, Diaz claims, "[a]mong other forms of injury, [he] lost employment, employment opportunities, and the wages and other compensation associated with said business, employment and opportunities, in that[he] was rendered unable to pursue gainful employment while defending himself against unjust charges and while unjustly incarcerated."

> * * *

> Without a harm to a specific business or property interest-a categorical inquiry typically determined by reference to state law-there is no injury to business or property within the meaning of RICO.

> * * *

> Contrary to the dissent's suggestion, our approach does not create RICO liability for every loss of wages resulting from a personal injury. * * *Diaz,* * * has alleged both the property interest and the financial loss. The harms he alleges amount to intentional interference with contract and interference with prospective business relations, both of which are established torts under California law. * * * And his claimed financial loss? He could not fulfill his employment contract or pursue valuable employment opportunities because he was in jail.

See also, Doe v. Roe, 958 F.2d 763 (7th Cir. 1992).

7. The Supreme Court in *Holmes v. SIPC*, 503 U.S. 258 (1992) ruled that common law ideas about proximate cause are to be applied under RICO: a fraudulent scheme injured the corporation and its clients, causing the plaintiff Securities Investor Protection Corporation (SIPC) to advance money to protect the clients. The Supreme Court concluded that the clients and the injured corporation were the proper plaintiffs rather than the indirectly

injured SIPC. "[D]irectly injured victims can generally be counted on to vindicate the law as private attorneys general, without any of the problems attendant upon suits by plaintiffs injured more remotely."

8. In *Beck v. Prupis*, 529 U.S. 494, 120 S.Ct. 1608 (2000), the Court adopted a limitation on the use of conspiracy to violate the RICO statute as a basis for a civil RICO action, concluding that a person does not have a RICO cause of action if the only injury to him/her was caused by an overt act in furtherance of the conspiracy. Petitioner's theory was that his injury was proximately caused by an overt act—namely, the termination of his employment—done in furtherance of respondents' conspiracy. Justice Thomas writing for the Court stated:

> This case turns on the combined effect of two provisions of RICO that, read in conjunction, provide a civil cause of action for conspiracy. Section 1964(c) states that a cause of action is available to anyone "injured ... by reason of a violation of section 1962." Section 1962(d) makes it unlawful for a person "to conspire to violate any of the provisions of subsection (a), (b), or (c) of this section." To determine what it means to be "injured ... by reason of" a "conspir[acy]," we turn to the well-established common law of civil conspiracy.[6]

> * * *

> By the time of RICO's enactment in 1970, it was widely accepted that a plaintiff could bring suit for civil conspiracy only if he had been injured by an act that was itself tortious. ...

> * * *

> The principle that a civil conspiracy plaintiff must claim injury from an act of a tortious character was so widely accepted at the time of RICO's adoption as to be incorporated in the common understanding of "civil conspiracy." ... We presume, therefore, that when Congress established in RICO a civil cause of action for a person "injured ... by reason of" a "conspir[acy]," it meant to adopt these well-established common-law civil conspiracy principles.

> * * *

> We conclude, therefore, that a person may not bring suit under § 1964(c) predicated on a violation of § 1962(d) for injuries caused by an overt act that is not an act of racketeering or otherwise unlawful under the statute.

9. The courts impose a standing requirement on RICO plaintiffs. For example, it has been held that injury to mere expectancy interests is not

---

6. Petitioner suggests that we should look to criminal, rather than civil, common-law principles to interpret the statute. We have turned to the common law of criminal conspiracy to define what constitutes a violation of § 1962(d), see *Salinas v. United States,* 522 U.S. 52, 63–65, 118 S.Ct. 469, 139 L.Ed.2d 352 (1997), a mere violation being all that is necessary for criminal liability. This case, however, does not present simply the question of what constitutes a violation of § 1962(d), but rather the meaning of a civil cause of action for private injury by reason of such a violation. In other words, our task is to interpret §§ 1964(c) and 1962(d) in conjunction, rather than § 1962(d) standing alone. The obvious source in the common law for the combined meaning of these provisions is the law of civil conspiracy.

sufficient to confer standing: Plaintiffs who were purchasers of sports trading cards in search of "chase cards" (rare and valuable collectibles inserted randomly in some packages) claimed that the defendant trading card company was running an illegal gambling operation and filed a RICO treble damage suit. *Price v. Pinnacle Brands*, 138 F.3d 602 (5th Cir.1998).

10. A state or local government is a proper civil RICO plaintiff and can use a civil treble damage suit in aid of enforcement of its tax laws. *Illinois Department of Revenue v. Phillips*, 771 F.2d 312 (7th Cir. 1985).

11. The European Community (on its own behalf and on behalf of member states) and the Republic of Colombia have been civil RICO plaintiffs. They filed a civil RICO suit against various tobacco companies alleging that they directed several schemes to smuggle contraband cigarettes into the plaintiffs' territories and in the process entered into conspiracies to commit mail and wire fraud, money laundering, misrepresentations to customs authorities, and various common law torts. Specifically it was alleged that—

> "the tobacco companies directed and facilitated contraband cigarette smuggling by studying smuggling routes, soliciting smugglers, and supplying them with cigarettes encased in packages that allowed the defendants to monitor and control the smuggling. The smugglers would then forge shipping documents and route the cigarettes so as to avoid paying the customs duties and excise taxes of the countries into which the cigarettes were smuggled. The profits from the smuggling were partially funneled into bonuses and kickbacks for defendants' executives. Facilitating the smuggling trade also enabled the tobacco companies to argue to the public and the EC that the high import taxes maintained by the EC's member states were fostering a black market in cigarettes."

Plaintiffs claimed that as a result they had suffered economic harm in the form of lost tax revenues and law enforcement costs. The district court dismissed the complaints, finding that because plaintiffs' claims were premised on purported violations of their tax laws, the court's consideration of the case violated the revenue rule, that is, it would require the court to interpret and enforce foreign revenue laws. The Second Circuit affirmed. *European Community v. RJR Nabisco, Inc.*, 355 F.3d 123 (2d Cir. 2004), The plaintiffs sought review in the Supreme Court. See *European Community v. RJR Nabisco, Inc.*, 125 S.Ct. 1968 (2005): The petition for certiorari was granted, the judgment was vacated and the case remanded to the Second Circuit "for further consideration in light of *Pasquantino v. United States*" [125 S.Ct. 1766 (2005)] (defendants had been convicted of wire fraud in connection with scheme to evade Canadian liquor importation taxes; Supreme Court held that the prosecution was not barred by the common law revenue rule). See the discussion of *Pasquantino*, supra, p. 212.

12. The United States was the defendant, in a civil RICO suit, at least for a short time, in *Marina Point Development Associates v. United States*, 364 F.Supp.2d 1144 (C.D. Cal. 2005). The lawsuit was brought by a developer, who for 20 years had been trying to build a condominium complex at Big Bear Lake in California. The suit alleged that three U.S. Forest Service employees and a local resident who played a key role in an environmental group opposed to the development had committed mail and wire fraud by distributing a report to various governmental agencies under the guise of it

being an official Forest Service report rather than it being the employee's personal work, as a result of which the plaintiffs allegedly were deprived of the honest services of the employees. The United States became a defendant in the case when it decided to represent the defendant federal employees and substituted for them. The district court first dismissed the case against the government and then against the remaining defendant, the local resident:

> "Plaintiff's core claim of injury is the "deprivation of the intangible right to honest governmental services." The entire Complaint rests on allegations that the Forest Service employees abused their official positions for private gain and that [the local resident defendant] ... went along with this "scheme." ... However, the deprivation of the right to honest governmental services is not a tangible and concrete financial loss, and so is not injury to "business or property" as required by section 1964(c). Plaintiff's claim of financial loss is completely dependent on, and flows from, this intangible injury. Thus ... [plaintiff] lacks statutory standing to bring a civil RICO action.
>
> ....[Plaintiff] also lacks statutory standing under civil RICO because any injury it might have suffered was not the direct result of, or proximately caused by, ... [the local resident's] alleged racketeering activity."

Subsequently, the judge ordered the law firm and two of its attorneys who had filed the RICO civil suit to pay $267,000 in sanctions for filing a "frivolous" lawsuit. See LA Times, August 16, 2005, B4.

13. A state or local government or one of its agencies has been held not to be a proper defendant in a civil RICO treble damage action. *Lancaster Community Hospital v. Antelope Valley Medical Group*, 940 F.2d 397 (9th Cir.1991), although the state or local governmental officials can be sued in their individual capacities, *Pelfresne v. Village of Rosemont*, 22 F.Supp.2d 756 (N.D.Ill.1998).

14. The defense of common law legislative immunity was recognized in a RICO civil suit against a former state legislator who was alleged to have sponsored and obtained the passage of legislation in exchange for bribes. The court's theory was that the acceptance of the bribes caused no injury to the plaintiff, who was only harmed by the passage of the legislation. Since the conduct that caused him injury was legislative, immunity attached and the plaintiff did not state a claim upon which relief could be granted. *Chappell v. Robbins*, 73 F.3d 918 (9th Cir.1996).

15. Can the doctrine of respondeat superior be used generally in civil RICO suits to impose liability on corporations for the acts of their agents? *Compare D & S Auto Parts v. Schwartz*, 838 F.2d 964 (7th Cir.1988) *with Brady v. Dairy Fresh Products Co.*, 974 F.2d 1149 (9th Cir. 1992) *and Davis v. Mutual Life Insurance Co. of New York*, 6 F.3d 367 (6th Cir.1993).

16. RICO provides not only for a civil damage remedy, but also for injunctive relief. Section 1964 (a) gives the district courts authority to prevent and restrain RICO violations but does not specify who is authorized to seek such relief. By way of contrast, subsection (b) authorizes the Attorney General to obtain equitable relief and subsection (c) provides a treble damage remedy for private plaintiffs. Some courts have held that

private plaintiffs cannot obtain injunctive relief under RICO, see, e.g., *Religious Tech. Center v. Wollersheim*, 796 F.2d 1076 (9th Cir.1986) and see *In re Fredeman Litigation*, 843 F.2d 821 (5th Cir.1988), while other courts have reserved judgment on the issue, see, e.g. *Price v. Pinnacle Brands, Inc.*, 138 F.3d 602 (5th Cir.1998). Should private plaintiffs be able to obtain equitable relief under RICO? Does the statute as written authorize such relief? In one of the circuit decisions in the NOW v. Scheidler series of cases, 267 F.3d 687 (7th Cir. 2001), the court ruled that private plaintiffs could obtain injunctive relief:

> Our study of Supreme Court decisions since the 1986 *Wollersheim* opinion convinces us that the approach of the Ninth Circuit (which relied almost exclusively on the legislative history of RICO to reach its result, as opposed to the actual language of the statute) no longer conforms to the Court's present jurisprudence, assuming for the sake of argument that it was a permissible one at the time. We are persuaded instead that the text of the RICO statute, understood in the proper light, itself authorizes private parties to seek injunctive relief.

The issue may eventually be resolved by the Supreme Court, possibly in connection with its impending decision in NOW III, see *supra*, pp. 239 and 245.

Civil equitable suits brought by the Attorney General are treated in the next section.

2. CIVIL RICO ACTIONS BROUGHT BY THE FEDERAL GOVERNMENT

The federal government has used the equitable remedy authority contained in § 1964 (b) in a number of noteworthy cases, mainly against labor unions but also against organized crime families and businesses and individuals allegedly involved in organized crime. The cases have certain common characteristics. Many of them go on for many years. The government frequently requests a monitor to oversee union activities and, on occasion, has obtained far-reaching injunctions and orders for disgorgement. See James B. Jacobs, GOTHAM UNBOUND: HOW NEW YORK CITY WAS LIBERATED FROM THE GRIP OF ORGANIZED CRIME (NYU Press 1999). Some illustrative cases are described below.

1. *United States v. Local 560*, 974 F.2d 315 (3d Cir.1992): The government's efforts were directed to purging this union local of the influence of organized crime. A trusteeship was imposed on the union for more than 10 years. Court orders were obtained enjoining corrupt individuals from participating in the union's affairs. The particular appeal in this case involved the government's efforts to obtain a permanent injunction to prevent a former president of the Union, Sciarra, from participating in the local's affairs. Among the provisions of the injunction were clauses that barred Sciarra from holding any position or performing any service for the union, attending or participating in any membership meeting, function or rally, and from frequenting the union hall except for certain limited purposes. The order of the district court granting the permanent injunction was affirmed.

2. *United States v. Carson*, 52 F.3d 1173 (2d Cir.1995): The district court in this case granted injunctive relief against Carson, the Secretary–Treasurer of a union local, an order to disgorge ill-gotten gains, and an order imposing $46,000 in costs. Carson claimed that the disgorgement was double jeopardy and the injunction was overbroad. The injunction barred Carson permanently from participating in the affairs of any labor union, even barring him from joining a union, and from visiting the site of any labor organization or communicating with any person at the site of any labor organization. Carson had been previously convicted of accepting kickbacks to maintain labor peace which he shared with associates of an organized crime family, and the district court in this case also found that he had embezzled money from the union and interfered with the democratic rights of the union's membership by maintaining a climate of fear. The circuit court affirmed the injunction but vacated the order of disgorgement, remanding to the district court with instructions to determine if the disgorgement ordered was designed "to prevent and restrain" future conduct, which the court indicated was the only legitimate function of such an order under the RICO statute.

3. In the Second Circuit decision in *United States v. Carson, supra* note 2, the court had concluded that while a claim brought by the government under 1964(a) was limited to orders "to prevent and restrain" RICO violations, disgorgement of ill-gotten gains might serve that purpose if there were a finding that "the gains are being used to fund or promote the illegal conduct, or constitute capital available for that purpose." The *Carson* approach was followed in *Richard v. Hoechst Celanese Chem. Group, Inc.*, 355 F.3d 345 (5th Cir. 2003). However, the D.C. Circuit has taken a different view, concluding that disgorgement is not under any circumstances an available remedy under § 1964(a). In *United States v. Philip Morris*, 396 F.3d 1190 (D.C.Cir. 2005), "the Government sought disgorgement of $280 billion that it traced to proceeds from Appellants' cigarette sales to the "youth addicted population" between 1971 and 2001. This population includes all smokers who became addicted before the age of 21, as measured by those who were smoking at least 5 cigarettes a day at that age." Regarding the disgorgement issue, the court stated:

> Section 1964(a) provides jurisdiction to issue a variety of orders "to prevent and restrain" RICO violations. This language indicates that the jurisdiction is limited to forward-looking remedies that are aimed at future violations. ... Divestment, injunctions against persons' future involvement in the activities in which the RICO enterprise had been engaged, and dissolution of the enterprise are all aimed at separating the RICO criminal from the enterprise so that he cannot commit violations *in the future*. Disgorgement, on the other hand, is a quintessentially backward-looking remedy focused on remedying the effects of past conduct to restore the status quo. ... It is measured by the amount of prior unlawful gains and is awarded without respect to whether the defendant will act unlawful-

ly in the future. Thus it is both aimed at and measured by *past conduct*.

... RICO ... provides for a comprehensive set of remedies. When Congress intended to award remedies that addressed past harms as well as those that offered prospective relief, it said as much. In a criminal RICO action the defendant must forfeit his interest in the RICO enterprise and unlawfully acquired proceeds, and may be punished with fines, imprisonment for up to twenty years, or both. 18 U.S.C. 1963(a). In a civil case the Government may request limited equitable relief under 1964(a). Individual plaintiffs are made whole and defendants punished through treble damages under 18 U.S.C. § 1964(c)

* * *

Congress' intent when it drafted RICO's remedies would be circumvented by the Government's broad reading of its 1964(a) remedies. The disgorgement requested here is similar in effect to the relief mandated under the criminal forfeiture provision, § 1963(a), without requiring the inconvenience of meeting the additional procedural safeguards that attend criminal charges, including a five-year statute of limitations, 18 U.S.C. § 3282, notice requirements, 18 U.S.C. § 1963(*l*), and general criminal procedural protections including proof beyond a reasonable doubt. Further, on the Government's view it can collect sums paralleling-perhaps exactly-the damages available to individual victims under 1964(c). Not only would the resulting overlap allow the Government to escape a statute of limitations that would restrict private parties seeking essentially identical remedies, *see Agency Holding Corp. v. Malley–Duff & Assoc., Inc.,* 483 U.S. 143, 156, 107 S.Ct. 2759, 97 L.Ed.2d 121 (1987), but it raises issues of duplicative recovery of exactly the sort that the Supreme Court said in *Holmes v. Securities Investor Protection Corp.,* 503 U.S. 258, 269, 112 S.Ct. 1311, 117 L.Ed.2d 532 (1992), constituted a basis for refusing to infer a cause of action not specified by the statute. Permitting disgorgement under 1964(a) would therefore thwart Congress' intent in creating RICO's elaborate remedial scheme.

Although the judge had not yet awarded damages in the case, the Department of Justice filed a petition for certiorari, seeking review of the above described circuit decision, July 18, 2005 (No. 05–92), arguing that the court of appeals' "erroneous" decision had undermined the "most important civil action that the government has ever brought" under the RICO statute and could have "far reaching implications for RICO cases generally" and would have "enormous consequences for the American public."

The filing of the petition for certiorari was preceded by a month long-furor triggered by the fact that the Department of Justice, at the close of the trial in the case, scaled down the damages it was seeking from $130 billion to $10 billion. Department of Justice officials stated that they had no choice given the circuit court opinion barring disgorgement, while suspicions were voiced in the media by members of the Congress and even by the judge in the case ("Perhaps it suggests that additional influences have been brought to bear on what the government's case is"—NY Times, June 14, 2005, A16) and by others, that the decision to reduce the damage claim so dramatically had been dictated by political considerations, with critics pointing to the tobacco industry contributions to the Bush Administration and its ties to some Justice Department officials. NY Times, July 9, 2005, A16.

The Justice Department defended its actions in a Letter to the Editor in the New York Times, June 17, 2005, A22 from the Department's Director of Public Affairs, contending that the $130 billion smoking cessation program "required modification to meet with the court's new standard . . . ," "that any remedies must be 'forward-looking' " and "must 'prevent and restrain' only future or continuing frauds."

If the Supreme Court does not grant review in the case or if it reviews the case but affirms the circuit decision, and if the case is not settled (newspaper reports suggested that the judge was taking steps to encourage settlement), eventually the judge will have to decide what kind of remedies meet the "forward-looking" standard established by the circuit court. Consider, for example, the following which are among the remedies sought at one point or another by the government.

Requiring the defendants to fund—

1) a 25 year program to help all smokers who want to quit.

2) a five year program to treat all smokers who become addicted in the near future.

3) a public education program on the ills of smoking and secondhand smoke.

Or imposing

4) a system of automatic fines if targets for reducing smoking by young people are not met.

5) a ban on price-cutting promotions of cigarettes.

4. *United States v. Allen*, 155 F.3d 35 (2d Cir.1998): This case began in 1989 when the government filed a RICO civil action against 112 defendants involved in the solid waste carting industry on Long Island. The defendants were alleged organized crime families, a trade association, a labor union, carting firms and their officers and directors and a number of municipal employees who were alleged to have taken bribes. The district court in 1997 had granted the government's motion for summary judgment, ordering disgorgement of all gains from the bribery scheme, enjoining one defendant from engaging in any activities in the waste removal industry, and subjecting other defendants to a monitorship program and ordering them to pay the reasonable cost of the monitorship. 'The circuit court reversed the order granting summary

judgment on the issue of RICO liability, concluding that with respect to various RICO legal issues, there were factual issues in dispute and therefore summary judgment was not appropriate.

5. In July, 2005, the U.S. Attorney for the Eastern District of New York announced the filing of a RICO civil suit against the International Longshoremen's Association, AFL–CIO (ILA), certain top ILA officials, including the ILA's long-time president, various ILA employee health, welfare and pension benefit plans, and three organized crime members, who had previously been convicted of criminal RICO violations. The press release announcing the suit asserted that the charges were based on decades of evidence relating to corruption and organized crime influence within the union and businesses operating on the New York/ New Jersey waterfront and the Port of Miami; that this was the first prosecution brought against the ILA under the RICO statute;, and that the remedies sought in the suit were the imposition of court-ordered trusteeships responsible for reforming and overseeing the union and its benefit plans, and the barring of current union officials and organized crime members from the waterfront and from managing or influencing the operations of the union and its benefit funds.

6. *United States v. Bonanno Organized Crime Family*, 879 F.2d 20 (2d Cir.1989): This case was quite unusual in that the government for the first time brought a legal action against an organized crime family. The government sought treble damages in the suit. The court ruled that the suit failed for two reasons. First the United States was not a "person" authorized to bring suit for treble damages under § 1964 (c). Second, the Bonnano crime family was not a "person" subject to suit under 1964 (c). Should the government be able to use the remedies of injunction against unions but not against an organized crime family? Do you agree that such a family is not a "person" within the meaning of the RICO statute? Should it be?

7. Query, would the establishment of a monitorship or trusteeship, see, supra, notes 1, 4 and 5, be an appropriate remedy in the tobacco industry case, supra, note 3.

F. THE RICO PROSECUTORIAL GUIDELINES

The U.S. Attorneys' Manual guidelines regarding RICO prosecutions are found in ¶¶ 9–110.010 et seq. (Aug. 1999).[a] We summarize and excerpt here pertinent provisions. In reviewing these provisions, consider whether all of the cases that you have examined in this Chapter appear to fall within the guidelines.

The guidelines state that "[n]o RICO criminal indictment or information or civil complaint shall be filed * * * without the prior approval of the Criminal Division." *Id.* at ¶ 9–110.101. They provide that a RICO

---

a. The United States Attorneys Manual is available on Westlaw in the "USAM" database.

charge should be sought only if one or more of the following requirements is present:

1. RICO is necessary to ensure that the indictment adequately reflects the nature and extent of the criminal conduct in a way that prosecution only on the underlying charges would not;

2. A RICO prosecution would provide the basis for an appropriate sentence under all the circumstances of the case in a way that prosecution only on the underlying charges would not;

3. A RICO charge could combine related offenses which would otherwise have to be prosecuted separately in different jurisdictions;

4. RICO is necessary for a successful prosecution of the government's case against the defendant or a co-defendant;

5. Use of RICO would provide a reasonable expectation of forfeiture which is proportionate to the underlying criminal conduct;

6. The case consists of violations of State law, but local law enforcement officials are unlikely or unable to successfully prosecute the case, in which the federal government has a significant interest;

7. The case consists of violations of State law, but involves prosecution of significant political or government individuals, which may pose special problems for the local prosecutor.

Id. at ¶ 9–110.310. The guidelines also indicate that "[s]ignificant organized crime involvement" is another ground for filing a RICO charge where the predicate acts consist only of state offenses. *Id.* at ¶ 9–110.330.

These guidelines make it clear that not every case in which the elements of a RICO violation technically exist will be approved for prosecution. One purpose of the guidelines is to reemphasize that the primary responsibility for enforcing state laws rests with the states. In the case of a RICO case that could be predicated on other federal charges, a RICO charge will not be added unless it serves some special RICO purpose. In general approval will not be granted when RICO is sought only to serve an evidentiary purpose.

In light of the general discretion wielded by the United States Attorneys, why do you think Criminal Division approval is required before RICO charges can be filed? Is this requirement justified? More justified in RICO cases than in other kinds of matters?

Chapter 12

ANTI–TERRORISM ENFORCEMENT

INTRODUCTION

Following the September 11, 2002 attacks on the World Trade Center and the Pentagon and the crash of the third airliner in Pennsylvania, a number of significant steps aimed at increasing the effectiveness of enforcement against terrorist activity were taken by the Congress and the federal government. For example, the USA PATRIOT ("Uniting and Strengthening America by Providing Appropriate Tools Required to Intercept and Obstruct Terrorism") Act was enacted. The Act included provisions dealing with electronic surveillance, broadened authority to obtain records, search warrant and grand jury secrecy, broadened authority to deal with money laundering and to address certain types of immigration matters and facilitating of information sharing between the intelligence and criminal prosecution arms of the federal government. [Note: A number of the PATRIOT Act provisions contained sunset clauses that terminated them unless renewed by December 31, 2005. In July, 2005, both the Senate and the House of Representatives approved bills that extended the life of these provisions, but some of the provisions of the two bills differed. Thus, e.g., the Senate extended for four years the authority to conduct roving wiretaps; the House adopted a 10 year period for the same authority. The differences between the two bills are to be ironed out in the Conference Committee.]

The PATRIOT Act effected only a limited number of changes in the substantive federal criminal law relating to terrorism. Numerous substantive crime provisions, found in Title 18, U.S.C. §§ 2331 et seq., aimed at terrorist activity had been enacted as part of earlier anti-terrorist legislative packages, especially the Antiterrorism and Effective Death Penalty Act (AEDPA), enacted in 1996.

Section A of this Chapter notes the variety of different crimes generally charged in terrorism cases and then focuses on two crimes that in the post 9/11 period have become the federal prosecutor's favorite offenses for prosecuting terrorism-related conduct, 18 U.S.C. § 2339A and § 2339B.

While this volume focuses on federal criminal prosecutions, in the aftermath of 9/11, the possibility has been opened up that persons who engage in terrorist activity might be detained and prosecuted within the military jurisdiction. Accordingly, section B deals with an alternative to prosecuting federal criminal charges in a civilian court, namely, prosecution of individuals in a military tribunal. Without departing from our main federal criminal mission, we believe it useful to present some materials relating to this alternate track. This subject is treated in depth in Norman Abrams, Anti-terrorism and Criminal Enforcement, 2nd Edition (Thomson/West, 2005).

Finally section C addresses the possible uses of the military in a law enforcement mode within the United States and the application of the Posse Comitatus statute.

A. CRIMINAL ENFORCEMENT AGAINST TERRORIST ACTIVITY

1. ILLUSTRATIVE OFFENSES*

Over the course of recent decades, while there had been a number of major terrorism events in, or directly involving the United States, prior to September 11, 2001, there had not been a large number of prosecutions arising out of such events nor a very large body of accumulated criminal case law related to such matters. Among the most well-known of the recent major instances of terrorism prior to September 11, 2001, and some of the prosecutions instituted in their wake were the 1995 Oklahoma City bombing [*See United States v. McVeigh*, 153 F.3d 1166 (10th Cir. 1998)]; the first World Trade Center bombing in 1993 [*see, e.g., United States v. Salameh, et al.*, 261 F.3d 271 (2d Cir. 2001 (2001)) and see the earlier opinion in the same case, 152 F.3d 88 (1998)]; the 1998 bombings of U.S. embassies in Nairobi, Kenya and Dar Es Salaam, Tanzania [*see United States v. Bin Laden et al.*, 92 F.Supp.2d 225 (S.D. N.Y. 2000)],

Post 9/11 some of the more prominent prosecutions of persons directly or indirectly involved in terrorism-related conduct included: the prosecution of Zacarias Moussaoui, in the Eastern District of Virginia, 2001, alleged to have been intended to be the so-called 20th terrorist in the 9/11 bombing of the World Trade Center, and the prosecutions of Richard Reid, the so-called shoe bomber; John Walker Lindh, the so-called American Taliban; the so-called Lackawanna six in upstate New York; and James Earnest Ujaama in the state of Washington. All of these cases . . . ended in pleas of guilty. . . .

Both terrorism crimes as well as more traditional federal crimes are often charged in such cases. They also illustrate a recurring phenomenon in federal criminal prosecutions—the charging in a single case of a

*This introduction is excerpted from NORMAN ABRAMS, ANTI-TERRORISM AND CRIMINAL ENFORCEMENT, 2ND EDITION, 120–121 (Thomson/West 2005).

multiplicity of different offenses, made possible by the overlapping nature of many crimes in the federal criminal code.

McVeigh, for example, was convicted of charges involving use of a weapon of mass destruction, 18 U.S.C. § 2332a, destruction by explosives, 18 U.S.C. § 844, and homicide offenses, 18 U.S.C. § 1111 and 1114. The convictions in the *Salameh* case similarly were based in 18 U.S.C. § 844 as well as using explosives to bomb automobiles used in interstate commerce, with reckless disregard for human life, 18 U.S.C. § 33, assaulting federal officers, § 111, using a destructive device in a crime of violence, 18 U.S.C. § 924, and traveling in interstate commerce with intent to commit certain crimes, 18 U.S.C. § 1952. In the Bin Laden prosecution, the charged offenses involved conspiring to kill U.S. nationals under 18 U.S.C. § 2332 and destruction of national defense facilities, 18 U.S.C. § 2155 as well as offenses that had been used in the earlier cases, namely, Title 18, U.S.C.§§ 844, 2332a and 1111, 1114.

Moussaoui was charged with conspiring to commit acts of terrorism transcending national boundaries, 18 U.S.C. § 2332b, to commit air piracy, 49 U.S.C. § 46502, to destroy aircraft, 18 U.S.C. 32, to use weapons of mass destruction, 18 U.S.C. § 2332a, to murder U.S. employees, 18 U.S.C. § 1114 and 1117, and to destroy property, 18 U.S.C. § 844.

2. 18 U.S.C. §§ 2339A AND 2339B

18 U.S.C. § 2339A makes it a federal crime to knowingly provide material support or resources in aid of specified federal crimes. § 2339B makes it a federal crime to knowingly provide material support or resources to a foreign terrorist organization. 2339B incorporates by reference the definition of material support or resources that is found in 18 U.S.C. § 2339A. 2339B provides that the designation of an organization as a "foreign terrorist organization" (i.e. one of elements of the 2339B offense) is made under the provisions of 8 U.S.C. § 1189.

Both of these sections, but especially 2339B, have been used as the basis for criminal charges in a wide range of different kinds of factual contexts. For example, 2339B has been used in the prosecution of an individual who volunteered to fight in a foreign army and ended up fighting against U.S. forces in Afghanistan, the Walker Lindh case, *United States v. Lindh, 212 F.Supp. 2d 541 (E.D. Va. 2002)*. It has also been to prosecute individuals who traveled to Afghanistan to participate in an alleged terrorist group training camp. See *United States v. Goba, 220 F.Supp.2d 182 (W.D.N.Y. 2002)* (the Lackawanna six case) and against an individual who allegedly was trying to set up a terrorist training facility in the state of Washington (the prosecution of Earnest James Ujaama). It has been used to prosecute individuals who allegedly transferred funds to a designated foreign terrorist organization (see *United States v. Afshari, 392 F.3d 1031 (9th Cir. 2004)*. And it has been used as the basis for charges against an attorney representing a federal prisoner charged with terrorism offenses where the government alleges that the attorney facilitated the passing of information to the prisoner's confederates. See *United States v. Sattar, infra.*

What makes these sections usable in prosecuting so many different kinds of conduct? A case that illustrates the ubiquitous quality and breadth of application of these statutes is *United States v. Sattar,* reproduced infra. The language of 2339A and § 2339B that was on the books at the time the *Sattar* case was decided is reproduced immediately below. Post-*Sattar*, the Intelligence Reform and Terrorism Prevention Act of 2004 (IRTPA) amended both statutory provisions. The new IRTPA language is reproduced in the Notes following the *Sattar* opinion, *infra,* p. 592.

§ 2339A. *Providing material support to terrorists*

(a) Offense.—Whoever provides material support or resources or conceals or disguises the nature, location, source, or ownership of material support or resources, knowing or intending that they are to be used in preparation for, or in carrying out, a violation of section 32, 37, 81, 175, 229, 351, 831, 842(m) or (n), 844(f) or (i), 930(c), 956, 1114, 1116, 1203, 1361, 1362, 1363, 1366, 1751, 1992, 1993, 2155, 2156, 2280, 2281, 2332, 2332a, 2332b, 2332c, or 2340A of this title, section 236 of the Atomic Energy Act of 1954 (*42 U.S.C. 2284*), or section 46502 or 60123(b) of title 49, or in preparation for, or in carrying out, the concealment or an escape from the commission of any such violation, or attempts or conspires to do such an act, shall be fined under this title, imprisoned not more than 15 years, or both, and, if the death of any person results, shall be imprisoned for any term of years or for life. A violation of this section may be prosecuted in any Federal judicial district in which the underlying offense was committed, or in any other Federal judicial district as provided by law.

(b) Definition.—In this section, the term "material support or resources" means currency or monetary instruments or financial securities, financial services, lodging, training, expert advice or assistance, safehouses, false documentation or identification, communications equipment, facilities, weapons, lethal substances, explosives, personnel, transportation, and other physical assets, except medicine or religious materials.

§ 2339B. *Providing material support or resources to designated foreign terrorist organizations*

(a) Prohibited activities.—

(1) Unlawful conduct.—Whoever, within the United States or subject to the jurisdiction of the United States, knowingly provides material support or resources to a foreign terrorist organization, or attempts or conspires to do so, shall be fined under this title or imprisoned not more than 15 years, or both, and, if the death of any person results, shall be imprisoned for any term of years or for life.

. . .

(g) Definitions.—As used in this section—

. . .

(4) the term "material support or resources" has the same meaning as in section 2339A;

((6) the term terrorist organization means an organization designated as a terrorist organization under section 219 of the Immigration and Nationality Act.

UNITED STATES v. SATTAR

314 F.Supp.2d 279 (S.D. N.Y. 2004).

KOELTL, DISTRICT JUDGE.

The defendants—Ahmed Abdel Sattar ("Sattar"), Lynne Stewart ("Stewart"), and Mohammed Yousry ("Yousry")—were charged in a seven-count superseding indictment ("S1 Indictment") filed on November 19, 2003. * * *

The S1 Indictment supersedes a five-count indictment filed on April 8, 2002 ("original indictment"). Count One of the original indictment charged Sattar, Stewart, Yousry, and Yassir Al–Sirri, a defendant not charged in the S1 Indictment, with conspiring to provide material support and resources to a foreign terrorist organization ("FTO") in violation of 18 U.S.C. § 2339B. Count Two charged the same defendants with providing and attempting to provide material support and resources to an FTO in violation of 18 U.S.C. §§ 2339B and 2. * * *

Sattar, Stewart, and Yousry moved to dismiss the original indictment on various grounds. The defendants argued, among other things, that Counts One and Two were unconstitutionally vague as applied to the conduct alleged against them in the original indictment. Counts One and Two charged the defendants with conspiring to provide, and providing, material support and resources to the Islamic Group, an organization led by Sheikh Abdel Rahman that had been designated an FTO by the Secretary of State. Section 2339B of Title 18 incorporates the definition of "material support or resources" from § 2339A, and the definition includes, among other things, "personnel" and "communications equipment." In an Opinion and Order dated July 22, 2003, the Court granted the defendants' motion to dismiss Counts One and Two of the original indictment as void for vagueness as applied to the allegations in the original indictment, where the defendants were alleged in part to have "provided" material support by providing themselves as "personnel" and to have provided "communications equipment" by using their own telephones.

The Government filed the S1 Indictment on November 19, 2003. Sattar and Stewart now move to dismiss the S1 Indictment on numerous grounds. They also move for a bill of particulars and various other relief.

The S1 Indictment alleges the following facts. From at least the early 1990's until in or about April 2002, Omar Ahmad Ali Abdel Rahman, a/k/a "the Sheikh," a/k/a "Sheikh Omar" ("Sheikh Abdel

Rahman''), an unindicted alleged co-conspirator in Counts One and Two, was an influential and high-ranking member of terrorist organizations based in Egypt and elsewhere. * * *

Sheikh Abdel Rahman allegedly supported and advocated jihad to, among other things: (1) overthrow the Egyptian government and replace it with an Islamic state; (2) destroy the nation of Israel and give the land to the Palestinians; and (3) oppose those governments, nations, institutions, and individuals, including the United States and its citizens, whom he perceived as enemies of Islam and supporters of Egypt and Israel.

Sheikh Abdel Rahman allegedly endorsed terrorism to accomplish his goals. * * *

* * * In October 1995, Sheikh Abdel Rahman was convicted of engaging in a seditious conspiracy to wage a war of urban terrorism against the United States, including the 1993 World Trade Center bombing and a plot to bomb other New York City landmarks. He was also found guilty of soliciting crimes of violence against the United States military and Egyptian president Hosni Mubarak. In 1996 Sheikh Abdel Rahman was sentenced to life imprisonment. His conviction was affirmed on appeal, and became final on January 10, 2000 when the United States Supreme Court refused to hear his case.

The S1 Indictment alleges that both prior to and after his arrest and imprisonment, Sheikh Abdel Rahman was a spiritual leader of an international terrorist group based in Egypt and known as the Islamic Group, a/k/a "Gama'a al-Islamiyya," a/k/a "IG," * * *

Since in or about 1997, Sheikh Abdel Rahman has been incarcerated in various facilities operated by the United States Bureau of Prisons, including the Federal Medical Center in Rochester, Minnesota. The S1 Indictment alleges that, following his arrest, Sheikh Abdel Rahman urged his followers to wage jihad to obtain his release from custody. * * *

The S1 Indictment charges that, after Sheikh Abdel Rahman's arrest, a coalition of alleged terrorists, supporters, and followers, including leaders and associates of the Islamic Group, al Qaeda, the Egyptian Islamic Jihad, and the Abu Sayyaf terrorist group in the Philippines threatened and committed acts of terrorism directed at obtaining the release of Sheikh Abdel Rahman from prison. The Islamic Group allegedly released, in response to the sentence of life imprisonment imposed on Sheikh Abdel Rahman, a statement that warned:

> "All American interests will be legitimate targets for our struggle until the release of Sheikh Omar Abdel Rahman and his brothers. As the American Government has opted for open confrontation with the Islamic movement and the Islamic symbols of struggle, [the Islamic Group] swears by God to its irreversible vow to take an eye for any eye." * * *

On or about November 17, 1997, six assassins shot and stabbed a group of tourists visiting an archaeological site in Luxor, Egypt, killing fifty-eight foreign tourists and four Egyptians. The S1 Indictment charges that, before making their exit, the assassins scattered leaflets espousing their support for the Islamic Group and calling for release of Sheikh Abdel Rahman, and inserted one of the leaflets into one victim's slit torso.

* * *

The S1 Indictment charges that at various times starting in or about July 1997, certain Islamic Group leaders and factions called for an "initiative," or cease-fire, in which the Islamic Group would suspend terrorist operations in Egypt in a tactical effort to persuade the Egyptian government to release Islamic Group leaders, members, and associates who were in prison in Egypt. The S1 Indictment further charges that, in or about February 1998, Usama Bin Laden and Taha, among others, issued a fatwah, a legal ruling issued by an Islamic scholar, that stated, among other things, "We in the name of God, call on every Muslim who believes in God and desires to be rewarded, to follow God's order and kill Americans and plunder their wealth wherever and whenever they find it." * * *

The S1 Indictment alleges that, beginning in or about April 1997, United States authorities, in order to protect the national security, limited certain of Sheikh Abdel Rahman's privileges in prison, including his access to the mail, the media, the telephone, and visitors. At that time, the Bureau of Prisons, at the direction of the Attorney General, imposed Special Administrative Measures ("SAMs") upon Sheikh Abdel Rahman. The alleged purpose of the SAMs was to protect "persons against the risk of death or serious bodily injury" that could result if Sheikh Abdel Rahman were free "to communicate (send or receive) terrorist information." Under the SAMs, Sheikh Abdel Rahman was permitted to call and receive visits only from his immediate family members or his attorneys and their translator. SAMs prohibited communication with any member or representative of the news media, and they required all of Sheikh Abdel Rahman's mail to be screened by federal authorities. The SAMs specifically provided that Sheikh Abdel Rahman's attorneys, before being allowed access to Sheikh Abdel Rahman, were obliged to sign an affirmation acknowledging that that they and their staff would abide fully by the SAMs. The attorneys agreed in the affirmations, among other things, to "only be accompanied by translators for the purpose of communicating with inmate Abdel Rahman concerning legal matters." Since at least in or about May 1998, the attorneys also agreed not to use "meetings, correspondence, or phone calls with Abdel Rahman to pass messages between third parties (including, but not limited to, the media) and Abdel Rahman."

Stewart was one of Sheikh Abdel Rahman's attorneys during his 1995 criminal trial and continued to act as one of his attorneys following his conviction. Yousry testified as a defense witness at Sheikh Abdel Rahman's 1995 criminal trial and, starting in or about 1997, acted as an Arabic interpreter for communications between Sheikh Abdel Rahman and his attorneys. The S1 Indictment charges that Sattar is a longtime associate of and surrogate for Sheikh Abdel Rahman. The S1 Indictment alleges that, following Sheikh Abdel Rahman's arrest, conviction, sentence, and the imposition of the SAMs, Sattar coordinated efforts to keep Sheikh Abdel Rahman in contact with his co-conspirators and followers. It also alleges that Stewart, through her continued access to Sheikh Abdel Rahman, enabled him to remain in contact with his co-conspirators and followers. And it alleges that Yousry, through his continued access to Sheikh Abdel Rahman and facilitated by Stewart, enabled Sheikh Abdel Rahman to remain in contact with his co-conspirators and followers.

Count One of the S1 Indictment alleges that, from in or about June 1997 through in or about April 2002, defendants Sattar, Stewart, and Yousry, as well as Sheikh Abdel Rahman and Taha, together with others known and unknown, in violation of 18 U.S.C. § 371, conspired to defraud the United States by obstructing the Department of Justice and the Bureau of Prisons in the administration and enforcement of the SAMs imposed on Sheikh Abdel Rahman. The S1 Indictment alleges a series of overt acts committed in furtherance of the alleged conspiracy. * * *

On or about May 16, 2000, Stewart signed an affirmation in which she agreed to abide by the terms of the SAMs then in effect on Sheikh Abdel Rahman. The S1 Indictment alleges that during a May 2000 prison visit to Sheikh Abdel Rahman by Stewart and Yousry, Yousry told Sheikh Abdel Rahman and Stewart about the kidnappings by the Abu Sayyaf terrorist group in the Philippines and the group's demand to free Sheikh Abdel Rahman. Stewart allegedly responded, "Good for them." During the same prison visit, Yousry allegedly read Sheikh Abdel Rahman an inflammatory statement by Taha that had recently been published in an Egyptian newspaper. Yousry also allegedly read to Sheikh Abdel Rahman, at Stewart's urging, a letter from Sattar. Sattar's letter allegedly sought Sheikh Abdel Rahman's comments on Sattar's communications with certain Islamic Group leaders, and it also allegedly sought Sheikh Abdel Rahman's endorsement of "the formation of a team that calls for cancellation of the peace initiative or makes threats or escalates things."

The S1 Indictment alleges that while Yousry read Taha's statement and Sattar's letter to Sheikh Abdel Rahman, Stewart actively concealed that fact from the prison guards, in part by instructing Yousry to make it look as if Stewart were communicating with Sheikh Abdel Rahman and Yousry were merely translating, by having Yousry look periodically at Stewart and Sheikh Abdel Rahman in turn, and by pretending to be participating in the conversation with Sheikh Abdel Rahman by making extraneous comments like "chocolate" and "heart attack." Stewart allegedly observed to Yousry that she could "get an award for" her acts, and Yousry allegedly agreed that Stewart should "get an award in acting." * * *

* * * The S1 Indictment also alleges that on or about June 14, 2000, Stewart released a statement to the press that quoted Sheikh Abdel Rahman as stating that he "is withdrawing his support for the cease-fire that currently exists."

* * *

On or about May 7, 2001, Stewart signed an affirmation in which she agreed to abide by the terms of the SAMs then in effect on Sheikh Abdel Rahman. The S1 Indictment charges that, on or about July 13, 2001, during a prison visit to Sheikh Abdel Rahman by Stewart and Yousry, Yousry told Sheikh Abdel Rahman that Sattar had been informed that the U.S.S. Cole had been bombed on Sheikh Abdel Rahman's behalf and that Sattar was asked to convey to the United States government that more terrorist acts would follow if the United States government did not release Sheikh Abdel Rahman from custody. While Yousry was speaking to Sheikh Abdel Rahman, Stewart allegedly actively concealed the conversation between Sheikh Abdel Rahman and Yousry from prison guards by, among other things, shaking a water jar and tapping on the table while stating that she was "just doing covering noise." The S1 Indictment further charges that on a second day of the prison visit by Stewart and Yousry, Yousry read letters to Sheikh Abdel Rahman and Sheikh Abdel Rahman dictated responsive letters to Yousry.

The S1 Indictment also alleges that on or about January 8, 2001, Sattar informed Stewart by telephone that a prison administrator where Sheikh Abdel Rahman was incarcerated had pleaded with Sheikh Abdel Rahman's wife to tell Sheikh Abdel Rahman to take insulin for his diabetes. Sattar and Stewart allegedly agreed that Sattar would issue a public statement falsely claiming that the Bureau of Prisons was denying medical treatment to Sheikh Abdel Rahman, even though Sattar and Stewart allegedly knew that Sheikh Abdel Rahman was voluntarily refusing to take insulin for his diabetes. Stewart allegedly expressed the opinion that this misrepresentation was "safe" because no one on the "outside" would know the truth. The S1 Indictment further alleges that Sattar and Al–Sirri thereafter wrote a statement falsely claiming that Sheikh Abdel Rahman was being denied insulin by the United States Government, a statement that Sattar and Al–Sirri disseminated to several news organizations, including Reuters, and on a website.

* * *

Count Four charges that, from in or about September 1999 through in or about April 2002, defendants Stewart and Yousry, together with others, conspired, in violation of 18 U.S.C. § 371, to violate 18 U.S.C. § 2339A. The alleged object of the conspiracy was to provide material support and resources, in the form of personnel, by making Sheikh Abdel Rahman available as a co-conspirator, and to conceal and disguise the nature, location, and source of personnel by concealing and disguising that Sheikh Abdel Rahman was a co-conspirator. The S1 Indictment charges that Stewart and Yousry carried out this conspiracy knowing and intending that such material support and resources were to be used in preparation for, and in carrying out, the conspiracy charged in Count Two of the S1 Indictment—namely, the conspiracy to kill and kidnap persons in a foreign country—and in preparation for, and in carrying out, the concealment of such violation. Count Four realleges various overt acts in furtherance of the alleged conspiracy. Count Five charges defendants Stewart and Yousry with committing the substantive offense of violating 18 U.S.C. § § 2339A and 2 that was the object of the conspiracy charged in Count Four.

Counts Six and Seven charge defendant Stewart with having made false statements in her affirmations submitted to the United States Attorney's Office for the Southern District of New York, in May 2000 and May 2001, respectively, stating that she would abide by the terms of the SAMs imposed on Sheikh Abdel Rahman, that the translators accompanying her on prison visits would be used only for communications concerning legal matters, and that she would not use any communication with Sheikh Abdel Rahman to pass messages between Sheikh Abdel Rahman and third parties, including, but not limited to, the media. The May 2001 affirmation is also alleged to be false in stating that Stewart "will only allow the meetings to be used for legal discussion between Abdel Rahman and [her]."

* * *

Stewart moves to dismiss Counts Four and Five on a number of grounds. Counts Four and Five charge Stewart and Yousry with conspiring to violate, and violating, 18 U.S.C. § 2339A.

* * *

Counts Four and Five charge that Stewart and Yousry conspired to provide, and did in fact provide, material support knowing or intending that it would be used in preparation for, or in carrying out, the conspiracy charged in Count Two—the conspiracy to kill and kidnap persons in a foreign country in violation of 18 U.S.C. § 956—by making Sheikh Abdel Rahman available as a co-conspirator in the Count Two conspiracy. The Counts also charge that Stewart and Yousry conspired to, and did in fact, conceal and disguise the nature, location, and source of Sheikh Abdel Rahman as personnel preparing for, or carrying out, the conspiracy charged in Count Two. The S1 Indictment alleges, among other things, that Stewart and Yousry used prison visits with Sheikh Abdel Rahman to pass messages between Sheikh Abdel Rahman and his alleged Count Two co-conspirators, including Sattar. It also alleges that Stewart and Yousry took steps to conceal their efforts to pass messages between Sheikh Abdel Rahman and the alleged Count Two co-conspirators.

The charges in Counts Four and Five of the S1 Indictment differ from those in Counts One and Two in the original indictment that the Court previously dismissed. While the factual allegations are similar, the critical statute is different, the elements of the offense, including scienter, are different, and the allegations as to how the defendants' conduct violated the statute are different.

Counts One and Two of the original indictment charged that Sattar, Stewart, and Yousry conspired to violate 18 U.S.C. § 2339B and committed a substantive violation of that statute by, among other means, providing themselves as "personnel" to a designated FTO and by providing "communications equipment" to an FTO by using their own telephones to further the goals of an FTO. Title 18 U.S.C. § 2339B, which was enacted about a year and a half after 18 U.S.C. § 2339A was enacted, makes it a crime to, in relevant part, "knowingly provide[ ] material support or resources to a foreign terrorist organization." Section 2339B incorporates the definition of "material support or resources" from 18 U.S.C. § 2339A, and that definition includes, among other things, "personnel" and "communications equipment." Title 18 U.S.C. § 2339A, at issue in the S1 Indictment, and which Stewart and Yousry are alleged to have violated, does not penalize the provision of material support or resources to an FTO, but rather makes it a crime to provide material support or resources or conceal or disguise the nature, location, or source of such material support or resources "knowing or intending that they are to be used in preparation for, or in carrying out, a violation" of specific violent crimes—in this case, a violation of 18 U.S.C. § 956, which prohibits a conspiracy to kill or kidnap persons in a foreign country. In the opinion dismissing Counts One and Two of the original indictment, the Court contrasted the intent requirements of the two statutes: "Section 2339B, which is alleged to have been violated [in the original indictment], requires only that a person 'knowingly' 'provides' 'material support or resources' to a 'foreign terrorist organization.' Section 2339A criminalizes the provision of 'material support or resources' 'knowing or intending that they are to be used in preparation for, or in carrying out,' a violation of various criminal statutes."

The Court dismissed Counts One and Two of the original indictment as unconstitutionally vague as applied to the conduct alleged in those counts. Concerning the "provision" of "communications equipment," the Court held that "by criminalizing the mere use of phones and other means of communication the statute provides neither notice nor standards for its application such that it is unconstitutionally vague as applied." The Court further concluded that by prohibiting the "provision" of "personnel," including oneself, to a "foreign terrorist organization," § 2339B could conceivably apply to someone engaging in advocacy on behalf of such an organization, conduct protected by the First Amendment. The Court noted that mere membership in an organization could not be prohibited without a requirement that the Government prove the defendants' specific intent to further the FTO's unlawful ends, ... but the statute provided no means to distinguish providing oneself to an organization from mere membership in the organization.

The S1 Indictment, on the other hand, which charges a violation of 18 U.S.C. § 2339A rather than § 2339B, no longer charges Stewart and

Yousry with providing themselves as personnel to an FTO, but rather with providing and conspiring to provide personnel—by making Sheikh Abdel Rahman, not themselves, available as a co-conspirator—to the conspiracy alleged in Count Two, namely the conspiracy to kill and kidnap persons in a foreign country. It also charges them with concealing and disguising the nature, location, and source of that personnel by disguising that Sheikh Abdel Rahman was a co-conspirator. These actions were allegedly done with the knowledge and intent that such personnel was to be used in preparation for, or in carrying out, the conspiracy to kill and kidnap persons in a foreign country. This is the heightened specific intent required by § 2339A.

Stewart argues that, despite the changes from the original indictment, the charges in Counts Four and Five of the S1 Indictment should be dismissed because 18 U.S.C. § 2339A should not be interpreted to reach the conduct alleged in Counts Four and Five, because § 2339A is unconstitutionally vague as applied to the allegations in the S1 Indictment, and because the statute is unconstitutionally overbroad.

Stewart argues initially that 18 U.S.C. § 2339A does not cover the conduct in which she allegedly engaged. The S1 Indictment charges that Stewart and Yousry "provided" "personnel" by "making Abdel Rahman available" as a co-conspirator in the conspiracy to kill and kidnap persons in a foreign country. Stewart alleges that "provides" should not be interpreted to include "makes available" and that "personnel" should not include Sheikh Abdel Rahman. Stewart contends that the term "making available" does not define the term "provides," but rather represents an impermissible attempt by the Government to expand the statute's reach. Stewart would limit the word "provides" to the physical transfer of an item.

The term "provides" is not defined in § 2339A. Where words in a statute are not defined, they "must be given their ordinary meaning." ... The plain and ordinary meaning of the transitive verb "provide" is "[t]o furnish; supply ... [t]o make ready ... [t]o make available; afford." *Webster's II: New Riverside University Dictionary* 948 (1994); ...

Moreover, statutory terms are to be interpreted in their context in light of their "placement and purpose in the statutory scheme. In this case, "provides" is the verb used for a variety of items defined as "material support or resources," including "financial services, lodging, training, ... [and] transportation...." 18 U.S.C. § 2339A(b). A defendant would reasonably be providing material support or resources by making these items or services available with the requisite knowledge or intent. Limiting the definition of "provides" to the physical transfer of an asset would result in a strained and untenable reading of the statute. * * *

Stewart also raises questions whether the meaning of "personnel" in the statute can be interpreted to include Sheikh Abdel Rahman. However, the Government is correct that, in using the term "personnel" in § 2339A, Congress plainly intended to refer to persons engaged in "prepar[ing] for" or "carry[ing] out" one of the crimes specified in § 2339A, or in "prepar[ing] for" or "carry[ing] out[ ] the concealment or an escape from the commission of any such" crime—that is, persons who are jointly involved in participating in those crimes. * * *

Stewart also argues that § 2339A is unconstitutionally vague in its proscription of "provid[ing]" material support or resources in the form of "personnel," and in its proscription of "conceal[ing] or disguis[ing] the nature, location, [or] source" of "personnel." Stewart contends that § 2339A does not provide fair notice of the acts that are prohibited by its proscription of providing personnel

* * *

In light of the plain meaning of the term "personnel" as used in the context of § 2339A, Stewart's reliance on cases, including this Court's prior opinion, that have found the term "personnel" in 18 U.S.C. § 2339B unconstitutionally vague is misplaced. Section 2339B makes it a crime to "provide[ ] material support or resources to a foreign terrorist organization" that has been designated as such by the Secretary of State. 18 U.S.C. § 2339B(a)(1), (g)(6). The statute's potential reach raises significant First Amendment concerns, because § 2339B's ban on providing personnel to a "foreign terrorist organization" could trench upon associational and expressive freedoms—including pure advocacy— protected by the First Amendment. The statute, as this Court explained, was particularly problematic as applied to the conduct of persons alleged-ly providing themselves as personnel to the organization. ... The Court of Appeals for the Ninth Circuit has held that these concerns are not displaced even when 18 U.S.C.§ 2339B is construed to include a require-ment that the accused knew of the organization's designation as an FTO or of the organization's unlawful activities that caused it to be so designated. *See Humanitarian Law Project v. U.S. Dept. of Justice,* 352 F.3d 382, 404–05 (9th Cir.2003).

The First Amendment concerns raised by the use of "personnel" in § 2339B, as applied to persons who provided themselves as "personnel" to an organization, are simply not present in this case. Section 2339A is being applied to persons who allegedly provided other personnel "know-ing and intending that [it is] to be used in preparation for, or in carrying out" a violation of specific statutes, in this case a conspiracy to kill or kidnap persons in a foreign country. The allegations in this case do not concern the scope of membership in an organization or the permissible extent of advocacy.

* * *

Stewart contends that the statute is unconstitutionally vague be-cause a conscientious lawyer representing her client could not avoid "making her client 'available' through ... services that a lawyer regular-ly and lawfully performs." Lawyers, including defense lawyers, are not immune from criminal liability arising out of offenses committed while representing clients, and indeed defense counsel conceded at argument that lawyers have no license to violate generally applicable criminal laws.

* * *

In this case, Stewart has not demonstrated that § 2339A, on its face or in actual fact, prohibits any constitutionally protected expression, much less that any possible overbreadth is "substantial" when judged in relation to the statute's plainly legitimate sweep. The motion to dismiss on overbreadth grounds is therefore denied.

Notes

1. On February 10, 2005, the jury in the above case found Lynne Stewart guilty of defrauding the government, conspiracy and providing material support for terrorist crimes. She is scheduled to be sentenced in February, 2006.

2. What advantages, if any, did the government gain by changing the offense charged from 2339B to 2339A?

3. Why do you think the government changed its theory of the nature of the "material support" that was "provided"? What was the exact nature of the change?

4. Does criminal liability under the material support/terrorism provisions sweep too broadly? § 2339B criminalizes the providing of various kinds of assistance to a criminal organization. Does that permit imposing serious criminal penalties when the aider is quite remote from the feared conduct? How does it compare with liability for conspiracy? § 2339A criminalizes providing material support to named offenses and defines specific categories of aid that are prohibited? How does it differ, if at all, from liability for complicity? Is the government interpreting too broadly the specific categories of material support defined in the statute? Are there reasons why the terms defining the specific categories of material support should not be construed more broadly than the normal meanings of the terms? See Norman Abrams, *The Material Support Terrorism Offenses*: *Perspectives Derived from the (Early) Model Penal Code,* 1 J.Nat.Sec.L. & Pol'y 5 (2005).

5. The Intelligence Reform and Terrorism Prevention Act of 2004, enacted into law on December 17, 2004 amended the definition of "material support" in § 2339A and made certain changes in 2339B as set forth below:

(b) Definitions.—Section 2339A(b) of title 18, United States Code, is amended to read as follows:

"(b) Definitions.—As used in this section—

"(1) the term 'material support or resources' means any property, tangible or intangible, or service, including currency or monetary instruments or financial securities, financial services, lodging, training, expert advice or assistance, safehouses, false documentation or identification, communications equipment, facilities, weapons, lethal substances, explosives, personnel (1 or more individuals who may be or include oneself), and transportation, except medicine or religious materials;

"(2) the term 'training' means instruction or teaching designed to impart a specific skill, as opposed to general knowledge; and

"(3) the term 'expert advice or assistance' means advice or assistance derived from scientific, technical or other specialized knowledge."

(c) Terrorist Organizations.—Section 2339B(a)(1) of title 18, United States Code, is amended—

* * *

(2) by adding at the end the following: "To violate this paragraph, a person must have knowledge that the organization is a designated terrorist organization (as defined in subsection (g)(6)), that the organization has engaged or engages in terrorist activity (as defined in section 212(a)(3)(B) of the Immigration and Nationality Act), or that the organization has engaged or engages in terrorism (as defined in section 140(d)(2) of the Foreign Relations Authorization Act, Fiscal Years 1988 and 1989))."

(e) * * *

(4) the term 'material support or resources' has the same meaning given that term in section 2339A (including the definitions of 'training' and 'expert advice or assistance' in that section).

(f) ... Section 2339B of title 18, United States Code, is amended by adding at the end the following:

(h) Provision of Personnel.—No person may be prosecuted under this section in connection with the term 'personnel' unless that person has knowingly provided, attempted to provide, or conspired to provide a foreign terrorist organization with 1 or more individuals (who may be or include himself) to work under that terrorist organization's direction or control or to organize, manage, supervise, or otherwise direct the operation of that organization. Individuals who act entirely independently of the foreign terrorist organization to advance its goals or objectives shall not be considered to be working under the foreign terrorist organization's direction and control.

(i) Rule of Construction.—Nothing in this section shall be construed or applied so as to abridge the exercise of rights guaranteed under the First Amendment to the Constitution of the United States.

6. What changes were effected by the amendment of the definition of "material support" in § 2339A(b) set forth in note 5 supra. Consult Abrams, op.cit.supra, note 4 at 32.

7. The addition of new mens rea language in § 2339B(a)(1) as set forth in note 5 supra, adopts the mens rea approach reflected in the opinion in Humanitarian Law Project v. U.S. Department of Justice, 352 F.3d 382 (9th Cir. 2003)(vacated by 382 F.3d 1154).

8. What is the purpose of subsection (h) which has been added to § 2339B, as set forth in note 5, supra?

9. The IRTPA statute also added a new section that made it a crime to receive military-type training from a foreign terrorist organization, 18 U.S.C.§ 2339D. Instances where individuals had gone abroad to receive such training had previously been prosecuted under § 2339B. Does the enactment of § 2339D mean that such cases no longer can be (should be?) prosecuted under § 2339B?

10. Another case that involves material support/terrorism charges as well as charges of conspiracy to murder people, Travel Act violations, RICO, immigration law violations, obstruction of justice and perjury is the prosecution of Sami Al–Arian, a former computer science professor at the University of South Florida. It is alleged that a think tank and charity established by Al Arian were used as fronts for fundraising for the Palestinian Islamic Jihad which perpetrated terrorist attacks in Israel, and that Al–Arian was involved with such attacks. See *United States v. Al–Arian,* 308 F.Supp.2d 1322 (M.D. Fla. 2004). Al-Arian was acquitted on some of the charges, and the jury disagreed on the remainder in December, 2005.

11. As mentioned earlier, the designation of an organization as a foreign terrorist organization for purposes of § 2339B is handled under another statute, 8 U.S.C. § 1189. Legal issues relating to the designation procedure have been addressed in a number of cases. See, e.g., *National Council of Resistance v. Department of State,* 251 F.3d 192 (D.C. Cir. 2001); *People's Mojahedin Organization v. Department of State,* 327 F.3d 1238 (D.C. Cir. 2003); *National Council of Resistance v. Department of State,* 373 F.3d 152 (D.C.Cir.2004). Section 1189(a)(8) provides that such a designation cannot be challenged by a defendant in a criminal prosecution. The legality of precluding such a challenge in a prosecution under § 2339B is addressed in *United States v. Afshari,* 392 F.3d 1031 (9th Cir. 2004).

B. A MILITARY ALTERNATIVE TO TRADITIONAL FEDERAL CRIMINAL ENFORCEMENT

In the wake of the events of September 11, 2001, the President issued a Military Order that provided for the detention and trial before military commissions of persons who are not U.S. citizens and are members of the organization known as al Qaida*, or who engage in acts of international terrorism that cause adverse effects on the United States or its citizens or knowingly harbor individuals who are members of al Qaida or who engage in international terrorism. Authority for the issuance of the Order was expressly based in the President's authority as Commander-in-Chief of the Armed Forces; the Joint Resolution passed by the Congress after 9/11; and §§ 821 and 836 of Title 10, United States Code.

The Order noted that members of al Qaida had carried out attacks against U.S. personnel and facilities abroad and in the United States "on

---

* This was the spelling used in the President's Military Order. Subsequently, the spelling al Qaeda was used, which except in this instance, is the spelling used in these materials.

a scale that has created a state of armed conflict that requires the use of the United States Armed Forces" ... that "an extraordinary emergency exists for national defense purposes ... and that issuance of this order is necessary to meet the emergency."

The government found support for its approach in the World War II decision of the Supreme Court in *Ex Parte Quirin*, 317 U.S. 1 (1942). *Quirin* involved Nazi saboteurs who had secretly entered country, were apprehended, tried before a military tribunal and sentenced to death. The Supreme Court upheld treating them as unlawful enemy combatants—"an enemy combatant who without uniform comes secretly through the lines for the purpose of waging war by destruction of life or property," who is not entitled to treatment as a prisoner of war, but who is an offender against the law of war and subject to trial before a military tribunal. The Court in *Quirin* also upheld treating a U.S. citizen as an unlawful enemy combatant.

Sometime after the President had issued his post–9/11 Military Order, the Secretary of Defense promulgated detailed regulations governing the procedures to be used in prosecutions before the military commissions and, still later, issued regulations that amounted to a mini-criminal code, describing the offenses that can be prosecuted before the commissions.

In May, 2002, Jose Padilla, a U.S. citizen, upon arrival by air from Pakistan, was arrested at Chicago's O'Hare Airport under a material witness warrant. Media reports indicated that the government believed that Padilla was involved in an al Qaeda plot to detonate a "dirty bomb" (that is, a conventional bomb sheathed in radioactive material that would spew the material over a wide area). A month later, the President issued an order designating Padilla as an "enemy combatant," citing in support of the action his authority as Commander-in-Chief and the Use of Force Resolution passed by the Congress. The President made findings that Padilla (1) "is closely associated with al Qaeda, an international terrorist organization with which the United States is at war;" (2) that he "engaged in ... hostile and war-like acts, including ... preparation for acts of international terrorism" against the United States; (3) that he "possesses intelligence" about al Qaeda that "would aid U. S. efforts to prevent attacks by al Qaeda on the United States"; and finally, (4) that he "represents a continuing, present and grave danger to the national security of the United States." Padilla was thereupon transferred from civilian criminal custody to military custody and sent to a naval brig in Charleston, South Carolina where he is still incarcerated.

Padilla's lawyer filed a habeas corpus petition in New York against the Secretary of Defense. When the case reached the Supreme Court, a majority of the justices ruled that Padilla had sued the wrong defendant in the wrong court and accordingly did not reach the merits of the petition. Rumsfeld v. Padilla, 542 U.S. 426 (2004). The four justice minority did address the merits, concluding that the government did not have authority to hold Padilla. The Padilla decision was handed down the same day that the Court decided: 1) that U.S. courts have jurisdiction to consider challenges to the legality of detention filed by individuals detained at Guantanamo Bay Naval Base in Cuba, most of whom had been seized on the battlefield in Afghanistan, Rasul v. Bush, 542 U.S. 466 (2004); and 2) that Yaser Hamdi, a person born in the United States and therefore a U.S. citizen, who had been seized on the battlefield in Afghanistan was entitled to a meaningful opportunity to test the factual basis for his detention as an enemy combatant, Hamdi v. Rumsfeld, 542 U.S. 507 (2004).

Subsequently, Padilla started his legal action again, this time seeking habeas corpus in the South Carolina. district where he was incarcerated.

PADILLA v. HANFT

389 F.Supp.2d 678 (D. S.C. 2005).

FLOYD, HENRY F., DISTRICT JUDGE

MEMORANDUM OPINION AND ORDER

This is a 28 U.S.C. § 2241 *habeas corpus* action. . . . Pending before the Court is Petitioner's Motion for Summary Judgment as to Counts One and Two. The sole question before the Court today is whether the President of the United States (President) is authorized to detain a United States citizen as an enemy combatant under the unique circumstances presented here.

* * *

This case was commenced on July 2, 2004, with the filing of the petition discussed herein. Respondent filed his Answer on August 30, 2004.

On October 20, 2004, Petitioner filed a Motion for Summary Judgment to Counts One and Two of his Petition, as well as his Memorandum of Law in Support of the Motion (Petitioner's Motion). . . .

Rule 56(c) of the Federal Rules of Civil Procedure provides that summary judgment "shall be rendered forthwith if the pleadings, depositions, answers to interrogatories and admissions on file, together with affidavits, if any, show that there is no genuine issue as to any material fact and that the moving party is entitled to a judgment as a matter of law."

* * *

Petitioner maintains that Congress has not authorized the indefinite detention without trial of citizens arrested in the United States. He also argues that the President's inherent constitutional powers do not allow him to subject United States citizens who are arrested in the United States to indefinite military detention.

Conversely, respondent contends that the President has the constitutional authority to detain Petitioner as an enemy combatant without charging him criminally. Furthermore, according to Respondent, the Non–Detention Act, 18 U.S.C. § 4001(a), does not constrain the President's authority to detain Petitioner as an enemy combatant.

* * *

Respondent maintains that the decisions of the Supreme Court in *Hamdi v. Rumsfeld,* 124 S.Ct. 2633 (2004) and *Quirin,* 317 U.S. 1 "reaffirm the military's long-settled authority—independent of and distinct from the criminal process—to detain enemy combatants for the duration of a given armed conflict, including the current conflict against al Qaeda.". According to Respondent, "[t]hose decisions squarely apply to this case." Petitioner, on the other hand, maintains that *Ex parte Milligan,* 71 U.S. (4 Wall) 2 (1866) is controlling. The Court will consider each case in turn.

The petitioner in *Hamdi* was an American citizen captured while on the battlefield in Afghanistan. In that case, the Supreme Court had before it the threshold question of "whether the Executive has the authority to detain citizens who qualify as 'enemy combatants.' "

While the Court noted that there was some debate and no full exposition by the Government of the proper scope of the term "enemy combatant," it was clear in *Hamdi* that, the "enemy combatant that [the Government was] seeking to detain [was] an individual who, it allege[d], was part of or supporting forces hostile to the United States or coalition partners in Afghanistan and who engaged in an armed conflict against the United States there." The Court also noted that, "the basis asserted for detention by the military is that Hamdi was *carrying a weapon against American troops on a foreign battlefield;* that is, that he was an enemy combatant."

Against this backdrop, the Supreme Court found that authority existed to detain Mr. Hamdi. The Court reasoned,

> [t]here is no bar to this Nation's holding one of its own citizens as an enemy combatant. . . . A citizen, no less than an alien, can be "part of or supporting forces hostile to the United States or coalition partners" and "engaged in an armed conflict against the United States"; such a citizen, if released, would pose the same threat of returning to the front during the ongoing conflict.
>
> In light of these principles, it is of no moment that the AUMF [ed. the congressional Joint Resolution] does not use specific language of detention. Because detention to prevent a combatant's return to the battlefield is a fundamental incident of waging war, in permitting the use of "necessary and appropriate force," Congress has clearly and unmistakably authorized detention *in the narrow circumstances considered here.*

Hamdi, 124 S.Ct. at 2640–41 (emphasis added).

Thus, it is true that, under some circumstances, such as those present in *Hamdi,* the President can indeed hold an United States citizen as an enemy combatant. Just because something is sometimes true, however, does not mean that it is always true. The facts in this action bear out that truth.

In the instant case, Respondent would have this Court find more similarities between Petitioner here and the petitioner in *Hamdi* than actually exist. As two other courts have already found, however, the differences between the two are striking.

The first to distinguish the difference was Judge Wilkinson when he noted that "[t]o compare this battlefield capture [in *Hamdi*] to the domestic arrest in *Padilla v. Rumsfeld* is to compare apples and oranges." *Hamdi v. Rumsfeld,* 337 F.3d 335, 344 (4th Cir. 2003) (Wilkinson, J., concurring). Not long thereafter, the Supreme Court, in responding to Justice Scalia's dissent, specifically noted "Justice Scalia largely ignores the context of *[Hamdi]:* a United States citizen captured in a *foreign* combat zone."

Nevertheless, Respondent would have the Court find that the place of capture is of no consequence in determining whether the President can properly hold Petitioner as an enemy combatant. According to that view, it would be illogical to find that Petitioner could evade his detention as an enemy combatant status just because he returned to the United States before he could be captured. The cogency of this argument eludes the Court.

In *Hamdi,* the petitioner was an American citizen who was captured on the battlefield. Petitioner is also an American citizen, but he was captured in an United States airport. He is, in some respects, being held for a crime that he is alleged to have planned to commit in this country.
* * *

It cannot be disputed that the circumstances in *Hamdi* comport with the requirement of the AUMF, which provides that "the President is authorized to use all *necessary and appropriate force* against those . . . persons, in order to prevent attacks by al Qaeda on the United States." That is, the President's use of force to capture Mr. Hamdi was necessary and appropriate. Here, that same use of force was not.

Again, Petitioner in this action was captured in the United States. His alleged terrorist plans were thwarted at the time of his arrest. There were no impediments whatsoever to the Government bringing charges against him for any one or all of the array of heinous crimes that he has been effectively accused of committing. Also at the Government's disposal was the material witness warrant. In fact, the issuance of a material witness warrant was the tool that the law enforcement officers used to thwart Petitioner's alleged terrorist plans. Therefore, since Petitioner's alleged terrorist plans were thwarted when he was arrested on the material witness warrant, the Court finds that the President's subsequent decision to detain Petitioner as an enemy combatant was neither necessary nor appropriate.

* * *

Quirin involves the *habeas* petitions of seven German soldiers, all of whom had lived in the United States at some point in their lives. The soldiers came to the United States bent on engaging in military sabotage. One of the seven, Haupt, claimed to be an American citizen.

In denying the soldiers' petitions, the Supreme Court held that "Citizenship in the United States of an enemy belligerent does not relieve him from the consequences of a belligerency which is unlawful because in violation of the law of war."

Respondent maintains that *Quirin* is wholly on point and, thus, for purposes of this motion, is controlling. The Court is unconvinced.

Although seemingly similar to the instant case, it is, in fact, like *Hamdi,* starkly different. As the Second Circuit has already noted, "the *Quirin* Court's decision to uphold military jurisdiction rested on the express congressional authorization of the use of military tribunals to try combatants who violated the law."

From the very beginning of its history this Court has recognized and applied the law of war as including that part of the law of nations which prescribes, for the conduct of war, the status, rights and duties of enemy nations as well as of enemy individuals. By the Articles of War, and especially Article 15, Congress has explicitly provided, so far as it may constitutionally do so, that military tribunals shall have jurisdiction to try offenders or offenses against the law of war in appropriate cases. Congress, in addition to making rules for the government of our Armed Forces, has thus exercised its authority to define and punish offenses against the law of nations by sanctioning, within constitutional limitations, the jurisdiction of military commissions to try persons for offenses which, according to the rules and precepts of the law of nations, and more particularly the law of war, are cognizable by such tribunals. And the President, as Commander in Chief, by his Proclamation in time of war has invoked that law. By his Order creating the present Commission he has undertaken to exercise the authority conferred upon him by Congress, and also such authority as the Constitution itself gives the Commander in Chief, to direct the performance of those functions which may constitutionally be performed by the military arm of the nation in time of war.

Quirin, 317 U.S. at 27–28.

Respondent goes to great lengths to argue that the Court is *Quirin* did not rest its decision on a "clear statement from Congress." The Court is unconvinced.

Contrary to Respondent's argument, it is clear from *Quirin* that the Court found that Congress had "explicitly provided, so far as it may constitutionally do so, that military tribunals shall have jurisdiction to try offenders or offenses against the law of war in appropriate cases." Therefore, since no such Congressional authorization is present here, Respondent's argument as to the application of *Quirin* must fail.[10]

Ex parte Milligan involves a United States citizen during the Civil War who was neither a resident of one of the Confederate states, nor a prisoner of war, but a citizen of Indiana for twenty years. He had never been in the military or naval service. Milligan was arrested while at home.

The Court held in *Milligan* that the military commission lacked any jurisdiction to try Milligan when the civilian "courts are open and their process unobstructed." The President may not unilaterally establish military commissions in wartime "because he is controlled by law, and has his appropriate sphere of duty, which is to execute, not to make, the laws."[11]

While not directly on point, and limited by *Quirin, Milligan's* greatest import to the case at bar is the same as that found in *Quirin:* the detention of a United States citizen by the military is disallowed without explicit Congressional authorization.

The Non–Detention Act, also referred to as the "Railsback Amendment," after its author Representative Railsback, provides that "No citizen shall be imprisoned or otherwise detained by the United States except pursuant to an Act of Congress." 18 U.S.C. § 4001(a).

Respondent asserts that the Non–Detention Act does not constrain the President's authority to detain Petitioner as an enemy combatant. He contends that 1) the Joint Resolution for Authorization for Use of Miliary Force (AUMF), passed by Congress on September 18, 2001, is an "Act of Congress" authorizing Petitioner's detention and 2) the Non–Detention Act does not apply to the military's detention of the military's wartime detention of enemy combatants to fulfill this statute [sic]. The

---

10. Other differences include, but are not limited to, the fact that:

    1) In *Quirin,* Mr. Quirin was charged with a crime and tried by a military tribunal. In the instant case, Petitioner has not been charged and has not been tried.

    2) *Quirin* involves a prisoner whose detention was punitive whereas Petitioner's detention is purportedly preventative.

    3) *Quirin* is concerned more with whether the petitioner was going to be tried by a military tribunal or a civilian court. The case at bar is concerned with whether Petitioner is going to be charged and tried at all.

    4) The decision in *Quirin* preceded the Non–Detention Act.

    5) *Quirin* involved a war that had a definite ending date. The present war on terrorism does not.

11. The court in *Hamdi,* 124 S.Ct. at 2642, observed, however, that the *Milligan* court made repeated reference to the fact that its inquiry into whether the military tribunal had jurisdiction to try and punish Milligan turned in large part on the fact that Milligan was not a prisoner of war, but a resident of Indiana arrested while at home there. That fact was central to its conclusion. Had Milligan been captured while he was assisting Confederate soldiers by carrying a rifle against Union troops on a Confederate battlefield, the holding of the Court might well have been different. The Court's repeated explanations that Milligan was not a prisoner of war suggest that had these different circumstances been present he could have been detained under military authority for the duration of the conflict, whether or not he was a citizen.

Court finds these contentions to be without merit. The AUMF provides, in relevant part, that

> [t]he President is authorized to use all *necessary and appropriate* force against those nations, organizations, or persons he determines planned, authorized, committed, or aided the terrorist attacks that occurred on September 11, 2001, or harbored such organizations or persons, in order to prevent any future acts of international terrorism against the United States by such nations, organizations or persons.

Joint Resolution 2(a).

... Contrary to Respondent's contentions otherwise, the Court finds that 1) the AUMF does not authorize Petitioner's detention and 2) Petitioner's present confinement is in direct contradiction to the mandate of the Non–Detention Act.

As the Second Circuit stated,

> While it may be possible to infer a power of detention from the Joint Resolution in the battlefield context where detentions are necessary to carry out the war, there is no reason to suspect from the language of the Joint Resolution that Congress believed it would be authorizing the detention of an American citizen already held in a federal correctional institution and not arrayed against our troops in the field of battle.

Padilla, 352 F.3d at 723

To be more specific, whereas it may be a necessary and appropriate use of force to detain a United States citizen who is captured on the battlefield, this Court cannot find, in narrow circumstances presented in this case, that the same is true when a United States citizen in arrested in a civilian setting such as an United States airport.

... In the case *sub judice,* there is no language in the AUMF that "clearly and unmistakably" grants the President the authority to hold Petitioner as an enemy combatant. Therefore, Respondent's argument must fail.

In arguing that the Non–Detention Act has no application to Petitioner, Respondent first maintains that the placement of the Act–in Title 18 ("Crimes and Criminal Procedure"), with directions regarding the Attorney General's control over federal prisons, and not in Title 10 ("Armed Forces") or Title 50 ("War and National Defense")—indicates that it speaks only to civilian detentions. Second, Respondent argues that the legislative history of the Non–Detention Act renders the same result. The Court is unpersuaded by either argument. Simply stated, the statute is clear, simple, direct and ambiguous. It forbids *any* kind of detention of an United States citizen, except that it be specifically allowed by Congress. Therefore, since Petitioner's detention has not been authorized by Congress, Respondent's argument must again fail.

Having found that the Non–Detention Act expressly forbids the President from holding Petitioner as an enemy combatant, and that the AUMF does not authorize such detention, neither explicitly nor by implication, the Court turns to the question of whether the President has the inherent authority to hold Petitioner.

Respondent states that

The Commander-in-Chief Clause grants the President the power to defend the Nation when it is attacked, and he "is bound to accept the challenge without waiting for any special legislative authority." *The Prize Cases*, 67 U.S. (2 Black) 635, 668 (1862). An essential aspect of the President's authority in this regard is to "determine what degree of force the crisis demands." *Id.* at 670; see *Campbell v. Clinton*, 203 F.3d 19, 27 (D.C. Cir.) (Silberman, J., concurring) ("[T]he President has independent authority to repel aggressive acts by third parties even without specific congressional authorization, and courts may not review the level of force selected."), cert. denied, 531 U.S. 815 (2000). The President's decision to detain petitioner as an enemy combatant represents a basic exercise of his authority as Commander in Chief to determine the level of force needed to prosecute the conflict against al Qaeda.

Respondent's Opposition at 10.

As a preliminary matter, the Court strongly agrees that "great deference is afforded the President's exercise of his authority as Commander-in-Chief." However, "[w]here the exercise of Commander-in-Chief powers, no matter how well intentioned, is challenged on the ground that it collides with the powers assigned by the Constitution to Congress, a fundamental role exists for the courts." *Padilla*, 352 F.3d at 713 ...Pursuant to the seminal case of *Youngstown Sheet & Tube v. Sawyer*, 343 U.S. 579 (1952), in a case such as this, where the President has taken steps that are inconsistent with the will of Congress—both express and implied—the President's authority is "at its lowest ebb, for then he can rely only upon his own constitutional powers minus any constitutional powers of Congress over the matter." *Youngstown*, 343 U.S. at 637.

Simply stated, Respondent has not provided, and this Court has not found, any law that supports the contention that the President enjoys the inherent authority pursuant to which he claims to hold Petitioner.
* * *

As Justice Jackson stated, "Congress, not the Executive, should control utilization of the war power as an instrument of domestic policy." *Youngstown*, 343 U.S. at 644 (Jackson, J., concurring). "There are indications that the Constitution did not contemplate that the title Commander-in-Chief of the Army and Navy will constitute [the President] also Commander-in-Chief of the country, its industries and its inhabitants. *Id.* at 643–44.

Accordingly, and limited to the facts of this case, the Court is of the firm opinion that it must reject the position posited by Respondent. To do otherwise would not only offend the rule of law and violate this country's constitutional tradition, but it would also be a betrayal of this Nation's commitment to the separation of powers that safeguards our democratic values and individual liberties.

... Pursuant to its interpretation, the Court finds that the President has no power, neither express nor implied, neither constitutional nor statutory, to hold Petitioner as an enemy combatant.

* * *

It is true that there may be times during which it is necessary to give the Executive Branch greater power than at other times. Such a granting of power, however, is in the province of the legislature and no one else—not the Court and not the President....

Simply stated, this is a law enforcement matter, not a military matter. The civilian authorities captured Petitioner just as they should have. At the time that Petitioner was arrested pursuant to the material arrest warrant, any alleged terrorist plans that he harbored were thwarted. From then on, he was available to be questioned—and was indeed questioned—just like any other citizen accused of criminal conduct. This is as it should be.

There can be no debate that this country's laws amply provide for the investigation, detention and prosecution of citizen and non-citizen terrorists alike. For example, in his dissenting opinion in *Hamdi,* 124 S.Ct. at 2664, Justice Scalia lists the following criminal statutes that are available to the Government in fighting terrorism: 18 U.S.C. § 2381(the modern treason statute which essentially tracks the language of the constitutional provision); 18 U.S.C. § 32 (destruction of aircraft or aircraft facilities); 18 U.S.C. § 2332a (use of weapons of mass destruction); 18 U.S.C. § 2332b (acts of terrorism transcending national boundaries); 18 U.S.C. § 2339A (providing material support to terrorists); 18 U.S.C. § 2339B (providing material support to certain terrorist organizations); 18 U.S.C. § 2382 (misprision of treason); 18 U.S.C. § 2383 (rebellion or insurrection); § 2384 (seditious conspiracy); 18 U.S.C. § 2390 (enlistment to serve in armed hostility against the United States); 31 CFR § 595.204 (2003) (prohibiting the "making or receiving of any contribution of funds, goods, or services" to terrorists); and 50 U.S.C. § 1705(b) (criminalizing violations of 31 CFR § 595.204). In his concurrence, in addition to these statutes, Justice Souter lists 18 U.S.C. § 3142(e) (pretrial detention).

[I]n declaring Padilla an enemy combatant, the President relied upon facts that would have supported charging Padilla with a variety of offenses. The government thus had the authority to arrest, detain, interrogate, and prosecute Padilla apart from the extraordinary authority it claims here. The difference between invocation of the criminal process and the power claimed by the President here, however, is one of accountability. The criminal justice system requires that defendants and witnesses be afforded access to counsel, imposes judicial supervision over government action, and places congressionally imposed limits on incarceration.

"The Privilege of the Writ of *Habeas Corpus* shall not be suspended, unless when in Cases of Rebellion or Invasion the public Safety may require it." Const. Art. 1, § 9, cl. 2. This power belongs solely to Congress. Since Congress has not acted to suspend the writ, and neither the President nor this Court have the ability to do so, in light of the findings above, Petitioner must be released.

If the law in its current state is found by the President to be insufficient to protect this country from terrorist plots, such as the one alleged here, then the President should prevail upon Congress to remedy the problem. For instance, if the Government's purpose in detaining Petitioner as an enemy combatant is to prevent him from "returning to the field of battle and taking up arms once again[,]" *Hamdi,* 124 S.Ct. at 2640, but the President thinks that the laws do not provide the necessary and appropriate measures to provide for that goal, then the President should approach Congress and request that it make proper modifications to the law. As Congress has already demonstrated, it stands ready to carefully consider, and often accommodate, such significant requests.

Accordingly, in light of the foregoing discussion and analysis, it is the judgment of this Court that Petitioner's Motion for Summary Judgment on Counts One and Two of the Petition, as well as his Petition for a writ of *habeas corpus* must be granted. Accordingly, Respondent is hereby directed to release Petitioner from his custody within forty-five (45) days of the entry of this Order.[14]

Notes

1. The decision in the principal case, supra, was reversed. *Padilla v. Hanft,* 423 F.3d 386 (4th Cir.2005), and a petition for certiorari was filed, 74 U.S.L.W. 3275 (2005). The circuit court opinion recounted additional facts regarding Padilla's sojourn in Afghanistan, that he received explosives training in an al Qaeda camp, that he served as an armed guard at a Taliban outpost, that he was on the facts presented "armed and present in a combat zone . . . ."

Then, on November 22, 2005, an indictment was unsealed charging Padilla with conspiracy to murder, maim and kidnap abroad. Charging him with crimes in a civilian court meant that Padilla was to be transferred from military to civilian custody and this probably forestalled Supreme Court review of the case. Why do you think the government adopted this course of action?

2. Padilla had been held in a naval brig since June, 2002, without indication of any plans to bring him to trial. If he were to be tried in a

---

14. Of course, if appropriate, the Government can bring criminal charges against Petitioner or it can hold him as a material witness.

military proceeding, it could not have occurred under the terms of the President's Military Order authorizing the military commissions because that Order only applies to persons who are not U.S. citizens. Either it would have been necessary to amend the Order or to develop some other military process for trying U.S. citizens.

3.   The legality of the use of military commissions to try non-citizens seized on the battlefield in Afghanistan was tested in the following case. Compare the issues discussed in this case with those addressed in Padilla v. Hanft, supra. What bearing does each case have on the other?

HAMDAN v. RUMSFELD

415 F.3d 33 (D.C. Cir. 2005).
Petition for cert. granted, 126 S.Ct. 622 (2005).

Before: RANDOLPH and ROBERTS, CIRCUIT JUDGES, and WILLIAMS, SENIOR CIRCUIT JUDGE.

Concurring opinion filed by SENIOR CIRCUIT JUDGE WILLIAMS.

RANDOLPH, CIRCUIT JUDGE.

Afghani militia forces captured Salim Ahmed Hamdan in Afghanistan in late November 2001. Hamdan's captors turned him over to the American military, which transported him to the Guantanamo Bay Naval Base in Cuba. The military initially kept him in the general detention facility, known as Camp Delta. On July 3, 2003, the President determined "that there is reason to believe that [Hamdan] was a member of al Qaeda or was otherwise involved in terrorism directed against the United States." This finding brought Hamdan within the compass of the President's November 13, 2001, Order concerning the Detention, Treatment, and Trial of Certain Non–Citizens in the War Against Terrorism, 66 Fed.Reg. 57,833. Accordingly, Hamdan was designated for trial before a military commission. . . .

In April 2004, Hamdan filed this petition for habeas corpus. While his petition was pending before the district court, the government formally charged Hamdan with conspiracy to commit attacks on civilians and civilian objects, murder and destruction of property by an unprivileged belligerent, and terrorism. The charges alleged that Hamdan was Osama bin Laden's personal driver in Afghanistan between 1996 and November 2001, an allegation Hamdan admitted in an affidavit. The charges further alleged that Hamdan served as bin Laden's personal bodyguard, delivered weapons to al Qaeda members, drove bin Laden to al Qaeda training camps and safe havens in Afghanistan, and trained at the al Qaeda-sponsored al Farouq camp. Hamdan's trial was to be before a military commission, which the government tells us now consists of three officers of the rank of colonel.

In response to the Supreme Court's decision in *Hamdi v. Rumsfeld*, 542 U.S. 507, 124 S.Ct. 2633, 159 L.Ed.2d 578 (2004), Hamdan received a formal hearing before a Combatant Status Review Tribunal. The Tribunal affirmed his status as an enemy combatant, "either a member of or affiliated with Al Qaeda," for whom continued detention was required.

On November 8, 2004, the district court granted in part Hamdan's petition. Among other things, the court held that Hamdan could not be tried by a military commission unless a competent tribunal determined that he was not a prisoner of war under the 1949 Geneva Convention governing the treatment of prisoners. The court therefore enjoined the Secretary of Defense from conducting any further military commission proceedings against Hamdan. This appeal followed.

* * *

In an argument distinct from his claims about the Geneva Convention, which we will discuss next, Hamdan maintains that the President violated the separation of powers inherent in the Constitution when he established military commissions. * * * In any event, on the merits there is little to Hamdan's argument.

The President's Military Order of November 13, 2001, stated that any person subject to the order, including members of al Qaeda, "shall, when tried, be tried by a military commission for any and all offenses triable by [a]. ... military commission that such individual is alleged to have committed "66 Fed.Reg. at 57,834. The President relied on four sources of authority: his authority as Commander in Chief of the Armed Forces, U.S. Const., art. II, § 2; Congress's joint resolution authorizing the use of force; 10 U.S.C. § 821; and 10 U.S.C. § 836. The last three are, of course, actions of Congress.

In the joint resolution, passed in response to the attacks of September 11, 2001, Congress authorized the President "to use all necessary and appropriate force against those nations, organizations, or persons he determines planned, authorized, committed, or aided" the attacks and recognized the President's "authority under the Constitution to take action to deter and prevent acts of international terrorism against the United States." Authorization for Use of Military Force, Pub.L. No. 107–40, 115 Stat. 224, 224 (2001). * * * *Id.* We think it no answer to say, as Hamdan does, that this case is different because Congress did not formally declare war. It has been suggested that only wars between sovereign nations would qualify for such a declaration. * * * Even so, the joint resolution "went as far toward a declaration of war as it might, and as far or further than Congress went in the Civil War, the Philippine Insurrection, the Boxer Rebellion, the Punitive Expedition against Pancho Villa, the Korean War, the Vietnam War, the invasion of Panama, the Gulf War, and numerous other conflicts." The plurality in *Hamdi v. Rumsfeld,* in suggesting that a military commission could determine whether an American citizen was an enemy combatant in the current conflict, drew no distinction of the sort Hamdan urges upon us.

Ex parte Quirin also stands solidly against Hamdan's argument. The Court held that Congress had authorized military commissions through Article 15 of the Articles of War. The modern version of Article 15 is 10

U.S.C. § 821, which the President invoked when he issued his military order. Section 821 states that court-martial jurisdiction does not "deprive military commissions . . . of concurrent jurisdiction with respect to offenders or offenses that by statute or by the law of war may be tried by military commissions." Congress also authorized the President, in another provision the military order cited, to establish procedures for military commissions. 10 U.S.C. § 836(a). Given these provisions * * *it is impossible to see any basis for Hamdan's claim that Congress has not authorized military commissions. * * *

We therefore hold that through the joint resolution and the two statutes just mentioned, Congress authorized the military commission that will try Hamdan.

This brings us to Hamdan's argument, accepted by the district court, that the Geneva Convention Relative to the Treatment of Prisoners of War, Aug. 12, 1949, 6 U.S.T. 3316 ("1949 Geneva Convention"), ratified in 1955, may be enforced in federal court.

"Treaties made, or which shall be made, under the Authority of the United States, shall be the supreme Law of the Land."U.S. CONST., art. VI, cl. 2. Even so, this country has traditionally negotiated treaties with the understanding that they do not create judicially enforceable individual rights. As a general matter, a "treaty is primarily a compact between independent nations," and "depends for the enforcement of its provisions on the interest and honor of the governments which are parties to it." If a treaty is violated, this "becomes the subject of international negotiations and reclamation," not the subject of a lawsuit. Thus, "[i]nternational agreements, even those directly benefitting private persons, generally do not create private rights or provide for a private cause of action in domestic courts."RESTATEMENT (THIRD) OF THE FOREIGN RELATIONS LAW OF THE UNITED STATES § 907 cmt. a, at 395 (1987). The district court nevertheless concluded that the 1949 Geneva Convention conferred individual rights enforceable in federal court. We believe the court's conclusion disregards the principles just mentioned and is contrary to the Convention itself. * * * The Supreme Court's *Rasul* decision did give district courts jurisdiction over habeas corpus petitions filed on behalf of Guantanamo detainees such as Hamdan. But *Rasul* did not render the Geneva Convention judicially enforceable. That a court has jurisdiction over a claim does not mean the claim is valid. The availability of habeas may obviate a petitioner's need to rely on a private right of action, *see Wang v. Ashcroft*, 320 F.3d 130, 140–41 & n. 16 (2d Cir.2003), but it does not render a treaty judicially enforceable.

We therefore hold that the 1949 Geneva Convention does not confer upon Hamdan a right to enforce its provisions in court

[The court went on to consider the question whether the provisions of the Geneva Convention, if it could be enforced, provided protections to the petitioner. The court concluded that Hamdan was not entitled to prisoner of war status nor to the protections of the Convention. Inter alia, the court made the following statement:

Another problem for Hamdan is that the 1949 Convention does not apply to al Qaeda and its members. The Convention appears to contemplate only two types of armed conflicts. The first is an international conflict. Under Common Article 2, the provisions of the Convention apply to "all cases of declared war or of any other armed conflict which may arise between two or more of the High Contracting Parties, even if the state of war is not recognized by one of them." Needless to say, al Qaeda is not a state and it was not a "High Contracting Party." There is an exception, set forth in the last paragraph of Common Article 2, when one of the "Powers" in a conflict is not a signatory but the other is. Then the signatory nation is bound to adhere to the Convention so long as the opposing Power "accepts and applies the provisions thereof." Even if al Qaeda could be considered a Power, which we doubt, no one claims that al Qaeda has accepted and applied the provisions of the Convention.]

Suppose we are mistaken about Common Article 3. Suppose it does cover Hamdan. Even then we would abstain from testing the military commission against the requirement in Common Article 3(1)(d) that sentences must be pronounced "by a regularly constituted court affording all the judicial guarantees which are recognized as indispensable by civilized peoples." Unlike his arguments that the military commission lacked jurisdiction, his argument here is that the commission's procedures-particularly its alleged failure to require his presence at all stages of the proceedings-fall short of what Common Article 3 requires. The issue thus raised is not *whether* the commission may try him, but rather *how* the commission may try him. That is by no stretch a jurisdictional argument. No one would say that a criminal defendant's contention that a district court will not allow him to confront the witnesses against him raises a jurisdictional objection. * * * Accordingly, comity would dictate that we defer to the ongoing military proceedings. If Hamdan were convicted, and if Common Article 3 covered him, he could contest his conviction in federal court after he exhausted his military remedies.

After determining that the 1949 Geneva Convention provided Hamdan a basis for judicial relief, the district court went on to consider the legitimacy of a military commission in the event Hamdan should eventually appear before one. In the district court's view, the principal constraint on the President's power to utilize such commissions is found in Article 36 of the Uniform Code of Military Justice, 10 U.S.C. § 836, which provides:

> Pretrial, trial, and post-trial procedures, including modes of proof, for cases arising under this chapter triable in courts-martial, military commissions and other military tribunals ... may be prescribed by the President by regulations which shall, so far as he considers practicable, apply the principles of law and the rules of evidence generally recognized in the trial of criminal cases in the United States district courts, *but which may not be contrary to or inconsistent with this chapter.*

(Emphasis added.)

The district court interpreted the final qualifying clause to mean that military commissions must comply in all respects with the requirements of the Uniform Code of Military Justice (UCMJ). This was an error.

Throughout its Articles, the UCMJ takes care to distinguish between "courts-martial" and "military commissions." *See, e.g.,* 10 U.S.C. § 821 (noting that "provisions of this chapter conferring jurisdiction upon courts-martial do not deprive military commissions . . . of concurrent jurisdiction"). The terms are not used interchangeably, and the majority of the UCMJ's procedural requirements refer only to courts-martial. The district court's approach would obliterate this distinction. A far more sensible reading is that in establishing military commissions, the President may not adopt procedures that are "contrary to or inconsistent with" the UCMJ's provisions governing military commissions. In particular, Article 39 requires that sessions of a "trial by *court-martial.* . . . shall be conducted in the presence of the accused." Hamdan's trial before a *military commission* does not violate Article 36 if it omits this procedural guarantee.

* * * The UCMJ thus imposes only minimal restrictions upon the form and function of military commissions, *see, e.g.,* 10 U.S.C. §§ 828, 847(a)(1), 849(d), and Hamdan does not allege that the regulations establishing the present commission violate any of the pertinent provisions. * * *

C. THE USE OF MILITARY FORCES IN A LAW ENFORCEMENT MODE WITHIN THE UNITED STATES

W. KENT DAVIS, SWORDS INTO PLOWSHARES: THE DANGEROUS POLITICIZATION OF THE MILITARY IN THE POST–COLD WAR ERA

33 Val. U. L. Rev. 61 (1998).

* * * The subordination of the military to the civilian authorities is an Anglo–American tradition that stretches back to the Magna Carta of 1215. Indeed, the strong interest in limiting military involvement in civilian affairs was recognized in the Declaration of Independence, which stated among its reasons for seeking liberty from Great Britain that the King "has affected to render the Military independent of and superior to the Civil power." Though the Constitution does not contain an explicit provision addressing the use of the military for domestic purposes, the Founding Fathers mandated civilian control of the military in the Federal Constitution through the government structure. The Supreme Court has recognized this concept in its decisions as well. General Douglas MacArthur's defiance of administration policy and President Truman's unceremonious sacking of the General during the Korean War silenced any further doubts about this tradition of civilian control of the military.

Despite this tradition, the government has used the military for domestic purposes as early as 1794 when President Washington called out the militia to quell the Whiskey Rebellion. In the ensuing years, troops have been periodically called to keep the peace, to provide humanitarian assistance to local communities, and to enforce the civilian laws. Early acts of Congress supported the use of the military for law enforcement, and public fear of the power of the military seemed to wane in the years between the Revolutionary and Civil Wars. The mid–1800's, however, saw a resurrection of the traditional fear of oppressive military power. One catalyst for this renewed apprehension was the Fugitive Slave Act of 1850, which allowed federal marshals to call on a posse comitatus to aid in returning slaves to their owners. After its passage, the Attorney General issued an advisory opinion that defined posse comitatus to include use of the military. During the Reconstruction era, the use of the military in Southern states heightened the public distaste for the use of troops in pursuing domestic duties. In the most extreme example, President Grant had authorized the use of federal troops as a posse comitatus to police polling stations in the South. Allegedly, troops were used to influence the outcome of the 1876 presidential election. Abuse of the military in these situations—some of the most central to a democracy—cried out for a statutory solution.

Congress formulated a solution to the growing public concern by passing the Posse Comitatus Act in 1878. Updated in 1956 to include the Air Force as part of its coverage, the Act now states the following:

> Whoever, except in cases and under circumstances expressly authorized by the Constitution or Act of Congress, willfully uses any part of the Army or the Air Force as a posse comitatus or otherwise to execute the laws shall be fined under this title or imprisoned not more than two years, or both. 18 U.S.C. § 1385 (1994).

The Posse Comitatus Act embodies the traditional separation of the military and civilian spheres. Accordingly, its intent is to restrict the direct and active use of the military for civilian law enforcement purposes. A few caveats are in order when discussing the Act, however. First, it only refers by direct reference to the Army and Air Force, and some courts have been reluctant to apply it to the sea services. However, Navy regulations have long applied the underlying principles to forbid the use of Navy and Marine Corps assets as a posse comitatus, but only as a matter of Department of Defense policy. Moreover, because the Act was not intended to limit the use of state militias, National Guard forces are not subject to the strictures of the Act while remaining under state control.

Despite its nature as a criminal statute, no reported court cases involving criminal prosecution of a person for violating the Posse Comitatus Act exist. In addition, the Act provides no private right of action. Instead, defendants, including the government itself, have raised alleged violations of the Act as defenses in court proceedings. From these proceedings, two clear procedural rules have emerged. First, the decisions have uniformly held that a violation of the Act by the government does not erase the trial court's jurisdiction over the person or the crimes alleged. Secondly, the exclusionary rule (barring introduction of evidence seized) does not apply when there has been a violation of the Act.

Perhaps surprising in light of the concerns that gave rise to it, there are many exceptions to the Posse Comitatus Act. First, as previously stated, the Act was meant to limit only direct and active use of troops— that is, actions of a "regulatory, proscriptive, or compulsory" nature— for civilian law enforcement. In other words, the indirect use of military assets, such as providing advice to civilian law enforcement officials and loaning military equipment to the police, would appear to be inherently acceptable. Other forms of indirect assistance that have not been held to violate the Act include the use of Air Force assets to fly surveillance missions for civilian law enforcement and military officers' advice in quelling civilian disorders. Even the direct and active use of troops is allowed in some circumstances under constitutional, statutory, and common law exceptions. As one authoritative source explains, "[t]he constitutional exceptions are (1) emergency authority to prevent loss of life or property destruction and (2) authority to protect federal property and functions when 'duly constituted local authorities are unable' to provide adequate protection." Many statutory exemptions allow the direct use of troops for domestic purposes as well. Three of these involve the use of federal troops for the suppression of civilian insurrection. A fourth statutory exception not only allows but also specifically requires that the military, upon request from the Secret Service, assist it in carrying out its duties to protect political figures and candidates from physical harm. The common law exceptions are two-fold: (1) No violation of the Act occurs when military personnel assist civilian police on their own initiative as private citizens; and (2) No violation occurs when military personnel assist civilian police "to achieve a military purpose and only incidentally enhance civilian law enforcement," such as protecting people on a military base from fleeing felons or investigating drug dealing by military personnel.

For almost 100 years following its passage, the Posse Comitatus Act was rarely a topic of discussion in the judicial system, prompting one court to describe it as "obscure and all-but-forgotten." * * * Interest in the Act rose in the 1980's, as the nation began to view the military as a potential asset in the famous "war on drugs" and reached a crescendo in the 1990's with the search for new post-Cold War roles for the military. . . .

* * *

The 1981 amendments to the Posse Comitatus Act have arguably made enforcement of the nation's drug laws more effective. However, they faced tough opposition both within Congress and from outside influences, including such unlikely partners as the Department of Defense itself, criminal defense lawyers, and civil libertarians. A quick look at one specific incident involving these amendments may illustrate the critics' concerns. Pursuant to the 1981 amendments, the Navy began embarking small teams of Coast Guard Tactical Enforcement Teams (TACLETs) on board its warships that patrolled known drug smuggling areas. On July 14, 1983, one such team aboard the Navy destroyer USS KIDD (DDG 993) sighted a suspicious fishing boat. When the boat refused a request by the Coast Guard officers to stop, the KIDD checked the registry of the vessel and found that the registry was fraudulent. The KIDD then ordered the boat to stop. When the boat refused to do so—in an amazing turn of events in naval history—the commanding officer of the destroyer ordered the raising of the Coast Guard ensign (essentially declaring the ship a Coast Guard law enforcement asset rather than a Navy warship) and gave chase. After firing warning shots (which were ignored), the KIDD fired directly at the fishing boat, disabling it and allowing the TACLET team to board. The TACLET team subsequently found almost 900 bales of marijuana aboard the fishing boat, and the crewmembers were later prosecuted in federal court. Incidents such as this prompted one observer in the mid–1980's to comment that ''[t]he 1981 amendments to the Posse Comitatus Act portend an increased military role in civil law enforcement.'' Time would prove him right.

Since the late 1980's and the diminishment of the Soviet threat, the legislative and executive branches have repeatedly expanded the military's role in the enforcement of drug laws. By 1989, Congress had even designated the Department of Defense as the ''single lead agency'' in the nation's drug interdiction efforts. In 1994, Congress firmly tied the drug issue to national security, thus formally legitimizing the use of the military in drug interdiction efforts, by enacting a statute with the following language: ''Personnel of the Department of Defense may not be detailed to another department or agency in order to implement the National Drug Control Strategy unless the Secretary of Defense certifies to Congress that the detail of such personnel is in the national security interest of the United States.''

This new linkage prompted one military officer to observe with concern that ''[g]ranting the military the responsibility for the general national welfare under the aegis of 'national security' is a major expansion of its customary function.'' Still, the drive to use the military in ever-increasing drug law enforcement roles continues. There have even been proposals to use military troops to patrol neighborhoods in Washington, D.C. in an effort to stop drug trafficking. The expanded military role became so pervasive by the mid 1990's that the Department of Defense had begun to establish entire military units dedicated solely to drug interdiction. One example can be found at Naval Air Station Atlanta. On November 18, 1995, for the first time in its history, the Navy commissioned a unit, Airborne Early Warning Squadron 77 (VAW–77), whose entire mission is to fight the war on drugs. Instead of training to fly its E–2C reconnaissance planes from the decks of aircraft carriers, this new Atlanta-based squadron will patrol the waters of the Caribbean looking for drug runners, a tremendous diversion of resources to law enforcement efforts.

* * *

The year 1993 ushered in a new potential domestic role for the military. At lunchtime on February 26, 1993, a bomb exploded in the parking garage beneath the World Trade Center, "immeasurably harm[ing] America's notions of security from terrorism." Two years later a truck bomb planted by Timothy McVeigh leveled the federal building in downtown Oklahoma City, shattering any remaining sense of security from terrorism that Americans had. * * * All of these incidents illustrated to Americans the danger from terrorist attacks that originate within the United States.

Although the United States had long had statutes dealing with such threats, Americans called for military intervention. Within one week of the Oklahoma City bombing, for example, President Clinton proposed an exception to the Posse Comitatus Act that would have allowed the military to assist civilian law enforcement agencies in cases involving "weapons of mass destruction." The exception would have been codified in the Counterterrorism Act of 1995. However, Congress deleted this exception to ensure the passage of the Counterterrorism Act against some heavy opposition in the House of Representatives. Still, one commentator asked, "Should military troops be used in responding to a terrorist threat, either at home or abroad" and "Should we be prepared to subject such defendants to military trials?" These incidents of terrorism and the subsequent legislative proposal by President Clinton paved the path for greater military involvement.

Lacking clear direction on its role in combating domestic terrorism, the Department of Defense has attempted to delineate the parameters of military involvement in this effort. Specifically, a 1994 Department directive addresses terrorism and other civil disturbances. It states that the president can order the deployment of troops in such emergencies but allows their deployment without presidential authority when necessary to "prevent loss of life or wanton destruction of property, or to restore government functioning and public order." The same directive, however, states that the Attorney General maintains his duty of directing federal response to acts of domestic terrorism and mandates that any troops used "remain under military command and control at all times." Using these and other guidelines, the government has deployed military troops in several recent situations to counter potential domestic terrorism; the 1996 Olympics in Atlanta is a prime example.[102]

* * *

102. The author of this paper was one of the military members who participated in the joint task force set up for the 1996 Olympics. Approximately 13,000 troops were deployed for the Olympics at a cost to taxpayers of $51 million, with the threat of terrorism as one of the motivating factors. *See* John J. Fialka, *Join the Army to See the World; Drive Athletes Around Atlanta*, Wall St. J., June 12, 1996, at B1. However, not

The preceding examples illustrate that the once-distinct line between the military and civilian spheres has blurred over the past few years, particularly since the demise of the Cold War. * * * Nowhere are these dangers more prevalent than in the use of the military for civilian law enforcement. Civilian supremacy over the military rests on the assumption that organization and maintenance of the military is separate from the local and more decentralized police forces of the nation. The paramount reason for the separation of these two entities is their fundamentally different roles and missions, resulting in distinct training methods. Police officers must recognize individual rights and seek to protect those rights. Prior to using force, police officers must try to de-escalate a situation, and they draw their weapons only when prepared to use them. On the other hand, members of the armed forces are trained to carry out the external mission of defending the nation. In doing so, troops do not focus on individual rights and may use deadly force without any prior aggression by the target. The traditional separation of the military and police forces warranted by these differing roles, however, is being steadily eroded by the growing exceptions to the Posse Comitatus Act, which could prove to have dire consequences. The most dangerous consequence is that using the military to seize civilians can expose civilian government to the threat of military rule and the suspension of constitutional liberties. As an Air Force officer has warned, "[t]he military's elevated standing, combined with other circumstances of the contemporary political landscape, invites an unprecedented insinuation of the military into American life," a situation which "challenges civilian control of the [military]." This danger is even more ominous when one considers that the peacetime military forces performing domestic duties before the Cold War were very small compared to the rest of American society, a situation that is very different today.

Undoubtedly, military involvement in the domestic sphere produces some benefits to pressing domestic problems. The need to fight the war on drugs, to deter illegal immigration and smuggling, and to combat domestic terrorism, however, are all serious problems that will only disappear with long-term social solutions. Austere budgets and the public desire for a quick-fix do not warrant the emergency use of the military in a nontraditional and dangerous role. The Supreme Court recognized this when it said "[e]mergency does not create power. Emergency does not increase granted power or remove or diminish the restrictions placed upon power granted or reserved." Delegating domestic duties to the military under the guise of an emergency can pose risks not only to individual liberty, but also to the history and the underlying structure of the United States. So far, Congress and the President have shown little interest in stemming the transfer of domestic duties to the military. If the trend continues, however, the courts will inevitably have

all of the troops were used for security purposes; some were used for such mundane tasks as watering field-hockey arenas and driving buses, which led Senator John McCain (R–Ariz.) to call the assignments "demeaning and degrading," to the troops. *Id.*

to restore the traditional subordination of the military to civilian control. Even the intervention of the courts might not be enough in the end, however. No better closing commentary can be made on this ultimate danger than the words of Colonel Charles J. Dunlap:

> In the final analysis, it is the American people who must make some hard decisions about the kind of nation in which they wish to live. If they continue to turn to the military for answers, if they abandon their attachment to the democratic process, if they fail to take the necessary action to reinvigorate civilian control, if they persist in exalting inflated notions of security over all other human values, then they will get, as it is often said, the government they deserve.... [J]ust as the military can keep a nation free, it can, without effective civilian control, enslave a nation as well.

Notes

1. One of the main fears of the author is that the military, because of their training, will respond more aggressively to a confrontation than would civilian police. Are these fears well founded? A dramatization of this scenario was presented in the movie "The Siege," starring Denzel Washington, Annette Bening, and Bruce Willis. In the movie, a group of Middle Eastern terrorists wreak havoc on New York City via a bombing campaign. Despite success by the FBI in preventing some attacks, other terrorists remain at large and the public clamors for more decisive action. As a result, the President declares a State of Emergency and sends in the army to impose military order. The army rounds up every male of Arab descent into Yankee stadium and even tortures one of the prime suspects in order to extract information on the next bombing. According to the promotions released by the studio, the movie poses the question "Faced with such grave danger, how will the members of a free society measure up?" How realistic is this scenario? Is the military more likely to disregard constitutional constraints than domestic law enforcement agencies? How well will ordinary checks and balances operate if the military is involved in law enforcement?

2. What standards should be used to determine whether military personnel went beyond the provision of indirect aid authorized by 10 U.S.C. §§ 371–76 and violated the Posse Comitatus Act? Several tests have been employed in the lower courts. In *United States v. Yunis*, 681 F.Supp. 891, 892 (D.D.C.1988), the district court described the prior cases:

> Because the proscriptions of the Act have been relied upon in various situations, several tests have been articulated to determine whether an individual's rights have been infringed upon through violations of the statute. In the litigation which arose out of the standoff between Native American Indians and federal law enforcement authorities at Wounded Knee, South Dakota, in 1973, United States Marshals, FBI agents, the National Guard, as well as Army and Air Force personnel were both visible and involved. The first test was whether civilian law enforcement agents made "direct active use" of military personnel to execute the laws. (The statute prohibits the "direct active use of Army or Air Force personnel and does not mean the use of Army or Air

Force equipment or materiel."). The second [test was] whether "use of any part of the Army or Air Force pervaded the activities" of the civilian law enforcement agents. (No one questioned that substantial amounts of Army material and equipment were used. But "it is the use of military personnel, not materiel, which is proscribed by 18 U.S.C. § 1385." Since there was reasonable doubt whether military personnel were involved enough to render their actions unlawful, the defendants were acquitted.). The third test is whether the military personnel subjected citizens to the exercise of military power which was regulatory, proscriptive, or compulsory in nature. *United States v. McArthur*, 419 F.Supp. 186 (D.N.D.1975), *aff'd sub nom. United States v. Casper*, 541 F.2d 1275 (8th Cir.1976). (In *McArthur*, military personnel were used, but it was "not material enough to taint the presumption that the law enforcement officers were acting in performance of their duties." "[T]he borrowing of highly skilled personnel, like pilots and highly technical equipment like aircraft and cameras, for a specific, limited, temporary purpose is far preferable to the maintenance of such personnel and equipment by the United States Marshals' Service.").

Finding that the Navy had played only a passive role in housing, transporting, and caring for the defendant while he was being transported to the United States for trial, the district court concluded that there had been no violation of the Posse Comitatus Act. The court of appeals affirmed. 924 F.2d 1086 (D.C.Cir.1991).

Which of these three tests is preferable? In *United States v. McArthur*, supra, the court expressed concern that the "direct active use" standard was too mechanical, while the "pervading" test was too vague. The court concluded:

> Returning to the posse comitatus statute with its mandate against the use of a part of the Army or Air Force to "execute" the law, execute implies an authoritarian act. I conclude that the feared use which is prohibited by the posse comitatus statute is that which is regulatory, prescriptive or compulsory in nature, and causes the citizens to be presently or prospectively subject to regulations, proscriptions, or compulsions by military authority.

3. There have been no reported cases of a criminal prosecution under the Posse Comitatus Act. How then are violations of the act litigated—if at all? Typically, criminal defendants have tried to get charges dismissed or evidence excluded based on an alleged violation of the Act. Most courts have avoided the remedial question by finding that no violation of the act occurred. The few cases that have reached the question of a remedy have almost uniformly denied relief, though several courts suggested that an exclusionary rule might be available if there were evidence of widespread and repeated violations. *See, e.g., United States v. Mendoza–Cecelia*, 963 F.2d 1467, 1478 nn. 8 & 9 (11th Cir.1992); *United States v. Yunis*, 924 F.2d 1086 (D.C.Cir.1991); *United States v. Hartley*, 796 F.2d 112, 115 (5th Cir. 1986); *United States v. Roberts*, 779 F.2d 565, 568 (9th Cir. 1986).

One of the rare examples which did work to the benefit of a criminal defendant comes from the Hawaiian Supreme Court, see *State v. Pattioay*, 78 Hawai'i 455, 896 P.2d 911 (1995). Army investigators, acting on a tip from a military dependent, went undercover to buy cocaine from a local civilian drug dealer. This evidence was then used by local law enforcement to obtain a search warrant and the seizure of evidence for use in trial. The trial court, however, held that

> [t]he military control and involvement was clearly pervasive and largely unregulated by civilian law enforcement officials based on evidence presented at the hearings herein.... In view of the foregoing, the need to deter the pattern of conduct hereinabove described is clear. Under the particular circumstances of this case, suppression is warranted.

Id. at 915. Furthermore, the court found that the nexus of the defendant with the military had been too tenuous to warrant the army's initial investigation.

The Hawaiian Supreme Court affirmed the trial court's decision. In his concurrence, Judge Mario Ramil emphasized the special relevance of the Posse Comitatus Act to Hawaii.

> Trepidation toward the notion of military involvement in civilian law enforcement is particularly prominent in the State of Hawai'i. Indeed, many of our citizens still remember the period during World War II when Hawai'i existed under martial law. The impact was felt by every citizen from the moment martial law was declared upon the Territory of Hawai'i on December 7, 1941, to the moment blackout and curfew were finally lifted on July 11, 1945. * * * During this time period, almost every aspect of civilian life was monitored and controlled by the new military regime.

Id. at 928.

4. The Department of Defense established the Joint Task Force 6 (JTF–6) in 1989 to coordinate missions between military and law enforcement agencies along the 2,000–mile Mexican border. The lead federal agency is the Border Patrol, while the Army, Marine Corps, and the National Guard conduct missions such as reconnaissance patrols, maintaining observation posts, and guarding and maintaining operation bases.[a] The purpose of the task force was to stop the flow of drugs and illegal aliens across the border. For nearly 7 years and 3000 missions, the cooperation between civilian law enforcement and the military worked well. Then, on May 20, 1997, tragedy struck.[b]

Esequiel Hernandez, an 18–year-old American citizen, was herding his family's flock of goats along the Mexican border. He had brought along his rifle in case of rattlesnake and for amusement. Unknown to Hernandez, a team of Marines, dressed in full camouflage, had been following him for about 20 minutes. The Marines suspected Hernandez might be an advance scout for a drug smuggler.

---

a. John Flock, *The Legality of United States Military Operations Along the United States–Mexico Border*, 5 Sw. J.L. & Trade Am. 453, 466 (Fall 1998).

b. The following information is drawn from accounts presented in Flock, *supra*

footnote a and Douglas Holt, *An Identity Crisis Most Deadly: A Goatherder Becomes the First U.S. Civilian Killed by the Military Since Kent State*, Chi. Trib., July 5, 1998 at 1 (available 1998 WL 2873325).

After Hernandez shot twice in the general direction of the soldiers, the team leader received permission to shoot Hernandez if he pointed the gun again toward the soldiers. Following the rules of military engagement, the soldiers did not identify themselves or try to question Hernandez. Shortly thereafter, Hernandez was shot, but did not die for 20 minutes. Even though one of the Marines had been trained as a medic, no aid was given, nor was a medivac helicopter called for until civilian law enforcement arrived on the scene.

Within a few days the Pentagon suspended the use of ground forces along the Mexican border for counter-drug missions and the Marine Corps began an investigation. The 13,000 page report, which was issued in mid–1998, concluded that the mission had been fraught with "systematic failures at every level of command." For example, the Border Patrol knew, but did not tell the Marines, that Hernandez often tended to his family's goats and brought along a rifle for safety and amusement. Furthermore, the report indicated that the Marines battlefield mentality and training were significantly out-of-place at an observation post on private property adjacent to a small U.S. community.

6. The expanded use of the military in civilian law enforcement is occurring at a time of rapid expansion in the scope of federal criminal law. What concerns do these parallel developments raise? What are the implications of a comprehensive national criminal code enforced, at least in part, by the military? Do the developments that have occurred to date threaten civil liberties? Or is this merely an issue to keep in mind if these trends continue?

7. Domestic use of the military can raise First Amendment issues. In *Laird v. Tatum*, 408 U.S. 1 (1972), a class action was brought seeking relief from alleged surveillance of civilian political activity by the Army based on a claimed chilling effect of such surveillance on the exercise of First Amendment rights. The intelligence system for such surveillance had been set up to secure information relating to potential or actual disorders after the Army had been called upon by local authorities to control civil disorders that arose in the late 1960's. The Supreme Court reinstated the district court action dismissing the suit on the ground that there was no claim of specific present objective harm or specific future harm that presented a justiciable controversy for the courts. Writing for the Court, Chief Justice Burger said:

The President is authorized by 10 USC § 331 to make use of the armed forces to quell insurrection and other domestic violence if and when the conditions described in that section obtain within one of the States.

* * *

The data-gathering system here involved is said to have been established in connection with the development of more detailed and specific contingency planning designed to permit the Army, when called upon to assist local authorities, to be able to respond effectively with a minimum of force. As the Court of Appeals observed,

"In performing this type function the Army is essentially a police force or the back-up of a local police force. To quell disturbances or to prevent further disturbances the Army needs the same tools and, most importantly, the same information to which local police forces have access. Since the Army is sent into territory almost invariably unfamiliar to most soldiers and their commanders, their need for information is likely to be greater than that of the hometown policeman.

"No logical argument can be made for compelling the military to use *blind* force. When force is employed it should be intelligently directed, and this depends upon having reliable information—in time. As Chief Justice John Marshall said of Washington, 'A general must be governed by his intelligence and must regulate his measures by his information. It is his duty to obtain correct information. . . .' So we take it as undeniable that the military, i.e., the Army, need a certain amount of information in order to perform their constitutional and statutory missions."

The system put into operation as a result of the Army's 1967 experience consisted essentially of the collection of information about public activities that were thought to have at least some potential for civil disorder, the reporting of that information to Army Intelligence headquarters at Fort Holabird, Maryland, the dissemination of these reports from headquarters to major Army posts around the country, and the storage of the reported information in a computer data bank located at Fort Holabird. The information itself was collected by a variety of means, but it is significant that the principal sources of information were the news media and publications in general circulation. Some of the information came from Army Intelligence agents who attended meetings that were open to the public and who wrote field reports describing the meetings, giving such data as the name of the sponsoring organization, the identity of speakers, the approximate number of persons in attendance, and an indication of whether any disorder occurred. And still other information was provided to the Army by civilian law enforcement agencies.

The material filed by the Government in the District Court reveals that Army Intelligence has field offices in various parts of the country; these offices are staffed in the aggregate with approximately 1,000 agents, 94% of whose time is devoted to the organization's principal mission, which is unrelated to the domestic surveillance system here involved.

We, of course, intimate no view with respect to the propriety or desirability, from a policy standpoint, of the challenged activities of the Department of the Army; our conclusion is a narrow one, namely, that on this record the respondents have not presented a case for resolution by the courts.

The concerns of the Executive and Legislative Branches in response to disclosure of the Army surveillance activities and indeed the claims alleged in the complaint reflect a traditional and strong resistance of Americans to any military intrusion into civilian affairs. That tradition has deep roots in our history and found early expression, for example, in the Third Amendment's explicit prohibition against quartering soldiers in private homes without consent and in the constitutional provisions for civilian control of the military. Those prohibitions are not directly presented by this case, but their philosophical underpinnings explain our traditional insistence on limitations on military operations in peacetime. Indeed, when presented with claims of judicially cognizable injury resulting from military intrusion into the civilian sector, federal courts are fully empowered to consider claims of those asserting such injury; there is nothing in our Nation's history or in this Court's decided cases, including our holding today, that can properly be seen as giving any indication that actual or threatened injury by reason of unlawful activities of the military would go unnoticed or unremedied.

408 U.S. at 3–15.

Justice Douglas joined by Justice Marshall wrote a strong dissent in which he stated:

If Congress had passed a law authorizing the armed services to establish surveillance over the civilian population, a most serious constitutional problem would be presented. There is, however, no law authorizing surveillance over civilians, which in this case the Pentagon concededly had undertaken. The question is whether such authority may be implied. One can search the Constitution in vain for any such authority.

The start of the problem is the constitutional distinction between the "militia" and the Armed Forces. By Art. I, § 8, of the Constitution the militia is specifically confined to precise duties: "to execute the Laws of the Union, suppress Insurrections and repel Invasions."

This obviously means that the "militia" cannot be sent overseas to fight wars. It is purely a domestic arm of the governors of the several States, save as it may be called under Art. I, § 8, of the Constitution into the federal service. Whether the "militia" could be given powers comparable to those granted the FBI is a question not now raised, for we deal here not with the "militia" but with "armies." The Army, Navy, and Air Force are comprehended in the constitutional term "armies." Art I, § 8, provides that Congress may "raise and support Armies," and "provide and maintain a Navy," and make "Rules for the Government and Regulation of the land and naval Forces." And the Fifth Amendment excepts from the requirement of a presentment or indictment of a grand jury "cases arising in the land or naval forces, or in the Militia, when in actual service in time of War or public danger."

Acting under that authority, Congress has provided a code governing the Armed Services. That code sets the procedural standards for the Government and regulation of the land and naval forces. It is difficult to imagine how those powers can be extended to military surveillance over civilian affairs.

Our tradition reflects a desire for civilian supremacy and subordination of military power. The tradition goes back to the Declaration of Independence in which it was recited that the King "has affected to render the Military independent of and superior to the Civil power." Thus, we have the "militia" restricted to domestic use, the restriction of appropriations to the "armies" to two years, Art I, § 8, and the grant of command over the armies and the militia when called into actual service of the United States to the President, our chief civilian officer. * * *

* * *

The act of turning the military loose on civilians even if sanctioned by an Act of Congress, which it has not been, would raise serious and profound constitutional questions. Standing as it does only on brute power and Pentagon policy, it must be repudiated as a usurpation dangerous to the civil liberties on which free men are dependent. * * *

This case is a cancer in our body politic. It is a measure of the disease which afflicts us. Army surveillance, like Army regimentation, is at war with the principles of the First Amendment. Those who already walk submissively will say there is no cause for alarm. But submissiveness is not our heritage. The First Amendment was designed to allow rebellion to remain as our heritage. The Constitution was designed to keep government off the backs of the people. The Bill of Rights was added to keep the precincts of belief and expression, of the press, of political and social activities free from surveillance. The Bill of Rights was designed to keep agents of government and official eavesdroppers away from assemblies of people. The aim was to allow men to be free and independent and to assert their rights against government. There can be no influence more paralyzing of that objective than Army surveillance. When an intelligence officer looks over every nonconformist's shoulder in the library or walks invisibly by his side in a picket line or infiltrates his club, the America once extolled as the voice of liberty heard around the world no longer is cast in the image which Jefferson and Madison designed, but more in the Russian image....

408 U.S. at 16–29.

Chapter 13

AN OVERVIEW OF RICO, CCE, AND THE OTHER FEDERAL STATUTES DEALING WITH ORGANIZATIONAL CRIME

A significant number of serious federal offenses involve organizational crime. We have dealt with many of them in the preceding chapters: Chapter 12, for example, dealt with providing material support to, that is, aiding, a foreign terrorist organization. RICO and conspiracy to commit a RICO violation were treated in Chapter 11. Chapter 9, which deals with drug offenses, examines another major organizational crime, continuing criminal enterprise (or CCE), 21 U.S.C. § 848; as discussed in Chapter 9 at p. 389, CCE is aimed at the top brass of drug enterprises, and it has enhanced penalties for super drug kingpins. And we should not overlook the first organizational crime statute—the Travel Act, 18 U.S.C. § 1952, discussed in Chapter 3, p. 103, criminalizes interstate activity intended to promote or carry on the activities of a "business enterprise" involving gambling, drug, liquor, or prostitution offenses. The federal criminal code also includes two other provisions dealing with organizational crime that have not been treated in the preceding pages, the gambling business statute, 18 U.S.C. § 1955, and the continuing financial crimes enterprise (CFCE), 18 U.S.C. § 225. CFCE, enacted in 1990, is the newest organizational crime statute. The gambling business statute and CFCE are reprinted at the end of this chapter.

Our purpose in this chapter is not simply to use this as a way to review complex material but also to explore the features these statutes share as well as those that distinguish them, and, hopefully, to shed additional light on the concepts, themes and doctrinal issues that different types of organizational crimes share in common.

Most of the initiatives in the criminalization of organizational behavior have developed first at the federal level, though many states subsequently enacted similar statutes. What accounts for the stress on organizational crime in the federal system? Is it a surrogate for criminality on such a large scale that it justifies federal enforcement efforts? If so, are the measures of large-scale criminality sufficient? Are there any other measures not presently in use that should be added?

In reviewing the materials on one or more of these offenses, consider the implications of the following structural features:

1. RICO, CCE, and CFCE are compound-complex crimes, that is, they require proof of a "pattern" or "series" of violations of other criminal statutes. The gambling business statute implicitly contains a similar requirement: proof of an illegal gambling business that either remained in operation for more than 30 days or had gross revenues in excess of $2,000 in a single day will ordinarily encompass multiple gambling offenses. The earliest of the organized crimes statutes, the Travel Act, contains no similar requirement, though the lower courts have generally agreed that the phrase "business enterprise" requires proof of a continuous course of conduct.[a] Although a single transaction will not ordinarily be sufficient to establish the requisite continuity, the cases have not prescribed any minimum number of acts necessary to meet this requirement. *See, e.g., United States v. Muskovsky,* 863 F.2d 1319 (7th Cir.1988).

What is the function of the pattern or series requirement that characterizes the compound-complex crimes? Are these essentially recidivist statutes? Or are they something more, and if so, what?

a.   One possibility—suggested by the judicial interpretation of the RICO pattern requirement—is that these statutes require not simply multiple offenses, but offenses that occur over a substantial period of time. In *H.J., Inc. v. Northwest Bell Telephone, supra* p. 528, the Supreme Court held that "Congress was concerned with long-term criminal conduct," and accordingly that a RICO pattern must demonstrate "continuity." Does this mean that RICO includes a minimum duration requirement? What would be the justification for establishing new higher penalties for persons who commit a pattern of offenses over an extended period of time? Is such conduct more detrimental to society than the same number of crimes committed over a short period of time? If duration by itself does not seem significant, is it a proxy for some other factor? Could it be a crude proxy for the threat of additional future crimes? In *H.J. Inc.* the Court said that "[p]redicate acts extending over a few weeks or months *and threatening no future criminal conduct do not satisfy [the continuity] requirement.*" For a description of the lower court decisions interpreting the RICO pattern requirement, see *supra* at pp. 538–545.

The question of minimum duration has received little attention under CCE, see *supra* p. 396, and there are as yet no reported cases under CFCE. Why has the issue generated so much more attention

---

a. The phrase "continuous course of conduct" originated in the testimony of Attorney General Robert Kennedy, who assured Congress that "[t]he target is organized crime * * *. Obviously we are not trying to curtail the sporadic, casual involvement in these offenses, but rather a course of conduct sufficient for it to be termed a business enterprise." S. Rep. No. 644, 87th Cong., 1st Sess. 3 (1961).

under RICO than CCE? Is the difference attributable to the large number of civil RICO actions—including *H.J. Inc.*—which litigate every conceivable issue? The fault could lie with the defense bar, which may not have pressed this issue in CCE cases. Or this may suggest that the federal courts take a different attitude in drug prosecutions, including CCE prosecutions, than in other criminal cases, dismissing issues that they might consider more substantial in another context. Do the materials in the drug chapter provide any evidence that either the rhetoric about the war on drugs or the sheer volume of drug cases has reduced the care given to the issues in drug cases?

b.   Perhaps Congress employs continuity as one of several measures of the seriousness of certain criminal conduct justifying aggravated penalties. The gambling business statute appears to take this approach. It requires the government to prove either the continuation of the gambling business over time—30 days—**or** its receipt of large gross revenues in a single day. CCE and CFCE include not only a "series" requirement but also a revenue requirement ($5 million within 24 months under CFCE, $10 million within 12 months for the enhanced CCE penalties, and "substantial income" for the standard CCE penalties). Do these alternative measures of the magnitude of the criminal activity guarantee that these statutes will be applied only to large-scale enterprises, and thus justify relatively relaxed treatment of the series requirement under CCE and CFCE? What is the effect of the amorphous "substantial income" requirement in standard CCE prosecutions? Do the cases interpreting the substantial income requirement, *supra* p. 396, ensure that only very large-scale enterprises are in fact prosecuted under CCE? If not, should the courts require a showing of continuity over a substantial period of time? What period? Would judicial recognition of a minimum duration requirement be consistent with Congress's failure to include such a requirement in these offenses?

Does this discussion suggest that CCE should be amended? Should Congress specify a minimum dollar amount for standard CCE offenses? Since Congress included minimum dollar amounts in the gambling business statute, CFCE, and the super drug kingpin section of CCE, § 848(b), can you think of any justification for failing to specify a minimum dollar amount for standard CCE offenses? What dollar amount would you suggest? Would you specify "income" or "gross receipts"? Should Congress add a minimum duration requirement to CCE instead of—or as an alternative to—greater specificity regarding the minimum standards for the proceeds?

What does this discussion suggest about the Travel Act, which is limited only by the continuity requirement generally thought to be implicit in the concept of a "business enterprise"? The Travel Act, passed in 1961, is the earliest federal statute aimed at organized crime. Now that Congress has adopted more specific standards in enacting other organizational crime statutes, is it time to add more precision to the Travel Act? Note that in the absence of such an amendment federal prosecutors may be able to bring gambling and drug cases under the

Travel Act even though the facts would not meet the more specific standards of CCE or the gambling business statute. On the other hand, the maximum penalty for a Travel Act violation—5 years—is substantially less than that under CCE. Do you favor amending the Travel Act, and—if so—what would you add? Note that the failure to amend (or even repeal) the Travel Act fits the federal legislative pattern: in general new statutes have simply been layered on over old statutes.

c.   Note also that the structure of compound-complex crimes which rely on proof of numerous predicate offenses inevitably raises double jeopardy concerns. See the discussion in connection with RICO, *supra* at p. 547 and CCE, supra at p. 397. CFCE will raise the same issues, though the dual sovereignty aspect of the problem will not arise since CFCE includes only federal predicate offenses. Although these issues have received less attention under the gambling business statute, they can arise there as well. Section 1955(b)(1)(i) requires proof of each defendant's participation in a gambling business that "is a violation of the law of a State or local political subdivision in which it is conducted." What result if one or more of the defendants in a gambling business prosecution have been acquitted on related counts in state court? Does the lack of specificity in the Travel Act avoid such problems?

2.   In general, these offenses aim at group criminality, though RICO is an important exception to this generalization.

a.   CCE, CFCE, and the gambling business statute require proof of the participation of a minimum number of individuals: CCE requires that the defendant supervise or manage 5 or more persons, CFCE requires that a defendant manage an enterprise consisting of at least 4 persons acting in concert, and the gambling business statute requires that the illegal gambling business involve at least 5 persons. The Travel Act, the forebear of these statutes, has no parallel requirement.

Although RICO contains no parallel requirement, and can be committed by an individual acting alone, certain classes of RICO cases typically involve group criminality. RICO criminalizes several different forms of conduct. Section 1962 (a) & (b) criminalize the infiltration of a legitimate business through a pattern of racketeering activity or through income gained from racketeering; these offenses can be committed by an individual acting alone. Most RICO prosecutions charge that the defendant conducted or participated in the affairs of an enterprise through a pattern of racketeering activity in violation of § 1962(c). A defendant acting alone may violate § 1962(c) if he conducts the affairs of a legitimate enterprise through his own acts of racketeering. Of course, the legitimate enterprise itself typically involves the activities of a group although an individual can be an enterprise under the definition in § 1961, and cases pursued on that basis pose special legal issues, see supra, p. 505.

The most common fact pattern under § 1962(c), however, involves an illegal enterprise and group criminality. The typical § 1962 prosecution involves a wholly criminal enterprise being conducted by a pattern of racketeering activity involving multiple actors. Thus even though the substantive RICO offenses do not require multiple actors, the most common factual scenario of cases prosecuted does involve such multiple actors. It should also be noted that RICO makes conspiring to commit one of the racketeering offenses a crime, and this necessarily involves group criminality.

Insofar as the organizational crimes aim at group criminality, how do they relate to the traditional offense of conspiracy? In general the new offenses carry far harsher penalties than the general conspiracy statute, 18 U.S.C. § 371, which is punishable by a maximum of 5 years imprisonment. In contrast, the maximum term under RICO is 20 years, and under CCE the maximum term is life and the *minimum* term is 20 years for a first offense.[b] The *minimum* sentence under the new continuing financial crimes enterprise statute is 10 years, and the maximum is life imprisonment. The gambling business statute is the only exception to this picture of extremely high penalties; the maximum sentence is 5 years. What is the justification for the severe penalties applicable to RICO, CCE, and CFCE? Is there a distinction between these statutes, on the one hand, and the gambling business statute, on the other hand?

b.   One possibility is that these new statutes are specialized conspiracy provisions tailored to a small number of serious substantive offenses. If so, this should be reflected in their treatment vis-a-vis the existing conspiracy provisions.

CCE is plainly not intended to serve *merely* as a drug conspiracy statute, since the federal code includes not only CCE but also two drug conspiracy provisions, 21 U.S.C. §§ 846 and 961. On the other hand, as discussed in greater detail below, in *Jeffers v. United States*, 432 U.S. 137 (1977), the Supreme Court treated CCE as if it were an aggravated drug conspiracy provision. The Court observed that the CCE penalty structure already took into account the additional dangers of group criminality, which serve as the justification for separate penalties for conspiracy. Accordingly, it was improper to impose cumulative punishments for both conspiracy to commit the predicate drug offenses and CCE. The Court also noted that CCE reflects a comprehensive penalty structure leaving no room for pyramiding penalties. Under this interpretation, 21 U.S.C. § 846, the drug conspiracy provision, is treated as a lesser included offense in relation to CCE. The Supreme Court confirmed this interpretation in *Rutledge v. United States*, 517 U.S. 292 (1996). [But in a successive prosecution context where the government later became aware of an entirely new dimension of criminal conduct implicating separate offenses although also involving an extension of the earlier CCE, the subsequent conduct can be pursued without violating the Double Jeopardy clause. See, e.g., *United States v. Cole*, 293 F.3d 153 (4th Cir. 2002).] CCE's "in concert" requirement parallels the agree-

b. Subsequent offenses are punishable by a minimum term of 30 years imprisonment. 21 U.S.C. § 848(a). In addition, the death penalty is available if for CCE-related murders. 21 U.S.C. § 848(e).

ment element of conspiracy, but CCE also requires proof of several additional elements: that the defendant supervised a minimum of 5 persons, that the group committed a "series" of drug offenses, and that the defendant derived substantial income from the violations. In this respect, CCE appears to function as a specialized drug conspiracy provision that focuses on the ringleader(s) of a large-scale conspiracy that is generating substantial income from the commission of multiple drug offenses. Since CFCE was modeled on CCE, it seems likely that it would receive a similar construction as an aggravated conspiracy provision.

Does this analysis apply with equal force to the gambling business statute? In *Iannelli v. United States*, 420 U.S. 770 (1975), the Supreme Court rejected the conclusion that the gambling business statute was the equivalent of a conspiracy statute. The question in *Iannelli* was whether a defendant could be convicted of both a violation of the gambling business statute, § 1955, and a conspiracy to violate § 1955. The Court concluded that both convictions could stand because the multiple actor requirement of § 1955 was intended merely to limit federal prosecutions to gambling activities of a sufficiently large scale that federal and not merely state and local interests were implicated. Since the requirement of concerted activity was directed to jurisdictional concerns, it was not intended to and did not displace the conspiracy provisions.

Jeffers distinguished *Iannelli* on the ground that the gambling business statute, unlike CCE, did not require an agreement or action in concert. Does this distinction between the treatment of the gambling business statute and CCE make any sense? Even if the multiple actor requirement in the gambling business statute was intended for jurisdictional purposes, Congress certainly took into account the danger of group criminality when it established the penalty under § 1955. Surely both CCE and the gambling business statute require action in concert.

On the other hand, the Court's disposition of *Iannelli* and *Jeffers* does make some sense if one considers the sentencing consequences. At the time it enacted CCE, Congress established high penalties for the substantive drug offenses and also enacted two separate drug conspiracy provisions carrying the same penalties as the object offenses. To allow punishment for not only the predicate offenses and CCE, but also for drug conspiracy,[c] would significantly pyramid the penalties. Because even a standard CCE offense is punishable by a minimum of 20 years and a maximum of life in prison, there seems to be no justification for piling on a conspiracy charge in addition to the predicate drug offenses and the CCE charge.

In contrast, the opportunities for pyramiding penalties—and the consequences of multiple charges—are far more modest under the gambling business statute. The predicate offenses under the gambling busi-

---

c. A later case, *Albernaz v. United States*, 450 U.S. 333 (1981), held that a defendant may be convicted of *two* drug conspiracies, under 21 U.S.C. §§ 846 and 961, for a single agreement to import and distribute drugs. This possibility obviously exacerbates the possibilities for pyramiding penalties.

ness statute are state and local, not federal, offenses. Accordingly, allowing convictions for both the gambling business statute and conspiracy to violate it permitted a maximum of two layers of federal penalties, not three as would be the case under CCE. Moreover, the lower penalties available under the gambling business statute mean that the maximum penalty available if the defendant is convicted of both § 1955 and conspiracy to violate § 1955 will be 10 years. In contrast, the maximum available if the government had succeeded in *Jeffers* would be 20 years to life for CCE, plus up to life imprisonment for both the conspiracy and each of the predicate drug offenses.

If the maximum penalty available under § 1955—5 years—is inadequate for a very large-scale gambling operation, or for top brass of such a structure, perhaps § 1955 should be amended to add a penalty enhancement provision, rather than allowing the pyramiding of a conspiracy charge based upon the transparent fiction that § 1955 does not require action in concert.

c. Should the *Jeffers* principle barring cumulative punishments for both the organizational crime and conspiracy be extended to RICO? As noted above, the only portion of the § 1962 statutory language that *requires* group activity is the RICO conspiracy provision, § 1962(d). Despite its origin in concerns regarding organized crime, the statutory language of RICO makes it clear that the substantive provisions of the statute are not simply specialized conspiracy provisions. To the contrary, Congress drew a clear distinction between the RICO conspiracy provision, § 1962(d), and the substantive RICO offenses in § 1962(a)-(c). Moreover, the predicate acts of racketeering also include many conspiracy offenses, see supra, p. 546, although not the basic federal conspiracy provision, 18 U.S.C. § 371. In light of this clear distinction between conspiracy and the substantive RICO offenses under § 1962(a)-(c), cumulative penalties should be available for conspiracy to commit a predicate offense and a substantive RICO offense under § 1962(a)-(c). Cumulative penalties should also be available for both RICO conspiracy and one or more of the RICO substantive offenses, in light of the general federal rule allowing cumulative penalties for both conspiracy and the object offense. *See United States v. Felix*, 503 U.S. 378 (1992).

Is there any point at which the *Jeffers* concerns about pyramiding penalties and offenses should come into play in RICO cases? As noted above, the gist of the most common RICO substantive charge under § 1962 is an allegation of a criminal enterprise involving multiple criminal actors. Should cumulative penalties be permitted for running a RICO enterprise under § 1962(c), and RICO conspiracy under § 1962(d), and conspiracy as a predicate offense? In *United States v. Licavoli*, 725 F.2d 1040 (6th Cir.1984), the court upheld convictions for 12 predicate conspiracies, for conducting a RICO enterprise under § 1962(c), and RICO conspiracy, § 1962(d). See, e.g., *United States v. Warneke*, 310 F.3d 542 (7th Cir. 2002) affirming agreement with the *Licavoli* decision. Is this double or triple use of conspiracy justified by the danger of group criminality? For a discussion of RICO conspiracy and predicate conspiracies, see *supra* pp. 549–558.

d. The Sentencing Guidelines introduce a new wrinkle into this analysis. In general the Guidelines reduce the opportunity for pyramiding penalties by adding multiple counts arising out of the same criminal activity. Note that U.S.S.G. § 2E1.1 (reprinted in the appendix, *infra* p. 1020), provides that the base offense level for RICO is either 19 or the applicable level for the underlying racketeering activity, whichever is greater. Note also that the Guidelines generally take account of each defendant's role in the offense, prescribing varying increases in the base level if the defendant was an "organizer or leader" or a "manager or supervisor;" the increases also vary depending upon the number of participants. *See* U.S.S.G. § 3B1.1. Finally, the Guidelines also make special provisions for sentencing a "career offender." *See* U.S.S.G. § 4B1.1.

3. Some, but not all of these statutes are aimed at the top brass or kingpins of crime. CCE and CFCE both require proof that the defendant organized, managed, or supervised a minimum number of participants, and CCE also includes a separate provision with enhanced penalties for the "principal administrators, organizers, or leaders" of a drug enterprise that received at least $10 million in gross revenues in one year. In contrast, the Supreme Court has recognized that the gambling business statute "proscribes any degree of participation in an illegal gambling business, except participation as a mere bettor." *Sanabria v. United States*, 437 U.S. 54, 70–71 n. 6 (1978).[d]

a. The Supreme Court's decision in *Reves v. Ernst & Young*, 507 U.S. 170 (1993), has introduced into the RICO statute the concept of only imposing criminal liability on those who "participate in the operation or management of the enterprise." This requirement may be viewed as the RICO analogue of the CCE statutory phrase, "organizer, a supervisory position or any other position of management," although not exactly the same, but the RICO phrase limits liability to management at some level. Recall that the Court in *Reves* declined to decide how far RICO liability extends down the ladder of operation. See pp. 520–524, for discussion of the case law that has addressed this issue in the wake of *Reves*. How does the interpretation of "operate or manage" under RICO compare with the comparable issues under the CCE? Does the government gain advantages by charging a drug enterprise under RICO that it does not obtain under CCE?

The overlap between RICO and CCE suggests a broader question. Because nearly all serious federal offenses are RICO predicates, RICO inevitably covers much of the same ground as CCE, CFCE, the Travel

---

d. This interpretation still requires the lower courts to determine whether peripheral actors have actually participated in the conduct of the enterprise. For example, various courts have struggled to determine whether one bookmaker who takes a few lay off bets for another bookmaker has participated in the conduct of the latter's gambling business. *See United States v. Pinelli*, 890 F.2d 1461, 1471 (10th Cir.1989) (collecting cases); *id.* at 1477–83 (on petition for rehearing).

Act, and the gambling business enterprise statute. What are the implications of this overlap? Do these statutes have sufficiently distinct functions that multiple prosecutions and cumulative penalties should be permitted? In particular, where a wholly criminal enterprise is the subject of a prosecution under § 1962(c) and the same enterprise is also subject to prosecution under one of the other organizational crime statutes, should cumulative penalties be permitted? What if the prosecutor also charges a RICO conspiracy under § 1962(d) in such a case?

b. The application of accomplice provisions to the kingpin statutes has caused some difficulty. The general federal accomplice liability provision, 18 U.S.C. § 2, provides that any aider and abettor is liable as a principal. If CCE is viewed as a substantive offense, one would expect accomplice liability to apply to it. This could mean that each of the minions who assists a kingpin would become liable as a CCE principal, with the serious penalties that attach to that status. In *United States v. Amen*, 831 F.2d 373 (2d Cir.1987), however, the court declined to apply the normal accomplice liability in this context, holding that because CCE represents a congressional decision to single out the ringleaders of large narcotics operations for special punishment, the statute does not apply to one who simply aids and abets a kingpin. Carried too far, the limitation of accomplice doctrine could cripple CCE if it required proof that the kingpin was a principal in a series of drug transactions. This could effectively shield the top layer—super kingpins—who are almost never involved in day to day transactions. Accordingly, in *United States v. Miskinis*, 966 F.2d 1263 (9th Cir.1992), the court held that CCE applies to one who is otherwise a kingpin but whose involvement in the predicate offenses consisted solely of aiding and abetting. *Cf. United States v. Pino-Perez*, 870 F.2d 1230 (7th Cir.1989) (en banc) (though language of § 848 precludes liability for subordinates, liability can extend to one who aids and abets a kingpin in some other capacity). For a more recent application of the *Amen* doctrine, see *United States v. Joyner*, 201 F.3d 61 (2d Cir. 2000).

The RICO analogue of this set of issues involves the question of whether accomplice theory can be used to impose RICO liability on one who did not operate or manage the enterprise. Under RICO, a different answer is given to that question depending on whether the context is a civil suit or a criminal prosecution. See p. 524, supra. Also, it appears that given the necessary mens rea, one who conspires to violate RICO may be held liable under § 1964(d), even though the conspirator did not operate or manage the enterprise. See supra, p. 557. Is there an analogue to that situation under the CCE?

How will all of these issues be handled under the CFCE? Recall that it is modeled on the CCE. There is still only a limited body of case law interpreting the CFCE. See, e.g., *United States v. Lefkowitz*, 289 F.Supp.2d 1076 (D. Minn. 2003) where the court considered whether jury unanimity was required as to which violations make up the series that provide the basis for the CFCE offense, under the doctrine of *Richardson v. United States*, 526 U.S. 813 (1999), which dealt with the same issue under the CCE. See the discussion of *Richardson, supra*, p. 396. Also see *United States v. Harris*, 79 F.3d 223 (2d Cir. 1996) and a later proceeding in the same case, 367 F.3d 74 (2d Cir. 2004).

c. The gambling business statute has raised another wrinkle of traditional accomplice doctrine. Upon occasion the government has charged a peripheral participant in a gambling business as an aider and abettor, rather than a principal. In light of the general provision making accomplices liable as principals,[e] does the designation of an individual as an accomplice in a gambling business case have any significance? The statute draws no distinction between the leaders of the enterprise and other participants, but it does require the participation of at least 5 persons. Is it permissible to count someone charged as an aider and abettor as one of the 5 persons? Following the traditional common law rule that a crime must have been committed before an aider and abettor can be held liable as a accomplice, an early case held that the 5–person requirement must be met without counting an aider and abettor. *United States v. Morris*, 612 F.2d 483 (10th Cir.1979). Does this analysis survive the Supreme Court decision in *Standefer v. United States*, 447 U.S. 10 (1980), which held that an accomplice can be convicted despite the earlier acquittal of the principal? If so, does it nonetheless depend on the incorrect premise that peripheral participants cannot be charged as principals in the first instance, in light of the general recognition that any degree of participation—other than as a mere bettor—is sufficient to support a finding that an individual "conduct[ed]" a gambling business?

---

18 U.S.C.

§ 1955. Prohibition of illegal gambling businesses

(a) Whoever conducts, finances, manages, supervises, directs, or owns all or part of an illegal gambling business shall be fined under this title or imprisoned not more than five years, or both.

(b) As used in this section—

(1) "illegal gambling business" means a gambling business which—

(i) is a violation of the law of a State or political subdivision in which it is conducted;

(ii) involves five or more persons who conduct, finance, manage, supervise, direct, or own all or part of such business; and

(iii) has been or remains in substantially continuous operation for a period in excess of thirty days or has a gross revenue of $2,000 in any single day.

---

e. 18 U.S.C. § 2.

(2) "gambling" includes but is not limited to pool-selling, book-making, maintaining slot machines, roulette wheels or dice tables, and conducting lotteries, policy, bolita or numbers games, or selling chances therein.

(3) "State" means any State of the United States, the District of Columbia, the Commonwealth of Puerto Rico, and any territory or possession of the United States.

(c) If five or more persons conduct, finance, manage, supervise, direct, or own all or part of a gambling business and such business operates for two or more successive days, then, for the purpose of obtaining warrants for arrests, interceptions, and other searches and seizures, probable cause that the business receives gross revenue in excess of $2,000 in any single day shall be deemed to have been established.

(d) Any property, including money, used in violation of the provisions of this section may be seized and forfeited to the United States. All provisions of law relating to the seizure, summary, and judicial forfeiture procedures, and condemnation of vessels, vehicles, merchandise, and baggage for violation of the customs laws; the disposition of such vessels, vehicles, merchandise, and baggage or the proceeds from such sale; the remission or mitigation of such forfeitures; and the compromise of claims and the award of compensation to informers in respect of such forfeitures shall apply to seizures and forfeitures incurred or alleged to have been incurred under the provisions of this section, insofar as applicable and not inconsistent with such provisions. Such duties as are imposed upon the collector of customs or any other person in respect to the seizure and forfeiture of vessels, vehicles, merchandise, and baggage under the customs laws shall be performed with respect to seizures and forfeitures of property used or intended for use in violation of this section by such officers, agents, or other persons as may be designated for that purpose by the Attorney General.

(e) This section shall not apply to any bingo game, lottery, or similar game of chance conducted by an organization exempt from tax under paragraph (3) of subsection (c) of section 501 of the Internal Revenue Code of 1954, as amended, if no part of the gross receipts derived from such activity inures to the benefit of any private shareholder, member, or employee of such organization except as compensation for actual expenses incurred by him in the conduct of such activity.

––––––––

18 U.S.C.

§ 225. Continuing financial crimes enterprise

(a) Whoever—

(1) organizes, manages, or supervises a continuing financial crimes enterprise; and

(2) receives $5,000,000 or more in gross receipts from such enterprise during any 24–month period, shall be fined not more than $10,000,000 if an individual, or $20,000,000 if an organization, and imprisoned for a term of not less than 10 years and which may be life.

(b) For purposes of subsection (a), the term "continuing financial crimes enterprise" means a series of violations under section 215, 656, 657, 1005, 1006, 1007, 1014, 1032, or 1344 of this title, or section 1341 or 1343 affecting a financial institution, committed by at least 4 persons acting in concert.

*

Part V

THE PROTECTION OF FEDERAL RIGHTS AND FUNCTIONS

Chapter 14

THE CRIMINAL CIVIL RIGHTS STATUTES

INTRODUCTION

The principal federal criminal civil rights statutes—18 U.S.C. §§ 241 and 242—were enacted in the post Civil War period and have had a lengthy history. They were initially intended to provide federal sanctions for misconduct directed at newly freed slaves, other blacks, and their supporters. After a long period of nonuse, they were rediscovered in the middle of this century, and in 1968, another civil rights provision, 18 U.S.C. § 245, was added to the federal penal code.

18 U.S.C.

§ 241. Conspiracy against rights

If two or more persons conspire to injure, oppress, threaten, or intimidate any person in any State, Territory, Commonwealth, Possession, or District in the free exercise or enjoyment of any right or privilege secured to him by the Constitution or laws of the United States, or because of his having so exercised the same; or

If two or more persons go in disguise on the highway, or on the premises of another, with intent to prevent or hinder his free exercise or enjoyment of any right or privilege so secured—

They shall be fined under this title or imprisoned not more than ten years, or both; and if death results from the acts committed in violation of this section or if such acts include kidnapping or an attempt to kidnap, aggravated sexual abuse or an attempt to commit aggravated sexual abuse, or an attempt to kill, they shall be fined under this title or imprisoned for any term of years or for life, or both, or may be sentenced to death.

18 U.S.C.

§ 242. Deprivation of rights under color of law

Whoever, under color of any law, statute, ordinance, regulation, or custom, willfully subjects any person in any State, Territory, Commonwealth, Possession, or District to the deprivation of any rights, privileges, or immunities secured or protected by the Constitution or laws of the United States, or to different punishments, pains, or penalties, on account of such person being an alien, or by reason of his color, or race, than are prescribed for the punishment of citizens, shall be fined under this title or imprisoned not more than one year, or both; and if bodily injury results from the acts committed in violation of this section or if such acts include the use, attempted use, or threatened use of a dangerous weapon, explosives, or fire, shall be fined under this title or imprisoned not more than ten years, or both; and if death results from the acts committed in violation of this section or if such acts include kidnapping or an attempt to kidnap, aggravated sexual abuse, or an attempt to commit aggravated sexual abuse, or an attempt to kill, shall be fined under this title, or imprisoned for any term of years or for life, or both, or may be sentenced to death.

Sections 241 and 242 are most often used today for traditional civil rights enforcement—to prosecute criminal conduct motivated by racial or similar prejudice or involving police brutality. These provisions have also been used, however, to prosecute in situations that do not fit the classic model—for example, against official corruption and other crimes committed by governmental agents or where witnesses have been assaulted or killed. In addressing the "new" uses of these statutes reflected in this chapter you should consider questions such as: Which constitutional right has the victim been deprived of in each case? Under what circumstances are offenses committed by police ordinary criminality which should more appropriately be prosecuted as ordinary crime? Are the civil rights offenses being used by the federal government as a type of catch-all crime? What factors have been contributing to the increasingly diversified use of the criminal civil rights statutes?

Civil rights prosecutions are sometimes initiated where there has been a prior state prosecution that failed to produce a conviction or resulted in a penalty deemed inadequate. Accordingly, civil rights prosecutions produce their share of cases in which a claim is made that there has been a violation of the prohibition against double jeopardy or the federal policy against multiple prosecutions. These issues are treated in Chapter 17, infra.

Prior to 1968, the maximum penalty for a violation of § 241 was a $5,000 fine and 10 years imprisonment while § 242 was a misdemeanor subject to a $1,000 fine and a maximum of one year imprisonment. In 1968, the maximum fine under § 241 was increased to $10,000 and the maximum penalty applicable to both provisions if death results from a violation was increased to imprisonment for any term of years or for life. Do you think that the change in the available penalties is likely to have affected the type of cases being prosecuted? The increase in possible penalties does not, of course, guarantee that heavy penalties are in fact always imposed.

A. ELEMENTS OF THE §§ 241, 242 OFFENSES

1. SPECIFIC INTENT

UNITED STATES v. EHRLICHMAN

546 F.2d 910 (D.C.Cir.1976), cert. denied, 429 U.S. 1120 (1977).

Wilkey, Circuit Judge:

John D. Ehrlichman was convicted by a jury of the United States District Court for the District of Columbia on one count of conspiracy to violate the civil rights of Dr. Louis Fielding, 18 U.S.C. § 241, and on two counts of perjury. 18 U.S.C. § 1623. The indictment and conviction arose out of the burglary of Dr. Fielding's office by members of the "Special Investigations" unit within the White House, over which Ehrlichman exercised general supervision, and out of statements made by Ehrlichman to the grand jury and the FBI, in the aftermath of the break-in.

* * *

Opinion for the Court filed by CIRCUIT JUDGE WILKEY.

Concurring opinion filed by CIRCUIT JUDGE LEVENTHAL, joined by JUDGE MERHIGE.

WILKEY, CIRCUIT JUDGE:

* * *

II. GOOD FAITH AS A DEFENSE TO "SPECIFIC
INTENT" UNDER 18 U.S.C. § 241

The most substantial argument advanced by defendant Ehrlichman on appeal from his conviction under 18 U.S.C. § 241 is that the District Court's mistaken legal view of the statute's "specific intent" requirement led the court to commit reversible error, both in ruling on the admissibility of certain evidence sought to be introduced by him and in instructing the jury on the basic elements of the offense. Not every conspiracy affecting a citizen's constitutional rights falls within the prohibition of section 241. It is settled law that "the offender must act with a specific intent to interfere with the federal rights in question...." Ehrlichman contends that he acted without the requisite "specific intent" to invade Dr. Fielding's Fourth Amendment rights, since he agreed to a search of the doctor's office in the good faith belief that it would involve no violation of the law, constitutional or otherwise.

Prior to trial Ehrlichman and his co-defendants presented this theory of the case to the District Court in connection with motions for discovery of certain national security information. They took the position that the information would provide factual support for their asserted belief in the legality of the Fielding operation. The District Court rejected the defendants' theory, and their motions, in the following language:

> Defendants contend that, even if the break-in was illegal, they lacked the specific intent necessary to violate section 241 because they reasonably *believed* that they had been authorized to enter and search Dr. Fielding's office. As explained above, however, such authorization was not only factually absent but also legally insufficient, and it is well established that a mistake of law is no defense in a conspiracy case to the knowing performance of acts which, like the unauthorized entry and search at issue here, are malum in se. As the Supreme Court said in *Screws v. United States*, 325 U.S. 91, 106 (1945), "[t]he fact that the defendants may not have been thinking in constitutional terms is not material [to a charge under § 242, a related specific intent statute,] where their aim was not to enforce local law but to deprive a citizen of a right and that right was protected by the Constitution." Here, defendants are alleged to have intended to search Dr. Fielding's office without a warrant, and their mistaken belief that such conduct did not offend the Constitution would not protect them from prosecution under section 241.

As a result of the District Court's ruling, Ehrlichman was restricted during the trial in his ability to obtain and introduce evidence of the national security circumstances surrounding the Fielding operation. At the end of the trial, the court rejected jury instructions which provided that belief in the legality of one's conduct could negate "specific intent" under section 241, and advised the jury that the requisite intent would be established under section 241 if the Prosecutor showed simply "that the object of the conspiracy and the purpose of each defendant was to carry out a warrantless entry into and search of Dr. Fielding's office without permission."

The trial judge's position, as set forth in both his pre-trial opinion and in his instructions to the jury, unquestionably states the law with regard to the vast majority of criminal conspiracies. Even though all such conspiracies are crimes of "specific intent"—in that the defendant must not only combine with others but also intend to commit unlawful acts—generally there is no requirement that the conspirator know those acts to be unlawful. A mistake as to the legality of the prohibited activity, therefore, is no defense.

The doctrine that a mistake of law will not excuse a crime normally applies in conspiracy cases even when the target offense itself has "specific intent" as an element. The reason for this is that the mental state required for most "specific intent" offenses does not involve knowledge of illegality. If the recognition of the unlawfulness of one's action is not an element of the substantive crime, neither is it a component of the offense of agreeing to commit the crime.

Significantly, however, some "specific intent" crimes can be committed only if the defendant performs the actus reus with an intention to violate the law, or without ground for believing his action is lawful. A good faith mistake as to the legality of his activity, or failure to act, is a valid defense to prosecution for such a crime. Equally important, such a mistake necessarily also constitutes a defense to a charge of conspiracy to commit this kind of "specific intent" crime.

In sum, whether the District Court properly rejected the good faith defense proffered by Ehrlichman is a question whose answer rests, in the first instance, on the mens rea required to commit the target offense under section 241. We examine the nature of that section's "specific intent" requirement in Subsection A. * * * Our conclusion is that under the circumstances of this case the District Court did not err in rejecting the defendant's good faith defense.

A. The "Specific Intent" Requirement of Section 241

1. *Screws v. United States*[a]

The substantive counterpart to section 241 is 18 U.S.C. § 242, which provides in pertinent part:

> Whoever, under color of any law, statute, ordinance, regulation, or custom, willfully subjects any inhabitant ... to the deprivation of any rights, privileges, or immunities secured or protected by the Constitution or laws of the United States, ... shall be fined not more than $1,000 or imprisoned not more than one year, or both; and if death results shall be subject to imprisonment for any term of years or for life.

The seminal case dealing with the element of *mens rea* under section 242 is *Screws v. United States.* The defendants in *Screws,* law enforcement officials who had beaten a prisoner to death, were charged with denying that individual various of his due process rights under the Fourth Amendment. They countered with an attack on the constitutionality of section 242—arguing that if it incorporated such a large body of changing and uncertain law as surrounds the concept of due process, the statute lacked the basic specificity essential to criminal statutes under our legal system.

The Court acknowledged that this "vagueness" challenge would be serious if the "customary standard" of guilt for statutory crimes were applied under section 242. The presence of the term "willfully" in the statute, however, afforded the Court, a convenient means for narrowing its potential reach—not only to fulfill the constitutional requirement of specificity but also to prevent the federal statute from becoming a "catchall" which might interfere with the traditional law enforcement role of the states. The Court noted, first, that precise construction of the word "willful" in a statute was dependent on its context. "But 'when used in a criminal statute it generally means an act done with a bad purpose.' "It requires a particular intent in addition to the performance of the act required by the statute.

a. *Screws* is reprinted, infra at p. 646.

The Court determined that for the purposes of section 242 acting "willfully" meant acting with "a purpose to deprive a person of a specific constitutional right," "made definite by decision or other rule of law." Such a construction, in the Court's view, would cure the problem of vagueness presented by the statute:

> One who does act with such specific intent is aware that what he does is precisely that which the statute forbids. He is under no necessity of guessing whether the statute applies to him ... for he either knows or acts in reckless disregard of its prohibition of the deprivation of a defined constitutional or other federal right.... The Act would then not become a trap for law enforcement agencies acting in good faith. "A mind intent upon willful evasion is inconsistent with surprised innocence." *United States v. Ragen*, [314 U.S. 513, 524 (1942).]

The Court observed that the indictment in *United States v. Classic*, an earlier case involving section 242, met the test of "specific intent" it had just laid down. That indictment charged the defendants with, inter alia, the willful alteration of ballots. Such alteration, the Court emphasized, clearly breached a right expressly guaranteed by the Constitution—viz., the right to vote. The indictment did not charge that the defendants had acted with the specific intent to deprive voters of their constitutional prerogatives. Nevertheless, the Court concluded:

> Such a charge is adequate since he who alters ballots or without legal justification destroys them would be acting willfully in the sense in which [§ 242] uses the term. *The fact that the defendants may not have been thinking in constitutional terms is not material where their aim was not to enforce local law but to deprive a citizen of a right and that right was protected by the Constitution. When they so act they at least act in reckless disregard of constitutional prohibitions or guarantees.*

Turning to the charge against the defendants in *Screws* itself, the Court observed, "Likewise, it is plain that basic to the concept of due process of law in a criminal case is a trial—a trial in a court of law, not a 'trial by ordeal.'""No allegation of intent to breach a constitutional right, therefore, was necessary. The Court held that the 'specific intent' requirement of section 242 would be met if the jury were instructed simply that to convict they must find the defendants had beaten their prisoner to death with the particular purpose of subjecting him to a trial by ordeal."

2. *The Meaning of Screws*

Although some of the language in *Screws* can be read more broadly, its holding essentially sets forth two requirements for a finding of "specific intent" under section 242. The first is a purely legal determination. Is the constitutional right at issue clearly delineated and plainly applicable under the circumstances of the case? If the trial judge concludes that it is, then the jury must make the second, factual, determination. Did the defendant commit the act in question with the particular purpose of depriving the citizen victim of his enjoyment of the interests protected by that federal right? If both requirements are met, even if the defendant did not in fact recognize the unconstitutionality of his act, he will be adjudged as a matter of law to have acted "willfully"—i.e., "in reckless disregard of constitutional prohibitions or guarantees."

These "specific intent" requirements, grafted by the Supreme Court onto the elements of a section 242 violation, met the Court's twin concerns of vagueness and federalism in *Screws*. On the one hand, the requirement that the constitutional right in question be clearly established provides the specificity needed for a criminal statute to meet minimal standards of due process. On the other hand, the requirement that the defendant have a purpose to infringe federally protected interests preserves the states' traditional prerogative to prosecute and punish those who commit ordinary crime. For example, as *Screws* illustrates, the Constitution clearly grants protection to a citizen's interests in not being punished by governmental officials without a trial. There is no violation of section 242, however, if a sheriff and his deputies commit a murder for purely personal, nongovernmental reasons. The state can, and should, deal with such crime. Section 242 comes into play only if the object of the murder was to punish a prisoner for past illegal acts, or for some other purpose stemming from the official position of those committing the homicide.

The same principles apply to prosecutions for conspiracy under section 241. Although the language of sections 241 and 242 is somewhat different—indeed, section 241 does not contain the word "willfully"—the Supreme Court has made clear since *Screws* that the "specific intent" requirements of section 242 are equally applicable (or derivatively applicable) to section 241. In *United States v. Guest*, decided in 1966, the Court reversed the dismissal of an indictment charging the defendants with violating section 241 by, inter alia, conspiring to intimidate blacks in the free exercise of the right of interstate travel. The Court observed, first, that the rights of equal utilization of public facilities and freedom of travel had been firmly established and repeatedly recognized; therefore, the requirement of constitutional clarity presented no difficulty. Second, the Court noted with reference to the right to travel that under *Screws* not every criminal conspiracy which incidentally interfered with that right is prohibited by section 241. A conspiracy to rob a private person who happens to be traveling interstate, for example, would not violate section 241, because it would entail no purpose to invade federally protected interests. On remand, therefore, the Court found that the prosecution would have to show the defendants conspired to intimidate an individual *because* he was traveling interstate.

Most recently, in *Anderson v. United States*, decided in 1974, the Court reaffirmed and further elucidated the "specific intent" requirements of section 241. Since the constitutional right in question was the right to an equal vote in a federal election, the defendants convicted of casting false votes could not be assailed on the ground that the federal interests involved were not clear and firmly established. Rather, the main issue was whether an intent to invade those federal interests had been proven, in view of the fact that the primary objective of the conspiracy was to influence a local election—even though false votes had been cast for candidates for federal office as well. The Court found adequate evidence of "specific intent," concluding:

> A single conspiracy may have several purposes but if one of them—whether primary or secondary—be the violation of federal law, the conspiracy is unlawful under federal law.

* * *

> That petitioners may have had no purpose to change the outcome of the federal election is irrelevant. The specific intent required under § 241 is not the intent to change the outcome of a federal election, but rather the intent to have false votes cast and thereby injure the right of all voters in a federal election to express their choice of a candidate and to have their expressions of choice given full value and effect, without being diluted or distorted by the casting of fraudulent ballots.

Screws and its progeny thus compel the conclusion that the specific intent required to violate section 241 is the purpose of the conspirators to commit acts which deprive a citizen of interests in fact protected by clearly defined constitutional rights. If that purpose was present, there is no "good faith" defense, such as Ehrlichman proffers, because of lack of awareness of the conspirators at the time they commit the proscribed acts that they are violating constitutional rights. There is no requirement under section 241 that a defendant recognize the unlawfulness of his acts.

* * *

[T]he violation of the Fourth Amendment in this case was clear. Ehrlichman cannot and does not argue that he should be allowed a defense based upon his reasonable reliance on an apparently valid statute or judicial decision, nor does his invocation of the claimed foreign affairs exception to the warrant requirement avail him, for even the claim of a foreign affairs exception has consistently been conditioned on specific approval by the President or the Attorney General. Ehrlichman was himself a high government official. He does not contend that specific judicial or Presidential approval was obtained for the Fielding break-in. He simply asserts that it was his belief that the break-in was lawful notwithstanding the absence of any such specific approval. Such a mistake of law can be no defense.

* * *

It is not a violation of section 241 for individuals who happen to be government agents to burglarize a doctor's office for purely personal gain. It *is* a civil rights conspiracy in violation of that section, however, if they enter his office in their capacity as government agents without proper authorization to secure information for an ostensible government purpose. The concern of Congress in enacting section 241 was to extend the federal police power to those who intentionally interfere with federally protected interests—e.g., officials whose specific purpose is to accomplish the governmental objectives of punishment or obtaining confessions or searching private premises, individuals who act with the particular intent of preventing other citizens' equal use of the polls or the interstate highways. The objective must be governmental even though section 241, unlike section 242, does not require that conspirators act under color of law. The states can deal with those who kill or mug or burglarize out of passion or greed for purely personal reasons.

* * *

Notes

1.   Is there a reason why the specific intent requirement under section 242 should be read into section 241?

2.   It has been suggested that *Screws* requires "that there be shown a specific intent to deprive the victim of his federal *rights*, not merely, for example, to beat or murder him." (emphasis in the original). Nat. Comm'n on Reform of Federal Criminal Laws, Study Draft of a New Federal Criminal Code, § 1501, Comment at 147 (1970). Is this a correct reading of *Screws?* Must the defendant have been thinking in terms of depriving the victim of a federal right? Thinking in terms of a constitutional right? *See e.g. United States v. McClean*, 528 F.2d 1250 (2d Cir.1976) and *United States v. Stokes*, 506 F.2d 771 (5th Cir.1975). In *McClean*, the court stated: "[The judge] * * * properly instructed the jury that if it found that each defendant knew and intended what he was doing and that his conduct deprived a person of his constitutional rights, it might conclude that the defendant acted with the 'intention to deprive the victims of that constitutional right'. [T]he clear intention of the defendants * * * was to extort money from their victims under color of their state authority and without adherence to the processes due under the law." 528 F.2d 1250, 1255.

If National Guardsmen fire shots into a protesting group of students because of a mistaken belief that an order to fire has been given, can they be guilty of a § 242 violation? Suppose they fired because they had some preexisting malice toward the students? *See United States v. Shafer*, 384 F.Supp. 496 (N.D.Ohio 1974). Is it helpful to distinguish between primary and secondary intent? *See Anderson v. United States*, 417 U.S. 211, 225–226 (1974).

For a thorough discussion of *Screws*, the history of the civil rights statutes and their interpretation, and an attempt to set forth a clear outline of the mens rea that should be required in different kinds of civil rights prosecutions, see Frederick M. Lawrence, *Civil Rights and Criminal Wrongs: The Mens Rea of Federal Civil Rights Crimes*, 67 Tul. L. Rev. 2113 (1993). For a critique of the decisions interpreting the specific intent requirement in §§ 241 and 242, see Edward F. Malone, *Comment, Legacy of the Reconstruction: The Vagueness of the Criminal Civil Rights Statutes*, 38 U.C.L.A. L. Rev. 163 (1990). For a discussion of cases regarding jury instructions on specific intent in the context of prosecutions for excessive force in the course of an arrest, see the notes following *Schatzle*, infra at p. 662.

3.   What difference does it make how the mens rea requirement set forth in *Screws* is interpreted? Does it determine whether the use of these sections is limited to classic civil rights matters or can be extended to more general kinds of criminal enforcement? Does the interpretation given to the mens rea requirement potentially affect the federal-state enforcement relationship as much as does the interpretation given to the "under color of law" formula or the deprivation of rights issue?

4.   When § 241 was challenged on First Amendment grounds in a cross burning case, the panel majority found the intent element crucial to sustaining the statute in *United States v. Lee*, 935 F.2d 952 (8th Cir.1991), though the chief judge dissented and the full court granted rehearing en banc on this issue. The panel majority stated:

> We hold that the governmental interest in supporting this regulation [§ 241] is unrelated to the suppression of free expression. Section 241 does not prohibit conspiracies to communicate offensive or racist messages; it does not prohibit conspiracies to simply burn a cross. Section 241 is a content neutral statute which prohibits conspiracies to threaten or intimidate others in the exercise of their federally guaranteed rights. As applied to the facts before us, *section 241 does not prohibit Lee from conspiring to burn a cross to convey an offensive message or a message of racial hatred. Rather, the statute prohibits Lee from conspiring to burn a cross to threaten or intimidate targeted individuals in the exercise of their federally guaranteed right to rent and occupy a dwelling.*

Id. at 955 (emphasis added). The panel majority also rejected the claim that § 241 is vague and overbroad, finding that "[v]iewed in the context of the statute and, thus, as a part of the complex scienter requirement, the meaning of the statute is not vague." *Id.* at 957. Chief Judge Arnold dissented, arguing that the statute as construed is not sufficiently narrowly tailored to justify the restrictions on expressive conduct protected by the First Amendment, *id.* at 958–60; and the en banc court granted review and vacated the panel's opinion regarding the charge under § 241. *Id.* at 952.

While the en banc court had *Lee* under submission, the Supreme Court decided *R.A.V. v. City of Saint Paul*, 505 U.S. 377 (1992), a cross-burning case in which it held a municipal hate crimes ordinance facially invalid under the First Amendment. Even construed as limited to fighting words, the ordinance violated the First Amendment because it discriminated by content and even by viewpoint, prohibiting only fighting words containing messages of bias-motivated hatred. The five-member majority concluded that "[s]electivity of this sort creates the possibility that the city is seeking to handicap the expression of particular ideas." 505 U.S. at 394. The majority also rejected the claim that the ordinance was justified by a compelling state interest in helping ensure the basic human rights of members of groups that have historically been subjected to discrimination. The majority acknowledged that these interests are compelling, but it concluded that the same benefits could be obtained by an ordinance without the content discrimination. The only interest distinctively served by the regulation in question was "that of displaying the city council's special hostility toward the particular biases thus singled out." 505 U.S. at 396.

After the decision in *R.A.V.* the en banc court reversed the conviction in *Lee* without producing a majority opinion. *United States v. Lee*, 6 F.3d 1297 (8th Cir.1993). Judge Gibson's plurality opinion reiterated Chief Judge Arnold's concern that the jury instructions had extended the statute to " 'criminalize a great deal of conduct, some of it pure speech, which does no more than forcefully state a view that others find revolting or appalling.' " 6 F.3d at 1301. The plurality concluded that on retrial Lee's conviction for cross burning could be sustained if the jury found either (1) Lee burned the cross with the intent to advocate force or violence and the burning was likely to produce such action, or (2) Lee intended to threaten the residents or at least intended to cause them reasonably to fear the imminent use of force or violence. 6 F.3d at 1304.

As applied to expressive conduct such as cross burning, is § 241 subject to the same analysis as the ordinance involved in *R.A.V.?* Unlike the St. Paul ordinance, § 241 does not specifically target expressive conduct. Rather, its focus is on conduct aimed at depriving individuals of their constitutional rights. Thus it seems likely that the analysis of § 241 will continue to focus on the issue of overbreadth. Chief Judge Arnold argued that the instruction in *Lee* did not require the jury to find either imminent actual force or threat of force, and thus that the statute was overbroad. 935 F.2d at 959–60. For other cases involving cross burnings prosecuted under § 241, *see United States v. Whitney*, 229 F.3d 1296 (10th Cir.2000), *United States v. Stewart*, 65 F.3d 918 (11th Cir.1995), *United States v. McDermott*, 29 F.3d 404 (8th Cir.1994), and *United States v. J.H.H.*, 22 F.3d 821 (8th Cir.1994). The Whitney, Stewart, and J.H.H. cases also involved prosecutions under 42 U.S.C. § 3631 which provides in pertinent part,

> Whoever, whether or not acting under color of law, . . . by threat of force . . . willfully . . . attempts to . . . intimidate . . . (a) any person because of his race [or] color . . . and because he is occupying . . . any dwelling . . . shall be fined . . . or imprisoned not more than one year, or both . . . . [but] if such acts include the use of fire . . . shall be fined . . . or imprisoned not more than ten years, or both . . . .

2.   UNDER COLOR OF LAW

SCREWS v. UNITED STATES

325 U.S. 91, 65 S.Ct. 1031, 89 L.Ed. 1495 (1945).

Mr. Justice Douglas announced the judgment of the Court and delivered the following opinion, in which the Chief Justice, Mr. Justice Black and Mr. Justice Reed concur.

This case involves a shocking and revolting episode in law enforcement. Petitioner Screws was sheriff of Baker County, Georgia. He enlisted the assistance of petitioner Jones, a policeman, and petitioner Kelley, a special deputy, in arresting Robert Hall, a citizen of the United States and of Georgia. The arrest was made late at night at Hall's home on a warrant charging Hall with theft of a tire. Hall, a young negro about thirty years of age, was handcuffed and taken by car to the court house. As Hall alighted from the car at the court house square, the three petitioners began beating him with their fists and with a solid-bar blackjack about eight inches long and weighing two pounds. They claimed Hall had reached for a gun and had used insulting language as he alighted from the car. But after Hall, still handcuffed, had been knocked to the ground they continued to beat him from fifteen to thirty minutes until he was unconscious. Hall was then dragged feet first through the court house yard into the jail and thrown upon the floor dying. An ambulance was called and Hall was removed to a hospital where he died within the hour and without regaining consciousness. There was evidence that Screws held a grudge against Hall and had threatened to "get" him.

An indictment was returned against petitioners—one count charging a violation of § 20 of the Criminal Code, 18 U.S.C. § 52, and another charging a conspiracy to violate § 20 contrary to § 37 of the Criminal Code, 18 U.S.C. § 88, 18 U.S.C. § 88, Sec. 20 provides:

> "Whoever, under color of any law, statute, ordinance, regulation, or custom, willfully subjects, or causes to be subjected, any inhabitant of any State, Territory, or District to the deprivation of any rights, privileges, or immunities secured or protected by the Constitution and laws of the United States, or to different punishments, pains, or penalties, on account of such inhabitant being an alien, or by reason of his color, or race, than are prescribed for the punishment of citizens, shall be fined not more than $1,000, or imprisoned not more than one year, or both."

The indictment charged that petitioners, acting under color of the laws of Georgia, "willfully" caused Hall to be deprived of "rights, privileges, or immunities secured or protected" to him by the Fourteenth Amendment—the right not to be deprived of life without due process of law; the right to be tried, upon the charge on which he was arrested, by due process of law and if found guilty to be punished in accordance with the laws of Georgia; that is to say that petitioners "unlawfully and wrongfully did assault, strike and beat the said Robert Hall about the head with human fists and a blackjack causing injuries" to Hall "which were the proximate and immediate cause of his death." A like charge was made in the conspiracy count.

The case was tried to a jury. The court charged the jury that due process of law gave one charged with a crime the right to be tried by a jury and sentenced by a court. On the question of intent it charged that

> "... if these defendants, without its being necessary to make the arrest effectual or necessary to their own personal protection, beat this man, assaulted him or killed him while he was under arrest, then they would be acting illegally under color of law, as stated by this statute, and would be depriving the prisoner of certain constitu-

tional rights guaranteed to him by the Constitution of the United States and consented to by the State of Georgia."

The jury returned a verdict of guilty and a fine and imprisonment on each count was imposed. The Circuit Court of Appeals affirmed the judgment of conviction, one judge dissenting. The case is here on a petition for a writ of certiorari which we granted because of the importance in the administration of the criminal laws of the questions presented.

* * *

It is said, however, that petitioners did not act "under color of any law" within the meaning of § 20 of the Criminal Code. We disagree. We are of the view that petitioners acted under "color" of law in making the arrest of Robert Hall and in assaulting him. They were officers of the law who made the arrest. By their own admissions they assaulted Hall in order to protect themselves and to keep their prisoner from escaping. It was their duty under Georgia law to make the arrest effective. Hence, their conduct comes within the statute.

Some of the arguments which have been advanced in support of the contrary conclusion suggest that the question under § 20 is whether Congress has made it a federal offense for a state officer to violate the law of his State. But there is no warrant for treating the question in state law terms. The problem is not whether state law has been violated but whether an inhabitant of a State has been deprived of a federal right by one who acts under "color of any law." He who acts under "color" of law may be a federal officer or a state officer. He may act under "color" of federal law or of state law. The statute does not come into play merely because the federal law or the state law under which the officer purports to act is violated. It is applicable when and only when some one is deprived of a federal right by that action. The fact that it is also a violation of state law does not make it any the less a federal offense punishable as such. Nor does its punishment by federal authority encroach on state authority or relieve the state from its responsibility for punishing state offenses.

We agree that when this statute is applied to the action of state officials, it should be construed so as to respect the proper balance between the States and the federal government in law enforcement. Violation of local law does not necessarily mean that federal rights have been invaded. The fact that a prisoner is assaulted, injured, or even murdered by state officials does not necessarily mean that he is deprived of any right protected or secured by the Constitution or laws of the United States. The Fourteenth Amendment did not alter the basic relations between the States and the national government. Our national government is one of delegated powers alone. Under our federal system the administration of criminal justice rests with the States except as Congress, acting within the scope of those delegated powers, has created offenses against the United States. As stated in *United States v. Cruikshank*, 92 U.S. 542, 553, 554, "It is no more the duty or within the power of the United States to punish for a conspiracy to falsely imprison or murder within a State, than it would be to punish for false imprisonment or murder itself." It is only state action of a "particular character" that is prohibited by the Fourteenth Amendment and against which the Amendment authorizes Congress to afford relief. *Civil Rights Cases*, 109 U.S. 3, 11, 13. Thus Congress in § 20 of the Criminal Code did not undertake to make all torts of state officials federal crimes. It brought within § 20 only specified acts done "under color" of law and then only those acts which deprived a person of some right secured by the Constitution or laws of the United States.

This section was before us in *United States v. Classic*, 313 U.S. 299, 326, where we said: "Misuse of power, possessed by virtue of state law and made possible only because the wrongdoer is clothed with the authority of state law, is action taken 'under color of' state law." In that case state election officials were charged with failure to count the votes as cast, alteration of the ballots, and false certification of the number of votes cast for the respective candidates. We stated that those acts of the defendants "were committed in the course of their performance of duties under the Louisiana statute requiring them to count the ballots, to record the result of the count, and to certify the result of the election." In the present case, as we have said, the defendants were officers of the law who had made an arrest and who by their own admissions made the assault in order to protect themselves and to keep the prisoner from escaping, i.e. to make the arrest effective. That was a duty they had under Georgia law. *United States v. Classic* is, therefore, indistinguishable from this case so far as "under color of" state law is concerned. In each officers of the State were performing official duties; in each the power which they were authorized to exercise was misused. We cannot draw a distinction between them unless we are to say that § 20 is not applicable to police officers. But the broad sweep of its language leaves no room for such an exception.

It is said that we should abandon the holding of the *Classic Case*. It is suggested that the present problem was not clearly in focus in that case and that its holding was ill-advised. A reading of the opinion makes plain that the question was squarely involved and squarely met. * * *

* * * We are not dealing here with a case where an officer not authorized to act nevertheless takes action. Here the state officers were authorized to make an arrest and to take such steps as were necessary to make the arrest effective. They acted without authority only in the sense that they used excessive force in making the arrest effective. It is clear that under "color" of law means under "pretense" of law. Thus acts of officers in the ambit of their personal pursuits are plainly excluded. Acts of officers who undertake to perform their official duties are included whether they hew to the line of their authority or overstep it. If, as suggested, the statute was designed to embrace only action which the State in fact authorized, the words "under color of any law" were hardly apt words to express the idea.

[JUSTICE RUTLEDGE concurred in the result. JUSTICE MURPHY, separately, and JUSTICE ROBERTS, in an opinion joined by JUSTICES FRANKFURTER and JACKSON, dissented.]

Notes

1. The Supreme Court has repeatedly sustained the power of Congress to employ criminal sanctions to enforce the rights guaranteed by the Due Process Clause of the Fourteenth Amendment. *See United States v. Price*, 383 U.S. 787, 789 (1966); *United States v. Williams*, 341 U.S. 70, 72 (1951); *Screws v. United States*, 325 U.S. 91, 100 (1945).

2. *Price* also held that § 241 could be used to prosecute a conspiracy under color of law to deprive a person of Fourteenth Amendment rights. In *Price* eighteen defendants were charged with violations of §§ 241 and 242 in connection with the murder in Mississippi of civil rights workers Schwerner, Chaney and Goodman. The district court held that the statutes did not reach the conduct of private persons, and dismissed the indictment. The Supreme Court reversed, stating:

> Private persons, jointly engaged with state officials in the prohibited action are acting "under color" of law for purposes of the statute. To act "under color" of law does not require that the accused be an officer of the State. It is enough that he is a willful participant in joint activity with the State or its agents.

383 U.S. at 794. For an account of the civil rights movement, these murders, and their aftermath, see SETH CAGIN & PHILIP DRAY, WE ARE NOT AFRAID : THE STORY OF GOODMAN, SCHWERNER, AND CHANEY AND THE CIVIL RIGHTS CAMPAIGN FOR MISSISSIPPI (1988). For a more recent case applying the theory that a private individual can be charged under § 241 if he conspires with state officials, see *United States v. Farmer*, 923 F.2d 1557 (11th Cir.1991), where investigators from the sheriff's department brought a suspect in for questioning and then stood by while the victim of the crime assaulted the suspect.

3. In some cases the question is whether a state officer or employee is acting under color of law or as a private citizen. Judge Lanier, infra p. 652, raised this argument, but the Supreme Court declined to consider it because it had not been addressed by the en banc court of appeals. Consider the following cases. Do you think they fall within the civil rights statutes?

a. In *United States v. Tarpley*, 945 F.2d 806 (5th Cir.1991), a deputy sheriff assaulted his wife's former lover with "sap gloves" filled with metal shot, put his service revolver in the victim's mouth, and threatened to kill the victim, saying that he could get away with it because he was a cop. The defendant then summoned a fellow officer; together they followed the victim's car out of town. Although the attack occurred in the defendant's home and the motive was an extra-marital affair, the court of appeals upheld the conviction under §§ 241 and 242, reasoning as follows:

> There was sufficient evidence in the record from which a rational juror could conclude that Tarpley was acting under color of law. Tarpley did more than simply use his service revolver and identify himself as a police officer. At several points during his assault of Vestal, he claimed

to have special authority for his actions by virtue of his official status. He claimed that he could kill Vestal because he was an officer of the law. Significantly, Tarpley summoned another police officer from the sheriff's station and identified him as a fellow officer and ally. The men proceeded to run Vestal out of town in their squad car. The presence of police and the air of official authority pervaded the entire incident. * * * 945 F.2d at 809.

b. In *United States v. Causey*, 185 F.3d 407 (5th Cir.1999), a divided court affirmed the conviction under §§ 241 and 242 of a New Orleans police officer who recruited a drug dealer and his associate to kill a citizen who had filed a complaint charging the officer with police brutality. A majority of the court stated that the test for the "color of law" requirement was whether (1) the officer had misused or abused his official power, (2) there was "a nexus between the victim, the improper conduct, and [the officer's] performance of official duties," and (3) the other defendants "jointly engaged with [the officer] in the prohibited action." 185 F.3d at 415. Two members of the court concluded that this test was met because the officer paged the other defendants during his shift to set up the killing, met with them at the police station, took them to the place for the killing in his patrol car, paged them again while patrolling to tell them the victim's location, and used his police radio to confirm that the murder had taken place. *Ibid.* The officer intended that the murder occur during his shift so that he could cover up his associates' connection to the murder. The court also noted that the motive for the crime arose from the defendant's official conduct. Judge DeMoss dissented on the ground that the officer was not exercising any actual or apparent authority. *Id.* at 424–26. (He was not, for example, even purporting to be making an arrest.)

c. In *United States v. Robinson*, 503 F.2d 208, 211–12 (7th Cir.1974), two Chicago police officers, Robinson and Tolliver and one Taylor, were charged with violations of 18 U.S.C. § 1201(a) (kidnapping) and §§ 241 and 242. The conduct on which the charges were based had resulted in the deaths of Smith and Beard. Robinson was convicted of all three crimes and sentenced to life imprisonment. Taylor was convicted of kidnapping and the § 242 charge and sentenced to life imprisonment. Tolliver was acquitted.

Pursuant to planning a big robbery, Robinson and others (including O'Neal who turned out to be an FBI informant) engaged in a "fundraising" effort to finance the robbery. Their fundraising included shakedowns of drug pushers and accepting "hit contracts" to murder designated individuals. Under one of these "contracts," they agreed to murder one McFerren, a witness in a state murder case. By mistake, while trying to kill McFerren, they killed Smith. Tolliver allegedly fired the fatal rifle shot from a moving car that Robinson was driving on a Chicago Expressway. Beard, a narcotics pusher, was the subject of another of these "contracts." Robinson picked up Beard, informed him that he had a warrant for his arrest and that he was going to take him to the stationhouse. Robinson handcuffed him and instead took him across the state line to Indiana where he shot and clubbed him to death.

Was the *Robinson* case an instance of abuse of official authority or was it simply ordinary criminality that happened to be performed by an official?

Was Robinson acting under "color of law" in connection with either of the killings? Were these "acts of officers in the ambit of their personal pursuits"?

Why were violations of §§ 241 and 242 charged? What did they add, given the availability of the kidnapping charge in connection with Beard's death? In connection with the killing of Smith, should it matter that there were police officers involved? In connection with the killing of Smith should it matter that McFerren was a state witness? Does it matter that the Smith killing occurred on the Expressway? Which of the two killings, Smith or Beard, involved a more questionable application of § 241 or § 242?

For further litigation arising out of the same facts as the *Robinson* decision, see *United States v. Robinson*, 585 F.2d 274 (7th Cir.1978), and Beard v. Mitchell, 604 F.2d 485 (7th Cir.1979).

3. THE DEPRIVATION OF "RIGHTS, PRIVILEGES, OR IMMUNITIES SECURED OR PROTECTED BY THE CONSTITUTION OR LAWS OF THE UNITED STATES"

UNITED STATES v. LANIER

520 U.S. 259, 117 S.Ct. 1219, 137 L.Ed.2d 432 (1997).

JUSTICE SOUTER DELIVERED THE OPINION OF THE COURT.

Respondent David Lanier was convicted under 18 U.S.C. § 242 of criminally violating the constitutional rights of five women by assaulting them sexually while Lanier served as a state judge. The Sixth Circuit reversed his convictions on the ground that the constitutional right in issue had not previously been identified by this Court in a case with fundamentally similar facts. The question is whether this standard of notice is higher than the Constitution requires, and we hold that it is.

I

David Lanier was formerly the sole state Chancery Court judge for two rural counties in western Tennessee. The trial record, read most favorably to the jury's verdict, shows that from 1989 to 1991, while Lanier was in office, he sexually assaulted several women in his judicial chambers. The two most serious assaults were against a woman whose divorce proceedings had come before Lanier and whose daughter's custody remained subject to his jurisdiction. When the woman applied for a secretarial job at Lanier's courthouse, Lanier interviewed her and suggested that he might have to reexamine the daughter's custody. When the woman got up to leave, Lanier grabbed her, sexually assaulted her, and finally committed oral rape. A few weeks later, Lanier inveigled the woman into returning to the courthouse again to get information about another job opportunity, and again sexually assaulted and orally raped her. On five other occasions Lanier sexually assaulted four other women: two of his secretaries, a Youth Services Officer of the juvenile court over which Lanier presided, and a local coordinator for a federal program who was in Lanier's chambers to discuss a matter affecting the same court.

Ultimately, Lanier was charged with 11 violations of § 242, each count of the indictment alleging that, acting willfully and under color of Tennessee law, he had deprived the victim of "rights and privileges which are secured and protected by the Constitution and the laws of the United States, namely the right not to be deprived of liberty without due process of law, including the right to be free from wilful sexual assault." Before trial, Lanier moved to dismiss the indictment on the ground that § 242 is void for vagueness. The District Court denied the motion.

The trial judge instructed the jury on the Government's burden to prove as an element of the offense that the defendant deprived the victim of rights secured or protected by the Constitution or laws of the United States:

> "Included in the liberty protected by the [Due Process Clause of the] Fourteenth Amendment is the concept of personal bodily integrity and the right to be free of unauthorized and unlawful physical abuse by state intrusion. Thus, this protected right of liberty provides that no person shall be subject to physical or bodily abuse without lawful justification by a state official acting or claiming to act under the color of the laws of any state of the United States when that official's conduct is so demeaning and harmful under all the circumstances as to shock one's consci[ence]. Freedom from such physical abuse includes the right to be free from certain sexually motivated physical assaults and coerced sexual battery. It is not, however, every unjustified touching or grabbing by a state official that constitutes a violation of a person's constitutional rights. The physical abuse must be of a serious substantial nature that involves physical force, mental coercion, bodily injury or emotional damage which is shocking to one's consci[ence]."

The jury returned verdicts of guilty on seven counts, and not guilty on three (one count having been dismissed at the close of the Government's evidence). It also found that the two oral rapes resulted in "bodily injury," for which Lanier was subject to 10–year terms of imprisonment on each count, in addition to 1–year terms under the other five counts of conviction, see § 242. He was sentenced to consecutive maximum terms totaling 25 years.

A panel of the Court of Appeals for the Sixth Circuit affirmed the convictions and sentence, but the full Court vacated that decision and granted rehearing en banc. On rehearing, the Court set aside Lanier's convictions for "lack of any notice to the public that this ambiguous criminal statute [i.e., § 242] includes simple or sexual assault crimes within its coverage." Invoking general canons for interpreting criminal statutes, as well as this Court's plurality opinion in *Screws v. United States*, 325 U.S. 91 (1945), the Sixth Circuit held that criminal liability may be imposed under § 242 only if the constitutional right said to have been violated is first identified in a decision of this Court (not any other federal, or state, court), and only when the right has been held to apply in "a factual situation fundamentally similar to the one at bar." The

Court of Appeals regarded these combined requirements as "substantially higher than the 'clearly established' standard used to judge qualified immunity" in civil cases under Rev. Stat. § 1979, 42 U.S.C. § 1983. Finding no decision of this Court applying a right to be free from unjustified assault or invasions of bodily integrity in a situation "fundamentally similar" to those charged, the Sixth Circuit reversed the judgment of conviction with instructions to dismiss the indictment. Two judges would not have dismissed the felony counts charging the oral rapes but concurred in dismissing the misdemeanor counts, while three members of the court dissented as to all dismissals.

We granted certiorari to review the standard for determining whether particular conduct falls within the range of criminal liability under § 242. We now reverse.

II

Section 242 is a Reconstruction Era civil rights statute making it criminal to act (1) "willfully" and (2) under color of law (3) to deprive a person of rights protected by the Constitution or laws of the United States. The en banc decision of the Sixth Circuit dealt only with the last of these elements, and it is with that element alone that we are concerned here.

The general language of § 242, referring to "the deprivation of any rights, privileges, or immunities secured or protected by the Constitution or laws of the United States," is matched by the breadth of its companion conspiracy statute, § 241, which speaks of conspiracies to prevent "the free exercise or enjoyment of any right or privilege secured to [any person] by the Constitution or laws of the United States." Thus, in lieu of describing the specific conduct it forbids, each statute's general terms incorporate constitutional law by reference, and many of the incorporated constitutional guarantees are, of course, themselves stated with some catholicity of phrasing. The result is that neither the statutes nor a good many of their constitutional referents delineate the range of forbidden conduct with particularity.

The right to due process enforced by § 242 and said to have been violated by Lanier presents a case in point, with the irony that a prosecution to enforce one application of its spacious protection of liberty can threaten the accused with deprivation of another: what Justice Holmes spoke of as "fair warning ... in language that the common world will understand, of what the law intends to do if a certain line is passed. To make the warning fair, so far as possible the line should be clear." " 'The ... principle is that no man shall be held criminally responsible for conduct which he could not reasonably understand to be proscribed.' "[5]

There are three related manifestations of the fair warning requirement. First, the vagueness doctrine bars enforcement of "a statute

5. The fair warning requirement also reflects the deference due to the legislature, which possesses the power to define crimes and their punishment.

which either forbids or requires the doing of an act in terms so vague that men of common intelligence must necessarily guess at its meaning and differ as to its application." Second, as a sort of "junior version of the vagueness doctrine," the canon of strict construction of criminal statutes, or rule of lenity, ensures fair warning by so resolving ambiguity in a criminal statute as to apply it only to conduct clearly covered. Third, although clarity at the requisite level may be supplied by judicial gloss on an otherwise uncertain statute, due process bars courts from applying a novel construction of a criminal statute to conduct that neither the statute nor any prior judicial decision has fairly disclosed to be within its scope. In each of these guises, the touchstone is whether the statute, either standing alone or as construed, made it reasonably clear at the relevant time that the defendant's conduct was criminal.

We applied this standard in *Screws v. United States*, 325 U.S. 91 (1945), which recognized that the expansive language of due process that provides a basis for judicial review is, when incorporated by reference into § 242, generally ill-suited to the far different task of giving fair warning about the scope of criminal liability. The *Screws* plurality identified the affront to the warning requirement posed by employing § 242 to place "the accused ... on trial for an offense, the nature of which the statute does not define and hence of which it gives no warning." At the same time, the same Justices recognized that this constitutional difficulty does not arise when the accused is charged with violating a "right which has been made specific either by the express terms of the Constitution or laws of the United States or by decisions interpreting them." When broad constitutional requirements have been "made specific" by the text or settled interpretations, willful violators "certainly are in no position to say that they had no adequate advance notice that they would be visited with punishment.... [T]hey are not punished for violating an unknowable something." Accordingly, *Screws* limited the statute's coverage to rights fairly warned of, having been "made specific" by the time of the charged conduct.[6]

The Sixth Circuit, in this case, added two glosses to the made-specific standard of fair warning. In its view, a generally phrased constitutional right has been made specific within the meaning of *Screws* only if a prior decision of this Court has declared the right, and then

---

6. This process of "making specific" does not, as the Sixth Circuit believed, qualify *Screws* as "the only Supreme Court case in our legal history in which a majority of the Court seems [to have been] willing to create a common law crime." Federal crimes are defined by Congress, not the courts, and *Screws* did not "create a common law crime"; it narrowly construed a broadly worded act of Congress, and the policies favoring strict construction of criminal statutes oblige us to carry out congressional intent as far as the Constitution will admit. Nor is § 242's pedigree as an act of Congress tainted by its birth at the hands of codifiers who arguably made substantive changes in the pre-existing law, as the Sixth Circuit concluded from the statutory history. The legislative intent of Congress is to be derived from the language and structure of the statute itself, if possible, not from the assertions of codifiers directly at odds with clear statutory language. Further, the Sixth Circuit's conclusion that Congress never intended § 242 to extend to "newly-created constitutional rights," is belied by the fact that Congress has increased the penalties for the section's violation several times since *Screws* was decided, without contracting its substantive scope.

only when this Court has applied its ruling in a case with facts "fundamentally similar" to the case being prosecuted. None of the considerations advanced in this case, however, persuades us that either a decision of this Court or the extreme level of factual specificity envisioned by the Court of Appeals is necessary in every instance to give fair warning.

First, contrary to the Court of Appeals, we think it unsound to read *Screws* as reasoning that only this Court's decisions could provide the required warning. Although the *Screws* plurality gave two examples involving decisions of the Court, their opinion referred in general terms to rights made specific by "decisions interpreting" the Constitution, and no subsequent case has held that the universe of relevant interpretive decisions is confined to our opinions. * * * It is also to the point, as we explain below, that in applying the rule of qualified immunity under 42 U.S.C. § 1983 and *Bivens v. Six Unknown Narcotics Agents*, 403 U.S. 388 (1971), we have referred to decisions of the Courts of Appeals when enquiring whether a right was "clearly established." Although the Sixth Circuit was concerned, and rightly so, that disparate decisions in various Circuits might leave the law insufficiently certain even on a point widely considered, such a circumstance may be taken into account in deciding whether the warning is fair enough, without any need for a categorical rule that decisions of the Courts of Appeals and other courts are inadequate as a matter of law to provide it.

Nor have our decisions demanded precedents that applied the right at issue to a factual situation that is "fundamentally similar" at the level of specificity meant by the Sixth Circuit in using that phrase. To the contrary, we have upheld convictions under § 241 or § 242 despite notable factual distinctions between the precedents relied on and the cases then before the Court, so long as the prior decisions gave reasonable warning that the conduct then at issue violated constitutional rights. *See United States v. Guest*, 383 U.S. 745, 759 n. 17 (1966) (prior cases established right of interstate travel, but later case was the first to address the deprivation of this right by private persons); *United States v. Saylor*, 322 U.S. 385 (1944) (pre-*Screws*; prior cases established right to have legitimate vote counted, whereas later case involved dilution of legitimate votes through casting of fraudulent ballots); *United States v. Classic*, 313 U.S. 299, 321–324 (1941) (pre-*Screws*; prior cases established right to have vote counted in general election, whereas later case involved primary election); see also *Screws*, *supra*, at 106 (stating that *Classic* met the test being announced).

But even putting these examples aside, we think that the Sixth Circuit's "fundamentally similar" standard would lead trial judges to demand a degree of certainty at once unnecessarily high and likely to beget much wrangling. This danger flows from the Court of Appeals' stated view that due process under § 242 demands more than the "clearly established" law required for a public officer to be held civilly liable for a constitutional violation under § 1983 or *Bivens*. This, we think, is error.

In the civil sphere, we have explained that qualified immunity seeks to ensure that defendants "reasonably can anticipate when their conduct may give rise to liability," by attaching liability only if "[t]he contours of the right [violated are] sufficiently clear that a reasonable official would understand that what he is doing violates that right." So conceived, the object of the "clearly established" immunity standard is not different from that of "fair warning" as it relates to law "made specific" for the purpose of validly applying § 242. The fact that one has a civil and the other a criminal law role is of no significance; both serve the same objective, and in effect the qualified immunity test is simply the adaptation of the fair warning standard to give officials (and, ultimately, governments) the same protection from civil liability and its consequences that individuals have traditionally possessed in the face of vague criminal statutes. To require something clearer than "clearly established" would, then, call for something beyond "fair warning."

This is not to say, of course, that the single warning standard points to a single level of specificity sufficient in every instance. In some circumstances, as when an earlier case expressly leaves open whether a general rule applies to the particular type of conduct at issue, a very high degree of prior factual particularity may be necessary. But general statements of the law are not inherently incapable of giving fair and clear warning, and in other instances a general constitutional rule already identified in the decisional law may apply with obvious clarity to the specific conduct in question, even though "the very action in question has [not] previously been held unlawful." As Judge Daughtrey noted in her dissenting opinion in this case, " '[t]he easiest cases don't even arise. There has never been ... a section 1983 case accusing welfare officials of selling foster children into slavery; it does not follow that if such a case arose, the officials would be immune from damages [or criminal] liability.' " In sum, as with civil liability under § 1983 or *Bivens*, all that can usefully be said about criminal liability under § 242 is that it may be imposed for deprivation of a constitutional right if, but only if, "in the light of pre-existing law the unlawfulness [under the Constitution is] apparent." Where it is, the constitutional requirement of fair warning is satisfied.

Because the Court of Appeals used the wrong gauge in deciding whether prior judicial decisions gave fair warning that respondent's actions violated constitutional rights, we vacate the judgment and remand for application of the proper standard.[7]

---

7. We also leave consideration of other issues that may remain open to the Court of Appeals on remand. Several of the arguments tendered by respondent here are, however, plainly without merit and need not be left open. First, Lanier's contention that *Screws* excluded rights protected by the Due Process Clause of the Fourteenth Amendment from the ambit of § 242 is contradicted by the language of *Screws* itself as well as later cases. Second, although

DeShaney v. Winnebago County Dept. of Social Servs., 489 U.S. 189 (1989), generally limits the constitutional duty of officials to protect against assault by private parties to cases where the victim is in custody, DeShaney does not hold, as respondent maintains, that there is no constitutional right to be free from assault committed by state officials themselves outside of a custodial setting. Third, contrary to respondent's claim,

Notes

The defendant's conduct in *Lanier* was egregious, and the Supreme Court's unanimous opinion suggests that this was an easy case. But was it? The government argued that " 'freedom from sexual assault' is a part of a general constitutional right against interference with 'bodily integrity' in a way that 'shocks the conscience.' " 73 F.3d 1380 at 1388. This constitutional right was said to be part of substantive due process. The en banc opinion in the court of appeals observed that in *Screws* the Supreme Court faced a choice "between declaring § 242 unconstitutional and adopting a 'saving construction' that would greatly narrow the statute to the deprivation of obvious, well-established and publicly known constitutional rights" of which the defendant would have adequate notice. *Id.* at 1392. To meet this standard, the majority concluded that § 242 must be confined:

> (1) to cases under § 242 in which the constitutional right "deprived" is specifically stated in the Constitution itself (e.g., unconstitutional searches or seizures) and understood by the literate public to be a well-settled constitutional right, and (2) to well-established procedural due process rights like the right to be tried before being punished by law enforcement officers.

Ibid.

The majority in the court of appeals held that the prosecution before it failed this test. Although there is a well known right not to be assaulted under state law, the right not to be assaulted is not listed in the Constitution, has never been declared to be a federal right by the Supreme Court, and is not a well-established right of procedural due process like the right to be tried before being punished. For a right not listed in the Constitution to be sufficiently well settled, the court reasoned that only a decision of the Supreme Court could provide sufficient notice under § 242. Moreover, the Supreme Court must "also hold that the right applies to a factual situation fundamentally similar to the one at bar." *Id.* at 1392–93. The majority concluded:

> * * * permitting federal prosecutions for "conscience shocking" simple and sexual assaults committed by federal, state and local employees or officials places unparalleled, unprecedented discretion in the hands of federal law enforcement officers, prosecutors and judges. In the absence of any definition or limitations on the extent of the crime—and given that such prosecutions are useful political weapons—permitting such discretion is a particular risk for due process. Many public officials and employees have recently been accused of similar deviant conduct, but no other case has been prosecuted. Such an unprecedented, selective application of the statute in this case was possible only by giving the broadest possible construction to the most ambiguous of federal criminal statutes.

Graham v. Connor, 490 U.S. 386, 394 (1989), does not hold that all constitutional claims relating to physically abusive government conduct must arise under either the Fourth or Eighth Amendments; rather, *Graham* simply requires that if a constitutional claim is covered by a specific constitutional provision, such as the Fourth or Eighth Amendment, the claim must be analyzed under the standard appropriate to that specific provision, not under the rubric of substantive due process.

The indictment in this case for a previously unknown, undeclared and undefined constitutional crime cannot be allowed to stand. Accordingly, the judgment of the court below is reversed and the Court is instructed to dismiss the indictment.

Id. at 1393–94. The majority rested its decision on "longstanding principles of federalism, separation of judicial and legislative powers, and the right to formal public notice when new crimes are enacted." *Id.* at 1394 n.13.

The Supreme Court's opinion swept aside these concerns. Why do you think a conservative Supreme Court unanimously approved this expansion of § 242 liability? Did the Court's decision mean that there is an established constitutional right to be free from sexual assault? Is freedom from sexual assault really a clear concept, in light of the ferment in state law regarding the definition of rape and sexual harassment? If not, what could have motivated the Court? Note that the defendant in the case was a state judge who used his official position to intimidate his victims, and the defendant's brother was the local prosecutor. 73 F.3d at 1403 (Wellford, concurring in part and dissenting in part). If a federal prosecution had not been possible, do you think there would have been a state prosecution?

B. SPECIAL USES OF §§ 241, 242

1. EXCESSIVE FORCE IN THE COURSE OF AN ARREST

In April, 1992 the Rodney King case in Los Angeles focused national attention on standards governing criminal liability for the use of excessive force when arrests are made, and the distinctions and interaction between state and federal law. State charges against the police officers who were videotaped beating King ended in acquittals on all but one of the charges, touching off rioting in Los Angeles that left scores dead and millions of dollars of property damage.

In August, 1992 the United States Attorney announced the indictment of the same officers for depriving King of his federally protected civil rights while acting under color of law in violation of 18 U.S.C. § 242. The indictment alleged that three of the defendants willfully and intentionally used unreasonable force in their arrest of King, and that the fourth defendant, an on-duty sergeant, willfully permitted and failed to take action to stop the assault. This section analyzes the legal principles that govern cases where civil rights charges under 18 U.S.C. §§ 241 or 242 are premised on allegations of the use of excessive force in the course of an arrest.

UNITED STATES v. SCHATZLE

901 F.2d 252 (2d Cir.1990).

OAKES, CHIEF JUDGE:

[The defendant was a secret service agent. During the 1988 presidential campaign he was driving a car in a motorcade taking Senator Albert Gore, then a candidate, through New York City. When a pedestrian, Gorayeb, tried to cross the street, defendant had to swerve to avoid striking him. As the car went by, Gorayeb cursed the defendant, who then stopped, left his car, and ran after Gorayeb. The government's witnesses testified that the defendant punched Gorayeb, breaking his nose, delivered a knee to his groin, and continued to punch and kick Gorayeb as he fell to the ground. The defendant then informed Gorayeb that he was under arrest. In contrast, the defendant testified that Gorayeb was the aggressor in the encounter which culminated in his arrest. The jury found the defendant guilty of depriving Gorayeb of his constitutional rights by subjecting him to excessive force under § 242, but not guilty of depriving him of his constitutional rights by subjecting him to a false arrest.]

* * *

Schatzle contends that the district court incorrectly instructed the jury concerning what it needed to find to conclude that Schatzle had used excessive force.

Several weeks before Schatzle's trial, the Supreme Court handed down *Graham v. Connor*, 490 U.S. 386, 109 S.Ct. 1865, 104 L.Ed.2d 443 (1989), in which it outlined the standard governing the right to be free from excessive force in the context of an investigatory stop or arrest. The Court explained that excessive force claims in arrest and investigatory stop contexts implicate the Fourth Amendment right to be free from unreasonable seizures and consequently are judged under the Fourth Amendment's reasonableness standard. Although noting that " '[t]he test of reasonableness under the Fourth Amendment is not capable of precise definition or mechanical application,' " the Court laid out several guideposts for measuring an excessive force claim. First, it instructed that evaluating whether a law enforcement officer has used excessive force

> requires careful attention to the facts and circumstances of each particular case, including the severity of the crime at issue, whether the suspect poses an immediate threat to the safety of the officers or others, and whether he is actively resisting arrest or attempting to evade arrest by flight.

The Court added that in judging whether an officer's actions are reasonable, a court looks "from the perspective of a reasonable officer on the scene, rather than with the 20/20 vision of hindsight."

Measured against this standard, we believe the district court's jury instructions were sound. The district court initially charged the jury as follows:

> Now, let me talk about excessive force under Count One.

> Even if Schatzle had the right to question or arrest Gorayeb, that would not necessarily mean that he had the right to use force or violence against him. On this issue, the question of whether Schatzle was entitled to use force, and if so, how much, depends on what Gorayeb's conduct was.

If an agent is authorized to arrest or detain someone, and the person resists, the agent is entitled to use a reasonable amount of force to overcome that resistance.

Also, if an agent is attacked by another person, the agent is entitled to use reasonable force to repel the attack and subdue the attacker.

How much force the agent is entitled to use depends upon how much force or resistance he encounters. The amount of force the agent may use is the amount that is reasonable to deal with the resistance or attack that he faces.

In short, the agent may use as much force as is reasonable to insure his own safety and accomplish his legitimate law enforcement objective. He may not use more, he may not use unreasonable or excessive force....

The fact that a police officer is entitled to use some force in a particular circumstance does not mean that he may use unlimited amounts of force. He may use that amount of force which is reasonable under the circumstances to accomplish his legitimate law enforcement objectives, protect himself and repel any attack.

In response to a request from the jury, the district court repeated the substance of its charge on the standard for excessive force and summarized the evidence presented by both parties relevant to the excessive force issue.

Schatzle offers a litany of passages from *Graham* and argues that the district court should have closely incorporated these particular passages directly into its charge. We disagree. The passages quoted to us by Schatzle do no more than reiterate the general notion that whether a particular use of force is excessive ultimately turns on its reasonableness. We cannot place the talismanic weight urged by Schatzle on *Graham*'s exact wording and do not believe the district court needed to echo the opinion paragraph by paragraph to convey adequately its import to the jury. *Graham* requires that the district court impress upon the jury the necessity of assessing whether the force employed by Schatzle was reasonable in light of the particular situation and dangers facing Schatzle at the time he encountered Gorayeb. Because the district court's instructions did just that, Schatzle's argument fails.[2]

* * *

2. While instructing the jury, the district court briefly summarized the pertinent evidence, noting the Government's theory that Schatzle attacked Gorayeb "in anger." Schatzle objects that the summarization led the jury to consider whether he had subjective malice towards Gorayeb, which, as *Graham* points out, is not relevant to evaluating the reasonableness of a use of force. We find no basis in Schatzle's claim that the district court's summarization of the evidence somehow led the jury to inject its assessment of his malice into its deliberation of his culpability.

Moreover, we note that the district court's inclusion of the Government's contention that Schatzle acted in anger was necessitated by Schatzle's insistence that the district court summarize for the jury his contention that he responded as his Secret Service training had taught him to

Notes

1. Prior to the Supreme Court's decision in *Graham* the lower federal courts had employed a four-part test that looked, inter alia, at whether the officers acted in good faith or maliciously and sadistically. The Supreme Court rejected this test, holding that the question under the fourth amendment is "whether the officers' actions are 'objectively reasonable' in light of the facts and circumstances confronting them, without regard to their underlying intent or motivation." 490 U.S. at 397.

2. Although the Fourth Amendment inquiry is an objective one, as discussed in Section A 1, *supra*, §§ 241 and 242 require a showing of specific intent to violate the arrestee's rights. The lower court decisions vary considerably on the question, what constitutes an adequate instruction on the requisite willfulness in excessive force cases. In *United States v. Messerlian*, 832 F.2d 778 (3d Cir.1987), the court affirmed the conviction of a state trooper who had beaten an arrestee's head with a flashlight while he was in the patrol car, causing his death. The court approved an instruction that "carefully defined for the jury the term 'willfulness' as requiring proof of an act 'done voluntarily and intentionally, and with specific intent to do something [that] the law forbids.' " 832 F.2d at 790. In dicta the court observed that "a violation of § 242 is established if a defendant acted in reckless disregard of the law as he understood it." *Id.* at 791. In contrast, in *United States v. Kerley*, 643 F.2d 299, 303 (5th Cir.1981), the court reversed a conviction where the jury had been instructed that it must find the defendant " 'knowingly and intentionally exerted force that he knew to be unlawful,' " because it had not also been instructed that willfully means acting "with a bad purpose or an evil motive."

3. *Graham* left open the question whether the Fourth Amendment provides continuing protection against the use of excessive physical force *after* the arrest ends and the defendant and pretrial detention begins. 490 U.S. at 395 n.10. The Court observed, however, that at a minimum the Due Process Clause protects a pretrial detainee against the use of excessive force that amounts to punishment. *Ibid.* In *United States v. Cobb*, 905 F.2d 784 (4th Cir.1990), the court of appeals applied this due process standard in a prosecution under § 242 against a group of police officers who beat a handcuffed pretrial detainee in a holding area for two hours with a slapjack. Since the question in the context of the Due Process Clause was whether the force amounted to punishment, the court of appeals approved an instruction that focused on whether the force was employed in good faith to maintain or restore discipline, or maliciously and sadistically for the purpose of causing harm. 905 F.2d at 789.

4. How do these standards apply to the case of the officers who were videotaped beating Rodney King? According to the evidence at the state trial, police observed King driving far in excess of the speed limit and he led them on a seven mile high-speed chase before he was apprehended by four white

react. Before accepting Schatzle's proposed instruction, the district court made clear that it intended to balance the charge by instructing the jury on the Government's contention that Schatzle acted in anger. Having assented at trial to this reasonable arrangement, Schatzle may not attack it on appeal.

Los Angeles police officers. King did not follow their orders to lie down and allow himself to be searched (though his passengers did), and he was shot with a non-lethal taser dart. As he lurched toward one of the officers, King was struck to the ground. A resident videotaped the officers striking King 56 times with a baton, kicking him, and shocking him with a stun gun. The officers claimed that they believed King was on PCP—which makes suspects extremely difficult to subdue—and also that they believed he was searching for a concealed weapon during the beating. No trace of PCP was found in King's bloodstream and he was unarmed, though he had consumed a large quantity of alcohol and was intoxicated. On the basis of this evidence, the state charged the four officers with assault with a deadly weapon or with force likely to produce great bodily injury, Cal. Penal Code § 245 (West 1992),[b] and unnecessary assault or beating by a public official, Cal. Penal Code § 149 (1992).[c] Because the defendants were armed while committing the offense, the state invoked a one-year sentence enhancement provision. In addition, two defendants were charged with the submission of a false police report. After a lengthy state trial, the defendants were acquitted of all charges except the § 149 excessive force charge against defendant Powell, on which the jury could not reach agreement.

As noted in the introduction to this section, following the state acquittals the defendants were indicted for violating 18 U.S.C. § 242. What did the federal prosecutors have to prove at the civil rights trial that was not at issue in the state trial?[d] At the conclusion of the federal trial Officers Briseno and Wind were acquitted, and Officer Powell and Sergeant Koon were convicted and sentenced to thirty months imprisonment. Powell and Koon appealed, and the government appealed their sentences. The court of appeals affirmed the convictions and vacated the sentences. *United States v. Koon*, 34 F.3d 1416 (9th Cir.1994). For a discussion of the jury instructions and the sufficiency of the evidence, see 34 F.3d at 1446–51. The Supreme Court granted certiorari and issued a major ruling on the scope of appellate review in departure cases, concluding that the district court had erred in both downward departures. *Koon v. United States*, 518 U.S. 81 (1996).

b. Section 245(a)(1) provided:

Every person who commits an assault upon the person of another with a deadly weapon or instrument other than a firearm or by means of force likely to produce great bodily injury is punishable by imprisonment in the state prison for two, three or four years, or in a county jail not exceeding one year, or by fine not exceeding ten thousand dollars ($10,000), or by both such a fine and imprisonment.

c. Section 145 provided:

Every public officer who, under color of authority, without lawful necessity, assaults or beats any person, is punishable by a fine not exceeding ten thousand dollars ($10,000), or by imprisonment in the state prison, or in a county jail not ex-

ceeding one year, or by both such fine and imprisonment.

d. Compare also the facts involved in the beating of white truck driver Reginald Denny. A few hours after the King acquittals he was dragged out of the cab of his truck by an angry mob protesting the King verdict. News cameras photographed and broadcast his savage beating by a group of young black men. One smashed a brick into Denny's head as he lay on the ground, and then seemed to do a victory dance. Denny was near death when good samaritans brought him to a hospital. State prosecutors charged three black men with attempted murder, mayhem, and torture. Since none of the defendants were acting under color of law, could civil rights charges be filed in this case? See Section C, discussing § 245.

2. OFFICIAL CORRUPTION OR OTHER CRIMINALITY

UNITED STATES v. SENAK

477 F.2d 304 (7th Cir.1973).

Before FAIRCHILD, PELL, and SPRECHER, CIRCUIT JUDGES.

PELL, CIRCUIT JUDGE.

In February 1972, a federal grand jury returned a five-count indictment against Nick Senak, a public defender for Lake County, Indiana. The indictment charged that Senak, while acting under color of law, "willfully and unlawfully exacted and took" money from various persons, thereby willfully depriving those persons of their right under the Fourteenth Amendment not to be deprived of property without due process of law, in violation of 18 U.S.C. § 242. More specifically, notwithstanding his appointment under Indiana law as a "pauper attorney," by virtue of which he was entitled to governmental compensation, Senak had allegedly exacted fees from a pauper "client" (Count I) and from friends or relatives of other impoverished "clients" (Counts II–V) by threatening inadequate legal representation of those he had been appointed to represent unless the extra sums were paid to him.

On March 27, 1972, the district court reluctantly sustained Senak's pre-trial motion to dismiss the indictment on the ground that the indictment failed to state an offense against the United States. The Government seeks reversal of the court's order dismissing the indictment.

* * *

* * * The elements of an 18 U.S.C. § 242 offense are: (1) the defendant's acts must have deprived someone of a right secured or protected by the Constitution or laws of the United States; (2) the defendant's illegal acts must have been committed under color of law; (3) the person deprived of his rights must have been an inhabitant of a State, Territory, or District; and (4) the defendant must have acted willfully. Only elements (1) and (2) are in dispute on this appeal.

Senak contends that a public defender is immune from liability under § 242 and that, once he is appointed in a given case, he does not act under color of state law but functions purely as a private attorney. For this proposition, Senak relies on *Brown v. Joseph*, 463 F.2d 1046 (3d Cir.1972), where the question was whether a Pennsylvania county public defender could be held liable for damages in an action brought by a former indigent client who alleged constitutional deprivations under 42 U.S.C. § 1983, the civil counterpart of 18 U.S.C. § 242. The district court there held that the complaint failed to state a claim upon which relief could be granted on the basis that the defendant was not acting under color of state law. On appeal, the Third Circuit decided it need not reach the "under color of any law" question. The court instead held that a county public defender enjoys immunity from liability under the Civil Rights Act.

Brown, supra, the one case Senak cites on this issue, is inapposite. The court's remarks about "color of law" are dicta. Further, an examination of the holding there reveals that the court was concerned with immunity for state judges, prosecutors, and public defenders "for acts done in the performance of [their] judicial function[s]...." 463 F.2d at 1048. The court recognized an exception to immunity where the officials' acts are clearly outside the scope of the officials' jurisdiction. *Id.* Also, the court emphasized certain policy considerations which are irrelevant to the charge in the indictment before us, e.g., the importance of encouraging the officials' "free exercise of professional discretion in the discharge of pre-trial, trial, and post-trial obligations." *Id.*

Senak provides neither binding precedent nor persuasive reasons to lead us to conclude that the Government would be unable, as a matter of law, to satisfy the "color of law" requirement. * * * At this juncture we do not know, for example, in what words Senak couched his alleged demands for money or what representations he made to the alleged "victims." Nor do we know all the conditions that attached to Senak's appointment as public defender, *i.e.*, the duties and ethical conduct required by law of someone assuming such a position. If the indictment is sufficient in other respects, the Government should be given the opportunity to try to establish that Senak acted "under color of ... law."

The district court's objections to the indictment centered on the supposed absence of the "deprivation of a constitutional right" element. Implicit in its discussion, however, were doubts about the "under color of any law" requirement. In the court's view, to hold that the defendant, by charging a fee, had deprived the named persons of property without due process of law was "to strain that concept well past its breaking point."

The "constitutional deprivation" element of the section 242 offense charged here consists of three concepts: the right to "property," a "deprivation," and "due process." It is clear that the right to acquire, enjoy, own, and dispose of property is protected by the Constitution. Each count of the indictment against Senak referred to the named person's right to property under the Fourteenth Amendment and specified the form of that property (money) and the approximate amount allegedly taken.

A more difficult problem is whether Senak's alleged conduct constituted a "deprivation" under the Constitution. The district court considered that term to import a "taking" in the sense of "a nonconsensual divestiture compelled by legal authority" and reluctantly concluded that the indictment failed to allege such a "taking".

* * *

In its prior opinion sustaining the motion to dismiss directed to the first indictment, which opinion was incorporated by reference in the second opinion, the district court stated: "There is no claim that those charged [a fee] were ever under any compulsion, legal *or otherwise,* to pay. . . ." (Emphasis added.)

It would seem obvious that there was no legal compulsion. Senak was being paid by the state and could not have successfully claimed any additional compensation from those he represented, either directly or vicariously. However, that he had no legal right to the money he supposedly collected or that the named "victims" might have asserted a successful defense to a suit by him for payment does not preclude the possibility that Senak "deprived" those persons of their property.

It appears to us that reality is ignored to say that there is no compulsion "otherwise" on an impoverished person who has supposedly been provided with legal representation or on his relatives and close friends when they are confronted with a demand from that counsel, ostensibly by virtue of his appointment "backed by the power of the state," for additional compensation if there is to be adequate representation. The constitutional right to appointed counsel does not contemplate any standard less than adequate representation.

We are not here dealing with the inherent variation in legal skills existing from lawyer to lawyer. Attorneys appointed to represent indigents, like retained counsel, undoubtedly will possess varying degrees of legal acumen; none, however, should be purposely inadequate. When the matter is baldly put as a choice between adequate representation possibly followed by an acquittal and inadequate representation which could reasonably assure a conviction, the choice is surely of the Hobson variety.

The litigant with means can choose his counsel. The pauper cannot, and his constitutional right to appointed counsel has not been extended to the point of affording him this privilege. That it has not been should be no basis for exposing him to the necessity of trying by some means to gather together funds to compensate the attorney whom he has not selected and who has told him that without those funds he would not be competently represented.

* * * The Government claims that Senak's official position enabled him to perpetrate a scheme of obtaining money to which he was not entitled. His being county public defender allegedly gave him the opportunity to make the demands and clothed him with the authority of the state in so doing.

In sum, we think that the district court construed the "deprivation" requirement too narrowly.

By emphasizing compulsion and coercion, the district court seemed to suggest that "deprivation" is a taking accomplished without adherence to proper procedures. The term "deprivation" by itself, however connotes neither legality nor illegality. The portion of the Fourteenth

Amendment with which we are concerned in this case—"nor shall any State deprive any person of life, liberty, or property, without due process of law"—indicates that the violation of due process standards makes a particular "deprivation" an objectionable, illegal "deprivation." That is, the Amendment focuses on the means by which the "deprivation" is achieved.

The Government argues that "the named victims possessed certain constitutional rights both before and after defendant's appointment [as public defender]; specifically, each citizen's basic, continuing right to use and control his own property until such time as he voluntarily disposes of it ... or it is taken from him through means consistent with due process standards...."

In our opinion, the indictment satisfactorily alleges a violation of that constitutional right.

* * *

* * * We do, however, understand the court's apprehension that the Government has opened a Pandora's box. We have held that the particular indictment before us adequately states an offense under 18 U.S.C. § 242; we intimate no opinion about the sufficiency of other possible indictments under section 242 involving different factual situations.

The order dismissing the February 1972 indictment is reversed, and the cause is remanded to the district court for further proceedings consistent with this opinion.

Reversed and remanded.

FAIRCHILD, CIRCUIT JUDGE (concurring).

While I agree that the instant indictment states an offense against the United States under 18 U.S.C. § 242, the legal theory upon which the indictment is grounded does not, in my view, satisfactorily grapple with the primary "deprivation" effected by defendant's alleged conduct.

The right of indigents to appointed counsel is guaranteed by the Sixth Amendment. *Gideon v. Wainwright*, 372 U.S. 335 (1963). And, the "essence of this right is the right to effective, competent and adequate representation." Thus, if an appointed attorney threatens to provide less than adequate legal services for an indigent defendant unless paid additional sums, he in effect subjects that defendant to a deprivation of his Sixth Amendment rights.

It is this subjection of an indigent to deprivation of his Sixth Amendment rights which is the real harm posed by defendant's alleged conduct. Accordingly, the indictment would be better framed if it focused upon this reality.

Notes

1. For a subsequent stage of the prosecution in *Senak*, see 527 F.2d 129 (7th Cir.1975).

2. In *United States v. O'Dell*, 462 F.2d 224, 226 (6th Cir.1972), seven Tennessee law enforcement officials and a private bondsman were charged with violating 18 U.S.C. §§ 242 and 241 respectively. The proof at trial showed that over a period of months the defendants arrested persons as they drove away from local taverns and charged them with drunk driving. In jail they were told that they could either make "bail" in amounts up to $350 or be sentenced up to a year of road work. It was explained to them that they would not receive a receipt for the bail money and they were not to return— for trial or otherwise. Thereupon when the bail money was paid, the charges were dropped. Were the victims of O'Dell and his cohorts deprived of a federal right by the defendants? What right? The right to be taken promptly before a magistrate? The right to bail? The right to non-excessive bail? The right to have Tennessee law complied with? The right to a fair trial?

3. Compare with the foregoing cases *United States v. McClean*, 528 F.2d 1250 (2d Cir.1976), where three New York City police detectives were convicted of having violated § 242 through the operation of a shakedown racket of persons apprehended for narcotics violations. The court ruled that under § 242, it "was sufficient to allege and prove that acting under color of their office appellants 'willfully appropriated property from their victims without due process,' "and "the record reveals that appellants did not act in a private capacity which might have precluded federal prosecution, but under color of law." *Id.* at 1255. Would it be relevant had all the property extorted from the victims in *McClean* been contraband? *See id.* at 1255– 1256.

4. Consider the constitutional rights involved in *United States v. Melendez*, 2004 WL 162937 (E.D. Mich. 2004) where the court described the facts as follows:

> This is a criminal case. Defendants are eighteen Detroit police officers who have been charged in a thirty-two count first superseding indictment with various offenses, including conspiring to violate constitutional rights, 18 U.S.C. § 241, deprivation of rights under color of law, 18 U.S.C. § 242, * * *

> The first superseding indictment alleges in Count One that all defendants "did willfully conspire and agree with each other and with various other unindicted coconspirators ... to injure, oppress, threaten and intimidate persons in the State of Michigan in the free exercise and enjoyment of the rights secured to them by the Constitution and laws of the United States" in violation of 18 U.S.C. § 241. Specifically, Count One alleges that defendants conspired to violate four rights: (1) the right to be free from unreasonable search and seizure, (2) the right to be free from the deprivation of liberty without due process of law, including the right not to have criminal charges based on fraudulent evidence or false information, (3) the right to be free from the deprivation of property without due process of law, and (4) the right to be free from the intentional use of unreasonable force.

> Count One * * *lists various general "manner and means by which the defendants and their co-conspirators sought to accomplish the objectives of their conspiracy," including, among other things, forcibly entering residences without a warrant or exigent circumstances, stealing

from individuals, detaining individuals without reasonable suspicion, falsifying police reports and committing perjury to cover up illegal actions, planting evidence, and intimidating individuals who were illegally detained with threats of violence or unlawful arrest. The indictment lists twenty-one specific overt acts committed by the various defendants.

5. The court in *Melendez*, supra, note 4, proceeded to discuss the specific constitutional rights that the defendants were alleged to have violated:

> The indictment alleges in ten of the substantive counts and ten of the overt acts relating to the conspiracy count that defendants deprived individuals of their rights to be free from unreasonable search and seizure under the Fourth Amendment. Defendants say that the indictment is deficient because it does not allege that the individuals whose Fourth Amendment rights were allegedly violated had standing to assert those rights at the time of the alleged violation. According to defendants, many of the alleged victims were merely trespassers or guests in the residences described and some of these residences were abandoned or temporary.

> Defendants are correct that an individual may only assert his Fourth Amendment rights if he has "standing," meaning that the person had a reasonable expectation of privacy in the property searched or the items seized. * * *

> The substantive counts in the indictment allege a violation of 18 U.S.C. § 242, the elements of which are a (1) willful (2) deprivation of a constitutional right (3) under color of law. Each count alleges that particular defendants unlawfully entered residences without exigent circumstances or obtaining a search warrant and subjected individuals to illegal searches and seizures. The indictment gives the address of each residence, states the date of each alleged constitutional violation, and identifies the alleged victims by name. The "element" that must be stated in the indictment is the deprivation of a constitutional right. Here, it is the Fourth Amendment right to be free from unreasonable search and seizure. As the government correctly points out, an occupant's expectation of privacy is merely one fact that must be proved to establish the second element of 18 U.S.C. § 242. Whether the government is able to prove the element will be determined at trial. The allegations in the indictment are plainly sufficient to allege the second element and fairly inform defendants of the charges against them.

> Further, the substantive counts allege that once inside the residences, defendants subjected the occupants to unlawful searches and seizures, which may constitute separate Fourth Amendment violations apart from the illegal entries. The indictment sets forth all of the elements necessary to constitute the offense.

> The indictment alleges in many of the substantive counts and overt acts that defendants denied various individuals the right to be free from the deprivation of liberty without due process of law, including the right not to have criminal charges based on fraudulent evidence or false information. The indictment alleges, among other things, that defen-

dants falsified police reports and committed perjury to cover up illegal searches and the planting of false evidence. Defendants again attack the indictment on the grounds that it fails to charge due process violations.

18 U.S.C. §§ 241 and 242 prohibit individuals from depriving, or conspiring to deprive, other persons of their constitutional rights. Instead of forbidding specific conduct, the statutes "incorporate constitutional law by reference." Because of the uncertainties in constitutional law, the Supreme Court has specified that in order to give fair warning to potential defendants, criminal liability "may be imposed for deprivation of a constitutional right if, but only if, in the light of preexisting law the unlawfulness under the Constitution is apparent." * * * The preexisting law may be found in appellate as well as lower court decisions and the facts of the decision need not be fundamentally similar to the case at hand. Often, the clearest constitutional violations will not be the subject of a judicial opinion; hence, "a general constitutional rule already identified in the decisional law may apply ... even though the very action in question has not previously been held unlawful."

Defendants say that there is no pre-existing law indicating that the use of false or fraudulent evidence in a criminal prosecution violates the Due Process Clause of the Fourteenth Amendment. According to defendants, due process is only violated when false or fraudulent evidence is willfully presented in court and is material to a conviction. * * * Because the Supreme Court has not held that the making of a false police report or the presentation of false evidence at trial is a due process violation by itself, the right is not established by preexisting law according to Lanier.

While the government acknowledges that the mere falsification of evidence by itself does not violate due process, it says that defendants have mischaracterized the allegations in the indictment. The indictment does not charge that due process rights were violated by the mere falsification of evidence. Rather, the substantive counts and overt acts allege that specific victims were deprived of their due process rights including "the right not to have criminal charges based on fraudulent evidence or false information" and "the right not to have false evidence intentionally presented against" them. According to the government, the evidence introduced at trial will show a "chain of events" including charges based on false police reports, individuals held in custody based on the fabricated charges, guilty pleas based on the false allegations, and false testimony at trial.

There is abundant analogous case law indicating that there is a right under the Due Process Clause not to be prosecuted on the basis of fraudulent evidence in the form of written reports or false testimony.

* * * The government says that the false evidence and false testimony are merely the beginning of a "chain of events" leading to prosecution that will establish a due process violation at trial.

Other courts have also found constitutional violations for conduct similar to the acts alleged in the indictment here.* * * . Two cases decided after defendants' conduct began in 2000 illustrate this point. See *Castellano v. Fragozo*, 352 F.3d 939 (5th Cir. 2003) ("causing charges to be filed without probable cause will not without more violate the Constitution" but "additional government acts that may attend the initiation of a criminal charge could give rise to claims of constitutional deprivation"); *Devereaux v. Abbey,* 263 F.3d 1070, 1075 (9th Cir. 2001) ("There is a clearly established constitutional due process right not to be subjected to criminal charges on the basis of false evidence that was deliberately fabricated by the government. Perhaps because the proposition is virtually self-evident, we are not aware of any prior cases that have expressly recognized this specific right, but that does not mean that there is no such right").

* * *

Based on these cases, the conduct alleged in the indictment is unlawful according to pre-existing law and satisfies the fair warning concern * * * The indictment alleges due process violations that are based in part on underlying conduct (filing false police reports and testifying falsely in court proceedings) that set in motion a "chain of events" including the bringing of criminal charges. The government says that it will show these actions resulted in individuals being held in custody, convicted, or induced to plead guilty. The indictment is sufficient to inform defendants of the charges against them. Again, the government bears the burden of proving the due process charges in the indictment at trial.

6. What about the use of civil rights laws as a response to abortion clinic violence? Although this theory met with some success in the lower courts in private actions brought under 42 U.S.C. § 1985(3), in *Bray v. Alexandria Women's Health Clinic,* 506 U.S. 263 (1993), the Supreme Court held, inter alia, that the civil rights laws do not protect the right to abortion from purely private conspiracies. In response to the Supreme Court's decision, Congress enacted 18 U.S.C. § 248, sometimes called FACEA (The Freedom of Access to Clinic Entrances Act). FACEA provides for criminal penalties, private civil actions, and civil actions brought by the Attorney General of the United States or state attorneys general as parens patriae. It defines the prohibited conduct to include the use of force, threats of force, or physical obstruction with the intent to intimidate or interfere with persons obtaining or providing reproductive health services. The penalty varies, depending upon the nature of the conduct. A lower penalty is provided for nonviolent physical obstruction, but if bodily injury occurs a term of imprisonment of up to 10 years is authorized, and if death results life imprisonment is authorized.

3. ATTACKS ON FEDERAL WITNESSES

UNITED STATES v. DINOME

954 F.2d 839 (2d Cir.1992).

WINTER, CIRCUIT JUDGE:

[The civil rights charges were part of a sixteen month trial on racketeering and other charges against a component of the Gambino organized crime family called the DeMeo Crew.]

* * *

One of the activities of the DeMeo Crew involved exporting late-model, stolen American cars to Kuwait. Ronald Falcaro and Khaled Daoud conducted a competing, but legitimate, venture of exporting cars to Kuwait. Noting the easy availability of vehicles to their competitor, Ronald Ustica, Daoud came to suspect that the DeMeo operation involved stolen cars and began copying down Vehicle Identification Numbers from cars in the DeMeo inventory. This was a fatal mistake because he was observed doing so by Ronald Ustica, the leader of the DeMeo stolen car scheme. Falcaro and Daoud were thereafter lured to a garage in Brooklyn by a false promise that Fred DiNome would sell them a portion of his excess inventory. Once inside the garage, Falcaro and Daoud were murdered by a group of men that included Joseph Testa and Anthony Senter.

Testa and Senter were convicted under 18 U.S.C. § 241 (1988) for Falcaro's murder as a violation of his civil right to be a witness in a federal proceeding. Testa and Senter argue on appeal that an element of proof of this offense was lacking, namely the requirement that Testa and Senter acted with the intent to interfere with Falcaro's right to be specifically a federal witness. Testa and Senter misconceive the nature of the proof required to establish a violation of 18 U.S.C. § 241.

Section 241 protects, inter alia, the right to provide information about federal crimes to authorities, and the right to be a witness in a federal proceeding. Whether Testa and Senter violated Falcaro's rights under Section 241 depends upon whether: (i) Falcaro possessed those civil rights and (ii) Testa and Senter intended to interfere with the exercise of those rights. It is not necessary, however, to show knowledge on their part that Falcaro possessed those specific civil rights or that Falcaro was actually likely to become specifically a federal witness. Rather, it need only be shown that Testa and Senter: (i) knew of facts that constituted a federal crime in which they were implicated whether or not they knew of its federal implications; (ii) knew that Falcaro possessed evidence regarding their criminality; and (iii) took action specifically to interfere with his providing that information to authorities or testifying as to that evidence anytime or anywhere whether or not there was imminent contact between Falcaro and federal authorities.

Falcaro clearly possessed the requisite right at the pertinent time. He knew of the scheme to export stolen automobiles to Kuwait, facts that constitute a federal crime. *See* 18 U.S.C. § 2312. The right to be a witness in a federal proceeding attaches at the time such a person is possessed of evidence sufficient to create the potential of becoming a federal witness. Testa and Senter knew of the facts constituting the federal crime and of Falcaro's sharing of that knowledge. Their murder of Falcaro was self-evidently intended to prevent him from disseminating his knowledge of those facts, including the provision of information to federal authorities or testimony as a witness in federal criminal proceedings. That Falcaro was at that time not in contact with federal officials neither diminishes his ongoing civil right to testify in a federal proceeding nor excuses Testa's and Senter's intent to prevent testimony anytime and anywhere. The evidence was thus sufficient to prove a violation of Section 241.

* * *

Notes

1.   What is the source of the right to be a federal witness that is being protected in *DiNome?* In *United States v. Pacelli,* 491 F.2d 1108, 1113 (2d Cir.1974), the court observed that not all rights "secured by the Constitution or laws of the United States" within the meaning of § 241 are explicitly mentioned in the Constitution or a statute. Certain rights are implicitly conferred by the creation of a national government, including "the right to testify at a federal trial in response to a request or demand of a federal district court." *Ibid.* Exclusive reliance on the states to enforce this right would tend to defeat the independence and supremacy of the federal government.

2.   Although § 241 prohibits a conspiracy to injure, threaten or intimidate any person in the exercise of protected federal rights, the section is violated by a conspiracy to intimidate even an unwilling witness who does not want to exercise this right to testify. Note that in *Pacelli* the court referred to the right to testify *in response to the demand of the district court.* Section 241 is applicable even if a witness is testifying pursuant to a subpoena, or has decided to testify only after being held in contempt. *United States v. Walker,* 710 F.2d 1062, 1071 (5th Cir.1983). What if the victim is unwilling to testify? What if she has not yet been subpoenaed?

3.   Federal criminal provisions dealing with obstruction of justice have also been used in cases of interference with federal witnesses. *See* 18 U.S.C. § 1503 et seq. In *United States v. Bufalino,* 518 F.Supp. 1190 (S.D.N.Y. 1981), for example, two defendants were charged in one count with conspiring to violate the civil rights of a federal witness under § 241 by plotting to kill him. One of them was also charged in a second count with obstruction of justice under 18 U.S.C. § 1503 in connection with the same conduct. The original indictment had charged as the first count a conspiracy to obstruct justice under § 1503 and 18 U.S.C. § 371. After noting that § 241 contains a harsher penalty than § 1503, the court stated:

> The government represents that the reason for bringing the superseding indictment is the dearth of evidence going to Rizzitello's awareness of Napoli's status as a federal witness. Proof of such an awareness is a necessary element under 18 U.S.C. § 1503, but not an element under 18 U.S.C. § 241.

Id. at 1193.

For a case in which the court upheld prosecution under § 1503 and § 241, see *United States v. Smith,* 623 F.2d 627 (9th Cir.1980).

4. In 1982, Congress enacted a new statute, The Victim and Witness Protection Act, P.L. 97–291, 96 Stat. 1248, which added provisions to the pre-existing obstruction of justice provisions that were specifically aimed at protecting federal witnesses, namely §§ 1512–1513, Title 18, United States Code. These provisions have since been amended to expand their applicability. They punish the killing or use of force against federal witnesses as well as the use of threats, intimidation or corrupt persuasion. In recent years, these provisions have been used, and there appears to be less use of the civil rights provisions, to protect federal witnesses than in the past. If this is the case, it is somewhat of a departure from the usual pattern: After a more specific federal crime is enacted, in addition to a more general provision which has been interpreted to provide a basis for enforcement in a particular substantive area, prosecutors typically charge both offenses in subsequent cases. What might account for the fact that federal prosecutors may be departing from the usual pattern in this instance? For detailed treatment of the use of obstruction of justice provisions and the witness protection provisions, see Chapter 16, *infra*.

5. For a case in which a RICO charge was combined with a charge under § 241, with the killing of a federal witness charged both as a predicate act—murder—under RICO and as the basis for the § 241 charge, see *United States v. Thevis*, 665 F.2d 616 (5th Cir.1982). *See also United States v. Kimble*, 719 F.2d 1253 (5th Cir.1983).

C. 18 U.S.C. § 245

§ 245. Federally protected activities

* * *

(b) Whoever, whether or not acting under color of law, by force or threat of force willfully injures, intimidates or interferes with, or attempts to injure, intimidate or interfere with—

> (1) any person because he is or has been, or in order to intimidate such person or any other person or any class of persons from—

>> (A) voting or qualifying to vote, qualifying or campaigning as a candidate for elective office, or qualifying or acting as a poll watcher, or any legally authorized election official, in any primary, special, or general election;

>> (B) participating in or enjoying any benefit, service, privilege, program, facility, or activity provided or administered by the United States;

>> (C) applying for or enjoying employment, or any perquisite thereof, by any agency of the United States;

>> (D) serving, or attending upon any court in connection with possible service, as a grand or petit juror in any court of the United States;

(E) participating in or enjoying the benefits of any program or activity receiving Federal financial assistance; or

(2) any person because of his race, color, religion or national origin and because he is or has been—

Race
Color
Religion
Nat. Origin.

(A) enrolling in or attending any public school or public college;

(B) participating in or enjoying any benefit, service, privilege, program, facility or activity provided or administered by any State or subdivision thereof;

(C) applying for or enjoying employment, or any perquisite thereof, by any private employer or any agency of any State or subdivision thereof, or joining or using the services or advantages of any labor organization, hiring hall, or employment agency;

(D) serving, or attending upon any court of any State in connection with possible service, as a grand or petit juror,

(E) traveling in or using any facility of interstate commerce, or using any vehicle, terminal, or facility of any common carrier by motor, rail, water, or air;

(F) enjoying the goods, services, facilities, privileges, advantages, or accommodations of any inn, hotel, motel, or other establishment which provides lodging to transient guests, or of any restaurant, cafeteria, lunchroom, lunch counter, soda fountain, or other facility which serves the public and which is principally engaged in selling food or beverages for consumption on the premises, or of any gasoline station, or of any motion picture house, theater, concert hall, sports arena, stadium, or any other place of exhibition or entertainment which serves the public, or of any other establishment which serves the public and (i) which is located within the premises of any of the aforesaid establishments or within the premises of which is physically located any of the aforesaid establishments, and (ii) which holds itself out as serving patrons of such establishments; or

(3) during or incident to a riot or civil disorder, any person engaged in a business in commerce or affecting commerce, including, but not limited to, any person engaged in a business which sells or offers for sale to interstate travelers a substantial portion of the articles, commodities, or services which it sells or where a substantial portion of the articles or commodities which it sells or offers for sale have moved in commerce; or

(4) any person because he is or has been, or in order to intimidate such person or any other person or any class of persons from—

(A) participating, without discrimination on account of race, color, religion or national origin, in any of the benefits or activities described in subparagraphs (1)(A) through (1)(E) or subparagraphs (2)(A) through (2)(F); or

(B) affording another person or class of persons opportunity or protection to so participate; or

(5) any citizen because he is or has been, or in order to intimidate such citizen or any other citizen from lawfully aiding or encouraging other persons to participate, without discrimination on account of race, color, religion or national origin, in any of the benefits or activities described in subparagraphs (1)(A) through (1)(E) or subparagraphs (2)(A) through (2)(F), or participating lawfully in speech or peaceful assembly opposing any denial of the opportunity to so participate—

shall be fined under this title, or imprisoned not more than one year, or both; and if bodily injury results from the acts committed in violation of this section or if such acts include the use, attempted use, or threatened use of a dangerous weapon, explosives, or fire shall be fined under this title, or imprisoned not more than ten years, or both; and if death results from the acts committed in violation of this section or if such acts include kidnapping or an attempt to kidnap, aggravated sexual abuse or an attempt to commit aggravated sexual abuse, or an attempt to kill, shall be fined under this title or imprisoned for any term of years or for life, or both, or may be sentenced to death. As used in this section, the term "participating lawfully in speech or peaceful assembly" shall not mean the aiding, abetting, or inciting of other persons to riot or to commit any act of physical violence upon any individual or against any real or personal property in furtherance of a riot. Nothing in subparagraph (2)(F) or (4)(A) of this subsection shall apply to the proprietor of any establishment which provides lodging to transient guests, or to any employee acting on behalf of such proprietor, with respect to the enjoyment of the goods, services, facilities, privileges, advantages, or accommodations of such establishment if such establishment is located within a building which contains not more than five rooms for rent or hire and which is actually occupied by the proprietor as his residence.

* * *

UNITED STATES v. BLEDSOE

728 F.2d 1094 (8th Cir.1984).

Ross, Circuit Judge.

The appellant, Raymond Bledsoe, was charged with a violation of 18 U.S.C. § 245(b)(2)(B). The case was tried to a jury and a guilty verdict was returned. The appellant was sentenced to life in prison and he appeals. We affirm.

Considered in the light most favorable to the government, the facts were these: On the evening of November 4, 1980, Raymond Bledsoe and two of his four roommates, Roy Loyd and James Graham, left their suburban house to go to Liberty Memorial Park in Kansas City, Missouri. A party was in progress at the time they left the house. The appellant and his companions regularly went to Liberty Park to "harass homosexuals." On his way out the appellant picked up a dowel rod and put it in the car. A baseball bat was already on the back seat. The appellant drove to the park.

At the park, the three went to the restrooms adjacent to a large baseball field. The appellant and Loyd entered the men's restroom and Graham stood by outside. Inside, the appellant began to wave the dowel rod at a white male who had been using the urinal. The appellant struck him on the back of the head with the dowel rod, breaking it in the process, and the man ran out of the bathroom. The appellant and Loyd followed him outside and watched him run away. The appellant did not give chase.

The appellant told his companions that somebody was in the other restroom and he and Loyd went into the women's bathroom. The appellant had the baseball bat in his hand. Stephen Harvey, a black man, was in the restroom sitting on a stool with his pants down to his knees. Loyd turned away as the appellant hit Harvey with the baseball bat. Harvey ran out of the restroom and the appellant pursued, continuously striking him with the baseball bat. Harvey, who had not been able to pull up his pants, made it out to the middle of the baseball field where he tripped and rolled over on his back. The appellant stood over Harvey and using an overhand swing, repeatedly struck him on the top of his head. The blows crushed Harvey's skull and caused his death.

Before leaving the park, the appellant checked to see if Stephen Harvey was breathing. He then told his companions "I think I killed him." The appellant drove back to the party and while crossing a bridge threw the baseball bat into a river. Loyd, Graham and the appellant made a "pact" never to say anything about the killing. Several people at the party saw the appellant arrive covered with blood. The appellant went into the bathroom and was followed by Gary Adams. In the bathroom the appellant told Adams he had killed a "black faggot," hitting the "black guy" on the head with a baseball bat, and that Loyd and Graham had to "pull him off from the guy while he was still hitting him".

Stephen Harvey was discovered in the park the next morning. The state police were unable to arrest anyone until February of 1981 when Gary Adams came forward and told the police about Loyd, Graham and the appellant's involvement. All three men were arrested but only the appellant was charged with murder. Loyd and Graham pled guilty to assault charges in exchange for testimony against the appellant. The appellant was acquitted after trial before a jury in the Missouri State Court System. A federal investigation followed the state trial and as a result the appellant was indicted for willfully interfering with Stephen L. Harvey because of his race and because he was enjoying privileges and facilities provided and administered by Kansas City, Missouri, a violation of 18 U.S.C. § 245(b) (1976). He was tried, convicted, and sentenced to life in prison.

* * *

The appellant argues that Congress relied on the fourteenth amendment in enacting section 245 and because the statute as applied reaches private action, this court must find that it is unconstitutional. The government argues that the question of whether Congress can reach purely private action under the fourteenth amendment has been answered by this court in *Action v. Gannon*, 450 F.2d 1227 (8th Cir.1971) (en banc).

In *Action*, supra, two private organizations concerned with the promotion of the economic welfare of black citizens conspired to systematically disrupt religious services at a Catholic cathedral. The church sued in federal district court under 42 U.S.C. § 1985(3) and requested an injunction prohibiting further disruptions. In concluding that Congress had the power to reach the conspiracy under sections 1 and 5 of the fourteenth amendment, the court noted: "We must answer two questions in order to reach this result: (1) Does the Fourteenth Amendment protect the First Amendment rights involved here, and (2) if so, does it protect those rights against state action only or against private actions as well?" *Id.* at 1233. This court, relying on *United States v. Guest*, 383 U.S. 745 (1966) answered both questions in the affirmative and allowed an injunction to issue.

* * *

In addition to the binding precedent which upholds congressional power to reach this type of activity under the fourteenth amendment, in our opinion the statute is constitutional as applied under the thirteenth amendment. It is abundantly clear that under this amendment Congress can reach purely private action. *Jones v. Mayer Co.*, 392 U.S. 409, 438–39 (1968). Nor can there be doubt that interfering with a person's use of a public park because he is black is a badge of slavery. * * * We therefore reject the appellant's argument and hold that 18 U.S.C. § 245(b) does not exceed the scope of power granted to Congress by the Constitution.

The appellant next contends that the instructions given to the jury did not set out the necessary elements of the crime with sufficient clarity, and that the conviction must be overturned on this basis. This issue centers on the question of motive. Section 245(b) clearly states that the interference must have been prompted by the victim's race. The following were among the instructions read to the jury:

> Instruction No. 16. Five essential elements are required to be proved beyond a reasonable doubt in order to establish the offense charged in the indictment.

* * *

Third: The defendant must have acted because Stephen Harvey was a black man and because he was or had been enjoying the facilities of Penn Valley Park, a public park administered by Kansas City, Missouri.

* * *

and Instruction No. 18:

* * *

You are instructed that every citizen, regardless of race, color, religion or national origin, has the right to enjoy the public parks. If you find beyond a reasonable doubt that Penn Valley Park was administered by the city of Kansas City, Missouri, and that the defendant willfully injured, intimidated, or interfered with Stephen Harvey because he was a black man and because he was using Penn Valley Park, this element of the offense would be established. Furthermore, if you find that the defendant had the motivation I have just described, the offense charged would be complete even if the defendant had other reasons for doing what he did, such as personal anger, or hatred for homosexuals, or a desire to commit robbery. In other words, the presence of other motives, given the existence of the defendant's motive to interfere with the victim's use of the park, does not make his conduct any less a violation of 18 United States Code 245.

The appellant argues that for a violation to be established under section 245 the substantial motivating factor for his actions must have been the victim's race and these instructions are inadequate because a conviction could be returned even if the interference was motivated only incidentally by race. We do not agree. The district court clearly stated that the prosecution must prove, beyond a reasonable doubt, that the appellant attacked Stephen Harvey because of his race. The clear implication from these instructions is that a substantial motivating factor must have been race. The additional information concerning the possible presence of other motivating factors simply restates the law on mixed motives.

The appellant also argues that the district court erred in denying his motion for judgment of acquittal. The appellant argues that the evidence established, if anything, that he beat Stephen Harvey to death because he believed him to be a homosexual and not because he was black. We do not agree. The government introduced a great deal of evidence which established that the appellant had a history of violently attacking blacks, and further, that this attack in particular was motivated by race hatred. The record contains several admissions made by the appellant:

He said that he had once killed a nigger queen.

And

A.   He told me that he had killed Stephen Harvey.

Q.   Did he tell you why?

A. Because he was a black fag and he made a pass at me.

In addition to the admissions, the government introduced circumstantial evidence of a highly probative nature. The white male the appellant believed to be a homosexual was assaulted and then allowed to escape after a single blow was struck. Stephen Harvey, on the other hand, was beaten, pursued, caught and killed. These disparate fates indicate that more than a hatred for homosexuals was operating when the appellant struck the blows which killed Stephen Harvey. When this evidence, together with the inferences which may fairly be drawn from it, is viewed in the light most favorable to the government, we must conclude that the motion was properly denied.

* * *

Notes

1. A number of federal prosecutions involving homicides that have a racial or ethnic motivation have been brought under § 245(b)(2). Some of these cases, like *Bledsoe*, were brought by federal authorities after state prosecutions had failed. For example, in *United States v. Ebens*, 800 F.2d 1422, 1423–25 (6th Cir.1986), the defendant and the victim were drinking at a nude dancing bar when the defendant began making racial and obscene remarks toward the victim, calling him "Nip," and "Chink," and making remarks about import cars that put American workers out of jobs. The defendant either mistook the victim, a Chinese–American, for a Japanese, or drew no distinction between the two. An altercation that started in the bar continued outside, and culminated in the defendant striking the victim repeatedly on the head with a baseball bat, causing his death. The federal charges were brought after the defendant pleaded guilty to manslaughter in state court and was placed on probation and fined $3,720. At that point, as the court of appeals noted:

> * * * [P]ublic outrage at the perceived lenity of the penalty [in the state court] was extensive, especially within the Chinese–American community. The case was accompanied by massive publicity at both the state and national levels and undoubtedly because of the activity on behalf of the Chinese–American community, the United States Department of Justice, overruling the decision of the local United States Attorney not to prosecute, instituted proceedings under the Civil Rights Act * * *.

800 F.2d at 1425.

The federal charges were brought first in *United States v. Franklin*, 704 F.2d 1183, 1185–87 (10th Cir.1983), the prosecution of an avowed racist who shot and killed two black men who were jogging with two white women. The defendant was convicted under § 245 (b)(2)(B), and he received two life sentences. He was then prosecuted by the state, which sought the death penalty for two counts of first degree murder arising from the same killings. When the state jury was unable to reach a unanimous verdict on the death penalty, he received two more life sentences.

For a discussion of the issues raised by duplicative federal and state prosecutions, see Chapter 17.

2.　United States v. Nelson, 277 F.3d 164 (2d Cir. 2002) arose out of tensions between the African American and Jewish communities in Brooklyn, N.Y. The events which ultimately led to the prosecution began with an auto accident in which two African American children (one of whom later died from the injuries) were struck by a car driven by a driver who was Jewish. A crowd gathered; harangued by hateful speech, it became a mob and went on a rampage, assaulting a Jewish couple and then a Jewish man before spotting in the street and attacking Rosenbaum, a bearded man in orthodox Jewish garb. In the course of this attack, the defendant stabbed Rosenbaum, and he died from the stab wounds. Judge Calabresi wrote a lengthy opinion upholding the charge under 18 U.S.C. § 245(b)(2)(B), for which Nelson had been convicted, but reversing the conviction because of error in empanelling the jury. He wrote:

> The Thirteenth Amendment to the United States Constitution provides:
>
> > Section 1. Neither slavery nor involuntary servitude, except as a punishment for a crime whereof the party shall have been duly convicted, shall exist within the United States, or any place subject to their jurisdiction.
> >
> > Section 2. Congress shall have power to enforce this article by appropriate legislation.
>
> > U.S. Const. amend. XIII.
>
> In the case at bar, the government asserts that this constitutional provision authorizes the application of § 245(b)(2)(B) to make a federal crime of concededly private, bias-motivated violence against a person because of that person's Jewishness and because that person was enjoying the use of a city street. In considering this contention, we focus on each of the two Sections of the Thirteenth Amendment in turn. * * *
>
> In contrast to Section One of the Fourteenth Amendment, which famously includes the language "No State shall ___," Section One of the Thirteenth Amendment eliminates slavery and involuntary servitude generally, and without any reference to the source of the imposition of slavery or servitude. Accordingly, it has been recognized from the Amendment's enactment that Congress powers under the Thirteenth Amendment are not limited by any analogue to the State Action Doctrine that was early deemed to restrict the Fourteenth Amendment. The Thirteenth Amendment, unlike the Fourteenth, in and of itself reaches purely private conduct.

* * *

> And the Supreme Court early on held that although "negro slavery alone was in the mind of the Congress which proposed the thirteenth article, it forbids any other kind of slavery, now or hereafter," and would apply equally to "Mexican peonage or the Chinese coolie labor system." *The Slaughter–House Cases*, 83 U.S. (16 Wall.) 36, 72, 21 L.Ed. 394 (1873). The Court, moreover, re-affirmed this sentiment roughly thirty years later, explaining that the Thirteenth Amendment "is the denunciation of a condition, and not a declaration in favor of a particular people. It reaches every race and every individual, and if in any

respect it commits one race to the nation, it commits every race and every individual thereof. Slavery or involuntary servitude of the Chinese, of the Italian, of the Anglo Saxon, are as much within its compass as slavery or involuntary servitude of the African." There can, therefore, be no doubt that the Thirteenth Amendment's prohibitions extend, at the least, to all race-based slavery or servitude.

Furthermore, "race" as used in Thirteenth Amendment jurisprudence is a term of art, whose meaning is not limited by today's usage.[12] The fact that Jews (the group to which the government seeks, through the application of § 245(b)(2)(B) * * *, to extend the protections of the Thirteenth Amendment) are today generally not considered a distinct race, therefore, does not rule out Jews from the shelter of the Thirteenth Amendment. * * * Indeed, the Supreme Court's case law firmly and clearly rules that Jews count as a "race" under certain civil rights statutes enacted pursuant to Congress's power under the Thirteenth Amendment. *See St. Francis Coll. v. Al–Khazraji*, 481 U.S. 604, 611, 107 S.Ct. 2022, 95 L.Ed.2d 582 (1987); *Shaare Tefila Congregation v. Cobb*, 481 U.S. 615, 617–18, 107 S.Ct. 2019, 95 L.Ed.2d 594 (1987). * * * [T]hese cases not only extend the protections of Reconstruction Era civil rights statutes, now codified at 42 U.S.C. §§ 1981 and 1982, to Jews understood as a "race," they also implicitly rule that the Thirteenth Amendment, the source of congressional power upon which the Court found that these statutes relied, protects Jews as a race.

* * *

St. Francis College and *Shaare Tefila* make clear that §§ 1981 and 1982 (and consequently the Thirteenth Amendment) extend to protect the Jewish "race." First, in *St. Francis College*, the Supreme Court unanimously held that the guarantees established by 42 U.S.C. § 1981 applied to a Caucasian of Arabian ancestry. In reaching this holding, the Court conducted an extensive investigation of mid-to-late nineteenth century dictionary and encyclopedia accounts of race, which revealed that, in addition to Arabs, Finns, Basques, Norwegians, Germans, Greeks, and many others, Jews (also known as Hebrews) were considered a distinct race at the time the Thirteenth Amendment was adopted. * * * In addition, the Court looked into the legislative history of 1981, which also revealed that the 1866 Congress considered Jews to be a distinct race. This research led the Court to conclude, concerning 1981, that Congress intended to protect from discrimination identifiable classes of persons who are subjected to intentional discrimination solely because of their ancestry or ethnic characteristics. Such discrimination is racial discrimination that Congress intended 1981 to forbid, whether or not it would be classified as racial in terms of modern scientific theory.

* * *

12. Of course, as the Supreme Court itself has noted, the modern usage may well itself be a fiction, in the sense that it groups people into what are no more than socially constructed categories. *See Saint Francis Coll. v. Al–Khazraji*, 481 U.S. 604, 610 n. 4, 107 S.Ct. 2022, 95 L.Ed.2d 582 (1987) (collecting references to biological and anthropological sources arguing that racial classifications are socio-political rather than biological).

Finally, there is strong precedent to support the conclusion that the Thirteenth Amendment extends its protections to religions directly, and thus to members of the Jewish religion, without the detour through historically changing conceptions of "race" that we have just taken. * * *

That the protections of the Thirteenth Amendment extend to private actions, and that Jews are entitled to the full measure of these protections, does not, however, settle the question now before us. It remains to be determined whether these protections (bestowed upon Jews or any other groups) suffice to authorize the congressional exercise of power at issue here—§ 245(b)(2)(B)'s criminalization of violence applied against a person on account of (a) his race (religion), and (b) his use of a public street. If the Thirteenth Amendment included only Section One, this would present an unsettled question. * * *

The existence of the Amendment's second section, however, renders consideration of the independent scope of Section One unnecessary. As the following discussion explains, Section Two grants Congress the power to enforce the Amendment by appropriate legislation, and it is clear from many decisions of the Supreme Court that Congress may, under its Section Two enforcement power, now reach conduct that is not directly prohibited under Section One. Furthermore, § 245(b)(2)(B), as applied in the case before us, falls comfortably within the limits of Congress's broad powers of enforcement under Section Two as these have been defined by controlling precedent.

* * *

Section 245(b)(2)(B), properly understood, * * * stops well short of creating a general, undifferentiated federal law of criminal assault and instead restricts its attention to acts of force or threat of force that involve two distinct kinds of discriminatory relationships with the victim—first, an animus against the victim on account of her race, religion, etc., that is, her membership in the *categories* the statute protects; and, second, an intent to act against the victim on account of her using public facilities, etc., that is, because she was engaging in an *activity* the statute protects.

It is important to understand that acts of violence or force committed against members of a hated class of people with the intent to exact retribution for and create dissuasion against their use of public facilities have a long and intimate historical association with slavery and its cognate institutions.

* * *

On the basis of the foregoing analysis, we similarly conclude that § 245(b)(2)(B)'s prohibition against private violence motivated by the victim's race, religion, etc., *and* because of the victim's use of a public facility, etc. falls comfortably within Congress's "power under the Thirteenth Amendment rationally to determine what are the badges and the incidents of slavery, and [its] authority to translate that determination into effective legislation." Accordingly, we find that § 245(b)(2)(B), as applied in the case at bar,[27] is a constitutional exercise of Congress's power under the Thirteenth Amendment.[28]

* * *

The defendants argue, next, that even if § 245(b)(2)(B) is constitutional, it does not reach the conduct for which they were tried and convicted.

* * *

Section 245(b)(2)(B) limits its scope to acts committed against victims because they are "participating in or enjoying any benefit, service, privilege, program, facility or activity provided or administered by any State or subdivision thereof." The defendants contend that their conduct does not come under the statute because Rosenbaum was not

27. We are mindful of the irony that attaches to applying the Thirteenth Amendment in this case. In doing so, we employ a constitutional provision enacted with the emancipation of black slaves in mind to uphold a criminal law as applied against black men who, the jury found, acted with racial motivations, but in circumstances in which they were, at least partly, responding to perceived discrimination against them. We make no effort to dissolve this irony, noting only that the post-Civil War amendments' specific historical focus on black Americans and the amendments' generally egalitarian language are all too often in tension.

28. Because we find that § 245(b)(2)(B) is a constitutional exercise of the powers granted Congress under the Thirteenth Amendment, we do not reach the alternative arguments—based on the Fourteenth Amendment and the Commerce Clause respectively—that the government has at various points in this litigation advanced. We note, however, that an important connection exists between the Thirteenth Amendment argument on which we uphold the constitutionality of § 245(b)(2)(B) and the suggestion that the statute is a constitutional exercise of Congress's powers under the Commerce Clause.

The Supreme Court has recently expressed a great reluctance to allow the Commerce Clause to grant Congress powers to regulate activities that are not directly economic. * * *And the activities regulated by § 245(b)(2)(B) unquestionably fall into this non-economic category.

But the dominant theme in *Lopez* and *Morrison* was to protect from federal interference activities that are local in character and, in particular, these cases reflect the fear that a broad reading of the commerce power that allowed Congress to regulate even non-economic activities whenever these substantially affected interstate commerce " 'would effectually obliterate the distinction between what is national and what is local and create a completely centralized government.' " It is in response to this worry that the Court has declined to adopt an expansive understanding of what might count as substantially affecting commerce. Under such a broad understanding, the Court opined, it would be "difficult to perceive any limitation on federal power, even in areas such as criminal law enforcement or education where States historically have been sovereign."

The Thirteenth Amendment argument presented in the main text reveals, however, that private violence motivated by a discriminatory animus against members of a race or religion, etc., who use public facilities, etc., is anything but intrinsically a matter of purely local concern. Instead, such violence has long been intimately connected to a system of slavery and involuntary servitude that the Thirteenth Amendment made centrally a matter of national concern. And for this reason, congressional action taken to regulate such activity is not likely to infringe impermissibly on local affairs. It follows that laws such as § 245(b)(2)(B) (if the activity regulated also involves substantial effects on interstate commerce) may well be constitutional directly under the Commerce Clause, even after *Lopez* and *Morrison*, and even without any independent resort to the Thirteenth Amendment. The fact that Congress may regulate an activity pursuant to its Thirteenth Amendment powers in itself indicates that the regulated activity is fundamentally national rather than local. And, as a result, Congress might also, separately, opt to regulate the activity pursuant to its Commerce Clause powers.

"participating in or enjoying any benefit, service, privilege, program, facility or activity" when he was attacked. In particular, the defendants argue that the Brooklyn city street on which Rosenbaum was attacked does not count as a "facility" within the meaning of § 245(b)(2)(B).

* * *

The defendants begin with the proposition that "facility" as used in § 245(b)(2)(B) is an ambiguous term, so that we must, in deciding the statute's meaning, look beyond statutory language. Proceeding from this premise, they contend that in light of the legislative history of the statute and also of the rule of lenity (which asserts that ambiguities in criminal statutes should be resolved in a defendant favor), we should find that a city street is not a "facility" for purposes of § 245(b)(2)(B). As a result, the defendants urge us to conclude that the fact that Rosenbaum was using a city street when the defendants attacked him is insufficient to sustain their convictions under the statute.

* * *

This argument need not detain us long, for it stumbles at its initial premise. As the defendants themselves concede, "the starting point in interpreting a statute is its language, for 'if the intent of Congress is clear, that is the end of the matter.' Therefore, if 245(b)(2)(B) is not ambiguous on its face, the defendants remaining contentions fall away.

Defendants' suggestions to the contrary notwithstanding, the term "facility" clearly and unambiguously includes city streets within its meaning. A "facility" is "something that promotes the ease of any action, operation, transaction, or course of conduct" or "something (as a hospital, machinery, plumbing) that is built, constructed, installed or established to perform some particular function or facilitate some particular end." *Webster Third International Dictionary* 812–13 (1966). And a city street undoubtedly "promotes the ease of" travel and transportation within the city and is "built" and "constructed" to "perform [the] function [and] facilitate [the] end" of such travel and transportation. It therefore unambiguously falls within the clear meaning of the text of § 245(b)(2)(B). Accordingly, as the district court correctly held, President Street in Brooklyn qualifies as a "facility" for purposes of § 245(b)(2)(B).

3. § 241 and § 245 are also used to prosecute "lesser" civil rights offenses. See, e.g., *United States v. Allen*, 341 F.3d 870 (9th Cir. 2003) where white supremacists were "patrolling" a public park, surrounded an Hispanic woman, an African American man and an Hispanic man who were socializing there, then wielding weapons and berating them with racial epithets, forced them out of the park. The court stated: "Although the actual "park patrol" occurred at a local park in Billings, the patrol was a racially motivated hate crime that interfered with the victims' exercise of their federally recognized and protected civil rights." In upholding the constitutionality of the statute, the court based its analysis more heavily on the commerce power than did Judge Calabresi in *Nelson*, supra, note 2, but also relied on the 13th Amendment, citing *Nelson* in support.

4. Section 245 does not reach all "hate crimes." In many cases, such as the murders of James Byrd, Jr., who was dragged to his death behind a pick up truck, and Matthew Shepard, the gay college student who was tied to a fence, beaten, and left to die, the defendants were not seeking to prevent the victim from exercising one of the federal rights enumerated in § 245(b), nor were they acting under color of law. Proposals to extend § 245 to cover a much wider range of hate crimes have been introduced repeatedly, and a bill passed in the Senate in 1999 but it was not adopted into law. One of these bills is included in Section D, *infra*.

5. Not all of the prosecutions under § 245 have involved racially motivated crimes. In *United States v. Fine*, 413 F.Supp. 728 (W.D.Wis.1976) the defendant was charged with five federal offenses in connection with the bombing and resulting death of a person at a research center at the University of Wisconsin: (1) injuring property of the U.S. (18 U.S.C. § 1361); (2) using a firearm to commit a felony prosecutable in a federal court (18 U.S.C. § 924(c)); (3) possessing an unregistered firearm (26 U.S.C. §§ 5861(d) and 5871); (4) conspiring to commit the foregoing crimes (18 U.S.C. § 371); and (5) interfering with a person's participation in a program receiving federal financial assistance (18 U.S.C. § 245). The last-mentioned count alleged that the defendant and named co-defendants:

> [D]id injure, intimidate, and interfere with the class of persons participating in a program at the University of Wisconsin, receiving Federal financial assistance and called Research In Application of Applied Mathematics because of the participation of that class of persons in that program.

> That is to say, that on or about August 24, 1970, the said defendants did willfully cause an explosion to occur at Sterling Hall at the University of Wisconsin, wherein the aforesaid class of persons participated in the said program, which explosion damaged Sterling Hall, injured three persons, and caused the death of Robert E. Fassnacht, and did thereby willfully and forcibly injure, intimidate, and interfere with and attempt to injure, intimidate, and interfere with the aforesaid class of persons because of their participation in a program receiving Federal financial assistance, in violation of Section 245(b)(1)(E), Title 18 United States Code.

Id. at 734.

6. In *United States v. Carvin*, 555 F.2d 1303 (5th Cir.1977), the defendant was charged with making oral telephone threats against President Ford, Vice President Rockefeller and Presidential candidate Reagan and with pointing an authentic-looking toy gun at Reagan during his campaigning. The court of appeals affirmed his conviction of violations of 18 U.S.C. § 245 (attempting to intimidate or interfere with a candidate campaigning for elective office); § 871(a) (threatening the President or Vice President); § 875(a) (interstate communication of ransom demand); and § 876 (mailing threatening communications).

7. In *United States v. Pacelli*, 491 F.2d 1108 (2d Cir.1974), the defendant argued that § 245 amended § 241 by implication by defining the rights protected by that section with greater specificity. The court rejected the argument stating:

The Congressional purpose in enacting § 245 was not to repeal § 241 but to remove any doubt as to the protection that would be extended against private interference with certain specific rights enumerated in § 245. Neither the language nor the legislative history of the new statute [§ 245] indicates the slightest intention to strip the national government of its existing ability under § 241 to protect * * * important interests * * *.

491 F.2d at 1114.

8. Subsection (a) of § 241 reflects a recognition that the offenses in question are typically prosecuted by state and local authorities, and it contains an unusual provision requiring certification at a very high level within the Justice Department before a prosecution may be instituted. It provides:

(a)(1) Nothing in this section shall be construed as indicating an intent on the part of Congress to prevent any State, any possession or Commonwealth of the United States, or the District of Columbia, from exercising jurisdiction over any offense over which it would have jurisdiction in the absence of this section, nor shall anything in this section be construed as depriving State and local law enforcement authorities of responsibility for prosecuting acts that may be violations of this section and that are violations of State and local law. No prosecution of any offense described in this section shall be undertaken by the United States except upon the certification in writing of the Attorney General, the Deputy Attorney General, the Associate Attorney General, or any Assistant Attorney General specially designated by the Attorney General that in his judgment a prosecution by the United States is in the public interest and necessary to secure substantial justice, which function of certification may not be delegated.

(2) Nothing in this subsection shall be construed to limit the authority of Federal officers, or a Federal grand jury, to investigate possible violations of this section.

Is this restriction either necessary or desirable? Can you think of other offenses for which a statutory restriction of this type should be enacted?

D. LEGISLATIVE PROPOSAL

Amendment No. 1324, Introduced July 22, 1999
145 Cong. Rec. S.9038

SEC. XX 01. SHORT TITLE.

This title may be cited as the "Hate Crimes Prevention Act of 1999".

SEC. XX 02. FINDINGS.

Congress finds that—

(1) the incidence of violence motivated by the actual or perceived race, color, national origin, religion, sexual orientation, gender, or disability of the victim poses a serious national problem;

(2) such violence disrupts the tranquility and safety of communities and is deeply divisive;

(3) existing Federal law is inadequate to address this problem;

(4) such violence affects interstate commerce in many ways, including—

(A) by impeding the movement of members of targeted groups and forcing such members to move across State lines to escape the incidence or risk of such violence; and

(B) by preventing members of targeted groups from purchasing goods and services, obtaining or sustaining employment or participating in other commercial activity;

(5) perpetrators cross State lines to commit such violence;

(6) instrumentalities of interstate commerce are used to facilitate the commission of such violence;

(7) such violence is committed using articles that have traveled in interstate commerce;

(8) violence motivated by bias that is a relic of slavery can constitute badges and incidents of slavery;

(9) although many State and local authorities are now and will continue to be responsible for prosecuting the overwhelming majority of violent crimes in the United States, including violent crimes motivated by bias, Federal jurisdiction over certain violent crimes motivated by bias is necessary to supplement State and local jurisdiction and ensure that justice is achieved in each case;

(10) Federal jurisdiction over certain violent crimes motivated by bias enables Federal, State, and local authorities to work together as partners in the investigation and prosecution of such crimes;

(11) the problem of hate crime is sufficiently serious, widespread, and interstate in nature as to warrant Federal assistance to States and local jurisdictions; and

(12) freedom of speech and association are fundamental values protected by the first amendment to the Constitution of the United States, and it is the purpose of this title to criminalize acts of violence, and threats of violence, carried out because of the actual or perceived race, color, religion, national origin, gender, sexual orientation, or disability of the victim, not to criminalize beliefs in the abstract.

SEC. XX 03. DEFINITION OF HATE CRIME.

In this title, the term "hate crime" has the same meaning as in section 280003(a) of the Violent Crime Control and Law Enforcement Act of 1994 (28 U.S.C. 994 note).

SEC. XX 04. PROHIBITION OF CERTAIN ACTS OF VIOLENCE.

Section 245 of title 18, United States Code, is amended—

(1) by redesignating subsections (c) and (d) as subsections (d) and (e), respectively; and

(2) by inserting after subsection (b) the following:

"(c)(1) Whoever, whether or not acting under color of law, willfully causes bodily injury to any person or, through the use of fire, a firearm, or an explosive device, attempts to cause bodily injury to any person, because of the actual or perceived race, color, religion, or national origin of any person—

"(A) shall be imprisoned not more than 10 years, or fined in accordance with this title, or both; and

"(B) shall be imprisoned for any term of years or for life, or fined in accordance with this title, or both if—

"(i) death results from the acts committed in violation of this paragraph; or

"(ii) the acts committed in violation of this paragraph include kidnapping or an attempt to kidnap, aggravated sexual abuse or an attempt to commit aggravated sexual abuse, or an attempt to kill.

"(2)(A) Whoever, whether or not acting under color of law, in any circumstance described in subparagraph (B), willfully causes bodily injury to any person or, through the use of fire, a firearm, or an explosive device, attempts to cause bodily injury to any person, because of the actual or perceived religion, gender, sexual orientation, or disability of any person—

"(i) shall be imprisoned not more than 10 years, or fined in accordance with this title, or both; and

"(ii) shall be imprisoned for any term of years or for life, or fined in accordance with this title, or both, if—

"(I) death results from the acts committed in violation of this paragraph; or

"(II) the acts committed in violation of this paragraph include kidnapping or an attempt to kidnap, aggravated sexual abuse or an attempt to commit aggravated sexual abuse, or an attempt to kill.

"(B) For purposes of subparagraph (A), the circumstances described in this subparagraph are that—

"(i) in connection with the offense, the defendant or the victim travels in interstate or foreign commerce, uses a facility or instrumentality of interstate or foreign commerce, or engages in any activity affecting interstate or foreign commerce; or

"(ii) the offense is in or affects interstate or foreign commerce.

"(3) No prosecution of any offense described in this subsection may be undertaken by the United States, except upon the certification in writing of the Attorney General, the Deputy Attorney General, the Associate Attorney General, or any Assistant Attorney General specially designated by the Attorney General that—

"(A) he or she has reasonable cause to believe that the actual or perceived race, color, national origin, religion, sexual orientation, gender, or disability of any person was a motivating factor underlying the alleged conduct of the defendant; and

"(B) that he or his designee or she or her designee has consulted with State or local law enforcement officials regarding the prosecution and determined that—

"(i) the State does not have jurisdiction or refuses to assume jurisdiction;

"(ii) the State has requested that the Federal Government assume jurisdiction; or

"(iii) actions by State and local law enforcement officials have or are likely to leave demonstratively unvindicated the Federal interest in eradicating bias-motivated violence."

SEC. XX 05. DUTIES OF FEDERAL SENTENCING COMMISSION.

(a) AMENDMENT OF FEDERAL SENTENCING GUIDELINES.— Pursuant to its authority under section 994 of title 28, United States Code, the United States Sentencing Commission shall study the issue of adult recruitment of juveniles to commit hate crimes and shall, if appropriate, amend the Federal sentencing guidelines to provide sentencing enhancements (in addition to the sentencing enhancement provided for the use of a minor during the commission of an offense) for adult defendants who recruit juveniles to assist in the commission of hate crimes.

(b) CONSISTENCY WITH OTHER GUIDELINES.—In carrying out this section, the United States Sentencing Commission shall—

(1) ensure that there is reasonable consistency with other Federal sentencing guidelines; and

(2) avoid duplicative punishments for substantially the same offense.

SEC. XX 06. GRANT PROGRAM.

(a) AUTHORITY TO MAKE GRANTS.—The Office of Justice Programs of the Department of Justice shall make grants, in accordance with such regulations as the Attorney General may prescribe, to State and local programs designed to combat hate crimes committed by juveniles, including programs to train local law enforcement officers in investigating, prosecuting, and preventing hate crimes.

(b) AUTHORIZATION OF APPROPRIATIONS.—There are authorized to be appropriated such sums as may be necessary to carry out this section.

SEC. XX 07. AUTHORIZATION FOR ADDITIONAL PERSONNEL TO ASSIST STATE AND LOCAL LAW ENFORCEMENT.

There are authorized to be appropriated to the Department of the Treasury and the Department of Justice, including the Community Relations Service, for fiscal years 2000, 2001, and 2002 such sums as are necessary to increase the number of personnel to prevent and respond to alleged violations of section 245 of title 18, United States Code (as amended by this title).

SEC. XX 08. SEVERABILITY.

If any provision of this title, an amendment made by this title, or the application of such provision or amendment to any person or circumstance is held to be unconstitutional, the remainder of this title, the amendments made by this title, and the application of the provisions of such to any person or circumstance shall not be affected thereby.

Note

Senate Democrats introduced this provision as an amendment to the Justice and Commerce Department appropriations bill. Similar provisions had been introduced in the previous Congress, which held hearings. *See Hate Crimes Prevention Act of 1998, Hearing on S.J. Res. 1529 Before the Senate Comm. on the Judiciary*, 105th Cong., 2d Sess. (1998). In contrast, Republicans sponsored a proposal to collect data on hate crimes and analyze trends, draft a model state hate crime statute in conjunction with groups such as the Commissions of Uniform State Laws, and provide assistance for state and local investigations and prosecutions of hate crimes. *See* Amendment 1320, 145 Cong. Rec. S9037 (July 22, 1999). Although the Senate appropriations bill included the Democratic hate crimes proposals, the House bill did not, and the final appropriations bill was adopted without these provisions. Note that this bill would add two sections to § 245. What forms of bias are covered by new section (c)(1), and what is the jurisdictional basis of this provision? Compare the coverage of (c)(2). Is there an adequate constitutional basis for the exercise of federal jurisdiction under each provision?

Similar legislation was introduced in later Congresses. See, e.g., Washington Post, September 17, 2004, A04, "Hate Crimes Initiative Probably Dead," reporting that a hate crimes bill which had been attached to the 2005 defense authorization bill was opposed by House Republicans reportedly, in part, on the ground that it improperly punishes thought rather than action. See Sara Sun Beale, *Federalizing Hate Crimes: Symbolic Politics, Expressive Law, or Tool for Criminal Enforcement*, 80 Boston U. L.Rev. 1227 (2000). Also see FREDERICK M. LAWRENCE, PUNISHING HATE: BIAS CRIMES UNDER AMERICAN LAW (1999) (proponent of bias crimes legislation, includes survey of existing hate crimes laws, history of federal civil rights statutes, analyzes First

Amendment issues and need for federal hate crime laws in addition to state laws), *with* JAMES B. JACOBS & KIMBERLY POTTER, HATE CRIMES: CRIMINAL LAW AND IDENTITY POLITICS (1998) (opponents of hate crime legislation, they argue that there has been no rise in hate crimes, and that hate crime laws are redundant to existing law, violative of the First Amendment, and detrimental to social cohesion because they promote divisive identity politics).

Chapter 15

PERJURY AND FALSE STATE-MENTS—18 U.S.C. §§ 1621-1623; 1001

INTRODUCTION

The crimes of perjury and making false statements within the jurisdiction of a federal agency are in many ways related. The crime of perjury provides a sanction designed to encourage witnesses in formal proceedings to be truthful when they testify under oath. As an offense, it has an ancient history going back to the Ninth of the Ten Commandments. But it also can provide a basis for prosecution when the government may have difficulty in proving the underlying crime(s) of a witness who is also a putative accused, and it is much easier to charge such a person with having lied under oath about her conduct; added to the underlying crimes, a perjury charge, where applicable, is also used to increase the possible penalties. Thus, perjury by itself is an important federal crime category. A study of perjury also provides useful insights about and contrasts with the crime of making a false statement.

We focus in this part both on the original federal perjury statute, 18 U.S.C. § 1621 and on § 1623, which applies only to false statements under oath before or in proceedings ancillary to a court or grand jury and which eliminates some of the traditional proof requirements applied under § 1621. The reader should be aware that the federal criminal code also contains a number of specialized perjury statutes applicable in certain kinds of proceedings or to certain types of documents. See, e.g., 18 U.S.C. § 152 (false oaths or declarations in bankruptcy proceedings; 18 U.S.C. § 7206 (false declarations in tax returns and other tax-related documents).

I. PERJURY

A. THE PERJURY STATUTES

§ 1621. Perjury generally

Whoever—

(1) having taken an oath before a competent tribunal, officer, or person, in any case in which a law of the United States authorizes

an oath to be administered, that he will testify, declare, depose, or certify truly, or that any written testimony, declaration, deposition, or certificate by him subscribed, is true, willfully and contrary to such oath states or subscribes any material matter which he does not believe to be true; or

(2) in any declaration, certificate, verification, or statement under penalty of perjury as permitted under section 1746 of title 28, United States Code, willfully subscribes as true any material matter which he does not believe to be true;

is guilty of perjury and shall, except as otherwise expressly provided by law, be fined under this title or imprisoned not more than five years, or both. This section is applicable whether the statement or subscription is made within or without the United States.

§ 1623.   False declarations before grand jury or court

(a) Whoever under oath (or in any declaration, certificate, verification, or statement under penalty of perjury as permitted under section 1746 of title 28, United States Code) in any proceeding before or ancillary to any court or grand jury of the United States knowingly makes any false material declaration or makes or uses any other information, including any book, paper, document, record, recording, or other material, knowing the same to contain any false material declaration, shall be fined under this title or imprisoned not more than five years, or both.

(b) This section is applicable whether the conduct occurred within or without the United States.

(c) An indictment or information for violation of this section alleging that, in any proceedings before or ancillary to any court or grand jury of the United States, the defendant under oath has knowingly made two or more declarations, which are inconsistent to the degree that one of them is necessarily false, need not specify which declaration is false if—

(1) each declaration was material to the point in question, and

(2) each declaration was made within the period of the statute of limitations for the offense charged under this section.

In any prosecution under this section, the falsity of a declaration set forth in the indictment or information shall be established sufficient for conviction by proof that the defendant while under oath made irreconcilably contradictory declarations material to the point in question in any proceeding before or ancillary to any court or grand jury. It shall be a defense to an indictment or information made pursuant to the first sentence of this subsection that the defendant at the time he made each declaration believed the declaration was true.

(d) Where, in the same continuous court or grand jury proceeding in which a declaration is made, the person making the declaration admits such declaration to be false, such admission shall bar prosecution under this section if, at the time the admission is made, the declaration has not substantially affected the proceeding, or it has not become manifest that such falsity has been or will be exposed.

(e) Proof beyond a reasonable doubt under this section is sufficient for conviction. It shall not be necessary that such proof be made by any particular number of witnesses or by documentary or other type of evidence.

§ 1622. Subornation of perjury

Whoever procures another to commit any perjury is guilty of subornation of perjury, and shall be fined under this title or imprisoned not more than five years, or both.

B. THE RELATIONSHIP BETWEEN § 1621 AND § 1623

UNITED STATES v. SHERMAN

150 F.3d 306 (3d Cir. 1998).

Before: ALITO, LEWIS* & MCKEE, CIRCUIT JUDGES.

MCKEE, CIRCUIT JUDGE.

The government appeals the order of the District Court for the Middle District of Pennsylvania dismissing a five-count indictment against Robert Sherman in which he was charged with committing perjury before a federal grand jury in violation of 18 U.S.C. § 1621. The district court held that the prosecution improperly charged Sherman under that general perjury statute rather than the more specific false declarations statute, 18 U.S.C. § 1623, thereby denying him the ability to assert the recantation defense available under 18 U.S.C. § 1623(d). For the reasons that follow, we will reverse and remand for further proceedings consistent with this opinion.

* * * The indictment stemmed from Sherman's testimony in the medical malpractice trial of Samuel and Gail Gassert v. Latif Awad, M.D. and Geisinger Medical Center. Sherman—a longtime obstetrician/gynecologist—had testified as the plaintiffs' medical expert in that trial. When cross examined about his qualifications as an expert, Sherman had testified that he was licensed to practice medicine in the District of Columbia, Virginia and Massachusetts and that none of his licenses had ever been revoked, suspended or restricted. He further testified that he had never been subject to any disciplinary proceedings by any hospital or medical society. He did, however, acknowledge that he had once been named in a medical malpractice case fifteen years earlier, involving a problem with a "D & C", but he described it as "routine." When Sherman provided that testimony, he knew that all of his licenses had

---

*Judge Lewis heard argument in this matter, but was unable to clear the opinion due to illness.

been revoked, and defense counsel ultimately elicited this admission from Sherman. Because that testimony is at the heart of this appeal, we will quote the relevant exchange at length:

Q: At the present time you are licensed to practice medicine in Virginia.

A: Yes.

Q: Over the course of your practice, which has been about how many years now?

A: Thirty years.

Q: Okay, over the course of your practice, how many states have you ever been licensed to practice in?

A: I was licensed in Massachusetts, Virginia, Maryland, and D.C.

Q: And you've continued to keep your license current in Virginia.

A: That's all.

Q: Do you remember at the time of your retirement in 1985, do you remember what states you had licenses in?

A: I don't have that handy at the moment.

Q: Well, were you licensed to practice medicine in Virginia in 1985?

A: Yes. yes.

Q: How about Massachusetts?

A: I moved away from Massachusetts so I didn't bother with that
. . . . .

Q: Did you ever have your privileges at any of those hospitals either revoked, suspended or restricted?

A: No.

. . . .

Q: Did you ever have any of your hospital privileges in Boston or in the Boston area revoked, suspended or restricted?

A: No.

Q: Have you ever been subject to any disciplinary proceedings by any—

(Objection and objection overruled)

Q: Dr. Sherman, have you ever been subject to any disciplinary proceedings by a hospital or medical society?

A: No.

Q: Have you ever been named as a defendant in a medical malpractice suit?

(Objection and objection overruled)

A: I had a malpractice case about 15 years ago myself, yes.

Q: Could you tell us what that was about?

A: It was settled somehow or other, but there was a routine case.

Q: Was that an OB/GYN case?

A: Yes.

Q: And it was routine?

A: Well, there was a D & C problem.

Q: You mentioned that over the course of your practice you were licensed in four states that you told us about. Have any of those licenses ever been revoked, suspended or restricted in any fashion?

A: No, I let them—I let them go because I had no intention of going back to active OB.

Q: So you let your license in Massachusetts lapse?

A: Yes.

Q: And you let your license in Maryland lapse?

A: Yes.

Q: And you let your license in the District of Columbia lapse?

A: Yes.

. . . .

Q: Go back to your licensures, Doctor. Isn't it true that you had your license to practice medicine in the District of Columbia revoked in 1977?

A: Yes, it was. Yes, but—

Q: Isn't it true that you had your license to practice medicine in Massachusetts revoked in 1983?

(Objection and objection overruled).

A: Yes.

Q: Isn't it true that you had your license to practice medicine in Virginia revoked in 1979?

A: But it was reinstated.

Q: The question to you, Doctor, is isn't' it true that your license to practice medicine in Virginia was revoked in 1979?

A: Yes.

Q: And it was not until 197—1993 that your license was reinstated in Virginia.

A: Yes.

Q: And wasn't you license in Virginia reinstated on a probationary status?

A: Yes.

* * *

Q: And according to the order of reinstatement you were not to engage in the practice of medicine until such time as you successfully passed the special purpose examination.

A: Yes.

Q: Did you pass that examination?

A: I have to take it on March 17th.

Q: Do you have plans to take it?

A: Yes.

Q: But you have not yet complied with that particular requirement.

A: Not yet.

Q: I see. If you have not complied with a particular term or condition of reinstatement, has your license in Virginia in fact been reinstated?

A: Has it been reinstated?

Q: Has it been actually reinstated?

A: It has been reinstated subject to that, yes.

Q: Could you go into the state of Virginia today and treat patients?

A: I don't treat any patients at the—

Q: If you wanted to, could you, with your restricted license, go into Virginia today and treat patients?

A: No.

Q: After your license was revoked in Massachusetts in March of 1983, you requested in 1992 reinstatement, did you not?

A: Yes.

Q: That was denied, wasn't it?

A: Yes.

Q: Didn't you have a license to practice in Maine?

A: Yes.

Q: And you made a license renewal to Maine in 1983 which was denied, didn't you?

A: At that time. It is under advisement for renewal at this time.

. . . .

Q: Doctor you told us that 15 years ago you were subject—you were a defendant in a routine medical malpractice suit, weren't you?

A: Yes.

Q: You know where I'm going, don't you, Doctor?

A: Yes.

Q: Do you remember a patient by the name of Rita McDowell?

A: Yes.

Q: Rita McDowell came into your clinic for an abortion, didn't she?

A: Yes.

Q: She was 16 years of age.

A: Yes.

Q: You performed an incomplete abortion on her

A: I did not.

Q: Doctor, as a result of the procedure that you performed on Rita McDowell, she died didn't she?

A: Absolutely not.

Q: Rita McDowell did not die?

A: She died at D.C. General Hospital as a result of a CVP line which perforated the lungs, and she died of cardiac arrest on that score.

Q: Doctor, the reason that your license was revoked in D.C. in 1977 was because of the Rita McDowell case, wasn't it?

A: Yes.

Q: And the reason that your license was revoked in D.C. was because you, as a practice, were performing incomplete septic abortions on your patients.

A: That is your opinion but not mine.

Sherman was subsequently indicted for perjury under 18 U.S.C. § 1621. * * *

The sole issue before us is whether the district court erred in dismissing the five-count indictment against Sherman. The court held that the government lacked the discretion to charge Sherman under the general perjury statute, 18 U.S.C. § 1621, rather than the false swearing statute, 18 U.S.C. § 1623, as the latter statute more specifically applied to his conduct, and not prosecuting under that statute improperly deprived Sherman of the defense of recantation which is available under 18 U.S.C. § 1623(d), but which does not apply to 18 U.S.C. § 1621.

We have previously noted the distinctions between the two statutes: 1) § 1623 does not require that the prosecution employ the "two-witness rule" for proving perjury; 2) § 1623 has a reduced mens rea requiring only that one "knowingly" commit perjury rather than "willfully," as is required under § 1621; and 3) § 1623 is restricted to testimony before grand juries and courts and is therefore more limited in reach than § 1621.

In United States v. Lardieri, 506 F.2d 319 (3d Cir. 1974), we examined the congressional intent behind these overlapping statutes. We stated:

It was the congressional judgment that the overall purpose of Section 1623, obtaining more truthful responses from witnesses before courts and grand juries, would be best accomplished by facilitating perjury convictions for those who had violated their oaths. In order to remove encumbrances from such convictions, Congress abandoned the two-witness rule, discontinued the requirement that the prosecutor prove the truth of one of two irreconcilable statements under oath, and required only a 'knowing' rather than a 'willful' state of mind. * * *

The congressional effort to improve truth telling in judicial proceedings was thus twofold. Congress magnified the deterrent role of the criminal law by easing the Government's path to perjury convictions and the emphasis here was plainly calculated to induce the witness to speak the truth at all times. Congress also extended absolution to perjurers who recant under prescribed conditions, admittedly an endeavor to secure truth through correction of previously false testimony. Each of these techniques has its own virtue, and it was, of course, the prerogative of Congress to put them to use; but it is evident that in some degree they unavoidably must work at cross-purposes. Recantation, for all its value in ultimately unveiling the truth, may well prove to be a disincentive to veracity in the first instance; to the extent that a perjurer can sidestep prosecution simply by recanting, he is hardly the more prompted to tell the truth in the beginning. By the same token, the deterrent effect of any statute punishing perjury is weakened in the same measure that recantation holds out the promise of possible escape. And indisputably, maximum deterrence of perjury is necessarily inconsistent with maximum range for recantation. United States v. Moore, 613 F.2d 1029, 1041.

* * *

When Sherman testified about his background, he violated 18 U.S.C. § 1621 as well as 18 U.S.C. § 1623. With certain exceptions, when conduct runs afoul of more than one prohibition of the criminal law, prosecutors have discretion to choose under which statute to prosecute.

* * *

However, notwithstanding the breadth of prosecutorial discretion, a prosecutor's charging decision cannot be "motivated solely by a desire to [achieve] a tactical advantage by impairing the ability of a defendant to mount an effective defense, [in such a case] a due process violation might be shown." Here, Sherman argues that the prosecution did just that. The district court accepted Sherman's argument that he was denied due process of the law because the prosecutor deliberately secured a tactical advantage in denying him a defense that he was entitled to assert by indicting him under § 1621 rather than § 1623. In dismissing the indictment, the district court stated: "we are of the view that allowing a prosecutor unbridled discretion to charge a defendant under section 1621 in all cases where a defendant might assert a recantation defense would eliminate the defense and is inappropriate." Accordingly, we must examine the defense of recantation and determine if Sherman's prosecution under 18 U.S.C. § 1621 improperly denied him a defense that he was entitled to assert.

Under 18 U.S.C. § 1623(d) the defense of recantation is available: 1) "if, at the time the admission is made, the declaration has not substantially affected the proceeding"; or 2) "it has not become manifest that such falsity has been or will be exposed." Here, the district court concluded that Sherman could have asserted the defense as his perjury had not substantially affected the proceeding when he recanted. Understandably, the court concluded that it was irrelevant that the perjury had been exposed prior to the recantation because the statute was drafted in the disjunctive so Sherman needed only to satisfy one of the two conditions, not both of them. The court held that the government's reliance upon 18 U.S.C. § 1621 deprived Sherman of the defense Congress wrote into § 1623 and that Sherman's right to due process of the law had therefore been violated.

The government contends that the district court erred in reading § 1623(d) in the disjunctive rather than the conjunctive, because both prongs must be met before a recantation defense is available. Since Sherman's perjury was exposed prior to his attempted recantation, the government argues that his right to due process of the law could not have been denied because he was not entitled to the recantation defense. Thus, our inquiry is focused upon whether Sherman was entitled to the defense of recantation under 18 U.S.C. § 1623(d).

* * *

18 U.S.C. § 1623(d) is deceptive in its apparent clarity. It says "or" and Sherman argues that Congress intended the statute to mean exactly that. However, reading the statute as Sherman argues we must results in a statute that is both inconsistent with, and frustrating to, Congress' twofold intent in enacting the legislation. If Sherman is correct, one could commit perjury with impunity. A witness could violate his or her oath in the comfort of knowing that no perjury prosecution was possible so long as he or she recanted as soon as it appeared the perjury would be disclosed. A recantation at that point, under Sherman's interpretation, would shield the conduct even if the judicial proceedings had been substantially affected by the false testimony. Similarly, a witness could escape prosecution even after the false nature of it had been disclosed and hope to successfully argue that the proceedings had not been substantially effected [sic] because there had been a recantation.

* * *

Thus, neither the text of the statute upon which § 1623(d) was modeled, nor the court decision that is codified by that statute support Sherman's position. They both require recantation before the perjury prejudices the investigation and before there is a reasonable likelihood that the perjury will be discovered.

Although there is not a wealth of legislative history available for § 1623, that which does exist reveals that Congress' intent was to encourage truthful testimony by witnesses appearing before federal courts and grand juries by facilitating perjury prosecutions and providing narrowed opportunity for recantation.

Only if both statutory conditions exist at the time of recantation will Congress' dual purpose of deterring perjury through more effective prosecutions and encouraging truthful testimony be furthered. Congress clearly did not intend to remove the twin impediments of the "two-witness" rule and the burden of proving which of two conflicting statements was actually false only to replace them with a "get out of jail free card." Accordingly, we conclude that Congress intended to limit the defense of recantation in 18 U.S.C. § 1623(d) only to those instances where the perjurer recants before the "declaration has not substantially affected the proceeding," and "it has not become manifest that such falsity has been or will be exposed."

Here, that did not happen. Sherman's revelation came too late to allow him to rely upon it to defend himself from prosecution under the general perjury statute. Accordingly, we must reject his argument that the prosecutor's decision to charge him under 18 U.S.C. § 1621 rather than 18 U.S.C. § 1623 deprived him of a defense in violation of his right to due process of the law.

The reasoning ... which we today adopt, is consistent with the decisions of the vast majority of courts of appeals that have addressed the overlap of these two statutes.

* * *

For the foregoing reasons, we will reverse the order of the district court dismissing the government's indictment against Sherman and remand for proceedings consistent with this opinion.[12]

Notes

1.   In the *Sherman* case, Judge Alito in footnote 12 was responding in part to a footnote to a portion of Judge McKee's opinion which was omitted above. The footnote (No.10) read as follows:

We note that, since we conclude that Sherman was not entitled to the defense of recantation under 18 U.S.C. § 1623(d), we need not address whether the Constitution would preclude the prosecutor from prosecuting under § 1621 and thereby depriving Sherman of a defense to which

---

12. Judge Alito concurs in this decision because he does not believe that the subsequent enactment of 18 U.S.C. § 1623 in any way affected 18 U.S.C. § 1621, and because he does not believe that the Constitution or any other rule of federal law requires that charges be brought under § 1623, rather than § 1621, in those cases in which alleged criminal conduct falls within the purview of both statutes.

he would have otherwise been entitled. It may well be, ...that such a decision would arouse due process concerns.

2. As noted in *Sherman*, the two-witness rule continues to be applicable to § 1621 but is not applied under § 1623. The rule has deep historical roots. See *Weiler v. United States*, 323 U.S. 606 (1945):

> This Court stated in *Hammer v. United States*, 271 U.S. 620, 626, that "The general rule in prosecutions for perjury is that the uncorroborated oath of one witness is not enough to establish the falsity of the testimony of the accused set forth in the indictment." The question here is whether it is reversible error to refuse to charge the jury to this effect.

* * *

First. The government asks that we reexamine and abandon the rule which bars a conviction of perjury on the uncorroborated testimony of a single witness. The argument is that while this quantitative rule as particularly applied to perjury cases may have been suited to the needs of the 18th Century, it has long since outlived its usefulness, that it is an incongruity in our modern system of justice, and that it raises an unjustifiable barrier to convictions for perjury.

Our system of justice rests on the general assumption that the truth is not to be determined merely by the number of witnesses on each side of a controversy. In gauging the truth of conflicting evidence, a jury has no simple formulation of weights and measures upon which to rely. The touchstone is always credibility; the ultimate measure of testimonial worth is quality and not quantity. Triers of fact in our fact-finding tribunals are, with rare exceptions, free in the exercise of their honest judgment to prefer the testimony of a single witness to that of many.

The special rule which bars conviction for perjury solely upon the evidence of a single witness is deeply rooted in past centuries. That it renders successful perjury prosecution more difficult than it otherwise would be is obvious, and most criticism of the rule has stemmed from this result. It is argued that since effective administration of justice is largely dependent upon truthful testimony, society is ill-served by an "anachronistic" rule which tends to burden and discourage prosecutions for perjury. Proponents of the rule, on the other hand, contend that society is well-served by such consequence. Lawsuits frequently engender in defeated litigants sharp resentments and hostilities against adverse witnesses, and it is argued, not without persuasiveness, that rules of law must be so fashioned as to protect honest witnesses from hasty and spiteful retaliation in the form of unfounded perjury prosecutions.

The crucial role of witnesses compelled to testify in trials at law has impelled the law to grant them special considerations. In order that witnesses may be free to testify willingly, the law has traditionally afforded them the protection of certain privileges, such as, for example, immunity from suits for libel springing from their testimony. Since equally honest witnesses may well have differing recollections of the same event, we cannot reject as wholly unreasonable the notion that a conviction for perjury ought not to rest entirely upon "an oath against an oath." The rule may originally have stemmed from quite different reasoning, but implicit in its evolution and continued vitality has been the fear that innocent witnesses might be unduly harassed or convicted in perjury prosecutions if a less stringent rule were adopted.

Whether it logically fits into our testimonial pattern or not, the government has not advanced sufficiently cogent reasons to cause us to reject the rule. As we said in *Hammer* v. *United States, supra,* 626–627.

> "The application of that rule in federal and state courts is well nigh universal. The rule has long prevailed, and no enactment in derogation of it has come to our attention. The absence of such legislation indicates that it is sound and has been found satisfactory in practice."

* * *

The refusal of the trial judge to instruct the jury as requested was error.

3. § 1623 also eliminated the traditional requirement that a perjury conviction could not rest on simply proving two irreconcilable statements, that it was necessary to prove the falsity of one of the statements (this requirement is still applicable to § 1621). Regarding the standard applicable under 1623, see *United States v. Flowers,* 813 F.2d 1320 (4th Cir. 1987):

> While § 1623(c) has eliminated the need for extrinsic evidence of falsity, the statutory language "irreconcilably contradictory" and "necessarily false" requires a variance in testimony that extends beyond mere vagueness, uncertainty, or equivocality. Even though two declarations may differ from one another, the § 1623(c) standard is not met unless, taking them in context, they are so different that if one is true there is no way that the other can also be true.

C. THE NATURE OF FALSITY UNDER THE PERJURY STATUTE

1. THE LITERALLY TRUE STATEMENT; THE NON–RESPONSIVE ANSWER

BRONSTON v. UNITED STATES

409 U.S. 352, 93 S.Ct. 595, 34 L.Ed.2d 568 (1973).

MR. CHIEF JUSTICE BURGER delivered the opinion of the Court.

We granted the writ in this case to consider a narrow but important question in the application of the federal perjury statute, 18 U. S. C. § 1621: whether a witness may be convicted of perjury for an answer, under oath, that is literally true but not responsive to the question asked and arguably misleading by negative implication.

Petitioner is the sole owner of Samuel Bronston Productions, Inc., a company that between 1958 and 1964, produced motion pictures in various European locations. For these enterprises, Bronston Productions opened bank accounts in a number of foreign countries; in 1962, for example, it had 37 accounts in five countries. As president of Bronston Productions, petitioner supervised transactions involving the foreign bank accounts.

In June 1964, Bronston Productions petitioned for an arrangement with creditors under Chapter XI of the Bankruptcy Act, 11 U. S. C. § 701 *et seq*. On June 10, 1966, a referee in bankruptcy held a § 21 (a) hearing to determine, for the benefit of creditors, the extent and location of the company's assets. Petitioner's conviction was founded on the answers given by him as a witness at that bankruptcy hearing, and in particular on the following colloquy with a lawyer for a creditor of Bronston Productions:

"Q. Do you have any bank accounts in Swiss banks, Mr. Bronston?

"A. No, sir.

"Q. Have you ever?

"A. The company had an account there for about six months, in Zurich.

"Q. Have you any nominees who have bank accounts in Swiss banks?

"A. No, sir.

"Q. Have you ever?

"A. No, sir."

It is undisputed that for a period of nearly five years, between October 1959 and June 1964, petitioner had a personal bank account at the International Credit Bank in Geneva, Switzerland, into which he made deposits and upon which he drew checks totaling more than $180,000. It is likewise undisputed that petitioner's answers were literally truthful. (a) Petitioner did not at the time of questioning have a Swiss bank account. (b) Bronston Productions, Inc., did have the account in Zurich described by petitioner. (c) Neither at the time of questioning nor before did petitioner have nominees who had Swiss accounts. The Government's prosecution for perjury went forward on the theory that in order to mislead his questioner, petitioner answered the second question with literal truthfulness but unresponsively addressed his answer to the company's assets and not to his own—thereby implying that he had no personal Swiss bank account at the relevant time.

At petitioner's trial, the District Court instructed the jury that the "basic issue" was whether petitioner "spoke his true belief." Perjury, the court stated, "necessarily involves the state of mind of the accused" and "essentially consists of willfully testifying to the truth of a fact which the defendant does not believe to be true"; petitioner's testimony could not be found "willfully" false unless at the time his testimony was given petitioner "fully understood the questions put to him but nevertheless gave false answers knowing the same to be false." The court further instructed the jury that if petitioner did not understand the question put to him and for that reason gave an unresponsive answer, he could not be convicted of perjury. Petitioner could, however, be convicted if he gave an answer "not literally false but when considered in the context in which it was given, nevertheless constitute[d] a false statement."[3] * * *

In the Court of Appeals, petitioner contended, as he had in post-trial motions before the District Court, that the key question was imprecise and suggestive of various interpretations. In addition, petitioner contended that he could not be convicted of perjury on the basis of testimony that was concededly truthful, however unresponsive. A divided Court of Appeals held that the question was readily susceptible of a responsive reply and that it adequately tested the defendant's belief in the veracity of his answer. The Court of Appeals further held that, "for the purposes of 18 U. S. C. § 1621, an answer containing half of the truth which also constitutes a lie by negative implication, when the answer is intentionally given in place of the responsive answer called for by a proper question, is perjury." In this Court, petitioner renews his attack on the specificity of the question asked him and the legal sufficiency of his answer to support a conviction for perjury. The problem of the ambiguity of the question is not free from doubt, but we need not reach that issue. Even assuming, as we do, that the question asked petitioner specifically focused on petitioner's personal bank accounts, we conclude that the federal perjury statute cannot be construed to sustain a conviction based on petitioner's answer.

* * *

There is, at the outset, a serious literal problem in applying § 1621 to petitioner's answer. The words of the statute confine the offense to the witness who "willfully ... states ... any material matter which he does not believe to be true." Beyond question, petitioner's answer to the crucial question was not responsive if we assume, as we do, that the first question was directed at personal bank accounts. There is, indeed, an implication in the answer to the second question that there was never a personal bank account; in casual conversation this interpretation might reasonably be drawn. But we are not dealing with casual conversation and the statute does not make it a criminal act for a witness to willfully

---

3. The District Court gave the following example "as an illustration only"

"If it is material to ascertain how many times a person has entered a store on a given day and that person responds to such a question by saying five times when in fact he knows that he entered the store 50 times that day, that person may be guilty of perjury even though it is technically true that he entered the store five times."

The illustration given by the District Court is hardly comparable to petitioner's answer; the answer "five times" is responsive to the hypothetical question and contains nothing

to alert the questioner that he may be sidetracked. Moreover, it is very doubtful that an answer which, in response to a specific quantitative inquiry, baldly understates a numerical fact can be described as even "technically true." Whether an answer is true must be determined with reference to the question it purports to answer, not in isolation. An unresponsive answer is unique in this respect because its unresponsiveness by definition prevents its truthfulness from being tested in the context of the question—unless there is to be speculation as to what the unresponsive answer "implies."

state any material matter that *implies* any material matter that he does not believe to be true.[4]

The Government urges that the perjury statute be construed broadly to reach petitioner's answer and thereby fulfill its historic purpose of reinforcing our adversary factfinding process. We might go beyond the precise words of the statute if we thought they did not adequately express the intention of Congress, but we perceive no reason why Congress would intend the drastic sanction of a perjury prosecution to cure a testimonial mishap that could readily have been reached with a single additional question by counsel alert—as every examiner ought to be—to the incongruity of petitioner's unresponsive answer. Under the pressures and tensions of interrogation, it is not uncommon for the most earnest witnesses to give answers that are not entirely responsive. Sometimes the witness does not understand the question, or may in an excess of caution or apprehension read too much or too little into it. It should come as no surprise that a participant in a bankruptcy proceeding may have something to conceal and consciously tries to do so, or that a debtor may be embarrassed at his plight and yield information reluctantly. It is the responsibility of the lawyer to probe; testimonial interrogation, and cross-examination in particular, is a probing, prying, pressing form of inquiry. If a witness evades, it is the lawyer's responsibility to recognize the evasion and to bring the witness back to the mark, to flush out the whole truth with the tools of adversary examination.

It is no answer to say that here the jury found that petitioner intended to mislead his examiner. A jury should not be permitted to engage in conjecture whether an unresponsive answer, true and complete on its face, was intended to mislead or divert the examiner; the state of mind of the witness is relevant only to the extent that it bears on whether "he does not believe [his answer] to be true." To hold otherwise would be to inject a new and confusing element into the adversary testimonial system we know. Witnesses would be unsure of the extent of their responsibility for the misunderstandings and inadequacies of examiners, and might well fear having that responsibility tested by a jury under the vague rubric of "intent to mislead" or "perjury by implication." The seminal modern treatment of the history of the offense concludes that one consideration of policy overshadowed all others during the years when perjury first emerged as a common-law offense: "that the measures taken against the offense must not be so severe as to discourage witnesses from appearing or testifying." Study of Perjury, reprinted in Report of New York Law Revision Commission, Legis. Doc. No. 60, p. 249 (1935).

---

4. Petitioner's answer is not to be measured by the same standards applicable to criminally fraudulent or extortionate statements. In that context, the law goes "rather far in punishing intentional creation of false impressions by a selection of literally true representations, because the actor himself generally selects and arranges the representations." In contrast, "under our system of adversary questioning and cross-examination the scope of disclosure is largely in the hands of counsel and presiding officer." A. L. I. Model Penal Code § 208.20, Comment (Tent. Draft No. 6, 1957, p. 124).

Addressing the same problem, Montesquieu took as his starting point the French tradition of capital punishment for perjury and the relatively mild English punishment of the pillory. He thought the disparity between the punishments could be explained because the French did not permit the accused to present his own witnesses, while in England "they admit of witnesses on both sides, and the affair is discussed in some measure between them; consequently false witness is there less dangerous, the accused having a remedy against the false witnesses, which he has not in France." Montesquieu, *THE SPIRIT OF THE LAWS*, quoted in Study of Perjury, *supra*.

Thus, we must read § 1621 in light of our own and the traditional Anglo–American judgment that a prosecution for perjury is not the sole, or even the primary, safeguard against errant testimony. While "the lower federal courts have not dealt with the question often," and while their expressions do not deal with unresponsive testimony and are not precisely in point, "it may be said that they preponderate against the respondent's contention." The cases support petitioner's position that the perjury statute is not to be loosely construed, nor the statute invoked simply because a wily witness succeeds in derailing the questioner—so long as the witness speaks the literal truth. The burden is on the questioner to pin the witness down to the specific object of the questioner's inquiry.

The Government does not contend that any misleading or incomplete response must be sent to the jury to determine whether a witness committed perjury because he intended to sidetrack his questioner. As the Government recognizes, the effect of so unlimited an interpretation of § 1621 would be broadly unsettling. It is said, rather, that petitioner's testimony falls within a more limited category of intentionally misleading responses with an especially strong tendency to mislead the questioner * * * [T]the Government isolates two factors which are said to require application of the perjury statute in the circumstances of this case: the unresponsiveness of petitioner's answer and the affirmative cast of that answer, with its accompanying negative implication.

This analysis succeeds in confining the Government's position, but it does not persuade us that Congress intended to extend the coverage of § 1621 to answers unresponsive on their face but untrue only by "negative implication." Though perhaps a plausible argument can be made that unresponsive answers are especially likely to mislead, any such argument must, we think, be predicated upon the questioner's being aware of the unresponsiveness of the relevant answer. Yet, if the questioner is aware of the unresponsiveness of the answer, with equal force it can be argued that the very unresponsiveness of the answer should alert counsel to press on for the information he desires. It does not matter that the unresponsive answer is stated in the affirmative, thereby implying the negative of the question actually posed; for again, by hypothesis, the examiner's awareness of unresponsiveness should lead him to press another question or reframe his initial question with greater precision. Precise questioning is imperative as a predicate for the offense of perjury.

It may well be that petitioner's answers were not guileless but were shrewdly calculated to evade. Nevertheless, we are constrained to agree with Judge Lumbard, who dissented from the judgment of the Court of Appeals, that any special problems arising from the literally true but unresponsive answer are to be remedied through the "questioner's acuity" and not by a federal perjury prosecution.

Reversed.

Notes

1.   See *United States v. Roberts,* 308 F.3d 1147 (11th Cir. 2002) where the defendant was charged with perjury based on his assertion in a 28 U.S.C. § 2255 filing that he had not previously filed a § 2255 motion. In fact he had previously filed such a motion; it had been denied; he filed a second motion in which he acknowledged having filed the first motion; it was denied; and he filed a third time, on this occasion asserting that he had not previously filed such a motion. The court stated:

> We review de novo whether a conviction for perjury should be reversed because the sworn statements were literally truthful. *United States v. Shotts,* 145 F.3d 1289, 1297 (11th Cir. 1998), * * * We reiterated in Shotts the Supreme Court's holding that a perjury conviction under § 1621 cannot be based upon a statement, "however misleading or incomplete, that is the 'literal truth.' " *Shotts,* 145 F.3d at 1297 (citing *Bronston v. United States,* 409 U.S. 352, 360, 93 S.Ct. 595, 34 L.Ed.2d 568 (1973)). "An answer to a question may be non-responsive, or may be subject to conflicting interpretations, or may even be false by implication. Nevertheless, if the answer is literally true, it is not perjury." Shotts, 145 F.3d at 1297.

* * *

> Appellant contends that because the pleading his attorney filed in the district court on April 25, 1997 was not styled as a § 2255 motion, and because he had not *personally* filed a § 2255 motion, his statements (in the instant habeas petition) that he had not done so were literally truthful. The district court, therefore, should have granted him a judgment of acquittal because a perjury conviction under § 1621 cannot be based upon a statement, however misleading or incomplete, that is the literal truth. As a lay person with no familiarity with the complex federal habeas corpus rules, he had no reason to believe that what his attorney filed on April 25, 1997, was a motion seeking § 2255 relief. Moreover, the inmate, Jorge Borjas, who prepared his petition, failed to inform him of the criminal penalties that might be imposed if he filed a petition containing the statements at issue here.

The court of appeals affirmed the conviction. How is *Roberts* different, if it is, from *Bronston?*

2. See Linda F. Harrrison, *The Law of Lying: The Difficulty of Pursuing Perjury under the Federal Perjury Statutes,* 35 U.Tol. L.Rev. 397 (2003) where the author reports the following facts relating to President Clinton's testimony regarding his relationship to Monica Lewinsky:

> . . . [W]hen President Clinton appeared at his deposition on January 17, 1998, he denied the existence of an affair with Monica Lewinsky and, in fact, referred to her falsely sworn affidavit in support of his denial.* * * During the deposition, the prosecution attempted to ask the President about the affair, which might have occurred with Ms. Lewinsky during his presidency. At that point, the President's lawyer objected to that line of questioning as based on innuendo, and referred to Ms. Lewinsky's sworn affidavit in support of his objection. He explained to Judge Wright that, in her affidavit, Ms. Lewinsky had sworn "that there is absolutely no sex of any kind in any manner, shape or form with [the] President." When asked about the affidavit, President Clinton stated that the affidavit was "absolutely true." Shortly after this deposition, the President publicly denied the relationship.
>
> After taping the lunch meeting between the two friends, the Independent Counsel confronted Ms. Lewinsky and eventually secured her cooperation in their investigation of the President. In exchange for immunity for making a false statement in her affidavit, Ms. Lewinsky agreed to testify truthfully before a grand jury, and to provide the prosecution with details of her affair and also with a blue dress on which she claimed she had discovered semen stains belonging to the President.
>
> After prosecutors secured Ms. Lewinsky's cooperation and obtained the blue dress and a detailed statement from her, President Clinton was called before the grand jury on August 17, 1998. In this appearance, the President admitted to engaging in "conduct that was wrong," but insisted that these "encounters did not consist of sexual intercourse" or "sexual relations as I understood that term to be defined at my January 17, 1998 deposition." When asked about Ms. Lewinsky's false affidavit submitted to the court during his deposition, Clinton replied, "in the present tense . . . that would be a completely accurate statement." When pressed to explain, Clinton said, "it depends on what the meaning of the word is is. If is means is and never has been, that is not—that is one thing. If it means there is none, that is a completely true statement." When pressed further on the issue, the President denied "trying to give . . . a cute answer," but argued that "generally speaking in the present tense, if someone said that, that would be true. And I don't know what [the prosecutor] had in his mind."

* * *

If Clinton's argument that he did not engage in sexual relations with Ms. Lewinsky because she performed oral sex on him, and not him on her, is valid, then his statement that he engaged in improper conduct is not inconsistent. He never denied that she had performed oral sex on him; he denied that he had sex with her. Clinton did not say that they had never had a relationship; rather, he denied that there was one currently. In fact, prior to his "improper conduct" statement in his grand jury testimony, there is no statement from Clinton describing his conduct at all, only hers. There are not two statements about the same thing here, only one statement about Lewinsky's conduct and one statement about his. The statements that Clinton made do not contradict at all and, therefore, do not need to be reconciled.

It would seem that the President apparently thought that under the doctrine of the *Bronston* case, he was speaking the literal truth in his testimony and therefore was not committing perjury. Is the issue of literal truth in connection with his testimony different from *Bronston*?

2. RESPONSE TO A QUESTION THAT CONTAINS AN AMBIGUITY

In *United States v. Farmer*, 137 F.3d 1265 (10th Cir. 1998), the defendant was prosecuted under § 1623 for having given a negative answer to the prosecutor's question on cross-examination. The defendant was testifying as a defense witness in the trial of a friend of hers who was being tried for possession of a firearm, having been previously convicted of a drug felony. The transcript of the testimony in question and the court's treatment of the matter follow:

Q. Prior to your coming to testify here today, did you speak to anyone about your testimony here today?

A. No, just the attorney asked me if I would—you know, verifying that I would come.

Q. When was that?

A. Well, I called the office this morning, which I didn't speak with him. Oh, I did too. I spoke with an investigator, a federal investigator.

Q. Who is that?

A. Well, I have got his name written down but I don't remember it. I believe it was Steve. I am not sure on that. I do have his name and number written down.

Q. When did you talk to this investigator?

A. I talked to him over the phone, I believe, a couple of weeks ago. He just basically, you know, asked me if Peter [McMahon] had been to my house and that was about it.

Q. Have you talked to Mr. McMahon, the Defendant about your testimony here today?

A. No.

Q. When is the last time you talked to Mr. McMahon?

A. I talked to him—well, I believe it was yesterday. I am not real sure. It was yesterday or the day before. He called and I talked to him briefly on the phone.

Q. What did you talk about?

A. Just—he just wanted to know if I was going to be here and I told him I was going to do my best. I have been working and, you know, I have two children, and that was about it.

In *Larranaga*, we held as a matter of law that the defendant did not violate § 1623(a) when he responded "yes" to an inquiry about whether the subpoenaed minutes of a corporate board meeting were complete. The prosecutor asked: "Are these all of the minutes of the Board of Directors' meeting or any other subcommittees of that board?" Although a second set of minutes and some rough notes of the meeting existed, Defendant responded: "Yes, sir." *Larranaga,* 787 F.2d at 496. We reasoned:

> Here the questioner could have precisely asked Larranaga if there were any related rough notes, memoranda or the like dealing with the meetings covered by the minutes. He could also have inquired whether there were any other minutes detailing the events of the same meetings in question. Leaving the matter as it was permitted the answer to be ambiguous in the context of these facts, and untrue by its "negative implication." We must agree that the theory that perjury was committed by Larranaga's one answer is untenable under the perjury statute as construed in *Bronston*.

Id. at 497. In so holding, we expressly rejected the Government's argument that the jury should determine whether the defendant knowingly gave a false answer to the prosecutor's question. We stated:

> We are mindful of the trial court's instruction which charged the jury that if it found a question was ambiguous, and that the defendant truthfully answered one reasonable interpretation of it, then the answer would not be false.... We do not feel that the instruction solved the problem. In these circumstances, the question asked left the matter in doubt and the finding of guilty on the perjury charge as to this theory rested on an impermissible negative implication and ambiguous circumstances.

Larranaga, 787 F.2d at 497 n.2.

* * *

[C]ourts reviewing perjury convictions have removed the issue of a question's meaning from the jury, where such question is "fundamentally ambiguous." These courts have applied a de novo standard of review and resolved the issue as a matter of law in favor of the defendant.

A question is fundamentally ambiguous when it " 'is not a phrase with a meaning about which men of ordinary intellect could agree, nor one which could be used with mutual understanding by a questioner and answerer unless it were defined at the time it were sought and offered as testimony.' The purpose of the rule of fundamental ambiguity is three-fold, namely, to (1) preclude convictions grounded on surmise or conjecture; (2) prevent witnesses from unfairly bearing the risks of inadequate examination; and (3) encourage witnesses to testify (or at least not discourage them from doing so). Unfortunately, line drawing is inevitable, for to precisely define the point at which a question becomes fundamentally ambiguous, and thus not amenable to jury interpretation, is impossible.

To be sure, in most instances, the meaning of a prosecutor's question and the truthfulness of a defendant's answer are best left to the jury. Fundamental ambiguity is the exception, not the rule. In other words, where a prosecutor's question is only "arguably ambiguous," a defendant's understanding of the question is for the jury to resolve in the first instance. * * * Where a defendant claims that the question is ambiguous or misunderstood, the context of the question and answer becomes critically important.

Where a question considered in proper context is only arguably ambiguous, courts reviewing perjury convictions have viewed the defense of ambiguity as an attack upon the sufficiency of the evidence. Applying a de novo but more deferential standard of review, these courts view the evidence in a light most favorable to the Government and ask whether any reasonable jury could have found all elements of the crime beyond a reasonable doubt. * * * Even under this more deferential standard, however, courts still require a perjury conviction to rest upon precise questioning.

Where a question admits of two reasonable interpretations, some evidence must show what the question meant to the defendant when she answered it. ("The principles underlying the Bronston decision also bar perjury convictions for arguably untrue answers to vague or ambiguous questions when there is insufficient evidence of how they were understood by the witness."). Otherwise, the Government has not provided the jury with enough evidence to conclude beyond a reasonable doubt that the defendant knowingly rendered false testimony, as required to obtain a conviction under § 1623(a). While a jury may guess correctly as to a defendant's understanding of a question, "it is not entitled to guess at all."

How we label the prosecutor's question in this case makes no difference. We need not decide whether the prosecutor's question: "Have you talked to Mr. McMahon, the Defendant about your testimony here today?" is fundamentally ambiguous or only arguably ambiguous for we would reach the same result regardless of any label. Undoubtedly, the question considered in isolation is ambiguous for it has two possible meanings. Whether the phrase "here today" refers to the word "talked" or the word "testimony," is patently unclear. Viewed in the context of her entire line of testimony, the question becomes no clearer. The phrase "here today" when considered in the context of the prosecutor's question: "Have you talked to Mr. McMahon, the Defendant about your testimony here today?" does not seem to be "a phrase with a meaning about which men of ordinary intellect could agree, nor one which could be used with mutual understanding by a questioner and answerer unless it were defined.' "

* * * In fact, the exchange between Defendant and the prosecutor immediately following her negative response to the question, buttresses her understanding of the question. The prosecutor next asked: "When is the last time you talked to Mr. McMahon?" Defendant responded that she had spoken with McMahon "yesterday or the day before." Defendant's response seems to follow logically if she understood the prosecutor's former question as she claims. In other words, Defendant indicated by her testimony that she had not spoken with McMahon on the day of the pretrial hearing but had spoken with him a day or two before the hearing.

Defendant did not deny speaking with McMahon prior to her testimony. When asked what she and McMahon talked about, Defendant stated that McMahon "just wanted to know if I was going to be here and I told him I was going to do my best." At this point, the prosecutor pressed no further, but ended his inquiry into the matter. While Defendant may have had the opportunity at the pretrial hearing to divulge all matters she and McMahon discussed in their telephone conversation, the burden was on the prosecutor to pin her down with specific questions. Precise examination, which the prosecutor failed to pursue in this case, rather than a perjury prosecution, is the primary safeguard against errant testimony.

The Government simply did not offer any evidence to suggest what the question meant to Defendant when she answered it. Only by surmise and conjecture could the jury conclude that Defendant understood the question as the prosecutor did. The evidence in this case is insufficient to establish beyond a reasonable doubt that Defendant knowingly rendered false testimony as charged in the indictment. Accordingly, Defendant's conviction under 18 U.S.C. § 1623(a) is reversed, and this cause is remanded for entry of a judgment of acquittal.

3. THE "I DO NOT RECALL" RESPONSE

Can a witness avoid a perjury charge by claiming that she does not remember? See *United States v. Abrams*, 568 F.2d 411 (5th Cir. 1978):

Second, appellant contends that there was no evidence introduced to show that she willfully and knowingly lied to the grand jury, that is, that she knew the charges were not incurred and remembered that fact. In this connection we are asked to ponder the thousands of cases which passed through, and the thousands of transactions taking place in, this busy, disorganized law office, all of which made it unreasonable for Abrams to remember the details of the Henry cost breakdown. There are several answers to this contention.

Abrams typed and signed on Davis' behalf the letters to the Florida Bar, and she—according to her grand jury testimony—

prepared the cost breakdown. This office work was necessary only because a very serious complaint about Davis had been lodged with the Bar. Abrams was an employee in a law office where such complaints should not have been an everyday occurrence and should not have been treated routinely or cavalierly. All the more so because Abrams was well aware in April 1974 that Davis had been the target of a recent investigation. Indeed, that investigation prompted a meeting of Davis' staff which Abrams attended and during which Davis instructed the staff to take certain actions.

In light of this background, the jury could have reasonably concluded that the Henry cost breakdown was not as forgettable as appellant contends and that Abrams knew full well that certain of her answers were false. This is especially so in light of the overwhelming evidence which could lead a jury to conclude that Abrams must have known or recalled that the $107.50 cost for investigation and photography was *never* incurred and that the $75 for conferences with Dr. Fox and the $35 for photographs were somehow fabricated in response to the Florida Bar inquiry.[46]

In the absence of a statement by the defendant, the falsity of an "I don't recall" answer must be proven by circumstantial evidence. This does not mean that proof is impossible. As another court has stated, "The jury must infer the state of a man's mind from the things he says and does. Such an inference may come from proof of the objective falsity itself, from proof of a motive to lie, and from other facts tending to show that the defendant really knew the things he claimed not to know" or recall.

In applying these principles, there was abundant proof—already detailed at length—of objective falsity and other facts tending to show that Abrams really knew or recalled that which she denied knowing or recalling. As to motive, the jury knew that Abrams was employed by Davis when she appeared before the grand jury and it was at liberty to draw reasonable inferences concerning motive from the employer-employee relationship, as well as from the grant of use immunity. The jury, properly instructed, resolved this issue against Abrams and we see no reason to disturb its verdict here.

II. FALSE STATEMENTS WITHIN THE JURISDICTION OF A FEDERAL AGENCY—18 U.S.C. § 1001

A. INTRODUCTION

In 1996, the False Statements Accountability Act was passed by the Congress, and the false statements statute, 18 U.S.C. § 1001, was amended to provide as follows:

---

46. It should be emphasized that several perjured answers did not involve "I don't know" or "I don't remember" responses. For example, Abrams stated unequivocally that the investigator prepared the Worldwide invoice for $107.50. The jury obviously believed Hallen's testimony to the contrary.

§ 1001. Statements or entries generally

(a) Except as otherwise provided in this section, whoever, in any matter within the jurisdiction of the executive, legislative, or judicial branch of the Government of the United States, knowingly and willfully—

(1) falsifies, conceals, or covers up by any trick, scheme, or device a material fact;

(2) makes any materially false, fictitious, or fraudulent statement or representation; or

(3) makes or uses any false writing or document knowing the same to contain any materially false, fictitious, or fraudulent statement or entry;

shall be fined under this title, imprisoned not more than 5 years or, if the offense involves international or domestic terrorism (as defined in section 2331 [18 USCS § 2331]), imprisoned not more than 8 years, or both.*

(b) Subsection (a) does not apply to a party to a judicial proceeding, or that party's counsel, for statements, representations, writings or documents submitted by such party or counsel to a judge or magistrate in that proceeding.

(c) With respect to any matter within the jurisdiction of the legislative branch, subsection (a) shall apply only to—

(1) administrative matters, including a claim for payment, a matter related to the procurement of property or services, personnel or employment practices, or support services, or a document required by law, rule, or regulation to be submitted to the Congress or any office or officer within the legislative branch; or

(2) any investigation or review, conducted pursuant to the authority of any committee, subcommittee, commission or office of the Congress, consistent with applicable rules of the House or Senate.

The prior version of § 1001 had provided as follows:

§ 1001. Statements or entries generally

Whoever, in any matter within the jurisdiction of any department or agency of the United States knowingly and willfully falsifies, conceals or covers up by any trick, scheme, or device a material fact, or makes any false, fictitious or fraudulent statements or representations, or makes or uses any false writing or document knowing the same to contain any false, fictitious or fraudulent statement or entry, shall be fined not more than $10,000 or imprisoned not more than five years, or both.

* The 8 year penalty provision in international or domestic terrorism cases was added by the Intelligence Reform and Terrorism Prevention Act of 2004.

We have reproduced the prior version of § 1001, above, because the cases in this chapter include decisions under the old law. In general, cases decided under the prior statute, are being followed in prosecutions under the new version of 1001. Specific issues relating to the applicability of earlier decisions under the new statute will be addressed in the specific contexts in which they arise.

Section 1001, both new and old versions, bears a superficial resemblance to a perjury provision although it lacks certain elements normally found in such an offense—that the statement be made under oath and that it be made in an official proceeding.

Violations of section 1001 can also be charged in a variety of contexts—for example, to prosecute conduct aimed at the defrauding of the federal government accompanied by the making of false statements. In that dimension, it supplements the many fraud provisions found in Title 18 as well as the crime of conspiracy to defraud, 18 U.S.C. § 371. Insofar as it does not require that the government be defrauded (compare, for example, 18 U.S.C. § 1013) or that there be any financial loss to the government, it may be viewed as a provision that punishes inchoate fraud.

Finally, insofar as the statute can be used to punish false statements made to law enforcement agents, it deals with conduct that has overtones of obstructing justice, and its coverage may be compared with provisions dealing expressly with that subject. See Chapter 16, infra. In this last-mentioned dimension, section 1001 provides to federal criminal investigators—the FBI as well as other agencies—a potent combination of an investigatory and prosecutorial tool.

B. ELEMENTS OF THE OFFENSE— IN GENERAL

UNITED STATES v. WHAB

355 F.3d 155 (2d Cir. 2004).

JUDGES: Before: CABRANES and RAGGI, CIRCUIT JUDGES, and MUKASEY, DISTRICT JUDGE.

The Honorable Michael B. Mukasey, Chief Judge of the United States District Court for the Southern District of New York, sitting by designation.

JOSE A. CABRANES, CIRCUIT JUDGE:

Defendant Usama Sadik Ahmed Abdel Whab appeals from a judgment entered on September 16, 2002 in the United States District Court for the Southern District of New York (Colleen McMahon, *Judge*) following a jury trial. Defendant was convicted on three counts: (1) making a false statement in an application for a United States passport, in violation of 18 U.S.C. §§ 1542 and 2; (2) making and using a false writing, specifically, a forged baptismal certificate, in support of his application for a passport, in violation of 18 U.S.C. § 1001; and (3) making a false statement to a federal agent, in violation of 18 U.S.C.

§ 1001. Defendant was sentenced principally to a term of 6 months' imprisonment, which he has now completed, to be followed by three years' supervised release.

We view the evidence presented at trial in the light most favorable to the government. In June 2001, defendant, an Egyptian-born citizen of Egypt, claimed in an application for a United States passport that he was born in Brooklyn, New York. After receiving a request for additional documentation supporting his claim that he was born in the United States, defendant submitted a forged baptismal certificate to the United States Passport Agency ("Passport Agency"). In October 2001, defendant was interviewed by a federal agent, and again falsely stated that he had been born in Brooklyn.

Defendant claims on appeal that (1) under the "willfulness" requirement of 18 U.S.C. § 1001, the Government was required to prove that defendant specifically knew that making a false statement to a federal agent was criminal, and failed to do so; (2) the Government failed to prove that his forged baptismal certificate was material to his passport application under 18 U.S.C. § 1001, in light of the baptismal certificate's recent date of issue; and (3) the District Court erred in refusing to instruct the jurors that they were not to consider the reasonableness of defendant's belief that he was born in Brooklyn. We affirm.

Defendant first argues that there was insufficient evidence to prove that he violated 18 U.S.C. § 1001 by making a false statement to a federal agent, because the Government was required, and failed, to prove that defendant specifically knew that it was unlawful to make a false statement to a federal agent. Defendant's argument, while cast in terms of a challenge to the sufficiency of the evidence, is in essence a claim that the District Court erred by failing to instruct the jury that the Government was required to prove that defendant knew that making a false statement to a federal agent was a crime.

Because defendant did not raise this argument below, we review for plain error. Before we can correct an error not raised at trial, "there must be (1) 'error,' (2) that is 'plain,' and (3) that 'affect[s] substantial rights.'" Where all three conditions are met, "an appellate court may then exercise its discretion to notice a forfeited error, but only if (4) the error 'seriously affect[s] the fairness, integrity, or public reputation of judicial proceedings.'"

* * *

We hold that, in the circumstances presented, this case does not require a resort to any such difficult or exceptional application of "plain error" review. Defendant was convicted of violating 18 U.S.C. § 1542 and § 1001, both of which prohibit knowingly and willfully making false statements to government agents or particular agencies. The District Court, in explaining the concept of knowing and willful conduct in connection with Count One of the indictment, the § 1542 offense, stated:

An act is done knowingly if it is done voluntarily and purposely and not because of mistake, accident, or some other reason. An act is done willfully if it is done knowingly, intentionally and with a bad purpose, a purpose to do something that the law forbids.

In determining whether a defendant has acted knowingly and willfully, it is not necessary for the Government to establish that the defendant knew that he was breaking any particular law or particular rule. He need only have been aware of the generally unlawful nature of his actions.

* * *

Where, as in this case, a district court provides a jury with the identical definition of key terms such as "knowingly" and "willfully" in its instructions on three separate counts of the indictment, it would be obvious to the jury that any amplifications of the definitions provided in the court's first discussion of their application necessarily pertain to subsequent applications as well. In short, tedious repetition was unnecessary to ensure an intelligible and accurate portrayal of the law. Reviewing the District Court's instructions as a whole, we are satisfied that they clearly charged the jury that, in order to find that defendant acted "willfully" under § 1001, the Government was required to show that he acted with a purpose to do something the law forbids, and with an awareness of the generally unlawful nature of his actions.

Defendant seems to argue that the requirement of § 1001 that a defendant act "willfully" in making a false statement includes something more: specific knowledge that lying to a federal agent is a crime. He contends that his conviction cannot stand in the absence of "evidence showing that [he] was told that it was a crime to make such a false statement." Defendant relies on *United States v. Wiener*, 96 F.3d 35, 40 (2d Cir. 1996), in which we rejected the "exculpatory no" doctrine, a judicially-created exception to § 1001, adopted by several courts, that made § 1001 inapplicable to "false statements that are essentially exculpatory denials of criminal activity.". In discussing the boundaries of criminal liability under § 1001, we noted:

> Arguably, to violate Section 1001, a person must know that it is unlawful to make such a false statement. The Supreme Court recently held that the word "willfully" in 31 U.S.C. § 5322(a) requires that a defendant "act [] with knowledge that his conduct was unlawful." (quoting *Ratzlaf v. United States*, 510 U.S. 135, 137, 126 L.Ed.2d 615, 114 S.Ct. 655 (1994)).

We immediately clarified however, that "we do not decide whether knowledge of unlawfulness is an element of this crime. . . ." The quoted passage from *Wiener* was thus explicitly identified as *dicta* in the text of *Wiener*, and defendant's position is therefore far from " 'clear under current law.' *Wiener*, therefore, does not suffice to render the District Court's jury instructions "plain error."

Moreover, we have, since *Wiener*, expressly repudiated the interpretation of *Ratzlaf v. United States*, 510 U.S. 135, 126 L.Ed.2d 615, 114 S.Ct. 655 (1994), that was suggested by the *dicta* in *Wiener.* * * * *United States v. Gabriel*, 125 F.3d 89, 100 (2d Cir. 1997).

* * *. [W]e are not aware of any appellate court that has held that "willfully" in § 1001—a term that has long been part of a venerable statute, requires proof that a defendant knew that his conduct was criminal.[3]

* * *

While we can find no basis for the claim that "willfully" in 18 U.S.C. § 1001 requires a defendant's specific knowledge that his conduct is criminal, we need not decide the issue, a matter of first impression in this Circuit. We merely hold that—in the absence of binding precedent from the Supreme Court or this Court—it was not "plain error" for the District Court to fail to instruct the jury that "willfully" under § 1001 required something more than that the defendant have been aware of the generally unlawful nature of his conduct. On the record before us, moreover, the jury's verdict that defendant violated § 1001 was not unreasonable.

Defendant next argues that the evidence at trial was insufficient to support his false statement conviction for submitting a forged baptismal certificate, because the Government failed to prove that the certificate was "materially false," as required by 18 U.S.C. § 1001. * * *

In challenging the sufficiency of the evidence, defendant "bears a heavy burden," We will uphold the jury's verdict if "*any* rational trier of fact could have found the essential elements of the crime beyond a reasonable doubt."

Defendant relies on a federal regulation providing that the Passport Agency will consider, as secondary evidence [of an applicant's birth in

---

3. Additionally, while we have not squarely addressed the issue, our decision in *Gabriel* strongly implied that, in a prosecution under § 1001, the government need not prove that the defendant specifically knew his conduct to be criminal. *Gabriel* addressed a defendant's liability under 18 U.S.C. § 2(b) for aiding and abetting the making of a materially false statement in violation of § 1001. Section 2(b) states that "whoever willfully causes an act to be done which if directly performed by him or another would be an offense against the United States, is punishable as a principal." The defendant in *Gabriel* argued that under *Ratzlaf*, "willfully" as used in § 2(b) requires the defendant's knowledge that his conduct was unlawful. As explained above, we rejected the defendant's argument, holding that *Ratzlaf's* interpretation of 31 U.S.C. § 5322(a) did not apply to 18 U.S.C. § 2(b). We noted that "the most natural interpretation of section 2(b) is that a defendant *with* the mental state necessary to violate the underlying section is guilty of violating that section if he *intentionally* causes another to commit the requisite act." We then concluded that "the government is not required to prove a knowing violation of the law under section 2(b)," and affirmed the defendant's conviction. Because the underlying crime, which the defendant was convicted of aiding and abetting, was making a false statement in violation of § 1001, our opinion properly indicated that the government need not prove the defendant's specific knowledge of unlawfulness under *either* § 2(b) *or* § 1001. In other words, if § 1001 had required a defendant to know that his false statement was a crime, then § 2(b) would have extended the same requirement to an alleged aider or abettor of a false statement—which, we held, it did not.

the United States], baptismal certificates, certificates of circumcision or other documentary evidence *created shortly after birth but not more than 5 years after birth.*" 22 C.F.R. § 51.43(b) (emphasis added). Defendant claims that in light of this provision, his forged baptismal certificate—with an issue date of June 20, 2001, more than five years after his birth—was, as a matter of law, not material, because the Passport Agency was not entitled to consider it.

We reject defendant's argument that 22 C.F.R. § 51.43(b) can only be construed to limit the Passport Agency's consideration of baptismal certificates to those issued within five years of birth. In instructing the Passport Agency to consider baptismal certificates "created shortly after birth but not more than 5 years after birth," the regulation focuses on when a record of baptism was *first created*—in other words, on the date of baptism. At trial, the Government offered the testimony of a priest at the church where defendant claimed he was baptized, who testified that once a baptism is performed, the church records the baptism, and at any subsequent time—including decades later—an individual may request an official certificate confirming the recorded date of baptism. A church that keeps track of baptisms will presumably record a baptism at or around the time of the baptism, and an official certificate based on that record will be probative of the date of baptism regardless of when the certificate is issued. Thus, Passport Agency officials could reasonably understand the regulation to contemplate their consideration of baptismal certificates showing that an applicant was *baptized* no more than five years after birth, because only such baptisms would be sufficiently probative of where the applicant was born. Indeed, a fraud prevention manager employed by the Passport Agency testified at trial that it is the date of the applicant's baptism, rather than the date that the certificate was issued, that matters to the Passport Agency.

Here, defendant's proffered baptismal certificate indicated that he was born on May 27, 1975, and baptized on July 5, 1975. The Passport Agency was therefore entitled to consider it as evidence of defendant's place of birth, and he cannot claim that his forgery was immaterial as a matter of law.

A false statement is material if it has a "natural tendency to influence, or is capable of influencing, the decision of the decisionmaking body to which it was addressed." Drawing all inferences in favor of the testimony offered by the Government as to the practices of the Passport Agency, we cannot say that no reasonable factfinder could have found defendant's forged baptismal certificate to be a material misstatement.

Defendant's third argument is that the District Court committed reversible error by failing to instruct the jury that, in determining whether defendant "willfully and knowingly" made a false statement in his passport application in violation of 18 U.S.C. § 1542, the reasonableness of his belief about where he was born was not to be considered. The District Court instructed the jury that the Government was required to prove beyond a reasonable doubt, among other things, that defendant *knew* that he was *not* born in Brooklyn. Under these instructions, if defendant *believed* he was born in Brooklyn—regardless of whether that belief was reasonable—the jury was required to acquit. Defendant argues that a district court must also specifically instruct the jury that the reasonableness of a defendant's beliefs about where he was born are not to be considered. We think an approach more consistent with the language of § 1542, which requires that a defendant act "willfully and knowingly" but does not mention reasonableness, is simply not to mention reasonableness at all in the jury instruction. The District Court's instruction—that the Government must prove beyond a reasonable doubt that defendant knew that he was not born in Brooklyn—properly stood on its own, avoiding the risk of confusion inherent in bringing the concept of "reasonableness" to the jury's attention, and then asking the jury to disregard it. The District Court's jury instruction was therefore without error.

Notes

1. As *Whab* indicates, materiality is one of the principal elements of a § 1001 violation. However, under the prior version of § 1001 the "materiality" term was expressly provided for in only one of the three false statements provisions, and the circuit courts had divided on whether materiality was an element of the other two kinds of false statement offenses. One of the principal changes made by the 1996 amendments was to add the term "material" to each of the three clauses of § 1001(a), making it clear that materiality was an element of all three kinds of false statements described in § 1001. The House Report accompanying the 1996 statute (H.R. Rep. No. 680, 104th Cong., 2d Sess. at 8 (1996) stated that "the Committee does not view the offenses defined in paragraphs (1), (2) and (3) as changing already existing case law as it relates to the elements of the offenses." It would seem therefore that the cases under the prior statute defining materiality are still good law. (The other principal change in the 1996 amendment was to respond to a decision of the Supreme Court holding that 1001 did not apply to false statements in judicial proceedings. *See infra*, p. 739 for a discussion of this issue.)

2. In *United States v. Gaudin*, 515 U.S. 506 (1995), the Supreme Court ruled that the issue of materiality of the false statement is a mixed question of law and fact that the judge is required to submit to the jury. The circuit court case law had been divided on the issue, although a majority of the decisions had treated the materiality issue as one of law to be resolved by the trial judge. Subsequent decisions ruled that *Gaudin* was to be applied retroactively to all cases pending on direct review or not yet final. *See, e.g., United States v. Rogers*, 118 F.3d 466 (6th Cir. 1997); United States v. Mandanici, 205 F.3d 519 (2d Cir. 2000).

3. What is the purpose of the materiality requirement and exactly what does materiality mean? Its purpose has been described as, "to insure that the reach of § 1001 is confined to reasonable bounds and not allowed to embrace trivial falsehoods." *United States v. Gafyczk*, 847 F.2d 685, 691

(11th Cir.1988). See, e.g., United States v. Robertson, 324 F.3d 1028 (8th Cir. 2003):

> Robertson contends that the government presented no evidence that any false statements he made were material. Robertson told Special Agent Grey Bear three falsehoods: (1) that he had used a BB gun, not a .22 caliber handgun; (2) that he was only joking; and (3) that the gun had been smashed and thrown into the trash. Robertson argues that his confession that he had pointed a BB gun at Cavanaugh was sufficient to support an assault charge, thus any false statements he told along the way were immaterial. We disagree. Robertson's false statements about the type of weapon used and what became of it were material to Special Agent Grey Bear's investigation. It is elementary that when police officers investigate a crime, they will seek out physical evidence, such as the weapon that was used. Materiality does not require proof that the government actually relied on the statement. A jury could reasonably conclude that Robertson's false statements had a natural tendency to influence the course of the investigation and thus were material to the investigation.

4. Suppose at the time the statement was made, the federal agent knew it was false. In *United States v. Sarihifard*, 155 F.3d 301 (4th Cir.1998), the defendant had made statements to government agents investigating the matter and the agents called him a "liar" after he told his version of the facts. Similarly when he had told the same story before the grand jury, the prosecutor had told the grand jury to disregard his testimony. Applying the standard, "A statement is material if it has a natural tendency to influence or is capable of influencing, the decision-making body to which it is addressed," the court ruled that the fact that the statement was disregarded or not relied upon by the government agents is irrelevant. *See also United States v. Johnson*, 139 F.3d 1359 (11th Cir.1998). The *Sarihifard* court also indicated that the capacity to influence is to be measured at the point in time when the statement was made. The fact that the relevant government agency did not rely on the statement is similarly not relevant provided the statement had the natural tendency to influence or capacity to influence. *United States v. Ross*, 77 F.3d 1525 (7th Cir.1996). Suppose it is proven that it was "impossible" for the agency to have been influenced in its actions. *See United States v. Valdez*, 594 F.2d 725 (9th Cir.1979) (impossibility of influencing government action no defense; "test is the intrinsic capabilities of the false statement itself, rather than the possibility of the actual attainment of its end as measured by collateral circumstances"). In *Brogan v. United States*, 522 U.S. 398 (1998), the Court wrote: t could be argued, perhaps, that a disbelieved falsehood does not pervert an investigation. But making the existence of this crime turn upon the credulousness of the federal investigator (or the persuasiveness of the liar) would be exceedingly strange.

5. Compare the approach to materiality under some of the specialized false statement statutes. See, e.g. *United States v. Biheiri*, 293 F.Supp.2d 656 (E.D. Va. 2003):

> For example, the Form N–400 Application for Naturalization asks applicants whether they have ever committed a crime for which they

have not been arrested. If an applicant answers "no" knowing that while in college, he drank a beer at a fraternity party before his 21st birthday, ... he would be in violation of § 1015(a). As such, this violation could serve as a predicate for conviction, and thus mandatory loss of citizenship, under § 1425(a). It may very well be that Congress never intended such a result or, more likely, simply never contemplated this possibility. In this respect, both §§ 1425(a) and 1015(a) differ significantly from 18 U.S.C. § 1014, the statute at issue in *United States v. Wells,* 519 U.S. 482, 137 L.Ed.2d 107, 117 S.Ct. 921 (1997). In *Wells,* the Supreme Court held that § 1014, which prohibits knowingly making false statements in loan applications to financial institutions for the purpose of influencing those institutions, did not include a materiality requirement, noting that a "statement made 'for the purpose of influencing' a bank will not usually be about something a banker would regard as trivial." Therefore, while § 1014 does not require materiality, its very language provides a mechanism to ensure that trivial and immaterial false statements do not result in conviction under the statute. Section 1425 includes no such language. As a policy matter, it may indeed be unwise to leave unchecked discretion in the hands of the executive branch to pursue prosecution for minor, immaterial misstatements under § 1425(a). This question, however, is for Congress to consider and decide.

6. *United States v. Stern,* 313 F.Supp.2d 155 (S.D.N.Y.2003):

Stern's final argument in favor of dismissal of the indictment is that he was set up—i.e., that he was the victim of what would be, in a grand jury context, a "perjury trap" because the FBI agent asked him questions knowing that he would lie so that he then could be prosecuted. This argument suffers from at least three defects. First, the perjury trap defense has never been recognized in this Circuit. See United States v. Regan, 103 F.3d 1072, 1079 (2d Cir. 1997) (noting that the defense has been discussed but never recognized). Second, even the discussion in Regan ... which Regan cites, took place in relation to false grand jury statements, not false statements to investigative agencies, where such considerations as the need to monitor during the pendency of an investigation the reliability of an informant always may be present, whereas such considerations may not be present during a grand jury investigation. Third, even in relation to false grand jury testimony, "the existence of a legitimate basis for an investigation and for particular questions answered falsely precludes any application of the 'perjury trap' doctrine.

7. Does the literal truth doctrine apply under § 1001? See *United States v. Kosth,* 257 F.3d 712 (7th Cir. 2001):

Kosth stresses, and we agree, that he cannot be convicted under § 1001 for statements that are literally true, see *United States v. Lozano,* 511 F.2d 1 (7th Cir. 1975), and that there is no harm if the owner of property transfers his entire interest in the property to a third party and then denies ownership of that property. We note at the outset that Kosth did not request a literal truth instruction or otherwise assert this defense at trial. Even if it was not waived, a full review of the record shows that the jury did not convict Kosth for literally true statements. The whole point of the government evidence was that, Kosth had *not* relinquished the benefits of owning the property at the time he completed the SBA application. To the contrary, he enjoyed all the real indicia of share ownership and he was actively managing both the board and the operations of the company. If, as we conclude it reasonably could have done based on the evidence before it, the jury determined that Terri Kosth nominal stock ownership was simply part of Daniel Kosth scheme to conceal the fact that he was the part-owner of Hillcrest Resort, Inc., then neither his claim that Terri Kosth was the owner of 30% of the Hillcrest stock, nor his claim that no Hillcrest manager had a criminal record was literally true.

8. Suppose it turns out that the false statements submitted pertained to matters outside of the agency's jurisdiction, indeed outside of federal law enforcement jurisdiction. *See United States v. DiFonzo*, 603 F.2d 1260 (7th Cir.1979): In the course of an SEC investigation into the defendant's operation of a business selling commodity options, the defendant made false statements. At the time, there were conflicting decisions in the district courts and courts of appeals as to whether discretionary trading accounts in commodity futures were "securities" subject to SEC jurisdiction. The government contended that the statutory jurisdiction of the SEC went "beyond the Commission's statutory authority to regulate and include[d] their authority to investigate to determine whether security laws [were] being violated." Concluding that there was a sufficient nexus between the subject matter of the SEC investigation and the SEC's regulatory authority the court stated:

> The SEC began an investigation in a field in which it arguably possessed regulatory authority and defendant submitted false statements to the SEC in the course of that investigation. To conclude that Section 1001 does not apply if a defendant ultimately can show that the false statements he submitted pertained to matters outside the regulatory jurisdiction of the SEC would cripple the SEC's preliminary investigatory capacities, thereby frustrating its ability to make an intelligent independent, assessment of whether it possesses regulatory authority over a given person's activities. Id. at 1265–1266.

Query: Were the false statements in *DiFonzo* material? If the SEC had not arguably possessed regulatory authority, could the false statement have had any tendency or capacity to influence the agency's official action?

9. It is not always necessary that the false statement be communicated to or provided to a federal official; it is sufficient that it affects federal functions and activities. The application of this principle in the context of false statements made to a state agency receiving federal funds has generated a split in the circuits in cases involving false statements made to obtain state unemployment benefits. State unemployment agencies receive federal funds only for administrative expenses. The Department of Labor monitors the agencies' compliance with federal administrative regulations, but not their award of benefits. The Ninth Circuit held that jurisdiction under § 1001 does not exist "unless a direct relationship obtains between the false statement and an authorized function of a federal agency or department,"

and such a direct relationship was lacking because the Department of Labor has no power to control the award of benefits. *United States v. Facchini*, 874 F.2d 638, 641 (9th Cir.1989) (en banc). *Accord: United States v. Holmes*, 111 F.3d 463 (6th Cir.1997). On similar facts the Eleventh Circuit affirmed a conviction under § 1001, concluding that use of federal funds by the state agency in question is sufficient to establish federal jurisdiction under § 1001. *United States v. Herring*, 916 F.2d 1543 (11th Cir.1990). Future prosecutions of this nature are unlikely because the Justice Department has determined that it is "inappropriate" for the Department of Labor to investigate false statements on state applications for unemployment benefits. *Herring v. United States*, 500 U.S. 946 (1991) (White, J., dissenting from the denial of certiorari). As Justice White observed, the Department's determination that future investigations would be "inappropriate" seems at odds with its position that the statements in *Herring* were in fact made within the jurisdiction of a federal agency.

10. For another illustration of the issue discussed in note 9 supra, see *United States v. Salman,* 189 F.Supp.2d 360 (E.D. Va. 2002):

> * * * At issue is whether the false statements alleged in the Indictment satisfy the jurisdictional requirement of 18 U.S.C. § 1001 in light of the fact that they were made to a state official acting under the direction of the United States Marshals Service (the "Marshals Service") pursuant to a valid contract, rather than being made directly to a federal official. Finding no case law on point from the United States Court of Appeals for the Fourth Circuit, and noting that other federal circuits have reached mixed conclusions with respect to similar issues, the Court will treat this case as presenting a matter of first impression within this Circuit.

> * * *

> [O]n or about November 29, 2001, Defendant arrived at the Alexandria Detention Center (the "Detention Center"), where his brother was housed as an inmate pursuant to an agreement between the Marshals Service and the Alexandria Sheriff, as authorized by federal law. See 18 U.S.C. § 4013 (permitting the Attorney General to contract with state or local governments for the housing of federal prisoners). Defendant falsely identified himself to the deputy sheriff on duty as a medical doctor summoned to render medical treatment to Hussein Addine Selmen. The deputy sheriff is not a federal employee.

> Defendant now seeks dismissal of Count II of the Indictment (the false statement charge), arguing that the false statement alleged to have been made by him at the Detention Center, even when accepted as true for purposes of this motion, fails to satisfy the jurisdictional requirement of 18 U.S.C. § 1001 because it was made to a state official.

> * * *

> The Bureau of Prisons has primary responsibility for the placement, care and subsistence of "all persons charged with or convicted of offenses against the United States." 18 U.S.C. § 4042(2). Merely because the Bureau of Prisons chose to delegate part of this responsibility to a state facility does not remove these matters from its jurisdiction.

Accordingly, the Court finds that the fact that the contract at issue in this case delegates many of the day-to-day functions to local officials is not dispositive of the federal jurisdictional issue in this case. Rather, . . . "it is the mere existence of the federal agency's supervisory authority that is important to determining jurisdiction." 8 F.3d at 929. Such supervisory authority clearly exists in this case, as evidenced by the language used in various sections of the contract itself. In addition, the Court believes that an approach based on the case-by-case parsing of contract language in order to determine the scope of § 1001's jurisdiction—as urged by Defendant—directly contradicts the Supreme Court's admonition in Rodgers that "the term 'jurisdiction' should not be given a narrow or technical meaning for purposes of § 1001." 466 U.S. at 480 (quoting *Bryson v. United States,* 396 U.S. 64, 24 L.Ed.2d 264, 90 S.Ct. 355 (1969)).

Finally, the Court notes that, at bottom, the Marshals Service has essentially done nothing more than rent bed space for approximately one hundred federal prisoners at the Alexandria Detention Center, presumably because of its close proximity to the federal courthouse in Alexandria. The Marshals Service still retains general supervisory control over these prisoners. While the contract leaves the day-to-day functioning of the prison to the discretion of local officials, these officials clearly remain accountable to the federal government. Accordingly, as with the Bureau of Prisons in Davis, a decision by the Marshals Service to delegate some of its responsibility to local officials "does not remove these matters from its jurisdiction" for purposes of determining the scope of criminal liability under § 1001.

11. Is recantation a defense to a charge under § 1001? See *United States v. Sebaggala,* 256 F.3d 59 (1st Cir. 2001):

The appellant has a fallback position: he points out that he admitted, the second time around, to carrying over $10,000 in currency equivalents. He treats this second declaration as "amending" the first and, analogizing to cases involving perjury, he says that this "amendment" negated his earlier false statement.

The analogy is not apt. Although an individual sometimes can avoid a perjury prosecution by recanting a prior false statement, that result flows from a specific statutory provision applicable only to perjury cases. The statute under which the appellant was charged and convicted is devoid of any comparable safe harbor; it simply provides for criminal consequences if a person "knowingly and willfully makes any materially false, fictitious, or fraudulent statement or representation" in a matter within the government's jurisdiction. 18 U.S.C. § 1001. The appellant cites no authority that would support transplanting the provisions of section 1623(d) into the unreceptive soil of section 1001. For our part, we see no basis for writing into section 1001 a recantation defense that Congress chose to omit.

* * *

We hasten to add that the appellant's argument would fail even if the criteria found in 18 U.S.C. § 1623(d) were imported into prosecutions brought under 18 U.S.C. § 1001. In order effectively to recant a prior perjurious statement, the declarant must make an outright retraction and repudiation. He also must "explain unambiguously and specifically" the respects in which his earlier answer was false. In this case, the appellant never tendered either an outright retraction or a meaningful explanation of his first false statement: he did nothing more than substitute a second false statement for it. The core purpose of the recantation provision is "to encourage truthful testimony." In light of this purpose, we do not believe that a person can recant simply by replacing one lie with another.

12.   Can an implied rather than an express false statement be a basis for a prosecution under § 1001? "While no case law is directly on point, we conclude that the body of law, in the aggregate, makes plain that implied falsity is a basis for conviction." *United States v. Brown*, 151 F.3d 476, 485 (6th Cir.1998). Must the government prove that the defendant knew that the statement was made "within the jurisdiction of any department or agency of the United States?" The Supreme Court considered this question in the next case.

UNITED STATES v. YERMIAN

468 U.S. 63, 104 S.Ct. 2936, 82 L.Ed.2d 53 (1984).

JUSTICE POWELL delivered the opinion of the Court.

It is a federal crime under 18 U.S.C. § 1001 to make any false or fraudulent statement in any matter within the jurisdiction of a federal agency. To establish a violation of § 1001, the Government must prove beyond a reasonable doubt that the statement was made with knowledge of its falsity. This case presents the question whether the Government also must prove that the false statement was made with actual knowledge of federal agency jurisdiction.

I

Respondent Esmail Yermian was convicted in the District Court of Central California on three counts of making false statements in a matter within the jurisdiction of a federal agency, in violation of § 1001. The convictions were based on false statements respondent supplied his employer in connection with a Department of Defense security questionnaire. Respondent was hired in 1979 by Gulton Industries, a defense contractor. Because respondent was to have access to classified material in the course of his employment, he was required to obtain a Department of Defense Security Clearance. To this end, Gulton's security officer asked respondent to fill out a "Worksheet For Preparation of Personnel Security Questionnaire."

In response to a question on the worksheet asking whether he had ever been charged with any violation of law, respondent failed to disclose that in 1978 he had been convicted of mail fraud, in violation of 18 U.S.C. § 1341. In describing his employment history, respondent falsely stated that he had been employed by two companies that had in fact never employed him. The Gulton security officer typed these false representations onto a form entitled "Department of Defense Personnel Security Questionnaire." Respondent reviewed the typed document for errors and signed a certification stating that his answers were "true, complete, and correct to the best of [his] knowledge" and that he understood "that any misrepresentation or false statement ... may subject [him] to prosecution under section 1001 of the United States Criminal Code."

After witnessing respondent's signature, Gulton's security officer mailed the typed form to the Defense Industrial Security Clearance Office for processing. Government investigators subsequently discovered that respondent had submitted false statements on the security questionnaire. Confronted with this discovery, respondent acknowledged that he had responded falsely to questions regarding his criminal record and employment history. On the basis of these false statements, respondent was charged with three counts in violation of § 1001.

At trial, respondent admitted to having actual knowledge of the falsity of the statements he had submitted in response to the Department of Defense Security Questionnaire. He explained that he had made the false statements so that information on the security questionnaire would be consistent with similar fabrications he had submitted to Gulton in his employment application. Respondent's sole defense at trial was that he had no actual knowledge that his false statements would be transmitted to a federal agency.[1]

Consistent with this defense, respondent requested a jury instruction requiring the Government to prove not only that he had actual knowledge that his statements were false at the time they were made, but also that he had actual knowledge that those statements were made in a matter within the jurisdiction of a federal agency. The District Court rejected that request and instead instructed the jury that the Government must prove that respondent "knew or should have known that the information was to be submitted to a government agency." Respondent's objection to this instruction was overruled, and the jury returned convictions on all three counts charged in the indictment.

The Court of Appeals for the Ninth Circuit reversed, holding that the District Court had erred in failing to give respondent's requested instruction. * * *

---

1. Respondent maintained this defense despite the fact that both the worksheet and the questionnaire made reference to the Department of Defense, and the security questionnaire signed by respondent was captioned "Defense Department." The latter document also contained a reference to the "Defense Industrial Security Clearance Office," stated that respondent's work would require access to "secret" material, and informed respondent that his signature would grant "permission to the Department of Defense to obtain and review copies of [his] medical and institutional records." Nevertheless, respondent testified that he had not read the form carefully before signing it and thus had not noticed either the words "Department of Defense" on the first page or the certification printed above the signature block.

II

The only issue presented in this case is whether Congress intended the terms "knowingly and willfully" in § 1001 to modify the statute's jurisdictional language, thereby requiring the Government to prove that false statements were made with actual knowledge of federal agency jurisdiction. The issue thus presented is one of statutory interpretation. Accordingly, we turn first to the language of the statute.

A

The relevant language of § 1001 provides:

"Whoever, in any matter within the jurisdiction of any department or agency of the United States knowingly and willfully ... makes any false, fictitious or fraudulent statements or representations, ... shall be fined...." 18 U.S.C. § 1001.

The statutory language requiring that knowingly false statements be made "in any matter within the jurisdiction of any department or agency of the United States" is a jurisdictional requirement. Its primary purpose is to identify the factor that makes the false statement an appropriate subject for federal concern. Jurisdictional language need not contain the same culpability requirement as other elements of the offense. Indeed, we have held that "the existence of the fact that confers federal jurisdiction need not be one in the mind of the actor at the time he perpetrates the act made criminal by the federal statute." *United States v. Feola*, 420 U.S. 671, 676–677, n. 9 (1975). Certainly in this case, the statutory language makes clear that Congress did not intend the terms "knowingly and willfully" to establish the standard of culpability for the jurisdictional element of § 1001. The jurisdictional language appears in a phrase separate from the prohibited conduct modified by the terms "knowingly and willfully." Any natural reading of § 1001, therefore, establishes that the terms "knowingly and willfully" modify only the making of "false, fictitious or fraudulent statements," and not the predicate circumstance that those statements be made in a matter within the jurisdiction of a federal agency. Once this is clear, there is no basis for requiring proof that the defendant had actual knowledge of federal agency jurisdiction. The statute contains no language suggesting any additional element of intent, such as a requirement that false statements be "knowingly made in a matter within federal agency jurisdiction," or "with the intent to deceive the federal government." On its face, therefore, § 1001 requires that the Government prove that false statements were made knowingly and willfully, and it unambiguously dispenses with any requirement that the Government also prove that those statements were made with actual knowledge of federal agency jurisdiction. Respondent's argument that the legislative history of the statute supports a contrary interpretation is unpersuasive.

* * *

[The Court here reviewed the predecessor enactments of § 1001 and accompanying legislative history.]

Respondent argues that absent proof of actual knowledge of federal agency jurisdiction, § 1001 becomes a "trap for the unwary," imposing criminal sanctions on "wholly innocent conduct." Whether or not respondent fairly may characterize the intentional and deliberate lies prohibited by the statute (and manifest in this case) as "wholly innocent conduct," this argument is not sufficient to overcome the express statutory language of § 1001. Respondent does not argue that Congress lacks the power to impose criminal sanctions for deliberately false statements submitted to a federal agency, regardless whether the person who made such statements actually knew that they were being submitted to the Federal Government. Cf. *Feola, supra*, 420 U.S., at 676 n. 9, That is precisely what Congress has done here. In the unlikely event that § 1001 could be the basis for imposing an unduly harsh result on those who intentionally make false statements to the Federal Government, it is for Congress and not this Court to amend the criminal statute.[2]

IV

Both the plain language and the legislative history establish that proof of actual knowledge of federal agency jurisdiction is not required under § 1001. Accordingly, we reverse the decision of the Court of Appeals to the contrary.

It is so ordered.

JUSTICE REHNQUIST, with whom JUSTICE BRENNAN, Justice Stevens AND Justice O'Connor JOIN, DISSENTING.

It is common ground that in a prosecution for the making of false statements the government must prove that the defendant actually knew that the statements were false at the time he made them. *See Bryson v. United States*, 396 U.S. 64, 68 0 (1969). The question presented here is whether the government must also prove that the defendant actually knew that his statements were made in a matter within he jurisdiction of any department or agency of the United States. The Court concludes that the plain language and the legislative history of 18 U.S.C. 1001 conclusively establish that the statute is intended to reach false state-

---

2. In the context of this case, respondent's argument that § 1001 is a "trap for the unwary" is particularly misplaced. It is worth noting that the jury was instructed, without objection from the prosecution, that the Government must prove that respondent "knew or should have known" that his false statements were made within the jurisdiction of a federal agency.

As the Government did not object to the reasonable foreseeability instruction, it is unnecessary for us to decide whether that instruction erroneously read a culpability requirement into the jurisdictional phrase. Moreover, the only question presented in this case is whether the Government must prove that the false statement was made with *actual* knowledge of federal agency jurisdiction. The jury's finding that federal agency jurisdiction was reasonably foreseeable by the defendant, combined with the requirement that the defendant had actual knowledge of the falsity of those statements, precludes the possibility that criminal penalties were imposed on the basis of innocent conduct.

ments made without actual knowledge of federal involvement in the subject matter of the false statements. I cannot agree.

The Court nonetheless proceeds on the assumption that *some* lesser culpability standard is required in 1001 prosecutions, but declines to decide what that lesser standard is. Even if I agreed with the Court that actual knowledge of federal involvement is not required here, I could not agree with the Court disposition of this case because it reverses the Court of Appeals without determining for itself, or remanding for the lower court to determine, whether the jury instructions in respondent case were proper. I think that our certiorari jurisdiction is best exercised to resolve conflicts in statutory construction, and not simply to decide whether a jury in a particular case was correctly charged as to the elements of the offense. But here the Court, in a remarkable display of left-footedness, accomplishes neither result: reading its opinion from beginning to end, one neither knows what the congressionally intended element of intent is, nor whether the jury was properly instructed in this case.

I

I think that in this case, "[a]fter 'seiz[ing] every thing from which aid can be derived,' *United States v. Fisher*, 2 Cranch [6 U.S.] 358, 386 (1805) (Marshall, C.J.), we are left with an ambiguous statute." *United States v. Bass*, 404 U.S. 336, 347 (1971). Notwithstanding the majority's repeated, but sparsely supported, assertions that the evidence of Congress' intent not to require actual knowledge is "convincing," and "unambiguous," I believe that the language and legislative history of § 1001 can provide "no more than a guess as to what Congress intended." I therefore think that the canon of statutory construction which requires that "ambiguity concerning the ambit of criminal statutes ... be resolved in favor of lenity," *Rewis v. United States*, 401 U.S. 808, 812, (1971), is applicable here. Accordingly, I would affirm the Court of Appeals' conclusion that actual knowledge of federal involvement is a necessary element for conviction under § 1001.

* * *

[The dissent here also reviewed the predecessor enactments and accompanying legislative history.]

* * * It seems to me highly unlikely that, without so much as a hint of explanation, Congress would have changed the statute from one intended to deter the perpetration of deliberate deceit on the federal government, to one intended to criminalize the making of even the most casual false statements so long as they turned out, unbeknownst to their maker, to be material to some federal agency function. The latter interpretation would substantially extend the scope of the statute even to reach, for example, false statements privately made to a neighbor if the neighbor then uses those statements in connection with his work for a federal agency.

Of course "[i]t is not unprecedented for Congress to enact [such] stringent legislation," *United States v. Feola*, 420 U.S. 671, 709 (Stewart, J., dissenting). But I cannot subscribe to the Court's interpretation of this statute in such a way as to "make a surprisingly broad range of unremarkable conduct a violation of federal law," *Williams v. United States*, 458 U.S. 279, 286 (1982), when the legislative history simply "fails to evidence congressional awareness of the statute's claimed scope." Thus, I would hold that the rule of lenity is applicable in this case and that it requires the government to prove that a defendant in a § 1001 prosecution had actual knowledge that his false statements were made in a matter within federal agency jurisdiction.

II

Seemingly aware of the broad range of conduct that § 1001 could sweep within its scope under today's interpretation, the Court apparently does not hold that the words "in any matter within the jurisdiction of any department or agency of the United States" are jurisdictional words *only* and that *no* state of mind is required with respect to federal agency involvement. Instead, the Court suggests that some lesser state of mind may well be required in § 1001 prosecutions in order to prevent the statute from becoming a "trap for the unwary." Accordingly, it expressly declines to decide whether the trial judge erred in its jury instructions in this case.

In my view, the Court has simply disregarded the clearest, albeit not conclusive, evidence of legislative intent and then has invited lower courts to improvise a new state of mind requirement, almost out of thin air, in order to avoid the unfairness of the Court's decision today. I think that the Court's opinion will engender more confusion than it will resolve with respect to the culpability requirement in § 1001 cases not before the Court. And, unfortunately, it tells us absolutely nothing about whether respondent Yermian received a proper jury instruction in the case that *is* before the Court.

Notes

1. Even if knowledge of the jurisdiction of a federal agency is not required, may it still have evidentiary value in a false statement prosecution? In *United States v. Montemayor*, 712 F.2d 104, 107–109 (5th Cir.1983), the defendant made false statements to a state agency to obtain birth certificates with the intent to use them to establish the citizenship of her children in U.S. immigration proceedings. The court held that a statement to a state agency can constitute a violation of § 1001 whether or not the defendant knows of the statement's ultimate federal purpose. The court suggested, however, that the defendant's knowledge of federal involvement might be relevant to the determination whether the statement was "within the jurisdiction" of a federal agency, since "[t]he term jurisdiction merely incorporates Congress's intent that the statute apply whenever false statements would result in the perversion of the authorized function of a federal department or agency." *Id.* at 108. The court continued:

* * * [W]hen a statement is not submitted directly to a federal agency, knowledge of federal involvement may be one circumstance to be considered in assessing the potential threat the statement may be to the proper functioning of the federal agency involved. This knowledge may be decisive when the involvement of the United States in the matter to which the statement relates is peripheral. In other instances, a showing that the defendant had actual knowledge of federal involvement might lessen the need for a detailed examination of the federal government's relationship to the statements.

Ibid.

2. In *United States v. Hildebrandt*, 961 F.2d 116 (8th Cir.1992), the defendant filed false IRS 1099 forms, which are used to report non-wage compensation paid to a taxpayer. Hildebrandt, a farmer whose property had been foreclosed, claimed payments to all of the persons whom he believed to have conspired to deprive him of his farm, including creditors, lenders, judges, and attorneys who had been involved in the foreclosure or other legal proceedings. Hildebrandt claimed that he acted in reliance on a package of taped and written materials that purported to inform farmers of their legal rights. The district court denied his requested for an instruction that he had not acted willfully if he had a good faith belief that he was not violating the law, though it instructed the jury that to convict it must find that Hildebrandt knew when he submitted the forms to the IRS that they contained a false, fictitious or fraudulent statement. The court of appeals upheld his conviction, holding that "[i]t is not necessary that the defendant act with the intent to deceive the United States or have actual knowledge that the statement was made in a matter within a federal agency's jurisdiction." *Id.* at 118–19. The court distinguished *Cheek v. United States*, 498 U.S. 192 (1991), which held that a defendant is entitled to such an instruction in a prosecution for tax evasion and failure to file. While certain tax offenses may require special treatment because of the complexity of the tax laws, the court held that this rationale did not extend to the willful making of a false statement.

3. There is a conflict between two circuit court decisions regarding the question of whether when a prosecutor charges a defendant under § 1001 and 18 U.S.C. § 2(b) ("willfully caus[ing] an act to be done which if directly performed by * * * another would be an offense against the United States") the prosecutor must prove that the defendant knew of the federal reporting obligations of the person whom he caused to file a false report and that the defendant knew his conduct was unlawful. Both cases involved defendants who caused treasurers of election campaign organizations to file false reports with the Federal Election Commission by providing false information regarding campaign contributions they had funneled to those organizations. In *United States v. Curran*, 20 F.3d 560 (3d Cir.1994), relying on *Ratzlaf v. United States*, 510 U.S. 135 (1994), *see supra* Chapter 10, pp. 435–436, the court held that the prosecutor was required to prove the defendant's awareness of the unlawfulness of his conduct. The U.S. Court of Appeals for the District of Columbia Circuit reached a contrary conclusion in *United States v. Hsia*, 176 F.3d 517 (D.C.Cir.1999). Should the prosecutor be required to prove the knowledge of the defendant of the unlawfulness of his or her conduct when the charge is causing someone else to make a false

statement but not when the defendant is directly charged with making the false statement?

C. LIMITATIONS

1. ACCORDING TO THE AGENCY OR AGENCY FUNCTION

UNITED STATES v. RODGERS

466 U.S. 475, 104 S.Ct. 1942, 80 L.Ed.2d 492 (1984).

JUSTICE REHNQUIST delivered the opinion of the Court.

Respondent Larry Rodgers was charged in a two-count indictment with making "false, fictitious or fraudulent statements" to the Federal Bureau of Investigation (FBI) and the United States Secret Service, in violation of 18 U.S.C. § 1001 (1982). Rodgers allegedly lied in telling the FBI that his wife had been kidnapped and in telling the Secret Service that his wife was involved in a plot to kill the President. Rodgers moved to dismiss the indictment for failure to state an offense on the grounds that the investigation of kidnappings and the protection of the President are not matters "within the jurisdiction" of the respective agencies, as that phrase is used in § 1001. The District Court for the Western District of Missouri granted the motion, and the United States Court of Appeals for the Eighth Circuit affirmed. We now reverse. The statutory language clearly encompasses criminal investigations conducted by the FBI and the Secret Service, and nothing in the legislative history indicates that Congress intended a more restricted reach for the statute.

On June 2, 1982, Larry Rodgers telephoned the Kansas City, Missouri, office of the FBI and reported that his wife had been kidnapped. The FBI spent over 100 agent hours investigating the alleged kidnapping only to determine that Rodgers' wife had left him voluntarily. Two weeks later, Rodgers contacted the Kansas City office of the Secret Service and reported that his "estranged girlfriend" (actually his wife) was involved in a plot to assassinate the President. The Secret Service spent over 150 hours of agent and clerical time investigating this threat and eventually located Rodgers' wife in Arizona. She stated that she left Kansas City to get away from her husband. Rodgers later confessed that he made the false reports to induce the federal agencies to locate his wife.

In granting Rodgers' motion to dismiss the indictment, the district court considered itself bound by a prior decision of the Eighth Circuit in *Friedman v. United States*, 374 F.2d 363 (1967). *Friedman* also involved false statements made to the FBI to initiate a criminal investigation. In that case, the Court of Appeals reversed the defendant's conviction under § 1001, holding that the phrase "within the jurisdiction," as used in that provision, referred only to "the power to make final or binding determinations."

The *Friedman* court noted that the current statutory language was first passed in 1934 at the urging of some of the newly created regulatory agencies. See S.Rep. 1202, 73d Cong., 2d Sess. (1934). A predecessor provision punished false statements only when made "for the purpose and with the intent of cheating and swindling or defrauding the Government of the United States." Act of Oct. 23, 1918, ch. 194, 40 Stat. 1015. In 1934, Congress deleted the requirement of a specific purpose and enlarged the class of punishable false statements to include false statements made "in any matter within the jurisdiction of any department or agency of the United States." Act of June 18, 1934, ch. 587, 48 Stat. 996. The "immediate and primary purpose" of this amendment, the Eighth Circuit surmised, was to curtail the flow of false information to the new agencies, which was interfering with their administrative and regulatory functions.

> "Though the statute was drafted in broad inclusive terms, presumably due to the numerous agencies and the wide variety of information needed, there is nothing to indicate that Congress intended this statute to have application beyond the purposes for which it was created." 374 F.2d, at 366.

Reading the term "jurisdiction" in this restrictive light, the Court of Appeals included within its scope the "power to make monetary awards, grant governmental privileges, or promulgate binding administrative and regulative determinations," while excluding "the mere authority to conduct an investigation in a given area without the power to dispose of the problems or compel action." The court concluded that false statements made to the FBI were not covered by § 1001 because the FBI "had no power to adjudicate rights, establish binding regulations, compel the action or finally dispose of the problem giving rise to the inquiry."

* * *

It seems to us that the interpretation of § 1001 adopted by the Court of Appeals for the Eighth Circuit is unduly strained. Section 1001 expressly embraces false statements made "in *any* matter within the jurisdiction of *any* department or agency of the United States." 18 U.S.C. § 1001 (emphasis supplied). A criminal investigation surely falls within the meaning of "any matter," and the FBI and the Secret Service equally surely qualify as "department[s] or agenc[ies] of the United States." The only possible verbal vehicle for narrowing the sweeping language Congress enacted is the word "jurisdiction." But we do not think that that term, as used in this statute, admits of the constricted construction given it by the Court of Appeals.

"Jurisdiction" is not defined in the statute. We therefore "start with the assumption that the legislative purpose is expressed by the ordinary meaning of the words used." *Richards v. United States*, 369 U.S. 1, 9 (1962). The most natural, nontechnical reading of the statutory language is that it covers all matters confided to the authority of an agency or department. Thus, Webster's Third New International Dictionary 1227 (1976) broadly defines "jurisdiction" as, among other things, "the limits or territory within which any particular power may be exercised: sphere of authority." A department or agency has jurisdiction, in this sense, when it has the power to exercise authority in a particular situation. *See United States v. Adler*, 380 F.2d, at 922 ("the word 'jurisdiction' as used in the statute must mean simply the power to act upon information when it is received"). Understood in this way, the phrase "within the jurisdiction" merely differentiates the official, authorized functions of an agency or department from matters peripheral to the business of that body.

There are of course narrower, more technical meanings of the term "jurisdiction." For example, an alternative definition provided by Webster's is the "legal power to interpret and administer the law." But a narrow, technical definition of this sort, limiting the statute's protections to judicial or quasi-judicial activities, clashes strongly with the sweeping, everyday language on either side of the term. It is also far too restricted to embrace some of the myriad governmental activities that we have previously concluded § 1001 was designed to protect. *See, e.g., Bryson v. United States*, 396 U.S. 64 (1969) (affidavit filed by union officer with NLRB falsely denying affiliation with Communist Party); *United States v. Bramblett*, 348 U.S. 503 (1955) (fraudulent representations by Member of Congress to Disbursing Office of House of Representatives); *United States v. Gilliland*, 312 U.S. 86 (1941) (false reports filed with Secretary of the Interior on the amount of petroleum produced from certain wells).

[I]n *United States v. Gilliland, supra*, 312 U.S., at 91, we rejected a defendant's contention that the reach of the statute was confined "to matters in which the Government has some financial or proprietary interest." We noted that the 1934 amendment, which added the current statutory language, was not limited by any specific set of circumstances that may have precipitated its passage.

> "The amendment indicated the congressional intent to protect the authorized functions of governmental departments and agencies from the perversion which might result from the deceptive practices described. We see no reason why this apparent intention should be frustrated by construction."

Discussing the same amendment in *United States v. Bramblett, supra*, 348 U.S., at 507, 75 S.Ct., at 507, we concluded: "There is no indication in either the committee reports or in the congressional debates that the scope of the statute was to be in any way restricted." And in *Bryson v. United States, supra*, 396 U.S., at 70–71, we noted the "valid legislative interest in protecting the integrity of official inquiries" and held that a "statutory basis for an agency's request for information provides jurisdiction enough to punish fraudulent statements under § 1001."[3]

---

3. Both respondent and the court below attempt to distinguish *Bryson* on the ground that the NLRB, unlike the FBI or the Secret Service, "is an agency with the power to adjudicate rights and establish regulations...." But it is undisputed that in the matter at issue in *Bryson*, the NLRB was neither adjudicating rights nor establishing regulations. It was conducting an "official inquiry" or investigation, just as the FBI and the Secret Service were doing in the instant case. Unless one is simply to read the phrase "*any* department or agency of the United States" out of the statute,

There is no doubt that there exists a "statutory basis" for the authority of the FBI and the Secret Service over the investigations sparked by respondent Rodgers' false reports. The FBI is authorized "to detect and prosecute crimes against the United States," including kidnapping. 28 U.S.C. § 533(1) (1982). And the Secret Service is authorized "to protect the person of the President." 18 U.S.C. § 3056 (1982). It is a perversion of these authorized functions to turn either agency into a Missing Person's Bureau for domestic squabbles. The knowing filing of a false crime report, leading to an investigation and possible prosecution, can also have grave consequences for the individuals accused of crime. There is, therefore, a "valid legislative interest in protecting the integrity of [such] official inquiries," an interest clearly embraced in, and furthered by, the broad language of § 1001.

Limiting the term "jurisdiction" as used in this statute to "the power to make final or binding determinations," as the Court of Appeals thought it should be limited, would exclude from the coverage of the statute most, if not all, of the authorized activities of many "departments" and "agencies" of the federal government, and thereby defeat the purpose of Congress in using the broad inclusive language which it did. If the statute referred only to courts, a narrower construction of the word "jurisdiction" might well be indicated; but referring as it does to "any department or agency" we think that such a narrow construction is simply inconsistent with the rest of the statutory language.

The Court of Appeals supported its failure to give the statute a "literal interpretation" by offering several policy arguments in favor of a more limited construction. For example, the court noted that § 1001 carries a penalty exceeding the penalty for perjury and argued that Congress could not have "considered it more serious for one to informally volunteer an untrue statement to an F.B.I. agent than to relate the same story under oath before a court of law." * * * The fact that the maximum possible penalty under § 1001 marginally exceeds that for perjury provides no indication of the particular penalties, within the permitted range, that Congress thought appropriate for each of the myriad violations covered by the statute. Section 1001 covers "a variety of offenses and the penalties prescribed were maximum penalties which gave a range for judicial sentences according to the circumstances and gravity of particular violations."

Perhaps most influential in the reasoning of the court below was its perception that "the spectre of criminal prosecution" would make citizens hesitant to report suspected crimes and thereby thwart "the important social policy that is served by an open line of communication between the general public and law enforcement agencies." But the justification for this concern is debatable. Section 1001 only applies to those who "knowingly and willfully" lie to the Government. It seems

there is no justification for treating the investigatory activities of one agency as within the scope of § 1001 while excluding the same activities performed by another agency.

likely that "individuals acting innocently and in good faith, will not be deterred from voluntarily giving information or making complaints to the F.B.I."[4]

Even if we were more persuaded than we are by these policy arguments, the result in this case would be unchanged. Resolution of the pros and cons of whether a statute should sweep broadly or narrowly is for Congress. Its decision that the perversion of agency resources and the potential harm to those implicated by false reports of crime justifies punishing those who "knowingly and willfully" make such reports is not so "absurd or glaringly unjust," *Sorrells v. United States*, 287 U.S. 435 (1932), as to lead us to question whether Congress actually intended what the plain language of § 1001 so clearly imports.

Finally, respondent urges that the rule of lenity in construing criminal statutes should be applied to § 1001, and that because the *Friedman* case has been on the books in the Eighth Circuit for a number of years a contrary decision by this Court should not be applied retroactively to him. The rule of lenity is of course a well-recognized principle of statutory construction, but the critical statutory language of § 1001 is not sufficiently ambiguous, in our view, to permit the rule to be controlling here. And any argument by respondent against retroactive application to him of our present decision, even if he could establish reliance upon the earlier *Friedman* decision, would be unavailing since the existence of conflicting cases from other courts of appeals made review of that issue by this Court and decision against the position of the respondent reasonably foreseeable.

The judgment of the Court of Appeals is reversed, and the case is remanded for further proceedings consistent with this opinion.

Notes

1. Do you think that the 1996 revision of § 1001 affected the decision in *Rodgers*? Note that under the 1996 revision, a false statement "in any matter within the jurisdiction of the executive ... branch" is covered by the statute while under the pre–1996 version of 1001, false statements "in any matter within the jurisdiction of any department or agency of the United States ..." are included.

---

4. The Eighth Circuit also expressed concern that a literal application of the statute would obviate the taking of oaths in judicial proceedings. "Since the Judiciary is an agency of the United States Government, a strict application of this statute would remove the time-honored and now necessary formality of requiring witnesses to testify under oath." *Friedman v. United States*, 374 F.2d, at 367. Several courts faced with that question have in fact held that 1001 does not reach false statements made under oath in a court of law. *See, e.g., United States v. Abrahams*, 604 F.2d 386 (C.A.5 1979); *United States v. D'Amato*, 507 F.2d 26 (C.A.2 1974) (holding limited to private civil actions); *United States v. Erhardt*, 381 F.2d 173 (C.A.6 1967) (per curiam). But they have mostly relied, not on a restricted construction of the term "jurisdiction," but rather on the phrase "department or agency." These courts have held that, although the federal judiciary is a "department or agency" within the meaning of 1001 with respect to its housekeeping or administrative functions, the judicial proceedings themselves do not so qualify. Abrahams, supra, at 392 93; *Erhardt, supra*, at 175. See also *Morgan v. United States*, 309 F.2d 234, 237 (C.A.D.C.), cert. denied, 373 U.S. 917 (1963). We express no opinion on the validity of this line of cases.

2. Suppose a person makes a false statement to an FBI agent but later claims that he did not know that the questioner was a federal agent? Suppose a person makes a false statement to a state or local plainclothes police officer unaware that he is a member of a federal-state-local task force conducting an investigation relating to drug offenses. *See United States v. Yermian, supra* p. 728. Is it significant that *Yermian* and *Rodgers* were argued on the same day; that Justice Rehnquist who wrote the Opinion of the Court in *Rodgers,* wrote a dissent in *Yermian;* and that while he rejected application of the rule of lenity in the one case, he invoked it in the other?

3. Before the Supreme Court's decision in *Rodgers* many circuits had rejected *Friedman* but developed other kinds of restrictions limiting the operation of § 1001 in relation to statements made to law enforcement agents. The material in the next section discusses other possible limitations on the application of § 1001. In connection with these materials, you should consider whether *Rodgers* had implications for any such limitations and whether any of these other doctrinal limitations would be a desirable way to limit § 1001.

4. A principal purpose of the 1996 revision of § 1001 was to "ensure that section 1001 applies to the judicial and legislative branches as well as the executive branch, thereby ensuring the integrity of legislative and judicial functions and proceedings." House Rep. No. 104–680, 104th Cong., 2d Sess. 1996. The House Report went on to state:

> In *Hubbard v. United States*, 514 U.S. 695, 115 S.Ct. 1754 (1995), the Supreme Court held that a Federal Court is not a "department" or "agency" within the meaning of section 1001, and that the statute, therefore, does not apply to false statements made in a judicial proceeding. * * * While the Court did not directly address the question of whether section 1001 still applies to Congress, * * * *Hubbard* is widely interpreted as leaving section 1001 covering only the executive branch, leaving Congress outside of its scope. * * * After *Hubbard*, Ethics in Government Act reports filed by officials within the Courts and Congress are no longer covered by section 1001.

* * *

> H.R. 3166 [which became the new version of 1001] applies section 1001 to all three branches of the U.S. Government, with two exceptions. First, the bill does not apply section 1001 "to a party to a judicial proceeding, or that party's counsel, for statements ... submitted ... to a judge in that proceeding."

* * *

> The second exception exempts from section 1001's scope certain representations that are made involving the legislative branch.

* * *

> Without such an exception, the criminal penalties of section 1001 would apply to all forms of communication to Congress. This would include, for example, opinions expressed through constituent correspondence and all forms of unsworn testimony.

5. What is the impact of the 1996 revision of § 1001 on the decision in *United States v. Poindexter*, 951 F.2d 369, 387 (D.C.Cir.1991)? The case involved John Poindexter who as National Security Advisor had been involved in the coverup of Oliver North's support of the Nicaraguan "Contras" and the shipment of arms to Iran in exchange for hostages. Pursuant to the coverup Poindexter sent letters containing false statements to the chairmen of two House committees and made false oral statements at meetings with both the House and Senate Intelligence Committees. Under the prior version of the statute, the court rejected his claim that these statements did not fall within § 1001:

> Poindexter * * * argues that the Congress, like a court, has other ways in which to protect itself against false statements; for example, it can force a person to testify under oath, thus subjecting him to the risk of prosecution for perjury if he lies. Second, he contends that application of § 1001 to the legislative context would chill "private discussion between representatives of the political branches." The latter problem is exacerbated, he argues, when § 1001 is applied to an untranscribed statement made by a person not under oath.

> We are not persuaded to carve out a broad legislative function exception to § 1001 * * *.

> Poindexter also argues that § 1001 should not apply to "private discussions between representatives of the political branches where, as here, no oath is administered and no verbatim transcript is maintained." In such circumstances, "proof literally becomes a matter of one person's word against another, even though neither may have heard or remembered with precision exactly what form of words was used in making an allegedly false statement." We have already held, however, that § 1001 may be applied to "statements [that were] not under oath [and were] not stenographically transcribed." The absence of such formal trappings is relevant, of course, to the difficulty of proving beyond a reasonable doubt exactly what the defendant said and whether he intended to deceive his audience as to a material question of fact; but these are issues of the sufficiency of the evidence in a particular case, not reasons for carving a categorical exception from the statute.

> Nor is our understanding of the statute altered because the false statement is made in a meeting between representatives of the political branches. Section 1001 requires that the statement be made to a government department; that it was here also made by the representative of another government department adds a political dimension to the relationship between speaker and auditor.

> Poindexter correctly points out that "[i]nformal powers and protections ... play a significant role" in the ongoing relationship between the political branches. "[A]n Administration or administrative official who lies to Congress can lose the political and personal trust that is essential to the effective operation of government at its highest levels." But that is hardly a reason for believing that the Congress did not intend that § 1001 also be applied to an Executive Branch representative who bears false witness before it; indeed, the contrary implication is more plausible.

2. ACCORDING TO THE TYPE OF STATEMENT

BROGAN v. UNITED STATES

522 U.S. 398, 118 S.Ct. 805, 139 L.Ed.2d 830 (1998).

[SCALIA, J., delivered the opinion of the Court, in which REHNQUIST, C. J., and O'CONNOR, KENNEDY, and THOMAS, JJ., joined, and in which SOUTER, J., joined in part. SOUTER, J., filed a statement concurring in part and concurring in the judgment. GINSBURG, J., filed an opinion concurring in the judgment, in which SOUTER, J., joined. STEVENS, J., filed a dissenting opinion, in which BREYER, J., joined.]

JUSTICE SCALIA delivered the opinion of the Court.

This case presents the question whether there is an exception to criminal liability under 18 U.S.C. § 1001 for a false statement that consists of the mere denial of wrongdoing, the so-called "exculpatory no."

I

While acting as a union officer during 1987 and 1988, petitioner James Brogan accepted cash payments from JRD Management Corporation, a real estate company whose employees were represented by the union. On October 4, 1993, federal agents from the Department of Labor and the Internal Revenue Service visited petitioner at his home. The agents identified themselves and explained that they were seeking petitioner's cooperation in an investigation of JRD and various individuals. They told petitioner that if he wished to cooperate, he should have an attorney contact the U.S. Attorney's Office, and that if he could not afford an attorney, one could be appointed for him.

The agents then asked petitioner if he would answer some questions, and he agreed. One question was whether he had received any cash or gifts from JRD when he was a union officer. Petitioner's response was "no." At that point, the agents disclosed that a search of JRD headquarters had produced company records showing the contrary. They also told petitioner that lying to federal agents in the course of an investigation was a crime. Petitioner did not modify his answers, and the interview ended shortly thereafter.

Petitioner was indicted for accepting unlawful cash payments from an employer in violation of 29 U.S.C. §§ 186(b)(1), (a)(2), (d)(2), and making a false statement within the jurisdiction of a federal agency in violation of 18 U.S.C. § 1001. He was tried, along with several co-defendants, before a jury in the United States District Court for the Southern District of New York, and was found guilty. The United States Court of Appeals for the Second Circuit affirmed the convictions. We granted certiorari on the issue of the "exculpatory no."

II

At the time petitioner falsely replied "no" to the Government investigators' question, 18 U.S.C. § 1001 (1988 ed.) provided:

"Whoever, in any matter within the jurisdiction of any department or agency of the United States knowingly and willfully falsifies, conceals or covers up by any trick, scheme, or device a material fact, or makes any false, fictitious or fraudulent statements or representations, or makes or uses any false writing or document knowing the same to contain any false, fictitious or fraudulent statement or entry, shall be fined not more than $10,000 or imprisoned not more than five years, or both."

By its terms, 18 U.S.C. § 1001 covers "any" false statement—that is, a false statement "of whatever kind." The word "no" in response to a question assuredly makes a "statement," see e.g., Webster's New International Dictionary 2461 (2d ed. 1950). ("That which is stated; an embodiment in words of facts or opinions"), and petitioner does not contest that his utterance was false or that it was made "knowingly and willfully." In fact, petitioner concedes that under a "literal reading" of the statute he loses.

Petitioner asks us, however, to depart from the literal text that Congress has enacted, and to approve the doctrine adopted by many Circuits which excludes from the scope of § 1001 the "exculpatory no." The central feature of this doctrine is that a simple denial of guilt does not come within the statute. There is considerable variation among the Circuits concerning, among other things, what degree of elaborated tale-telling carries a statement beyond simple denial. In the present case, however, the Second Circuit agreed with petitioner that his statement would constitute a "true 'exculpatory no' as recognized in other circuits," but aligned itself with the Fifth Circuit (one of whose panels had been the very first to embrace the "exculpatory no" see *Paternostro v. United States*, 311 F.2d 298 (C.A.5 1962)) in categorically rejecting the doctrine, see *United States v. Rodriguez–Rios*, 14 F.3d 1040 (C.A.5 1994) (en banc).

Petitioner's argument in support of the "exculpatory no" doctrine proceeds from the major premise that § 1001 criminalizes only those statements to Government investigators that "pervert governmental functions"; to the minor premise that simple denials of guilt to government investigators do not pervert governmental functions; to the conclusion that 1001 does not criminalize simple denials of guilt to Government investigators. Both premises seem to us mistaken. As to the minor: We cannot imagine how it could be true that falsely denying guilt in a Government investigation does not pervert a governmental function. Certainly the investigation of wrongdoing is a proper governmental function; and since it is the very purpose of an investigation to uncover the truth, any falsehood relating to the subject of the investigation perverts that function. It could be argued, perhaps, that a disbelieved falsehood does not pervert an investigation. But making the existence of this crime turn upon the credulousness of the federal investigator (or the persuasiveness of the liar) would be exceedingly strange; such a defense to the analogous crime of perjury is certainly unheard-of. Moreover, as we shall see, the only support for the "perversion of governmental functions" limitation is a statement of this Court referring to the possibility (as opposed to the certainty) of perversion of function—a possibility that exists whenever investigators are told a falsehood relevant to their task.

In any event, we find no basis for the major premise that only those falsehoods that pervert governmental functions are covered by § 1001. Petitioner derives this premise from a comment we made in *United States v. Gilliland*, 312 U.S. 86 (1941), a case involving the predecessor to § 1001. That earlier version of the statute subjected to criminal liability " 'whoever shall knowingly and willfully . . . make or cause to be made any false or fraudulent statements or representations, or make or use or cause to be made or used any false bill, receipt, voucher, roll, account, claim, certificate, affidavit, or deposition, knowing the same to contain any fraudulent or fictitious statement or entry, in any matter within the jurisdiction of any department or agency of the United States . . .' ". The defendant in *Gilliland*, relying on the interpretive canon ejusdem generis, argued that the statute should be read to apply only to matters in which the Government has a financial or proprietary interest. In rejecting that argument, we noted that Congress had specifically amended the statute to cover " 'any matter within the jurisdiction of any department or agency of the United States,' " thereby indicating "the congressional intent to protect the authorized functions of governmental departments and agencies from the perversion which might result from the deceptive practices described." Petitioner would elevate this statement to a holding that § 1001 does not apply where a perversion of governmental functions does not exist. But it is not, and cannot be, our practice to restrict the unqualified language of a statute to the particular evil that Congress was trying to remedy—even assuming that it is possible to identify that evil from something other than the text of the statute itself. The holding of *Gilliland* certainly does not exemplify such a practice, since it rejected the defendant's argument for a limitation that the text of the statute would not bear. And even the relied-upon dictum from *Gilliland* does not support restricting text to supposed purpose, but to the contrary acknowledges the reality that the reach of a statute often exceeds the precise evil to be eliminated. There is no inconsistency whatever between the proposition that Congress intended "to protect the authorized functions of governmental departments and agencies from the perversion which might result" and the proposition that the statute forbids all "the deceptive practices described."

The second line of defense that petitioner invokes for the "exculpatory no" doctrine is inspired by the Fifth Amendment. He argues that a literal reading of § 1001 violates the "spirit" of the Fifth Amendment because it places a "cornered suspect" in the "cruel trilemma" of admitting guilt, remaining silent, or falsely denying guilt. * * * This "trilemma" is wholly of the guilty suspect's own making, of course. An innocent person will not find himself in a similar quandary (as one commentator has put it, the innocent person lacks even a "lemma.") And even the honest and contrite guilty person will not regard the third prong of the "trilemma" (the blatant lie) as an available option. The bon mot "cruel trilemma" first appeared in Justice Goldberg's opinion for the Court in *Murphy v. Waterfront Comm'n of N.Y. Harbor*, 378 U.S. 52 (1964), where it was used to explain the importance of a suspect's Fifth Amendment right to remain silent when subpoenaed to testify in an official inquiry. Without that right, the opinion said, he would be exposed "to the cruel trilemma of self-accusation, perjury or contempt." In order to validate the "exculpatory no," the elements of this "cruel trilemma" have now been altered—ratcheted up, as it were, so that the right to remain silent, which was the liberation from the original trilemma, is now itself a cruelty. We are not disposed to write into our law this species of compassion inflation.

Whether or not the predicament of the wrongdoer run to ground tugs at the heart strings, neither the text nor the spirit of the Fifth Amendment confers a privilege to lie. "Proper invocation of the Fifth Amendment privilege against compulsory self-incrimination allows a witness to remain silent, but not to swear falsely." Petitioner contends that silence is an "illusory" option because a suspect may fear that his silence will be used against him later, or may not even know that silence is an available option. As to the former: It is well established that the fact that a person's silence can be used against him—either as substantive evidence of guilt or to impeach him if he takes the stand—does not exert a form of pressure that exonerates an otherwise unlawful lie. And as for the possibility that the person under investigation may be unaware of his right to remain silent: In the modern age of frequently dramatized "*Miranda*" warnings, that is implausible. Indeed, we found it implausible (or irrelevant) 30 years ago, unless the suspect was "in custody or otherwise deprived of his freedom of action in any significant way."

Petitioner repeats the argument made by many supporters of the "exculpatory no," that the doctrine is necessary to eliminate the grave risk that § 1001 will become an instrument of prosecutorial abuse. The supposed danger is that overzealous prosecutors will use this provision as a means of "piling on" offenses—sometimes punishing the denial of wrongdoing more severely than the wrongdoing itself. The objectors' principal grievance on this score, however, lies not with the hypothetical prosecutors but with Congress itself, which has decreed the obstruction of a legitimate investigation to be a separate offense, and a serious one. It is not for us to revise that judgment. Petitioner has been unable to demonstrate, moreover, any history of prosecutorial excess, either before or after widespread judicial acceptance of the "exculpatory no." And finally, if there is a problem of supposed "overreaching" it is hard to see how the doctrine of the "exculpatory no" could solve it. It is easy enough for an interrogator to press the liar from the initial simple denial to a more detailed fabrication that would not qualify for the exemption.

III

A brief word in response to the dissent's assertion that the Court may interpret a criminal statute more narrowly than it is written: Some of the cases it cites for that proposition represent instances in which the Court did not purport to be departing from a reasonable reading of the text. In the others, the Court applied what it thought to be a background interpretive principle of general application. *Staples v. United States*, 511 U.S. 600, 619 (1994) (construing statute to contain common-law requirement of mens rea); *Sorrells v. United States*, 287 U.S. 435, 446 (1932) (construing statute not to cover violations produced by entrapment); *United States v. Palmer*, 16 U.S. 610, 3 Wheat. 610, 631 (1818) (construing statute not to apply extraterritorially to noncitizens). Also into this last category falls the dissent's correct assertion that the present statute does not "make it a crime for an undercover narcotics agent to make a false statement to a drug peddler." Criminal prohibitions do not generally apply to reasonable enforcement actions by officers of the law. It is one thing to acknowledge and accept such well defined (or even newly enunciated), generally applicable, background principles of assumed legislative intent. It is quite another to espouse the broad proposition that criminal statutes do not have to be read as broadly as they are written, but are subject to case-by-case exceptions. The problem with adopting such an expansive, user-friendly judicial rule, is that there is no way of knowing when, or how, the rule is to be invoked. As to the when: The only reason JUSTICE STEVENS adduces for invoking it here is that a felony conviction for this offense seems to him harsh. Which it may well be. But the instances in which courts may ignore harsh penalties are set forth in the Constitution, and to go beyond them will surely leave us at sea. And as to the how: There is no reason in principle why the dissent chooses to mitigate the harshness by saying that § 1001 does not embrace the "exculpatory no," rather than by saying that § 1001 has no application unless the defendant has been warned of the consequences of lying, or indeed unless the defendant has been put under oath. We are again at sea.

* * *

In sum, we find nothing to support the "exculpatory no" doctrine except the many Court of Appeals decisions that have embraced it. * * * Courts may not create their own limitations on legislation, no matter how alluring the policy arguments for doing so, and no matter how widely the blame may be spread. Because the plain language of § 1001 admits of no exception for an "exculpatory no," we affirm the judgment of the Court of Appeals.

It is so ordered.

JUSTICE SOUTER, concurring in part and concurring in the judgment.

I join the opinion of the Court except for its response to petitioner's argument premised on the potential for prosecutorial abuse of 18 U.S.C. § 1001 as now written On that point I have joined JUSTICE GINSBURG's opinion espousing congressional attention to the risks inherent in the statute's current breadth.

Justice Ginsburg, with whom Justice Souter joins, concurring in the judgment.

Because a false denial fits the unqualified language of 18 U.S.C. § 1001, I concur in the affirmance of Brogan's conviction. I write separately, however, to call attention to the extraordinary authority Congress, perhaps unwittingly, has conferred on prosecutors to manufacture crimes. I note, at the same time, how far removed the "exculpatory no" is from the problems Congress initially sought to address when it proscribed falsehoods designed to elicit a benefit from the Government or to hinder Government operations.

This case is illustrative. Two federal investigators paid an unannounced visit one evening to James Brogan's home. The investigators already possessed records indicating that Brogan, a union officer, had received cash from a company that employed members of the union Brogan served. (The agents gave no advance warning, one later testified, because they wanted to retain the element of surprise.) When the agents asked Brogan whether he had received any money or gifts from the company, Brogan responded "No." The agents asked no further questions. After Brogan just said "No," however, the agents told him: (1) the Government had in hand the records indicating that his answer was false; and (2) lying to federal agents in the course of an investigation is a crime. Had counsel appeared on the spot, Brogan likely would have received and followed advice to amend his answer, to say immediately: "Strike that; I plead not guilty." But no counsel attended the unannounced interview, and Brogan divulged nothing more. Thus, when the interview ended, a federal offense had been completed—even though, for all we can tell, Brogan's unadorned denial misled no one.

* * *

At oral argument, the Solicitor General forthrightly observed that § 1001 could even be used to "escalate completely innocent conduct into a felony." More likely to occur, "if an investigator finds it difficult to prove some elements of a crime, she can ask questions about other elements to which she already knows the answers. If the suspect lies, she can then use the crime she has prompted as leverage or can seek prosecution for the lies as a substitute for the crime she cannot prove." If the statute of limitations has run on an offense—as it had on four of the five payments Brogan was accused of accepting—the prosecutor can endeavor to revive the case by instructing an investigator to elicit a fresh denial of guilt. Prosecution in these circumstances is not an instance of Government "punishing the denial of wrongdoing more severely than the wrongdoing itself"; it is, instead, Government generation of a crime when the underlying suspected wrongdoing is or has become nonpunishable.

II

It is doubtful Congress intended § 1001 *to cast so large a net.*

* * *

* * * [T]he core concern persists: "The function of law enforcement is the prevention of crime and the apprehension of criminals. Manifestly, that function does not include the manufacturing of crime." The Government has not been blind to this concern. Notwithstanding the prosecution in this case and the others, the Department of Justice has long noted its reluctance to approve § 1001 indictments for simple false denials made to investigators. Indeed, the Government once asserted before this Court that the arguments supporting the "exculpatory no" doctrine "are forceful even if not necessarily dispositive."

In *Nunley*, we vacated a § 1001 conviction and remanded with instructions to dismiss the indictment, at the Solicitor General's suggestion. *Nunley v. United States*, 434 U.S. 962 (1977). The Government urged such a course because the prosecution had been instituted without prior approval from the Assistant Attorney General, and such permission was "normally refused" in cases like Nunley's, where the statements "essentially constituted mere denials of guilt."

Since *Nunley*, the Department of Justice has maintained a policy against bringing § 1001 prosecutions for statements amounting to an "exculpatory no." At the time the charges against Brogan were filed, the United States Attorneys' Manual firmly declared: "Where the statement takes the form of an 'exculpatory no,' 18 U.S.C. § 1001 does not apply regardless who asks the question." United States Attorneys' Manual ¶ 9–42.160 (Oct. 1, 1988). After the Fifth Circuit abandoned the "exculpatory no" doctrine in *United States v. Rodriguez–Rios*, 14 F.3d 1040 (1994) (en banc), the manual was amended to read: "It is the Department's policy that it is not appropriate to charge a Section 1001 violation where a suspect, during an investigation, merely denies his guilt in response to questioning by the government." United States Attorneys' Manual ¶ 42.160 (Feb. 12, 1996).[6]

These pronouncements indicate, at the least, the dubious propriety of bringing felony prosecutions for bare exculpatory denials informally made to Government agents. Although today's decision holds that such prosecutions can be sustained under the broad language of § 1001, the Department of Justice's prosecutorial guide continues to caution restraint in each exercise of this large authority.

IV

The Court's opinion does not instruct lower courts automatically to sanction prosecution or conviction under § 1001 in all instances of false denials made to criminal investigators. The Second Circuit, whose judgment the Court affirms, noted some reservations. That court left open the question whether "to violate Section 1001, a person must know that

6. While this case was pending before us, the Department of Justice issued yet another version of the manual, which deleted the words "that it is" and "appropriate" from the sentence just quoted. The new version reads: "It is the Department's policy not to charge a Section 1001 violation in situations in which a suspect, during an investigation, merely denies guilt in response to questioning by the government." United States Attorneys' Manual ¶ 9–42.160 (Sept. 1997).

it is unlawful to make such a false statement." *United States v. Wiener,* 96 F.3d 35, 40 (1996). And nothing that court or this Court said suggests that "the mere denial of criminal responsibility would be sufficient to prove such [knowledge]." *Ibid.* Moreover, "a trier of fact might acquit on the ground that a denial of guilt in circumstances indicating surprise or other lack of reflection was not the product of the requisite criminal intent," and a jury could be instructed that it would be permissible to draw such an inference. Finally, under the statute currently in force, a false statement must be "material" to violate § 1001. *See* False Statements Accountability Act of 1996.

The controls now in place, however, do not meet the basic issue, i.e., the sweeping generality of § 1001's language. Thus, the prospect remains that an overzealous prosecutor or investigator—aware that a person has committed some suspicious acts, but unable to make a criminal case—will create a crime by surprising the suspect, asking about those acts, and receiving a false denial. Congress alone can provide the appropriate instruction.

Congress has been alert to our decisions in this area, as its enactment of the False Statements Accountability Act of 1996 (passed in response to our decision in *Hubbard v. United States,* 514 U.S. 695 (1995)) demonstrates. Similarly, after today's decision, Congress may advert to the "exculpatory no" doctrine and the problem that prompted its formulation.

The matter received initial congressional consideration some years ago. Legislation to revise and recodify the federal criminal laws, reported by the Senate Judiciary Committee in 1981 but never enacted, would have established a "defense to a prosecution for an oral false statement to a law enforcement officer" if "the statement was made 'during the course of an investigation of an offense or a possible offense and the statement consisted of a denial, unaccompanied by any other false statement, that the declarant committed or participated in the commission of such offense.'" S. Rep. No. 97–307, p. 407 (1981). In common with the "exculpatory no" doctrine as it developed in the lower courts, this 1981 proposal would have made the defense "available only when the false statement consists solely of a denial of involvement in a crime." *Ibid.* It would not have protected a denial "if accompanied by any other false statement (e.g., the assertion of an alibi)."

The 1981 Senate bill covered more than an "exculpatory no" defense; it addressed frontally, as well, unsworn oral statements of the kind likely to be made without careful deliberation or knowledge of the statutory prohibition against false statements. The bill would have criminalized false oral statements to law enforcement officers only "where the statement is either volunteered (e.g., a false alarm or an unsolicited false accusation that another person has committed an offense) or is made after a warning, designed to impress on the defendant the seriousness of the interrogation and his obligation to speak truthfully."

More stringent revision, following the lead of the Model Penal Code and the 1971 proposal of a congressionally chartered law reform commission, would excise unsworn oral statements from § 1001 altogether. *See* ALI, Model Penal Code §§ 241.3, 241.4, 241.5 (1980); National Commission on Reform of Federal Criminal Laws, Final Report §§ 1352, 1354 (1971). A recodification proposal reported by the House Judiciary Committee in 1980 adopted that approach. It would have applied the general false statement provision only to statements made in writing or recorded with the speaker's knowledge, see H. R. Rep. No. 96–1396, pp. 181–183 (1980); unsworn oral statements would have been penalized under separate provisions, and only when they entailed misprision of a felony, false implication of another, or false statements about an emergency. The 1971 law reform commission would have further limited § 1001; its proposal excluded from the false statement prohibition all "information given during the course of an investigation into possible commission of an offense unless the information is given in an official proceeding or the declarant is otherwise under a legal duty to give the information." National Commission on Reform of Federal Criminal Laws, Final Report § 1352(3).

In sum, an array of recommendations has been made to refine § 1001 to block the statute's use as a generator of crime while preserving the measure's important role in protecting the workings of Government. I do not divine from the Legislature's silence any ratification of the "exculpatory no" doctrine advanced in lower courts. The extensive airing this issue has received, however, may better inform the exercise of Congress' lawmaking authority.

Notes

1. Under the Sentencing Guidelines, the fact that a convicted defendant had obstructed justice in connection with his case by giving false testimony is a basis for increasing the sentence. Does the exculpatory no doctrine apply in this context? See *United States v. Aguilar–Portillo*, 334 F.3d 744 (8th Cir. 2003):

> "If a defendant objects to an obstruction of justice enhancement based on perjury, the district court 'must review the evidence and make independent findings' that the defendant willfully gave false testimony concerning a material matter in the case." The district court refused to make such a finding here, noting, among other things, several contradictions in various witnesses' testimony, a probable lie by one of the prosecution's witnesses, the fact that the jury deliberated for a day and a half, the fact that Mr. Aguilar–Portillo did not look evasive, and the fact that he merely made unembellished denials.
>
> The government contends that an enhancement for obstruction was warranted because Mr. Aguilar–Portillo's denials pertained to material matters, were not caused by "confusion, mistake, or faulty memory," and, because they were contrary to the jury verdict, were necessarily false. The government argues that the district court erroneously created

a so-called "exculpatory no" exception to obstruction enhancements for false testimony, pointing to statements by the district court at the sentencing hearing such as "I don't know what [Mr. Aguilar–Portillo] might have said, but he—if he was making an outright fabrication in addition to what he had—just a plain no he said here, then I would certainly be having a problem."

The "exculpatory no" exception enjoyed a long pedigree as a judicially-created exception to the prohibitions of the False Statements Act, 18 U.S.C. § 1001. *See Brogan v. United States*, 522 U.S. 398, 401, 139 L.Ed.2d 830, 118 S.Ct. 805 (1998). The central feature of this doctrine [was] that a simple denial of guilt does not come within the statute. But the Supreme Court in *Brogan* rejected this exception, concluding that a simple denial of guilt could be a false statement under the Act.

Although we agree with the government that there can be no such thing as an "exculpatory no" defense when the question before the district court is whether the defendant has obstructed justice, since a simple denial of guilt can be as perjurious as any other false statement as long the defendant willfully intended to provide false testimony, we disagree with the government's characterization of the district court's determination here. Our careful examination of the transcript of the sentencing hearing leads us to conclude that the district court was merely of the view that Mr. Aguilar–Portillo's "no's" were not perjurious, not that a simple denial of guilt without more was not perjurious as a matter of law. In other words, we think that the district court believed that the government did not prove by a preponderance of the evidence that Mr. Aguilar–Portillo was lying.

2. How significant is it that a false statement is oral and unsworn? In *United States v. Massey*, 550 F.2d 300, 305 (5th Cir.1977), the defendant argued "that since the statements are untranscribed they were unreliable as a starting point for a false statement prosecution because they are merely the recollection of a federal policeman." This argument has usually been rejected. *See United States v. Massey, supra*; *United States v. Isaacs*, 493 F.2d 1124 (7th Cir.1974); *United States v. Ratner*, 464 F.2d 101 (9th Cir.1972). *But see United States v. Levin*, 133 F.Supp. 88 (D.Colo.1953) and consider the following excerpt from *United States v. Ehrlichman*, 379 F.Supp. 291, 292 (D.D.C.1974):

> The principal difficulty with invoking § 1001 to punish those who lie to the F.B.I. when there is no legal obligation to respond to its inquiry is that the prosecution can thereafter demand sanctions as onerous as those imposed under the general perjury statute, 18 U.S.C. § 1621, without affording those suspected of criminal conduct with any of the safeguards normally provided under that statute. There is no requirement of an oath, no strict rule of materiality, and no guarantee that the proceeding will be transcribed or reduced to memorandum. In short, the F.B.I. interview may occur—as it did here—under extremely informal circumstances which do not sufficiently alert the person interviewed to the danger that false statements may lead to a felony conviction. * * *

This informality is particularly serious in light of the Supreme Court's recent decision in *Bronston v. United States*, 409 U.S. 352 (1973), in which the Court held that an incomplete, misleading or deceptive statement does not constitute perjury so long as it is literally true. If this principle is not applied to prosecutions under § 1001, then it constitutes one more significant safeguard that can be avoided by the application of that statute to F.B.I. interviews. On the other hand, if the *Bronston* literal-truth test *is* applied to allegedly false representations under § 1001, which would appear to be the more reasonable result, then the absence of a transcript would make application of that test nearly impossible. In the instant case, defendant Ehrlichman was faced with the difficult task of arguing that his statements to the F.B.I. were literally true on the sole basis of the agent's sketchy notes, which do not purport to be a verbatim record of either the questions or the answers at issue and which were not even shown to him until shortly before trial.

For a case overturning a § 1001 conviction because the oral evidence of the federal agents was "too fragile to support a guilty verdict," see *United States v. Poutre*, 646 F.2d 685 (1st Cir.1980).

3. *Brogan* is analyzed and critiqued in Lauren C. Hennessey, *No Exception for "No": Rejection of the Exculpatory No Doctrine*, 89 J. CRIM. L. & CRIMINOLOGY 905 (1999), and *The Supreme Court 1997 Term—Leading Cases*, 112 HARV. L. REV. 345 (1998).

D. § 1001 AND OTHER CRIMES

UNITED STATES v. WOODWARD

469 U.S. 105, 105 S.Ct. 611, 83 L.Ed.2d 518 (1985).

Per Curiam.

* * *

Woodward was indicted on charges of making a false statement to an agency of the United States, 18 U.S.C. § 1001, and willfully failing to report that he was carrying in excess of $5,000 into the United States, 84 Stat. 1121, 1122, 31 U.S.C. §§ 1058, 1101 (1976 ed.).[7] The same con-

---

7. Title 31 U.S.C. § 1101(a) (1976 ed.) provides in pertinent part:

"Except as provided in subsection (c) of this section, whoever, whether as principal, agent, or bailee, or by an agent or bailee, knowingly—

"(1) transports or causes to be transported monetary instruments—

"(A) from any place within the United States or through any place outside the United States, or

"(B) to any place within the United States or through any place outside the United States, or

"(2) receives monetary instruments at the termination of their transportation to the United States from or through any place outside the United States in an amount exceeding $5,000 on any one occasion shall file a report or reports in accordance with subsection (b) of this section."

Title 31 U.S.C. § 1058 (1976 ed.) provides:

"Whoever willfully violates any provision of this chapter or any regulation under this chapter shall be fined not more than $1,000, or imprisoned not more than one year, or both."

Sections 1058 and 1101 were recently recodified without substantive change at 31 U.S.C. §§ 5322(a) and 5316. See Pub.L. 97–258, 96 Stat. 877 et seq.

duct—answering "no" to the question whether he was carrying more than $5,000 into the country—formed the basis of each count. A jury convicted Woodward on both charges; he received a sentence of six months in prison on the false statement count, and a consecutive three-year term of probation on the currency reporting count. During the proceedings in the District Court, the respondent never asserted that Congress did not intend to permit cumulative punishment for conduct violating the false statement and the currency reporting statutes.

The United States Court of Appeals for the Ninth Circuit, after inviting briefs on the subject, held that respondent's conduct could not be punished under both 18 U.S.C. § 1001 and 31 U.S.C. §§ 1058, 1101 (1976 ed.). The court applied the rule of statutory construction contained in *Blockburger v. United States,* 284 U.S. 299, 304 (1932)—" 'whether each provision requires proof of a fact which the other does not' "—and held that the false statement felony was a lesser included offense of the currency reporting misdemeanor. In other words, every violation of the currency reporting statute necessarily entails a violation of the false statement law.[8] The court reasoned that a willful failure to file a required report is a form of concealment prohibited by 18 U.S.C. § 1001. Concluding that Congress presumably intended someone in respondent position to be punished only under the currency reporting misdemeanor, the Court of Appeals reversed respondent felony conviction for making a false statement.

The Court of Appeals plainly misapplied the *Blockburger* rule for determining whether Congress intended to permit cumulative punishment; proof of a currency reporting violation does not necessarily include proof of a false statement offense. Section 1001 proscribes the nondisclosure of a material fact only if the fact is "conceal[ed] ... by any *trick, scheme, or device.*" (Emphasis added.)[9] A person could, without employing a trick, scheme or device, simply and willfully fail to file a currency disclosure report. A traveler who enters the country and passes through Customs prepared to answer questions truthfully, but is never asked whether he is carrying over $5,000 in currency, might nonetheless be subject to conviction under 31 U.S.C. § 1058 (1976 ed.) for willfully transporting money without filing the required currency report. However, because he did not conceal a material fact by means of a trick, scheme, or device, (and did not make any false statement) his conduct would not fall within 18 U.S.C. § 1001.

There is no evidence in 18 U.S.C. § 1001 and 31 U.S.C. §§ 1058, 1101 (1976 ed.) that Congress did not intend to allow separate punishment for the two different offenses. *See generally Albernaz v. United*

---

8. The converse is clearly not true; 31 U.S.C. §§ 1058, 1101 (1976 ed.), but not 18 U.S.C. § 1001, involve the failure to file a currency disclosure report.

9. In Woodward's case, the Government did not have to prove the existence of a trick, scheme, or device. Woodward was charged with violating § 1001 because he made a false statement on the Customs form. This type of affirmative misrepresentation is proscribed under the statute even if not accompanied by a trick, scheme or device.

States, *450 U.S. 333, 340 (1981);* Missouri v. Hunter, *459 U.S. 359, 367 (1983). Sections 1058 and 1101 were enacted by Congress in 1970 as part of the Currency and Foreign Transactions Reporting Act, Pub.L. 91–508, Tit. II, 84 Stat. 1118 et seq. Section 203(k) of that Act expressly provided:*

> "For the purposes of section 1001 of title 18, United States Code, the contents of reports required under any provision of this title are statements and representations in matters within the jurisdiction of an agency of the United States." 31 U.S.C. § 1052(k) (1976 ed.)[10]

It is clear that in passing the currency reporting law, Congress' attention was drawn to 18 U.S.C. § 1001, but at no time did it suggest that the two statutes could not be applied together. We cannot assume, therefore, that Congress was unaware that it had created two different offenses permitting multiple punishment for the same conduct. *See Albernaz, supra.*

Finally, Congress' intent to allow punishment under both 18 U.S.C. § 1001 and 31 U.S.C. §§ 1058, 1101 (1976 ed.), is shown by the fact that the statutes "are directed to separate evils." The currency reporting statute was enacted to develop records that would "have a high degree of usefulness in criminal, tax, or regulatory investigations." 31 U.S.C. § 1051 (1976 ed.). The false statement statute, on the other hand, was designed "to protect the authorized functions of governmental departments and agencies from the perversion which might result from the deceptive practices described."

All guides to legislative intent reveal that Congress intended respondent's conduct to be punishable under both 18 U.S.C. § 1001, and 31 U.S.C. §§ 1058, 1101 (1976 ed.). Accordingly, the petition for a writ of certiorari is granted, and that part of the Court of Appeals' judgment reversing respondent's 18 U.S.C. § 1001 conviction is reversed.

It is so ordered.

Notes

1.   The holding in *Woodward* does not necessarily extend to all federal statutes that penalize false statements in particular contexts. In *United States v. Avelino,* 967 F.2d 815 (2d Cir.1992), the court distinguished *Woodward* and held that the same conduct could not be punished under both § 1001 and 18 U.S.C. § 542, which proscribes false statements to United States Customs officials. Applying the *Blockburger* analysis, the court concluded that every element under § 1001 was also an element under § 542. The court stated:

> To be convicted for false statements under Section 542, a defendant must: (1) attempt to import merchandise into the United States (2) "by

---

10. When Title 31 was recodified in 1982, this provision was eliminated as "[u]nnecessary" because "Section 1001 ap-   plies unless otherwise provided." H.R.Rep. No. 97–651, p. 301 (1982).

means of" a false statement (3) without reasonable cause to believe the truth of such statement or practice. * * * The elements under Section 1001 are, however, also elements under Section 542: (1) the knowing element of a Section 1001 false statement will always be encompassed by the lack of a reasonable cause to believe element of Section 542; (2) Section 1001's materiality requirement is redundant because false statements under Section 542 are necessarily material because the importation must be "by means of [the] false statement"; (3) importation of merchandise implicates Customs, a department or agency of the United States. Finally, neither the statutory language nor the legislative history demonstrate a "clear intent" by Congress to punish the same offense under these two statutory provisions.

Id. at 817.

2. *Woodward* is concerned with the possibility that the government will obtain multiple convictions for the same conduct by charging the defendant under more than one statute. A related issue arises when the government charges the defendant with multiple counts under § 1001. What is the proper analysis if the defendant repeats his false statement? Is each repetition a separate violation of § 1001? In *United States v. Olsowy*, 836 F.2d 439 (9th Cir.1987), a Secret Service agent asked the defendant the same question three times, and the defendant's three denials lead to his conviction for three counts of violating § 1001. He argued that the government should not be able to pile on multiple convictions by repeatedly asking the same question to a criminal suspect. The court of appeals responded:

> * * * [I]n *Gebhard v. United States*, 422 F.2d 281 (9th Cir.1970), we considered a very similar contention in the context of multiple perjury convictions for repeating the same lie to a grand jury in response to the same question. *Gebhard* reasoned that there was no chance the grand jury could be hindered in its investigation by each repetition of the false utterance. Therefore, we held that the government should not be able to obtain multiple perjury convictions.
>
> We hold our reasoning in *Gebhard* applicable here. Olsowy made exactly the same oral denial to the same Secret Service agent twice and then signed a document embodying the very same denial. The repetition of Olsowy's initial false statement did not further impair the operations of the government. Once he misled the agent, repeating the lie adds little or nothing to the harm caused to the Secret Service's inquiry. Therefore, we hold that where identical false statements, in either oral or written form, are made in response to identical questions, the declarant may be convicted only once.

Id. at 443. Later the same year another panel of the Ninth Circuit upheld two convictions under § 1001 for the repetition of a false statement to two different customs officers. *United States v. Salas–Camacho*, 859 F.2d 788 (9th Cir.1988). The court concluded that the defendant's second denial that he had goods to declare did further impair the operations of the government because the second statement was made to a separate official with different duties than the first official. While the first inspector was responsible for making only a preliminary examination, the official at the secondary inspection area was responsible for making a more searching examination, including a computer search to determine any prior violations. Accordingly, the court concluded that the false statement to the second official constituted an additional impairment of his governmental function. Accord: *United States v. Newton*, 2002 WL 1285361 (S.D.N.Y.) aff'd on other grounds, 72 Fed.Appx. 855 (2d Cir.2003).

3. The high profile prosecution of Martha Stewart illustrates the use of § 1001 along with an obstruction of justice count in lieu of prosecuting her for the underlying conduct that had originally triggered federal interest— suspected insider trading. She was convicted in 2004 of § 1001 false statements, obstruction and conspiracy. The false statement counts were based on Stewart's statements during an interview with the FBI, SEC and the United States Attorney's office. The false statements alleged in the indictment included Stewart's description of her conversations with her broker and also her statement that she did not recall certain subjects being discussed. The obstruction of justice count covered much the same ground. The indictment had also included a securities fraud count alleging insider trading, but the trial judge dismissed that count before trial. See *United States v. Stewart*, 305 F.Supp.2d 368 (S.D.N.Y. 2004), and see generally, Kathleen F. Brickey, *Mostly Martha,* 44 Washburn L.J. 517 (2005).

Query: Would it have been appropriate to charge the false statement and obstruction charges and not charge the insider trading count? Once the trial judge dismissed the insider trading count, should the government be permitted to continue with the false statement and obstruction charges? Should it make any difference what the basis was for the dismissal of the insider trading charge? Suppose the basis was that there was no basis for federal jurisdiction in the matter? In other recent high profile corporate fraud-complex accounting cases, the government has been prosecuting using ancillary charges like obstruction, perjury and false statements sometimes in addition to, and sometimes rather than charging the underlying fraud. It is often much easier to prove such ancillary charges than to engage in a long-drawn out trial involving complex accounting and corporate business matters. Is this a sufficient justification for the government to adopt this type of litigation strategy? See Stuart P. Green, *Uncovering the Cover-up Crimes,* 42 Am. Crim. L.Rev. 9 (2005); Daniel C. Richman & William J. Stuntz, *Al Capone's Revenge: an Essay on the Political Economy of Pretextual Prosecution,* 105 Colum. L.Rev. 583 (2005); Harry Litman, *Pretextual Prosecution,* 92 Geo. L.J. 1135 (2004); Norman Abrams, *The New Ancillary Offenses,* 1 Crim.L. Forum 1 (1989), and see Chapter 16 infra.

Chapter 16

OBSTRUCTION OF JUSTICE: INTERFERENCE WITH WITNESSES

INTRODUCTION

Because obstruction of justice can involve activities that take so many different forms, it presents a special challenge in statutory drafting. There are two basic approaches: A general catchall-type provision might be used, or a series of specific statutes might be enacted. The approach adopted in 18 U.S.C. §§ 1503–1515 reflects both approaches. The result is that there is a large number of different federal statutory provisions that deal expressly with this subject. The court in *Catrino v. United States*, 176 F.2d 884, 887 (9th Cir.1949) aptly characterized the relationship between this statutory scheme and the different forms that obstruction of justice can take:

> The obstruction of justice statute is an outgrowth of Congressional recognition of the variety of corrupt methods by which the proper administration of justice may be impeded or thwarted, a variety limited only by the imagination of the criminally inclined.

The crime of obstructing justice can also be used to address conduct covered by, and which therefore overlaps with other categories of crime, for example, perjury or suborning perjury, making false statements or, even, engaging in murderous, assaultive or threatening conduct against witnesses, sources of information, parties, or officials involved in the administration of justice.

Prior to 1982, the provisions expressly dealing with obstruction of justice were found in Title 18, §§ 1503–1510. In 1982, the Victim and Witness Protection Act, P.L. 97–291, 96 Stat. 1249 was enacted which modified somewhat the content of some of these provisions. Language relating to interference with, or attempts to influence witnesses was deleted from §§ 1503 and 1505, but these sections were otherwise left intact, and a new § 1512 was added containing provisions relating to tampering with federal witnesses, potential witnesses or informants by intimidation, physical force, threats, misleading conduct or harassment

757

as well as altering or destroying documents. Two other provisions were added: § 1513 which prohibits retaliation against a federal witness, and § 1514 which provides for the issuance of restraining orders to prevent harassment of witnesses. Some of these provisions were subsequently amended in various details from their original 1982 version. Of particular note are amendments to § 1512 effected by the Sarbanes–Oxley Act of 2002.

We focus in this chapter primarily on § 1503 and § 1512, the two provisions that are most frequently invoked in obstruction contexts, 1503, because of its generality and consequent applicability to a wide variety of situations and 1512, because of its detailed and wide-ranging coverage in regard to interference with witnesses and destruction of documents. § 1503 is reproduced at the beginning of section A, infra, which addresses issues of interpretation and application under the section. The current version of § 1512 is reproduced at the beginning of section B, infra, which similarly deals with some issues of interpretation of particular clauses of this lengthy statutory provision. Both sections A and B focus primarily on various mens rea-type issues under 1503 and 1512. Section C focuses on the varying types of conduct that can be prosecuted under 1503 and 1512. The question whether interference with witnesses can be prosecuted under both 1503 and 1512 is addressed in section D, and section E reproduces the other obstruction of justice statutory provisions.

A. § 1503, THE OMNIBUS PROVISION: KNOWLEDGE OF JUDICIAL PROCEEDINGS AND ANALOGOUS ELEMENTS—THE "NEXUS" REQUIREMENT

18 U.S.C. § 1503

§ 1503. Influencing or injuring officer or juror generally

(a) Whoever corruptly, or by threats or force, or by any threatening letter or communication, endeavors to influence, intimidate, or impede any grand or petit juror, or officer in or of any court of the United States, or officer who may be serving at any examination or other proceeding before any United States magistrate judge or other committing magistrate, in the discharge of his duty, or injures any such grand or petit juror in his person or property on account of any verdict or indictment assented to by him, or on account of his being or having been such juror, or injures any such officer, magistrate judge, or other committing magistrate in his person or property on account of the performance of his official duties, or corruptly or by threats or force, or by any threatening letter or communication, influences, obstructs, or impedes, or endeavors to influence, obstruct, or impede, the due administration of justice, shall be punished as provided in subsection (b). If the offense under this section occurs in connection with a trial of a criminal case, and the act in violation of this section involves the threat of physical force or physical force, the maximum term of imprisonment which may be imposed for the offense shall be the higher of that otherwise provided by law or the maximum term that could have been imposed for any offense charged in such case.

(b) The punishment for an offense under this section is—

(1) in the case of a killing, the punishment provided in sections 1111 and 1112;

(2) in the case of an attempted killing, or a case in which the offense was committed against a petit juror and in which a class A or B felony was charged, imprisonment for not more than 20 years, a fine under this title, or both; and

(3) in any other case, imprisonment for not more than 10 years, a fine under this title, or both.

UNITED STATES v. AGUILAR

515 U.S. 593, 115 S.Ct. 2357, 132 L.Ed.2d 520 (1995).

CHIEF JUSTICE REHNQUIST delivered the opinion of the Court.

A jury convicted United States District Judge Robert Aguilar of one count of endeavoring to obstruct the due administration of justice in violation of § 1503. A panel of the Court of Appeals for the Ninth Circuit* * * reversed the conviction under § 1503. * * * We granted certiorari to resolve a conflict among the Federal Circuits over whether § 1503 punishes false statements made to potential grand jury witnesses * * * .

Many facts remain disputed by the parties. Both parties appear to agree, however, that a motion for postconviction relief filed by one Michael Rudy Tham represents the starting point from which events bearing on this case unfolded. Tham was an officer of the International Brotherhood of Teamsters, and was convicted of embezzling funds from the local affiliate of that organization. In July 1987, he filed a motion under 28 U.S.C. § 2255 to have his conviction set aside. The motion was assigned to Judge Stanley Weigel. Tham, seeking to enhance the odds that his petition would be granted, asked Edward Solomon and Abraham Chalupowitz, a.k.a. Abe Chapman, to assist him by capitalizing on their respective acquaintances with another judge in the Northern District of California, respondent Aguilar. Respondent knew Chapman as a distant relation by marriage and knew Solomon from law school. Solomon and Chapman met with respondent to discuss Tham's case, as a result of which respondent spoke with Judge Weigel about the matter.

Independent of the embezzlement conviction, the Federal Bureau of Investigation (FBI) identified Tham as a suspect in an investigation of labor racketeering. On April 20, 1987, the FBI applied for authorization to install a wiretap on Tham's business phones. Chapman appeared on the application as a potential interceptee. Chief District Judge Robert

Peckham authorized the wiretap. The 30–day wiretap expired by law on May 20, 1987, but Chief Judge Peckham maintained the secrecy of the wiretap after a showing of good cause. During the course of the racketeering investigation, the FBI learned of the meetings between Chapman and respondent. The FBI informed Chief Judge Peckham, who, concerned with appearances of impropriety, advised respondent in August 1987 that Chapman might be connected with criminal elements because Chapman's name had appeared on a wiretap authorization.

Five months after respondent learned that Chapman had been named in a wiretap authorization, he noticed a man observing his home during a visit by Chapman. He alerted his nephew to this fact and conveyed the message (with an intent that his nephew relay the information to Chapman) that Chapman's phone was being wiretapped. Respondent apparently believed, in error, both that Chapman's phones were tapped in connection with the initial application and that the initial authorization was still in effect. Chief Judge Peckham had in fact authorized another wiretap on Tham's phones effective from October 1987 through the period in which respondent made the disclosure, but there is no suggestion in the record that the latter had any specific knowledge of this reauthorization.

At this point, respondent's involvement in the two separate Tham matters converged. Two months after the disclosure to his nephew, a grand jury began to investigate an alleged conspiracy to influence the outcome of Tham's habeas case. Two FBI agents questioned respondent. During the interview, respondent lied about his participation in the Tham case and his knowledge of the wiretap. The grand jury returned an indictment; a jury convicted Aguilar of one count of disclosing a wiretap, 18 U.S.C. § 2232(c), and one count of endeavoring to obstruct the due administration of justice, § 1503.

On rehearing en banc, the Court of Appeals reversed both convictions for the reason that the conduct * * * was not covered by the statutory language. * * * The Court of Appeals also found that respondent had not interfered with a pending judicial proceeding under § 1503. It first noted that the grand jury had not authorized or directed the FBI investigation. It then held that merely uttering false statements does not " 'corruptly influence' " within the meaning of the statute. It drew this conclusion, in part, from 1988 amendments to § 1512, which added a prohibition on corrupt persuasion of witnesses. The court read the corrupt persuasion prohibited by § 1512 to require an active attempt to persuade a witness to tell a false story, and used the language in § 1512 as a guide to interpret the omnibus clause of § 1503 narrowly.

* * *

The statute is structured as follows: first it proscribes persons from endeavoring to influence, intimidate, or impede grand or petit jurors or court officers in the discharge of their duties; it then prohibits injuring grand or petit jurors in their person or property because of any verdict or indictment rendered by them; it then prohibits injury of any court officer, commissioner, or similar officer on account of the performance of his official duties; finally, the "Omnibus Clause" serves as a catchall, prohibiting persons from endeavoring to influence, obstruct, or impede the due administration of justice. The latter clause, it can be seen, is far more general in scope than the earlier clauses of the statute. Respondent was charged with a violation of the Omnibus Clause, to wit: with "corruptly endeavoring to influence, obstruct, and impede the . . . grand jury investigation."

The first case from this Court construing the predecessor statute to § 1503 was *Pettibone v. United States*, 148 U.S. 197 (1893). There we held that "a person is not sufficiently charged with obstructing or impeding the due administration of justice in a court unless it appears that he knew or had notice that justice was being administered in such court." The Court reasoned that a person lacking knowledge of a pending proceeding necessarily lacked the evil intent to obstruct. Recent decisions of Courts of Appeals have likewise tended to place metes and bounds on the very broad language of the catchall provision. The action taken by the accused must be with an intent to influence judicial or grand jury proceedings; it is not enough that there be an intent to influence some ancillary proceeding, such as an investigation independent of the court's or grand jury's authority. Some courts have phrased this showing as a "nexus" requirement—that the act must have a relationship in time, causation, or logic with the judicial proceedings. In other words, the endeavor must have the " 'natural and probable effect' "of interfering with the due administration of justice. This is not to say that the defendant's actions need be successful; an "endeavor" suffices. But as in *Pettibone*, if the defendant lacks knowledge that his actions are likely to affect the judicial proceeding, he lacks the requisite intent to obstruct.

Although respondent urges various broader grounds for affirmance, we find it unnecessary to address them because we think the "nexus" requirement developed in the decisions of the Courts of Appeals is a correct construction of § 1503. We have traditionally exercised restraint in assessing the reach of a federal criminal statute, both out of deference to the prerogatives of Congress, *Dowling v. United States*, 473 U.S. 207 (1985), and out of concern that "a fair warning should be given to the world in language that the common world will understand, of what the law intends to do if a certain line is passed," *McBoyle v. United States*, 283 U.S. 25, 27 (1931). We do not believe that uttering false statements to an investigating agent—and that seems to be all that was proved here—who might or might not testify before a grand jury is sufficient to make out a violation of the catch-all provision of § 1503.

The Government did not show here that the agents acted as an arm of the grand jury, or indeed that the grand jury had even summoned the testimony of these particular agents. The Government argues that respondent "understood that his false statements would be provided to the grand jury" and that he made the statements with the intent to thwart the grand jury investigation and not just the FBI investigation.

The Government supports its argument with a citation to the transcript of the recorded conversation between Aguilar and the FBI agent at the point where Aguilar asks whether he is a target of a grand jury investigation. The agent responded to the question by stating:

> "There is a Grand Jury meeting. Convening I guess that's the correct word. Um some evidence will be heard I'm ... I'm sure on this issue."

Because respondent knew of the pending proceeding, the Government therefore contends that Aguilar's statements are analogous to those made directly to the grand jury itself, in the form of false testimony or false documents.

We think the transcript citation relied upon by the Government would not enable a rational trier of fact to conclude that respondent knew that his false statement would be provided to the grand jury, and that the evidence goes no further than showing that respondent testified falsely to an investigating agent. Such conduct, we believe, falls on the other side of the statutory line from that of one who delivers false documents or testimony to the grand jury itself. Conduct of the latter sort all but assures that the grand jury will consider the material in its deliberations. But what use will be made of false testimony given to an investigating agent who has not been subpoenaed or otherwise directed to appear before the grand jury is far more speculative. We think it cannot be said to have the "natural and probable effect" of interfering with the due administration of justice. Justice Scalia criticizes our treatment of the statutory language for reading the word "endeavor" out of it, inasmuch as it excludes defendants who have an evil purpose but use means that would "only unnaturally and improbably be successful." This criticism is unwarranted. Our reading of the statute gives the term "endeavor" a useful function to fulfill: It makes conduct punishable where the defendant acts with an intent to obstruct justice, and in a manner that is likely to obstruct justice, but is foiled in some way. Were a defendant with the requisite intent to lie to a subpoenaed witness who is ultimately not called to testify, or who testifies but does not transmit the defendant's version of the story, the defendant has endeavored to obstruct, but has not actually obstructed, justice. Under our approach, a jury could find such defendant guilty.

Justice Scalia also apparently believes that any act, done with the intent to "obstruct ... the due administration of justice," is sufficient to impose criminal liability. Under the dissent's theory, a man could be found guilty under § 1503 if he knew of a pending investigation and lied to his wife about his whereabouts at the time of the crime, thinking that an FBI agent might decide to interview her and that she might in turn be influenced in her statement to the agent by her husband's false account of his whereabouts. The intent to obstruct justice is indeed present, but the man's culpability is a good deal less clear from the statute than we usually require in order to impose criminal liability.

* * *

Notes

1. In *Aguilar*, there was a pending grand jury proceeding at the time the defendant made false statements to the FBI investigating agent and the evidence showed that defendant was told about it by the federal agent interviewing him. In *United States v. Frankhauser*, 80 F.3d 641 (1st Cir. 1996), the defendant advised a potential witness, the mother of the target of the grand jury investigation, to dispose of evidence that might be used against her son. Held: No violation of § 1503. The defendant knew that the FBI was investigating the suspect, but there was no evidence that the defendant knew that the investigation was connected to a grand jury proceeding (there was in fact a pending grand jury proceeding). Both *Aguilar* and *Frankhauser* reach the same result. Are the rationales the same in the two cases? Compare with the results in *Aguilar* and *Frankhauser*, the decision in *United States v. Brenson*, 104 F.3d 1267 (11th Cir. 1997) where a grand juror disclosed information about the content of the grand jury proceedings and its planned actions and agreed to provide information about further actions to the target of the grand jury investigation; inter alia, the grand juror was charged under the omnibus clause of § 1503. Held: It was reasonably foreseeable that the defendant's actions would have the probable effect of obstructing the due administration of justice; conviction affirmed.

2. For an application of the Aguilar doctrine but with a proviso in certain circumstances, see *United States v. Fassnacht,* 332 F.3d 440 (7th Cir. 2003):

> The dispute in this case essentially comes down to the question of the intended object of Fassnacht's and Malanga's obstructive efforts. The defendants argue that the government offered evidence which showed that, while they were aware of the grand jury proceeding, they only acted with an intent to mislead the *IRS investigation*. The government contends that there was sufficient evidence from which the jury could have concluded that the *grand jury investigation* was an object of the defendants' efforts. We agree with the government.

> This Court has previously held that conviction under § 1503's "corruptly endeavors" language requires, as an element of the offense, the specific intent to impede, obstruct, or interfere with a judicial proceeding. * * *

> A grand jury investigation constitutes the "due administration of justice" for purposes of § 1503, but an IRS investigation, standing alone, does not. * * *

> Further complicating the distinction between judicial proceedings and investigative efforts, we have held that an investigation by a government agency undertaken in direct support of a grand jury investigation constitutes the "due administration of justice." For example, in *United States v. Furkin*, the defendant failed to report income from certain gambling machines on his federal tax returns and was convicted of conspiracy to defraud the IRS; he was also convicted of obstruction of justice under § 1503 for his efforts to impede the criminal investigation into his tax evasion. 119 F.3d 1276, 1278–79 (7th Cir. 1997). In challeng-

ing his conviction under § 1503, Furkin argued that the evidence against him indicated, at most, an intent to impede the IRS investigation, but not the grand jury investigation. We disagreed, noting that the evidence demonstrated that "Furkin was also aware that the IRS was *integrally involved* in the grand jury investigation. . . . The IRS investigation was not some 'ancillary proceeding' unrelated to the grand jury investigation. Indeed, the IRS investigation and the grand jury investigation were *one and the same*, and the evidence established that Furkin understood this fact."

Like the situation in *Furkin*, there was sufficient evidence presented in this case for the jury to have rationally concluded that Fassnacht and Malanga were aware of the grand jury investigation into their tax returns and that they understood that the IRS agents were "integrally involved" in that grand jury investigation or, at the least, that the IRS agents would provide to the grand jury the information they garnered from the defendants.

* * *

Taking this evidence in the light most favorable to the government, as we must when reviewing the denial of a motion for judgment of acquittal, we believe that a jury could have rationally concluded that Fassnacht and Malanga intended that their conduct would have the "natural and probable effect" of impeding the investigation by the grand jury.

The evidence offered at trial—including Newell's testimony, the tape-recorded conversations, and other documentary evidence—indicated that after Fassnacht and Malanga became aware that a federal grand jury was involved in the investigation of their tax returns, they continued to stick with the finder's fee cover story, repeatedly making false statements to the IRS Criminal Investigation Division agents and creating fictitious documents to back up their false statements. References to the grand jury interspersed among the defendants' conversations in which they continued to refine their cover story provide a rational basis on which the jury could have concluded that the defendants were more than merely aware of the grand jury investigation, but that the grand jury was in fact an object of their obstructive efforts. In addition, even if it believed that the defendants' obstructive efforts were primarily aimed at the IRS agents, the jury was entitled to make the rational inference that Fassnacht and Malanga understood that the IRS agents were acting as the "arm of the grand jury," and that impeding the agents' efforts necessarily meant obstructing the grand jury.

3. Suppose the charge is conspiring to violate § 1503. What is the requisite mental state for such a charge after *Aguilar*? *See United States v. Vaghela*, 169 F.3d 729 (11th Cir.1999): Defendant and another drafted a backdated contract to conceal illegal kickbacks. At the time there was no pending grand jury inquiry. The government argued that "it is enough for the government to prove that the conspirators undertook to obstruct the due administration of justice in a federal proceeding that they anticipated would commence in the future." Held: The government need not always show that a judicial proceeding existed at the time the defendants formed the conspira-

cy, but "must demonstrate that the actions the conspirators agreed to take were directly intended to prevent or otherwise obstruct the processes of a specific judicial proceeding in a way that is more than merely speculative." The court also stated:

> In a broad and colloquial sense, every criminal act is an obstruction of justice, as is every effort to conceal that criminal act. However, as we noted earlier, such a broad and literal reading of the definition of this criminal offense is inconsistent with *Aguilar*.

4. In *Vaghela, supra* note 3, the court cited *United States v. Messerlian* 832 F.2d 778 (3d Cir.1987) as an illustration of a case where a conspiracy to obstruct justice charge would lie even though there was no pending grand jury proceeding because the defendants were found to have taken steps and agreed to prevent a future grand jury investigation into the specific matter: "[T]he direct object of the actions agreed to by the conspirators * * * was to prevent or otherwise obstruct the commencement of a grand jury investigation into circumstances surrounding the * * * death * * *."

5. See *United States v. Schwarz*, 283 F.3d 76 (2d Cir. 2002), a federal civil rights prosecution in which there was also a charge of conspiracy to obstruct justice. The facts in the case involved a brutal sodomization of an arrested person by police officers using a broom handle in a stationhouse bathroom. The victim had been arrested in an incident involving a street fight among patrons of a night club. [For a fuller statement of the facts in the same case, see *United States v. Bruder,* 103 F.Supp.2d 155 (E.D. NY. 2000).] The defendant police officer, Bruder, among other police officers, had told conflicting stories about what transpired in the stationhouse. Although Bruder was involved in the arrest, he was not himself present or involved in the bathroom incident. Bruder was served with a grand jury document subpoena two days before he made allegedly false statements to federal investigators and prosecutors. The court stated:

> The government argues that Aguilar is inapposite because it concerned the sufficiency of the evidence to support a conviction for a substantive § 1503 violation, whereas here only a conspiracy was charged so that the government was not obligated to prove that the conduct at issue violated § 1503. But to prove a conspiracy, the government must show that the defendants "knowingly engaged in the conspiracy with the specific intent to commit the offense[] that [was] the object[] of the conspiracy." * * *This the government has failed to do.

* * *

> At oral argument before us, the government urged that this case is distinguishable from Aguilar because Bruder initiated a meeting with the federal investigators and prosecutors that had served him with a federal grand jury subpoena for his documents. The government contends that Bruder's conduct was sufficient to demonstrate that he intended to influence the grand jury. The government in Aguilar made a similar argument—namely, that because the judge had been informed that there was a pending grand jury investigation into the matter, the judge " 'understood that his false statements would be provided to the grand jury' and that he made the statements with the intent to thwart

the grand jury investigation." However, the Supreme Court rejected this argument on the ground that the judge's mere knowledge of the pending grand jury investigation "would not enable a rational trier of fact to conclude that respondent knew that his false statement would be provided to the grand jury," We must do so here for the same reason.

We see no meaningful distinction between this case and Aguilar. The fatal defect in the government's case is that there was no showing that Bruder, who had been subpoenaed only for his memo book, knew that the allegedly false statements he made to the federal investigators on November 8, 1997 would be conveyed to the federal grand jury. Bruder had not himself been called to testify and there is no evidence that the investigators gave him any indication that they would repeat his statements to the grand jury. He may have hoped that they would be provided to the grand jury, and surely there was that possibility; but there was insufficient evidence to "enable a rational trier of fact to conclude that [Bruder] knew" that this would happen or that he entertained any expectations on that score that were based on such knowledge. At best, the government proved that Bruder, knowing of the existence of a federal grand jury investigation, lied to federal investigators regarding issues pertinent to the grand jury's investigation. The government has therefore failed to offer sufficient evidence of Bruder's intent to obstruct the federal grand jury for if the defendant lacks knowledge that his actions are likely to affect the judicial proceeding, he lacks the requisite intent to obstruct."

6. What circumstances might be sufficient to prove that Bruder knew that his false statements would be communicated to the grand jury? Must the federal investigators tell him that they are going to convey his statements to the grand jury? Is the import of the decision in *Schwarz* that in order to support a charge under § 1503 the investigator must give warnings somewhat parallel to the *Miranda* warnings—they might be called *Aguilar* warnings—telling the individual that anything he/she says "may"(?) "will" (?) be communicated to the grand jury.

7. Is the court in *Schwarz* applying Aguilar too strictly? Bruder not only knew that the grand jury was investigating the matter; he knew that the grand jury was interested in obtaining certain kinds of information from him; he had received a grand jury subpoena for documents.

Is there another explanation for *Aguilar*, which itself seemed to adopt a rather strict view of the type of knowledge required to impose criminal liability? Recall that both Aguilar and Bruder were prosecuted under the omnibus clause of 1503. Both were being prosecuted for false statements made in the course of an interview by investigating agents. Might there be some judicial reluctance to use the broad language of the omnibus clause to prosecute this type of conduct, and this reluctance produces a rather strict interpretation of the statute in such contexts. (Compare Chapter 15, supra, where some judicial decisions interpreting 18 U.S.C. § 1001, may be viewed as reflecting a similar kind of judicial reluctance but where the statute is much more specific.)

8. Is the approach taken by the court in *Schwarz* consistent with the decision in *Fassnacht*, supra, note 2.

9. The preceding notes describe cases that hold that under § 1503 there need not be a pending grand jury proceeding where the charge is conspiracy and there is a specific intent to obstruct the processes of a specific proceeding. Might a similar result be reached in the absence of a conspiracy, that is, where a single individual is involved, and he or she has the type of specific intent described above? What language in § 1503 bears on the answer to this question?

10. Compare the interpretation of the "nexus" requirement in applying § 1503 with the application of a similar requirement under § 1512, infra.

11. Construing the term "corruptly" in § 1503, the court in *United States v. Russo*, 104 F.3d 431 (D.C.Cir.1997), stated:

> Anyone who intentionally lies to a grand jury is on notice that he may be corruptly obstructing the grand jury's investigation. Whatever the outer limits of "corruptly" in 1503, * * * acts of perjury * * * [are] near its center. * * * As we said [in a prior case], "very few non-corrupt ways to or reason for intentionally obstructing a judicial proceeding leap to mind."

Also see *United States v. Thompson*, 76 F.3d 442 (2d Cir.1996), which adopted the view expounded by earlier cases that "corruptly" in § 1503 means "motivated by an improper purpose."

B. § 1512: DOCUMENT DESTRUCTION AS OB-STRUCTION OF JUSTICE: "CORRUPTLY PER-SUADES"; THE NEXUS REQUIREMENT

The current version of § 1512, Title 18, U.S.C. is reproduced below. The statute was amended in 2002 by the 21st Century Department of Justice Appropriations Act and the Sarbanes Oxley Act.

§ 1512.   Tampering with a witness, victim, or an informant

(a) (1) Whoever kills or attempts to kill another person, with intent to—

> (A) prevent the attendance or testimony of any person in an official proceeding;

> (B) prevent the production of a record, document, or other object, in an official proceeding; or

> (C) prevent the communication by any person to a law enforcement officer or judge of the United States of information relating to the commission or possible commission of a Federal offense or a violation of conditions of probation, parole, or release pending judicial proceedings;

shall be punished as provided in paragraph (3).

(2) Whoever uses physical force or the threat of physical force against any person, or attempts to do so, with intent to—

(A) influence, delay, or prevent the testimony of any person in an official proceeding;

(B) cause or induce any person to—

(i) withhold testimony, or withhold a record, document, or other object, from an official proceeding;

(ii) alter, destroy, mutilate, or conceal an object with intent to impair the integrity or availability of the object for use in an official proceeding;

(iii) evade legal process summoning that person to appear as a witness, or to produce a record, document, or other object, in an official proceeding; or

(iv) be absent from an official proceeding to which that person has been summoned by legal process; or

(C) hinder, delay, or prevent the communication to a law enforcement officer or judge of the United States of information relating to the commission or possible commission of a Federal offense or a violation of conditions of probation, supervised release, parole, or release pending judicial proceedings;

shall be punished as provided in paragraph (3).

(3) The punishment for an offense under this subsection is—

(A) in the case of murder (as defined in section 1111 [18 USCS § 1111]), the death penalty or imprisonment for life, and in the case of any other killing, the punishment provided in section 1112 [18 USCS § 1112];

(B) in the case of—

(i) an attempt to murder; or

(ii) the use or attempted use of physical force against any person;

imprisonment for not more than 20 years; and

(C) in the case of the threat of use of physical force against any person, imprisonment for not more than 10 years.

(b) Whoever knowingly uses intimidation, threatens or corruptly persuades another person, or attempts to do so, or engages in misleading conduct toward another person, with intent to—

(1) influence, delay or prevent the testimony of any person in an official proceeding;

(2) cause or induce any person to—

(A) withhold testimony, or withhold a record, document, or other object, from an official proceeding;

(B) alter, destroy, mutilate, or conceal an object with intent to impair the object's integrity or availability for use in an official proceeding;

(C) evade legal process summoning that person to appear as a witness, or to produce a record, document, or other object, in an official proceeding; or

(D) be absent from an official proceeding to which such person has been summoned by legal process; or

(3) hinder, delay, or prevent the communication to a law enforcement officer or judge of the United States of information relating to the commission or possible commission of a Federal offense or a violation of conditions of probation, supervised release, parole, or release pending judicial proceedings;

shall be fined under this title or imprisoned not more than ten years, or both.

(c) Whoever corruptly—

(1) alters, destroys, mutilates, or conceals a record, document, or other object, or attempts to do so, with the intent to impair the object's integrity or availability for use in an official proceeding; or

(2) otherwise obstructs, influences, or impedes any official proceeding, or attempts to do so,

shall be fined under this title or imprisoned not more than 20 years, or both.

(d) Whoever intentionally harasses another person and thereby hinders, delays, prevents, or dissuades any person from—

(1) attending or testifying in an official proceeding;

(2) reporting to a law enforcement officer or judge of the United States the commission or possible commission of a Federal offense or a violation of conditions of probation, supervised release, parole, or release pending judicial proceedings;

(3) arresting or seeking the arrest of another person in connection with a Federal offense; or

(4) causing a criminal prosecution, or a parole or probation revocation proceeding, to be sought or instituted, or assisting in such prosecution or proceeding;

or attempts to do so, shall be fined under this title or imprisoned not more than one year, or both.

(e) In a prosecution for an offense under this section, it is an affirmative defense, as to which the defendant has the burden of proof by a preponderance of the evidence, that the conduct consisted solely of lawful conduct and that the defendant's sole intention was to encourage, induce, or cause the other person to testify truthfully.

(f) For the purposes of this section—

(1) an official proceeding need not be pending or about to be instituted at the time of the offense; and

(2) the testimony, or the record, document, or other object need not be admissible in evidence or free of a claim of privilege.

(g) In a prosecution for an offense under this section, no state of mind need be proved with respect to the circumstance—

(1) that the official proceeding before a judge, court, magistrate, grand jury, or government agency is before a judge or court of the United States, a United States magistrate [United States magistrate judge], a bankruptcy judge, a Federal grand jury, or a Federal Government agency; or

(2) that the judge is a judge of the United States or that the law enforcement officer is an officer or employee of the Federal Government or a person authorized to act for or on behalf of the Federal Government or serving the Federal Government as an adviser or consultant.

(h) There is extraterritorial Federal jurisdiction over an offense under this section.

(i) A prosecution under this section or section 1503 [18 USCS § 1503] may be brought in the district in which the official proceeding (whether or not pending or about to be instituted) was intended to be affected or in the district in which the conduct constituting the alleged offense occurred.

(j) If the offense under this section occurs in connection with a trial of a criminal case, the maximum term of imprisonment which may be imposed for the offense shall be the higher of that otherwise provided by law or the maximum term that could have been imposed for any offense charged in such case.

(k) Whoever conspires to commit any offense under this section shall be subject to the same penalties as those prescribed for the offense the commission of which was the object of the conspiracy.

———

The Enron scandal and the subsequent prosecution of a major accounting firm which had been the auditor of Enron highlighted the usefulness, from the government's perspective, of the obstruction of justice statutes in the investigation and prosecution of complex financial transactions. In 2001, Enron, one of the world's largest electricity and natural gas traders, first announced a $618 million third quarter loss, and then announced that it had overstated its earnings by $567 million since 1997. Shortly thereafter it filed for bankruptcy and announced 4000 layoffs. These events triggered an SEC investigation and eventually a criminal investigation into the labyrinth of complex accounting procedures Enron had used to obscure its financial situation.

The first prosecutions did not focus on the underlying transactions. Instead prosecutors targeted the Arthur Andersen accounting firm and focused on its conduct in seeking to block the earliest stages of the investigation. No SEC or criminal proceeding had been instituted at the time of the events in question, so § 1503 was not available as a basis for prosecution. Instead, Andersen was charged under § 1512(b). The case reached the Supreme Court in the 2004–2005 term. (Note: Andersen was prosecuted under the year 2000 version of the statute. The amendments of § 1512 reflected in the language reproduced supra, were enacted in 2002, subsequent to the initiation of the prosecution of the case. Accordingly, the amended language was not before the Court. A question to be addressed below is whether if subsection (c) which was added in 2002 had been in effect at the time, would it have changed the result in the *Andersen* case?

ARTHUR ANDERSEN LLP v. UNITED STATES

__ U.S. __, 125 S.Ct. 2129, 161 L.Ed.2d 1008 (2005).

CHIEF JUSTICE REHNQUIST delivered the opinion of the Court.

As Enron Corporation's financial difficulties became public in 2001, petitioner Arthur Andersen LLP, Enron's auditor, instructed its employees to destroy documents pursuant to its document retention policy. A jury found that this action made petitioner guilty of violating 18 U.S.C. §§ 1512(b)(2)(A) and (B). These sections make it a crime to "knowingly us[e] intimidation or physical force, threate[n], or corruptly persuad[e] another person ... with intent to ... cause" that person to "withhold" documents from, or "alter" documents for use in, an "official proceeding."[1] The Court of Appeals for the Fifth Circuit affirmed. We hold that the jury instructions failed to convey properly the elements of a "corrup[t] persuas[ion]" conviction under § 1512(b), and therefore reverse.

Enron Corporation, during the 1990's, switched its business from operation of natural gas pipelines to an energy conglomerate, a move that was accompanied by aggressive accounting practices and rapid growth. Petitioner audited Enron's publicly filed financial statements and provided internal audit and consulting services to it. Petitioner's "engagement team" for Enron was headed by David Duncan. Beginning in 2000, Enron's financial performance began to suffer, and, as 2001 wore on, worsened. On August 14, 2001, Jeffrey Skilling, Enron's Chief Executive Officer (CEO), unexpectedly resigned. Within days, Sherron Watkins, a senior accountant at Enron, warned Kenneth Lay, Enron's newly reappointed CEO, that Enron could "implode in a wave of accounting scandals." She likewise informed Duncan and Michael Odom, one of petitioner's partners who had supervisory responsibility over Duncan, of the looming problems.

On August 28, an article in the Wall Street Journal suggested improprieties at Enron, and the SEC opened an informal investigation. By early September, petitioner had formed an Enron "crisis-response"

---

1. We refer to the 2000 version of the statute, which has since been amended by Congress.

team, which included Nancy Temple, an in-house counsel.[3] On October 8, petitioner retained outside counsel to represent it in any litigation that might arise from the Enron matter. The next day, Temple discussed Enron with other in-house counsel. Her notes from that meeting reflect that "some SEC investigation" is "highly probable."

On October 10, Odom spoke at a general training meeting attended by 89 employees, including 10 from the Enron engagement team. Odom urged everyone to comply with the firm's document retention policy.[4] He added: " '[I]f it's destroyed in the course of [the] normal policy and litigation is filed the next day, that's great..... [W]e've followed our own policy, and whatever there was that might have been of interest to somebody is gone and irretrievable.' " On October 12, Temple entered the Enron matter into her computer, designating the "Type of Potential Claim" as "Professional Practice–Government/Regulatory Inv[estigation]." Temple also e-mailed Odom, suggesting that he " 'remin[d] the engagement team of our documentation and retention policy.' "

On October 16, Enron announced its third quarter results. That release disclosed a $1.01 billion charge to earnings. The following day, the SEC notified Enron by letter that it had opened an investigation in August and requested certain information and documents. On October 19, Enron forwarded a copy of that letter to petitioner.

On the same day, Temple also sent an e-mail to a member of petitioner's internal team of accounting experts and attached a copy of the document policy. On October 20, the Enron crisis-response team held a conference call, during which Temple instructed everyone to "[m]ake sure to follow the [document] policy." On October 23, Enron CEO Lay declined to answer questions during a call with analysts because of "potential lawsuits, as well as the SEC inquiry." *Ibid.* After the call, Duncan met with other Andersen partners on the Enron engagement team and told them that they should ensure team members were complying with the document policy. Another meeting for all team members followed, during which Duncan distributed the policy and told everyone to comply. These, and other smaller meetings, were followed by substantial destruction of paper and electronic documents.

---

3. A key accounting problem involved Enron's use of "Raptors," which were special purpose entities used to engage in "off-balance-sheet" activities. Petitioner's engagement team had allowed Enron to "aggregate" the Raptors for accounting purposes so that they reflected a positive return. This was, in the words of petitioner's experts, a "black-and-white" violation of Generally Accepted Accounting Principles. Brief for United States 2.

4. The firm's policy called for a single central engagement file, which "should contain only that information which is relevant to supporting our work." The policy stated that, "in cases of threatened litigation, ... no related information will be destroyed." It also separately provided that, if petitioner is "advised of litigation or subpoenas regarding a particular engagement, the related information should not be destroyed. See Policy Statement No. 780–Notification of Litigation." Policy Statement No. 780 set forth "notification" procedures for whenever "professional practice litigation against [petitioner] or any of its personnel has been commenced, has been threatened or is judged likely to occur, or when governmental or professional investigations that may involve [petitioner] or any of its personnel have been commenced or are judged likely."

On October 26, one of petitioner's senior partners circulated a New York Times article discussing the SEC's response to Enron. His e-mail commented that "the problems are just beginning and we will be in the cross hairs. The marketplace is going to keep the pressure on this and is going to force the SEC to be tough." On October 30, the SEC opened a formal investigation and sent Enron a letter that requested accounting documents.

Throughout this time period, the document destruction continued, despite reservations by some of petitioner's managers. On November 8, Enron announced that it would issue a comprehensive restatement of its earnings and assets. Also on November 8, the SEC served Enron and petitioner with subpoenas for records. On November 9, Duncan's secretary sent an e-mail that stated: "Per Dave—No more shredding.... We have been officially served for our documents." *Id.*, at 10. Enron filed for bankruptcy less than a month later. Duncan was fired and later pleaded guilty to witness tampering.

In March 2002, petitioner was indicted in the Southern District of Texas on one count of violating §§ 1512(b)(2)(A) and (B). The indictment alleged that, between October 10 and November 9, 2001, petitioner "did knowingly, intentionally and corruptly persuade ... other persons, to wit: [petitioner's] employees, with intent to cause" them to withhold documents from, and alter documents for use in, "official proceedings, namely: regulatory and criminal proceedings and investigations." A jury trial followed. When the case went to the jury, that body deliberated for seven days and then declared that it was deadlocked. The District Court delivered an *"Allen* charge," *Allen v. United States,* 164 U.S. 492, 17 S.Ct. 154, 41 L.Ed. 528 (1896), and, after three more days of deliberation, the jury returned a guilty verdict. The District Court denied petitioner's motion for a judgment of acquittal.

The Court of Appeals for the Fifth Circuit affirmed. 374 F.3d, at 284. It held that the jury instructions properly conveyed the meaning of "corruptly persuades" and "official proceeding"; that the jury need not find any consciousness of wrongdoing; and that there was no reversible error. Because of a split of authority regarding the meaning of § 1512(b), we granted certiorari.

Chapter 73 of Title 18 of the United States Code provides criminal sanctions for those who obstruct justice. Sections 1512(b)(2)(A) and (B), part of the witness tampering provisions, provide in relevant part:

> "Whoever knowingly uses intimidation or physical force, threatens, or corruptly persuades another person, or attempts to do so, or engages in misleading conduct toward another person, with intent to ... cause or induce any person to ... withhold testimony, or withhold a record, document, or other object, from an official proceeding [or] alter, destroy, mutilate, or conceal an object with intent to impair the object's integrity or availability for use in an official proceeding ... shall be fined under this title or imprisoned not more than ten years, or both."

In this case, our attention is focused on what it means to "knowingly . . . corruptly persuad[e]" another person "with intent to . . . cause" that person to "withhold" documents from, or "alter" documents for use in, an "official proceeding."

We have traditionally exercised restraint in assessing the reach of a federal criminal statute, both out of deference to the prerogatives of Congress, , and out of concern that 'a fair warning should be given to the world in language that the common world will understand, of what the law intends to do if a certain line is passed,'.

Such restraint is particularly appropriate here, where the act underlying the conviction—"persua[sion]"—is by itself innocuous. Indeed, "persuad[ing]" a person "with intent to . . . cause" that person to "withhold" testimony or documents from a Government proceeding or Government official is not inherently malign. Consider, for instance, a mother who suggests to her son that he invoke his right against compelled self-incrimination, , or a wife who persuades her husband not to disclose marital confidences, ...

Nor is it necessarily corrupt for an attorney to "persuad[e]" a client "with intent to . . . cause" that client to "withhold" documents from the Government. * * *

"Document retention policies," which are created in part to keep certain information from getting into the hands of others, including the Government, are common in business. See generally Chase, To Shred or Not to Shred: Document Retention Policies and Federal Obstruction of Justice Statutes, 8 Ford. J. Corp. & Fin. L. 721 (2003). It is, of course, not wrongful for a manager to instruct his employees to comply with a valid document retention policy under ordinary circumstances.

Acknowledging this point, the parties have largely focused their attention on the word "corruptly" as the key to what may or may not lawfully be done in the situation presented here. Section 1512(b) punishes not just "corruptly persuad[ing]" another, but "*knowingly* corruptly persuad[ing]" another. (Emphasis added.) The Government suggests that "knowingly" does not modify "corruptly persuades," but that is not how the statute most naturally reads. It provides the *mens rea*—"knowingly"—and then a list of acts—"uses intimidation or physical force, threatens, or corruptly persuades." We have recognized with regard to similar statutory language that the *mens rea* at least applies to the acts that immediately follow, if not to other elements down the statutory chain. * * * The Government suggests that it is "questionable whether Congress would employ such an inelegant formulation as 'knowingly . . . corruptly persuades.' "Long experience has not taught us to share the Government's doubts on this score, and we must simply interpret the statute as written.

The parties have not pointed us to another interpretation of "knowingly . . . corruptly" to guide us here. In any event, the natural meaning of these terms provides a clear answer "[K]nowledge" and "knowingly" are normally associated with awareness, understanding, or consciousness. See Black's Law Dictionary 888 (8th ed.2004) (hereinafter Black's); Webster's Third New International Dictionary 1252–1253 (1993) (hereinafter Webster's 3d); American Heritage Dictionary of the English Language 725 (1981) (hereinafter Am. Hert.). "Corrupt" and "corruptly" are normally associated with wrongful, immoral, depraved, or evil. See Black's 371; Webster's 3d 512; Am. Hert. 299–300. Joining these meanings together here makes sense both linguistically and in the statutory scheme. Only persons conscious of wrongdoing can be said to "knowingly ... corruptly persuad[e]." And limiting criminality to persuaders conscious of their wrongdoing sensibly allows § 1512(b) to reach only those with the level of "culpability ... we usually require in order to impose criminal liability." *United States v. Aguilar,* 515 U.S., at 602, 115 S.Ct. 2357;

The outer limits of this element need not be explored here because the jury instructions at issue simply failed to convey the requisite consciousness of wrongdoing. Indeed, it is striking how little culpability the instructions required. For example, the jury was told that, "even if [petitioner] honestly and sincerely believed that its conduct was lawful, you may find [petitioner] guilty." App. JA–213. The instructions also diluted the meaning of "corruptly" so that it covered innocent conduct.

The parties vigorously disputed how the jury would be instructed on "corruptly." The District Court based its instruction on the definition of that term found in the Fifth Circuit Pattern Jury Instruction for § 1503. This pattern instruction defined "corruptly" as " 'knowingly and dishonestly, with the specific intent to subvert or undermine the integrity' " of a proceeding. The Government, however, insisted on excluding "dishonestly" and adding the term "impede" to the phrase "subvert or undermine." *Ibid.* (internal quotation marks omitted). The District Court agreed over petitioner's objections, and the jury was told to convict if it found petitioner intended to "subvert, undermine, or impede" governmental factfinding by suggesting to its employees that they enforce the document retention policy.

These changes were significant. No longer was any type of "dishonest[y]" necessary to a finding of guilt, and it was enough for petitioner to have simply "impede[d]" the Government's factfinding ability. As the Government conceded at oral argument, " 'impede' " has broader connotations than " 'subvert' " or even " 'undermine,' ", and many of these connotations do not incorporate any "corrupt[ness]" at all. The dictionary defines "impede" as "to interfere with or get in the way of the progress of" or "hold up" or "detract from." Webster's 3d 1132. By definition, anyone who innocently persuades another to withhold information from the Government "get[s] in the way of the progress of" the Government. With regard to such innocent conduct, the "corruptly" instructions did no limiting work whatsoever.

The instructions also were infirm for another reason. They led the jury to believe that it did not have to find *any* nexus between the "persua [sion]" to destroy documents and any particular proceeding. In resisting any type of nexus element, the Government relies heavily on § 1512(e)(1), which states that an official proceeding "need not be pending or about to be instituted at the time of the offense." It is, however, one thing to say that a proceeding "need not be pending or about to be instituted at the time of the offense," and quite another to say a proceeding need not even be foreseen. A "knowingly ... corrup[t] persaude[r]" cannot be someone who persuades others to shred documents under a document retention policy when he does not have in contemplation any particular official proceeding in which those documents might be material.

We faced a similar situation in *Aguilar*. Respondent Aguilar lied to a Federal Bureau of Investigation agent in the course of an investigation and was convicted of " 'corruptly endeavor[ing] to influence, obstruct, and impede [a] ... grand jury investigation' " under § 1503. All the Government had shown was that Aguilar had uttered false statements to an investigating agent "who might or might not testify before a grand jury." We held that § 1503 required something more—specifically, a "nexus" between the obstructive act and the proceeding. "[I]f the defendant lacks knowledge that his actions are likely to affect the judicial proceeding," we explained, "he lacks the requisite intent to obstruct."

For these reasons, the jury instructions here were flawed in important respects. The judgment of the Court of Appeals is reversed, and the case is remanded for further proceedings consistent with this opinion.

It is so ordered.

Notes

1. For pre-*Andersen* case law dealing with the interpretation of "corruptly" and the nexus requirement under § 1512 (b)(2), see *United States v. Frankhauser*, 80 F.3d 641 (1st Cir.1996). See note 1, supra, p. 763 for the facts in the case. The court stated:

> Because an official proceeding need not be pending * * *, the statute obviously cannot require actual knowledge of a pending proceeding. On the other hand, the defendant must act knowingly and with the intent to impair an object's availability for use in a particular official proceeding * * *.

> There was no dispute that * * * [on the date in question] Frankhauser knew that the FBI was investigating Brian Clayton. His warnings to Mrs. Clayton that her son could go to jail unless she followed his instructions * * * [was] direct evidence that he in fact expected a grand jury investigation and/or a trial in the foreseeable future, and that his intent was to make the items unavailable for use in such a proceeding. * * * His prior conviction for participating in a conspiracy to obstruct justice by advising destruction of documents gave him notice that his advice to Mrs. Clayton was illegal, thus establishing that he acted with corrupt intent to violate the law.

Compare with *Frankhauser* the ruling in *United States v. Farrell*, 126 F.3d 484, 488 (3d Cir.1997):

> Thus, we are confident that both attempting to bribe someone to withhold information and attempting to persuade someone to provide false information to federal investigators constitute "corrupt persuasion" punishable under § 1512(b).... [W]e are similarly confident that the "culpable conduct" that violates § 1512(b)(3) "corruptly persuades" clause does not include a noncoercive attempt to persuade a coconspirator who enjoys a Fifth Amendment right not to disclose self-incriminating information about the conspiracy to refrain, in accordance with that right, from volunteering information to investigators.

For a case presenting a fact situation similar to that addressed in the first sentence of the quotation from *Farrell*, supra, see *United States v. Khatami*, 280 F.3d 907 (9th Cir. 2002), where the underlying criminal conduct involved falsely claiming that she had no independent sources of income in order to receive social security disability benefits over a seven year period—in fact she earned a living baby sitting children in her neighborhood. The defendant allegedly asked two of the people who employed her as a babysitter to lie and tell the government agent that they had not been compensating her for her services.

Suppose the defendant attempts to persuade a person not to speak with federal agents in a situation where that person has relevant incriminating information, and that person has no fifth amendment right since there is nothing in what he might say that would tend to incriminate him. See *United States v. Shotts*, 145 F.3d 1289 (11th Cir. 1998) (conviction affirmed).

2. Suppose Arthur Andersen had been prosecuted under § 1512(c), supra, p. 769, the new subsection added by Sarbanes Oxley. Would the prosecution have been more successful than in the actual case?

3. The nexus issue, which is addressed at the end of the *Andersen* opinion, has posed some problems of application under § 1512. For example, see *United States v. Gabriel*, 125 F.3d 89 (2d Cir.1997): Defendant was charged with witness tampering under § 1512 (b)(1) which makes it a crime to "corruptly persuade another person * * * or engage in misleading conduct toward another person with intent to * * * influence * * * the testimony of any person in an official proceeding." The government's theory was that the defendant told a potential witness a false story intending that the witness believe the story and testify to it before the grand jury. Defendant argued that there was insufficient evidence that the potential witness was likely to testify (he was in Australia and beyond the grand jury's subpoena power). The court ruled:

> * * * [T]he government was not required to prove that Mealing was likely to testify or that Gabriel actions were likely to affect Mealing testimony. Rather, the government was required to prove only that Gabriel endeavored corruptly to persuade or mislead Mealing with the intent of influencing Mealing potential testimony before a grand jury. *Id.* at 103.

In *Gabriel*, the court ruled that under § 1512 (b)(1), there is no requirement that the actions of the defendant be "likely to affect" a judicial proceeding, while in *Aguilar*, the Court imposed a "likely to affect" requirement with regard to the omnibus clause of § 1503. What are the grounds for distinguishing between the two provisions?

4.   In *United States v. Veal*, 153 F.3d 1233 (11th Cir.1998), the defendants were charged with a violation of § 1512 (b)(3) (engaging in misleading conduct toward another person "with intent to * * * hinder * * * the communication to a law enforcement officer or judge of the United States of information relating to the commission * * * of a Federal offense * * *.") The defendants, all local police officers, misled state investigators, "thereby precluding their communicating ... [the actual] facts [regarding the death of a drug dealer, the victim of police-involved use of force] to the Federal Bureau of Investigation...." Three days after the defendants made their statements to state investigators, a federal civil rights investigation was initiated. Held: the conduct of the defendants falls within the language of 1512(b)(3).

C. KINDS OF CONDUCT CONSTITUTING AN OBSTRUCTION OF JUSTICE

1.   The materials in the previous section provide some illustrations of the different kinds of conduct that can constitute an obstruction of justice under one or more of the relevant statutory provisions. In this section, we illustrate further the point made in the Introduction to this Chapter, regarding the different kinds of conduct that can constitute an obstruction, "a variety limited only by the imagination of the criminally inclined."

2.   In *United States v. Collis*, 128 F.3d 313 (6th Cir.1997), a fabricated letter allegedly written by the defendant's employer in support of leniency was submitted by defendant's lawyer to the judge in a supervised release parole violation hearing. The judge gave the defendant a lenient sentence. It was learned that the letter was a forgery. At defendant's trial for violating § 1503, his lawyer in the earlier matter testified the defendant had given him the letter. Defendant's conviction under § 1503 was affirmed.

3.   In *United States v. Cueto*, 151 F.3d 620 (7th Cir.1998), the defendant was a lawyer who was charged with obstruction of justice under § 1503. Defendant acted as a legal advisor to V, an individual who was subsequently indicted and convicted on federal racketeering charges relating to an illegal gambling business. A state investigator, R, had assumed an undercover role for the FBI as a corrupt liquor agent in an attempt to gather evidence against V and his company. At one point, R solicited a bribe from V, indicating that he could avoid further investigations of his illegal gambling operation. Acting on the defendant's advice, it was arranged for the defendant's law partner to report to the state investigating agency that R had solicited a bribe and a letter was drafted by the defendant and V accusing R of corrupt conduct and delivered to the local prosecutor. The defendant filed a complaint against R in state court alleging that R was a corrupt agent, and served him with a

subpoena which required him to appear in 15 minutes for an injunction hearing in state court on the question of whether a restraining order should be issued, enjoining him from extortion and interfering with V's business. At the hearing, R was questioned by the defendant about the FBI's covert investigation, and the state court issued a preliminary injunction. Subsequently, the injunction was dissolved by the federal district court.

The evidence in defendant's obstruction of justice trial showed that he had developed more than a professional attorney-client relationship with V, having entered into various financial transactions and business deals, some of which involved secret partnerships. The theory of the obstruction of justice charge was that the defendant corruptly endeavored to use his office as an attorney to obstruct the administration of justice in various court proceedings involving the prosecution of V, by filing various pleadings against R, by his attempts to persuade the local prosecutor to indict R, and by preparing and filing and urging defense counsel to prepare and file false pleadings and court papers in connection with the racketeering case. The court in affirming defendant's conviction stated:

> There is little case authority directly on point to consider whether an attorney acting in his professional capacity could be criminally liable under the omnibus clause of § 1503 for traditional litigation-related conduct that results in an obstruction of justice.

> * * *

> An amicus brief file by the National Association of Criminal Defense Lawyers * * * also questions the proper scope of the omnibus clause of § 1503, and the Association articulates its fears that if we affirm * * * [defendant] conviction * * *, criminal defense attorneys will be subject to future prosecutions not only for actual misconduct, but also for apparent and inadvertent wrongdoing, notwithstanding a lawyer's good faith advocacy. * * * [W]e are also concerned with the flip side of * * * [the Association's] argument. If lawyers are not punished for their criminal conduct and corrupt endeavors to manipulate the administration of justice, the result would be * * * the weakening of an ethical adversarial system and the undermining of just administration of the law.

> We cannot ignore * * * [defendant's] corrupt endeavors to manipulate the administration of justice and his clear criminal violations of the law. *Id.* at 631–32.

4. Numerous questions regarding possible obstruction of justice charges were raised in connection with the allegations that President Clinton attempted to cover up an affair with Ms. Monica Lewinsky. President Clinton's critics charged that he (or someone acting on his behalf) transferred Lewinsky to a Pentagon position to prevent her discovery by counsel for Paula Jones who was suing the President and whose lawyer was seeking to prove a pattern of misconduct on the part

of the President vis-a-vis female employees. Assume that the critics' allegations can be proved. Was the President's conduct violative of any federal obstruction of justice provisions? Which ones? Assume further that the allegation could be proved that the President had his secretary retrieve the gifts he had given Lewinsky so that Lewinsky could truthfully deny having anything in her possession that would be responsive to a subpoena. Would that constitute witness tampering? Under which provision (s)?

5. *United States v. Weber* 320 F.3d 1047 (9th Cir. 2003) further illustrates the broad uses to which § 1503 can be put. Weber had been convicted of wire fraud and sentenced to 33 months of incarceration and three years of supervised release. During the period of supervised release, he fled the country and the judge in his case issued an arrest warrant. During the course of his travels abroad, he telephoned the Secret Service agent who had originally arrested him between 20 and 40 times and telephoned his Probation Officer a dozen times. During one of these calls, among other wild statements punctuated by cursing, he stated: "... I'm gonna shoot a * * * federal judge right in the * * * head. ... I'll take * * * Singleton [the judge in his case] out with a high powered Russian rifle. You understand." He was indicted on one count of threatening an act of terrorism in violation of 18 U.S.C. § 2332(a)(2) and one count of obstructing justice in violation of § 1503. His conviction was affirmed. Also see *United States v. Fleming*, 215 F.3d 930 (9th Cir. 2000) where the basis for a 1503 charge were harassing acts against the district judge who had dismissed the defendant's law suit against the State Bar of California and the American Bar Association (in which he sought a judgment that the practice of law should not be limited to lawyers). The acts of harassment involved trying to file a lien on real property owned by the judge and his wife and leaving a copy of the lien in the judge's mail box.

6. Destruction of documents may be charged under § 1503 as well as under § 1512. See, e.g., *United States v. Triumph Capital Group, Inc.*, 260 F.Supp.2d 470 (D.Conn. 2003).

7. *United States v. Jackson,* 204 F.Supp.2d 1126 (N.D. Ill. 2002) upheld the use of a 1503 charge, added to a criminal contempt of court violation, against a person who, having been a percipient witness to a criminal assault, refused, after having been granted immunity, to give a videotaped deposition to be used as his testimony before the grand jury investigating the assault.

8. For cases in which a violation of 1512 is charged based on allegations that the defendant murdered a witness to keep the witness from testifying or providing information, see, e.g., *United States v. Rose*, 362 F.3d 1059 (8th Cir. 2004); *United States v. Veal*, 153 F.3d 1233 (11th Cir. 1998); *United States v. Jefferson*, 149 F.3d 444 (6th Cir. 1998).

9. In some of the witness homicide or threats against witnesses cases, there is a question whether there is a sufficient federal nexus. Was the witness going to testify in a federal matter? See, e.g. *United States v.*

Veal, supra note 8; *United States v. Lopez,* 372 F.3d 86 (2d Cir. 2004); *United States v. Cross,* 258 F.Supp.2d 432 (E.D. Va. 2003). In the *Cross* case, for example, the accused had assaulted his girlfriend; she told the responding officers that the accused had drugs and firearms at his residence. The officers obtained a search warrant and searched and found the drugs and firearms. State arrest warrants were issued for the accused. The DEA was notified and interviewed the girl friend on July 12, 2002, and on that date a DEA investigation of the accused was initiated. On August 10, 2002, the accused threatened his girl friend, "You're going to testify against Antoine, you better have your life insurance and your son's life insurance paid up," and then assaulted her. The accused was charged with assault and battery in a state court on August 10 and obstruction of justice was added on August 13, 2002, and he was found guilty of the assault and battery charge on October 15, 2002. The obstruction charge was forwarded to a state grand jury. On December 18, 2002, the accused was charged with a violation of 18 U.S.C. § 1512(b)(1). The state warrants were nolle prossed on December 2, 2002 and the state charges were nolle prossed on December 19, 2002. A federal information was filed against him on January 31, 2003 and a federal indictment was issued on January 22, 2003 charging witness tampering and witness retaliation. The court stated:

> In the affidavit attached to the criminal complaint filed in this case on December 18, 2002, Agent Parker did not delineate his interactions with Lewis. However, the testimony and evidence presented at the hearing on April 3, 2003, established that Agent Parker interviewed Lewis on July 12, 2002, prior to the alleged assault of Lewis by Cross on August 10, 2002, and that a DEA investigation against Goodman was underway at the time of the assault. Furthermore, the investigation against Goodman did culminate in federal drug charges being brought against him. Under the statute, the federal proceeding need not be pending or about to be instituted, § 1512(e), and state of mind need not be proven as to the federal character of the proceedings, § 1512(f). Therefore, as Lewis was a witness in a federal investigation, which led to federal charges, the criteria are met for the charge of witness tampering under 18 U.S.C. § 1512(b)(1).

D. THE RELATIONSHIP BETWEEN CHARGES UNDER § 1503 AND § 1512

UNITED STATES v. LESTER

749 F.2d 1288 (9th Cir.1984).

Before BROWNING, MERRILL, and SNEED, CIRCUIT JUDGES.

SNEED, CIRCUIT JUDGE:

These consolidated appeals follow the government's successful prosecution of Gary Lester and Leroy McGill for violations of 18 U.S.C. § 371 (conspiracy to obstruct justice and to obstruct a criminal investigation), 18 U.S.C. § 1503 (obstruction of justice), and 18 U.S.C. § 1510 (obstruction of a criminal investigation). The jury returned guilty verdicts against both defendants on all counts. Acting under Fed. R. Crim. P. 29(c), the district judge entered judgments of acquittal as to the two substantive counts for Lester and the conspiracy count for McGill. The government appeals from the judgments of acquittal for both defendants. Lester appeals from his conviction on the conspiracy count. We affirm Lester's conviction for conspiracy, set aside the judgments of acquittal as to both defendants, and reinstate the guilty verdicts.

I.

BACKGROUND

This case involves a conspiracy to prevent Leslie Brigham from testifying in a federal prosecution of Felix Mitchell, the alleged leader of an Oakland narcotics gang. In April 1983, the Oakland police department arrested Brigham for murder. While in custody, Brigham began cooperating with federal authorities as they prepared to prosecute Mitchell. Mitchell had been arrested in February 1983.

On April 17, 1983, while still in custody, Brigham was approached by Mitchell's attorney. The attorney urged Brigham not to cooperate with the federal authorities. In addition, she showed Brigham a note, authored by Mitchell, which directed him to refrain from testifying against Mitchell or speaking to the Justice Department Strike Force Attorney.

On or about April 15, 1983, Lester met with McGill and others to arrange Brigham's release from jail. This meeting apparently followed up a prior meeting in February 1983, attended by Lester and Mitchell, where Mitchell expressed concern that his own arrest was imminent and that Brigham might cooperate with the authorities. At the April 15 meeting, Lester said that the gang should get Brigham out of jail "because he [Brigham] was going to talk against Felix Mitchell." Accordingly, Lester approved the use of the gang's money for the purpose of securing Brigham's release; he instructed McGill to take $1000 to post as the cash part of Brigham's bail.

Before Lester or McGill could arrange Brigham's release, however, the Oakland police released Brigham into the temporary protection of the FBI. On April 18, 1983, the FBI checked Brigham and his wife into a San Francisco motel. Two days later, the couple left the motel and went to Brigham's sister's home in Oakland. There, Brigham called Tony Mitchell, Felix Mitchell's brother, and left a message that he was at his sister's home. A short time later, Lester called Brigham's sister and found to his surprise that Brigham was there. Apparently frightened, Brigham immediately called the Justice Department Attorney. While he was on the phone, however, Lester, Lester's brother Tony, and Tony Mitchell walked in. Brigham pretended he was talking to someone other than the Justice Department Attorney, and he abruptly cut off the conversation. After some discussion and a telephone conversation with Mitchell, the parties agreed that Brigham should leave town for a time.

Brigham, accompanied by Lester's brother, then went to a motel in Alameda. Lester's brother paid for the room and left Brigham $300 in cash. He told Brigham to wait there until McGill came by in the morning.

McGill met Brigham the next day. The two stayed with their wives at another Alameda motel for three days. Needing money, Brigham and McGill drove to the house of Annie MacDonald, who gave McGill $500.

Brigham, McGill, and their wives then departed for San Diego, where they stayed for roughly three weeks. One of Mitchell's girlfriends paid for the accommodations in cash. While in San Diego, McGill periodically received money from Oakland, which he divided with Brigham. Evidence suggested that Lester's brother sent the money. On returning to Oakland, Brigham was arrested by the FBI.

* * *

The primary issue raised by these appeals is whether 15 U.S.C. § 1503 covers witness tampering of the sort suggested by the facts in the present case. In addition, Lester and McGill dispute whether there was sufficient evidence to convict either of them of the conspiracy count and to convict Lester of the substantive counts. McGill also disputes the applicability of 18 U.S.C. § 1510 (obstructing a criminal investigation) to the conduct charged. * * *

III.

APPLICABILITY OF SECTION 1503

A. *Statutory Coverage*

* * * Lester and McGill contend that by enacting the Victim and Witness Protection Act of 1982, Pub.L. No. 97–291, 96 Stat. 1248, Congress intended to remove witness tampering from section 1503 and to consolidate all such offenses in a new provision, 18 U.S.C. § 1512. The government argues that the omnibus clause in section 1503—which prohibits "endeavors to influence, obstruct, or impede, the due administration of justice"—reaches witness tampering of the type presented in this case.

Prior to the enactment of 18 U.S.C. § 1512, section 1503 prohibited influencing or intimidating "any witness ... any grand or petit juror, or officer in or of any court of the United States" or injuring any of them for discharging their duties in court. The Act removed from section 1503 all references to witnesses and enacted section 1512 to protect witnesses, victims, and informants. The Act, however, left the omnibus provision of section 1503 intact. Lester and McGill argue that the Act evinces a congressional intent to redress all forms of witness tampering under section 1512, leaving section 1503 to remedy only tampering with court officers and jurors. We disagree.

As originally enacted, section 1503 had two objectives: " 'It [was] designed to protect witnesses in Federal courts and also to prevent a miscarriage of Justice by corrupt methods.' " *Catrino v. United States*, 176 F.2d 884, 887 (9th Cir.1949). Undeniably, Congress passed the Act "to strengthen existing legal protections for victims and witnesses of Federal crimes." S.Rep. No. 532, 97th Cong., 2d Sess. 9 (1982), *reprinted in* 1982 U.S.Code Cong. & Ad.News 2515, 2515. And Congress may well have intended to remove the protection of witnesses from section 1503. It by no means follows, however, that Congress intended to reduce the effectiveness of section 1503 in combating "miscarriage[s] of Justice by corrupt methods." Yet this is precisely the result to which the defendants' urged construction would lead. If witness tampering should fall exclusively under section 1512, and if the accused used a method other than one prescribed in section 1512 (intimidation, physical force, threats, harassment, or misleading conduct), that conduct would no longer be prohibited. Neither section 1503 nor section 1512 would cover it * * *.

An examination of the scope of section 1512 and the scope of section 1503 prior to the enactment of section 1512 makes this clear. The witness tampering reached by section 1512 involves the use of force or coercion. Section 1512(a) proscribes knowing use of intimidation, physical force, threats, or misleading conduct to "cause or induce any person to ... be absent from an official proceeding to which such person has been summoned by legal process...." 18 U.S.C. § 1512(a)(2)(D). With the exception of misleading conduct, which is not alleged in the present case, all of the activities proscribed by the provision involve some element of coercion. Similarly, section 1512(b) prohibits intentional harassment that "hinders, delays, prevents, or dissuades any person from ... attending or testifying in an official proceeding...." 18 U.S.C. § 1512(b)(1). Although section 1512(b) apparently requires less force or intimidation than does section 1512(a), the gist of the offense is coercive conduct. As the Senate report notes, section 1512(b) "covers any conduct that maliciously hinders, delays, prevents, or dissuades a witness or victim from ... attending or testifying in an official proceeding ... *if the conduct is done with intent to intimidate, harass, harm, or injure another person.*" S.Rep. No. 532, 97th Cong., 2d Sess. 17 (1982), *reprinted in* 1982 U.S.Code Cong. & Ad.News 2515, 2523 (discussing section 1512(a)(2), the precursor of section 1512(b)) (emphasis added); see also 128 Cong.Rec. H8469 (daily ed. Oct. 1, 1982) (remarks of Congressman Rodino) ("[T]he Senate amendment adds a new subsection describing a misdemeanor offense of intentionally harassing another person and thereby intentionally preventing any person from attending or testifying in an official proceeding.... The Senate language will reach thinly-veiled threats that create justifiable apprehension in a victim or witness. It does not reach mere annoyance, however, nor does it reach conduct, for example, that is not intended ... to prevent the witness from testifying....").

The omnibus clause of section 1503, by contrast, is broader. It reaches conduct that "corruptly ... endeavors to influence, obstruct, or impede, the due administration of justice." In decisions prior to the enactment of section 1512, this court consistently has rejected the argument that the omnibus provision covers only activities obstructing justice that involve force, threats, or intimidation. This provision includes noncoercive witness tampering, and in *United States v. Gates*, 616 F.2d 1103 (9th Cir.1980), we upheld a conviction under section 1503 where the defendant had provided a witness with a false story to give to a grand jury. *See also United States v. Vesich*, 724 F.2d 451, 453–58 (pre-section 1512 case upholding obstruction of justice conviction for attempting to persuade a potential grand jury witness to testify falsely), *reh'g denied*, 726 F.2d 168 (5th Cir.1984).

So interpreted, section 1503 embraces the conduct of Lester and McGill who are charged, inter alia, with conspiracy to obstruct justice by hiding the witness Brigham to prevent his appearance at the trial of Felix Mitchell. Their efforts to secrete Brigham, manifestly done with the purpose of preventing his testimony, constitute a corrupt endeavor to obstruct justice in violation of section 1503, at least as that provision stood prior to the Act. *See United States v. Schaffner*, 715 F.2d 1099, 1102–03 (6th Cir.1983) (pre-section 1512 case holding that section 1503 covers efforts to hide a witness). We do not believe Congress intended to change this result. * * **

First, we cannot assume that when the Act was passed Congress was unaware of the wide assortment of cases extending the reach of section 1503 to noncoercive conduct, including noncoercive witness tampering. On that assumption, it would be improper to hold that Congress silently decriminalized noncoercive, but nevertheless corrupt, efforts to interfere with witnesses. Rather, we believe that Congress enacted section 1512 to prohibit specific conduct comprising various forms of coercion of witnesses, leaving the omnibus provision of section 1503 to handle more imaginative forms of criminal behavior, including forms of witness tampering, that defy enumeration.

The legislative history supports this view.

In the present case, Lester and McGill hid a witness from the authorities to prevent his testimony at the Mitchell trial. Both Lester and McGill strenuously assert that no one coerced Brigham to go to San Diego. Taking that assertion at face value, their conduct lies outside "intimidation and harassment of witnesses"; however, it falls precisely within the residual omnibus clause of section 1503. Here it is not the witness but the "administration of justice" that stands in need of protection. Extending that protection is the province of section 1503, not section 1512.

* * *

Notes

1. The circuits are in conflict over whether witness intimidation can be prosecuted under § 1503 as well as under § 1512. Most of the circuits that

have considered the issue have concluded that prosecutions can proceed under both sections, but the Second Circuit has held that § 1512 is the exclusive vehicle for prosecution of witness tampering. *United States v. Masterpol*, 940 F.2d 760 (2d Cir.1991). See also *United States v. Hernandez*, 730 F.2d 895 (2d Cir.1984), cited in the principal case, where the defendant was convicted of violation of 18 U.S.C. §§ 1503 and 1512 based upon his conduct in threatening a witness. The court concluded that threatening a witness in order to obtain documentary evidence (stolen checks that the defendant had used to pay his bills) is no longer covered by § 1503. However, also see *United States v. Bruno,* 383 F.3d 65 (2d Cir. 2004) in which the court stated:

> On appeal, the Government asks us to affirm the District Court waiver analysis or, alternatively, to overrule our decision in *Masterpol* (whose reasoning has been rejected by every other federal court of appeals that has considered the issue). We decline to reach these arguments, given our conclusion below that the evidence supporting the obstruction-of-justice convictions is legally insufficient.

In *United States v. Ladum*, 141 F.3d 1328 (9th Cir. 1998), the Ninth Circuit concluded that the amendment of § 1512 in 1988 to cover non-coercive witness tampering did not repeal the application of the omnibus clause of § 1503 to witness tampering. Other circuits which subscribe to the Ninth Circuit view include the Fourth, *United States v. Kenny*, 973 F.2d 339 (4th Cir. 1992); the Sixth, *United States v. Tackett*, 113 F.3d 603 (6th Cir.1997); and the Eleventh, *United States v. Moody*, 977 F.2d 1420 (11th Cir.1992).

2.   Sections 1503, 1505, 1510, 1512, and 1513 serve to protect witnesses and other participants in federal proceedings. Consider whether any of these provisions can or should be applied to state witnesses or other participants in state proceedings. Should the federal government assume responsibility for protection of state witnesses, judges or jurors, or for preventing other types of obstruction of justice of state laws? Is there a case for assuming such responsibility based upon the fact that the federal government frequently prosecutes local corruption? Can any other federal crimes that you have studied in previous chapters be used to prosecute in state witness tampering cases? Is it desirable to enact a general provision, comparable to § 1503 and § 1512, but applicable to state proceedings? Note that § 1511 under certain circumstances makes criminal a conspiracy to obstruct enforcement of state or local criminal laws "with the intent to facilitate an illegal gambling business." Is there any reason to provide such federal protection with respect to gambling violations and not in other areas? Also see note 9, p. 780 supra, where a case involving the application of the federal obstruction provisions to a situation where federal officers are not yet very much involved is presented.

E. OTHER OBSTRUCTION OF JUSTICE PROVISIONS

§ 1505. Obstruction of proceedings before departments, agencies, and committees

Whoever, with intent to avoid, evade, prevent, or obstruct compliance, in whole or in part, with any civil investigative demand duly and properly made under the Antitrust Civil Process Act [15 USCS §§ 1311 et seq.], willfully withholds, misrepresents, removes from any place, conceals, covers up, destroys, mutilates, alters, or by other means falsifies any documentary material, answers to written interrogatories, or oral testimony, which is the subject of such demand; or attempts to do so or solicits another to do so; or

Whoever corruptly, or by threats or force, or by any threatening letter or communication influences, obstructs, or impedes or endeavors to influence, obstruct, or impede the due and proper administration of the law under which any pending proceeding is being had before any department or agency of the United States, or the due and proper exercise of the power of inquiry under which any inquiry or investigation is being had by either House, or any committee of either House or any joint committee of the Congress—

Shall be fined under this title, imprisoned not more than 5 years or, if the offense involves international or domestic terrorism (as defined in section 2331), imprisoned not more than 8 years, or both.

§ 1510. Obstruction of criminal investigations

(a) Whoever willfully endeavors by means of bribery to obstruct, delay, or prevent the communication of information relating to a violation of any criminal statute of the United States by any person to a criminal investigator shall be fined under this title, or imprisoned not more than five years, or both.

(b)(1) Whoever, being an officer of a financial institution, with the intent to obstruct a judicial proceeding, directly or indirectly notifies any other person about the existence or contents of a subpoena for records of that financial institution, or information that has been furnished to the grand jury in response to that subpoena, shall be fined under this title or imprisoned not more than 5 years, or both.

(2) Whoever, being an officer of a financial institution, directly or indirectly notifies—

(A) a customer of that financial institution whose records are sought by a grand jury subpoena; or

(B) any other person named in that subpoena;

about the existence or contents of that subpoena or information that has been furnished to the grand jury in response to that subpoena, shall be fined under this title or imprisoned not more than one year, or both.

(3) As used in this subsection—

(A) the term "an officer of a financial institution" means an officer, director, partner, employee, agent, or attorney of or for a financial institution; and

(B) the term "subpoena for records" means a Federal grand jury subpoena or a Department of Justice subpoena (issued under section 3486 of title 18), for customer records that has been served relating to a violation of, or a conspiracy to violate—

(i) section 215, 656, 657, 1005, 1006, 1007, 1014, 1344, 1956, 1957, or chapter 53 of title 31; or

(ii) section 1341 or 1343 affecting a financial institution.

(c) As used in this section, the term "criminal investigator" means any individual duly authorized by a department, agency, or armed force of the United States to conduct or engage in investigations of or prosecutions for violations of the criminal laws of the United States.

(d)(1) Whoever—

(A) acting as, or being, an officer, director, agent or employee of a person engaged in the business of insurance whose activities affect interstate commerce, or

(B) is engaged in the business of insurance whose activities affect interstate commerce or is involved (other than as an insured or beneficiary under a policy of insurance) in a transaction relating to the conduct of affairs of such a business,

with intent to obstruct a judicial proceeding, directly or indirectly notifies any other person about the existence or contents of a subpoena for records of that person engaged in such business or information that has been furnished to a Federal grand jury in response to that subpoena, shall be fined as provided by this title or imprisoned not more than 5 years, or both.

(2) As used in paragraph (1), the term "subpoena for records" means a Federal grand jury subpoena for records that has been served relating to a violation of, or a conspiracy to violate, section 1033 of this title.

§ 1511. Obstruction of State or local law enforcement

(a) It shall be unlawful for two or more persons to conspire to obstruct the enforcement of the criminal laws of a State or political subdivision thereof, with the intent to facilitate an illegal gambling business if—

(1) one or more of such persons does any act to effect the object of such a conspiracy;

(2) one or more of such persons is an official or employee, elected, appointed, or otherwise, of such State or political subdivision; and

(3) one or more of such persons conducts, finances, manages, supervises, directs, or owns all or part of an illegal gambling business.

(b) As used in this section—

(1) "illegal gambling business" means a gambling business which—

(i) is a violation of the law of a State or political subdivision in which it is conducted;

(ii) involves five or more persons who conduct, finance, manage, supervise, direct, or own all or part of such business; and

(iii) has been or remains in substantially continuous operation for a period in excess of thirty days or has a gross revenue of $2,000 in any single day.

(2) "gambling" includes but is not limited to pool-selling, bookmaking, maintaining slot machines, roulette wheels, or dice tables, and conducting lotteries, policy, bolita or numbers games, or selling chances therein.

(3) "State" means any State of the United States, the District of Columbia, the Commonwealth of Puerto Rico, and any territory or possession of the United States.

(c) This section shall not apply to any bingo game, lottery, or similar game of change conducted by an organization exempt from tax under paragraph (3) of subsection (c) of section 501 of the Internal Revenue Code of 1954, as amended, if no part of the gross receipts derived from such activity inures to the benefit of any private shareholder, member, or employee of such organization, except as compensation for actual expenses incurred by him in the conduct of such activity.

(d) Whoever violates this section shall be punished by a fine under this title or imprisonment for not more than five years, or both.

§ 1513.   Retaliating against a witness, victim, or an informant

(a)(1) Whoever kills or attempts to kill another person with intent to retaliate against any person for—

(A) the attendance of a witness or party at an official proceeding, or any testimony given or any record, document, or other object produced by a witness in an official proceeding; or

(B) providing to a law enforcement officer any information relating to the commission or possible commission of a Federal offense or a violation of conditions of probation, supervised release, parole, or release pending judicial proceedings, shall be punished as provided in paragraph (2).

(2) The punishment for an offense under this subsection is—

(A) in the case of a killing, the punishment provided in sections 1111 and 1112 [18 USCS §§ 1111 and 1112]; and

(B) in the case of an attempt, imprisonment for not more than 20 years.

(b) Whoever knowingly engages in any conduct and thereby causes bodily injury to another person or damages the tangible property of another person, or threatens to do so, with intent to retaliate against any person for—

(1) the attendance of a witness or party at an official proceeding, or any testimony given or any record, document, or other object produced by a witness in an official proceeding; or

(2) any information relating to the commission or possible commission of a Federal offense or a violation of conditions of probation, supervised release, parole, or release pending judicial proceedings given by a person to a law enforcement officer;

or attempts to do so, shall be fined under this title or imprisoned not more than ten years, or both.

(c) If the retaliation occurred because of attendance at or testimony in a criminal case, the maximum term of imprisonment which may be imposed for the offense under this section shall be the higher of that otherwise provided by law or the maximum term that could have been imposed for any offense charged in such case.

(d) There is extraterritorial Federal jurisdiction over an offense under this section.

(e) Whoever knowingly, with the intent to retaliate, takes any action harmful to any person, including interference with the lawful employment or livelihood of any person, for providing to a law enforcement officer any truthful information relating to the commission or possible commission of any Federal offense, shall be fined under this title or imprisoned not more than 10 years, or both.

[(f)](e)* Whoever conspires to commit any offense under this section shall be subject to the same penalties as those prescribed for the offense the commission of which was the object of the conspiracy.

§ 1515. Definitions for certain provisions; general provision

(a) As used in sections 1512 and 1513 of this title and in this section—

(1) the term "official proceeding" means—

* [Two subsection (e)'s were enacted.]

(A) a proceeding before a judge or court of the United States, a United States magistrate, a bankruptcy judge, a judge of the United States Tax Court, a special trial judge of the Tax Court, a judge of the United States Claims Court, or a Federal grand jury;

(B) a proceeding before the Congress;

(C) a proceeding before a Federal Government agency which is authorized by law; or

(D) a proceeding involving the business of insurance whose activities affect interstate commerce before any insurance regulatory official or agency or any agent or examiner appointed by such official or agency to examine the affairs of any person engaged in the business of insurance whose activities affect interstate commerce;

(2) the term "physical force" means physical action against another, and includes confinement;

(3) the term "misleading conduct" means—

(A) knowingly making a false statement;

(B) intentionally omitting information from a statement and thereby causing a portion of such statement to be misleading, or intentionally concealing a material fact, and thereby creating a false impression by such statement;

(C) with intent to mislead, knowingly submitting or inviting reliance on a writing or recording that is false, forged, altered, or otherwise lacking in authenticity;

(D) with intent to mislead, knowingly submitting or inviting reliance on a sample, specimen, map, photograph, boundary mark, or other object that is misleading in a material respect; or

(E) knowingly using a trick, scheme, or device with intent to mislead;

(4) the term "law enforcement officer" means an officer or employee of the Federal Government, or a person authorized to act for or on behalf of the Federal Government or serving the Federal Government as an adviser or consultant—

(A) authorized under law to engage in or supervise the prevention, detection, investigation, or prosecution of an offense; or

(B) serving as a probation or pretrial services officer under this title;

(5) the term "bodily injury" means—

(A) a cut, abrasion, bruise, burn, or disfigurement;

(B) physical pain;

(C) illness;

(D) impairment of the function of a bodily member, organ, or mental faculty; or

(E) any other injury to the body, no matter how temporary; and

(6) the term "corruptly persuades" does not include conduct which would be misleading conduct but for a lack of a state of mind.

(b) As used in section 1505, the term "corruptly" means acting with an improper purpose, personally or by influencing another, including making a false or misleading statement, or withholding, concealing, altering, or destroying a document or other information.

(c) This chapter does not prohibit or punish the providing of lawful, bona fide, legal representation services in connection with or anticipation of an official proceeding.

Notes

1. Section 1515 contains two clauses that provide some further statutory definition of the term "corruptly." Section 1515(a) (6) provides:

(6) the term "corruptly persuades" does not include conduct which would be misleading conduct but for a lack of a state of mind.

Section 1515 (b) provides:

(b) As used in section 1505, the term "corruptly" means acting with an improper purpose, personally or by influencing another, including making a false or misleading statement, or withholding, concealing, altering, or destroying a document or other information.

2. In *United States v. Poindexter*, 951 F.2d 369 (D.C. Cir. 1991), the court ruled that the term "corruptly" in § 1505 was unconstitutionally vague and failed to provide constitutionally adequate notice as applied to the conduct alleged, namely lying to Congress. Note that the definition in § 1515 regarding the meaning of the term "corruptly" in § 1505 was enacted after the decision in *Poindexter*. Does it affect the significance of that decision?

Part VI

THE CONSEQUENCES OF JURISDICTIONAL OVERLAP

Chapter 17

THE CHOICE BETWEEN FEDERAL OR STATE PROSECUTION, OR DUPLICATIVE PROSECUTIONS

INTRODUCTION

As the number of federal crimes that largely duplicate or cover the same ground as state offenses has multiplied, the possibility of prosecuting a defendant for either a state or federal crime—or both—has also increased. The state-federal choice issue should by this time be familiar since it appears in various forms throughout these materials. This chapter considers two related issues. First, we survey the factors that influence the choice between federal and state prosecutions. Second, we explore the potential for prosecutions in both federal and state court arising out of the same course of conduct.

The choice whether to bring federal rather than state charges is one particular feature of the discretion exercised by prosecutors. For a general discussion of prosecutorial discretion in the federal system, see Chapter 4. The state-federal choice issue adds another dimension to the discretionary decision whether to prosecute—one that does not exist in countries that do not have a federal system or does not apply in situations where there is no overlapping state-federal criminal coverage. In situations where the state-federal prosecutorial choice is available, it gives to a prosecutor a much wider range of options regarding crimes to be charged, applicable penalties, procedural rules, and the like. Of course, even within a single jurisdiction, state or federal, there are usually options—whether to proceed civilly or criminally, which crimes of those available to charge, etc. Whatever the normally available options are, however, they increase significantly when a choice between state and federal prosecution is available.

Note, however, that even where there are good reasons for prosecuting a case in one jurisdiction rather than the other, and even where based upon such reasons one jurisdiction declines to prosecute in favor of another, there is no guarantee that the first prosecution will be successful. Although one study of federal prosecutors' decisionmaking found that deferring to state prosecution was the most common specific reason for federal declinations, the study also noted that it was "very unlikely ... that even one half of the cases declined in favor of state prosecution were actually successfully prosecuted in the state system." Richard S. Frase, *The Decision to File Federal Criminal Charges: A Quantitative Study of Prosecutorial Discretion*, 47 U. OF CHI. L. REV. 246, 262, 272, 278 (1980). A more recent study showed that, laying aside various evidentiary concerns, prosecution by other authorities was the most common individual reason for declining prosecutions, being cited as the reason for 23% of declinations. A less frequent but still significant reason cited was minimal federal interest (8%), and at least some of these cases were likely referred to state and local authorities. *See* Michael Edmund O'Neill, *Understanding Federal Prosecutorial Declinations: An Empirical Analysis of Predictive Factors*, 41 AM. CRIM. L. REV. 1439, 1458–61 (2004).

While Section A considers the issues raised when a choice is made between bringing a federal or a state prosecution, Section B considers the issues raised when prosecutions arising from the same course of conduct are instituted in *both* the federal and state courts. We examine various questions related to such duplicative prosecutions: Are they permissible under the U.S. Constitution? Under other provisions of federal law? Under state law? If such prosecutions are permissible as a matter of law, are there any other restrictions? Do such prosecutions occur frequently? And, finally, should additional limitations be imposed and, if so, what kinds?

A.　THE CHOICE BETWEEN FEDERAL OR STATE PROSECUTION

How is the choice made whether to bring a federal or state prosecution? In this section we first survey some of the factors that affect the choice of forum. We then focus on a particularly important consideration that may affect the choice: the relative advantage of prosecuting a case in the federal or state system. Finally, policy formulations relating to that choice are reviewed.

1.　CONSIDERATIONS AFFECTING THE CHOICE BETWEEN A FEDERAL OR STATE FORUM

Many different kinds of factors may affect the choice of the jurisdiction, state or federal, in which to prosecute when that choice is presented. A number of such factors are reviewed below. In addition, in Chapter 9, *supra* at pp. 375–88, we explore in detail the factors affecting the determination of the choice of jurisdiction for drug charges. As you read the following material, think about whether the factors that drive the choice of jurisdiction in drug prosecutions are the same as those that are determinative in other types of cases. What about other specific categories of cases, such as those involving white collar crime or political corruption?

a. Primary Investigative Jurisdiction and the Practice of Cross–Designation

The most significant determinant of whether a case is prosecuted in the state or the federal system, where it could be prosecuted in either, is often the amount of investigatory work done by the respective jurisdictions. *See* John Kaplan, *The Prosecutorial Discretion? A Comment*, 60 Nw.U.L.Rev. 174, 192 (1965) ("In the absence of other considerations, the assistant [U.S. Attorney] prosecuted where most of the investigatory work was done by federal agents and declined in favor of state prosecution whenever the state officials had 'built' the case.")

The practice of cross-designation, whereby a federal prosecutor may receive a special, temporary appointment as a state prosecutor, or vice versa, can be used to permit the person who was involved in the development of the case to pursue the prosecution under the laws of and in the courts of the other jurisdiction. *See e.g.* 5 U.S.C. §§ 3371–3376. The familiarity that comes from being involved in the investigation of a case and the accompanying pride of "possession" can thus be retained while enabling the choice of where to prosecute to be made based upon other kinds of factors.

b. Custody of the Suspect

A second related factor assuming the offender to be charged has already been arrested, is whether he or she is in state or federal custody. Custody gives the custodial jurisdiction a measure of control over the choice of the forum, at least in the first instance. When other jurisdictions wish to proceed, they are ordinarily able to negotiate with the jurisdiction that originally obtained custody. But what if the negotiations are unsuccessful, and the custodial jurisdiction refuses to cooperate? For a case in which the federal court refused to order the United States to turn over a witness to state prosecutors, see *Special Prosecutor of the State of New York v. United States Attorney for the S.D. of N.Y.*, 375 F. Supp. 797, 799 (S.D.N.Y. 1974). Rudolph Giuliani is listed as one of the Assistant United States Attorneys who briefed this case.

c. The Possibility of a Duplicative Prosecution

Of course the fact that one jurisdiction decides to prosecute may not prevent the other from also prosecuting, even for essentially the same conduct. As discussed later in this chapter, 807–21, there is no federal constitutional bar to such successive prosecutions. There are, however, statutes or constitutional provisions in many states prohibiting a prosecution for conduct previously prosecuted in another jurisdiction, and there is a policy against such prosecutions in the federal system. These matters are treated later in this chapter at 821–35. Insofar as a duplicative prosecution is possible, the choice may not be between state or federal prosecution but rather which jurisdiction takes the first crack at the individual.

d. *Collaborative Investigations*

There appears to be an increasing trend toward collaborative investigations by state and federal law enforcement agents. Sometimes there is a formal umbrella, such as a joint drug task force. Oftentimes, however, it involves ad hoc arrangements between law enforcement agents from the different agencies, cooperating at the operational level. The fact of state-federal cooperation in the investigation of a case may remove the informal preference for the investigating jurisdiction, and leave the choice open and subject to negotiation between the agents and prosecutors of the respective jurisdictions. It thus creates an environment where other factors can be taken into account, particularly the jurisdiction of legal advantage consideration, discussed later in this section.

e. *The Big Case Factor*

The office of prosecutor, state or federal, has sometimes been a springboard to a political career. Whether because of this factor or for other reasons, there may be a keen competition between state and federal offices to prosecute notorious cases that are the subject of much media attention. In the wake of the sniper attacks that terrorized the Washington, D.C. area in 2002, a feud reportedly erupted between two politically ambitious prosecutors, the Maryland U.S. Attorney and the chief prosecutor for Montgomery County, Maryland, over who would be first to prosecute the suspects. *See* Katherine Shaver, *Montgomery Prosecutor Gains the Spotlight; Gansler's Decision to File Murder Charges First Creates Some Backlash*, WASH. POST, Oct. 28, 2002 at A10.

Sometimes there is a similar competition between local and state prosecutors or between U.S. Attorney offices in two or more federal districts. Upon occasion, for example, the press has publicized disputes between the U.S. attorneys in the Southern and Eastern Districts of New York. *See* Howard Kurtz, *Prosecutors Vie in N.Y. Crime Wars; U.S. Attorneys in Brooklyn and Manhattan Keep Eye on Bad Guys—And Each Other*, WASH. POST, Aug. 12, 1988 at A25; Alexander Stille, *A Dynamic Prosecutor Captures the Headlines*, NAT'L L.J., June 17, 1985, at 1, 49–50. Prosecutors in the Southern District of New York have also competed with the Eastern District of Virginia, particularly over the prosecution of terrorism cases. After a dispute over where to try Zacarias Moussaoui, the only suspect prosecuted for the September 11, 2001 attacks, a compromise was reached wherein the trial would take place in Virginia but the lead prosecutor would be brought in from New York. The decision by Attorney General John Ashcroft to bring the case in Virginia was a blow to the U.S. Attorney's Office for the Southern District of New York, which considered itself to play a "critical role in prosecuting terrorism." Benjamin Weiser, *New Federal Prosecutor Inherits Old Priority*, N.Y. TIMES, Jan. 7, 2002, at B4. Note that where there is a state-federal conflict, there may be no official who has the legal authority to resolve the dispute, although the prosecutor with the greater degree of political "clout" will often "win." Disputes between two U.S. Attorneys, however, may be resolved by the Justice Department.

f. *Caseload and Resources*

Caseload factors may affect the prosecutor's decision whether to pursue a case or refer it to another jurisdiction. Lack of resources helps explain a puzzling finding in a recent study of federal prosecutions. Although common sense says the likelihood of prosecution should increase as the size of the loss increases, the study found just the opposite. Federal prosecutors declined fraud cases involving high dollar losses more frequently than they declined those involving low dollar losses. Lack of resources was often cited as a reason for declining the large dollar loss cases. Although they generally have greater resources than their state counterparts, this study suggests that federal prosecutors still do not have adequate resources to prosecute complex fraud cases, which involve expensive forensic analysis and expert witnesses. *See* Michael Edmund O'Neill, *Understanding Federal Prosecutorial Declinations: An Empirical Analysis of Predictive Factors*, 41 AM. CRIM. L. REV. 1439, 1457, 1469 (2004). Sometimes, too, the fact that another jurisdiction is better equipped or has personnel more familiar with the type of matter involved may influence choice of the jurisdiction, although, of course, perceptions regarding such matters within any two prosecution offices may differ.

g. *Inter–Agency Relationships and Relations Among Agents*

The formal and informal network and working relationships between law enforcement and prosecutorial agencies and their personnel can play an important role in the choice of the forum of prosecution. Where the relationships are positive, the choice is more likely to be made based upon the respective advantages of prosecuting in one or the other jurisdiction or similar factors. Some notion of sharing appropriately in the prosecutorial pie may also be taken into account. Where there is hostility between individuals or intense competition between agencies, the choice is more likely to be made by the jurisdiction which builds the case first or has the offender(s) in custody.

h. *Policy Considerations*

Policy considerations may influence the choice of the forum. For example, whether the crime is deemed of special federal interest may be a factor. Enforcement priorities which are crime-specific or focus on particular types of conduct, (see pp. 144–45 *supra*) may also affect the choice. Thus one would expect a federal prosecutor to be unlikely to refer for state prosecution a matter involving a reputed organized crime figure or involving a large drug conspiracy, whereas one would expect more frequent referral to the state or local prosecutor of interstate transportation of stolen motor vehicle cases, at least since the Department of Justice decided to de-emphasize such cases. Regarding Department of Justice enforcement priorities, see pp. 125–56 *supra*. Of course, similar kinds of enforcement policies may exist on the state and local levels as well.

i. *Legal Advantage*

Often the choice of the forum is dictated by legal advantages available there that are not available in the other jurisdiction. This subject is treated in the next section, and also explored in the context of drug prosecutions *supra* at pp. 375–81.

2. THE JURISDICTION OF LEGAL ADVANTAGE

In addition to the type of considerations mentioned in the previous section, the choice of state or federal prosecution is often heavily influenced by the fact that it may be legally more advantageous to file charges in one rather than the other jurisdiction. Sometimes it may be clear that because of legal constraints a prosecution cannot succeed in one of the two jurisdictions; most often, however, the advantage will be relative only. Consider, for example, the following case, in which the court explicitly discusses prosecutorial "forum shopping":

> The present case involves evidence collected by state officers, in a search incident to an arrest for a state traffic law, when the arrest violated constraints imposed by state law. The evidence was turned over to a federal prosecutor, for use in a federal court, even though federal agents would not have had a basis for initiating the arrest that produced the evidence.

> Under the law of this Circuit, federal prosecutors have free reign to make use of evidence obtained in violation of state law that federal officers would not have been able to obtain on their own, and that would have been suppressed in state court.

> Some courts have questioned whether the hand off of evidence on the proverbial "silver platter" from state officials to federal officials really occurs. But why would a federal prosecutor decline to prosecute a case under federal drug laws if the major defect in the case is not recognized by the federal courts? Forum shopping is not a myth.

> When the substantive laws overlap, there is an increasing motive for federal prosecutors to take advantage of evidence unlawfully obtained by state officers, in a way that undermines the exclusionary consequence states impose to discourage such illegalities.

> This Court continues to hope that the Fifth Circuit will revisit the federalism issues raised by the use in federal court of evidence unlawfully seized by state officers, especially when federal officers could not have obtained the evidence on their own.

United States v. Coleman, 162 F.Supp.2d 582, 587–91 (N.D. Tex. 2001).

Is this type of forum-shopping appropriate in criminal cases, and if so, is it desirable? In general, we have no qualms about plaintiffs' lawyers who bring suit in a favorable forum in order to gain a legal advantage. Is forum shopping in criminal cases really any different? Should the government be more restrained than private parties when it seeks to gain a legal advantage over its citizens? Do you see any difference in trying to deprive a civil or criminal defendants of the protections they would receive in their home jurisdiction?

The constraints that may affect the relative legal advantage of prosecuting in the state or federal systems include:

1. *Substantive law*—e.g. definitions of offenses; statutes of limitation; defenses; and other general criminal law doctrines.

2. *Penalties*—e.g. relative severity; availability of mandatory minimum and penalty enhancement provisions; probation and parole provisions; diversion and juvenile procedures; forfeiture; the death penalty.

3. *Procedures*—e.g. extradition v. removal; joinder; Speedy Trial requirements; availability of grand jury; use of preliminary hearing; bail rules; subpoena power; the scope of defense discovery.

4. *Rules of evidence*

5. *Constitutional and other doctrines and statutory provisions which affect investigation techniques and evidence gathering*—e.g. doctrines relating to search and seizure, interrogation, and pre-trial identification; immunity; electronic surveillance; entrapment.

6. *Judicial attitudes* in interpreting and applying the foregoing.

The Department of Justice has recognized the "powerful advantages" prosecutors have in the federal system, and advocates that cases be brought in the federal system to take advantage of various differences between federal and state law. Nat'l Inst. of Justice, U.S. Dep't of Justice, Fighting Urban Crime: The Evolution of Federal–Local Collaboration 3 (Dec. 2003). This report lists a variety of procedural and evidentiary advantages to bringing a prosecution in the federal system: the long duration and national subpoena power of the federal grand jury; limited, rather than blanket, immunity for grand jury witnesses; lower standards for obtaining search warrants; the availability of preventive detention; the lower burden of proof required for electronic surveillance; a well-developed witness protection program; the ability to use uncorroborated accomplice testimony; and more favorable discovery rules. *See also* John C. Jeffries, Jr. & John Gleeson, *The Federalization of Organized Crime: Advantages of Federal Prosecution*, 46 Hastings L.J. 1095, 1103–1125 (1995) (arguing that several features of the federal law make it the jurisdiction of legal advantage for organized crime prosecutions).

This type of state-federal comparison regarding particular legal advantages will vary, of course, depending upon the particular context and the law of the state involved. Any one of 50 different comparisons can thus be made depending on the place where the crime was committed. To the extent, too, that there are differences among approaches taken in the several federal circuits, sometimes amounting to "a conflict among the circuits," not yet resolved by the Supreme Court, the state-federal comparison may also be affected by which federal district and circuit is involved.

What does all of this really mean? Try to come up with specific illustrations drawn from the materials in this volume, the material of other courses you have studied in law school or your general knowledge involving differences between state and federal law under each of the foregoing headings. For example, how do these factors affect the choice of forum in drug cases? *See supra* at pp. 375–88. In drug cases—or cases of any kind—is the difference from the federal law common to all or most of the 50 states, or does the law vary from state to state? Where you have identified a difference between state and federal law that may make one or the other a more advantageous forum, which is the more advantageous? And how great do think the advantage is?

Note that there may be various tradeoffs between relative advantages. For example, suppose in jurisdiction A there is a much higher penalty for the offense involved—which makes it an attractive forum for the prosecutors—but the definition of the offense in A makes it more difficult to obtain a conviction than it would be in jurisdiction B.

Note also that state law is often modeled after the federal law (or sometimes vice versa), and in other cases they both use a common source as the model. Consider, for example, that 41 states have now adopted the Federal Rules of Evidence in various forms. For a discussion of the influence of federal law on state criminal procedure, see Jerold Israel, *Federal Criminal Procedure as a Model for the States*, 543 ANNALS AM. ACAD. POL. & SOC. SCI. 130, 141–43 (1996). Is it desirable to move in the direction of greater uniformity among the states, and between the states and the federal system, with respect to the various legal rules and doctrines mentioned above so as to avoid having such factors affect the choice of the forum jurisdiction? Or is the variability in the present state of affairs desirable? Are there other reasons why such uniformity would be undesirable?

If there is a long-term trend in the direction of making the federal system a legally more advantageous jurisdiction in which to prosecute, should this be viewed as a desirable or undesirable development? *See* Dennis E. Curtis, *The Effect of Federalization on the Defense Function*, 543 ANNALS AM. ACAD. POL. & SOC. SCI. 85, 91–95 (1996) (arguing, inter alia, that defendants who might be prosecuted in either the federal system or a state are more likely to be convicted in a federal prosecution because of prosecution-oriented federal rules of procedural, and federal prosecutors' power to coerce guilty pleas because of their greater control over sentencing).

There is one final wrinkle on the jurisdiction of legal advantage issue. Forum shopping can occur in some federal criminal cases even when there is no overlapping state crime that could be charged, because the case could be brought in more than one federal district. The Eastern District of Virginia has become the favored venue for trying terrorism cases, because of its reputation as the "rocket docket" for its speed and efficiency, and because it is considered conservative, pro-prosecution, and pro-death penalty. Also, the EDVA is in the Fourth Circuit, which many regard as the most conservative federal appellate court. For example, the decision was made to prosecute Zacarias Moussaoui for the September 11, 2001 attacks on the World Trade Center and the Pentagon in the Eastern District of Virginia, rather than in the Southern District of New York, in part because the courts and juries in Virginia are more pro-death penalty and because the of the likelihood of a transfer of venue out of Manhattan. *See* Don Van Natta, Jr. & Benjamin Weiser, *Compromise Settles Debate Over Tribunal*, N.Y. Times, Dec. 12, 2001, at B1. Does forum shopping within the federal system raise the same issues as forum shopping between the state and federal systems?

An example of a case where there was competition between both federal and state prosecutors and between prosecutors in different states is the prosecution of John Muhammad and Lee Malvo, the Washington, D.C., area snipers. Many of the factors discussed in this section played a role in determining the jurisdiction that would first prosecute the shooters. Attacks occurred in both Virginia and Maryland, and a regional task force was formed to investigate the cases. Although they were arrested on federal warrants, the FBI, the Maryland State Police, and the Montgomery County police were all involved in their capture.

As the press accounts reveal, each of the prosecutors involved badly wanted to prosecute Muhammad and Malvo. Six of the ten sniper slayings were committed in Maryland, and a seventh victim who was killed in Virginia was a Maryland resident. Moreover, the arrests occurred in Maryland, and the men were initially held in custody in a county jail. But ultimately the United States controlled the decision, and it chose Virginia.

The defendants were arrested pursuant to federal warrants, and thus arraigned in federal court after a brief period of detention in a county facility. That physical custody pursuant to the original charges put the United States in the driver's seat to prosecute or decide which state should do so. Of course murder is not a federal offense, but by this point in the course you should realize that a determined federal prosecutor can usually find some way to reach criminal conduct. In this case, the mechanism was the Hobbs Act. There had been a demand for $10 million dollars to stop the killings, and this was the basis for the Hobbs Act extortion charges. Although the charges included the commission of murder in the course of extortion, and some of the charges carried the potential for the death penalty, there were problems with keeping the case in the federal system. In the first place, the evidence connecting the defendants to the murders was much stronger than the evidence connecting the defendants to the extortion note. Moreover, the heart of the federal case had to be extortion, rather than murder, and federal law did not allow the execution of juveniles. In fact, it appears that the final decision turned on where it was most likely that both defendants could be executed. Maryland's governor had imposed a moratorium on carrying out death sentences, and its law too barred the execution of juveniles. Virginia law, in contrast, permitted the execution of juveniles, and Virginia has been one of the leading states in terms of the number of executions carried out. So Attorney General John Ashcroft made the decision to allow Virginia to take the cases. How was this accomplished? The defendants were in federal custody, and they were moved from a federal facility in Maryland to one in Virginia, from which they were released into the custody of Virginia state officials. The Maryland prosecutors (and the victims they represented) were left out in the cold.

For an interesting account of the jurisdictional battle, see Sari Horwitz & Michael E. Fuane, *Jurisdictions Vied to Prosecute Pair*, WASH. POST, Oct. 9, 2003, at A1, *available online at* 2003 WL 62221661.

3. POLICY FORMULATIONS

General policies have, on occasion, been formulated that focus directly on the choice of state or federal prosecution issue. In its most generalized form, such a policy might simply refer to a commitment to the notion that primary responsibility for law enforcement and prosecution in this country should be in the hands of state and local law enforcement agencies. This translates into a notion that federal prosecutorial resources should be devoted largely to matters in which there is a special federal interest and that the federal role in areas of overlapping jurisdiction should be, in the main, viewed as aiding state and local governments in their primary role. *See generally* L.B. Schwartz, *Federal Criminal Jurisdiction and Prosecutors' Discretion*, 13 LAW & CONTEMP. PROB. 64 (1948); Norman Abrams, *Consultant's Report on Jurisdiction*, 1 WORKING PAPERS, NATIONAL COMMISSION ON REFORM OF FEDERAL CRIMINAL LAWS 33 (1970). Such an approach can be relied upon to justify federal deference to state prosecution in particular crime areas. See, e.g., Note, *Discretion to Prosecute Federal Civil Rights Crimes*, 74 YALE L.J. 1297, 1301 (1965).

Consider the following formulations of a general policy approach to the state-federal choice issue:

a. L.B. Schwartz, Federal Criminal Jurisdiction and Prosecutors' Discretion, 13 Law & Contemp. Prob. 64, 73 (1948)

* * * [I]n general it can be said that federal action is justified in the presence of one or more of the following circumstances: (1) When the states are unable or unwilling to act; (2) when the jurisdictional feature, e.g., use of the mails, is not merely incidental or accidental to the offense, but an important ingredient of its success; (3) when, although the particular jurisdictional feature is incidental, another substantial federal interest is protected by the assertion of federal power; (4) when the criminal operation extends into a number of states, transcending the local interests of any one; (5) when it would be inefficient administration

to refer to state authorities a complicated case investigated and developed on the theory of federal prosecution. * * *

b. *Final Report, National Commission on Reform of Federal Criminal Laws at 19–20 (1971)*

§ 207. Discretionary Restraint in Exercise of Concurrent Jurisdiction.

Notwithstanding the existence of concurrent jurisdiction, federal law enforcement agencies are authorized to decline or discontinue federal enforcement efforts whenever the offense can effectively be prosecuted by nonfederal agencies and it appears that there is no substantial Federal interest in further prosecution or that the offense primarily affects state, local or foreign interests. A substantial federal interest exists in the following circumstances, among others:

(a) the offense is serious and state or local law enforcement is impeded by interstate aspects of the case;

(b) federal enforcement is believed to be necessary to vindicate federally-protected civil rights;

* * *

(d) an offense apparently limited in its impact is believed to be associated with organized criminal activities extending beyond state lines;

(e) state or local law enforcement has been so corrupted as to undermine its effectiveness substantially.

Where federal law enforcement efforts are discontinued in deference to state, local or foreign prosecution, federal agencies are directed to cooperate with state, local or foreign agencies, by providing them with evidence already gathered or otherwise, to the extent that this is practicable without prejudice to federal law enforcement. The Attorney General is authorized to promulgate additional guidelines for the exercise of discretion in employing federal criminal jurisdiction.* * *

c. *Jamie S. Gorelick and Harry Litman, Prosecutorial Discretion and the Federalization Debate, 46 Hastings L.J. 967, 976–77 (1995)*[a]

The Department's prosecutorial policy emphasizes two elements: (1) allocation of criminal justice resources according to the comparative advantage of the federal, state, and local governments; and (2) cooperation between federal and state or local law enforcement officials to promote the most efficient use of criminal justice resources.

The comparative advantage approach rests on the idea that each agency or level of government ideally should handle those aspects of a

---

a. At the time this article was prepared, Ms. Gorelick was Deputy Attorney General, and Mr. Litman was Deputy Assistant Attorney General, Office of Policy Development.

law enforcement problem that it is best equipped to handle. The federal government's advantages may vary according to the case, but they typically include inter-jurisdictional investigative capabilities, victim-and witness-assistance programs, expertise in traditionally federal areas of law such as organized crime or environmental crime, and favorable procedures, such as preventive detention. The availability of stiffer penalties in the federal system is also a potential comparative advantage, particularly in multiple-offender cases, where the prospect of a long sentence may induce a low-level figure to plead guilty and cooperate in the prosecution of the most culpable offenders.

The comparative advantage approach does not imply that a federal prosecution should be brought whenever the federal government has a comparative advantage. Rather, federal law enforcement resources should be deployed in the way that federal, state, and local actors jointly believe would be most effective. For example, federal investigative resources or witness-and victim-protection programs can be made available to state authorities in a case in which a state prosecution is brought. This approach can maximize the effectiveness of state and federal criminal justice resources. * * *

d. United States Attorneys Manual Chapter 9–27.000 Principles of Federal Prosecution (August 2002)

9–27.240 Initiating and Declining Charges—Prosecution in Another Jurisdiction

A. In determining whether prosecution should be declined because the person is subject to effective prosecution in another jurisdiction, the attorney for the government should weigh all relevant considerations, including:

1. The strength of the other jurisdiction's interest in prosecution;

2. The other jurisdiction's ability and willingness to prosecute effectively; and

3. The probable sentence or other consequences if the person is convicted in the other jurisdiction.

B. Comment. * * * [T]hese factors are illustrative only, and the attorney for the government should also consider any others that appear relevant to his/her in a particular case.

1. **The Strength of the Jurisdiction's Interest.** The attorney for the government should consider the relative Federal and state characteristics of the criminal conduct involved. Some offenses, even though in violation of Federal law, are of particularly strong interest to the authorities of the state or local jurisdiction in which they occur, either because of the nature of the offense, the identity of the offender or victim, the fact that the investigation was conducted primarily by state or local investigators, or some other circumstance. Whatever the reason, when it appears that the Federal interest in prosecution is less substan-

tial than the interest of state or local authorities, consideration should be given to referring the case to those authorities rather than commencing or recommending a Federal prosecution.

2. **Ability and Willingness to Prosecute Effectively.** In assessing the likelihood of effective prosecution in another jurisdiction, the attorney for the government should also consider the intent of the authorities in that jurisdiction and whether that jurisdiction has the prosecutorial and judicial resources necessary to undertake prosecution promptly and effectively. Other relevant factors might be legal or evidentiary problems that might attend prosecution in the other jurisdiction. In addition, the Federal prosecutor should be alert to any local conditions, attitudes, relationships, or other circumstances that might cast doubt on the likelihood of the state or local authorities conducting a thorough and successful prosecution.

3. **Probable Sentence Upon Conviction.** The ultimate measure of the potential for effective prosecution in another jurisdiction is the sentence, or other consequence, that is likely to be imposed if the person is convicted. In considering this factor, the attorney for the government should bear in mind not only the statutory penalties in the jurisdiction and sentencing patterns in similar cases, but also, the particular characteristics of the offense or, of the offender that might be relevant to sentencing. He/she should also be alert to the possibility that a conviction under state law may, in some cases result in collateral consequences for the defendant, such as disbarment, that might not follow upon a conviction under Federal law.

Notes

1. Review these formulations of state-federal prosecutorial policy and try to spot the differences among them. Are you convinced that each of the criteria mentioned warrant federal prosecution (or state prosecution) as the case may be? Can you think of any additional considerations not mentioned in these formulations? Assuming that the right issues are on the table, other issues arise.

All of the provisions excerpted above are stated in very general terms. Is a policy statement at this level of generality useful in making the decision whether to prosecute a case federally or in the state courts? General statements will not ordinarily dictate clear outcomes in particular cases. How then can we achieve the goals of making the best use of limited federal resources and treating similar cases alike? Is it feasible to introduce more detail into such policy statements? One option is to have much more detailed statements, which might be adopted on a nationwide basis, or—more likely—in each U.S. Attorney's Office. Many U.S. Attorneys have promulgated such internal guidelines. If greater specificity is not the answer, there are other options. Is an administrative review process the answer, or should a defendant be able to litigate the propriety of the decision to bring federal charges?

Consider also the sources of the rules. Does it matter whether the policy is incorporated into a statutory provision or is promulgated administratively? Note also that these proposals deal with only one side of the coin. Is it feasible to formulate comparable policies at the state level?

2.   Some commentators have suggested that federal prosecutors should consider the availability of state or local resources as affecting the prospect of successful investigation or prosecution. Should that factor be taken into account where the offense is not a major offense? Consider a policy which in 1985 was being implemented by then-U.S. Attorney Rudy Giuliani in the Southern District of New York. One day a week a large number of federal prosecutions of neighborhood drug pushers arrested by local police were filed "because the state court system was slow and overloaded . . . [and] to create a Russian roulette effect . . . not letting anyone know which day cases would be brought to the U.S. Attorney's office." Alexander Stille, *A Dynamic Prosecutor Captures the Headlines*, NAT'L L.J., June 17, 1985, at 1, 48. Assume that the potential of a quicker trial and a longer sentence in the federal courts might have at least some deterrent effect on crime. Is there any reason for a federal prosecutor not to adopt a "federal day" policy for some–or all–of the state offenses that could conceivably be brought into federal court? Why or why not?

B.   DUPLICATIVE PROSECUTIONS

What if the choice is made, either deliberately or inadvertently, to prosecute the defendant in both the federal and state systems for essentially the same conduct? We now turn to the question of the constitutional and statutory limits on dual prosecutions. We then discuss the current administrative approach–termed the *Petite* Policy. And finally, we explore other possible approaches, including preemption.

1.   CONSTITUTIONAL AND STATUTORY LIMITS

Many readers will remember the videotape of the arresting officers beating motorist Rodney King, and may also recall that the state prosecution of the officers ended in an acquittal followed by riots which killed at least 45 people, destroyed more than 5,000 buildings, and caused at least $750 million in property damage, and later by a second federal trial that ended in the conviction of two of the officers for civil rights violations. This section first explores the constitutional doctrine that permits such successive prosecutions—the "dual sovereignty" limitation on the Double Jeopardy Clause—and then notes the statutory provisions that bar successive prosecutions in many states.

In 1959 the Supreme Court handed down two decisions that established the modern constitutional foundations for the dual sovereignty doctrine. In *Bartkus v. Illinois*, 359 U.S. 121, 138–39 (1959), the Court upheld the state prosecution of a defendant who had already been acquitted of the same offense in federal court, rejecting the claim that such a successive prosecution would amount to a denial of Due Process under the Fourteenth Amendment. *Abbate v. United States*, 359 U.S. 187, 195–96 (1959), extended this rationale to the Double Jeopardy Clause of the Fifth Amendment, holding that a federal prosecution commenced after a state conviction based on the same conduct was not a violation of that protection.

The defendant in *Bartkus* had already been acquitted of the robbery of a federally insured savings and loan association by the District Court for the Northern District of Illinois when an Illinois grand jury indicted him. While the facts listed in the Illinois indictment were "substantially identical" to those listed in the federal indictment, the trial court refused to dismiss the indictment and the Illinois Supreme Court affirmed. The Court rejected Bartkus's argument that the Due Process Clause barred such successive prosecutions. The Court began by quoting from an earlier opinion stating the principle of dual sovereignty, and then turned to the policies served by that principle:

> "Every citizen of the United States is also a citizen of a State or territory. He may be said to owe allegiance to two sovereigns, and may be liable to punishment for an infraction of the laws of either. The same act may be an offence or transgression of the laws of both."

* * *

> A practical justification for rejecting such a reading of due process also commends itself in aid of this interpretation of the Fourteenth Amendment. In *Screws v. United States*, 325 U.S. 91, defendants were tried and convicted in a federal court under federal statutes with maximum sentences of a year and two years respectively. But the state crime there involved was a capital offense. Were the federal prosecution of a comparatively minor offense to prevent state prosecution of so grave an infraction of state law, the result would be a shocking and untoward deprivation of the historic right and obligation of the States to maintain peace and order within their confines. It would be in derogation of our federal system to displace the reserved power of States over state offenses by reason of prosecution of minor federal offenses by federal authorities beyond the control of the States.

* * *

> Precedent, experience, and reason alike support the conclusion that Alfonse Bartkus has not been deprived of due process of law by the State of Illinois.

359 U.S. at 131–39.

Justice Black dissented, arguing that the "supposed 'requirements' of 'federalism'" should not be relied upon to cut back on important procedural safeguards:

> The Court apparently takes the position that a second trial for the same act is somehow less offensive if one of the trials is conducted by the Federal Government and the other by a State. Looked at from the standpoint of the individual who is being prosecuted, this notion is too subtle for me to grasp. If double

punishment is what is feared, it hurts no less for two "Sovereigns" to inflict it than for one. If danger to the innocent is emphasized, that danger is surely no less when the power of State and Federal Governments is brought to bear on one man in two trials, than when one of these "Sovereigns" proceeds alone. In each case, inescapably, a man is forced to face danger twice for the same conduct.

359 U.S. at 155.

In *Abbate* (decided the same day as *Bartkus*) the order of the proceedings was reversed: the defendants challenged a federal prosecution brought after a successful state prosecution for the same conduct. The defendants had already pled guilty in Illinois to conspiracy to dynamite a telephone company facility located in Mississippi and had been sentenced to three months when they were indicted for the same crime in local federal court. After their federal conviction on the basis of the same conduct relied upon in the state prosecution, the Supreme Court granted certiorari to consider their claim that such successive prosecutions violated the Double Jeopardy Clause of the Fifth Amendment. Writing for the Court, Justice Brennan placed primary reliance on the principal of dual sovereignty. The Court described earlier opinions that acknowledged the principle of dual sovereignty and quoted its opinion in *United States v. Lanza*, 260 U.S. 377, 382 (1922), which upheld successive prosecutions for liquor violations under state and federal law:

> "We have here two sovereignties, deriving power from different sources, capable of dealing with the same subject-matter within the same territory. * * * Each government in determining what shall be an offense against its peace and dignity is exercising its own sovereignty, not that of the other.
>
> "It follows that an act denounced as a crime by both national and state sovereignties is an offense against the peace and dignity of both and may be punished by each. The Fifth Amendment, like all the other guaranties in the first eight amendments, applies only to proceedings by the federal government, * * * and the double jeopardy therein forbidden is a second prosecution under authority of the federal government after a first trial for the same offense under the same authority."

The *Abbate* Court then declined to overrule its dual sovereignty cases, reasoning as follows:

> [I]f the States are free to prosecute criminal acts violating their laws, and the resultant state prosecutions bar federal prosecutions based on the same acts, federal law enforcement must necessarily be hindered. For example, the petitioners in this case insist that their Illinois convictions resulting in three months' prison sentences should bar this federal prosecution which could result in a sentence of up to five years. Such a disparity will very often arise when, as in this case, the defendants' acts impinge more seriously on a federal

interest than on a state interest. But no one would suggest that, in order to maintain the effectiveness of federal law enforcement, it is desirable completely to displace state power to prosecute crimes based on acts which might also violate federal law. This would bring about a marked change in the distribution of powers to administer criminal justice, for the States under our federal system have the principal responsibility for defining and prosecuting crimes. Thus, unless the federal authorities could somehow insure that there would be no state prosecutions for particular acts that also constitute federal offenses, the efficiency of federal law enforcement must suffer if the Double Jeopardy Clause prevents successive state and federal prosecutions. Needless to say, it would be highly impractical for the federal authorities to attempt to keep informed of all state prosecutions which might bear on federal offenses.

The conclusion is therefore compelled that the prior Illinois conviction of the petitioners did not bar the instant federal prosecution.

359 U.S. at 195–96.

In the following case, the Supreme Court had the opportunity to discuss the dual sovereignty doctrine as it applies to successive prosecutions by two different states, rather than federal and state prosecutions.

HEATH v. ALABAMA

474 U.S. 82 (1985).

Justice O'Connor delivered the opinion of the Court.

* * *

In August 1981, petitioner, Larry Gene Heath, hired Charles Owens and Gregory Lumpkin to kill his wife, Rebecca Heath, who was then nine months pregnant; for a sum of $2,000. On the morning of August 31, 1981, petitioner left the Heath residence in Russell County, Alabama, to meet with Owens and Lumpkin in Georgia, just over the Alabama border from the Heath home. Petitioner led them back to the Heath residence, gave them the keys to the Heaths' car and house, and left the premises in his girlfriend's truck. Owens and Lumpkin then kidnaped Rebecca Heath from her home. The Heath car, with Rebecca Heath's body inside, was later found on the side of a road in Troup County, Georgia. The cause of death was a gunshot wound in the head. The estimated time of death and the distance from the Heath residence to the spot where Rebecca Heath's body was found are consistent with the theory that the murder took place in Georgia, and respondent does not contend otherwise.

* * *

[Heath was prosecuted first in Georgia for "malice" murder under Ga. Code Ann. § 16–5–1 (1984). After Georgia notified Heath of its intention to seek the death penalty, he pleaded guilty in exchange for a sentence of life imprisonment (which could involve his serving as few as seven years in prison). Shortly thereafter an Alabama grand jury indicted Heath for the capital offense of murder during a kidnaping. The Alabama state courts rejected both Heath's Double Jeopardy arguments and his claim that Alabama lacked jurisdiction because the crime occurred in Georgia. The courts relied on Ala. Code § 15–2–3 (1982), which provided that Alabama had jurisdiction of a crime commenced within the state, regardless of where the crime is consummated. The Alabama jury convicted petitioner of murder during a kidnaping in the first degree and recommended the death penalty. The trial judge accepted the jury's recommendation, finding that the aggravating factor, that the capital offense was "committed while the defendant was engaged in the commission of a kidnaping," outweighed the mitigating factor that the "defendant was convicted of the murder of Rebecca Heath in the Superior Court of Troup County, Georgia, . . . and received a sentence of life imprisonment in that court." The Alabama Supreme Court affirmed the conviction and death penalty, relying on the dual sovereignty exception to the Double Jeopardy Clause. The Supreme Court granted certiorari to consider the application of successive prosecutions under the laws of different states.]

The dual sovereignty doctrine is founded on the common law conception of crime as an offense against the sovereignty of the government. When a defendant in a single act violates the "peace and dignity" of two sovereigns by breaking the laws of each, he has committed two distinct "offences." *United States v. Lanza*, 260 U.S. 377, 382 (1922). * * *

In applying the dual sovereignty doctrine, then, the crucial determination is whether the two entities that seek successively to prosecute a defendant for the same course of conduct can be termed separate sovereigns. This determination turns on whether the two entities draw their authority to punish the offender from distinct sources of power. *See, e.g., United States v. Wheeler*, 435 U.S. 313, (1978). Thus, the Court has uniformly held that the States are separate sovereigns with respect to the Federal Government because each State's power to prosecute is derived from its own "inherent sovereignty," not from the Federal Government. * * *

The States are no less sovereign with respect to each other than they are with respect to the Federal Government. Their powers to undertake criminal prosecutions derive from separate and independent sources of power and authority originally belonging to them before admission to the Union and preserved to them by the Tenth Amendment. The States are equal to each other "in power, dignity and authority, each competent to exert that residuum of sovereignty not delegated to the United States by the Constitution itself." Thus, "[e]ach has the power, inherent in any sovereign, independently to determine what shall be an offense against its authority and to punish such offenses, and in doing so each " 'is exercising its own sovereignty, not that of the other.' "

* * *

Petitioner invites us to restrict the applicability of the dual sovereignty principle to cases in which two governmental entities, having concurrent jurisdiction and pursuing quite different interests, can demonstrate that allowing only one entity to exercise jurisdiction over the defendant will interfere with the unvindicated interests of the second entity and that multiple prosecutions therefore are necessary for the satisfaction of the legitimate interests of both entities. This balancing of interests approach, however, cannot be reconciled with the dual sovereignty principle. This Court has plainly and repeatedly stated that two identical offenses are not the "same offence" within the meaning of the Double Jeopardy Clause if they are prosecuted by different sovereigns. *See, e.g., United States v. Lanza*, 260 U.S. 377 (1922) (same conduct, indistinguishable statutes, same "interests"). If the States are separate sovereigns, as they must be under the definition of sovereignty which the Court consistently has employed, the circumstances of the case are irrelevant.

Petitioner, then, is asking the Court to discard its sovereignty analysis and to substitute in its stead his difficult and uncertain balancing of interests approach. The Court has refused a similar request on at least one previous occasion, *see Abbate v. United States*, 359 U.S. 187 (1959); *id.*, at 196 (BRENNAN, J., separate opinion), and rightfully so. The Court's express rationale for the dual sovereignty doctrine is not simply a fiction that can be disregarded in difficult cases. It finds weighty support in the historical understanding and political realities of the States' role in the federal system and in the words of the Double Jeopardy Clause itself, "nor shall any person be subject for the same offence to be twice put in jeopardy of life or limb." U.S. Const., Amdt. 5.

It is axiomatic that "[i]n America, the powers of sovereignty are divided between the government of the Union, and those of the States. They are each sovereign, with respect to the objects committed to it, and neither sovereign with respect to the objects committed to the other." It is as well established that the States, "as political communities, [are] distinct and sovereign, and consequently foreign to each other." The Constitution leaves in the possession of each State "certain exclusive and very important portions of sovereign power." THE FEDERALIST No. 9, p. 55 (J. Cooke ed. 1961). Foremost among the prerogatives of sovereignty is the power to create and enforce a criminal code. To deny a State its power to enforce its criminal laws because another State has won the race to the courthouse "would be a shocking and untoward deprivation of the historic right and obligation of the States to maintain peace and order within their confines." *Bartkus*, 359 U.S., at 137, 79 S. Ct., at 685.

Such a deprivation of a State's sovereign powers cannot be justified by the assertion that under "interest analysis" the State's legitimate penal interests will be satisfied through a prosecution conducted by another State. A State's interest in vindicating its sovereign authority through enforcement of its laws by definition can never be satisfied by another State's enforcement of its own laws. Just as the Federal Government has the right to decide that a state prosecution has not vindicated a violation of the "peace and dignity" of the Federal Government, a State must be entitled to decide that a prosecution by another State has not satisfied its legitimate sovereign interest. In recognition of this fact, the Court consistently has endorsed the principle that a single act constitutes an "offence" against each sovereign whose laws are violated by that act. The Court has always understood the words of the Double Jeopardy Clause to reflect this fundamental principle, and we see no reason why we should reconsider that understanding today.

The judgment of the Supreme Court of Alabama is affirmed.

It is so ordered.

* * *

JUSTICE MARSHALL, with whom Justice BRENNAN joins, dissenting.

* * *

The dual sovereignty theory posits that where the same act offends the laws of two sovereigns, "it cannot be truly averred that the offender has been twice punished for the same offence; but only that by one act he has committed two offences, for each of which he is justly punishable." Therefore, "prosecutions under the laws of separate sovereigns do not, in the language of the Fifth Amendment, 'subject [the defendant] for the same offence to be twice put in jeopardy.'" Mindful of the admonitions of Justice Black, we should recognize this exegesis of the Clause as, at best, a useful fiction and, at worst, a dangerous one. *See Bartkus v. Illinois*, 359 U.S. 121, 158 (1959) (BLACK, J., dissenting). No evidence has ever been adduced to indicate that the Framers intended the word "offense" to have so restrictive a meaning.

* * *

This strained reading of the Double Jeopardy Clause has survived and indeed flourished in this Court's cases not because of any inherent plausibility, but because it provides reassuring interpretivist support for a rule that accommodates the unique nature of our federal system. Before this rule is extended to cover a new class of cases, the reasons for its creation should therefore be made clear.

Under the constitutional scheme, the Federal Government has been given the exclusive power to vindicate certain of our Nation's sovereign interests, leaving the States to exercise complementary authority over matters of more local concern. The respective spheres of the Federal Government and the States may overlap at times, and even where they do not, different interests may be implicated by a single act. *See, e.g., Abbate v. United States*, 359 U.S. 187 (1959) (conspiracy to dynamite telephone company facilities entails both the destruction of property and disruption of federal communications network). Yet were a prosecution by a State, however zealously pursued, allowed to preclude further prosecution by the Federal Government for the same crime, an entire range of national interests could be frustrated. The importance of those federal interests has thus quite properly been permitted to trump a defendant's interest in avoiding successive prosecutions or multiple punishments for the same crime. *See Screws v. United States*, 325 U.S. 91, 108–110, and n. 10 (1945) (plurality opinion). Conversely, because "the States under our federal system have the principal responsibility for defining and prosecuting crimes," it would be inappropriate in the absence of a specific congressional intent to preempt state action pursuant to the Supremacy Clause to allow a federal prosecution to preclude state authorities from vindicating "the historic right and obligation of the States to maintain peace and order within their confines," *Bartkus v. Illinois, supra*, at 137.

The complementary nature of the sovereignty exercised by the Federal Government and the States places upon a defendant burdens commensurate with concomitant privileges. Past cases have recognized that the special ordeal suffered by a defendant prosecuted by both federal and state authorities is the price of living in a federal system, the cost of dual citizenship. Every citizen, the Court has noted, "owes allegiance to the two departments, so to speak, and within their respective spheres must pay the penalties which each exacts for disobedience to its laws. In return, he can demand protection from each within its own jurisdiction."

* * *

Where two States seek to prosecute the same defendant for the same crime in two separate proceedings, the justifications found in the federal-state context for an exemption from double jeopardy constraints simply do not hold. Although the two States may have opted for different policies within their assigned territorial jurisdictions, the sovereign concerns with whose vindication each State has been charged are identical. Thus, in contrast to the federal-state context, barring the second prosecution would still permit one government to act upon the broad range of sovereign concerns that have been reserved to the States by the Constitution. The compelling need in the federal-state context to subordinate double jeopardy concerns is thus considerably diminished in cases involving successive prosecutions by different States. Moreover, from the defendant's perspective, the burden of successive prosecutions cannot be justified as the quid pro quo of dual citizenship.

* * *

Even where the power of two sovereigns to pursue separate prosecutions for the same crime has been undisputed, this Court has barred both governments from combining to do together what each could not constitutionally do on its own. *See Murphy v. Waterfront Comm'n*, 378 U.S. 52 (1964); *Elkins v. United States*, 364 U.S. 206 (1960). And just as the Constitution bars one sovereign from facilitating another's prosecution by delivering testimony coerced under promise of immunity or evidence illegally seized, I believe that it prohibits two sovereigns from combining forces to ensure that a defendant receives only the trappings of criminal process as he is sped along to execution.

* * *

While no one can doubt the propriety of two States cooperating to bring a criminal to justice, the cooperation between Georgia and Alabama in this case went far beyond their initial joint investigation. Georgia's efforts to secure petitioner's execution did not end with its acceptance of his guilty plea. Its law enforcement officials went on to play leading roles as prosecution witnesses in the Alabama trial. Indeed, had the Alabama trial judge not restricted the State to one assisting officer at the prosecution's table during trial, a Georgia officer would have shared the honors with an Alabama officer. Although the record does not reveal the precise nature of the assurances made by Georgia authorities that induced petitioner to plead guilty in the first proceeding against him, I cannot believe he would have done so had he been aware that the officials whose forbearance he bought in Georgia with his plea would merely continue their efforts to secure his death in another jurisdiction.

Even before the Fourteenth Amendment was held to incorporate the protections of the Double Jeopardy Clause, four Members of this Court registered their outrage at "an instance of the prosecution being allowed to harass the accused with repeated trials and convictions on the same evidence, until it achieve[d] its desired result of a capital verdict." *Ciucci v. Illinois*, 356 U.S. 571, 573 (1958). Such "relentless prosecutions," they asserted, constituted "an unseemly and oppressive use of a criminal trial that violates the concept of due process contained in the Fourteenth Amendment, whatever its ultimate scope is taken to be." The only differences between the facts in *Ciucci* and those in this case are that here the relentless effort was a cooperative one between two States and that petitioner sought to avoid trial by pleading guilty. Whether viewed as a violation of the Double Jeopardy Clause or simply as an affront to the due process guarantee of fundamental fairness, Alabama's prosecution of petitioner cannot survive constitutional scrutiny. I therefore must dissent.

Notes

The successive federal and state prosecutions of Terry Nichols provide another example of some of the issues raised in *Heath*. Nichols was convicted in federal court of one count of conspiracy (with Timothy McVeigh) to use a weapon of mass destruction, and eight counts of involuntary manslaughter relating to federal personnel killed in the Oklahoma City bombing. After the federal court sentenced Nichols to multiple life sentences with no possibility of release, the state of Oklahoma charged him with 168 counts of murder and sought the death penalty. A state jury convicted Nichols of 161 counts of first-degree murder, but deadlocked on the death penalty. After the state judge imposed additional life sentences, Nichols was returned to federal prison.

The state charges have been controversial. Critics emphasized that the state prosecution cost Oklahoma millions of dollars but did nothing to change Nichols' prison status. (Indeed, by 2005 the state had paid over 4 million dollars just for Nichols' defense.) Legal experts also questioned whether the state conviction would hold up in light of the federal district court's earlier decision moving the federal trials to Denver on the ground that Nichols and McVeigh could not receive a fair trial in Oklahoma.

1. **Explaining the persistence of the dual sovereignty rule:** *Bartkus* and *Abbate* were met with a barrage of critical commentary, and many authorities predicted that both cases would be overruled in short order. These predictions seemed reasonable in light of the general trend of Supreme Court decisions in the decade following *Bartkus* and *Abbate,* when the Warren Court frequently struck the balance between the rights of the individual accused and institutional considerations in favor of the accused. Specific decisions of the Court also seemed to be portents of a doctrinal change. The Supreme Court rejected the concept of dual sovereignty in the context of the Fourth and Fifth Amendments,[b] and it showed great sensitivity to Double Jeopardy concerns in a series of opinions.[c]

But as *Heath v. Alabama* demonstrates, the Supreme Court has not repudiated *Bartkus* and *Abbate,* despite numerous opportunities to do so. To the contrary, the Court reaffirmed and extended the dual sovereignty doctrine in *Heath* and in *United States v. Wheeler,* 435 U.S. 313 (1978), which held that a Navajo Tribal prosecution under the Tribal Code was the action of a separate sovereign, and that the Double Jeopardy clause did not bar a subsequent federal prosecution based on the same conduct.[d]

---

b. *United States v. Halper,* 490 U.S. 435 (1989).

c. *See Ashe v. Swenson,* 397 U.S. 436 (1970) (concluding collateral estoppel is part of Double Jeopardy); *Benton v. Maryland,* 395 U.S. 784 (1969) (incorporating Double Jeopardy into Fourteenth Amendment); *Murphy v. Waterfront Commission of New York Harbor,* 378 U.S. 52 (1964) (rejecting dual sovereignty limitation in context of immunity from self incrimination); *Waller v. Florida,* 397 U.S. 387 (1970) (refusing to apply dual sovereignty doctrine to successive prosecutions by municipal and state courts).

d. An interesting wrinkle on the basic dual sovereignty problem arose in *United States v. Lara,* 541 U.S. 193 (2004). The defendant, a member of the Turtle Mountain Band of Chippewa Indians, assaulted a federal officer while on the Spirit Lake Tribe's reservation. After Lara pled guilty in the Spirit Lake Tribal Court for "violence to a policeman," he was charged with assault on a federal officer under 18 U.S.C. § 111(a)(1). Lara argued that the second prosecution was barred by Double Jeopardy, because the tribal court had been exercising federal power delegated by Congress under the Indian Civil Rights Act, not the inherent jurisdiction of the sovereign tribe. The jurisdictional provision under which he was prosecuted in the tribal court had been enacted by Congress in response to an earlier decision of the Supreme Court holding that tribal courts lacked jurisdiction to try nonmembers. A divided Court rejected this argument, concluding that the statute in question merely affirmed the inherent power of the tribes as sovereigns. Exercising its powers to legislate with respect to Indian tribes, Congress had first placed limitations on the exercise of tribal jurisdiction–leading to the Court's earlier ruling that there was no jurisdiction over nonmembers–and then had lifted or relaxed those restrictions. Thus the power exercised by the tribal court was the tribe's own inherent sovereign power, not federal power delegated by Congress. Accordingly, the case was governed by *Wheeler,* and the dual sovereignty doctrine was applicable.

What accounts for the surprising persistence of the dual sovereignty doctrine in the context of Double Jeopardy, when the Supreme Court has rejected the doctrine in the context of the Fourth and Fifth Amendments? There is certainly some bite to Justice Black's argument that a second trial and punishment has the same impact on the defendant and is equally unfair whether one or two sovereigns are involved. Why then did the Warren Court fail to extend the so-called criminal procedural revolution to this aspect of Double Jeopardy jurisprudence?

One possibility is that the dual sovereignty doctrine serves some purpose that the Warren Court valued just as highly as it valued fairness to individual criminal defendants. Recall that another hallmark of the Warren Court was its supports of civil rights (which may be seen, for example, in cases requiring school desegregation). It seems possible that the Court saw the dual sovereignty doctrine as an important safeguard in the move toward equal rights in the South. In a number of cases state and local authorities had failed to bring to justice those accused of the assault or murder of civil rights demonstrators, and in some cases state officials were themselves implicated in the violence. In situations of that nature, there was a real danger that state authorities could thwart federal interests by a state prosecution that ended in an acquittal or a "slap on the wrist." Indeed, two of the Supreme Court's major civil rights cases in the 1960s involved federal civil rights prosecutions brought after the failure of state murder prosecutions. *See United States v. Guest*, 383 U.S. 745, 748 n.1 (1966) (noting that defendants, members of the Klu Klux Klan, had previously been found not guilty of murder of Col. Lemuel Penn by a state jury); *United States v. Price*, 383 U.S. 787 (1966) (affirming convictions of local officials and their co-conspirators for the murders of civil rights workers Michael Schwerner, Andrew Goodman, and James Chaney).

Recently, there has been a resurgence of both state and federal prosecutions for civil rights era racial violence. One example is the 2003 federal trial of Ernest Avants for the 1966 murder of Ben Chester White, a sixty-seven-year-old black man, in Natchez, Mississippi. Avants and two other Klansmen abducted White, shot him multiple times, and dumped his body in a creek in the Homochitto National Forest, in an effort to lure Dr. Martin Luther King, Jr. to Mississippi to be assassinated. Avants was acquitted in state court in 1967, and no one was convicted of the murder. In 2000, after learning from a television news broadcast that the murder took place in a national forest, federal prosecutors indicted Avants, the only living suspect, citing federal jurisdiction over the national forest. Avants was convicted in 2003 and died in prison in 2004 at the age of 72. *See* Rick Bragg, *Former Klansman Is Found Guilty of 1966 Killing*, N.Y. TIMES, May 1, 2003, at A12. For a comprehensive discussion of the recent renewed prosecutions of civil rights era cases of racial violence, see Anthony V. Alfieri, *Retrying Race*, 101 MICH. L. REV. 1141, 1165 (2003).

Is the civil rights justification sufficient to support the dual sovereignty doctrine across the board? If not, does it warrant a narrower exception to Double Jeopardy for federal prosecutions for civil rights violations? Would such an exception make doctrinal sense? It has been suggested that because the Fourteenth Amendment was adopted after the Fifth Amendment Double Jeopardy Clause, the Equal Protection Clause and the Congressional enforcement authority under that Amendment might be understood to create an exception to Double Jeopardy.

In thinking about the survival of the dual sovereignty doctrine in the context of Double Jeopardy, it is also worth noting that the stakes are higher from the government's perspective in the context of Double Jeopardy than in the Fourth and Fifth Amendments. A robust interpretation of the Fourth and Fifth Amendments does not absolutely bar the successful prosecution of a defendant whose rights are found to have been violated. If there has been an illegal search or a confession elicited without *Miranda* warnings, it is still possible to convict the defendant if the government develops other evidence by constitutional means. In contrast, once a court finds a violation of the Double Jeopardy Clause, there is an absolute bar to a reprosecution for "the same offense." Without the dual sovereignty doctrine, a failed state prosecution could bar forever a federal prosecution for a serious crime, even if federal interests seemed to outweigh the state's interest. In light of the Supreme Court's evident concern for the policy implications of the dual sovereignty doctrine, it seems likely that the Court was sensitive to this factor.

2. **Criticism of the dual sovereignty doctrine:** In general, scholars have attacked the dual sovereignty doctrine. *See, e.g.,* Akhil Reed Amar & Jonathan L. Marcus, *Double Jeopardy Law After Rodney King*, 95 COLUM. L. REV. 1 (1995); Daniel A. Braun, *Praying to False Sovereigns: The Rule Permitting Successive Prosecutions in the Age of Cooperative Federalism*, 20 AM. J. CRIM. L. 1, 7–11 (1992); Susan N. Herman, *Double Jeopardy All Over Again: Dual Sovereignty, Rodney King, and the ACLU*, 41 UCLA L. REV. 609, 618–19 n.32 (1994) (collecting and digesting a dozen articles); George C. Thomas III, *Islands in the Stream of History: An Institutional Archeology of Dual Sovereignty*, Ohio St. J. Crim. L. 345, 346 (2003) ("Dual sovereignty is an acid that destroys all double jeopardy protection."). For a comprehensive analysis of dual sovereignty, see ADAM HARRIS KURLAND, SUCCESSIVE CRIMINAL PROSECUTIONS : THE DUAL SOVEREIGNTY EXCEPTION TO DOUBLE JEOPARDY IN STATE AND FEDERAL COURTS (2001).

Some recent critics have suggested that changes in circumstances warrant reconsideration of the dual sovereignty doctrine. Professor Sandra Guerra has argued that in the area of drug enforcement it is no longer accurate to assume that the federal and state government operate as separate sovereigns. After a rich description of the multi-jurisdictional model of law enforcement brought about by federal funding and cooperative programs including the DEA State and Local Task Forces and the Organized Crime Drug Enforcement Task Forces she concludes:

> Theory and reality diverge in double jeopardy law as it relates to successive or dual prosecutions, especially in the context of multijurisdictional drug law enforcement. Since federal law and state codes now respond to the same drug offenses, every drug offense is likely to violate two penal codes. For example, possession of cocaine is a crime in every state and under federal law. This parallel coding raises the possibility of multiple prosecutions in all drug cases.

* * *

* * * The multijurisdictional paradigm of drug law enforcement suggests that federal and state law enforcement and prosecuting authorities work together as one team with one mutual goal—the elimination of illicit drugs from our society. When two jurisdictions join forces in this way, the reasons for granting each sovereign the power to enforce its laws disappear. The two sovereignties in effect act as one sovereign; that they represent two governments becomes insignificant.

Sandra Guerra, *The Myth of Dual Sovereignty: Multijurisdictional Drug Law Enforcement and Double Jeopardy*, 73 N.C. L. REV. 1159, 1192, 1207 (1995).

Judge Guido Calabresi has also argued that changes in the federal role in law enforcement warrant a reassessment of the dual sovereignty doctrine. In a concurring opinion in *United States v. All Assets of G.P.S. Automotive Corp.*, 66 F.3d 483, 498–99 (2d Cir. 1995), he wrote:

* * * When *Bartkus* and *Abbate* were decided in 1959, the scope of federal criminal law was still very narrow, and the overlap of federal and state criminal jurisdiction was quite small. The risk to individual rights posed by successive prosecutions by state and federal officials was therefore necessarily limited. Under such circumstances, it was not implausible to believe that these risks could be contained through prosecutorial rules, and by the development of a significant and dynamic "sham or cover" exception such as that which *Bartkus*, by negative implication, could be read to countenance.

In recent years, however, the scope of federal criminal law has expanded enormously. And the number of crimes for which a defendant may be made subject to both a state and a federal prosecution has become very large. At the same time, the *Bartkus* exception has been defined extremely narrowly. It follows that today defendants in an enormous number of cases can be subjected to dual prosecutions. And this can happen even when state and federal officials, in practice, join together to take a second bite at the apple. As Judge Adams stated prophetically for the Third Circuit in *United States v. Grimes*, 641 F.2d 96 (3d Cir. 1981), at a time when the growth of federal criminal law had not yet reached its present extremes, "the recent expansion of federal criminal ... jurisdiction magnifies the impact of *Bartkus* and *Abbate*, thus rendering a reassessment of those decisions timely from a practical standpoint as well," since "permitting successive state-federal prosecutions for the same act [appears] inconsistent with what is a most ancient principle in western jurisprudence—that the government may not twice place a person in jeopardy for the same offense."

Among recent important examples of successive federal-state prosecution are (1) the federal prosecution of the Los Angeles police officers accused of using excessive force on motorist Rodney King after their acquittal on state charges, (2) the federal prosecution of an African–American youth accused of murdering a Hasidic Jew in the Crown Heights section of Brooklyn, New York, after his acquittal on state charges, and (3) the Florida state prosecution—seeking the death penalty—of the anti-abortion zealot who had been convicted and sentenced to life imprisonment in federal court for killing an abortion doctor. While I express no opinion whatsoever about these particular cases or about the applicability of the Double Jeopardy Clause to them, there can be no doubt that all of these cases involved re-prosecutions in emotionally and politically charged contexts. It was to avoid political pressures for re-prosecution that the Double Jeopardy Clause was adopted. And it is especially troublesome that the dual sovereignty doctrine keeps the Double Jeopardy Clause from protecting defendants whose punishment, after an acquittal or an allegedly inadequate sentence, is the object of public attention and political concern.

The degree of cooperation between state and federal officials in criminal law enforcement has, moreover, reached unparalleled levels in the last few years, especially in the context of the "war on drugs." This cooperation, which undoubtedly fosters effective enforcement of the criminal law, is surely to be encouraged. Still, this same cooperation should cause one to wonder whether it makes much sense to maintain the fiction that federal and state governments are so separate in their interests that the dual sovereignty doctrine is universally needed to protect one from the other.

The Supreme Court has recently shown its willingness to re-consider supposedly well-settled landmarks of double jeopardy jurisprudence with respect to its definition of what constitutes prosecutions for the "same offense." And the Supreme Court's decision earlier this year in *United States v. Lopez* has similarly revealed the Court's willingness to give serious and renewed thought to issues of federalism at the foundation of our constitutional system, and to do so in the context of the enormous expansion of federal criminal law. In that light, a new look by the High Court at the dual sovereignty doctrine and what it means today for the safeguards the Framers sought to place in the Double Jeopardy Clause would surely be welcome.

See also William Van Alstyne, *Dual Sovereignty, Federalism and National Criminal Law: Modernist Constitutional Doctrine and the Nonrole of the Supreme Court*, 26 Am. Crim. L. Rev. 1740, 1750–57 (1989). At least one court has rejected the argument that such a "joint sovereign" exception exists. *United States v. Claiborne*, 92 F.Supp.2d 503, 508 (E.D. Va. 2000).

3. **Is there a sham exception to the dual sovereignty doctrine?:** Dicta from the *Bartkus* opinion has generally been interpreted as creating a "sham" exception to the dual sovereignty doctrine. The Court stated the state prosecution was undertaken by state officials within their own discretion on the basis of evidence of conduct that violated the Illinois criminal code. The Court concluded that the cooperation in that case between the federal and state authorities was merely "the conventional practice between the two sets of prosecutors throughout the country," which did not support the defendant's claim "the state prosecution was a sham and a cover for a federal prosecution, and thereby in essential fact another federal prosecution." 359 U.S. at 123–24.

But as the court explained in *United States v. Figueroa–Soto*, 938 F.2d 1015 (9th Cir. 1991):

As a practical matter, however, under the criteria established by *Bartkus* itself it is extremely difficult and highly unusual to prove that a prosecution by one government is a tool, a sham or a cover for the other government. * * *

As *Bartkus* makes plain, there may be very close coordination in the prosecutions, in the employment of agents of one sovereign to help the other sovereign in its prosecution, and in the timing of the court proceedings so that the maximum assistance is mutually rendered by the sovereigns. None of this close collaboration amounts to one government being the other's "tool" or providing a "sham" or "cover." Collaboration between state and federal authorities is "the conventional practice." No constitutional barrier exists to this norm of cooperative effort.

938 F.2d at 1019–20. *See also United States v. All Assets of G.P.S. Automotive Corp.,* 66 F.3d 483, 495–96 (2d Cir. 1995) (Calabresi, J. concurring) (agreeing that federal-state cooperation and even cross designation of a prosecutor does not establish a sham prosecution, but suggesting that sham exception should apply where state prosecutors persuade federal officials to institute federal forfeiture after state conviction if the state will receive a disproportionate share of the proceeds).

4. **Prohibiting successive prosecutions by statute or treaty:** Many states have statutes prohibiting a state prosecution after a prior prosecution by the federal authorities or another state. A 2001 survey of state law found that a majority of states have some statutory or state constitutional provision limiting successive prosecutions after prior prosecution in another jurisdiction, but cautions that the state approaches are confusing and vary markedly on determining which prior prosecutions are barred. *See* ADAM HARRIS KURLAND, SUCCESSIVE CRIMINAL PROSECUTIONS: THE DUAL SOVEREIGNTY EXCEPTION TO DOUBLE JEOPARDY IN STATE AND FEDERAL COURTS (2001). The Model Penal Code includes a provision barring a second prosecution by a different jurisdiction when the subsequent prosecution is based on the same conduct unless "the offense of which the defendant was formerly convicted or acquitted and the offense for which he is subsequently prosecuted each requires proof of a fact not required by the other and the law defining each of such offenses is intended to prevent a substantially different harm or evil * * *." MODEL PENAL CODE § 1.10.

Should Congress pass a statute limiting successive prosecutions? Shortly after the decisions in *Bartkus* and *Abbate,* a bill was introduced in Congress that would have generally barred prosecution by the federal government if a state had previously prosecuted, but it died in Committee. *See* H.R. 6176, 86th Cong., 1st Sess. (1959). What are the advantages of accomplishing such an end through legislation rather than by constitutional decision? A statute can readily include exceptions, and it can be amended or repealed if necessary. Would that make it more or less desirable from your point of view?

In a few instances, provisions defining specific federal crimes provide for a plea in bar where there has been a prior conviction or acquittal "on the merits" under state law. *See* 18 U.S.C.A. § 659 (theft from interstate shipment); § 660 (embezzlement of funds accruing from or used in commerce); § 2117 (breaking and entering carrier facilities). It is not clear, at least in some cases, why Congress chose to bar a duplicative federal prosecution for these particular crimes. Is a crime-by-crime approach desirable? If so, what factors would justify a bar on reprosecution for particular offenses? Is there a danger of reprosecution for improper or insufficient reasons for certain offenses? Is there a lesser federal interest in certain federal offenses?

In 1992 the United States became a signatory to the International Covenant on Civil and Political Rights (ICCPR), which includes a prohibition on double jeopardy. ICCPR Article 14(7). Although the U.S. submitted a reservation to this provision indicating its desire to preserve the dual sovereignty doctrine, it has been suggested that the U.S. will to come under international pressure to reexamine this position in the future. Paul Hoffman, *Double Jeopardy Wars: The Case for a Civil Rights "Exception,"* 41 UCLA L. Rev. 649, 654 (1994). Do you think Congress is likely to bow to international pressure on this issue?

2.   THE *PETITE* POLICY APPROACH

In the absence of constitutional or statutory limits, how does and should the federal government employ its authority to bring successive prosecutions?

In 1959, shortly after the Supreme Court's decisions in *Abbate* and *Bartkus,* Attorney General William Rogers issued a press release announcing what has come to be known as the *Petite* Policy. The press release stated that "After a state prosecution there should be no federal trial for the same act or acts unless the reasons are compelling."

The *Petite* Policy gained more attention (and derived its name) the following year when the Supreme Court considered *Petite v. United States*, 361 U.S. 529 (1960). In *Petite* the government filed a motion asking the Supreme Court to remand the case with directions to dismiss the indictment on the ground that "it is the general policy of the federal government 'that several offenses arising out of a single transaction should be alleged and tried together and should not be made the basis of multiple prosecutions, a policy dictated by considerations both of fairness to defendants and of efficient and orderly law enforcement.'" 361 U.S. at 530. The Solicitor General represented this policy as closely related to the policy against duplicative federal-state prosecutions announced by the press release noted above. The Supreme Court granted the government's motion.

Ever since the decision in *Petite,* the phrase *Petite* Policy has been used to refer to both (1) the policy restricting dual federal-state prosecutions and (2) the policy to try together several federal offenses arising out of a single transaction. The current version, reprinted below, continues the general presumption against successive prosecutions and enforces it through the requirement that each dual prosecution be approved in advance by the appropriate assistant attorney general.

UNITED STATES ATTORNEYS MANUAL CHAPTER 9–2.000
AUTHORITY OF THE UNITED STATES ATTORNEY IN
CRIMINAL DIVISION MATTERS/PRIOR APPROVALS

June 2005

9–2.031   Dual and Successive Prosecution Policy ("Petite Policy")

A.   Statement of Policy. This policy establishes guidelines for the exercise of discretion by appropriate officers of the Department of

Justice in determining whether to bring a federal prosecution based on substantially the same act(s) or transactions involved in a prior state or federal proceeding. *See Rinaldi v. United States*, 434 U.S. 22, 27, (1977); *Petite v. United States*, 361 U.S. 529 (1960). Although there is no general statutory bar to a federal prosecution where the defendant's conduct already has formed the basis for a state prosecution, Congress expressly has provided that, as to certain offenses, a state judgment of conviction or acquittal on the merits shall be a bar to any subsequent federal prosecution for the same act or acts. *See* 18 U.S.C. §§ 659, 660, 1992, 2101, 2117; *see also* 15 U.S.C. §§ 80a–36, 1282.

The purpose of this policy is to vindicate substantial federal interests through appropriate federal prosecutions, to protect persons charged with criminal conduct from the burdens associated with multiple prosecutions and punishments for substantially the same act(s) or transaction(s), to promote efficient utilization of Department resources, and to promote coordination and cooperation between federal and state prosecutors.

This policy precludes the initiation or continuation of a federal prosecution, following a prior state or federal prosecution based on substantially the same act(s) or transaction(s) unless three substantive prerequisites are satisfied: first, the matter must involve a substantial federal interest; second, the prior prosecution must have left that interest demonstrably unvindicated; and third, applying the same test that is applicable to all federal prosecutions, the government must believe that the defendant's conduct constitutes a federal offense, and that the admissible evidence probably will be sufficient to obtain and sustain a conviction by an unbiased trier of fact. In addition, there is a procedural prerequisite to be satisfied, that is, the prosecution must be approved by the appropriate Assistant Attorney General.

Satisfaction of the three substantive prerequisites does not mean that a proposed prosecution must be approved or brought. The traditional elements of federal prosecutorial discretion continue to apply. *See Principles of Federal Prosecution*, USAM 9–27.110.

In order to insure the most efficient use of law enforcement resources, whenever a matter involves overlapping federal and state jurisdiction, federal prosecutors should, as soon as possible, consult with their state counterparts to determine the most appropriate single forum in which to proceed to satisfy the substantial federal and state interests involved, and, if possible, to resolve all criminal liability for the acts in question.

B. Types of Prosecution to which This Policy Applies. This policy applies only to charging decisions; it does not apply to pre-charge investigations. Yet, where a prior prosecution has been brought based on substantially the same act(s) or transaction(s), a subsequent federal investigation should, generally speaking, initially focus on evidence relevant to determining whether a subsequent federal prosecution would be warranted in light of the three substantive prerequisites previously listed.

Keeping in mind the distinction between charging decisions and precharge investigations, this policy applies whenever the contemplated federal prosecution is based on substantially the same act(s) or transaction(s) involved in a prior state or federal prosecution.

This policy constitutes an exercise of the Department's prosecutorial discretion, and applies even where a prior state prosecution would not legally bar a subsequent federal prosecution under the Double Jeopardy Clause because of the doctrine of dual sovereignty (*see Abbate v. United States*, 359 U.S. 187 (1959)), or a prior prosecution would not legally bar a subsequent state or federal prosecution under the Double Jeopardy Clause because each offense requires proof of an element not contained in the other. *See United States v. Dixon*, 509 U.S. 688 (1993); *Blockburger v. United States*, 284 U.S. 299 (1932).

This policy does not apply, and thus prior approval is not required, where the prior prosecution involved only a minor part of the contemplated federal charges. For example, a federal conspiracy or RICO prosecution may allege overt acts or predicate offenses previously prosecuted as long as those acts or offenses do not represent substantially the whole of the contemplated federal charge, and, in a RICO prosecution, as long as there are a sufficient number of predicate offenses to sustain the RICO charge if the previously prosecuted offenses were excluded.

This policy does not apply, and thus prior approval is not required, where the contemplated federal prosecution could not have been brought in the initial federal prosecution because of, for example, venue restrictions, or joinder or proof problems.

Please note that when there is no need for prior approval because this policy does not apply, all other approval requirements remain in force. One example of another approval requirement is the one requiring Criminal Division approval of all RICO indictments.

C. Stages of Prosecution at which Policy Applies. This policy applies whenever there has been a prior state or federal prosecution resulting in an acquittal, a conviction, including one resulting from a plea agreement, or a dismissal or other termination of the case on the merits after jeopardy has attached.

Once a prior prosecution reaches one of the above-listed stages this policy applies, and approval is required before a federal prosecution can be initiated or continued, even if an indictment or information already has been filed in the federal prosecution.

An exception occurs, and this policy does not apply, if the federal trial has commenced and the prior prosecution subsequently reaches one of the above-listed stages. When, however, a federal trial results in a mistrial, dismissal, or reversal on appeal, and, in the interim, a prior prosecution has reached one of the above listed stages, this policy applies.

D. Substantive Prerequisites for Approval of a Prosecution Governed by this Policy. As previously stated there are three substantive prerequisites that must be met before approval will be granted for the initiation or a continuation of a prosecution governed by this policy.

The first substantive prerequisite is that the matter must involve a substantial federal interest. This determination will be made on a case-by-case basis, applying the considerations applicable to all federal prosecutions. *See Principles of Federal Prosecution*, USAM 9–27.230. Matters that come within the national investigative or prosecutorial priorities established by the Department are more likely than others to satisfy this requirement.

The second substantive prerequisite is that the prior prosecution must have left that substantial federal interest demonstrably unvindicated. In general, the Department will presume that a prior prosecution, regardless of result, has vindicated the relevant federal interest. That presumption, however, may be overcome when there are factors suggesting an unvindicated federal interest.

The presumption may be overcome when a conviction was not achieved because of the following sorts of factors: first, incompetence, corruption, intimidation, or undue influence; second, court or jury nullification in clear disregard of the evidence or the law; third, the unavailability of significant evidence, either because it was not timely discovered or known by the prosecution, or because it was kept from the trier of fact's consideration because of an erroneous interpretation of the law; fourth, the failure in a prior state prosecution to prove an element of a state offense that is not an element of the contemplated federal offense; and fifth, the exclusion of charges in a prior federal prosecution out of concern for fairness to other defendants, or for significant resource considerations that favored separate federal prosecutions.

The presumption may be overcome even when a conviction was achieved in the prior prosecution in the following circumstances: first, if the prior sentence was manifestly inadequate in light of the federal interest involved and a substantially enhanced sentence—including forfeiture and restitution as well as imprisonment and fines—is available through the contemplated federal prosecution, or second, if the choice of charges, or the determination of guilt, or the severity of sentence in the prior prosecution was affected by the sorts of factors listed in the previous paragraph. An example might be a case in which the charges in the initial prosecution trivialized the seriousness of the contemplated federal offense, for example, a state prosecution for assault and battery in a case involving the murder of a federal official.

The presumption also may be overcome, irrespective of the result in a prior state prosecution, in those rare cases where the following three conditions are met: first, the alleged violation involves a compelling federal interest, particularly one implicating an enduring national priority; second, the alleged violation involves egregious conduct, including that which threatens or causes loss of life, severe economic or physical harm, or the impairment of the functioning of an agency of the federal government or the due administration of justice; and third, the result in the prior prosecution was manifestly inadequate in light of the federal interest involved.

The third substantive prerequisite is that the government must believe that the defendant's conduct constitutes a federal offense, and that the admissible evidence probably will be sufficient to obtain and sustain a conviction by an unbiased trier of fact. This is the same test applied to all federal prosecutions. *See Principles of Federal Prosecution*, USAM 9–27.200 *et seq*. This requirement turns on the evaluation of the admissible evidence that will be available at the time of trial. The possibility that, despite the law and the facts, the fact-finder may acquit the defendant because of the unpopularity of some factor involved in the prosecution, or because of the overwhelming popularity of the defendant, or his or her cause, is not a factor that should preclude a proposed prosecution. Also, when in the case of a prior conviction the unvindicated federal interest in the matter arises because of the availability of a substantially enhanced sentence, the government must believe that the admissible evidence meets the legal requirements for such sentence.

E. Procedural prerequisite for Bringing a Prosecution Governed by This Policy. Whenever a substantial question arises as to whether this policy applies to a prosecution, the matter should be submitted to the appropriate Assistant Attorney General for resolution. Prior approval from the appropriate Assistant Attorney General must be obtained before bringing a prosecution governed by this policy. The United States will move to dismiss any prosecution governed by this policy in which prior approval was not obtained, unless the Assistant Attorney General retroactively approves it on the following grounds: first, that there [are] unusual or overriding circumstances justifying retroactive approval, and second, that the prosecution would have been approved had approval been sought in a timely fashion. Appropriate administrative action may be initiated against prosecutors who violate this policy.

F. Reservation and Superseding Effect: for Internal Guidance Only, No Substantive or Procedural Rights Created. This policy has been promulgated solely for the purpose of internal Department of Justice guidance. It is not intended to, does not, and may not be relied upon to create any rights, substantive or procedural, that are enforceable at law by any party in any matter, civil or criminal, nor does it place any limitations on otherwise lawful litigative prerogatives of the Department of Justice.

All of the federal circuit courts that have considered the question have held that a criminal defendant can not invoke the Department's policy as a bar to federal prosecution. * * * The Supreme Court, in analogous contexts, has concluded that Department policies governing its internal operations do not create rights which may be enforced by defendants against the Department. *See United States v. Caceres*, 440 U.S. 741 (1979); *Sullivan v. United States*, 348 U.S. 170 (1954).

This policy statement supersedes all prior Department guidelines and policy statements on the subject.

Notes

1. Why do you think the Department promulgated the *Petite* Policy? As noted above, the policy was first announced in 1959, a few months after the Supreme Court's dual sovereignty decisions in *Abbate* and *Bartkus*. It has been suggested that the policy was a response to concern that the Court would reverse itself if it believed that the practice of bringing successive prosecutions was being abused.

The *Petite* Policy has been through several revisions. For example, in 1977 Attorney General Griffin Bell announced an exception to the policy for civil rights cases which "necessarily involve compelling federal interests." *See* Joseph S. Allerhand, Note, *The Petite Policy: An Example of Enlightened Prosecutorial Discretion*, 66 GEO. L.J. 1137, 1141 n.19 (1978). It appears that the most recent revision by Attorney General Janet Reno was prompted in part by questions raised in connection with the federal prosecution after the state acquittal of the police officers who beat Los Angeles motorist Rodney King. For a discussion of the new policy and related state laws, see Beth M. Bollinger, *Defending Dual Prosecutions: Learning How to Draw the Line*, 10 CRIM. JUST. 16 (Fall 1995).

2. Two Department of Justice attorneys involved in Attorney General Reno's revision of the *Petite* Policy have written about the amendment of the policy, and have also provided some statistics about the Department's approval of duplicative prosecutions:

The Department of Justice recently completed a revision of the *Petite* Policy. The revised statement of the policy precludes a federal prosecution following a state prosecution based on "substantially the same act(s) or transaction(s)" unless a "substantial federal interest" has been "demonstrably unvindicated" by the prior prosecution. The policy implements this substantive standard through the extraordinary procedural requirement that a dual prosecution be approved by the appropriate assistant attorney general.

The policy dictates that a prior prosecution, regardless of its result, will be presumed to have vindicated the federal interests involved, except when specified standards are met. [The federal interest may be unvindicated if the prior prosecution was flawed by one of several factors, including the unavailability of evidence or an incompetent prosecutor or judge. Even if the prior proceeding resulted in a conviction, the presumption may be overcome if the prior sentence was manifestly inadequate in light of the federal interest involved and a substantially enhanced sentence would be available through federal prosecution. Regardless of the result of the prior prosecution, in "rare" cases the presumption can be overcome, if the case involves a "compelling federal interest, particularly one implicating an enduring national priority" and "egregious conduct," and the result of the previous prosecution was "manifestly inadequate in light of the federal interest involved." The policy also sets up a procedural framework, requiring, first, that federal prosecutors coordinate with their state counterparts at the earliest possible time to determine the most appropriate forum, and, second, that if a federal prosecutor determines that there is a substantial question as to whether the policy applies, the case cannot be prosecuted unless it is approved by the appropriate assistant attorney general.]

Statistics on dual prosecutions reflect the selectivity that the *Petite* Policy has produced. Dual prosecutions are quite rare. The Justice Department's 94 U.S. Attorney's Offices and litigating divisions together typically bring fewer than 150 dual prosecutions each year. This represents a tiny fraction of the total number of state prosecutions that, because of overlapping federal and state jurisdiction, could be reprosecuted in the federal system, and a small fraction of the approximately 65,000 annual federal prosecutions.

Harry Litman & Mark D. Greenberg, *Dual Prosecutions: A Model For Concurrent Federal Jurisdiction*, 543 ANNALS AM. ACAD. POL. & SOC. SCI. 72, 75–77 (1996). In a footnote the authors note that the Civil Rights Division had approved fewer than fifty dual prosecutions over the last 15 years. *Id.* at 84 n.15.

3. In cases like *Petite*, where the government discovers after conviction that a prosecution does not comply with the policy, the government will move to vacate the conviction. (See subsection E, *supra* at p. 826.) Although the Supreme Court granted the government's motion in the *Petite* case and in several subsequent cases, the Court's authority to do so is not entirely clear, and several justices have expressed opposition to this practice. Other justices have agreed that the Court has the authority to grant such motions, but have expressed the view that it should exercise its own discretion in determining whether to grant the government's request that it do so in particular cases.

In *Petite,* the Court issued a per curiam opinion stating "[t]he case is remanded to the Court of Appeals to vacate its judgment and to direct the District Court to vacate its judgment and to dismiss the indictment. In the interest of justice, the Court is clearly empowered thus to dispose of the matter, 28 U.S.C. § 2106." 361 U.S. at 531. Chief Justice Warren concurred as follows:

> Authority to grant this type of motion is one thing, however, and determination of the considerations relevant to a proper exercise of that authority is another. As I believe that the Court should not deny all such motions peremptorily, so do I believe that we should not automatically grant them through invocation of the policy of avoiding decision of constitutional issues. There are circumstances in which our responsibility of definitively interpreting the law of the land and of supervising its judicial application would dictate that we dispose of a case on its merits. In a situation, for example, where the invalidity of the judgment is clear and the motion to vacate and remand is obviously a means of avoiding an adjudication, I think we would be remiss in our duty were we to grant the motion.

361 U.S. at 532. Justice Brennan joined by Justices Black and Douglas also concurred, agreeing that the Court should review the merits of each case before granting the government's motion. However, in *Watts v. United States*, 422 U.S. 1032 (1975), Chief Justice Burger, joined by Justices White and Rehnquist, dissented, arguing that the Court should not vacate convictions when the government belatedly discovers that it failed to comply with the *Petite* Policy.

　　4. What about the other side of the coin, where *the defendant* seeks judicial enforcement of the *Petite* Policy, arguing that the government has failed to comply. Subsection F, *supra* at p. 826, states that the policy is intended "solely" to provide internal guidance to the Justice Department, and that it is not enforceable by any party. Defendants have alleged *Petite* violations in many cases, and the courts have universally refused to grant relief. Indeed, most courts have refused even to consider the merits of the question whether the policy was violated.

　　In denying relief, the courts have generally reasoned that the *Petite* Policy is not constitutionally mandated and by its own terms confers no rights upon the accused. A number of courts have indicated that the determination of the presence of a sufficient federal interest to warrant a second prosecution is not an appropriate subject for judicial evaluation. Some courts have also suggested that enforcement would intrude into the internal affairs of the Justice Department in violation of the separation of powers doctrine. And, as noted in the policy itself (*supra* at p. 827), the Supreme Court has ruled that other internal department policies are not judicially enforceable. For example, in *United States v. Caceres*, 440 U.S. 741, 743–44 (1979), the Court held that an internal IRS policy requiring advance approval before recording conversations with taxpayers would not be judicially enforced.

　　Is the courts' refusal to enforce the *Petite* Policy appropriate, or should there be at least some judicial review and control available? Recall that the policy requires the government to move to vacate a conviction if it discovers that the necessary approval was not given under the policy, but it also provides for retroactive approval in cases where unusual circumstances justify retroactive approval and approval would have been granted if sought in a timely manner. *See* section E, *supra* at p. 826. So disputes arise only in cases in which the Department takes the position that the policy has (at least belatedly) been followed. What do you think would happen if the courts began vacating convictions in such cases over the objections of the Department? In the *Caceres* case noted above, the Supreme Court suggested that judicial enforcement over the objection of the IRS might lead the IRS to rescind or restrict its policy, which was intended to be protective of taxpayers. 440 U.S. at 755–56. Could that happen to the *Petite* Policy?

　　If application and interpretation of the policy were subject to judicial review, what scope of review would be appropriate? Wouldn't a deferential standard of review meet some or all of the concerns that have been used to justify the courts' refusal to review decisions under the *Petite* Policy? For an article arguing for heightened judicial review of violations of the *Petite* Policy, and Department of Justice guidelines in general, see Ellen S. Podgor,

Department of Justice Guidelines: Balancing "Discretionary Justice," 13 CORNELL J.L. & PUB. POL'Y 167 (2004).

5. For a policy which was first promulgated almost 50 years ago, we have surprisingly little information about how frequently the *Petite* policy is invoked, and about how it is being interpreted and applied. No statistical data has been published on the number of times a *Petite* issue has arisen in connection with a federal prosecution, though Department attorneys Litman and Greenberg (writing in 1996) stated that approximately 150 duplicate prosecutions are approved per year under the policy. The only other index of frequency is the reported cases where a *Petite* issue is or could have been raised. Writing in 1995, Professor Sandra Guerra cited eight cases from the previous two decades as examples in which the policy had been "violated," and suggested that perhaps it was "honored more often in the breach." Sandra Guerra, *The Myth of Dual Sovereignty: Multijurisdictional Drug Law Enforcement and Double Jeopardy*, 73 N.C. L. REV. 1159, 1210 n.178 (1995). Assuming that the policy was violated in all of these cases, does that establish lax enforcement? This may depend on what baseline you use. Although Guerra's list does not purport to be exhaustive, it is still worth noting that it includes less than one case per year out of the total federal caseload. Since the total caseload during the period covered by Guerra's list was never less than 28,000 (and generally was far higher), less than one violation per year might suggest that enforcement of the policy is actually quite stringent. On the other hand, the reported cases may be just the tip of the iceberg. After all, more than 90% of federal convictions rest on a guilty plea; in these cases few if any of the possible issues are litigated, and fewer still are the subject of reported opinions.

6. Although many of the specifics of how the policy is being interpreted are not available and perhaps unknown, certain substantive aspects of the policy can be identified.

The revised *Petite* Policy bars a successive federal prosecution unless the prior state prosecution "left that substantial federal interest demonstrably unvindicated." There is a presumption that a prior state prosecution vindicated the federal interests, but this presumption may be overcome. Note that suggesting the kinds of facts sufficient to overcome this presumption the policy distinguishes between cases in which the prior prosecution resulted in an acquittal and where it resulted in a conviction. For example, the presumption can be overcome by a showing that an acquittal resulted from incompetence, corruption, intimidation, undue influence; by court or jury nullification in clear disregard of the evidence or the law; or by a showing that a conviction resulted in a "manifestly inadequate" sentence. And regardless of the outcome of the first prosecution, the presumption against a successive federal prosecution may be overcome when three criteria are met:

> first, the alleged violation involves a compelling federal interest, particularly one implicating an enduring national priority; second, the alleged violation involves egregious conduct, including that which threatens or causes loss of life, severe economic or physical harm, or the impairment of the functioning of an agency of the federal government or the due administration of justice; and third, the result in the prior prosecution was manifestly inadequate in light of the federal interest involved.

Evaluate the revised *Petite* Policy. Does it identify the proper considerations, and strike the right balance between the government's interest in prosecuting and punishing serious anti-social conduct and the individual's need to be free from the strain and burden of repetitive prosecutions? Does it provide sufficient guidance to prosecutors in the field?

3. OTHER APPROACHES

a. *In General*

A variety of other approaches for dealing with the duplicative prosecution issue have been suggested. As you read these suggestions, consider whether you think they would be practical, and whether they would create any new difficulties of their own:

1.   Whenever there is a federal crime that parallels a state crime, try both crimes together in state court. Federal investigators and prosecutors could still be used, but the state courts would have jurisdiction. In special cases where this approach might not work, allow either party to petition the federal court to have the case tried in a federal court. *See* Guido Calabresi, *Federal and State Courts: Restoring a Workable Balance*, 78 N.Y.U. L. Rev. 1293, 1298 (2003).

2.   Allow the defendant to decide whether to be prosecuted for the federal crime. Under this scheme, choice of the federal forum would bar the state from subsequently prosecuting but not the contrary. If the federal forum were chosen, but federal authorities declined to prosecute, the state could try the defendant. *See* Walter L. Fisher, *Double Jeopardy and Federalism*, 50 Minn. L. Rev. 607, 610–613 (1966).

3.   Empower federal officials to enjoin a state prosecution where the federal interests are sufficiently great to require federal prosecution. This suggestion is closely related to the concept of preemption, which is discussed *infra* at p. 832.

4.   Authorize the prosecution of both state and federal crimes in a single trial in a state court or in a federal court. *See* Note, *Double Prosecution By State and Federal Governments: Another Exercise in Federalism*, 80 Harv. L. Rev. 1538, 1554 (1967).

5.   Generally prohibit the second prosecution but introduce some flexibility into the system through allowing a second prosecution when each prosecution vindicates a "separate interest." Note, *Double Prosecution By State and Federal Governments: Another Exercise in Federalism*, 80 Harv. L. Rev. 1538, 1561 (1967).

6.   Permit federal prosecution after state conviction but require that the penalty imposed by the state be subtracted from any federal punishment. *See* Note, *Preemption by Federal Criminal Statutes*, 55 Colum. L. Rev. 83, 94 (1955).

7.   Require federal and state prosecutors to coordinate their interests before either begins prosecution, perhaps with the guidance and approval of a judge. See James E. King, Note, *The Problem of Double Jeopardy in Successive Federal–State Prosecutions: A Fifth Amendment*

Solution, 31 STAN. L. REV. 477, 496–97 (1979). A variation on the foregoing would impose a requirement of consultation but give the federal prosecutor the right of first refusal. How would federal prosecutors know that a state prosecution affecting federal interests is being undertaken? Compare: "[A] system of notification, either formal or informal, could be established under which federal authorities would be informed of all anticipated state prosecutions concerning activities which state officials reasonably believe might also violate federal law." Note, *Double Prosecution By State and Federal Governments: Another Exercise in Federalism*, 80 HARV. L. REV. 1538, 1551 (1967). How practicable a proposal is this?

Why do you think that Congress has never adopted any of these proposals? Apparently, it is satisfied with the status quo under the *Petite* Policy. If you had the authority to do so and were considering the adoption of one of these suggestions, which do you think has the most promise? In your judgment, would it be preferable to the *Petite* Policy?

b. *Federal Preemption*

It might seem that the easiest way to eliminate duplicative state and federal criminal prosecutions in matters of concurrent jurisdiction would be for one jurisdiction to assert exclusive authority to prosecute. Congress indeed has the authority to enact legislation that supersedes and preempts a state statute that deals with matters otherwise within the purview of both jurisdictions. However, Congress has rarely enacted laws that unambiguously preempt state legislation, and it has usually been left to the courts to decide whether to give a federal statute preemptive effect.

Much of the decisional law on preemption has arisen in connection with complex schemes of regulation, particularly under the Commerce Clause. For a review of various approaches to preemption found in Supreme Court opinions in the Commerce-regulatory scheme cases and shifts that have occurred in those approaches under the influence of notions of cooperative federalism, see Erwin Chemerinsky, *Empowering States When it Matters*, 69 BROOK. L. REV. 1313 (2004); Mary J. Davis, *Unmasking the Presumption in Favor of Preemption*, 53 S.C. L. REV. 967 (2002); Karen A. Jordan, *The Shifting Preemption Paradigm: Conceptual and Interpretative Issues*, 51 VAND. L. REV. 1149 (1998); and Susan Raeker–Jordan, *The Pre–Emption Presumption That Never Was: Pre–Emption Doctrine Swallows the Rule*, 40 ARIZ. L. REV. 1379 (1998). For a case in which the Commerce Clause and preemption jurisprudence were applied to a state statute criminalizing the sale within one state of another state's lottery tickets, see *Pic–A–State PA, Inc. v. Commonwealth*, 42 F.3d 175, 176 (3d Cir. 1994) (concluding that state statute was not precluded by 18 U.S.C. § 1301, which makes conduct of a business that sells another state's lottery a federal offense).

The only criminal case not involving a regulatory scheme in which the Supreme Court has ruled that a federal criminal statute superseded state criminal legislation is *Pennsylvania v. Nelson*, 350 U.S. 497 (1956). In *Nelson* the Court held that the federal Smith Act, which prohibited knowing advocacy of the overthrow of the U.S. Government by force or violence, superseded the Pennsylvania Sedition Act, which prohibited the same conduct. The Court applied three tests derived from prior cases to determine whether the state law was preempted: (1) whether the scheme of federal regulation is so pervasive as to make reasonable the inference that Congress left no room for the States to supplement it; (2) whether the federal statute touches a field in which the federal interest is so dominant that the federal system must be assumed to preclude enforcement of state laws on the same subject; and (3) whether the enforcement of state law presents a serious danger of conflict with the administration of the federal program. 350 U.S. at 501–506. Applying these tests, the Court determined that the state statute in question was preempted. Indeed, the Court observed that since 1939 federal authorities had urged local authorities not to intervene in such matters, but to turn over to the federal authorities immediately and unevaluated all information concerning subversive activities "in order to avoid a hampering of uniform enforcement of its program by sporadic local prosecutions." 350 U.S. at 505–06.

The Court also emphasized the limitations of its decision. After noting that its decision was not applicable to the concurrent jurisdiction to enforce prohibition under the Eighteenth Amendment, the Court continued:

> Neither does it limit the right of the State to protect itself at any time against sabotage or attempted violence of all kinds. Nor does it prevent the State from prosecuting where the same act constitutes both a federal offense and a state offense under the police power, as was done in *Fox v. Ohio*, 5 How. 410, 46 U.S. 410, 12 L.Ed. 213, and *Gilbert v. Minnesota*, 254 U.S. 325, 41 S. CT. 125, 65 L.Ed. 287, relied upon by petitioner as authority herein. In neither of those cases did the state statute impinge on federal jurisdiction. In the *Fox* case, the federal offense was counterfeiting. The state offense was defrauding the person to whom the spurious money was passed. In the *Gilbert* case this Court, in upholding the enforcement of a state statute, proscribing conduct which would "interfere with or discourage the enlistment of men in the military or naval forces of the United States or of the State of Minnesota," treated it not as an act relating to "the raising of armies for the national defense, nor to rules and regulations for the government of those under arms (a constitutionally exclusive federal power). It (was) simply a local police measure.* * * "

350 U.S. at 500–501.

Although nearly a half century has passed since the decision in *Nelson*, the Supreme Court has not returned to the subject of preemption in the context of criminal prosecutions. *Nelson* is still good law, but it has not been read broadly. The contemporary assumption is that absent an explicit statutory provision to the contrary federal criminal statutes will seldom, if ever, preempt state criminal law. In the criminal context there is a clear understanding that Congress ordinarily intends to supplement state law, rather than to regulate comprehensively and occupy the field.[e] Since *Nelson*, claims have occasionally been raised regarding the preemptive effect of federal criminal statutes, but these have typically been rejected by the lower courts. *See, e.g., United States v. Ruthstein*, 414 F.2d 1079 (7th Cir. 1969).

In *Jones v. United State*, 529 U.S. 848 (2000), the court held that the arson statute applies only to property that is actively "used" in interstate commerce, and hence the statute does not reach the arson of an owner-occupied private residence. In a concurring opinion, Justice Stevens discussed the presumption against preemption. Professor Susan R. Klein pointed out the implications of the statement that federal criminal laws should not displace state policy choices:

> In *Jones v. United States*, Justice Stevens argued that "presumption against federal pre-emption of state law" dictated interpreting the federal statute to apply only to arsons of businesses, as otherwise the federal criminal statute, which authorizes a sentence of thirty-five years, would displace the state "policy choice" to punish home arson with a ten-year maximum. *Jones v. United States*, 529 U.S. 848, 859 (2000) (Stevens, J., with Thomas, J., concurring). The implication here is that a clear statement by Congress that 18 U.S.C. § 844 (1998) applies to arsons of private residences would mean that the federal arson statute would preempt the Indiana state statute. This is strange, given that every federal criminal statute displaces state policy choices unless the federal and state statutes are identical in punishment and procedure, yet the Court has not held that any of these federal criminal statutes preempt state criminal statutes.

Susan R. Klein, *Independent-Norm Federalism in Criminal Law*, 90 CAL. L. REV. 1541, 1554 n.62 (2000).

Does the federal power to preempt completely imply the power to preempt on an ad hoc basis? Consider 18 U.S.C. § 351, which makes it a federal crime to kill, kidnap or assault designated federal officials including Members of Congress, heads of government departments, the Director or Deputy Director of the CIA or Justices of the United States. Subsection (f) of § 351 provides:

> If Federal investigative or prosecutive jurisdiction is asserted for a violation of this section, such assertion shall suspend the exercise of jurisdiction by a State or local authority, under any applicable State or local law, until Federal action is terminated.

e. This is consistent with a broad general trend in preemption law . For a general discussion of preemption law, see 3 CHESTER J. ANTIEU & WILLIAM J. RICH, MODERN CONSTITUTIONAL LAW §§ 43.17–43.20 (1997); *id.* § 43.20 at 45 ("The Court has become progressively more protective of state authority to adopt concurrent regulations.") *See also* JOHN E. NOWAK & RONALD D. ROTUNDA, CONSTITUTIONAL LAW § 9.2 (7th ed. 2004) (describing *Nelson* test and its application).

Who is authorized to "assert" federal jurisdiction under this provision? See S.1437, 95th Cong. 2d Session (1978) (a bill which was not enacted), which in a similar provision authorized the Attorney General to assert federal jurisdiction. S.1437 also contained a long list of "federal interest" crimes over which exclusive federal jurisdiction could be asserted. Would it be desirable to extend the applicability of a provision such as § 351(f) to other crimes? Would this be a desirable way to deal with the problem of duplicative prosecutions? Would it be a desirable development in the relations between federal and state criminal enforcement? Compare with the foregoing the suggestion made earlier that congressional legislation barring the states from prosecuting after a prior federal conviction or acquittal might be sustained based upon the preemption power.

In the absence of legislative provisions of the type contained in § 351(f) does the U.S. Attorney General or any of his subordinates have the legal authority to stop a state investigation that is deemed to be interfering with a federal inquiry?

*

Part VII

SENTENCING GUIDELINES AND FORFEITURE

Chapter 18

THE SENTENCING GUIDELINES

INTRODUCTION

It is no exaggeration to say that the Sentencing Guidelines revolutionized federal sentencing. Prior to the adoption of the Guidelines in 1987 the sentencing judge had largely uncontrolled discretion to set an individual sentence anywhere within the broad sentencing ranges established for most offenses, and appellate review was not available. Sentences for the same conduct varied considerably from judge to judge and from district to district. Moreover, federal sentences were generally indeterminate, and the actual release date was determined by the Parole Commission. Widespread dissatisfaction with this state of affairs led to the passage of the Sentencing Reform Act, which abolished the Parole Commission and adopted a new system of determinate sentencing intended to eliminate or reduce unwarranted sentencing disparities. The Act established the United States Sentencing Commission with the mandate to promulgate federal sentencing guidelines. The resulting Guidelines are long, detailed, and complex. Not surprisingly, they have generated an extensive body of case law.

The federal sentencing revolution entered a new phase in 2005, when the Supreme Court held the legislation authorizing the Guidelines unconstitutional. In *United States v. Booker*, 543 U.S. 220 (2005), excerpted at 854–69, the five member majority held that the Guidelines procedure violated the Sixth Amendment right to trial by jury and the requirement of proof beyond a reasonable doubt. The Guidelines are not, however, gone. In a separate remedial majority opinion five members of the Court held that the Guidelines would continue to apply in an advisory fashion. No one knows how long this regime of advisory Guidelines will continue. Indeed, the Court recognized the likelihood that Congress might prefer a different remedy to adapt sentencing to the requirements of the Fifth and Sixth Amendments.

In the post-*Booker* world, then, federal sentencing is Guidelines plus (or, some would argue, Guidelines minus). The task for students is to master the basics of the Guidelines, no easy task given their complexity, and then see how courts are responding to their new authority to treat the Guidelines as only advisory. And, finally, it is useful to consider how Congress may respond.

Section A provides an overview of the history and function of the Guidelines. Section B contains a general introduction to the mechanics of Guidelines application, beginning with a step by step description of the process and then following the steps in a hypothetical case. The *Booker* opinion and its lower court progeny are considered in Section C. Finally, Section D provides an overview of proposed post-*Booker* alternatives to Guidelines reform.

A. OVERVIEW OF THE HISTORY AND FUNCTION OF THE SENTENCING GUIDELINES

The Sentencing Reform Act of 1984—which was intended to bring about a fundamental "reform" of federal sentencing—created the United States Sentencing Commission and authorized it to promulgate guidelines to govern federal sentencing. The initial Guidelines adopted by the Commission became effective on November 1, 1987, and the constitutionality of the Commission itself and the Guidelines it produced were immediately challenged by defendants in virtually every federal judicial district. In *Mistretta v. United States*, 488 U.S. 361 (1989), the Supreme Court held that creation of the Sentencing Commission did not constitute an unconstitutional delegation of legislative authority, nor did it violate the constitutional separation of powers. The following portion of the Court's opinion provides a good introduction to the Sentencing Reform Act:

> For almost a century, the Federal Government employed in criminal cases a system of indeterminate sentencing. Statutes specified the penalties for crimes but nearly always gave the sentencing judge wide discretion to decide whether the offender should be incarcerated and for how long, whether he should be fined and how much, and whether some lesser restraint, such as probation, should be imposed instead of imprisonment or fine. This indeterminate-sentencing system was supplemented by the utilization of parole, by which an offender was returned to society under the "guidance and control" of a parole officer.

> Both indeterminate sentencing and parole were based on concepts of the offender's possible, indeed probable, rehabilitation, a view that it was realistic to attempt to rehabilitate the inmate and thereby to minimize the risk that he would resume criminal activity upon his return to society. It obviously required the judge and the parole officer to make their respective sentencing and release decisions upon their own assessments of the offender's amenability to rehabilitation. As a result, the court and the officer were in positions to exercise, and usually did exercise, very broad discretion. This led almost inevitably to the conclusion on the part of a reviewing court that the sentencing judge "sees more and senses more" than the

appellate court; thus, the judge enjoyed the "superiority of his nether position," for that court's determination as to what sentence was appropriate met with virtually unconditional deference on appeal. The decision whether to parole was also "predictive and discretionary." The correction official possessed almost absolute discretion over the parole decision.

Historically, federal sentencing—the function of determining the scope and extent of punishment—never has been thought to be assigned by the Constitution to the exclusive jurisdiction of any one of the three Branches of government. Congress, of course, has the power to fix the sentence for a federal crime, and the scope of judicial discretion with respect to a sentence is subject to congressional control. Congress early abandoned fixed-sentence rigidity, however, and put in place a system of ranges within which the sentencer could choose the precise punishment. Congress delegated almost unfettered discretion to the sentencing judge to determine what the sentence should be within the customarily wide range so selected. This broad discretion was further enhanced by the power later granted the judge to suspend the sentence and by the resulting growth of an elaborate probation system. Also, with the advent of parole, Congress moved toward a "three-way sharing" of sentencing responsibility by granting correction personnel in the Executive Branch the discretion to release a prisoner before the expiration of the sentence imposed by the judge. Thus, under the indeterminate-sentence system, Congress defined the maximum, the judge imposed a sentence within the statutory range (which it usually could replace with probation), and the Executive Branch's parole official eventually determined the actual duration of imprisonment.

* * *

[The Senate Report] referred to the "outmoded rehabilitation model" for federal criminal sentencing, and recognized that the efforts of the criminal justice system to achieve rehabilitation of offenders had failed. It observed that the indeterminate-sentencing system had two "unjustifi[ed]" and "shameful" consequences. The first was the great variation among sentences imposed by different judges upon similarly situated offenders. The second was the uncertainty as to the time the offender would spend in prison. Each was a serious impediment to an evenhanded and effective operation of the criminal justice system. The Report went on to note that parole was an inadequate device for overcoming these undesirable consequences. This was due to the division of authority between the sentencing judge and the parole officer who often worked at cross purposes; to the fact that the Parole Commission's own guidelines did not take into account factors Congress regarded as important in sentencing, such as the sophistication of the offender and the role the offender played in an offense committed with others, and to the fact that the Parole Commission had only limited power to adjust a sentence imposed by the court.

Before settling on a mandatory-guideline system, Congress considered other competing proposals for sentencing reform. It rejected strict determinate sentencing because it concluded that a guideline system would be successful in reducing sentence disparities while retaining the flexibility needed to adjust for unanticipated factors arising in a particular case. The Judiciary Committee rejected a proposal that would have made the sentencing guidelines only advisory.

The Act, as adopted, revises the old sentencing process in several ways:

1. It rejects imprisonment as a means of promoting rehabilitation, and it states that punishment should serve retributive, educational, deterrent, and incapacitative goals.

2. It consolidates the power that had been exercised by the sentencing judge and the Parole Commission to decide what punishment an offender should suffer. This is done by creating the United States Sentencing Commission, directing that Commission to devise guidelines to be used for sentencing, and prospectively abolishing the Parole Commission.

3. It makes all sentences basically determinate. A prisoner is to be released at the completion of his sentence reduced only by any credit earned by good behavior while in custody.

4. It makes the Sentencing Commission's guidelines binding on the courts, although it preserves for the judge the discretion to depart from the guideline applicable to a particular case if the judge finds an aggravating or mitigating factor present that the Commission did not adequately consider when formulating guidelines. The Act also requires the court to state its reasons for the sentence imposed and to give "the specific reason" for imposing a sentence different from that described in the guideline.

5. It authorizes limited appellate review of the sentence. It permits a defendant to appeal a sentence that is above the defined range, and it permits the Government to appeal a sentence that is below that range. It also permits either side to appeal an incorrect application of the guideline.

Thus, guidelines were meant to establish a range of determinate sentences for categories of offenses and defendants according to various specified factors, "among others." The maximum of the range ordinarily may not exceed the minimum by more than the greater of 25% or six months, and each sentence is to be within the limit provided by existing law.

Justice Scalia, the only dissenter, argued that the Court had erred in failing to recognize that the Sentencing Reform Act created "a sort of junior-varsity Congress."

B. HOW THE GUIDELINES WORK

1. A STEP BY STEP TOUR OF THE GUIDELINES

With this background in mind, we turn to the question how the guidelines actually work. The following excerpt provides an excellent roadmap to the steps of guideline application.

UNITED STATES SENTENCING COMMISSION, SPECIAL REPORT TO CONGRESS: MANDATORY MINIMUM PENALTIES IN THE FEDERAL CRIMINAL JUSTICE SYSTEM, PP. 20–26 (1991)

A. The Guideline Principle of Varying Punishment in Light of Case–Specific Offense and Offender Characteristics

* * * [T]he Sentencing Reform Act was prompted in large measure by Congress's concern that the lack of a comprehensive and systematic approach to sentencing in the federal courts permitted unwarranted sentencing disparity. Congress wanted the Sentencing Commission to reduce unwarranted sentencing disparity by developing a rational sentencing structure that would channel judicial sentencing discretion.

Starting with the premise that treating similar offenses and similar offenders alike forms the basis of a just and rational sentencing policy, the Sentencing Commission created guidelines that take into account both the seriousness of the offense, including relevant offense characteristics, and important information about the offender, such as the offender's role in the offense and prior record. Using this information, the guidelines prescribe proportional individual sentences that, for example, punish the recidivist criminal substantially more than the first offender, and the organizer of a criminal enterprise substantially more than his minions. To understand how the guidelines system functions, and how that system contrasts with mandatory minimum sentencing, a description of the way in which a sentence is determined under the guidelines is helpful.

Step One: Determining the Base Offense Level

The starting point for sentencing an individual defendant under the guidelines system is the determination of the base offense level. Federal law contains over 2,000 separate criminal offenses. Rather than construct a complex and potentially unmanageable system containing a separate guideline for each offense, the Sentencing Commission created generic guidelines that group offenses by offense type. The guidelines carefully rank these offense categories according to severity by assigning them base offense levels, varying from 4 to 43. In this way the guidelines not only ensure that like offenses are treated alike, but also that a logical, proportionate relationship exists among offenses according to their relative seriousness.[65]

---

65. Thus, to cite one of countless examples, the base offense level for rape is higher than the base offense level for a nonsexual assault, which, in turn, is higher than that for a threatening communication.

Step Two: Examining the Specific Offense Characteristics

After determining the base offense level, the court determines whether certain attributes common to that type of offense are present in the case. These specific offense characteristics are specified in the applicable guideline and help establish the seriousness of the offense. When present in a case, specific offense characteristics require an adjustment in the offense level.[66] The robbery guideline provides, for example, a 3–level increase if a firearm was possessed, a 5–level increase if a firearm was discharged, a 6–level increase if life-threatening bodily injury occurred, and increases of zero to seven levels depending on the value of the property taken.

Similarly, the fraud guideline directs the sentencing court to consider specific offense characteristics and a range of adjustments relevant to that offense. Any fraud that results in loss to the victim exceeding $2,000 requires an increase in the offense level corresponding to the amount of loss caused. Evidence of more than minimal planning, creating a risk of serious bodily injury, or jeopardizing the safety and soundness of a financial institution also require increases of varying amounts.

Step Three: Applying the Chapter Three Adjustments

After determining the base offense level and the specific offense characteristics identified by the relevant guideline for that type of offense, the court considers whether certain generic adjustments to the offense level apply. The application of these adjustments (called "Chapter Three adjustments" because they appear in Chapter Three of the Guideline Manual) is not limited to a particular offense or group of offenses, but rather can apply to any offense. Chapter Three adjustments act to further individualize the sentence. They require determinations, for example, as to whether the offense involved a vulnerable victim (2–level addition to the base offense level); whether the victim was a law enforcement or corrections officer (a 3–level increase); and whether the defendant willfully obstructed justice (a 2–level increase).

Importantly, Chapter Three adjustments require the court to consider the defendant's role in the offense. A finding that the defendant played a reduced role in the offense results in a decrease of up to four levels. The adjustments for role in the offense assure, for example, that the kingpin who organized a drug distribution ring and received the bulk of its illicit profits will receive a substantially greater sentence than a one-time drug courier or "mule," who had limited involvement in the crime.

Step Four: Counting Multiple Counts

Because of a potential for irrational and disproportionate results absent detailed guidance when a defendant is to be sentenced for

---

66. On average, each offense level increment changes the sentence by about 12 percent. Thus, a 4–level enhancement equates to about a 50 percent increase in sentence; an 8–level enhancement effectively doubles the sentence.

multiple counts of conviction, the guidelines carefully prescribe specific rules for sentencing in multiple count cases. One potential problem in multiple count cases is how to increase the sentence when the multiplicity of counts does in fact reflect multiple harms. The Guideline Manual describes this problem as follows:

> The difficulty is that when a defendant engages in conduct that causes several harms, each additional harm, even if it increases the extent to which punishment is warranted, does not necessarily warrant a proportionate increase in punishment. A defendant who assaults others during a fight, for example, may warrant more punishment if he injures ten people than if he injures one, but his conduct does not necessarily warrant ten times the punishment.

The guidelines resolve this problem by directing that incremental amounts for each offense involving a distinct harm be added to the base offense level that corresponds to the most serious offense in the group. Thus, for example, two separate bank robberies will not result in a doubling of the offense level for one bank robbery, but will generally require a 2–level increase in the applicable offense level. Grouping counts in this manner increases punishment where there is increased harm and culpability, but avoids disproportionate punishment when more than one count has been charged.

A second problem with multiple count cases that the guidelines address occurs when multiple counts do not particularly reflect the presence of multiple harms. Some offenses, although technically distinct under federal law, are so closely related that they result in essentially the same harm. Embezzling money from a bank and falsifying the records, for example, are two ways federal statutory law recognizes what can be essentially the same criminal conduct. In cases such as these, the guidelines group the offenses and apply the offense level for the most serious offense without adding levels for the closely-related offenses. In this way the seriousness of the offense is captured but without artificial increases for non-existent additional harms.

In other types of cases, such as drug distribution, it is the total quantity of drugs distributed that should influence the sentence, and not whether the government elects to charge the offense as several counts of distribution or one larger conspiracy. The guideline grouping rules assure this desired result as well.

Step Five: Acceptance of Responsibility

The sentencing guidelines credit the defendant for certain post-offense conduct. If the defendant "demonstrates a recognition and affirmative acceptance of personal responsibility for his criminal conduct," the sentencing court may reduce the base offense level by two levels. The guidelines detail the possible actions an offender can take that indicate acceptance of responsibility:

> (a) voluntary termination or withdrawal from criminal conduct or associations;

(b) voluntary payment of restitution prior to adjudication of guilt;

(c) voluntary and truthful admission to authorities of involvement in the offense and related conduct;

(d) voluntary surrender to authorities promptly after commission of the offense;

(e) voluntary assistance to authorities in the recovery of the fruits and instrumentalities of the offense;

(f) voluntary resignation from the office or position held during the commission of the offense; and

(g) the timeliness of the defendant's conduct in manifesting acceptance of responsibility.

Because of the judge's unique ability to assess this factor, the decision whether to award credit for acceptance of responsibility is left more substantially to the judge's discretion than other guideline sentence determinants for which judicial fact-finding is key but the operation of discretion is more limited. Guideline commentary states that "[e]ntry of a plea of guilty prior to the commencement of trial combined with truthful admission of involvement in the offense and related conduct will constitute significant evidence of acceptance of responsibility...."

Step Six: Assessing the Defendant's Criminal History

Because a defendant's prior record is relevant to such important sentencing goals as general deterrence, just punishment, and the need to protect the public from the defendant's propensity to commit crimes, the guidelines evaluate criminal history with some care and complexity. Points are assigned to account for the severity of the prior criminal conduct (e.g., three points for more serious offenses committed as an adult, down to one point for less serious offenses resulting in probation). Additional points are added if the defendant committed the offense within two years after release from imprisonment or while under any criminal justice sentence, including probation, work release, or escape status. These factors reflect a need for heightened punishment due to the recency of the prior criminal conduct and the defendant's disregard for the earlier sanction.

The guidelines account for patterns of prior criminal conduct that warrant especially serious treatment. When a defendant is at least 18 years old at the time of the current offense, the offense is a violent felony or involved a controlled substance, and the defendant has at least two prior felony convictions involving a violent crime or a controlled substance, the defendant qualifies as a career offender. The guidelines establish a special set of offense levels for the career offender that are calibrated, in conjunction with the highest criminal history category, to correspond to the maximum sentences authorized by statute for the instant offense.

After the defendant's entire record has been examined and the appropriate points assigned, the points are converted into criminal history categories ranging from I to VI. The career offender is always assigned the highest criminal history category, Category VI.

Step Seven: Determining the Applicable Sentencing Range

To determine the sentencing range for the particular offense involved, the sentencing judge turns to a sentencing table. Offense levels are set out in the vertical column of the table and criminal history categories are displayed in the horizontal column, forming a grid that contains the various sentencing ranges. By matching the applicable offense level and criminal history category, the court finds the guideline sentencing range that applies to the individual offender before the court. The court has discretion to pick the sentence from any point in the range. The ranges are relatively narrow. By statute, the maximum of a sentencing range providing for imprisonment may not exceed the minimum by more than 25 percent.

Summary

In sum, the sentencing guidelines seek to address all key aspects of the sentencing decision where the unguided judicial discretion of the past allowed unwarranted disparities to occur.

- Similar offenses are grouped together and assigned the same offense level, thus minimizing the chance that sentences will differ simply because a defendant is charged and convicted under one statute rather than another.

- Specific offense characteristics are considered to help determine the seriousness of the particular offense.

- Chapter Three adjustments are made to further gauge offense seriousness and individualize the punishment. Importantly, the defendant's role in the offense is measured to assure that the sentence properly accounts for the defendant's degree of culpability, and incremental increases are provided for multiple convictions involving significant additional criminal conduct.

- To credit the individual defendant who is truly remorseful and accepts responsibility for his or her crime (usually manifested by a truthful admission as part of a guilty plea), the guidelines permit a consistent, 2–level adjustment in the appropriate circumstances.

- And, in order to increase punishment when the defendant has a significant record of prior criminal activity or qualifies as a career criminal, the guidelines provide the means for proportionate increases in the sentence that reflect these reasons as well.

- The guidelines provide a range of appropriate sentences within which the sentencing judge may consider such factors as family ties, community involvement, and degree of sophistication. As sentence exposure increases at the higher offense levels, the 25 percent within-range differential can result in considerable latitude for judges. For example, at level 30 there is a 24–month difference between the top and bottom of the guideline range.

Finally, as Congress expressly intended, the guidelines recognizes that doing justice in individual cases require a margin of flexibility. Even the most finely-tuned system cannot anticipate every factual situation. Accordingly, the sentencing judge retains flexibility through the guidelines' departure provisions. In the unusual instance that the sentencing judge finds "an aggravating or mitigating circumstance of a kind, or to a degree, not adequately taken into consideration" in the guidelines, the judge, for valid reasons stated in open court, may depart from the otherwise applicable guideline range, subject to review on appeal.

Through these various mechanisms, the guidelines seek to provide for sentences that are certain, substantial, proportionate, and fair. The guidelines represent a sophisticated, comprehensive, calibrated system that begins with a specified base penalty for particular offenses and modifies above and below for a variety of factors, without whose consideration, disparity would result.

This is the grid, or Sentencing Table, that establishes the authorized sentencing range for each offender.

SENTENCING TABLE
(in months of imprisonment)

Offense Level	Criminal History Category (Criminal History Points)					
	I (0 or 1)	**II** (2 or 3)	**III** (4, 5, 6)	**IV** (7, 8, 9)	**V** (10, 11, 12)	**VI** (13 or more)
1	0-6	0-6	0-6	0-6	0-6	0-6
2	0-6	0-6	0-6	0-6	0-6	1-7
3	0-6	0-6	0-6	0-6	2-8	3-9
4	0-6	0-6	0-6	2-8	4-10	6-12
5	0-6	0-6	1-7	4-10	6-12	9-15
6	0-6	1-7	2-8	6-12	9-15	12-18
7	0-6	2-8	4-10	8-14	12-18	15-21
8	0-6	4-10	6-12	10-16	15-21	18-24
9	4-10	6-12	8-14	12-18	18-24	21-27
10	6-12	8-14	10-16	15-21	21-27	24-30
11	8-14	10-16	12-18	18-24	24-30	27-33
12	10-16	12-18	15-21	21-27	27-33	30-37
13	12-18	15-21	18-24	24-30	30-37	33-41
14	15-21	18-24	21-27	27-33	33-41	37-46
15	18-24	21-27	24-30	30-37	37-46	41-51
16	21-27	24-30	27-33	33-41	41-51	46-57
17	24-30	27-33	30-37	37-46	46-57	51-63
18	27-33	30-37	33-41	41-51	51-63	57-71
19	30-37	33-41	37-46	46-57	57-71	63-78
20	33-41	37-46	41-51	51-63	63-78	70-87
21	37-46	41-51	46-57	57-71	70-87	77-96
22	41-51	46-57	51-63	63-78	77-96	84-105
23	46-57	51-63	57-71	70-87	84-105	92-115
24	51-63	57-71	63-78	77-96	92-115	100-125
25	57-71	63-78	70-87	84-105	100-125	110-137
26	63-78	70-87	78-97	92-115	110-137	120-150
27	70-87	78-97	87-108	100-125	120-150	130-162
28	78-97	87-108	97-121	110-137	130-162	140-175
29	87-108	97-121	108-135	121-151	140-175	151-188
30	97-121	108-135	121-151	135-168	151-188	168-210
31	108-135	121-151	135-168	151-188	168-210	188-235
32	121-151	135-168	151-188	168-210	188-235	210-262
33	135-168	151-188	168-210	188-235	210-262	235-293
34	151-188	168-210	188-235	210-262	235-293	262-327
35	168-210	188-235	210-262	235-293	262-327	292-365
36	188-235	210-262	235-293	262-327	292-365	324-405
37	210-262	235-293	262-327	292-365	324-405	360-life
38	235-293	262-327	292-365	324-405	360-life	360-life
39	262-327	292-365	324-405	360-life	360-life	360-life
40	292-365	324-405	360-life	360-life	360-life	360-life
41	324-405	360-life	360-life	360-life	360-life	360-life
42	360-life	360-life	360-life	360-life	360-life	360-life
43	life	life	life	life	life	life

Zone A (Offense Levels 1–8)
Zone B (Offense Levels 9–10)
Zone C (Offense Levels 11–12)
Zone D (Offense Levels 13–43)

Commentary to Sentencing Table

Application Notes:

1.   *The Offense Level (1-43) forms the vertical axis of the Sentencing Table. The Criminal History Category (I-VI) forms the horizontal axis of the Table. The intersection of the Offense Level and Criminal History Category displays the Guideline Range in months of imprisonment. "Life" means life imprisonment. For example, the guideline range applicable to a defendant with an Offense Level of 15 and a Criminal History Category of III is 24-30 months of imprisonment.*

2.   *In rare cases, a total offense level of less than 1 or more than 43 may result from application of the guidelines. A total offense level of less than 1 is to be treated as an offense level of 1. An offense level of more than 43 is to be treated as an offense level of 43.*

3.   *The Criminal History Category is determined by the total criminal history points from Chapter Four, Part A, except as provided in §§4B1.1 (Career Offender) and 4B1.4 (Armed Career Criminal). The total criminal history points associated with each Criminal History Category are shown under each Criminal History Category in the Sentencing Table.*

<u>Historical Note</u>: Effective November 1, 1987. Amended effective November 1, 1989 (<u>see</u> Appendix C, amendment 270); November 1, 1991 (<u>see</u> Appendix C, amendment 418); November 1, 1992 (<u>see</u> Appendix C, amendment 462).

2. APPLYING THE GUIDELINES—AN EXAMPLE

As explained in the Commission report excerpted above, the Guidelines analysis begins with the determination of the base offense level. The base offense level is adjusted first on the basis of specific offense characteristics and then by other factors that individualize the offense (such as the special status of the victim). To see how this works, we'll apply U.S.S.G. § 2B1.1, reprinted at 997–1005, as well as the Sentencing Table reprinted on page 848, to the following hypothetical:

> Elmo Gantry was convicted of mail fraud in connection with his solicitation of donations for what he claimed to be a scholarship fund for children whose parents were killed while serving in Iraq. There was, in fact, no scholarship fund, and Gantry planned to pocket all of the donations. He sent out one hundred letters asking for $1,000 donations. Gantry sent the letters to members of a church for which he had briefly done clerical work, using a membership list he had taken, without authority, from the church office. Although Gantry's scheme was discovered immediately, and no one lost any money, the government claims that the (anticipated) loss was $100,000. Gantry has never been in trouble with the law before, and has no criminal history.

Look at the sentencing table (*supra* 848). As you see, it has two axes. The horizontal axis is criminal history. Because Gantry has no criminal history, he would be in Criminal History Category I on the horizontal axis. His Guidelines sentencing range will be calculated by determining the offense level, and then finding the box on the table where the base offense level and criminal history category intersect.

Here are the steps that would be followed to determine Gantry's offense level on the vertical axis.

- The base offense level: U.S.S.G. § 2B1.1 (*infra* 997 et seq.) applies to mail and wire fraud cases as well as embezzlement, theft, and other offenses. Under § 2B1.1(a)(1), the base offense level is either 6 or 7, depending on the statutory penalty for the offense in question. Because mail fraud is punishable by a maximum sentence of 20 years (or more if the victim is a financial institution), the base offense level is 7. The Sentencing Chart provides that for a defendant with Criminal History Category I, this is **0–6 months**.

- Adjustment for specific offense characteristics: U.S.S.G. § 2B1.1(b) sets out a list of specific offense characteristics. The most important adjustment come under the loss table in (b)(1), where the largest losses can increase the sentence by 30 levels. Since the $100,000 is more than $70,000 but less than $120,000, the sentence is increased by 8 levels. At level 15 (7 + 8), the sentence for a Category I offender is **18–24 months**. What about the fact that no one *actually* lost any money, because the fraud was discovered so quickly? Application Note 3(A) (*infra* at 1000–01) provides that the loss for this purpose is the greater of the actual or intended loss.

Note that the Guidelines make it much less important whether the prosecutor filed multiple mail or wire fraud counts. Under U.S.S.G. § 1B1.3(a)(2) (reprinted *infra* at 989–90) all acts and omissions involving "the same course of conduct or common plan or scheme" are combined. This provision applies not only to fraud, but also to drugs. Rather than count the number of mailings or drug sales, the Guideline focuses on the amounts involved in the whole course of conduct or scheme. (Of course the sentence for a single count cannot exceed the maximum sentence under the statute, in this case 20 years.)

The other adjustments under U.S.S.G. § 2B1.1 involve a wide variety of factors, including the number of victims of the scheme, whether the misrepresentation involved a claim that the defendant was acting on behalf of a charitable, religious, or political entity, and whether the offense imperiled a financial institution. Because Gantry falsely represented that he was acting on behalf of a charitable organization, the offense would be increased by 2 levels under U.S.S.G. § 2B1.1(b)(8)(A), or level 17 (15 + 2) **(24–30 months)**.

- Chapter 3 adjustments: Chapter 3 provides for a variety of additional adjustments. Some are related the victim of the offense, others to the defendant's role in the offense, the number of different counts in the case, and the defendant's acceptance of responsibility. For example, if the defendant knew or should have known that the victim of the offense was "vulnerable," then U.S.S.G. § 3A1.1(b)(1) provides for a 2 level enhancement. The government might claim that Gantry knew or should have known that many of the church members he solicited were elderly and living on fixed incomes. If the court finds that the offense involves vulnerable victims, the 2 level adjustment would take Gantry to level 19 (**30–37 months**).[a]

The defendant's role in the offense can serve to either aggravate (if, for example, he was an organizer or leader), or a mitigate (if the defendant was a minor or minimal participant) the sentence. *See* U.S.S.G. §§ 3B1.1 and 3B1.2. If there was an abuse of a position of public or private trust, or of a special skill, to facilitate or conceal the offense, U.S.S.G. § 3B1.3 provides for a two level upward adjustment. If the misuse of the church's membership roster qualifies as the abuse of a private trust, that would take our Gantry to level 21 (**37–46 months**).

• Acceptance of responsibility: Under U.S.S.G. §§ 3E1.1 (reprinted *infra* at 994–97), a defendant can get a 2 (or sometimes a 3) level reduction for "acceptance of responsibility." If he has reached level 21, pleading guilty and getting a two level adjustment for accepting responsibility would take Gantry back down to level 19 (**30–37 months**).

• Criminal history: As noted above, we have assumed that Gantry had no criminal history, and was in criminal history category I. If, however, he were in category III, his sentence at level 19 would be increased to **37–46 months**. At the highest level, category VI, the sentence for level 19 is **63–78 months**.

After all of these adjustments, the court would calculate the sentencing range. In our hypothetical at criminal history category I, the sentencing range would be **30–37 months** with a guilty plea and acceptance of responsibility, or **37–46 months** without acceptance. Note that every step in the calculations up to this point has been mandatory. If the court finds that the loss was a certain amount, then it is required by law to adjust the sentence as provided by the loss table. Similarly, the court is required to make each of the other adjustments discussed above. The purpose of the system is to eliminate unjustified sentencing disparities, ensuring that defendants with the same criminal record who committed the same offense in the same way will receive the same sentence.

But the Guidelines do also permit some degree of individualization. This individualization comes in two ways. First, the court has the discretion under the Guidelines to determine what sentence to give the defendant within the range (in this case within the range of 30–37

---

a. U.S.S.G. § 2B1.1(b) also provides for an adjustment based upon the number of victims and the means by which they were contacted. Under § 2B1.1(b)(2) the government might claim that the offense was committed by "mass marketing," which would warrant a 2 level upward adjustment, and that the scheme involved 50 or more victims, which causes a 4 level upward adjust-ment. (Note that if both provisions were applicable, the court would apply the greater adjustment.) But was this mass marketing? And were there any victims, since no one lost any money? The sentencing court would have to resolve these interpretative issues in order to calculate the Guideline sentence.

SENTENCING GUIDELINES AND FORFEITURE

months, if Gantry accepted responsibility, or 37–46 months if he did not). Second, the Guidelines themselves provide that the court also has the discretion, under certain circumstances, to "depart" from the Guideline sentence, either upward or downward.

- <u>Departures</u>: Under U.S.S.G. § 5K2.0(a) the court may depart from the Guideline sentence if it finds that there exists in the case an "aggravating or mitigating circumstance . . . of a kind, or to a degree, not adequately taken into consideration" by the Commission in formulating the Guidelines.[b] This can involve an unusual factor that was not considered at all by the Commission, or one that was considered but presents itself in a particular case in a way that is unusual. In our hypothetical case, for example, the government might seek to show that Gantry's fraudulent scheme caused unique harms not contemplated by the Guidelines, or that the monetary loss understated the true damage to the victims. On the other hand, the defense might try to establish some unusual mitigating circumstance.

- <u>Substantial assistance departures</u>: The Sentencing Reform Act and the Guidelines also provide for one particularly important departure, for rendering "substantial assistance" to the authorities in the investigation and prosecution of other persons who have committed offenses. U.S.S.G. § 5K1.1. Neither the statute nor the Guideline limits the amount of the departure in substantial assistance cases.

Substantial assistance departures are unique for two reasons. First, the Sentencing Reform Act and the Guidelines both provide that this departure is available if and only if the government files a motion with the court requesting a departure on this ground. Second, if a defendant assists the authorities and the prosecution moves for a substantial assistance departure, then the court can not only depart from the Guidelines range, *it can also sentence the defendant below any statutorily prescribed mandatory minimum sentence.* All other downward departures are subject any mandatory minimum sentencing statutes.

Obviously it would be a great advantage for Gantry—or any other defendant—if he could provide substantial assistance and gain a government motion in his favor. Gantry would have a great incentive to cooperate if he knew enough to provide substantial assistance. Of course he may not have any information about others, especially if he was acting alone, or if he was a peripheral low level operative with little or no knowledge of an overall scheme or the role played by others. Since Gantry was acting alone, he'd be out of luck. Substantial assistance departures are discussed *infra* at 887–90.

---

b. Under U.S.S.G. §§ 5K2.0(a)(1)(B) and (b), a different, and more restricted, departure standard applies in cases involving "child crimes and sexual offenses."

- <u>Other offender characteristics</u>: What about facts such as the defendant's general good character, his job history, his rehabilitative potential, or the harm that will occur to his family if he is sentenced to incarceration? Under the Guidelines these facts are "not ordinarily relevant." As noted in the excerpt from *Mistretta*, the Sentencing Reform Act generally rejected rehabilitation as a standard for sentencing, and instead of sentencing based on the *offender's* characteristics (other than criminal history), it focuses on the *offense*. In exceptional cases, however, some of these factors *might* provide a basis for a departure. See *infra* at 876 to 98.

There are other factors that we have not discussed, but this should be enough to give you a general idea how the system works. The central idea is to eliminate unjustified disparity, and to insure that a defendant who does the crime does the time–by providing a series of detailed adjustments based on a host of factors regarding the defendant's criminal history and the facts of the case. Note that *none* of the factors noted above—as you know from reading Chapter 5–constitute elements of mail or wire fraud. (For example, while a scheme to defraud is required, it is not necessary to show that there was any loss, or to prove the amount of the loss.)

The Guidelines provide that a defendant's sentence is to be based on the "relevant conduct," and recognize that relevant conduct includes "[c]onduct that is not formally charged or is not an element of the offense of conviction." U.S.S.G. § 1B1.3 (Background). What if the defendant disputes the amount of the loss, or whether he knew the victim was vulnerable, or whether he falsely represented that he was acting for a charitable "institution"? If the defendant plead guilty, his plea would not establish these facts. If he went to trial, the jury would make no findings on these issues. But they are critically important in determining the sentence. Indeed, in the case of a defendant who went to trial and could not claim acceptance of responsibility the findings above–none of which were elements of the offense of mail fraud—would increase the defendant's Guideline sentence from a range of 0–6 months up to 37–46 months.

Under the Sentencing Reform Act, these findings were to be made at sentencing by the district court–not the jury–applying the preponderance standard, rather than beyond a reasonable doubt. In *Booker*, reprinted below, the Supreme Court took up the question whether this scheme was compatible with the Fifth and Sixth Amendments. The Court issued two majority opinions (each commanding five votes). The first opinion (on the "merits") holds that key provisions of the Sentencing Reform Act violate the Fifth and Sixth Amendments. The second opinion grapples with the remedy for these constitutional violations, and comes to a rather surprising conclusion.

C. *BOOKER* AND ITS OFFSPRING

UNITED STATES v. BOOKER

543 U.S. 220, 125 S.Ct. 738, 160 L.Ed.2d 621 (2005).

JUSTICE STEVENS delivered the opinion of the Court in part.*

The question presented in each of these cases is whether an application of the Federal Sentencing Guidelines violated the Sixth Amendment. In each case, the courts below held that binding rules set forth in the Guidelines limited the severity of the sentence that the judge could lawfully impose on the defendant based on the facts found by the jury at his trial. In both cases the courts rejected, on the basis of our decision in *Blakely v. Washington,* 542 U.S. 296, 124 S.Ct. 2531 (2004), the Government's recommended application of the Sentencing Guidelines because the proposed sentences were based on additional facts that the sentencing judge found by a preponderance of the evidence. We hold that both courts correctly concluded that the Sixth Amendment as construed in *Blakely* does apply to the Sentencing Guidelines. In a separate opinion authored by Justice BREYER, the Court concludes that in light of this holding, two provisions of the Sentencing Reform Act of 1984 (SRA) that have the effect of making the Guidelines mandatory must be invalidated in order to allow the statute to operate in a manner consistent with congressional intent.

It has been settled throughout our history that the Constitution protects every criminal defendant "against conviction except upon proof beyond a reasonable doubt of every fact necessary to constitute the crime with which he is charged." *In re Winship,* 397 U.S. 358, 364 (1970). It is equally clear that the "Constitution gives a criminal defendant the right to demand that a jury find him guilty of all the elements of the crime with which he is charged." These basic precepts, firmly rooted in the common law, have provided the basis for recent decisions interpreting modern criminal statutes and sentencing procedures.

In *Blakely v. Washington,* 542 U.S. 296, 124 S.Ct. 2531 (2004), we dealt with a determinate sentencing scheme similar to the Federal Sentencing Guidelines. There the defendant pleaded guilty to kidnaping, a class B felony punishable by a term of not more than 10 years. Other provisions of Washington law, comparable to the Federal Sentencing Guidelines, mandated a "standard" sentence of 49–to–53 months, unless the judge found aggravating facts justifying an exceptional sentence. Although the prosecutor recommended a sentence in the standard range, the judge found that the defendant had acted with " 'deliberate cruelty' "and sentenced him to 90 months.

For reasons explained in [*Apprendi v. New Jersey,* 530 U.S. 466 (2000) and related cases], the requirements of the Sixth Amendment

---

* Justice SCALIA, Justice SOUTER, Justice THOMAS, and Justice GINSBURG join this opinion.

were clear. The application of Washington's sentencing scheme violated the defendant's right to have the jury find the existence of " 'any particular fact' " that the law makes essential to his punishment. That right is implicated whenever a judge seeks to impose a sentence that is not solely based on "facts reflected in the jury verdict or admitted by the defendant." We rejected the State's argument that the jury verdict was sufficient to authorize a sentence within the general 10–year sentence for Class B felonies, noting that under Washington law, the judge was *required* to find additional facts in order to impose the greater 90–month sentence. Our precedents, we explained, make clear "that the 'statutory maximum' for *Apprendi* purposes is the maximum sentence a judge may impose *solely on the basis of the facts reflected in the jury verdict or admitted by the defendant.*" The determination that the defendant acted with deliberate cruelty, like the determination in *Apprendi* that the defendant acted with racial malice, increased the sentence that the defendant could have otherwise received. Since this fact was found by a judge using a preponderance of the evidence standard, the sentence violated Blakely's Sixth Amendment rights.

As the dissenting opinions in *Blakely* recognized, there is no distinction of constitutional significance between the Federal Sentencing Guidelines and the Washington procedures at issue in that case. This conclusion rests on the premise, common to both systems, that the relevant sentencing rules are mandatory and impose binding requirements on all sentencing judges.

If the Guidelines as currently written could be read as merely advisory provisions that recommended, rather than required, the selection of particular sentences in response to differing sets of facts, their use would not implicate the Sixth Amendment. We have never doubted the authority of a judge to exercise broad discretion in imposing a sentence within a statutory range. Indeed, everyone agrees that the constitutional issues presented by these cases would have been avoided entirely if Congress had omitted from the SRA the provisions that make the Guidelines binding on district judges; it is that circumstance that makes the Court's answer to the second question presented possible. For when a trial judge exercises his discretion to select a specific sentence within a defined range, the defendant has no right to a jury determination of the facts that the judge deems relevant.

The Guidelines as written, however, are not advisory; they are mandatory and binding on all judges. While subsection (a) of § 3553 of the sentencing statute lists the Sentencing Guidelines as one factor to be considered in imposing a sentence, subsection (b) directs that the court "*shall* impose a sentence of the kind, and within the range" established by the Guidelines, subject to departures in specific, limited cases. Because they are binding on judges, we have consistently held that the Guidelines have the force and effect of laws.

The availability of a departure in specified circumstances does not avoid the constitutional issue, just as it did not in *Blakely* itself.

Importantly, however, departures are not available in every case, and in fact are unavailable in most. In most cases, as a matter of law, the Commission will have adequately taken all relevant factors into account, and no departure will be legally permissible. In those instances, the judge is bound to impose a sentence within the Guidelines range. It was for this reason that we rejected a similar argument in *Blakely*, holding that although the Washington statute allowed the judge to impose a sentence outside the sentencing range for " 'substantial and compelling reasons,' " that exception was not available for Blakely himself. The sentencing judge would have been reversed had he invoked the departure section to justify the sentence.

Booker's case illustrates the mandatory nature of the Guidelines. The jury convicted him of possessing at least 50 grams of crack in violation of 21 U.S.C. § 841(b)(1)(A)(iii) based on evidence that he had 92.5 grams of crack in his duffel bag. Under these facts, the Guidelines specified an offense level of 32, which, given the defendant's criminal history category, authorized a sentence of 210–to–262 months. See USSG § 2D1.1(c)(4). Booker's is a run-of-the-mill drug case, and does not present any factors that were inadequately considered by the Commission. The sentencing judge would therefore have been reversed had he not imposed a sentence within the level 32 Guidelines range.

Booker's actual sentence, however, was 360 months, almost 10 years longer than the Guidelines range supported by the jury verdict alone. To reach this sentence, the judge found facts beyond those found by the jury: namely, that Booker possessed 566 grams of crack in addition to the 92.5 grams in his duffel bag. The jury never heard any evidence of the additional drug quantity, and the judge found it true by a preponderance of the evidence. Thus, just as in *Blakely*, "the jury's verdict alone does not authorize the sentence. The judge acquires that authority only upon finding some additional fact." There is no relevant distinction between the sentence imposed pursuant to the Washington statutes in *Blakely* and the sentences imposed pursuant to the Federal Sentencing Guidelines in these cases.

In his dissent, Justice BREYER argues on historical grounds that the Guidelines scheme is constitutional across the board. He points to traditional judicial authority to increase sentences to take account of any unusual blameworthiness in the manner employed in committing a crime, an authority that the Guidelines require to be exercised consistently throughout the system. This tradition, however, does not provide a sound guide to enforcement of the Sixth Amendment's guarantee of a jury trial in today's world.

It is quite true that once determinate sentencing had fallen from favor, American judges commonly determined facts justifying a choice of a heavier sentence on account of the manner in which particular defendants acted. In 1986, however, our own cases first recognized a new trend in the legislative regulation of sentencing when we considered the significance of facts selected by legislatures that not only authorized, or even mandated, heavier sentences than would otherwise have been imposed, but increased the range of sentences possible for the underlying crime. Provisions for such enhancements of the permissible sentencing range reflected growing and wholly justified legislative concern about the proliferation and variety of drug crimes and their frequent identification with firearms offences.

The effect of the increasing emphasis on facts that enhanced sentencing ranges, however, was to increase the judge's power and diminish that of the jury. It became the judge, not the jury, that determined the upper limits of sentencing, and the facts determined were not required to be raised before trial or proved by more than a preponderance.

As the enhancements became greater, the jury's finding of the underlying crime became less significant. And the enhancements became very serious indeed. *See, e.g., Jones,* 526 U.S., at 230 (judge's finding increased the maximum sentence from 15 to 25 years); respondent Booker (from 262 months to a life sentence); respondent Fanfan (from 78 to 235 months); *United States v. Rodriguez,* 73 F.3d 161, 162–163 (C.A.7 1996) (Posner, C.J., dissenting from denial of rehearing en banc) (from approximately 54 months to a life sentence); *United States v. Hammoud,* 381 F.3d 316, 361–362 (C.A.4 2004) (en banc) (Motz, J., dissenting) (actual sentence increased from 57 months to 155 years).

As it thus became clear that sentencing was no longer taking place in the tradition that Justice BREYER invokes, the Court was faced with the issue of preserving an ancient guarantee under a new set of circumstances. The new sentencing practice forced the Court to address the question how the right of jury trial could be preserved, in a meaningful way guaranteeing that the jury would still stand between the individual and the power of the government under the new sentencing regime. And it is the new circumstances, not a tradition or practice that the new circumstances have superseded, that have led us to the answer first considered in *Jones* and developed in *Apprendi* and subsequent cases culminating with this one. It is an answer not motivated by Sixth Amendment formalism, but by the need to preserve Sixth Amendment substance.

We recognize that in some cases jury factfinding may impair the most expedient and efficient sentencing of defendants. But the interest in fairness and reliability protected by the right to a jury trial—a common-law right that defendants enjoyed for centuries and that is now enshrined in the Sixth Amendment—has always outweighed the interest in concluding trials swiftly.

Accordingly, we reaffirm our holding in *Apprendi:* Any fact (other than a prior conviction) which is necessary to support a sentence exceeding the maximum authorized by the facts established by a plea of guilty or a jury verdict must be admitted by the defendant or proved to a jury beyond a reasonable doubt.

JUSTICE BREYER delivered the opinion of the Court in part.*

We here turn to the second question presented, a question that concerns the remedy. We must decide whether or to what extent, "as a matter of severability analysis," the Guidelines "as a whole" are "inapplicable ... such that the sentencing court must exercise its discretion to sentence the defendant within the maximum and minimum set by statute for the offense of conviction."

We answer the question of remedy by finding the provision of the federal sentencing statute that makes the Guidelines mandatory, 18 U.S.C.A. § 3553(b)(1), incompatible with today's constitutional holding. We conclude that this provision must be severed and excised, as must one other statutory section, § 3742(e), which depends upon the Guidelines' mandatory nature. So modified, the Federal Sentencing Act makes the Guidelines effectively advisory. It requires a sentencing court to consider Guidelines ranges, see 18 U.S.C.A. § 3553(a)(4), but it permits the court to tailor the sentence in light of other statutory concerns as well, see § 3553(a).

We answer the remedial question by looking to legislative intent. We seek to determine what "Congress would have intended" in light of the Court's constitutional holding. In this instance, we must determine which of the two following remedial approaches is the more compatible with the legislature's intent as embodied in the 1984 Sentencing Act.

One approach, that of Justice STEVENS' dissent, would retain the Sentencing Act (and the Guidelines) as written, but would engraft onto the existing system today's Sixth Amendment "jury trial" requirement. The addition would change the Guidelines by preventing the sentencing court from increasing a sentence on the basis of a fact that the jury did not find (or that the offender did not admit).

The other approach, which we now adopt, would (through severance and excision of two provisions) make the Guidelines system advisory while maintaining a strong connection between the sentence imposed and the offender's real conduct—a connection important to the increased uniformity of sentencing that Congress intended its Guidelines system to achieve.

In today's context—a highly complex statute, interrelated provisions, and a constitutional requirement that creates fundamental change—we cannot assume that Congress, if faced with the statute's invalidity in key applications, would have preferred to apply the statute in as many other instances as possible. Neither can we determine likely congressional intent mechanically. We cannot simply approach the problem grammatically, say, by looking to see whether the constitutional requirement and the words of the Act are linguistically compatible.

---

* THE CHIEF JUSTICE, Justice O'CONNOR, Justice KENNEDY, and Justice GINSBURG join this opinion. [Justice Breyer also wrote an opinion for the four members of the Court who dissented from the portion of the majority opinion authored by Justice Stevens. Justice Ginsburg did not join that opinion.]

Nor do simple numbers provide an answer. It is, of course, true that the numbers show that the constitutional jury trial requirement would lead to additional decisionmaking by juries in only a minority of cases. Prosecutors and defense attorneys would still resolve the lion's share of criminal matters through plea bargaining, and plea bargaining takes place without a jury. Many of the rest involve only simple issues calling for no upward Guidelines adjustment. And in at least some of the remainder, a judge may find adequate room to adjust a sentence within the single Guidelines range to which the jury verdict points, or within the overlap between that range and the next highest.

But the constitutional jury trial requirement would nonetheless affect every case. It would affect decisions about whether to go to trial. It would affect the content of plea negotiations. It would alter the judge's role in sentencing. Thus we must determine likely intent not by counting proceedings, but by evaluating the consequences of the Court's constitutional requirement in light of the Act's language, its history, and its basic purposes.

While reasonable minds can, and do, differ about the outcome, we conclude that the constitutional jury trial requirement is not compatible with the Act as written and that some severance and excision are necessary.

Several considerations convince us that, were the Court's constitutional requirement added onto the Sentencing Act as currently written, the requirement would so transform the scheme that Congress created that Congress likely would not have intended the Act as so modified to stand. First, the statute's text states that "[t]he court" when sentencing will consider "the nature and circumstances of the offense and the history and characteristics of the defendant." 18 U.S.C.A. § 3553(a)(1). In context, the words "the court" mean "the judge without the jury," not "the judge working together with the jury." . . .

Second, Congress' basic statutory goal—a system that diminishes sentencing disparity—depends for its success upon judicial efforts to determine, and to base punishment upon, the *real conduct* that underlies the crime of conviction. That determination is particularly important in the federal system where crimes defined as, for example, "obstruct[ing], delay[ing], or affect[ing] commerce or the movement of any article or commodity in commerce, by . . . extortion," 18 U.S.C. § 1951(a), or, say, using the mail "for the purpose of executing" a "scheme or artifice to defraud," § 1341, can encompass a vast range of very different kinds of underlying conduct. But it is also important even in respect to ordinary crimes, such as robbery, where an act that meets the statutory definition can be committed in a host of different ways. Judges have long looked to real conduct when sentencing. Federal judges have long relied upon a presentence report, prepared by a probation officer, for information (often unavailable until *after* the trial) relevant to the manner in which the convicted offender committed the crime of conviction.

To engraft the Court's constitutional requirement onto the sentencing statutes, however, would destroy the system. It would prevent a judge from relying upon a presentence report for factual information, relevant to sentencing, uncovered after the trial. In doing so, it would, even compared to pre-Guidelines sentencing, weaken the tie between a sentence and an offender's real conduct. It would thereby undermine the sentencing statute's basic aim of ensuring similar sentences for those who have committed similar crimes in similar ways.

Several examples help illustrate the point. Imagine Smith and Jones, each of whom violates the Hobbs Act in very different ways. See 18 U.S.C. § 1951(a) (forbidding "obstruct[ing], delay[ing], or affect[ing] commerce or the movement of any article or commodity in commerce, by ... extortion"). Smith threatens to injure a co-worker unless the co-worker advances him a few dollars from the interstate company's till; Jones, after similarly threatening the co-worker, causes far more harm by seeking far more money, by making certain that the co-worker's family is aware of the threat, by arranging for deliveries of dead animals to the co-worker's home to show he is serious, and so forth. The offenders' behavior is very different; the known harmful consequences of their actions are different; their punishments both before, and after, the Guidelines would have been different. But, under the dissenters' approach, unless prosecutors decide to charge more than the elements of the crime, the judge would have to impose similar punishments.

[Justice Breyer provided several other illustrations supporting his argument that the relationship between the real conduct and the sentence imposed would be weakened under the system proposed by the dissent.]

This point is critically important. Congress' basic goal in passing the Sentencing Act was to move the sentencing system in the direction of increased uniformity. That uniformity does not consist simply of similar sentences for those convicted of violations of the same statute—a uniformity consistent with the dissenters' remedial approach. It consists, more importantly, of similar relationships between sentences and real conduct, relationships that Congress' sentencing statutes helped to advance and that Justice STEVENS' approach would undermine. In significant part, it is the weakening of this real-conduct/uniformity-in-sentencing relationship, and not any "inexplicabl[e]" concerns for the "*manner* of achieving uniform sentences," that leads us to conclude that Congress would have preferred *no* mandatory system to the system the dissenters envisage.

Third, the sentencing statutes, read to include the Court's Sixth Amendment requirement, would create a system far more complex than Congress could have intended. Would the indictment in a mail fraud case have to allege the number of victims, their vulnerability, and the amount taken from each? How could a judge expect a jury to work with the Guidelines' definitions of, say, "relevant conduct," which includes "all acts and omissions committed, aided, abetted, counseled, commanded, induced, procured, or willfully caused by the defendant; and [in the case of a conspiracy] all reasonably foreseeable acts and omissions of others in furtherance of the jointly undertaken criminal activity"? §§ 1B1.3(a)(1)(A)-(B). How would a jury measure "loss" in a securities fraud case—a matter so complex as to lead the Commission to instruct judges to make "only ... a reasonable estimate"? § 2B1.1, comment., n. 3(C). How would the court take account, for punishment purposes, of a defendant's contemptuous behavior at trial—a matter that the Government could not have charged in the indictment? § 3C1.1.

Fourth ... [b]ecause plea bargaining inevitably reflects estimates of what would happen at trial, plea bargaining too under such a system would move in the wrong direction. That is to say, in a sentencing system modified by the Court's constitutional requirement, plea bargaining would likely lead to sentences that gave greater weight, not to real conduct, but rather to the skill of counsel, the policies of the prosecutor, the caseload, and other factors that vary from place to place, defendant to defendant, and crime to crime. Compared to pre-Guidelines plea bargaining, plea bargaining of this kind would necessarily move federal sentencing in the direction of diminished, not increased, uniformity in sentencing. It would tend to defeat, not to further, Congress' basic statutory goal.

Such a system would have particularly troubling consequences with respect to prosecutorial power. Until now, sentencing factors have come before the judge in the presentence report. But in a sentencing system with the Court's constitutional requirement engrafted onto it, any factor that a prosecutor chose not to charge at the plea negotiation would be placed beyond the reach of the judge entirely. Prosecutors would thus exercise a power the Sentencing Act vested in judges: the power to decide, based on relevant information about the offense and the offender, which defendants merit heavier punishment.

Fifth, Congress would not have enacted sentencing statutes that make it more difficult to adjust sentences *upward* than to adjust them *downward.* As several United States Senators have written in an *amicus* brief, "the Congress that enacted the 1984 Act did not conceive of— much less establish—a sentencing guidelines system in which sentencing judges were free to consider facts or circumstances not found by a jury or admitted in a plea agreement for the purpose of adjusting a base-offense level *down,* but not *up,* within the applicable guidelines range. Such a one-way lever would be grossly at odds with Congress's intent." Yet that is the system that the dissenters' remedy would create.

For all these reasons, Congress, had it been faced with the constitutional jury trial requirement, likely would not have passed the same Sentencing Act. It likely would have found the requirement incompatible with the Act as written. Hence the Act cannot remain valid in its entirety. Severance and excision are necessary.

We now turn to the question of *which* portions of the sentencing statute we must sever and excise as inconsistent with the Court's constitutional requirement. [W]e must retain those portions of the Act that are (1) constitutionally valid, (2) capable of "functioning independently," and (3) consistent with Congress' basic objectives in enacting the statute.

Application of these criteria indicates that we must sever and excise two specific statutory provisions: the provision that requires sentencing courts to impose a sentence within the applicable Guidelines range (in the absence of circumstances that justify a departure), see 18 U.S.C. § 3553(b)(1), and the provision that sets forth standards of review on appeal, including *de novo* review of departures from the applicable Guidelines range, see § 3742(e) (see Appendix, *infra* 988–89, for text of both provisions). With these two sections excised (and statutory cross-references to the two sections consequently invalidated), the remainder of the Act satisfies the Court's constitutional requirements.

The remainder of the Act "function[s] independently." Without the "mandatory" provision, the Act nonetheless requires judges to take account of the Guidelines together with other sentencing goals. See 18 U.S.C.A. § 3553(a). The Act nonetheless requires judges to consider the Guidelines "sentencing range established for . . . the applicable category of offense committed by the applicable category of defendant," § 3553(a)(4), the pertinent Sentencing Commission policy statements, the need to avoid unwarranted sentencing disparities, and the need to provide restitution to victims, §§ 3553(a)(1), (3), (5)-(7). And the Act nonetheless requires judges to impose sentences that reflect the seriousness of the offense, promote respect for the law, provide just punishment, afford adequate deterrence, protect the public, and effectively provide the defendant with needed educational or vocational training and medical care. § 3553(a)(2).

Moreover, despite the absence of § 3553(b)(1), the Act continues to provide for appeals from sentencing decisions (irrespective of whether the trial judge sentences within or outside the Guidelines range in the exercise of his discretionary power under § 3553(a)). We concede that the excision of § 3553(b)(1) requires the excision of a different, appeals-related section, namely § 3742(e), which sets forth standards of review on appeal. That section contains critical cross-references to the (now-excised) § 3553(b)(1) and consequently must be severed and excised for similar reasons.

Excision of § 3742(e), however, does not pose a critical problem for the handling of appeals. That is because, as we have previously held, a statute that does not *explicitly* set forth a standard of review may nonetheless do so *implicitly*. We infer appropriate review standards from related statutory language, the structure of the statute, and the "sound administration of justice." And in this instance those factors, in addition to the past two decades of appellate practice in cases involving departures, imply a practical standard of review already familiar to appellate courts: review for "unreasonable [ness]." 18 U.S.C. § 3742(e)(3).

We do not doubt that Congress, when it wrote the Sentencing Act, intended to create a form of mandatory Guidelines system. But, we repeat, given today's constitutional holding, that is not a choice that remains open. Hence we have examined the statute in depth to determine Congress' likely intent *in light of today's holding*. And we have concluded that today's holding is fundamentally inconsistent with the judge-based sentencing system that Congress enacted into law. In our view, it is more consistent with Congress' likely intent in enacting the Sentencing Reform Act (1) to preserve important elements of that system while severing and excising two provisions (§§ 3553(b)(1) and 3742(e)) than (2) to maintain all provisions of the Act and engraft today's constitutional requirement onto that statutory scheme.

Ours, of course, is not the last word: The ball now lies in Congress' court. The National Legislature is equipped to devise and install, long-term, the sentencing system, compatible with the Constitution, that Congress judges best for the federal system of justice.

It is so ordered.

APPENDIX

Title 18 U.S.C.A. § 3553(a) (main ed. and Supp.2004) provides:

"Factors to be considered in imposing a sentence.—The court shall impose a sentence sufficient, but not greater than necessary, to comply with the purposes set forth in paragraph (2) of this subsection. The court, in determining the particular sentence to be imposed, shall consider—

"(1) the nature and circumstances of the offense and the history and characteristics of the defendant;

"(2) the need for the sentence imposed—

"(A) to reflect the seriousness of the offense, to promote respect for the law, and to provide just punishment for the offense;

"(B) to afford adequate deterrence to criminal conduct;

"(C) to protect the public from further crimes of the defendant; and

"(D) to provide the defendant with needed educational or vocational training, medical care, or other correctional treatment in the most effective manner;

"(3) the kinds of sentences available;

"(4) the kinds of sentence and the sentencing range established for—

"(A) the applicable category of offense committed by the applicable category of defendant as set forth in the guidelines—

"(i) issued by the Sentencing Commission pursuant to section 994(a)(1) of title 28, United States Code, subject to any amendments made to such guidelines by act of Congress (regardless of whether such amendments have yet to be incorporated by the Sentencing Commission into amendments issued under section 994(p) of title 28); and

"(ii) that, except as provided in section 3742(g), are in effect on the date the defendant is sentenced; or

"(B) in the case of a violation of probation or supervised release, the applicable guidelines or policy statements issued by the Sentencing Commission pursuant to section 994(a)(3) of title 28, United States Code, taking into account any amendments made to such guidelines or policy statements by act of Congress (regardless of whether such amendments have yet to be incorporated by the Sentencing Commission into amendments issued under section 994(p) of title 28);

"(5) any pertinent policy statement—

"(A) issued by the Sentencing Commission pursuant to section 994(a)(2) of title 28, United States Code, subject to any amendments made to such policy statement by act of Congress (regardless of whether such amendments have yet to be incorporated by the Sentencing Commission into amendments issued under section 994(p) of title 28); and

"(B) that, except as provided in section 3742(g), is in effect on the date the defendant is sentenced.

"(6) the need to avoid unwarranted sentence disparities among defendants with similar records who have been found guilty of similar conduct; and

"(7) the need to provide restitution to any victims of the offense."

[Justice Breyer's Appendix also reprinted 18 U.S.C. §§ 3551(b)(1) and 3742(e) at this point. These provisions are reprinted *infra* at 988–89.]

JUSTICE STEVENS, with whom JUSTICE SOUTER joins, and with whom JUSTICE SCALIA joins, dissenting in part.[a]

Neither of the two Court opinions that decide these cases finds any constitutional infirmity inherent in any provision of the Sentencing Reform Act of 1984 (SRA) or the Federal Sentencing Guidelines. Specifically, neither 18 U.S.C.A. § 3553(b)(1), which makes application of the Guidelines mandatory, nor § 3742(e), which authorizes appellate review of departures from the Guidelines, is even arguably unconstitutional. Neither the Government, nor the respondents, nor any of the numerous *amici* has suggested that there is any need to invalidate either provision in order to avoid violations of the Sixth Amendment in the administra-

a. Justice Scalia noted that he did not not join the portions of Justice Steven's opinion relying on legislative history and referring to the application of the decision to pending cases.

tion of the Guidelines. The Court's decision to do so represents a policy choice that Congress has considered and decisively rejected. While it is perfectly clear that Congress has ample power to repeal these two statutory provisions if it so desires, this Court should not make that choice on Congress' behalf. I respectfully dissent from the Court's extraordinary exercise of authority.

[I]t is appropriate to explain how the violation of the Sixth Amendment that occurred in Booker's case could readily have been avoided without making any change in the Guidelines. Booker received a sentence of 360 months' imprisonment. His sentence was based on four factual determinations: (1) the jury's finding that he possessed 92.5 grams of crack (cocaine base); (2) the judge's finding that he possessed an additional 566 grams; (3) the judge's conclusion that he had obstructed justice; and (4) the judge's evaluation of his prior criminal record. Under the jury's 92.5 grams finding, the maximum sentence authorized by the Guidelines was a term of 262 months. See United States Sentencing Commission, Guidelines Manual § 2D1.1(c)(4) (Nov.2003) (USSG).

If the 566 gram finding had been made by the jury based on proof beyond a reasonable doubt, that finding would have authorized a guidelines sentence anywhere between 324 and 405 months—the equivalent of a range from 27 to nearly 34 years—given Booker's criminal history. § 2D1.1(c)(2). Relying on his own appraisal of the defendant's obstruction of justice, and presumably any other information in the presentence report, the judge would have had discretion to select any sentence within that range. Thus, if the two facts, which in this case actually established two separate crimes, had both been found by the jury, the judicial factfinding that produced the actual sentence would not have violated the Constitution. In other words, the judge could have considered Booker's obstruction of justice, his criminal history, and all other real offense and offender factors without violating the Sixth Amendment. Because the Guidelines as written possess the virtue of combining a mandatory determination of sentencing ranges and discretionary decisions within those ranges, they allow ample latitude for judicial factfinding that does not even arguably raise any Sixth Amendment issue.

The principal basis for the Court's chosen remedy is its assumption that Congress did not contemplate that the Sixth Amendment would be violated by depriving the defendant of the right to a jury trial on a factual issue as important as whether Booker possessed the additional 566 grams of crack that exponentially increased the maximum sentence that he could receive. I am not at all sure that that assumption is correct, but even if it is, it does not provide an adequate basis for volunteering a systemwide remedy that Congress has already rejected and could enact on its own if it elected to.

When one pauses to note that over 95% of all federal criminal prosecutions are terminated by a plea bargain, and the further fact that in almost half of the cases that go to trial there are no sentencing enhancements, the extraordinary overbreadth of the Court's unprecedented remedy is manifest. It is, moreover, unique because, under the Court's reasoning, if Congress should decide to reenact the exact text of the two provisions that the Court has chosen to invalidate, that reenactment would be unquestionably constitutional. In my judgment, it is therefore clear that the Court's creative remedy is an exercise of legislative, rather than judicial, power.

Regardless of how the Court defines the standard for determining when a facial challenge to a statute should succeed, it is abundantly clear that the fact that a statute, or any provision of a statute, is unconstitutional in a portion of its applications does not render the statute or provision invalid, and no party suggests otherwise. The Government conceded at oral argument that 45% of federal sentences involve no enhancements. And, according to two U.S. Sentencing Commissioners who testified before Congress shortly after we handed down our decision in *Blakely v. Washington,* the number of enhancements that would actually implicate a defendant's Sixth Amendment rights is even smaller. Simply stated, the Government's submissions to this Court and to Congress demonstrate that the Guidelines could be constitutionally applied in their entirety, without any modifications, in the "majority of the cases sentenced under the federal guidelines." On the basis of these submissions alone, this Court should have declined to find the Guidelines, or any particular provisions of the Guidelines, facially invalid.

As the majority concedes, only a tiny fraction of federal prosecutions ever go to trial. See Estimate 2 ("In FY02, 97.1 percent of cases sentenced under the guidelines were the result of plea agreements"). If such procedures were followed in the future, our holding that *Blakely* applies to the Guidelines would be consequential only in the tiny portion of prospective sentencing decisions that are made after a defendant has been found guilty by a jury.

[I]n the remaining fraction of cases that result in a jury trial, I am confident that those charged with complying with the Guidelines—judges, aided by prosecutors and defense attorneys—could adequately protect defendants' Sixth Amendment rights without this Court's extraordinary remedy. In many cases, prosecutors could avoid an *Apprendi* problem simply by alleging in the indictment the facts necessary to reach the chosen Guidelines sentence. Following our decision in *Apprendi,* and again after our decision in *Blakely,* the Department of Justice advised federal prosecutors to adopt practices that would enable them "to charge and prove to the jury facts that increase the statutory maximum—for example, drug type and quantity for offenses under 21 U.S.C. 841." Enhancing the specificity of indictments would be a simple matter, for example, in prosecutions under the federal drug statutes (such as Booker's prosecution). The Government has already directed its prosecutors to allege facts such as the possession of a dangerous weapon or "that the defendant was an organizer or leader of criminal activity that involved five or more participants" in the indictment and prove them to the jury beyond a reasonable doubt.

[E]ven in those trials in which the Guidelines require the finding of facts not alleged in the indictment, such factfinding by a judge is not unconstitutional *per se*. To be clear, our holding that *Blakely* applies to the Guidelines does not establish the "impermissibility of judicial factfinding." Instead, judicial factfinding to support an offense level determination or an enhancement is *only unconstitutional when that finding raises the sentence beyond the sentence that could have lawfully been imposed by reference to facts found by the jury or admitted by the defendant*. This distinction is crucial to a proper understanding of why the Guidelines could easily function as they are currently written.

Rather than rely on traditional principles of facial invalidity or severability, the majority creates a new category of cases in which this Court may invalidate any part or parts of a statute (and add others) when it concludes that Congress would have preferred a modified system to administering the statute in compliance with the Constitution. This is entirely new law.

Rather than engage in a wholesale rewriting of the SRA, I would simply allow the Government to continue doing what it has done since this Court handed down *Blakely*—prove any fact that is *required* to increase a defendant's sentence under the Guidelines to a jury beyond a reasonable doubt. As I have already discussed, a requirement of jury factfinding for certain issues can be implemented without difficulty in the vast majority of cases.

[I]n order to justify "excising" 18 U.S.C.A. §§ 3553(b)(1) and 3742(e), the Court has the burden of showing that Congress would have preferred the remaining system of discretionary Sentencing Guidelines to not just the remedy I would favor, but also to *any* available alternative, including the alternative of total invalidation, which would give Congress a clean slate on which to write an entirely new law. The Court cannot meet this burden because Congress has already considered and overwhelmingly rejected the system it enacts today. In doing so, Congress revealed both an unmistakable preference for the certainty of a binding regime and a deep suspicion of judges' ability to reduce disparities in federal sentencing. A brief examination of the SRA's history reveals the gross impropriety of the remedy the Court has selected.

[Justice Stevens then reviewed the legislative history of the SRA in detail, arguing that it cannot be squared with the conclusion that Congress would have preferred advisory guidelines rather than alternative remedies. In the years prior to the passage of the SRA, Congress repeatedly rejected proposals for advisory guidelines. During the debate over the passage of the SRA Congress again explicitly discussed and rejected discretionary guidelines. It rejected the House bill, which authorized the creation of discretionary guidelines, replacing it with the Senate bill, which provided for binding guidelines and *de novo* appellate review to ensure compliance. Justice Stevens included many citations to statements in the Senate Report and floor debate indicating the importance that Congress placed upon making the guidelines mandatory and enforcing compliance. The lack of confidence in the judiciary's willingness and ability to root out sentencing disparity was also reflected in the debate over who would write the guidelines. The House bill, proposing the Guidelines be written by the Judicial Conference of the United States, was defeated by the Senate. The inference, Justice Stevens argued, was clear: Congress believed that judges could not be trusted to impose uniform sentences. In Justice Stevens' view subsequent developments reinforce the conclusion that Congress is strongly committed to binding guidelines. Specifically, the Prosecutorial Remedies and Other Tools to End the Exploitation of Children Today Act of 2003 (PROTECT Act) limited the number of available departures, and expanded *de novo* review of departures.]

This Court clearly had the power to adopt a remedy that both complied with the Sixth Amendment and also preserved a determinate sentencing regime in which judges make regular factual determinations regarding a defendant's sentence. It has chosen instead to exaggerate the constitutional problem and to expand the scope of judicial invalidation far beyond that which is even arguably necessary. Our holding that *Blakely* applies to the Sentencing Guidelines did not dictate the Court's unprecedented remedy.

As a matter of policy, the differences between the regime enacted by Congress and the system the Court has chosen are stark. Were there any doubts about whether Congress would have preferred the majority's solution, these are sufficient to dispel them. First, Congress' stated goal of uniformity is eliminated by the majority's remedy. True, judges must still *consider* the sentencing range contained in the Guidelines, but that range is now nothing more than a suggestion that may or may not be persuasive to a judge when weighed against the numerous other considerations listed in 18 U.S.C.A. § 3553(a). The result is certain to be a return to the same type of sentencing disparities Congress sought to eliminate in 1984. Prior to the PROTECT Act, rates of departure from the applicable Guidelines sentence (via upward or downward departure) varied considerably depending upon the Circuit in which one was sentenced. *See* Sourcebook 53–55 (Table 26) (showing that 76.6% of sentences in the Fourth Circuit were within the applicable Guidelines range, whereas only 48.8% of sentences in the Ninth Circuit fell within the range). Those disparities will undoubtedly increase in a discretionary system in which the Guidelines are but one factor a judge must consider in sentencing a defendant within a broad statutory range.

Congress' demand in the PROTECT Act that departures from the Guidelines be closely regulated and monitored is eviscerated—for there can be no "departure" from a mere suggestion. How will a judge go about determining how much deference to give to the applicable Guidelines range? How will a court of appeals review for reasonableness a district court's decision that the need for "just punishment" and "adequate deterrence to criminal conduct" simply outweighs the considerations contemplated by the Sentencing Commission? What if a sentencing judge determines that a defendant's need for "educational or vocational training, medical care, or other correctional treatment in the most effective manner," § 3553(a)(2)(D), requires disregarding the stiff Guidelines range Congress presumably preferred? These questions will arise in every case in the federal system under the Court's system. Regrettably, these are exactly the sort of questions Congress hoped that sentencing judges would not ask after the SRA.

Unlike a rule that would merely require judges and prosecutors to comply with the Sixth Amendment, the Court's systematic overhaul turns the entire system on its head *in every case,* and, in so doing, runs contrary to the central purpose that motivated Congress to act in the first instance. Moreover, by repealing the right to a determinate sentence that Congress established in the SRA, the Court has effectively eliminated the very constitutional right *Apprendi* sought to vindicate.

I respectfully dissent.

Notes

1. *Booker* was a bombshell. Although many observers had predicted that the Court would extend the constitutional analysis of *Blakely* to the Guidelines, virtually no one predicted the remedial portion of the opinion. In his dissenting opinion Justice Scalia noted the irony of a remedial choice that "[i]n order to rescue from nullification a statutory scheme designed to eliminate discretionary sentencing, discards the provisions that eliminate discretionary sentencing." Under *Booker* the guidelines are preserved but transformed from mandatory to advisory standards that must be "considered" by the sentencing courts, subject to appellate review for reasonableness, unless and until Congress intervenes.

Look again at the analysis of the remedial opinion. A great deal of Justice Breyer's argument turns on the importance of preserving "real offense" sentencing. It's important to understand what he meant, and why he thought it was so important to preserve real offense sentencing, even though the cost was making the Guidelines only advisory.

The Guidelines definition of "relevant conduct" incorporates more than just the elements of the offense, looking at many characteristics of the "real offense" that are not part of the statutory definition of the offense. Sometimes this means facts that were never presented to a jury, or even included in the indictment. But note that this can and does go even further. Indeed, *United States v. Watts,* 519 U.S. 148 (1997) (per curiam), held that it was proper to increase the defendants' Guidelines offense levels on the basis of the judges' finding, by a preponderance of the evidence, that the defendants had committed drug and weapons offenses of which their juries had just *acquitted* them, because the actions in question were part of the "real offenses" of which the juries did convict them. Many people find that shocking. But in Justice Breyer's view, if a defendant did use a gun, or did traffic in large quantities of a drug, it's vital to consider those facts at sentencing to insure that truly similar cases receive similar sentences—even if that issue was never presented to a jury, or the proof that was presented fell short of the reasonable doubt standard, as long as it is enough to meet the preponderance standard.[b] The central insight of the merits opinion, however, is that a defendant is entitled to have a jury determine, beyond a reasonable doubt, whether he did use a gun or traffic in larger quantities of a drug (and so forth) before these facts can provide a basis for an increase in his sentence. The system can't require a judge to increase a defendant's sentence on the basis of such facts without the usual procedural safeguards of trial by jury or proof beyond a reasonable doubt.

The remedial majority preserves real offense sentencing but avoids trial by jury and proof beyond a reasonable doubt by concluding that the Guidelines no longer *require* an increase in the defendant's sentence based on the judge's finding that he possessed a gun or was involved in a larger transaction—they just *recommend* an increase on the basis of those facts. The remedial majority argues that's what judges were doing before the passage of the Guidelines, and that nothing in the Fifth or Sixth Amendments is offended by this traditional practice.

2. *Booker* left open a lot of questions that the lower courts are beginning to answer. What does it mean to make the Guidelines "advisory"? Although the Guidelines were mandatory, the courts had the authority to "depart" from the Guidelines. What's the difference between the departure authority and the courts authority under the new advisory system? How do you square the Congressional goal of avoiding unjustified disparities with the courts' greater discretion under an advisory system? And what do you call these new *Booker* sentences? They aren't really the same as the departures authorized by the Guidelines, so some other term seems to be needed. Some courts use the term "variance," and others refer to them as § 3553(a) (or statutory) sentences or "non-Guidelines" sentences.

The Commission is monitoring post-*Booker* sentencing decisions in an effort to provide Congress and the Commission itself with a overview.[c] The 64 thousand dollar question is whether the rate of sentences outside the Guidelines range will change dramatically, and, if so, how. Based upon the statistics as of September 30, 2005 (nine months after the decision in

---

b. Judge—now Justice—Breyer was one of the original Sentencing Commissioners, and shortly after the promulgation of the Guidelines he wrote an article explaining the Commission's decision key decisions. He explained that a charge offense system "tends to overlook the fact that particular crimes may be committed in different ways, which in the past have made, and still should make, an important difference in terms of the punishment imposed." Stephen Breyer, *The Federal Sentencing Guidelines And The Key Compromises Upon Which They Rest*, 17 HOFSTRA L.REV. 1, 8 (1988):

A bank robber, for example, might, or might not, use a gun; he might take a little, or a lot, of money; he might, or might not, injure the teller. The typical armed robbery statute, however, does not distinguish among these different ways of committing the crime. Nor does such a statute necessarily distinguish between

how cruelly the defendant treated the victims, whether the victims were especially vulnerable as a result of their age, or whether the defendant, though guilty, acted under duress. Thus, unless the statutes are rewritten to make such distinctions, the sentencing court is asked to look, at least in part, at what really happened under the particular factual situation before it.

Given Justice Breyer's heavy involvement in the drafting of the Guidelines, and particularly in the decision to incorporate real offense sentencing, some commentators have suggested that he should have recused himself from the decision in *Booker*.

c. The discussion that follows is based upon U.S. Sentencing Comm'n, Special Post-*Booker* Coding Project (Oct. 13, 2005), *available at* http://www.ussc.gov/Blakely/PostBooker_101305.pdf.

Booker), the answer is that there has been a change, but whether it's significant (or good or bad) may be in the eye of the beholder. In the two prior years for which statistics were available, the rate of within Guidelines sentences ranged from 65% to 69.4%. In contrast, in the post-*Booker* period the rate of within Guidelines sentences fell to 61.9%. Both above-range and below-range sentences increased after *Booker*. There were also changes in the kinds of below-range sentences. The percentage of cases where the below-range sentence was based on substantial assistance to the authorities decreased after *Booker*, and the percentage of below-range cases that were not initiated by or agreed to by the government increased. Thus there were some cases in which the defendants got harsher sentences, but in many more cases the courts used their expanded discretion to decrease sentences. Reasonable people can (and do) differ on the question whether the size of the change is significant, and whether the way the courts are using their expanded discretion fulfills the intent underlying 18 U.S.C. § 3553(a). Moreover, another cut at the data seems to reveal a different story: sentences have been as high or higher after *Booker* as before. The same Commission report compares the actual sentences imposed for the four most common guideline categories (drug trafficking, unlawful entry into the U.S., firearms, and theft/fraud) over time, and reveals that both the average and median sentence imposed for all of these guidelines was the same or higher in the nine months after *Booker* as it was in the last year for which we have pre-*Booker* statistics.

The Commission's data also reflects the fact that in practice there is no bright line between the categories. Many courts refer to both their departure authority and their authority under *Booker* as justifications for below- and above-Guideline sentences. In fact, one of clearest trends is that the courts now refer far less frequently to their authority to depart. It seems that courts are using their *Booker*/§ 3553(a) authority in cases in they would previously have labeled as departures.

3. Individual courts have taken quite different approaches to the question what it means to "consider" the guidelines. At one end of the spectrum, in *United States v. Wilson (Wilson I)*, 350 F. Supp. 2d 910 (D. Utah 2005), the court concluded that the guidelines should be given "heavy weight" in order to implement the congressionally mandated purposes behind criminal sentences and avoid unjustified disparity. Accordingly, the court would deviate from the guideline sentence only in unusual cases for clearly identified reasons. In *United States v. Wilson (Wilson II)*, 355 F. Supp. 2d 1269 (D. Utah 2005), the court reviewed and then rejected decisions reading the district courts' authority more broadly. The author of *Wilson* opinions, Judge Paul Cassell, develops his points in detail with a great deal of supporting authority, and the opinions are worth studying in detail. Here is the kernel of his argument in *Wilson II*:

> In [*Wilson I*], this court concluded that the recommended Guidelines sentence should receive considerable weight. Guidelines sentences typically achieve congressional objectives. They appear to track the public's view as to just punishment and are well-designed to incapacitate serious offenders and deter would-be criminals. Finally, the Guidelines are the only available common standard for judges to use in crafting sentences. Heavy reliance on the Guidelines is thus the only way to

implement the congressional directive for courts to "avoid unwarranted sentencing disparities among defendants with similar records who have been found guilty of similar conduct...." [18 U.S.C. § 3553(a)(6).]

... As *Booker* explains, Congress' "basic statutory goal in enacting the Guidelines was to provide a sentencing system that diminishes sentencing disparity" and "to move the sentencing system in the direction of increased uniformity."

If the court were to vary from the Guidelines with any frequency, it would be impossible to achieve this congressional objective. As explained in the earlier opinion in this case:

> The only way of avoiding gross disparities in sentencing from judge-to-judge and district-to-district is for sentencing courts to apply some uniform measure in all cases. The only standard currently available is the Sentencing Guidelines. If each district judge follows his or her own views of "just punishment" and "adequate deterrence," the result will be a system in which prison terms will "depend on 'what the judge ate for breakfast' on the day of sentencing" and other irrelevant factors.

> ... On a procedural level, it is critical for courts to follow the "old 'departure' methodology." *Booker* commands that "[t]he district courts, while not bound to apply the Guidelines, must consult those Guidelines and take them into account when sentencing." Departure provisions are, of course, part of "the Guidelines" that the court must take "into account" when imposing sentence. Unless the court calculates and then considers what the Guidelines advise as to a particular sentence in a particular case—that is, the initial Guideline sentence adjusted by any applicable departures—the court is not in a position to follow *Booker*'s requirements. Today, the Second Circuit reached this conclusion, holding that district judges should decide whether to impose a sentence "within the applicable Guidelines range *or within permissible departure authority*," as opposed to a non-Guidelines sentence. As the Circuit explained, a " 'departure' [is] not a sentence within the applicable Guidelines range, but it [is] nonetheless a 'Guidelines sentence,' *i.e.*, imposed pursuant to the departure provisions of the policy statements in the Guidelines, as well as the departure authority of subsection 3553(b)(1)."

It is important for courts to follow the traditional departure methodology for substantive reasons as well. Because the departure methodology guides the exercise of discretion—both as to whether to depart and as to the extent of any departure—use of that standard methodology by courts around the country will help to minimize unwarranted sentencing disparity. [Otherwise], different courts will surely give different weights to the broadly-worded factors listed in the Sentencing Reform Act. The result will almost inevitably be that defendants sentenced in the Eastern District of Wisconsin will serve different sentences for the same offense than similarly-situated defendants sentenced in the District of Utah. This would produce the "discordant symphony" of "excessive sentencing disparities" that the *Booker* majority stated would *not* be a consequence of its decision.

... In recent years, unwarranted sentencing disparity arising from judicial discretion has been dramatically reduced because of the Guidelines. In a country committed to equal justice under the law—with a sentencing statute that mandates similar outcomes for similar crimes committed by similar offenders—this part of the court's business must continue. The only realistic way to insure this is to follow generally the Guidelines.

Other courts such as *United States v. Ranum,* 353 F. Supp. 2d 984 (D. Iowa 2005), have disagreed, saying that *Booker* was not an invitation to business as usual, and that the guidelines should be considered along with the other factors identified in § 3553(a). In the decision that follows, the district judge explores at length the reasons she rejects the narrow approach in *Wilson I* and *II,* and she departs downward, inter alia, to avoid disparity with sentence of more culpable co-felon.

UNITED STATES v. JABER

362 F.Supp.2d 365 (D. Mass. 2005).

GERTNER, D.J.

Issa Jaber ("Jaber") and Philip Momoh ("Momoh") were charged with conspiracy to possess or distribute pseudoephedrine, possession or distribution of pseudoephedrine with the knowledge that it would be used to manufacture a controlled substance, and conspiracy to commit money laundering. Jaber pled guilty to all counts of the indictment. Momoh, named only in four counts of the indictment, also pled guilty. Before I discuss their sentences, I address the applicable legal framework in light of *United States v. Booker,* 125 S.Ct. 738 (2005).

On January 12, 2005, the United States Supreme Court in *Booker* concluded that the Federal Sentencing Guidelines (hereinafter "Guidelines") were unconstitutional. The Court found that the Guidelines violated the Sixth Amendment because they were not "guidelines" in any meaningful sense of the word. They obligated judges to find facts with specific consequences, consequences which were pre-ordained by the United States Sentencing Commission (hereinafter "Commission") and which increased a defendant's sentence beyond the range required by a jury's verdict or a plea of guilty. This constitutional defect required severance of the provisions of the Sentencing Reform Act of 1984 (hereinafter "SRA"), 28 U.S.C. § 994 et seq., 18 U.S.C. § 3551 et seq., that made the Guidelines mandatory, namely, 18 U.S.C. § 3553(b)(1). The Guidelines are now to be deemed "advisory," such that courts are to "consider" Guidelines ranges, *see* § 3553(a)(4), but are permitted to tailor sentences in light of other statutory concerns.

* * * As I describe in greater detail below, "advisory" does not mean a regime without rules, or a return to the standardless sentencing which preceded the SRA. Nor does it mean slavish application of the Guidelines under the guise of fair "consideration," an approach which is

now unconstitutional. "Advisory" means something in-between, which I articulate below.

* * *

A. THE ADVISORY FRAMEWORK

One way to identify what is permissible in an advisory framework is first to identify what is impermissible. Sentencing approaches can now be tracked along a continuum. At one end lies the mandatory extreme. To the extent that judges enforce the federal sentencing guidelines without exercising any discretion, i.e., as if they are "mandatory," the *Blakely-Booker* line of cases suggest that judges are behaving in an unconstitutional manner. They are arrogating to themselves fact-finding decisions which appropriately belong to juries.

On the other end of the continuum is what I have come to describe as the "free at last" regime, or a return to pre–1984 indeterminate sentencing. Put another way, this end describes an approach to sentencing in which judges feel free to disagree about the fundamental premises of sentencing, to implement their own perceptions of what policies should drive punishment. The "free at last" mentality is characterized by comments like, "I won't sentence according to the Guidelines because I simply don't agree that sale of marijuana deserves such severe penalties."

Advisory guidelines should fall somewhere in-between these poles; they should constitute a regime based on rules of general application— what many have described as a common law of sentencing, supplementing, not supplanting, judges. To be sure, in this regime, the existing set of rules—the Guidelines—are very important, but they cannot be outcome-determinative without running afoul of *Booker*.

I agree with the Second Circuit in *United States v. Crosby,* 397 F.3d 103 (2d Cir. 2005), that it is not useful to determine in advance the weight that sentencing judges should give to applicable Guidelines ranges. Rather, in *Crosby,* the Court concluded that it is "more consonant with the day to day role of district judges in imposing sentences and the episodic role of appellate judges in reviewing sentences ... to permit the concept of 'consideration' in the context of the applicable Guideline range to evolve...."

At the same time, I have concerns about the approach in *United States v. Wilson,* 350 F.Supp.2d 910 (D.Utah 2005) (*Wilson I*), and *United States v. Wilson,* 355 F.Supp.2d 1269, 2005 WL 273168 (D.Utah Feb.2, 2005) (*Wilson II*). In *Wilson,* the court noted that the Guidelines are entitled to "heavy" weight, and that deviation from Guidelines ranges is only appropriate in unusual cases, for clearly identified and persuasive reasons.

I have concerns about such an approach, both as a matter of law and fact. As a practical matter, the *Wilson* method comes perilously close to the mandatory regime found to be constitutionally infirm in *Booker*.

Guidelines ranges had always been the presumptive sentences, and perhaps became even more compulsory after the amendments of the Prosecutorial Remedies and Tools Against the Exploitation of Children Today (PROTECT) Act. *See* Pub.L. No. 108–21, 117 Stat. 650, 667 (codified in scattered sections of 18 and 42 U.S.C., with the Feeney Amendment set forth in a note to 18 U.S.C. § 3553). Deviations from the Guidelines for certain facts were permitted only in "extraordinary" circumstances. In fact, departure authority was always framed in the terms used by the Court in *Wilson*.

Furthermore, I have concerns about the legal premises on which the *Wilson* approach is based. In *Wilson* I (reaffirmed in *Wilson* II), the Court noted that the Guidelines are entitled to "heavy" weight for a number of reasons: 1) they were promulgated by an "expert agency," 2) that expert agency promulgated "comprehensive guidelines", and 3) these Guidelines directly reflected the congressionally-mandated purposes of the SRA.[15] From the Court's perspective, there was nothing more a trial judge could do to effectuate the purposes of the statute in a given case than to impose the Guidelines sentence. The Commission, with Congress' concurrence, had done it all. As the *Wilson* court noted:

> It would be startling to discover that while Congress had created an expert agency, approved the agency's members, directed the agency to promulgate Guidelines, allowed those Guidelines to go into effect, and adjusted those Guidelines over a period of fifteen years, that the resulting Guidelines did not well serve the underlying congressional purposes. The more likely conclusion is that the Guidelines reflect precisely what Congress believes is the punishment that will achieve its purposes in passing criminal statutes.

Apart from congressional approval, the [*Wilson*] Court found that the Guidelines *in fact* achieved the statutory purposes: They achieved just punishment because they precisely reflected society's views about punishment, as described in the Commission's own studies, and they achieved the goal of deterrence, enumerated in § 3553(a), by their impact on crime rates. Crime rates, the Court noted, had declined since the inauguration of the Guidelines. Indeed, relative to the sentencing experts on the Commission, courts were poorly suited to consider "elasticities and other factors that would go into a sensible deterrence calculation," particularly with respect to classes of crimes. In contrast to the courts, "the Sentencing Commission with its ability to collect sentencing data, monitor crimes rates, and conduct statistical analyses, is perfectly situated to evaluate deterrence arguments."

While I have considerable respect for the United States Sentencing Commission, and as the sentences below suggest, for the Guidelines it has promulgated, the Court in *Wilson* overstates the case for deference to the Commission, particularly in individual cases.

---

15. The *Wilson* court concluded that Congress had ratified each and every Guideline because it "had an opportunity both to review the initial Guidelines and all subsequent amendments to insure that they fulfill congressional purposes."

1. The Guidelines Were Not in Fact, and Could Not Be, Comprehensive. Under 28 U.S.C. § 991(b)(1), the Sentencing Commission was directed to establish policies that would "[a]void[ ] unwarranted sentencing disparities among defendants with similar records who have been found guilty of similar criminal conduct *while maintaining sufficient flexibility to permit individualized sentences when warranted by mitigating or aggravating factors not taken into account in the establishment of general sentencing practices.*" 28 U.S.C. § 991(b)(1)(B) (emphasis added). The original Commission recognized that its understanding of the factors that could legitimately affect sentencing was not exhaustive. In part, the Commission was limited by a regime in its preliminary stages. In part, and this is particularly relevant today, the Commission conceded the inherent complexity of the sentencing enterprise. It acknowledged "the difficulty of foreseeing and capturing a single set of guidelines that encompasses the vast range of human conduct potentially relevant to a sentencing decision." U.S.S.G. ch. I, pt. A, intro. cmt. 4(b). Indeed, it saw that "[c]ircumstances that may warrant departure from the guideline range ... cannot, by their very nature, be comprehensively listed and analyzed in advance." U.S.S.G. § 5K2.0(a) (prior to amendment). With few exceptions, the Commission refused to "limit the kind of factors (whether or not mentioned anywhere else in the Guidelines) that could constitute grounds for departure in an unusual case." U.S.S.G. ch. I, pt. A, intro. cmt. 4(b).

The Commission's concerns, and its approach, apply with particular force today after the Supreme Court's decision in *Booker.* From the start, the Guidelines were intended to advance both the goals of uniformity and proportionality. Congress did not seek to impose a regime with absolutely uniform sentences across the country. It sought to eliminate only "unwarranted" disparities, while enabling judges to consider those factors that cannot be tallied in advance, but that may create "warranted" disparities in sentencing.

Indeed, the drafters of the Guidelines regime envisioned an important role for judges in articulating what those factors might be. As judges applied the Guidelines, they were supposed to highlight issues and concerns that the Guidelines had not addressed, in effect, to create a common law of sentencing in the interstices of the Guidelines. As one scholar noted: "[t]he notion of judicial development of a 'common law of sentencing' was a fundamental component of the guidelines model which hoped to take advantage of 'the interlocking substantive lawmaking competencies of the commission and judiciary.'" [Douglas A. Berman, *Balanced and Purposeful Departures: Fixing a Jurisprudence that Undermines the Federal Sentencing Guidelines,* 76 Notre Dame L.Rev. 21, 34 (2000).] Judges were to articulate the purposes of sentencing, and to "consider what impact, if any, each particular purpose should have on the sentence in each case." STREP. No. 98–225, at 77 (1983), *reprinted in* 1984 ISKCON 3182, 3260. In short, the drafters understood that fairness in the individual case meant something other than rote application of the Guidelines.

This approach is not only consistent with the SRA and the Guidelines, but also, I would argue, is now compelled by *Booker*. (Indeed, had the Guidelines been interpreted more consistently with this early vision, perhaps *Booker* would have had a different outcome.)

2. The Guidelines Do Not Implement the Purposes of Sentencing. Indeed, the Commission made no effort to implement the statutory purposes of sentencing. The first Commission noted that choosing among purposes would be "difficult," that the selection of purposes was often "irrelevant," and that, therefore, it would simply not identify its purposes at all (or would claim that *all* purposes were relevant to all cases). In effect, the purposes enumerated under § 3553(a) became irrelevant to the Guideline enterprise. This is so even as the Guidelines have been amended over the years.[18]

3. The Commission Has Not Functioned as a Sentencing Expert in the Way the Statute Envisioned. The Commission's mandate was to develop Guidelines that "reflect, to the extent practicable, advancement in knowledge of human behavior as it relates to the criminal justice process." 28 U.S.C. § 991(b)(1)(C). Moreover, it was to "develop means of measuring the degree to which the sentencing, penal, and correctional practices are effective in meeting the purposes of sentencing as set forth in section 3553(a)(2)." 28 U.S.C. § 991(b)(2). One can imagine these directives leading to scientific studies on the efficacy of different guidelines, how they relate to crime control objectives, to what extent they deter crime, or, to quote one judge, "what works."

But, with few exceptions, the Commission has done no such analysis. Without an agreement on the purposes of sentencing, there was no way for the Commission to measure sentences against particular objectives. Even after the Guidelines were promulgated, all discussions of delay for "field testing" were rebuffed. Instead, the Commission simply took the average national sentences for a given offense, and then increased them, without explanation, much less scientific study.

The Commission did not try to justify its Guidelines in any meaningful way either. It did not have to. Like other administrative agencies' rules, the Commission's proposed rules become law unless disapproved by Congress. But, unlike other rule making agencies of the federal government, the Commission is not subject to the Administrative Procedure Act. Since the Guidelines could not be challenged as "arbitrary" or "capricious," the Commission faced no pressure to provide explanations.

4. Congress Has Approved the Guidelines Generally—Not Their Use In Any Particular Case. Proposed Guidelines become law unless disapproved by legislation. To disapprove a proposed guideline,

---

18. Indeed, the assumption that the Commission must have thought about purposes—when it did not—is responsible in part for the overly rigid enforcement of the Guidelines. *See* Paul J. Hofer & Mark Allenbaugh, *The Reason Behind the Rules: Finding and Using The Philosophy of the* *Federal Sentencing Guidelines,* 40 Am. Crim. L.Rev. 19, 22 (2003) ("Mechanical judging fails to subject the rules to the ongoing critical scrutiny needed when applying them to the particular circumstances of individual defendants.")

Congress must pass a bill. If the president vetoes that bill, it can become law only by a two-thirds vote of both Houses of Congress. If Congress does not adopt disapproval legislation within 180 days, any Guideline becomes legally binding. *See* 28 U.S.C. § 994(a, p) (1994). It is no surprise that, with some exceptions, Congress has not played an active role in the promulgation of individual Guidelines.

5. While the Guidelines May Reflect Public Opinion to a Degree, They Do Not Reflect the Public's View of Individual Cases. In fact, the studies cited in *Wilson I* found that, while there was agreement between the Guidelines and the public in ranking crimes, the general consensus did not extend to the length of the sentence in an individual case, which is precisely the decision that judges have to make. As the authors note, "on the level of sentences given to individual vignettes, there was only a very modest amount of agreement between the sentences given by individual respondents and those prescribed by the guidelines." Peter H. Ross & Richard A. Berk, *Just Punishment: Federal Guidelines and Public Views Compared* 208 (1997). Moreover, there were "major departures" from "close agreement" with respect to crimes, such as drug trafficking, that the Commission had determined required lengthy sentences. In short, it is not at all clear that the public would agree with mechanistically-derived Guidelines outcomes, if it had all the information that judges possess, instead of just sound bytes or incendiary headlines.

6. There Is Substantial Debate about the Role of the Federal Sentencing Guidelines in Crime Rate Reduction. Even assuming that incarceration contributes heavily to the drop in crime, federal sentencing comprises only a fraction of the sentences meted out in courts around the country every year. In 2001, 59,363 defendants were convicted of felonies in federal court. *See* BUREAU OF JUSTICE STATISTICS, SOURCE-BOOK OF CRIMINAL JUSTICE STATISTICS ONLINE ("Sourcebook Online"), Table 5.18, "Federal defendants convicted in U.S. District Courts" (fiscal year 2001), *available at* http:// www.albany.edu/sourcebook/pdf/t518.pdf. In contrast, in 2000, fully 924,700 felony convictions took place in state courts. *See* Sourcebook Online, Table 5.44, "Felony convictions in State courts" (2000), *available at:* http:// www.albany.edu/source-book/pdf/t544.pdf. Furthermore, state sentencing policies vary widely from federal sentencing policy. Some states have guideline systems, some do not, and others use hybrid structures.

Indeed, most studies attribute falling crime rates to factors other than incarceration rates, much less to the Federal Sentencing Guidelines. *See e.g.,* Henry Ruth & Kevin R. Reitz, *The Challenge of Crime: Rethinking Our Response* 5, 15–18 (2003). In fact, although drug offenders are incarcerated for longer and longer periods, the drug crime rate has increased. *See id.* at 211–214; *see also* Jeffrey A. Roth, *Review of an Analysis of Non–Violent Drug Offenders with Minimal Criminal Histories,* 7 Fed. Sent. Rep. 18, at 4–5 (1994).

But, having said all of the above, I have absolutely no doubt that, however one characterizes the Guidelines, their advantages and their flaws, the Guidelines will continue to play an important part in sentencing. They have shaped the vocabulary we use to describe sentences, and the standards we use to evaluate and compare cases. Since there were no alternative rules prior to the Sentencing Guidelines—no empirical studies linking particular sentences to particular crime control objectives, no common law of sentencing—and there have been none since, the Guidelines will continue to have a critical impact. At the same time, as I describe below, the only way for courts to truly "consider" the Guidelines, rather than to follow them by rote, is to do in each case just what the Commission failed to do—to explain, correlate to the purposes of sentencing, cite to authoritative sources, and be subject to appellate review. As for the Commission, it can now return to what it was supposed to do as well—to studying the impact of sentences on crime control, as well as monitoring disparity. *See e.g.,* Barbara M. Vincent, *Research in Sentencing,* 6 Fed. Sent. Rep. 22 (1993).

In the final analysis, the SRA sought to eliminate "unwarranted disparity" between "similarly situated offenders." It did not call for *identical* sentences from one end of the country to another. Differences justified by "differences among offenses or offenders" are *warranted* differences. STREP. No. 98–225, at 38 (1984), *reprinted in* 1984 ISKCON 3183, 3221–29 ("Sentencing disparities that are not justified by differences among offenses or offenders are unfair both to offenders and to the public."). Differences in the treatment of offenders based on identifiable, sustainable standards, spelled out in decisions, statements of reasons, or transcripts, and subject to review, or even testing, are not "unwarranted."

The devil, however, is in the details to which I now turn. I begin a discussion of my two sentencing decisions in the cases of Issa Jaber and Philip Momoh with a review of the Guidelines—an effort to interpret them, to determine what factors each guideline comprised and, to the extent possible, why these factors are important. I then review the sentences that resulted with a view to the statutory purposes of sentencing. In my judgment, each of these sentences could be described as "Guidelines" sentences, as they hark back to the original statute and intended approach.

II.　Issa Jaber and Philip Momoh

Issa Jaber ("Jaber") and Philip Momoh ("Momoh") were charged in an eight count superceding indictment alleging conspiracy to possess or distribute a list I chemical, namely pseudoephedrine, in violation of 21 U.S.C. § 846 (Count 1), possession or distribution of a listed chemical knowing that it would be used to manufacture a controlled substance, in violation of 21 U.S.C. 841(c)(2) (Counts 2–7), and conspiracy to commit money laundering, in violation of 18 U.S.C. § 1965(h) (Count 8). Jaber is named in all counts, to which he pled guilty. Momoh is named in Counts 1, 4, 7 and 8, to which he also pled guilty.

The nub of the offense according to the indictment was the charge that, from January 2000 until July 2000, Jaber, working through a phony pharmaceutical wholesale business, illegally diverted pseudoephedrine for use in methamphetamine trafficking organizations. Momoh was his employee, essentially a functionary. Jaber had been introduced to the business by Khalid Abu–Lawi ("Abu–Lawi"), who was not a defendant in this case.

But the indictment and the pleas only told part of the story. I requested Abu–Lawi's presentence report to learn more about the scope of the charges than what was framed by the Momoh–Jaber indictment. The presentence report revealed that Jaber's operation was a very small part of a much larger conspiracy, and that Abu–Lawi was more than simply a facilitator of an illegal Massachusetts operation.

Abu–Lawi was indicted with 26 co-defendants in the Southern District of Florida. The indictment charged a conspiracy beginning over nine months before Jaber's introduction, namely, beginning in April of 1999. The conspiracy was national in scope, including transactions in Florida, California, Oregon, Chicago, and Houston. As the Abu–Lawi presentence report described:

> The investigation revealed a structured network of individuals, international in scope, involved in providing pseudoephedrine to various methamphetamine organizations in the United States. Individuals would acquire pseudoephedrine through the use of 'front' business. Bulk quantities of the drug were then shipped to California for further distribution to those involved in the manufacture of methamphetamine.

> The acquisition of quantities necessary to make even small amounts of methamphetamine is difficult due to limitation on the retail sale of pseudoephedrine [which is an ingredient in common over the counter cold medications.] Therefore, organizations that have formed to procure and illegally divert pseudoephedrine are critically important to the criminal organizations that actually distribute methamphetamine.

The leader of the organization was Habes Habbas ("Habbas"), now a fugitive. He supplied pseudoephedrine to Tarek Zaki Abu–Lawi ("Zaki"), also a fugitive. Since Zaki is Abu–Lawi's uncle, Abu–Lawi was plainly an insider. He played a significant role in the business, obtaining bulk quantities of the drug through a number of front groups, and then diverting it to methamphetamine manufacturers on the West Coast. In effect, he franchised his operation to others, whose "fronts" would purchase the drug for him. He provided them with money, tips on obtaining a Drug Enforcement Administration ("DEA") registration, money laundering, shipping sources, purchasers, pill size, etc.

In effect, Jaber was one such franchisee. Abu–Lawi encouraged Jaber to set up his own pseudoephedrine business, told him how to do it, and gave him cash to get started. He even tutored Jaber about the use of pseudoephedrine and its manufacture. From October 1, 1999, Jaber did what Abu–Lawi suggested. He set up a phony company, obtained a DEA license, opened accounts, and started to purchase pseudoephedrine from legitimate distributors. In November 1999, Abu–Lawi sent Jaber money, as well as the telephone numbers of additional distributors from whom to purchase the drug. When Abu–Lawi had a buyer, he provided Jaber with the address, taking the lion's share of the profits. To use just one example, from the first sale, Abu–Lawi received $80,000; Jaber received $20,000.

Jaber met Momoh when Momoh was purchasing furniture at Jaber's father's business. A naturalized citizen, Momoh was a married man with three (soon to be four, at the time of sentencing) small children and an ill wife. While he had an advanced degree from the University of Massachusetts, he was unable to get a job commensurate with his skills. He began working for Jaber in January 2000 for $350 per week; his salary was later raised to $500.

In June 2000, Abu–Lawi and Jaber had a falling out. For a very short time thereafter, until some time in July 2000, Jaber and Momoh worked directly with a customer in California.

But the Jaber operation began to fall apart as well. On July 29, 2000, agents seeking a different suspect searched Jaber's residence in Florida. The fruits of that search, receipts for purchases of pseudoephedrine, led the DEA agents to Jaber's business address in Massachusetts. By August 3, 2000, Jaber told Momoh to dispose of their inventory and then to pretend that there had been a break-in. (Jaber reports that the reason for destroying the drugs was because their inability to find a buyer.) Momoh complied. The business was over.

On July 30, 2002, Jaber was arrested. In a sealed document, counsel outlined his considerable efforts to cooperate with the government—four proffers, meetings in Florida. These efforts were not considered substantial enough in Massachusetts, and were ignored in Florida.

Momoh was arrested on August 1, 2002. He immediately tried to cooperate too, but unlike Jaber, he had no basis—no contacts.

Abu–Lawi had been arrested earlier, on July 31, 2000. He pled guilty and cooperated with the government, offering up all of the individuals, including Jaber and Momoh, whom he set up in the business in the first place. Notwithstanding the scope of his participation in these charges, his Guidelines sentence, initially set at 135 months, was first reduced to 78 months and, finally, to 51 months. The government sought a sentence of 87 months for Jaber, and 70 months for Momoh.

I now turn to an analysis of the Guidelines, their application to this case, and the relationship between the Guideline categories and the statutory purposes of federal sentencing. The sentences I imposed *are* Guideline sentences, reflecting how many originally conceived of the Guideline regime.

A. JABER

1. Guideline Analysis

The government and the defendant agreed that a base offense level of 30 reflected the amount of pseudoephedrine in Jaber's possession. In addition, the money laundering charge yielded a base offense level of 29. The parties also agreed that the defendant was entitled to a three-level adjustment for "acceptance of responsibility" under U.S.S.G. § 3E1.1(a) and (b).

* * *

Both the issue of "role" and "drug quantity" should have raised serious Guideline questions, even pre-*Booker,* given the relationship between the instant charges and the Abu–Lawi prosecution. In one sense, considering the breadth of Abu–Lawi's case is nothing more than a variation on the theme of "real offense" sentencing—looking beyond the four corners of the charge to what the conduct truly comprised.[25] If the government had indicted these defendants in an East Coast conspiracy, Jaber's participation would have been minor relative to the others.[26]

Section 3B1.1 of the Guidelines provides for an increase in the offense level when the defendant was: (a)"an organizer or leader of a criminal activity that involved five or more participants or that was otherwise extensive" (an increase of four levels), (b) "a manager or supervisor (but not an organizer or leader) and the criminal activity involved five or more participants or was otherwise extensive" (an increase of three levels), or (c) "an organizer, leader, manager, or supervisor in any criminal activity other than that described in (a) or (b)" (an increase of two levels). *See* U.S.S.G. § 3B1.1(a-c). Unlike other sections, the role adjustment provision does connect this enhancement to concerns about culpability, public safety, and recidivism:

> This adjustment is included primarily because of concerns about relative responsibility. However, it is also likely that persons who exercise a supervisory or managerial role in the commission of an offense tend to profit more from it and present a greater danger to the public and/or are more likely to recidivate. The Commission's intent is that this adjustment should increase with both the size of the organization and the degree of defendant's responsibility.

U.S.S.G. § 3 B1.1, cmt. (backg'd). While the significance of the enhancement varies, depending on the seriousness of the offense, there is no commentary suggesting how the Commission arrived at those fixed enhancement scores (2, 3, or 4 levels) or why it chose that approach rather than some other.

---

25. As Justice Breyer noted, the Guideline system "that diminishes sentencing disparity—depends for its success upon judicial efforts to determine, and to base punishment upon, the real conduct that underlies the crime of conviction."

26. The government claims that joining Jaber and Abu–Lawi in a single conspiracy would have been wrong. But whether or not the cases can be formally joined is irrelevant. A "real offense" approach entitles me to consider both.

Section 3B1.1 does direct the court to look at the "real offense" and consider a number of factors, including (but obviously not limited to): "the exercise of decision making authority, the nature of participation in the commission of the offense, the recruitment of accomplices, the claimed right to a larger share of the fruits of the crime, the degree of participation in planning or organizing the offense, the nature and scope of the illegal activity, and the degree of control and authority exercised over others." U.S.S.G. § 3 B1.1, cmt. n.4.

Jaber had no criminal record before his encounter with Abu–Lawi. He had had no contacts with, or even information about, pseudoephedrine and its uses. He did essentially what Abu–Lawi directed him to do during most of his involvement with the organization. When he was on his own, he fell on his face. The operation ended in August of 2000.

Between that date and the date of his arrest, he never tried to restart the business. While he may have garnered profits from the operation, his portion pales in comparison to Abu–Lawi's.

Measuring the relative culpability of the participants against the scope of the Abu–Lawi operation suggests that Jaber should receive no enhancement. Moreover, this conclusion is buttressed by the other concerns, reflected in the Guidelines—danger to the public and recidivism.

With respect to the amount of drugs in Jaber's possession—what largely drove the Guidelines sentence—I concluded that the amount did not accurately reflect his culpability. Sometimes quantity is an entirely appropriate proxy for culpability. At other times, it is not. All other things being equal, one who distributes a greater amount of illegal drugs is more culpable than one who distributes a lesser amount. But, as Judge Lynch noted in *United States v. Emmenegger,* 329 F.Supp.2d 416, 427 (S.D.N.Y.2004), a case dealing with fraud amounts, "[i]n many cases ... the amount stolen is a relatively weak indicator of the moral seriousness of the offense or the need for deterrence." Drug quantity may well be a kind of accident, depending on the fortuities of law enforcement or even the market, as much as it reflects the defendant's culpability.

Jaber did not set out to distribute a particular quantity of pseudoephedrine. At first, from January to July, he purchased only the quantities that Abu–Lawi required; nothing more, and nothing less. Then, when he started out on his own, he purchased ten cases of pseudoephedrine, or 62 kilograms, in a single transaction, which he paid for in three installments, but then could not sell. While the quantity may be an appropriate indicator of culpability for Abu–Lawi, it is not for Jaber. It does not, in short, reflect the true "nature and circumstances" of Jaber's offense.

With respect to Jaber's cooperation and acceptance of responsibility, Jaber labored mightily to cooperate with the government. In a sealed affidavit, the defendant revealed his considerable efforts to do so. In Florida, his cooperation did not produce any prosecutions, ostensibly because of a change in personnel in the United States Attorney's office. I cannot give Jaber "credit" for that cooperation simply because I do not have all of the information in the government's possession. Nevertheless, Jaber's repeated efforts to help law enforcement surely bear on his extraordinary acceptance of responsibility, which is both a Guidelines factor and something that impacts on the likelihood of recidivism.

The aforementioned factors suggest that a departure is warranted. However, they do not suggest the appropriate amount of departure, to which I now turn.

2.   18 U.S.C. § 3553(a)

Jaber's counsel requested a sentence of "time served." I rejected that suggestion. Congress and the Commission have expressed their deep concern that pseudoephedrine offenses be treated seriously. I am not free to reject that approach based on my personal predilection (what I have earlier called the "free at last" regime). Whatever his role vis-a-vis Abu–Lawi, Jaber knew what he was doing; he knew that he had embarked on an illegal career that promised substantial rewards.

Jaber's Guideline sentence, computed as I have set out, would have been a base offense level of 27 with a criminal history of I, or 70–87 months. But to arrive at a sentence under *Booker,* I must go beyond the Guideline framework, directly to the purposes of sentencing under 18 U.S.C. § 3553(a). Ironically, in this case, the Guidelines concerns about "unwarranted disparity among defendants with similar records who have been found guilty of similar conduct," 18 U.S.C. § 3553(a)(6), call for an out-of-Guidelines adjustment. Ordinarily, the Guidelines do not permit me to make adjustments as between co-defendants in a single case, much less between defendants in separate indictments. However, in the instant case, there is something troubling about the extent to which differences in sentencing were driven not by differences in the crime, but by the happenstance of the way the government indicted, the jurisdictions of indictment, and who ran to cooperate first. Because of Abu–Lawi's prominence, and the timing of his cooperation, the government had virtually all it needed before it got to Jaber. Some adjustment is essential to reduce unwarranted disparity in the case at bar.

With respect to public safety and recidivism, 18 U.S.C. § 3553(A)(2)(c), I conclude that it is exceedingly unlikely that Jaber (or Momoh, as I describe below) will re-offend. They were marginal players at the outset. This experience surely capped their illegal career.

Following the Guidelines template, I departed downward four levels for Jaber, sentencing him to 51 months, roughly equivalent to the sentence of Abu–Lawi.

B.   Momoh

1.   *Guidelines Analysis*

With respect to Philip Momoh, all the parties agree that at the outset of his employment with Jaber, he had absolutely no idea that he was involved in an illegal operation. Plainly, that changed at some point during the eight months of the Jaber operation. The government maintains that the sentence it seeks already reflects these circumstances because it dismissed two counts dating from the period when Momoh did not know what he had gotten into. The government suggests that I need do no more. I disagree.

Momoh is entitled to three points for acceptance of responsibility and, perhaps even more, for extraordinary efforts.[28] He did everything he could to help the government, but like the defendant in *United States v. Jurado–Lopez,* 338 F.Supp.2d 246 (D.Mass.2004), he did not have much to offer.

His base offense level was 30, minus two for his minor role, and minus three for acceptance of responsibility.[29] Grouping the offenses as probation had done leads to 25 as the final offense level. His Guideline range is 57 to 71 months.

Under the Guidelines strictly construed, Momoh would not be eligible for any further reductions. The safety valve,[a] *see* 18 U.S.C. § 3553(f)(1)(5), which allows for further reductions, is reserved for individuals subject to a mandatory minimum sentence.[30] There is no mandatory minimum for pseudoephedrine; the Guideline drafters simply excluded that substance from the provision describing the safety valve. Had the 57–71 months of the Guidelines range been a 60 month mandatory minimum, he would have qualified for safety valve relief.

But, at the very least, Momoh's situation reflects the concerns that animated the enactment of the "safety valve," which enabled certain low-level drug offenders to escape out from under mandatory minimum drug sentences, provided the offenders met fairly rigorous criteria. Prior to the safety valve's passage, a high level offender would offer to cooperate with the government against his subordinates. The subordinates—particularly those at the bottom—were unable to cooperate meaningfully because they knew nothing. It was not at all unlikely that the subordinates would be sentenced to terms longer than that of the "kingpin."

---

28. Significantly, probation characterized Momoh's cooperation as extraordinary. Indeed, it recommended that he receive an acceptance of responsibility departure even while also recommending an enhancement for obstruction of justice (a recommendation probation offered pre-*Booker*).

29. Jaber's and Momoh's offense levels are the same because the pseudoephedrine Guidelines are at such a high level that it does not take much to trigger a higher category.

a. For a discussion of the safety valve statute, see *supra* at 353. *See also* note 6, *infra* at 896, discussing a bill that would substantially restrict the safety valve.

30. U.S.S.G. § 5C1.2, entitled "Limitation on Applicability of Statutory Minimum Sentences in Certain Cases," instructs the court to impose "a sentence in accordance with the applicable guidelines *without regard to any statutory minimum sentence,* if the court finds that the defendant meets the criteria in 18 U.S.C. § 3553(f)(1)-(5)...." U.S.S.G. § 5C1.2(a) (emphasis added). The cross-listed safety valve provision, entitled "Limitation on applicability of statutory minimums in certain cases," also directs that "the court shall impose a sentence pursuant to guidelines promulgated by the United States Sentencing Commission ... *without regard to any statutory minimum sentence....*" 18 U.S.C. § 3553(f) (emphasis added).

That is precisely the situation in the case at bar. Abu–Lawi got 51 months; Momoh was facing 57–71 months.

2.   18 U.S.C. § 3553(a)

While the government believes that the Guidelines are entirely adequate to reflect Momoh's culpability and the appropriate sentence, I do not agree. The two-level minor role adjustment does not begin to reflect his position in this enterprise—an employee, on a salary, taking directions from Jaber. Moreover, if the drug quantity did not adequately reflect Jaber's culpability, it surely does not reflect Momoh's.

Momoh was a functionary. Although his responsibilities were growing, he still did not take a profit; he was on salary. He had even less control over the direction of the enterprise than Jaber. He took orders from Jaber. The amount of pseudoephedrine that passed through his hands reflects someone else's decisions, not his own. Even in a Guidelines regime, I would have concluded that Momoh's sentence falls outside of the heartland of like offenders.

Moreover, between 2000 and the date of Momoh's arrest in 2002, there is no evidence that he engaged in any criminal acts. Indeed, just the opposite: He worked as a mental health worker in Lowell. He counseled individuals on a crisis hotline and gave referrals to hospitals. His hours were from 11:00 p.m. to 7:00 a.m. In addition, Momoh worked at the University of Massachusetts Memorial Health Alliance Hospital in the same capacity.

On pretrial release until sentencing, his record was perfect. This was especially significant given the stressors in his life—a wife who was hospitalized and dysfunctional, with Momoh effectively taking over the care of four young children.[31] His residence was foreclosed; he was unable to find a meaningful job. Measuring a departure for "extraordinary family obligations" now in the light of *Booker* and the purposes of sentencing (particularly the likelihood of recidivism), I would find that Momoh qualified for a downward departure on these grounds as well.

None of the purposes of sentencing outlined in 18 U.S.C. § 3553(a) were served by Momoh's incarceration. Accordingly, I sentenced Momoh to two years of probation, six months of which were to be spent in home detention.

III.   Conclusion

The sentences of Philip Momoh and Issa Jaber are essentially Guideline sentences informed by the teachings of *Booker*. Each Guideline provision was interpreted with a view to the statutory purposes of sentencing, and their application to the cases at bar. In addition, each

31. Momoh's wife has diabetes, high blood pressure and panic attacks. She refused to drive a car and has been suffering from depression. In June of 2003, she was hospitalized for pancreatitis, and underwent surgery to remove her gallbladder. Momoh has essentially assumed responsibility for the care of the children.

composite sentence was evaluated against the same statutory purposes. Such a common law process lies at the heart of judging.

Notes

1. **Understanding the *Jaber* Sentences.** It seems pretty clear that Jaber and Momoh could not have received these sentences before *Booker*, nor could these sentences be justified under *Wilson I and II*. It's worth exploring why that's the case, and then seeing how that illuminates the different approaches being taken in the lower courts.

Most courts agree that the first step after *Booker* is to calculate the Guideline sentence, following the same steps described *supra* at 842–46 and 849–53. The district judge did that here. After determining the base offense level, the major adjustments in this case were for the drug type (pseudoephedrine) and quantity. Drug quantity is, of course, one of the key measures used by Congress to set mandatory minimum sentences, and by the Commission to set offense levels under the Guidelines. And it doesn't take much pseudoephedrine to get a high offense level. But in this case Judge Gertner concluded drug quantity is a poor measure of Jaber's culpability, especially relative to Abu–Lawi, the supplier and brains of the operation, who recruited and supervised Jaber. Yet Jaber's Guideline sentence would be 70–87 months, while the more culpable Abu–Lawi had already been sentenced to only 51 months.

Why was Abu–Lawi's sentence so relatively low? He was the first one arrested, and he cooperated with the authorities, providing them with substantial assistance in the prosecution of other defendants, including Jaber and Momoh. Note that Jaber and Momoh also tried to cooperate with the authorities, but they were not successful in obtaining a government sponsored § 5K1.1 motion. Although Jaber "labored mightily to cooperate with the government" and detailed these efforts for the court in a sealed affidavit, the court notes two reasons that the government did not support a downward departure for him, *supra* at 883. First, there was a change in personnel in the U.S. Attorney's office,[a] and second "[b]ecause of Abu–Lawi's prominence, and the timing of his cooperation, the government had virtually all it needed before it got to Jaber." Similarly, in Momoh's case, the problem was that Momoh didn't know much, and so "did not have much to offer." As a mere "functionary" who did not even know initially that he was involved in illegal activity, Momoh couldn't provide the kind of information that the government got from Abu–Lawi, the ringleader. Jaber and Momoh did, however, get a downward adjustment for acceptance of responsibility.

In Judge Gertner's view, giving Jaber and Momoh longer sentences than Abu–Lawi would be an unjustified sentencing disparity. The Guidelines, however, make no provision for departure to avoid disparities between the sentences of co-defendants or co-conspirators, and indeed the substantial assistance departure under § 5K1.1 virtually ensures that such disparities

---

a. The court doesn't explain why this would have made a difference, so we can only speculate. Possibly Jaber was working with a prosecutor who left, and no one else cared to follow up the leads she was developing. Or new supervisors might have changed the policy on § 5K1.1 motions, or simply decided not to pursue some cases that were being investigated.

will occur. Ordinarily the government does not need assistance from all of the participants in a particular criminal transaction. To the contrary, it generally uses the § 5K1.1 motion as an incentive to convince one participant to provide information leading to the conviction of other participants. If a cooperator has the same level of culpability as those upon whom he informs, he will get a lower sentence. And, as in the case of Abu–Lawi, the government may find it advantageous to seek cooperation from someone in the upper echelons of a criminal enterprise, who will be able to provide extremely valuable information about everyone in the enterprise. In such a case, the reward for substantial assistance can bring the sentence of a kingpin below that of some of the lackeys. Congress provided for substantial assistance departures by statute (and as noted above limited them to cases in which the Department of Justice moves for a downward departure on this ground) in order to provide prosecutors with a valuable tool to fight crime.

Looking at the § 3553(a) statutory factors of public safety and recidivism, Judge Gertner concluded that it was highly unlikely that either Jaber or Momoh would reoffend. And, in Momoh's case, the court noted that extraordinary family responsibilities also warrant a departure. (Note that under the Guidelines, family ties and responsibilities are "not ordinarily relevant" at sentencing. *See infra* at 896–98).

2. **Perspectives on the *Jaber* Sentences.** There are several different ways to think about the difference in approach between the *Wilson* and *Jaber* courts. Which approach is more consistent with the Supreme Court's opinion in *Booker*? The problem, of course, is that *Booker* says almost nothing about how much leeway courts will have under advisory Guidelines. Judge Cassell says if we let every district judge have the latitude that Judge Gertner favors this will lead right back to the unjustified disparities that Congress was seeking to eliminate when it passed the Sentencing Reform Act. Maybe so, but there are at least two responses. First, the Supreme Court held that the Sentencing Reform Act unconstitutional. Unless it rewrites the Act, Congress can't have mandatory Guidelines, even if those are the best way to avoid disparity. As a constitutional matter, judges must have more leeway under the advisory Guidelines than they did under the mandatory system. Is there really any difference between the approach Judge Cassell advocates in *Wilson I and II* and pre-*Booker* departures? They were, after all, available for extraordinary and unusual cases. Second, what does disparity mean? In Judge Gertner's view, she is eliminating, not creating, disparity. And as long as we consider only the Abu–Lawi gang, that seems to be right. But what about comparing Jaber and Momoh to other defendants who were responsible for the same amount of pseudoephedrine? Isn't there a good argument that Judge Gertner has created unjustified disparity among pseudoephedrine cases?

Another way to think about this is to consider it from Congress's point of view. In the 2003 PROTECT Act (discussed in *Booker, supra* at 854, and *Jaber, supra* at 875), Congress made a variety of statutory changes to restrict departures, and also directed the Commission to tighten up the Guidelines to "ensure that the incidence of downward departures are *substantially reduced....*" 18 U.S.C. § 3553(c). Since Congress has been trying to reduce departures, does this support the view that sentencing courts should seldom if ever use their *Booker* authority to depart below the

Guidelines? Or is it irrelevant in light of the remedial opinion's conclusion that the Guidelines cannot constitutionally be mandatory?

What about the Justice Department's perspective? The Department's greatest concern is preserving the incentive created by the substantial assistance departure. Of course the departure still exists, but Judge Gertner's approach makes it much less valuable. She lowered the sentences for Jaber and Momoh even though they were not able to provide substantial assistance. Defendants are generally reluctant to cooperate; they don't wish to inculpate their associates and often fear they will suffer retribution. But if that's the only way to get a sentence reduction, it's a very strong incentive. That incentive is much less if defendants believe they can get reductions without cooperating. The Department has also opposed greater discretion on the part of district judges, which has generally been employed in recent years to lower, rather than raise sentences. Does that mean that *Jaber* is wrong? Or is it just a reason that the Department may support a legislative change? Note that for many critics one of the principal problems with the Guidelines before *Booker* was that they transferred discretion from the sentencing judge–a neutral party who acted on the record–to the prosecutor. Not only did federal prosecutors still have a wide range of discretion–whether to charge, what to charge, whether to accept a plea bargain, and whether to move for downward departure for substantial assistance–but prosecutors did not have to explain the reason for their actions on the record, and they were not subject to judicial review. Not everyone felt comfortable putting that much unreviewable discretion in the hands of the government, especially when that could mean a young and relatively inexperienced prosecutor.

3. **Post-*Booker* Appellate Review.** We don't know much yet about how the appellate courts will exercise their authority to review these sentences for reasonableness. In *Booker*, Justice Scalia wrote separately to express his concerns about appellate review. The reasonableness standard of appellate review will do nothing to fix the disparities that will, in his view, be the inevitable result of instructing the district courts to consider a variety of unranked priorities under the SRA and the guidelines. If the courts of appeals hold deviation from the Guidelines *per se* unreasonable, that will be a thinly disguised mandatory system. If, at the other extreme, courts of appeals approve every sentencing decision that falls within the statutory range, the result would be the discretionary sentencing the Guidelines attempted to eliminate. Moreover, he predicted that different courts would adopt different standards:

> What I anticipate will happen is that "unreasonableness" review will produce a discordant symphony of different standards, varying from court to court and judge to judge, giving the lie to the remedial majority's sanguine claim that "no feature" of its avant-garde Guidelines system will "ten[d] to hinder" the avoidance of "excessive sentencing disparities."

Justice Breyer, writing for the majority, did not share these "fears," and he argued that discord and disparity should be viewed "with a comparative eye." Although a reasonableness standard will not provide the same degree of uniformity as a mandatory system, the system of mandatory guidelines enforced by appellate review is "no longer an open choice." The majority's remedy, he noted, at least preserved a form of appellate review to help iron out differences from court to court.

The courts of appeals have been busy hearing appeals concerning the impact of *Booker* on cases already in the pipeline (which raise knotty issues such as the application of the plain error rule), but they are now just receiving the first appeals involving sentences imposed under *Booker*. Do you think they will uphold the approach in *Jaber*? What about *Wilson I and II*? Is it possible that both are reasonable? What about sentences that are within the Guidelines range–are they necessarily "reasonable"?

4. **Disparity Before and After *Booker*.** How big a concern would disparity from circuit to circuit, or district to district, really be? If there is disparity, does that mean that Congress needs to step in? Before you answer that question, it's important to know there was a great deal of disparity in different districts and circuits before *Booker*. For example, the rate of substantial assistance departures varied enormously from district to district. In fiscal 2003 (the most recent year for which statistics are available), nationally 15.9% of defendants received downward departures for substantial assistance. But more than 30% received such departures in five districts, and fewer than 10% received such departures in sixteen other districts. A few years earlier a Sentencing Commission study revealed significant differences in what different districts defined as substantial assistance, and it appears that these differences have persisted.

But it's not only prosecutorial practices that differed from one district (or circuit) to another: it appears that the sentencing environment was radically different from place to place within the federal system, notwithstanding the fact that all were operating under the same formal system. This is perhaps seen best by comparing the total percentage of within-Guideline sentences, which excludes upward departures and all downward departures for substantial assistance or any other factor. In 2003, prior to *Booker*, nationwide 69.4% of offenders received within-Guideline sentences. But in the Second Circuit, only 50.6% of sentences were within the Guidelines, compared with 77% in the Fourth Circuit. In individual districts, the range was even wider, from a low of 41% within the Guidelines to a high of 89%. In some districts bordering Mexico, the low within-Guideline rates were the result of a large number of cases involving illegal aliens. These aliens were offered special "fast track" plea bargains combining below-Guideline sentences and deportation following the service of the sentence. But in other places the main reason for the disparity seems to be the development of localized legal cultures.[b]

This level of disparity seems pretty shocking in a system that was intended to reduce if not eliminate inter-district, as well as inter-judge disparity. Of course the types of cases found in each district will vary, but it's hard to imagine that the caseload variations are sufficient to account for all of the differences noted above. But is the problem as great as it seems?

b. For an interesting discussion of the effects of judicial culture on two similar neighboring districts, see Lisa M. Farabee, *Disparate Departures Under the Federal Sentencing Guidelines: A Tale of Two Districts, Summary*, 15 FED. SENT. R. 207 (2003).

Maybe not. Some commentators have cautioned that it's misleading to compare districts based upon a single measure, such as § 5K1.1 departures, because other districts may use another procedure, such as systematic charge bargaining, that yields roughly similar sentences.[c]

It would not be surprising to find similar patterns emerging post-*Booker*. Should we just accept this as a fact of life, or is it a serious problem? If it's a problem, who should fix it: the Commission, the courts, or Congress? (And of course the Department of Justice has a role to play in any of these scenarios.) We turn now to the question of the legislative response to *Booker*.

D. POST *BOOKER* LEGISLATIVE REFORMS

Congress can preempt the judicial responses to *Booker* by legislation. Whether–or when–it will do so is anybody's guess, and there is no agreement about what shape that legislative response should take. In this section we begin with brief descriptions of several of the major reform proposals, and then turn to some of the key issues raised by the proposals. For an excellent overview of the reform options, see Steven L. Chanenson, *The Next Era of Sentencing Reform*, 54 EMORY L. J. 377 (2005).

1. TOPLESS (OR TOPS OFF) GUIDELINES

This approach, first suggested by Professor Frank Bowman,[d] would raise the top of each sentencing range to the statutory maximum for the offense in question, while leaving the bottom of the range unchanged. If the Guideline range for every conviction of an offense was the statutory maximum, then the conviction or guilty plea would establish all of the facts necessary for that maximum sentence. This approach seems to satisfy *Booker* (at least at a formal level), but it creates enormously broad sentencing ranges. For example, a first-time offender convicted of one count of mail fraud for defrauding a single victim of $4,500 would have a pre-*Booker* Guideline range of zero to six months in prison, but under the topless Guideline approach the applicable Guideline range would be zero to twenty years. Although this proposal had some support immediately after *Blakely*—at least as an interim measure—it seems unlikely that Congress would move from the current advisory system to a topless system that created such enormous discretion.

2. INVERTED GUIDELINES

This approach would turn the Guidelines upside down, starting the presumptive sentence in each case at the statutory maximum, and

---

c. Laura Storto, *Getting Behind the Numbers: A Report on Four Districts and What They Do "Below the Radar Screen," Summary*, 15 FED. SENT. R. 204 (2003). *See also* Panel II: The Effect of Region, Circuit, Caseload and Prosecutorial Policies on Disparity, 15 FED. SENT. R. 165–78 (2003) (describing panelists' various points of view).

d. *See* Frank O. Bowman, *Memorandum Presenting A Proposal For Bringing the Federal Sentencing Guidelines into Conformity with Blakely v. Washington*, 16 FED. SENT. R. 364 (2004). Professor Bowman no longer supports topless guidelines.

allowing the judge to make findings on facts that could reduce the sentence.[e] In other words, instead of starting at a low base offense level and *increasing* the sentence on the basis of a variety of facts (such as whether a weapon was used, the amount of the fraud, or whether there was a vulnerable victim), this approach would set the base offense level as high as it could be, and then consider whether the sentence should be *decreased*. These reductions could be based on factors similar to those in the present Guidelines, though they would have a reverse effect. For example, proof of a smaller fraud loss could result in a sentence reduction. Most or all of the current aggravating factors could be inverted (the defendant was not a leader in the criminal enterprise, there were no vulnerable victims, etc.).

The inverted Guideline proposal avoids the enormously wide ranges that would be produced under the topless system, and it conforms–technically–to *Booker*, since the court would not be *increasing* the defendant's sentence on the basis of any facts not established by a jury verdict or guilty plea. Its constitutional validity rests on the continued vitality of *Harris v. United States*, 536 U.S. 545 (2002), a 5 to 4 decision in which the Supreme Court held that mandatory minimum sentences do not have to be submitted to the jury and proved beyond a reasonable doubt. Is *Harris* still good law? The *Booker* Court did not overrule it, and as a formal matter there is a clear difference between a factor that raises the maximum sentence and one that merely increases the minimum sentence to which a defendant is subject. But inverting the entire system would place a very severe strain on this formal distinction, since it would deprive the defendants of the constitutional protections at issue in the line of cases culminating in *Booker*. From the defendant's point of view, precisely the same interests are at stake in an inverted guideline system as in the system that was held to be constitutionally deficient in *Booker*. Not surprisingly, proposals to satisfy *Booker* by inverting the Guidelines have been controversial on both policy and constitutional grounds.

This basic inversion proposal could, however, be modified to place controls on the judge's discretion to mitigate down, and to reduce the strain on the formal distinction. It would, for example, be possible to establish a rebuttable presumption in favor of mitigation once a defendant raises an issue, which would require the government to disprove the mitigating factor.

3. *BOOKER*–IZED GUIDELINES[f]

As all members of the Court recognized in *Booker*, there's no constitutional problem with mandatory Guidelines if the facts that serve as a basis for upward departures are submitted to a jury and proved beyond a reasonable doubt. Some states have taken this tack. The key virtue of this approach is that it delivers on the promise of the merits

e. For further discussion of how this option would work and the constitutional issues it poses, see Chanenson, *supra* page 891, at 414–416.

f. Several commentators referred to ''*Blakely*izing'' the Guidelines before the *Booker* decision, and we simply adapt this idea to the post-*Booker* era.

opinion in *Booker*: the key facts that raise a defendant's sentence would be proved beyond a reasonable doubt to a jury. One of the disagreements between the *Booker* majority and dissent was whether it was feasible to adapt the federal Guidelines to a jury trial/reasonable doubt process. The five justices who made up the majority for the remedial opinion took the position that it would be difficult (and unwise) to do so. Congress could side with the dissenters and reenact the provisions that make the Guidelines mandatory, making any other changes necessary to adapt to jury trial and proof beyond a reasonable doubt.

Most supporters of this approach also favor simplifying the Guidelines to reduce the number of issues that would have to be presented to the jury (thus making the federal Guidelines more like the simpler state guidelines).[g] For example, the American Bar Association supports simplified Guidelines that identify critical culpability factors to be treated as elements of the offense and submitted to the jury.[h]

Would this be a good idea? Justice Breyer argued that presenting Guidelines issues at trial would disadvantage many defendants by requiring them to focus on issues that would not appropriately be considered at the same time as guilt or innocence. For example, a defendant who claimed that he was not involved in a drug deal would not want to appear to concede his involvement by litigating at trial issues such as whether his role was major, minor or minimal (or disputing whether a second transaction was part of the same relevant conduct). In addition, some issues might be difficult for juries to understand. The computation of loss under the fraud table is a common example; indeed the application notes recognize the difficulty of the task and require only that the court make "a reasonable estimate of the loss." *See* U.S.S.G. § 2B1.1, application note 3(C), *infra* at 1002. On the other hand, what sense does it make to base an elaborate sentencing analysis on unreliable factfind-

---

g. *See, e.g.*, Blakely v. Washington *and the Future of the Federal Sentencing Guidelines: Hearing Before the Senate Comm. on the Judiciary*, 108th Cong. (2004) (statement of Rachel E. Barkow), *available at* < http://judiciary.senate.gov/print _testimony.cfm?id=1260 & wit_id=3684 >.

A creative version of *Booker*-ized Guidelines would "supersize" the Guidelines ranges to three times their current size (a "3x solution"). *See* Mark Osler, *The* Blakely *Problem and the 3X Solution*, 16 Fed. Sent. Rep. 344 (2004). If paired with some simplification of the Guidelines, the larger ranges would give judges discretion to do additional factfinding and tailoring of sentences within range. The problem, of course, is that with such large ranges it would be difficult to ensure uniformity.

h. The ABA's position is two pronged. Its first recommendation is that Congress leave the advisory guidelines in place, and

study the issue over time before taking any action. However, if Congress determines that advisory guidelines result in unwarranted disparities, the ABA House of Delegates then urges Congress to consider the following actions:

1. Simplify the guidelines either by adding a limited number of critical culpability factors as elements of each offense to be determined by the jury, or by directing the Commission to identify sentencing factors to be determined by the jury;

2. Revise the 25% rule to allow expanded sentencing ranges derived from the jury verdicts; [and]

3. Permit downward departures from these ranges under the same standard applicable to existing guidelines * * * .

ABA Resolution, Feb. 14, 2005, *available at* http://www.abanet.org/crimjust/policy/my05301.pdf .

ing, or factfinding that does not comply with traditional norms of procedural fairness?

Note that there are also possible procedural solutions to these issues, including bifurcating the guilt innocence and sentencing proceedings (as is done in capital cases). Note also that more than 90 percent of federal criminal defendants plead guilty, waiving their right to jury trial and proof beyond a reasonable doubt. Defendants could also waive *Booker* rights as part of the guilty plea/plea bargaining process.

4. MANDATORY MINIMUM GUIDELINES

Although the Justice Department has not yet taken an official position on the proper Congressional response to *Booker*, the Attorney General has spoken repeatedly in favor of mandatory minimum guidelines as an adjunct to the current system of advisory guidelines. This proposal appears to be modeled on the mandatory minimum sentences now found in a variety of current federal statutes, most notably the drug and gun laws. The new mandatory minimum guidelines would set the floor, and then the advisory guideline system would operate as it does now to determine where individual sentences should fall above that floor. The only exception to the mandatory minimum would presumably be in the case of a government motion on behalf of a defendant who provided substantial assistance in the prosecution of other cases. As in the case of inverted guidelines, this approach assumes the continued validity of the distinction drawn in *Harris v. United States* between sentencing factors that increase the top of the range, and those that merely establish the floor.[i] In practical terms, the impact of such provisions would turn to a significant degree on how high the new mandatory minimum sentences would be.

The Attorney General argues that mandatory minimum Guidelines are a good way to reduce unjustified disparity and keep crime rates low. They would also help preserve the incentive for defendants to provide substantial assistance, which in turn helps the government to prosecute other cases successfully. Critics of the existing mandatory minimum sentencing laws–which the Sentencing Commission has consistently opposed—argue that they are unduly rigid and they shift enormous power to prosecutors, disrupting the balance of the adversary system and imposing unjust sentences.[j]

* * *

i. For an example of the Attorney General's approach, see Prepared Remarks of Attorney General Alberto Gonzales, Sentencing Guidelines Speech, Washington, D.C., June 21, 2005, *available at* http://www.usdoj.gov/ag/speeches/2005/06212005victimsofcrime.htm.

j. For an argument that the focus on drug quantity in the Guidelines and the mandatory minimum sentencing laws has shifted so much power to prosecutors that it has damaged the adversary system and wrought real injustice, see Ian Weinstein, *Fifteen Years After The Federal Sentencing Revolution: How Mandatory Minimums Have Undermined Effective and Just Narcotics Sentencing*, 40 Am. Crim. L. Rev. 87 (2003).

The last two proposals–which are diametrically opposed–differ from those already discussed because both rest more firmly on the view (express or implied) that the Guidelines were seriously flawed prior to *Booker*. Thus they seek not only to conform the Guidelines to *Booker*, but to change federal sentencing by enhancing or reducing judicial discretion.

5. LESS COMPLEX GUIDELINES, MORE JUDICIAL DISCRETION

As noted above, many proponents of *Booker*-izing the Guidelines argue that the Guidelines could be simplified sufficiently to make it practical to submit the key issues to the jury for findings beyond a reasonable doubt. There is also support for Guideline simplification in its own right. If the Guidelines were simplified, this could (and most proponents believe it should) be coupled with greater judicial discretion. Supporters of this approach argue that the federal Guidelines—which are much more complex than comparable state provisions—tie the courts' hands unnecessarily, and hamper, rather than promote, sentences that are proportional to each defendant's culpability.

For example, this is the position of the Constitution Project's Sentencing Initiative:[k]

> The federal sentencing guidelines, as applied prior to *United States v. Booker*, have several serious deficiencies:
>
> A. The guidelines are overly complex. They subdivide offense conduct into too many categories and require too many detailed factual findings.
>
> B. The guidelines are overly rigid. This rigidity results from the combination of a complex set of guidelines and significant legal strictures on judicial departures. It is exacerbated by the interaction of the guidelines with mandatory minimum sentences for some offenses.
>
> C. The guidelines place excessive emphasis on quantifiable factors such as monetary loss and drug quantity, and not enough emphasis on other considerations such as the defendant's role in the criminal conduct. They also place excessive emphasis on conduct not centrally related to the offense of conviction.
>
> The basic design of the guidelines, particularly their complexity and rigidity, has contributed to a growing imbalance among the institutions that create and enforce federal sentencing law and has inhibited the development of a more just, effective, and efficient federal sentencing system.

k. The full text of the Sentencing Initiative's Recommendations is available at http://www.constitutionproject.org/si/Principles.doc. The quotation in the text is taken from principles 11 and 12; the numbers are omitted.

6.　LESS JUDICIAL DISCRETION, MORE RIGID GUIDELINES

In contrast, some members of Congress supported restricting judicial discretion prior to *Booker* (see *supra* at 868), and they continue to believe the problem is too much judicial discretion, not too little.

Legislation has been proposed in the House that would drastically restrict the district courts' sentencing discretion. Section 12 of H.R.1528, Defending America's Most Vulnerable: Safe Access to Drug Treatment and Child Protection Act of 2005, lists 34 different factors and provides that they may be considered *only* in determining the sentence within the range established by the guidelines. The list is so extensive that it appears to cover most—if not all—possible grounds for departures or non-guideline sentences under the factors listed in § 3553(a). It includes family ties and responsibilities, mental condition, disadvantaged upbringing, role in the offense, the sentence which the defendant would have received under state law, the defendant's likelihood of recidivism, the effect of his incarceration on others, restitution, and more than 20 other factors. The bill also provides for heightened procedural requirements if the court is considering a sentence below the applicable guideline range, involving 20 days written notice and briefing, proof by clear and convincing evidence, and a detailed written statement by the court explaining how the sentence avoids unwarranted disparities with other defendants with similar records who have been found guilty of similar crimes. These procedures are not applicable, however, when the government moves for a substantial assistance or fast track departure. Other portions of the bill radically restrict the safety valve provisions and add new or increased mandatory minimum sentences.

This approach raises an obvious constitutional issue. If the procedures in this bill were adopted, would they convert the Guidelines back into a mandatory system? In what way would the system still be advisory?

7.　KEY ISSUES—WHAT DO YOU THINK?

How do you think federal sentencing should work? The notes above have already introduced one of the most important issues—how much discretion there should be in the system, and who should have it (prosecutors vs. courts). As you think about that fundamental issue, consider also the following questions:

a.　*Offender characteristics.* First, should there be more emphasis on offender characteristics, such as age, family responsibilities, and rehabilitative potential? The Guidelines generally give these factors very little weight, generally stating that they are "not ordinarily relevant." *See* U.S.S.G. §§ 5H.1.1 (age), 5H1.2 (education and vocational skills), 5H1.4 (drug or alcohol dependence), 5H1.5 (employment record), 5H1.6 (family ties and responsibilities), and 5H1.11(military, civic, charitable, or public service).

Why did the Guidelines take this position, which was a clear break with the past? As to rehabilitative potential, one reason was a belief that it's difficult if not impossible to rehabilitate people or predict who will be rehabilitated. Moreover, rehabilitative potential and many of the other characteristics, such as having a stable family or a good work history and a job waiting for you, are correlated to other factors, such as socioeconomic status and race. That's another reason the Commission decided not to emphasize these factors. Indeed, with the exception of criminal history, the Commission concentrated on the offense, rather than the offender. In theory anyone who does the same crime—in the same way—gets the same sentence as others with the same criminal history.

Note, however, that theory often diverged from practice, but much more in some districts than others. Downward departures on the basis of offender characteristics was one of the factors causing the disparity in rates of within-Guideline sentences before *Booker*. It's not hard to find cases where districts courts departed down in sympathetic cases, finding that defendants had "extraordinary" family responsibilities on the basis of facts that would not have been the basis for a departure in most other jurisdictions. *See, e.g., United States v. Galante*, 111 F.3d 1029 (2d Cir. 1997) (upholding departure despite dissent citing contrary decisions from other circuits).

As a normative matter, how much of a role should these factors play in federal sentencing? Critics like Professor Myrna Raeder charge that the Guidelines have "backfired, wreaking havoc in the lives of female offenders and their children." Myrna S. Raeder, *Gender and Sentencing: Single Moms, Battered Women, and Other Sex–Based Anomalies in the Gender–Free World of the Federal Sentencing Guidelines*, 20 PEPP. L. REV. 905, 910 (1993). Raeder notes that about three quarters of female inmates have children, and about two thirds of these are single parents; she argues that incarcerating these single mothers takes a terrible toll on them and on their children. In most cases the children's father does not take custody. In some cases another family member takes custody, and in other cases the children are placed in foster care. Children seldom see their incarcerated mothers, especially in the federal system, which has only a small number of prisons nationwide that can house female offenders. Not surprisingly, in these situations children suffer emotional harms that have long term effects. Accordingly, Raeder argues that the Guidelines should be amended to provide for a downward departure for single parents, which could be denied where warranted by factors such as the seriousness of the defendant's crime, or the availability of the other parent to care for the children.[1] For a counter argument, see Ilene H. Nagel & Barry L. Johnson, *The Role of Gender in a Structured Sentencing System: Equal Treatment, Policy Choices, and the Sentencing of Female Offenders Under the United States Sentencing Guidelines*, 85 J. CRIM. L. & CRIMINOLOGY 181 (1994). Nagel—one of the original mem-

---

1. *See also* Sean B. Berberian, *Protecting Children: Explaining Disparities in the Female Offender's Pretrial Process, and Policy Issues Surrounding Lenient Treatment of Mothers*, 10 HASTINGS WOMEN'S L.J. 369 (1999); Nancy Gertner, *Women Offenders and the Sentencing Guidelines*, 14 YALE J. L. & FEMINISM, 291, 291–300 (2002); and *Developments in the Law, Alternative Sanctions for Female Offenders*, 111 HARV. L. REV. 1921 (1998).

bers of the Sentencing Commission—and Johnson argue that the Sentencing Reform Act and the Guidelines adopt just desert and crime control principles, and that "exogenous utilitarian concerns" such as the impact of sentencing on children "are rarely sufficient to outweigh either culpability or crime control considerations in the allocation of sentences." *Id.* at 207.[m] The debate between Raeder and Nagel can be characterized as a normative question about whether the special harm that a single mother and her children will suffer as a result of incarceration should be considered in determining whether she is similarly situated to another defendant who has committed the same crime but has no children.

b. *The relative importance of various sentencing factors.* More generally, some critics think that the Guidelines place far too much emphasis on some factors, such as drug quantity and weight, and too little on others, with the result that they treat fundamentally different cases the same, promoting a false illusion of equality.[n] On this view, placing so much emphasis on a factor such as drug quantity, and so little on other factors means that a defendant like Momoh (*see supra* at 884–86) will get the same sentence as others who dealt with the same amount of pseudoephedrine under very different circumstances.[o] This mechanistic uniformity defeats rather than enhances justice. A related argument is that this excessive–and misplaced–rigidity was creating pressure to ignore and evade the Guidelines.[p] Under this view, it is not surprising that at least some districts and circuits had low within-Guideline sentencing rates, *see supra* at 890, nor that the actors in the system used their discretion to find ways around drug sentences they viewed as unnecessarily high, *see supra* at 354–55.

c. *Complexity.* How detailed and complex should the Guidelines be? The federal Guidelines are substantially more complex than any of the

---

m. *But see* Berberian, *supra* n. l at 401, noting that the Commission readily departed from the just deserts philosophy by authorizing downward departures for defendants who provided substantial assistance to the authorities, but refused to do so in order to prevent harm to children.

n. For an articulate statement of this argument, see Albert W. Alschuler, *Failure of Sentencing Guidelines: A Plea for Less Aggregation*, 58 U. Chi. L. Rev. 901, 916 (1991). For a recent case in which the court explains why the amount of loss is often a weak indicator of the seriousness of an offense, see United States v. Emmenegger, 329 F. Supp.2d 416, 427–28 (S.D.N.Y. 2004).

o. *See* David M. Zlotnick, *Shouting Into the Wind: District Court Judges and Federal Sentencing Policy*, 9 Roger Williams U. L. Rev. 645, 651–66 (collecting cases) (2004); Shimica Gaskins, Note, *"Women of Circumstance"—The Effects of Mandatory Mini-*

mum Sentencing on Women Minimally Involved in Drug Crimes, 41 Am. Crim. L. Rev. 1533 (2004) (describing cases, including that of a college student with no prior record who received a 24 year sentence despite her minimal involvement and other mitigating factors, including her fear of the kingpin who had physically abused her and killed someone he thought was an informer), and Weinstein, *supra* note j.

p. For example, one study shortly after the adoption of the Guidelines concluded that evasion of the Guidelines may occur in 20–35% of cases. Stephen J. Schulhofer, *Assessing the Federal Sentencing Process: The Problem is Uniformity, Not Disparity*, 29 Am. Crim. L. Rev. 833 (1992). There is considerable evidence that all of the parties feel pressure to avoid draconian sentences in drug cases, and that they take various actions to avoid what they regard as unjust results. This issue is discussed in Chapter 9, *supra* at 354–55, and in Zlotnick, *supra* note o, at 666–680.

state sentencing guidelines. The federal Guidelines have 43 offense levels, in contrast to 10 or 11 for comparable state guidelines. *See* Marc Miller, *True Grid: Revealing Sentencing Policy*, 25 U.C. DAVIS L. REV. 587, 588–90 (1992). On the other axis of the federal Guidelines grid there are six criminal history categories, yielding a total of 258 sentencing boxes. By determining the base offense level, any adjustments, and the criminal history, the sentencing court calculates which of the 258 boxes each offender falls into. This box states the applicable sentencing range for that offender. In contrast, the Minnesota guidelines have 60 sentence boxes, and Oregon has 99. *Id.* at 614–15. The federal Guidelines differ from state guidelines in two other ways: they include many factors not incorporated into state guidelines, and they make provision for each factor in much greater detail than do state guidelines.

Although Justice Breyer (a member of the original Sentencing Commission) has argued that the complexity is a necessary outgrowth of the directives provided by Congress, the complexity of the federal criminal code, and the lack of political consensus on the federal level,[q] the Commission made numerous choices that greatly increased the length and complexity of the guidelines. The statutory directives did not require such a complex grid; indeed, a grid with only 7 offense levels and 42 sentencing boxes would have satisfied the statutory mandate. *Id.* at 596–604. The Commission deliberately chose a methodology that fostered greater complexity, rejecting the "usual case" methodology employed by the states in favor of a "base offense" approach, which assigns a point value to every aggravating and mitigating circumstance. *See* Kay A. Knapp & Denis J. Hauptly, *State and Federal Sentencing Guidelines: Apples and Oranges*, 25 U.C. DAVIS L. REV. 679, 685–86 (1992). Moreover, the federal guidelines include many factors not included in state guidelines, and give "long and detailed answers to questions that state guidelines asked and answered more simply." Ronald F. Wright, *Complexity and Distrust in Sentencing Guidelines*, 25 U.C. DAVIS L. REV. 617, 618–22 (1992). As Professor Wright put it, the complexity of the federal guidelines was "a choice, not a fate." *Id.* at 619 (capitalization omitted).

This complexity means that the Guidelines require a large number of factual and legal determinations in each case. To make the system administratively practical the Commission assigned this fact finding to the judge, and that decision led to *Booker*. Indeed, one of the subjects of disagreement between the majority and dissent in that case was whether it would be practical—or even possible—for juries to make all of the findings required by the Guidelines. In the wake of *Booker*, some of the states with simpler guidelines have adopted jury fact finding with no apparent difficulties. Resolving multiple factual and legal issues is time consuming, and risks an increased error rate. Of course the Sentencing

---

q. Stephen Breyer, *The Federal Sentencing Guidelines and the Key Compromises Upon Which They Rest*, 17 HOFSTRA L. REV. 1, 3–4 (1988) (noting that Minnesota and Washington have only 251 and 108 crimes to which their guidelines are applicable, whereas the federal guidelines initially applied to 688 crimes).

Reform Act provided for appellate review, but there are costs associated with appellate review, especially on a large scale.

What do you think—should the Guidelines be simplified, or will that lead right back to unjustified disparity because factors that really will make a difference will be ignored, or treated inconsistently?

8. KEEPING UP WITH POST–BOOKER DEVELOPMENTS

As you can tell from the foregoing review of lower court decisions following *Booker* and the proposals for legislative reform, this is an area where new developments are happening almost daily. Fortunately, Professor Douglas Berman has an outstanding blog that keeps track of the developments, http://sentencing.typepad.com/, and it's the first place to go to keep up to date. In addition to providing links to new judicial opinions, articles, testimony before Congress and the Commission, etc., Professor Berman offers his own commentary and provides a forum for debating issues. The Federal Defender's Office's web site provides another valuable resource; it has been tracking, abstracting, and indexing all of the lower court decisions following *Booker*. *See* http://www.fd.org/blakely_main.htm. Finally, the Sentencing Commission's site has provided periodic statistical analyses of the post-*Booker* cases, as well as links to other related material. *See* http://www.ussc.gov/bf.HTM .

Chapter 19

FORFEITURE

INTRODUCTION

The history of federal forfeiture law

In 1970 Congress created two new organizational crimes—RICO and CCE—and provided that each was punishable by criminal forfeiture of certain property. Though civil forfeiture had long been employed in connection with customs and revenue offenses, from 1790 to 1970 the federal criminal code had made no provision for criminal forfeiture.[a] The new federal criminal forfeiture provisions were a significant innovation. Indeed, one commentator has called the RICO and CCE forfeiture provisions "the first new punishment for crime since the rise of the penitentiary in the early nineteenth century."[b] Congress saw forfeiture as a means of striking directly at the economic roots of organized crime. RICO forfeiture was intended to provide a means of disentangling organized crime from legitimate businesses that had been infiltrated. But more generally, forfeiture was intended to remove the profit from organized crime by separating the criminal from the illegal profits.

Congress displayed a strong continuing interest in forfeiture, and as a result expanded the scope of criminal forfeiture and adopted procedures intended to facilitate it. Forfeiture was first extended to a small number of additional crimes: all felony drug offenses, money laundering, trafficking in pornography, and bank-related offenses. More recently, Congress expanded the availability of criminal forfeiture to the vast majority of federal offenses, including the over 250 specified unlawful activities listed in 18 U.S.C. § 1956. In addition, the range of property subject to forfeiture was expanded to include the "proceeds" of racketeering and "substitute assets" (lawfully acquired property that substitutes if forfeitable property is put beyond the reach of law enforcement).

---

a. S. Rep. No. 98–225, at 82 (1983) states:

> While there is one indication that the concept of criminal forfeiture was used in the colonies, the First Congress by Act of April 20, 1790 abolished forfeiture of estate and corruption of blood, including

such punishment in cases of treason. From that time until 1970 there was no criminal forfeiture provision in the United States Code.

b. David J. Fried, *Rationalizing Criminal Forfeiture*, 79 J. Crim. L. & Criminology 328, 330 (1988).

The most significant procedural change was the codification of the "relation-back" theory of forfeiture, under which title to the forfeitable property vests in the government at the moment the criminal act is committed, potentially making all later transfers voidable. Other procedural provisions dealt with pretrial restraint of assets and the burden of proof in forfeiture proceedings. Congress also provided for equitable sharing of forfeited assets with state, local, and foreign law enforcement authorities who participated in joint investigations leading to forfeitures. This asset-sharing program serves as a potent force encouraging cooperation among federal, state, local, and foreign law enforcement agencies.

The government initially pursued both civil and criminal forfeiture aggressively.[c] Between 1985 and 1990 the number of asset seizures grew at an average rate of 59 percent annually. The amount forfeited in the Department of Justice Asset Forfeiture Fund between 1985 and 1994 was more than $3.8 billion, and by the end of 1994 the inventory of seized assets consisted of cash and property valued at nearly $1.4 billion. This did not include an additional $10.9 million in cash being held as evidence.

Since the initial period of growth, the government has continued to derive significant revenues from asset forfeitures and to share these revenues with state and local law enforcement agencies. There are two major funds that receive forfeited assets, one for the Department of Justice and the other in the Treasury Department. Net revenues for the DOJ Assets Forfeiture Fund from 1996 to 2004 totaled almost $4 billion. In 2004, the DOJ seized approximately 36,000 items with a total value of about $521.3 million, and $281.8 million was expended for equitable sharing and joint law enforcement operations.[d] In the same year the Treasury Forfeiture Fund showed $289.2 million in gross revenues, and $101.4 million from that fund was shared with state, local, and foreign law enforcement agencies.[e]

Forfeiture's financial incentives

Some commentators believe that forfeitures have given law enforcement a hidden financial stake that is now driving criminal justice policy. Eric Blumenson and Eva Nilsen argue that the actual and potential revenues from forfeiture are reshaping law enforcement:

> First, these programs have distorted governmental policymaking and law enforcement. During the past decade, law enforcement agencies increasingly have turned to asset seizures and drug enforcement grants to compensate for budgetary shortfalls, at the expense of other criminal justice goals. We believe the strange shape of the criminal justice system today—the law enforcement agenda

---

c. This information is derived from the 1990 Annual Report of the Department of Justice Asset Forfeiture Program.

d. U.S. Department of Justice Assets Forfeiture Fund and Seized Asset Deposit Fund Financial Statement Fiscal Year 2004.

e. Treasury Forfeiture Fund Accountability Report Fiscal Year 2004.

that targets assets rather than crime, the 80 percent of seizures that are unaccompanied by any criminal prosecution, the plea bargains that favor drug kingpins and penalize the "mules" without assets to trade, the reverse stings that target drug buyers rather than drug sellers, the overkill in agencies involved even in minor arrests, the massive shift towards federal jurisdiction over local law enforcement—is largely the unplanned by-product of this economic incentive structure.

Second, the forfeiture laws in particular are producing self-financing, unaccountable law enforcement agencies divorced from any meaningful legislative oversight. There are numerous examples of such semi-independent agencies targeting assets with no regard for the rights, safety, or even lives of the suspects. Such dire results should prompt reform, particularly because a single measure—one mandating that forfeited assets be deposited in the Treasury's General Fund rather than retained by the seizing agency—would cure the forfeiture law of its most corrupting effects. But thus far the forfeiture industry has enjoyed an astonishing immunity from scrutiny by lawmakers and the courts.

Eric Blumenson & Eva Nilsen, *Policing for Profit: The Drug War's Hidden Economic Agenda*, 65 U. Chi. L. Rev. 35, 40–41 (1998). To date, although Congress has enacted other forfeiture reforms discussed below, it has taken no action to eliminate these incentives. However, several states have enacted legislation intended to eliminate the incentives of forfeiture by redirecting assets to purposes such as drug treatment and education, and by prohibiting state law enforcement officials from evading these limitations by turning over seized assets for federal forfeiture.[f]

The targets of forfeiture

Though in the 1980's and 1990's it was used primarily as a tool in the war on drugs, forfeiture can also be used to combat terrorism. Professor Sandra Guerra Thompson suggests that as the "war on drugs" wanes, tools such as multi-jurisdictional cooperation fueled by the financial incentives of asset forfeiture will not disappear, but will be implemented to fight the new "war on terrorism." Sandra Guerra Thompson, *Did the War of Drugs Die with the Birth of the War on Terrorism?: A Closer Look at Civil Forfeiture and Racial Profiling After 9/11*, 14 Fed. Sent. Rep. 147 (2002). Recent cases show that the government has used the USA PATRIOT Act of 2001 to go after terrorist financing. In the first prosecution under the new 18 U.S.C. § 2339B, which prohibits providing material support to designated terrorist organizations, Mohamad Youseff Hammoud and Chawki Youseff Hammoud were found

---

f. Eric C. Blumenson & Eva Nilsen, *The Next Stage of Forfeiture Reform*, 14 Fed. Sent. Rep. 76, 81 (2001). Professors Blumenson and Nilsen also argue that the conflict of interest implicit in the "forfeiture reward scheme" rises to the level of a Due Process violation in cases where (1) asset-rich defendants have been selectively prosecuted, (2) drug buyers are selected for reverse stings in order to allow seizure of the buyer's cash, or (3) very wealthy defendants receive disparate plea offers or sentences because of the assets available for forfeiture. *Id.* at 76–79.

guilty of conspiring to provide material support to the terrorist group Hezbollah through a cigarette smuggling and credit card fraud scheme in North Carolina. The indictment sought forfeiture of funds held in several bank accounts where illicit funds were held, as well as other property. Forfeiture has also been used in prosecutions under 18 U.S.C. § 1960; this section criminalizes unlicensed money transfer businesses, which may be used to funnel clean money to terrorist organizations abroad. For example, a forfeiture count was included in the indictment of Mohamed Hussein, who was convicted under 18 U.S.C. § 1960 and was suspected of using his business, Barakaat North America, to send funds to Osama bin Laden's terrorist network.

The USA PATRIOT Act added 18 U.S.C. § 981(a)(1)(G), which authorizes the seizure of all assets of anyone engaged in terrorism, any property affording any person a "source of influence" over a terrorist organization, and any property derived from or used to commit a terrorist act. Note the breadth of this language. It does not require any nexus between the property in question and any terrorism offense. Instead, it provides that the government can seize and forfeit any and all assets of any person, entity, or organization that is engaged in terrorism against the United States or its citizens, residents, or their property. *See generally* Stephan D. Cassella, *Forfeiture of Terrorist Assets Under the USA Patriot Act of 2001*, 34 LAW & POL'Y INT'L BUS. 7 (2002). For a general discussion of federal terrorism legislation, see Chapter 12 *infra*.

Forfeiture also has the potential to yield very large revenues in white-collar crime prosecutions. One example is the prosecution of John Rigas, founder of the nation's sixth largest cable company, Adelphia Communications Corp., who along with his three sons, was involved in a complex fraud scheme in which they hid over $2 billion of debt from shareholders and regulators and diverted company funds for personal use. The Rigases resigned from the company after the debt was disclosed, and were charged with both criminal and civil fraud. In a settlement, the Rigases agreed to forfeit over $1.5 billion derived from the fraud, including their interest in several cable companies. Adelphia itself will obtain title in the companies and must pay $715 million to a victim restitution fund. Rigas and his son Timothy were convicted of criminal charges in 2005 and sentenced to 15 yeas and 20 years in prison, respectively. For a discussion of the extensive, and profitable, prosecution of the Bank of Credit and Commerce International (BCCI), which netted $1.2 billion in assets in the U.S. alone, see *infra* at p. 941.

How forfeiture works—civil and criminal forfeiture

Federal law authorizes both civil and criminal forfeitures. Although many issues are common to both kinds of forfeitures, there are also some important procedural differences. Criminal forfeiture is now available for a very wide variety of federal offenses, but only as part of a larger criminal case against the owner of the property. If the defendant is convicted, forfeiture may be part of the criminal sentence. The burden of proof for the conviction is, of course, proof beyond a reasonable doubt.

However, because forfeiture is a part of the sentencing rather than an element of the offense, the Supreme Court held in *Libretti v. United States*, 516 U.S. 29 (1995), that neither proof beyond a reasonable doubt nor a jury finding is required. To date, that holding has survived the Supreme Court's more recent decisions on the procedural requirements applicable to Guidelines sentencing, discussed *supra* at 854 to 69.

Civil forfeiture, in contrast, is an in rem—rather than an in personam—action. This means that the defendant in the civil proceeding is the property the government seeks to forfeit, which can lead to rather unusual case names, referring to, for example, a shipment of crab, a minivan, and a moon rock.[g] Because of its in rem nature, civil forfeiture is available in a variety of situations when criminal forfeiture would not be, including cases where the government cannot bring a prosecution because it does not know who committed a crime or it cannot acquire jurisdiction over the perpetrator, and also cases in which the defendant is not the owner of the property that the government seeks to forfeit. Other procedural differences have also played a role in the government's election to use civil or criminal forfeiture. Until relatively recently, the government's burden of proof in civil forfeiture cases was extremely low: anyone who opposed the government's claim had to bear the burden of proving that the property in question was not forfeitable, and to bear all of the costs of litigating the issue. In 2000 Congress enacted the Civil Asset Forfeiture Reform Act (CAFRA), which provided various procedural protections for third parties opposing civil forfeitures, including the requirement that the government must establish by a preponderance of the evidence that property is forfeitable.

CAFRA not only imposed procedural requirements making it more difficult for the government to forfeit property civilly, it also made criminal forfeiture available for a wider range of offenses. This led to predictions that the government would increase its reliance on criminal as opposed to civil forfeiture, and there are some indications that this has occurred. Though other factors may also have played a role,[h] the proportion of civil and criminal forfeitures shifted immediately after the

---

g. *United States v. 144,744 Pounds of Blue King Crab*, 410 F.3d 1131 (9th Cir. 2005); *United States v. Dodge Caravan Grand SE/Sport Van*, 387 F.3d 758 (8th Cir. 2004); *United States v. One Lucite Ball Containing Lunar Material*, 252 F. Supp. 2d 1367 (S.D. Fla. 2003).

h. Among other things, there has been an increased emphasis on using criminal forfeiture whenever possible since the double jeopardy challenges in the early and mid–1990's, discussed *infra* at p. 928 n. k. That emphasis continued after the double jeopardy question was resolved in the government's favor by the *Ursery* decision. Many USAO forfeiture units were moved from the civil to the criminal division of their offices during that period, and many have stayed since they were moved, in order

to make it easier for the forfeiture units to interact with and assist other prosecutors. When there is a criminal prosecution and the subject property belongs to the criminal defendant, criminal forfeiture is more efficient, because it can be effected as part of the criminal case, without the need for a separate civil proceeding. Most criminal cases end in guilty pleas, and the forfeiture is typically included as part of the plea. In addition, particularly since September 11, 2001, non-terrorism-related resources have been strained, and the relatively small number of forfeiture specialist AUSAs have been spread thin, making it even more important for them to encourage their colleagues to prosecute forfeitures criminally wherever appropriate.

enactment of CAFRA. Prior to CAFRA, civil forfeiture filings exceeded criminal filings. In the first year post-CAFRA, however, the number of criminal cases with forfeiture counts exceeded the number of civil forfeiture actions filed, and criminal filings have continued to exceed civil filings each year since the passage of CAFRA.[i] Moreover, the number of civil filings has remained stagnant, but criminal forfeiture filings have risen steeply each year. Between 2000 and 2004, the number of criminal cases including forfeiture counts more than doubled.[j] It should be noted, however, that cases including criminal forfeiture counts still represent only a small percentage of the total number of criminal filings. In 2004, the total number of criminal cases filed by U.S. Attorneys' offices was 61,443. Only 3,785 of those, about six percent, included forfeiture counts.

Aside from civil and criminal judicial forfeitures, the government may also forfeit property administratively. We will not deal with administrative forfeitures—because lawyers don't—but a large percentage of forfeitures are handled through these uncontested administrative proceedings. If an asset is seized on a valid basis, notice is published, and no one claims the property, it is forfeited. Though property must be under $500,000 to be forfeited administratively, these "small" forfeitures add up to a lot. In 2004, administrative forfeitures accounted for almost $294 million, almost half of the total dollar amount forfeited by Department of Justice agencies.

The materials that follow explore some of the questions raised by the contemporary emphasis on forfeiture. Section A considers the scope of criminal forfeiture, focusing primarily on forfeiture under the drug statute. Section B considers recent constitutional issues raised by forfeiture. When can civil forfeiture be viewed as punishment? And under what conditions does forfeiture become constitutionally excessive? In light of the Sixth Amendment right to counsel, are fees needed to retain defense counsel exempt from forfeiture? Section C considers the "relation back" doctrine and the bona fide purchaser and innocent owner defenses. Throughout, our major focus is on criminal forfeiture, though we refer as well to some civil cases, especially where the criminal and civil statutes have parallel language and courts construe them in tandem.

i. This statistical information is derived from the United States Attorneys' Annual Statistical Reports for 1999, 2001, 2002, 2003, and 2004. Note that in addition to the U.S. Attorneys' offices, some forfeiture cases are handled by the Department of Justice Asset Forfeiture and Money Laundering Section. The data discussed here do not include those cases.

j. The picture is less clear, however, upon examination of another set of data. Statistics from the Department of Justice asset tracking database measure the number and dollar amount of assets forfeited rather than the number of cases filed. Though not inconsistent with the filing data, this information does not show as strong a shift to criminal forfeitures. Between 1998 and 2003, more assets were forfeited criminally than civilly every year except 2000. However, the difference between the two has increased since 2000. Looking at the dollar amounts, no discernable pattern emerges, which makes sense considering that one extremely large dollar value asset could skew the data.

The statutory provisions governing drug and RICO forfeiture are now lengthy and complex. Excerpts of the drug forfeiture statute are reprinted below, and RICO forfeiture provisions are excerpted *supra* at pp. 481–82. The complete text of these provisions is reprinted in the appendix at pp. 971–88.

21 U.S.C. § 853

Criminal forfeitures

(a) Property subject to criminal forfeiture

Any person convicted of a violation of this subchapter or subchapter II of this chapter punishable by imprisonment for more than one year shall forfeit to the United States, irrespective of any provision of State law—

    (1) any property constituting, or derived from, any proceeds the person obtained, directly or indirectly, as the result of such violation;

    (2) any of the person's property used, or intended to be used, in any manner or part, to commit, or to facilitate the commission of, such violation; and

    (3) in the case of a person convicted of engaging in a continuing criminal enterprise in violation of section 848 of this title, the person shall forfeit, in addition to any property described in paragraph (1) or (2), any of his interest in, claims against, and property or contractual rights affording a source of control over, the continuing criminal enterprise.

The court, in imposing sentence on such person, shall order, in addition to any other sentence imposed pursuant to this subchapter or subchapter II of this chapter, that the person forfeit to the United States all property described in this subsection. In lieu of a fine otherwise authorized by this part, a defendant who derives profits or other proceeds from an offense may be fined not more than twice the gross profits or other proceeds.

(b) Meaning of term "property"

Property subject to criminal forfeiture under this section includes—

    (1) real property, including things growing on, affixed to, and found in land; and

    (2) tangible and intangible personal property, including rights, privileges, interests, claims, and securities.

(c) Third party transfers

All right, title, and interest in property described in subsection (a) of this section vests in the United States upon the commission of the act giving rise to forfeiture under this section. Any such property that is subsequently transferred to a person other than the defendant may be the subject of a special verdict of forfeiture and thereafter shall be ordered forfeited to the United States, unless the transferee establishes in a hearing pursuant to subsection (n) of this section that he is a bona fide purchaser for value of such property who at the time of purchase was reasonably without cause to believe that the property was subject to forfeiture under this section.

(d) Rebuttable presumption

There is a rebuttable presumption at trial that any property of a person convicted of a felony under this subchapter or subchapter II of this chapter is subject to forfeiture under this section if the United States establishes by a preponderance of the evidence that—

(1) such property was acquired by such person during the period of the violation of this subchapter or subchapter II of this chapter or within a reasonable time after such period; and

(2) there was no likely source for such property other than the violation of this subchapter or subchapter II of this chapter.

* * *

(o) Construction

The provisions of this section shall be liberally construed to effectuate its remedial purposes.

(p) Forfeiture of substitute property

(1) In general

Paragraph (2) of this subsection shall apply, if any property described in subsection (a), as a result of any act or omission of the defendant—

(A) cannot be located upon the exercise of due diligence;

(B) has been transferred or sold to, or deposited with, a third party;

(C) has been placed beyond the jurisdiction of the court;

(D) has been substantially diminished in value; or

(E) has been commingled with other property which cannot be divided without difficulty;

(2) Substitute property

In any case described in any of subparagraphs (A) through (E) of paragraph (1), the court shall order the forfeiture of any other property of the defendant, up to the value of any property described in subparagraphs (A) through (E) of paragraph (1), as applicable.

(3) Return of property to jurisdiction

In the case of property described in paragraph (1)(C), the court may, in addition to any other action authorized by this subsection, order the defendant to return the property described to the jurisdiction of the court so that the property may be seized and forfeited.

A. THE SCOPE OF FORFEITURE

Though criminal forfeiture was at one time only available for a limited number of offenses with forfeiture provisions, such as drug trafficking, RICO, and money laundering, criminal forfeiture is now available for a wide range of offenses. *See* 28 U.S.C. § 2461(c) (authorizing criminal forfeiture for any offense for which civil forfeiture is available). In addition to offenses with specific forfeiture provisions, this includes the over 250 specified unlawful activities (SUAs) listed in 18 U.S.C. § 1956, which is reprinted above at 440–45. Criminal forfeiture can be sought in a conviction for any of these offense, even if not charged as money laundering. For a comprehensive list of the forfeiture statutes and the specified unlawful activities, see U.S. Dep't of Justice Asset Forfeiture & Money Laundering Section, Selected Federal Asset Forfeiture Statutes (2004).

The scope of forfeiture under the current statutes is extremely broad. For example, 21 U.S.C. § 853, reprinted *supra* at pp. 907–08, which authorizes forfeiture in felony drug cases, provides for the forfeiture of:

> • the "proceeds" of the crime, and any property "derived from" the proceeds of the crime (§ 853(a)(1)), and

> • any of the defendant's property "used * * * in any manner or part, to commit, or to facilitate the commission" of the crime (§ 853(a)(2)), and

> • "substitute property" in lieu of any of the above that cannot be located with due diligence, or has been transferred, placed beyond the jurisdiction of the court, diminished in value, or commingled with other property (§ 853(p)).

The term "property" is also defined expansively to include not only real property and tangible personal property, but also intangible property "including rights, privileges, interests, claims, and securities." 21 U.S.C. § 853 (b)(2). Under these provisions a wide variety of property has been forfeited, including a law firm, fraternity houses, farms, a drug store, apartment houses, public housing leases, life insurance annuities, diamond rings, cars, boats, and horses.

The breadth of these provisions raises several questions. What does "facilitate" mean? Or, to put the question another way, how much of a connection is required between the property in question and the offense? And how does one define the "property"? What if there is a farm, and marijuana is grown on only one of the several fields? Or an apartment house, and only one of the apartments is used for the distribution of cocaine? May the government forfeit the whole, or only a part of the property? These questions are considered in the next case and the notes that follow it.

UNITED STATES v. WILTON MANORS

175 F.3d 1304 (11th Cir. 1999).

TJOFLAT, CIRCUIT JUDGE:

* * *

I.

Charles Howerin was arrested by city police in October 1991 for selling cocaine out of his home in Wilton Manors, Florida. He was convicted in Florida court on drug possession and trafficking charges. Subsequent to the state conviction, the United States brought an in rem action against Howerin's property seeking forfeiture pursuant to 21 U.S.C. § 881(a)(7) (1994). Howerin filed a claim of ownership on the property, and then answered the Government's complaint. * * *

The Government moved for summary judgment. The district court granted the motion as to Lot 56, but held that the Government had not shown a substantial connection between Lot 1 and the criminal activity and therefore denied the motion as to that parcel. After a bench trial, the district court again held that the Government had not shown the necessary connection between Lot 1 and the criminal activity, and entered final judgment in favor of Howerin. Both parties appeal.

II.

* * *

The dispute in this case centers on the proper interpretation of 21 U.S.C. § 881(a)(7), which states that "[a]ll real property ... which is used, or intended to be used, in any manner or part, to commit, or to facilitate the commission of, a violation of this subchapter" shall be subject to forfeiture. The Government contends that the word "property" in the statute should be defined by reference to the deed used to convey the land to the owner. Thus, if a given area of land is used to facilitate the commission of a drug crime, forfeiture should be granted as to all of the land included in the deed conveying that area of land. Howerin contends that "property" should be defined by reference to descriptions in local land records. Thus, if a given area of land is used to facilitate the commission of a drug crime, forfeiture should be granted as to all of the land included in the descriptive unit (for example, a lot in a subdivision) containing that area of land.

Each side has cases from other circuits that support its position. The Government's position is supported by the Fourth and Eighth Circuits.[3]

---

3. Other circuits have reached similar, but distinguishable, conclusions. *See United States v. Smith*, 966 F.2d 1045, 1053–54 (6th Cir. 1992) (using deed to define "property" in 21 U.S.C. § 853(a)(2), a criminal forfeiture statute); *see also United States v.* *Plat 20, Lot 17*, 960 F.2d 200, 205–06 (1st Cir. 1992) (holding that, for purposes of initial seizure warrant in forfeiture action, the Government may seize land according to the description contained in the deed). The Ninth Circuit has stated that the deed

See United States v. Bieri, 21 F.3d 819, 824 (8th Cir. 1994) (holding that the deed, and not the historical description of the land, determines what land constitutes the forfeitable "property"); *United States v. Reynolds*, 856 F.2d 675, 677 (4th Cir. 1988) (holding that scope of property subject to forfeiture is defined by "the instrument creating an interest in the property"). Howerin's position is supported by the Second Circuit. *See United States v. 19 & 25 Castle St.*, 31 F.3d 35, 41 (2d Cir. 1994) (holding that "parcels of property separately described in the local land records, whether or not conveyed to an owner by a single instrument, should be considered separately for forfeiture purposes" except in certain unusual circumstances).

The question is one of first impression in this court. We feel that the technical approaches offered by the parties, although they have the advantage of ease of application, are unjustly arbitrary. Under either approach, two identical pieces of land would be treated very differently under forfeiture law depending on the timing of the conveyance or the lines on a subdivision map. Furthermore, each of these approaches encourages opportunistic behavior by drug dealers—a sophisticated dealer could either purchase his land in numerous small parcels or seek to purchase land in areas with small lot divisions.

We instead conclude that the definition of "property" under 21 U.S.C. § 881(a)(7) must be determined on a case-by-case basis. Specifically, the court must examine the character of the land on which the criminal activity took place, and determine whether all of the land sought by the Government can be considered to be of that same character. For instance, if the Government seeks forfeiture of farmland used for growing marijuana, it may acquire all of the land that can reasonably be considered part of the farm. If, however, the claimant owns two farms, the Government may acquire only the farm on which marijuana was grown—even if the farms are adjacent and were conveyed in a single deed. Likewise, if the Government seeks forfeiture of commercial real estate used as a front for drug distribution, it may acquire all of the land that can reasonably be considered part of the front business. Again, if the claimant owns two businesses, and only one is used for criminal purposes, only that business is to be forfeited. While deeds and local land records will undoubtedly be probative evidence in this inquiry, they will not be conclusive.

This test fits well with the conceptual underpinnings of forfeiture; the thing used in the commission of the offense—for example, a farm or a business—is the thing that is surrendered to the Government. This test also fits well with common-sense notions of property—one speaks of owning a "farm," a "house," a "business," and so forth; one does not speak in deed-like terms of owning "the west 118 feet of the east 621 feet of Lot 56, except the west 61 feet of. . . ." On its face, a case-by-case test of this sort might appear to introduce too much ambiguity into the

presumptively defines the property to be seized, but that other evidence, including descriptions in local land records, may re- but that presumption. *See United States v. 6380 Little Canyon Rd.*, 59 F.3d 974, 986 n. 15 (9th Cir. 1995).

law of forfeiture. In the overwhelming majority of cases, however, the test should be simple to apply.

This is one of those simple cases. The character of the land on which the cocaine sales took place is undisputedly residential. Lot 1 was part of the residence—namely, the front yard. Lot 1 was therefore subject to forfeiture along with Lot 56.

* * *

Notes

1. Note that *Wilton Manors* involved civil forfeiture under the drug laws, and that the court cited both civil and criminal precedents. On this point at least—the definition of property subject to seizure—the courts have not drawn a distinction between civil and criminal forfeiture.

2. As indicated in the opinion, *Wilton Manors'* "common-sense" approach towards defining the forfeitable property tracks new ground. Many courts look for guidance in state property law. For example, in *United States v. Smith*, 966 F.2d 1045 (6th Cir. 1992), the defendant was convicted of growing marijuana on his farm. He had obtained his interest in the farm by four separate conveyances of four tracts to Smith and his former wife, Linda, on four dates between 1978 and 1984. The four tracts were taxed separately and were the subject of separate deeds of trust. Smith and Linda divorced in 1985, at which time Linda conveyed all of her interest in all four tracts to Smith by a single quitclaim deed, which Smith recorded. The government argued that in light of the quitclaim deed, which conveyed all four tracts as one single unit, the entire farm constituted the "property" subject to forfeiture. The court rejected that argument, finding that under the Tennessee law Linda's transfer of her interest in the four tracts did not create Smith's interest in the land. Rather, Smith obtained his interest in the farm by the four separate deeds that created four separate tenancies by the entirety.

Why did the court apply state rather than federal law? The court observed that since " '[f]orfeiture proceedings implicate property rights which have traditionally been measured in terms of state law,' and * * * section 853 contains no rule for determining the scope of property rights, 'it is appropriate to refer to state law in determining the nature of the property interest' involved in a forfeiture proceeding." 966 F.2d at 1054 n.10.

3. The determination in *Smith* that the four tracts were separate properties set the stage for the final question: which of the four tracts was forfeitable? Tract 1, on which the officers discovered the marijuana patch in the cornfield, and Tract 2, which contained a marijuana seed bed, were clearly forfeitable. Tract 4, on which no marijuana grew, posed a more difficult issue. but the court held that it was forfeitable as well:

> The government argues that, because the cornfield in which the officers located the large marijuana patch extended across Tract 1 and Tract 4, Tract 4 "facilitated" the commission of the offense by concealing the patch on Tract 1. To "facilitate" the commission of the offense under section 853, the property in question must bear a "sufficient nexus" or

"substantial connection" to the underlying criminal activity. We hold that, when the defendant uses real property to actually physically conceal the commission of the offense on adjacent property, the nexus is sufficient to support a finding that the property "facilitated" commission of the offense under section 853(a)(2). The district court found that Tract 4 helped to actually physically conceal the marijuana patch on Tract 1, and the evidence supports this finding. We thus find no error in the district court's determination that Tract 4 facilitated commission of the offense.

966 F.2d at 1055. On the other hand, the court rejected the government's attempt to forfeit Tract 3, on which defendant's residence was located. The court found that no evidence had been presented that Tract 3 was used to guard or conceal the growing marijuana, and it rejected the government's argument that as a matter of law the legitimate use of adjacent property would facilitate the offense by concealing it. 966 F.2d at 1055–56. Judge Guy dissented from this conclusion:

> Forfeiture is intended to be a harsh sanction. It is intended not only to take the profit out of drug dealing but also to make persons give serious consideration prospectively as to whether the potential gain is worth the downside risk. I would not try to formulate any type of per se rule relative to forfeitures, but simply analyze each situation on a case-by-case basis. Here, the defendant had a relatively small farm, with a farmhouse located on the property. I would treat the property as one entity, notwithstanding how it was acquired historically, and declare it all forfeitable. For all practical purposes, the property was treated as a unit, and the house certainly was the "command post" for whatever was occurring on the property, be it growing marijuana or legitimate activities. There well may be a point at which a defendant's constitutional rights will mandate that the proportionality of the forfeiture to the offense be considered. This case is far short of such a point, however.

966 F.2d at 1056.

4. The issue regarding Tracts 3 and 4 in *Smith* was whether they "facilitate[d]" the drug offenses. As the following case indicates, the *Smith* court's relatively broad interpretation of that term is typical. In *United States v. Heldeman*, 402 F.3d 220 (1st Cir. 2005), the defendant, a 72-year-old dermatologist whose business cards advertised him as "Dr. Marvin, The Bodybuilder's Friend," wrote prescriptions for steroids and addictive pain medication to people he had never met or treated, in return for sexual services. The court upheld the forfeiture of the defendant's residence on a facilitation theory, rejecting the argument that the home did not facilitate the offense because he could have committed the offense in another location:

> Whatever the exact degree of connection required by the criminal forfeiture statute, the evidence provided to the district court in this case amply supported the forfeiture. All six of the drug offenses with which Heldeman was charged involved prescriptions written in his apartment. His apartment served as a base of operations for his crime just as surely as does a residence where drugs are actually delivered or stored.

> Nor is it any defense to claim (as Heldeman does) that his activities could have been undertaken elsewhere. The statute requires only that

the property "facilitate[]" the offense. Heldeman's proffered reading would cripple the statute and defeat the evident congressional intent to forfeit property used in committing the crime. It would also be at odds with our prior case law on civil forfeiture, which contains no suggestion that the property must be the only means of achieving the defendant's criminal goals in order to merit forfeiture. Heldeman may not be what the average person thinks of when speaking of a "drug dealer," but he does not dispute that his acts are within section 841 so the forfeiture provision applies.

402 F.3d at 222.

5. Before CAFRA made criminal forfeiture available for the vast majority of federal offenses, prosecutors had an extra incentive to add a money laundering count or two to provide a basis for forfeiture. Even post-CAFRA there is still an advantage to charging money laundering as well as predicate offenses in order to enlarge the scope of forfeiture.

The statute authorizing forfeiture in money laundering cases reaches property "involved in" the offense, 18 U.S.C. § 982(a). But money is fungible. So if tainted and untainted funds are commingled, how can the tainted funds be identified for forfeiture? Indeed, if both tainted and untainted funds have been deposited in an account and some funds have been withdrawn, how can the court tell whether there are any tainted funds left in the account? In many cases, courts have permitted the government to forfeit the entire account on the grounds that the legitimate funds facilitated the money laundering by hiding the dirty money. Although § 982 does not use the term facilitate, the courts assume funds that facilitate a money laundering offense are "involved in" it. That means that the government may be able to forfeit much more than the proceeds of the offense.

United States v. McGauley, 279 F.3d 62 (1st Cir. 2002), is a good example of the power of money laundering to expand the scope of forfeiture. The defendant was a convicted of mail fraud and money laundering for a scheme in which she stole thousands of dollars worth of clothes from retail stores. She returned the clothes for $55,000 in refunds, which she deposited into several bank accounts containing clean money. After police searched her home, she began withdrawing money from these accounts, transferring over $300,000 into new accounts she owned jointly with her parents, from which she then made substantial withdrawals. The defendant was ordered to forfeit more than $243,000 contained in her personal accounts. She argued that the forfeiture should be limited to the $55,000 she obtained in refunds. The court upheld the forfeiture of the entire amount, because "the commingling of tainted funds (mail fraud proceeds) with legitimate funds is enough to expose the legitimate funds to forfeiture, if the commingling was done for the purpose of concealing the nature or source of the tainted funds (that is, if the commingling was done to facilitate money laundering)." *Id.* at 76. For a description of other such cases and a discussion of how forfeiture is used to fight money laundering, see Stephan D. Cassella, *The Forfeiture of Property Involved in Money Laundering Offenses*, 7 BUFF. CRIM. L. REV. 583 (2004). For a critique of these cases, see Jon E. Gordon, *Prosecutors Who Seize Too Much and the Theories They Love: Money Laundering, Facilitation, and Forfeiture*, 44 Duke L. J. 744 (1995).

When funds from a tainted account are transferred to a second account, does the taint carry over? If so, how far do you think this theory could be carried?

Congress has also provided for special rules applicable to civil forfeitures of "fungible property" in currency reporting, structuring, and money laundering cases. Since cash is fungible, the statute permits the government to forfeit any cash found in a place forfeitable property was kept, without showing that the particular cash was itself tainted. 18 U.S.C. § 984 provides that "it shall not be necessary for the Government to identify the specific property involved in the offense that is the basis for the forfeiture," and "it shall not be a defense that the property involved in such an offense has been removed and replaced by identical property." 18 U.S.C. § 984(b)(1). In other words, "any identical property found in the same place or account as the property involved in the offense that is the basis for the forfeiture shall be subject to forfeiture under this section." 18 U.S.C. § 984(b)(2). This section is subject to only two additional limitations: the forfeiture action must be commenced within one year of the offense, and funds held in an "interbank account" are not subject to forfeiture unless the financial institution holding the account knowingly engaged in the offense. Has Congress gone too far in responding to the difficulty of showing that fungible property is tainted?

For a discussion of money laundering, see Chapter 10.

6. Many of the forfeiture statutes, including § 853, authorize the forfeiture of "property." But what exactly counts as property for this purpose? Is a license property? Does it matter what kind of license it is? Are the considerations the same as when the courts try to determine whether a scheme to defraud deprived the victim of property for purposes of the mail and wire fraud statutes? For an interesting discussion of these issues see Wesley M. Oliver, *A Round Peg in a Square Hole: Federal Forfeiture of State Professional Licenses*, 28 Am. Crim. L. Rev. 179 (2001). Oliver discusses *United States v. Dicter*, 198 F.3d 1284 (11th Cir. 1999), which upheld the forfeiture of the medical license of a physician who had unlawfully dispensed narcotics without a valid medical purpose. Oliver (who represented Dr. Dicter) concedes that the medical license facilitated the offense, but notes that the doctor's medical school degree did so as well. He argues that the forfeiture of professional licenses "is part of a disturbing trend of federal usurpation of matters traditionally left to the states"—in this case, the sort of hearing that a professional is entitled to before he is prohibited from engaging in his profession, and the proper authorities to determine eligibility to practice. Should federal prosecutors and juries determine who is qualified to practice medicine . . . or law?

7. What is the scope of RICO forfeiture? RICO forfeiture is exclusively a criminal remedy. (The courts do, however, have significant remedial authority in civil RICO actions brought by the government, see *supra* at 573–77.) Section 1963(a)(2) provides for forfeiture of "any interest in * * * any enterprise which [the defendant] has established, operated, controlled, conducted, or participated in the conduct of, in violation of section 1962." In *United States v. Busher*, 817 F.2d 1409 (9th Cir. 1987), the court commented:

Section 1963 was designed to totally separate a racketeer from the enterprise he operates. Thus, forfeiture is not limited to those assets of a RICO enterprise that are tainted by use in connection with racketeering activity, but rather extends to the convicted person's entire interest in the enterprise.

817 F.2d at 1413. In addition, Section 1963(a)(1) provides for the forfeiture of "any interest * * * acquired or maintained in violation of Section 1962," and 1963(a)(3) provides for the forfeiture of "any property constituting, or derived from, any proceeds which the person obtained, directly or indirectly, from racketeering activity." RICO also provides for the forfeiture of substitute assets when appropriate.

8. Under the Employee Retirement Income Security Act (ERISA), an employee's individual retirement annuity is termed "nonforfeitable." *See* 26 U.S.C. § 408(b)(4). Does this prevent the government from seizing a convicted criminal's pension fund? This issue was addressed in *United States v. Infelise*, 159 F.3d 300 (7th Cir. 1998), in which the government sought the defendant's life insurance annuity following a RICO conviction. Infelise argued, quite simply, that "[n]on-forfeitable means nonforfeitable." *Id.* at 303. The court, however, held that this reading was too literal: words have multiple meanings that must be understood within the context of the statute. In this case, nonforfeitable, under ERISA, indicated that the account was vested in the owner; thus, an employer cannot retake the money even if an employee is caught embezzling funds. However, the statute does not prevent the government from obtaining forfeiture of the account upon demonstrating that the fund was tainted with criminal proceeds.

B. THE CONSTITUTIONALITY OF CIVIL AND CRIMINAL FORFEITURE

Since the beginning of the Government's fascination with the forfeiture laws, defendants have been questioning the right of the Government to seize their property. In addition to raising procedural issues, persons from whom property was seized have challenged the magnitude and the punitiveness of both criminal and civil forfeitures.

One foundational issue that faced the Supreme Court was determining what constitutional provisions are applicable to criminal and civil forfeiture. In *Alexander v. United States*, 509 U.S. 544 (1993), the Supreme Court concluded that criminal forfeitures are governed by the Excessive Fines Clause of the Eighth Amendment. Why isn't criminal forfeiture governed by the Cruel and Unusual Punishment Clause? *Alexander* explained that the latter "is concerned with matters such as the duration or conditions of confinement," while the Excessive Fines Clause " 'limits the government's power to extract payments, whether in cash or in kind, as punishment for some offense.' " 509 U.S. at 558. The *Alexander* Court concluded that an in personam criminal forfeiture "is a form of monetary punishment no different, for Eighth Amendment purposes, from a traditional fine." *Id.* The Court declined to address the question whether the forfeiture of petitioner's property was excessive, since the courts below had not considered that question. The Court remanded for consideration of the excessiveness issue without providing any guidance to the lower court on the standard to be applied.

The materials that follow explore the constitutional standard for excessiveness, and the whether the Sixth Amendment right to counsel limits the forfeiture of attorney's fees.

1. THE CONSTITUTIONAL MEASURE OF EXCESSIVENESS

The lower courts disagreed on the proper measure of excessiveness under the Excessive Fines Clause, with some courts adopting an instrumentality test that focused on the degree to which the property was employed in the commission of the offense, and others a proportionality analysis that compared the severity of the forfeiture and the seriousness of the crime. That issue was resolved by the Supreme Court in next case.

UNITED STATES v. BAJAKAJIAN

524 U.S. 321 (1998).

JUSTICE THOMAS delivered the opinion of the Court.

I

On June 9, 1994, respondent, his wife, and his two daughters were waiting at Los Angeles International Airport to board a flight to Italy; their final destination was Cyprus. Using dogs trained to detect currency by its smell, customs inspectors discovered some $230,000 in cash in the Bajakajians' checked baggage. A customs inspector approached respondent and his wife and told them that they were required to report all money in excess of $10,000 in their possession or in their baggage. Respondent said that he had $8,000 and that his wife had another $7,000, but that the family had no additional currency to declare. A search of their carry-on bags, purse, and wallet revealed more cash; in all, customs inspectors found $357,144. The currency was seized and respondent was taken into custody.

A federal grand jury indicted respondent on three counts. * * *

Respondent pleaded guilty to the failure to report in Count One; the Government agreed to dismiss the false statement charge in Count Two; and respondent elected to have a bench trial on the forfeiture in Count Three. After the bench trial, the District Court found that the entire $357,144 was subject to forfeiture because it was "involved in" the offense. The court also found that the funds were not connected to any other crime and that respondent was transporting the money to repay a lawful debt. The District Court further found that respondent had failed to report that he was taking the currency out of the United States because of fear stemming from "cultural differences": Respondent, who had grown up as a member of the Armenian minority in Syria, had a "distrust for the Government."

Although § 982(a)(1) directs sentencing courts to impose full forfeiture, the District Court concluded that such forfeiture would be "extraordinarily harsh" and "grossly disproportionate to the offense in question," and that it would therefore violate the Excessive Fines Clause. The court instead ordered forfeiture of $15,000, in addition to a sentence of three years of probation and a fine of $5,000—the maximum fine under the Sentencing Guidelines—because the court believed that the maximum Guidelines fine was "too little" and that a $15,000 forfeiture would "make up for what I think a reasonable fine should be."

The United States appealed, seeking full forfeiture of respondent's currency as provided in § 982(a)(1). The Court of Appeals for the Ninth Circuit affirmed. * * *

II

The Eighth Amendment provides: "Excessive bail shall not be required, nor excessive fines imposed, nor cruel and unusual punishments inflicted." U.S. Const., Amdt. 8. This Court has had little occasion to interpret, and has never actually applied, the Excessive Fines Clause. We have, however, explained that at the time the Constitution was adopted, "the word 'fine' was understood to mean a payment to a sovereign as punishment for some offense." The Excessive Fines Clause thus "limits the government's power to extract payments, whether in cash or in kind, 'as punishment for some offense.'" *Austin v. United States,* 509 U.S. 602, 609–610 (1993) (emphasis deleted). Forfeitures—payments in kind—are thus "fines" if they constitute punishment for an offense.

We have little trouble concluding that the forfeiture of currency ordered by § 982(a)(1) constitutes punishment. The statute directs a court to order forfeiture as an additional sanction when "imposing sentence on a person convicted of" a willful violation of § 5316's reporting requirement. The forfeiture is thus imposed at the culmination of a criminal proceeding and requires conviction of an underlying felony, and it cannot be imposed upon an innocent owner of unreported currency, but only upon a person who has himself been convicted of a § 5316 reporting violation.

The United States argues, however, that the forfeiture of currency under § 982(a)(1) "also serves important remedial purposes." The Government asserts that it has "an overriding sovereign interest in controlling what property leaves and enters the country." It claims that full forfeiture of unreported currency supports that interest by serving to "dete[r] illicit movements of cash" and aiding in providing the Government with "valuable information to investigate and detect criminal activities associated with that cash." Deterrence, however, has traditionally been viewed as a goal of punishment, and forfeiture of the currency here does not serve the remedial purpose of compensating the Government for a loss. Although the Government has asserted a loss of information regarding the amount of currency leaving the country, that loss would not be remedied by the Government's confiscation of respondent's $357,144.

* * *

The Government specifically contends that the forfeiture of respondent's currency is constitutional because it involves an "instrumentality" of respondent's crime. According to the Government, the unreported cash is an instrumentality because it "does not merely facilitate a violation of law," but is " 'the very sine qua non of the crime.' "The Government reasons that "there would be no violation at all without the exportation (or attempted exportation) of the cash."

Acceptance of the Government's argument would require us to expand the traditional understanding of instrumentality forfeitures. This we decline to do. Instrumentalities historically have been treated as a form of "guilty property" that can be forfeited in civil in rem proceedings. In this case, however, the Government has sought to punish respondent by proceeding against him criminally, in personam, rather than proceeding in rem against the currency. It is therefore irrelevant whether respondent's currency is an instrumentality; the forfeiture is punitive, and the test for the excessiveness of a punitive forfeiture involves solely a proportionality determination.

III

Because the forfeiture of respondent's currency constitutes punishment and is thus a "fine" within the meaning of the Excessive Fines Clause, we now turn to the question of whether it is "excessive."

A

The touchstone of the constitutional inquiry under the Excessive Fines Clause is the principle of proportionality: The amount of the forfeiture must bear some relationship to the gravity of the offense that it is designed to punish. Until today, however, we have not articulated a standard for determining whether a punitive forfeiture is constitutionally excessive. We now hold that a punitive forfeiture violates the Excessive Fines Clause if it is grossly disproportional to the gravity of a defendant's offense.

The text and history of the Excessive Fines Clause demonstrate the centrality of proportionality to the excessiveness inquiry; nonetheless, they provide little guidance as to how disproportional a punitive forfeiture must be to the gravity of an offense in order to be "excessive." Excessive means surpassing the usual, the proper, or a normal measure of proportion. See 1 N. WEBSTER, AMERICAN DICTIONARY OF THE ENGLISH LANGUAGE (1828) (defining excessive as "beyond the common measure or proportion"); S. JOHNSON, A DICTIONARY OF THE ENGLISH LANGUAGE 680 (4th ed. 1773) ("[b]eyond the common proportion"). The constitutional question that we address, however, is just how proportional to a criminal offense a fine must be, and the text of the Excessive Fines Clause does not answer it.

Nor does its history. The Clause was little discussed in the First Congress and the debates over the ratification of the Bill of Rights. As we have previously noted, the Clause was taken verbatim from the English Bill of Rights of 1689. That document's prohibition against excessive fines was a reaction to the abuses of the King's judges during the reigns of the Stuarts, but the fines that those judges imposed were described contemporaneously only in the most general terms. * * *

We must therefore rely on other considerations in deriving a constitutional excessiveness standard, and there are two that we find particularly relevant. The first, which we have emphasized in our cases interpreting the Cruel and Unusual Punishments Clause, is that judgments about the appropriate punishment for an offense belong in the first instance to the legislature. The second is that any judicial determination regarding the gravity of a particular criminal offense will be inherently imprecise. Both of these principles counsel against requiring strict proportionality between the amount of a punitive forfeiture and the gravity of a criminal offense, and we therefore adopt the standard of gross disproportionality articulated in our Cruel and Unusual Punishments Clause precedents. *See, e.g., Solem v. Helm*, 463 U.S. 277, 288 (1983); *Rummel v. Estelle*, 445 U.S. 263, 271 (1980).

In applying this standard, the district courts in the first instance, and the courts of appeals, reviewing the proportionality determination de novo, must compare the amount of the forfeiture to the gravity of the defendant's offense. If the amount of the forfeiture is grossly disproportional to the gravity of the defendant's offense, it is unconstitutional.

B

Under this standard, the forfeiture of respondent's entire $357,144 would violate the Excessive Fines Clause. Respondent's crime was solely a reporting offense. It was permissible to transport the currency out of the country so long as he reported it. Section 982(a)(1) orders currency to be forfeited for a "willful" violation of the reporting requirement. Thus, the essence of respondent's crime is a willful failure to report the removal of currency from the United States.[12] Furthermore, as the

---

12. Contrary to the dissent's contention, the nature of the nonreporting offense in this case was not altered by respondent's "lies" or by the "suspicious circumstances" surrounding his transportation of his currency." A single willful failure to declare the currency constitutes the crime, the gravity of which is not exacerbated or mitigated by "fable[s]" that respondent told one month, or six months, later. The Government indicted respondent under 18 U.S.C. § 1001 for "lying," but that separate count did not form the basis of the nonreporting offense for which § 982(a)(1) orders forfeiture. Further, the District Court's finding that respondent's lies stemmed from a fear of the Government because of

"cultural differences," does not mitigate the gravity of his offense. We reject the dissent's contention that this finding was a "patronizing excuse" that "demeans millions of law-abiding American immigrants by suggesting they cannot be expected to be as truthful as every other citizen." We are confident that the District Court concurred in the dissent's incontrovertible proposition that "[e]ach American, regardless of culture or ethnicity, is equal before the law." Ibid. The District Court did nothing whatsoever to imply that "cultural differences" excuse lying, but rather made this finding in the context of establishing that respondent's willful failure to report the currency was unrelated to any other crime—a finding

District Court found, respondent's violation was unrelated to any other illegal activities. The money was the proceeds of legal activity and was to be used to repay a lawful debt. Whatever his other vices, respondent does not fit into the class of persons for whom the statute was principally designed: He is not a money launderer, a drug trafficker, or a tax evader.[13] And under the Sentencing Guidelines, the maximum sentence that could have been imposed on respondent was six months, while the maximum fine was $5,000. Such penalties confirm a minimal level of culpability.[14]

The harm that respondent caused was also minimal. Failure to report his currency affected only one party, the Government, and in a relatively minor way. There was no fraud on the United States, and respondent caused no loss to the public fisc. Had his crime gone undetected, the Government would have been deprived only of the information that $357,144 had left the country. The Government and the dissent contend that there is a correlation between the amount forfeited and the harm that the Government would have suffered had the crime gone undetected. We disagree. There is no inherent proportionality in such a forfeiture. It is impossible to conclude, for example, that the harm respondent caused is anywhere near 30 times greater than that caused by a hypothetical drug dealer who willfully fails to report taking $12,000 out of the country in order to purchase drugs.

Comparing the gravity of respondent's crime with the $357,144 forfeiture the Government seeks, we conclude that such a forfeiture would be grossly disproportional to the gravity of his offense. It is larger than the $5,000 fine imposed by the District Court by many orders of magnitude, and it bears no articulable correlation to any injury suffered by the Government.

* * *

highly relevant to the determination of the gravity of respondent's offense. The dissent's charge of ethnic paternalism on the part of the District Court finds no support in the record, nor is there any indication that the District Court's factual finding that respondent "distrust[ed] . . . the Government," was clearly erroneous.

13. Nor, contrary to the dissent's repeated assertion, is respondent a "smuggler." Respondent owed no customs duties to the Government, and it was perfectly legal for him to possess the $357,144 in cash and to remove it from the United States. His crime was simply failing to report the wholly legal act of transporting his currency.

14. In considering an offense's gravity, the other penalties that the Legislature has authorized are certainly relevant evidence. Here, as the Government and the dissent stress, Congress authorized a maximum fine of $250,000 plus five years' imprisonment for willfully violating the statutory reporting requirement, and this suggests that it did not view the reporting offense as a trivial one. That the maximum fine and Guideline sentence to which respondent was subject were but a fraction of the penalties authorized, however, undercuts any argument based solely on the statute, because they show that respondent's culpability relative to other potential violators of the reporting provision—tax evaders, drug kingpins, or money launderers, for example—is small indeed. This disproportion is telling notwithstanding the fact that a separate Guideline provision permits forfeiture if mandated by statute. That Guideline, moreover, cannot override the constitutional requirement of proportionality review.

For the foregoing reasons, the full forfeiture of respondent's currency would violate the Excessive Fines Clause. The judgment of the Court of Appeals is

Affirmed.

JUSTICE KENNEDY, with whom THE CHIEF JUSTICE, JUSTICE O'CONNOR, and JUSTICE SCALIA join, dissenting.

For the first time in its history, the Court strikes down a fine as excessive under the Eighth Amendment. The decision is disturbing both for its specific holding and for the broader upheaval it foreshadows. At issue is a fine Congress fixed in the amount of the currency respondent sought to smuggle or to transport without reporting. If a fine calibrated with this accuracy fails the Court's test, its decision portends serious disruption of a vast range of statutory fines. The Court all but says the offense is not serious anyway. This disdain for the statute is wrong as an empirical matter and disrespectful of the separation of powers. The irony of the case is that, in the end, it may stand for narrowing constitutional protection rather than enhancing it. To make its rationale work, the Court appears to remove important classes of fines from any excessiveness inquiry at all. This, too, is unsound; and with all respect, I dissent.

I

A

In striking down this forfeiture, the majority treats many fines as "remedial" penalties even though they far exceed the harm suffered. Remedial penalties, the Court holds, are not subject to the Excessive Fines Clause at all. Proceeding from this premise, the majority holds customs fines are remedial and not at all punitive, even if they amount to many times the duties due on the goods. In the majority's universe, a fine is not a punishment even if it is much larger than the money owed. This confuses whether a fine is excessive with whether it is a punishment.

This novel, mistaken approach requires reordering a tradition existing long before the Republic and confirmed in its early years. The Court creates its category to reconcile its unprecedented holding with a six-century-long tradition of in personam customs fines equal to one, two, three, or even four times the value of the goods at issue. * * *

In order to sweep all these precedents aside, the majority's remedial analysis assumes the settled tradition was limited to "reimbursing the Government for" unpaid duties. The assumption is wrong. Many offenses did not require a failure to pay a duty at all. See, e.g., Act of Mar. 3, 1863, § 1, 12 Stat. 738 (importing under false invoices); Act of Mar. 3, 1823, ch. 58, S 1, 3 Stat. 781 (failing to deliver ship's manifest); Act of Mar. 2, 1799, § 28, 1 Stat. 648 (transferring goods from one ship to another); Act of Aug. 4, 1790, § 14, 1 Stat. 158 (same); 5 Rich. II, st. 1, ch. 2 (1381) (Eng.) (exporting gold or silver without a license). None of these in personam penalties depended on a compensable monetary loss to the government. True, these offenses risked causing harm but so does smuggling or not reporting cash. A sanction proportioned to potential rather than actual harm is punitive, though the potential harm may make the punishment a reasonable one. The majority nonetheless treats the historic penalties as nonpunitive and thus not subject to the Excessive Fines Clause, though they are indistinguishable from the fine in this case. (It is a mark of the Court's doctrinal difficulty that we must speak of nonpunitive penalties, which is a contradiction in terms.)

Even if the majority's typology were correct, it would have to treat the instant penalty as nonpunitive. In this respect, the Court cannot distinguish the case on which it twice relies, *One Lot Emerald Cut Stones v. United States*, 409 U.S. 232 (1972) (per curiam). *Emerald Stones* held forfeiture of smuggled goods plus a fine equal to their value was remedial and not punitive, for purposes of double jeopardy, because the fine "serves to reimburse the Government for investigation and enforcement expenses." The logic, however, applies with equal force here. Forfeiture of the money involved in the offense would compensate for the investigative and enforcement expenses of the Customs Service. There is no reason to treat the cases differently, just because a small duty was at stake in one and a disclosure form in the other. *See Bollinger's Champagne*, 3 Wall. 560, 564, 18 L.Ed. 78 (1865) (holding falsehoods on customs forms justify forfeiture even if the lies do not affect the duties due and paid). The majority, in short, is not even faithful to its own artificial category of remedial penalties.

* * *

II

Turning to the question of excessiveness, the majority states the test: A defendant must prove a gross disproportion before a court will strike down a fine as excessive. This test would be a proper way to apply the Clause, if only the majority were faithful in applying it. The Court does not, however, explain why in this case forfeiture of all of the cash would have suffered from a gross disproportion. The offense is a serious one, and respondent's smuggling and failing to report were willful. The cash was lawful to own, but this fact shows only that the forfeiture was a fine; it cannot also prove that the fine was excessive.

The majority illuminates its test with a principle of deference. Courts "should grant substantial deference to the broad authority that legislatures necessarily possess" in setting punishments. Again, the principle is sound but the implementation is not. The majority's assessment of the crime accords no deference, let alone substantial deference, to the judgment of Congress. Congress deems the crime serious, but the Court does not. Under the congressional statute, the crime is punishable by a prison sentence, a heavy fine, and the forfeiture here at issue. As the statute makes clear, the Government needs the information to investigate other serious crimes, and it needs the penalties to ensure compliance.

A

By affirming, the majority in effect approves a meager $15,000 forfeiture. The majority's holding purports to be narrower, saying only that forfeiture of the entire $357,144 would be excessive. This narrow holding is artificial in constricting the question presented for this Court's review. The statute mandates forfeiture of the entire $357,144. *See* 18 U.S.C. § 982(a)(1). The only ground for reducing the forfeiture, then, is that any higher amount would be unconstitutional. The majority affirms the reduced $15,000 forfeiture on de novo review, which it can do only if a forfeiture of even $15,001 would have suffered from a gross disproportion. Indeed, the majority leaves open whether the $15,000 forfeiture itself was too great. Money launderers, among the principal targets of this statute, may get an even greater return from their crime.

The majority does not explain why respondent's knowing, willful, serious crime deserves no higher penalty than $15,000. It gives only a cursory explanation of why forfeiture of all of the money would have suffered from a gross disproportion. The majority justifies its evisceration of the fine because the money was legal to have and came from a legal source. This fact, however, shows only that the forfeiture was a fine, not that it was excessive. * * *

B

1

In assessing whether there is a gross disproportion, the majority concedes, we must grant " 'substantial deference' " to Congress' choice of penalties. Yet, ignoring its own command, the Court sweeps aside Congress' reasoned judgment and substitutes arguments that are little more than speculation.

Congress considered currency smuggling and non-reporting a serious crime and imposed commensurate penalties. It authorized punishments of five years' imprisonment, a $250,000 fine, plus forfeiture of all the undeclared cash. Congress found the offense standing alone is a serious crime, for the same statute doubles the fines and imprisonment for failures to report cash "while violating another law of the United States." Congress experimented with lower penalties on the order of one year in prison plus a $1,000 fine, but it found the punishments inadequate to deter lucrative money laundering. The Court today rejects this judgment.

The Court rejects the congressional judgment because, it says, the Sentencing Guidelines cap the appropriate fine at $5,000. The purpose of the Guidelines, however, is to select punishments with precise proportion, not to opine on what is a gross disproportion. In addition, there is no authority for elevating the Commission's judgment of what is prudent over the congressional judgment of what is constitutional. The majority, then, departs from its promise of deference in the very case announcing the standard.

The Court's argument is flawed, moreover, by a serious misinterpretation of the Guidelines on their face. The Guidelines do not stop at the $5,000 fine the majority cites. They augment it with this vital point: "Forfeiture is to be imposed upon a convicted defendant as provided by statute." United States Sentencing Commission, Guidelines Manual § 5E1.4 (Nov.1995). The fine thus supplements the forfeiture; it does not replace it. Far from contradicting congressional judgment on the offense, the Guidelines implement and mandate it.

2

The crime of smuggling or failing to report cash is more serious than the Court is willing to acknowledge. The drug trade, money laundering, and tax evasion all depend in part on smuggled and unreported cash. Congress enacted the reporting requirement because secret exports of money were being used in organized crime, drug trafficking, money laundering, and other crimes. Likewise, tax evaders were using cash exports to dodge hundreds of millions of dollars in taxes owed to the Government.

The Court does not deny the importance of these interests but claims they are not implicated here because respondent managed to disprove any link to other crimes. Here, to be sure, the Government had no affirmative proof that the money was from an illegal source or for an illegal purpose. This will often be the case, however. By its very nature, money laundering is difficult to prove; for if the money launderers have done their job, the money appears to be clean. The point of the statute, which provides for even heavier penalties if a second crime can be proved, is to mandate forfeiture regardless. * * *

In my view, forfeiture of all the unreported currency is sustainable whenever a willful violation is proven. The facts of this case exemplify how hard it can be to prove ownership and other crimes, and they also show respondent is far from an innocent victim. For one thing, he was guilty of repeated lies to Government agents and suborning lies by others. Customs inspectors told respondent of his duty to report cash. He and his wife claimed they had only $15,000 with them, not the $357,144 they in fact had concealed. He then told customs inspectors a friend named Abe Ajemian had lent him about $200,000. Ajemian denied this. A month later, respondent said Saeed Faroutan had lent him $170,000. Faroutan, however, said he had not made the loan and respondent had asked him to lie. Six months later, respondent resurrected the fable of the alleged loan from Ajemian, though Ajemian had already contradicted the story. As the District Court found, respondent "has lied, and has had his friends lie." He had proffered a "suspicious and confused story, documented in the poorest way, and replete with past misrepresentation."

Respondent told these lies, moreover, in most suspicious circumstances. His luggage was stuffed with more than a third of a million dollars. All of it was in cash, and much of it was hidden in a case with a false bottom.

The majority ratifies the District Court's see-no-evil approach. The District Court ignored respondent's lies in assessing a sentence. It gave him a two-level downward adjustment for acceptance of responsibility, instead of an increase for obstruction of justice. It dismissed the lies as stemming from "distrust for the Government" arising out of "cultural differences." While the majority is sincere in not endorsing this excuse, it nonetheless affirms the fine tainted by it. This patronizing excuse demeans millions of law-abiding American immigrants by suggesting they cannot be expected to be as truthful as every other citizen. Each American, regardless of culture or ethnicity, is equal before the law. Each has the same obligation to refrain from perjury and false statements to the Government.

In short, respondent was unable to give a single truthful explanation of the source of the cash. The multitude of lies and suspicious circumstances points to some form of crime. Yet, though the Government rebutted each and every fable respondent proffered, it was unable to adduce affirmative proof of another crime in this particular case.

Because of the problems of individual proof, Congress found it necessary to enact a blanket punishment. One of the few reliable warning signs of some serious crimes is the use of large sums of cash. So Congress punished all cash smuggling or non-reporting, authorizing single penalties for the offense alone and double penalties for the offense coupled with proof of other crimes. The requirement of willfulness, it judged, would be enough to protect the innocent. The majority second-guesses this judgment without explaining why Congress' blanket approach was unreasonable.

Money launderers will rejoice to know they face forfeitures of less than 5% of the money transported, provided they hire accomplished liars to carry their money for them. Five percent, of course, is not much of a deterrent or punishment; it is comparable to the fee one might pay for a mortgage lender or broker. It is far less than the 20–26% commissions some drug dealers pay money launderers. Since many couriers evade detection, moreover, the average forfeiture per dollar smuggled could amount, courtesy of today's decision, to far less than 5%. In any event, the fine permitted by the majority would be a modest cost of doing business in the world of drugs and crime.

Given the severity of respondent's crime, the Constitution does not forbid forfeiture of all of the smuggled or unreported cash. Congress made a considered judgment in setting the penalty, and the Court is in serious error to set it aside.

III

The Court's holding may in the long run undermine the purpose of the Excessive Fines Clause. One of the main purposes of the ban on excessive fines was to prevent the King from assessing unpayable fines to keep his enemies in debtor's prison. Concern with imprisonment may explain why the Excessive Fines Clause is coupled with, and follows right after, the Excessive Bail Clause. While the concern is not implicated here—for of necessity the money is there to satisfy the forfeiture—the Court's restrictive approach could subvert this purpose. Under the Court's holding, legislators may rely on mandatory prison sentences in lieu of fines. Drug lords will be heartened by this, knowing the prison terms will fall upon their couriers while leaving their own wallets untouched.

At the very least, today's decision will encourage legislatures to take advantage of another avenue the majority leaves open. The majority subjects this forfeiture to scrutiny because it is in personam, but it then suggests most in rem forfeitures (and perhaps most civil forfeitures) may not be fines at all. The suggestion, one might note, is inconsistent or at least in tension with *Austin v. United States*, 509 U.S. 602 (1993). In any event, these remarks may encourage a legislative shift from in personam to in rem forfeitures, avoiding mens rea as a predicate and giving owners fewer procedural protections. By invoking the Excessive Fines Clause with excessive zeal, the majority may in the long run encourage Congress to circumvent it.

IV

The majority's holding may not only jeopardize a vast range of fines but also leave countless others unchecked by the Constitution. Non-remedial fines may be subject to deference in theory but overbearing scrutiny in fact. So-called remedial penalties, most in rem forfeitures, and perhaps civil fines may not be subject to scrutiny at all. I would not create these exemptions from the Excessive Fines Clause. I would also accord genuine deference to Congress' judgments about the gravity of the offenses it creates. I would further follow the long tradition of fines calibrated to the value of the goods smuggled. In these circumstances, the Constitution does not forbid forfeiture of all of the $357,144 transported by respondent. I dissent.

Notes

1. *Bajakajian* establishes a gross disproportionality test under the Excessive Fines clause, but—as the dissent emphasizes—this test will not be applied unless the forfeiture in question is found to be punitive rather than remedial. What kinds of criminal forfeitures will be characterized as remedial? Note that the majority rejected the government's claim that the currency was an instrumentality of the crime. Can the forfeiture of an instrumentality ever be grossly disproportionate? What about the forfeiture under RICO of the defendant's interest in the "enterprise" she established, participated in or controlled in violation of the act? What about the "proceeds" of a drug offense? The broader the treatment of the category of remedial forfeitures, the less bite the excessiveness standard articulated in *Bajakajian* will have.

2. On the other hand, the *Bajakajian* test is applicable to at least some civil forfeitures. In *Austin v. United States*, 509 U.S. 602 (1993), the

Supreme Court held that civil forfeiture, like criminal forfeiture, is subject to the limitations imposed by the Excessive Fines Clause of the Eighth Amendment. Why is *civil* forfeiture governed by the Excessive Fines Clause—which previously applied only to criminal sanctions? Writing for five members of the Court in *Austin*, Justice Blackmun reasoned that civil forfeiture can be imposed as punishment, and when civil forfeiture can only be explained as serving *in part* as punishment,[k] it is governed by the Excessive Fines Clause. The majority noted that the Excessive Fines Clause, unlike some of the other provisions of the Bill of Rights, is not expressly limited to criminal cases. The purpose of the Excessive Fines Clause is to limit the government's power to extract payments, in cash or in kind, as punishment for some offense, and he concluded that the notion of punishment " 'cuts across the division between civil and criminal law.' " 509 U.S. at 610 (quoting *United States v. Halper*, 490 U.S. 435, 447–48 (1989)).

Accordingly, the *Austin* Court turned to the question whether the forfeiture in question was punishment. Recognizing that sanctions frequently serve more than one purpose, the majority stated that the court must determine whether a forfeiture that is partly remedial "can only be explained as serving in part to punish." 509 U.S. at 610. The Court noted that the structure of the statute and legislative history of the civil drug forfeiture provisions in the case, 21 U.S.C. §§ 881(a)(4) and (7), revealed a Congressional intent to punish those involved in drug trafficking and to exempt innocent owners. Even assuming that the forfeitures were intended in part to serve the remedial purposes cited by the government (the removal of dangerous instruments of the drug trade and the compensation of the government for law enforcement and social expenditures necessitated by the drug trade), the Court found that the forfeiture must be deemed punishment because it could not be said to serve *solely* a remedial purpose. Four members of the Court concurred on narrower grounds.

3.   In attempting to apply *Bajakajian*'s test of gross disproportionality, the lower courts have generally looked at three factors: (a) the culpability of the claimant; (b) the seriousness of the claimant's actions; and (c) the ratio of the size of the forfeiture to the fine suggested by the Sentencing Guidelines. For example, in *One 1995 Toyota Pick-Up Truck v. District of Columbia*, 718 A.2d 558 (D.C. 1998), the claimant was convicted of a first offense of soliciting a prostitute, an offense which carried only a statutory $300 maximum fine (of which the claimant was only fined $150). The city sought forfeiture of the defendant's $15,000 truck, but the D.C. Court of Appeals determined that the forfeiture violated the Excessive Fines Clause under *Bajakajian*. The statute in question was labeled a civil forfeiture, but relying

---

k. By recognizing that civil forfeiture constitutes "punishment" in a constitutional sense, *Austin* sowed the seeds of a Double Jeopardy argument. How then could civil and criminal forfeiture for the same offense be imposed in successive proceedings? Double jeopardy issues spread like wild fire throughout the lower courts, and the circuits were deeply divided. However, in *United States v. Ursery*, 518 U.S. 267 (1996), the court brought the expansive readings of *Austin* to an abrupt halt, sharply restricting it to the Excessive Fines Clause. In *Hudson v. United States*, 522 U.S. 93 (1997), the Court signaled a further retreat from an expansive interpretation of the Double Jeopardy Clause, repudiating its decision in *United States v. Halper*, 490 U.S. 435 (1989). The Double Jeopardy defense to civil forfeiture is now considered a dead letter.

on the presence of key features generally associated with criminal forfeiture (a provision exempting innocent owners and a legislative history indicating importance of deterrence), the court concluded that it was subject to the Excessive Fines Clause. *Id.* at 562–63. The court then applied the *Bajakajian* factors, finding that a first-time solicitation offense was historically considered to be a minor offense, and that a forfeiture 100 times higher than the fine was constitutionally excessive. *Id.* at 564–65.

On the other hand, the court in *Yskamp v. Drug Enforcement Admin.*, 163 F.3d 767 (3rd Cir. 1998), upheld the constitutionality, under the Excessive Fines Clause, of the forfeiture of a Lear jet appraised at $1 million. In *Yskamp*, the claimant had purchased the jet for use in a charter operation. A few years later, the DEA, while tracking some suspects, observed the suspects unloading luggage from a truck into Yskamp's jet. After obtaining permission to search the jet, the DEA agents found 300 kg of cocaine in the luggage. Yskamp acknowledged that the flight had seemed odd because "the bulk of the payment was in cash, the travelers had significantly more luggage in one direction that the other, and the turn-around time was short." 163 F.3d at 769. The DEA concluded, at a forfeiture hearing, that Yskamp had not "taken reasonable steps to assure that the jet was not used for conveying illegal drugs," and confiscated the jet. 163 F.3d at 769–70. Yskamp's insurer, CIGNA, paid for the loss under Yskamp's insurance policy. After *Bajakajian* came out, Yskamp and CIGNA challenged the forfeiture as a violation of the Excessive Fines Clause. The court, however, was not sympathetic:

> We conclude that the forfeiture here was not excessive. The federal statute clearly authorized the forfeiture of aircraft used in the transportation of drugs. The amount of cocaine to be transported in the jet was comparatively large for a drug case. Indeed, an offense involving 150 kgs or more of cocaine has been placed in the highest base offense level under the Sentencing Guidelines. *See* U.S.S.G. § 2D1.1(c). Furthermore, the DEA found CIGNA culpable because it failed to assure that the jet was not used for improper purposes. CIGNA has not contended that it had no duty to take reasonable precautions to prevent Yskamp's use of the airplane for illegal cargo. The DEA noted that CIGNA's insurance policy reimbursed a claimant even though the property seized was used in illegal drug trafficking, which effectively insulated criminals from the loss consequences of their crimes. Consequently, the forfeiture of the jet does not violate the constitutional ban on excessive fines.

163 F.3d at 773.

What are the key differences between *Yskamp*, where the court upheld the forfeiture, and *Bajakajian* and *One 1995 Toyota Pick-Up*, where the forfeitures were held to be grossly disproportionate? Do you see any basis for the dissent's charge in *Bajakajian* that the courts are simply overriding legislative judgements of the relative seriousness of various offenses? Or is there a principled basis for the distinctions the courts are drawing?

Although the court in *Yskamp* did not discuss this issue, it could be argued that the forfeiture in question was remedial, rather than punitive, because the airplane was an instrumentality of the crime. It appears under *Bajakajian* that this would be the end of the matter for constitutional purposes, regardless of the amount of drugs that were being carried, or the fact that the plane was worth $1 million. Do you see why the dissent in *Bajakajian* was concerned about exempting a potentially large category of forfeitures from any limitations under the Excessive Fines Clause?

4. In response to *Bajakajian*, Congress enacted a new bulk cash smuggling statute as part of the USA PATRIOT Act. 31 U.S.C. § 5332 makes it a crime to knowingly conceal more than $10,000 in currency or other monetary instruments and transport or transfer it or attempt to transport of transfer it out of the United States, and authorizes civil forfeiture of any property "involved in" the currency smuggling offense. The Court in *Bajakajian* emphasized that the offense giving rise to the forfeiture was merely a reporting offense, as transporting the currency was not a crime. Section 5332 makes the transfer itself the crime, rather than just the failure to report. *See* JIMMY GURULÉ ET AL., THE LAW OF ASSET FORFEITURE § 7–3(d) (2004).

Would *Bajakajian* have a different result under the new statute? Maybe not. In *United States v. $293,316 in United States Currency*, 349 F. Supp. 2d 638 (E.D.N.Y. 2004), the three defendants were convicted under § 5332(a) for concealing over $10,000 and attempting to transfer it out of the country, while attempting to board a plane to Pakistan with $515,583 between them. The government sought forfeiture of the entire amount seized, but the court determined that the forfeiture would violate the Excessive Fines Clause. At their criminal trial, the court found that the money was "intended to help families in Pakistan with money earned legally in the United States, not to fund terrorist activity or for any other illegal purpose." Relying on *Bajakajian*, the court found that, though civil, the forfeiture was punitive because it was predicated on a crime and could not be imposed on innocent owners, and therefore the forfeiture was subject to review under the Excessive Fines Clause. In considering whether the forfeiture was grossly disproportional, the court looked to the factors in *Bajakajian*, as well as extensive statistics regarding the practice of federal courts nationwide in setting forfeiture amounts for currency reporting and bulk cash smuggling violations. Despite the fact that most of the courts used a 100% forfeiture rate, the court found that in this case forfeiture of the entire amount would be grossly disproportionate. The court stressed that it would have been legal to transport the currency had they complied with the reporting requirement and that the defendants did not fit into the class of persons for whom the statute was designed.

5. *Bajakajian* articulates a gross disproportionality test under the Excessive Fines Clause that appears, at first blush, to be parallel to the gross disproportionality standard applied to terms of imprisonment under the Cruel and Unusual Punishment Clause of the Eight Amendment. The Supreme Court's application of the two standards, however, has been quite different. In *Bajakajian*, the court found forfeiture of $357,144 grossly disproportional to the gravity of the offense. In contrast, in *Lockyer v. Andrade*, 538 U.S. 63 (2003), and *Ewing v. California*, 538 U.S. 11 (2003), the Court upheld life sentences under California's Three Strikes Law for defendants convicted of shoplifting nine video tapes and of stealing three golf clubs, respectively. Though the Court purportedly applies the same standard, the gross disproportionality test used for terms of imprisonment has more teeth when applied to forfeiture. For an article arguing that the Supreme Court has not shown the same concern for proportionality of prison sen-

tences as it has to forfeiture of property and arguing for a consistent approach to proportionality, see Rachel A. Van Cleave, *"Death is Different," Is Money Different? Criminal Punishments, Forfeitures, and Punitive Damages—Shifting Constitutional Paradigms for Assessing Proportionality*, 12 S. CAL. INTERDISC. L.J. 217 (2003).

Why was the Court willing to reject the judgment of Congress in *Bajakajian*, but reluctant to second guess the California legislature? Does it seem appropriate to prioritize money over prison time? For an argument that deprivations of liberty are more serious and deserve higher scrutiny than deprivations of property in the context of civil punitive damage awards, see Adam M. Gershowitz, Note, *The Supreme Court's Backwards Proportionality Jurisprudence: Comparing Judicial Review of Excessive Criminal Punishment and Excessive Punitive Damages Awards*, 86 VA. L. REV. 1249, 1288–91 (2000).

2. FORFEITURE OF ATTORNEY'S FEES?

What happens if the government claims the right to forfeit assets that a defendant wishes to use to pay counsel to defend him against the very criminal charges upon which the claim of forfeiture is based? In *Caplin v. Drysdale, Chartered v. United States*, 491 U.S. 617 (1989), the Supreme Court, in a 5–4 decision, rejected Sixth Amendment right to counsel and Due Process challenges to the drug forfeiture statute. In a previous proceeding, the defendant pled guilty to drug kingpin charges under the CCE statute, 21 U.S.C. § 848, and, under § 853, agreed to forfeit specified assets listed in the indictment. The law firm that had represented the defendant before the grand jury and in the criminal proceedings claimed that its legal fees—amounting to $190,000—were exempt from forfeiture. Noting that the defendant's statutory argument had been rejected in the companion decision in *Monsanto*,[1] the Court turned to the constitutional issues. The attorneys claimed that § 853 infringed on the defendant's Sixth Amendment right to counsel of choice and violated the Due Process Clause of the Fifth Amendment by upsetting the balance of power between the government and the accused.

Responding to the Sixth Amendment challenge, the Court distinguished the case from one in which the government asks "a court to prevent a defendant's chosen counsel from representing the accused." Instead, here the argument is that the forfeiture of assets the defendant intended to use to pay his attorney may prevent him from retaining counsel of his choice. The Court pointed out that this burden is limited, as defendants can still use nonforfeitable assets and may be able to find attorneys who will represent them now for fees paid at some future point. However, even in cases where a defendant cannot retain the attorney he would have if his assets were not forfeited, the Court stated this does not rise to the level of a Sixth Amendment violation:

1. *See infra* at 937.

Whatever the full extent of the Sixth Amendment's protection of one's right to retain counsel of his choosing, that protection does not go beyond "the individual's right to spend his own money to obtain the advice and assistance of ... counsel." A defendant has no Sixth Amendment right to spend another person's money for services rendered by an attorney, even if those funds are the only way that that defendant will be able to retain the attorney of his choice. A robbery suspect, for example, has no Sixth Amendment right to use funds he has stolen from a bank to retain an attorney to defend him if he is apprehended. The money, though in his possession, is not rightfully his; the Government does not violate the Sixth Amendment if it seizes the robbery proceeds and refuses to permit the defendant to use them to pay for his defense. "[N]o lawyer, in any case, ... has the right to ... accept stolen property, or ... ransom money, in payment of a fee.... The privilege to practice law is not a license to steal."

* * *

There is no constitutional principle that gives one person the right to give another's property to a third party, even where the person seeking to complete the exchange wishes to do so in order to exercise a constitutionally protected right. While petitioner and its supporting amici attempt to distinguish between the expenditure of forfeitable assets to exercise one's Sixth Amendment rights, and expenditures in the pursuit of other constitutionally protected freedoms, * * * there is no such distinction between, or hierarchy among, constitutional rights. If defendants have a right to spend forfeitable assets on attorney's fees, why not on exercises of the right to speak, practice one's religion, or travel? The full exercise of these rights, too, depends in part on one's financial wherewithal; and forfeiture, or even the threat of forfeiture, may similarly prevent a defendant from enjoying these rights as fully as he might otherwise. Nonetheless, we are not about to recognize an antiforfeiture exception for the exercise of each such right; nor does one exist for the exercise of Sixth Amendment rights.

The Court reasoned that the government has more than a modest interest in forfeitable assets, because the goal of forfeiture is more than dispossessing a criminal of the proceeds of his crime. First, the government has a pecuniary interest in forfeiture, because the profits are used to fund law enforcement programs. Second, the government has an interest in returning property to the rightful owners from whom it was wrongfully taken. Finally, the Court discussed the government's interest in removing the economic benefit from crime:

Finally, as we have recognized previously, a major purpose motivating congressional adoption and continued refinement of the racketeer influenced and corrupt organizations (RICO) and CCE forfeiture provisions has been the desire to lessen the economic power of organized crime and drug enterprises. This includes the use of such economic power to retain private counsel. As the Court of Appeals put it: "Congress has already underscored the compelling public interest in stripping criminals such as Reckmeyer of their undeserved economic power, and part of that undeserved power may be the ability to command high-priced legal talent." The notion that the Government has a legitimate interest in depriving criminals of economic power, even insofar as that power is used to retain counsel of choice, may be somewhat unsettling. But when a defendant claims that he has suffered some substantial impairment of his Sixth Amendment rights by virtue of the seizure or forfeiture of assets in his possession, such a complaint is no more than the reflection of "the harsh reality that the quality of a criminal defendant's representation frequently may turn on his ability to retain the best counsel money can buy." *Morris v. Slappy*, 461 U.S. 1, 23 (1983) (Brennan, J., concurring in result). Again, the Court of Appeals put it aptly: "The modern day Jean Valjean must be satisfied with appointed counsel. Yet the drug merchant claims that his possession of huge sums of money ... entitles him to something more. We reject this contention, and any notion of a constitutional right to use the proceeds of crime to finance an expensive defense."

These interests override any Sixth Amendment interest in permitting criminals to use forfeitable assets to pay for an attorney.

The Court also rejected the Fifth Amendment Due Process argument that forfeiture of attorneys fees upsets the balance between the government and the accused, reasoning that this argument adds nothing, as the fair trial guaranteed by the Due Process Clause is defined through the provisions of the Sixth Amendment. Any due process claims would only arise in specific cases of prosecutorial misconduct, and the fact that this tool, like many others available, may be abused by prosecutors in some cases does not render the statute unconstitutional. Such cases of abuse can be dealt with by lowers courts as they may arise.

Writing for a four-person dissent, Justice Blackmun stressed the importance of the right to private counsel of choice and the effect that the forfeiture of attorneys fees has on the adversarial system of justice. On an individual level, the right to private counsel of choice fosters trust between the attorney and client, a trust which is lost when counsel is appointed by the government. Even if a defendant does find a private attorney to take his case, the attorney-client relationship is undermined by the forfeiture statute:

Perhaps the attorney will be willing to violate ethical norms by working on a contingent-fee basis in a criminal case. But if he is not—and we should question the integrity of any criminal-defense attorney who would violate the ethical norms of the profession by doing so—the attorney's own interests will dictate that he remain ignorant of the source of the assets from which he is paid. Under § 853(c), a third-party transferee may keep assets if "the transferee establishes ... that he is a bona fide purchaser for value of such property who at the time of purchase was reasonably without cause to believe that the property was subject to forfeiture under this section." The less an attorney knows, the greater the likelihood that he can claim to have been an "innocent" third party. The attorney's interest in knowing nothing is directly adverse to his client's interest in full disclosure. The result of the conflict may be a less vigorous investigation of the defendant's circumstances, leading in turn to a failure to recognize or pursue avenues of inquiry necessary to the defense. Other conflicts of interest are also likely to develop. The attorney who fears for his fee will be tempted to make the Government's waiver of fee forfeiture the sine qua non for any plea agreement, a position which conflicts with his client's best interests. * * *

491 U.S. at 650.

Looking at the broader institutional ramifications, Justice Blackmun emphasized that the right to private counsel also keeps in balance the powers of the government and the accused. Without this right, "the Government too readily could defeat its adversaries simply by outspending them." The loss of the right to private counsel, he reasoned, would give the government too much power, weakening the criminal defense bar and subordinating the needs of individual defendants to the needs to the system:

> Perhaps most troubling is the fact that forfeiture statutes place the Government in the position to exercise an intolerable degree of power over any private attorney who takes on the task of representing a defendant in a forfeiture case. The decision whether to seek a restraining order rests with the prosecution, as does the decision whether to waive forfeiture upon a plea of guilty or a conviction at trial. *The Government will be ever tempted to use the forfeiture weapon against a defense attorney who is particularly talented or aggressive on the client's behalf—the attorney who is better than what, in the Government's view, the defendant deserves. The specter of the Government's selectively excluding only the most talented defense counsel is a serious threat to the equality of forces necessary for the adversarial system to perform at its best.* * * *

> The long-term effects of the fee-forfeiture practice will be to decimate the private criminal-defense bar. As the use of the forfeiture mechanism expands to new categories of federal crimes and spreads to the States, only one class of defendants will be free routinely to retain private counsel: the affluent defendant accused of a crime that generates no economic gain. As the number of private clients diminishes, only the most idealistic and the least skilled of young lawyers will be attracted to the field, while the remainder seek greener pastures elsewhere. * * *

> In short, attorney's-fee forfeiture substantially undermines every interest served by the Sixth Amendment right to chosen counsel,

on the individual and institutional levels, over the short term and the long haul.

491 at 650–51 (emphasis added).

Notes

1. What did the Court mean in *Caplin & Drysdale* when it stated that the government has an interest in stripping organized criminals of their undeserved economic power to hire high-priced legal talent? Professor Pamela Karlan has suggested that there are two possible interpretations:

> One might view this power as consisting of the ability to buy goods and services with the proceeds of criminal activity. The residential real estate that Reckmeyer and Monsanto purchased with the profits of their drug dealing is an example of this kind of undeserved economic power. One might view the ability to purchase lawyers' services as very much like the ability to acquire any other market commodity. Just as we strip Reckmeyer and Monsanto of the ability to buy fancy houses, so, too, we deny them the right to hire fancy lawyers.

> But there is an alternative conception of "undeserved economic power" under which lawyers are a very different kind of good. Under this conception, economic power serves as an instrumentality of criminal activity as well as a proceed from it. The complex criminal enterprise's wealth gives the enterprise opportunities for criminal activity that poorer entities do not have and gives it opportunities to evade liability that less affluent criminals lack. If the outcome of a criminal proceeding is positively correlated to the caliber of counsel appearing on a defendant's behalf, and if the caliber of counsel is positively related to the " 'ability to retain the best counsel money can buy' "—both common assumptions—then the economic power acquired by a complex enterprise may enable the enterprise to stay in business by avoiding convictions and forfeitures. Economic power not only constitutes a benefit to the criminal; it also lessens her costs (because it lowers the probability that she will be detected or successfully prosecuted). The power to buy fancy lawyers may in fact be worse than the power to buy fancy houses, because the latter does not facilitate the commission of further crimes as the former can.

> Forfeiture of assets increases the government's chances of prevailing in a prosecution and decreases the defendant's chances of escaping conviction. The *Caplin & Drysdale* Court seemed to approve of this pro-conviction tilt. But whether the tilt is good or bad depends, to a significant degree, on whether it increases or decreases the accuracy of criminal adjudication. Eliminating guilty defendants' ability to engage high-priced lawyers will decrease the risk of false negatives. At the same time, however, we might expect that eliminating innocent defendants' ability to engage high-priced lawyers will increase the number of false positives. It is difficult to evaluate the merits of this pro-conviction tilt, because one cannot know ex ante whether the defendants are guilty or innocent—all have been indicted under the same standard of probable cause.

Pamela Karlan, *Discrete and Relational Criminal Representation: The Changing Vision of the Right to Counsel*, 105 HARV. L. REV. 670, 709–10 (1992).

2. The United States Attorneys Manual includes detailed guidelines regarding the forfeiture of assets that have been transferred to an attorney for the payment of legal fees. The Manual includes the following statement of departmental policy:

> While there are no constitutional or statutory prohibitions to application of the third party forfeiture provisions to attorneys fees, the Department recognizes that attorneys, who among all third parties uniquely may be aware of the possibility of forfeiture, may not be able to meet the statutory requirements for relief for third party transferees without hampering their ability to represent their clients. In particular, requiring an attorney to bear the burden of proving lack of reasonable cause to believe that an asset was subject to forfeiture may prevent the free and open exchange of information between an attorney and a client. The Department recognizes that the proper exercise of prosecutorial discretion dictates that this be taken into consideration in applying the third party forfeiture provisions to attorney fees. Accordingly, it is the policy of the Department that application of the forfeiture provisions to attorney fees be carefully reviewed and that they be uniformly and fairly applied.

U.S. ATTORNEYS MANUAL 9–119.200 (Dec. 2002). To ensure this careful review, the Manual provides that the prior approval of the Assistant Attorney General, Criminal Division, is required before any civil or criminal proceedings may be instituted to forfeit an asset transferred to an attorney as fees for legal services. *Id.* at 9–119.202, 9–119.203.

Additional guidance relating to attorney fee forfeiture is included in the Justice Department's Criminal Resource Manual (CRM) (which is available online at http://www.usdoj.gov/usao/eousa/foia_reading_room/usam/title9/crm00000.htm.) The Criminal Resource Manual states that an asset transferred to an attorney as payment for legal fees in a criminal matter may be forfeited "where there are reasonable grounds to believe that the attorney had actual knowledge that the asset was subject to forfeiture at the time of the transfer." CRM at 2307. However, "such reasonable grounds must be based on facts and information other than compelled disclosures of confidential communications made during the course of the representation." *Id.* (In contrast, if the asset was transferred to pay for civil representation, forfeiture is allowed if the attorney knew or had "reasonable cause to know" the asset was subject to forfeiture at the time of transfer. *Id.* at 2306.) In a criminal case, the attorney must have knowledge that a particular asset is subject to forfeiture, not merely that some of a client's assets are or might be subject to forfeiture. *Id.* at 2310. An inference of such actual knowledge arises from the lawyer's knowledge that either (1) the government has asserted that the asset is subject to forfeiture, or (2) the particular asset is the product of criminal misconduct. *Id.* Note that these guidelines are set forth solely to provide internal guidance within the department, and that they "are not intended to, do not, and may not be relied upon to create any rights, substantive or procedural, enforceable at law by any party * * * ." *Id.* at 2304.

How significant do you think these guidelines are? Are they mere window dressing, or do they provide significant protection for the constitutional and policy concerns raised by attorney fee forfeiture? In making that assessment, one key question is how seriously to take internal guidelines that are not judicially enforceable. What do you think?

3. If assets that the defendant wishes to use to pay defense counsel are subject to forfeiture, may the court freeze these assets prior to trial to preserve them? In *United States v. Monsanto*, 491 U.S. 600 (1989), a companion case to *Caplin & Drysdale*, the Supreme Court concluded that the federal drug forfeiture statute authorizes a district court to enter a pretrial order freezing assets in a defendant's possession, even where the defendant seeks to use those assets to pay an attorney.

Monsanto claimed that freezing the assets in question before he was convicted—and before they were finally adjudged to be forfeitable—raised distinct constitutional concerns not addressed in *Caplin & Drysdale*. The Court rejected this contention, concluding that assets in a defendant's possession may be restrained prior to trial based on a finding of probable cause to believe that the assets are forfeitable. The Court observed that once probable cause has been established its prior decisions authorized both pretrial *seizure*—not merely restraint—of property subject to forfeiture and pretrial arrest to ensure the defendant's appearance at trial. *Caplin & Drysdale* established that the holding of these prior cases could be extended to funds that the defendant wished to use to employ counsel. As the Court explained:

> if the Government may, post-trial, forbid the use of forfeited assets to pay an attorney, then surely no constitutional violation occurs when, after probable cause is adequately established, the Government obtains an order barring a defendant from frustrating that end by dissipating his assets prior to trial.

In a footnote, however, the Court left open an important procedural question: whether the Due Process Clause requires that the court conduct a pretrial adversarial hearing on the legality of restraining such assets.

4. As the Supreme Court recognized in *Caplin & Drysdale*, forfeiture of assets can prevent defendants from retaining their choice of defense counsel. One commentator has argued that the proper response to this situation is to relax the traditional ban on contingent fee representation in criminal cases. *See* Lindsey N. Godfrey, Note, *Rethinking the Ethical Ban on Criminal Contingent Fees: A Commonsense Approach to Asset Forfeiture*, 79 Tex. L. Rev. 1699 (2001). The ABA's current rules assume contingent fees are per se unreasonable in criminal cases. Why should that be so, given that they are common in civil cases? The main objection seems to be that a lawyer whose fee depends upon an acquittal will have a strong incentive to discourage a guilty plea, even if it would be in the client's best interest. One might ask whether this is

really much different from the pressures felt by defense counsel in many other contexts, particularly those faced by public defenders and lawyers who represent indigents, on a contract basis. In each case, the lawyer has only minimal resources to conduct the defense, and will surely have an economic incentive to plead a defendant guilty, rather than undergo a costly and lengthy trial. Yet there is no ethical ban on such pressures. In any event, Godfrey argues that a relaxation of the absolute ban on contingent fees is justified in response to forfeitures that may leave the defendant in a complex case with an inadequately prepared and funded public defender.

C. THIRD PARTY CLAIMS

When the government seeks forfeiture from a criminal defendant, or civil forfeiture based upon property's relationship to a criminal offense, there are often third parties who claim an interest in the property in question. These interests can arise in many ways, and depend to some degree on the government's theory of forfeiture.

In the case of property that the government claims to be the "proceeds" of an offense, third parties often claim that they purchased the property from the defendant, or obtained a full or partial interest in it by various legal means. These claimants include not only purchasers, but also creditors who took a security interest, unsecured creditors, and even parties injured by the defendant who want to use the property to satisfy a tort judgment. These parties typically claim that the property is not subject to forfeiture because they—not the defendant—are the owners, or that their interest should be superior to the government's forfeiture claim. As explained below, some—but not all—of these third party interests will be exempt from forfeiture. Note that in addition to genuine transactions, there can also be sham transactions and transactions specifically designed to disguise the source or ownership of property. For example, in *United States v. Corchado–Peralta, supra* at 445–449, a drug trafficker sought to obscure his connection to drug proceeds by making a $700,000 "loan" to an associate who then sent him monthly loan repayments. The associate was convicted of money laundering. (For a discussion of money laundering, see Chapter 10.)

Cases in which the government claims that the property was used to "facilitate" an offense often involve the interests of the record owner of the property. These cases may involve efforts to forfeit residential properties owned by the defendant's spouse or parents, or residential property held in the defendant's name which serves as the primary residence for family members not involved in criminal activity. Other cases involve a roommate, employer, or a friend who allowed the defendant to use his house, business, car, or boat. These record owners typically claim they did not know of—or consent to—the illegal use of their property.

The civil and criminal forfeiture statutes deal with these third party claims in several ways, and the relevant doctrines and concepts—relation back, bona fide purchaser, and innocent owner—tend to overlap. These doctrines are discussed below. In addition, in cases in which third parties are unable to prove that they have a legal claim that defeats forfeiture, they may petition the Attorney General for relief in the interests of justice. *See, e.g.,* 21 U.S.C. § 853(i), reprinted *infra* at 974. Note however that relief on this ground is discretionary, not a matter of legal right. Thus a third party is much better off if she can establish that she is a bona fide purchaser or innocent owner.

1. THE "RELATION–BACK" DOCTRINE

Each of the principal forfeiture statutes now contains a "relation back" provision. The relation back doctrine is intended to perfect the government's interest in forfeitable property at the earliest possible moment—by making the government's title "relate back" to an earlier time—in order to invalidate the later claims of third party transferees. The criminal drug forfeiture provision, 21 U.S.C. § 853(c), provides that title to forfeitable property "vests in the United States upon the commission of the act giving rise to forfeiture under this section." Virtually identical language may be found in the provisions authorizing RICO forfeiture (18 U.S.C. § 1963(c)), civil drug forfeiture (21 U.S.C. § 881(h)), money laundering FIRREA forfeiture (18 U.S.C. §§ 982(b) and 981(f)), and civil and criminal forfeiture arising out of the sexual exploitation of minors (18 U.S.C. §§ 2253(b) and 2254(g)). As a result of changes adopted in 2000 that broadened the availability of forfeiture to the over 250 specified unlawful activities listed in 18 U.S.C. § 1956(c)(7), the relation back provisions apply to civil and criminal forfeitures arising out of most crimes.

However, even if the government's title does relate back, it will not necessarily defeat the claims of third parties who can establish that they are bona fide purchasers for value or innocent owners, as discussed below.

2. CRIMINAL CASES—BONA FIDE PURCHASERS FOR VALUE

In criminal cases, the relation back theory is intended to work in tandem with the provisions regarding bona fide purchasers for value (BFPs). 21 U.S.C. § 853(c), which governs criminal drug forfeitures, provides that the interest of a bona fide purchaser (BFP) for value is exempt from forfeiture:

> Any such property that is subsequently transferred to a person other than the defendant may be the subject of a special verdict of forfeiture and thereafter shall be ordered forfeited to the United States, unless the transferee establishes in a hearing pursuant to subsection (n) of this section that *he is a bona fide purchaser for value of such property who at the time of purchase was reasonably*

without cause to believe that the property was subject to forfeiture under this section. (Emphasis added.)

Similar provisions are found in the other federal criminal forfeiture statutes.

The concept of a BFP is derived from commercial law. Normally when property is transferred the receiver takes no greater title than the transferor has to give. Following that logic, as a result of the relation back doctrine a person whose property is subject to forfeiture cannot give good title. However, commercial law adopted the BFP concept as a means of protecting—and encouraging—good faith commercial transactions where the transferee has given money, goods, or services in exchange for the transferred property. Under commercial law, if a transferee who provides valuable consideration has no notice of a defect in the title, he generally takes good title as a BFP. Congress intended to incorporate this commercial law concept into the criminal forfeiture laws, and the courts have generally used commercial law cases to help flesh out the meaning of BFP in this context.

There are two elements to the definition of a BFP. First, the BFP must be a good faith purchaser for value. In this context, the concept of "purchase" generally includes an exchange of goods or services. But not every legal claim or transaction will be treated as a purchase. For example, American Express Bank sought to characterize itself as a BFP when it exercised a state law right of "set off" against $23 million of the assets of a financial institution that had defaulted on a series of foreign currency exchanges and an uncollateralized loan. After the government ordered forfeiture of the assets of the financial institution held at American Express Bank, American Express Bank transferred over $199 million of assets, but sought to retain the $23 million owed to it by the defaulting institution. The court adjudicating the forfeiture proceeding against the defaulting financial institution rejected the claim that American Express had made a purchase, concluding that a state law right to set off against accounts for debts owed was "both functionally and legally different from the purchase of a tangible asset. ... All the bank acquired through its contractual dealings ... was a cause of action for breach of contract and a right of set off under New York law." The acquisition of these legal rights was not a purchase within the meaning of Subsection (1)(6)(B). *United States v. BCCI Holdings*, 961 F.Supp. 287 (D.D.C. 1997).

Assuming that there has been a good faith purchase for value, the second requirement is that the third party claiming BFP status did not have reason to believe that the property was subject to forfeiture at the time of the purchase. The standard is whether at that time a reasonable person would have been on notice that the property was subject to forfeiture, based on personal knowledge, as well as other information—including legal actions such as the listing of the property in an indictment or restraining order, and even media reports.

Although many forfeitures involve relatively small sums, others are very large and involve numerous third party claimants. The most spectacular example to date was the arose from a RICO prosecution of BCCI Holdings, an international banking network with branches in 69 countries. The "largest bank failure in history" led to the forfeiture of $1.2 billion in assets in the U.S., and 175 third party claims, most of which fell into five categories: (1) liquidators of the BCCI overseas branches, who tried to obtain BCCI property in the U.S. for distribution to their local creditors; (2) depositors who wanted to recover their deposits abroad from BCCI property in the U.S.; (3) commercial banks whose wire transfers through BCCI had been interrupted by the initial federal seizure; (4) tort claimants against BCCI; and (5) trade creditors. *See United States v. BCCI Holdings (Luxembourg), S.A.*, 69 F. Supp. 2d 36 (D.D.C. 1999). This decision, which represents the court's final order of forfeiture for the criminal case against BCCI, summarizes the major events and holdings that occurred throughout the "longest-running forfeiture proceeding in the history of federal racketeering law."

The *BCCI* court held that unsecured creditors are not bona fide purchasers "because they did not acquire an interest in the defendant's property, they acquired only a contractual debt." Congress subsequently endorsed this approach in civil cases. *See* 18 U.S.C. § 983(d)(6)(B).

Claimants who did not acquire property through a purchase or sale cannot qualify as BFPs, even if they might have a good argument, as a matter of policy, that they should be entitled to some of the assets the government is seeking to forfeit. For example, in *United States v. Lavin*, 942 F.2d 177 (3rd Cir. 1991), the victim of an embezzlement scheme claimed to be a BFP when the embezzler was convicted of drug trafficking and the government sought to forfeit the drug proceeds. The victim had previously won a default judgment against the defendant for the embezzlement, and now claimed an interest in the defendant's assets. The court rejected this claim, noting that the BFP provisions were enacted to promote and encourage voluntary commercial dealings, not to protect the interests of all third parties. The victim of the embezzlement had not voluntarily engaged in a commercial exchange with the drug trafficker, and thus could not claim the protection afforded to BFPs.

3. CIVIL CASES—INNOCENT OWNERS

Unlike the BFP concept, which applies to property transferred AFTER the crime occurs, the innocent owner concept was originally associated with cases where the third party's interest predated the criminal offense. The paradigm case involves the defendant's use of a third party's property to "facilitate" a drug offense. Many of the cases concern real property where drug transactions occurred, and cars, boats, or planes that were used to transfer drugs. Since this property is owned by a third party, the issue arises in civil forfeiture cases in which the government proceeds directly against the property. To understand why this issue arises in *civil* forfeiture proceedings, think again about the difference between civil forfeiture, where the government brings suit against the asset itself, and a criminal case, where the court exercises personal jurisdiction over one or more individual defendants. Since the court has jurisdiction over a defendant in a criminal case, its judgment can include imprisonment, a fine, or criminal forfeiture. But only property of which the defendant is the owner—in whole or part—can be forfeited in a criminal case. The court has no jurisdiction over property owned by third parties, even if the defendant used it to facilitate an offense. If the government wants to forfeit the property in this situation, it must use civil forfeiture.

In 2000 Congress enacted the Civil Asset Forfeiture Reform Act (CAFRA), which adopted a uniform definition of "innocent owner" (with only a small number of minor forfeiture provisions carved out). It clarifies and extends the innocent owner concept, and adopts a bifurcated definition. 18 U.S.C. § 983(d).

a. The Core Innocent Owner Provisions

The first prong of the CAFRA definition applies in the traditional innocent owner situation. It defines an innocent owner as one who either—

> (i) did not know of the conduct giving rise to the forfeiture; or

> (ii) upon learning of the conduct giving rise to the forfeiture, did all that reasonably could be expected under the circumstances to terminate such use of the property.

18 U.S.C. § 983(d)(2)(A). CAFRA also describes conduct that may constitute such reasonable steps as (1) giving timely notice to a law enforcement agency, *and* (2) in a timely fashion revoking or attempting to revoke permission to use the property or taking reasonable efforts to discourage illegal use of the property in consultation with a law enforcement agency. 18 U.S.C. § 983(d)(2)(B). Finally, CAFRA provides that a person is not required to take any steps that he or she reasonably believes would likely to subject someone to physical danger. *Id.* This prong of the innocent owner defense allows the parents whose child committed drug offenses in the family home to avoid forfeiture if the parents were aware of that conduct, but only if they gave notice to law enforcement authorities and took steps to terminate the illegal use of their home. *Compare United States v. Two Parcels of Property Located at 19 and 25 Castle Street*, 31 F.3d 35 (2d Cir. 1994) (pre CAFRA case holding that parents took insufficient action to prevent their children from using parents' apartment for drug dealing because they failed to undertake "every reasonable means," including conducting searches of the premises to check for narcotics). On the other hand, CAFRA also makes clear that a wife who has been the victim of domestic abuse by a husband who is selling drugs from their home need not risk her physical safety to avoid the forfeiture of her home or other property, even if she knows that the property is being used to facilitate drug trafficking.

The innocent owner defense is also relevant in a variety of commercial contexts, and the potential for forfeiture can affect routine commercial transactions. If a bank lends money to a person who is subsequently identified as drug dealer, the collateral securing the loan may be forfeited unless the bank can qualify as an innocent owner. As noted above, CAFRA requires that one who seeks to qualify as an innocent owner must establish that the illegality occurred without his knowledge, but it may not be sufficient for a bank to show that it did not know the borrower was involved in drug trafficking. The applicable Treasury regulations deny the innocent owner defense to a party who "should have known of the illegal use" to which his property was put unless the lender can show that it "did what reasonably could be expected to prevent the violation." 19 C.F.R. § 171.52(c)(1)(iii) (2005). This provision echoes the Supreme Court's comment in *Calero-Toledo v. Pearson Yacht Leasing Co.*, 416 U.S. 663, 688 (1974), that the application of forfeiture provisions to lessors, bailors, and secured creditors who are themselves innocent of wrongdoing "may have the desirable effect of inducing them to exercise greater care in transferring their property." It also raises the question whether it is good policy to shift part of the burden for waging the war on drugs to commercial lenders. For an argument that this policy will have a negligible effect on drug dealing while substantially increasing the cost of credit, see Michael D. Weiss, Note, *The Poor Tax Revisited: The Effects of Shifting the Burden of Investigating Drug Crime to Lenders*, 70 Tex. L. Rev. 717 (1992). For an exploration of the tension between forfeiture and commercial and bankruptcy law, and a discussion of the effect of forfeiture on secured and unsecured creditors, see Steven L. Schwarcz & Alan E. Rothman, *Civil Forfeiture: A Higher Form of Commercial Law?*, 62 Fordham L. Rev. 287 (1993).

b. Extending the "Innocent Owner" Concept to Include Some BFPs

The second prong of CAFRA's innocent owner defense breaks new ground by extending the concept to cases in which the owner acquired an interest in property *after* the illegal conduct occurred, defining a class of BFPs as innocent owners in civil cases. Prior to the adoption of this provision, civil forfeiture law had no BFP provision. CAFRA adopts a BFP provision for civil cases, but does so by a bit of legal alchemy, defining a BFP as an "innocent owner" for purposes of civil forfeiture. To meet this prong of the innocent owner definition, a claimant must first establish that he was a "bona fide purchaser or seller for value (including a purchaser or seller of goods or services for value)" and that he did not know and was reasonably without cause to believe that the property was subject to forfeiture. 18 U.S.C. § 983(d)(3)(A). By adopting this provision, CAFRA ensures that a third party whose rights would be protected in criminal forfeiture will also be protected in civil forfeiture proceedings.

c. Special Provisions for Residential Property

In addition, this prong of CAFRA also creates a narrow new class of innocent owner/BFPs applicable solely to cases in which the government is seeking to forfeit residential property. Even though this group did not give anything of value in exchange for the property, CAFRA defines them as BFP-innocent owners if the property in question is the claimant's primary residence, depriving her of the property would deprive her of reasonable shelter in the community for her and her dependents, the property is not—and is not traceable to—the proceeds of a criminal offense, and the claimant acquired her interest in the property through marriage, divorce, inheritance, or probate. *Id.* at (d)(3)(B). Although the intent of this provision is to protect vulnerable spouses and children, the requirements are so narrowly drafted that it is not likely to provide relief in many cases, particularly since the party claiming innocent owner status must establish that the property in question was not purchased with funds traceable to the proceeds of any criminal offense.

Prior to the adoption of CAFRA, Professor Sandra Guerra wrote about the general unwillingness of courts to apply the innocent owner defense to parents and spouses, and argued that these cases are a sign of misplaced government values:

> To the extent that forfeitures of drug-related assets remove drug proceeds from drug offenders, they may further the goal of crippling large-scale drug operations. But the forfeiture of homes used to "facilitate" drug offenses does not further this goal. The Supreme Court observed that such forfeitures of real property serve primarily to punish, not to divest a person of ill-gotten gains. Forfeitures of family homes used as the site of a drug transaction therefore punish uninvolved property owners as well as other uninvolved residents of the home. In most cases, the innocent victims of family home forfeitures are working-class, single mothers raising two generations of children, or the wives and young children of men involved in the drug trade. None of the cases have involved rich drug "kingpins."

> We have lived with the present law long enough to see its unfortunate results. Drug law enforcement has been pursued at the expense of another essential goal: the preservation of the family. In weighing the costs and benefits of the current system, it seems clear that the time has come to put the family first.

Sandra Guerra, *Family Values?: The Family as an Innocent Victim of Civil Drug Asset Forfeiture*, 81 CORNELL L. REV. 343, 391 (1996). Does CAFRA go far enough to meet these objections? If not, should Congress go further to protect families?

APPENDIX

I. CIVIL RIGHTS STATUTES

18 U.S.C. § 245. Federally protected activities

(a)(1) Nothing in this section shall be construed as indicating an intent on the part of Congress to prevent any State, any possession or Commonwealth of the United States, or the District of Columbia, from exercising jurisdiction over any offense over which it would have jurisdiction in the absence of this section, nor shall anything in this section be construed as depriving State and local law enforcement authorities of responsibility for prosecuting acts that may be violations of this section and that are violations of State and local law. No prosecution of any offense described in this section shall be undertaken by the United States except upon the certification in writing of the Attorney General, the Deputy Attorney General, the Associate Attorney General, or any Assistant Attorney General specially designated by the Attorney General that in his judgment a prosecution by the United States is in the public interest and necessary to secure substantial justice, which function of certification may not be delegated.

(2) Nothing in this subsection shall be construed to limit the authority of Federal officers, or a Federal grand jury, to investigate possible violations of this section.

(b) Whoever, whether or not acting under color of law, by force or threat of force willfully injures, intimidates or interferes with, or attempts to injure, intimidate or interfere with—

(1) any person because he is or has been, or in order to intimidate such person or any other person or any class of persons from—

(A) voting or qualifying to vote, qualifying or campaigning as a candidate for elective office, or qualifying or acting as a poll watcher, or any legally authorized election official, in any primary, special, or general election;

(B) participating in or enjoying any benefit, service, privilege, program, facility, or activity provided or administered by the United States;

(C) applying for or enjoying employment, or any perquisite thereof, by any agency of the United States;

(D) serving, or attending upon any court in connection with possible service, as a grand or petit juror in any court of the United States;

(E) participating in or enjoying the benefits of any program or activity receiving Federal financial assistance; or

(2) any person because of his race, color, religion or national origin and because he is or has been—

(A) enrolling in or attending any public school or public college;

(B) participating in or enjoying any benefit, service, privilege, program, facility or activity provided or administered by any State or subdivision thereof;

(C) applying for or enjoying employment, or any perquisite thereof, by any private employer or any agency of any State or subdivision thereof, or joining or using the services or advantages of any labor organization, hiring hall, or employment agency;

(D) serving, or attending upon any court of any State in connection with possible service, as a grand or petit juror,

(E) traveling in or using any facility of interstate commerce, or using any vehicle, terminal, or facility of any common carrier by motor, rail, water, or air;

(F) enjoying the goods, services, facilities, privileges, advantages, or accommodations of any inn, hotel, motel, or other establishment which provides lodging to transient guests, or of any restaurant, cafeteria, lunchroom, lunch counter, soda fountain, or other facility which serves the public and which is principally engaged in selling food or beverages for consumption on the premises, or of any gasoline station, or of any motion picture house, theater, concert hall, sports arena, stadium, or any other place of exhibition or entertainment which serves the public, or of any other establishment which serves the public and (i) which is located within the premises of any of the aforesaid establishments or within the premises of which is physically located any of the aforesaid establishments, and (ii) which holds itself out as serving patrons of such establishments; or

(3) during or incident to a riot or civil disorder, any person engaged in a business in commerce or affecting commerce, including, but not limited to, any person engaged in a business which sells or offers for sale to interstate travelers a substantial portion of the articles, commodities, or services which it sells or where a substantial portion of the articles or commodities which it sells or offers for sale have moved in commerce; or

(4) any person because he is or has been, or in order to intimidate such person or any other person or any class of persons from—

(A) participating, without discrimination on account of race, color, religion or national origin, in any of the benefits or activities described in subparagraphs (1)(A) through (1)(E) or subparagraphs (2)(A) through (2)(F); or

(B) affording another person or class of persons opportunity or protection to so participate; or

(5) any citizen because he is or has been, or in order to intimidate such citizen or any other citizen from lawfully aiding or encouraging other persons to participate, without discrimination on account of race, color, religion or national origin, in any of the benefits or activities described in subparagraphs (1)(A) through (1)(E) or subparagraphs (2)(A) through (2)(F), or participating lawfully in speech or peaceful assembly opposing any denial of the opportunity to so participate—

shall be fined under this title, or imprisoned not more than one year, or both; and if bodily injury results from the acts committed in violation of this section or if such acts include the use, attempted use, or threatened use of a dangerous weapon, explosives, or fire shall be fined under this title, or imprisoned not more than ten years, or both; and if death results from the acts committed in violation of this section or if such acts include kidnapping or an attempt to kidnap, aggravated sexual abuse or an attempt to commit aggravated sexual abuse, or an attempt to kill, shall be fined under this title or imprisoned for any term of years or for life, or both, or may be sentenced to death. As used in this section, the term "participating lawfully in speech or peaceful assembly" shall not mean the aiding, abetting, or inciting of other persons to riot or to commit any act of physical violence upon any individual or against any real or personal property in furtherance of a riot. Nothing in subparagraph (2)(F) or (4)(A) of this subsection shall apply to the proprietor of any establishment which provides lodging to transient guests, or to any employee acting on behalf of such proprietor, with respect to the enjoyment of the goods, services, facilities, privileges, advantages, or accommodations of such establishment if such establishment is located within a building which contains not more than five rooms for rent or hire and which is actually occupied by the proprietor as his residence.

(c) Nothing in this section shall be construed so as to deter any law enforcement officer from lawfully carrying out the duties of his office; and no law enforcement officer shall be considered to be in violation of this section for lawfully carrying out the duties of his office or lawfully enforcing ordinances and laws of the United States, the District of Columbia, any of the several States, or any political subdivision of a State. For purposes of the preceding sentence, the term "law enforcement officer" means any officer of the United States, the District of Columbia, a State, or political subdivision of a State, who is empowered by law to conduct investigations of, or make arrests because of, offenses against the United States, the District of Columbia, a State, or a political subdivision of a State.

(d) For purposes of this section, the term "State" includes a State of the United States, the District of Columbia, and any commonwealth, territory, or possession of the United States.

II. CURRENCY REPORTING STATUTES

31 U.S.C. § 5313(a)

(a) When a domestic financial institution is involved in a transaction for the payment, receipt, or transfer of United States coins or currency (or other monetary instruments the Secretary of the Treasury prescribes), in an amount, denomination, or amount and denomination, or under circumstances the Secretary prescribes by regulation, the institution and any other participant in the transaction the Secretary may prescribe shall file a report on the transaction at the time and in the way the Secretary prescribes. A participant acting for another person shall make the report as the agent or bailee of the person and identify the person for whom the transaction is being made.

31 U.S.C. § 5316(a)

(a) Except as provided in subsection (c) of this section, a person or an agent or bailee of the person shall file a report under subsection (b) of this section when the person, agent, or bailee knowingly—

(1) transports, is about to transport, or has transported, monetary instruments of more than $10,000 at one time—

(A) from a place in the United States to or through a place outside the United States; or

(B) to a place in the United States from or through a place outside the United States; or

(2) receives monetary instruments of more than $10,000 at one time transported into the United States from or through a place outside the United States.

(b) A report under this section shall be filed at the time and place the Secretary of the Treasury prescribes. The report shall contain the following information to the extent the Secretary prescribes:

(1) the legal capacity in which the person filing the report is acting.

(2) the origin, destination, and route of the monetary instruments.

(3) when the monetary instruments are not legally and beneficially owned by the person transporting the instruments, or if the person transporting the instruments personally is not going to use them, the identity of the person that gave the instruments to the person transporting them, the identity of the person who is to receive them, or both.

(4) the amount and kind of monetary instruments transported.

(5) additional information.

(c) This section or a regulation under this section does not apply to a common carrier of passengers when a passenger possesses a monetary instrument, or to a common carrier of goods if the shipper does not declare the instrument.

(d) Cumulation of closely related events.—The Secretary of the Treasury may prescribe regulations under this section defining the term "at one time" for purposes of subsection (a). Such regulations may permit the cumulation of closely related events in order that such events may collectively be considered to occur at one time for the purposes of subsection (a).

III. DRUG STATUTES

21 U.S.C. § 841. Prohibited acts

(a) Unlawful acts

Except as authorized by this subchapter, it shall be unlawful for any person knowingly or intentionally—

(1) to manufacture, distribute, or dispense, or possess with intent to manufacture, distribute, or dispense, a controlled substance; or

(2) to create, distribute, or dispense, or possess with intent to distribute or dispense, a counterfeit substance.

(b) Penalties

Except as otherwise provided in section 859, 860, or 861 of this title, any person who violates subsection (a) of this section shall be sentenced as follows:

(1)(A) In the case of a violation of subsection (a) of this section involving—

(i) 1 kilogram or more of a mixture or substance containing a detectable amount of heroin;

(ii) 5 kilograms or more of a mixture or substance containing a detectable amount of—

(I) coca leaves, except coca leaves and extracts of coca leaves from which cocaine, ecgonine, and derivatives of ecgonine or their salts have been removed;

(II) cocaine, its salts, optical and geometric isomers, and salts of isomers;

(III) ecgonine, its derivatives, their salts, isomers, and salts of isomers; or

(IV) any compound, mixture, or preparation which contains any quantity of any of the substances referred to in subclauses (I) through (III);

(iii) 50 grams or more of a mixture or substance described in clause (ii) which contains cocaine base;

(iv) 100 grams or more of phencyclidine (PCP) or 1 kilogram or more of a mixture or substance containing a detectable amount of phencyclidine (PCP);

(v) 10 grams or more of a mixture or substance containing a detectable amount of lysergic acid diethylamide (LSD);

(vi) 400 grams or more of a mixture or substance containing a detectable amount of N-phenyl-N-[1–(2–phenylethyl)–4–piperidinyl] propanamide or 100 grams or more of a mixture or substance containing a detectable amount of any analogue of N-phenyl-N-[1–(2–phenylethyl)–4–piperidinyl] propanamide;

(vii) 1000 kilograms or more of a mixture or substance containing a detectable amount of marijuana, or 1,000 or more marijuana plants regardless of weight; or

(viii) 50 grams or more of methamphetamine, its salts, isomers, and salts of its isomers or 500 grams or more of a mixture or substance containing a detectable amount of methamphetamine, its salts, isomers, or salts of its isomers;

such person shall be sentenced to a term of imprisonment which may not be less than 10 years or more than life and if death or serious bodily injury results from the use of such substance shall be not less than 20 years or more than life, a fine not to exceed the greater of that authorized in accordance with the provisions of Title 18, or $4,000,000 if the defendant is an individual or $10,000,000 if the defendant is other than an individual, or both. If any person commits such a violation after a prior conviction for a felony drug offense has become final, such person shall be sentenced to a term of imprisonment which may not be less than 20 years and not more than life imprisonment and if death or serious bodily injury results from the use of such substance shall be sentenced to life imprisonment, a fine not to exceed the greater of twice that authorized in accordance with the provisions of Title 18, or $8,000,000 if the defendant is an individual or $20,000,000 if the defendant is other than an individual, or both. If any person commits a violation of this subparagraph or of section 849, 859, 860, or 861 of this title after two or more prior convictions for a felony drug offense have become final, such person shall be sentenced to a mandatory term of life imprisonment without release and fined in accordance with the preceding sentence. Notwithstanding section 3583 of title 18, any sentence under this subparagraph shall, in the absence of such a prior conviction, impose a term of supervised release of at least 5 years in addition to such term of imprisonment and shall, if there was such a prior conviction, impose a term of supervised release of at least 10 years in addition to such term of imprisonment. Notwithstanding any other provision of law, the court shall not place on probation or suspend the sentence of any person sentenced under this subparagraph. No person sentenced under this subparagraph shall be eligible for parole during the term of imprisonment imposed therein.

(B) In the case of a violation of subsection (a) of this section involving—

(i) 100 grams or more of a mixture or substance containing a detectable amount of heroin;

(ii) 500 grams or more of a mixture or substance containing a detectable amount of—

(I) coca leaves, except coca leaves and extracts of coca leaves from which cocaine, ecgonine, and derivatives of ecgonine or their salts have been removed;

(II) cocaine, its salts, optical and geometric isomers, and salts of isomers;

(III) ecgonine, its derivatives, their salts, isomers, and salts of isomers; or

(IV) any compound, mixture, or preparation which contains any quantity of any of the substances referred to in subclauses (I) through (III);

(iii) 5 grams or more of a mixture or substance described in clause (ii) which contains cocaine base;

(iv) 10 grams or more of phencyclidine (PCP) or 100 grams or more of a mixture or substance containing a detectable amount of phencyclidine (PCP);

(v) 1 gram or more of a mixture or substance containing a detectable amount of lysergic acid diethylamide (LSD);

(vi) 40 grams or more of a mixture or substance containing a detectable amount of N-phenyl-N-[1–(2–phenylethyl)–4–piperidinyl] propanamide or 10 grams or more of a mixture or substance containing a detectable amount of any analogue of N-phenyl-N-[1–(2–phenylethyl)–4–piperidinyl] propanamide;

(vii) 100 kilograms or more of a mixture or substance containing a detectable amount of marijuana, or 100 or more marijuana plants regardless of weight; or

(viii) 5 grams or more of methamphetamine, its salts, isomers, and salts of its isomers or 50 grams or more of a mixture or substance containing a detectable amount of methamphetamine, its salts, isomers, or salts of its isomers;

such person shall be sentenced to a term of imprisonment which may not be less than 5 years and not more than 40 years and if death or serious bodily injury results from the use of such substance shall be not less than 20 years or more than life, a fine not to exceed the greater of that authorized in accordance with the provisions of Title 18, or $2,000,000 if the defendant is an individual or $5,000,000 if the defendant is other than an individual, or both. If any person commits such a violation after a prior conviction for a felony drug offense has become final, such person shall be sentenced to a term of imprisonment which may not be less than 10 years and not more than life imprisonment and if death or serious bodily injury results from the use of such substance shall be sentenced to life imprisonment, a fine not to exceed the greater of twice that authorized in accordance with the provisions of Title 18, or $4,000,000 if the defendant is an individual or $10,000,000 if the defendant is other than an individual, or both. Notwithstanding section 3583 of Title 18, any sentence imposed under this subparagraph shall, in the absence of such a prior conviction, include a term of supervised release of at least 4 years in addition to such term of imprisonment and shall, if there was such a prior conviction, include a term of supervised release of at least 8 years in addition to such term of imprisonment. Notwithstanding any other provision of law, the court shall not place on probation or suspend the sentence of any person sentenced under this subparagraph. No person sentenced under this subparagraph shall be eligible for parole during the term of imprisonment imposed therein.

(C) In the case of a controlled substance in schedule I or II, gamma hydroxybutyric acid (including when scheduled as an approved drug product for purposes of section 3(a)(1)(B) of the Hillory J. Farias and Samantha Reid Date–Rape Drug Prohibition Act of 2000), or 1 gram of flunitrazepam, except as provided in subparagraphs (A), (B), and (D), such person shall be sentenced to a term of imprisonment of not more than 20 years and if death or serious bodily injury results from the use of such substance shall be sentenced to a term of imprisonment of not less than twenty years or more than life, a fine not to exceed the greater of that authorized in accordance with the provisions of Title 18, or $1,000,000 if the defendant is an individual or $5,000,000 if the defendant is other than an individual, or both. If any person commits such a violation after a prior conviction for a felony drug offense has become final, such person shall be sentenced to a term of imprisonment of not more than 30 years and if death or serious bodily injury results from the use of such substance shall be sentenced to life imprisonment, a fine not to exceed the greater of twice that authorized in accordance with the provisions of Title 18, or $2,000,000 if the defendant is an individual or $10,000,000 if the defendant is other than an individual, or both. Notwithstanding section 3583 of Title 18, any sentence imposing a term of imprisonment under this paragraph shall, in the absence of such a prior conviction, impose a term of supervised release of at least 3 years in addition to such term of imprisonment and shall, if there was such a prior conviction, impose a term of supervised release of at least 6 years in addition to such term of imprisonment. Notwithstanding any other provision of law, the court shall not place on probation or suspend the sentence of any person sentenced under the provisions of this subparagraph which provide for a mandatory term of imprisonment if death or serious bodily injury results, nor shall a person so sentenced be eligible for parole during the term of such a sentence.

(D) In the case of less than 50 kilograms of marihuana, except in the case of 50 or more marihuana plants regardless of weight, 10 kilograms of hashish, or one kilogram of hashish oil or in the case of any controlled substance in schedule III (other than gamma hydroxybutyric acid), or 30 milligrams of flunitrazepam, such person shall, except as provided in paragraphs (4) and (5) of this subsection, be sentenced to a term of imprisonment of not more than 5 years, a fine not to exceed the greater of that authorized in accordance with the provisions of Title 18, or $250,000 if the defendant is an individual or $1,000,000 if the defendant is other than an individual, or both. If any person commits such a violation after a prior conviction for a felony drug offense has become final, such person shall be sentenced to a term of imprisonment of not more than 10 years, a fine not to exceed the greater of twice that authorized in accordance with the provisions of Title 18, or $500,000 if the defendant is an individual or $2,000,000 if the defendant is other than an individual, or both. Notwithstanding section 3583 of Title 18, any sentence imposing a term of imprisonment under this paragraph shall, in the absence of such a prior conviction, impose a term of supervised release of at least 2 years in addition to such term of imprisonment and shall, if there was such a prior conviction, impose a term of supervised release of at least 4 years in addition to such term of imprisonment.

(2) In the case of a controlled substance in schedule IV, such person shall be sentenced to a term of imprisonment of not more than 3 years, a fine not to exceed the greater of that authorized in accordance with the provisions of Title 18, or $250,000 if the defendant is an individual or $1,000,000 if the defendant is other than an individual, or both. If any person commits such a violation after one or more prior convictions of him for an offense punishable under this paragraph, or for a felony under any other provision of this subchapter or subchapter II of this chapter or other law of a State, the United States, or a foreign country relating to narcotic drugs, marihuana, or depressant or stimulant substances, have become final, such person shall be sentenced to a term of imprisonment of not more than 6 years, a fine not to exceed the greater of twice that authorized in accordance with the provisions of Title 18, or $500,000 if the defendant is an individual or $2,000,000 if the defendant is other than an individual, or both. Any sentence imposing a term of imprisonment under this paragraph shall, in the absence of such a prior conviction, impose a term of supervised release of at least one year in addition to such term of imprisonment and shall, if there was such a prior conviction, impose a term of supervised release of at least 2 years in addition to such term of imprisonment

(3) In the case of a controlled substance in schedule V, such person shall be sentenced to a term of imprisonment of not more than one year, a fine not to exceed the greater of that authorized in accordance with the provisions of Title 18, or $100,000 if the defendant is an individual or $250,000 if the defendant is other than an individual, or both. If any person commits such a violation after one or more convictions of him for an offense punishable under this paragraph, or for a crime under any other provision of this subchapter or subchapter II of this chapter or

other law of a State, the United States, or a foreign country relating to narcotic drugs, marihuana, or depressant or stimulant substances, have become final, such persons shall be sentenced to a term of imprisonment of not more than 2 years, a fine not to exceed the greater of twice that authorized in accordance with the provisions of Title 18, or $200,000 if the defendant is an individual or $500,000 if the defendant is other than an individual, or both.

(4) Notwithstanding paragraph (1)(D) of this subsection, any person who violates subsection (a) of this section by distributing a small amount of marihuana for no remuneration shall be treated as provided in section 844 of this title and section 3607 of Title 18.

(5) Any person who violates subsection (a) of this section by cultivating a controlled substance on Federal property shall be imprisoned as provided in this subsection and shall be fined any amount not to exceed–

(A) the amount authorized in accordance with this section;

(B) the amount authorized in accordance with the provisions of Title 18;

(C) $500,000 if the defendant is an individual; or

(D) $1,000,000 if the defendant is other than an individual;

or both.

(6) Any person who violates subsection (a), or attempts to do so, and knowingly or intentionally uses a poison, chemical, or other hazardous substance on Federal land, and, by such use–

(A) creates a serious hazard to humans, wildlife, or domestic animals,

(B) degrades or harms the environment or natural resources, or

(C) pollutes an aquifer, spring, stream, river, or body of water,

shall be fined in accordance with title 18, United States Code, or imprisoned not more than five years, or both.

(7) Penalties for distribution.

(A) In general. Whoever, with intent to commit a crime of violence, as defined in section 16 of Title 18 (including rape), against an individual, violates subsection (a) of this section by distributing a controlled substance to that individual without that individual's knowledge, shall be imprisoned not more than 20 years and fined in accordance with Title 18.

(B) Definitions. For purposes of this paragraph, the term "without that individual's knowledge" means that the individual is unaware that a substance with the ability to alter that individual's ability to appraise conduct or to decline participation in or communicate unwillingness to participate in conduct is administered to the individual.

(c) Offenses involving listed chemicals

Any person who knowingly or intentionally—

(1) possesses a listed chemical with intent to manufacture a controlled substance except as authorized by this subchapter;

(2) possesses or distributes a listed chemical knowing, or having reasonable cause to believe, that the listed chemical will be used to manufacture a controlled substance except as authorized by this subchapter; or

(3) with the intent of causing the evasion of the recordkeeping or reporting requirements of section 830 of this title, or the regulations issued under that section, receives or distributes a reportable amount of any listed chemical in units small enough so that the making of records or filing of reports under that section is not required;

shall be fined in accordance with Title 18 or imprisoned not more than 20 years in the case of a violation of paragraph (1) or (2) involving a list I chemical or not more than 10 years in the case of a violation of this subsection other than a violation of paragraph (1) or (2) involving a list I chemical, or both.

(d) Boobytraps on Federal property; penalties; "boobytrap" defined

(1) Any person who assembles, maintains, places, or causes to be placed a boobytrap on Federal property where a controlled substance is being manufactured, distributed, or dispensed shall be sentenced to a term of imprisonment for not more than 10 years and shall be fined not more than $10,000.

(2) If any person commits such a violation after 1 or more prior convictions for an offense punishable under this subsection, such person shall be sentenced to a term of imprisonment of not more than 20 years and shall be fined not more than $20,000.

(3) For the purposes of this subsection, the term "boobytrap" means any concealed or camouflaged device designed to cause bodily injury when triggered by any action of any unsuspecting person making contact with the device. Such term includes guns, ammunition, or explosive devices attached to trip wires or other triggering mechanisms, sharpened stakes, and lines or wires with hooks attached.

(e) Ten-year injunction as additional penalty

In addition to any other applicable penalty, any person convicted of a felony violation of this section relating to the receipt, distribution, manufacture, exportation, or importation of a listed chemical may be enjoined from engaging in any transaction involving a listed chemical for not more than ten years.

(f) Wrongful distribution or possession of listed chemicals

(1) Whoever knowingly distributes a listed chemical in violation of this subchapter (other than in violation of a recordkeeping or

reporting requirement of section 830 of this title) shall be fined under Title 18 or imprisoned not more than 5 years, or both.

(2) Whoever possesses any listed chemical, with knowledge that the recordkeeping or reporting requirements of section 830 of this title have not been adhered to, if, after such knowledge is acquired, such person does not take immediate steps to remedy the violation shall be fined under Title 18 or imprisoned not more than one year, or both.

21 U.S.C. § § 848. Continuing criminal enterprise

(a) Penalties; forfeitures

Any person who engages in a continuing criminal enterprise shall be sentenced to a term of imprisonment which may not be less than 20 years and which may be up to life imprisonment, to a fine not to exceed the greater of that authorized in accordance with the provisions of Title 18, or $2,000,000 if the defendant is an individual or $5,000,000 if the defendant is other than an individual, and to the forfeiture prescribed in section 853 of this chapter; except that if any person engages in such activity after one or more prior convictions of him under this section have become final, he shall be sentenced to a term of imprisonment which may not be less than 30 years and which may be up to life imprisonment, to a fine not to exceed the greater of twice the amount authorized in accordance with the provisions of Title 18, or $4,000,000 if the defendant is an individual or $10,000,000 if the defendant is other than an individual, and to the forfeiture prescribed in section 853 of this chapter.

(b) Conditions for life imprisonment for engaging in continuing criminal enterprise

Any person who engages in a continuing criminal enterprise shall be imprisoned for life and fined in accordance with subsection (a) of this section if—

(1) such person is the principal administrator, organizer, or leader of the enterprise or is one of several such principal administrators, organizers, or leaders; and

(2)(A) the violation referred to in subsection (c)(1) of this section involved at least 300 times the quantity of a substance described in subsection 841(b)(1)(B) of this title, or

(B) the enterprise, or any other enterprise in which the defendant was the principal or one of several principal administrators, organizers, or leaders, received $10 million dollars in gross receipts during any twelve-month period of its existence for the manufacture, importation, or distribution of a substance described in section 841(b)(1)(B) of this title.

(c) Continuing criminal enterprise defined

For purposes of subsection (a) of this section, a person is engaged in a continuing criminal enterprise if—

(1) he violates any provision of this subchapter or subchapter II of this chapter the punishment for which is a felony, and

(2) such violation is a part of a continuing series of violations of this subchapter or subchapter II of this chapter—

(A) which are undertaken by such person in concert with five or more other persons with respect to whom such person occupies a position of organizer, a supervisory position, or any other position of management, and

(B) from which such person obtains substantial income or resources.

(d) Suspension of sentence and probation prohibited

In the case of any sentence imposed under this section, imposition or execution of such sentence shall not be suspended, probation shall not be granted, and the Act of July 15, 1932 (D.C.Code, secs. 24–203 to 24–207), shall not apply.

(e) Death penalty

(1) In addition to the other penalties set forth in this section—

(A) any person engaging in or working in furtherance of a continuing criminal enterprise, or any person engaging in an offense punishable under section 841(b)(1)(A) or section 960(b)(1) who intentionally kills or counsels, commands, induces, procures, or causes the intentional killing of an individual and such killing results, shall be sentenced to any term of imprisonment, which shall not be less than 20 years, and which may be up to life imprisonment, or may be sentenced to death; and

(B) any person, during the commission of, in furtherance of, or while attempting to avoid apprehension, prosecution or service of a prison sentence for, a felony violation of this subchapter or subchapter II of this chapter who intentionally kills or counsels, commands, induces, procures, or causes the intentional killing of any Federal, State, or local law enforcement officer engaged in, or on account of, the performance of such officer's official duties and such killing results, shall be sentenced to any term of imprisonment, which shall not be less than 20 years, and which may be up to life imprisonment, or may be sentenced to death.

(2) As used in paragraph (1)(b), the term "law enforcement officer" means a public servant authorized by law or by a Government agency or Congress to conduct or engage in the prevention, investigation, prosecution or adjudication of an offense, and includes those engaged in corrections, probation, or parole functions.

(g) Hearing required with respect to the death penalty

A person shall be subjected to the penalty of death for any offense under this section only if a hearing is held in accordance with this section.

(h) Notice by the Government in death penalty cases

(1) Whenever the Government intends to seek the death penalty for an offense under this section for which one of the sentences provided is death, the attorney for the Government, a reasonable time before trial or acceptance by the court of a plea of guilty, shall sign and file with the court, and serve upon the defendant, a notice—

(A) that the Government in the event of conviction will seek the sentence of death; and

(B) setting forth the aggravating factors enumerated in subsection (n) of this section and any other aggravating factors which the Government will seek to prove as the basis for the death penalty.

(2) The court may permit the attorney for the Government to amend this notice for good cause shown.

(i) Hearing before court or jury

(1) When the attorney for the Government has filed a notice as required under subsection (h) of this section and the defendant is found guilty of or pleads guilty to an offense under subsection (e) of this section, the judge who presided at the trial or before whom the guilty plea was entered, or any other judge if the judge who presided at the trial or before whom the guilty plea was entered is unavailable, shall conduct a separate sentencing hearing to determine the punishment to be imposed. The hearing shall be conducted—

(A) before the jury which determined the defendant's guilt;

(B) before a jury impaneled for the purpose of the hearing if—

(i) the defendant was convicted upon a plea of guilty;

(ii) the defendant was convicted after a trial before the court sitting without a jury;

(iii) the jury which determined the defendant's guilt has been discharged for good cause; or

(iv) after initial imposition of a sentence under this section, redetermination of the sentence under this section is necessary; or

(C) before the court alone, upon the motion of the defendant and with the approval of the Government.

(2) A jury impaneled under paragraph (1)(B) shall consist of 12 members, unless, at any time before the conclusion of the hearing, the parties stipulate with the approval of the court that it shall consist of any number less than 12.

(j) Proof of aggravating and mitigating factors

Notwithstanding rule 32(c) of the Federal Rules of Criminal Procedure, when a defendant is found guilty of or pleads guilty to an offense under subsection (e) of this section, no presentence report shall be prepared. In the sentencing hearing, information may be presented as to matters relating to any of the aggravating or mitigating factors set forth in subsections (m) and (n) of this section, or any other mitigating factor or any other aggravating factor for which notice has been provided under subsection (h)(1)(B) of this section. Where information is presented relating to any of the aggravating factors set forth in subsection (n) of this section, information may be presented relating to any other aggravating factor for which notice has been provided under subsection (h)(1)(B) of this section. Information presented may include the trial transcript and exhibits if the hearing is held before a jury or judge not present during the trial, or at the trial judge's discretion. Any other information relevant to such mitigating or aggravating factors may be presented by either the Government or the defendant, regardless of its admissibility under the rules governing admission of evidence at criminal trials, except that information may be excluded if its probative value is substantially outweighed by the danger of unfair prejudice, confusion of the issues, or misleading the jury. The Government and the defendant shall be permitted to rebut any information received at the hearing and shall be given fair opportunity to present argument as to the adequacy of the information to establish the existence of any of the aggravating or mitigating factors and as to appropriateness in that case of imposing a sentence of death. The Government shall open the argument. The defendant shall be permitted to reply. The Government shall then be permitted to reply in rebuttal. The burden of establishing the existence of any aggravating factor is on the Government, and is not satisfied unless established beyond a reasonable doubt. The burden of establishing the existence of any mitigating factor is on the defendant, and is not satisfied unless established by a preponderance of the evidence.

(k) Return of findings

The jury, or if there is no jury, the court, shall consider all the information received during the hearing. It shall return special findings identifying any aggravating factors set forth in subsection (n) of this section, found to exist. If one of the aggravating factors set forth in subsection (n)(1) of this section and another of the aggravating factors set forth in paragraphs (2) through (12) of subsection (n) of this section is found to exist, a special finding identifying any other aggravating factor for which notice has been provided under subsection (h)(1)(B) of this section, may be returned. A finding with respect to a mitigating factor may be made by one or more of the members of the jury, and any member of the jury who finds the existence of a mitigating factor may consider such a factor established for purposes of this subsection, regardless of the number of jurors who concur that the factor has been established. A finding with respect to any aggravating factor must be unanimous. If an aggravating factor set forth in subsection (n)(1) of this section is not found to exist or an aggravating factor set forth in subsection (n)(1) of this section is found to exist but no other aggravating factor set forth in subsection (n) of this section is found to exist, the court shall impose a sentence, other than death, authorized by law. If an aggravating factor set forth in subsection (n)(1) of this section and one or more of the other aggravating factors set forth in subsection (n) of this section are found to exist, the jury, or if there is no jury, the court, shall then consider whether the aggravating factors found to exist sufficiently outweigh any mitigating factor or factors found to exist, or in the absence of mitigating factors, whether the aggravating factors are themselves sufficient to justify a sentence of death. Based upon this consideration, the jury by unanimous vote, or if there is no jury, the court, shall recommend that a sentence of death shall be imposed rather than a sentence of life imprisonment without possibility of release or some other lesser sentence. The jury or the court, regardless of its findings with respect to aggravating and mitigating factors, is never required to impose a death sentence and the jury shall be so instructed.

(*l*) Imposition of sentence

Upon the recommendation that the sentence of death be imposed, the court shall sentence the defendant to death. Otherwise the court shall impose a sentence, other than death, authorized by law. A sentence of death shall not be carried out upon a person who is under 18 years of age at the time the crime was committed. A sentence of death shall not be carried out upon a person who is mentally retarded. A sentence of death shall not be carried out upon a person who, as a result of mental disability—

(1) cannot understand the nature of the pending proceedings, what such person was tried for, the reason for the punishment, or the nature of the punishment; or

(2) lacks the capacity to recognize or understand facts which would make the punishment unjust or unlawful, or lacks the ability to convey such information to counsel or to the court.

(m) Mitigating factors

In determining whether a sentence of death is to be imposed on a defendant, the finder of fact shall consider mitigating factors, including the following:

(1) The defendant's capacity to appreciate the wrongfulness of the defendant's conduct or to conform conduct to the requirements of law was significantly impaired, regardless of whether the capacity was so impaired as to constitute a defense to the charge.

(2) The defendant was under unusual and substantial duress, regardless of whether the duress was of such a degree as to constitute a defense to the charge.

(3) The defendant is punishable as a principal (as defined in section 2 of Title 18) in the offense, which was committed by another, but the defendant's participation was relatively minor,

regardless of whether the participation was so minor as to constitute a defense to the charge.

(4) The defendant could not reasonably have foreseen that the defendant's conduct in the course of the commission of murder, or other offense resulting in death for which the defendant was convicted, would cause, or would create a grave risk of causing, death to any person.

(5) The defendant was youthful, although not under the age of 18.

(6) The defendant did not have a significant prior criminal record.

(7) The defendant committed the offense under severe mental or emotional disturbance.

(8) Another defendant or defendants, equally culpable in the crime, will not be punished by death.

(9) The victim consented to the criminal conduct that resulted in the victim's death.

(10) That other factors in the defendant's background or character mitigate against imposition of the death sentence.

(n) Aggravating factors for homicide

If the defendant is found guilty of or pleads guilty to an offense under subsection (e) of this section, the following aggravating factors are the only aggravating factors that shall be considered, unless notice of additional aggravating factors is provided under subsection (h)(1)(B) of this section:

(1) The defendant—

(A) intentionally killed the victim;

(B) intentionally inflicted serious bodily injury which resulted in the death of the victim;

(C) intentionally engaged in conduct intending that the victim be killed or that lethal force be employed against the victim, which resulted in the death of the victim;

(D) intentionally engaged in conduct which—

(i) the defendant knew would create a grave risk of death to a person, other than one of the participants in the offense; and

(ii) resulted in the death of the victim.

(2) The defendant has been convicted of another Federal offense, or a State offense resulting in the death of a person, for which a sentence of life imprisonment or a sentence of death was authorized by statute.

(3) The defendant has previously been convicted of two or more State or Federal offenses punishable by a term of imprisonment of

more than one year, committed on different occasions, involving the infliction of, or attempted infliction of, serious bodily injury upon another person.

(4) The defendant has previously been convicted of two or more State or Federal offenses punishable by a term of imprisonment of more than one year, committed on different occasions, involving the distribution of a controlled substance.

(5) In the commission of the offense or in escaping apprehension for a violation of subsection (e) of this section, the defendant knowingly created a grave risk of death to one or more persons in addition to the victims of the offense.

(6) The defendant procured the commission of the offense by payment, or promise of payment, of anything of pecuniary value.

(7) The defendant committed the offense as consideration for the receipt, or in the expectation of the receipt, of anything of pecuniary value.

(8) The defendant committed the offense after substantial planning and premeditation.

(9) The victim was particularly vulnerable due to old age, youth, or infirmity.

(10) The defendant had previously been convicted of violating this subchapter or subchapter II of this chapter for which a sentence of five or more years may be imposed or had previously been convicted of engaging in a continuing criminal enterprise.

(11) The violation of this title in relation to which the conduct described in subsection (e) of this section occurred was a violation of section 859 of this title.

(12) The defendant committed the offense in an especially heinous, cruel, or depraved manner in that it involved torture or serious physical abuse to the victim.

(*o*) Right of the defendant to justice without discrimination

(1) In any hearing held before a jury under this section, the court shall instruct the jury that in its consideration of whether the sentence of death is justified it shall not consider the race, color, religious beliefs, national origin, or sex of the defendant or the victim, and that the jury is not to recommend a sentence of death unless it has concluded that it would recommend a sentence of death for the crime in question no matter what the race, color, religious beliefs, national origin, or sex of the defendant, or the victim, may be. The jury shall return to the court a certificate signed by each juror that consideration of the race, color, religious beliefs, national origin, or sex of the defendant or the victim was not involved in reaching his or her individual decision, and that the individual juror would have made the same recommendation regarding a sentence for the crime in question no matter what the race, color, religious

beliefs, national origin, or sex of the defendant, or the victim, may be.

(2) Not later than one year from November 18, 1988, the Comptroller General shall conduct a study of the various procedures used by the several States for determining whether or not to impose the death penalty in particular cases, and shall report to the Congress on whether or not any or all of the various procedures create a significant risk that the race of a defendant, or the race of a victim against whom a crime was committed, influence the likelihood that defendants in those States will be sentenced to death. In conducting the study required by this paragraph, the General Accounting Office shall—

(A) use ordinary methods of statistical analysis, including methods comparable to those ruled admissible by the courts in race discrimination cases under title VII of the Civil Rights Act of 1964 [42 U.S.C.A. § 2000e et seq.];

(B) study only crimes occurring after January 1, 1976; and

(C) determine what, if any, other factors, including any relation between any aggravating or mitigating factors and the race of the victim or the defendant, may account for any evidence that the race of the defendant, or the race of the victim, influences the likelihood that defendants will be sentenced to death. In addition, the General Accounting Office shall examine separately and include in the report, death penalty cases involving crimes similar to those covered under this section.

(p) Sentencing in capital cases in which death penalty is not sought or imposed

If a person is convicted for an offense under subsection (e) of this section and the court does not impose the penalty of death, the court may impose a sentence of life imprisonment without the possibility of parole.

(q) Appeal in capital cases; counsel for financially unable defendants

(1) In any case in which the sentence of death is imposed under this section, the sentence of death shall be subject to review by the court of appeals upon appeal by the defendant. Notice of appeal must be filed within the time prescribed for appeal of judgment in section 2107 of Title 28. An appeal under this section may be consolidated with an appeal of the judgment of conviction. Such review shall have priority over all other cases.

(2) On review of the sentence, the court of appeals shall consider the record, the evidence submitted during the trial, the information submitted during the sentencing hearing, the procedures employed in the sentencing hearing, and the special findings returned under this section.

(3) The court shall affirm the sentence if it determines that—

(A) the sentence of death was not imposed under the influence of passion, prejudice, or any other arbitrary factor; and

(B) the information supports the special finding of the existence of every aggravating factor upon which the sentence was based, together with, or the failure to find, any mitigating factors as set forth or allowed in this section.

In all other cases the court shall remand the case for reconsideration under this section. The court of appeals shall state in writing the reasons for its disposition of the review of the sentence.

(4)(A) Notwithstanding any other provision of law to the contrary, in every criminal action in which a defendant is charged with a crime which may be punishable by death, a defendant who is or becomes financially unable to obtain adequate representation or investigative, expert, or other reasonably necessary services at any time either—

(i) before judgment; or

(ii) after the entry of a judgment imposing a sentence of death but before the execution of that judgment;

shall be entitled to the appointment of one or more attorneys and the furnishing of such other services in accordance with paragraphs (5), (6), (7), (8), and (9).

(B) In any post conviction proceeding under section 2254 or 2255 of Title 28, seeking to vacate or set aside a death sentence, any defendant who is or becomes financially unable to obtain adequate representation or investigative, expert, or other reasonably necessary services shall be entitled to the appointment of one or more attorneys and the furnishing of such other services in accordance with paragraphs (5), (6), (7), (8), and (9).

(5) If the appointment is made before judgment, at least one attorney so appointed must have been admitted to practice in the court in which the prosecution is to be tried for not less than five years, and must have had not less than three years experience in the actual trial of felony prosecutions in that court.

(6) If the appointment is made after judgment, at least one attorney so appointed must have been admitted to practice in the court of appeals for not less than five years, and must have had not less than three years experience in the handling of appeals in that court in felony cases.

(7) With respect to paragraphs (5) and (6), the court, for good cause, may appoint another attorney whose background, knowledge, or experience would otherwise enable him or her to properly represent the defendant, with due consideration to the seriousness of the possible penalty and to the unique and complex nature of the litigation.

(8) Unless replaced by similarly qualified counsel upon the attorney's own motion or upon motion of the defendant, each attorney so appointed shall represent the defendant throughout every subsequent stage of available judicial proceedings, including pretrial proceedings, trial, sentencing, motions for new trial, appeals, applications for writ of certiorari to the Supreme Court of the United States, and all available post-conviction process, together with applications for stays of execution and other appropriate motions and procedures, and shall also represent the defendant in such competency proceedings and proceedings for executive or other clemency as may be available to the defendant.

(9) Upon a finding that investigative, expert, or other services are reasonably necessary for the representation of the defendant, whether in connection with issues relating to guilt or the sentence, the court may authorize the defendant's attorneys to obtain such services on behalf of the defendant and, if so authorized, shall order the payment of fees and expenses therefor under paragraph (10). No ex parte proceeding, communication, or request may be considered pursuant to this section unless a proper showing is made concerning the need for confidentiality. Any such proceeding, communication, or request shall be transcribed and made a part of the record available for appellate review." for "Upon a finding in ex parte proceedings that investigative, expert or other services are reasonably necessary for the representation of the defendant, whether in connection with issues relating to guilt or sentence, the court shall authorize the defendant's attorneys to obtain such services on behalf of the defendant and shall order the payment of fees and expenses therefore, under paragraph (10). Upon a finding that timely procurement of such services could not practicably await prior authorization, the court may authorize the provision of and payment for such services nunc pro tunc.

(10)(A) Compensation shall be paid to attorneys appointed under this subsection at a rate of not more than $125 per hour for in-court and out-of-court time. Not less than 3 years after April 24, 1996, the Judicial Conference is authorized to raise the maximum for hourly payment specified in the paragraph up to the aggregate of the overall average percentages of the adjustments in the rates of pay for the General Schedule made pursuant to section 5305 of Title 5 on or after such date. After the rates are raised under the preceding sentence, such hourly range may be raised at intervals of not less than one year, up to the aggregate of the overall average percentages of such adjustments made since the last raise under this paragraph.

(B) Fees and expenses paid for investigative, expert, and other reasonably necessary services authorized under paragraph (9) shall not exceed $7,500 in any case, unless payment in excess of that limit is certified by the court, or by the United States magistrate judge, if the services were rendered in connection with the case disposed of entirely before such magistrate judge, as necessary to provide fair compensation for services of an unusual character or duration, and the amount of the excess payment is approved by the chief judge of the circuit. The chief judge of the circuit may delegate such approval authority to an active circuit judge.

(C) The amounts paid under this paragraph for services in any case shall be disclosed to the public, after the disposition of the petition.

(r) Refusal to participate by State and Federal correctional employees

No employee of any State department of corrections or the Federal Bureau of Prisons and no employee providing services to that department or bureau under contract shall be required, as a condition of that employment, or contractual obligation to be in attendance at or to participate in any execution carried out under this section if such participation is contrary to the moral or religious convictions of the employee. For purposes of this subsection, the term "participation in executions" includes personal preparation of the condemned individual and the apparatus used for execution and supervision of the activities of other personnel in carrying out such activities.

IV.   STATUTES REGULATION USE OF THE MILITARY IN LAW ENFORCEMENT

10 U.S.C. § 371. Use of information collected during military operations

(a) The Secretary of Defense may, in accordance with other applicable law, provide to Federal, State, or local civilian law enforcement officials any information collected during the normal course of military training or operations that may be relevant to a violation of any Federal or State law within the jurisdiction of such officials.

(b) The needs of civilian law enforcement officials for information shall, to the maximum extent practicable, be taken into account in the planning and execution of military training or operations.

(c) The Secretary of Defense shall ensure, to the extent consistent with national security, that intelligence information held by the Department of Defense and relevant to drug interdiction or other civilian law enforcement matters is provided promptly to appropriate civilian law enforcement officials.

10 U.S.C. § 372. Use of military equipment and facilities

(a) In general.—The Secretary of Defense may, in accordance with other applicable law, make available any equipment (including associated supplies or spare parts), base facility, or research facility of the Department of Defense to any Federal, State, or local civilian law enforcement official for law enforcement purposes.

(b) Emergencies involving chemical and biological agents.—(1) In addition to equipment and facilities described in subsection (a), the Secretary may provide an item referred to in paragraph (2) to a Federal, State, or local law enforcement or emergency response agency to prepare for or respond to an emergency involving chemical or biological agents if the Secretary determines that the item is not reasonably available from another source. The requirement for a determination that an item is not reasonably available from another source does not apply to assistance provided under section 382 of this title pursuant to a request of the Attorney General for the assistance.

(2) An item referred to in paragraph (1) is any material or expertise of the Department of Defense appropriate for use in preparing for or responding to an emergency involving chemical or biological agents, including the following:

(A) Training facilities.

(B) Sensors.

(C) Protective clothing.

(D) Antidotes.

10 U.S.C. § 373. Training and advising civilian law enforcement officials

The Secretary of Defense may, in accordance with other applicable law, make Department of Defense personnel available—

(1) to train Federal, State, and local civilian law enforcement officials in the operation and maintenance of equipment, including equipment made available under section 372 of this title; and

(2) to provide such law enforcement officials with expert advice relevant to the purposes of this chapter.

10 U.S.C. § 374. Maintenance and operation of equipment

(a) The Secretary of Defense may, in accordance with other applicable law, make Department of Defense personnel available for the maintenance of equipment for Federal, State, and local civilian law enforcement officials, including equipment made available under section 372 of this title.

(b)(1) Subject to paragraph (2) and in accordance with other applicable law, the Secretary of Defense may, upon request from the head of a Federal law enforcement agency, make Department of Defense personnel available to operate equipment (including equipment made available under section 372 of this title) with respect to—

(A) a criminal violation of a provision of law specified in paragraph (4)(A); or

(B) assistance that such agency is authorized to furnish to a State, local, or foreign government which is involved in the enforcement of similar laws.

(C) a foreign or domestic counter-terrorism operation; or

(D) a rendition of a suspected terrorist from a foreign country to the United States to stand trial.

(2) Department of Defense personnel made available to a civilian law enforcement agency under this subsection may operate equipment for the following purposes:

(A) Detection, monitoring, and communication of the movement of air and sea traffic.

(B) Aerial reconnaissance.

(C) Aerial reconnaissance.

(D) Interception of vessels or aircraft detected outside the land area of the United States for the purposes of communicating with such vessels and aircraft to direct such vessels and aircraft to go to a location designated by appropriate civilian officials.

(E) Operation of equipment to facilitate communications in connection with law enforcement programs specified in paragraph (4)(A).

(F) Subject to joint approval by the Secretary of Defense and the Attorney General (and the Secretary of State in the case of a law enforcement operation outside of the land area of the United States)—

(i) the transportation of civilian law enforcement personnel along with any other civilian or military personnel who are supporting, or conducting, a joint operation with civilian law enforcement personnel;

(ii) the operation of a base of operations for civilian law enforcement and supporting personnel; and

(iii) the transportation of suspected terrorists from foreign countries to the United States for trial (so long as the requesting Federal law enforcement agency provides all security for such transportation and maintains custody over the suspect through the duration of the transportation).

(3) Department of Defense personnel made available to operate equipment for the purpose stated in paragraph (2)(C) may continue to operate such equipment into the land area of the United States in cases involving the pursuit of vessels or aircraft where the detection began outside such land area.

(4) In this subsection:

(A) The term "Federal law enforcement agency" means a Federal agency with jurisdiction to enforce any of the following:

(i) The Controlled Substances Act (21 U.S.C. 801 et seq.) or the Controlled Substances Import and Export Act (21 U.S.C. 951 et seq.).

(ii) Any of sections 274 through 278 of the Immigration and Nationality Act (8 U.S.C. 1324–1328).

(iii) A law relating to the arrival or departure of merchandise (as defined in section 401 of the Tariff Act of 1930 (19 U.S.C. 1401) into or out of the customs territory of the United States (as defined in general note 2 of the Harmonized Tariff Schedule of the United States) or any other territory or possession of the United States.

(iv) The Maritime Drug Law Enforcement Act (46 U.S.C.App. 1901 et seq.)

(v) Any law, foreign or domestic, prohibiting terrorist activities.

(B) The term "land area of the United States" includes the land area of any territory, commonwealth, or possession of the United States.

(c) The Secretary of Defense may, in accordance with other applicable law, make Department of Defense personnel available to any Federal, State, or local civilian law enforcement agency to operate equipment for purposes other than described in subsection (b)(2) only to the extent that such support does not involve direct participation by such personnel in a civilian law enforcement operation unless such direct participation is otherwise authorized by law.

10 U.S.C. § 375. Restriction on direct participation by military personnel

The Secretary of Defense shall prescribe such regulations as may be necessary to ensure that any activity (including the provision of any equipment or facility or the assignment or detail of any personnel) under this chapter does not include or permit direct participation by a member of the Army, Navy, Air Force, or Marine Corps in a search, seizure, arrest, or other similar activity unless participation in such activity by such member is otherwise authorized by law.

10 U.S.C. § 376. Support not to affect adversely military preparedness

Support (including the provision of any equipment or facility or the assignment or detail of any personnel) may not be provided to any civilian law enforcement official under this chapter if the provision of such support will adversely affect the military preparedness of the United States. The Secretary of Defense shall prescribe such regulations as may be necessary to ensure that the provision of any such support does not adversely affect the military preparedness of the United States.

10 U.S.C. § 377. Reimbursement

(a) To the extent otherwise required by section 1535 of title 31 (popularly known as the "Economy Act") or other applicable law, the

Secretary of Defense shall require a civilian law enforcement agency to which support is provided under this chapter to reimburse the Department of Defense for that support.

(b) An agency to which support is provided under this chapter is not required to reimburse the Department of Defense for such support if such support—

(1) is provided in the normal course of military training or operations; or

(2) results in a benefit to the element of the Department of Defense providing the support that is substantially equivalent to that which would otherwise be obtained from military operations or training.

10 U.S.C. § 378. Nonpreemption of other law

Nothing in this chapter shall be construed to limit the authority of the executive branch in the use of military personnel or equipment for civilian law enforcement purposes beyond that provided by law before December 1, 1981.

10 U.S.C. § 379. Assignment of Coast Guard personnel to naval vessels for law enforcement purposes

(a) The Secretary of Defense and the Secretary of Homeland Security shall provide that there be assigned on board every appropriate surface naval vessel at sea in a drug-interdiction area members of the Coast Guard who are trained in law enforcement and have powers of the Coast Guard under title 14, including the power to make arrests and to carry out searches and seizures.

(b) Members of the Coast Guard assigned to duty on board naval vessels under this section shall perform such law enforcement functions (including drug-interdiction functions)—

(1) as may be agreed upon by the Secretary of Defense and the Secretary of Homeland Security; and

(2) as are otherwise within the jurisdiction of the Coast Guard.

(c) No fewer than 500 active duty personnel of the Coast Guard shall be assigned each fiscal year to duty under this section. However, if at any time the Secretary of Homeland Security, after consultation with the Secretary of Defense, determines that there are insufficient naval vessels available for purposes of this section, such personnel may be assigned other duty involving enforcement of laws listed in section 374(b)(4)(A) of this title.

(d) In this section, the term "drug-interdiction area" means an area outside the land area of the United States (as defined in section 374(b)(4)(B) of this title) in which the Secretary of Defense (in consultation with the Attorney General) determines that activities involving smuggling of drugs into the United States are ongoing.

V. FORFEITURE STATUTES

21 U.S.C. § 853. Criminal forfeitures

(a) Property subject to criminal forfeiture

Any person convicted of a violation of this subchapter or subchapter II of this chapter punishable by imprisonment for more than one year shall forfeit to the United States, irrespective of any provision of State law—

(1) any property constituting, or derived from, any proceeds the person obtained, directly or indirectly, as the result of such violation;

(2) any of the person's property used, or intended to be used, in any manner or part, to commit, or to facilitate the commission of, such violation; and

(3) in the case of a person convicted of engaging in a continuing criminal enterprise in violation of section 848 of this title, the person shall forfeit, in addition to any property described in paragraph (1) or (2), any of his interest in, claims against, and property or contractual rights affording a source of control over, the continuing criminal enterprise.

The court, in imposing sentence on such person, shall order, in addition to any other sentence imposed pursuant to this subchapter or subchapter II of this chapter, that the person forfeit to the United States all property described in this subsection. In lieu of a fine otherwise authorized by this part, a defendant who derives profits or other proceeds from an offense may be fined not more than twice the gross profits or other proceeds.

(b) Meaning of term "property"

Property subject to criminal forfeiture under this section includes—

(1) real property, including things growing on, affixed to, and found in land; and

(2) tangible and intangible personal property, including rights, privileges, interests, claims, and securities.

(c) Third party transfers

All right, title, and interest in property described in subsection (a) of this section vests in the United States upon the commission of the act giving rise to forfeiture under this section. Any such property that is subsequently transferred to a person other than the defendant may be the subject of a special verdict of forfeiture and thereafter shall be ordered forfeited to the United States, unless the transferee establishes in a hearing pursuant to subsection (n) of this section that he is a bona fide purchaser for value of such property who at the time of purchase was reasonably without cause to believe that the property was subject to forfeiture under this section.

(d) Rebuttable presumption

There is a rebuttable presumption at trial that any property of a person convicted of a felony under this subchapter or subchapter II of this chapter is subject to forfeiture under this section if the United States establishes by a preponderance of the evidence that—

(1) such property was acquired by such person during the period of the violation of this subchapter or subchapter II of this chapter or within a reasonable time after such period; and

(2) there was no likely source for such property other than the violation of this subchapter or subchapter II of this chapter.

(e) Protective orders

(1) Upon application of the United States, the court may enter a restraining order or injunction, require the execution of a satisfactory performance bond, or take any other action to preserve the availability of property described in subsection (a) of this section for forfeiture under this section—

(A) upon the filing of an indictment or information charging a violation of this subchapter or subchapter II of this chapter for which criminal forfeiture may be ordered under this section and alleging that the property with respect to which the order is sought would, in the event of conviction, be subject to forfeiture under this section; or

(B) prior to the filing of such an indictment or information, if, after notice to persons appearing to have an interest in the property and opportunity for a hearing, the court determines that—

(i) there is a substantial probability that the United States will prevail on the issue of forfeiture and that failure to enter the order will result in the property being destroyed, removed from the jurisdiction of the court, or otherwise made unavailable for forfeiture; and

(ii) the need to preserve the availability of the property through the entry of the requested order outweighs the hardship on any party against whom the order is to be entered:

Provided, however, That an order entered pursuant to subparagraph (B) shall be effective for not more than ninety days, unless extended by the court for good cause shown or unless an indictment or information described in subparagraph (A) has been filed.

(2) A temporary restraining order under this subsection may be entered upon application of the United States without notice or opportunity for a hearing when an information or indictment has not yet been filed with respect to the property, if the United States demonstrates that there is probable cause to believe that the property with respect to which the order is sought would, in the event of

conviction, be subject to forfeiture under this section and that provision of notice will jeopardize the availability of the property for forfeiture. Such a temporary order shall expire not more than ten days after the date on which it is entered, unless extended for good cause shown or unless the party against whom it is entered consents to an extension for a longer period. A hearing requested concerning an order entered under this paragraph shall be held at the earliest possible time and prior to the expiration of the temporary order.

(3) The court may receive and consider, at a hearing held pursuant to this subsection, evidence and information that would be inadmissible under the Federal Rules of Evidence.

(4) Order to repatriate and deposit

(A) In general

Pursuant to its authority to enter a pretrial restraining order under this section, the court may order a defendant to repatriate any property that may be seized and forfeited, and to deposit that property pending trial in the registry of the court, or with the United States Marshals Service or the Secretary of the Treasury, in an interest-bearing account, if appropriate.

(B) Failure to comply

Failure to comply with an order under this subsection, or an order to repatriate property under subsection (p) of this section, shall be punishable as a civil or criminal contempt of court, and may also result in an enhancement of the sentence of the defendant under the obstruction of justice provision of the Federal Sentencing Guidelines.

(f) Warrant of seizure

The Government may request the issuance of a warrant authorizing the seizure of property subject to forfeiture under this section in the same manner as provided for a search warrant. If the court determines that there is probable cause to believe that the property to be seized would, in the event of conviction, be subject to forfeiture and that an order under subsection (e) of this section may not be sufficient to assure the availability of the property for forfeiture, the court shall issue a warrant authorizing the seizure of such property.

(g) Execution

Upon entry of an order of forfeiture under this section, the court shall authorize the Attorney General to seize all property ordered forfeited upon such terms and conditions as the court shall deem proper. Following entry of an order declaring the property forfeited, the court may, upon application of the United States, enter such appropriate restraining orders or injunctions, require the execution of satisfactory performance bonds, appoint receivers, conservators, appraisers, accountants, or trustees, or take any other action to protect the interest of the United States in the property ordered forfeited. Any income accruing to or derived from property ordered forfeited under this section may be used to offset ordinary and necessary expenses to the property which are required by law, or which are necessary to protect the interests of the United States or third parties.

(h) Disposition of property

Following the seizure of property ordered forfeited under this section, the Attorney General shall direct the disposition of the property by sale or any other commercially feasible means, making due provision for the rights of any innocent persons. Any property right or interest not exercisable by, or transferable for value to, the United States shall expire and shall not revert to the defendant, nor shall the defendant or any person acting in concert with him or on his behalf be eligible to purchase forfeited property at any sale held by the United States. Upon application of a person, other than the defendant or a person acting in concert with him or on his behalf, the court may restrain or stay the sale or disposition of the property pending the conclusion of any appeal of the criminal case giving rise to the forfeiture, if the applicant demonstrates that proceeding with the sale or disposition of the property will result in irreparable injury, harm, or loss to him.

(i) Authority of the Attorney General

With respect to property ordered forfeited under this section, the Attorney General is authorized to—

(1) grant petitions for mitigation or remission of forfeiture, restore forfeited property to victims of a violation of this subchapter, or take any other action to protect the rights of innocent persons which is in the interest of justice and which is not inconsistent with the provisions of this section;

(2) compromise claims arising under this section;

(3) award compensation to persons providing information resulting in a forfeiture under this section;

(4) direct the disposition by the United States, in accordance with the provisions of section 881(e) of this title, of all property ordered forfeited under this section by public sale or any other commercially feasible means, making due provision for the rights of innocent persons; and

(5) take appropriate measures necessary to safeguard and maintain property ordered forfeited under this section pending its disposition.

(j) Applicability of civil forfeiture provisions

Except to the extent that they are inconsistent with the provisions of this section, the provisions of section 881(d) of this title shall apply to a criminal forfeiture under this section.

(k) Bar on intervention

Except as provided in subsection (n) of this section, no party claiming an interest in property subject to forfeiture under this section may—

(1) intervene in a trial or appeal of a criminal case involving the forfeiture of such property under this subchapter; or

(2) commence an action at law or equity against the United States concerning the validity of his alleged interest in the property subsequent to the filing of an indictment or information alleging that the property is subject to forfeiture under this section.

(*l*) Jurisdiction to enter orders

The district courts of the United States shall have jurisdiction to enter orders as provided in this section without regard to the location of any property which may be subject to forfeiture under this section or which has been ordered forfeited under this section.

(m) Depositions

In order to facilitate the identification and location of property declared forfeited and to facilitate the disposition of petitions for remission or mitigation of forfeiture, after the entry of an order declaring property forfeited to the United States, the court may, upon application of the United States, order that the testimony of any witness relating to the property forfeited be taken by deposition and that any designated book, paper, document, record, recording, or other material not privileged be produced at the same time and place, in the same manner as provided for the taking of depositions under Rule 15 of the Federal Rules of Criminal Procedure.

(n) Third party interests

(1) Following the entry of an order of forfeiture under this section, the United States shall publish notice of the order and of its intent to dispose of the property in such manner as the Attorney General may direct. The Government may also, to the extent practicable, provide direct written notice to any person known to have alleged an interest in the property that is the subject of the order of forfeiture as a substitute for published notice as to those persons so notified.

(2) Any person, other than the defendant, asserting a legal interest in property which has been ordered forfeited to the United States pursuant to this section may, within thirty days of the final publication of notice or his receipt of notice under paragraph (1), whichever is earlier, petition the court for a hearing to adjudicate the validity of his alleged interest in the property. The hearing shall be held before the court alone, without a jury.

(3) The petition shall be signed by the petitioner under penalty of perjury and shall set forth the nature and extent of the petitioner's right, title, or interest in the property, the time and circumstances of the petitioner's acquisition of the right, title, or interest

in the property, any additional facts supporting the petitioner's claim, and the relief sought.

(4) The hearing on the petition shall, to the extent practicable and consistent with the interests of justice, be held within thirty days of the filing of the petition. The court may consolidate the hearing on the petition with a hearing on any other petition filed by a person other than the defendant under this subsection.

(5) At the hearing, the petitioner may testify and present evidence and witnesses on his own behalf, and cross-examine witnesses who appear at the hearing. The United States may present evidence and witnesses in rebuttal and in defense of its claim to the property and cross-examine witnesses who appear at the hearing. In addition to testimony and evidence presented at the hearing, the court shall consider the relevant portions of the record of the criminal case which resulted in the order of forfeiture.

(6) If, after the hearing, the court determines that the petitioner has established by a preponderance of the evidence that—

(A) the petitioner has a legal right, title, or interest in the property, and such right, title, or interest renders the order of forfeiture invalid in whole or in part because the right, title, or interest was vested in the petitioner rather than the defendant or was superior to any right, title, or interest of the defendant at the time of the commission of the acts which gave rise to the forfeiture of the property under this section; or

(B) The petitioner is a bona fide purchaser for value of the right, title, or interest in the property and was at the time of purchase reasonably without cause to believe that the property was subject to forfeiture under this section;

the court shall amend the order of forfeiture in accordance with its determination.

(7) Following the court's disposition of all petitions filed under this subsection, or if no such petitions are filed following the expiration of the period provided in paragraph (2) for the filing of such petitions, the United States shall have clear title to property that is the subject of the order of forfeiture and may warrant good title to any subsequent purchaser or transferee.

(o) Construction

The provisions of this section shall be liberally construed to effectuate its remedial purposes.

(p) Forfeiture of substitute property

(1) In general

Paragraph (2) of this subsection shall apply, if any property described in subsection (a), as a result of any act or omission of the defendant—

(A) cannot be located upon the exercise of due diligence;

(B) has been transferred or sold to, or deposited with, a third party;

(C) has been placed beyond the jurisdiction of the court;

(D) has been substantially diminished in value; or

(E) has been commingled with other property which cannot be divided without difficulty.

(2) Substitute property

In any case described in any of subparagraphs (A) through (E) of paragraph (1), the court shall order the forfeiture of any other property of the defendant, up to the value of any property described in subparagraphs (A) through (E) of paragraph (1), as applicable.

(3) Return of property to jurisdiction

In the case of property described in paragraph (1)(C), the court may, in addition to any other action authorized by this subsection, order the defendant to return the property to the jurisdiction of the court so that the property may be seized and forfeited.

(q) Restitution for cleanup of clandestine laboratory sites

The court, when sentencing a defendant convicted of an offense under this subchapter or subchapter II of this chapter involving the manufacture of amphetamine or methamphetamine, shall—

(1) order restitution as provided in sections 3612 and 3664 of Title 18;

(2) order the defendant to reimburse the United States, the State or local government concerned, or both the United States and the State or local government concerned for the costs incurred by the United States or the State or local government concerned, as the case may be, for the cleanup associated with the manufacture of amphetamine or methamphetamine by the defendant; and

(3) order restitution to any person injured as a result of the offense as provided in section 3663A of Title 18.

21 U.S.C. § 881. Forfeitures

(a) Property subject

The following shall be subject to forfeiture to the United States and no property right shall exist in them:

(1) All controlled substances which have been manufactured, distributed, dispensed, or acquired in violation of this subchapter.

(2) All raw materials, products, and equipment of any kind which are used, or intended for use, in manufacturing, compounding, processing, delivering, importing, or exporting any controlled substance or listed chemical in violation of this subchapter.

(3) All property which is used, or intended for use, as a container for property described in paragraph (1), (2), or (9).

(4) All conveyances, including aircraft, vehicles, or vessels, which are used, or are intended for use, to transport, or in any manner to facilitate the transportation, sale, receipt, possession, or concealment of property described in paragraph (1), (2), or (9).

(5) All books, records, and research, including formulas, microfilm, tapes, and data which are used, or intended for use, in violation of this subchapter.

(6) All moneys, negotiable instruments, securities, or other things of value furnished or intended to be furnished by any person in exchange for a controlled substance in violation of this subchapter, all proceeds traceable to such an exchange, and all moneys, negotiable instruments, and securities used or intended to be used to facilitate any violation of this subchapter, except that no property shall be forfeited under this paragraph, to the extent of the interest of an owner, by reason of any act or omission established by that owner to have been committed or omitted without the knowledge or consent of that owner.

(7) All real property, including any right, title, and interest (including any leasehold interest) in the whole of any lot or tract of land and any appurtenances or improvements, which is used, or intended to be used, in any manner or part, to commit, or to facilitate the commission of, a violation of this subchapter punishable by more than one year's imprisonment, except that no property shall be forfeited under this paragraph, to the extent of an interest of an owner, by reason of any act or omission established by that owner to have been committed or omitted without the knowledge or consent of that owner.

(8) All controlled substances which have been possessed in violation of this subchapter.

(9) All listed chemicals, all drug manufacturing equipment, all tableting machines, all encapsulating machines, and all gelatin capsules, which have been imported, exported, manufactured, possessed, distributed, dispensed, acquired, or intended to be distributed, dispensed, acquired, imported, or exported, in violation of this subchapter or subchapter II of this chapter.

(10) Any drug paraphernalia (as defined in section 863 of this title).

(11) Any firearm (as defined in section 921 of Title 18) used or intended to be used to facilitate the transportation, sale, receipt, possession, or concealment of property described in paragraph (1) or (2) and any proceeds traceable to such property.

(b) Seizure procedures

Any property subject to forfeiture to the United States under this section may be seized by the Attorney General in the manner set forth in section 981(b) of Title 18.

(c) Custody of Attorney General

Property taken or detained under this section shall not be repleviable, but shall be deemed to be in the custody of the Attorney General, subject only to the orders and decrees of the court or the official having jurisdiction thereof. Whenever property is seized under any of the provisions of this subchapter, the Attorney General may—

(1) place the property under seal;

(2) remove the property to a place designated by him; or

(3) require that the General Services Administration take custody of the property and remove it, if practicable, to an appropriate location for disposition in accordance with law.

(d) Other laws and proceedings applicable

The provisions of law relating to the seizure, summary and judicial forfeiture, and condemnation of property for violation of the customs laws; the disposition of such property or the proceeds from the sale thereof; the remission or mitigation of such forfeitures; and the compromise of claims shall apply to seizures and forfeitures incurred, or alleged to have been incurred, under any of the provisions of this subchapter, insofar as applicable and not inconsistent with the provisions hereof; except that such duties as are imposed upon the customs officer or any other person with respect to the seizure and forfeiture of property under the customs laws shall be performed with respect to seizures and forfeitures of property under this subchapter by such officers, agents, or other persons as may be authorized or designated for that purpose by the Attorney General, except to the extent that such duties arise from seizures and forfeitures effected by any customs officer.

(e) Disposition of forfeited property

(1) Whenever property is civilly or criminally forfeited under this subchapter the Attorney General may—

(A) retain the property for official use or, in the manner provided with respect to transfers under section 1616a of Title 19, transfer the property to any Federal agency or to any State or local law enforcement agency which participated directly in the seizure or forfeiture of the property;

(B) except as provided in paragraph (4), sell, by public sale or any other commercially feasible means, any forfeited property which is not required to be destroyed by law and which is not harmful to the public;

(C) require that the General Services Administration take custody of the property and dispose of it in accordance with law;

(D) forward it to the Drug Enforcement Administration for disposition (including delivery for medical or scientific use to any Federal or State agency under regulations of the Attorney General); or

(E) transfer the forfeited personal property or the proceeds of the sale of any forfeited personal or real property to any foreign country which participated directly or indirectly in the seizure or forfeiture of the property, if such a transfer—

(i) has been agreed to by the Secretary of State;

(ii) is authorized in an international agreement between the United States and the foreign country; and

(iii) is made to a country which, if applicable, has been certified under section 2291j (b) of Title 22.

(2)(A) The proceeds from any sale under subparagraph (B) of paragraph (1) and any moneys forfeited under this title shall be used to pay—

(i) all property expenses of the proceedings for forfeiture and sale including expenses of seizure, maintenance of custody, advertising, and court costs; and

(ii) awards of up to $100,000 to any individual who provides original information which leads to the arrest and conviction of a person who kills or kidnaps a Federal drug law enforcement agent.

Any award paid for information concerning the killing or kidnapping of a Federal drug law enforcement agent, as provided in clause (ii), shall be paid at the discretion of the Attorney General.

(B) The Attorney General shall forward to the Treasurer of the United States for deposit in accordance with section 524(c) of Title 28, any amounts of such moneys and proceeds remaining after payment of the expenses provided in subparagraph (A), except that, with respect to forfeitures conducted by the Postal Service, the Postal Service shall deposit in the Postal Service Fund, under section 2003(b)(7) of Title 29, such moneys and proceeds.

(3) The Attorney General shall assure that any property transferred to a State or local law enforcement agency under paragraph (1)(A)—

(A) has a value that bears a reasonable relationship to the degree of direct participation of the State or local agency in the law enforcement effort resulting in the forfeiture, taking into account the total value of all property forfeited and the total law enforcement effort with respect to the violation of law on which the forfeiture is based; and

(B) will serve to encourage further cooperation between the recipient State or local agency and Federal law enforcement agencies.

(4)(A) With respect to real property described in subparagraph (B), if the chief executive officer of the State involved submits to the Attorney General a request for purposes of such subparagraph, the authority established in such subparagraph is in lieu of the authority established in paragraph (1)(B).

(B) In the case of property described in paragraph (1)(B) that is civilly or criminally forfeited under this subchapter, if the property is real property that is appropriate for use as a public area reserved for recreational or historic purposes or for the preservation of natural conditions, the Attorney General, upon the request of the chief executive officer of the State in which the property is located, may transfer title to the property to the State, either without charge or for a nominal charge, through a legal instrument providing that—

(i) such use will be the principal use of the property; and

(ii) title to the property reverts to the United States in the event that the property is used otherwise.

(f) Forfeiture and destruction of schedule I or II substances

(1) All controlled substances in schedule I or II that are possessed, transferred, sold, or offered for sale in violation of the provisions of this subchapter; all dangerous, toxic, or hazardous raw materials or products subject to forfeiture under subsection (a)(2) of this section; and any equipment or container subject to forfeiture under subsection (a)(2) or (3) of this section which cannot be separated safely from such raw materials or products shall be deemed contraband and seized and summarily forfeited to the United States. Similarly, all substances in schedule I or II, which are seized or come into the possession of the United States, the owners of which are unknown, shall be deemed contraband and summarily forfeited to the United States.

(2) The Attorney General may direct the destruction of all controlled substances in schedule I or II seized for violation of this subchapter; all dangerous, toxic, or hazardous raw materials or products subject to forfeiture under subsection (a)(2) of this section; and any equipment or container subject to forfeiture under subsection (a)(2) or (3) of this section which cannot be separated safely from such raw materials or products under such circumstances as the Attorney General may deem necessary.

(g) Plants

(1) All species of plants from which controlled substances in schedules I and II may be derived which have been planted or cultivated in violation of this subchapter, or of which the owners or

cultivators are unknown, or which are wild growths, may be seized and summarily forfeited to the United States.

(2) The failure, upon demand by the Attorney General or his duly authorized agent, of the person in occupancy or in control of land or premises upon which such species of plants are growing or being stored, to produce an appropriate registration, or proof that he is the holder thereof, shall constitute authority for the seizure and forfeiture.

(3) The Attorney General, or his duly authorized agent, shall have authority to enter upon any lands, or into any dwelling pursuant to a search warrant, to cut, harvest, carry off, or destroy such plants.

(h) Vesting of title in United States

All right, title, and interest in property described in subsection (a) of this section shall vest in the United States upon commission of the act giving rise to forfeiture under this section.

(i) Stay of civil forfeiture proceedings

The provisions of section 981(g) of Title 18 regarding the stay of a civil forfeiture proceeding shall apply to forfeitures under this section.

(j) Venue

In addition to the venue provided for in section 1395 of Title 28 or any other provision of law, in the case of property of a defendant charged with a violation that is the basis for forfeiture of the property under this section, a proceeding for forfeiture under this section may be brought in the judicial district in which the defendant owning such property is found or in the judicial district in which the criminal prosecution is brought.

(*l*) Agreement between Attorney General and Postal Service for performance of functions

The functions of the Attorney General under this section shall be carried out by the Postal Service pursuant to such agreement as may be entered into between the Attorney General and the Postal Service.

18 U.S.C. § 1963. Criminal penalties

(a) Whoever violates any provision of section 1962 of this chapter shall be fined under this title or imprisoned not more than 20 years (or for life if the violation is based on a racketeering activity for which the maximum penalty includes life imprisonment), or both, and shall forfeit to the United States, irrespective of any provision of State law—

(1) any interest the person has acquired or maintained in violation of section 1962;

(2) any—

(A) interest in;

(B) security of;

(C) claim against; or

(D) property or contractual right of any kind affording a source of influence over;

any enterprise which the person has established, operated, controlled, conducted, or participated in the conduct of in violation of section 1962; and

(3) any property constituting, or derived from, any proceeds which the person obtained, directly or indirectly, from racketeering activity or unlawful debt collection in violation of section 1962.

The court, in imposing sentence on such person shall order, in addition to any other sentence imposed pursuant to this section, that the person forfeit to the United States all property described in this subsection. In lieu of a fine otherwise authorized by this section, a defendant who derives profits or other proceeds from an offense may be fined not more than twice the gross profits or other proceeds.

(b) Property subject to criminal forfeiture under this section includes—

(1) real property, including things growing on, affixed to, and found in land; and

(2) tangible and intangible personal property, including rights, privileges, interests, claims and securities.

(c) All right, title, and interest in property described in subsection (a) vests in the United States upon the commission of the act giving rise to forfeiture under this section. Any such property that is subsequently transferred to a person other than the defendant may be the subject of a special verdict of forfeiture and thereafter shall be ordered forfeited to the United States, unless the transferee establishes in a hearing pursuant to subsection (l) that he is a bona fide purchaser for value of such property who at the time of purchase was reasonably without cause to believe that the property was subject to forfeiture under this section.

(d)(1) Upon application of the United States, the court may enter a restraining order or injunction, require the execution of a satisfactory performance bond, or take any other action to preserve the availability of property described in subsection (a) for forfeiture under this section—

(A) upon the filing of an indictment or information charging a violation of section 1962 of this chapter and alleging that the property with respect to which the order is sought would, in the event of conviction, be subject to forfeiture under this section; or

(B) prior to the filing of such an indictment or information, if, after notice to persons appearing to have an interest in the property and opportunity for a hearing, the court determines that—

(i) there is a substantial probability that the United States will prevail on the issue of forfeiture and that failure to enter the order will result in the property being destroyed, removed from the jurisdiction of the court, or otherwise made unavailable for forfeiture; and

(ii) the need to preserve the availability of the property through the entry of the requested order outweighs the hardship on any party against whom the order is to be entered:

Provided, however, That an order entered pursuant to subparagraph (B) shall be effective for not more than ninety days, unless extended by the court for good cause shown or unless an indictment or information described in subparagraph (A) has been filed.

(2) A temporary restraining order under this subsection may be entered upon application of the United States without notice or opportunity for a hearing when an information or indictment has not yet been filed with respect to the property, if the United States demonstrates that there is probable cause to believe that the property with respect to which the order is sought would, in the event of conviction, be subject to forfeiture under this section and that provision of notice will jeopardize the availability of the property for forfeiture. Such a temporary order shall expire not more than ten days after the date on which it is entered, unless extended for good cause shown or unless the party against whom it is entered consents to an extension for a longer period. A hearing requested concerning an order entered under this paragraph shall be held at the earliest possible time, and prior to the expiration of the temporary order.

(3) The court may receive and consider, at a hearing held pursuant to this subsection, evidence and information that would be inadmissible under the Federal Rules of Evidence.

(e) Upon conviction of a person under this section, the court shall enter a judgment of forfeiture of the property to the United States and shall also authorize the Attorney General to seize all property ordered forfeited upon such terms and conditions as the court shall deem proper. Following the entry of an order declaring the property forfeited, the court may, upon application of the United States, enter such appropriate restraining orders or injunctions, require the execution of satisfactory performance bonds, appoint receivers, conservators, appraisers, accountants, or trustees, or take any other action to protect the interest of the United States in the property ordered forfeited. Any income accruing to, or derived from, an enterprise or an interest in an enterprise which has been ordered forfeited under this section may be used to offset ordinary and necessary expenses to the enterprise which are required by law, or which are necessary to protect the interests of the United States or third parties.

(f) Following the seizure of property ordered forfeited under this section, the Attorney General shall direct the disposition of the property by sale or any other commercially feasible means, making due provision for the rights of any innocent persons. Any property right or interest not exercisable by, or transferable for value to, the United States shall expire and shall not revert to the defendant, nor shall the defendant or any person acting in concert with or on behalf of the defendant be eligible to purchase forfeited property at any sale held by the United States. Upon application of a person, other than the defendant or a person acting in concert with or on behalf of the defendant, the court may restrain or stay the sale or disposition of the property pending the conclusion of any appeal of the criminal case giving rise to the forfeiture, if the applicant demonstrates that proceeding with the sale or disposition of the property will result in irreparable injury, harm or loss to him. Notwithstanding 31 U.S.C. 3302(b), the proceeds of any sale or other disposition of property forfeited under this section and any moneys forfeited shall be used to pay all proper expenses for the forfeiture and the sale, including expenses of seizure, maintenance and custody of the property pending its disposition, advertising and court costs. The Attorney General shall deposit in the Treasury any amounts of such proceeds or moneys remaining after the payment of such expenses.

(g) With respect to property ordered forfeited under this section, the Attorney General is authorized to—

(1) grant petitions for mitigation or remission of forfeiture, restore forfeited property to victims of a violation of this chapter, or take any other action to protect the rights of innocent persons which is in the interest of justice and which is not inconsistent with the provisions of this chapter;

(2) compromise claims arising under this section;

(3) award compensation to persons providing information resulting in a forfeiture under this section;

(4) direct the disposition by the United States of all property ordered forfeited under this section by public sale or any other commercially feasible means, making due provision for the rights of innocent persons; and

(5) take appropriate measures necessary to safeguard and maintain property ordered forfeited under this section pending its disposition.

(h) The Attorney General may promulgate regulations with respect to—

(1) making reasonable efforts to provide notice to persons who may have an interest in property ordered forfeited under this section;

(2) granting petitions for remission or mitigation of forfeiture;

(3) the restitution of property to victims of an offense petitioning for remission or mitigation of forfeiture under this chapter;

(4) the disposition by the United States of forfeited property by public sale or other commercially feasible means;

(5) the maintenance and safekeeping of any property forfeited under this section pending its disposition; and

(6) the compromise of claims arising under this chapter.

Pending the promulgation of such regulations, all provisions of law relating to the disposition of property, or the proceeds from the sale thereof, or the remission or mitigation of forfeitures for violation of the customs laws, and the compromise of claims and the award of compensation to informers in respect of such forfeitures shall apply to forfeitures incurred, or alleged to have been incurred, under the provisions of this section, insofar as applicable and not inconsistent with the provisions hereof. Such duties as are imposed upon the Customs Service or any person with respect to the disposition of property under the customs law shall be performed under this chapter by the Attorney General.

(i) Except as provided in subsection (*l*), no party claiming an interest in property subject to forfeiture under this section may—

(1) intervene in a trial or appeal of a criminal case involving the forfeiture of such property under this section; or

(2) commence an action at law or equity against the United States concerning the validity of his alleged interest in the property subsequent to the filing of an indictment or information alleging that the property is subject to forfeiture under this section.

(j) The district courts of the United States shall have jurisdiction to enter orders as provided in this section without regard to the location of any property which may be subject to forfeiture under this section or which has been ordered forfeited under this section.

(k) In order to facilitate the identification or location of property declared forfeited and to facilitate the disposition of petitions for remission or mitigation of forfeiture, after the entry of an order declaring property forfeited to the United States the court may, upon application of the United States, order that the testimony of any witness relating to the property forfeited be taken by deposition and that any designated book, paper, document, record, recording, or other material not privileged be produced at the same time and place, in the same manner as provided for the taking of depositions under Rule 15 of the Federal Rules of Criminal Procedure.

(*l*)(1) Following the entry of an order of forfeiture under this section, the United States shall publish notice of the order and of its intent to dispose of the property in such manner as the Attorney General may direct. The Government may also, to the extent practicable, provide direct written notice to any person known to have alleged an interest in the property that is the subject of the order of forfeiture as a substitute for published notice as to those persons so notified.

(2) Any person, other than the defendant, asserting a legal interest in property which has been ordered forfeited to the United States pursuant to this section may, within thirty days of the final publication of notice or his receipt of notice under paragraph (1), whichever is

earlier, petition the court for a hearing to adjudicate the validity of his alleged interest in the property. The hearing shall be held before the court alone, without a jury.

(3) The petition shall be signed by the petitioner under penalty of perjury and shall set forth the nature and extent of the petitioner's right, title, or interest in the property, the time and circumstances of the petitioner's acquisition of the right, title, or interest in the property, any additional facts supporting the petitioner's claim, and the relief sought.

(4) The hearing on the petition shall, to the extent practicable and consistent with the interests of justice, be held within thirty days of the filing of the petition. The court may consolidate the hearing on the petition with a hearing on any other petition filed by a person other than the defendant under this subsection.

(5) At the hearing, the petitioner may testify and present evidence and witnesses on his own behalf, and cross-examine witnesses who appear at the hearing. The United States may present evidence and witnesses in rebuttal and in defense of its claim to the property and cross-examine witnesses who appear at the hearing. In addition to testimony and evidence presented at the hearing, the court shall consider the relevant portions of the record of the criminal case which resulted in the order of forfeiture.

(6) If, after the hearing, the court determines that the petitioner has established by a preponderance of the evidence that—

> (A) the petitioner has a legal right, title, or interest in the property, and such right, title, or interest renders the order of forfeiture invalid in whole or in part because the right, title, or interest was vested in the petitioner rather than the defendant or was superior to any right, title, or interest of the defendant at the time of the commission of the acts which gave rise to the forfeiture of the property under this section; or

> (B) the petitioner is a bona fide purchaser for value of the right, title, or interest in the property and was at the time of purchase reasonably without cause to believe that the property was subject to forfeiture under this section;

the court shall amend the order of forfeiture in accordance with its determination.

(7) Following the court's disposition of all petitions filed under this subsection, or if no such petitions are filed following the expiration of the period provided in paragraph (2) for the filing of such petitions, the United States shall have clear title to property that is the subject of the order of forfeiture and may warrant good title to any subsequent purchaser or transferee.

(m) If any of the property described in subsection (a), as a result of any act or omission of the defendant—

> (1) cannot be located upon the exercise of due diligence;

(2) has been transferred or sold to, or deposited with, a third party;

(3) has been placed beyond the jurisdiction of the court;

(4) has been substantially diminished in value; or

(5) has been commingled with other property which cannot be divided without difficulty;

the court shall order the forfeiture of any other property of the defendant up to the value of any property described in paragraphs (1) through (5).

VI. SENTENCING STATUTES AND GUIDELINES

Sentencing Statutes–*Booker* Appendix

The following two provisions were included in the Appendix to Justice Breyer's opinion for the majority on the remedial issues in *United States v. Booker*. For the remainder of Justice Breyer's opinion and accompanying Appendix, see 854–64.

Title 18 U.S.C.A. § 3553(b)(1) (Supp.2004)

(b) Application of guidelines in imposing a sentence.—

(1) In general.—Except as provided in paragraph (2), the court shall impose a sentence of the kind, and within the range, referred to in subsection (a)(4) unless the court finds that there exists an aggravating or mitigating circumstance of a kind, or to a degree, not adequately taken into consideration by the Sentencing Commission in formulating the guidelines that should result in a sentence different from that described. In determining whether a circumstance was adequately taken into consideration, the court shall consider only the sentencing guidelines, policy statements, and official commentary of the Sentencing Commission. In the absence of an applicable sentencing guideline, the court shall impose an appropriate sentence, having due regard for the purposes set forth in subsection (a)(2). In the absence of an applicable sentencing guideline in the case of an offense other than a petty offense, the court shall also have due regard for the relationship of the sentence imposed to sentences prescribed by guidelines applicable to similar offenses and offenders, and to the applicable policy statements of the Sentencing Commission."

Title 18 U.S.C.A. § 3742(e) (main ed. and Supp.2004)

(e) Consideration.—Upon review of the record, the court of appeals shall determine whether the sentence—

(1) was imposed in violation of law;

(2) was imposed as a result of an incorrect application of the sentencing guidelines;

(3) is outside the applicable guideline range, and

(A) the district court failed to provide the written statement of reasons required by section 3553(c);

(B) the sentence departs from the applicable guideline range based on a factor that—

(i) does not advance the objectives set forth in section 3553(a)(2); or

(ii) is not authorized under section 3553(b); or

(iii) is not justified by the facts of the case; or

(C) the sentence departs to an unreasonable degree from the applicable guidelines range, having regard for the factors to be considered in imposing a sentence, as set forth in section 3553(a) of this title and the reasons for the imposition of the particular sentence, as stated by the district court pursuant to the provisions of section 3553(c); or

(4) was imposed for an offense for which there is no applicable sentencing guideline and is plainly unreasonable.

The court of appeals shall give due regard to the opportunity of the district court to judge the credibility of the witnesses, and shall accept the findings of fact of the district court unless they are clearly erroneous and, except with respect to determinations under subsection (3)(A) or (3)(B), shall give due deference to the district court's application of the guidelines to the facts. With respect to determinations under subsection (3)(A) or (3)(B), the court of appeals shall review de novo the district court's application of the guidelines to the facts.

§ 1B1.3. Relevant Conduct (Factors that Determine the Guideline Range)

(a) *Chapters Two (Offense Conduct) and Three (Adjustments).* Unless otherwise specified, (i) the base offense level where the guideline specifies more than one base offense level, (ii) specific offense characteristics and (iii) cross references in Chapter Two, and (iv) adjustments in Chapter Three, shall be determined on the basis of the following:

(1)(A) all acts and omissions committed, aided, abetted, counseled, commanded, induced, procured, or willfully caused by the defendant; and

(B) in the case of a jointly undertaken criminal activity (a criminal plan, scheme, endeavor, or enterprise undertaken by the defendant in concert with others, whether or not charged as a conspiracy), all reasonably foreseeable acts and omissions of others in furtherance of the jointly undertaken criminal activity,

that occurred during the commission of the offense of conviction, in preparation for that offense, or in the course of attempting to avoid detection or responsibility for that offense;

(2) solely with respect to offenses of a character for which § 3D1.2(d) would require grouping of multiple counts, all acts and

omissions described in subdivisions (1)(A) and (1)(B) above that were part of the same course of conduct or common scheme or plan as the offense of conviction;

(3) all harm that resulted from the acts and omissions specified in subsections (a)(1) and (a)(2) above, and all harm that was the object of such acts and omissions; and

(4) any other information specified in the applicable guideline.

(b) *Chapters Four (Criminal History and Criminal Livelihood) and Five (Determining the Sentence).* Factors in Chapters Four and Five that establish the guideline range shall be determined on the basis of the conduct and information specified in the respective guidelines.

Commentary

1. Application Notes:

1. The principles and limits of sentencing accountability under this guideline are not always the same as the principles and limits of criminal liability. Under subsections (a)(1) and (a)(2), the focus is on the specific acts and omissions for which the defendant is to be held accountable in determining the applicable guideline range, rather than on whether the defendant is criminally liable for an offense as a principal, accomplice, or conspirator.

2. A "jointly undertaken criminal activity" is a criminal plan, scheme, endeavor, or enterprise undertaken by the defendant in concert with others, whether or not charged as a conspiracy.

In the case of a jointly undertaken criminal activity, subsection (a)(1)(B) provides that a defendant is accountable for the conduct (acts and omissions) of others that was both:

(i) in furtherance of the jointly undertaken criminal activity; and

(ii) reasonably foreseeable in connection with that criminal activity.

Because a count may be worded broadly and include the conduct of many participants over a period of time, the scope of the criminal activity jointly undertaken by the defendant (the "jointly undertaken criminal activity") is not necessarily the same as the scope of the entire conspiracy, and hence relevant conduct is not necessarily the same for every participant. In order to determine the defendant's accountability for the conduct of others under subsection (a)(1)(B), the court must first determine the scope of the criminal activity the particular defendant agreed to jointly undertake (*i.e.*, the scope of the specific conduct and objectives embraced by the defendant's agreement). The conduct of others that was both in furtherance of, and reasonably foreseeable in connection with, the criminal activity jointly undertaken by the defendant is relevant conduct under this provision. The conduct of others that was not in furtherance of the criminal activity jointly undertaken by the defendant, or was not reasonably foreseeable in connection with that criminal activity, is not relevant conduct under this provision.

In determining the scope of the criminal activity that the particular defendant agreed to jointly undertake (*i.e.*, the scope of the specific conduct and objectives embraced by the defendant's agreement), the court may consider any explicit agreement or implicit agreement fairly inferred from the conduct of the defendant and others.

Note that the criminal activity that the defendant agreed to jointly undertake, and the reasonably foreseeable conduct of others in further-ance of that criminal activity, are not necessarily identical. For example, two defendants agree to commit a robbery and, during the course of that robbery, the first defendant assaults and injures a victim. The second defendant is accountable for the assault and injury to the victim (even if the second defendant had not agreed to the assault and had cautioned the first defendant to be careful not to hurt anyone) because the assaultive conduct was in furtherance of the jointly undertaken criminal activity (the robbery) and was reasonably foreseeable in connection with that criminal activity (given the nature of the offense).

With respect to offenses involving contraband (including controlled substances), the defendant is accountable for all quantities of contraband with which he was directly involved and, in the case of a jointly undertaken criminal activity, all reasonably foreseeable quantities of contraband that were within the scope of the criminal activity that he jointly undertook.

The requirement of reasonable foreseeability applies only in respect to the conduct (*i.e.*, acts and omissions) of others under subsection (a)(1)(B). It does not apply to conduct that the defendant personally undertakes, aids, abets, counsels, commands, induces, procures, or will-fully causes; such conduct is addressed under subsection (a)(1)(A).

A defendant's relevant conduct does not include the conduct of members of a conspiracy prior to the defendant joining the conspiracy, even if the defendant knows of that conduct (*e.g.*:, in the case of a defendant who joins an ongoing drug distribution conspiracy knowing that it had been selling two kilograms of cocaine per week, the cocaine sold prior to the defendant joining the conspiracy is not included as relevant conduct in determining the defendant's offense level). The Commission does not foreclose the possibility that there may be some unusual set of circumstances in which the exclusion of such conduct may not adequately reflect the defendant's culpability; in such a case, an upward departure may be warranted.

Illustrations of Conduct for Which the Defendant is Accountable

* * *

9. "Common scheme or plan" and "same course of conduct" are two closely related concepts.

(A) *Common scheme or plan.* For two or more offenses to constitute part of a common scheme or plan, they must be substantially connected to each other by at least one common factor, such as common victims, common accomplices, common purpose, or similar *modus operandi.* For example, the conduct of five defendants who together defrauded a group of investors by computer manipulations that unlawfully transferred funds over an eighteen-month period would qualify as a common scheme or plan on the basis of any of the above listed factors; *i.e.,* the commonality of victims (the same investors were defrauded on an ongoing basis), commonality of offenders (the conduct constituted an ongoing conspiracy), commonality of purpose (to defraud the group of investors), or similarity of *modus operandi* (the same or similar computer manipulations were used to execute the scheme).

(B) *Same course of conduct.* Offenses that do not qualify as part of a common scheme or plan may nonetheless qualify as part of the same course of conduct if they are sufficiently connected or related to each other as to warrant the conclusion that they are part of a single episode, spree, or ongoing series of offenses. Factors that are appropriate to the determination of whether offenses are sufficiently connected or related to each other to be considered as part of the same course of conduct include the degree of similarity of the offenses, the regularity (repetitions) of the offenses, and the time interval between the offenses. When one of the above factors is absent, a stronger presence of at least one of the other factors is required. For example, where the conduct alleged to be relevant is relatively remote to the offense of conviction, a stronger showing of similarity or regularity is necessary to compensate for the absence of temporal proximity. The nature of the offenses may also be a relevant consideration (*e.g.*:, a defendant's failure to file tax returns in three consecutive years appropriately would be considered as part of the same course of conduct because such returns are only required at yearly intervals).

10. In the case of solicitation, misprision, or accessory after the fact, the conduct for which the defendant is accountable includes all conduct relevant to determining the offense level for the underlying offense that was known, or reasonably should have been known, by the defendant.

Background: This section prescribes rules for determining the applicable guideline sentencing range, whereas § 1B1.4 (Information to be Used in Imposing Sentence) governs the range of information that the court may consider in adjudging sentence once the guideline sentencing range has been determined. Conduct that is not formally charged or is not an element of the offense of conviction may enter into the determination of the applicable guideline sentencing range. The range of information that may be considered at sentencing is broader than the range of information upon which the applicable sentencing range is determined.

Subsection (a) establishes a rule of construction by specifying, in the absence of more explicit instructions in the context of a specific guideline, the range of conduct that is relevant to determining the applicable offense level (except for the determination of the applicable offense guideline, which is governed by § 1B1.2(a)). No such rule of construction is necessary with respect to Chapters Four and Five because the guidelines in those Chapters are explicit as to the specific factors to be considered.

Subsection (a)(2) provides for consideration of a broader range of conduct with respect to one class of offenses, primarily certain property, tax, fraud and drug offenses for which the guidelines depend substantially on quantity, than with respect to other offenses such as assault, robbery and burglary. The distinction is made on the basis of § 3D1.2(d), which provides for grouping together (*i.e.*, treating as a single count) all counts charging offenses of a type covered by this subsection. However, the applicability of subsection (a)(2) does not depend upon whether multiple counts are alleged. Thus, in an embezzlement case, for example, embezzled funds that may not be specified in any count of conviction are nonetheless included in determining the offense level if they were part of the same course of conduct or part of the same scheme or plan as the count of conviction. Similarly, in a drug distribution case, quantities and types of drugs not specified in the count of conviction are to be included in determining the offense level if they were part of the same course of conduct or part of a common scheme or plan as the count of conviction. On the other hand, in a robbery case in which the defendant robbed two banks, the amount of money taken in one robbery would not be taken into account in determining the guideline range for the other robbery, even if both robberies were part of a single course of conduct or the same scheme or plan. (This is true whether the defendant is convicted of one or both robberies.)

Subsections (a)(1) and (a)(2) adopt different rules because offenses of the character dealt with in subsection (a)(2) (*i.e.*, to which § 3D1.2(d) applies) often involve a pattern of misconduct that cannot readily be broken into discrete, identifiable units that are meaningful for purposes of sentencing. For example, a pattern of embezzlement may consist of several acts of taking that cannot separately be identified, even though the overall conduct is clear. In addition, the distinctions that the law makes as to what constitutes separate counts or offenses often turn on technical elements that are not especially meaningful for purposes of sentencing. Thus, in a mail fraud case, the scheme is an element of the offense and each mailing may be the basis for a separate count; in an embezzlement case, each taking may provide a basis for a separate count. Another consideration is that in a pattern of small thefts, for example, it is important to take into account the full range of related conduct. Relying on the entire range of conduct, regardless of the number of counts that are alleged or on which a conviction is obtained, appears to be the most reasonable approach to writing workable guidelines for these offenses. Conversely, when § 3D1.2(d) does not apply, so that convictions on multiple counts are considered separately in determining the guideline sentencing range, the guidelines prohibit aggregation of quantities from other counts in order to prevent "double counting" of the conduct and harm from each count of conviction. Continuing offenses present similar practical problems. The reference to § 3D1.2(d), which provides for grouping of multiple counts arising out of a continuing offense when the offense guideline takes the continuing nature into account, also prevents double counting.

Subsection (a)(4) requires consideration of any other information specified in the applicable guideline. For example, § 2A1.4 (Involuntary Manslaughter) specifies consideration of the defendant's state of mind; § 2K1.4 (Arson; Property Damage By Use of Explosives) specifies consideration of the risk of harm created.

§ 3E1.1. Acceptance of Responsibility

(a) If the defendant clearly demonstrates acceptance of responsibility for his offense, decrease the offense level by **2** levels.

(b) If the defendant qualifies for a decrease under subsection (a), the offense level determined prior to the operation of subsection (a) is level **16** or greater, and upon motion of the government stating that the defendant has assisted authorities in the investigation or prosecution of his own misconduct by timely notifying authorities of his intention to enter a plea of guilty, thereby permitting the government to avoid preparing for trial and permitting the government and the court to allocate their resources efficiently, decrease the offense level by 1 additional level.

Commentary

Application Notes:

1. In determining whether a defendant qualifies under subsection (a), appropriate considerations include, but are not limited to, the following:

(a) truthfully admitting the conduct comprising the offense(s) of conviction, and truthfully admitting or not falsely denying any additional relevant conduct for which the defendant is accountable under § 1B1.3 (Relevant Conduct). Note that a defendant is not required to volunteer, or affirmatively admit, relevant conduct beyond the offense of conviction in order to obtain a reduction under subsection (a). A defendant may remain silent in respect to relevant conduct beyond the offense of conviction without affecting his ability to obtain a reduction under this subsection. However, a defendant who falsely denies, or frivolously contests, relevant conduct that the court determines to be true has acted in a manner inconsistent with acceptance of responsibility;

    (b) voluntary termination or withdrawal from criminal conduct or associations;

    (c) voluntary payment of restitution prior to adjudication of guilt;

    (d) voluntary surrender to authorities promptly after commission of the offense;

    (e) voluntary assistance to authorities in the recovery of the fruits and instrumentalities of the offense;

    (f) voluntary resignation from the office or position held during the commission of the offense;

    (g) post-offense rehabilitative efforts (e.g., counseling or drug treatment); and

    (h) the timeliness of the defendant's conduct in manifesting the acceptance of responsibility.

    2. This adjustment is not intended to apply to a defendant who puts the government to its burden of proof at trial by denying the essential factual elements of guilt, is convicted, and only then admits guilt and expresses remorse. Conviction by trial, however, does not automatically preclude a defendant from consideration for such a reduction. In rare situations a defendant may clearly demonstrate an acceptance of responsibility for his criminal conduct even though he exercises his constitutional right to a trial. This may occur, for example, where a defendant goes to trial to assert and preserve issues that do not relate to factual guilt (e.g., to make a constitutional challenge to a statute or a challenge to the applicability of a statute to his conduct). In each such instance, however, a determination that a defendant has accepted responsibility will be based primarily upon pre-trial statements and conduct.

    3. Entry of a plea of guilty prior to the commencement of trial combined with truthfully admitting the conduct comprising the offense of conviction, and truthfully admitting or not falsely denying any additional relevant conduct for which he is accountable under § 1B1.3 (Relevant Conduct) (see Application Note 1(a)), will constitute significant evidence of acceptance of responsibility for the purposes of subsection (a). However, this evidence may be outweighed by conduct of the defendant that is inconsistent with such acceptance of responsibility. A defendant who enters a guilty plea is not entitled to an adjustment under this section as a matter of right.

    4. Conduct resulting in an enhancement under § 3C1.1 (Obstructing or Impeding the Administration of Justice) ordinarily indicates that the defendant has not accepted responsibility for his criminal conduct. There may, however, be extraordinary cases in which adjustments under both §§ 3C1.1 and 3E1.1 may apply.

5. The sentencing judge is in a unique position to evaluate a defendant's acceptance of responsibility. For this reason, the determination of the sentencing judge is entitled to great deference on review.

6. Subsection (a) provides a 2–level decrease in offense level. Subsection (b) provides an additional 1–level decrease in offense level for a defendant at offense level 16 or greater prior to the operation of subsection (a) who both qualifies for a decrease under subsection (a) and who has assisted authorities in the investigation or prosecution of his own misconduct by taking the steps set forth in subsection (b). The timeliness of the defendant's acceptance of responsibility is a consideration under both subsections, and is context specific. In general, the conduct qualifying for a decrease in offense level under subsection (b) will occur particularly early in the case. For example, to qualify under subsection (b), the defendant must have notified authorities of his intention to enter a plea of guilty at a sufficiently early point in the process so that the government may avoid preparing for trial and the court may schedule its calendar efficiently.

Because the Government is in the best position to determine whether the defendant has assisted authorities in a manner that avoids preparing for trial, an adjustment under subsection (b) may only be granted upon a formal motion by the Government at the time of sentencing. See section 401(g)(2)(B) of Public Law 108–21.

Background: The reduction of offense level provided by this section recognizes legitimate societal interests. For several reasons, a defendant who clearly demonstrates acceptance of responsibility for his offense by taking, in a timely fashion, the actions listed above (or some equivalent action) is appropriately given a lower offense level than a defendant who has not demonstrated acceptance of responsibility.

Subsection (a) provides a 2–level decrease in offense level. Subsection (b) provides an additional 1–level decrease for a defendant at offense level 16 or greater prior to operation of subsection (a) who both qualifies for a decrease under subsection (a) and has assisted authorities in the investigation or prosecution of his own misconduct by taking the steps specified in subsection (b). Such a defendant has accepted responsibility in a way that ensures the certainty of his just punishment in a timely manner, thereby appropriately meriting an additional reduction. Subsection (b) does not apply, however, to a defendant whose offense level is level 15 or lower prior to application of subsection (a). At offense level 15 or lower, the reduction in the guideline range provided by a 2–level decrease in offense level under subsection (a) (which is a greater proportional reduction in the guideline range than at higher offense levels due to the structure of the Sentencing Table) is adequate for the court to take into account the factors set forth in subsection (b) within the applicable guideline range.

Section 401(g) of Public Law 108–21 directly amended subsection (b), Application Note 6 (including adding the last paragraph of that application note), and the Background Commentary, effective April 30, 2003.

§ 2B1.1.   Larceny, Embezzlement, and Other Forms of Theft; Offenses Involving Stolen Property; Property Damage or Destruction; Fraud and Deceit; Forgery; Offenses Involving Altered or Counterfeit Instruments Other than Counterfeit Bearer Obligations of the United States

(a) Base Offense Level:

(1) **7**, if (A) the defendant was convicted of an offense referenced to this guideline; and (B) that offense of conviction has a statutory maximum term of imprisonment of 20 years or more; or

(2) **6**, otherwise

(b) Specific Offense Characteristics

(1) If the loss exceeded $5,000, increase the offense level as follows:

	Loss (Apply the Greatest)	Increase in Level
(A)	$5,000 or less	no increase
(B)	More than $5,000	add **2**
(C)	More than $10,000	add **4**
(D)	More than $30,000	add **6**
(E)	More than $70,000	add **8**
(F)	More than $120,000	add **10**
(G)	More than $200,000	add **12**
(H)	More than $400,000	add **14**
(I)	More than $1,000,000	add **16**
(J)	More than $2,500,000	add **18**
(K)	More than $7,000,000	add **20**
(L)	More than $20,000,000	add **22**
(M)	More than $50,000,000	add **24**
(N)	More than $100,000,000	add **26**
(O)	More than $200,000,000	add **28**
(P)	More than $400,000,000	add **30**.

(2) (Apply the greatest) If the offense—

(A) (i) involved 10 or more victims; or (ii) was committed through mass-marketing, increase by **2** levels;

(B) involved 50 or more victims, increase by **4** levels; or

(C) involved 250 or more victims, increase by **6** levels.

(3) If the offense involved a theft from the person of another, increase by **2** levels.

(4) If the offense involved receiving stolen property, and the defendant was a person in the business of receiving and selling stolen property, increase by **2** levels.

(5) If the offense involved misappropriation of a trade secret and the defendant knew or intended that the offense would benefit a

foreign government, foreign instrumentality, or foreign agent, increase by **2** levels.

(6) If the offense involved theft of, damage to, or destruction of, property from a national cemetery, increase by **2** levels.

(7) If (A) the defendant was convicted of an offense under 18 U.S.C. § 1037; and (B) the offense involved obtaining electronic mail addresses through improper means, increase by **2** levels

(8) If the offense involved (A) a misrepresentation that the defendant was acting on behalf of a charitable, educational, religious, or political organization, or a government agency; (B) a misrepresentation or other fraudulent action during the course of a bankruptcy proceeding; (C) a violation of any prior, specific judicial or administrative order, injunction, decree, or process not addressed elsewhere in the guidelines; or (D) a misrepresentation to a consumer in connection with obtaining, providing, or furnishing financial assistance for an institution of higher education, increase by **2** levels. If the resulting offense level is less than level **10**, increase to level **10.**

(9) If (A) the defendant relocated, or participated in relocating, a fraudulent scheme to another jurisdiction to evade law enforcement or regulatory officials; (B) a substantial part of a fraudulent scheme was committed from outside the United States; or (C) the offense otherwise involved sophisticated means, increase by **2** levels. If the resulting offense level is less than level **12**, increase to level **12**.

(10) If the offense involved (A) the possession or use of any (i) device-making equipment, or (ii) authentication feature; (B) the production or trafficking of any (i) unauthorized access device or counterfeit access device, (ii) or authentication feature; or (C)(i) the unauthorized transfer or use of any means of identification unlawfully to produce or obtain any other means of identification; or (ii) the possession of 5 or more means of identification that unlawfully were produced from, or obtained by the use of, another means of identification, increase by **2** levels. If the resulting offense level is less than level **12**, increase to level **12**.

(11) If the offense involved an organized scheme to steal vehicles or vehicle parts, and the offense level is less than level **14**, increase to level **14**.

(12) If the offense involved (A) the conscious or reckless risk of death or serious bodily injury; or (B) possession of a dangerous weapon (including a firearm) in connection with the offense, increase by **2** levels. If the resulting offense level is less than level **14**, increase to level **14**.

(13) (Apply the greater) If—

(A) the defendant derived more than $1,000,000 in gross receipts from one or more financial institutions as a result of the offense, increase by **2** levels; or

(B) the offense (i) substantially jeopardized the safety and soundness of a financial institution; (ii) substantially endangered the solvency or financial security of an organization that, at any time during the offense, (I) was a publicly traded company; or (II) had 1,000 or more employees; or (iii) substantially endangered the solvency or financial security of 100 or more victims, increase by **4** levels.

(C) The cumulative adjustments from application of both subsections (b)(2) and (b)(12)(B) shall not exceed **8** levels, except as provided in subdivision (D)

(D) If the resulting offense level determined under subdivision (A) or (B) is less than level **24**, increase to level **24**.

(14)(A) (Apply the greatest) If the defendant was convicted of an offense under:

(i) 18 U.S.C. § 1030, and the offense involved (I) a computer system used to maintain or operate a critical infrastructure, or used by or for a government entity in furtherance of the administration of justice, national defense, or national security; or (II) an intent to obtain personal information, increase by **2** levels.

(ii) 18 U.S.C. § 1030(a)(5)(A)(i), increase **4** levels.

(iii) 18 U.S.C. § 1030, and the offense caused a substantial disruption of a critical infrastructure, increase by **6** levels.

(B) If subdivision (A)(iii) applies, and the offense level is less than level 24, increase to level **24**.

(15) If the offense involved—

(A) a violation of securities law and, at the time of the offense, the defendant was (i) an officer or a director of a publicly traded company; (ii) a registered broker or dealer, or a person associated with a broker or dealer; or (iii) an investment adviser, or a person associated with an investment adviser; or

(B) a violation of commodities law and, at the time of the offense, the defendant was (i) an officer or a director of a futures commission merchant or an introducing broker; (ii) a commodities trading advisor; or (iii) a commodity pool operator, increase by **4** levels.

(c) Cross References

(1) If (A) a firearm, destructive device, explosive material, or controlled substance was taken, or the taking of any such item was an object of the offense; or (B) the stolen property received, trans-

ported, transferred, transmitted, or possessed was a firearm, destructive device, explosive material, or controlled substance, apply § 2D1.1 (Unlawful Manufacturing, Importing, Exporting, or Trafficking (Including Possession with Intent to Commit These Offenses); Attempt or Conspiracy), § 2D2.1 (Unlawful Possession; Attempt or Conspiracy), § 2K1.3 (Unlawful Receipt, Possession, or Transportation of Explosive Materials; Prohibited Transactions Involving Explosive Materials), or § 2K2.1 (Unlawful Receipt, Possession, or Transportation of Firearms or Ammunition; Prohibited Transactions Involving Firearms or Ammunition), as appropriate.

(2) If the offense involved arson, or property damage by use of explosives, apply § 2K1.4 (Arson; Property Damage by Use of Explosives), if the resulting offense level is greater than that determined above.

(3) If (A) neither subdivision (1) nor (2) of this subsection applies; (B) the defendant was convicted under a statute proscribing false, fictitious, or fraudulent statements or representations generally (e.g., 18 U.S.C. § 1001, § 1341, § 1342, or § 1343); and (C) the conduct set forth in the count of conviction establishes an offense specifically covered by another guideline in Chapter Two (Offense Conduct), apply that other guideline.

(4) If the offense involved a cultural heritage resource, apply § 2B1.5 (Theft of, Damage to, or Destruction of, Cultural Heritage Resources; Unlawful Sale, Purchase, Exchange, Transportation, or Receipt of Cultural Heritage Resources), if the resulting offense level is greater than that determined above.

Commentary

Statutory Provisions: 7 U.S.C. §§ 6, 6b, 6c, 6h, 6o, 13, 23; 15 U.S.C. §§ 50, 77e, 77q, 77x, 78j, 78ff, 80b–6, 1644, 6821; 18 U.S.C. §§ 38, 225, 285–289, 471–473, 500, 510, 553(a)(1), 641, 656, 657, 659, 662, 664, 1001–1008, 1010–1014, 1016–1022, 1025, 1026, 1028, 1029, 1030(a)(4)-(5), 1031, 1341–1344, 1348, 1350, 1361, 1363, 1702, 1703 (if vandalism or malicious mischief, including destruction of mail, is involved), 1708, 1831, 1832, 1992, 1993(a)(1), (a)(4), 2113(b), 2312–2317, 2332b(a)(1); 29 U.S.C. § 501(c); 42 U.S.C. § 1011; 49 U.S.C. §§ 30170, 46317(a), 60123(b). For additional statutory provision(s), see Appendix A (Statutory Index).

Application Notes:

[The application notes are very extensive. Only a few selected provisions are included here.]

*   *   *

3. *Loss Under Subsection (b)(1).*—This application note applies to the determination of loss under subsection (b)(1).

(ii) In a case involving collateral pledged or otherwise provided by the defendant, the amount the victim has recovered at the time of sentencing from disposition of the collateral, or if the collateral has not been disposed of by that time, the fair market value of the collateral at the time of sentencing.

* * *

19. *Departure Considerations.*—

(A) *Upward Departure Considerations.*—There may be cases in which the offense level determined under this guideline substantially understates the seriousness of the offense. In such cases, an upward departure may be warranted. The following is a non-exhaustive list of factors that the court may consider in determining whether an upward departure is warranted:

(i) A primary objective of the offense was an aggravating, non-monetary objective. For example, a primary objective of the offense was to inflict emotional harm.

(ii) The offense caused or risked substantial non-monetary harm. For example, the offense caused physical harm, psychological harm, or severe emotional trauma, or resulted in a substantial invasion of a privacy interest (through, for example, the theft of personal information such as medical, educational, or financial records).

(iii) The offense involved a substantial amount of interest of any kind, finance charges, late fees, penalties, amounts based on an agreed-upon return or rate of return, or other similar costs, not included in the determination of loss for purposes of subsection (b)(1).

(iv) The offense created a risk of substantial loss beyond the loss determined for purposes of subsection (b)(1).

(v) In a case involving stolen information from a "protected computer", as defined in 18 U.S.C. § 1030(e)(2), the defendant sought the stolen information to further a broader criminal purpose.

(vi) In a case involving access devices or unlawfully produced or unlawfully obtained means of identification:

(I) The offense caused substantial harm to the victim's reputation or credit record, or the victim suffered a substantial inconvenience related to repairing the victim's reputation or a damaged credit record.

(II) An individual whose means of identification the defendant used to obtain unlawful means of identification is erroneously arrested or denied a job because an arrest record has been made in that individual's name.

(III) The defendant produced or obtained numerous means of identification with respect to one individual and essentially assumed that individual's identity.

(B) *Upward Departure for Debilitating Impact on a Critical Infrastructure.*—An upward departure would be warranted in a case in which subsection (b)(14)(iii) applies and the disruption to the critical infrastructure(s) is so substantial as to have a debilitating impact on national security, national economic security, national public health or safety, or any combination of those matters.

(C) *Downward Departure Consideration.*—There may be cases in which the offense level determined under this guideline substantially overstates the seriousness of the offense. In such cases, a downward departure may be warranted.

Background: This guideline covers offenses involving theft, stolen property, property damage or destruction, fraud, forgery, and counterfeiting (other than offenses involving altered or counterfeit bearer obligations of the United States). It also covers offenses involving altering or removing motor vehicle identification numbers, trafficking in automobiles or automobile parts with altered or obliterated identification numbers, odometer laws and regulations, obstructing correspondence, the falsification of documents or records relating to a benefit plan covered by the Employment Retirement Income Security Act, and the failure to maintain, or falsification of, documents required by the Labor Management Reporting and Disclosure Act.

Because federal fraud statutes often are broadly written, a single pattern of offense conduct usually can be prosecuted under several code sections, as a result of which the offense of conviction may be somewhat arbitrary. Furthermore, most fraud statutes cover a broad range of conduct with extreme variation in severity. The specific offense characteristics and cross references contained in this guideline are designed with these considerations in mind.

The Commission has determined that, ordinarily, the sentences of defendants convicted of federal offenses should reflect the nature and magnitude of the loss caused or intended by their crimes. Accordingly, along with other relevant factors under the guidelines, loss serves as a measure of the seriousness of the offense and the defendant's relative culpability and is a principal factor in determining the offense level under this guideline.

Theft from the person of another, such as pickpocketing or non-forcible purse-snatching, receives an enhanced sentence because of the increased risk of physical injury. This guideline does not include an enhancement for thefts from the person by means of force or fear; such crimes are robberies and are covered under § 2B3.1 (Robbery).

A minimum offense level of level 14 is provided for offenses involving an organized scheme to steal vehicles or vehicle parts. Typically, the scope of such activity is substantial, but the value of the property may be particularly difficult to ascertain in individual cases because the stolen property is rapidly resold or otherwise disposed of in the course of the offense. Therefore, the specific offense characteristic of "organized scheme" is used as an alternative to "loss" in setting a minimum offense level.

Use of false pretenses involving charitable causes and government agencies enhances the sentences of defendants who take advantage of victims' trust in government or law enforcement agencies or the generosity and charitable motives of victims. Taking advantage of a victim's self-interest does not mitigate the seriousness of fraudulent conduct; rather, defendants who exploit victims' charitable impulses or trust in government create particular social harm. In a similar vein, a defendant who has been subject to civil or administrative proceedings for the same or similar fraudulent conduct demonstrates aggravated criminal intent and is deserving of additional punishment for not conforming with the requirements of judicial process or orders issued by federal, state, or local administrative agencies.

Offenses that involve the use of financial transactions or financial accounts outside the United States in an effort to conceal illicit profits and criminal conduct involve a particularly high level of sophistication and complexity. These offenses are difficult to detect and require costly investigations and prosecutions. Diplomatic processes often must be used to secure testimony and evidence beyond the jurisdiction of United States courts. Consequently, a minimum offense level of level 12 is provided for these offenses.

§ 2B3.1. Robbery

(a) Base Offense Level: **20**

(b) Specific Offense Characteristics

(1) If the property of a financial institution or post office was taken, or if the taking of such property was an object of the offense, increase by **2** levels.

(2) (A) If a firearm was discharged, increase by **7** levels; (B) if a firearm was otherwise used, increase by **6** levels; (C) if a firearm was brandished or possessed, increase by **5** levels; (D) if a dangerous weapon was otherwise used, increase by **4** levels; (E) if a dangerous weapon was brandished or possessed, increase by **3** levels; or (F) if a threat of death was made, increase by **2** levels.

(3) If any victim sustained bodily injury, increase the offense level according to the seriousness of the injury:

Degree of Bodily Injury	Increase in Level
(A) Bodily Injury	add **2**
(B) Serious Bodily Injury	add **4**
(C) Permanent or Life–Threatening Bodily Injury	add **6**

Degree of Bodily Injury — Increase in Level

(D) If the degree of injury is between that specified in subdivisions (A) and (B), — add **3** levels; or

(E) If the degree of injury is between that specified in subdivisions (B) and (C), — add **5** levels.

Provided, however, that the cumulative adjustments from (2) and (3) shall not exceed **11** levels.

(4) (A) If any person was abducted to facilitate commission of the offense or to facilitate escape, increase by **4** levels; or (B) if any person was physically restrained to facilitate commission of the offense or to facilitate escape, increase by **2** levels.

(5) If the offense involved carjacking, increase by **2** levels.

(6) If a firearm, destructive device, or controlled substance was taken, or if the taking of such item was an object of the offense, increase by *1* level.

(7) If the loss exceeded $10,000, increase the offense level as follows:

Loss (Apply the Greatest)	Increase in Level
(A) $10,000 or less	no increase
(B) More than $10,000	add **1**
(C) More than $50,000	add **2**
(D) More than $250,000	add **3**
(E) More than $800,000	add **4**
(F) More than $1,500,000	add **5**
(G) More than $2,500,000	add **6**
(H) More than $5,000,000	add **7**

(c) Cross Reference

(1) If a victim was killed under circumstances that would constitute murder under 18 U.S.C. § 1111 had such killing taken place within the territorial or maritime jurisdiction of the United States, apply § 2A1.1 (First Degree Murder).

Commentary

Statutory Provisions: 18 U.S.C. §§ 1951, 2113, 2114, 2118(a). For additional statutory provision(s), see Appendix A (Statutory Index).

Application Notes:

1. "Firearm," "destructive device," "dangerous weapon," "otherwise used," "brandished," "bodily injury," "serious bodily injury," "permanent or life-threatening bodily injury," "abducted," and "physically restrained" are defined in the Commentary to § 1B1.1 (Application Instructions).

"Carjacking" means the taking or attempted taking of a motor vehicle from the person or presence of another by force and violence or by intimidation.

2. When an object that appeared to be a dangerous weapon was brandished, displayed, or possessed, treat the object as a dangerous weapon for the purposes of subsection (b)(2)(E).

3. Valuation of loss is discussed in the Commentary to § 2B1.1 (Larceny, Embezzlement, and Other Forms of Theft).

4. The combined adjustments for weapon involvement and injury are limited to a maximum enhancement of 11 levels.

5. If the defendant intended to murder the victim, an upward departure may be warranted; see § 2A2.1 (Assault With Intent to Commit Murder; Attempted Murder).

6. "A threat of death," as used in subsection (b)(2)(F), may be in the form of an oral or written statement, act, gesture, or combination thereof. Accordingly, the defendant does not have to state expressly his intent to kill the victim in order for the enhancement to apply. For example, an oral or written demand using words such as "Give me the money or I will kill you", "Give me the money or I will pull the pin on the grenade I have in my pocket", "Give me the money or I will shoot you", "Give me your money or else (where the defendant draws his hand across his throat in a slashing motion)", or "Give me the money or you are dead" would constitute a threat of death. The court should consider that the intent of this provision is to provide an increased offense level for cases in which the offender(s) engaged in conduct that would instill in a reasonable person, who is a victim of the offense, a fear of death.

Background: Possession or use of a weapon, physical injury, and unlawful restraint sometimes occur during a robbery. The guideline provides for a range of enhancements where these factors are present.

Although in pre-guidelines practice the amount of money taken in robbery cases affected sentence length, its importance was small compared to that of the other harm involved. Moreover, because of the relatively high base offense level for robbery, an increase of 1 or 2 levels brings about a considerable increase in sentence length in absolute terms. Accordingly, the gradations for property loss increase more slowly than for simple property offenses.

The guideline provides an enhancement for robberies where a victim was forced to accompany the defendant to another location, or was physically restrained by being tied, bound, or locked up.

§ 2B3.2. Extortion by Force or Threat of Injury or Serious Damage

(a) Base Offense Level: **18**

(b) Specific Offense Characteristics

(1) If the offense involved an express or implied threat of death, bodily injury, or kidnapping, increase by **2** levels.

(2) If the greater of the amount demanded or the loss to the victim exceeded $10,000, increase by the corresponding number of levels from the table in § 2B3.1(b)(7).

(3) (A)(i) If a firearm was discharged, increase by **7** levels; (ii) if a firearm was otherwise used, increase by **6** levels; (iii) if a firearm was brandished or possessed, increase by **5** levels; (iv) if a dangerous weapon was otherwise used, increase by **4** levels; or (v) if a dangerous weapon was brandished or possessed, increase by **3** levels; or

(B) If the offense involved preparation to carry out a threat of (i) death, (ii) serious bodily injury, (iii) kidnapping, or (iv) product tampering; or if the participant(s) otherwise demonstrated the ability to carry out such threat, increase by **3** levels.

(4) If any victim sustained bodily injury, increase the offense level according to the seriousness of the injury:

Degree of Bodily Injury	Increase in Level
(A) Bodily Injury	add **2**
(B) Serious Bodily Injury	add **4**
(C) Permanent or Life–Threatening Bodily Injury	add **6**
(D) If the degree of injury is between that specified in subdivisions (A) and (B),	add **3** levels; or
(E) If the degree of injury is between that specified in subdivisions (B) and (C),	add **5** levels.

Provided, however, that the cumulative adjustments from (3) and (4) shall not exceed **11** levels.

(5) (A) If any person was abducted to facilitate commission of the offense or to facilitate escape, increase by **4** levels; or (B) if any person was physically restrained to facilitate commission of the offense or to facilitate escape, increase by **2** levels.

(c) Cross References

(1) If a victim was killed under circumstances that would constitute murder under 18 U.S.C. § 1111 had such killing taken place within the territorial or maritime jurisdiction of the United States, apply § 2A1.1 (First Degree Murder).

(2) If the offense was tantamount to attempted murder, apply § 2A2.1 (Assault with Intent to Commit Murder; Attempted Murder) if the resulting offense level is greater than that determined above.

Commentary

Statutory Provisions: 18 U.S.C. §§ 875(b), 876, 877, 1030(a)97), 1951. For additional statutory provision(s), see Appendix A (Statutory Index).

Application Notes:

1. "Firearm," "dangerous weapon," "otherwise used," "brandished," "bodily injury," "serious bodily injury," "permanent or life-

threatening bodily injury," "abducted," and "physically restrained" are defined in the Commentary to § 1B1.1 (Application Instructions).

2. This guideline applies if there was any threat, express or implied, that reasonably could be interpreted as one to injure a person or physically damage property, or any comparably serious threat, such as to drive an enterprise out of business. Even if the threat does not in itself imply violence, the possibility of violence or serious adverse consequences may be inferred from the circumstances of the threat or the reputation of the person making it. An ambiguous threat, such as "pay up or else," or a threat to cause labor problems, ordinarily should be treated under this section.

3. Guidelines for bribery involving public officials are found in Part C, Offenses Involving Public Officials. "Extortion under color of official right," which usually is solicitation of a bribe by a public official, is covered under § 2C1.1 unless there is use of force or a threat that qualifies for treatment under this section. Certain other extortion offenses are covered under the provisions of Part E, Offenses Involving Criminal Enterprises and Racketeering.

4. The combined adjustments for weapon involvement and injury are limited to a maximum enhancement of 11 levels.

5. "Loss to the victim," as used in subsection (b)(2), means any demand paid plus any additional consequential loss from the offense (e.g., the cost of defensive measures taken in direct response to the offense).

6. In certain cases, an extortionate demand may be accompanied by conduct that does not qualify as a display of a dangerous weapon under subsection (b)(3)(A)(v) but is nonetheless similar in seriousness, demonstrating the defendant's preparation or ability to carry out the threatened harm (e.g., an extortionate demand containing a threat to tamper with a consumer product accompanied by a workable plan showing how the product's tamper-resistant seals could be defeated, or a threat to kidnap a person accompanied by information showing study of that person's daily routine). Subsection (b)(3)(B) addresses such cases.

7. If the offense involved the threat of death or serious bodily injury to numerous victims (e.g., in the case of a plan to derail a passenger train or poison consumer products), an upward departure may be warranted.

8. If the offense involved organized criminal activity, or a threat to a family member of the victim, an upward departure may be warranted.

Background: The Hobbs Act, 18 U.S.C. § 1951, prohibits extortion, attempted extortion, and conspiracy to extort. It provides for a maximum term of imprisonment of twenty years. 18 U.S.C. §§ 875–877 prohibits communication of extortionate demands through various means. The maximum penalty under these statutes varies from two to twenty years. Violations of 18 U.S.C. § 875 involve threats or demands transmitted by interstate commerce. Violations of 18 U.S.C. § 876 involve the use of the

United States mails to communicate threats, while violations of 18 U.S.C. § 877 involve mailing threatening communications from foreign countries. This guideline also applies to offenses under 18 U.S.C. § 1030(a)(7) involving a threat to impair the operation of a "protected computer."

§ 2B3.3. Blackmail and Similar Forms of Extortion

(a) Base Offense Level: **9**

(b) Specific Offense Characteristic

(1) If the greater of the amount obtained or demanded (A) exceeded $2,000 but did not exceed $5,000, increase by 1 level; or (B) exceeded $5,000, increase by the number of levels from the table in § 2B1.1 (Theft, Property Destruction, and Fraud) corresponding to that amount.

(c) Cross References

(1) If the offense involved extortion under color of official right, apply § 2C1.1 (Offering, Giving, Soliciting, or Receiving a Bribe; Extortion Under Color of Official Right).

(2) If the offense involved extortion by force or threat of injury or serious damage, apply § 2B3.2 (Extortion by Force or Threat of Injury or Serious Damage).

Commentary

Statutory Provisions: 18 U.S.C. §§ 873, 875–877, 1951. For additional statutory provision(s), see Appendix A (Statutory Index).

Application Note:

1. This section applies only to blackmail and similar forms of extortion where there clearly is no threat of violence to person or property. "Blackmail" (18 U.S.C. § 873) is defined as a threat to disclose a violation of United States law unless money or some other item of value is given.

Background: Under 18 U.S.C. § 873, the maximum term of imprisonment authorized for blackmail is one year. Extortionate threats to injure a reputation, or other threats that are less serious than those covered by § 2B3.2, may also be prosecuted under 18 U.S.C. §§ 875–877, which carry higher maximum sentences.

Amendment & Reason: 2B3.3(b) is amended because the Commission struck section 2F1.1, and moved its provisions to 2B1.1.

§ 2C1.1. Offering, Giving, Soliciting, or Receiving a Bribe; Extortion Under Color of Official Right; Fraud Involving the Deprivation of the Intangible Right to Honest Services of Public Officials; Conspiracy to Defraud by Interference with Governmental Functions

(a) Base Offense Level:

(1) **14**, if the defendant was a public official; or

(2) **12**, otherwise.

(b) Specific Offense Characteristics

(1) If the offense involved more than one bribe or extortion, increase by **2** levels.

(2) If the value of the payment, the benefit received or to be received in return for the payment, the value of anything obtained or to be obtained by a public official or others acting with a public official, or the loss to the government from the offense, whichever is greatest, exceeded $5,000, increase by the number of levels from the table in § 2B1.1 (Theft, Property Destruction, and Fraud) corresponding to that amount.

(3) If the offense involved an elected public official or any public official in a high-level decision-making or sensitive position, increase by **4** levels. If the resulting offense level is less than level **18**, increase to level **18**.

(4) If the defendant was a public official who facilitated (A) entry into the United States for a person, a vehicle, or cargo; (B) the obtaining of a passport or a document relating to naturalization, citizenship, legal entry, or legal resident status; or (C) the obtaining of a government identification document, increase by **2** levels.

(c) Cross References

(1) If the offense was committed for the purpose of facilitating the commission of another criminal offense, apply the offense guideline applicable to a conspiracy to commit that other offense, if the resulting offense level is greater than that determined above.

(2) If the offense was committed for the purpose of concealing, or obstructing justice in respect to, another criminal offense, apply § 2X3.1 (Accessory After the Fact) or § 2J1.2 (Obstruction of Justice), as appropriate, in respect to that other offense, if the resulting offense level is greater than that determined above.

(3) If the offense involved a threat of physical injury or property destruction, apply § 2B3.2 (Extortion by Force or Threat of Injury or Serious Damage), if the resulting offense level is greater than that determined above.

(d) Special Instruction for Fines—Organizations

(1) In lieu of the pecuniary loss under subsection (a)(3) of § 8C2.4 (Base Fine), use the greatest of: (A) the value of the unlawful payment; (B) the value of the benefit received or to be received in return for the unlawful payment; or (C) the consequential damages resulting from the unlawful payment.

Commentary

Statutory Provisions: 15 U.S.C. §§ 78dd–1, 78dd–2, 78dd–3; 18 U.S.C. §§ 201(b)(1), (2), 371 (if conspiracy to defraud by interference with governmental functions), 872, 1341 (if the scheme or artifice to defraud was to deprive another of the intangible right of honest services of a public official), 1342 (if the scheme or artifice to defraud was to deprive another of the intangible right of honest services of a public official), 1343 (if the scheme or artifice to defraud was to deprive another of the intangible right of honest services of a public official), 1951. For additional statutory provision(s), see Appendix A (Statutory Index).

Application Notes:

    1. Definitions.—For purposes of this guideline:

"Government identification document" means a document made or issued by or under the authority of the United States Government, a State, or a political subdivision of a State, which, when completed with information concerning a particular individual, is of a type intended or commonly accepted for the purpose of identification of individuals.

"Payment" means anything of value. A payment need not be monetary.

"Public official" shall be construed broadly and includes the following:

    (A) "Public official" as defined in 18 U.S.C. § 201(a)(1).

    (B) A member of a state or local legislature. "State" means a State of the United States, and any commonwealth, territory, or possession of the United States.

    (C) An officer or employee or person acting for or on behalf of a state or local government, or any department, agency, or branch of government thereof, in any official function, under or by authority of such department, agency, or branch of government, or a juror in a state or local trial.

    (D) Any person who has been selected to be a person described in subdivisions (A), (B), or (C), either before or after such person has qualified.

    (E) An individual who, although not otherwise covered by subdivisions (A) through (D): (i) is in a position of public trust with official responsibility for carrying out a government program or policy; (ii) acts under color of law or official right; or (iii) participates so substantially in government operations as to possess de facto authority to make governmental decisions (e.g., which may include a leader of a state or local political party who acts in the manner described in this subdivision).

    2. More than One Bribe or Extortion.—Subsection (b)(1) provides an adjustment for offenses involving more than one incident of either bribery or extortion. Related payments that, in essence, constitute a single incident of bribery or extortion (e.g., a number of installment payments for a single action) are to be treated as a single bribe or extortion, even if charged in separate counts.

In a case involving more than one incident of bribery or extortion, the applicable amounts under subsection (b)(2) (i.e., the greatest of the value of the payment, the benefit received or to be received, the value of anything obtained or to be obtained by a public official or others acting with a public official, or the loss to the government) are determined separately for each incident and then added together.

3. Application of Subsection (b)(2).—"Loss", for purposes of subsection (b)(2)(A), shall be determined in accordance with Application Note 3 of the Commentary to § 2B1.1 (Theft, Property Destruction, and Fraud). The value of 'the benefit received or to be received' means the net value of such benefit. Examples: (A) A government employee, in return for a $500 bribe, reduces the price of a piece of surplus property offered for sale by the government from $10,000 to $2,000; the value of the benefit received is $8,000. (B) A $150,000 contract on which $20,000 profit was made was awarded in return for a bribe; the value of the benefit received is $20,000. Do not deduct the value of the bribe itself in computing the value of the benefit received or to be received. In the preceding examples, therefore, the value of the benefit received would be the same regardless of the value of the bribe.

4. Application of Subsection (b)(3).—

(A) Definition.—"High-level decision-making or sensitive position" means a position characterized by a direct authority to make decisions for, or on behalf of, a government department, agency, or other government entity, or by a substantial influence over the decision-making process.

(B) Examples.—Examples of a public official in a high-level decision-making position include a prosecuting attorney, a judge, an agency administrator, and any other public official with a similar level of authority. Examples of a public official who holds a sensitive position include a juror, a law enforcement officer, an election official, and any other similarly situated individual.

5. Application of Subsection (C) .—For the purposes of determining whether to apply the cross references in this section, the "resulting offense level" means the final offense level (i.e., the offense level determined by taking into account both the Chapter Two offense level and any applicable adjustments from Chapter Three, Parts A–D). See § 1B1.5(d); Application Note 2 of the Commentary to § 1B1.5 (Interpretation of References to Other Offense Guidelines).

6. Inapplicability of § 3B1.3.—Do not apply § 3B1.3 (Abuse of Position of Trust or Use of Special Skill).

7. Upward Departure Provisions.—In some cases the monetary value of the unlawful payment may not be known or may not adequately reflect the seriousness of the offense. For example, a small payment may be made in exchange for the falsification of inspection records for a shipment of defective parachutes or the destruction of evidence in a major narcotics case. In part, this issue is addressed by the enhance-

ments in § 2C1.1(b)(2) and (c)(1), (2), and (3). However, in cases in which the seriousness of the offense is still not adequately reflected, an upward departure is warranted. See Chapter Five, Part K (Departures).

In a case in which the court finds that the defendant's conduct was part of a systematic or pervasive corruption of a governmental function, process, or office that may cause loss of public confidence in government, an upward departure may be warranted. See § 5K2.7 (Disruption of Governmental Function).

Background: This section applies to a person who offers or gives a bribe for a corrupt purpose, such as inducing a public official to participate in a fraud or to influence such individual's official actions, or to a public official who solicits or accepts such a bribe.

The object and nature of a bribe may vary widely from case to case. In some cases, the object may be commercial advantage (e.g., preferential treatment in the award of a government contract). In others, the object may be issuance of a license to which the recipient is not entitled. In still others, the object may be the obstruction of justice. Consequently, a guideline for the offense must be designed to cover diverse situations.

In determining the net value of the benefit received or to be received, the value of the bribe is not deducted from the gross value of such benefit; the harm is the same regardless of value of the bribe paid to receive the benefit. In a case in which the value of the bribe exceeds the value of the benefit, or in which the value of the benefit cannot be determined, the value of the bribe is used because it is likely that the payer of such a bribe expected something in return that would be worth more than the value of the bribe. Moreover, for deterrence purposes, the punishment should be commensurate with the gain to the payer or the recipient of the bribe, whichever is greater.

Under § 2C1.1(b)(3), if the payment was for the purpose of influencing an official act by certain officials, the offense level is increased by 4 levels.

Under § 2C1.1(c)(1), if the payment was to facilitate the commission of another criminal offense, the guideline applicable to a conspiracy to commit that other offense will apply if the result is greater than that determined above. For example, if a bribe was given to a law enforcement officer to allow the smuggling of a quantity of cocaine, the guideline for conspiracy to import cocaine would be applied if it resulted in a greater offense level.

Under § 2C1.1(c)(2), if the payment was to conceal another criminal offense or obstruct justice in respect to another criminal offense, the guideline from § 2X3.1 (Accessory After the Fact) or § 2J1.2 (Obstruction of Justice), as appropriate, will apply if the result is greater than that determined above. For example, if a bribe was given for the purpose of concealing the offense of espionage, the guideline for accessory after the fact to espionage would be applied.

Under § 2C1.1(c)(3), if the offense involved forcible extortion, the guideline from § 2B3.2 (Extortion by Force or Threat of Injury or Serious Damage) will apply if the result is greater than that determined above.

Section 2C1.1 also applies to offenses under 15 U.S.C. §§ 78dd–1, 78dd–2, and 78dd–3. Such offenses generally involve a payment to a foreign public official, candidate for public office, or agent or intermediary, with the intent to influence an official act or decision of a foreign government or political party. Typically, a case prosecuted under these provisions will involve an intent to influence governmental action.

Section 2C1.1 also applies to fraud involving the deprivation of the intangible right to honest services of government officials under 18 U.S.C. §§ 1341–1343 and conspiracy to defraud by interference with governmental functions under 18 U.S.C. § 371. Such fraud offenses typically involve an improper use of government influence that harms the operation of government in a manner similar to bribery offenses.

Offenses involving attempted bribery are frequently not completed because the offense is reported to authorities or an individual involved in the offense is acting in an undercover capacity. Failure to complete the offense does not lessen the defendant's culpability in attempting to use public position for personal gain. Therefore, solicitations and attempts are treated as equivalent to the underlying offense.

Historical Note: Effective November 1, 1987. Amended effective January 15, 1988 (see Appendix C, amendment 18); November 1, 1989 (see Appendix C, amendments 120–122); November 1, 1991 (see Appendix C, amendments 367 and 422); November 1, 1997 (see Appendix C, amendment 547); November 1, 2001 (see Appendix C, amendment 617); November 1, 2002 (see Appendix C, amendment 639); November 1, 2003 (see Appendix C, amendment 653); November 1, 2004 (see Appendix C, amendment 666).

§ 2C1.2. Offering, Giving, Soliciting, or Receiving a Gratuity

(a) Base Offense Level:

(1) **11**, if the defendant was a public official; or

(2) **9**, otherwise.

(b) Specific Offense Characteristics

(1) If the offense involved more than one gratuity, increase by **2** levels.

(2) If the value of the gratuity exceeded $5,000, increase by the number of levels from the table in § 2B1.1 (Theft, Property Destruction, and Fraud) corresponding to that amount.

(3) If the offense involved an elected public official or any public official in a high-level decision-making or sensitive position, increase by **4** levels. If the resulting offense level is less than level **15**, increase to level **15**.

(4) If the defendant was a public official who facilitated (A) entry into the United States for a person, a vehicle, or cargo; (B) the obtaining of a passport or a document relating to naturalization, citizenship, legal entry, or legal resident status; or (C) the obtaining of a government identification document, increase by **2** levels.

(c) Special Instruction for Fines—Organizations

(1) In lieu of the pecuniary loss under subsection (a)(3) of § 8C2.4 (Base Fine), use the value of the unlawful payment.

Commentary

Statutory Provisions: 18 U.S.C. §§ 201(c)(1), 212–214, 217. For additional statutory provision(s), see Appendix A (Statutory Index).

Application Notes:

1. Definitions.—For purposes of this guideline:

"Government identification document" means a document made or issued by or under the authority of the United States Government, a State, or a political subdivision of a State, which, when completed with information concerning a particular individual, is of a type intended or commonly accepted for the purpose of identification of individuals.

"Public official" shall be construed broadly and includes the following:

(A) "Public official" as defined in 18 U.S.C. § 201(a)(1).

(B) A member of a state or local legislature. "State" means a State of the United States, and any commonwealth, territory, or possession of the United States.

(C) An officer or employee or person acting for or on behalf of a state or local government, or any department, agency, or branch of government thereof, in any official function, under or by authority of such department, agency, or branch of government, or a juror.

(D) Any person who has been selected to be a person described in subdivisions (A), (B), or (C), either before or after such person has qualified.

(E) An individual who, although not otherwise covered by subdivisions (A) through (D): (i) is in a position of public trust with official responsibility for carrying out a government program or policy; (ii) acts under color of law or official right; or (iii) participates so substantially in government operations as to possess de facto authority to make governmental decisions (e.g., which may include a leader of a state or local political party who acts in the manner described in this subdivision).

2. Application of Subsection (b)(1).—Related payments that, in essence, constitute a single gratuity (e.g., separate payments for airfare

and hotel for a single vacation trip) are to be treated as a single gratuity, even if charged in separate counts.

3.   Application of Subsection (b)(3).—

(A)   Definition.—"High-level decision-making or sensitive position" means a position characterized by a direct authority to make decisions for, or on behalf of, a government department, agency, or other government entity, or by a substantial influence over the decision-making process.

(B)   Examples.—Examples of a public official in a high-level decision-making position include a prosecuting attorney, a judge, an agency administrator, a law enforcement officer, and any other public official with a similar level of authority. Examples of a public official who holds a sensitive position include a juror, a law enforcement officer, an election official, and any other similarly situated individual.

4.   Inapplicability of § 3B1.3.—Do not apply the adjustment in § 3B1.3 (Abuse of Position or Trust or Use of Special Skill).

Background: This section applies to the offering, giving, soliciting, or receiving of a gratuity to a public official in respect to an official act. It also applies in cases involving (1) the offer to, or acceptance by, a bank examiner of a loan or gratuity; (2) the offer or receipt of anything of value for procuring a loan or discount of commercial bank paper from a Federal Reserve Bank; and (3) the acceptance of a fee or other consideration by a federal employee for adjusting or cancelling a farm debt.

Historical Note: Effective November 1, 1987. Amended effective November 1, 1989 (see Appendix C, amendment 121); November 1, 1991 (see Appendix C, amendment 422); November 1, 1995 (see Appendix C, amendment 534); November 1, 2001 (see Appendix C, amendment 617); November 1, 2004 (see Appendix C, amendment 666).

§ 2D1.1. Unlawful Manufacturing, Importing, Exporting, or Trafficking (Including Possession with Intent to Commit These Offenses); Attempt or Conspiracy

(a)   Base Offense Level (Apply the greatest):

(1) **43**, if the defendant is convicted under 21 U.S.C. § 841(b)(1)(A), (b)(1)(B), or (b)(1)(C), or 21 U.S.C. § 960(b)(1), (b)(2), or (b)(3), and the offense of conviction establishes that death or serious bodily injury resulted from the use of the substance and that the defendant committed the offense after one or more prior convictions for a similar offense; or

(2) **38**, if the defendant is convicted under 21 U.S.C. § 841(b)(1)(A), (b)(1)(B), or (b)(1)(C), or 21 U.S.C. § 960(b)(1), (b)(2), or (b)(3), and the offense of conviction establishes that death or serious bodily injury resulted from the use of the substance; or

(3) the offense level specified in the Drug Quantity Table set forth in subsection (c), except that if (A) the defendant receives an adjustment under § 3B1.2 (Mitigating Role); and (B) the base offense level under subsection (c) is (i) level **32**, decrease by 2 levels; (ii) level **34** or level **36**, decrease by 3 levels; or level **38**, decrease by 4 levels.

(b) Specific Offense Characteristics

(1) If a dangerous weapon (including a firearm) was possessed, increase by **2** levels.

(2) If the defendant unlawfully imported or exported a controlled substance under circumstances in which (A) an aircraft other than a regularly scheduled commercial air carrier was used to import or export the controlled substance, or (B) the defendant acted as a pilot, copilot, captain, navigator, flight officer, or any other operation officer aboard any craft or vessel carrying a controlled substance, increase by **2** levels. If the resulting offense level is less than level **26**, increase to level **26.**

(3) If the object of the offense was the distribution of a controlled substance in a prison, correctional facility, or detention facility, increase by **2** levels.

(4) If (A) the offense involved the importation of amphetamine or methamphetamine or the manufacture of amphetamine or methamphetamine from listed chemicals that the defendant knew were imported unlawfully, and (B) the defendant is not subject to an adjustment under § 3B1.2 (Mitigating Role), increase by **2** levels.

(5) If the defendant, or a person for whose conduct the defendant is accountable under § 1B1.3 (Relevant Conduct), distributed a controlled substance through mass-marketing by means of an interactive computer service, increase by **2** levels.

(6) (Apply the greater):

(A) If the offense involved (i) an unlawful discharge, emission, or release into the environment of a hazardous or toxic substance; or (ii) the unlawful transportation, treatment, storage, or disposal of a hazardous waste, increase by **2** levels.

(B) If the offense (i) involved the manufacture of amphetamine or methamphetamine; and (ii) created a substantial risk of harm to (I) human life other than a life described in subdivision (C); or (II) the environment, increase by **3** levels. If the resulting offense level is less than level **27**, increase to level **27.**

(C) If the offense (i) involved the manufacture of amphetamine or methamphetamine; and (ii) created a substantial risk of harm to the life of a minor or an incompetent, increase by 6 levels. If the resulting offense level is less than level **30**, increase to level **30.**

(7) If the defendant meets the criteria set forth in subdivisions (1)-(5) of subsection (a) of § 5C1.2 (Limitation on Applicability of Statutory Minimum Sentences in Certain Cases), decrease by **2** levels.

* * *

[The drug quantity tables, including drug equivalency tables, are too lengthy to be reproduced here.]

Amendment & Reason: Section 2D1.1(a)(3) is amended by striking "below." and inserting ", except that if the defendant receives an adjustment under § 3B1.2 (Mitigating Role), the base offense level under this subsection shall be not more than level 30."

§ 2D1.2. Drug Offenses Occurring Near Protected Locations or Involving Underage or Pregnant Individuals; Attempt or Conspiracy

(a) Base Offense Level (Apply the greatest):

(1) **2** plus the offense level from § 2D1.1 applicable to the quantity of controlled substances directly involving a protected location or an underage or pregnant individual; or

(2) **1** plus the offense level from § 2D1.1 applicable to the total quantity of controlled substances involved in the offense; or

(3) **26**, if the offense involved a person less than eighteen years of age; or

(4) **13**, otherwise.

Commentary

Statutory Provisions: 21 U.S.C. §§ 859 (formerly 21 U.S.C. § 845), 860 (formerly 21 U.S.C. § 845a), 861 (formerly 21 U.S.C. § 845b).

Application Note:

1. Where only part of the relevant offense conduct directly involved a protected location or an underage or pregnant individual, subsections (a)(1) and (a)(2) may result in different offense levels. For example, if the defendant, as part of the same course of conduct or common scheme or plan, sold 5 grams of heroin near a protected location and 10 grams of heroin elsewhere, the offense level from subsection (a)(1) would be level 16 (2 plus the offense level for the sale of 5 grams of heroin, the amount sold near the protected location); the offense level from subsection (a)(2) would be level 17 (1 plus the offense level for the sale of 15 grams of heroin, the total amount of heroin involved in the offense).

Background: This section implements the direction to the Commission in Section 6454 of the Anti–Drug Abuse Act of 1988.

§ 2D1.5. Continuing Criminal Enterprise; Attempt or Conspiracy

(a) Base Offense Level (Apply the greater):

(1) **4** plus the offense level from § 2D1.1 applicable to the underlying offense; or

(2) **38**.

Commentary

Statutory Provision: 21 U.S.C. § 848.

Application Notes:

1. Do not apply any adjustment from Chapter Three, Part B (Role in the Offense).

2. If as part of the enterprise the defendant sanctioned the use of violence, or if the number of persons managed by the defendant was extremely large, an upward departure may be warranted.

3. Under 21 U.S.C. § 848, certain conduct for which the defendant has previously been sentenced may be charged as part of the instant offense to establish a "continuing series of violations." A sentence resulting from a conviction sustained prior to the last overt act of the instant offense is to be considered a prior sentence under § 4A1.2(a)(1) and not part of the instant offense.

4. Violations of 21 U.S.C. § 848 will be grouped with other drug offenses for the purpose of applying Chapter Three, Part D (Multiple Counts).

Background: Because a conviction under 21 U.S.C. § 848 establishes that a defendant controlled and exercised authority over one of the most serious types of ongoing criminal activity, this guideline provides a minimum base offense level of 38. An adjustment from Chapter Three, Part B is not authorized because the offense level of this guideline already reflects an adjustment for role in the offense.

Title 21 U.S.C. § 848 provides a 20–year minimum mandatory penalty for the first conviction, a 30–year minimum mandatory penalty for a second conviction, and a mandatory life sentence for principal administrators of extremely large enterprises. If the application of the guidelines results in a sentence below the minimum sentence required by statute, the statutory minimum shall be the guideline sentence. See § 5G1.1(b).

§ 2E1.1. Unlawful Conduct Relating to Racketeer Influenced and Corrupt Organizations

(a) Base Offense Level (Apply the greater):

(1) **19**; or

(2) the offense level applicable to the underlying racketeering activity.

Commentary

Statutory Provisions: 18 U.S.C. §§ 1962, 1963.

Application Notes:

1. Where there is more than one underlying offense, treat each underlying offense as if contained in a separate count of conviction for the purposes of subsection (a)(2). To determine whether subsection (a)(1) or (a)(2) results in the greater offense level, apply Chapter Three, Parts A, B, C, and D to both (a)(1) and (a)(2). Use whichever subsection results in the greater offense level.

2. If the underlying conduct violates state law, the offense level corresponding to the most analogous federal offense is to be used.

3. If the offense level for the underlying racketeering activity is less than the alternative minimum level specified (i.e., 19), the alternative minimum base offense level is to be used.

4. Certain conduct may be charged in the count of conviction as part of a "pattern of racketeering activity" even though the defendant has previously been sentenced for that conduct. Where such previously imposed sentence resulted from a conviction prior to the last overt act of the instant offense, treat as a prior sentence under § 4A1.2(a)(1) and not as part of the instant offense. This treatment is designed to produce a result consistent with the distinction between the instant offense and criminal history found throughout the guidelines. If this treatment produces an anomalous result in a particular case, a guideline departure may be warranted.

§ 2H1.1. Offenses Involving Individual Rights

(a) Base Offense Level (Apply the Greatest):

(1) the offense level from the offense guideline applicable to any underlying offense;

(2) **12**, if the offense involved two or more participants;

(3) **10**, if the offense involved (A) the use or threat of force against a person; or (B) property damage or the threat of property damage; or

(4) **6**, otherwise.

(b) Specific Offense Characteristic

(1) If (A) the defendant was a public official at the time of the offense; or (B) the offense was committed under color of law, increase by **6** levels.

Commentary

Statutory Provisions: 18 U.S.C. §§ 241, 242, 245(b), 246, 247, 248, 1091; 42 U.S.C. § 3631.

Application Notes:

1. "Offense guideline applicable to any underlying offense" means the offense guideline applicable to any conduct established by the offense of conviction that constitutes an offense under federal, state, or local law (other than an offense that is itself covered under Chapter Two, Part H, Subpart 1).

In certain cases, conduct set forth in the count of conviction may constitute more than one underlying offense (e.g., two instances of assault, or one instance of assault and one instance of arson). In such cases, use the following comparative procedure to determine the applicable base offense level: (i) determine the underlying offenses encompassed within the count of conviction as if the defendant had been charged with a conspiracy to commit multiple offenses. See Application Note 5 of § 1B1.2 (Applicable Guidelines); (ii) determine the Chapter Two offense level (i.e., the base offense level, specific offense characteristics, cross references, and special instructions) for each such underlying offense; and (iii) compare each of the Chapter Two offense levels determined above with the alternative base offense level under subsection (a)(2), (3), or (4). The determination of the applicable alternative base offense level is to be based on the entire conduct underlying the count of conviction (i.e., the conduct taken as a whole). Use the alternative base offense level only if it is greater than each of the Chapter Two offense levels determined above. Otherwise, use the Chapter Two offense levels for each of the underlying offenses (with each underlying offense treated as if contained in a separate count of conviction). Then apply subsection (b) to the alternative base offense level, or to the Chapter Two offense levels for each of the underlying offenses, as appropriate.

2. "Participant" is defined in the Commentary to § 3B1.1 (Aggravating Role).

3. The burning or defacement of a religious symbol with an intent to intimidate shall be deemed to involve the threat of force against a person for the purposes of subsection (a)(3)(A).

4. If the finder of fact at trial or, in the case of a plea of guilty or nolo contendere, the court at sentencing determines beyond a reasonable doubt that the defendant intentionally selected any victim or any property as the object of the offense because of the actual or perceived race, color, religion, national origin, ethnicity, gender, disability, or sexual orientation of any person, an additional 3–level enhancement from § 3A1.1(a) will apply. An adjustment from § 3A1.1(a) will not apply, however, if a 6–level adjustment from § 2H1.1(b) applies. See § 3A1.1(c).

5. If subsection (b)(1) applies, do not apply § 3B1.3 (Abuse of Position of Trust or Use of Special Skill).

§ 2H2.1. Obstructing an Election or Registration

(a) Base Offense Level (Apply the greatest):

(1) **18**, if the obstruction occurred by use of force or threat of force against person(s) or property; or

(2) **12**, if the obstruction occurred by forgery, fraud, theft, bribery, deceit, or other means, except as provided in (3) below; or

(3) **6**, if the defendant (A) solicited, demanded, accepted, or agreed to accept anything of value to vote, refrain from voting, vote for or against a particular candidate, or register to vote, (B) gave false information to establish eligibility to vote, or (C) voted more than once in a federal election.

Commentary

Statutory Provisions: 18 U.S.C. §§ 241, 242, 245(b)(1)(A), 592, 593, 594, 597; 42 U.S.C. §§ 1973i, 1973j(a), (b). For additional statutory provision(s), see Appendix A (Statutory Index).

Application Note:

1. If the offense resulted in bodily injury or significant property damage, or involved corrupting a public official, an upward departure may be warranted. See Chapter Five, Part K (Departures).

Background: Alternative base offense levels cover three major ways of obstructing an election: by force, by deceptive or dishonest conduct, or by bribery. A defendant who is a public official or who directs others to engage in criminal conduct is subject to an enhancement from Chapter Three, Part B (Role in the Offense).

§ 2S1.1. Laundering of Monetary Instruments; Engaging in Monetary Transactions in Property Derived from Unlawful Activity

(a) Base Offense Level:

(1) The offense level for the underlying offense from which the laundered funds were derived, if (A) the defendant committed the underlying offense (or would be accountable for the underlying offense under subsection (a)(1)(A) of § 1B1.3 (Relevant Conduct)); and (B) the offense level for that offense can be determined; or

(2) **8** plus the number of offense levels from the table in § 2B1.1 (Theft, Property Destruction, and Fraud) corresponding to the value of the laundered funds, otherwise.

(b) Specific Offense Characteristics

(1) If (A) subsection (a)(2) applies; and (B) the defendant knew or believed that any of the laundered funds were the proceeds of, or were intended to promote (i) an offense involving the manufacture, importation, or distribution of a controlled substance or a listed chemical; (ii) a crime of violence; or (iii) an offense involving firearms, explosives, national security, terrorism, or the sexual exploitation of a minor, increase by 6 levels.

(2) (Apply the Greatest):

    (A) If the defendant was convicted under 18 U.S.C. § 1957, increase by **1** level.

    (B) If the defendant was convicted under 18 U.S.C. § 1956, increase by **2** levels.

    (C) If (i) subsection (a)(2) applies; and (ii) the defendant was in the business of laundering funds, increase by **4** levels.

    (3) If (A) subsection (b)(2)(B) applies; and (B) the offense involved sophisticated laundering, increase by **2** levels.

Commentary

Statutory Provisions: 18 U.S.C. §§ 1956, 1957. For additional statutory provision(s), see Appendix A (Statutory Index).

Application Notes:

    1. Definitions. For purposes of this guideline:

"Crime of violence" has the meaning given that term in subsection (a)(1) of § 4B1.2 (Definitions of Terms Used in Section 4B1.1).

"Criminally derived funds" means any funds derived, or represented by a law enforcement officer, or by another person at the direction or approval of an authorized Federal official, to be derived from conduct constituting a criminal offense.

"Laundered funds" means the property, funds, or monetary instrument involved in the transaction, financial transaction, monetary transaction, transportation, transfer, or transmission in violation of 18 U.S.C. § 1956 or § 1957.

"Laundering funds" means making a transaction, financial transaction, monetary transaction, or transmission, or transporting or transferring property, funds, or a monetary instrument in violation of 18 U.S.C. § 1956 or § 1957.

"Sexual exploitation of a minor" means an offense involving (A) promoting prostitution by a minor; (B) sexually exploiting a minor by production of sexually explicit visual or printed material; (C) distribution of material involving the sexual exploitation of a minor, or possession of material involving the sexual exploitation of a minor with intent to distribute; or (D) aggravated sexual abuse, sexual abuse, or abusive sexual contact involving a minor. "Minor" means an individual under the age of 18 years.

    2. Application of Subsection (a)(1).

    (A) Multiple Underlying Offenses. In cases in which subsection (a)(1) applies and there is more than one underlying offense, the offense level for the underlying offense is to be determined under the procedures set forth in Application Note 3 of the Commentary to § 1B1.5 (Interpretation of References to Other Offense Guidelines).

(B) Defendants Accountable for Underlying Offense. In order for subsection (a)(1) to apply, the defendant must have committed the underlying offense or be accountable for the underlying offense under § 1B1.3(a)(1)(A). The fact that the defendant was involved in laundering criminally derived funds after the commission of the underlying offense, without additional involvement in the underlying offense, does not establish that the defendant committed, aided, abetted, counseled, commanded, induced, procured, or willfully caused the underlying offense.

(C) Application of Chapter Three Adjustments. Notwithstanding § 1B1.5(c), in cases in which subsection (a)(1) applies, application of any Chapter Three adjustment shall be determined based on the offense covered by this guideline (i.e., the laundering of criminally derived funds) and not on the underlying offense from which the laundered funds were derived.

3. Application of Subsection (a)(2).

(A) In General. Subsection (a)(2) applies to any case in which (i) the defendant did not commit the underlying offense; or (ii) the defendant committed the underlying offense (or would be accountable for the underlying offense under § 1B1.3(a)(1)(A)), but the offense level for the underlying offense is impossible or impracticable to determine.

(B) Commingled Funds. In a case in which a transaction, financial transaction, monetary transaction, transportation, transfer, or transmission results in the commingling of legitimately derived funds with criminally derived funds, the value of the laundered funds, for purposes of subsection (a)(2), is the amount of the criminally derived funds, not the total amount of the commingled funds, if the defendant provides sufficient information to determine the amount of criminally derived funds without unduly complicating or prolonging the sentencing process. If the amount of the criminally derived funds is difficult or impracticable to determine, the value of the laundered funds, for purposes of subsection (a)(2), is the total amount of the commingled funds.

(C) Non–Applicability of Enhancement. Subsection (b)(2)(B) shall not apply if the defendant was convicted of a conspiracy under 18 U.S.C. § 1956(h) and the sole object of that conspiracy was to commit an offense set forth in 18 U.S.C. § 1957.

4. Enhancement for Business of Laundering Funds.

(A) In General. The court shall consider the totality of the circumstances to determine whether a defendant who did not commit the underlying offense was in the business of laundering funds, for purposes of subsection (b)(2)(C).

(B) Factors to Consider. The following is a non-exhaustive list of factors that may indicate the defendant was in the business of laundering funds for purposes of subsection (b)(2)(C):

(i) The defendant regularly engaged in laundering funds.

(ii) The defendant engaged in laundering funds during an extended period of time.

(iii) The defendant engaged in laundering funds from multiple sources.

(iv) The defendant generated a substantial amount of revenue in return for laundering funds.

(v) At the time the defendant committed the instant offense, the defendant had one or more prior convictions for an offense under 18 U.S.C. § 1956 or § 1957, or under 31 U.S.C. § 5313, § 5314, § 5316, § 5324 or § 5326, or any similar offense under state law, or an attempt or conspiracy to commit any such federal or state offense. A conviction taken into account under subsection (b)(2)(C) is not excluded from consideration of whether that conviction receives criminal history points pursuant to Chapter Four, Part A (Criminal History).

(vi) During the course of an undercover government investigation, the defendant made statements that the defendant engaged in any of the conduct described in subdivisions (i) through (iv).

5.   (A) Sophisticated Laundering under Subsection (b)(3). For purposes of subsection (b)(3), "sophisticated laundering" means complex or intricate offense conduct pertaining to the execution or concealment of the 18 U.S.C. § 1956 offense. Sophisticated laundering typically involves the use of—

(i) fictitious entities;

(ii) shell corporations;

(iii) two or more levels (i.e., layering) of transactions, transportation, transfers, or transmissions, involving criminally derived funds that were intended to appear legitimate; or

(iv) offshore financial accounts.

(B) Non–Applicability of Enhancement. If subsection (b)(3) applies, and the conduct that forms the basis for an enhancement under the guideline applicable to the underlying offense is the only conduct that forms the basis for application of subsection (b)(3) of this guideline, do not apply subsection (b)(3) of this guideline.

6.   Grouping of Multiple Counts. In a case in which the defendant is convicted of a count of laundering funds and a count for the underlying offense from which the laundered funds were derived, the counts shall be grouped pursuant to subsection (c) of § 3D1.2 (Groups of Closely–Related Counts).

§ 2S1.2.   Deleted (Consolidated with 2S1.1 on 11/01/2001)

Reason for Amendment: The 2001 amendment consolidates the money laundering guidelines, §§ 2S1.1 (Laundering of Monetary Instruments) and 2S1.2 (Engaging in Monetary Transactions in Property Derived from Specified Unlawful Activity), into one guideline that applies to convictions under 18 U.S.C. § 1956 or § 1957, or 21 U.S.C. § 854. The amendment responds in several ways to concerns that the penalty structure existing prior to this amendment for such offenses did not reflect adequately the culpability of the defendant or the seriousness of the money laundering conduct because the offense level for money laundering was determined without sufficient consideration of the defendant's involvement in, or the relative seriousness of, the underlying offense. The amendment promotes proportionality by providing increased penalties for defendants who launder funds derived from more serious underlying criminal conduct, such as drug trafficking, crimes of violence, and fraud offenses that generate relatively high loss amounts, and decreased penalties for defendants who launder funds derived from less serious underlying criminal conduct, such as basic fraud offenses that generate relatively low loss amounts.

First, the amendment ties offense levels for money laundering more closely to the underlying conduct that was the source of the criminally derived funds by separating money laundering offenders into two categories for purposes of determining the base offense level. For direct money launderers (offenders who commit or would be accountable under § 1B1.3(a)(1)(A) (Relevant Conduct) for the underlying offense which generated the criminal proceeds), subsection (a)(1) sets the base offense level at the offense level in Chapter Two (Offense Conduct) for the underlying offense (i.e., the base offense level, specific offense characteristics, cross references, and special instructions for the underlying offense). For third party money launderers (offenders who launder the proceeds generated from underlying offenses that the defendant did not commit or would not be accountable for under § 1B1.3(a)(1)(A)), subsection (a)(2) sets the base offense level at level 8, plus an increase based on the value of the laundered funds from the table in subsection (b)(1) of § 2B1.1 (Theft, Fraud, Property Destruction).

Second, in addition to the base offense level calculation, the amendment provides an enhancement designed to reflect the differing seriousness of the underlying conduct that was the source of the criminally derived funds. Subsection (b)(1) provides a six-level enhancement for third party money launderers who knew or believed that any of the laundered funds were the proceeds of, or were intended to promote, certain types of more serious underlying criminal conduct; specifically, drug trafficking, crimes of violence, offenses involving firearms, explosives, national security, terrorism, and the sexual exploitation of a minor. The Commission determined that defendants who knowingly launder the proceeds of these more serious underlying offenses are substantially more culpable than third party launderers of criminally derived proceeds of less serious underlying offenses.

Third, the amendment provides three alternative enhancements, with the greatest applicable enhancement to be applied. These enhancements are designed to (1) ensure that all direct money launderers receive additional punishment for committing both the money laundering offense and the underlying offense, and (2) reflect the differing seriousness of money laundering conduct depending on the nature and sophistication of the offense. Specifically, subsection (b)(2)(A) provides a one-level increase if the defendant was convicted under 18 U.S.C. § 1957, and subsection (b)(2)(B) provides a two-level increase if the defendant was convicted under 18 U.S.C. § 1956. The one-level difference between these two enhancements reflects the fact that 18 U.S.C. § 1956 has a statutory maximum penalty (20 years' imprisonment) that is twice as long as the statutory maximum penalty for violations of 18 U.S.C. § 1957 (10 years' imprisonment). In addition, subsection (b)(3) provides an additional two-level increase if subsection (b)(2)(B) applies and the offense involved sophisticated laundering such as the use of fictitious entities, shell corporations, two or more levels of transactions, or offshore financial accounts. The Commission determined that, similar to fraud and tax offenses that involve sophisticated means, see subsection (b)(8) of § 2B1.1 (Theft, Property Destruction, and Fraud), subsection (b)(2) of § 2T1.1 (Tax Evasion; Willful Failure to File Return, Supply Information, or Pay Tax; Fraudulent or False Returns, Statements, or Other Documents), violations of 18 U.S.C. § 1956 that involve sophisticated laundering warrant additional punishment because such offenses are more difficult and time consuming for law enforcement to detect than less sophisticated laundering. As a result of the enhancements provided by subsections (b)(2)(A), (b)(2)(B), and (b)(3), all direct money launderers will receive an offense level that is one to four levels greater than the Chapter Two offense level for the underlying offense, depending on the statute of conviction and sophistication of the money laundering offense conduct.

With respect to third party money launderers, subsection (b)(2)(C) provides a four level enhancement if the defendant is "in the business" of laundering funds. The Commission determined that, similar to a professional "fence", see § 2B1.1(b)(4)(B), defendants who routinely engage in laundering funds on behalf of others, and who gain financially from engaging in such transactions, warrant substantial additional punishment because they encourage the commission of additional criminal conduct.

Finally, this amendment provides that convictions under 18 U.S.C. § 1960 are referenced to § 2S1.3 (Structuring Transactions to Evade Reporting Requirements).

Operation of money transmitting businesses without an appropriate license is proscribed by 18 U.S.C. § 1960, as are failures to comply with certain reporting requirements issued under 31 U.S.C. § 5330. The Commission determined that offenses involving these regulatory requirements serve many of the same purposes as Currency Transaction Reports, Currency and Monetary Instrument Reports, Reports of Foreign Bank and Financial Accounts, and Reports of Cash Payments over $10,000 Received in a Trade or Business, violations regarding which currently are referenced to § 2S1.3, and that, therefore, violations of 18 U.S.C. § 1960 also should be referenced to § 2S1.3.

§ 2S1.3. Structuring Transactions to Evade Reporting Requirements; Failure to Report Cash or Monetary Transactions; Failure to File Currency and Monetary Instrument Report; Knowingly Filing False Reports; Bulk Cash Smuggling; Establishing or Maintaining Prohibited Accounts

(a) Base Offense Level:

(1) 8, if the defendant was convicted under 31 U.S.C. § 5318 or § 5318A; or (2) 6 plus the number of offense levels from the table in § 2B1.1 (Theft, Property Destruction, and Fraud) corresponding to the value of the funds, if subsection (a)(1) does not apply.

(b) Specific Offense Characteristics

(1) If (A) the defendant knew or believed that the funds were proceeds of unlawful activity, or were intended to promote unlawful activity; or (B) the offense involved bulk cash smuggling, increase by **2** levels.

(2) If the defendant (A) was convicted of an offense under subchapter II of chapter 53 of title 31, United States Code; and (B) committed the offense as part of a pattern of unlawful activity involving more than $100,000 in a 12–month period, increase by **2** levels.

(3) If (A) subsection (a)(2) applies and subsections (b)(1) and (b)(2) do not apply; (B) the defendant did not act with reckless disregard of the source of the funds; (C) the funds were the proceeds of lawful activity; and (D) the funds were to be used for a lawful purpose, decrease the offense level to level **6**.

(c) Cross Reference

(1) If the offense was committed for the purposes of violating the Internal Revenue laws, apply the most appropriate guideline from Chapter Two, Part T (Offenses Involving Taxation) if the resulting offense level is greater than that determined above.

Commentary

Statutory Provisions: 18 U.S.C. § 1960; 26 U.S.C. §§ 7203 (if a violation based upon 26 U.S.C. § 6050I), 7206 (if a violation based upon 26 U.S.C. § 6050I); 31 U.S.C. §§ 5313, 5314, 5316, 5318, 5318A(b), 5322, 5324, 5326, 5331, 5332. For additional statutory provision(s), see Appendix A (Statutory Index).

Application Notes:

1. Definition of "Value of the Funds". For purposes of this guideline, "value of the funds" means the amount of the funds involved in the structuring or reporting conduct. The relevant statutes require monetary

reporting without regard to whether the funds were lawfully or unlawfully obtained.

2. Bulk Cash Smuggling. For purposes of subsection (b)(1)(B), "bulk cash smuggling" means (A) knowingly concealing, with the intent to evade a currency reporting requirement under 31 U.S.C. § 5316, more than $10,000 in currency or other monetary instruments; and (B) transporting or transferring (or attempting to transport or transfer) such currency or monetary instruments into or outside of the United States. "United States" has the meaning given that term in Application Note 1 of the Commentary to § 2B5.1 (Offenses Involving Counterfeit Bearer Obligations of the United States).

3. Enhancement for Pattern of Unlawful Activity. For purposes of subsection (b)(2), "pattern of unlawful activity" means at least two separate occasions of unlawful activity involving a total amount of more than $100,000 in a 12–month period, without regard to whether any such occasion occurred during the course of the offense or resulted in a conviction for the conduct that occurred on that occasion.

Background: Some of the offenses covered by this guideline relate to records and reports of certain transactions involving currency and monetary instruments. These reports include Currency Transaction Reports, Currency and Monetary Instrument Reports, Reports of Foreign Bank and Financial Accounts, and Reports of Cash Payments Over $10,000 Received in a Trade or Business.

This guideline also covers offenses under 31 U.S.C. §§ 5318 and 5318A, pertaining to records, reporting and identification requirements, prohibited accounts involving certain foreign jurisdictions, foreign institutions, and foreign banks, and other types of transactions and types of accounts.

Amendment & Reason: § 2S1.3 was amended to incorporate new money laundering provisions created by the PATRIOT Act. Specifically, the amendment provides an alternative base offense level of level 8 in § 2S1.3(a) in order to incorporate offenses under 31 U.S.C. §§ 5318 and 5318A. The base offense level of level 8 recognizes the heightened due diligence requirements placed on financial institutions with respect to payable-through accounts, correspondent accounts, and shell banks.

The amendment also amends § 2S1.3(b)(1), relating to the promotion of unlawful activity, to provide an alternative prong if the offense involved bulk cash smuggling. This amendment addresses 31 U.S.C. § 5332, added by section 371 of the PATRIOT Act, which prohibits concealing, with intent to evade a currency reporting requirement under 31 U.S.C. § 5316, more than $10,000 in currency or other monetary instruments and transporting or transferring such currency or monetary instruments into or outside of the United States.

Findings set forth in that section of the PATRIOT Act indicate that bulk cash smuggling typically involves the promotion of unlawful activity. The amendment also provides an enhancement in § 2S1.3(b) to give effect to the enhanced penalty provisions under 31 U.S.C. § 5322(b) for offenses under subchapter II of chapter 53 of title 31, United Stated Code, if such offenses were committed as part of a pattern of unlawful activity involving more than $100,000 in a 12–month period.

§ 2X1.1. Attempt, Solicitation, or Conspiracy (Not Covered by a Specific Offense Guideline)

(a) Base Offense Level: The base offense level from the guideline for the substantive offense, plus any adjustments from such guideline for any intended offense conduct that can be established with reasonable certainty.

(b) Specific Offense Characteristics

(1) If an attempt, decrease by **3** levels, unless the defendant completed all the acts the defendant believed necessary for successful completion of the substantive offense or the circumstances demonstrate that the defendant was about to complete all such acts but for apprehension or interruption by some similar event beyond the defendant's control.

(2) If a conspiracy, decrease by **3** levels, unless the defendant or a co-conspirator completed all the acts the conspirators believed necessary on their part for the successful completion of the substantive offense or the circumstances demonstrate that the conspirators were about to complete all such acts but for apprehension or interruption by some similar event beyond their control.

(A) If a solicitation, decrease by **3** levels unless the person solicited to commit or aid the substantive offense completed all the acts he believed necessary for successful completion of the substantive offense or the circumstances demonstrate that the person was about to complete all such acts but for apprehension or interruption by some similar event beyond such person's control.

(B) If the statute treats solicitation of the substantive offense identically with the substantive offense, do not apply subdivision (A) above; i.e., the offense level for solicitation is the same as that for the substantive offense.

(c) Cross Reference

(1) When an attempt, solicitation, or conspiracy is expressly covered by another offense guideline section, apply that guideline section.

(d) Special Instruction

(1) Subsection (b) shall not apply to

(A) Any of the following offenses, if such offense involved, or was intended to promote, a federal crime of terrorism as defined in 18 U.S.C. § 2332b(g)(5):

18 U.S.C. § 81;

18 U.S.C. § 930(c);

18 U.S.C. § 1362;

18 U.S.C. § 1363;

18 U.S.C. § 1992;

18 U.S.C. § 2339A;

18 U.S.C. § 2340A;

49 U.S.C. § 46504;

49 U.S.C. § 46505; and

49 U.S.C. § 60123(b).

(B) Any of the following offenses:

18 U.S.C. § 32;

18 U.S.C. § 1993; and

18 U.S.C. § 2332a.

Commentary

Statutory Provisions: 18 U.S.C. §§ 371, 372, 2271. For additional statutory provision(s), see Appendix A (Statutory Index).

Application Notes:

1. Certain attempts, conspiracies, and solicitations are expressly covered by other offense guidelines.

Offense guidelines that expressly cover attempts include:

§§ 2A2.1, 2A3.1, 2A3.2, 2A3.3, 2A3.4, 2A4.2, 2A5.1;

§§ 2C1.1, 2C1.2;

§§ 2D1.1, 2D1.2, 2D1.5, 2D1.6, 2D1.7, 2D1.8, 2D1.9, 2D1.10, 2D1.11, 2D1.12, 2D1.13, 2D2.1, 2D2.2, 2D3.1, 2D3.2;

§ 2E5.1;

§ 2M6.1

§ 2N1.1;

§ 2Q1.4.

Offense guidelines that expressly cover conspiracies include:

§ 2A1.5;

§§ 2D1.1, 2D1.2, 2D1.5, 2D1.6, 2D1.7, 2D1.8, 2D1.9, 2D1.10, 2D1.11, 2D1.12. 2D1.13, 2D2.1, 2D2.2, 2D3.1, 2D3.2;

§ 2H1.1;

§ 2M6.1

§ 2T1.9.

Offense guidelines that expressly cover solicitations include:

§ 2A1.5;

§ 2C1.1, 2C1.2;

§ 2E5.1.

2. "Substantive offense," as used in this guideline, means the offense that the defendant was convicted of soliciting, attempting, or conspiring to commit. Under § 2X1.1(a), the base offense level will be the same as that for the substantive offense. But the only specific offense

characteristics from the guideline for the substantive offense that apply are those that are determined to have been specifically intended or actually occurred. Speculative specific offense characteristics will not be applied. For example, if two defendants are arrested during the conspiratorial stage of planning an armed bank robbery, the offense level ordinarily would not include aggravating factors regarding possible injury to others, hostage taking, discharge of a weapon, or obtaining a large sum of money, because such factors would be speculative. The offense level would simply reflect the level applicable to robbery of a financial institution, with the enhancement for possession of a weapon. If it was established that the defendants actually intended to physically restrain the teller, the specific offense characteristic for physical restraint would be added. In an attempted theft, the value of the items that the defendant attempted to steal would be considered.

3. If the substantive offense is not covered by a specific guideline, see § 2X5.1 (Other Offenses).

4. In certain cases, the participants may have completed (or have been about to complete but for apprehension or interruption) all of the acts necessary for the successful completion of part, but not all, of the intended offense. In such cases, the offense level for the count (or group of closely related multiple counts) is whichever of the following is greater: the offense level for the intended offense minus 3 levels (under § 2X1.1(b)(1), (b)(2), or (b)(3)(A)), or the offense level for the part of the offense for which the necessary acts were completed (or about to be completed but for apprehension or interruption). For example, where the intended offense was the theft of $800,000 but the participants completed (or were about to complete) only the acts necessary to steal $30,000, the offense level is the offense level for the theft of $800,000 minus 3 levels, or the offense level for the theft of $30,000, whichever is greater.

In the case of multiple counts that are not closely related counts, whether the 3–level reduction under § 2X1.1(b)(1), (b)(2), or (b)(3)(A) applies is determined separately for each count.

Background: In most prosecutions for conspiracies or attempts, the substantive offense was substantially completed or was interrupted or prevented on the verge of completion by the intercession of law enforcement authorities or the victim. In such cases, no reduction of the offense level is warranted. Sometimes, however, the arrest occurs well before the defendant or any co-conspirator has completed the acts necessary for the substantive offense. Under such circumstances, a reduction of 3 levels is provided under § 2X1.1(b)(1) or (2).

Amendment & Reason: In response to terrorist attacks, the amendment affecting § 2X1.1 (Attempt, Solicitation, or Conspiracy) required that the three level reduction in § 2X1.1(b) does not apply to these offenses when committed for a terrorist objective.

§ 5K1.1. Substantial Assistance to Authorities (Policy Statement)

Upon motion of the government stating that the defendant has provided substantial assistance in the investigation or prosecution of another person who has committed an offense, the court may depart from the guidelines.

(a) The appropriate reduction shall be determined by the court for reasons stated that may include, but are not limited to, consideration of the following:

(1) the court's evaluation of the significance and usefulness of the defendant's assistance, taking into consideration the government's evaluation of the assistance rendered;

(2) the truthfulness, completeness, and reliability of any information or testimony provided by the defendant;

(3) the nature and extent of the defendant's assistance;

(4) any injury suffered, or any danger or risk of injury to the defendant or his family resulting from his assistance;

(5) the timeliness of the defendant's assistance.

Commentary

Application Notes:

1. Under circumstances set forth in 18 U.S.C. § 3553(e) and 28 U.S.C. § 994(n), as amended, substantial assistance in the investigation or prosecution of another person who has committed an offense may justify a sentence below a statutorily required minimum sentence.

2. The sentencing reduction for assistance to authorities shall be considered independently of any reduction for acceptance of responsibility. Substantial assistance is directed to the investigation and prosecution of criminal activities by persons other than the defendant, while acceptance of responsibility is directed to the defendant's affirmative recognition of responsibility for his own conduct.

3. Substantial weight should be given to the government's evaluation of the extent of the defendant's assistance, particularly where the extent and value of the assistance are difficult to ascertain.

Background: A defendant's assistance to authorities in the investigation of criminal activities has been recognized in practice and by statute as a mitigating sentencing factor. The nature, extent, and significance of assistance can involve a broad spectrum of conduct that must be evaluated by the court on an individual basis. Latitude is, therefore, afforded the sentencing judge to reduce a sentence based upon variable relevant factors, including those listed above. The sentencing judge must, however, state the reasons for reducing a sentence under this section. 18 U.S.C. § 3553(c). The court may elect to provide its reasons to the defendant in camera and in writing under seal for the safety of the defendant or to avoid disclosure of an ongoing investigation.

VII. FINAL REPORT OF THE NATIONAL COMMISSION ON REFORM OF THE FEDERAL CRIMINAL LAW (1971)

Section 201 Common Jurisdictional Bases

Federal jurisdiction to penalize an offense under this Code exists under the circumstances which are set forth as the jurisdictional base or bases for that offense.

Bases commonly used in the Code are as follows:

(a) the offense is committed with the special maritime and territorial jurisdiction of the United States as defined in section 210.

(b) The offense is committed in the course of committing or in immediate flight from the commission of any other offenses defined in this Code over which federal jurisdiction exists.

(c) the victim is a federal public servant engaged in the performance of his official duties or is the President of the United States, the President-elect, the Vice President, or, if there is no Vice President, the officer next in the order of succession to the office of President of the United States, the Vice President-elect, or any individual who is acting as President under the Constitution and laws of the United States, a candidate for the President or Vice President, or any member or member-designate of the President's cabinet, or a member of Congress, or a federal judge, or a head of a foreign nation or a foreign minister, ambassador or other public minister;

(d) the property which is the subject of the offense is owned by or in the custody or control of the United States or is being manufactured, constructed or stored for the United States;

(e) the United States mails or facility in interstate foreign commerce is used in the commission or consummation of the offense;

(f) the offense is against a transportation, communication or power facility of interstate or foreign commerce or against a United States mail facility;

(g) the offense affects interstate or foreign commerce;

(h) movement of any person across a state or United States boundary occurs in the commission or consummation of the offense;

(i) the property which is the subject of the offense is moving in interstate or foreign commerce or constitutes or is a part of an interstate or foreign shipment;

(j) the property which is the subject of the offense is moved across a state or United States boundary in the commission or consummation of the offense;

(k) the property which is the subject of the offense is owned by or in the custody of a national credit institution;

(l) the offense is committed under circumstances amounting to piracy, as prescribed in section 212.

When no base is specified for an offense, federal jurisdiction exists if the offense is committed anywhere within the United States, or within the special maritime and territorial jurisdiction of the United States.

*

Index

References are to pages

ABORTION PROTESTS
Freedom of Access to Clinic Entrances Act
  (FACEA), 504, 671
Hobbs Act prosecutions, 243 et seq., 245
RICO prosecutions, 499 et seq.

ARREST
See Enforcement of Laws, this index

ATTORNEY GENERAL
See Justice Department, this index

ATTORNEYS
  See also Counsel, Right to, this index
Forfeiture of fees
    Ethical conflicts, 931 et seq.
    Fees recoupment hazard, 931 et seq.
    Prosecutorial policies, 936 et seq.
Obstruction of justice offenses, 778–79
RICO liability of attorney adviser, 522

BANK SECRECY ACT (BSA)
See Currency Reporting Offenses, this index

BRIBERY
  Generally, 276 et seq.
Campaign contributions, 294 et seq.
Commercial bribery
    Generally, 88 et seq.
    Extortion compared, 242
Conjugal visit as thing of value, 297 et seq.
Federal program bribery
    Generally, 296 et seq.
    Constitutional challenges, 302–04
    Embezzlement, 296 n., 306–07
    Fraud activities, 296 n., 306–07
    Gratuities, 305
    Intent, 305
    Monetary threshold, 302
    Nexus, 297 et seq.
    Official bribery statute applied to,
      293–94
    Scope, 302 et seq.
Fees for legitimate services, 294 et seq.
Gifts, 286
Gratuities distinguished
    Generally, 279 et seq.
    Federal program bribery, 305
    Low level bribery, prosecution choices as
      to, 314 et seq.

BRIBERY—Cont'd
Official bribery statute
    Generally, 276 et seq.
    Campaign contributions, 294 et seq.
    Corrupt intent, 289
    Elements, 276, 282
    Federal officials, limitation to, 277,
      293–94
    Fees for legitimate services, 294 et seq.
    Future employment as thing of value,
      291–92
    Gifts, excepted, 286
    Gratuities distinguished, 279 et seq.
    Immunity defenses, 290
    Intangible benefits, 291
    Plea bargain, application to, 292
    Public official requirement, 293
    Quid pro quo requirement, 279 et seq.
    Scope, 277
    State and local officials
        Generally, 293–94, 296 et seq.,
          308 et seq.
        Federal aid administration, 293–94
        Reform legislation proposals, 319 et
          seq.
    Thing of value, 291
    Witness in federal prosecution, applica-
      tion to, 292
Plea bargain, application of official bribery
    statute to, 292
Political corruption
    Generally, 308 et seq.
    Low level bribery, prosecution choices as
      to, 314 et seq.
    Reform legislation proposals, 319 et seq.
Quid pro quo requirement, 279 et seq.
State and local officials
    Generally, 293–94, 296 et seq., 308 et
      seq.
    Reform legislation proposals, 319 et seq.
Travel Act, this index

CAMPAIGN CONTRIBUTIONS
Official bribery statute prosecutions, 294 et
  seq.

CIVIL RIGHTS OFFENSES
  Generally, 636 et seq.
Arrest, use of excessive force, 659 et seq.

1037

†